# Computation Structures

**The MIT Electrical Engineering and Computer Science Series**

Harold Abelson and Gerald Jay Sussman with Julie Sussman, *Structure and Interpretation of Computer Programs*, 1985.

William McC. Siebert, *Circuits, Signals, and Systems*, 1986.

Berthold Klaus Paul Horn, *Robot Vision*, 1986.

Barbara Liskov and John Guttag, *Abstraction and Specification in Program Development*, 1986.

Thomas H. Cormen, Charles E. Leiserson, and Ronald L. Rivest, *Introduction to Algorithms*, 1990.

Stephen A. Ward and Robert H. Halstead, Jr., *Computation Structures*, 1990.

Stephen A. Ward
Robert H. Halstead, Jr.

# Computation Structures

The MIT Press
Cambridge, Massachusetts  London, England

McGraw-Hill Book Company
New York  St. Louis  San Francisco  Montreal  Toronto

This book is one of a series of texts written by faculty of the Electrical Engineering and Computer Science Department at the Massachusetts Institute of Technology. It was edited and produced by The MIT Press under a joint production-distribution arrangement with the McGraw-Hill Book Company.

Ordering Information:

*North America*
Text orders should be addressed to the McGraw-Hill Book Company. All other orders should be addressed to The MIT Press.

*Outside North America*
All orders should be addressed to The MIT Press or its local distributor.

This book was printed and bound by Halliday Lithograph in the United States of America.

Library of Congress Cataloging-in-Publication Data

Ward, Stephen A.
  Computation structures / Stephen A. Ward, Robert H. Halstead, Jr.
    p.    cm.—(The MIT electrical engineering and computer science series)
    ISBN 0-262-23139-5 (MIT Press).—ISBN 0-07-068147-3 (McGraw-Hill)
    1. Computers—Circuits. 2. Logic design. 3. Computer
architecture.    I. Halstead, Robert H.    II. Title.    III. Series.
TK7888.4.W37    1989
621.39′2—dc20                                             89-12961
                                                              CIP

# Contents

**6**

**7**

**8**

**9**

**10**

**11**

## 18

### Processes and Processor Multiplexing *533*

## 19

### Process Synchronization *559*

## 20

### Interrupts, Priorities, and Real Time *587*

**21**

**A1**

**A2**

# Preface

This text approaches the field of digital systems architecture with a particular bias, one kindled during years of observation of M.I.T. students and speculation about the factors that distinguish outstanding engineers from the merely very competent majority. We bring to the project a conviction that the distinction reflects attitudes and perspectives that are at most subtle by-products of the usual technical education: subliminal lessons occasionally administered to students by virtue of accidental discovery rather than deliberate pedagogy. The organization and approach of *Computation Structures* is geared to the explicit cultivation of these characteristics in every student and reader.

## Scope and Mission

As computer systems become increasingly complex, their study inevitably relies upon more specific areas of specialization. We compartmentalize specific technologies—logic elements, processors, compilers, operating systems—as subdisciplines to be treated by separate courses, texts, and intellectual tools. Interfaces between the subdisciplines are powerful engineering abstractions that allow, for example, the designer of a processor to deal entirely in the domain of digital logic, naively exploiting the electronic circuitry in the abstraction below and providing interpretive services to software in the abstraction above.

The abstractions work sufficiently well that our curricula (and, for that matter, our job descriptions) accommodate specialists whose understanding of computer systems is cripplingly incomplete. We confer computer science degrees on theorists who may be helpless when programming is required, on hardware designers to whom the high-level structure of the system to which they contribute is mystery, and on programmers who lack a clear understanding of how or why their programs make real things happen. Often what passes for technical breadth takes the form of multiple specialties: Students exhibit pockets of local facility, unable to connect them into an effective understanding of the system as a whole. Such people can and do perform useful functions, but their potential for creativity is limited by their acceptance of the boundaries of their specialties. They shy from the challenge to venture beyond familiar approaches, to reshape problems, to develop new interfaces and revise existing ones; they accept the mysterious rather than unveiling it, oversensitized to their own limitations. They are, in effect, imprisoned by the abstractions they have been taught.

Outstanding students, in contrast, somehow develop a perspective that illuminates the interfaces between technologies, rather than the technologies themselves, as the most important structural elements of their discipline. They view the interfaces with respect but not reverence; they examine both sides of an abstraction, treating it as an object of study rather than a boundary between the known and the intractably mystical. They have discovered the power of their own universality; typically they have built complete systems, often with meager resources, and made them work. They have the sophistication, and most importantly the self-assurance, to explore new abstractions and to appreciate the role and costs of existing ones.

*Computation Structures* is intended to produce renaissance engineers of this latter category. To this end, it deliberately telescopes much of computer science into a bottom-up progression that builds simple electronics into representative computer systems. The student is catapulted through one layer after another of implementation technology, an experience that accentuates technological interfaces and the structure induced by them. The breadth of coverage of the book reflects our compulsion to demystify its subject matter. We are unwilling to ask students to accept a technology on faith, or to postpone its penetration to some more advanced course. The spectrum of implementation technology is laid before them as a challenge to sample, to uncover, to discover their capacity to master its entirety.

The ultimate mission of *Computation Structures* is not so much to convey facts as to catalyze personal discoveries by each student: the ability to master a wide range of technical details, the self-assurance to dive through a technological boundary, the power to grab a wire-wrap gun or CAD tool or body of code and create new structures. The considerable volume of technical detail is present largely to serve this goal; it is not the subject of the book, but rather a tool by which we convey its more important lesson.

## The Text

*Computation Structures* does not presume to replace the many excellent texts that focus on established subtopics such as logic design or operating systems; nor is it intended for an elite audience capable of digesting four semesters of course work in a single term. It covers topics that every engineer—certainly every computer scientist—should be aware of, in sufficient detail to establish a concrete connection between each topic and practical reality. In many cases that connection is provided by the MAYBE computer, a simple microarchitecture that we use as a running example throughout the text. The MAYBE is presented in sufficient detail to allow its actual construction and operation, an activity required of M.I.T. students; even in the absence of such experience, it provides a subject for close scrutiny and a context for concrete discussions and questions.

The text is introductory, presuming no formal background in digital systems; however, it generally assumes a level of technical sophistication consistent with that of an undergraduate engineering student. The text makes repeated connections to related technical areas. These should enrich the presentation for students with appropriate backgrounds, but are inessential to the sequel; for example, early chapters include a few circuit diagrams whose appreciation requires an Ohm's-law level of circuit sophistication. Programming ideas and constructs are introduced with a lack of fanfare that presumes some previous exposure to computers and programming on the part of the student. A subset of the C language, used for sample programs, is presented in a terse appendix; we have found that students easily attain a level of C fluency that allows them to read and understand the examples.

The text does not make extensive use of real-world case studies, relying instead on the more coherent framework designed into our real but parochial example machines. Connections to the technical literature and to industrial practice are identified primarily in sections entitled Context; these provide pointers for deeper investigation of technical issues, links to adjacent fields, and occasional historical perspective.

## Role at M.I.T.

*Computation Structures* is used at M.I.T. as the text for 6.004, a one-term, 15-hour-per-week sophomore "core" course required of all electrical engineering and computer science undergraduates. Three of the fifteen student hours are allocated to laboratory activities; the remainder are spent in classes and homework. Typical students have previously taken 6.001, a LISP-based programming course that uses Abelson and Sussman [1985] as a text, and 6.002, an introductory circuits course. The role of 6.002 is primarily to prepare the student for the 6.004 laboratory component, in which (for example) familiarity with an oscilloscope is assumed. 6.001 provides a first exposure to many ideas that recur in 6.004—programs, stacks, memory locations—albeit in quite a quite different context and often following a different idiom.

6.004 is a fast-moving course, stretching to accommodate the subject in its tightly packed single-term syllabus. Major topics are dealt with in about 25 lectures, which generally follow the order of the text and average one or two lectures per chapter. Substantial pruning is required to provide coherent if somewhat superficial coverage in lectures: While the major topics of the text are each dealt with in some depth, many of their ramifications and issues raised in the text are not addressed explicitly. Many of the optional (starred) sections are omitted, although the mix varies somewhat from one term to the next.

The big picture emerging from the lectures is embellished by smaller section meetings held twice weekly, by homework, and by laboratory assignments. These components provide a vehicle for sampling underlying technical detail, stimulating each student to relate the lecture topic with at least one example of practical reality. The cultivation of this connection is a key element of the course and this text. Rather than presenting a stack frame in abstract terms, for example, we encourage each student to come to grips with the entire set of nested implementation technologies that make it real—machine language, microcode, circuit diagrams, logic gates. Frequent probes to concrete reality reinforce the two major lessons of the course: first, the value of abstractions as a tool for structuring complex systems; and second, the capacity of the individual student to master *any* aspect of a system he or she cares to focus on.

## Laboratory Work

These key lessons of *Computation Structures* are reinforced by the laboratory component of the course. Each student is required to construct, debug, and program a working MAYBE computer from simple components (at the level of ROMs and registers). Several machine architectures—stack and general-register machines—are implemented and programmed using a common microarchitecture.

Students' computers are constructed from reusable take-home kits. The kits have a selection of logic components as well as integral prototyping board, power supply, and very primitive input/output provisions. Workstations (with a variety of support programs) and oscilloscopes are available in the laboratory. Although the wiring and much of the debugging can be performed by students at home, final checkout and subsequent program development require the use of facilities in the lab.

The laboratory is structured as about eight assignments, each directed at a fairly tightly constrained set of goals. The directedness of the assignments differentiates the activity from more advanced "project" laboratories, which emphasize initiative and creativity; however, each assignment contains some nugget of creative challenge, such as the design of a machine instruction. A major creative outlet takes the form of an optional design contest, held at the end of each term, in which students are given a relatively free hand to modify their machines to improve performance on a benchmark program that is not revealed until the day of the contest. Each entrant is constrained to use only parts from the lab kit, although we allow $n$-student teams to combine $n$ lab kits, normalizing the performance of such entries by a factor of $n$. (The best performance by this metric has come from two-kit entries.)

In order to make the student computer construction tractable and reasonably fail-safe, we have developed a set of printed-circuit modules (compatible with protoboard construction techniques) and a staged approach to construction whose early phases involve the use of a kernel subset of the machine to debug its incremental improvements. This methodology, involving the use of bootstrapping and scaffolding to develop complex systems, is among the major lessons of the course; it is one we have found no way to teach without hands-on experience.

The integration of a "complete" laboratory with a broad-spectrum architecture course makes an ambitious package, but one that produces students whose technical maturity and self-assurance is based on that ultimate educator: They have each built a computer and made it work. We enthusiastically recommend the approach.

While we value the *omniware* breadth of the laboratory, much of its pedagogy can be captured by somewhat less extreme programs. The majority of the laboratory activity involves coding at some level, and can be carried out effectively using simulation software rather than hardware implementations. Several simulators and related system software (available both for UNIX workstations and for PCs) provide a convenient development test bed for microcode and software, even where the alternative of a hardware MAYBE machine exists. Since the architectural personality of our machine is largely dictated by the contents of a control ROM, the range of architectural options that can be explored using reprogramming and simulation techniques is relatively unconstrained. An effective laboratory can thus be fashioned using only commonly available computing resources.

In the absence of such resources, the complete implementations presented here can still be explored in a kind of ersatz laboratory whose medium is paper rather than machinery, that is, in assignments that probe, modify, and analyze the given structures. This approach was used at M.I.T. in years prior to the 6.004 laboratory; while the latter has clear advantages, a paper laboratory devoted to all levels of a single coherent example accomplishes many of the demystification and perspective-building goals of our current course.

## Alternative Paths through the Text

The subject of the text lends itself well to subsetting by suppression of detail, and we expect individual courses and readers to deemphasize or omit selected subtopics to suit their needs and backgrounds. The (widely varying) dependencies among topics are mapped crudely by the following graph:

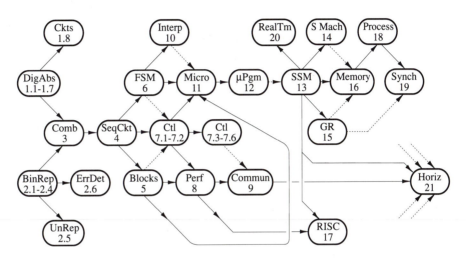

Relatively inessential dependencies are shown as dotted edges. The level of detail shown in the diagram ignores certain subtleties, often bundling essential and optional issues together as single nodes. Some additional guidance to topic selection is provided by observing sections marked with an asterisk, indicating digressions that can be skipped without compromising subsequent (nonasterisked) coverage.

Topic selection and path through the text may be adjusted to accommodate a number of different course needs. A two-term undergraduate sequence based on the text would allow careful and relaxed treatment of its entire coverage and, given sufficient student time, is an attractive alternative to the single-term firehose-style course offered at M.I.T. An introductory graduate course might augment the text by selected readings from the literature; candidates appear in the Context sections and in the bibliography. Certain of the exercises appearing at the end of each chapter are marked with one or two asterisks to indicate that they may be challenging for an introductory undergraduate course. A single asterisk suggests that the marked problem requires more than routine application of the principles of the chapter; double asterisks identify problems that should challenge graduate students.

## Acknowledgments

*Computation Structures* reflects the ideas, influence, and efforts of literally dozens of people who have contributed to 6.004 and its ancestors over the years. This lineage begins with the seminal course 6.032, which was developed in the late 1960s by Jack Dennis and subsequently evolved under the auspices of Jon Allen and Bob Gallager. The book owes its name and much of its sense of direction to these early roots; it conveys, to a considerable extent, lessons that have been taught its authors by their predecessors.

The current course began to take shape during the spring of 1980, when the authors collaborated with Dave Reed in an effort to modernize 6.032 and its course notes. Subsequent years saw a succession of significant revisions to the course, each accompanied by a rewrite of the notes, exploring a variety of pedagogic formulae. The birth of the MAYBE in 1984 marks the point at which the book's current content and focus began to jell; the efforts of Dan Nussbaum and Chris Terman played a significant role during this formative period. Subsequent maturation of the laboratory work included substantial contributions to the MAYBE by Mike Blair, Ken Mackenzie, and Henry Houh.

During this long history, the course and its notes were scrutinized by dozens of course staff and thousands of students, whose contributions to the surviving text are real but generally so diffused as to be unidentifiable. Exceptions, whose impact is more conspicuous, include Tom Anderson, Andy Ayers, Dave Goddeau, Mark Johnson, Rob Kassel, Ken Mackenzie, Rishiyur Nikhil, Dan Nussbaum, Jon Powell, Gill Pratt, Jerry Saltzer, Chris Terman, and John Wolfe. Valuable discussions, critique, and feedback on the text have been provided by Anant Agarwal, Bill Dally, Jacob Katzenelson, Jim Kirtley, Al Mok, Bruce Musicus, Steve Seda, Gerry Sussman, Rich Zippel, and many others.

Particular credit is due John Wolfe for the massive effort he devoted to conversion of the source manuscript to TeX, to Eva Tervo and Sharon Thomas for the help they lent and the aggravation they sustained in preparing the manuscript, to Larry Cohen for his skilled and tireless editing, and to the Harris Corporation, whose HCX-9 was used to format the book with blazing speed. And to Don Knuth, that premier computer scientist whose contributions have been varied, prolific, and influential, we are indebted for TeX, which deserves simultaneous recognition as the text formatter of choice and the most idiosyncratic programming language known to us. It is impossible to account for the prenatal debt incurred by the book to the authors' wives, Debbie and Louise, whose loving encouragement nursed it through its long gestation.

The authors are grateful to M.I.T. for providing an environment that led to *Computation Structures*, to the Department of Electrical Engineering and Computer Science for support of the course development surrounding the text, and to Hewlett-Packard and Tektronix for their donations to the 6.004 laboratory. Finally, a decade of 6.004 and 6.032 students deserve sympathy and thanks for their role as subjects of a long succession of educational experiments as well as credit for the result. They, after all, are more than an influence; they are the reason.

# Computation Structures

# 1    The Digital Abstraction

The key to the orderly design of complex systems, digital or otherwise, lies in the decomposition of their function into modules whose behavior can be independently and concisely specified. To encourage this functional modularity and simplify the specifications for each module, we adopt a variety of engineering disciplines and agree to abide by the constraints they impose; in programming, for example, conventions for the representation of data and for passing parameters are typical self-imposed constraints. Each such discipline involves a set of primitive elements, each performing some prescribed basic function, together with rules for the construction of new elements by the composition of existing ones. The power of an engineering discipline derives from its simplification of the functional specifications of each module by the abstraction of essential function from nonessential detail; the description of a square-root procedure, for example, must confront the arithmetic relationship between its input and output but need not deal with the patterns of bits used to represent them.

We can observe two broad classes of activities in the structuring of complex systems. The first and more common of these involves working within a single discipline, enriching its repertoire by combining existing functions to define new ones. The appropriate software analogy is the construction, within the framework of a particular programming language, of a library of procedures to perform various useful functions. The second and more radical structuring activity involves the use of the modules of one discipline to define and support a new, higher-level abstraction with its own primitive elements and composition rules. In software design, such radical structuring typically involves the use of a lower-level language (together with its library of support procedures) to implement a higher-level language whose primitives and composition rules are in some (perhaps application-dependent) sense more powerful. The major characteristic of the new level is that it isolates its user from the underlying implementation technology, as opposed to simply adding new options to it.

Typically the structure of complex systems shows an alternation between these two activities. Functional extensions are made to some discipline until its complexity becomes unwieldy, at which point it is used to support a new abstraction with a manageable number of higher-level primitives and composition rules.

Such abstractions and the disciplines that support them are the central theme of computer science. Every significant digital system involves many levels of discipline, each implementing a more powerful set of primitive elements and composition rules than the ones that underlie it. This chapter presents the fundamental abstraction that bridges the gap between the domain of the circuit designer (whose primitive elements are electronic components) and that of the computer architect.

## 1.1 Information and the Digital Abstraction

The primary use of electronic devices is the processing of information. Major appliances such as televisions and computers serve to translate information from one format to another—from an encoded radio frequency input to an output picture, or from a string of input symbols to a corresponding string of output symbols. Each such complex information processor is synthesized from components that transform, combine, store, and manipulate representations of information. Thus we can dissect a television and identify the information-processing functions of its major subsystems, specifying the way in which the input and output information of each is encoded into electronic signals. We might further scrutinize each subsystem, documenting the function performed by each component in information-handling terms, down to the level of fundamental circuit elements.

A capacitor, for example, is an energy storage device; in typical applications, its stored energy may be viewed as the electronic representation of stored information (such as elapsed time, in an RC timer circuit).[1]   While the electronic representations of information in a television typically involve continuous variables (such as voltages or frequencies), the symbolic information processed by a computer consists of discrete units such as binary digits.

Digital systems, in general, are based on technology for the electronic representation of discrete information units; they offer the important advantage that the information content of each electronic signal is easy to quantify. They illustrate a powerful and important engineering principle: the pursuit of simplicity through constraint. Digital engineering involves a self-imposed design discipline that allows systems to be analyzed in the simple, abstract domain of logic rather than the vastly more complicated domain of underlying electronic principles. The advantages and mechanism of this abstraction are explored briefly in the following paragraphs.

The amount of information carried in a discrete-valued signal $s$ may be defined as $\log_2 N_v$, where $N_v$ is the number of distinct values of $s$ that can be reliably set and measured. It is conventional to take the logarithm in base 2 and express the result in *bits*, or binary digits, of information. We might propose, for example, to communicate each decimal digit $d$ by means of a $d$-volt signal on a particular wire, so that $N_v$ is 10. If our measurement technology is accurate enough to distinguish reliably between the ten values, the information conveyed by each signal is $\log_2 10 = 3.322$ bits. If our measurement tells us only whether or not the

---

[1] There are situations in which this view is inappropriate, such as applications in which a capacitor is used as a storage medium for energy to power other devices.

signal is below 5 V, however, $N_v$ is 2 and the amount of information conveyed is $\log_2 2$ or 1 bit.

A single bit is the minimum amount of information necessary to distinguish reliably between two values; it is the smallest convenient quantum for discrete information representations and serves as the basic unit of information storage and communication in most digital systems. It is noteworthy that 1 bit is exactly the information content of a single digit in a binary number system, which makes binary (rather than, say, decimal) an attractive and popular choice for the representation of numbers in digital systems.

Electronic parameters such as voltages are, to a good first approximation, continuous variables; we quantify them by real numbers rather than by integers. Each such parameter can in theory assume infinitely many distinct values, even over a bounded range; a voltage between 0 and 1 V may be 0.23 V or 0.6713 V or 0.6713456278 V. If we were able to set and measure such a voltage exactly, it would carry an infinite amount of information (since $N_v$ would be infinite). Of course, noise and other physical realities limit our ability to constrain and measure physical parameters. A measurement of 0.23 V indicates that 0.23 V is a more likely value than, say, 0.3 V, which in turn is more likely than 0.4 V. The actual amount of information conveyed by our measurement is awkward to quantify exactly; it depends on the accuracy and reliability characteristics of the measuring device as well as electrical noise and other detriments to the validity of the signal itself. A typical signal level might carry 10 or 12 bits of useful information, on the average, with moderate reliability. Such representations are ideally suited to applications (such as television) involving large volumes of information flow and in which occasional errors are not catastrophic. The synthesis and analysis techniques used in these situations typically assume that each signal represents the corresponding real number to an acceptable accuracy, thus avoiding the need for precise quantification of its information content.

## 1.2 Representation of Discrete Variables

In many applications, it is convenient to use components whose behavior can be simply and precisely characterized in informational terms. A printer device connected to a computer can take as input the representation of a character to be printed, from an alphabet of, say, 128 possible characters. We would like the communication from the computer to the printer to be highly reliable: The printer must be able to determine precisely the character to be printed from the signals it receives. The amount of information conveyed to the printer is thus $\log_2 128 = 7$ bits for each character printed. The communication technique used will of course involve wires carrying continuously variable signals (such as voltages), but to reach our reliability goals we may be willing to sacrifice much of the information-carrying potential of each signal. A typical *parallel* printer interface, for example, involves seven independent wires, each carrying 1 bit of information encoded as a voltage. Each wire selects one of two alternative values (say, a 1 or 0 as the value of a corresponding binary digit), and the seven-wire aggregate thus identifies one of

$2^7 = 128$ possible characters.

The reliable translation between a discrete variable such as a binary digit and its representation as the approximate value of a continuous variable such as a voltage provides the key to what we call the *digital abstraction*. It allows us to use conventional circuit elements to build a family of *digital devices* whose information-processing characteristics can be specified as a simple logical function involving discrete inputs and outputs.

## 1.3 Combinational Devices

The simplest and most fundamental abstraction in the repertoire of the digital engineer is the *combinational device*, which we formalize as follows:

. . . . . . . . . . . . . . . . . . . . . . . . . . . . . . . . . . . . . . . . . . . . . . . . . . . . . . . .

*A **combinational device*** is a circuit element having the following properties:

- one or more discrete-valued *input* terminals;
- one or more discrete-valued *output* terminals;
- a *functional specification*, detailing the value of each output for each of the possible combinations of input values; and
- a *timing specification*, consisting (at minimum) of an upper bound $t_{\mathrm{pd}}$ on the time required for the device to compute the specified output values from an arbitrary set of input values.

. . . . . . . . . . . . . . . . . . . . . . . . . . . . . . . . . . . . . . . . . . . . . . . . . . . . . . . .

The usual interpretation of the *propagation delay* $t_{\mathrm{pd}}$ is that whenever a particular combination of input values is applied to the device and maintained for at least $t_{\mathrm{pd}}$ seconds, a corresponding set of output values will appear. Moreover, these output values will remain at the output terminals (at least) until the inputs change. Thus a set of input values applied for $t$ seconds results in corresponding output values for a period of at least $t - t_{\mathrm{pd}}$ seconds. Note that $t_{\mathrm{pd}}$ is a *maximum* time required for new input values to be reflected at the output terminals; in general, the *minimum* such time is assumed to be zero.[2] One result of the latter assumption is that output values are contaminated immediately by any change at the inputs, regardless of $t_{\mathrm{pd}}$.

An important feature of combinational devices is the simplicity with which they may be interconnected to synthesize new combinational functions. In particular, new combinational devices may be created by combining combinational elements in acyclic circuits, so long as care is taken not to connect outputs together.

More precisely, we can construct a combinational device by exploiting the basic rule of composition:

---

[2] A refinement of this assumption, in which a nonzero *contamination delay* becomes part of the device specification, is occasionally used in the design of performance-critical circuitry.

*The Digital Abstraction*

***Combinational composition***    A circuit is a combinational device if it consists of interconnected circuit elements such that

- each circuit element is itself combinational,

- every node of the circuit is either designated as an input to the circuit or connects to exactly one output terminal of a circuit element, and

- the circuit contains no directed cycles (that is, every path through the circuit that traverses elements only in the input-to-output direction visits each circuit node at most once).

Any of the circuit nodes may be designated as outputs of the new device.

It is easy to verify that this construction yields devices that conform to our combinational criteria. The acyclic constraint allows us to proceed systematically from the circuit's input terminals through successive circuit elements, assigning to each node both a functional specification (as a function of the input values) and a time bound. The functional specification of each noninput node is derived from the specification of the element driving that node together with the functional specification assigned to that element's inputs; similarly, the propagation delay associated with such a node is computed by adding the element's $t_{\mathrm{pd}}$ to the maximum of the delays associated with its input nodes. In general, $t_{\mathrm{pd}}$ for the constructed device becomes the *maximum* cumulative propagation delay encountered on a path from any input to any output.

## 1.4 The Static Discipline: Logic Levels

The fact that we can synthesize arbitrarily complicated combinational devices using acyclic circuits of combinational elements gives us a bootstrapping technique for extending the usefulness of a primitive initial set of such devices; this is vaguely analogous to the induction step of an inductive proof. A remaining task is the development of a basis—an initial set of combinational elements from which we can synthesize more ambitious ones. Clearly we must begin with at least one combinational device that is defined in terms of technologies other than combinational devices. It is in the design of these basic elements that fundamental decisions regarding the representation of the discrete values of our abstraction are confronted.

Suppose, for example, that we are to represent a binary (or *logical*) variable $d$ using a voltage $v$ that can be varied between 0 and 5 V. We might choose to represent $d = 0$ by a voltage of 0 and $d = 1$ by 5 V. The efficacy of this representation then depends on our ability to set and measure $v$ with sufficient reliability that the representation of $d = 0$ is never mistaken for the representation of $d = 1$ and vice versa, a reasonably easy demand to meet. We can afford to be fairly sloppy about setting and measuring $v$ and still deduce the correct value of $d$. If we guarantee that $v$ will be set to a value below 1 V when $d = 0$ and above

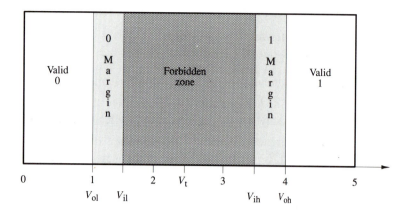

**Figure 1.1** Mapping of logic levels to voltage.

4 V when $d = 1$, and if we ensure that our measurement of $v$ will be accurate to within 0.5 V, we shall always measure a voltage greater than 3.5 V when $d = 1$ and below 1.5 V when $d = 0$. We might distinguish between the two cases by comparing the measured voltage with a 2.5-V threshold voltage $V_t$ and assuming a logical 1 as the value of $d$ if the measured value is above the threshold and a logical 0 if it is below.

Figure 1.1 shows the mapping of the continuous variable $v$ onto the discrete (binary digit) $d$. If the measured voltage is near or at the 2.5-V threshold, we will be unable to distinguish reliably between the two values of $d$. We avoid this embarrassing circumstance by outlawing it; we designate the region between 1.5 V and 3.5 V as a *forbidden zone* that does not correspond to the valid representation of a binary variable. Since we can reliably discriminate between voltages below 1.5 V and those above 3.5 V, adhering to the discipline that $v$ must be set above 4 V or below 1 V ensures that forbidden values are avoided. In fact, we have allowed an extra half-volt margin for error on each side of the forbidden zone; these *noise margins* allow our scheme to function in the presence of a certain amount of noise or other unanticipated error.

In general, the reliable representation of discrete variables using continuously variable physical quantities requires such ranges of excluded values between valid representations. This gives rise to the possibility of *invalid signals* that correspond to none of the logical values; a wire carrying $V_t$ represents neither a logical 1 nor a logical 0 by the convention outlined above. Such invalid signals are foreign to the digital abstraction and are unaccounted for in the analysis and synthesis methodologies commonly used by the digital engineer.

In order to protect digital designers from unanticipated invalid signals in their circuits, logic elements are commonly designed to conform to a *static discipline*:

.........................................................

*A **static discipline*** is a guarantee that, given logically valid inputs, every circuit element will (after an appropriate propagation delay) deliver logically valid outputs.

.........................................................

The interpretation of "logically valid" is relative to a particular representation convention, which in turn varies with the implementation technology. Typically, however, a single representation convention applies throughout an entire digital system. A static discipline offers a measure of assurance that invalid signals will not arise spontaneously in a well-designed combinational circuit: If the inputs to each device are well behaved, each device's outputs will also be well behaved after some bounded delay.

Noise margins amount to imposing a more stringent validity requirement on output signals from a device than apply to its inputs, ensuring that marginally valid input signals are restored to unquestionable signals at the output. The threshold $V_{il}$ represents the highest input voltage that must be interpreted as a logical 0; it is higher than $V_{ol}$, the highest output voltage that can be asserted to indicate a 0. This ensures that every valid output 0 will be interpreted as a 0 at connected inputs, even after some degradation. A similar relationship holds between $V_{ih}$ (the lowest input representing a valid 1) and $V_{oh}$ (the lowest output asserted to indicate a 1).

## 1.5 Rate of Information Flow

The representation scheme we have developed provides for the *static* transmission of a fixed amount of information—a single bit—as an electric signal over a wire. In general, we expect this value to change from time to time; if it *never* changes, as would occur if the value communicated is a constant, the need for the wire should be questioned! Thus, while at any instant a signal might convey only a single bit of information, it typically carries a *sequence* of bits over a period of time. If we make provisions for changing a signal to represent a new bit of information every second on the second, that signal may be viewed as carrying a *flow* of information at the rate of 1 bit/s; it could be used to transmit a 100-bit binary number in 100 s.

Any scheme we choose for communicating discrete variables places practical limits on the frequency with which we can change their values and thereby constrains the rate of information flow. Rates of information flow in digital systems are often specified in *baud*, or value transitions per second, a parameter that is constrained by the communication *bandwidth* of the underlying (analog) communication medium. A fundamental theorem by Nyquist places an upper bound on a communication channel's useful baud rate of twice its bandwidth, even in the absence of noise. In the case of binary representations, where each value is a binary digit, 1 baud is equivalent to 1 bit/s. Thus the theoretical maximum rate of information flow over a 3000-Hz voice-grade line carrying binary values as two different voltage levels is 6000 bits/s. This limit can be exceeded, in theory, by the use of more than two discrete values at a baud rate of less than 3000 changes per second; using four voltages, for example, raises the theoretical limit of our voice-grade line to 12,000 bits/s.

Of course, the effective rate of information flow can always be increased by using multiple signals; a 100-bit number can be transmitted in 1 s *serially* using a single 100-baud binary signal or *in parallel* by means of a hundred 1-baud binary signals, each encoding a single digit. Such choices are faced frequently by designers of digital systems, and a judgment typically depends strongly on underlying technological issues. For example, digital communication between geographically distant subsystems, such as terminals of an airline's flight reservation system, might rely on leased telephone lines whose bandwidth characteristics limit transmitted signals to audio frequencies. Reliable digital communication over such a line is limited to a few thousand baud, but increasing the communication rate by using multiple lines is expensive. Since communication cost is likely to be a dominant factor in the design of such systems, it is worthwhile devoting considerable effort to minimizing the required communication rates.

Even in localized systems, communication costs are an important design consideration. As logic elements become cheaper and perform more complex functions, the cost of running wires (or other media) to interconnect them becomes an increasingly important element of system costs. Although nearby modules of a system can communicate at rates measured in hundreds of megabaud by using many parallel wires, such high bandwidth is expensive in device terminals and interconnections and is not to be squandered. Even within a single integrated-circuit chip, where the economies are based largely on space (chip area), interconnection costs often dominate: More of the chip area is devoted to lines transmitting signals from one logic element to another than to the logic elements themselves.

## 1.6 Transitions and Validity

In a dynamic system, where logical variables change in value from time to time, we cannot in practice avoid brief excursions through the forbidden zone. Because of stray capacitance and other such physical constraints, the voltage representing a logical variable $v$ cannot be changed instantaneously from one valid logic representation to the other, although the transition may be quite fast—a few nanoseconds is typical.

We therefore enforce on ourselves an additional discipline: We avoid asking whether $v$ represents a logical 1 or 0 at about the time when it may be making a transition between values. This in turn requires that the beholders of $v$—those devices to which $v$ is an input—each have available information about when $v$ might change. Most commonly this requirement is met by constructing *synchronous systems*, in which logic values are constrained to make transitions only at prescribed times (for example, every microsecond on the microsecond) keyed to a globally available clock signal. For truly asynchronous systems, it is impossible to guarantee that no logic level will be sampled at an inauspicious time (for example, during a transition); however, such events can be made quite improbable in practice. This general topic is visited again in section 4.5.2.

*The Digital Abstraction*

## 1.7  Logic Families

Some of the parameters in figure 1.1 seem arbitrary. The association of low voltage with logical 0 and high voltage with logical 1 is a convention termed *positive logic*; the dual convention, *negative logic*, represents logical 0 by the higher of the two voltages. This choice may be made arbitrarily to suit one's taste; a digital system can be analyzed in terms of positive logic, negative logic, or a mixture of the two.

Other parameters, such as the choice of logically valid voltage ranges and threshold voltages, typically reflect a combination of design goals and characteristics of the implementation technology. Several distinct "families" of digital devices have been developed over the years, each with its own set of characteristics and parameters for mapping continuous electronic variables (usually voltage) onto logic (nearly always binary) values. Each such family includes a set of rules for the valid representation of logical values; each device in the family has the property that, so long as its inputs obey the rules, its outputs will also. They provide in each case a set of Tinkertoy-like modules that can be simply plugged together to build arbitrarily complex logical systems, with relative disregard for the underlying electronics. The resulting simplicity is an enormous advantage to the designer, who can deal with the concise logical characterization of devices whose specification in electrical terms would be nearly intractable.

## 1.8  Digital-Circuit Implementation

Figure 1.2(a) depicts a simple logic device from an early implementation technology called *resistor-transistor logic*, or RTL. The device is an *inverter*; its logical output at $C$ is 1 if its input (at $A$) is 0, and 0 if its input is 1. The transistor in the circuit of figure 1.2(b) may be viewed roughly as a switch controlled by its base (input) current, which in turn depends on the voltage at $A$. If the voltage at input $A$ is high (representing, using positive logic, a logical 1 input), then the switch is closed (the collector and emitter are short-circuited) and the output $C$ is effectively connected to ground (yielding a logical 0 output). If the input voltage is close to 0 (logical 0 input), the switch is open, leaving $C$ connected to the supply voltage $V_{CC}$ through a small resistor; this results in a logical 1 output.

### 1.8.1  Logic Levels and Noise

A slightly more sophisticated model of the transistor yields the voltage-transfer characteristics shown in figure 1.3 for our simple inverter.

Over a portion of its input-voltage range, the device behaves like an amplifier with a negative gain (proportional to the slope of the center segment of the plot). This is termed the *active* or *linear* region of operation. When the input voltage is sufficiently low, the transistor is said to be at *cutoff* and effectively presents an open circuit between its emitter and collector. When the input voltage is sufficiently high, the transistor becomes *saturated* and effectively short-circuits its emitter to its collector. Details of the sizes of each region of operation (cutoff, active, and saturation) and the exact placement of the "knees" of the transfer characteristic

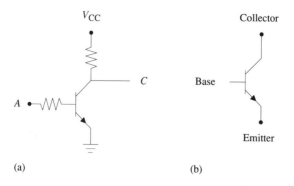

**Figure 1.2**  Resistor-transistor logic: (a) RTL inverter; (b) NPN transistor.

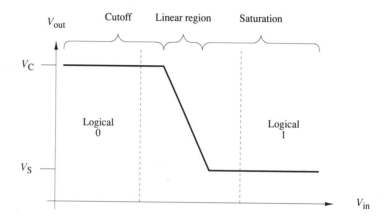

**Figure 1.3**  Voltage-transfer characteristics of an RTL inverter.

depend on parameters of the transistor (such as its gain) as well as on values of the resistors in the device. The ranges of voltages specified for valid logic levels of 0 and 1, in turn, reflect these details and hence constrain their choice.

It is important, for example, that the design parameters be such that a valid logic level at the input places the transistor either in the cutoff or saturation region of operation; this avoidance of the active region guarantees reliable performance in the presence of noise. In its active region, the circuit behaves like an amplifier with high gain; if, for example, a valid logical 1 at the input to the device biases the transistor into its linear region, it will amplify small perturbations of the input. Thus a 10-mV noise spike at the input might (assuming a gain of 10) become an 0.1-V noise spike at the output, as sketched in figure 1.4.

The output signal presumably connects to the input of other devices, where its noise component may be amplified further, until the resulting voltages become invalid representations of logic values.

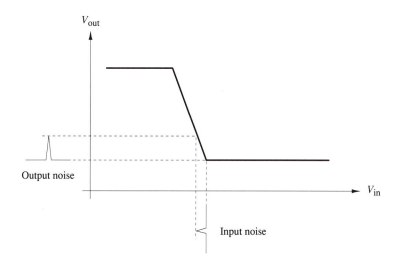

**Figure 1.4** Amplification of a noise spike.

Thus we constrain input voltages representing valid logic values to fall well within the cutoff and saturation regions, where the output voltage will be relatively insensitive to small perturbations of the input. In general, we leave a gap between each range of valid logic levels and the active region of the transistor in order to provide noise margins.

In the RTL logic family, the standard supply voltage $V_{CC}$ is 3.6 V. Valid logical 0 must be below 1 V, and logical 1 must be above 2.5 V; the resulting noise margins are each about 0.5 V.

### 1.8.2 Fanout Restrictions

It is necessary to define the valid logic levels so as to include the device's output values when it has logically valid inputs. Having insisted that valid inputs will result in either saturated or cutoff transistor behavior, we find that this reduces to a requirement that the cutoff output voltage $V_C$ and the saturation output voltage $V_S$ be included as valid logical 1 and 0 levels, respectively.

Unfortunately, the characteristic plotted in figure 1.3 oversimplifies the behavior of our device in several ways. One of these is the assumption, made for the purposes of the preceding discussion, that the load on the output of the device imposed by external devices connected to terminal $C$ is negligible. In fact, the voltage drops across the collector resistor and the transistor itself are functions of the output current; the effect of a heavy load on the output of the inverter is, roughly, to move the cutoff voltage $V_C$ and the saturation voltage $V_S$ toward each other and hence toward the forbidden zone between valid logic representations. As a result of this effect, each family of logic implementations imposes a restriction on the number of device inputs to which each device output can be connected; this is called the *fanout* limitation. In the case of RTL, device fanout is only about 5. This is primarily due to the voltage drop across the collector resistor while the

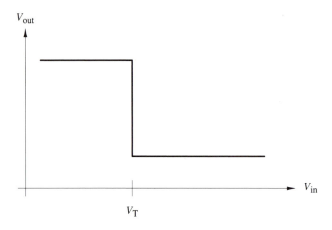

**Figure 1.5** Ultra-high-gain switching device.

transistor is at cutoff (in the logical 1 state), which lowers the output voltage as the fanout (and hence the output current) is increased.

### 1.8.3 Nonlinearities and Gain

We have seen that the continuous range of voltages between minimum (zero or ground, in our example) and maximum (the supply voltage $V_{CC}$) is divided into several regions: The valid logic levels are at the extremes, a forbidden zone occupies the center portion, and the remaining two gaps constitute the noise margins. It is generally desirable to center the forbidden zone between the valid logic levels, yielding comparable noise margins for logical 0 and 1 values; it is the *minimum* of the noise margins that dictates the maximum tolerable electrical noise level for a logic family.

The reader may have noticed that the active region of the transistor, which constitutes its useful range in linear applications (such as in a high-fidelity amplifier) is a positive annoyance in digital applications. The fact that it must be avoided in the assignment of valid logic levels motivates us to minimize its size, thereby allowing more freedom to assign logic levels and noise margins. From this standpoint, an ideal transistor for digital purposes has an infinitesimal linear region, as depicted in figure 1.5.

In this hypothetical device, the linear range is reduced to a vertical line, corresponding to a (negative) infinite gain at a single threshold voltage $V_T$.

The gain of active elements such as transistors plays a crucial role in digital logic, in that it allows a device with marginally valid input levels to produce output levels that are well within the valid ranges. It is possible to build logic devices using only passive devices such as diodes or even resistors, but the outputs of such devices will in general be closer to the forbidden zone than the inputs. Hence a logic signal passing through several such devices will gradually deteriorate until it is no longer valid. A passive device fails to guarantee that every valid input produces a valid

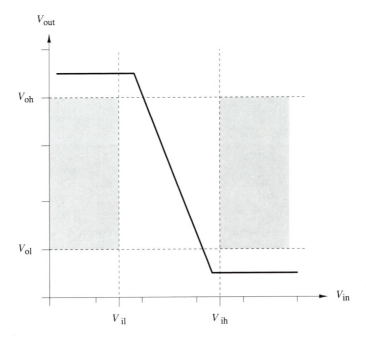

**Figure 1.6** Forbidden $V_{\text{in}}$-$V_{\text{out}}$ regions.

output; one can always find a marginally valid input value for which the output value is forbidden. Such a device fails to meet the static discipline unless the validity standards applied to its output signals are less rigorous than those applied to its inputs.

In order to apply a set of validity constraints such as those depicted in figure 1.1 uniformly to both inputs and outputs of a combinational device, we need an active device exhibiting both gain and nonlinearity.

Consider figure 1.6, which shows the static voltage-transfer curve of an inverter. The shaded regions of the diagram represent valid inputs that generate invalid outputs and are excluded by the static discipline. Consequently, the transfer curve of the inverter must enter the center rectangle at the top and leave it at the bottom, in order to constrain invalid outputs to occur only on invalid inputs. Since the width $V_{\text{ih}} - V_{\text{il}}$ of this rectangle is less than its height $V_{\text{oh}} - V_{\text{ol}}$ by the sum of the noise margins, the slope of the transfer characteristic—hence the gain—must be greater than 1 (in magnitude) over this center section of the curve. Moreover, since the difference between the maximum and minimum input values is at least as great as the difference between the maximum and minimum output values, the *average* gain over the entire transfer curve is at most 1; this implies that the gain outside of the central forbidden region must be less than 1. Thus differing slopes are required along various regions of the transfer characteristic, dictating a nonlinear input/output relationship.

These considerations lead us to the inescapable conclusion that only *nonlinear*

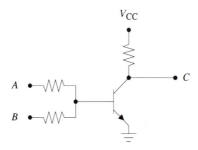

**Figure 1.7** Inferior RTL NOR gate.

devices are suitable for the implementation of logic families. Linear devices, whose DC gain is constant over their entire operating range, will result in logic elements that fail to meet the static discipline for certain values.

Passive and linear devices are occasionally used to perform logic functions, although this practice requires that active ("restoring") logic elements be interspersed to restore marginal signals to valid logic values. This technique amounts to a change of logic-level representations between the inputs to a device and its outputs, choosing in the latter case an ad hoc representation that accommodates the signal deterioration imposed by the device (such as lower signal levels due to low gain).

### 1.8.4 Input Gating

A logic family must provide devices that effect logical functions of several input variables. Devices that combine logical values in elementary ways are often called *gates*, a name that stems from the early days of switching theory. As the name suggests, gating can be viewed as a mechanism by which one logical signal can be blocked or passed, depending on the value of another signal.

In the RTL family, the simplest such device to implement is the two-input *NOR gate*. This device has the property that its output is a logical 0 (using positive logic) if either or both of its inputs are logical 1s; its output is 1 if and only if both inputs are 0s. An early implementation strategy for such devices used resistors to take a linear combination of the two input voltages and directed the result to a transistor with a strategically placed active region. Figure 1.7 shows such a circuit, and figure 1.8 shows a plausible voltage-transfer characteristic.

Note that the input circuitry (resistors) produces a weighted sum of the input voltages; the weights are made equal because of the symmetry of the operands to the logical NOR function. The effect is to select the transistor's input from one of three equally spaced values, corresponding to input combinations containing zero, one, or two logical 1s, respectively.

This implementation strategy is an example of *threshold logic*, in which a logic function is computed by comparison of a weighted sum of binary inputs against a fixed threshold value. The inherent weakness of this approach stems from the way

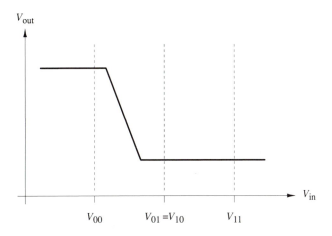

**Figure 1.8** NOR gate voltage-transfer characteristic.

that *fanin*, or number of inputs, compromises its noise-immunity characteristics. Referring to figure 1.8, we note that the transistor now has three valid input ranges rather than two; there is consequently less room between any two of them to squeeze both the forbidden zone (including the active transistor region) and noise margins. As the number of inputs is increased, the problem clearly gets worse, until the fundamental limit is reached in which pairs of distinct linear combinations of valid inputs are separated by less than the active range of the transistor. Primarily as a result of these considerations, the NOR gate implementation shown in figure 1.7 was abandoned early in the history of RTL.

The problem with this circuit stems from its use of linear circuit elements—namely resistors—to combine logic values. Although it was resolved in the case of RTL by moving from *input gating* (in which transistor inputs are combined) to the *output gating* strategy described in the next section, modern logic families use input gating extensively. The difference is that they use nonlinear circuit elements to combine the inputs. Diode-transistor logic (DTL) uses input diodes to effect logic functions, and the popular transistor-transistor logic (TTL) families use multiemitter transistors to perform input gating. It should be noted that input gating typically involves passive devices such as diodes or resistors and hence must be followed by an active "restoring" device to ensure unambiguous output values despite possibly marginal inputs.

### 1.8.5 Output Gating: Wired-OR

An alternative implementation of multi-input RTL gates is shown in figure 1.9. This circuit has noise characteristics similar to those of the inverter of figure 1.2, since the inputs are combined by the nonlinear output transistors rather than by the linear input resistors. A reasonable understanding of its operation may be obtained by viewing the transistors as switches connected in parallel, so that either or both

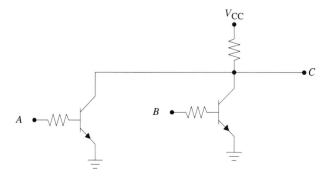

**Figure 1.9**  Improved RTL NOR gate.

switches being closed effectively connects the output $C$ to ground. While there are second-order effects that limit potential fanin with this approach, they are much less serious than those inherent in threshold logic techniques.

The NOR circuit of figure 1.9 differs only slightly from the result of connecting the outputs of two RTL inverters together; the difference is simply a reduction of the collector resistance in the latter case. In fact, the interconnection of outputs is common practice when using RTL and certain other amenable logic families. The technique has come to be known as *wired-OR*, although in the present case (RTL positive logic) *wired-AND* would be a more appropriate term. Thus two RTL logic levels $A$ and $B$, each the output of some RTL device, can be simply wired together to yield their logical conjunction $A$ AND $B$ (or $AB$, using the usual Boolean algebraic notation).

There are, of course, limits to the number of outputs that can be wired together. If $n$ RTL 1 levels are connected to a single RTL 0 level, for example, then one saturated transistor must carry the sum of the currents flowing through the $n + 1$ collector resistors. This increased current not only degrades the output voltage (moves it closer to the forbidden zone) but may, for sufficiently large $n$, approach the current limits of the output transistor.

### 1.8.6 Timing Considerations

If we use a rectangular voltage waveform such as the $V_{in}$ in figure 1.10 as input to an inverter, we are likely to observe an output waveform similar to that plotted as $V_{out}$.

We notice first that, in contrast to the "ideal" rectangular shape of the $V_{in}$ curve, the corners of the output waveform have become rounded and the rising and falling edges are not vertical. These effects reflect fundamental physical properties, such as capacitive effects, of the device. In order to make a transition between the valid logic levels, electrical charge must be moved—for example, to and from transistor junctions. This motion of charge constitutes work (in the sense of physics), and since we are constrained to apply finite power to the device, the transitions require finite amounts of time. While very fast logic families such as emitter-coupled

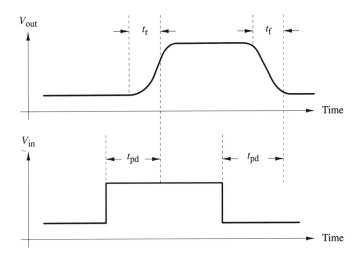

**Figure 1.10** Signal timing.

logic (ECL) attempt to minimize the amounts of stored charge to be moved and maximize the amount of power used to move it, in practice transitions between valid logic levels are not instantaneous. The time $t_r$ taken for a transition from low to high logic level is called *rise time*, and the time $t_f$ for the reverse transition is called *fall time*. Typical rise and fall times are measured in very small numbers of nanoseconds. They are dependent not only on the technology of particular logic families, but on the load placed on particular signals; higher load tends to add capacitance and hence prolong transitions. A pleasant characteristic of rise and fall times is their resistance to accumulation as a signal passes through a number of cascaded logic devices. Thus the waveform at the end of a long string of series-connected inverters will have rise and fall times similar to that of a single inverter. This is attributable to the high gains of the transistors, each of which tends to increase the slope of its input transitions.

The output waveform is delayed from the input by an approximately constant interval, corresponding to the propagation delay $t_{pd}$ of the device. This delay also reflects the time necessary for the motion of charge that accompanies transitions and is thus closely related to the rise and fall times. However, propagation delay *does* accumulate through cascaded devices. Thus, if the propagation delay of an RTL inverter is 12 ns, the output of $n$ series-connected inverters will be delayed (with respect to its input) by $12n$ ns. Of course, the output will be inverted if $n$ is odd and will be a delayed replica of the input if $n$ is even. Propagation delay is an important characteristic of digital devices, leading ultimately to performance limitations (in the sense of the number of computations that can be executed per unit of time) in complex digital systems.

### 1.8.7 Propagation and Contamination Delays

The delay involved in a complex digital computation is typically determined by the *longest* time necessary for signals to propagate from the inputs of a system to its outputs. As a consequence, digital designers often compute the total propagation delay along each signal path (adding the delays of each device it includes) to determine the limiting *critical path* of information flow. The usefulness of $t_{pd}$ specifications for component devices, then, stems from their validity as an *upper bound* on the delay of data through each device: System designers need a guarantee that the time taken by signals to propagate along each path is no longer than the value they compute from device specifications. An overly conservative $t_{pd}$ specification may cause a system to be designed for suboptimal performance, but it will operate as its designer predicts; an optimistic $t_{pd}$ specification is likely to cause faulty operation. To optimize performance, it is valuable to have the tightest possible bounds on propagation delays in order to know precisely when signals are valid; however, we must insist that these bounds be conservative.

Very aggressive designs sometimes require us to pin down signal validity periods even more precisely. Glancing back at figure 1.10, we note that the output voltage remains in a logically valid range for a brief period after the input changes; this reflects our acceptance of a *range* of valid voltages as well as the physical propagation time of the leading edge of the input signal. This delay represents an additional period of output signal validity that can be exploited in carefully engineered designs: A designer might assume that the output of a gate remains valid for a nanosecond or two *after* its input changes, in contrast to the more conservative assumption that output validity is immediately corrupted by an input change. To facilitate such highly engineered designs, the specification of a combinational device might include, in addition to the usual propagation delay $t_{pd}$, a *contamination delay $t_{cd}$*.[3] The contamination delay of a combinational device is the minimum interval following an input change during which the validity of previous outputs is guaranteed to remain intact.

While $t_{pd}$ is an *upper* bound on a period of output *invalidity*, $t_{cd}$ is a *lower* bound on a period of output *validity*. Like propagation delay, the contamination delay specifications must be conservative; however, a conservative $t_{cd}$ is *smaller* than necessary, whereas a conservative $t_{pd}$ is *larger* than necessary. Like propagation delays, contamination delays can be specified independently for each input-to-output path of a device. The contamination delay between an input-output pair reflects the *fastest* path between that input and output; the propagation delay reflects the *slowest* path. The contamination delay is always less than the corresponding propagation delay; typically, it is much less.

Designs that substantively exploit nonzero contamination delays are rare, and for good reason. Squeezing the last nanosecond out of a path requires painstaking timing analysis and effectively returns the engineer to the analog domain of

---

[3] Contamination delays are occasionally referred to as *minimum* propagation delays, which is misleading. Propagation and contamination generally happen at different times, contamination being earlier.

continuous variables and physical effects. It also tends to compromise system manufacturability by depending on subtle characteristics that are quite variable from device to device. Unless otherwise noted, we shall assume zero contamination delays throughout the remainder of this text.

### 1.8.8 Speed and Power

A major weakness of RTL stems from its use of a collector resistor (called a *pullup resistor*) to establish its high-voltage output level. First, this resistor limits collector current and hence prolongs the time necessary to charge stray capacitances associated with a low-to-high transition, yielding poor rise times and consequently high propagation delays. Second, it provides a substantially poorer path for current flow to $V_{CC}$ than a saturated transistor provides to ground; hence it introduces an asymmetry between the rise and fall times of the device.

Adjustments in the value of the pullup resistor affect both the switching speed and the power dissipated by the gate. For a resistance $R$ and total stray capacitance $C$, the switching times are on the order of $RC$ seconds; hence halving the value of the pullup resistor speeds up the device. However, the power dissipated by the resistor on a low-voltage output is roughly

$$P = \frac{(V_{CC})^2}{R}.$$

Thus the product of the switching time and the power dissipation, often cited as the *speed-power product*, is relatively independent of the value of $R$ and is approximately constant for a particular logic family or implementation strategy. Speed and power dissipation are important parameters in digital-system design decisions, and the speed-power product is sometimes used as a measure of efficiency by which alternative families are compared.

The asymmetry between the resistive pullup and saturated transistor pulldown tends to make opposite-going transitions propagate at differing rates through RTL devices, yielding in effect separate propagation delays for rising and falling edges. Aside from its other disadvantages, this disparity complicates enormously the conceptual model of the devices necessary to use them effectively; in particular, it casts suspicious light on our lumping of propagation delay into a simple single parameter. Figure 1.11 illustrates the more symmetrical output circuitry used in TTL logic.

The two output transistors are stacked in a *totem-pole output* configuration, arranged so that valid output levels are asserted by one transistor being saturated while the other is cut off. When the $A$ input is low, the input transistor is cut off. As a result, the base of the upper (pullup) output transistor is pulled high and that transistor saturates, while the base of the lower (pulldown) output transistor is pulled low and that transistor is cut off. Consequently, the voltage at the output terminal $C$ rises close to the collector supply voltage $V_{CC}$. Conversely, when the $A$ input is high, the input transistor saturates. The bases of the two output transistors are effectively wired together and pulled to a low voltage by current going into the base of the pulldown transistor, which saturates. The diode in series with the

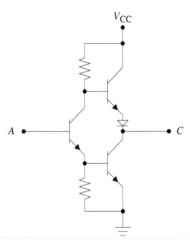

**Figure 1.11** Simplified TTL inverter.

pullup transistor's emitter causes the voltage at that emitter to be higher than the voltage at $C$ by the voltage drop across a conducting silicon diode (typically 0.7 V). As a result, the pullup transistor's emitter is at a high enough potential, relative to its base, that the transistor cuts off, and the voltage at $C$ drops to nearly zero.

Viewing the transistors as switches, we find that the circuit can provide a valid high output voltage if it connects $C$ to $V_{CC}$ about as definitively as it can short $C$ to ground to force it low. The passive resistive pullup of RTL logic has effectively been replaced by an active switch (transistor), resulting in a faster device with more similar rise and fall times.

A disadvantage of this scheme is that it rules out wired-OR interconnection of outputs, since the interconnection of a high to a low output would result in a low impedance path (through two saturated transistors) between $V_{CC}$ and ground. This constraint is partially alleviated by the availability of *three-state drivers* (often called *tristate drivers*), which feature a logic-level *enable* input. When *enable* carries a logical 1, the driver behaves as a normal TTL driver; when *enable* carries a logical 0, both of the totem-pole output transistors are cut off, leaving the output terminal floating. The symbol for a three-state driver is shown in figure 1.12. Several three-state outputs may be connected, so long as the logic that drives their enable inputs is designed to guarantee that at most one connected driver is enabled at any time. Of course, a line connected only to disabled three-state drivers is left floating and should generally be considered to carry an invalid logic level.

The goal of fast transitions dictates that the pair of totem-pole output transistors change between cutoff and saturation as nearly simultaneously as possible; thus there tends to be a brief period during each transition when both transistors are conducting. This in turn presents (momentarily) a nearly short-circuit path between $V_{CC}$ and ground, tending to generate annoying supply voltage spikes that can interfere with other logic devices sharing the same power supply. For this reason, it is common practice to proliferate small filtering capacitors in TTL designs to

*The Digital Abstraction*

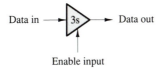

Data in → [3s] → Data out

Enable input

**Figure 1.12**  Three-state driver.

smooth out supply-voltage variations.

### 1.8.9 Saturation Charge

It has already been noted that electric charge stored in semiconductor junctions and stray capacitances requires both time and power to move, and hence limits the performance of digital circuits. This effect is due in large part to charge (and hence delay) associated with switching a transistor in and out of saturation. Several techniques have been developed to avoid delays stemming from *saturation charge*; in each case, output transistors remain in their active region rather than becoming saturated. This leads to faster switching times, generally at the cost of increased power consumption.

*Schottky TTL* is similar in design to (and compatible with) standard TTL, except for the incorporation of a very fast diode (a *Schottky diode*) between the base and collector of each transistor. This diode prevents the transistor from saturating and effectively provides nonlinearity at the low-voltage end of its voltage-transfer characteristic, but with greatly reduced charge storage.

*Emitter-coupled logic* (ECL) avoids nonlinearities at the saturation end of transistor voltage-transfer curves altogether. Instead, it combines input transistors with output transistors in such a way that either input or output transistors are cut off, thus using the relatively fast cutoff nonlinearities to stabilize both logical output values. This results in very fast switching times (on the order of a nanosecond) and ensures that each gate will provide some current path to ground at all times, thus increasing power dissipation.

### 1.8.10 Power and Density

The density at which logic gates can be packed onto a silicon chip is an important factor in both cost and performance. Integrated circuits that can be reliably manufactured involve a marginal production cost that is relatively independent of the complexity of the circuit they contain. Thus, to a first approximation, a small-scale integrated circuit containing a few dozen gates might have a price similar to that of a complete computer chip in high-volume production. Moreover, for a variety of reasons, electric signals take longer to propagate between chips than to propagate between gates on the same chip. Thus a complete single-chip computer is likely to outperform one that distributes the same technology among several chips, because of the increased interchip communication time. These and other factors have stimulated a strong push to increase the densities of integrated circuits; these

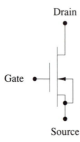

**Figure 1.13** n-channel FET.

have improved from the level of a few gates per chip in the mid-1960s to numbers in the hundreds of thousands by the late 1980s.

Density, however, is limited by several factors. Among these is the optical technology used to inscribe circuits on silicon, which limits (currently to a micron or so) the width of the on-chip lines that make up the circuit. Clearly the complexity of the basic gate design further limits the number of gates on a chip. Finally, the power consumed by each gate, coupled with the physical constraints on the amount of heat an integrated-circuit package can dissipate, is a fundamental limitation and provides a principal motivation for our concern with power dissipation as a parameter of gate technology.

Currently the highest densities are obtainable using *metal-oxide semiconductor* (MOS) technologies. The basic switching element in an MOS gate is a *field-effect transistor*, or FET, whose principal characteristic is its very high input impedance: An input to an FET draws virtually no current and hence consumes virtually no power. The combination of very low power consumption and a very simple gate design allows high densities and hence very complex functions on a single integrated circuit. Nearly all of the single-chip computers, for example, use MOS technologies.

MOS transistors, like bipolar ones, come in two polarities, called *n-channel* and *p-channel*, respectively. Figure 1.13 shows an n-channel FET. Note that it is a three-terminal device, which for our purposes can be viewed as a voltage-controlled switch. So long as the *drain* has a positive voltage with respect to the *source*, current flows from the drain to the source when the *gate* voltage is high (approaching the drain voltage) but not when the gate voltage is low (near the source voltage).

A common digital MOS technology—NMOS—uses n-channel FETs as the basic switching element. The basic NMOS gate (figure 1.14) is similar to the RTL gate, using a resistive pullup[4] and an active pulldown; the big difference between NMOS

---

[4] In fact, since resistors are very awkward to implement using NMOS technology, a fixed-bias *depletion-mode FET* is used as the pullup. To a good first approximation, the depletion-mode pullup may be viewed as a resistor.

*The Digital Abstraction*

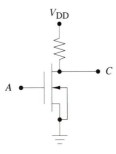

**Figure 1.14**   NMOS inverter.

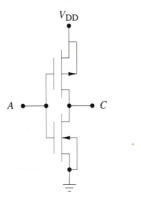

**Figure 1.15**   CMOS inverter.

and RTL gates is the much greater currents (and lower resistances) of the latter.

An MOS technology using active pullups, called *CMOS* (for complementary MOS), combines n- and p-channel FETs to form a gate with very low power dissipation. A CMOS gate may be viewed as two series-connected switches (similar to the totem-pole outputs of TTL), arranged so that one switch or the other is always open.

Thus a quiescent CMOS gate provides no path for current to flow between $V_{DD}$ and ground; furthermore, because of the high impedances of FET inputs, negligible amounts of current are drawn by other CMOS devices connected to its output. The result is that CMOS logic consumes very little power except during transitions, leading to a speed-power product several orders of magnitude better than those of other logic families. CMOS offers high noise immunity, allows a wide range of power-supply voltages, and is generally easy to design with; for these reasons, it has become the technology of choice for large-scale integrated circuits.

Each of the MOS technologies requires relatively complex buffers to interface the very-high-impedance MOS gates to external (off-chip) logic. As a result, they are generally used only for complex functions (such as calculator chips and microprocessors) where the number of external connections is small compared with the number of MOS gates involved.

## 1.9 Summary

The technology discussed in this chapter provides the basis for the fundamental abstraction of digital systems. It allows systems to be constructed by designers who are largely ignorant of the underlying electronics, who deal with the primitive elements (such as gates) strictly in the digital domain, and who agree to abide by the simple rules (such as fanout and synchrony) upon which we insist.

It should be emphasized that our goal has not been to deal seriously with the topic of logic gate design. Although the examples given were based on electronic implementations, the reader should recognize that the fundamental issues are not electronic; they apply equally to the realization of digital values as mechanical tension, fluid pressures, or any other continuously variable physical parameter. In each case nonlinearities, gain, and the "forbidden zone" will play essential roles. Each will involve speed-power trade-offs, noise, and propagation delays. An appreciation of the electronic details of the preceding examples is not essential to the understanding or even the effective design of digital systems; indeed, the degree of naivete they allow their users is precisely their value as an abstraction. It *is* important, however, to recognize the limits to the abstraction and the physical constraints from which they derive.

## 1.10 Context

The RTL and NMOS logic families were the progenitors of logic ICs (early 1960s) and VLSI (early 1970s), respectively, but each is now obsolete. Surviving families of off-the-shelf logic chips include ECL and the still ubiquitous TTL; the venerated *TTL Data Book* [TI 1984] will provide the uninitiated reader with a glimpse of the Tinkertoy-set world that has been available to the digital designer for a quarter century. Many contemporary textbooks on digital design, such as Hill and Peterson [1987], treat the subject of this and the following several chapters at a more detailed but still introductory level.

Logic implementation issues are treated in the context of NMOS technology in the classic Mead and Conway [1980], which precipitated something of a revolution by popularizing VLSI design beyond the engineering elite. Weste and Eshraghian [1985] perform a similar service for CMOS, the current vogue among custom chip design technologies.

*The Digital Abstraction*

### Problem 1.1  Logic Functions:

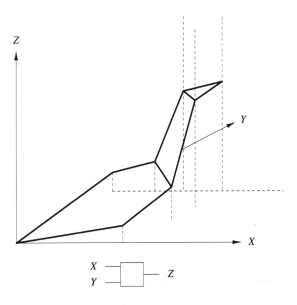

A. Using suitable values for valid logic levels and noise margins, what logic function does the device with the above transfer characteristic compute? Assume the convention of positive logic.

B. What function is computed by the above device if we assume negative logic?

### Problem 1.2  Base 3 Numbering:

*Ternary* is a term referring to the number system in base 3. Consider a convention in which a ternary digit is represented as an electric voltage between 0 and 10 V. Let 0–1 V represent a valid "0" output, 4–6 V a valid "1" output, and 9–10 V a valid "2" output.

A. Assuming noise margins 1 V wide, show the mapping of logic levels to voltages for this ternary system. Include valid logic-level outputs, noise margins, and forbidden zones. Your result should resemble figure 1.1.

B. Graph the transfer characteristic for a device capable of acting as a ternary logic *buffer*, that is, a device that produces at its output the same logic level present at its input, as shown below:

| IN | OUT |
|----|-----|
| 0  | 0   |
| 1  | 1   |
| 2  | 2   |

C. Can a device with the following transfer characteristic be used as a ternary logic buffer? Why or why not?

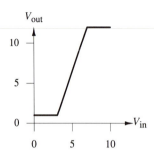

D. How many bits of information are carried in a ternary signal on a single wire?

E. How many different combinations of valid logic levels can be encoded on three ternary wires? How many bits of information does this represent? How many wires would be needed to carry this same amount of information in binary?

F. What is the information flow in bits per second for three ternary wires if a new set of values is sent every 10 ms?

G. What is the information flow in bits per second for three *binary* wires if a new set of values is sent every 10 ms?

## Problem 1.3  RTL Logic:

An RTL inverter circuit has the transfer characteristic diagrammed below:

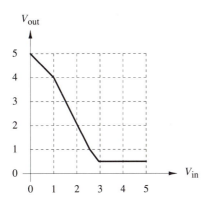

For suitable values of the threshold voltages $V_1$, $V_2$, $V_3$, and $V_4$ in the figure below, this RTL inverter obeys the static discipline.

| Valid 0 out | Noise margin | Forbidden zone | Noise margin | Valid 1 out |
|---|---|---|---|---|

0V    $V_1$         $V_2$                        $V_3$         $V_4$    5V

A. What is the smallest possible width for the forbidden zone (that is, what is the smallest possible value of $V_3 - V_2$) if the noise margins are each at least 0.5 V wide? Give values of $V_1$, $V_2$, $V_3$, and $V_4$ corresponding to this minimum width. Why can't the forbidden zone be made any smaller than this?

The above transfer characteristic is for an *unloaded* RTL inverter, that is, an inverter with no other logic circuits connected to its output. If other logic circuits are connected to this output, they will draw current from it and affect the shape of the transfer characteristic. Some of these altered transfer characteristics are shown below.

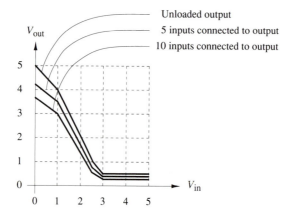

B. Pick threshold voltages $V_1$, $V_2$, $V_3$, and $V_4$, as before, so that the static discipline is obeyed where individual inverters have a fanout of no more than 5. In other words, the transfer curve of any individual inverter may be that of an unloaded inverter, or an inverter loaded with five logic inputs, or anywhere in between. Continue to allow noise margins of at least 0.5 V. Briefly explain the constraints on your selection (such as "$V_1$ cannot be greater than 2 V because...").

C. If the fanout of some inverters is increased to 10, is it still possible to pick $V_1$, $V_2$, $V_3$, and $V_4$ to allow noise margins of 0.5 V? Why or why not?

### Problem 1.4   Transfer Characteristics:

Is it possible to assign valid logic level and noise margin boundaries so that a device with the following transfer characteristic would serve as an inverter? Briefly explain your reasoning.

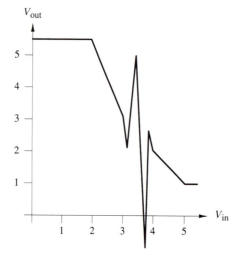

## Problem 1.5 Transfer Characteristics II:

Is it possible to assign valid logic levels and noise margin boundaries so that a device with the following transfer characteristic would serve as an inverter? Briefly explain your reasoning.

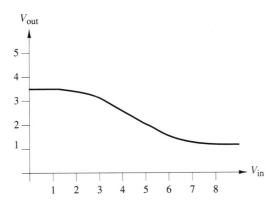

## Problem 1.6 Barracks Logic:

*Barracks logic* is built out of sleeping soldiers covered by electric blankets. Each blanket has a control switch with discrete control settings ranging in 5-degree (Fahrenheit) intervals from 0 to 50 degrees. The temperature of a soldier covered by one or more electric blankets will be the sum of the ambient temperature in the barracks plus the setting on the controller for each blanket.

Each soldier has a preferred sleeping temperature, which varies from individual to individual but is always within the range of 60 to 80 degrees, inclusive. If a soldier's temperature departs from his preferred temperature, he will wake up once every minute and adjust the control by one 5-degree increment in the direction he would like his temperature to be modified (if he is cold, he will increase the setting on his control, and vice versa). He will continue these adjustments by 5-degree increments until he once again reaches his preferred temperature (and goes to sleep) or runs out of settings (in which case he grumbles angrily in bed).

If every soldier is allowed to control his own blanket, each will soon reach his preferred temperature and slide into nocturnal bliss (assuming a suitable ambient temperature). The interesting aspects of barracks logic result from switching the controls of the various blankets to different soldiers. Inputs to the system are accomplished by placing a few controls in the hands of outsiders, and outputs are read from the control settings of certain soldiers designated by the logic designer.

A. Draw the graph of output control setting vs. input control setting for a typical soldier in steady state. Assume an ambient temperature of 40 degrees. Mark your graph with good choices of the valid regions for the two logical values, the forbidden zone, and the noise margins. Let logical 0 be when a control is completely off and logical 1 be when the control is completely on (or at the highest setting).

B. List some sources of noise that justify the need for noise margins.

C. Even though it is the middle of February, a sudden warm spell raises the ambient temperature in our barracks logic system to 55 degrees. Sketch a new graph of output control setting vs. input control setting in the warmer barracks.

D. Over what range of ambient temperatures will barracks logic function reliably?

E. Does the following arrangement perform a useful function? What is it?

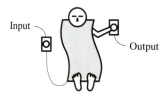

F. A model HOT-1 electric blanket control can power 1200 W of blankets. A model HOT-BED electric blanket requires 275 W. What is the fanout of a HOT-1? What might happen if this rating is exceeded? Is there more danger of exceeding the rating at an output value of logical 0 or logical 1?

G. To create a system with multiple inputs, we allow several blankets to be placed over a single soldier. What is the maximum fanin possible in barracks logic if 170 degrees is the highest temperature a soldier can tolerate without his characteristics being permanently altered?

H. Show how to build a NOR gate and an AND gate in barracks logic.

I. Explain what causes rise time, fall time, and propagation delay in barracks logic. Give worst-case numerical values for each of these parameters for the barracks logic inverter. (Let *rise time* be the time from when an output leaves the valid logical 0 range until it enters the valid logical 1 range, and vice versa for fall time. For propagation delay, use the time from when the input switches to a valid logic level to the time when the output switches to a valid logic level.)

## Problem 1.7

An inverter has propagation delay $t_d$ and rise time $t_r$. What is the propagation delay and rise time of three inverters connected in series?

## Problem 1.8

Consider a family of logic in which

$$
\begin{aligned}
V_{ol} &= 0.6 \text{ V}, \\
V_{oh} &= 2.8 \text{ V}, \\
V_{il} &= 1.0 \text{ V}, \\
V_{ih} &= 2.2 \text{ V}.
\end{aligned}
$$

A. How wide are the 0 and the 1 noise margins (in volts)?

B. What is the smallest average voltage gain that a buffer in this family must exhibit over the range $V_{il} < V_{in} < V_{ih}$? (Recall that a buffer is a combinational device that asserts on its output the same logical value that it senses at its input.)

## Problem 1.9

Consider a logic buffer (output logic value = input logic value) in a family of logic parameterized by the following mapping of voltages to logic levels:

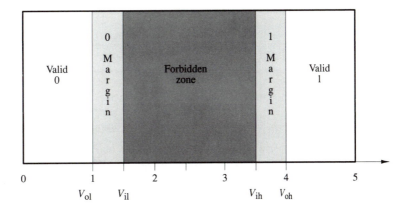

A. What is the minimum gain a *buffer* must exhibit over the forbidden zone in order to obey the static discipline with this convention?

B. Sketch the voltage-transfer characteristic of a buffer in this logic family.

C. Let $V_f$ be a voltage that, when applied to the inverter's input terminal, yields $V_f$ at the buffer's output. Give a range of possible values for $V_f$.

## Problem 1.10  *Propagation Delay and Rise Time:*

Assume that all gates have a propagation delay $t_{pd}$ and a rise time $t_r$. What is the maximum propagation delay and rise time of the following circuit?

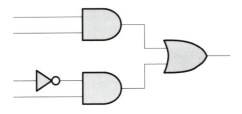

## Problem 1.11

Suppose we have an inverter with the following transfer characteristic, where $V_{oh}$, $V_{ih}$, $V_{ol}$, and $V_{il}$ are defined as in figure 1.1.

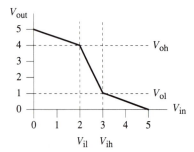

A. What are the sizes of the noise margins for this inverter?

B. Consider a single inverter having the above transfer characteristic, conventionally diagrammed as shown below. To what value could IN drop before OUT would cease to be a valid low output?

C. Now consider three cascaded inverters, each having the transfer characteristic shown above:

To what value could IN drop before OUT would cease to be a valid low output?

D. Suppose we put a box around these three cascaded inverters and called the box a NEW INVERTER. If $V_{oh} = 4$ V and $V_{ol} = 1$ V, what are the noise margins for this NEW INVERTER?

E. Give two reasons why this type of cascading is not a good way to increase noise margins.

# 2 Binary Representations and Notation

We shall now wholeheartedly accept the digital abstraction and move (with only occasional relapses) from the world of continuous voltages, currents, magnetic fields, and such to the world of discrete logic levels. Although we have seen how logic levels can be represented by physical quantities, the task of using logic levels to represent higher-level objects (such as numbers) remains before us. We approach this task in terms of *binary variables*, each of which can take on one of two values, which we call (arbitrarily) 0 and 1. These values correspond to the two logic levels supported by digital hardware. A single binary variable represents 1 *bit* (*binary digit*) of information.

A single bit is incapable of representing any quantity that can take on more than two values. Most quantities used in real computations must therefore be represented using groups, or sequences, of bits. The process of representing a number, character, or anything else in terms of bits involves establishing a correspondence between sequences of bits and possible values of the quantity being represented. Each bit in a group of $n$ bits can be independently assigned as either 0 or 1, so $2^n$ different sequences are possible. *A quantity that can take on $2^n$ values cannot be represented using fewer than $n$ bits.* In real computer systems the terms *byte* and *word*, among others, are used to denote bit sequences of particular sizes. A *byte* is an 8-bit quantity. The number of bits in a *word* is system-dependent; typical values are 16, 32, or 48 bits.

The correspondence between binary strings and particular data is in principle arbitrary; we could, for example, choose 0101 to represent the number 1, 1010 to represent 2, and 1100 to represent 3. Several standards have evolved in order to facilitate common operations on the data (such as addition and multiplication of numbers) and enhance the transportability of data between systems. Two common standards for representation of characters are the EBCDIC and ASCII codes, excerpts of which are shown in table 2.1.

The existence of standard codes makes it possible to construct character input/output devices, such as terminals and printers, that can be connected to a wide variety of machines. (Regrettably, there is not just *one* standard code, which would promote even greater interchangeability.) These codes have other advantages over randomly selected codes. For example, the *collating sequence* of each code, in which all the characters are ordered by the numerical value of their binary representation (numerical values of binary strings are discussed below), contains all the

**Table 2.1**  Two standard character codes.

| Character | EBCDIC code | ASCII code |
|-----------|-------------|------------|
| A | 11000001 | 01000001 |
| B | 11000010 | 01000010 |
| C | 11000011 | 01000011 |
| D | 11000100 | 01000100 |
| E | 11000101 | 01000101 |
| F | 11000110 | 01000110 |
| G | 11000111 | 01000111 |
| H | 11001000 | 01001000 |
| I | 11001001 | 01001001 |
| J | 11010001 | 01001010 |
| 0 | 11110000 | 00110000 |
| 1 | 11110001 | 00110001 |
| 2 | 11110010 | 00110010 |
| 3 | 11110011 | 00110011 |

letters in alphabetical order. This simplifies alphabetical sorting of character data represented in these codes.

## 2.1 Representation of Numbers

A few standard binary representations for numbers have also evolved. These are distinguished by their wide acceptance and the ease with which common arithmetic operations can be performed in them. Number representations are commonly called upon to provide for

- integer and fraction representations,
- positive and negative designations, and
- floating-point (or "scientific") representations.

The usual representation for positive integers using sequences of bits gives a numerical weight to each bit position as follows:

| $n-1$ | $n-2$ | | 1 | 0 | $\leftarrow$ bit place $i$ |
|-------|-------|---|---|---|---|
| $2^{n-1}$ | $2^{n-2}$ | | $2^1$ | $2^0$ | |

The value of the integer represented by these $n$ bits is

$$\sum_{i=0}^{n-1} b_i \cdot 2^i, \tag{2.1}$$

where $b_i$ is the value (0 or 1) of the bit in the $i$th place ($0 \leq i \leq n-1$). This is most commonly known as the *unsigned integer representation*.

To represent a positive fraction, the weight distribution can be changed to

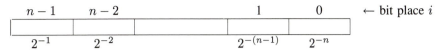

yielding the value

$$\sum_{i=0}^{n-1} b_i \cdot 2^{i-n}.$$

Note that this "unsigned fraction value" is simply equal to the unsigned integer value of the same bit string, scaled by a factor of $2^{-n}$. This corresponds to moving the "binary point" (analogous to the decimal point in decimal integers and fractions) to the left by $n$ places, from a position just to the right of the least significant bit in the integer representation to a position just to the left of the most significant bit in the fraction representation. These two formats are collectively called *fixed-point representations*, and a single arithmetic circuit (such as an adder) can compute appropriate results for either form. In fact, the binary point can be placed anywhere within, or even several places to the left or right of, the entire binary number without changing this principle, as long as the relevant scale factors are properly accounted for when performing arithmetic. The binary point is, indeed, illusory: Its position is not explicitly stored in the word. Rather, the position of the binary point is an important concept for *us* in deciding what number is represented by some particular bit string. For example, the bit string 0101 might have any of the following meanings, among others, depending on where we place the binary point:

```
0101.      5
010.1      2.5
01.01      1.25
0.101      0.625
.0101      0.3125
```

### 2.1.1 Fixed-Point Arithmetic

The operations of addition and multiplication on positive integers in binary notation are analogous to the corresponding operations in the more familiar decimal notation. The main difference is that in binary notation there are only two possibilities for each digit position, so the basic addition and multiplication tables are very simple. For binary addition of two single-bit quantities, there are only four possibilities:

```
  0          0          1          1
 +0         +1         +0         +1
 ──         ──         ──         ──
  0          1          1         10
```

To add multiple-bit quantities, individual bits are summed, working from right to left and propagating carries:

```
    111    ← carries
  10101                        21
 +  111                      +  7
 ──────                      ────
  11100                        28
```

Note that when carries are being propagated, the additional rule $1 + 1 + 1 = 11$ is necessary (along with other obvious extensions such as $1 + 1 + 0 = 10$).

The binary multiplication table is even simpler than the addition table:

$$
\begin{array}{cccc}
0 & 0 & 1 & 1 \\
\underline{\times 0} & \underline{\times 1} & \underline{\times 0} & \underline{\times 1} \\
0 & 0 & 0 & 1
\end{array}
$$

Multiple-bit quantities are multiplied using the same kind of scheme as is used for multiple-digit decimal numbers:

```
    10101              21
×     101            ×  5
   ───────            ────
    10101             105
   00000
  10101
 ───────
 1101001
```

Partial products are constructed by multiplying the multiplicand by each bit of the multiplier in turn. These partial products, properly aligned, are then summed to obtain the final product.

Subtraction can similarly be defined by analogy with decimal arithmetic, with "borrows" propagated to the left, as in

```
  1111      ← borrows
  10100                  20
−   111                − 7
 ───────               ────
  01101                 13
```

Likewise, "long division" can be performed on binary numbers, with the pleasant simplification that, since each quotient digit is either 0 or 1, the multiplications to determine what to subtract next from the dividend are trivial:

```
         1001                 9
    ──────────           ──────
 101│110001           5│49
     101                  45
    ──────                ──
     0010                 4
     000
    ──────
      1001
       101
      ──────
       100
```

## 2.1.2 Range of Number Representations

Not every possible integer can be represented in an $N$-bit positive integer representation. Only $2^N$ different integers can be represented by a string of $N$ bits, and we can see from equation (2.1) that the unsigned integer representation picks these from the range 0 through $2^N - 1$. Thus there is the possibility that the result of operating on two $N$-bit numbers will not fall within this range and hence will not be representable in $N$ bits using the same scheme. This eventuality is termed *overflow* and can lead to incorrect results if not detected and accounted for.

The $N$-bit unsigned fraction representation we have discussed covers the range 0 through $1 - 2^{-N}$ in increments of $2^{-N}$ (once again, giving a total of $2^N$ distinct values). Here, too, there is the possibility of overflow, as when the fraction 3/4 is added to itself to produce 3/2, which is outside the representable range. There is also another kind of arithmetic imprecision, *loss of significance*, that occurs when a result is within the representable range but is not one of the specifically representable values. For example, the 2-bit unsigned fraction representation of 3/4 is .11; if we multiply this by itself, we get .1001, the 4-bit positive fraction representation of 9/16. To represent this result in 2 bits we can make our "best guess" .10, which represents 1/2. The error introduced by such approximations is called *rounding error* or *truncation error*, depending on which strategy is used to construct the approximation. These errors usually occur without any notification that they are taking place; if not guarded against, they can build up to significant magnitude in long chains of numerical computations. Note that loss of significance can occur in integer arithmetic as well. For example, if we view the result of a division as a real number, rather than an integer quotient and an integer remainder, that result may have to be truncated or rounded off in order to be representable as an integer.

### 2.1.3 Signed Integer Representations

Three major conventions have been developed for representing signed numbers. These are 2's complement, 1's complement, and sign/magnitude. In all three schemes, the high-order bit position of the word is reserved to indicate the sign. A 0 sign bit indicates a positive number, and a 1 signifies a negative number.

Furthermore, in all three schemes, a positive number contains simply its unsigned integer representation, as discussed above, in the remaining bits. The schemes differ in the meaning attached to the remaining bits when the number is negative. The most straightforward of the three is the sign/magnitude representation, in which the remaining bits just carry the magnitude of the number, in the unsigned integer representation discussed above. Thus the 4-bit sign/magnitude representation of the integer +5 would be 0101, and of −5, 1101. The value of an $N$-bit sign/magnitude number can be expressed in terms of its constituent bits $b_{N-1}, b_{N-2}, ..., b_1, b_0$ as

$$(1 - 2 \cdot b_{N-1}) \sum_{i=0}^{N-2} b_i \cdot 2^i.$$

Unfortunately, arithmetic operations on sign/magnitude numbers are relatively complicated to perform.

The *1's complement representation* of a negative number carries the unsigned integer representation of its magnitude in the low-order bits, but with all 1s changed to 0s and vice versa; thus the 4-bit 1's complement representation of −5 would be 1010. In general, the value of an $N$-bit 1's complement number can be expressed as

$$-b_{N-1} \cdot (2^{N-1} - 1) + \sum_{i=0}^{N-2} b_i \cdot 2^i.$$

This apparently bizarre representation turns out to simplify considerably the process of adding two numbers. Positive 1's complement numbers can be added just as though they were in the unsigned integer representation defined previously, the only qualification being that if there is a carry into the sign bit position (meaning the result is too large to be represented as a 1's complement integer of that length), overflow occurs and the sum is incorrect. Interestingly, we can handle the addition of two negative numbers, or of one positive and one negative number, in exactly the same way as the addition of two positive numbers if we include one little wrinkle in the algorithm: The numbers are added as though they were unsigned integers, except that whenever there is a carry out of the most significant bit position, the sum is incremented by 1 to produce the final result. We illustrate this *end-around carry* trick with two examples:

$$
\begin{array}{rr}
\phantom{-}1 & \\
\phantom{-}0011 & +3 \\
-1010 & -5 \\
\hline
\phantom{-}1101 & -2 \\
\end{array}
$$

$$
\begin{array}{rr}
1 & \\
\phantom{-}1100 & -3 \\
-1011 & -4 \\
\hline
10111 & -7 \\
\phantom{-100}1 & \\
\hline
\phantom{-}1000 & \\
\end{array}
$$

The reader is invited to ponder, in terms of our definition of 1's complement, why this procedure always yields the correct result.

The existence of a simple addition procedure that works on both positive and negative numbers is an important advantage. It avoids the case analysis that is necessary when doing sign/magnitude arithmetic and means that any addition circuit can easily be made to perform subtraction simply by complementing one of the operands first. In fact, this is how subtraction is most commonly performed in digital systems.

In both the sign/magnitude and the 1's complement representations, the maximum integer that can be represented using $N$ bits is $2^{N-1} - 1$, and the minimum is $-(2^{N-1} - 1)$. Since this range contains only $2^N - 1$ values and there are $2^N$ different strings of $N$ bits, some integer must be represented twice. In fact, both representations have two distinct bit strings corresponding to $+0$ and $-0$. Having two representations for semantically the same quantity is a constant irritation when using these representations; it is avoided by the *2's complement representation*, in which the bit string corresponding to a negative number is calculated by forming the 1's complement representation of the number and then adding 1. For example, the 4-bit 2's complement representation of $-5$ is 1011. From this procedure we can deduce an expression for the integer value corresponding to a 2's complement representation. It is

$$-b_{N-1} \cdot 2^{N-1} + \sum_{i=0}^{N-2} b_i \cdot 2^i.$$

The 1's complement representation of $-0$, 1111, becomes 10000 after adding 1. Discarding the carry out past the fourth bit, we are left with 0000, the unique 2's complement representation of zero. As a pleasant additional benefit, the addition and subtraction procedures for 2's complement integers are exactly the same as those for unsigned integers. No end-around carry is needed; any carry out of the most significant position is simply discarded. For these reasons, the 2's complement representation is used almost exclusively in modern computers.

Although 2's complement integers can be added in the same fashion as unsigned integers, it does not follow that *any* operation on 2's complement numbers can be performed as though the operands were unsigned integers. For example, multiplication must be performed differently. The reader is invited to discover why and speculate as to the best strategy for multiplying 2's complement integers.

## 2.2 Floating-Point Representations

Many computers provide the means, either in software or in hardware, to deal with numbers in floating-point (as opposed to fixed-point), or "scientific," notation. In this format, the computer word (or, often, a group of several words) is divided into bit groups or fields:

| sign | exponent | fraction |
|------|----------|----------|

This format represents the value $(2^{\text{exponent}}) \cdot (\text{fraction})$. In some machines, the 2 is replaced by 16, which amounts to a scaling of the exponent. Both the exponent and the fraction are signed; the exponent field carries its own sign, and the explicit sign bit (the leftmost bit of the entire floating-point representation) belongs to the fraction. There are a number of strategies for deciding which, if any, bits of the floating-point number should be complemented if the sign of the fraction is negative.

Floating-point representation provides a large dynamic range in number size and permits a constant level of significance to be maintained over this range. These advantages are counterbalanced by the greater complexity of performing most arithmetic operations on floating-point numbers. Furthermore, floating-point arithmetic is particularly susceptible to loss-of-significance errors at places where they might not be expected by the uninitiated.

## 2.3 Other Representations

As mentioned above, the primary criteria for a representation are that it contain

**Table 2.2** Three-bit Gray code representation.

| Number | Gray code representation |
|--------|--------------------------|
| 0 | 000 |
| 1 | 001 |
| 2 | 011 |
| 3 | 010 |
| 4 | 110 |
| 5 | 111 |
| 6 | 101 |
| 7 | 100 |

sufficient bits to represent all the values of interest and that it be amenable to the operations that must be performed on it. The number representations discussed above are the ones most commonly used because they lend themselves to the ordinary arithmetic operations. Other representations are used, however, for specialized applications. For example, the *Gray code* representation of a number has the property that between any two consecutive integers at most 1 bit of the representation changes. This property is convenient in building mechanical shaft encoders that translate the angular position of a shaft into digital form. Table 2.2 shows a 3-bit Gray code.

A representation often used in business data processing is *binary-coded decimal*, or BCD, in which a number is stored as a sequence of decimal digits, each of which uses the unsigned integer representation:

| 3 | 9 | 5 | ← decimal number |
|------|------|------|------|
| 0011 | 1001 | 0101 | ← BCD representation |

This representation expedites input and output operations, which are common in business applications, at the expense of greater complexity in arithmetic operations.

Finally, many times a representation will include *parity bits* or other forms of redundancy, designed to help detect errors that may occur in transmission or processing of values.

## 2.4 Hexadecimal Notation

Although modern digital computers predominantly use binary (radix 2) representations of numeric data, humans tend to find binary numbers tedious. Consequently, programming languages commonly allow programmers to specify integers (for example) in familiar decimal form, like 109, rather than in the computer-acceptable binary equivalent, 1101101. Such languages translate the decimal representations to binary, a process that bored most of us during our early mathematics education.

**Table 2.3**  Decimal values in binary and hexadecimal.

| Decimal | Binary | Hexadecimal | Decimal | Binary | Hexadecimal |
|---------|--------|-------------|---------|--------|-------------|
| 0 | 0b0 | 0x0 | 8 | 0b1000 | 0x8 |
| 1 | 0b1 | 0x1 | 9 | 0b1001 | 0x9 |
| 2 | 0b10 | 0x2 | 10 | 0b1010 | 0xA |
| 3 | 0b11 | 0x3 | 11 | 0b1011 | 0xB |
| 4 | 0b100 | 0x4 | 12 | 0b1100 | 0xC |
| 5 | 0b101 | 0x5 | 13 | 0b1101 | 0xD |
| 6 | 0b110 | 0x6 | 14 | 0b1110 | 0xE |
| 7 | 0b111 | 0x7 | 15 | 0b1111 | 0xF |

While the decimal notation is both familiar and concise, there are occasions when details of the binary representation are important to the programmer. In such circumstances, it is common to use *hexadecimal*, or *radix 16*, *notation* as an alternative to binary. The major advantage of hexadecimal (or *hex*, for short) is that it is both concise and easy to convert (mentally) to and from binary. The latter property stems from its use of $2^4$ ($= 16$) as a base. This allows the digits of a binary number to be treated as a smaller number of 4-bit groups, each of which corresponds to a hexadecimal digit. Each 4-bit group can be converted to its hexadecimal digit independently of the others; since there are only 16 such groups, most programmers quickly memorize the binary representation corresponding to each hexadecimal digit. The familiar decimal digits, 0 through 9, are used as the first ten hex digits; the letters A through F are pressed into service as the remaining six.

To distinguish between decimal, binary, and hexadecimal numbers in our programs (and occasionally in the text) we adopt the convention of the C programming language: Integers are decimal by default, but may be prefixed by 0b or 0x to specify binary or hexadecimal representations, respectively. Table 2.3 gives the hexadecimal digits in binary and decimal.

The binary representation 0b1001010010111101 is equivalent to 0x94BD in hexadecimal, as can be verified by parsing its binary digits as 1001-0100-1011-1101 and separately translating each 4-bit group to hex. The reader should become familiar with the mechanics of converting in both directions.

## 2.5 *Unrepresentable Values

An infinite variety of data can be represented on a digital computer once we establish conventions for translation into sequences of bits. Various programming tricks, using data structures of variable size, can even establish representations for infinite sets of data such as the integers or rational numbers. (A finite computer cannot simultaneously hold the representations for the infinitely many integers, but it can support a representation convention capable of dealing with any of them, within the limits of its memory capacity.)

Certain other sets of mathematical objects, such as the real numbers, are less amenable to such representation. The uncountability of such sets makes it impossible to establish a correspondence between their elements and finite bit strings. For this reason, representations such as the floating-point format necessarily approximate the values of real numbers rather than representing them precisely. Similar restrictions apply to functions of integers, sets of bit strings, and other uncountably infinite sets.

It is important to recognize that this limitation is due to the intractable size of each set, rather than to the characteristics of individual elements. One can, for example, arbitrarily decide that the string 011010 represents the exact ratio of circumference to diameter. Indeed, it is quite possible to devise a system that represents the irrational number $\pi$, or the set of all prime numbers, as long as the number of objects to be represented remains at most countably infinite (thereby excluding the possibility of representing *all* irrational numbers or all sets of numbers).

## 2.6 Error Detection and Correction

The digital abstraction entices the engineer to assume completely reliable signaling of binary information, but there are circumstances under which this assumption is not practically tenable because of noise or other potential failures. Unreliable signals are most commonly associated with communication functions, such as the communication of data over telephone lines, but they can arise in other contexts as well. As memory densities are pushed toward physical limits, for example, the reliability with which each bit of memory can be recalled tends to decrease. Consequently there is a trade-off between memory cost and memory reliability, and every real digital memory system effects some compromise between these criteria. Fortunately, it is possible to compensate *within the digital abstraction* for unreliability inherent in the underlying implementation technology. The trick is to choose digital representations that comprise more bits than are strictly necessary to represent the essential data to be communicated. These extra bits provide a measure of redundancy—in effect, a consistency check by which a receiver can detect or even correct data corrupted by signaling errors. While these important techniques are largely beyond the scope of this book, we provide a glimpse of them in this section.

### 2.6.1 Parity Bits and Checksums

A modest goal in the promotion of system reliability is simply to *detect* errors, either alerting the operator to a subsystem malfunction or resorting to some established recovery scheme. In the context of data communication via telephone lines, for example, the detection of an error during transmission of a file might trigger— manually or automatically—retransmission of the file.

A simple and commonly used approach to error detection involves the addition to each binary data word of a *parity bit* whose value is chosen so that the total number of 1s in each augmented word (including parity bits) is, say, odd.[1] The receiver of a such a word recalculates its parity, by determining whether the number of 1s is odd, and signals a *parity error* if it is not correct.

Parity bits provide *single-bit error detection*, in that corruption of a word that changes a single bit (either a data bit or the parity bit) will result in a parity error. Two changed bits within a single word will maintain correct parity and thus go undetected. Assuming that errors are infrequent and tend to corrupt individual bits independently, parity bits can provide effective detection since the probability of two errors in the same word is small. However, a *burst error*, which tends to randomize an entire word, will accidentally generate correct parity about half the time, leading to a substantial number of undetected errors.

The error-detection characteristics of a coding scheme can be improved by increasing the number of redundant bits, thereby decreasing the chances that corrupted data will appear valid by accident. In order to diminish the communication or storage overhead imposed by these additional bits, they are often associated with blocks of data comprising a number of words. A common scheme for blocks of data is to add a single $k$-bit *checksum* word to each block of $n$ $k$-bit data words, with the value of the checksum word computed by taking the $k$-bit binary sum of the data words.[2] The receiver of the block recalculates the checksum and compares the result with the transmitted checksum; any discrepancy stimulates a *checksum error*.

Checksums clearly detect single-bit errors within the block; moreover, they detect a substantial majority (all but 1 in $2^k$) of the possible multiple-bit errors. Thus they provide much more robust error detection than parity bits, albeit at the cost of dealing with large data blocks rather than with individual words. This trade-off between data block size and the effectiveness of error-correction and error-detection schemes per added bit is fundamental and tends to bias communication and storage technologies toward the use of large data blocks.

### 2.6.2 Single-Bit Error Correction

Although parity and checksum techniques signal the presence of errors, they provide little clue as to which portion of the data has been corrupted or what the original value was. Fortunately, the use of additional redundant bits can lead to an *error-correcting code* whose error diagnosis contains sufficient information to correct certain corrupted data. Single-bit error correction can be implemented by means of multiple parity bits. As a simple example, consider a code that deals with blocks of $n$ $n$-bit words. Each such block can be viewed as a square ($n$ by $n$) matrix of single bits. If we associate a parity bit with each row and column of the matrix,

---

[1] This convention is termed *odd parity*; *even parity* is the straightforward alternative. Odd parity has the advantage that a continuous stream of 0s—often a common failure mode—appears as an error condition.

[2] The use of binary addition to compute the redundant word is somewhat arbitrary; other functions can be used, although the choice affects the statistical properties of the error-detection scheme. Such functions have come to be termed *cyclic redundancy checks*.

any single error among the $n^2$ bits will generate two parity errors: one for the affected row and one for the affected column. This pair of parity errors (or the *error syndrome bits*, in the jargon of error correction) uniquely identifies the bit position of the error, which can be flipped to restore the original data value.

More sophisticated allocation of parity bits minimizes the number of redundant bits necessary for the correction of single-bit errors; such schemes generally require a number of additional bits that grows logarithmically with the size of the data block.

## 2.7 Context

This chapter has barely introduced the topic of data representations, itself the subject of textbooks and courses. While the discussion has been confined to simple representations of numbers, representation conventions extend to data structures, text, symbolic information, computer instructions, and an infinite variety of other forms of information. Subsequent chapters provide glimpses of many of these, as representation questions arise in the course of program examples and discussions of architectural support.

Even the representation of numeric data admits infinite variety and provokes controversy. Variable-precision integer representations convey exact values of arbitrarily large integers; similar techniques allow exact representation of arbitrary rationals (rather than the approximate representation obtained using floating-point conventions). Floating-point representations are themselves a complex topic that remains controversial despite an IEEE-sponsored standardization effort. The reader is referred to Hill and Peterson [1987] for an introduction to floating-point representations and operations; more detail is available in Coonen [1980] and Cody [1981], among others. The general topic of numeric data representation and arithmetic manipulation is treated in Waser and Flynn [1982].

Error detection and correction is a similarly complex topic with a substantial body of literature and continuing developments. Hamming [1980] covers these techniques, along with other important representation approaches designed to "compact" or minimize the number of bits necessary to represent a class of data. The general topic of fault tolerance is discussed again in section 21.2.3.

## 2.8 Problems

### Problem 2.1
What decimal integer does the 8-bit 2's complement number 11110101 represent?

### Problem 2.2
A positive number is added to a negative number using 2's complement arithmetic. The result has a 1 in the sign bit. Does this indicate that overflow occurred?

## Problem 2.3
Give the 6-bit 2's complement representation of the following decimal numbers:

$27, 21, 15, -6, -15, -21, -13, -7$

## Problem 2.4
Calculate the following using 6-bit 2's complement arithmetic. Show your work.

$13 + 10$
$15 + (-18)$
$27 + (-6)$
$(-6) + (-15)$
$21 + (-21)$

## Problem 2.5
Which of the following proposals will work for taking the 2's complement of a binary number?

A. Invert all bits; add 1 to the result.

B. Invert all bits; subtract 1 from the result.

C. Subtract 1; invert all bits of the result.

D. Add 1, invert all bits of the result.

E. Examine every bit in sequence, starting with the least significant bit. When the first 1 is found, invert every subsequent bit encountered (not including that first 1) up to and including the most significant bit.

## Problem 2.6
What are the most positive and most negative integers that can be expressed using a $k$-bit 2's complement representation?

## Problem 2.7
Using a total of 6 bits, how many different numbers can be represented in each of the following representations?

A. Unsigned binary.

B. 2's complement.

C. 1's complement.

D. Sign/magnitude.

## Problem 2.8
A baseball umpire's meter has four displays: *Balls, Strikes, Outs,* and *Inning.* There are four values for the *Balls* display (0, 1, 2, and 3), three for *Strikes* (0, 1, 2), three for *Outs* (0, 1, 2), and ten for *Inning* (1, 2, ..., 10). What is the minimum number of bits required to hold the information recorded by the meter? Explain.

### Problem 2.9

Devise a scheme for representing integers, independently of size, as binary strings. Briefly describe algorithms for performing addition and comparison using your scheme.

### Problem 2.10

Devise a scheme for representing rational numbers as binary strings. Briefly describe algorithms for performing addition and comparison using your scheme.

### Problem 2.11

Devise a scheme for representing rational numbers *and* rational multiples of $\pi$ as binary strings. Comment on the implementability of arithmetic operations using your representation.

# 3 Combinational Devices and Circuits

Chapter 1 introduced the combinational device as an abstraction of our most fundamental digital elements and observed that acyclic circuits whose elements are combinational devices are themselves combinational devices. The present chapter introduces some basic notational and analytic tools that are useful for the synthesis of arbitrary combinational circuits from a small fixed repertoire of basic combinational devices.

## 3.1 Boolean Functions and Truth Tables

Functions from $n$ binary input variables to a single binary output variable are called *Boolean functions*. An arbitrary Boolean function with $n$ input variables can always be defined by a *truth table* with $2^n$ entries in which output values are given for each of the $2^n$ possible combinations of $n$ input values (figure 3.1). The tabular representation becomes unwieldy for a function with a large number of input values, but it has the advantage of conceptual simplicity. It corresponds to the basic definition of a function as a mapping from a domain to a range, and it specifies that mapping in detail.

An interesting attribute of Boolean algebra is that, since each variable can take on only a finite number of values, it is possible to characterize a function completely by writing its truth table. Since the values of Boolean functions are also binary, there are only a finite number of possible truth tables, and hence only a finite number of distinct Boolean functions of any particular number of variables. For example, there are only sixteen different Boolean functions of two variables, as shown in figure 3.2.

Some of the functions in figure 3.2 have been given mnemonic names because of their utility. Thus the function defined by column 1 is called AND since the value of the function is 1 only if both *A and B* have the value 1. Similarly column 7 defines the function OR whose value is 1 if either *A or B* (inclusive) has the value 1. Column 6 defines the function XOR (exclusive or) whose value is 1 if either *A or B*, but not both, has the value 1. The elements 1 and 0 are often thought of as representing the truth values *true* and *false*, respectively, which helps explain the special role of 1 (true) in the definition of the mnemonics AND and OR. This truth-value interpretation also leads to the common practice of calling the functions in figure 3.2 *logical functions* or *logical operations*.

| $A$ | $B$ | $C$ | $f(A,B,C)$ |
|---|---|---|---|
| 0 | 0 | 0 | 0 |
| 0 | 0 | 1 | 1 |
| 0 | 1 | 0 | 0 |
| 0 | 1 | 1 | 1 |
| 1 | 0 | 0 | 1 |
| 1 | 0 | 1 | 1 |
| 1 | 1 | 0 | 0 |
| 1 | 1 | 1 | 0 |

**Figure 3.1**  Truth-table definition of a function $f$.

| | | AND | | | | | | XOR | OR | NOR | | | | | | NAND | |
|---|---|---|---|---|---|---|---|---|---|---|---|---|---|---|---|---|---|---|
| $A$ | $B$ | 0 | 1 | 2 | 3 | 4 | 5 | 6 | 7 | 8 | 9 | 10 | 11 | 12 | 13 | 14 | 15 |
| 0 | 0 | 0 | 0 | 0 | 0 | 0 | 0 | 0 | 0 | 1 | 1 | 1 | 1 | 1 | 1 | 1 | 1 |
| 0 | 1 | 0 | 0 | 0 | 0 | 1 | 1 | 1 | 1 | 0 | 0 | 0 | 0 | 1 | 1 | 1 | 1 |
| 1 | 0 | 0 | 0 | 1 | 1 | 0 | 0 | 1 | 1 | 0 | 0 | 1 | 1 | 0 | 0 | 1 | 1 |
| 1 | 1 | 0 | 1 | 0 | 1 | 0 | 1 | 0 | 1 | 0 | 1 | 0 | 1 | 0 | 1 | 0 | 1 |

**Figure 3.2**  The sixteen possible Boolean functions of two variables.

The functions AND and OR are usually represented by the infix operators $\cdot$ and $+$, respectively. Thus $A \cdot B$ means the same thing as AND($A$,$B$), and $A + B$ means OR($A, B$). The use of $+$ to represent logical OR rather than addition is somewhat confusing but is well established. Sometimes the symbols $\wedge$ and $\vee$ are used in place of $\cdot$ and $+$, respectively.

A very useful one-argument (unary) function, NOT, is defined on logical variables by

| $A$ | NOT($A$) |
|---|---|
| 0 | 1 |
| 1 | 0 |

NOT is usually represented by a bar over the argument and sometimes by the prefix symbol $\neg$. Thus NOT($A$), $\overline{A}$, and $\neg A$ all mean the same thing. (Other forms sometimes seen are $\sim A$, $A'$, and $A-$.) The NOT function and the various functions of figure 3.2 can be related to each other through functional composition. For example, the function NAND in column 14 takes the value 1 just when AND has the value 0, so that

$$\text{NAND}(A, B) = \text{NOT}(\text{AND}(A, B)) = \overline{A \cdot B}.$$

This equation illustrates the visual advantage of using infix operators and over-bars to represent functions. In the same vein, the NOR function of column 8 is represented by

$$\text{NOR}(A, B) = \text{NOT}(\text{OR}(A, B)) = \overline{A + B}.$$

Each of the functions in figure 3.2 can, in fact, be represented as functional compositions of the three functions AND, OR, and NOT. Moreover, OR can be represented as a functional composition of AND and NOT:

$$\text{OR}(A, B) = \text{NOT}(\text{AND}(\text{NOT}(A), \text{NOT}(B))) = \overline{\overline{A} \cdot \overline{B}}.$$

Similarly, AND can be represented in terms of OR and NOT:

$$A \cdot B = \overline{\overline{A} + \overline{B}}.$$

Thus AND and NOT (or OR and NOT) provide a *complete* set of operations, in terms of which all the others can be represented.

One can also represent all the functions in terms of the single function NAND or the single function NOR. To see this for NAND, note that

$$\overline{A} = \text{NAND}(A, A),$$
$$A \cdot B = \text{NAND}(\text{NAND}(A, B), \text{NAND}(A, B)).$$

Since all the other functions can be represented in terms of NOT and AND, this completes the demonstration. Thus the range of logical operations directly provided in a programming environment (beyond a complete set) is merely a question of convenience and speed.

### 3.1.1 Logical Expressions

It can be verified directly from the definitions of AND and OR that the infix operators $\cdot$ and $+$ are associative:

$$A \cdot (B \cdot C) = (A \cdot B) \cdot C,$$
$$A + (B + C) = (A + B) + C.$$

In particular, $A \cdot (B \cdot C)$ has the value 1 if and only if $A$ has the value 1, $B$ has the value 1, and $C$ has the value 1. Since $(A \cdot B) \cdot C$ represents the same function, the expressions are equivalent. Because of this equivalence, there is no ambiguity in omitting the parentheses and representing this function by $A \cdot B \cdot C$. Such an expression is called a *term* or a *product*.

In the same way, the parentheses can be omitted from $A + (B + C)$, so that $A + B + C$ represents the function whose value is 1 if and only if one or more of the variables $A$, $B$, $C$ have the value 1. Such an expression is called a *sum*.

| $A$ | $B$ | $C$ | $g(A, B, C)$ |
|---|---|---|---|
| 0 | 0 | 0 | 0 |
| 0 | 0 | 1 | 0 |
| 0 | 1 | 0 | 0 |
| 0 | 1 | 1 | 1 |
| 1 | 0 | 0 | 0 |
| 1 | 0 | 1 | 0 |
| 1 | 1 | 0 | 0 |
| 1 | 1 | 1 | 0 |

**Figure 3.3** Truth table for $g(A, B, C) = \overline{A} \cdot B \cdot C$.

It also follows directly from their truth-table definitions that $\cdot$ and $+$ are commutative:

$$A \cdot B = B \cdot A,$$
$$A + B = B + A.$$

They also obey distributive laws:

$$A \cdot (B + C) = (A \cdot B) + (A \cdot C),$$
$$A + (B \cdot C) = (A + B) \cdot (A + C).$$

With the exception of the second distributive law, these rules are the same as those for ordinary arithmetic. This analogy to arithmetic can be carried one step further by introducing a parenthesizing convention between $\cdot$ and $+$; thus $A \cdot B + C$ will mean $(A \cdot B) + C$ rather than $A \cdot (B + C)$. The analogy is often carried to the point of omitting the dot denoting AND and simply juxtaposing the ANDed expressions, writing $A \cdot B$ as $AB$, but in this text we shall generally resist the temptation to be quite that laconic.

We are now in a position to represent an arbitrary Boolean function on $n$ variables, defined in table form, by a logical expression. First, consider the special case of a function whose value is 1 only for a single table entry. Such a function is represented by a single term that contains each variable. Each variable has an overbar or no overbar, depending on whether the value of the variable in the given table entry is 0 or 1, respectively. For example, the function $g$ in figure 3.3 has the value 1 only for the entry in which $A$ is 0, $B$ is 1, and $C$ is 1, leading to the expression $\overline{A} \cdot B \cdot C$.

In the general case, one can generate a term, as above, for each table entry for which the function has the value 1; a logical expression representing the function is the sum of those terms. This rule, applied to the function $f$ defined in figure 3.1, leads to the logical expression

$$f(A, B, C) = \overline{A} \cdot \overline{B} \cdot C + \overline{A} \cdot B \cdot C + A \cdot \overline{B} \cdot \overline{C} + A \cdot \overline{B} \cdot C.$$

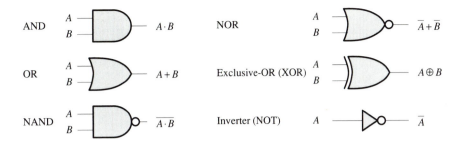

**Figure 3.4** Standard IEEE gate symbols.

It is easy to see why this rule works, since one term in the sum has the value 1 for each combination of input values for which the function has the value 1. Any combination of input values for which the function is 0 leads to the value 0 for every term in the sum. There is one special case in which the rule is not explicit: When the function is 0 for *all* combinations of input values, 0 is the simple logical expression that represents the function.

A logical expression resulting from the above procedure is called a *canonical sum-of-products expression* for the function. An alternative logical expression, called the *canonical product of sums*, is generated from the table representation of a function in a similar way: For each table entry with the value 0, we generate a sum whose value is 1 *except* for the combination of input values corresponding to the given entry. Such a sum contains each input variable, with an overbar or not depending on whether the value of that input variable is 1 or 0, respectively. The canonical product of sums is the product of all the sums so generated. For the function $f$ in figure 3.1, the canonical product-of-sums expression is

$$f(A, B, C) = (A + B + C) \cdot (A + \overline{B} + C) \cdot (\overline{A} + \overline{B} + C) \cdot (\overline{A} + \overline{B} + \overline{C}).$$

## 3.2 Elementary Gate Circuits

Figure 3.4 shows the standard IEEE symbols for several common logic gates. This set of symbols covers more than a complete set of operations, but all of these elements are frequently used in practice. The circuits corresponding to the operations AND, OR, NAND, NOR, and exclusive-OR (often designated XOR) are called *gates*, while the circuit realizing negation (NOT) is called an *inverter*. In general, any electronic circuit with one Boolean output that is a logical function of its $n$ inputs (logical values) is called a gate; thus gates are just the basic combinational circuits that are used to implement logical expressions. Note that negation is represented in two ways: by means of inverters, or by a small circle at the gate output.

"Negation circles" can also be used on input lines to denote input signals that are inverted before being used in the logical function specified by the shape of the gate body, as shown in figure 3.5.

**Figure 3.5** Negation circles.

**Figure 3.6** Buffers.

Another basic circuit that is sometimes seen on circuit diagrams is the noninverting buffer, whose symbol is the same as an inverter without the negation circle (figure 3.6). These buffers are used solely for power gain or delay and have no logical function. The same effect can, of course, be achieved with AND or OR.

### 3.2.1 Conversion from Logical Representation to Gates

We have seen how different forms for representing Boolean functions can be converted into Boolean expressions involving the AND, OR, and NOT operations. It is straightforward to translate such expressions to combinational circuits using the corresponding gate symbols. Some examples are given in figure 3.7.

To get from a combinational circuit diagram to an actual physical circuit, one must choose physical devices to implement the gates (taking into consideration speed, power, cost, and convenience), provide power to the devices, and package them in some way. We shall ignore those problems since they are highly dependent on a rapidly changing technology and are separable from questions of logical representation. There are often restrictions, however, on the types of gates that can be used in a combinational circuit and on the number of levels of gates in the circuit. These restrictions can be dealt with by using Boolean algebra (described below) to derive an equivalent logical expression that can be directly realized in a circuit satisfying the given constraints.

### 3.2.2 Manipulation of Logical Expressions

Boolean algebra is a system of identities that are useful in manipulating logical expressions; in addition to the commutative, associative, and distributive laws discussed above, other useful identities include

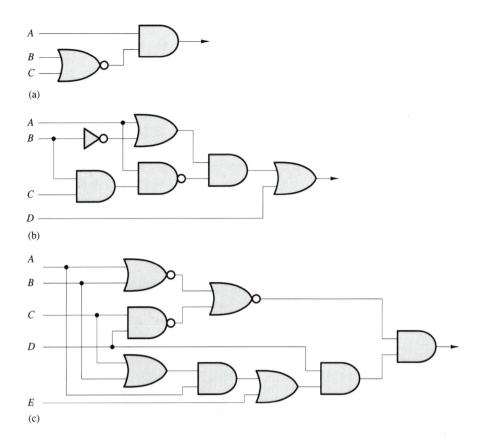

**Figure 3.7** Combinational circuits derived directly from logical expressions: (a) $A \cdot \overline{B + C}$; (b) $(A + \overline{B}) \cdot \overline{A \cdot B \cdot C} + D$; (c) $\overline{\overline{A + B} + \overline{C \cdot D}} \cdot D \cdot (E + A \cdot (B + C))$.

$$X + 1 = 1 \qquad\qquad X \cdot 0 = 0$$
$$X + 0 = X \qquad\qquad X \cdot 1 = X$$
$$X + \overline{X} = 1 \qquad\qquad X \cdot \overline{X} = 0 \qquad\qquad \text{(complement)}$$
$$X + X = X \qquad\qquad X \cdot X = X \qquad\qquad \text{(idempotence)}$$

$$X + (X \cdot Y) = X \qquad\qquad X \cdot (X + Y) = X \qquad\qquad \text{(absorption)}$$
$$X + (\overline{X} \cdot Y) = X + Y \qquad\qquad X \cdot (\overline{X} + Y) = X \cdot Y \qquad\qquad \text{(absorption)}$$

$$\overline{X_1 + X_2 + \cdots + X_n} = \qquad \overline{X_1 \cdot X_2 \cdots X_n} = \qquad\qquad \text{(DeMorgan's law)}$$
$$\overline{X_1} \cdot \overline{X_2} \cdots \overline{X_n} \qquad\qquad \overline{X_1} + \overline{X_2} + \cdots + \overline{X_n}$$

Each of these identities can be verified by constructing truth tables for the expressions on each side of the equals sign and verifying that these tables are the same. The identities are grouped in pairs to reflect the important principle of *duality*: Any identity between logical expressions remains an identity if simultaneously all 0s are changed to 1s, all 1s to 0s, all · operators to +, and all + operators to · (the parenthesizing must also be changed to reflect the precedence between + and · ).

The principle of duality can be understood in another light. In a physical digital circuit, any particular wire can be in one of two states, corresponding to the two logic levels in the system. The convention of *positive logic* arbitrarily assigns the meaning "1" to the higher (voltage or current) level and "0" to the lower, but we could as easily adopt the reverse, *negative logic* convention. Duality tells us that if we change between the positive and negative logic conventions, thereby interchanging 1s and 0s, all AND functions will be changed to OR functions and vice versa. To avoid the confusion that can arise when it is not clear which convention is being used, many manufacturers' data sheets for logic circuits use the symbols H and L for the high and low logic levels, respectively, leaving to the user the assignment of 1s and 0s to these levels. Often a complex logic circuit uses positive logic conventions for some signals and negative logic for others. Such signal lines may be identified as *active high* and *active low*, specifying local positive and negative representation conventions.

The identities above remain valid, of course, when their variables are replaced by arbitrary logical expressions. As an initial example of using Boolean algebra for simplification, consider the canonical sum-of-products expression for the function in figure 3.1:

$$f_0(A, B, C) = \overline{A} \cdot \overline{B} \cdot C + \overline{A} \cdot B \cdot C + A \cdot \overline{B} \cdot \overline{C} + A \cdot \overline{B} \cdot C$$

$$= \overline{A} \cdot C \cdot (\overline{B} + B) + A \cdot \overline{B} \cdot (\overline{C} + C)$$

$$= \overline{A} \cdot C + A \cdot \overline{B}.$$

Here we have used the associative, commutative, and distributive laws and then applied the complement identity. As a second example,

$$A \cdot \overline{(B + C) \cdot \overline{A}} + \overline{B + \overline{A}} = A \cdot (\overline{B + C} + A) + \overline{B} \cdot A = A + \overline{B} \cdot A = A.$$

Here we have used DeMorgan's law twice, then absorption on the first term and finally absorption on what was left.

## 3.3 Synthesis of Logic Circuits

We illustrate logic-circuit synthesis with five examples; in each, we assume that both the inputs and their complements are directly available.

*Example 1*
Synthesize $f_1 = A + B \cdot (C + \overline{D})$ with NAND gates. The general approach to finding a NAND gate realization is to use DeMorgan's law to eliminate all the OR operators in the logical expression. In cases like the one here, this leads directly to a NAND gate realization; in other cases, one must implement some additional

*Combinational Devices and Circuits*

NOT operators by tying together the inputs of NAND gates. Here

$$f_1 = A + B \cdot (C + \overline{D})$$
$$= A + B \cdot \overline{\overline{C} \cdot D}$$
$$= \overline{\overline{A} \cdot \overline{B \cdot \overline{\overline{C} \cdot D}}},$$

where we have applied DeMorgan's law first to $C + \overline{D}$ and then to the entire expression. The combinational circuit is

Note that by DeMorgan's law, $\overline{A} + \overline{B} = \overline{A \cdot B}$; hence the following two symbols represent the same gate function, which is in both cases a NAND function:

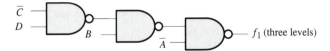

In general, DeMorgan's law can be applied to any gate symbol with an AND- or OR-type body by changing each AND-type body to an OR-type body (and vice versa), removing negation circles wherever present at the inputs or output, and adding negation circles wherever they were not present. Such transformations are often helpful in visualizing the operation of a logic circuit. Using the alternative symbol for NAND gates, the circuit for $f_1$ can be redrawn as

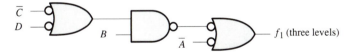

This gives a somewhat clearer picture of the purpose being served by each component in the circuit. Note that this is not a new circuit that implements the same function but rather a new diagram for the same circuit: All gates are still NAND gates, and they are interconnected in precisely the same way. However, by redrawing the diagram we have paired inverter circles so that every internal wire either has no circles on it or has one on each end. Then, using the fact that $\overline{\overline{A}} = A$, we can derive an equivalent (but not identical in the sense of having exactly the same components) circuit by removing the circles at each end of wires that have paired circles, yielding

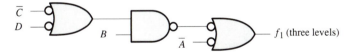

Finally, we can absorb inverter circles appearing at inputs by complementing the input variables themselves, yielding

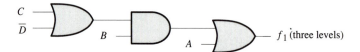

which is the naive implementation of the original expression for $f_1$. This process could also be carried out in reverse, of course, to synthesize the NAND-gate-only realization of $f_1$ from the naive gate circuit. In fact, this pictorial application of DeMorgan's law to gate circuits is probably much more popular than the more formal approach we use here.

*Example 2*

Synthesize $f_2 = (\overline{A} + B) \cdot (A + C)$ with NAND gates. Proceeding as above, we obtain

$$f_2 = \overline{\overline{A \cdot \overline{B}} \cdot \overline{\overline{A} \cdot \overline{C}}} = \overline{\overline{\overline{A \cdot \overline{B} \cdot \overline{A} \cdot \overline{C}}}}.$$

The combinational circuit is shown below, with its final NAND gate used to implement a NOT function.

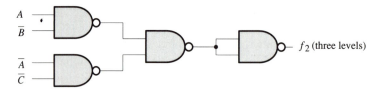

Using the alternative symbol for NAND gates, we can redraw this circuit as

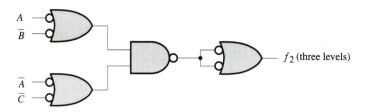

From this point on, we shall use the dual representations of NAND gates and other gates interchangeably.

The function above can be realized somewhat more efficiently by using the identity

$$(\overline{A} + B) \cdot (A + C) = A \cdot B + \overline{A} \cdot C,$$

which can be verified using truth tables. Thus

$$f_2 = \overline{\overline{A \cdot B} \cdot \overline{\overline{A} \cdot C}}.$$

*Combinational Devices and Circuits*

This leads to the realization

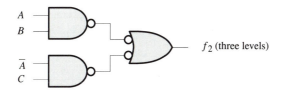

$f_2$ (three levels)

*Example 3*

Synthesize $f_1 = A + B \cdot (C + \overline{D})$ with two levels of NAND gates. The general approach when synthesizing two-level NAND-gate circuits is to obtain a sum-of-products logical expression and then apply DeMorgan's law.

$$f_1 = A + B \cdot C + B \cdot \overline{D}$$
$$= \overline{\overline{A} \cdot \overline{B \cdot C} \cdot \overline{B \cdot \overline{D}}}.$$

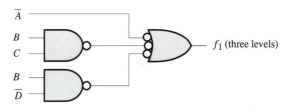

$f_1$ (three levels)

Note that this realization uses a three-input NAND gate. Most logic families include such multi-input gates. The functions realized by such gates are given below for the inputs $A_1, A_2, ..., A_n$:

| Type | Output |
|------|--------|
| AND | $A_1 \cdot A_2 \cdots A_n$ |
| OR | $A_1 + A_2 + \cdots + A_n$ |
| NAND | $\overline{A_1 \cdot A_2 \cdots A_n}$ |
| NOR | $\overline{A_1 + A_2 \cdots + A_n}$ |

*Example 4*

Synthesize $f_3 = A + B \cdot C \cdot \overline{D}$ with two-input NOR gates. The approach for NOR-gate synthesis is the dual of that for NAND gates; we use DeMorgan's law to replace AND operators with OR operators:

$$f_3 = A + B \cdot \overline{\overline{C} + D} = A + \overline{\overline{B} + \overline{\overline{C} + D}} = A + \overline{\overline{B} + \overline{\overline{C} + D}}.$$

*Example 5*

Synthesize $f = A \cdot B \cdot C + D$ and $g = A \cdot B \cdot C + \overline{D}$ with two levels of NAND gates. We already know how to synthesize $f$ and $g$ separately, but it is often possible when synthesizing several functions to share the gates for common subexpressions, as shown below.

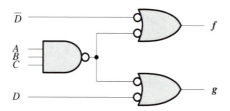

### 3.3.1 Karnaugh Maps

We have now discussed several representations of Boolean functions: truth tables, logical expressions, and combinational gate circuits. The Karnaugh map is yet another representation. It is a two-dimensional tabular array in which the input variables are divided into two sets. The possible values for the first set are listed on the horizontal axis, and the values for the second set are listed on the vertical axis. Each cell in the array corresponds to a particular set of values for the input variables, and the corresponding values of the function are given inside the array.

Figure 3.8 shows Karnaugh maps for the functions AND, OR, and NOT and for the function $f$ of figure 3.1. Note the unusual labeling of the columns in part (d). Karnaugh maps are always labeled so that between any pair of horizontally or vertically adjacent cells, only one of the corresponding input variables changes value. This property, which is reminiscent of the Gray code for integers, is true even for pairs of cells that are adjacent by "wrapping around" the Karnaugh map from bottom to top or right to left. In a three-variable Karnaugh map such as that of figure 3.8(d), this labeling (which is *the* novel feature of Karnaugh maps) has the effect that all the input combinations for which $B = 1$ appear in the center four cells of the array, and all combinations for which $A = 1$ appear in the rightmost four cells. Similar properties apply to other convenient combinations. This provides a powerful visual aid to the simplification of logical expressions. Figure 3.8(e) shows an equivalent but more compact notation in which the regions where $A = 1$, $B = 1$, and $C = 1$ are indicated by the letters surrounded by markers.

A Karnaugh map can be used, like a truth table, to construct a canonical sum-of-products expression for a function by simply reading off the terms that correspond to the cells containing 1s in the map. The Karnaugh map can also be used directly to read off simplified sum-of-products expressions. Any pair of adjacent cells, either vertically or horizontally, corresponds to a term with one of the variables missing. For example, the two rightmost cells in figure 3.8(e) correspond to the situation in which $A = 1$, $B = 0$, and $C$ is either 1 or 0, that is, to the term $A \cdot \overline{B}$. Similarly, any rectangle with four cells (either $1 \times 4$ or $2 \times 2$) corresponds to a term

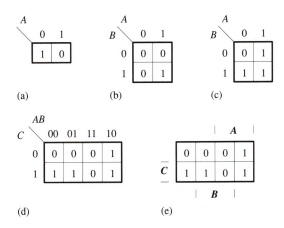

**Figure 3.8** Karnaugh maps: (a) NOT($A$); (b) AND($A,B$); (c) OR($A,B$); (d) the function $f$ from figure 3.1; (e) an alternate labeling scheme.

with two variables missing; thus the leftmost four cells in figure 3.8(e) correspond to the term $\overline{A}$. In general, any rectangle in a Karnaugh map containing $2^n$ cells corresponds to a term with $n$ variables missing. This property is a direct result of the labeling scheme, in which only one input value changes between any pair of adjacent cells. By finding such rectangles of $2^n$ adjacent cells containing only 1s, a simplified sum-of-products expression can rapidly be read off. The reader should note, in this connection, that in order to find a rectangle it may be necessary to "wrap around" the edges of the Karnaugh map. For example, the "rectangle" for the term $\overline{B}$, containing all cells for which $B = 0$, consists of the outer two columns in figure 3.8(e). For this reason, it is often useful to think of the edges of a Karnaugh map as being connected as in a torus.

The two 1s in the lower left corner of figure 3.8(e) indicate that the function has the value 1 when $A$ is 0 (left side), $C$ is 1 (lower row), and $B$ is either 0 or 1. Thus these two 1s (by themselves) correspond to the logical expression $\overline{A} \cdot C$. Similarly, the two 1s on the right side of the Karnaugh map correspond to the expression $A \cdot \overline{B}$. The function is represented by the sum of these two expressions:

$$f(A, B, C) = \overline{A} \cdot C + A \cdot \overline{B}.$$

This is the same logical expression we found earlier. The advantage of the Karnaugh map is that it makes it easy to spot contiguous sets of 1s in the map that can be combined into single terms.

Let us formalize slightly what we have done. A *literal* is a variable or a variable with an overbar, and an *implicant* of a function is a product of literals with the property that the function has the value 1 whenever the product has the value 1. For a function of three variables, each 1 in the Karnaugh map corresponds to an implicant with three literals. Each pair of contiguous 1s (including end around) corresponds to an implicant with two literals, and each rectangle of four 1s

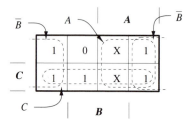

**Figure 3.9** A Karnaugh map with don't cares and prime implicants.

corresponds to an implicant with one literal. For example, the two-literal implicants of $f$ are $\overline{A} \cdot C$, $A \cdot \overline{B}$, and $\overline{B} \cdot C$. A *prime implicant* of a function is an implicant with the property that no other implicant consists of a subset of the literals in the given implicant. In the Karnaugh map, the prime implicants correspond to the largest rectangles of 1s that form implicants. A function is equal to the sum of its prime implicants; for the function $f$ in figure 3.8(e), this yields

$$f = \overline{A} \cdot C + A \cdot \overline{B} + \overline{B} \cdot C.$$

We can now concisely state the role of Karnaugh maps in simplifying logical expressions. Given the Karnaugh map corresponding to a logical expression, we can find the prime implicants by inspection. We then represent the function by the sum of enough of the prime implicants to cover all the 1s in the Karnaugh map.

In some cases, all of the prime implicants will be needed. In others, some of the prime implicants may be omitted. For example, the prime implicant $\overline{B} \cdot C$ is redundant in the function $f$ above and may be omitted, yielding the expression

$$f = \overline{A} \cdot C + A \cdot \overline{B}.$$

Often a Karnaugh map is used to construct a simplified sum-of-products expression for a logical function with "don't care" values, that is, a function whose output is immaterial for certain sets of input values. For example, a circuit that takes a 4-bit unsigned integer between 0 and 9 as input and generates output to display the corresponding digit on a seven-segment readout need not generate anything recognizable for input combinations outside the range from 0 to 9. Similarly, a tens-of-minutes readout on a digital clock would never need to handle any digits outside the range 0 to 5. Figure 3.9 shows a Karnaugh map for this latter design problem. The cells corresponding to input values $ABC = 110$ and 111 are labeled with the "don't care" symbol X to indicate that a synthesized function will be acceptable no matter what outputs it generates for these input combinations.

The procedure for constructing a reduced sum-of-products expression from a Karnaugh map with don't cares is as follows:

a. Identify the prime implicants, treating all don't cares as 1s.

b. Use just enough of the prime implicants found in step a as are necessary to cover all the 1s in the Karnaugh map (but not necessarily enough to cover any or all of the Xs).

Intuitively, we start out by treating Xs as 1s so that we can obtain the largest possible prime implicants (which will therefore have the fewest literals), but we do not include in the final expression any prime implicants whose sole purpose would be to turn on cells containing Xs and which therefore would make no further contribution to the goal of turning on all the 1s. In figure 3.9 the three prime implicants are $A$, $\overline{B}$, and $C$. Just $\overline{B}$ and $C$, however, suffice to cover all the 1s; hence $A$ is not needed. The resulting logical expression is $\overline{B} + C$; note that it produces a 1 for the don't care input $ABC = 111$, but a 0 for the other don't care input $ABC = 110$. Figure 3.10 illustrates the synthesis of logical expressions from Karnaugh maps for several examples and shows how Karnaugh maps are constructed for functions of four and five variables. In Karnaugh maps with more than three variables, both left-to-right and top-to-bottom wraparound are necessary; note particularly the implicant consisting of the four corners in figure 3.10(c). Beyond four variables, Karnaugh maps quickly become clumsy, and additional kinds of "internal wraparound" are necessary to connect all the implicants in figure 3.10(d).

When some of the prime implicants can be omitted in a sum-of-products expression for a function, it is sometimes interesting to ask which should be omitted to achieve the simplest expression. Texts on switching theory (such as Hill and Peterson [1981]) treat this problem in depth, but as we shall illustrate below, the simplest sum-of-products expression for a given function is not necessarily the simplest logical expression for the function, nor the most desirable starting point for an implementation.

There is a dual procedure for constructing product-of-sums expressions from Karnaugh maps by looking for blocks of contiguous 0s. The details are illustrated in figure 3.10(b).

## 3.4 Temporal Considerations in Combinational Circuits

Up to this point, we have characterized combinational circuits only in terms of their logical properties. No mention of temporal behavior has been made, and we have regarded the outputs as *immediate* functions of the input variables. All physical circuits, however, take time to respond to changes in the input variable values, and typical propagation delays for contemporary single-level gates range from 1 to 20 nanoseconds (ns) and more. In addition, these delays can vary over time, and wiring delays (approximately 1 ns per foot of wire) can also affect the circuit performance. The logic designer must take care that combinational circuit modules perform logically correctly, and also within a time appropriate to the overall speed required.

A combinational circuit, taken *by itself*, will always produce the correct output values eventually, after all changes have propagated through the circuit. It is important, however, to allow enough time for such settling, and such allowances are often the critical performance limitation in high-speed computers. The more *levels* of gating that are present in a circuit, the greater the *delay* through that

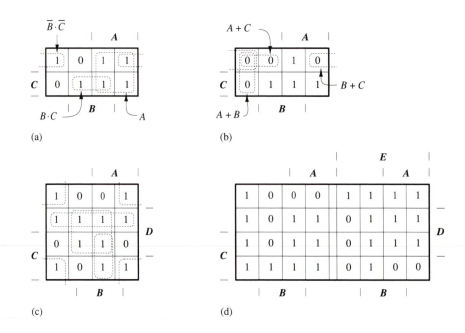

**Figure 3.10** Karnaugh maps and their logical expressions: (a) construction of a sum of products, $A + B \cdot C + \overline{B} \cdot \overline{C}$; (b) construction of a product of sums, $(A+B) \cdot (B+C) \cdot (C+A)$; (c) a four-variable map, $\overline{B} \cdot \overline{D} + \overline{C} \cdot D + B \cdot D + A \cdot B \cdot C$ or $(\overline{B} + C + D) \cdot (B + \overline{C} + \overline{D}) \cdot (A + \overline{B} + D)$; (d) a five-variable map, $A \cdot D + C \cdot \overline{D} \cdot \overline{E} + \overline{A} \cdot \overline{B} \cdot \overline{E} + \overline{C} \cdot \overline{D} \cdot E + \overline{A} \cdot B \cdot E$.

circuit, but shorter delay is often achieved only at the expense of additional circuit complexity.

A classic example of this trade-off in combinational circuits is the *parity* function, which is the worst possible function for two-level realization with respect to the resultant number of gates. Given $n$ logical variables, an *odd-parity* function generates a 1 if and only if the number of 1s among the $n$ input variables is odd. The Karnaugh map for this function will show a checkerboard pattern of 1s and 0s with no possibilities for combining implicants, as the reader can verify. A two-level odd-parity function over eight variables requires 129 NAND gates. While there are only two levels of delay, the cost of 129 gates will usually be prohibitive, and the designer may choose to tolerate more delay in order to reduce the number of gates. For example, using a cascade of several XOR gates, we can implement an odd-parity circuit as follows:

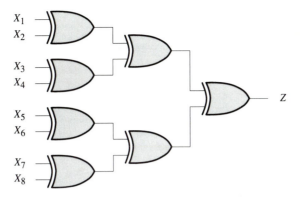

In turn, each XOR gate can be implemented using three NANDs and two inverters:

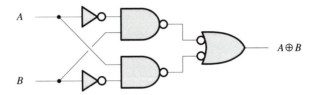

Thus the XOR implementation of odd parity for eight variables requires 21 NAND gates and 14 inverters but has nine levels of gating, counting an inverter as a level of gating. Thus no one technique will automatically give an "optimal" solution, and the choice of a circuit must be based on the constraints it must meet.

While a combinational circuit will always produce the correct output after a sufficient settling time, undesired output transitions can occur during that time. These transitions, which can cause malfunctions in certain circuits that utilize the combinational output, are called *hazards*. Hazards can arise even in very simple circuits and are characteristic of the gate configuration rather than the logical function itself. Figure 3.11 shows a circuit that computes the function

$$H = \overline{Y_2} \cdot Y_1 + Y_2 \cdot Y_3.$$

When $Y_1$, $Y_2$, and $Y_3$ are each 1, the output of gate 1 is 0 and the output of gate 2 is 1, so that the steady output $H$ is 1. Now let $Y_2$ change from 1 to 0. The inverter delays and inverts this change, and during this short delay the output of the inverter is still 0, so the output of gate 1 remains 0. But the new value of $Y_2$ arrives at gate 2 immediately, changing its output to 0, so that for a brief period the output of gate 3 may dip to 0. This sequence of events is shown in the timing diagram of figure 3.11(c), where the horizontal separations between dotted lines each represent one gate propagation delay time.

In this particular example, the input variables change from one set of values to another set that yields the same output, namely a 1. Because of variations in delay along different paths in the circuit, however, the input change induces temporary fluctuations in the output. Similar fluctuations can occur when an output is supposed to remain at 0, or even when a transition in output is supposed to occur, as shown in figure 3.12.

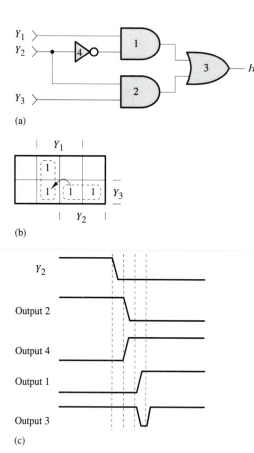

(a)

(b)

(c)

**Figure 3.11**  An output circuit with a hazard.  In (b), the arrow indicates the hazard-producing transition.

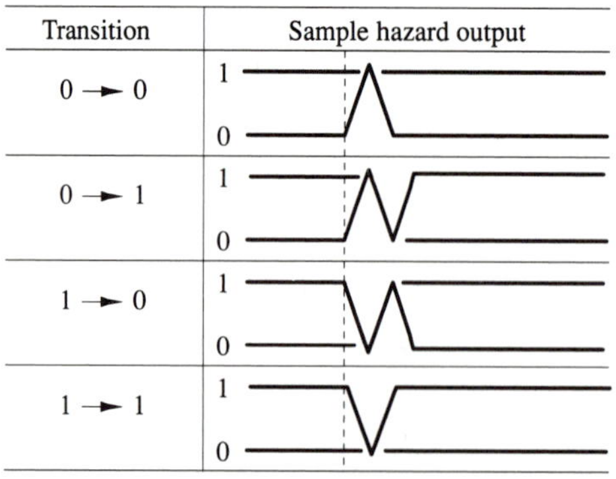

| Transition | Sample hazard output |
|---|---|
| 0 → 0 | |
| 0 → 1 | |
| 1 → 0 | |
| 1 → 1 | |

**Figure 3.12**  Examples of hazards.

A hazard is thus the result of *skew* in which the consequences of a change in an input value propagate at varying speeds through a circuit, leading to momentary "glitches" in gate outputs. Delay in logic elements is unfortunately a fact of life; furthermore, propagation delays generally vary between different types of components, between different components of the same type, and even from time to time for the same component, as the component is affected by temperature, aging, supply voltage, and other factors. It is therefore unwise to design circuits that depend for their correct operation on some critical relationship of component delay times.

The extreme form of this "speed-independent" design methodology is to design a circuit to operate correctly *no matter how long or short the individual propagation delays are*. Thus if we are trying to design circuits without output glitches, we would like a design that is glitch-free for any combination of individual component delays. This ideal can be achieved, in general, only if we restrict input variables to change just one at a time and if no new input transitions occur until all activity caused by previous transitions has subsided.

Except in certain special cases, it is impossible to construct speed-independent designs that are glitch-free when several inputs change state simultaneously. Thus, referring back to the logical function of figure 3.11, we do not hope for a design that would be glitch-free during a transition from $Y_1 = Y_2 = Y_3 = 1$ to $Y_1 = 1, Y_2 = Y_3 = 0$, but we do hope to find a design that will be immune to such fluctuations when only one input changes at a time.

The blocks in the map of figure 3.11(b) indicate the two terms in the sum-of-products circuit of part (a) and show that the hazard is produced by a transition that "jumps" from one block to the other. The hazard can be removed by adding the prime implicant $Y_1 \cdot Y_3$ to the sum, as shown in figure 3.13. The circuit implements the logical expression

$$H = (\overline{Y_2} \cdot Y_1) + (Y_1 \cdot Y_3) + (Y_2 \cdot Y_3).$$

This technique is in fact general, and one can always construct a hazard-free circuit for any given function by implementing the sum of all its prime implicants.

The details of why hazards occur and how to avoid them are beyond the scope of this book, but two further points should be made. First, the pulses and fluctuations that may occur in the outputs of a circuit with hazards *can* cause a circuit using those outputs to misbehave if it is sensitive to such momentary fluctuations in its input. Sometimes this is the case, but more often it is not. Thus it would be incorrect to conclude that all logic circuits must be made hazard-free. Indeed, such a design practice would add substantially to the cost of most computing hardware.

Second, even though in many cases it is possible to ignore hazards that may be present in a circuit, the existence of hazards serves to remind us of the limitations of our abstractions. Viewing gate circuits as delayless elements that implement Boolean functions is a useful simplification for the design and analysis of combinational logic, but in the physical world we must always bear in mind the potential impacts of noise and delay on the validity of this abstraction.

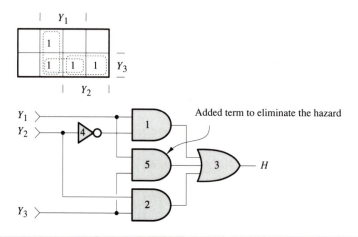

**Figure 3.13** Application of an additional gate to remove a hazard.

## 3.5 Context

The topics of this chapter fall squarely within the traditional headings of *digital design* and *switching theory*, the subject of classic texts such as Hill and Peterson [1981] and Peatman [1980]. The classic approach to logic design, which emphasizes gate-level synthesis and manual optimization of circuits (using, for example, Karnaugh maps) is, however, gradually evolving under the pressure of new technological parameters. The simple gate no longer plays quite the critical role it once held as the single inviolate abstraction on which systems are based: Board-level logic designers deal with more substantial primitives (such as those discussed in chapter 5), while design approaches at the chip level frequently trespass across gate boundaries in the interests of efficiency. In both arenas, computer-based tools are automating the design process, shifting emphasis from human-oriented to computer-oriented algorithms for optimization and analysis.

## 3.6 Problems

### Problem 3.1
Give a canonical sum-of-products expression for the Boolean function described by each truth table in figure 3.14.

### Problem 3.2
Give a simplified sum-of-products expression for the Boolean function described by each truth table in figure 3.14.

### Problem 3.3
Give a truth table for each of the following logical expressions.

A. $A \cdot \overline{B + C}$.

| $A$ | $B$ | $C$ | $F(A, B, C)$ |
|---|---|---|---|
| 0 | 0 | 0 | 1 |
| 0 | 0 | 1 | 0 |
| 0 | 1 | 0 | 0 |
| 0 | 1 | 1 | 0 |
| 1 | 0 | 0 | 1 |
| 1 | 0 | 1 | 1 |
| 1 | 1 | 0 | 0 |
| 1 | 1 | 1 | 1 |

(a)

| $A$ | $B$ | $C$ | $G(A, B, C)$ |
|---|---|---|---|
| 0 | 0 | 0 | 0 |
| 0 | 0 | 1 | 0 |
| 0 | 1 | 0 | 0 |
| 0 | 1 | 1 | 1 |
| 1 | 0 | 0 | 0 |
| 1 | 0 | 1 | 1 |
| 1 | 1 | 0 | 1 |
| 1 | 1 | 1 | 1 |

(b)

**Figure 3.14**  Two truth tables.

B. $(A + \overline{B}) \cdot \overline{A \cdot B \cdot C} + D$.

C. $A + B \cdot (C + \overline{D})$.

D. $(\overline{A} + B) \cdot (A + C)$.

E. $A + B \cdot C \cdot \overline{D}$.

F. $\overline{B} + \overline{(C + \overline{(D + C + A)})} + \overline{(\overline{D} + B + \overline{A})}$.

G. $\overline{(\overline{A} + B \cdot \overline{D}) \cdot (B + \overline{C}) \cdot \overline{\overline{B} \cdot C \cdot D}}$.

H. $A \cdot B + \overline{A} \cdot (C + D)$.

### Problem 3.4
Give a simplified sum-of-products expression for each expression in problem 3.3.

### Problem 3.5
Synthesize a circuit using only NAND gates for each expression in problem 3.3. (Omit expressions C and D, whose synthesis appears as example 3 in this chapter.)

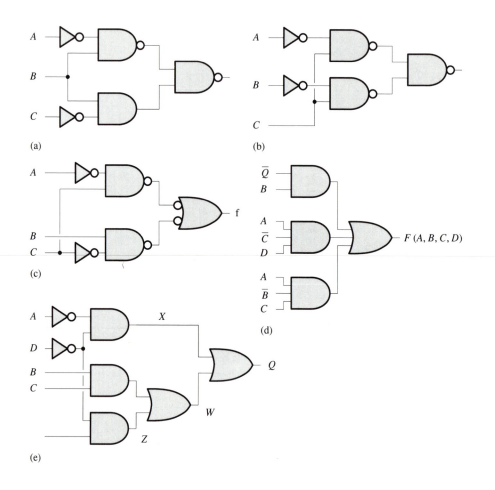

**Figure 3.15** Logic circuits.

### Problem 3.6
Synthesize a circuit using only NOR gates for each expression in problem 3.3. (Omit expression E, whose synthesis appears as example 4 in this chapter.)

### Problem 3.7
Give a truth table for each circuit in figure 3.15.

### Problem 3.8
Give a logical expression for each circuit in figure 3.15.

### Problem 3.9
For each circuit in figure 3.15, draw a circuit that computes the same logic function but contains only OR gates and inverters.

### Problem 3.10
Do the following for each circuit in figure 3.15:

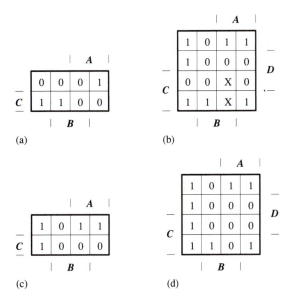

**Figure 3.16** Karnaugh maps.

- Draw a Karnaugh map, circling all prime implicants.
- Write a minimal sum-of-products expression, including only as many prime implicants as necessary.
- Synthesize a logic circuit based on this expression, using only AND gates, OR gates, and inverters.
- Identify hazards, if any, in the circuit drawn in the previous answer, indicating the hazard-producing transitions on your Karnaugh map.
- For each circuit containing one or more hazards, synthesize a hazard-free circuit that computes the same logic function.

## Problem 3.11

For each Karnaugh map in figure 3.16, show the minimum number of prime implicants needed to cover all the 1s in the function. Indicate any hazards that are present if only the prime implicants that you identified are used.

## Problem 3.12

Repeat problem 3.10, starting with the logical expressions in figure 3.10 instead of the circuits in figure 3.15.

## Problem 3.13  *Timing and Hazards:*

Consider the following combinational circuit:

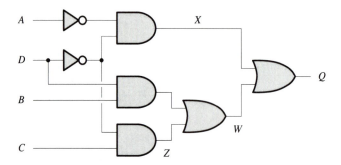

A. Suppose that each component in the circuit has a propagation delay of exactly 10 ns and negligible rise and fall times. Suppose initially that all four inputs are at 1 for a long time, and then the input $D$ changes to 0. Fill in the following waveforms, and circle any glitches in the output $Q$ due to hazards.

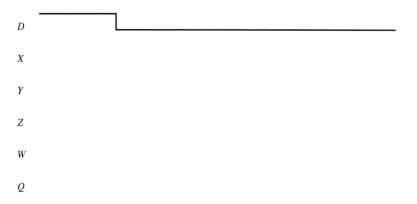

B. Show how to eliminate the hazard(s) using a Karnaugh map and adding the least number of prime implicant(s).

C. Redraw the circuit and show the least additional hardware needed to implement the hazard-correcting implicants, using only NOTs and two-input ANDs and ORs.

D. Explain in words from your circuit diagram why any glitches of the original circuit have been eliminated.

### Problem 3.14

How many Boolean functions of four variables are there? Of $n$ variables?

### Problem 3.15

Suppose you need to implement the function $\overline{A \cdot B}$, but all you have available is a three-input NAND. To what should the third input be connected so the output is still $\overline{A \cdot B}$ ?

*Combinational Devices and Circuits*

### Problem 3.16

A certain two-input gate computes the exclusive-OR function using *negative* logic. What function does the same gate compute using positive logic?

### Problem 3.17

Is there a Boolean function that cannot be realized using only AND and OR gates? If so, give a simple example; if not, explain.

### Problem 3.18

Is it possible for a one-input, one-output combinational circuit built entirely of two-input NAND gates to contain a hazard? Either draw such a circuit or explain why one cannot be built.

### Problem ★3.19

Is it possible for a combinational circuit built entirely of AND and OR gates to contain a hazard? Either draw such a circuit or explain why one cannot be built.

### Problem 3.20

Suppose you are shown this circuit:

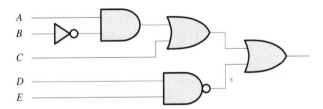

Without any analysis—just by looking at the circuit—you should be able to tell whether it does or does not have a hazard. Explain how you can do this and indicate whether or not this circuit has a hazard. (You can assume that each individual gate is hazard-free.)

### Problem ★3.21

Recall the discussion of the completeness of the NAND and NOR functions.

A. Referring to figure 3.2, identify which other two-argument Boolean functions are complete in the same sense. (*Hint:* Could a function be complete if its outputs are independent of one or both of its inputs?) Since NAND is complete, we can demonstrate the completeness of another Boolean function $f$ by showing how to implement NAND using only $f$ and the constants 1 and 0. Use the notation $f_n$ to denote the function numbered $n$ in figure 3.2. For example, the completeness of the NOR function, $f_8$, can be demonstrated as follows:

$$\text{NAND}(A, B) = f_8(f_8(f_8(A, 0), f_8(B, 0)), 0).$$

B. Give a definition of NAND in terms of each of the other complete functions. Do the same for NOR.

C. Which of the sixteen two-input Boolean functions are complete assuming that constants are *not* available?

D. If you had to build a computer out of just one type of gate, would the NAND gate be preferred over the AND gate? Why or why not?

## Problem 3.22  Binary Decoder:

A binary-to-seven-segment decoder takes 4 bits of input and produces seven outputs, one for each "segment" in a standard display:

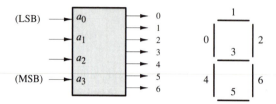

Given the appropriate binary input, this display produces outputs that light up the display in the following manner:

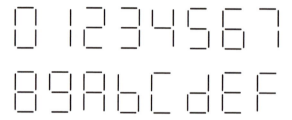

We are interested in the circuit that produces the signal for the segment numbered 3 (a 1 turns a segment on; a 0 turns it off):

A. Construct a Karnaugh map for segment 3.

B. Write a minimal sum-of-products expression for segment 3 in terms of the inputs $a_0$, $a_1$, $a_2$, and $a_3$.

C. Draw a circuit that implements this expression using AND and OR gates and inverters.

D. Does your circuit contain hazards? If so, indicate the transitions on which these hazards occur on the Karnaugh map of part A.

## Problem 3.23  Binary Adder:

A common approach to the addition of $n$-bit binary numbers uses $n$ cascaded combinational modules, each a 1-bit adder (conventionally called a *full adder*). Full-adder modules can be combined as follows to implement a circuit that adds the $n$-bit unsigned binary value $A$ to the $n$-bit unsigned binary value $B$, yielding the $n$-bit sum $S$ ($A_0$ designates the low-order bit of $A$, and $A_{n-1}$ the high-order bit):

*Combinational Devices and Circuits*

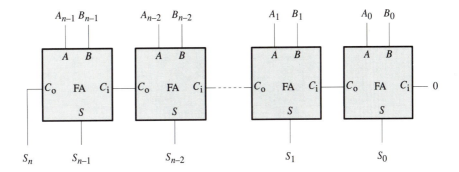

A. What information is carried by the $C_i$ input to each full adder? By the $C_o$ output?

B. Suppose the $C_i$ input to the low-order full adder is connected to logical 1 rather than logical 0. Describe the relationship of the binary number $S$ to the input numbers $A$ and $B$ under these circumstances.

C. Give truth tables for each of the outputs $S$ and $C_o$ for the full-adder module in terms of its inputs $A$, $B$, and $C_i$. Draw Karnaugh maps for each output.

D. Draw a circuit diagram for a full-adder module, using AND, OR, NAND, XOR, and inverter modules. Try to minimize the number of component modules in your design. (*Hint:* You'll find an XOR gate useful.)

E. Assuming a $t_{pd}$ of 10 ns for each module, what propagation delay should be specified for the full adder? For the $n$-bit adder?

F. Propose an addition to the circuit to produce a single output bit $U$ that carries a 1 if and only if the addition of the unsigned numbers $A$ and $B$ overflows the $n$-bit result $S$.

G. What modifications are necessary to make the $n$-bit adder properly add two *signed* numbers represented in 2's complement binary? Explain.

H. Propose an addition to your (perhaps modified) circuit to produce an output $V$ that carries a 1 if and only if the addition of the *signed* numbers $A$ and $B$ overflows the $n$-bit result $S$.

### Problem 3.24   Charlie on the MBTA:

The Massachusetts Bay Transportation Authority (MBTA) has just awarded you a contract to revamp the signaling system on its Green Line. You have decided upon the following basic approach: Each section of track will have a sensor to determine whether there is a train in that section and a signal with red, yellow, and green lights. You want the light in a track section to show *red* if there is a train in the very next section, *yellow* if there is no train in the next section but the section after that is occupied, and *green* otherwise. You decide to place a logic module, shown schematically below, under each section of track:

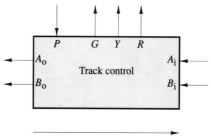

Direction of train movement

Tracks are one-way only, and trains move left to right relative to the track control module. The outputs $G$, $Y$, and $R$ should be a 1 to light the green, yellow, and red signals, respectively, for this section of track. The input $P$ is 1 if there is a train in this section. The signals $A_i$ and $B_i$ are received from the next section, and outputs $A_o$ and $B_o$ are passed back to the previous section. You may do with these what you like, but there are only two wires available, and you may not add more.

A. Design the logic for this box to implement the signaling function. Describe what use you have made of lines $A$ and $B$.

B. Under switches that merge two incoming tracks into one outgoing track, you will need to put a special kind of module:

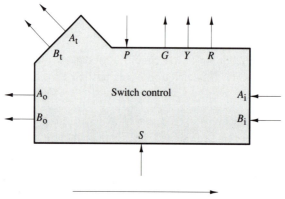

Direction of train movement

This module operates like a regular track control module except that it signals *red* in the previous section (and *yellow* in the section before that) to trains coming from the direction the switch is *not* currently set to accept. The input $S$ is 1 if the switch is set straight, 0 if it is turned. Give a logic diagram for this new module. You need not worry about logic modules for switches that split one incoming track into two outgoing tracks.

*Combinational Devices and Circuits*

# 4    Sequences and State

The digital circuits presented thus far perform operations that can be characterized logically (ignoring timing and other analog aspects of behavior) by a simple truth table. The truth table specifies an output value for each combination of input values; systems thus characterized are referred to as *combinational* systems.

Much of the power and simplicity of combinational logic comes from its finite nature. We can easily enumerate the combinational functions of $n$ inputs for any $n$; we can determine the logical equivalence of two combinational elements by exhaustive comparison of their truth tables; and we can utilize finite arrays of programmable logic elements, such as the read-only memories to be discussed in chapter 5, to implement arbitrary combinational functions of $n$ inputs. Moreover, acyclic circuits containing only combinational elements are themselves combinational; this affords a simple engineering discipline by which arbitrarily complex combinational systems can be constructed using a small repertoire of basic gates.

Unfortunately, strictly combinational systems are awkward for many applications. Consider the requirements of an adding machine that will be used to maintain a checkbook balance. A strictly combinational adding machine would require several inputs to be simultaneously present in order to produce valid output; in the extreme case, adding a column of $n$ numbers would require $n$ simultaneous inputs. Such an approach would require that the number of addends be limited to the number of input ports to the machine, constraining unnecessarily its range of uses. Faced with such a machine, the resourceful user would quickly develop a *sequential* mode of operation, in which an arbitrarily long summation is broken down into a sequence of two-input add operations. The user would maintain an imaginary balance, adding each successive addend sequentially.

Real adding machines, of course, are designed to operate in a sequential rather than a combinational fashion. A column of numbers to be added is entered in a sequence of suboperations through a single input port, and the result becomes available only after the entire sequence of inputs has been presented. The adding machine is a sequential digital system.

Unlike combinational circuits, the output of a sequential circuit may depend on variable factors other than the current inputs to that circuit; in an adding machine, for example, the current output will be the accumulated sum of all previous inputs. We refer collectively to these additional variables as the *state* of the system. The current output of a sequential system may reflect the state of the system as well as

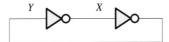

**Figure 4.1**  Two-inverter ring.

its current inputs, and each input may cause the state of the system to change. We may thus view a system's state as a collection of internal variables that are implicitly both inputs and outputs of the system. The state of a digital system reflects the entire history of its inputs; the state of our adding machine, for example, is the sum of all previous inputs.

In general, the state of a digital system may comprise arbitrarily large amounts of information. Although we frequently deal with abstract models with an unbounded capacity for information (pushdown stacks, for example), such systems are unrealistic in practice: Every realizable system has a finite limit on the amount of information reflected in its state. This fact leads to an important subclass of sequential systems called *finite-state machines*, whose state can be viewed as corresponding to an integer variable capable of assuming one of finitely many values.

This chapter is devoted to the development of finite-state machines, a key element in the technology of digital systems. We proceed in bootstrap fashion by (1) using combinational elements to synthesize a rudimentary two-state circuit called a *flip-flop*, (2) combining flip-flops to yield $n$-bit *registers*, each with $2^n$ states, and (3) developing a technique for synthesizing arbitrary finite-state machines using registers and combinational logic.

## 4.1  Feedback and State

A combinational circuit can be statically analyzed by assigning variable names to its inputs and deducing expressions for successive output nodes using the functional specification of each logic element. We can always deduce an upper bound on the time requirements of a combinational circuit from the time bounds specified for its individual components, again by a series of steps that establish the timing of the inputs of each element before deducing the timing of its output. This input-to-output analysis technique depends on the *acyclic* nature of combinational circuits: No input to an element is derived in any way from an output of that element. Thus a straightforward enumeration will necessarily consider *every* path from an input to an output.

The introduction of feedback paths in a logic circuit complicates both functional and timing analyses. Consider the simple circuit of figure 4.1. This circuit defies analysis by any technique that considers every path from an input to an output, primarily because its cyclic nature leads to infinitely many such paths (and secondarily, in this particular example, because there are no inputs).

We can, however, observe some constraints this circuit imposes on the logic values assumed at its nodes. In particular, each of the inverters produces at its

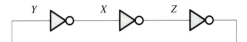

**Figure 4.2** Three-inverter ring.

output a value that is the inverse of its input; each constrains the value of one of the nodes to be the inverse of the other. These constraints can be summarized as

$$X = \overline{Y},$$

$$Y = \overline{X}.$$

Assuming that the inverters obey their specifications, any combination of logic values we find on nodes $X$ and $Y$ must obey these equations. However, the equations *underspecify* the $X$ and $Y$ logic values: There are two consistent solutions, namely $X = 1, \quad Y = 0$ and $X = 0, \quad Y = 1$. Neither assignment of values violates the relationships of our digital abstraction; indeed, within the digital abstraction we can find no reason for preferring one solution over the other. The circuit of figure 4.1 is in fact a simple *bistable* logic element: It has two stable *states* (corresponding to the two solutions to its *state equations*, above) and, once put in either state, will remain there indefinitely.

A slight variation of figure 4.1 is the ring of three inverters shown in figure 4.2. Again, each of the circuit elements constrains the logic values of one node to be a function of the values on the others; summarizing the constraints, we have

$$X = \overline{Y},$$

$$Y = \overline{Z},$$

$$Z = \overline{X}.$$

In contrast to the bistable circuit, however, the set of Boolean equations derived from the three-inverter ring has *no* consistent solution in the logic domain. The equations dictate that $X = \overline{Y} = \overline{\overline{Z}} = \overline{\overline{\overline{X}}} = \overline{X}$, which is a contradiction. We conclude from this analysis that the three-inverter ring has no stable equilibrium in the logic domain.

This conclusion is supported experimentally. A three-inverter ring will typically oscillate between valid logic levels, with a period on the order of six times the propagation delay of a single inverter. Such *astable* behavior is intuitively reasonable: If we assume that $X = 0$ at some time $t$, for example, it follows that after one propagation delay (at time $t + t_{\mathrm{pd}}$) $Z$ will be 1. This will cause $Y$ to be 0 at time $t + 2t_{\mathrm{pd}}$, whence $X$ will become 1 at time $t + 3t_{\mathrm{pd}}$. The value of $X$ will change again (back to 0) in another three propagation delays or so, yielding a full cycle over six propagation delays.

We can generalize these two examples to rings of $n$ inverters where $n > 1$: Such rings are bistable for even $n$ and astable for odd $n$. Odd-sized inverter rings are occasionally used as a digital time base in noncritical applications and are often constructed to measure the propagation delay of a logic family. We shall explore variations on the even-$n$ theme in the next section.

It is important to recognize that the modicum of analysis exhibited in the above examples—specifically, the derivation of systems of Boolean equations and scrutiny of their solutions—does not constitute a general or foolproof technique for predicting the behavior of logic circuits. Lest the reader misconstrue the power of our deductions, consider a logic circuit consisting of a single node $X$, implemented perhaps as a wire. We might characterize the logic-domain behavior of this absurd circuit by the Boolean tautology $X = X$, an equation whose solution set contains $X = 0$ and $X = 1$. It is obviously silly for us to expect only valid $X = 0$ or $X = 1$ values on our wire; do we look for TTL values of 0 or 5 V? How does the wire know that it is an elementless TTL circuit rather than an elementless ECL circuit?

The Boolean equations we derive from the circuit topology and the specifications of its elements are constraints that must be met by any assignment of valid logic values to circuit nodes, but the existence of a solution guarantees neither the logical validity nor the stability of the actual values. The fact that solutions of state equations of nontrivial logic circuits usually correspond to stable states reflects characteristics of logic elements that must be explained in the analog domain; their gain, for example, tends to produce valid outputs from invalid inputs. Such characteristics provide the engineer with a measure of practical assurance that, for example, valid logic levels will be found at the nodes of a two-inverter ring, but there remains the haunting possibility of anomalous behavior of various kinds. The reader is invited to explore the plausibility of oscillation in a two-inverter ring whose components are modeled by ideal finite-delay inverters for which $t_{\mathrm{pd}} = t_{\mathrm{cd}}$ and whose state is constrained to the initial values $X = 0$, $Y = 0$.

## 4.2 Latches, Flip-Flops, and Registers

A pair of cross-coupled inverters can exist in two stable states and therefore can be used as a primitive memory element to hold 1 bit of information. The problem with the circuit is that it cannot be forced into any particular state. This problem is solved by the simple circuit shown in figure 4.3, called an *R-S latch*. $S$ and $R$ are called the *set* and *reset* inputs, respectively, and $Q$ is the output.

When $S = 0$ and $R = 0$, this circuit is logically equivalent to the cross-coupled inverter circuit; it has two stable states and can act as a memory. If $S$ and $R$ are changed, however, the value stored by this circuit can be altered. If $S$ becomes 1 while $R = 0$, the signal $X$ will be forced to 0. With $X = 0$ and $R = 0$, the output $Q$ becomes 1. With $Q$ now 1, the value of $X$ will remain 0, independent of the value of $S$. Returning $S$ to 0 puts the circuit back into the memory state with $Q = 1$ (see figure 4.4). Similarly, pulsing $R$ from 0 to 1 and back to 0 forces the circuit into the state with $Q = 0$. Times during which a new value asserted on $S$ or $R$ is propagating through the circuit to set a new value on $Q$ are called *transition times*.

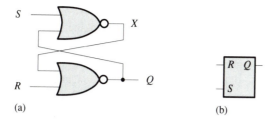

(a)

(b)

**Figure 4.3**  $R$-$S$ latch: (a) the circuit; (b) a shorthand diagram.

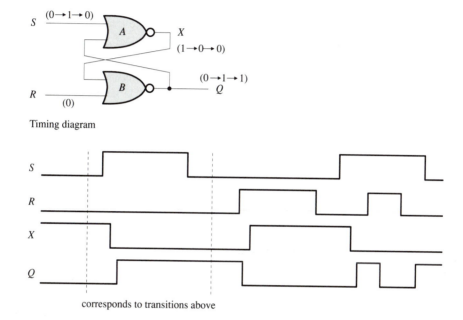

Timing diagram

corresponds to transitions above

**Figure 4.4**  Dynamics of the $R$-$S$ latch.

When $S = R = 0$, the circuit remembers which of $S$ or $R$ was high more recently. If $S$ was high more recently, then $Q$ will be 1 (set). If $R$ was high more recently, then $Q$ will be 0 (reset). If $S = R = 1$, $Q$ will remain 0 until such time as $S = 1$ and $R = 0$ (thus reset "overrides" set).

If both $R$ and $S$ change from 1 to 0 at the same time, gates $A$ and $B$ in the figure will both try to drive their outputs ($X$ and $Q$, respectively) to logical 1. This results in what is called a *race condition*, a term describing a situation in which the behavior of a circuit depends upon the relative transit times of two signals over combinational paths. If, for some reason, the new $R$ value propagates through the lower gate (yielding $Q = 1$) and drives an input to the upper gate fast enough to prevent the $S$ transition from driving $X$ to 1, the resulting state might be $Q = 1$. If the $S$ transition propagates much faster along its path, a $Q = 0$ state might

*Sequences and State*

79

result. Note that this race involves two paths that both go through the same pair of gates (albeit through different inputs), making it unlikely that either transition will emerge as a clear winner. In any case, the outcome of the race is beyond the control of the digital designer.

A more serious problem occurs if the propagation delays along the two paths are very close. In the race scenario described above, the output of the $R$-$S$ latch is a valid level, either 1 or 0, once the two signals in question have propagated along their respective paths. If there is no clear winner of the race, however, the propagation of each signal can compromise the validity of the other in a way that results in invalid logic levels that persist for an indefinite period of time. In this situation the circuit is said to be in a *metastable state*, an unstable equilibrium that inevitably exists in bistable devices. This topic is discussed in more depth in section 4.6; for the present, we observe that care must be taken to avoid nearly simultaneous negative transitions on $R$ and $S$.

Generally we shall adopt engineering disciplines that allow us to avoid dealing with timing details at this level. Our approach is to confront the timing problems in the simple context of *clocked* bistable devices (flip-flops) and then to confine our sequential system designs to stages of combinational circuitry separated by the clocked devices. Since the flip-flops are designed to provide no combinational path from data inputs to data outputs, they effectively constrain the propagation of information to occur only at discrete times, when they are allowed to assume new states. In so doing, they eliminate the need to consider the complex dynamics introduced by uncontrolled feedback paths. The rest of this section develops these ideas further.

### 4.2.1 The Transparent Latch

*Clocked* circuits contain a special input that constrains the time at which a state transition can take place. A simple example of a clocked circuit is the *transparent* or *D latch*, depicted in figure 4.5. The tranparent latch has two inputs, designated $D$ (data) and $G$ (gate); like the $R$-$S$ latch, it is a bistable device capable of storing a single bit of information for an arbitrary period of time. So long as $G = 0$, the $Q$ output of the latch remains constant; while $G = 1$, however, the output $Q$ follows the value at the input $D$ after a short propagation delay. The state of the latch (the "remembered" bit) can thus be changed by applying a new value to the $D$ input and raising $G$ momentarily. The timing diagram of figure 4.5 shows the response of a transparent latch to a sequence of inputs.

The transparent latch can be implemented quite simply by combining an $R$-$S$ latch with several gates, resulting in the circuit of figure 4.6. Note that the right half of this diagram is identical to the $R$-$S$ latch of figure 4.3. Its $S$ and $R$ inputs are generated from $G$ and $D$ so as to guarantee that $S = G \cdot D$ and $R = G \cdot \overline{D}$. Thus, while $G = 0$, $R = S = 0$ and the latch maintains its state; when $G = 1$, $S = D$ and $R = \overline{D}$, causing the $Q$ output to follow $D$.

We might try to improve on the implementation of the transparent latch by resorting to a cyclic circuit involving gates, rather than building on the $R$-$S$ latch as a base. While this approach can be followed (as, for example, in our earlier

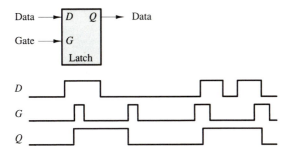

Figure 4.5 Transparent latch operation.

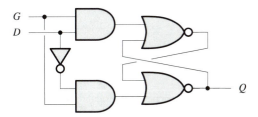

Figure 4.6 Transparent latch implementation.

development of the $R$-$S$ latch), it is fraught with subtle difficulties. Consider the faulty implementation attempt depicted in figure 4.7(b). Simple logic-domain analysis of this circuit confirms that when $G = 0$ it, like the $R$-$S$ latch, reduces to the bistable two-inverter ring; the Boolean equations describing the circuit admit $Q = 0$ and $Q = 1$ solutions independently of the value on $D$. When $G = 1$, $Q$ is forced to agree with the $D$ input, independently of the value on the feedback path labeled $X$.

This analysis, while sound at the level of Boolean algebra, is unfortunately naive when one considers timing details. In particular, it illustrates the importance of *hazards* in the synthesis of sequential circuits directly from combinational elements. Ignoring for the moment the feedback path in the circuit of figure 4.7 to the gate input marked $X$, we see that what remains is an (acyclic) combinational circuit that computes the state $Q$ from inputs $D$, $G$, and a newly created input $X$. We can view this combinational circuit as the heart of the device; it effectively computes a new value for the state $Q$, given inputs $D$, $G$, and an old state $X$; this view is developed further in section 4.5. However, careful scrutiny of the circuit shows a hazard on a $1 \rightarrow 0$ transition of $G$ when $X$ and $D$ are held at 1, as shown in the Karnaugh map of figure 4.7.

Suppose that a constant 1 is applied to the $D$ input of the faulty latch and that $G$ undergoes a transition from 1 to 0. Proper transparent latch operation should force $Q = 1$ while $G$ is 1 and maintain $Q = 1$ during and following the transition. The hazard in this circuit opens the possibility that a momentary 0 glitch will appear at

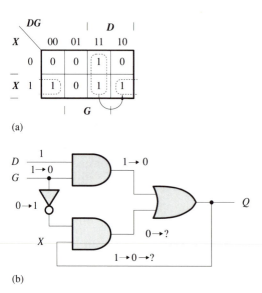

(a)

(b)

**Figure 4.7** Faulty implementation of a transparent latch: (a) a Karnaugh map showing the hazard; (b) the faulty implementation with a hazard.

$Q$ shortly after the transition and that the latch might actually remain in the $Q = 0$ state following the transition. The reader is encouraged to analyze the possible misbehavior of this circuit as component timing characteristics are varied. Briefly, the $1 \rightarrow 0$ transition on $G$ propagates through the topmost AND gate and the output OR gate, potentially causing a $1 \rightarrow 0$ transition at the $Q$ output. The same $1 \rightarrow 0$ transition on $G$ propagates through the inverter, bottom AND gate, and output OR gate, forcing $Q$ to the value at $X$. Assuming $Q = X = 1$, the upper two-gate path might force $Q$ to 0 a few nanoseconds before the lower three-gate path forces $Q$ back to 1, yielding a momentary output glitch. If, however, the lower path is much slower than the upper one (for example, if the delay through the inverter is long compared with other gate delays), the $Q = 0$ glitch from the upper path might propagate around the feedback loop before the effect of the $1 \rightarrow 0$ $G$ transition progresses along the bottom path; this would leave the latch in the $Q = 0$ state, constituting a serious malfunction.

Such simple complications can be circumvented by identifying and curing hazards, using additional terms in the sum-of-products expression on which the implementation is based; unfortunately, designing sequential circuits at this level becomes unmanageably awkward as their complexity increases. More commonly, the digital designer avoids them entirely by using a small repertoire of carefully designed sequential building blocks, combined with additional combinational circuitry, to create complex sequential systems.

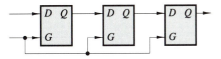

**Figure 4.8**  Naive interconnection of latches.

## 4.3 Edge-Triggered Flip-Flops and Registers

The name *transparent latch* reflects the fact that the latch transmits its input directly to its output while its gate signal is asserted (high, in our example). In this state, there is effectively a combinational path from $D$ input to $Q$ output: Asynchronous changes in the input are reflected at the output after a propagation delay. This feature of the $D$ latch can lead to a problem if several $D$ latches are *cascaded* together to form a chain, as in figure 4.8, with the intention of shifting data one stage to the right at each assertion of $G$. When $G$ is asserted in such a circuit, the combinational path extends the full length of the chain. The input to the chain may propagate through more than one level of latch while $G$ is asserted; indeed, the extent of such propagation depends upon the interval for which $G = 1$. We might attempt to solve the problem by applying a narrow pulse to the $G$ inputs, but this approach makes the circuit sensitive to analog timing variations that are difficult to control; this is generally considered bad engineering practice except under very special circumstances. Instead, we turn to one of several digital-domain circuit techniques that keep combinational paths short, allow ample time to accommodate every combinational propagation delay, and thereby avoid dependence on the exact values of propagation times.

Our approach involves the use of the *edge-triggered* family of flip-flops, which avoids combinational input-to-output paths altogether by separating the copying of input to output into two steps. Upon sensing a $0 \rightarrow 1$ transition on the clock, the flip-flop stops sampling its input.[1]  A short time (propagation delay) after the edge occurs, the output changes to the last value sampled on the input. Narrow clock pulses—necessary in the case of latches to prevent unwanted propagation of data through more than one level of latch during a single clock pulse—are not required by edge-triggered flip-flops. Often, edge-triggered flip-flops have an additional *load enable* input whose value at the time of an active clock edge specifies whether the flip-flop is to be loaded.

The clock input to an edge-triggered flip-flop effectively signals *events*, or points in time, via its active edges; in contrast, the gate input to a latch signals *intervals* during which the latch output is to be frozen. This is a basic difference in dimensionality, akin to the difference between points and lines: Transitions signal *events*, whereas levels signal *periods*. The signaling of events plays an important

---

[1] This is for a *positive* edge-triggered flip-flop; for a *negative* edge-triggered flip-flop, it would be a $1 \rightarrow 0$ transition.

**Figure 4.9** Two representations of an edge-triggered $D$ flip-flop.

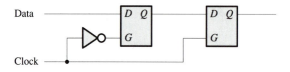

**Figure 4.10** Edge-triggered flip-flop.

role in the control of the dynamics of digital systems, a topic explored in detail in chapter 7.

Figure 4.9 shows two symbols for the edge-triggered $D$ flip-flop. A triangle is often used to indicate the clock input of edge-triggered devices, as in the second symbol. Figure 4.10 shows one implementation of a positive edge-triggered flip-flop. Note the use of two latches whose gate signals are complementary; for either value of the clock input, exactly one of the latches is transparent, while the other is holding. While the clock input is low, the left latch follows the input data and the right latch holds the previous output value constant; when the clock input is high, the left latch freezes its output and the right latch becomes transparent. Thus there is never a combinational path through the flip-flop; the effect is that stable input data at the time of a positive clock edge are "sampled" and propagate through to the output, where the data remain constant until the next positive clock edge. This analysis ignores analog issues such as the propagation delay through the inverter; the analysis of an edge-triggered flip-flop involves careful attention to such timing details to ensure that a combinational path through the device is avoided on both edges. Often this involves adjusting the $G = 1$ threshold of each gate input to ensure nonoverlap, even with unforeseen circuit delays.

Using two out-of-phase clock signals is an alternative to edge triggering that is common practice in VLSI designs. Nonoverlapping signals are generated and used alternately to control the transparency of successive logic stages in much the same fashion as the pair of latches in figure 4.10. Two-phase clocking generally requires fewer components per stage since, in effect, it allows the use of latches rather than the more complex edge-triggered devices to hold data. However, its extra engineering complexity (and the requirement for two clock pins rather than one) renders it awkward, in comparison with edge-triggered clocking, for chip-level building blocks.

Edge-triggered flip-flops are used in constructing *registers*, which are sets of flip-flops that can be read from and written into simultaneously. Figure 4.11 shows a

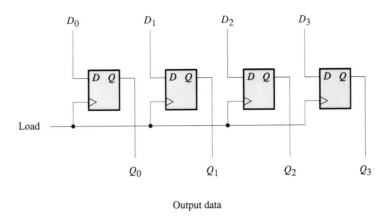

**Figure 4.11**  Register built out of *D* flip-flops.

4-bit register. On each positive edge of the clock signal, the input data are sampled and copied to the output data.

## 4.4 Register Timing

It is usual to specify the timing of inputs and outputs of edge-triggered devices relative to the active clock edge. Thus a flip-flop or register specification typically cites a *clock-to-Q* propagation delay $t_{\mathrm{p}C-Q}$ that bounds the interval between a clock edge and valid outputs.

The timing of other inputs (such as data and load enable) to an edge-triggered device is often specified in terms of *setup* and *hold* times relative to the active clock edge. To guarantee that an input is not sampled while invalid, the device specification insists on a period of validity extending slightly before and after the active edge; that is, it requires that the clock edge occur during a period of input stability. Specification of a setup time $t_{\mathrm{s}}$ and hold time $t_{\mathrm{h}}$ dictates that device inputs must be valid and stable during a period that begins $t_{\mathrm{s}}$ *before* the active clock edge and ends $t_{\mathrm{h}}$ *after* the edge.

Observe that the manufacturer of a clocked device can trade off between $t_{\mathrm{s}}$ and $t_{\mathrm{h}}$ simply by delaying the inputs or clock. The more essential constraint is the sum $t_{\mathrm{s}} + t_{\mathrm{h}}$, which dictates the size of the validity interval required by the device— effectively the amount of time taken to sample data inputs reliably. Typically, $t_{\mathrm{s}}$ and $t_{\mathrm{h}}$ are small compared with other delays in a system; we shall informally assume them to be zero except when otherwise specified.

Like combinational logic, clocked edge-triggered device specifications can cite *contamination delays* for use in highly optimized designs. Unlike combinational logic, however, a nonzero contamination delay is routinely assumed between the

*Sequences and State*                                                                                          85

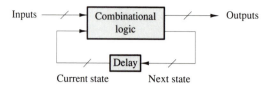

Inputs → Combinational logic → Outputs

Delay

Current state    Next state

**Figure 4.12** Fundamental model for sequential circuits.

clock and data outputs. More particularly, the contamination delay of a register is assumed to be greater than its hold time, giving it the important property that its inputs and outputs can be read and written simultaneously (that is, by similar devices sharing the same clock input). As a special case of this assumption, consider a register whose outputs are connected to its inputs. Assuming a nonzero hold time $t_h$ and a clock-to-$Q$ contamination delay $t_{cC-Q}$, such a circuit will meet the hold-time specifications only if $t_{cC-Q} > t_h$. While it is unusual to exploit contamination delays otherwise, the $t_{cC-Q} > t_h$ assumption is almost universally applied to clocked registers and is accommodated by commercially available devices. Often this is arranged simply by adjusting timing so that $t_h$ becomes zero. Indeed, $t_h$ can even be made *negative*, allowing input data to become invalid *prior* to an active clock edge.

## 4.5 Models of Sequential Circuits

A general implementation model for sequential circuits is shown in figure 4.12. Note that lines in this figure are marked with a short slash; this standard notation abbreviates a number of lines carrying parallel data, and often the slash is annotated to specify the number of lines in the bundle.

One set of signals called *state variables* encode the current state of the system; a sequential circuit with $N$ binary state variables has $2^N$ possible states. A block of combinational logic (having no feedback paths) takes as inputs the current state variables and the external input signals and computes the external output signals and the next state of the machine. The next state outputs pass through a set of delay elements and are fed into the combinational logic as the (now) current state. The nature of the delay element varies with the type of sequential circuit; in general, the delay is an analog circuit element whose output waveform is simply its input waveform delayed by some constant time interval. The simplest delay element is just a wire, in which case the model of figure 4.12 reduces to that shown in figure 4.13. Note that this is the model used for the analysis of the faulty transparent latch of figure 4.7.

All sequential circuits, including the memory elements we have discussed in this chapter, can be cast into the form of figure 4.12. The fundamental model lends itself to an analysis of these circuits in analog terms, so that we can deal with voltage waveforms in continuous time rather than with binary variables and discrete steps. Such analysis is tedious, particularly if it deals carefully with circuit details and

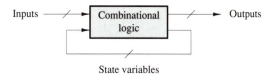

**Figure 4.13**  Implicit delay model for sequential circuits.

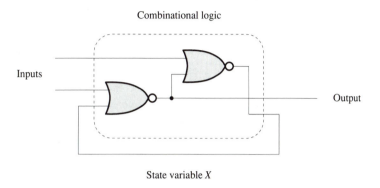

**Figure 4.14**  *R-S* latch as an asynchronous sequential circuit.

physical phenomena that affect stability and dynamics. Often careful analysis of a simple bistable circuit reveals a remarkable variety of unanticipated behavior, such as dynamic equilibria. Fortunately, the digital designer can largely avoid the tedium of asynchronous analysis by confining designs to the use of *clocked* or *synchronous* circuits and the appropriate design discipline.

### 4.5.1 Asynchronous Sequential Devices

Certain simple devices, such as the *R-S* latch of figure 4.14, do not fit the clocked circuit model and must be dealt with as asynchronous devices, in fundamental terms. Since the dynamic behavior of such a device is extraordinarily complex, its careful analysis is used to derive a *partial* description of its behavior that is useful to the digital engineer, even if it is incomplete.

We might characterize the *R-S* latch as an *asynchronous sequential device* whose inputs are the voltages $V_R(t)$ and $V_S(t)$ applied to the reset and set inputs and whose defined states are $Q = 0$ and $Q = 1$. Given a reasonable interval for $t_w$, the next-state criteria might be as follows:

$Q[t] = 0$ if either

- $Q[t - t_w] = 0$ and $V_S(\tau) < V_{il}$ for $(t - t_w) < \tau < t$, or
- $V_S(\tau) < V_{il}$ and $V_R(\tau) > V_{ih}$ for $(t - t_w) < \tau < t$.

$Q[t] = 1$ if either

- $Q[t - t_w] = 1$ and $V_R(\tau) < V_{il}$ for $(t - t_w) < \tau < t$, or
- $V_R(\tau) < V_{il}$ and $V_S(\tau) > V_{ih}$ for $(t - t_w) < \tau < t$.

This specification guarantees enough about the $R$-$S$ latch to ensure some useful traits: Under conditions realizable in practice, it will maintain its state as long as its inputs are held to valid 0, and state changes can be effected by appropriate manipulation of one input or the other. Reactions to many pathological conditions are left unspecified, however, including simultaneous or overlapping $S$ and $R$ signals, *runt pulses* on $S$ or $R$ that reach a valid 1 but hold it for a time shorter than $t_w$, and logically invalid input voltages. Where $Q[t]$ is left unspecified by the next-state criteria, we assume it to be in the undefined state $S_?$.

Of course, a more complicated specification could dictate more completely the behavior of the device. However, it is impossible for an unambiguous specification to be both complete and accurate; we can't specify *exactly* the minimum voltage on the $S$ input that causes the $R$-$S$ latch to set, for the same reason that we can't specify exactly the moment at which a gate decides that its input carries a 1 rather than a 0. The incompleteness of our specification plays the same role as the forbidden zone in the logic representations we design: Given inputs that are subject to misinterpretation, we avoid making *any* promises about behavior.

We formalize this level of abstraction as our most primitive model of a sequential system:

. . . . . . . . . . . . . . . . . . . . . . . . . . . . . . . . . . . . . . . . . . . . . . . . . . . . . . . .

### An asynchronous sequential device has

- a finite set of time-varying analog (continuous valued) inputs $I_1(t), I_2(t), ..., I_j(t)$;
- a finite set of discrete *defined states* $S_1, S_2, ..., S_k$, in addition to an *undefined state* $S_?$;
- a discrete, time-varying *state variable* $Q[t]$, ranging over $S_1, S_2, ..., S_k, S_?$;
- a finite time "window" or interval $t_w$; and
- a set of disjoint *next-state criteria*, $C_1, C_2, ..., C_k$, each $C_i$ specifying a *sufficient* condition to guarantee $Q[t] = S_i$, given a specified $Q[t - t_w]$ and some property of the input values during the interval between times $t - t_w$ and $t$.

. . . . . . . . . . . . . . . . . . . . . . . . . . . . . . . . . . . . . . . . . . . . . . . . . . . . . . . .

The asynchronous sequential device provides a link between the analog world of continuous variables and the digital domain by relating discrete states to the recent history of analog inputs. Note that the description of the inputs involves both continuously variable values (like voltages) and continuous time, while the state takes on a succession of discrete values as a function of (continuous) time. Like all abstractions, the asynchronous sequential device allows us to specify critical aspects of behavior of a device while leaving unspecified the inessential detail.

It is important that digital designers avoid building systems that rely upon unspecified aspects of component behavior. Such conservatism is sometimes more subtle than it appears. It is easy—but naive—to assume that even unspecified input combinations to the $R$-$S$ latch lead to one of the defined ($Q = 0$ or $Q = 1$) states. This fallacy and its consequences form the subject of section 4.6. For reasons discussed in that section, we assume that all unspecified inputs lead an asynchronous sequential circuit to the *undefined state* $S_?$, where it remains until some next-state criterion forces it to one of the defined states.

The undefined state $S_?$ is not a single, recognizable state; it is a token of our ignorance of behavior in unspecified cases. As we shall see in section 4.6, it can exhibit oscillation, invalid logic values, or some other unanticipated behavior pattern; $S_?$ may be identical to any of the defined states, or it may be none of them. By pessimistically assuming $Q[t] = S_?$, we relinquish any assumptions about the state of the circuit and its outputs at time $t$ and for an arbitrary period thereafter, depending on subsequent inputs.

### 4.5.2 Clocked Devices and the Dynamic Discipline

The complications of asynchronous circuit analysis motivate the use of clocked flip-flops and associated timing constraints to guarantee that undefined states are avoided. The goal is to constrain the timing of state changes so that they happen only when some next-state criterion is certain to apply, avoiding altogether transitions to the undefined state. In this way we return the analysis of sequential circuits to the digital domain of discrete *values*; moreover, by identifying a sequence of instants at which state changes can occur, we introduce the idea of *discrete time*.

Our approach parallels the development of the digital abstraction in chapter 1, involving both a circuit element—the *clocked sequential device*—whose behavior is specified largely in digital terms and an associated engineering discipline. We begin with the device.

. . . . . . . . . . . . . . . . . . . . . . . . . . . . . . . . . . . . . . . . . . . . . . . . . . . . . . .

*A **clocked sequential device*** is a circuit element having

- one or more discrete-valued *input* terminals;
- a *clock* input that identifies a sequence of times at which state transitions are to occur;
- one or more discrete-valued *output* terminals;
- a finite set of discrete *states* $S_1, S_2, ..., S_k$;
- a *next-state* criterion that specifies, for each choice of current state and input values, a successor state;
- an *output* specification that details the value of each output for each choice of current state and input values;
- an *input timing* specification, consisting (at minimum) of setup and hold times $t_s$ and $t_h$; and
- an *output timing* specification, consisting of an upper bound $t_{pd}$ on the time required for the output values to become valid following a state transition and

a lower bound $t_{cd}$ on the interval following a state transition for which the previous outputs remain valid.

· · · · · · · · · · · · · · · · · · · · · · · · · · · · · · · · · · · · · · · · · · · · · · · · · · · · · · · · · · · · · · ·

The operation of a clocked sequential device is simple and is specified largely in digital terms: At each active clock signal, a new state is assumed according to the current inputs and state transition rules. After the propagation delay $t_{pd}$ elapses, the values dictated by the next state, the current inputs, and the output specification appear at the output terminals. The *contamination delay* $t_{cd}$ plays a role analogous to that of contamination delays in combinational circuits. Unless otherwise specified, we assume $t_h = t_{cd} = 0$. Most clocked devices are viewed in these simple digital terms rather than in the more primitive asynchronous characterization used for the $R$-$S$ latch. Relative to the digital domain, their behavior as clocked devices is *completely* specified, provided certain conditions are met; these conditions give rise to the discipline to be developed presently.

Of course, elementary clocked devices, such as edge-triggered flip-flops, can be analyzed as asynchronous sequential devices; indeed, the justification of their characterization as clocked devices is that it conforms to a special case of asynchronous behavior of the underlying fundamental model. In asynchronous sequential terms, the behavior of an edge-triggered $D$ flip-flop whose setup and hold times are $t_s$ and $t_h$ might reflect next-state criteria that require valid and stable $D$ input during an interval $t_w$ sufficient to include $t_s$, $t_h$, and an intervening period containing an active clock edge. The $t_w$ "window" is thus broken into three periods: a setup time, during which the clock must be valid and (say) low; a transition time; and a hold time, during which the clock must be valid and high. A simple asynchronous flip-flop specification might thus include a constant $t_w$ and criteria such as

$Q[t] = 0$ if

- $V_C(\tau) < V_{il}$ for $(t - t_w) < \tau < (t - t_w + t_s)$, and
- $V_C(\tau) > V_{ih}$ for $(t - t_h) < \tau < t$, and
- $V_D(\tau) < V_{il}$ for $(t - t_w) < \tau < t$,

where $V_C(\tau)$ is the voltage applied to the clock input and $V_D(\tau)$ is the voltage applied to the data input.

The above fragment guarantees a $Q = 0$ state under particular circumstances, requiring that the clock transition occur within a bounded interval (to wit, $t_w - t_s - t_h$). This restriction is not entirely unrealistic: Edge-triggered devices often specify bounded rise times for their clock inputs. In other ways, however, the fragment is an oversimplification; it neglects clock-to-$Q$ propagation delay, for example, presuming that $t_{pC-Q} \leq t_h$.

Additional criteria ensure stability of the flip-flop state in the absence of active clock edges. For example, we might specify that

$Q[t] = 0$ if $Q[t_1] = 0$ for some previous time $t_1 < t$ and one of the following conditions applies in the interval $t_1 \leq \tau \leq t$:

- $V_C(\tau) < V_{il}$ for $t_1 \leq \tau \leq t$, or
- $V_C(\tau) > V_{ih}$ for $t_1 \leq \tau \leq t$, or
- $V_C(\tau) \leq V_C(\tau_1)$ for every $\tau_1$ such that $t_1 \leq \tau \leq \tau_1 \leq t$.

This fragment deals with the problem of maintaining the $Q = 0$ state while the clock is inactive (at either valid level) or monotonically falling (presuming a positive active edge). This criterion, in combination with the previous one, is sufficient to ensure that our flip-flop will assume and maintain a $Q = 0$ state under limited but practically realizable circumstances. Additional criteria must be supplied to deal with the $Q = 1$ state; moreover, practical issues (such as the propagation delay noted earlier) are likely to complicate the partial specification considerably.

The derivation of a simpler digital characterization of the flip-flop's behavior involves an analysis to verify that (1) in either of its defined states, the device maintains its current state as long as no $0 \rightarrow 1$ transition appears on the clock input and (2) a valid and stable $D$ input in the vicinity of an active clock edge causes the device to assume the state corresponding to that input.

. . . . . . . . . . . . . . . . . . . . . . . . . . . . . . . . . . . . . . . . . . . . . . . . . . . . . . . . . . . . . . . .

***The dynamic discipline*** requires that a digital circuit

- consist entirely of clocked sequential devices and combinational devices;
- be free from combinational cycles—that is, every cyclic path must contain at least one register;
- provide, at the clock input of each clocked device, a signal dictating the times of state transitions at intervals sufficiently long to conform to the clock specification of the device; and
- provide, at all other inputs to each clocked device, logic levels that are stable and valid for a period surrounding each specified transition that conforms to the input timing specification of the device.

. . . . . . . . . . . . . . . . . . . . . . . . . . . . . . . . . . . . . . . . . . . . . . . . . . . . . . . . . . . . . . . .

The dynamic discipline confines us to the use of clocked rather than asynchronous sequential devices, ruling out combinational cycles (which can effect asynchronous sequential devices such as the $R$-$S$ latch). Moreover, it requires that the circuit be engineered so as to guarantee that no input to a clocked device be invalid or transient near the time when the device makes a state transition; as with the forbidden zone and the static discipline, these constraints guarantee logically valid outputs given well-behaved inputs. Much as the static discipline establishes a forbidden zone in the voltage dimension, the dynamic discipline establishes a forbidden zone in the time dimension.

The following subsection presents a simple approach to the construction of sequential circuits that obey the dynamic discipline; a wider range of approaches is explored in chapter 7. Section 4.6 deals with the consequences of failure to obey the dynamic discipline.

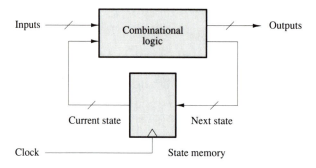

**Figure 4.15**   Clocked sequential circuit model.

### 4.5.3 Clocked Circuit Model

A simple implementation model for *clocked sequential circuits* is shown in figure 4.15. The approach is to use a clocked memory device, such as a register composed of edge-triggered $D$ flip-flops, as a replacement for the delay element of the fundamental model of figure 4.12. At each clock edge, the next state is loaded into the state flip-flops and becomes the current state. The clocked *state-memory* output lines hold binary state variables whose values change only following state transitions dictated by active edges of the clock input.

Given a sufficiently long clock period (for example, one somewhat longer than the propagation delay through the combinational logic) and appropriate constraints on the timing of transitions on the inputs, the inputs to the state memory can be guaranteed to be stable at the each transition time.

Note that the dynamic discipline, and hence the reliable operation of this circuit, depends on the assumptions that

- the clock period is longer than the sum of the delay through the combinational logic, the setup time of the memory, and the propagation delay $t_{\mathrm{p}C-Q}$ through the memory;
- the circuit's input lines are stable and valid for a sufficient period surrounding each active clock edge to accommodate both the propagation delay through the combinational logic and the setup time of the memory; and
- contamination delays around the cycle exceed the hold-time requirement of the memory, as discussed in section 4.4.

Clocked sequential circuits are easy to design, and glitches on the outputs of the combinational logic can generally be ignored. Figure 4.15 provides an implementation model for the finite-state machine, an important abstraction of sequential circuits that will be discussed in chapter 6.

One other distinction made among models of sequential circuits concerns the generation of the outputs. In one model, the outputs are functions of both the current state and the input variables. Circuits of this type are called *Mealy machines*. In another type of model, the *Moore machine*, the outputs are functions of the current

*Sequences and State*

state only. This is primarily a distinction of form; a Moore machine can be built to perform the same function as any Mealy machine, although the Moore machine may require more states and have delayed outputs relative to the Mealy machine. With few exceptions, the remainder of this text will use the Moore machine model since it is simpler to analyze and implement.

## 4.6 Synchronization and State

In this section we motivate the use of the dynamic discipline, presented in section 4.5.2, by exploring the consequences of failure to adhere to it. The dynamic discipline requires that we avoid sampling signals during a transition (that is, making decisions based on their logical values), since otherwise invalid logic levels and hence undefined behavior may result. In *synchronous* systems this restriction is met by means of a single master clock signal (typically a high-frequency square wave) from which all timing relationships are derived. Although there can be a variety of control signals to clocked devices (such as registers), each is derived in a fixed way from the master clock by such means as counters and combinational logic. The circuit can be designed, for example, so that the sampling edge of the clock signal to an edge-triggered flip-flop will occur sufficiently long after the data inputs have changed that they are guaranteed to be at valid logic levels. We have seen in figure 4.15 an example of a simple synchronous organization in which a single clock is used to latch simultaneously all combinational outputs that are to become combinational inputs during the next clock period. The principal requirement of such *single-clock* systems is that the clock period be slow enough to ensure that all signals propagate reliably through the combinational circuitry during a single clock cycle.

An *asynchronous* system is one containing two or more independent clock signals. So long as each clock drives independent logic circuitry, such a system is effectively a collection of independent synchronous systems. The logical combination of signals derived from independent clocks, however, poses difficulty because of the unpredictability of their phase relationship. In this section we briefly explore this problem and discuss its consequences.

### 4.6.1 Arbiters

An *arbiter* is a device that can be used to decide the winner of two-person races. It is housed in a box featuring two buttons, marked $B_0$ and $B_1$, and two logic-level outputs $W_0$ and $W_1$. The box is placed at the finish line of the race, and each contestant is instructed to press an assigned button on crossing the line; the first button pressed sets the output to 1, thus specifying the winner. A reasonable design specification for the arbiter might require the following conditions:

- A *reset* input to the arbiter causes both outputs to become 0, where they remain until one or both buttons are pressed.

- The pressing of either or both buttons causes, after an interval of at most $t_d$ seconds, exactly one of the output lines to become a valid 1 and the other to become a valid 0; these output levels persist until the next *reset* input.

- If $B_0$ is pressed $t_a$ seconds or more before $B_1$ is pressed, then $W_0$ will be the 1 output, reflecting the fact that the contestant assigned to $B_0$ is the winner; similarly, if $B_1$ is pressed $t_a$ seconds or more before $B_0$ is pressed, then the $W_1$ output will be 1 and $W_0$ will be 0.

- If $B_0$ and $B_1$ are pressed within $t_a$ seconds of each other, then one output line—we don't care which—will be a valid 1, and the other will be a valid 0, after the $t_d$-second interval.

The parameter $t_d$ is chosen to allow time for the logic within the box to make an acceptable decision and reflects necessary propagation delays for the internal logic. The arbitration time $t_a$ allows a margin for error on photo finishes; in close races we allow an arbitrary decision to be made. With suitable values for $t_d$ and $t_a$, the arbiter appears eminently constructible: It is easy to derive logic signals from the buttons; for example, a pair of $R$-$S$ latches could be arranged so that it is set by the one input and simultaneously disables the other input. However, the plausibility of such a scheme belies a remarkable and somewhat unnerving fact:

. . . . . . . . . . . . . . . . . . . . . . . . . . . . . . . . . . . . . . . . . . . . . . . . . . . . . . . . . . . . . . . . . . . . . .

***The asynchronous arbiter problem***   Even with perfectly reliable logic devices, for *no* choice of values for $t_a$ and $t_d$ is it possible to construct an absolutely reliable arbiter that meets the above specifications!

. . . . . . . . . . . . . . . . . . . . . . . . . . . . . . . . . . . . . . . . . . . . . . . . . . . . . . . . . . . . . . . . . . . . . .

In order to understand why the arbiter is unrealizable, we must recognize that we have introduced continuous variables—the times at which the buttons are pressed—into our discrete model. Let $t_0$ and $t_1$ be the times at which $B_0$ and $B_1$, respectively, are pressed. Then the function of the arbiter is to make a binary choice (either $W_0$ or $W_1$) based on the value of the continuously variable $t_0 - t_1$: If the difference is negative, $W_0$ is to be 1 and $W_1$ is to be 0; otherwise $W_0$ is to be 0 and $W_1$ is to be 1.

Figure 4.16 graphs the output value $W_0$ (a plot of $W_1$ would be the inverse) as a function of this time difference and corresponds roughly to the characteristic we would expect to realize if we constructed an arbiter by the strategy we have outlined. The output is a well-defined, valid logic level when $t_0$ is appreciably less than or greater than $t_1$; the trouble arises when they are nearly the same and the output is not well defined. Both the specifications and the plot in figure 4.16 are perfectly symmetric about the point where $t_0 = t_1$. The specifications allow an arbitrary choice to be made at this point but give no rules for making the choice. Indeed, there is no mechanism in our repertoire of digital functions for making an arbitrary choice; hence any arbiter we propose to construct using those functions will have a point at which its output is undefined. Note that this problem arises whenever we undertake to map a continuous variable onto a discrete

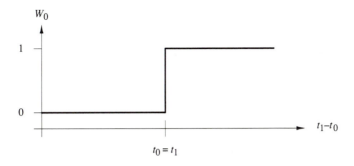

**Figure 4.16** Arbiter characteristic.

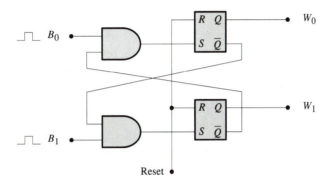

**Figure 4.17** A defective arbiter circuit.

one; in general, such mappings confront points of symmetry at which the value of the discrete variable is undefined. In the mapping of continuous voltages onto logic levels, we solved the problem by introducing a forbidden zone that excludes the ambiguous points from the range of possible inputs. Unfortunately, we cannot impose the same discipline here since we have no control over the timing of the inputs.

Figure 4.17 shows the circuit of a naively designed arbiter. The inputs are logic levels that normally carry 0s but become 1 when the corresponding button is pressed. The *reset* line serves to clear both latches so that each $Q$ output is 0 and each $\overline{Q}$ output is 1. When either button is pressed, the corresponding latch is set so that its $Q$ output is 1; its $\overline{Q}$ output becomes 0, disabling (via an AND gate) the other button. The reader should verify that this circuit conforms to the arbiter specification as long as there is a sufficient interval between the rising edges of the $B_0$ and $B_1$ inputs. If the $B_0$ and $B_1$ inputs are nearly coincident, signals can propagate to *both* $S$ latch inputs before either $\overline{Q}$ output has propagated to its AND gate. Thus both latches will be set, and both outputs will be 1s; two "winners" will be selected, in violation of the specified arbiter behavior.

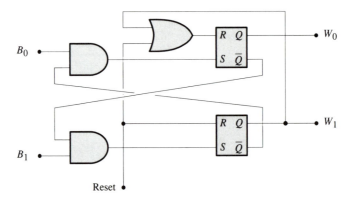

**Figure 4.18** An improved arbiter circuit.

In order to correct this problem, we try revising the circuit as shown in figure 4.18. The arbiter now has a connection between the $Q$ output of one latch and the $R$ input of the other (through an OR gate), guaranteeing that the two $Q$ outputs will not simultaneously carry 1s. If the "two-winner" state of the previous circuit ever arises, it will now cause the upper latch to be reset and declare $W_1$ the winner.

It is quite easy to convince oneself that this improved arbiter meets the specifications, as long as one assumes that every line always carries a valid logic level. Unfortunately, this assumption is wrong. Suppose, for example, that the rising edge of $B_0$ propagates through to the $S$ input of its latch while $B_1$ is 0; suppose further that the falling edge of $\overline{Q}$ (caused by setting the upper latch) arrives at the lower AND gate just as the rising edge of $B_1$ arrives at the same gate. Depending on the details of the timing of the two signals, the output of the AND gate might be a continuous 0, a momentary rise to 1 and return to 0 (sufficient to set the lower latch), or a "runt" pulse that is almost—but not quite—enough to set the lower latch. Most of the time, the latch would either be set or remain in its reset state; however, there is an inescapable possibility that a runt pulse of just the right magnitude will send the device into a limbo between these two stable states. This phenomenon is called *synchronization failure*, and this limbo is termed the *metastable state*. It is the bane of asynchronous digital systems. The problems it causes are not insurmountable, but they introduce costs and performance limitations that influence the organization of systems in important ways; in particular, they constrain the level to which asynchronous techniques can be employed in practice.

### 4.6.2 The Metastable State

To understand the metastable-state phenomenon, let us reconsider the $R$-$S$ latch composed of NOR gates shown in figure 4.13. Figure 4.19 shows this same circuit, slightly reorganized and with the connection from the output of one NOR gate to the input of the other replaced by a dotted line.

Ignoring this line for the moment, and assuming that both $R$ and $S$ inputs are connected to logical 0, we may view the result as a combinational circuit whose

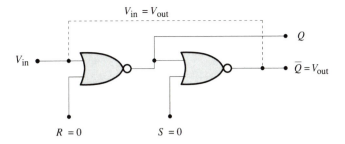

**Figure 4.19**  A NOR-based $R$-$S$ latch.

input is a logic level at $V_{in}$ and whose output is a logic level at $V_{out}$. Note that the input at $V_{in}$ becomes inverted as it passes through the leftmost NOR gate and is reinverted as it passes through the rightmost one. We have in effect cascaded two inverters (as long as the $R$ and $S$ inputs remain 0), and the output is simply a delayed replica of the input. If we were to examine the voltage-transfer characteristic ($V_{out}$ versus $V_{in}$), we would expect to find roughly the three-segment line in figure 4.20: a horizontal segment corresponding to 0s at both input and output, a nearly vertical active region (in the forbidden input zone), and a horizontal segment corresponding to 1s at both input and output.

If we now reintroduce the feedback path denoted by the dotted line in figure 4.19, we in effect add the constraint that $V_{in} = V_{out}$. This additional equation appears in figure 4.20 as a diagonal line. The intersections between these curves—the transfer characteristic of the cascaded gates and the $V_{in} = V_{out}$ line—correspond to voltages that simultaneously satisfy the imposed voltage constraints. Two of these represent the solutions to the logic equations derived in our previous analysis of the $R$-$S$ latch and are stable equilibria. Near either of these points, minor perturbations of $V_{out}$ or $V_{in}$ (such as might be caused by noise) are resisted by the tendency of the transfer characteristic to return to the point of intersection. The reader should verify this stability by picking an arbitrary point along the diagonal line as $V_{in}$, deducing from the cascaded gate characteristic the corresponding $V_{out}$, moving back to an input voltage identical to the new output voltage, and repeating the process until an equilibrium point is reached.

The middle intersection is not predicted by our logic equations since it involves voltages that are not valid logic levels. This metastable point represents an *unstable* equilibrium; a small perturbation in either direction will cause the system to scramble back to one of the stable points. This point can be reached in practice by a marginal set or clear pulse, which imparts barely enough energy to leave one stable state but not quite enough to complete the transition in a definite fashion. The instability of the equilibrium at that point, coupled with the inevitable sources of noise in real systems, eventually returns the system to one stable state or the other. Unfortunately, noise is undependable stuff, and the restoration of valid logic levels may take an arbitrarily long time.

We can visualize the situation using the mechanical analog in figure 4.21, which

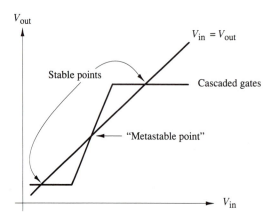

**Figure 4.20** *R-S* voltage constraints.

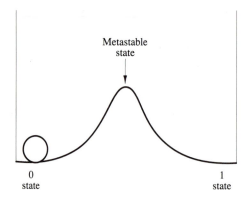

**Figure 4.21** A bistable mechanical system.

shows a well with steep walls, containing a hill in the middle and a ball that is free to roll around (constrained, of course, by the walls and gravity). This is clearly a bistable system: If we place the ball either to the left of the hill or to its right, it will not cross to the opposite side, even with a considerable wind (analogous to electrical noise in our *R-S* circuit). We can force a transition from the left to the right sides, however, by giving the ball a sufficiently large push to roll it past the top of the hill, whereupon it gravitates to the other stable point and remains there.

In theory we can also give the ball a weak push so that it has exactly zero momentum when it reaches the very top of the hill. At this metastable point, any additional push (from wind, for example) is likely to upset the delicate balance and send it down one side of the hill or the other. In fact, unless we place it *exactly* at the top of the hill (an event with infinitesimal probability), it will gradually gather momentum even in a dead calm; clearly, the closer to the exact equilibrium point we put it, the longer this will take.

We can reduce the average time required to roll down from the vicinity of the metastable equilibrium by making the sides of the hill steeper, leaving a sharp point at the top; this corresponds to increasing the gain of the transistors in the latch. While increased gain is of practical use in improving the average performance (and hence the odds against failure) of arbiters, it does not lead to an upper bound on the decision time. Even with *infinite*-gain switching devices, an arbiter may take arbitrarily long to select one of two nearly coincident inputs.

### 4.6.3 Asynchrony versus Arbitration

Not every logical operation that deals with asynchronous signals constitutes an arbitration problem; specific engineering disciplines, such as the ones we shall discuss in sections 7.2.3 and 7.6, allow the design of asynchronous systems that avoid arbitration problems and thus operate reliably. Arbitration problems occur whenever it is necessary to distinguish which of two asynchronous events occurs first; however, a number of useful operations can be performed on asynchronous digital signals without making such decisions.

We have observed that transitions can be used to signal *events*. Assume that we have two lines, $x$ and $y$, each of which has a single $0 \rightarrow 1$ transition during a specified interval. Even if these signals are completely asynchronous with respect to one another, we may take their logical AND and OR to yield new asynchronous signals that reliably have useful properties. The OR of the two signals, $x + y$, will have a single $0 \rightarrow 1$ transition at a time slightly after the *earlier* of the two transitions; the AND of the two signals will have a transition following the *later* of the two. Thus, given two asynchronous digital events, we can generate a new event that follows the earlier or the later by a small (bounded) amount, namely the propagation delay of the gate we use to combine the signals representing them.

Note that both of these operations carefully avoid making "which came first" decisions between asynchronous events; this is the key to evading arbitration problems. The most common way of avoiding such decisions is to avoid pairs of asynchronous events by using a single time base as the source of all events. More adventurous designers will allow asynchronous signals but carefully constrain the operations used to combine them. Both approaches are discussed in chapter 7.

### 4.6.4 Arbitration in Practice

Many strategies for constructing reliable arbiters have been devised, shown to be defective, and discarded. The reader might be tempted, for example, to think of ways to bias a latch toward one state or another so as to make it recover from the metastable state within a bounded time; but such cures simply move the metastable point from one voltage to another and offer no real improvement. Similarly, any attempt to build additional circuitry to detect and correct the metastable state (for example, by forcing a 0 state) simply substitutes one metastable difficulty for another; the detection circuitry can decide to force a 0 just as the original latch chooses to come out of its limbo with a 1. The metastable state is an inevitable consequence of the specifications of the arbiter; there is simply no way to avoid it entirely if an arbitration problem must indeed be solved. Sophisticated design engineers recognize this and avoid arbitration problems or adapt to their consequences.

In fact, latches *do* recover from metastable states given enough time, and arbiters can be made as reliable as desired by increasing the amount of time allowed them. An arbiter that allows, say, a few hundred nanoseconds for its state to stabilize (the time depends considerably on the implementation technology) reduces the probability of synchronization errors to the order of the probability of component failure, presumably a tolerable level.

## 4.7 Context

Sequential circuits are an abstraction that seems deceptively simple to maintain, since naive digital-domain analysis of cyclic circuits using combinational gates neatly hides the trouble spots involving synchronization and metastable states. The digital abstraction is so strongly ingrained among digital designers that many are still incredulous that a well-designed latch will misbehave for arbitrarily long periods if clocked at an inauspicious time; as a result, the arbitration problem has only grudgingly become recognized as a serious design issue.

A classic treatment of simple latches appears in Hill and Peterson [1981] and its predecessor. Metastable states and the arbitration problem are addressed by a still-growing corpus of literature, including Couranz and Wann [1975], Pechoucek [1976], Chaney [1979], Veendrick [1980], Mead and Conway [1980], and Stewart and Ward [1988].

## 4.8 Problems

### Problem 4.1  Timing of Sequential Circuits:

Consider the general model of a clocked sequential circuit shown in figure 4.12. Suppose that the building blocks are governed by the following parameters:

$$
\begin{aligned}
T &= \text{clock period,} \\
t_{\text{pd}} &= \text{maximum propagation delay through combinational logic,} \\
t_{\text{cd}} &= \text{contamination delay through combinational logic,} \\
t_{\text{p}C-Q} &= \text{propagation delay of registers implementing state,} \\
t_{\text{s}} &= \text{setup time for registers implementing state,} \\
t_{\text{h}} &= \text{hold time for registers implementing state.}
\end{aligned}
$$

A. What is the minimum clock period that will ensure correct operation of the circuit?

B. By how long must any change in inputs precede the next clock edge?

C. How long after the clock edge must the inputs be held valid?

D. What is the smallest time after the clock edge that outputs can be expected to be valid?

## Problem 4.2  Muller C-Element:

Consider the implementation shown below of the *Muller C-element* circuit, a simple circuit with state that appears frequently in the literature.

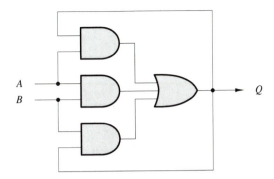

A. Give the Boolean equation relating $A$, $B$, and $Q$ that must be satisfied by any stable state of the $C$-element. Your answer should have the form $Q = f(A, B, Q)$.

B. What sets of values $(A, B, Q)$ are solutions to your equation? For which values of $A$ and $B$ is there more than one possible value for $Q$?

C. Copy the following timing diagram and fill in the behavior of $Q$:

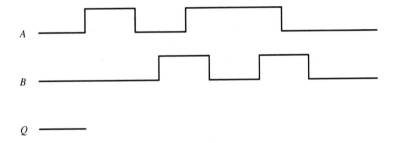

D. Explain briefly in words how the output $Q$ of the $C$-element is related to the present or past values of the inputs $A$ and $B$.

## Problem 4.3

An edge-triggered flip-flop $F_1$ has setup and hold times of $t_s$ and $t_h$, respectively. The flip-flop $F_2$ is constructed by adding a delay of $t_d$ to the data *input* of $F_1$. (Consider a delay to be a buffer with $t_{pd} = t_{cd} = t_d$.) What are the setup and hold times of $F_2$?

### Problem 4.4

Consider the following circuit:

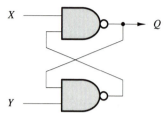

A. Complete the following timing diagram:

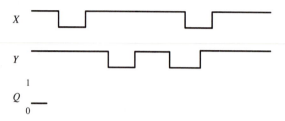

B. Can the above circuit enter a metastable state? If so, describe the input sequence that leads to metastable behavior. If not, explain why not.

### Problem 4.5  Basketball Metastability:

Consider a device that takes analog inputs describing the trajectory of a basketball and decides whether the ball has gone through or missed the net. Will such a device necessarily be unreliable because of its metastable state?

### Problem 4.6  Collision Avoidance:

The Federal Aviation Administration is evaluating proposals for an electronic box that would be installed on every airplane to help prevent midair collisions. The box would communicate directly with a similar box on any aircraft that seemed to be on a collision course. Together, the boxes would choose a course of action (such as "plane A goes left, plane B goes right") for the pilots to take to avoid collision.

A. Given what you know about metastable states, is it possible to build these boxes so that they operate with perfect reliability? Explain.

B. If your answer to first part is "no," estimate the probability that the boxes would actually fail to make a correct decision in time to prevent a collision. Explain your estimate. (We are not looking for a numerical estimate here, but a qualitative one, such as "very high," "very low," etc.)

## Problem 4.7  Pulse Synchronizer:

The circuit below is a type of pulse synchronizer. The $R$-$S$ latch is the kind shown in the text, and the $D$ flip-flops are positive edge-triggered flip-flops.

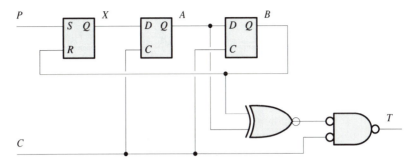

A. Give the waveforms at $X$, $A$, $B$, $Z$, and $T$ for the following input waveforms. Assume that all flip-flops are initially reset.

B. This circuit has several arbitration problems. Explain the arbitration problem remaining if we restrict $P$ so that the maximum width of a pulse on $P$ is one clock period and the minimum number of clock pulses between pulses on $P$ is eight.

C. Which circuit element performs the arbitration?

D. If the exclusive-OR gate is replaced with some function $f$ of $A$ and $B$, and $f$ is implemented with hazards, will those hazards affect the output $T$? Explain.

## Problem ★4.8  The Metastable State:

This exercise is designed to illustrate the behavior of devices in a metastable state.

Consider the following model of the behavior of a positive edge-triggered $D$ flip-flop. (This model is a reasonable first approximation and suffices for our purposes, but is not exact.)

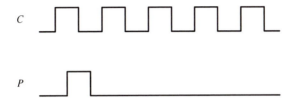

Assume that a logical 1 (true) is represented by 5 V and a logical 0 (false) is represented by 0 V. Assume further that whenever the rising edge of the clock passes 2.5 V, the "state" of the flip-flop (which is the voltage on the $Q$ output pin)

is instantaneously set to be equal to the voltage $V$ on the $D$ input pin. The value copied from the $D$ pin is an arbitrary voltage between 0 and 5 V. At all other times (when the clock is not rising past the 2.5-V trigger point), the state of the flip-flop evolves under control of the differential equation

$$\frac{dQ}{dt} = \begin{cases} 0 & \text{if } Q = 0 \quad \text{or} \quad Q = 5 \text{ V}, \\ \frac{(Q-Q^*)}{\tau} & \text{if } 0 < Q < 5 \text{ V}. \end{cases}$$

Here $Q^*$ is the metastable point of the system; if the system is set to $Q = Q^*$ exactly, it will remain forever in this state. Here $\tau$ is a function of the gain internal to the flip-flop and associated $RC$ delay constants; for the purposes of this exercise, we shall assume that $\tau = 1$ ns (about one gate delay).

A. Solve the differential equation above and give a simple closed-form expression for $Q$ in terms of the initial state $Q_0$, $Q^*$, $\tau$, and $t$. (You may ignore the boundary conditions if you wish and give a formula that lets $Q$ diverge to $+\infty$ or $-\infty$ as $t \to \infty$.)

B. Assume now that $Q^* = 2.5$ V. Suppose that $Q_0 = Q^* + \epsilon$ for some small, positive $\epsilon$. Give a precise formula for $\delta$ as a function of $\tau$ and $\epsilon$, where $\delta$ is the time taken by the system to reach $Q = 5$ V.

C. Suppose that we run our computer system at a clock rate of $f$ cycles/second. On each clock cycle, our $D$ flip-flop is used to sense the voltage on an input wire. (Assume that the system only has one such asynchronous input wire.) Assume that the voltages on the input wire are uniformly distributed between 0 and 5 V. What is the fastest clock rate we can have and still be confident that our $D$ flip-flop will converge to 0 or 5 V within one clock period with probability of at least $1 - 10^{-15}$? At this rate, what is the mean time between synchronization failures?

# 5 Synthesis of Digital Systems

Having introduced the technology that underlies the design of elementary gates and flip-flops, we turn to techniques for combining such elements into systems of arbitrary size and complexity. The most direct approach to the creation of large systems involves the synthesis of relatively complex new modules from combinations of more elementary ones, exploiting new abstractions at each step as described at the start of chapter 1. The efficacy of this traditional engineering approach depends considerably on the judgment of the engineer, whose taste and intuition strongly influence the choice of abstractions to be pursued. Engineering cleverness is expensive, however. As technological improvements have lowered the cost of elementary digital devices, they have increased the pressure to replace human engineering resources with automated procedures. The latter pressures have motivated the development of engineering approaches that use regular arrays of devices with systematic interconnections, eliminating most of the human costs from their design. In this chapter, we sample some common digital "building blocks" and explore several devices based on regular array structures.

## 5.1 Building Blocks for Logic Design

In the past, gate circuits were frequently constructed out of discrete components—transistors, diodes, and resistors. A circuit design at the gate level then went through a further expansion to become an actual electronic-circuit schematic diagram, from which the physical circuit would be constructed. As technology evolved, it became possible to *integrate* several discrete components onto a single "chip" of silicon. Thus entire logic gates, and ultimately groups of logic gates, could be fabricated on a single integrated-circuit (IC) chip. Within wide limits, the cost of one of these chips is dictated principally by packaging considerations and the economics of mass production, and is essentially independent of the complexity of the circuit on the chip. As technology has progressed, chips have been classified somewhat arbitrarily into the categories of small-scale integration (SSI), medium-scale integration (MSI), large-scale integration (LSI), and now very-large-scale integration (VLSI), based on the number of elementary gates or components they contain. IC chips can be further classified according to their "logic family," that is, according to the conventions used for representing 1s and 0s, and the kinds of electronic circuits

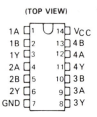

(TOP VIEW)

| | |
|---|---|
| 1A — 1 | 14 — V<sub>CC</sub> |


1A [1    14] V_CC
1B [2    13] 4 B
1Y [3    12] 4 A
2A [4    11] 4 Y
2B [5    10] 3 B
2Y [6     9] 3 A
GND [7    8] 3 Y

logic diagram (positive logic)

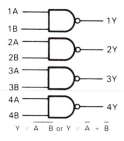

$$Y = \overline{A\ B} \text{ or } Y = \overline{A} + \overline{B}$$

| INPUTS | | OUTPUT |
|---|---|---|
| A | B | Y |
| H | H | L |
| L | X | H |
| X | L | H |

**Figure 5.1**   The 7400 IC chip.

used to implement the simple Boolean functions. Within each logic family, whole series of chips are available to implement different logic functions.

The building blocks used by a board-level engineer typically correspond to individual IC packages and thereby strongly reflect the level of integration and hence the state of the underlying technology. The early days of ICs offered the designer single gates and flip-flops in each package, while modern chips flaunt processors comprising hundreds of thousands of gates.

Increasing numbers of digital engineers have the resources to design in silicon rather than on printed circuit boards. As custom-chip design tools and support technologies develop, the ability to violate chip boundaries and redefine building blocks offers enticing new possibilities.

An early logic family that remains ubiquitous in board-level designs is the 7400 series of TTL logic. Perhaps the simplest SSI chip in the 7400 series is the 7400 chip itself (figure 5.1), which contains four independent two-input NAND gates. Standard digital IC packages range from 14 to as many as 64 pins. Cost does rise somewhat with the number of pins; larger packages with more pins cost more to manufacture and also to use (they occupy more space on circuit boards). Little is saved, though, in shrinking a package below about 14 pins. Thus instead of making a single NAND gate on a five-pin chip (two inputs, one output, and two power-supply pins), for about the same cost four independent gates can be manufactured on one chip, and their inputs and outputs can be brought out to separate pins. Many other simple logic gates are available, similarly packaged, on 7400 series chips.

Given that pin count and package size, along with the economics of mass production, are the primary determinants of chip cost, it is natural for chip designers to try to identify larger interconnections of gate circuits that would be generally useful and can be integrated into a single MSI chip without an unreasonably large number of pins. This effort has been spectacularly successful, and as a result the art of circuit design using 7400 series TTL or other similar families has become largely the art of selecting the right MSI building blocks from the 7400 series repertoire so that they can be combined using a minimum of SSI interface logic to perform the desired function.

In the early days of logic design, a great deal of research effort was expended on algorithms for implementing logic functions using the fewest number of gates. Today this is largely irrelevant; what counts in TTL design is minimizing the number of *packages*, which is frequently accomplished by using MSI units that have more gates. We shall see several examples of this as we proceed. In some other applications of logic design, such as the actual layout of circuits to be manufactured on IC chips, the notion of "package count" is not applicable. However, in this case the designer is striving to minimize power consumption and the area occupied by a circuit on the chip, and it is still true that this is often achieved by circuits that do not minimize the number of gates.

Besides reducing the package count of circuits constructed using ICs, the use of prefabricated functional units has at least one other benefit: It imposes a certain structure and discipline on the design process. As systems grow in complexity, this becomes an increasingly important consideration. In this chapter we shall survey a few of these building blocks that are useful in constructing combinational logic and study their impact on the practice of logic design.

### 5.1.1 Multiplexers

One common function in computer systems is the selection of a value from among a variety of possibilities. (For example, there may be four possible sources for the input a module is to operate on.) An IC building block that performs this function is called a *selector*, or *multiplexer* (since it "multiplexes" many signals onto one line). A typical multiplexer chip, the 74151, is shown in figure 5.2.

The 74151 has eight data inputs, $D_0$ through $D_7$, and four control inputs, $A$, $B$, $C$, and $S$. The output appears in inverted form at $W$ and in noninverted form at $Y$. By appropriately choosing $A$, $B$, and $C$, any of the eight data inputs can be made to appear at $Y$, or $Y$ can be unconditionally forced to 0 by setting the strobe input $S$ to 1.

From inspection of figure 5.2, we can write the logic equation

$$
\begin{aligned}
Y = {} & \overline{C} \cdot \overline{B} \cdot \overline{A} \cdot \overline{S} \cdot D_0 + \overline{C} \cdot \overline{B} \cdot A \cdot \overline{S} \cdot D_1 + \overline{C} \cdot B \cdot \overline{A} \cdot \overline{S} \cdot D_2 \\
& + \overline{C} \cdot B \cdot A \cdot \overline{S} \cdot D_3 + C \cdot \overline{B} \cdot \overline{A} \cdot \overline{S} \cdot D_4 + C \cdot \overline{B} \cdot A \cdot \overline{S} \cdot D_5 \\
& + C \cdot B \cdot \overline{A} \cdot \overline{S} \cdot D_6 + C \cdot B \cdot A \cdot \overline{S} \cdot D_7,
\end{aligned}
$$

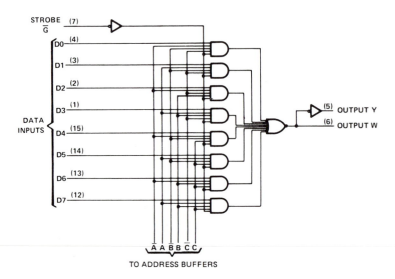

TO ADDRESS BUFFERS

FUNCTION TABLE

| INPUTS | | | | OUTPUTS | |
|--------|--|--|--|---------|--|
| SELECT | | | STROBE | | |
| C | B | A | $\overline{G}$ | Y | W |
| X | X | X | H | L | H |
| L | L | L | L | D0 | $\overline{D0}$ |
| L | L | H | L | D1 | $\overline{D1}$ |
| L | H | L | L | D2 | $\overline{D2}$ |
| L | H | H | L | D3 | $\overline{D3}$ |
| H | L | L | L | D4 | $\overline{D4}$ |
| H | L | H | L | D5 | $\overline{D5}$ |
| H | H | L | L | D6 | $\overline{D6}$ |
| H | H | H | L | D7 | $\overline{D7}$ |

**Figure 5.2** The 74151 multiplexer chip. In the function table, H indicates high, L low, and X irrelevant.

but this only begins to hint at the many ways of using a multiplexer chip. The most obvious, of course, is as a selector. For example, a computer with eight internal processor registers might have 3 bits in each instruction word to indicate the register to be used in that operation. These 3 bits would be fed into inputs $A$, $B$, and $C$ of a bank of multiplexers, while the contents of the registers would be supplied to the respective $D$ inputs. The value of the currently selected register would then be available at the $Y$ outputs of the bank of multiplexers. The resulting configuration, for the simple case of 2-bit registers, is shown in figure 5.3.

Our approach to this selector circuit illustrates several aspects of the design practices we shall study. First, notice that we did not explicitly use Boolean algebra in the design of this circuit. Although Boolean algebra is an important tool for understanding the behavior of logic circuits at the lowest level, it is too strong a magnifying glass for many system-design applications. Often, as in this case, it is preferable to deal directly with higher-level abstractions, such as the

*Synthesis of Digital Systems*

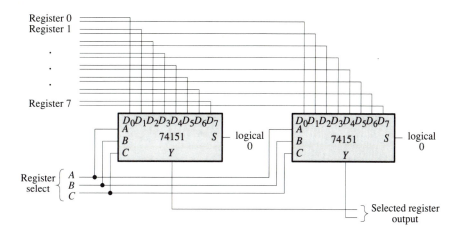

**Figure 5.3**　Two-bit-wide multiplexer.

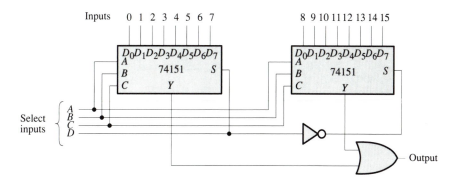

**Figure 5.4**　Sixteen-way multiplexer.

multiplexing function performed by the 74151 IC, viewed as a "black box" whose internal structure is not considered.

Second, note that we have built a new functional unit, a 2-bit-wide multiplexer, not itself available on a single chip, out of smaller functional units, namely 1-bit-wide multiplexers that *are* available on chips. This motif of building larger functional units out of smaller ones is very important and will recur. A modicum of care in the design of a functional unit can greatly enhance its usefulness in building larger units. In figure 5.3, the 2-bit-wide multiplexer could be constructed out of 1-bit-wide multiplexers by wiring together the corresponding select inputs, and it is obvious how this approach could be extended to achieve any desired width. Suppose, however, that instead of combining two 1-by-8 multiplexers into a 2-by-8 multiplexer, we desired instead to construct a 1-by-16 multiplexer. This can be done using the strobe inputs, as shown in figure 5.4.

Note that the 1-by-16 multiplexer defined in figure 5.4 does not itself have a

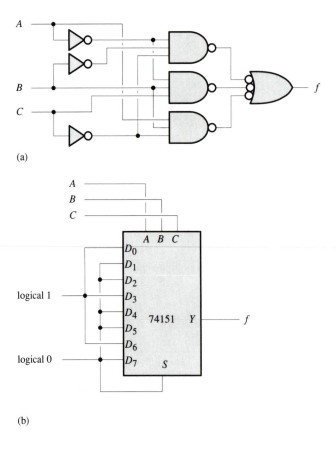

(a)

(b)

**Figure 5.5** Two implementations of $f(A, B, C) = \overline{A} \cdot \overline{B} \cdot \overline{C} + \overline{A} \cdot B \cdot C + A \cdot B \cdot \overline{C}$. Part (a) uses NAND gates; part (b) uses a multiplexer.

strobe input and therefore cannot be used to build a 1-by-32 multiplexer using an extension of the same philosophy. The reader is invited to remedy this deficiency, as well as to think about some of the other ways multiplexers can be combined into larger multiplexers.

Up to this point we have been viewing a multiplexer as having *data inputs* $D_0$ through $D_7$ and *control inputs* $A$, $B$, $C$, and $S$. This treatment is suggested by the terms *selector* and *multiplexer*, but it represents only one point of view: The logic equations and circuits for multiplexers make no distinction between one kind of input and another. We are thus free to call any input a data input or a control input as convenient. One common use of multiplexers is quite different in this respect from the data-selection applications discussed above. Suppose we wish to implement the logical function

$$f(A, B, C) = \overline{A} \cdot \overline{B} \cdot \overline{C} \;+\; \overline{A} \cdot B \cdot C \;+\; A \cdot B \cdot \overline{C}.$$

Figure 5.5(a) shows the straightforward sum-of-products realization using NAND gates, and figure 5.5(b) shows an alternative realization using a multiplexer.

In figure 5.5(b), the data inputs $A$, $B$, and $C$ have been applied to the select inputs of the multiplexer and used to choose one value from what is effectively a truth table for the function $f$, supplied at the inputs $D_0$ through $D_7$. Thus the multiplexer is used essentially as a programmable logic box capable of computing any Boolean function of the data inputs $A$, $B$, and $C$. The function computed is controlled by the values supplied at the inputs $D_0$ through $D_7$. It is, in fact, a primitive example of a *read-only memory*, a topic to be visited shortly.

Figure 5.5 represents an interpretation of control vs. data inputs that is diametrically opposed to that used earlier, underscoring the point that such interpretations are merely in the mind of the beholder and are not intrinsic properties of functional units. We shall see other cases in which treating control information as data, or using data as control information, is useful. Figure 5.5 also illustrates a practical design technique for implementing functions such as $f$ that do not lend themselves to simple gate implementations. Using multiplexers in such cases both reduces the package count and leads to a less obscure (and more easily modified) circuit.

### 5.1.2 Arithmetic Circuits

The addition of two $n$-bit numbers to produce their $(n+1)$-bit sum is a fundamental arithmetic operation. The basic procedure for doing this is described in section 2.1.1. In order to design a circuit to perform the addition of two $n$-bit numbers, we must implement the algorithm for adding two binary digits for each bit position. The addition algorithm, however, must also provide for a carry bit from the bit position to the right. We call this bit the *carry in* or $C_I$ bit. The addition algorithm at each bit position must generate the sum ($S$) and carry out ($C_O$) bits from the two input data bits ($A$ and $B$) and the $C_I$ bit. A circuit that implements these two Boolean functions is called a *full adder*, and its truth table is given in figure 5.6. The equations

$$S = \overline{A} \cdot \overline{B} \cdot C_I + A \cdot \overline{B} \cdot \overline{C_I} + A \cdot B \cdot C_I + \overline{A} \cdot B \cdot \overline{C_I},$$
$$C_O = A \cdot B + B \cdot C_I + A \cdot C_I,$$

describe the function performed by the full adder. These equations can be implemented in many ways; figure 5.7 shows some alternatives.

Once the basic full-adder circuit is available, it is a simple matter to build an $n$-bit adder by iteratively connecting full adders, one for each bit position, as shown in figure 5.8. Note that although the circuit is combinational, so that all bits from each of the two input data words are available simultaneously, the circuit *action* proceeds sequentially from right to left. Independent full adders are available on chips, as are groups of four full adders with internal carry connections already made. Although our discussion here centers on adders, various other arithmetic modules, such as magnitude comparators, are also available as prepackaged modules on chips.

The parallel $n$-bit adder described above becomes quite slow for large $n$ because of the propagation of carries from right to left. In fact, from the carry in at the right to the carry out at the left, there are $2n$ levels of logic. Frequently it is desirable to avoid this slow operation by using *carry look-ahead* circuits. The idea here is

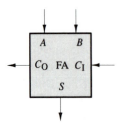

| | | | Carry | Sum |
|---|---|---|---|---|
| $A$ | $B$ | $C_I$ | $C_O$ | $S$ |
| 0 | 0 | 0 | 0 | 0 |
| 0 | 0 | 1 | 0 | 1 |
| 0 | 1 | 0 | 0 | 1 |
| 0 | 1 | 1 | 1 | 0 |
| 1 | 0 | 0 | 0 | 1 |
| 1 | 0 | 1 | 1 | 0 |
| 1 | 1 | 0 | 1 | 0 |
| 1 | 1 | 1 | 1 | 1 |

**Figure 5.6** Full-adder function.

to reduce the number of logic levels between the initial carry in and the first carry out. Let $C_i$ be the carry out from the $i$th stage of an $n$-bit adder and $C_{i-1}$ be its carry in (see figure 5.8). We then have

$$C_i = A_i \cdot B_i + (A_i + B_i) \cdot C_{i-1}.$$

Let $P_i = A_i + B_i$ and $G_i = A_i \cdot B_i$, so that

$$C_i = G_i + P_i \cdot C_{i-1}.$$

This equation can also be used to give $C_{i-1}$ in terms of $C_{i-2}$. Substituting this for the factor $C_{i-1}$ above, we have

$$C_i = G_i + P_i \cdot G_{i-1} + P_i \cdot P_{i-1} \cdot C_{i-2}.$$

Substituting again for $C_{i-2}$ and then for $C_{i-3}$, we get

$$C_i = G_i + P_i \cdot G_{i-1} + P_i \cdot P_{i-1} \cdot G_{i-2} + P_i \cdot P_{i-1} \cdot P_{i-2} \cdot G_{i-3}$$
$$+ P_i \cdot P_{i-1} \cdot P_{i-2} \cdot P_{i-3} \cdot C_{i-4}.$$

If a 4-bit parallel adder is built using the above formula for $C_4$ in terms of $C_0$, there will be only two levels of logic between $C_4$ and $C_0$. We can then build a

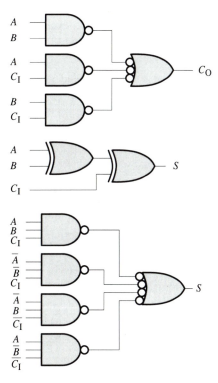

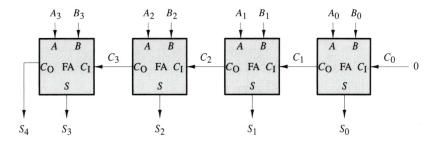

**Figure 5.7** Implementations of full-adder functions.

**Figure 5.8** A parallel 4-bit adder that will compute $(S_4S_3S_2S_1S_0) = (A_3A_2A_1A_0) + (B_3B_2B_1B_0)$.

$4n$-bit parallel adder using such 4-bit adders as modules with only $2n$ levels of logic between $C_{4n}$ and $C_0$, instead of the $8n$ levels of logic we would get using the design of figure 5.8. Commercially available ICs for 4-bit adders generally incorporate such a carry look-ahead circuit.

The use of carry look-ahead can be extended even further. The last equation can be rewritten in the form $C_i = G_i' + P_i' \cdot C_{i-4}$, where $G_i'$ and $P_i'$ are functions of $A_{i-3}, \ldots, B_{i-3}, \ldots, B_i$. This has the same form as the second equation above, and by repeating our substitutions there, we can express $C_i$ as a two-level logic function of $C_{i-16}$. Integrated circuits that perform this extended carry look-ahead operation are available commercially.

More powerful circuits are also available as single IC chips. All computers have an arithmetic-logic unit (ALU) that computes logical and arithmetic functions of input data words. Figure 5.9 shows the logic diagram for the 74181 TTL integrated-circuit ALU, which performs any of the 16 possible bit-wise logical operations or any of 16 arithmetic operations on two 4-bit parallel operands, as dictated by the mode control input $M$ and the four function select inputs $S_0$ through $S_3$. Figure 5.10 shows the 74181's truth table. Groups of 74181 chips can be interconnected to perform arithmetic on numbers larger than 4 bits; an on-chip look-ahead carry generator reduces carry propagation time in this case. The reader is invited to trace some of the signal paths in figure 5.9 to gain a deeper understanding of how the chip works.

The 74181 circuit contains over 75 equivalent gates on one IC chip, and iterated sequences of this circuit make up the *entire* ALU of many modern computers, aside from operand selection multiplexing and output destination demultiplexing. This ALU module is another good example of the utility of MSI circuits, which provide the computer designer with highly optimized functional units that deliver a high level of performance (in both speed and efficiency) while saving many hours of design time.

### 5.1.3 The Serial Adder

As an alternative to the spatial replication of circuitry characteristic of, say, an array of 74181s put together to perform arithmetic on wide data words, sequential circuits can be used to build more economical implementations of computational functions. By breaking a task down into a number of steps executed sequentially, the same circuitry can be reused in each step, thus replacing *spatial* replication of functions with *temporal* replication. For example, two $n$-bit binary numbers can be added together using $n$ full adders. But the addition of two $n$-bit numbers can also be performed in $n$ steps by repeated use of just one full adder.

In order to do this, we must encode the two $n$-bit numbers in serial form. That is, on each clock pulse, a new pair of bits from the two addends must be presented at the $X$ and $Y$ inputs. In the particular serial encoding we consider here, the less significant bits are presented first. (Under other circumstances, the most significant bit might come first.) Figure 5.11 shows how two inputs, 5 and 7, would be encoded.

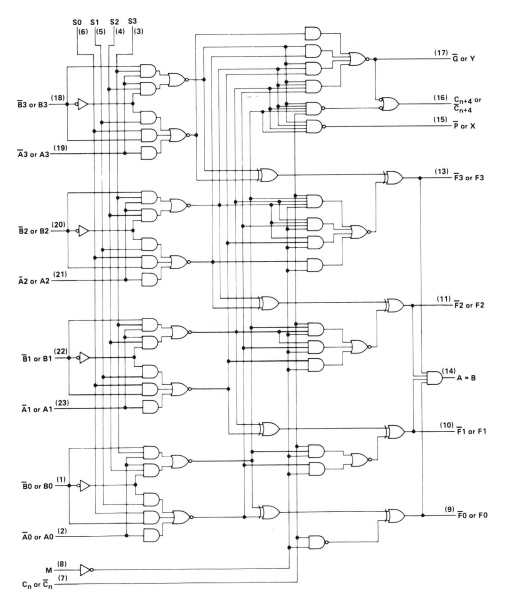

**Figure 5.9**  74181 IC logical diagram.

To initialize the adder, we hold a third input $L$ high to indicate the least significant bit. The $Z$ output of the serial adder is a serial representation of the sum, with each sum bit appearing shortly after the corresponding input bits are presented and being held until the next clock pulse.

The adder is constructed as shown in figure 5.12. To generate the next sum bit, we store the carry out of the previous place in flip-flop $K$. The $L$ input reinitializes the circuit by inhibiting the feedback of the carry from the previous stage.

Note that the serial adder has constant cost, no matter what the size of the inputs

*Synthesis of Digital Systems*

| SELECTION | | | | ACTIVE-LOW DATA | | |
|---|---|---|---|---|---|---|
| | | | | M = H | M = L; ARITHMETIC OPERATIONS | |
| S3 | S2 | S1 | S0 | LOGIC FUNCTIONS | $C_n$ = L (no carry) | $C_n$ = H (with carry) |
| L | L | L | L | F = $\overline{A}$ | F = A MINUS 1 | F = A |
| L | L | L | H | F = $\overline{AB}$ | F = AB MINUS 1 | F = AB |
| L | L | H | L | F = $\overline{A}$ + B | F = A$\overline{B}$ MINUS 1 | F = A$\overline{B}$ |
| L | L | H | H | F = 1 | F = MINUS 1 (2's COMP) | F = ZERO |
| L | H | L | L | F = $\overline{A + B}$ | F = A PLUS (A + $\overline{B}$) | F = A PLUS (A + $\overline{B}$) PLUS 1 |
| L | H | L | H | F = $\overline{B}$ | F = AB PLUS (A + $\overline{B}$) | F = AB PLUS (A + $\overline{B}$) PLUS 1 |
| L | H | H | L | F = A $\oplus$ B | F = A MINUS B MINUS 1 | F = A MINUS B |
| L | H | H | H | F = A + $\overline{B}$ | F = A + $\overline{B}$ | F = (A + $\overline{B}$) PLUS 1 |
| H | L | L | L | F = $\overline{A}$B | F = A PLUS (A + B) | F = A PLUS (A + B) PLUS 1 |
| H | L | L | H | F = A $\oplus$ B | F = A PLUS B | F = A PLUS B PLUS 1 |
| H | L | H | L | F = B | F = A$\overline{B}$ PLUS (A + B) | F = A$\overline{B}$ PLUS (A + B) PLUS 1 |
| H | L | H | H | F = A + B | F = (A + B) | F = (A + B) PLUS 1 |
| H | H | L | L | F = 0 | F = A PLUS A‡ | F = A PLUS A PLUS 1 |
| H | H | L | H | F = A$\overline{B}$ | F = AB PLUS A | F = AB PLUS A PLUS 1 |
| H | H | H | L | F = AB | F = A$\overline{B}$ PLUS A | F = A$\overline{B}$ PLUS A PLUS 1 |
| H | H | H | H | F = A | F = A | F = A PLUS 1 |

| SELECTION | | | | ACTIVE-HIGH DATA | | |
|---|---|---|---|---|---|---|
| | | | | M = H | M = L; ARITHMETIC OPERATIONS | |
| S3 | S2 | S1 | S0 | LOGIC FUNCTIONS | $\overline{C}_n$ = H (no carry) | $\overline{C}_n$ = L (with carry) |
| L | L | L | L | F = $\overline{A}$ | F = A | F = A PLUS 1 |
| L | L | L | H | F = $\overline{A + B}$ | F = A + B | F = (A + B) PLUS 1 |
| L | L | H | L | F = $\overline{A}$B | F = A + $\overline{B}$ | F = (A + $\overline{B}$) PLUS 1 |
| L | L | H | H | F = 0 | F = MINUS 1 (2's COMPL) | F = ZERO |
| L | H | L | L | F = $\overline{AB}$ | F = A PLUS A$\overline{B}$ | F = A PLUS A$\overline{B}$ PLUS 1 |
| L | H | L | H | F = $\overline{B}$ | F = (A + B) PLUS A$\overline{B}$ | F = (A + B) PLUS A$\overline{B}$ PLUS 1 |
| L | H | H | L | F = A $\oplus$ B | F = A MINUS B MINUS 1 | F = A MINUS B |
| L | H | H | H | F = A$\overline{B}$ | F = A$\overline{B}$ MINUS 1 | F = A$\overline{B}$ |
| H | L | L | L | F = $\overline{A}$ + B | F = A PLUS AB | F = A PLUS AB PLUS 1 |
| H | L | L | H | F = $\overline{A \oplus B}$ | F = A PLUS B | F = A PLUS B PLUS 1 |
| H | L | H | L | F = B | F = (A + $\overline{B}$) PLUS AB | F = (A + $\overline{B}$) PLUS AB PLUS 1 |
| H | L | H | H | F = AB | F = AB MINUS 1 | F = AB |
| H | H | L | L | F = 1 | F = A PLUS A† | F = A PLUS A PLUS 1 |
| H | H | L | H | F = A + $\overline{B}$ | F = (A + B) PLUS A | F = (A + B) PLUS A PLUS 1 |
| H | H | H | L | F = A + B | F = (A + $\overline{B}$) PLUS A | F = (A + $\overline{B}$) PLUS A PLUS 1 |
| H | H | H | H | F = A | F = A MINUS 1 | F = A |

**Figure 5.10** 74181 IC truth table.

and outputs. Here we have a clear example of a trade-off between quantity of hardware and time. By taking more time, we can reduce the amount of hardware needed to perform the addition.

### 5.1.4 Conversion between Parallel and Serial Data Representations

If a parallel adder is replaced by a serial adder, we might need to convert inputs from parallel to serial form and outputs back to parallel form. These conversions can be performed by devices called *shift registers*.

The basic shift-register structure is shown in figure 5.13; it is a series of $D$ flip-flops with a common clock input and with the output of one connected as input to the next. In this configuration, the shift register simply provides a delayed copy of

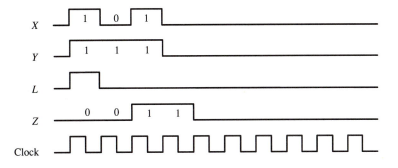

Figure 5.11 Timing diagram for adding 5 and 7.

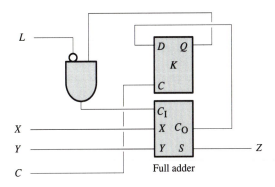

Figure 5.12 Circuit for a serial adder.

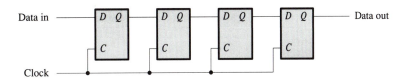

Figure 5.13 Shift register.

its inputs as output. If there are $n$ flip-flops in the shift register, the delay will be $n$ times the clock period.

A *serial-in, parallel-out* shift register has additional outputs, such that the last $n$ bits read in to the shift register can be input in parallel to some other circuit (see figure 5.14). The serial-in, parallel-out shift register is typically used for serial-to-parallel data conversion. If an $n$-bit serial-in, parallel-out shift register were connected to the $Z$ output of the serial adder above, after $n$ clock times the sum would be expressed in binary on the outputs of the shift register.

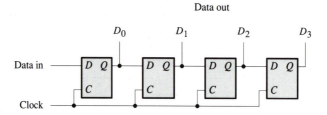

Figure 5.14   Serial-in, parallel-out shift register.

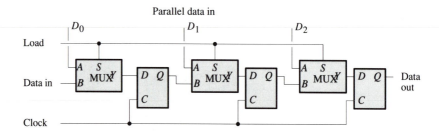

Figure 5.15   Parallel-in, serial-out shift register.

A *parallel-in, serial-out* shift register allows the input to each $D$ flip-flop to be obtained either from the adjacent flip-flop's output (as in other shift registers) or from one of a set of parallel inputs. Such a shift register is shown in figure 5.15. If the load input is high, the next clock transition causes the inputs to be taken from the parallel data inputs. If the load input is low, the shift register shifts one place, as in the garden-variety shift register.

The parallel-in, serial-out shift register is commonly used for parallel-to-serial conversion. We could allow data to be presented in parallel to our serial adder by loading the two addends into shift registers and then shifting the data one bit at a time through the adder. The output could then, if desired, be returned to parallel form, as discussed above. Shift registers are another common kind of MSI building block, and TTL units such as the 74194 and 74198 provide 4- or 8-bit-long shift registers with full parallel-in or parallel-out, left and right shift capabilities, all in one package.

### 5.1.5 Counters

Another important element used in the construction of digital circuits is a *counter*. The basic counter has a clock input and a set of parallel outputs that cycle through a sequence of values. The unsigned binary number represented by a binary counter's outputs increases by 1 at each clock time. When the counter reaches its maximum value, its next state is 0.

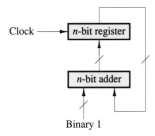

**Figure 5.16**   Counter.

A simple $n$-bit counter can be built out of an $n$-bit register and a combinational $n$-bit adder set up to add 1 to the present value of the register, as in figure 5.16. Since one input to the adder is fixed at 1, the full generality of an $n$-bit adder is not really needed here; commercially available counters substitute simpler circuitry that is only capable of incrementing its input by 1.

Typical counters include additional inputs that allow initialization of the counter state (*clear* or *init*) and control which of the clock pulses are counted (*count*).

In addition to counting selected clock pulses, a counter is often used to divide its clock frequency by some constant, giving a derived clock signal of some submultiple of that frequency. A binary counter whose cycle is $2^n$ (that is, an $n$-bit binary counter) can be used to derive a clock whose frequency is $f/2^n$ from a clock whose frequency is $f$ by using the most significant bit of the counter output as the derived clock signal. For the first $2^{n-1}$ clock pulses of the counter's cycle, this bit is 0, and for the second $2^{n-1}$ it is 1. Thus there is one output pulse per $2^n$ input clock pulses. If the duty cycle of the derived clock must be other than 50 percent, some combinational function of the counter outputs can be used to generate pulses of the desired shape (but this is an application in which avoiding glitches in the output is normally important, so that hazard-free design will be in order).

Commercially available TTL circuits such as the 74161, 74163, 74190, and 74191 provide 4-bit counters with parallel clear and load facilities, and often the choice of counting up or down, all in one package.

## 5.2  Regular Structures

In section 5.1.1 we discussed the use of a multiplexer to implement a logical function from its truth table. This technique is quite useful but has limitations. For example, suppose we wish to implement some function $f$ of eight variables using a single IC multiplexer. Such a multiplexer would have to have eight select inputs and $2^8 = 256$ data inputs (one for each row of the truth table for $f$). For several technological reasons, this is an unworkably large number of pins for one chip. Of course, several multiplexers could be cascaded together to synthesize

**Figure 5.17**  Pulldown symbol.

this large multiplexer; but for the purposes of implementing logical functions via multiplexers, there are preferable alternatives.

### 5.2.1 Read-Only Memories

Note that, in the example of section 5.1.1, only a constant value (either 1 or 0) is supplied at each data input. We can save on pins if each of these values is programmed, or prewired to the appropriate value, directly on the chip itself. Then only the eight select inputs and the output need be brought off the chip. Chips of this sort actually exist and are called *read-only memories*, or ROMs, because the select lines are effectively addressing bits of information stored in the ROM chip. Thus ROMs operate much like traditional read/write memories, except that there is no provision for changing the information stored in a ROM.

Many different kinds of ROMs are available, some containing as many as a million bits or more on one chip. Several combinations of speed, size, and cost can be obtained. Beyond these differences, three broad categories of ROMs can be distinguished, based on the way in which the information is programmed into the chip. *Mask-programmed* or *mask-programmable* ROMs are manufactured with an encoded bit pattern that cannot be changed. This pattern is determined by the particular circuit interconnections laid out on the chip. *Field-programmable ROMs*, or PROMs, can be programmed by the user by applying specified signals to certain pins. In one technology, these voltages burn out fusible links on the chip, so that the programming process is irreversible. Also available are *erasable PROMs*, or EPROMs, which can be restored to their original state by exposure to ultraviolet light and then reprogrammed. In a sense, PROMs are ROMs that can also be written; however, the writing process is orders of magnitude slower than the reading process, and thus a PROM is effectively a ROM once it is installed in a logic circuit.

In practice, large ROMs are not constructed simply as multiplexers with inputs fixed as 1s or 0s; rather, a two-dimensional organization is used, both because it is easier to lay out on an integrated circuit and because it reduces the total number of components that are needed. Unfortunately, logic circuits using traditional logic symbols are not adequate to depict this architecture. ROMs can be manufactured using a variety of different technologies, so rather than drawing an electric circuit diagram, which would apply to only one logic family, we introduce a new piece of notation, shown in figure 5.17.

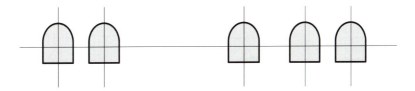

**Figure 5.18** An open-collector bus.

This symbol describes a *pulldown* with the following behavior: If the wire aligned with the long dimension of the AND-gate body (the vertical line in figure 5.17) carries a logical 0, then the horizontal wire is forced to 0; otherwise the horizontal wire is free to seek its own level, depending on the other connections to it. If a wire is subject to one or more pulldowns and none of them is active, it will assume a state of logical 1.

A wire subject to several pulldowns, as shown in figure 5.18, will assume a state that is the logical AND of all the pulldown control wires. Pulldowns are frequently implemented using a transistor whose collector is connected only to the wire being pulled down and not to any other part of the pulldown circuit; the term *open collector* is frequently used to describe this implementation, and the horizontal wire in figure 5.18 is often called an *open-collector bus*.

A ROM is implemented as a rectangular array of pulldowns, with address and decoding circuitry along the edges. Besides pulldowns and multiplexers, which we have already seen, the other kind of functional module in a ROM is a *decoder*. An $n$-bit decoder has $n$ inputs and $2^n$ outputs; thus there is one output corresponding to each possible combination of $n$ logic values at the inputs. Every output of a decoder is a logical 1, except for the output corresponding to the set of values currently present at the inputs; that output is a logical 0. (Sometimes the complementary formulation is used, in which all outputs are 0, except for one that is 1.) A decoder can be implemented as a simple collection of independent NAND gates sharing a common set of inputs, as in the three-line to eight-line decoder depicted in figure 5.19. Incidentally, decoders, in addition to being used inside ROMs and other circuits, are themselves available as IC chips.

In the ROM depicted in figure 5.20(a), there are a total of $m + n$ address inputs to select the desired bit. Of these, $n$ are applied to a decoder whose $2^n$ outputs drive the pulldowns in the array. A total of $2^m$ lines run perpendicularly to these and can be forced to 0 by pulldowns at the intersections. These $2^m$ lines feed into a multiplexer using the other $m$ address bits as select inputs. The output of the multiplexer has the value of the desired bit in the ROM.

Figure 5.20(b) is a more concrete example, showing a 64-bit ROM containing the primality function of the address inputs: If a prime number is given as an address, the ROM output will be a 1; otherwise the output will be 0. At any time, exactly one of the outputs of the decoder, determined by the top three address bits, will be 0. This line will pull down every vertically drawn bus wire that has a pulldown at its intersection with the selected decoder output. The value on one of

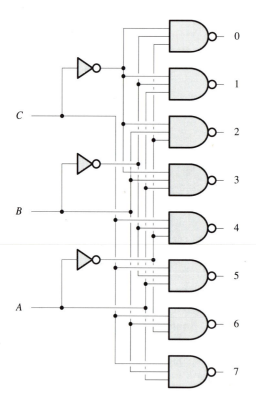

**Figure 5.19**   Three-line to eight-line decoder.

these buses, in turn, is selected by the bottom three address bits to be the output of the multiplexer and hence of the ROM.

Note that this arrangement requires a pulldown to be placed at every intersection corresponding to a 0 bit stored in the ROM, and no pulldown to be placed where a 1 is to be stored. Since only the presence or absence of pulldowns at intersections determines the content of the ROM, it is easy to imagine how localized and easy-to-describe changes to an IC layout will suffice to program a desired pattern into a ROM. The regularity and easy modifiability of a ROM layout is another reason for preferring it to gate-style combinational logic, even *within* IC chips, where pin count and package count considerations are not explicitly present.

In the real world, one or more of the signal lines shown in figure 5.20 may be inverted (carry the NOT of the signal shown), and other details may also differ. The basic principle of operation, however, is as we have discussed. Another common permutation on the design we have shown is that many ROM chips have more than one output—they effectively contain several ROMs sharing common address lines. This is easily accomplished by adding more arrays of pulldowns, each with its own multiplexer but sharing the outputs from the decoder.

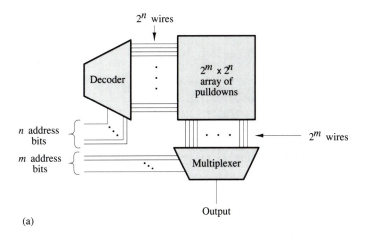

(a)

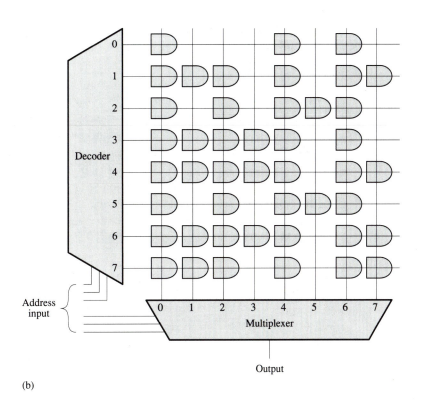

(b)

**Figure 5.20** Read-only memories: (a) general layout of a $2^{m+n}$-bit ROM; (b) a 64-bit ROM storing the primality function.

**Figure 5.21**   Notation for a pullup.

### 5.2.2 Programmable Logic Arrays

In many cases, a ROM is considerably superior to an ad hoc gate circuit for realizing a given combinational logic function. This is particularly true when the logic function in question has relatively little "structure" or regularity—when it cannot be broken down into a small number of elementary gate functions. However, it is sometimes necessary to implement a function with a considerable number of input variables that has some regularity, but not enough to lead to a simple gate implementation. The fact that the number of input variables is considerable means that a fairly large ROM would be required, since $n$ input variables imply a $2^n$-bit ROM. The fact that there is some regularity is a hint that, somehow, we ought to be able to do better. A technique for doing better does exist and is called the *programmable* (or *programmed*) *logic array*, or PLA.

Essentially, a PLA is a systematic way to implement a sum-of-products form of one or more logical functions of some set of input variables. Before we can describe how this is achieved, though, we must introduce one more piece of notation.

A *pullup*, drawn as in figure 5.21, is the dual of the pulldown. If the wire aligned with the long dimension of the OR-gate body (the vertical line in figure 5.21) is at logical 1, the other wire will be forced to logical 1; otherwise, it is free to assume whatever value is dictated by the other influences on it. A wire subject to one or more pullups will assume a state of logical 0 if none of the pullups is active; thus the logic value on such a wire is the OR of the values on all of its pullups.

The gross structure of a PLA is shown in figure 5.22(a). The two major constituents are an AND plane, in which conjunctions (ANDs) of relevant combinations of the input variables and their complements are computed, and an OR plane, in which disjunctions (ORs) of the terms applied from the AND plane are formed and provided as outputs. A third, minor constituent, a set of inverters and drivers capable of supplying the true and complemented value of each input variable, is shown just below the AND plane in figure 5.22(a).

The design of a PLA begins with sum-of-products expressions for each desired output variable. The AND plane must be designed to produce each term of each sum-of-products expression, but it need produce only one copy of any term that occurs in several different expressions. This can be one important source of economy in using PLAs. The OR plane is designed to generate each desired output variable by ORing together the appropriate terms generated in the AND plane. Our description of PLAs illustrates the overall principles of operation common to all PLAs; however, as in the case of ROMs, particular signal lines in actual PLAs

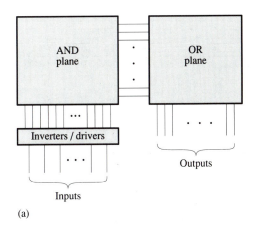

(a)

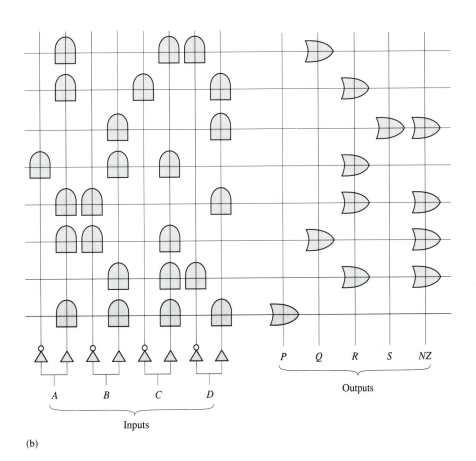

$A$ $B$ $C$ $D$

Inputs

$P$ $Q$ $R$ $S$ $NZ$

Outputs

(b)

**Figure 5.22** Programmable logic arrays: (a) gross structure of a PLA; (b) PLA for a 2-bit by 2-bit multiplier.

| Inputs | | | | Outputs | | | | |
|---|---|---|---|---|---|---|---|---|
| $A$ | $B$ | $C$ | $D$ | $P$ | $Q$ | $R$ | $S$ | $NZ$ |
| 0 | 0 | 0 | 0 | 0 | 0 | 0 | 0 | 0 |
| 0 | 0 | 0 | 1 | 0 | 0 | 0 | 0 | 0 |
| 0 | 0 | 1 | 0 | 0 | 0 | 0 | 0 | 0 |
| 0 | 0 | 1 | 1 | 0 | 0 | 0 | 0 | 0 |
| 0 | 1 | 0 | 0 | 0 | 0 | 0 | 0 | 0 |
| 0 | 1 | 0 | 1 | 0 | 0 | 0 | 1 | 1 |
| 0 | 1 | 1 | 0 | 0 | 0 | 1 | 0 | 1 |
| 0 | 1 | 1 | 1 | 0 | 0 | 1 | 1 | 1 |
| 1 | 0 | 0 | 0 | 0 | 0 | 0 | 0 | 0 |
| 1 | 0 | 0 | 1 | 0 | 0 | 1 | 0 | 1 |
| 1 | 0 | 1 | 0 | 0 | 1 | 0 | 0 | 1 |
| 1 | 0 | 1 | 1 | 0 | 1 | 1 | 0 | 1 |
| 1 | 1 | 0 | 0 | 0 | 0 | 0 | 0 | 0 |
| 1 | 1 | 0 | 1 | 0 | 0 | 1 | 1 | 1 |
| 1 | 1 | 1 | 0 | 0 | 1 | 1 | 0 | 1 |
| 1 | 1 | 1 | 1 | 1 | 0 | 0 | 1 | 1 |

**Figure 5.23**   Truth table for a multiplier PLA.

may be inverted with respect to those shown here. Thus PLAs in different logic families may have two NOR planes or two NAND planes, rather than AND and OR planes, as shown here.

As an example of PLA design, figure 5.22(b) shows a PLA that generates the product of two 2-bit binary numbers, along with an auxiliary output that indicates whether the product is nonzero. Figure 5.23 gives the truth table for our function, which multiplies the integers $AB$ and $CD$ to produce the product $PQRS$ and the nonzero indication $NZ$.

The sum-of-products equations used in the PLA are

$$P = A \cdot B \cdot C \cdot D,$$
$$Q = A \cdot \overline{B} \cdot C + A \cdot C \cdot \overline{D},$$
$$R = A \cdot \overline{B} \cdot D + A \cdot \overline{C} \cdot D + \overline{A} \cdot B \cdot C + B \cdot C \cdot \overline{D},$$
$$S = B \cdot D,$$
$$NZ = B \cdot D + A \cdot \overline{B} \cdot C + A \cdot \overline{B} \cdot D + B \cdot C \cdot \overline{D}.$$

These equations are all in minimal sum-of-products form, except for the equation for $NZ$, which was crafted to reuse implicants already needed for $P$, $Q$, $R$, or $S$. The conversion from these equations to the PLA layout shown in figure 5.22(b) is straightforward and consists merely of drawing the right number of wires in each direction and placing pullup and pulldown symbols at the appropriate intersections. Note how a PLA allows implicants to be shared among output variables.

As is the case with ROM configurations, PLA configurations can be determined at manufacturing time, by making local alterations to the IC masks so that pullups and pulldowns are properly placed. Or PLAs can be manufactured so that the user, by applying certain voltages to special pins, can program any desired configuration.

Both ROMs and PLAs are higher-level examples of the basic philosophy of design simplification through constraint that underlies all digital systems. Each offers a stylized way of implementing logical functions that lacks the flexibility of designing with individual gate circuits. In return, each is efficiently implementable in a variety of logic families and offers the additional advantage of being much less sensitive than random combinational logic-gate circuits to minor perturbations of design specifications. Finally, the gross structural features of a ROM or PLA of some given size are independent of the logical function programmed into it. Thus it is feasible to manufacture standard ROMs and PLAs that the user can customize.

The choice between a ROM or a PLA to implement some particular logical function depends on the nature of the function. In many cases, either approach will work fine, but for a function of a large number of variables that exhibits a certain degree of regularity, a PLA may be much more economical. Additionally, it is possible to implement hazard-free circuits as PLAs but not, in general, as ROMs.

Although our sample ROMs and PLAs have implemented, for motivational reasons, functions related to arithmetic, the main applications of ROMs and PLAs are in fact to the implementation of functions associated with the control of computing hardware, particularly in the combinational parts of various clocked sequential circuits. Because of the special nature of arithmetic functions and the considerable degree of commonality among arithmetic operations required in different digital systems, specialized building blocks for arithmetic exist.

### 5.2.3 Read/Write Memories

In addition to read-only memories and PLAs, many digital systems contain some form of addressable *read/write* memory. These provide a flexible way to store intermediate results of calculations. All read/write memories consist of a set of *cells* selected by distinct *addresses*. Individual cells can be read or written by specifying the proper address on the address inputs to the memory, and then either reading the data on the data outputs or presenting data on the data inputs. Memory organizations differ with respect to whether multiple reads can proceed simultaneously and the technique used to address the data.

Figure 5.24 shows how an $8 \times 1$-bit memory can be constructed using an octal decoder, an octal multiplexer, and eight edge-triggered $D$ flip-flops. The multiplexer is used to select which of the outputs from the eight flip-flops is presented on the data output. The decoder is used to select which of the flip-flops will be loaded from the data input when a pulse is received on the load input. Note that it is perfectly plausible to add another multiplexer, allowing two separate cells to be read simultaneously, while a third one is being written.

By using $n$ copies of the circuit in figure 5.24, we can make a register file consisting of 8 $n$-bit registers (an $8 \times n$-bit memory). Figure 5.25 shows how

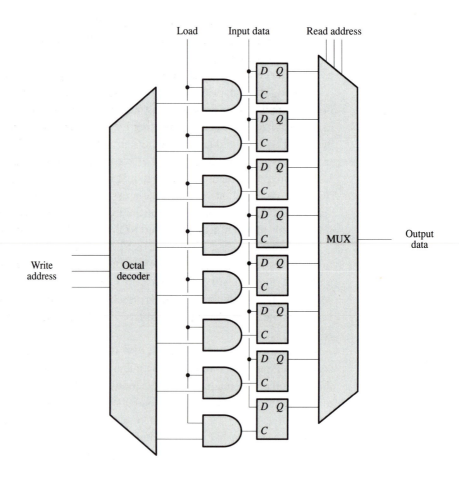

**Figure 5.24** An 8 × 1-bit memory. MUX = multiplexer.

this can be constructed (each box in the figure represents one module of the kind depicted in figure 5.24).

Small memories are often built in this way, out of flip-flops with addressing logic. When larger memories are needed, other technologies are generally used. For a long time, the common way to provide large, fast memories was to use arrays of magnetic cores. Here the polarity of magnetization is used to represent a 0 or 1. Contemporary technology in large, fast semiconductor memories uses the charge on a small capacitor to represent a bit of information, with specialized circuitry that selectively reads and writes information to individual capacitors in a large array. The major difference between such memories and the register file above is that simultaneous read and write is typically not possible. The term *random-access memory*, or RAM, is commonly used to refer to read/write memories (as distinguished from ROMs, which are read-only). We shall discuss such memories in more detail later.

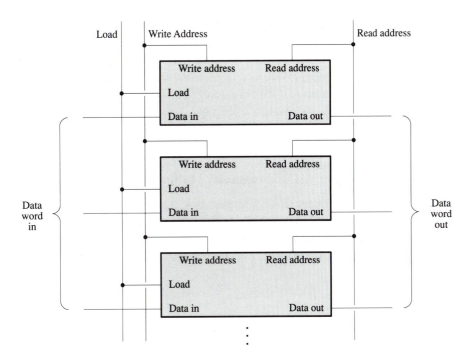

**Figure 5.25** An $8 \times n$-bit memory.

### 5.2.4 Other Logic Arrays

The ROM and PLA structures are bases for *semicustom* devices in which minor (and relatively inexpensive) design changes can yield arbitrary logic functions. A number of similar alternative structures exist, offering much the same advantage at various cost/performance levels.

Semicustom *gate arrays* feature a fixed pattern of one or more simple types of devices, which can be interconnected in various ways simply by specifying the mask for a final metal layer in the fabrication process. Although such devices are not competitive with carefully engineered custom designs in either performance or density, they represent a practical compromise between designs using off-the-shelf ICs and the much greater cost of custom chip design. Companies fabricating gate arrays typically automate the interconnect design through computer programs that take logic equations or other higher-level specifications as input.

The *programmed array logic*, or PAL, is a close relative of the PLA that has become a staple of the modern board-level engineer. The PAL is field-programmable (like a PROM) by electrically fusing links; the related *hard array logic*, or HAL, is a mask-programmed version. Like a PLA, the PAL has an AND plane driving an OR plane; however, in a PAL the arrangements of pullups in the OR plane is fixed, while the AND plane is programmable. A small PAL might have four inputs and four outputs, with 16 term lines going from the AND to the OR plane. Such a device would drive each output with a four-input OR gate, dividing the term lines equally among the outputs. Available PAL devices vary in their logic details, pin count, and miscellaneous features; some offer XOR gates or registers on their outputs. They are reasonably priced, accessible (requiring an inexpensive computer-based programmer), and fast performers. PALs and their relatives have nearly replaced gate-level SSI (such as the 7400 quad NAND gate illustrated earlier in this chapter) as the logic "glue" that interconnects complex components such as processors, arithmetic units, and memories.

## 5.3 Design Example: A Combinational Multiplier

Section 2.1.1 described how to multiply numbers in binary notation: Form partial products by ANDing the multiplicand with successive bits of the multiplier, align the products properly, and then sum. Thus the product of the 2-bit numbers $a_1 a_0$ and $b_1 b_0$ would be generated as

$$
\begin{array}{ccccc}
 & & & & a_1 a_0 \\
 & & & \times & b_1 b_0 \\
\hline
 & & a_1 b_0 & & a_0 b_0 \\
 & a_1 b_1 & a_0 b_1 & & \\
\hline
S_3 & S_2 & S_1 & & S_0
\end{array}
$$

Here the sum bits $S_3 S_2 S_1 S_0$ represent the final answer. In general, $m + n$ bits may be needed to express the product of an $m$-bit number and an $n$-bit number, and we see that this is the case here.

One approach to constructing a combinational multiplier circuit would be to work out the Boolean expression for each result bit $S_i$ and then design gate circuits (or ROMs or PLAs) to implement each expression. In fact, a 2-bit by 2-bit multiplier was precisely the example used to illustrate PLAs. For larger multiplications, using a single PLA to implement the entire multiplication quickly becomes impossibly cumbersome.

What is needed is an approach that takes advantage of the peculiar structure of the computation we are trying to implement. Using a string of full adders, as shown in figure 5.26(b), we can build a circuit that will add *two* partial products, but we need to add $n$ partial products, where $n$ is the number of bits in the multiplier. What we must do is generate *partial sums* along the way, such that the $(i + 1)$st partial sum is calculated by adding the $i$th partial sum and the $(i + 1)$st partial product. We can then build a combinational multiplier as a pile of identical modules, as shown in figure 5.26(a). Each module takes in a partial product formed using the appropriate multiplier bit to give a new partial sum at the bottom. The carry out generated in each module is shown emanating at the left-hand end; it becomes the most significant bit of the partial product generated. Note that successive modules are offset to produce the proper alignment of partial products. Note also that 0s are supplied as the 0th partial sum.

Figure 5.26(b) shows the structure of each module. Note that the full multiplicand $a_{n-1} \cdots a_1 a_0$ is used in each module, though the wiring to make this available

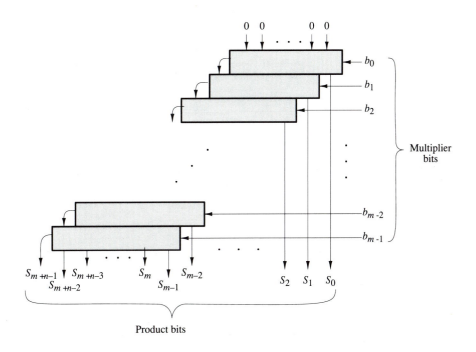

(a)

(b)

**Figure 5.26** Design of a combinational multiplier: (a) overall layout; (b) structure of an individual module.

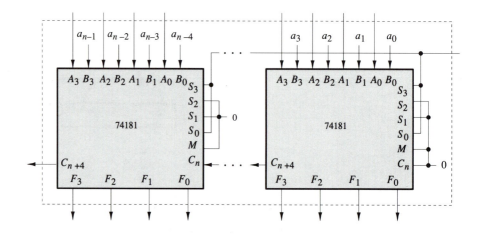

**Figure 5.27** Alternative implementation of the combinational multiplier module.

is not explicitly shown in figure 5.26(a). The row of AND gates computes the partial product used in the module, and the row of full adders combines this with the old partial sum, appearing at the top, thereby producing the new partial sum at the bottom and a carry out at the left.

An alternative implementation of the combinational multiplier module, illustrating some of the flexibility of the 74181 ALU chip, is shown in figure 5.27. Each 74181 subsumes the function of four full adders, and the AND gates are eliminated by applying the multiplier bits to selected *mode control* inputs of the 74181. A 0 multiplier bit selects the function $F = A$ (just pass through the partial sum from above), and a 1 bit selects the operation $F = A + B$ (add the multiplicand to the partial sum from above). Thus an entire combinational multiplier can be built out of nothing but 74181 chips, appropriately interconnected.

With the multiplier implementation of figure 5.25, the maximum propagation delay from any input to any output is $n + 2(m - 1)$ full-adder delays (assuming that the delay from any input to any output of a full adder is the same). The worst case occurs when a change in $b_0$ (or $a_0$) must be reflected in the value of $S_{m+n-1}$. The path through which this change is effected may be as sinuous as that shown in figure 5.28, where a change in, say, $b_0$ must travel through two adders on each of the first $m - 1$ levels and through all $n$ adders on the last level. The reader can find many other paths from $b_0$ to $S_{m+n-1}$ that are equally lengthy.

The delay of the combinational multiplier can be reduced by using carry lookahead within each bank of adders, but the magnitude of the reduction depends on exactly how the look-ahead is implemented. If the maximum delay from any input to any output of the bank of adders becomes $\tau$, then the $n$ full-adder delays counted above will be reduced to $\tau$. Additional time savings may be realized if the look-ahead circuitry allows changes in the multiplier or multiplicand bits to propagate more quickly to the relevant sum outputs of an adder bank. This would reduce the $2(m - 1)$ full-adder delays counted above. However, the delay will still include a term proportional to $m$, since, in general, a change in an input may have

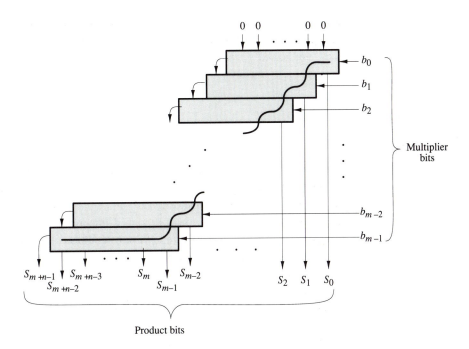

**Figure 5.28** Worst-case path through a combinational multiplier.

to percolate through $m$ banks of adders. Because of the vagaries of accounting correctly for the benefits obtained using carry look-ahead, as well as the fact that (assuming that $m$ and $n$ are of the same order of magnitude) the benefits are at most the reduction of the multiply time by a constant factor, we shall say nothing further about these benefits here. We do note, however, that techniques other than carry look-ahead can also be used to improve the performance of a combinational multiplier.

In our original combinational multiplier, we were able to obtain a multiply time (for multiplication of an $n$-bit number by an $m$-bit number) proportional to $n + 2(m-1)$ using a number of components proportional to $m \cdot n$. Radically different organizations would lead to different points in the cost-performance space. For example, we could implement the multiplier as a ROM, which would be addressed using a concatenation of the multiplier and multiplicand bits. Such a ROM would be able to perform a multiplication in essentially constant time (ignoring difficulties in scaling ROMs to large sizes) but would contain $2^{m+n}$ result words, each $m+n$ bits long, for a total component count proportional to $(m+n)2^{m+n}$; similar results would attend a PLA implementation.

These are two examples of cost-performance trade-offs available to implementors of the same logical function. With techniques to be introduced later on, several other trade-offs can be made for this same function. The important lesson for engineers of digital systems is that they must be constantly aware of the cost constraints and performance requirements of each application, both for the system as a whole and for each of its components. Often, a variety of approaches with differing cost and performance characteristics will be needed to construct a balanced, well-engineered system.

## 5.4 Context

The evolutionary trend mentioned in section 3.5 has raised the functional level of the digital engineer's primitive components from the gate level in the 1960s to the complexity and sophistication of single-chip processors in the 1980s. The designer constrained to use mass-produced integrated circuits rather than custom designs is offered an extensive repertoire of complex designs, with the dual effect that (1) more functionality can be provided with fewer parts (and hence at lower cost) and (2) architectural flexibility is increasingly constrained by the selection of functions made by the manufacturer of each component. This latter constraint has resulted in two visible reactions: (1) a movement toward custom VLSI by digital designers and (2) increased interest in "general-purpose" or "customizable" chips at the complex end of the mass-produced IC spectrum.

The emergence of custom VLSI as a popular design medium has reawakened interest in low-level design issues, although the gate has been deemphasized somewhat as an abstraction in favor of models that expose switches and charge storage as primitives. Automation of design, by means of sophisticated computer tools, compensates for the additional burden placed on designers by the more primitive components of their designs. In certain ways, this trend is analogous to the RISC movement discussed in chapter 17, which substitutes sophisticated compilers for sophisticated interpretive hardware. See Mead and Conway [1980] and Weste and Eshraghian [1985] for discussion of VLSI design.

The general-purpose integrated circuits include ROMs and RAMs, PLAs, and gate arrays of various kinds. Gate-level integrated circuits are yielding to PALs [Monolithic Memories 1985], and various suppliers of gate arrays are making semicustom devices increasingly accessible to even the casual designer. A recent innovation along these lines is gate arrays that are field-programmable via RAM cells [Xilinx 1986] rather than by metal masks or fusible links.

## 5.5 Problems

### Problem 5.1

A. Show the Boolean equation for the function $F$ described by the following circuit:

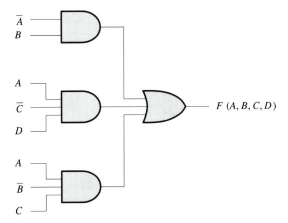

B. Implement $F$ using the $8 \times 1$ multiplexer shown below by specifying $I_0$ through $I_7$. The multiplexer selects input $I_j$ when the 3-bit binary number formed by the select inputs $A_2 A_1 A_0$ is equal to $j$. For example, $I_1$ is selected when $A_2 A_1 A_0 = 001$.

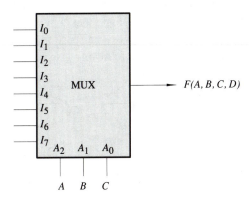

## Problem 5.2

Consider the circuit shown below. Each of the control inputs, $C_0$ through $C_3$, must be tied to a constant, either 0 or 1.

A. What are the values of $C_1$ through $C_3$ that would cause $F$ to be the *exclusive* OR of $A$ and $B$?

B. Can any arbitrary Boolean function of $A$ and $B$ be realized through appropriate wiring of the control signals?

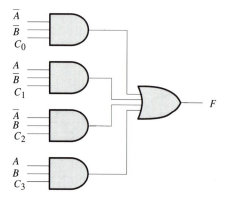

## Problem 5.3  Seven-Segment Display:

In most calculators the internal representation of numbers is a sequence of decimal digits represented as 4-bit binary numbers; this representation is known as *binary-coded decimal* (BCD). The calculator converts its internal representation into signals that light the proper parts of a seven-segment display in such a way that slow, nondigital humans can recognize the number easily. In this problem you are to design a block of combinational logic that converts a 4-bit number (positive only) into a seven-segment display code. The space to build this circuit is limited, and it is desirable to use as few of the following gate packages (chips) as possible.

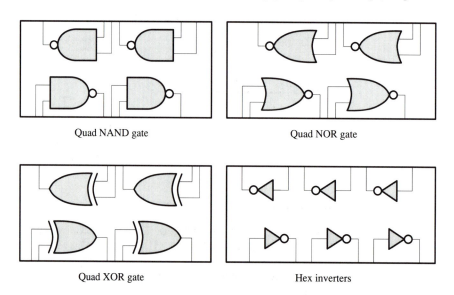

Quad NAND gate                     Quad NOR gate

Quad XOR gate                     Hex inverters

Here is the seven-segment display and the numbers that are to be represented. You need only represent these numbers and can assume any convenient output values for other combinations of input.

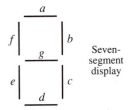

Seven-segment display

Numbers to be represented

A. Show the truth table taking 4 bits of input and generating 7 bits of output.

B. Write the Boolean functions for each segment ($F_a$–$F_g$).

C. Implement the decoder using as few gate packages as possible. Do not be a mindless slave to efficiency, though: Solutions do exist that use five packages, but you can feel satisfied if you have managed to do it using seven or so.

D. Draw the logic diagram of your implementation for maximum clarity. You do not need to keep gates from the same package together as packages or to give pin-number designations. Do label each gate to tell which package it is from—for example, NAND #1 or NOR #3.

### Problem ★5.4   PLA Implementation of the Seven-Segment Display:

Implement the seven-segment display described in problem 5.3 by using a PLA similar to those discussed in this chapter.

### Problem 5.5   Digital Stopwatch:

In this problem you will design a digital stopwatch with the following characteristics: Its display will consist of two two-digit decimal numbers representing minutes and seconds. The smallest display will be 00:00, the largest 59:59. The decimal digits will be seven-segment displays. The user will have three buttons available: a RESET button, which causes the time display to return to 00:00; a STOP button, which causes the stopwatch to freeze if it is running; and a GO button, which causes the stopwatch to start running if it is frozen. Pushing RESET while the stopwatch is running should set the time to 00:00 but not freeze it.

In addition to the seven-segment display module discussed previously, you have available modulo-6 and modulo-10 counters. In your design you should use the following symbols:

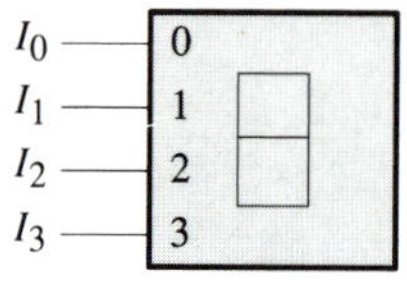


Seven–segment display

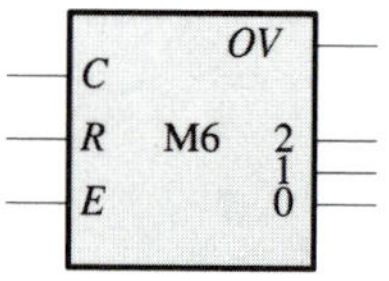


Modulo–6 counter

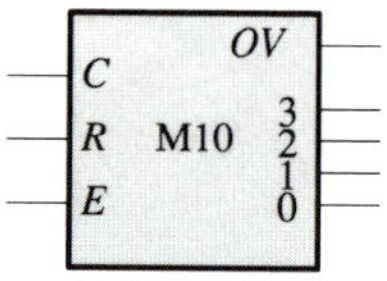


Modulo–10 counter

A *modulo-N counter* is a sequential circuit having $N$ states corresponding to the binary numbers 0 through $N - 1$. When enabled, the counter sequences from one state to the next on every clock pulse; thus the outputs of an enabled modulo-6 counter cycle through the sequence 000, 001, 010, 011, 100, 101, 000,.... Section 5.1.5 contains some comments on the implementation of counters.

The counter modules you are to use in this problem have outputs for the current counter state (numbered from most to least significant bit, bit 0 being the least significant) and several other terminals. The line labeled $C$ is the *clock* input to the counter (you may assume that it is positive edge-triggered). $R$ is a *reset* input, which, if 1, will force the counter state to 0 at the next clock pulse. $E$ is the *enable* input; counting will be inhibited if $E$ is 0. Finally, $OV$ is an overflow output, which is 1 only when $E$ is 1 and the counter state is at the maximum $(N - 1)$. In other words, $OV$ is 1 if the next clock pulse would take the counter from state $N - 1$ to state 0. *Note:* Do not assume that $OV$ is hazard-free; it may glitch momentarily after clock transitions.

A. Draw a circuit diagram for the digital stopwatch. You may use the modules discussed above and any other modules discussed in section 5.1. Your circuit will have a clock input with pulses supplied at 1-s intervals and RESET, STOP, and GO inputs that are 1 whenever the corresponding buttons are pressed. You may assume that each button remains pressed long enough to overlap at least one clock pulse; hence you need not worry about latching these inputs. Try to use as many building-block modules as possible and a minimum of ad hoc gate circuitry. One solution uses four seven-segment displays, two modulo-10 counters, two modulo-6 counters, one edge-triggered $D$ flip-flop, one two-input multiplexer, and one inverter. Give a short verbal description of how your circuit works, along with the circuit itself.

B. Are there any circumstances under which your stopwatch could function incorrectly because of metastable states? If so, describe them. How likely would these be to cause incorrect operation in practice? Explain your reasoning.

### *Problem 5.6 Comparator Cells:*

Digital Widgets Co. has introduced a new logic IC consisting of two comparator cells in a 14-pin package. A comparator cell, as drawn below, has four inputs and two outputs.

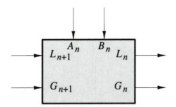

The inputs are labeled $A_n$, $B_n$, $G_{n+1}$, and $L_{n+1}$, and the outputs are labeled $G_n$ and $L_n$. The $G$ and $L$ signals have the meanings "$A$ greater than $B$" and "$A$ less than $B$," respectively. If both $G$ and $L$ are false, the meaning is $A = B$. $G$ and $L$ are never both true. Two $k$-bit numbers $A$ and $B$ may be compared using a circuit such as the following:

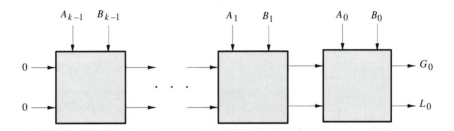

The most significant bits are supplied as $A_{k-1}$ and $B_{k-1}$, and the least significant bits are $A_0$ and $B_0$.

The output of a comparison is taken from the $G$ and $L$ outputs of the lowest-order cell ($G_0$ and $L_0$). $G_{n+1}$ and $L_{n+1}$ of the highest-order cell are connected to logical 0 to indicate that the numbers are assumed to be equal until some difference is found between a pair of bits $A_i$ and $B_i$.

If the $G_{n+1}$ and $L_{n+1}$ inputs indicate that higher-order bits have established $A > B$ or $A < B$, then cell $n$ must propagate that result to $G_n$ and $L_n$. However, if $G_{n+1}$ and $L_{n+1}$ indicate that the higher-order bits are equal, then cell $n$ must compare its bit of $A$ and $B$ to determine if $A > B$, $A < B$, or $A = B$ and must signal that result appropriately at $G_n$ and $L_n$.

A. Draw a logic diagram for an implementation of the Digital Widgets comparator cell.

B. Since there is delay associated with the propagation of the $G$ and $L$ signals through each cell, we could make the comparator work faster by redesigning the basic cell to compare two bits at a time, halving the number of stages through which the $G$ and $L$ signals will need to propagate.

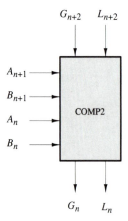

Work out expressions for $G_n$ and $L_n$ as functions of $G_{n+2}$, $L_{n+2}$, $A_{n+1}$, $B_{n+1}$, $A_n$, and $B_n$. Express your answers in the form

$$G_n = G_{n+2} + \overline{L_{n+2}} \cdot f(A_{n+1}, B_{n+1}, A_n, B_n),$$
$$L_n = L_{n+2} + \overline{G_{n+2}} \cdot g(A_{n+1}, B_{n+1}, A_n, B_n).$$

C. What is the significance of the functions $f$ and $g$? (How does the function they compute relate to the properties of the original numbers $A$ and $B$?)

D. Given a reasonable implementation of the equations for $G_n$ and $L_n$ derived in part B, how does the delay from a change in $G_{n+2}$ and $L_{n+2}$ to the appearance of correct outputs at $G_n$ and $L_n$ compare with the corresponding delay for a circuit composed of a cascade of two of the cells developed in part A? Assume that all $A$ and $B$ inputs remain unchanged throughout.

*Note:* The reason for our interest in the propagation delay of the $G$ and $L$ signals, specifically, is that in a chain of $N$ comparators, every extra gate delay in the $G$–$L$ path will penalize total performance by $N$ gate delays. The time it takes for a change in an $A$ or $B$ input to be reflected in the corresponding $G$ or $L$ output is also important, but improvements here can at best result in decreasing total delay by some constant amount.

### Problem 5.7  *Number Conversion Hardware:*

In this problem digital "building blocks," such as multiplexers, decoders, and adders, will be used to convert the representation of a value. We start with a 16-bit 2's complement number. We number the bits from the least significant bit ($b_0$) to the most significant bit ($b_{15}$) for reference. (Recall from chapter 2 that if $b_{15}$ is 0, the value is positive, and if it is 1, the value is negative.)

A. Design a box whose input is a 16-bit 2's complement integer and whose outputs are the 16-bit magnitude of the input and a single bit that is 1 if the input is negative. Use some 4-bit adders and some XOR gates. This is an *absolute-value box.*

| $I_7$ | $I_6$ | $I_5$ | $I_4$ | $I_3$ | $I_2$ | $I_1$ | $I_0$ | $A_2$ | $A_1$ | $A_0$ | $E_0$ |
|---|---|---|---|---|---|---|---|---|---|---|---|
| 1 | x | x | x | x | x | x | x | 1 | 1 | 1 | 0 |
| 0 | 1 | x | x | x | x | x | x | 1 | 1 | 0 | 0 |
| 0 | 0 | 1 | x | x | x | x | x | 1 | 0 | 1 | 0 |
| 0 | 0 | 0 | 1 | x | x | x | x | 1 | 0 | 0 | 0 |
| 0 | 0 | 0 | 0 | 1 | x | x | x | 0 | 1 | 1 | 0 |
| 0 | 0 | 0 | 0 | 0 | 1 | x | x | 0 | 1 | 0 | 0 |
| 0 | 0 | 0 | 0 | 0 | 0 | 1 | x | 0 | 0 | 1 | 0 |
| 0 | 0 | 0 | 0 | 0 | 0 | 0 | 1 | 0 | 0 | 0 | 0 |
| 0 | 0 | 0 | 0 | 0 | 0 | 0 | 0 | 0 | 0 | 0 | 1 |

**Figure 5.29**  Truth table for an 8-bit priority encoder.

B. A device known as an *8-bit priority encoder* has the truth table shown in figure 5.29. Using two 8-bit priority encoders and other digital building blocks as required, show an implementation for a 16-bit priority encoder.

C. We would like to use the circuits in parts A and B to convert a 16-bit 2's complement integer $b_{15}...b_0$ to a sign bit $S$, a 3-bit exponent $E$, and a 4-bit mantissa $M$, where

$$|b| = M \cdot 4^{E-1},$$
$$\text{sign}(b) = S,$$
$$0 \le E \le 7,$$
$$8 \le M < 16 \quad \text{if} \quad E \ne 0,$$
$$0 \le M < 16 \quad \text{if} \quad E = 0.$$

Note the use of a base of 4 for $E$, in contrast to the more customary base of 2 in floating-point representations. Here is an example:

| $b$ | | | | $S$ | $M$ | $E$ |
|---|---|---|---|---|---|---|
| 0000 | 0000 | 0010 | 0010 | 0 | 1000 | 010 |
| 1111 | 1111 | 1111 | 1000 | 1 | 1000 | 001 |
| 0001 | 0010 | 1100 | 1010 | 0 | 0100 | 110 |
| 1111 | 1111 | 1111 | 1111 | 1 | 0100 | 000 |

How can we use the priority-encoder circuit in part B in a circuit to find the base-4 exponent corresponding to an input number $b$?

D. Draw the circuit to produce $S$, $E$, and $M$ from the input $b$. Draw the circuits designed in parts A and C as "building-block" boxes. Use other building blocks as needed.

## Problem 5.8

How large a ROM is necessary for the implementation of an arbitrary $N$-input Boolean function?

## Problem 5.9

How many bits of information are stored in a ROM having $n$ inputs and $m$ outputs?

## Problem 5.10   Priority Encoder:

Using a PLA, implement the priority-encoder function described by the abbreviated truth table in figure 5.28. *Hint:* With this many inputs, Karnaugh maps are counterproductive.

# 6 Finite-State Machines

The combinational circuit, introduced in chapter 1, provides a model for the behavior of memoryless digital circuits. The finite-state machine, which is a similarly fundamental model of clocked sequential circuits, constitutes another basic intellectual tool of the digital engineer.

Consider the sequential circuit shown in figure 6.1. While the circuit diagram dictates the behavior of the device at a reasonably low level, it is often useful to deal with descriptions of abstract behavior without concern for circuit details. To this end, we may view the circuit as one of several possible implementations of a particular finite-state machine. Each FSM has a finite set of discrete *states* as well as finitely many digital inputs and outputs and a set of digital rules that govern its behavior. An FSM operates in discrete time: Its behavior is characterized as a sequence of steps that occur at regular intervals. An FSM's inputs, outputs, and state are assumed to be constant during each interval, changing only at the boundaries between consecutive intervals. We can summarize as follows:

. . . . . . . . . . . . . . . . . . . . . . . . . . . . . . . . . . . . . . . . . . . . . . . . . . . . . . . . . . . .

*A finite-state machine* is a digital device having

- a finite set of *states* $S_1$, $S_2$, ..., $S_k$ (where $k$ is the number of states). Optionally one of these, $S_I$, is distinguished as the *initial state* of the FSM;
- a finite number of binary inputs $I_1$, $I_2$, ..., $I_m$ (where $m$ is the number of inputs);
- a finite number of binary outputs $O_1$, $O_2$, ..., $O_n$ (where $n$ is the number of outputs);
- a set of *state-transition rules* specifying, for each choice of current state $S_s$ and input values $I_1$, $I_2$, ..., $I_m$, a *next state* $S_{s'}$; and
- a set of *output rules* specifying, for each choice of current state $S_s$ and input values $I_1$, $I_2$, ..., $I_m$, the binary value at each output.

. . . . . . . . . . . . . . . . . . . . . . . . . . . . . . . . . . . . . . . . . . . . . . . . . . . . . . . . . . . .

In a *Moore machine*, the FSM's outputs are functions of the current state alone. The behavior of such a machine can be specified by giving the rules for making transitions between states and the set of output values corresponding to each state.

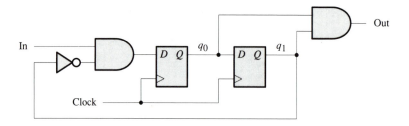

**Figure 6.1** Sequential circuit.

The alternative model, called a *Mealy machine*, allows outputs to reflect current inputs as well as current state. As discussed at the end of section 4.5, the behavior of every FSM can be described using either model, although the number of states and timing details will generally differ. The initial state of an FSM can be specified as a conventional starting point for the application of a sequence of inputs. Practical FSM implementations typically reserve a *reset* input, which returns the FSM to a prescribed initial state, and arrange for the machine to be reset before a new input sequence is applied (for example, when the system containing the FSM is turned on). Such an input makes specification of an initial state unnecessary.

Returning to the circuit of figure 6.1, we can identify its discrete states by tabulating combinations of values of its state variables. If we use $q_0$ and $q_1$ to denote the values of the state variables in the current state, and $Q_0$ and $Q_1$ to denote the values in the succeeding state, the equations describing this circuit are

$$Q_0 = in \cdot \overline{q_1},$$

$$Q_1 = q_0,$$

$$out = q_1 \cdot q_0.$$

We can capture both the state-transition and output rules in the simple truth table shown in figure 6.2, which lists all possible combinations of current state and input variables on the left side, and the next state the machine should enter on the right side along with the corresponding output. These tables can be easily obtained from the implementation of the FSM. For example, if in the circuit above, $q_0 = 0$, $q_1 = 0$, and $in = 0$, then the next state that results is $q_0 = 0$, $q_1 = 0$. If $in = 1$, the next state will be $q_0 = 1$, $q_1 = 0$.

The state-transition table immediately suggests a ROM implementation of the FSM, the left-hand side of the table being the address of the ROM and the right-hand columns being data outputs.

The final and most abstract representation for a finite-state machine is a *state-transition diagram*. In such a diagram, states are shown as circles. Outputs associated with the state are given inside the circle. Transitions between states are represented as directed arcs from one circle to another. The input combination that causes a given transition is written along the arc. Since we are dealing with clocked sequential machines, transitions only occur on clock edges, and for this reason the clock is not explicitly shown on state-transition diagrams. Figure 6.3 gives the state-transition diagram for the FSM discussed above.

| Current state | | Next state | |
| $q_1 q_0$ | Input | $Q_1 Q_0$ | Output |
| --- | --- | --- | --- |
| 00 | 0 | 00 | 0 |
| 00 | 1 | 01 | 0 |
| 01 | 0 | 10 | 0 |
| 01 | 1 | 11 | 0 |
| 10 | 0 | 00 | 0 |
| 10 | 1 | 00 | 0 |
| 11 | 0 | 10 | 1 |
| 11 | 1 | 10 | 1 |

**Figure 6.2**   State-transition truth table.

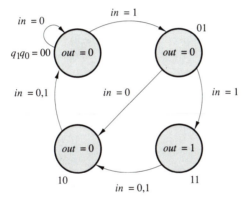

**Figure 6.3**   State-transition diagram.

## 6.1 Synthesis of Finite-State Machines

The synthesis and implementation of clocked sequential circuits is a fairly straight-forward process having four main steps. Most of the work comes in transforming from one representation of the FSM to another.

The first step is to draw a state-transition diagram for the FSM. This is often the most difficult step since it requires thinking very precisely about what the FSM is supposed to do. Next, determine the number of state variables (and therefore state flip-flops) from the number of states in the state-transition diagram and assign a binary encoding to each state. This assignment can be done arbitrarily.

Then, based on the state-transition diagram, build a state-transition table. It is important that the table cover all possible input combinations for each possible state. From the table, the circuit can be directly implemented with ROMs. If another implementation is required (logic gates, for example), develop Karnaugh maps

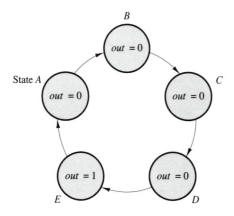

State A

B
out = 0

C
out = 0

out = 0

out = 1

out = 0

E

D

**Figure 6.4** State-transition diagram for the divide-by-5 counter.

| Transition table | | | Output table | |
| --- | --- | --- | --- | --- |
| Current state | Current state | Next state | State | Output |
| A | 000 | 001 | 000 | 0 |
| B | 001 | 010 | 001 | 0 |
| C | 010 | 011 | 010 | 0 |
| D | 011 | 100 | 011 | 0 |
| E | 100 | 000 | 100 | 1 |

**Figure 6.5** State-transition table for the divide-by-5 counter.

from the state-transition table for each next-state variable and each output variable. Finally, find a reduced sum-of-products expression for each and implement with appropriate combinational logic.

Consider the design of a simple FSM whose one output goes high every five clock times and remains high for one clock period. The frequency of the output pulses is one-fifth that of the clock. This type of circuit is called a *divide-by-5 counter*. This machine has no external inputs. Its state-transition diagram is shown in figure 6.4. (An arc with no input conditions next to it means that the transition always occurs.) A state assignment and a state-transition table for this counter are shown in figure 6.5.

## 6.2 Synchronous FSM Circuit Models

Although it is possible (and quite interesting) to base FSM implementations on self-timed and other timing disciplines, the vast majority of FSMs are engineered to use a simple, synchronous, single-clock scheme. A general sketch of an implementation strategy using the Moore machine model (in which outputs are functions only of

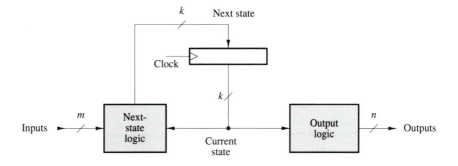

**Figure 6.6**  FSM (Moore machine) implementation.

current state, independently of current inputs) is shown in figure 6.6. Note the use of a clocked register to hold the current state information, the remainder of the circuit being combinational. A typical realization of this design might put both the output and next-state logic into a single ROM, PLA, or PAL.[1]

The circuit of figure 6.6 assumes that the timing of the inputs is synchronous with the FSM's clock, as would be the case if the FSM were a component of a larger, single-clock system. If the inputs are allowed to change asynchronously with respect to the clock, then this approach will fail for at least two reasons. First, the dynamic discipline is not obeyed: Asynchronous input transitions will yield asynchronous transitions at the output of the next-state logic, which can cause metastable behavior of the register. But the problem is much worse: Even without metastable states, an active clock occurring soon after an input transition (while its effects are still propagating through the next-state logic) is almost certain to load nonsense into the register.

We can accommodate asynchronous inputs by clocking them (along with the new state) into a register, as shown in figure 6.7. This revision guarantees that the inputs to the state register are stable at each active clock edge, assuming of course that the propagation delay along the combinational path through the logic is shorter than the clock period. Moreover, although metastable behavior of the input register remains a possibility, it has a clock period (minus the next-state propagation delay) to become valid before it corrupts the contents of the state register. Thus, for sufficiently long clock periods, this latter design should be arbitrarily reliable.

It is important to recognize that the implementations of figures 6.6 and 6.7 behave slightly differently, owing to the extra clock delay in the inputs of figure 6.7. Given identical next-state logic, identical input sequences will yield output sequences delayed by one clock cycle in the second approach.

---

[1] Single-chip field-programmable PALs are available with registers incorporated on their outputs, allowing simple FSMs to be implemented using a single off-the-shelf chip. This is a widely used approach to the implementation of control systems for board-level designs.

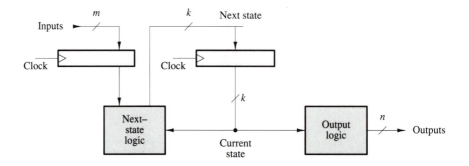

**Figure 6.7**  FSM for asynchronous inputs.

## 6.3 States and Bits

Most real digital systems are finite-state machines, yet the view and techniques introduced in this chapter are not appropriate in every circumstance. The binary encoding of an FSM's state allows at most $2^k$ states to be represented in $k$ bits of state variables, and in general about $k$ flip-flops are required to hold the state of a $2^k$-state machine. Adding a single flip-flop to a machine potentially doubles its number of states. This exponential relationship between the number of states and the amount of physical hardware in a sequential circuit leads the FSM model to become awkward in dealing with sequential circuits having more than a few bits of storage. A 10-bit register, for example, would be quite difficult to characterize by a state-transition diagram; the number of states of a supercomputer is inconceivably large.

Typically, such systems are viewed in terms of memory cells and registers, partitioning the enormous state into more tractable units. It is important to recognize that sequential circuits may be viewed either in *state* or in *bit* terms, that the two are exponentially related, and that it is often useful to vacillate between these views.

## 6.4 *Equivalence of FSMs

The input/output behavior of two FSMs may be identical even though the machines have different transition and output rules or even different numbers of states. As a degenerate example, consider two single-input FSMs whose output remains constant, independent of their state. From external observations it is impossible to distinguish between the states of such machines—one might have one state and the other nine, yet the machines are externally indistinguishable. We call FSMs *equivalent* if they are indistinguishable; for all practical purposes, equivalent FSMs are interchangeable.

Of course, a simple FSM is generally preferable to a complex equivalent, for cost and other reasons. It is therefore useful to develop the notion of equivalence together with engineering tools for reducing a specified FSM to a simpler equivalent. This section provides a fleeting glimpse of this heavily studied area. We begin with the concept of state equivalence.

. . . . . . . . . . . . . . . . . . . . . . . . . . . . . . . . . . . . . . . . . . . . . . . . . . . . . . . . . . . . . . . . . . . . .

***State equivalence***   Let $s_1$ and $s_2$ be particular states of FSMs $M_1$ and $M_2$, respectively. State $s_1$ of $M_1$ is *equivalent* to state $s_2$ of $M_2$ if and only if for *every* finite sequence of inputs, the outputs resulting from the application of that sequence to $M_1$ in $s_1$ are identical to the outputs resulting from the application of the same sequence to $M_2$ in $s_2$.

. . . . . . . . . . . . . . . . . . . . . . . . . . . . . . . . . . . . . . . . . . . . . . . . . . . . . . . . . . . . . . . . . . . . .

Thus two states are *not* equivalent only if there exists a finite input sequence that leads them to produce distinct outputs. We shall use the notation $M\!:\!s$ to specify state $s$ of machine $M$. Note that state equivalence is reflexive, transitive, and symmetric.[2]   We can elaborate slightly as follows.

. . . . . . . . . . . . . . . . . . . . . . . . . . . . . . . . . . . . . . . . . . . . . . . . . . . . . . . . . . . . . . . . . . . . .

***FSM equivalence***   Let $s_1$ and $s_2$ be initial states of FSMs $M_1$ and $M_2$, respectively. Then the machines $M_1$ and $M_2$ are *equivalent* if and only if $M_1\!:\!s_1$ is equivalent to $M_2\!:\!s_2$.

. . . . . . . . . . . . . . . . . . . . . . . . . . . . . . . . . . . . . . . . . . . . . . . . . . . . . . . . . . . . . . . . . . . . .

Given an FSM that solves some practical problem, we are often interested in finding the smallest equivalent FSM in order to minimize costs. While several measures of "smallest" might be proposed, a natural candidate (and usual choice) is the number of FSM states. Thus we seek to perform a *state reduction* on a given FSM $M_1$ to yield an equivalent $M_2$ having fewer states. In general, we may do this by detecting and merging equivalent states within $M_1$.

We could, for example, look for pairs $M_1\!:\!s_i$ and $M_1\!:\!s_j$ that are equivalent. When such a pair is found, we simply combine them into a single state, yielding an equivalent FSM with one fewer state. We then continue looking for equivalent states in the new FSM. The process terminates when a pair of equivalent states can no longer be found. This is an example of a *relaxation algorithm*, in which a set of reduction rules is repeatedly applied to reduce a structure until it can be reduced no more. It begins with a pessimistic but working model of the desired FSM and iteratively improves the cost while maintaining equivalence and hence usability.

This scheme has the disadvantage that the equivalence of two states can be difficult to detect. Fortunately, there is a variant that is simple and effective. Rather than incrementally improving an initial pessimistic model, the *optimistic relaxation* approach begins with the assumption that *all* of the states of $M_1$ are equivalent (yielding a one-state machine). The relaxation iteratively discovers pairs

---

[2] Section 7.3.2 defines reflexivity and transitivity; a relation $\equiv$ is *symmetric* if $A \equiv B$ implies $B \equiv A$ for all $A$ and $B$.

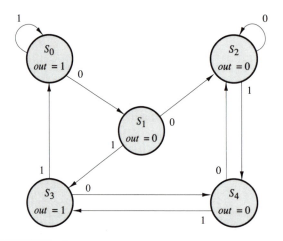

**Figure 6.8** Five-state FSM.

of presumed equivalent states that cannot in fact be equivalent and grudgingly splits them into their components. This scheme is based on the detection of state *non*equivalence through two rules:

- If states $s_i$ and $s_j$ have different outputs, then they are nonequivalent.
- If, for some input combination $v_1, v_2, \ldots, v_m$, state $s_{i_1}$ goes to state $S_{i_2}$ and state $s_{j_1}$ goes to state $S_{j_2}$, where $S_{i_2}$ and $S_{j_2}$ are nonequivalent, then $s_{i_1}$ and $s_{j_1}$ are nonequivalent.

Beginning with the unrealistic assumption that all states are equivalent, iteration of the above rules will uncover more and more nonequivalent pairs of states until every pair that has not been shown nonequivalent is in fact equivalent.

Consider, for example, the FSM diagrammed in figure 6.8. We begin our search for a reduced equivalent by constructing a truth table for output and transition rules for a one-state equivalent:

|  |  | Transitions | |
| --- | --- | --- | --- |
| New state | Output | 0 | 1 |
| $S_0 = S_1 = S_2 = S_3 = S_4$ | $X$ | | |

In the course of building the table, we check that each output and next-state value for a merged state is consistent with each of the component states from the original FSM. In this first step, we immediately detect an inconsistency: We can't put a value in the output column for our single combined state that is consistent with all five component states. We are thus forced to split our aggregate state for the next iteration into two new states, with output values of 0 and 1. We partition our five-state aggregate into one state corresponding to the original $S_0$ and $S_3$ states with a 1 output, and a second state corresponding to the original states with a 0 output. We then attempt to fill out the truth table:

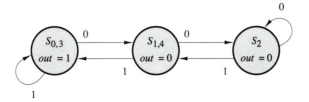

**Figure 6.9** Reduced equivalent FSM.

|  |  | Transitions | |
| --- | --- | --- | --- |
| New state | Output | 0 | 1 |
| $S_0 = S_3$ | 1 | $S_1 = S_4$ | $S_0$ |
| $S_1 = S_2 = S_4$ | 0 | $S_2$ | $X$ |

This time we can nearly complete the table. We encounter a single inconsistency in trying to assign a transition for the $S_1 = S_2 = S_4$ state on a 1 input: In the original machine, $S_1$ and $S_4$ both go to $S_3$ in this case, while $S_2$ goes to $S_4$. Since the respective next states $S_3$ and $S_4$ are not equivalent, we are forced to split $S_2$ out into a separate state. This leads to

|  |  | Transitions | |
| --- | --- | --- | --- |
| New state | Output | 0 | 1 |
| $S_0 = S_3$ | 1 | $S_1 = S_4$ | $S_0$ |
| $S_1 = S_4$ | 0 | $S_2$ | $S_3$ |
| $S_2$ | 0 | $S_2$ | $S_4$ |

The corresponding state-transition diagram is shown in figure 6.9. The reader should verify that this reduced FSM is equivalent to the original.

While simple optimistic relaxation gives optimal reductions in the case of completely specified FSMs, optimal solutions to interesting variations of the FSM reduction problem are known to be computationally intractable. For example, optimal reduction of an incompletely specified FSM, in the sense that *any* values are acceptable for certain outputs and/or transitions, is NP-hard.[3]   The development of good heuristic approaches to this and related optimization problems remains a topic of research.

## 6.5 *Regular Expressions and Nondeterministic FSMs

*Regular expressions* are a commonly used notation for describing simple classes

---

[3] *NP-hard* problems are suspected of being computationally intractable, in the sense that they require computation time that grows exponentially with the size of their input. However, this suspicion—the notorious $P = NP$? question—remains to be proved. The interested reader is referred to Garey and Johnson [1979] for details.

of strings of symbols. For the purposes of this section we shall use the following regular-expression syntax for describing strings of uppercase letters:

1. Finite strings of symbols (letters), including the empty string (which we write as $\epsilon$), are regular expressions. Thus $A$, $\epsilon$, and $ABCAABCAAABB$ are valid regular expressions, each denoting a set containing only the specified string of zero or more letters.

2. If $p$ and $q$ are regular expressions, then $pq$ is a regular expression denoting the set of strings formed by concatenating a string from $p$ with a string from $q$.

3. If $p$ and $q$ are regular expressions, then $p|q$ is a regular expression denoting the set of strings that includes both the strings denoted by $p$ and the strings denoted by $q$. Thus $A|B$ is a regular expression defining a set containing the strings $A$ and $B$.

4. If $p$ is a regular expression, then $(p)$ is a regular expression denoting the same set of strings; we use parentheses to disambiguate—for example, to distinguish $(AB)|C$ from $A(B|C)$.

5. If $p$ is a regular expression, then $p^*$ is a regular expression denoting all strings that are concatenations of finitely many (zero or more) strings denoted by $p$. Thus $A^*$ denotes the set of strings containing the empty string as well as every string consisting of finitely many $A$s; $A(A|B)^*B$ denotes the set of all strings of $A$s and $B$s that begin with $A$ and end with $B$.

An interesting property of regular expressions is that each regular expression defines a set of strings that can be *recognized* by a finite-state machine. We assume that the input to the FSM is a sequence of symbols (in this case, encoded uppercase letters) and that each consecutive input symbol can cause a transition from the current FSM state to a new state. At any time when the sequence of input symbols corresponds to a string to be recognized, the FSM is in a distinguished state marked $R$; we may allow several states to be so marked. We mark the starting state with an $S$. The following FSM, for example, recognizes the strings $B(AB)^*$:

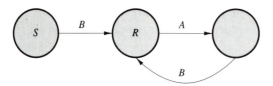

Note that we omit transitions corresponding to input strings that are not recognized (such as those containing the letter $C$). Our convention is that such strings cause implicit transitions to a BAD state, which causes the entire input sequence to be rejected.

Although every regular expression denotes a set of strings recognizable by an FSM, the systematic derivation of an FSM recognizer from a regular expression is not entirely trivial. A useful conceptual tool in dealing with regular expressions is the *nondeterministic FSM* (NFSM), whose state-transition diagram is *ambiguous* in the sense that it may indicate several possible transitions on a given input symbol.

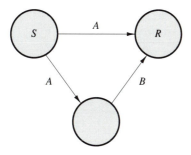

**Figure 6.10**   Nondeterministic FSM.

The simple NFSM in figure 6.10 recognizes the strings $A|(AB)$.

We can view the NFSM as being in several states simultaneously. We can emulate its behavior by hand, using tokens that we move about on the state-transition diagram to record active states. We begin with a token on the starting state. At each input symbol, we place tokens on each state at the arrow end of a transition from a marked state and remove the tokens that were there previously. Note that we need place at most one token in each state. Whenever one or more states marked $R$ contains a token, the input string is accepted (recognized) by the NFSM.

It is possible to construct a deterministic FSM that recognizes any regular expression, but the construction becomes cumbersome when an expression of the form $\alpha|\beta$ is encountered. In effect, the FSM under construction must entertain the two alternative forms $\alpha$ and $\beta$ as possible inputs until some input symbol rules one or both forms out; this may require a number of states, each corresponding to some combination of a tentative parse of form $\alpha$ or an alternative parse of form $\beta$. In contrast, the NFSM provides direct accommodation for alternative input forms by means of ambiguous transitions. The dual paths between the $S$ and $R$ states of figure 6.10, for example, correspond directly to the alternative input forms $A$ and $AB$.

As a further convenience in the construction of NFSMs from regular expressions, we allow the use of transitions on the *empty* input string; such transitions are taken spontaneously by the NFSM. In our token model, whenever there is an empty transition from a state marked by a token, we mark the target of the empty transition as well. Figure 6.11 shows how we might use empty transitions, designated by $\epsilon$, to convert our $A|(AB)$ NFSM, for example, to recognize $(A|(AB))^*$.

Nondeterministic FSMs are, in an important sense, no more powerful than deterministic FSMs: The same set of strings (the ones that can be described by regular expressions) can be recognized by each. NFSMs, however, provide a primitive model of parallelism because of their ability to model several discrete states simultaneously. While NFSMs and FSMs perform the same computations, a deterministic FSM may require exponentially many states compared to the equivalent NFSM.

The nondeterministic FSM, although not directly realizable in hardware, can be

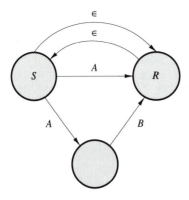

**Figure 6.11** NFSM that recognizes strings of form $(A|(AB))^*$.

an important tool in the synthesis of realizable deterministic FSMs that perform useful computations. The synthesis of an FSM to recognize strings described by the regular expression $(A|(AB))^*$, for example, might be approached by the straightforward synthesis of the NFSM of figure 6.11 followed by the derivation of an equivalent (but less intuitive) deterministic FSM using a computer-based algorithm. These ideas are explored further in the problems for this chapter.

## 6.6 Context

Finite-state machines are simulaneously a mathematical abstraction that has recieved considerable attention from theorists and a practical engineering tool of enormous consequence to the designer of digital systems. These roles are not independent; the formal study of FSMs has significantly enriched the repertoire of optimizations and techniques available to the engineer, while their practical significance stimulates continued attention by theorists.

FSMs are treated as a formalism in Hopcroft and Ullman [1979], along with other simple automata and their correspondence to formal languages. Wulf, Shaw, and Hilfinger [1981] offer a quite different perspective, emphasizing control and data structures, to the same topics. Hill and Peterson [1981] provide thorough coverage of FSMs as an engineering tool.

## 6.7 Problems

### Problem 6.1
Consider the combination of an $n$-state FSM with an $m$-state FSM. What can we deduce about the number of states of the new machine?

### Problem 6.2
Consider an FSM constructed from $m$ edge-triggered flip-flops and an arbitrary number of two-input NAND gates, having an arbitrary number of inputs and containing no combinational cycles. What is the maximum number of states that can be exhibited by this FSM?

### Problem 6.3
An $n$-state FSM is to have only a clock input and a single output $D$ whose value is 1 if and only if the number of active clock edges is a multiple of 5. The FSM is to be implemented using only a single $r$-bit register and a $2^k \times w$-bit ROM. What are the minimal ROM dimensions $k$ and $w$? How many states are required for this FSM?

### Problem 6.4
An $n$-state FSM is to have only a clock input and a single output $D$ whose value is 1 if and only if the number of active clock edges is either a multiple of 3 or a multiple of 2. How many states are required for this FSM?

### Problem 6.5   E Module:
We are interested in the behavior of the following FSM, called the *E module*:

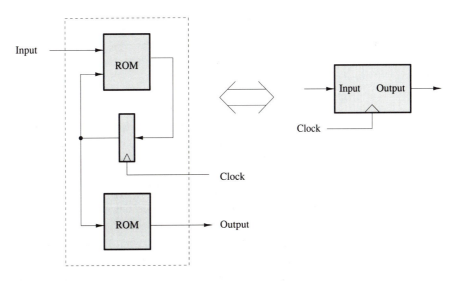

The propagation delay of each ROM is 100 ns, and the contamination delay is 0 ns. The register is defined by the following criteria:

$$t_\text{s} = 25 \text{ ns}, \quad t_\text{h} = 5 \text{ ns}, \quad t_{\text{c}C-Q} = 5 \text{ ns}, \quad t_{\text{p}C-Q} = 25 \text{ ns}.$$

The timing specifications for the input and output are characterized by three parameters: $t_{es}$ is the setup time of the element, $t_{eh}$ is the hold time of the element, and $t_{C-out}$ is the delay from the clock edge to a valid output. These parameters are illustrated below:

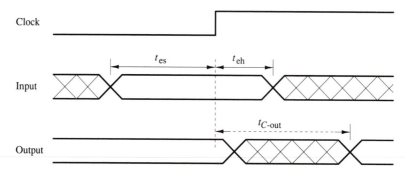

A. What is the minimum value that can be specified for $t_{es}$?

B. What is the minimum value that can be specified for $t_{eh}$?

C. What is the minimum value that can be specified for $t_{C-out}$?

D. What is the minimum allowable clock period for the E module that will ensure proper operation, assuming that the above timing specifications for the input are met?

E. Is it possible for the register in the E module to exhibit metastable behavior? Explain briefly, giving circumstances, if any, under which this might happen.

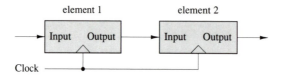

F. Suppose that two or more E modules are chained together as shown above. What is the minimum allowable clock period that will ensure proper operation of both E modules in this cascade configuration?

## Problem 6.6 FSM Design Philosophies:

The text has mentioned two basic designs for FSMs: the Mealy machine and the Moore machine. Figure 4.15 gives a general diagram for a Mealy machine, and figure 6.6 gives a general diagram for a Moore machine. Note that the key difference between the two designs is that in the Mealy machine the outputs are functions of both the current state and the input, whereas in the Moore machine the outputs are functions only of the current state.

We wish to investigate the advantages and disadvantages of the two designs. In order to simplify the design process, we shall make the (conservative) assumption that, in general, any output of a block of combinational logic can depend on any input and that there is one maximum propagation-delay parameter ($t_{pdc}$) for the entire block. That is, none of the outputs of the block can be said to be valid until $t_{pdc}$ after the last input to the block has settled. The timing characteristics of the registers that implement state memory are specified by a setup time $t_s$, a hold time $t_h$, and a propagation delay $t_{pC-Q}$. For this problem, we assume that $t_s$, $t_h$, and $t_{pC-Q}$ are all greater than zero.

A. Which design is likely to require fewer parts to produce?

B. Which design is more flexible, in terms of the values the outputs can take on? Explain.

Consider integration of an FSM into a larger system. It is often useful to treat such submodules as monolithic circuit components described by truth tables or state-transition tables plus timing requirements.

C. For each design, draw a timing diagram for the design, including inputs, outputs, current state, next state, and the system clock. Be sure to label all setup times, hold times, and propagation delays. Which of the two designs has the simpler timing specifications?

Now consider a larger system composed of some number of FSMs hooked up together.

D. In which of these designs can FSMs be hooked up in an arbitrary fashion without violating the dynamic discipline? What is the problem with the other design?

E. In which of these designs can an arbitrarily large number of FSMs be hooked up in series (as in problem 6.5F) without our having to worry about the clock period? What is the problem with the other design?

### Problem 6.7 *Manchester Encoding:*

*Manchester encoding* can be used to transmit a stream of bits over a single data wire, with no auxiliary clock information. Each bit is represented by one of the following patterns, where $T$ is the period of the clock used to encode the signal. Note that a Manchester-encoded signal always changes value in the middle of each bit cell.

A block diagram of a Manchester *decoder* is shown below. The decoder is a clocked sequential machine whose state memory consists of just two edge-triggered $D$ flip-flops.

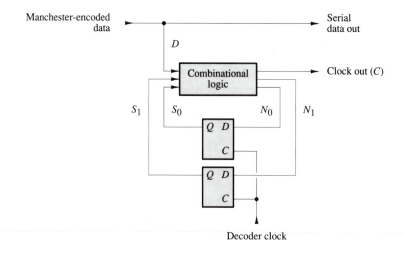

Manchester-encoded data

Serial data out

$D$

Combinational logic

Clock out ($C$)

$S_1$  $S_0$  $N_0$  $N_1$

$Q$ $D$

$C$

$Q$ $D$

$C$

Decoder clock

The combinational portion of the decoder has as inputs the Manchester-encoded signal and the current state of the two flip-flops. The combinational logic outputs the next state $N_1$ and $N_0$ for the two flip-flops and the clock signal $C$ generated for the stream of serial data. The truth table of the combinational logic is as follows:

| $S_1$ | $S_0$ | $D$ | $N_1$ | $N_0$ | $C$ |
|---|---|---|---|---|---|
| 0 | 0 | 0 | 0 | 1 | 1 |
| 0 | 0 | 1 | 0 | 1 | 1 |
| 0 | 1 | 0 | 1 | 0 | 0 |
| 0 | 1 | 1 | 1 | 1 | 0 |
| 1 | 0 | 0 | 1 | 0 | 0 |
| 1 | 0 | 1 | 0 | 0 | 0 |
| 1 | 1 | 0 | 0 | 0 | 0 |
| 1 | 1 | 1 | 1 | 1 | 0 |

Note that the serial data out from the decoder is just a copy of the Manchester-encoded data in. Thus the decoder must place positive transitions in its clock output $C$ timed to correspond to the correct logic values *already present* in the Manchester-encoded stream. The positive-going edge of each clock pulse must occur while the Manchester-encoded data has the proper value for the serial output; but there is no particular restriction that the clock output must return to zero before the Manchester-encoded input changes value, or that all output clock pulses be of the same duration or evenly spaced in time. The sample timing diagram below shows an original stream of serial input data and its clock, the result of Manchester-encoding that stream, and a clock output waveform that meets the conditions stated. (This is not intended to imply that the specific "clock out" signal shown would actually be generated by the above circuit.)

*Finite-State Machines*

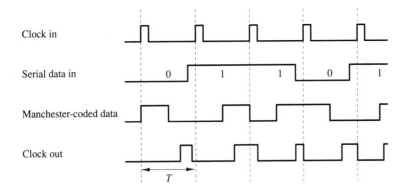

The period of the "decoder clock" that drives the $D$ flip-flops need not be $T$; in general, it will be faster.

A. When the decoder is properly "in synchronization" with the Manchester-encoded input data, it will be either in state 10 or in state 11 when the data make the transition in the middle of a bit cell. The decoder will enter state 00 (causing a positive transition on the clock output $C$) at the next decoder-clock pulse. Assuming that the decoder starts out in synchronization, what is the *longest* decoder-clock period for which the decoder is guaranteed to operate correctly? (State your answer as a fraction of $T$.)

B. What is the *shortest* decoder-clock period for which the decoder is guaranteed to operate correctly? (State your answer as a fraction of $T$.) Again, assume that the decoder starts out in synchronization.

C. Assume that the decoder-clock period is within the valid range you identified above. Give an input signal that will get the decoder in synchronization within a time $2T$, no matter what state the decoder is in initially. Don't worry about what pulses are output on the clock output $C$ during this synchronization process.

D. Describe a scenario that might result in your circuit's being driven into a metastable state.

## Problem 6.8

A divide-by-2 counter has the following specification:

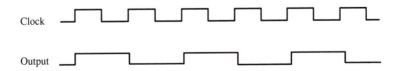

Design a divide-by-2 (that is, 1-bit) counter using only one $D$ flip-flop. You may also include any combinational logic you wish in your design, but try to minimize the additional logic used.

## Problem 6.9

An $N$-bit up/down counter is a sequential circuit with a clock input and an up/down control input. When control is 1, the circuit counts up, modulo $2^N$, on each rising edge of the clock. In other words, the present-state outputs of the circuit, interpreted as a positive binary integer, increase by 1 on each clock pulse; the next count after $2^N - 1$ goes back to 0. When the control signal is 0, the circuit decrements, or counts down, modulo $2^N$ on each rising edge of the clock.

A. Draw a state-transition diagram for a 2-bit up/down counter. You should have one state for each of the possible output integers. Label each arc with the value of the control input that causes that transition.

B. Think of the up/down counter of part A as a clocked sequential circuit of the form given in figure 4.15. Derive the truth table for the combinational logic, giving the next-state functions, $N_1$ and $N_0$, as functions of the present states, $S_1$ and $S_0$, and the control input.

C. Draw the Karnaugh maps and give Boolean equations for the next-state functions $N_1$ and $N_0$ derived in part B.


## Problem 6.10    State-Transition Diagram:

Consider the following state-transition diagram:

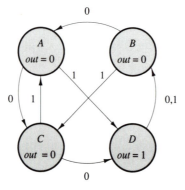

For each of the following questions, assume that the machine starts in state $A$.

A. Give the sequence of states visited, and the sequence of outputs produced, if a machine described by the above state-transition diagram is presented with the input string 00110.

B. What is the only string of inputs that will yield an output string composed entirely of 0s?

C. The state-transition diagram is implemented in a clocked sequential machine, shown below, consisting of a register of positive edge-triggered $D$ flip-flops and a "Q module," which is purely combinational logic. How many state variables are needed?

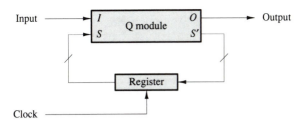

D. Give a truth table for the Q module such that the sequential machine sketched above implements the desired state-transition diagram. Make sure that the initial state $(A)$ corresponds to all state variables being zero.

E. Reproduce the diagram below and fill in the line for the output for the sequential machine using the Q module and $D$ flip-flops. You may neglect propagation delays in the logic, assuming them to be zero.

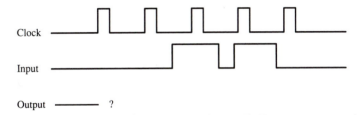

F. In the arrangement of Q modules shown below, what outputs will be produced at $X_1$–$X_5$ and $Y$?

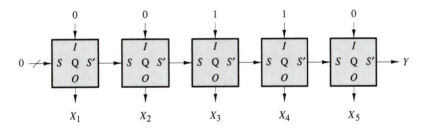

### Problem 6.11   Traffic Light:

This problem concerns a traffic light placed on a stretch of road where there is no cross traffic, but where pedestrians often cross. There are two sets of lights, one facing each direction of traffic, and two pedestrian buttons, one on each side of the road. Pushing either button while the light is green causes the light to turn yellow for 10 seconds, then red for 20 seconds, and back to green. Pushing buttons while the light is yellow or while the light has been red for 10 seconds or less has no effect. Pushing a button while the light has less than 10 seconds to go before it turns green will cause the light to stay red for at least 10 seconds more than it would otherwise. We want to design a sequential circuit for the traffic light controller.

A. Show a state-transition diagram and a state-transition table for the traffic light. Let the input be the state of the buttons (1 if either button has been pushed, 0 otherwise), and assume that a clock pulse occurs once every 10 seconds. (In other words, no state transition can occur except at 10-second intervals; every 10 seconds, the input is examined and a state transition, if called for, is made.)

B. How many $D$ flip-flops will you need to represent the states you have defined? Indicate the correspondence you have made between states in your answer to part A and the states of your set of $D$ flip-flops. Show truth tables and Boolean equations describing the next state of each flip-flop, based on the current state of the circuit and any other appropriate inputs.

C. Draw the circuit. Assume that two input lines are available: a clock line, which gives a short pulse once every 10 seconds, and a button line, which is high if a button is pushed. Your circuit should have three output lines controlling the lights; label the lines "red," "yellow," and "green."

D. It would be nice if the pedestrian did not have to lean on the button until a transition occurred. Your circuit currently has this property, unless you have departed from the clocked sequential-machine synthesis procedure suggested in the previous steps and described in the text. Give a modification of your circuit that solves this problem, and explain why it works.

## Problem 6.12   Data Transmission:

Data transmissions that leave the computer room are usually serial, that is, sent as a series of values on a single wire. One of the problems with serial transmission is the regrouping of bits into fixed-length characters. The problem is determining where the boundary between characters lies.

For example,

...0110001010011001101110...

can be divided as

...0110001   0100110   0110111   0...

or as

...01   1000101   0011001   101110...

and several other ways as well.

To help solve this problem we might send a special character several times in succession before transmitting data or control information. By examining the bit stream for occurrences of this character, we can determine where to begin counting off sets of bits as characters.

For our purposes, a character will be 7 bits long. The special synchronization character will be denoted SYN. SYN has the bit representation 0010110. Our transmission system sends the least significant bit first (right to left as we write character representations; you can think of the bit stream moving from left to right as it slides into the transmitter).

Searching for a SYN in a data stream requires knowledge of state since it requires remembering up to six of the past bits.

A. Draw a state-transition diagram for the SYN recognizer. One of the states should be labeled "Start" and another should be labeled "SYN found." A failure at some point in the recognition sequence should not always return to Start. Consider the bit stream 0010110110. Consider also 10010110010110, which should reach SYN found only once, since finding a SYN implies a character boundary, and hence the second character in this stream (which, remember, is to the *left* of the first) is really 1001011.

We now explore two ways of implementing the recognizer. In order to construct a recognizer, we must know when to sample the input. An additional input, Clock, is provided for this purpose. The rising edge of Clock will occur near the center of the time during which a single input value is valid.

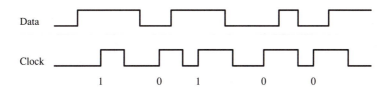

B. Figure 4.15 shows a clocked sequential circuit model we can use. One implementation strategy is to use a register of $D$ flip-flops for the state memory and a ROM for the combinational next-state and output determination. What is the minimum number of flip-flops needed in the state memory to represent all the states uniquely? How many inputs (excluding Clock) and outputs are there? Give the truth table for the ROM. Label the address inputs $I_0$ through $I_{j-1}$, the current states $CS_0$ through $CS_{n-1}$, the outputs $O_0$ through $O_{k-1}$, and the next states $NS_0$ through $NS_{n-1}$.

C. A serial-in, parallel-out shift register is shown in figure 5.14. Consider this shift register a sequential building block represented as

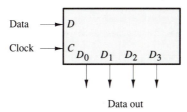

Two of these shift registers can be used to remember the last 8 data bits. Show how to use shift registers and gates or combinational building blocks to build the SYN recognizer.

D. Contrast the approaches of parts B and C. Give the advantages of each, particularly in terms of circuit complexity, package count, time to design, ease of modification, and performance.


### Problem 6.13   Divide-by-3 Circuits:

Digital Widgets Co. part number 3333 is a module that can be used to build a circuit that divides a positive binary integer by 3, as shown below:

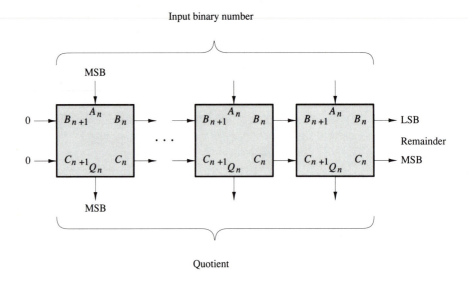

MSB and LSB are the most and least significant bits, respectively. Each box shown is a 3333. This circuit will compute the proper quotient and remainder from division of the input number by 3, if each 3333 module performs as follows:

- $Q_n$ is the 1-bit quotient that results from dividing the 3-bit binary number $(C_{n+1}B_{n+1}A_n)$ by 3.

- $(C_nB_n)$ is the 2-bit binary remainder of dividing $(C_{n+1}B_{n+1}A_n)$ by 3.

The input combination $C_{n+1} = B_{n+1} = 1$ will never occur (why?), so it does not matter what outputs the 3333 generates in this case. Convince yourself that the above interconnection of 3333s really performs the divide-by-3 function. (*Hint:* Consider how the answer would be computed by binary long division.)

A. Give Boolean equations for the 3333 module outputs $Q_n$, $C_n$, and $B_n$ in terms of the inputs $C_{n+1}$, $B_{n+1}$, and $A_n$.

B. A *serial* circuit that divides its input by 3 can be constructed using a *single* 3333 and a couple of edge-triggered $D$ flip-flops, as shown below:

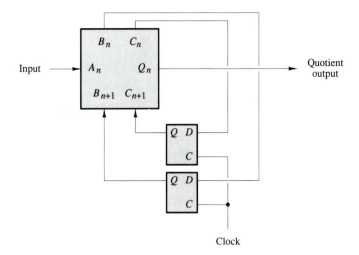

Draw a state-transition diagram for this circuit. (Do not include any details of clocking.) Be sure to indicate how the output bit is determined in each state.

C. To calculate the proper quotient and remainder, which bit of the input number should be fed into the serial circuit first: the most significant bit or the least significant? Why?

D. Where can the remainder be found when the serial circuit is used?

E. What states should the $D$ flip-flops initially be in so that a correct quotient and remainder will be calculated?

F. *Briefly* explain the relative advantages and disadvantages of the two divide-by-3 circuits we have shown here.

### Problem 6.14  FSM Synthesis:

Suppose we wish to measure the traffic at a point on a railroad track, counting the axle crossings in each direction. We set up a light beam just above the rails and place two photocells $A$ and $B$ some inches apart, as shown (looking from above):

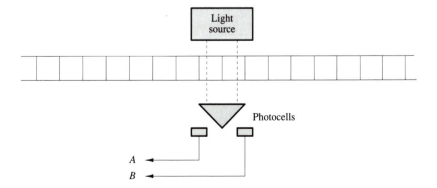

When the beam shines on a photocell, it produces a 0, and when the beam is interrupted, it produces a 1. Thus, when an axle crosses straight through from left to right, we read the following signals from $A$ and $B$:

$$00 \rightarrow 10 \rightarrow 11 \rightarrow 01 \rightarrow 00$$

(and the reverse for the opposite direction). Unfortunately, not all axles cross straight through, and an axle may turn back after going part way through. An axle may move back and forth within the scope of the beam.

We wish to construct a synchronous finite-state machine taking its two inputs from $A$ and $B$ and producing two outputs $X$ and $Y$ such that

- normally, both outputs are 0;
- when an axle has crossed completely from left to right, $X$ becomes 1 for exactly one clock period;
- when an axle has crossed completely from right to left, $Y$ becomes 1 for exactly one clock period.

(The pulses generated by $X$ and $Y$ could drive two counters, for example.) Assume that the only things that interrupt the light beams are axles, and that the clock is fast enough that we do not miss any transitions.

A. Draw a state-transition diagram for this FSM. Clearly label the inputs and outputs.

B. Construct the state-transition table for your FSM.

C. Show an implementation for this FSM using $D$ flip-flops and a ROM.

D. Suppose we need to notify the maintenance department periodically about wear and tear on the track, and further that $X$ and $Y$ drive another FSM with one output that goes from 0 to 1 after every 100,000 axle crossings (total, both directions). How many states must that FSM have? How many $D$ flip-flops would be needed to implement that FSM?

### Problem ⋆6.15

Ben Bitdiddle is exploring finite-state machines of the following form:

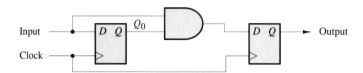

A. Draw a state-transition diagram for the FSM. Assume that you start in the state $Q_0 = 0, \text{Output} = 1$.

B. Assume that you start in the state $Q_0 = 0, \text{Output} = 0$. Does there exist an equivalent three-state finite-state machine?

C. Ben has also been experimenting with finite-state machines of the form shown below, where $F$ is an arbitrary two-input Boolean function. How many different (nonequivalent) finite-state machines can he generate this way?

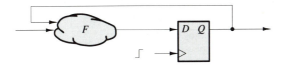

### Problem 6.16

Given an $n$-state FSM and an $m$-state FSM, what is the maximum number of states possible in a circuit built from the two FSMs connected as shown below?

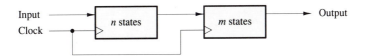

### Problem ★★6.17 Firing-Line Synchronization:

In this classic problem, you are to design a single finite-state machine S that will be connected in an arbitrarily long one-dimensional string as follows:

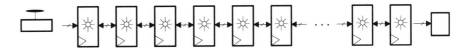

Each FSM in the string is connected by $k$ wires to its left and right neighbors; the wires can carry information in both directions between each pair. All FSMs share a common clock and make state transitions on active edges based on their current state and signals from their left and right neighbors. Connections to the left and right ends are such that the leftmost and rightmost FSMs can recognize their special positions.

Each FSM has a red light that is on only when the FSM is in a designated "fire" state; initially, the lights are all off. During some clock cycle, a *start* signal is applied to the inputs of the leftmost S module. The required behavior of the system is that the lights are all to remain off until some subsequent clock cycle, when all lights go on simultaneously and remain on. Note that the delay between the *start* signal and the "firing" of the FSMs can be arbitrarily long; it may, for example, depend on the number of modules in the string. However, all modules must be identical; their design (and the number of states) is independent of the length of the string.

This is a challenging problem. Unless you are unusually ambitious, you should stop short of a detailed design, which is tedious; just develop a convincing argument that your approach will work.

### Problem ★★6.18 Firing-Mob Synchronization:

Here is a similarly challenging variant of the firing-line synchronization problem. Consider an arbitrary network of identical M machines, each an FSM with three

$k$-wire bidirectional ports. Every port of an M module must connect to another port of an M module, although two ports of a single module may also be connected. A sample "firing mob" is diagrammed below:

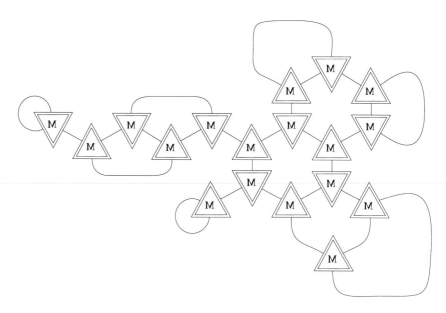

All modules make transitions synchronously with a shared clock. On some clock edge, exactly one module is forced into a *trigger* state by means of an external input (say, by pressing a button); on some subsequent clock edge, all modules are simultaneously to enter a *fire* state. (*Hint:* Solve the firing-squad synchronization problem before tackling this one.)

### Problem ★6.19
Draw a state-transition diagram for an FSM that recognizes strings denoted by the regular expression $A^*BB^*C$.

### Problem ★6.20
Draw the state-transition diagram for a *deterministic* FSM that recognizes the strings $A|(AB)$. Take care not to accept any other strings, such as $ABB$.

### Problem ★6.21
Draw the state-transition diagram for a nondeterministic FSM that recognizes the strings $A((ABC)|(ACB))^*A$.

### Problem ★6.22
Describe (in English) a general procedure for deriving an NFSM recognizer from a regular expression. Your procedure description will doubtless be recursive and should be based on the regular-expression syntax given in section 6.5.

### Problem ★★6.23
Because NFSMs do not correspond directly to any realizable hardware implementation, their generation from regular expressions does not completely solve the

problem of systematic construction of regular-expression recognizers. To bridge the gap between an NFSM and a real implementation, we explore the problem of deriving an equivalent (deterministic) FSM from a specified NFSM.

A. Draw the state-transition diagram for a *deterministic* FSM that is equivalent to the NFSM you constructed in problem 6.21, which recognizes the strings $A((ABC)|(ACB))^*A$.

B. Is the amount of state information associated with an NFSM at any moment always finite? If so, can you place a bound on the state information required for operation of an $n$-state NFSM? What does your answer imply about the number of states required by an equivalent deterministic FSM? (*Hint:* Consider the token-based model of NFSM operation in section 6.5.)

C. Describe a general procedure for the systematic derivation of a deterministic FSM from a given nondeterministic one. Explain the relationship between states of the deterministic FSM and states of the NFSM from which it is derived.

# 7    Control Structures
   and Disciplines

In this chapter, we begin to explore the construction of digital systems with complex behavior. Such systems frequently need closer control over the sequencing of operations and the flow of data than is available in a simple combinational implementation. An attractive design approach is to separate a system into *data paths*, where calculations are performed and data are stored, and *control circuitry*, which regulates the timing of operations in the data paths. The control circuitry must be designed to cope with propagation delays and other constraints imposed by the data paths. After initially exploring the problems and opportunities presented by various control strategies, and developing some relevant techniques and terminology, we examine by means of a case study several ways in which performance can be traded off against cost by using different data path and control organizations. A key idea throughout the chapter is that whenever a number of potentially concurrent operations of the same type must be performed, there is a spectrum of possible implementations ranging from serial reuse of a single module (the low-cost option) to concurrent use of many modules (the high-performance option).

The dynamic discipline requires that we establish some method of tracking when each signal in a system is valid, to avoid metastable behavior and the propagation of invalid signals. In effect, these low-level validity concerns force us to adopt an engineering discipline that allows us to deal with times in discrete rather than continuous terms. We view each wire in a circuit as carrying a sequence of valid logic values, punctuated by transient periods of invalidity; the first requirement of our control circuitry is thus to avoid sampling data (as in clocking into a register) at inauspicious times. We facilitate this by adhering to one of several alternative *timing disciplines*.

A timing discipline allows us to deal with sequences of operations in discrete time, avoiding analog problems associated with low-level synchronization issues. However, it does not necessarily dictate the order in which operations of a sequence are to be performed, or the extent to which operations can overlap in time rather than being performed sequentially. In general, we view these latter specifications as the *control structure* of our design and separate them from the lower-level timing issues addressed by the chosen timing discipline. The control structure can take a variety of forms, depending on the timing discipline chosen. It can be quite rigid, in effect wiring control decisions into the hardware; or it can be highly dynamic, making decisions regarding the sequencing of events during the actual operation of the circuit. It can be expressed as a *microprogram* detailing an operation sequence, or it can be simply a loose set of ordering constraints sufficient to guarantee proper operation of the system.

## 7.1 Timing Disciplines

Typically the number of timing constraints that must be obeyed by a sequential circuit grows faster than linearly with the size of the circuit, making the ad hoc approach unwieldy. A number of engineering disciplines have been proposed to control this complexity, and many of them work satisfactorily; the choice among them reflects the style and experience of the engineer as well as such considerations as the trade-off between engineering costs and system performance. Timing disciplines distinguish themselves along two major dimensions:

- *synchronous* vs. *asynchronous* disciplines, reflecting the extent to which state changes are constrained to a common (systemwide) clock signal; and
- *local* vs. *global* specification of timing constraints, reflecting the extent to which each subsystem dictates the timing of operations.

In general, *synchronous* systems establish a systemwide discrete view of time, based on intervals corresponding to the period of a global clock signal. The result is that "interesting" computational events, such as the loading of values into registers, happen only on active edges of the common clock signal. Each operation performed by a system component begins at some clock edge and finishes at some subsequent edge of the same clock, taking an integral number of clock periods for the computation performed. *Asynchronous* systems, in contrast, allow operations to begin and end at times that are continuously variable within some constraints, usually dictated by control signals specific to each operation. Since the time required by each operation is not constrained to be a multiple of a common clock period, asynchronous systems can often be tuned to higher performance than can synchronous ones (at some cost in complexity of engineering, circuitry, or both).

*Globally timed* systems fix the timing of each operation (for example, when it starts and finishes) in a static, systemwide scheme. The time taken by each operation is viewed as a constant (presumably reflected in the specifications for the component or subsystem that performs the operation) and designed into the system timing. Typically the control and timing circuitry of a globally timed system is localized and constitutes an identifiable subsystem. *Locally timed* (or *self-timed*) systems, in contrast, allow each module to control the time it spends on individual operations by means of additional control signals. A multiplier module, for example, might have a control *input* that dictates when to start an operation and a control *output* by which it announces the completion of an operation. The multiplier might require 100 ns in the general case, but only 10 ns if one of its input data is zero. A locally timed system would exploit the faster operation by using the output control signal to begin subsequent operations early when possible, resulting in improved system performance, while a globally timed system would ignore the output control signal and conservatively assume the multiplication time to be a constant 100 ns. Typically, locally timed systems *distribute* control circuitry among the modules performing actual data operations, rather than separating it as a control and timing subsystem.

These two distinctions give rise to four general classes of timing disciplines:

- *Synchronous globally timed* (SGT) *systems*, whose timing signals are digitally derived from a single common clock and whose operations follow a rigid pattern. SGT systems are easily constructed from combinational logic and registers; indeed, the finite-state machines in chapter 6 exemplify this approach. The primitive simplicity of the SGT discipline, in both engineering and implementation terms, accounts for its widespread use.

- *Asynchronous globally timed* (AGT) *systems*, whose timing signals are generated by analog means (such as delay lines or monostable multivibrators) in an ad hoc way. This approach seriously compromises the advantages of the digital abstraction and is generally considered a poor engineering choice.

- *Synchronous locally timed* (SLT) *systems*, whose components have dedicated control signals synchronized to a common clock. SLT systems have the flexibility to exploit variable timing of operations, but constrain each operation to take an integral number of clock periods. SLT modules and systems can be synthesized using digital engineering techniques and primitive logic elements (combinational logic and registers); SLT modules can also be easily combined to make new SLT modules.

- *Asynchronous locally timed* (ALT) *systems*, whose components have dedicated asynchronous control signals. At the system level, this approach offers complete timing flexibility: An ALT module can be started at any time and can announce its completion at any subsequent time. While ALT modules can be readily combined to form new ALT modules, the generation of ALT modules from primitive logic requires some additional engineering to deal with the continuously variable timing of control signals without violating the dynamic discipline.

This chapter develops the engineering principles underlying these timing disciplines. Section 7.2 elaborates the notion of *synchrony*, identifying basic clocking strategies used in well-behaved control structures. Section 7.3 provides terminology and notation for dealing abstractly with the relationships that must be imposed by a control structure—that is, for dealing with such relationships independently of the clocking strategy to be used. Sections 7.4–7.6 use the principles of sections 7.2 and 7.3 to build SGT, SLT, and ALT control structures.

## 7.2 Degrees of Synchrony

Taken literally, "synchronous" systems constrain computational events to happen at the same time, whereas "asynchronous" systems do not. In practice, the terms are often used to distinguish events that have some known timing relationship from those that have none; the output of a register, for example, is viewed as changing synchronously with respect to the register's clock input despite the clock-to-$Q$ delay it incurs. Specifically, we use the term *synchronous* in this text to distinguish systems whose clock signals are all digitally derived from a common time base: A synchronous system is one in which all events have a fixed, integral timing relationship modulo (bounded) propagation delays. In practice, synchronous systems often use a high-frequency signal source as a clock to drive counters and other FSMs to yield several lower-frequency clock signals for use in timing events. Although such a system has several clock signals, their fixed integral relationship ensures that all events are timed synchronously with the higher-frequency generating clock (modulo bounded propagation delays), and hence that the system is viewed as synchronous. Indeed, we can find a variety of clocking disciplines that fall within this "synchronous" classification, including some quite intricate ones. Any of these can serve as the basis for SGT or SLT control structures.

There is a similar spectrum of "asynchronous" clocking strategies, all sharing the characteristic that events have continuously variable timing relationships. It is important to distinguish asynchronous clocking schemes that can lead to the synchronization failures discussed in chapter 4 from those that avoid such failures, since only the latter are appropriate as the basis of reliable ALT control structures.

The types of timing relationships that can be imposed on a digital system thus vary from Spartan adherence to simultaneity (modulo propagation delays) to anarchic freedom from constraint. We sketch in the following subsections three important points along this spectrum; the first, and most disciplined, is the basis for our SGT and SLT examples in this and following chapters.

### 7.2.1 Single-Clock Synchronous Systems

At the extreme of the synchronous timing disciplines is an organizational approach that should be in every engineer's repertoire.

. . . . . . . . . . . . . . . . . . . . . . . . . . . . . . . . . . . . . . . . . . . . . . . . . . . . . . . . . . . .

*The single-clock synchronous system*    A sequential system organized around the single-clock synchronous discipline obeys the following rules:

- The entire system is composed of combinational devices and clocked registers.
- The circuit is free from combinational cycles; that is, every cyclic path contains at least one register.
- A single periodic *clock* signal, of period $t_{cl}$, is routed to the clock input of *every* register in the system.
- The cumulative propagation delay along any combinational path between two registers must be less than the clock period.

. . . . . . . . . . . . . . . . . . . . . . . . . . . . . . . . . . . . . . . . . . . . . . . . . . . . . . . . . . . .

Readers should convince themselves that this single-clock discipline ensures that register inputs are stable near active clock edges, and hence that the dynamic discipline is met.

The single-clock discipline outlaws such shady practices as gating clock signals and using delay lines to adjust the timing of clock edges and accommodate local requirements. In the extreme form given above, it imposes strong constraints on the engineer. Yet it has much to recommend it because of the engineering simplicity it affords. Note that synchronous FSMs such as those developed in chapter 6 easily accommodate the single-clock discipline: They can be fashioned using a ROM (or combinational gates) wired to a single register wide enough to hold state variables and inputs.

On first glance, the single-clock discipline would seem to specify the control circuitry entirely: The only control signal is a single, periodic clock that goes to every clock input. However, the single-clock discipline allows the combinational generation of nonclock signals whose levels, at each active clock edge, control the routing of data about the system. Examples include load-enable inputs to registers, which enable/disable a load operation at the next active clock edge; multiplexer *select* inputs; and three-state *output enables*. Although we can (and will) view these signals as control rather than data, they must conform to the same timing constraints as other nonclock signals in our single-clock system. A common engineering approach, illustrated in subsequent sections (and repeatedly in following chapters) is to generate such select and enable signals using a simple, stylized FSM clocked by the (single) system clock.

### 7.2.2 Multiple-Clock Systems

Complete abandonment of low-level synchrony constraints between modules of a system leads to multiple asynchronous clocks, each a free-running oscillator generating local clock edges independently of the others. This relationship is common among large, independently designed subsystems; as an extreme example, the interconnection of two separate computers (each of which may run synchronously with its single clock) constitutes a system with at least two unsynchronized clocks. Multiple independent clocks often appear within modules of a single system; the central processor and memory subsystems of a computer may, for example, be based on different clock signals.

The use of independently chosen clock frequencies for various subsystems has the obvious engineering advantage that it separates the choice of timing parameters of one module from that of another, thereby isolating engineering subproblems from one another. Unfortunately, it leads to a situation in which computational events of different subsystems have absolutely no known timing relationship: the $i$th clock edge $CA_i$ of system $A$ might occur before or after the $j$th edge $CB_j$ of the clock used by system $B$. Synchronization problems, that is, the inevitable possibility of the metastable behavior described in chapter 4, complicate communication between such independently clocked modules.

Consider, for example, communication to module $B$ of a value developed by module $A$ on its $i$th clock edge. Since the value changes synchronously with respect to $A$'s clock, its change is necessarily asynchronous with respect to $B$'s; if it is simply routed to the data input of a register clocked by $CB$, the result is a string of arbitration problems. For each edge $CB_j$ of $B$'s clock, the new value is to be loaded if $CA_i$ precedes $CB_j$. If the $CA$ and $CB$ edges happen at inauspicious times, the register setup and hold times will not be obeyed, and metastable register output may contaminate $B$'s data paths.

The usual solution to this problem allows sufficient delay for metastable effects to settle, thus burdening the time costs of communication between independently clocked modules with a substantial overhead. Typically, the delay is effected by routing the (possibly metastable) output of $B$'s register through a series of one or more additional registers also clocked by $CB$, decreasing the probability of metastable behavior by a large factor at each stage. While this approach can reduce the probability of synchronization failure to within any specified limit (for example, below the probability of spontaneous failure of the register), its cost is a clock period delay for each stage.

Some of this time penalty can, in theory, be recovered by means of sophisticated timing circuitry. Where $CA$ and $CB$ are independent but periodic, the timing relationship between their edges is predictable arbitrarily far into the future from accurate frequency and phase information. This predictability can be used, to varying extents, to anticipate close arbitration contests and decide them in advance. As a simple example, consider clocks $CA$ and $CB$ with periods of 2 and 3, respectively. If the $i$th edge of $CA$ is nearly coincident with a $CB$ edge, it follows that the $(i + 1)$st edge of $CB$ will fall about midway between two $CA$ edges, while the $(i + 2)$nd $CB$ edge will again be dangerously close to $CA$. Sophisticated intermodule communication circuitry might exploit this information, circumventing synchronization delays on edges known to be safely timed with respect to incoming data transitions. Of course, the decision as to whether a pair of edges will be "dangerously close" is itself an arbitration problem; but the periodicity of the clock signals (and hence the predictability of their timing relationship) allows that decision to be made sufficiently far in advance of the edges themselves that metastable behavior in the decision circuitry has ample time to settle out. Even if the decision to transmit data between the asynchronous modules is made shortly before the edges in question, this *anticipatory arbitration* strategy will have already chosen whether to pass the data on the $i$th or $(i + 1)$st clock edge.

### 7.2.3 Controlled Asynchrony

There is a spectrum of engineering possibilities between the simple rigidity of synchronous systems and the failure-prone proliferation of independent, free-running clocks. The design of reliable asynchronous locally timed systems, in particular, involves the use of modules that *begin* their computation synchronously with an externally supplied start signal; in order to avoid arbitration problems, no local clock can be running at the time start is expected. However, an active edge on start may enable a local oscillator that generates local clock events thereafter; the period of the local clock is independent of external system timing as long as it can be started synchronously with the start input. On completion of the module's computation, a finish output signal may be asserted synchronously with the local clock, so that the latter is stopped pending a start edge for a new computation.

Synchronization failure can be avoided in such a system as long as each module is prepared to accept an asynchronous start and the circuitry surrounding each module

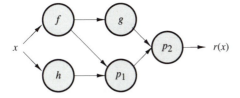

**Figure 7.1** Combinational implementation of $r(x) = p(g(f(x)), p(f(x), h(x)))$.

is prepared to accept an asynchronous finish. The key to avoiding arbitration contests is that no module should have an independent clock running during periods when it is sensitive to asynchronous inputs. In the scenario described above, only a single clock is running at any time. While a module is idle, it awaits an asynchronous start signal with no local clock running. When it is invoked, it assumes responsibility for generating clock signals while its invoker suspends its clock, awaiting the (asynchronous) finish signal.

One is tempted to conclude, from this sketch, that this approach uses a single clock whose period changes depending on which module is active; the responsibility for clock generation is passed between modules as the computation progresses. In fact, controlled asynchrony extends to the application of multiple simultaneous clocks as long as arbitration ("which came first") contests are carefully avoided. It is possible to invoke a number of asynchronous, locally timed modules simultaneously and wait for all to complete before proceeding; no arbitration is needed. Recall from chapter 4 that AND and OR operations can be performed on asynchronous monotonic signals (such as the start and finish signals described above) to generate new, well-behaved asynchronous monotonic signals; in particular, given a set of asynchronous control signals, each conveying the timing of some event, it is possible to derive a clean signal that follows the *latest* event. Where the operations performed by two or more modules are to proceed simultaneously, they can be supplied with identical start signals and the system clock can be suspended pending the conjunction of their finish signals. It is possible for each of the modules to start a local clock for its own internal timing uses, including the generation of its finish signal.

## 7.3 Constraints on Control Structure

Suppose we want to compute the value

$$r(x) = p(g(f(x)), p(f(x), h(x))),$$

using as circuit components modules that compute the separate functions $p$, $g$, $f$, and $h$. If the modules are combinational, we can combine them in a straightforward way to compute $r(x)$, as shown in figure 7.1.

Note that the subexpression $f(x)$ occurs twice in the definition of $r(x)$, but it needs to be computed only once. The two different applications of the $p$ function require separate $p$ modules in the combinational implementation, however, since they take different inputs. If we view the subcomputation performed by each module as an *operation*, we require a single $f$ operation but two $p$ operations. We distinguish the $p$ operations, as well as the combinational modules that perform them, by subscripts; thus

$$r(x) \; = \; p_2(g(f(x)), p_1(f(x), h(x))).$$

The combinational implementation has the engineering advantage that it requires no control structure. But it requires that (1) the component modules themselves be combinational, (2) a separate module be dedicated to each operation, and (3) successive $r(x)$ computations not overlap in time. In order to circumvent these restrictions (as well as to implement systems whose behavioral specifications explicitly require memory), we consider alternatives involving sequential implementation.

### 7.3.1 Data Paths and Operations

The functionality of a combinational circuit is completely dictated by the design of its data paths. Most sequential system designs, in contrast, involve data paths that are capable of performing a variety of different computations, depending on the sequence of control signals supplied to them. Extreme examples include the *universal* data paths of the general-purpose processors we shall explore in subsequent chapters, which are designed to provide for a wide range of functionality through programmability.

Even reasonably application-specific data paths leave some flexibility to the control-structure design. Consider the data paths of figure 7.2, a plausible vehicle for the sequential implementation of $r(x)$. Note that this design employs a single *three-state bus*, which at a given time can be driven by any one of the operator modules and whose data can be loaded into one of two registers. Assuming that the component operator modules ($f$, $g$, $h$, and $p$) are combinational, the control-signal inputs to this circuit consist of the register load enables and the three-state drive enables, in addition to the register clock signals. (Three-state drivers were discussed in conjunction with figure 1.12.) The use of sequential operator modules would typically involve additional control signals, such as the signals that cause each module to begin its subcomputation.

Unlike the combinational implementation, the data paths of figure 7.2 require only a single $p$ module, which must be reused for the two $p$ operations involved in the computation of $r(x)$.

At different times during the course of a computation, data will be transferred between the output of some module and either or both of the $A$ and $B$ registers by asserting the appropriate drive-enable and load-enable signals. For example, the subcomputation $f(x)$ can be implemented by a sequence of events that (1) load $x$ into the $A$ register, (2) begin operation of the $f$ module and awaits its completion, and (3) load the output of the $f$ module into, say, the $B$ register. Steps 1 and 3 are effected by asserting load- and drive-enable signals; for a combinational $f$ module, step 2 is satisfied simply by allowing sufficient time to elapse between

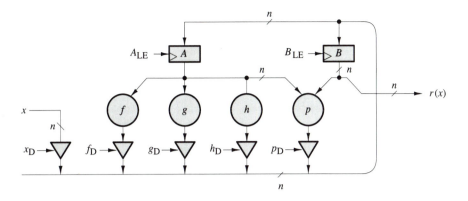

**Figure 7.2** Data paths for $r(x)$ computation.

steps 1 and 3. The entire computation of $r(x)$ can be resolved into a sequence of similar low-level computational events.

### 7.3.2 Precedence Relations

Although a variety of different sequences of control signals can be employed to compute $r(x)$ using the data paths of figure 7.2, there are some strong constraints on the order in which events may take place. For example, the operation $g$ in our $r(x)$ computation cannot start prior to completion of the operation $f$, since $g$ requires as input the output from $f$. In order to express such constraints concisely, we give the names $f^S$ and $f^F$ to the *events*, or points in time, that correspond to the start and finish of an operation $f$. Using this notation, we write the constraint that $g$ cannot start until $f$ has finished as $f^F \preceq g^S$. This *precedence relation* is read "$f^F$ precedes $g^S$" and may be viewed as a simple numerical inequality between the instants in time at which the operation $f$ finishes and $g$ starts. In particular, $\alpha \preceq \beta$ dictates that the event $\alpha$ must occur *no later than* the event $\beta$; thus $\alpha \preceq \beta$ can be satisfied by making $\alpha$ and $\beta$ simultaneous. Hence $\preceq$ is *reflexive*, meaning that $\alpha \preceq \alpha$ for every event $\alpha$, and *transitive*, meaning that $\alpha \preceq \beta$ and $\beta \preceq \gamma$ imply $\alpha \preceq \gamma$.

Although the precedence relation orders *instants*, it extends naturally to ordering entire *operations*, each of which corresponds to an *interval* during which that operation takes place. We abbreviate the statement $f^F \preceq g^S$ to $f \preceq g$, meaning that the entire $f$ operation must precede the entire $g$ operation. Note that, in general, $f \preceq g$ (where $f$ and $g$ are operations) implies that $f$ and $g$ cannot proceed concurrently; at most, the last event $f^F$ of $f$ might be simultaneous with the first event $g^S$ of $g$. Thus $f \preceq f$ is not true in general for any *operation* $f$, despite the reflexivity of $\preceq$ when restricted to events.

Precedence relations can be used as a simple descriptive tool. For example, we might analyze the operation of a system and observe that some event $\alpha$ (for example, the loading of a register or the start of an operation) is always earlier

**Table 7.3** Data dependencies for $r(x)$.

| | | |
|---|---|---|
| $r^S \preceq f$ | $f \preceq g$ | $g \preceq p_2$ |
| $r^S \preceq h$ | $f \preceq p_1$ | $p_1 \preceq p_2$ |
| $p_2 \preceq r^F$ | $h \preceq p_1$ | |

than another event $\beta$, so that $\alpha \preceq \beta$. More commonly, we shall use such relations as a prescriptive device to reflect constraints that must be accommodated by the timing of control signals in order to ensure proper operation. An example is the situation described earlier in which the $f$ operation must precede the $g$ operation; in this case, we refer to $f \preceq g$ as a *precedence constraint* on our system.

Broadly speaking, there are three sources of constraints on control structure. *Data dependencies* reflect the essential structure of the computation and the flow of information among its operations. *Device specifications* reflect the physical constraints imposed by the component timing restrictions. These two classes are *essential precedence constraints* in that they are unavoidable consequences of implementing the given algorithm using the specified repertoire of components. The third class consists of constraints imposed by the choice of data-path topology; these are *nonessential* in the sense that such constraints reflect the architectural choices made for a particular design.

### 7.3.3 Data Dependencies

Data dependencies are perhaps the most fundamental category of control-structure constraint, since they are inherent in the algorithm being used. A *data-dependency constraint* $r \preceq s$ exists between operations $r$ and $s$ whenever some value produced by $r$ is required as an input to $s$.

For the computation of

$$r(x) = p_2(g(f(x)), p_1(f(x), h(x))),$$

we enumerate the data dependencies between operations as table 7.3. The constraints involving $r^S$ simply express the requirement that neither $f$ nor $h$ can begin until the start of the $r$ operation itself, at which time the input $x$ is presumed to be available. Each of the constraints whose left-hand operation is $f$ reflects an operation that requires $f$'s output and hence must follow it; similarly for the remaining constraints. The constraint $p_2 \preceq r^F$ dictates that the $r$ operation cannot be considered to have finished until the $p_2$ operation, which produces the output $r(x)$, has completed.

### 7.3.4 Precedence Graphs

The precedence relation defined on a set $S$ of operations constitutes a *partial ordering* since it orders (in the sense of $f \preceq g$) some but not necessarily all of the elements of $S$. There may, for example, be pairs of *unordered* operations $h$ and $g$,

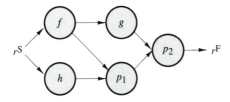

**Figure 7.4**  Precedence graph.

where neither of the constraints $h \preceq g$ nor $g \preceq h$ applies. We may view such unordered operations as a degree of freedom in the design of control circuitry; we may choose to have $h$ execute before $g$, $g$ execute before $h$, or $h$ and $g$ execute simultaneously.

It is often convenient to represent a partial ordering of a set $S$ by a directed graph containing a node for each member of $S$ and an arrow going from the node representing $x$ to the node representing $y$ for each pair of members $x$ and $y$ such that $x \preceq y$.

Figure 7.4 shows the graph of the set of precedence constraints enumerated in table 7.3. Note that we omit constraints such as $f \preceq p_2$ that are deducible from the given ones by the transitivity of $\preceq$.

A precedence graph provides a useful means for visualizing the potential concurrency allowed by a set of precedence constraints. Glancing at figure 7.4, we note that although $f$ must precede both $g$ and $p_1$, the latter two operations are unordered and consequently may take place concurrently. Similarly, $f$ is unordered with respect to $h$, suggesting additional potential parallelism to be exploited.

### 7.3.5  Data-Dependency Graphs

A *data-dependency graph* is a precedence graph depicting only the constraints due to data dependencies, as in figure 7.4. We may deduce such data-dependency constraints systematically from the algorithm and data-path diagram. Informally, we simply walk through the algorithm identifying operations in some sensible execution sequence and giving them unique names (perhaps using subscripts). For each operation $t$ encountered, we trace the source of its inputs; whenever an input to $t$ is traced back to the output of some operator $s$, we assert a precedence constraint $s \preceq t$ between the relevant instance of $s$ (which we must already have encountered and given a unique name) and $t$. Dependencies on inputs to the data-path diagram itself are recorded as dependencies on $r^S$, the "start" event at which the data-path inputs are presumed valid. Finally, for each operation $t$ whose output is an output from the data-path diagram, the constraint $t \preceq r^F$ (where $r^F$ is the "finish" event) is added, ensuring that the output will be valid when the operation is considered finished.

Using this data-dependency graph together with suitable information about the timing behavior of the operators and the topology of the circuit, we can pick an operation order for the computation of $r(x)$. We can view this process as adding further precedence constraints to the essential constraints given in the data-dependency graph.

### 7.3.6 Device Specifications

We now return to the discussion of essential precedence constraints, having identified data dependencies as one important class. A second class of essential precedence constraints reflects the timing properties of individual components ("operators") such as adders, registers, gates, and counters. In general, we can assert for each operation $f$ the constraint that $f^S \preceq f^F$, which simply specifies that the operation cannot finish until it has begun. Moreover, an operator that performs a sequence of operations $f_1$, $f_2$, ... will typically impose the constraint that at most one of its operations must be in progress at any time; hence, for all $i$, $f_i^F \preceq f_{i+1}^S$. *Pipelined* operators, discussed in chapter 8, are an exception to this rule.

We need additional information about the timing of each operator $r$ in order to guarantee that its output is available in time for subsequent uses. In particular, we need some handle on $r^F$ if we are to make any use of its result. There are three common ways to supply this information:

- The component specifications for a module $f$ can specify an upper bound $t_f$ on the amount of time taken by an execution of $f$. Such a bound justifies an assertion that $f^F \preceq f^S + t_f$. This approach, which is taken almost exclusively when dealing with combinational and other low-level components, is consistent with globally timed (combinational and SGT) timing disciplines.

- The specification for a *clocked* component can specify the required computation time in terms of clock periods rather than actual time units. This approach, which can be viewed as a discrete-time version of the previous specification, is characteristic of components of SGT systems that are themselves constructed using an SGT discipline.

- The component can supply a control *output* that specifies—for example, by a positive transition—when its computation is completed and valid output data are available. Thus the timing details of each component are determined dynamically and by circuitry local to the component, rather than being incorporated into a global control structure as absolute constants. This is the approach taken by components in the locally timed (SLT and ALT) disciplines.

The locally timed disciplines offer important structural and performance advantages in many applications. First, they delay fixing timing details until actual execution, allowing actual timing to be data-dependent. A multiplier component might, for example, recognize when one of its operands is zero and yield a result much faster than in the general case. A fixed time-bound scheme would have to allow the *worst-case* time for *all* multiplications, while a self-timed control structure might use the multiplier's "done" signal to get a substantial head start on the next step in the computation. Second, the self-timed structure allows local design changes to be made without reconsideration of global timing relationships. A faster (or slower) multiplier can be substituted in a self-timed circuit, for example, resulting in improved (or degraded) performance but without endangering any external assumptions about the timing behavior of the multiplier.

Often the specifications of a sequential component will require that data be valid for some period of time (the setup time) before the component receives its start signal, or that input data remain valid for some time (the hold time) afterward. Even when a component's setup and hold times are specified to be zero, input data must be valid in the neighborhood of the start signal to provide some margin for settling of signals and minor timing discrepancies; in practice, a nonzero valid interval must be provided for input sampling. Although these times must be accounted for in the detailed design of a system, they are often so small compared with operation times that their effect on performance parameters is negligible; under such circumstances, it is convenient to ignore their effect in analyses intended to support architectural decisions. We thus assume in our examples that setup and hold time requirements are zero.

### 7.3.7 Data-Path Topology

A third source of constraints on control structures arises not from the inherent data dependencies of the computation nor from the timing properties of individual components, but from the number and kind of components and the way in which they are interconnected. Often these topological constraints are difficult to express formally and fully in our language of precedence relations, and nontrivial deduction may be needed to derive them.

Consider, for example, the data paths shown in figure 7.2. Since this circuit has a single (combinational) $p$ module, it clearly imposes the constraint that only a single $p$ subcomputation can be in progress at any time; that is, $p_1$ and $p_2$ cannot proceed concurrently. In our particular example, this is not a serious drawback since data dependencies require that $p_1 \preceq p_2$. Slightly more subtle is the requirement that at most one value can be driven onto the three-state bus at any time; the results produced by the $f$ and $h$ modules, for example, must be loaded into registers at different times. Again, this may not be a serious practical drawback if the time duration of each transfer (the clock period in an SGT implementation) is short. The most serious constraints imposed by the design of figure 7.2 stem from its Spartan economy of registers: For example, the $A$ register is shared as an input register by all of the operator modules, disallowing concurrent operation by these modules on different input values.

As these examples suggest, the principal cause of constraints arising from the data-path topology is conflict over resources. The most common forms of conflict involve:

- *functional units* that are reused for several computations,
- *registers* that are used to store intermediate results, and
- *buses* through which values are communicated from one part of the data paths to another.

Not all control-structure constraints are precedence relations. For example, as discussed above, the computations $p_1$ and $p_2$ cannot proceed concurrently, since there is only one $p$ module. However, either ordering ($p_1 \preceq p_2$ or $p_2 \preceq p_1$) could be accommodated by the data paths in a computation such as $p_3(p_1(x), p_2(x))$. This *mutual-exclusion constraint* typically arises from conflicts over shared resources, such as the $p$ operator in our example. (Thus mutual-exclusion constraints are frequently due to the data-path topology.) A convenient notation for a mutual-exclusion constraint between operations $f$ and $g$ is $f \succeq g$, which means that either $f \preceq g$ or $g \preceq f$ (or, more precisely, either $f^F \preceq g^S$ or $g^F \preceq f^S$).

Although a precedence graph is a good aid in visualizing a set of precedence constraints, such graphs have no notation for representing mutual-exclusion constraints. Thus it is difficult to use a precedence graph to depict the constraints imposed by a particular data-path topology, although if every mutual-exclusion constraint $f \succeq g$ imposed by a topology is arbitrarily resolved to mean one of $f \preceq g$ or $g \preceq f$, the resulting set of precedence constraints (which only express a subset of the possibilities allowed by the topology) can, of course, be represented as a precedence graph.

### 7.3.8 Serializations

One straightforward approach to implementation of a computation is to perform its operations in a strict sequence without concurrency. In general, there may be several different sequences of operator execution that are consistent with the essential precedence constraints of a computation, and the *serialization* of a computation may be viewed as the imposition of additional precedence constraints so that the operations become totally ordered. For example, the serializations consistent with the data dependencies of figure 7.4 are

$$r^S \preceq f \preceq g \preceq h \preceq p_1 \preceq p_2 \preceq r^F,$$

$$r^S \preceq f \preceq h \preceq g \preceq p_1 \preceq p_2 \preceq r^F,$$

$$r^S \preceq f \preceq h \preceq p_1 \preceq g \preceq p_2 \preceq r^F,$$

$$r^S \preceq h \preceq f \preceq g \preceq p_1 \preceq p_2 \preceq r^F,$$

$$r^S \preceq h \preceq f \preceq p_1 \preceq g \preceq p_2 \preceq r^F.$$

Restricting our implementation choices to strictly serial execution of operations would be a serious limitation of our options, which at first glance would seem to undermine interest in an enumeration of serial sequences. However, it is interesting to observe that the complete set of serializations of events in a precedence graph conveys exactly the same information as the graph itself: $s \preceq t$ is implied by a precedence graph if and only if $s \preceq t$ in every serialization consistent with that precedence graph. Thus the introduction of new precedence constraints—for example, through limitations imposed by the data-path design—can be characterized by enumerating the serializations ruled out by the new constraints.

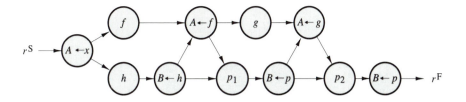

**Figure 7.5** Precedence graph with register loads.

### 7.3.9 Optimizing Data-Path Topology

In order to evaluate the impact of our data-path design on the timing of control signals, it is useful to consider in detail the timing of each register load operation in the context of our emerging precedence constraints. We can extend the precedence graph of figure 7.4 to include operations of the form $\alpha \leftarrow \beta$, signifying the loading of register $\alpha$ with the output of module $\beta$; in practice, this will be realized in our design by asserting the load enable of $\alpha$ while simultaneously asserting the enable input to the driver $\beta$. Because a single data bus is shared as the input to both registers, at most one value can be loaded into a register at any time; thus we have implicit mutual-exclusion constraints between operations $\alpha \leftarrow \beta$ and $\gamma \leftarrow \delta$ unless $\beta$ and $\delta$ are identical.

Figure 7.5 depicts the precedence constraints resulting from the data dependencies of figure 7.4 and the additional constraints imposed by the data paths of figure 7.2. Each operation is preceded by the loading of its inputs into the appropriate register, and each is followed by the loading of its result into some register for access by a subsequent operation.

The multiple use of the $A$ register leads to two subtle nonessential constraints in figure 7.5. Since $h$ and $f$ both require the input $x$, their sharing of $A$ as an input register causes no conflict. However, the output of the $f$ operation must also be loaded into the $A$ register for access by $g$ and $p_1$; yet loading a new value into $A$ immediately contaminates the output of the $h$ module. Thus we have the constraint that the loading of $B \leftarrow h$, which secures the output of $h$ in the $B$ register, must precede any change in the contents of $A$. For similar reasons, the output of $p_1$ must be saved in $B$ prior to the loading of $A$ with the output of $g$. The latter constraint is relatively harmless, since it simply orders two operations that both must precede $p_2$ for other reasons; it costs little, performancewise, to load both registers immediately prior to the start of $p_2$.[1]

The requirement that $B \leftarrow h$ must precede $A \leftarrow f$ is potentially more serious. Since $A \leftarrow f$ must precede $g$, the result is a new constraint $h \preceq g$ between two

---

[1] As noted earlier, the registers cannot be loaded simultaneously; thus the additional precedence constraint between the operations $B \leftarrow p$ and $A \leftarrow g$ dictates that both register loads follow, in sequence, the $p_1$ operation. This rules out the possibility of overlapping the $A \leftarrow g$ load with $p_1$, at the possible cost of the time required for a register load operation. We assume, however, that the duration of a load operation—one clock cycle—is short compared with the time taken by operations.

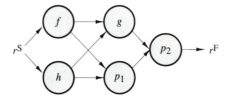

**Figure 7.6**  Effective precedence constraints.

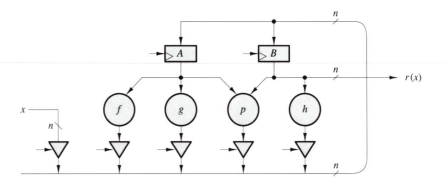

**Figure 7.7**  Improved data paths for $r(x)$ computation.

previously unordered operations, as shown in figure 7.6.

The additional constraint may be of little consequence if, for example, $h$ is fast compared with $f$; but it can incur a time penalty approaching a factor of two if the computation is dominated by time spent in the $h$ and $g$ operations. Without the extra constraint, $h$ and $g$ can be performed concurrently; with it, they must be serialized.

A minor variation in the data-path design eliminates one reason for the $h \preceq g$ constraint, with consequent opportunities for improved performance. The diagram of figure 7.7 differs from that of figure 7.2 only in that the $h$ operator takes its input from $B$ rather than $A$, thereby isolating $h$ from the effects of reloading $A$ before $h$ has completed. The resulting precedence graph, shown in figure 7.8, imposes no nonessential constraints among the operations $f$, $h$, $g$, $p_1$, and $p_2$. However, this relaxed precedence graph leaves the two load operations $B \leftarrow h$ and $A \leftarrow f$ unordered, despite the requirement observed earlier for their mutual exclusion. Thus, while figure 7.8 reflects *only* constraints that the control structure must satisfy, it does not reflect *all* such constraints: Control structures designed to meet these constraints must also ensure the mutual exclusion of load operations.

### 7.3.10 Determinacy

The design criteria for a digital system usually require that each of its outputs be

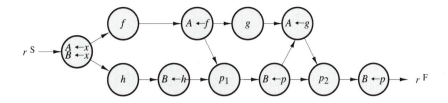

**Figure 7.8** Precedence graph using improved architecture.

some specified function of its inputs. In the case of systems whose specifications include internal state information (such as the running sum in a circuit designed to add consecutively entered binary numbers), we may view this information as an additional input. Thus with rare exceptions (such as a system designed to generate random numbers), a module's outputs are intended to be completely determined by its inputs. Systems that have this property are said to be *determinate*.

There are a variety of ways in which a system can misbehave. It may be determinate, for example, but simply compute the wrong function of its inputs. Such a problem often reflects a fundamental error in the design, such as a "bug" in the algorithm on which it is based. Many subtle problems, however, lead to indeterminate behavior of the implementation. Indeterminacy can be exasperatingly hard to find and correct, since its symptoms are often inconsistent, nonrepeatable, and generally dependent on elusive and transient parameters of the test environment (such as temperature and minor timing variations).

Indeterminacy in systems constructed of determinate components always reflects a failure to enforce to one or more precedence constraints. Given the constraints diagrammed in figure 7.8, a failure to ensure that $h^F$ precedes $B \leftarrow h$ would allow unspecified values to be loaded into $B$, yielding an indeterminate input to $p_1$ that could propagate through as an indeterminate $r(x)$ value.[2]   Similarly, a failure to observe the additional mutual-exclusion constraint between $B \leftarrow h$ and $A \leftarrow f$, which is *not* reflected in figure 7.8, would, by allowing multiple bus drivers to be simultaneously enabled, cause indeterminate results.

## 7.4 Synchronous Globally Timed Control

Globally timed control structures are based on the assumption that the time taken by each operation is a constant to be designed into the system; such structures must accommodate any timing variability by taking conservative (worst-case) values. Because device timings are presumed constant, the sequence and relative timing of computational events are frozen in the design; in effect, a single serialization of the events is chosen by the designer, consistent with essential precedence constraints, and the control machinery is built around this static choice. Note that the

---

[2] It is possible, of course, for $r(x)$ to be determinate despite indeterminacy in an intermediate value such as the input to $p_1$. The $p$ module might, for example, ignore its second input.

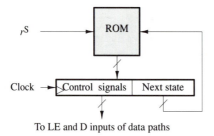

**Figure 7.9** SGT controller for the data paths of figure 7.7.

serialization of a sequence of *events* need not rule out concurrent operations. A sequence $f^S \preceq h^S \preceq f^F \preceq h^F$, for example, allows $f$ and $h$ to overlap in time.

Because of their inflexibility with respect to ordering of events, globally timed system designs are generally simpler but less flexible than locally timed alternatives. The simplicity of SGT control structures is, however, a powerful asset; it often enables engineering optimizations that result in better performance than locally timed designs. As a result, SGT control structures dominate digital system designs across the cost/performance spectrum.

To illustrate a simple SGT control structure, we return to the data paths used in figure 7.7 to compute $r(x)$. Assume that the period of the global system clock is one time unit and that combinational $f$, $h$, $g$, and $p$ modules have propagation delays of 2, 4, 5, and 3 time units, respectively. We assume that register times are negligible. The control circuit can take the form of the familiar ROM-based finite-state machine shown in figure 7.9. The controller is driven by the same clock signal that is furnished to the data paths, thus ensuring synchronous operation of the entire machine. The controller has only two parts: a ROM and a register. On every cycle, the register is loaded from the ROM location addressed by the previous contents of the "next-state" field in the register. The "control-signals" field of the register contains the $\alpha_D$ and $\alpha_{LE}$ signals for the data paths.

The controller has a single input, $r^S$, which signals the start of the $r$ computation; its outputs are the three-state drive ($\alpha_D$) and register load-enable ($\alpha_{LE}$) control signals for the drivers and registers of figure 7.7. All control signals are presumed to be asserted in the logical 1 state; thus, to load $A \leftarrow f$ at the end of a clock cycle, both $f_D$ and $A_{LE}$ must have the value 1 during that cycle. The computation of $r(x)$ is to begin after a cycle on which $r^S$ becomes 1 and is to complete after some fixed number of clock cycles that will be determined shortly.

The remaining piece of the design is to develop a truth table for the ROM of figure 7.9 that generates a sequence of control signals consistent with both the precedence constraints of figure 7.8 and the device specifications given above. Figure 7.10 presents such a truth table, annotated (in its leftmost columns) to expose its relationship to the events of the precedence graph. The table uses an asterisk in the $R^S$ input column to denote either 0 or 1 for that input; thus a line containing an asterisk is really an abbreviation for two truth-table lines with 0

| Annotations | | | ROM inputs | | ROM outputs | | | | | | | |
|---|---|---|---|---|---|---|---|---|---|---|---|---|
| Events | Loads | Time | $r^S$ | Current state | $x_D$ | $F_D$ | $g_D$ | $p_D$ | $h_D$ | $A_{LE}$ | $B_{LE}$ | Next state |
| $r^S = f^S, h^S$ | $A, B \leftarrow x$ | 0 | * | 0 | 1 | | | | | 1 | 1 | 1 |
| | | 1 | * | 1 | | | | | | | | 2 |
| $f^F, g^S$ | $A \;\leftarrow\; f$ | 2 | * | 2 | | 1 | | | | 1 | | 3 |
| | | 3 | * | 3 | | | | | | | | 4 |
| $h^F, p^S$ | $B \;\leftarrow\; h$ | 4 | * | 4 | | | | | 1 | | 1 | 5 |
| | | 5 | * | 5 | | | | | | | | 6 |
| | | 6 | * | 6 | | | | | | | | 7 |
| $g^F, p_1^F$ | $B \;\leftarrow\; p$ | 7 | * | 7 | | | | 1 | | | 1 | 8 |
| $p_2^S$ | $A \;\leftarrow\; g$ | 8 | * | 8 | | | 1 | | | 1 | | 9 |
| | | 9 | * | 9 | | | | | | | | 10 |
| | | 10 | * | 10 | | | | | | | | 11 |
| $p_2^F$ | $B \;\leftarrow\; p$ | 11 | * | 11 | | | | 1 | | | 1 | 12 |
| $r^F$ | | 12 | 0 | 12 | | | | | | | | 12 |
| | | | 1 | 12 | | | | | | | | 0 |

**Figure 7.10**  SGT control-ROM truth table.

and 1, respectively, in the indicated column. Missing entries in the output columns default to 0. Note that the next-state output of the ROM simply increments through successive states, in the fixed sequence consistent with a selected serialization of the computation events denoted in the leftmost column. In this respect, our FSM is quite uninteresting; its transition diagram has only a single path through its states. (Indeed, a reasonable implementation alternative would be to use a counter to hold the state information, eliminating the need for state variables at the input and output of the ROM.) Note that the FSM gravitates to state 12 (the designated "start" or "idle" state), where it awaits the $r^S$ input signaling a new $r(x)$ computation; following this stimulus, it progresses from state 0 to state 12 on the next 13 consecutive clock edges. The time column of the table notes the time, in clock cycles, since the start of the computation; by virtue of our state assignment, this value is identical to the state encoding in each case.

The second column of the table gives the load operation, if any, to be performed at the end of the corresponding clock cycle. Note that this entry dictates the choice of drive and load-enable signals to be output by the ROM during that cycle, as reflected in the output columns to the right.

The specification of the timing of control signals within an SGT system necessitates a *program* of sorts and partially dictates the function performed by the associated data paths. This style of building controllers is called *microprogramming*, since the ROM contents resemble a primitive program. The data paths of figure 7.7 contain a number of features that are obviously motivated by the particular application (such as the selection of operators and the placement of the $h$ module); nevertheless, like most programmable devices, this device can be programmed to perform other computations involving the same operations. Thus the data paths of figures 7.2 and 7.7 only partially specify the desired computation; in each case, a program dictating the sequence of control signals is required to complete the specification. One important difference between programs written to control our data paths and programs written in conventional programming languages is that a program for our data paths can deal with *concurrency*, such as a multiplication and an addition occurring at the same time, whereas most conventional programming languages are strictly sequential.

## 7.5 Synchronous Locally Timed Control

The globally timed controller of figures 7.9 and 7.10 adheres to a rigidly timed sequence of control signals built into its ROM contents. This inflexibility may be awkward for two reasons: (1) it fails to exploit data-dependent device timings (for example, $h$ may complete in one cycle when its argument value is zero); and (2) changing the timing specification of a component (for example, to exploit a faster $g$ module) requires redesign (or at least reprogramming) of the controller. We can avoid both problems by using modules that announce their completion via explicit finish signals and making the controller sensitive to such signals. In doing so, we move to a *locally timed control discipline*, also referred to as *self-timed control*. In locally timed systems, the timing parameters relevant to each device are determined by a mechanism within that device and instantiated as control signals; globally timed systems, in contrast, fix the timing of each module via constants in a systemwide timing scheme.

Locally timed components feature control inputs corresponding to start events and control outputs corresponding to finish events. In a simple synchronous locally timed system, these signals may take the form of levels to be sampled at clock edges: $f^S$ asserted prior to a clock edge signals valid inputs and the start of $f$'s computation, while $f^F$ asserted before an edge signals $f$'s completion and the availability of its output. We adopt the convention that $f^S$ remains asserted during $f$'s computation; thus $f^S$ is only deasserted while $f$ is idle. Further, we require that $f^F$ remain asserted by $f$ until $f^S$ is dropped.

Figure 7.9 can be extended in a straightforward way to provide for the additional inputs and outputs characteristic of locally timed modules; an additional output $r^F$ is required to make the $r$ module itself be a useful component in locally timed systems. Figure 7.11 shows a state-transition diagram that might be used as the basis for such an SLT controller. Note that certain transitions are marked with

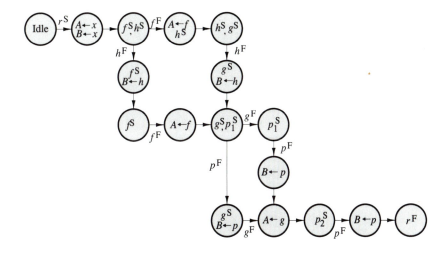

**Figure 7.11**  A synchronous locally timed controller.

control inputs, signifying the conditions under which they are taken; unmarked transitions are always taken at the next clock edge. Transitions corresponding to multiple simulaneous inputs are missing from the diagram (see problem 7.5).

States in figure 7.11 are marked with control outputs (such as $f^S$) and register load operations (such as $A \leftarrow f$) that abbreviate combinations of control outputs. Note that $p_1^S$ and $p_2^S$ are in fact the same output signal; the subscript is simply for notational convenience.

Several paths through figure 7.11 are possible, depending on the details of operator timing. This added flexibility automatically and transparently takes advantage of timing sophistication within each module, yielding nearly optimal $r(x)$ times for every combination of operation times. It also has the effect of isolating the system timing from the underlying period of the common clock. Unlike the previous SGT control example, where idle FSM states were used to ensure that device timing specifications were met, the SLT control FSM can be clocked with a period that is fast compared with operation times without changing its behavior. Our design assumes ordinary (not self-timed) registers and drivers, however; thus the clock period must be sufficiently long to accommodate register and bus driving times. Since unconditioned transitions—used to ensure certain precedence constraints— occur at the clock rate, it is advantageous to make the clock period short compared with operation times.

## 7.6 Asynchronous Locally Timed Control

The synchronous (SGT and SLT) control disciplines discussed thus far depend on the availability of a clock signal common to all system modules. Synchrony with a common clock has many advantages: It provides a basis of discrete time at a low level, allowing higher-level system engineering to be done in simple digital

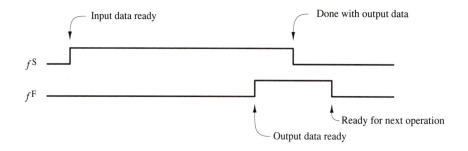

**Figure 7.12** Typical asynchronous protocol.

terms. However, synchronous systems are occasionally impractical for a variety of reasons, including:

- *Timing granularity.* Synchronous disciplines force events to occur at clock edges, thereby wasting occasional fractions of clock periods (for example, by rounding $f^F$ conservatively to the next clock edge).

- *Clock skew.* In physically large systems, it is difficult to share a single, globally consistent clock signal because of transmission delays.

- *Wire costs.* The expense of additional wiring to carry the common clock signal must be considered in the case of physically distant modules.

- *Noise and radiation.* A common clock signal is typically both the most powerful and the highest-frequency signal in a system; thus it is a major contributor to radiofrequency pollution and interference problems.

By careful attention to signal cleanliness, freedom from hazards and glitches, and related issues, start and finish events can be signaled asynchronously using transitions rather than synchronously using levels sampled at a common clock. The result is an *asynchronous locally timed discipline*, capable in theory of offering the greatest flexibility in the timing of operations and other events.

A typical asynchronous locally timed protocol is shown in figure 7.12. We have chosen (arbitrarily) to have both lines carry 0s in the normal (idle) state; positive transitions on each line signal $f^S$ and $f^F$, asserted by the external circuit and by the module, respectively. Note that a positive transition on either line signals the presence of valid data at either the module's inputs (in the case of the start control line) or at its outputs (in the case of the finish control line). The negative transitions also carry information: On the start line, a negative transition reports to the module that it no longer needs to maintain valid output data (presumably because the output data have been latched by external circuitry); the negative transition on the finish line simply reports that the module is ready to accept the next operation. Our convention thus requires a module to hold its results at the output terminals until the negative transition on its start line.

The use of two transitions on each signal line for each transaction limits the number of transactions per second to half the rate at which transitions can be

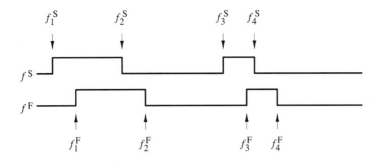

**Figure 7.13**  Bipolar transition signaling.

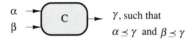

**Figure 7.14**  Transition signaling using a Muller C-element.

carried on each line. An alternative is *bipolar transition signaling*, in which every transition on a given line signifies a particular event, as shown in figure 7.13.

This scheme again uses a pair of lines to signal $f^S$ and $f^F$ events to and from the module $f$, but it uses positive and negative transitions interchangeably (indeed, alternately) to signal each. Note that by examining the state of the control lines to and from $f$, we can determine its state: If they carry identical logic values, then $f$ is idle; otherwise $f$ is busy computing, since we must be between some $f^S$ and its corresponding $f^F$.

Since bipolar transition signaling offers no extra transitions to signal "done with data" times, it is useful only in conjunction with additional conventions to establish how long data lines must be held valid by modules driving them. We address this need by requiring that each module's inputs be held valid until that module signals a finish event; conversely, the module must hold its outputs valid until it receives its next start signal.

The start and finish signals of ALT modules can be combined using ad hoc logic to enforce various precedence constraints. Of particular use in this regard is the *Muller C-element*, a fundamental bistable device described in problem 4.2. The C-element assumes a new state $Q$ whenever all of its inputs carry the value $Q$. So long as the inputs to a C-element disagree, its output remains at the last value on which the inputs have agreed.

Given two lines whose positive (or negative) transitions convey events $\alpha$ and $\beta$, for example, the circuit of figure 7.14 generates a line whose positive (negative) transition is guaranteed to follow $\alpha$ and $\beta$.

*Control Structures and Disciplines*                                              *193*

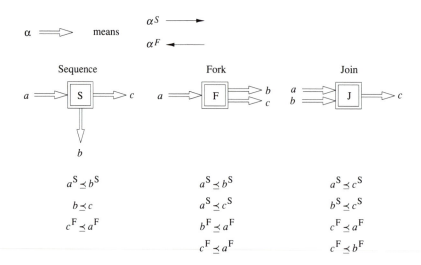

$$a^S \preceq b^S$$
$$b \preceq c$$
$$c^F \preceq a^F$$

$$a^S \preceq b^S$$
$$a^S \preceq c^S$$
$$b^F \preceq a^F$$
$$c^F \preceq a^F$$

$$a^S \preceq c^S$$
$$b^S \preceq c^S$$
$$c^F \preceq a^F$$
$$c^F \preceq b^F$$

**Figure 7.15**  Control-structure modules.

### 7.6.1  *Modular Control Structure

It is convenient to deal, at least conceptually, with primitives that allow us to structure control systems without resorting to the level of detail at which individual events are ordered.[3]   In particular, it is appealing to be able to start with two operations, say $a$ and $b$, and define a new operation $c$ that corresponds to the execution of $a$ and $b$ in sequence; alternatively, we might wish to define a new operation consisting of the concurrent execution of $a$ and $b$. The critical aspect of these constructions that is missing from bottom-level analysis of detailed precedence constraints is the *composition* of simple operations to define more complex ones, which in turn can be themselves combined.

A traditional repertoire of composition operators consists of *sequence*, *fork*, and *join operators* whose functions are to serialize operations, to split an operation into concurrent suboperations, and to merge concurrent suboperations into a single operation, respectively. If we bundle the start and finish control lines of each module into a *control link*, as diagrammed at the top of figure 7.15, we may view (or even implement) these three operators as control circuitry components whose inputs and outputs are control links. Control circuit symbols for the operators, together with the precedence constraints enforced by each, are shown in figure 7.15.

Each control link corresponds to a conceptual operation whose beginning and end are well-defined events. Thus ALT operator modules (such as adders, multipliers, or the $f$, $g$, $h$, and $p$ of our example) each have a control link in addition to their normal data-path inputs and outputs; ALT control modules have only control links as their input and output ports and are used as circuitry to interconnect the control

---

[3] This section follows the classic development by Dennis [1972] of ALT control modules based on transition signaling.

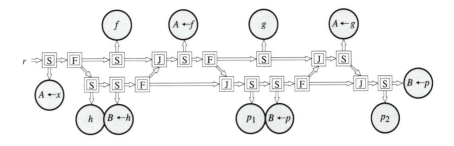

**Figure 7.16**  Modular control structure.

links of operator modules in a control structure. Each control module *defines* a new operation at each of its input links and *invokes* an operation at each of its output links. Note that each operation defined by a module includes each operation invoked by that module completely, in the sense that (1) no operation is invoked until a start is received on every input link and (2) no finish signal is reported on any input link until a module has received finish signals on every output link.

Figure 7.16 shows a modular control structure that enforces the precedence constraints of figure 7.5. Unlike the case of previous control structures, we assume here that the load operations are each implemented as locally timed modules. Figure 7.16 is suboptimal in that it contains control-structure modules that correspond to redundant precedence constraints in the graph of figure 7.5, such as the constraint that $B{\leftarrow}h$ precedes $p_1$, which is implied by $(B{\leftarrow}h) \preceq (A{\leftarrow}f) \preceq p_1$.

The sequence, fork, and join modules shown in figure 7.15 deal with simultaneously imposed precedence constraints, which can be accommodated by simply waiting for each of a collection of events (such as transitions) to occur. No module must make "which came first" decisions between asynchronous events. Thus each can be implemented in a way that avoids metastable behavior, since none of these modules is confronted with an arbitration problem. Conversely, a control structure implemented using these modules cannot address an arbitration problem, such as the mutual-exclusion constraint that only one of the operations $B{\leftarrow}h$ and $A \leftarrow f$ can occur at any given time. While the modules of figure 7.15 can be used to implement any set of constraints of the form $\alpha \preceq \beta$ and hence any given precedence graph, they are inadequate to implement the constraint $\alpha \succeq \beta$, which is equivalent to the requirement that either $\alpha \preceq \beta$ or $\beta \preceq \alpha$. As a consequence, we must explicitly prescribe in the control structure either $\alpha \preceq \beta$ or $\beta \preceq \alpha$ in order to ensure that $\alpha$ and $\beta$ do not occur concurrently. Indeed, the modules of figure 7.15 could be used to implement the precedence graph of figure 7.8, leaving the load operations $B{\leftarrow}h$ and $A{\leftarrow}f$ unordered. If no additional constraints were imposed, the resulting system would be indeterminate because 0 drivers could be simultaneously enabled onto the bus.

We can address the need for mutual exclusion by adding an *arbiter* module, shown in figure 7.17, to our repertoire of control modules. Note that the arbiter control module has a pair of input links and a corresponding pair of output links, simply defining an operation at each input link to be identical to the operation on

Arbiter

$a \Longrightarrow$ [ A ] $\Longrightarrow a'$
$b \Longrightarrow$ $\Longrightarrow b'$

Constraints enforced:

$$a^{\mathrm{S}} \preceq a'^{\mathrm{S}} \preceq a'^{\mathrm{F}} \preceq a^{\mathrm{F}}$$
$$b^{\mathrm{S}} \preceq b'^{\mathrm{S}} \preceq b'^{\mathrm{F}} \preceq b^{\mathrm{F}}$$

either $a' \preceq b'$ or $b' \preceq a'$

**Figure 7.17**  Arbiter control-structure module.

the matching output link. However, it imposes the additional constraint that the operations on the output links not proceed concurrently. The intention is that an input $a$ or $b$ operation be translated to an outgoing $a'$ or $b'$ operation without undue delay so long as the other input operation is inactive; if both are requested at nearly the same time, the output operations are serialized in some order. Thus the mutual-exclusion constraint between the two unordered load operations of figure 7.8 could be imposed by splicing an arbiter module in the control links to the respective load operations.

Clearly the construction of an effective module with this behavior confronts an arbitration problem, since the module must select a "winner" from among closely timed start events. Consequently, the arbiter cannot behave reliably if it is required to respond in bounded time. Fortunately, constant bounds on response times are foreign to ALT control structures, allowing construction (at least in theory) of reliable asynchronous arbiters that wait for stable decisions before beginning either output operation.

## 7.7  Context

The design of timing and control circuitry is one of the most complex and error-prone facets of digital engineering, particularly when approached in a haphazard fashion. This chapter has explored a spectrum of disciplines that lend structure to the timing of a system and make its control tractable. In practice, one often finds hybrids between the approaches taken here, minor compromises and transgressions, or even complete abandonment of structure in favor of ad hoc timing relationships.

The amount of structure to impose on the design of a system is one of the intuitive judgments an experienced engineer learns to make. Too little structure will result in a chaotic system that is likely never to work correctly; too much structure may impose constraints that lead to inefficiency. A first-rate engineer follows a course between these extremes, ultimately guided by a plan for a system structure that *guarantees* correct operation. Such a system can be proved to function correctly, based on device specifications and precedence constraints. While a practical engineer may omit details of the proof from a design for reasons of expediency, their omission is justified by the engineer's confidence that they can be generated if the design is challenged.

## 7.8 Problems

### Problem 7.1
Augment the statement of the single-clock synchronous discipline in section 7.2.1 to accommodate nonzero setup and hold times of the registers.

### Problem 7.2
We want to design a sequential circuit to compute

$$r(x) = g(g(f(x), h(x)), f(h(x))),$$

using modules that compute $g(x, y), f(x)$ and $h(x)$.

A. Draw a data-dependency graph for $r(x)$.

B. Suppose you are allowed to use at most one $g(x, y)$ module in your design for the circuit to compute $r(x)$. Does this limitation require the addition of nonessential precedence constraints to the precedence graph for one computation of $r(x)$? Briefly explain.

C. Suppose you are allowed to use at most one $f(x)$ module in your design. Does this limitation require the addition of nonessential precedence constraints to the precedence graph for one computation of $r(x)$? Briefly explain.

### Problem 7.3
Develop a ROM truth table to cause the data paths of figure 7.7 to compute

$$t(x) = f(h(p(g(x), p(x, h(x))))).$$

### Problem 7.4
Consider the following circuit:

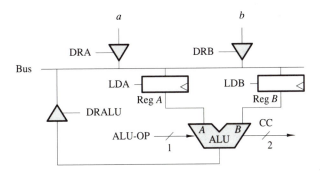

The ALU can perform only two operations, based on a single control, ALU-OP:

- ALU-OP $= 0 \Rightarrow A - B$,
- ALU-OP $= 1 \Rightarrow B - A$.

The CC bits indicate whether the ALU operation has produced a positive, negative, or zero result.

- $CC = 00 \Rightarrow$ result $= 0$,
- $CC = 01 \Rightarrow$ result positive,
- $CC = 10 \Rightarrow$ result negative.

Your job is to build a controller that will cause the circuit to execute the following algorithm, which computes the greatest common divisor of two inputs:

```
while a ≠ b do
    if a > b then a ← a-b
                 else b ← b-a
```

The controller will be a state machine that takes 2 bits of input (CC) and produces control signals for the data paths (DRA, DRB, LDA, LDB, ALU-OP, DRALU).

A. Draw a state diagram for the controller. Outputs from your FSM should depend only on the current state. Use symbolic notation for the outputs (for example, $A \leftarrow B - A$).

B. Supply a truth table for the ROM that implements your state-transition diagram.

## Problem 7.5

The state-transition diagram of figure 7.11 is incomplete, in that it omits transitions corresponding to multiple inputs changing at once. Fill in the missing transitions.

## Problem 7.6

Give a state-transition diagram for an SLT controller designed to cause the data paths of figure 7.7 to compute

$$t(x) = f(h(p(g(x), p(x, h(x))))).$$

## Problem ★★7.7

Design implementations of each of the modules shown in figure 7.15, assuming bipolar transition signaling. (*Hint:* Use Muller C-elements for the fork and join modules; the sequence module requires only wires.)

## Problem ★★7.8

Design implementations of each of the modules shown in figure 7.15, assuming the signaling conventions shown in figure 7.12.

## Problem ★7.9

Verify that each of the precedence constraints of figure 7.5 is enforced by the control structure of figure 7.16.

## Problem ★7.10

Redraw the modular control structure of figure 7.16 to eliminate redundant control modules.

## Problem ⋆7.11

Develop a modular control structure to cause the data paths of figure 7.7 to compute

$$t(x) = f(h(p(g(x), p(x, h(x))))).$$

## Problem ⋆⋆7.12

Propose an implementation technique by which the load operations of figures 7.8 and 7.7 can be treated as locally timed asynchronous operators. Assume constant setup, hold, and clock-to-$Q$ delays for registers, as well as constant bus driver turn-on time. You may assume the availability of delay lines that simply delay their input signal by a specified constant interval.

## Problem ⋆7.13

Develop a modular control structure that enforces the constraints of figure 7.8 in addition to the necessary mutual-exclusion constraints. Use a minimum number of control modules.

## Problem ⋆⋆7.14

Sketch a design for an ALT arbiter control module that uses transition signaling.

## Problem ⋆7.15  Data Dependencies and FSMs:

In this problem we consider the construction of a sequential circuit that computes $q(x) = r(f(g(x)), h(p(x)))$ from an input $x$. We are supplied component modules $r$, $f$, $g$, $h$, and $p$ (one of each module), from which we construct the data paths for our $q$ module; we are left with the problem of designing control circuitry for $q$. Each of the component modules is itself sequential; each takes an input control signal that causes the module to begin its computation. These input control signals are labeled $r^S$, $f^S$, $g^S$, $h^S$, and $p^S$, respectively. In addition, each module provides a finish output signal that goes high (and remains high) when the module's calculation is completed; these signals are labeled $r^F$, $f^F$, $g^F$, $h^F$, and $p^F$. The $q$ module will have similar self-timed control signals $q^S$ and $q^F$.

A. Draw a data-dependency graph showing the essential constraints that must be met by the control circuit. Include in your graph $q^S$ and $q^F$, the start and finish of the $q$ module's computation.

Our approach to the control circuitry will be to design an FSM whose state transitions are dictated by control-signal inputs (to the FSM). The FSM produces selected control signals as outputs at each state. We represent such an FSM by a state-transition diagram whose transitions are labeled with the input signals and whose states are labeled with the names of the output signals to be generated.

B. Assume that the modules $r$, $h$, and $g$ always require exactly 200 ns to perform their computation, while $f$ and $p$ always require 100 ns. Draw a state-transition diagram for the *simplest* FSM that will cause the $q$ module to compute $q(x)$ in the shortest possible time.

C. Under the timing assumptions of part B, are the sequence and relative timing of the output signals from your FSM always the same? Would a synchronous clocked FSM be an appropriate implementation technique for this case? Explain.

D. Now assume that the time required for each module's computation is data-dependent but that the *maximum* time required by $r$, $h$, and $g$ is 200 ns and that required by $f$ and $p$ is 100 ns. Would your previous FSM still give correct results? Would a simple synchronous clocked FSM controller introduce nonessential precedence constraints? Explain.

E. Draw a *nondeterministic* state-transition diagram for an NFSM controller that results in the fastest possible computation of $q(x)$ regardless of the particular times required by component modules.

F. From your NFSM, derive the state-transition diagram of a deterministic FSM controller that computes $q(x)$ in the shortest possible time.

G. Design an actual implementation of the control circuit dictated by the DFSM of part F. Use a ROM (give a table showing its contents) as well as registers. Clearly indicate the relationship between control signals and the ROM's address and data bits. You may assume the availability of a system clock whose frequency is high relative to that of the control signals; thus your DFSM implementation may be synchronous at negligible performance cost.

H. Generalize the technique you used to construct your NFSM controller. Describe, in a few sentences, how an arbitrary data-dependency graph can be used to define an NFSM controller for self-timed modules that exploits maximal concurrency among subcomputations.

# 8  Performance Measures and Trade-offs

The foregoing discussion of control structures has mentioned some ways in which the performance of a circuit can be traded for cost. The choices between combinational and sequential, serial and parallel circuits, and sequential reuse of one module vs. concurrent use of several modules can have important impacts on the cost and performance of an implementation. In order to discuss the trade-offs involved in making these various choices, we need a more precise understanding of how performance can be quantified.

As a first approximation, we can view a digital circuit as a "black box" like the one in figure 8.1. We can associate with this black box a "propagation delay," or *computation latency*, much as we can associate a characteristic propagation delay with an individual logic gate. Intuitively, the computation latency is the time that elapses from when a set of values is presented at the inputs of a digital circuit until the correct results appear at the outputs and can be calculated from the component characteristics and control structure of the digital circuit; but this is an oversimplification in many cases.

With purely combinational logic, a computation latency is not difficult to calculate and corresponds roughly to the longest total gate propagation delay over any path from some input to some output. A conservative assumption is that when modules are connected in series, their computation latencies add. Thus the four-input adder circuit shown in figure 8.2 has a computation latency of $3d$ if the latency of each adder element is $d$.

We say that the latency is $3d$ because in the worst case (inputs $C$ and $D$), an input signal may have to propagate through three adder elements. Even in this simple case, however, the latencies are not uniform: The latency from input $A$ to the output is only $d$, and the latency from input $B$ is only $2d$. These variations in latency can affect the analysis of some configurations that use this circuit if really tight performance figures are required.

Consider the proposed implementation of an adder module shown in figure 8.3 (note that we have assumed arithmetic on 4-bit numbers). If the latency of a full-adder circuit is $t$, then the latency $d$ of the adder module will be $4t$, since in the worst case a signal at one of the low-order input bits may have to travel through all four full adders to affect the high-order output bit. Thus, if our four-input adder is built out of the modules shown in figure 8.3, leading to the configuration in figure 8.4, we might expect the total latency to be $3d = 12t$.

**Figure 8.1** Basic digital circuit model.

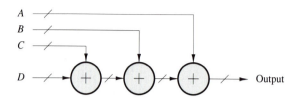

**Figure 8.2** Simple four-input adder.

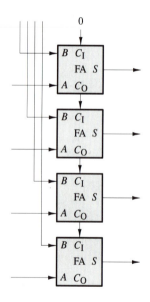

**Figure 8.3** Possible implementation of an adder module.

On closer inspection, however, the longest path we can find from any input to any output goes through six full adders, for a maximum latency of $6t$, only half of what we had calculated. The cause of this discrepancy is that, in our particular interconnection, once a signal has suffered a long propagation delay in one stage, it appears at an output that suffers little further delay in subsequent stages.

The purpose of this analysis is not to discredit the idea of measuring performance; indeed, performance measures are crucial if we are to make any meaningful comparison between implementations. Rather, it is to underscore the point that

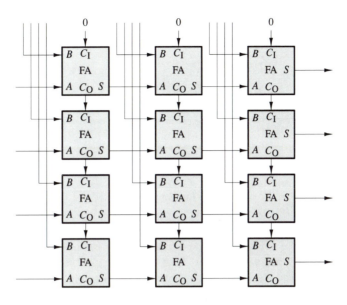

**Figure 8.4** Detail of four-input adder.

performance is a tricky subject that must be approached with care. Many different perspectives on performance are possible, and we shall see several of them in the pages to come.

The first of these perspectives is the notion of maximum latency. An upper bound on the latency of a serial connection of modules can always be obtained by summing the maximum latencies of the individual modules, although more detailed analysis may reveal the actual latency to be less. Returning to our four-input adder circuit, let us assume that the adder modules are implemented using carry look-ahead or other techniques so that the maximum latency of the module is a good representation of the delay from any input to any output. Then if the latency of an adder module is $d$, the maximum latency of the four-input adder really will be $3d$. Is there any way of improving on this performance?

One improvement that can be made is to reorganize the circuit into a tree structure as shown in figure 8.5. By equalizing the latencies from all the inputs, this circuit reduces the maximum latency to $2d$. In general, a tree of depth $n$, composed of $2^n - 1$ adder modules, is capable of adding $2^n$ numbers with a latency $nd$. For comparison, the linear arrangement requires the same amount of hardware but has a maximum latency of $(2^n - 1) \cdot d$.

For purposes of making comparisons such as these, which focus not just on the behavior of two particular configurations but on the behavior of two *families* of configurations generated using competing design approaches, each of which can be applied to problems of different sizes, it is convenient to introduce a new notation. If the latency of a circuit designed to process inputs of size $n$ is $c \cdot n^2$ for some constant $c$, we can say that the latency of that circuit is "of order $n^2$," or $\Theta(n^2)$. More generally, if there exist positive constants $c_1$ and $c_2$ such that $c_1 \cdot f(n) \leq$

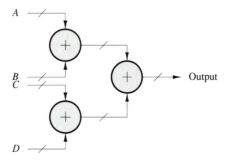

**Figure 8.5** Tree-structured four-input adder.

$g(n) \leq c_2 \cdot f(n)$ for all but a finite number (possibly none) of nonnegative values of $n$, we can say that $g(n)$ is of order $f(n)$, or $g(n) = \Theta(f(n))$.[1] This $\Theta(n)$ notation is useful when we wish to gloss over constant factors, such as the adder latency $d$ in the example above, and focus on the *scaling* behavior of some design philosophy when applied to larger and larger problems.

We can now restate our previous observations concerning adder circuits as follows: A linear arrangement of adders is capable of adding $N$ numbers using $\Theta(N)$ hardware with a maximum latency of $\Theta(N)$. A tree-shaped adder circuit can add $N$ numbers, also using $\Theta(N)$ hardware, but with maximum latency $\Theta(\log_2 N)$. (It is usually convenient, when analyzing digital circuit and computer algorithm performance, to use logarithms to the base 2, as is done here. Therefore the reader should assume all logarithms to be base 2 unless explicitly indicated otherwise. However, in the notation $\Theta(\log N)$ it does not really matter what base is used, since the difference will amount to only a constant factor.)

## 8.1 Pipelining

The reader may wonder whether further improvements can be made to the performance of the $N$-input adder. It can be shown that no arrangement of adder modules with a fixed fanin can be constructed with a maximum latency less than $\Theta(\log N)$, but a change in perspective may help us improve on this performance in certain cases. If we imagine a tree-shaped $N$-input adder and present all $N$ inputs simultaneously, the ensuing changes will propagate through the circuit as a "wave" until they reach the output $d \log N$ time units later (see figure 8.6).

The wave front takes $d$ time units to traverse each stage of the adder. Note that once the wave front has passed a stage, that stage is no longer performing any computation—it is merely holding its outputs at an already determined value,

---

[1] The more commonly used $g(n) = O(f(n))$ implies the second inequality but not the first; thus the symmetric relationship $g(n) = \Theta(f(n))$ places $f(n)$ and $g(n)$ on the *same* order, while the asymmetric $g(n) = O(f(n))$ establishes $f(n)$ as an *upper bound* on the growth of $g(n)$.

*Performance Measures and Trade-offs*

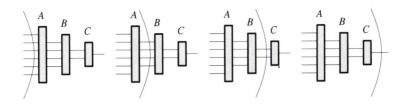

**Figure 8.6**   Signal propagation in an $N$-input adder.

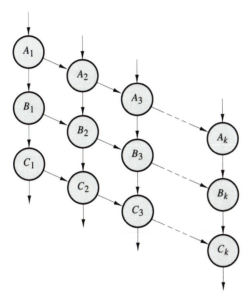

**Figure 8.7**   Data-dependency graph for the $N$-input adder.

waiting for the wave to propagate through the rest of the circuit. The larger the circuit, the more underutilized each module is, since it is "busy" only for $1/\log N$ of the total latency of the circuit.

If we have a steady stream of sets of $N$ values to be summed, then the conservative way to use our adder circuit is to present one set of $N$ values, wait long enough for their sum to appear at the output, extract that sum, and then present the next set of $N$ values. Used in this way, our circuit will exhibit a *throughput* of $1/(d \log N)$ sets of values, or *samples*, per unit time. This throughput of 1/latency is always achievable with any circuit, but a way of improving on it should be obvious to anyone who has ever had a lot of laundry to do and only one washer and dryer to do it in: You don't wait for each load of clothing to be washed *and* dried before starting on the next; you put a new load into the washer as soon as you've extracted the previous load and put it into the dryer.

More formally, figure 8.7 shows the data-dependency graph for the $N$-input adder. We use $A_i$ to denote the operation of processing the $i$th sample by the bank

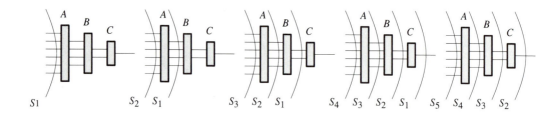

**Figure 8.8** Signal propagation in a pipelined $N$-input adder.

of adders labeled $A$ in figure 8.6; similarly, $B_i$ and $C_i$ denote the processing of the $i$th sample by adder banks $B$ and $C$.

The conservative approach to using the adder shown in figure 8.6 amounts to imposing the additional set of precedence constraints $C_i \preceq A_{i+1}$, which is not implied by any data dependency. In pursuit of higher performance, we could try presenting input samples to an $N$-input adder circuit more frequently—for example, by starting operation $A_{i+1}$ as soon as operation $A_i$ has finished. With a basic latency of $d$ time units for each operator, new samples could be supplied as often as one every $d$ time units, leading in the ideal case to the signal-propagation pattern depicted in figure 8.8.

In this model, as soon as a module has had $d$ time units to compute the output corresponding to its current set of inputs, it is presented with new inputs, for which valid outputs will be expected $d$ time units later. Thus computations proceed across the circuit in waves, like batches of laundry, and an original sample is long gone from the input by the time the corresponding sum becomes available at the output of the circuit. With a small amount of logic to pick off output values as they emerge and identify the input samples to which they each pertain, a serviceable adder with a throughput of $1/d$ samples per unit time can be constructed. This technique is known as *pipelining*.

With pipelining, the throughput of an $N$-input adder can be improved from $\Theta(1/\log N)$ to $\Theta(1)$, that is, a constant independent of the number of input lines. This is all done with a hardware investment that remains $\Theta(N)$, but there are several technical details that bear closer examination. First of all, the scenario depicted in figure 8.8, with data progressing through the adder modules in orderly waves, is difficult to obtain in practice using only combinational logic. The latencies along all paths through an adder module must be carefully balanced and the latencies of different adder modules closely matched; otherwise, some signals will "get ahead" of others, causing wave fronts to become distorted as they pass through the circuit. Ultimately, the distortions come to have the same magnitude as the packets of information traveling through the circuit. When this happens, individual packets lose their identity and errors occur.

When ordinary designs are used for circuit modules, this problem of *skew* becomes severe quite rapidly. The kind of engineering that generates the required balance among propagation delays is critical but rarely practiced. Instead, *registers*

*Performance Measures and Trade-offs*

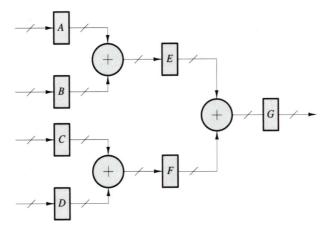

**Figure 8.9**  Pipelined four-input adder with registers.

are used to limit the regions over which skew can accumulate, as shown in figure 8.9.

Data are clocked into the registers at intervals of $d$ time units (the intervals are actually somewhat longer to allow for propagation delays through the registers themselves). Thus, at time 0, an input sample is clocked into registers $A$, $B$, $C$, and $D$. At time $d$, the sums $A + B$ and $C + D$ have been computed and are clocked into registers $E$ and $F$. Simultaneously, the next input sample is clocked into $A$, $B$, $C$, and $D$. At time $2d$, the sum $E + F$ is available and is clocked into register $G$. It will be available at the output of register $G$ from time $2d$ until time $3d$, when it will be replaced by the sum of the next input sample. Thus packets of information march through the circuit, advancing from one register to the next at every clock pulse.

The use of registers in pipelining adds somewhat to the hardware cost and reduces throughput by adding the register propagation delay to the time that must be allowed for each sample; but it has two important engineering advantages. First, the registers eliminate the need for fine-tuning delays in the combinational logic, which is likely to be a more expensive project than adding the registers. Second, they make the design much more robust against variations in component characteristics. Without registers, it is difficult to engineer a pipelined circuit that will not require frequent adjustment in order to continue working. With registers, a very reliable circuit can be designed easily, provided only that the clock period is long enough to ensure that all module outputs have settled to their final values before being latched. If allowance is made for the worst-case deviations of component timing from the norm, every circuit constructed using the design should operate reliably without any special tuning. It should be noted, though, that the need for this kind of design conservatism reduces the performance of pipelined circuits from what one might imagine to be achievable in the best case.

Consider now the slight modification of our four-input adder shown in figure 8.10. This circuit is intended to compute $f(A, B, C, D) = A \cdot B + C \cdot D$.

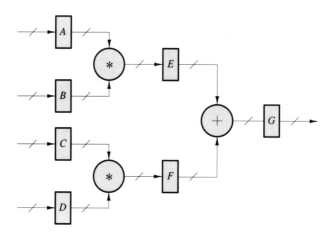

**Figure 8.10**　A pipelined circuit to compute $A \cdot B + C \cdot D$.

Assuming that the multiplier operators in the figure are combinational, nonpipelined implementations, the clock period for moving data through the pipeline registers will have to be the longer of the multiplier and adder latencies (the multiplier latency is the most likely). Otherwise, data will not be ready at all outputs when they must be latched. This brings up an important point: *The throughput of every operator in a pipeline must be the same.* In this sense, data flowing through a pipeline behaves like an incompressible fluid.

In a pipeline composed of modules with different performance figures, the throughput of the pipeline will be that of the module with the lowest throughput. This suggests an improvement for the circuit in figure 8.10. The longer *latency* of a multiplier module compared with an adder module is no particular problem as long as its *throughput* is no less. One way of improving the multiplier modules' throughput is to pipeline the multiplier modules themselves, in stages small enough that the throughput of the resulting modules is comparable with that of a simple adder module. There are other possibilities, but the important point is that if the components of a pipeline are not matched in throughput, then the components with greater throughput will not be used most effectively.

Another design consideration in constructing pipelined circuits is illustrated in figure 8.11. All parallel branches of a pipeline must be equally long, in the sense of having the same number of stages of registers. The circuit in figure 8.11 fails to meet this criterion, and hence the input value $C$ will get ahead of the inputs $A$ and $B$ from the same sample and will be mistakenly summed with inputs $A$ and $B$ of the previous sample. This error can be corrected by *padding* $C$'s branch of the pipeline with the extra register $C'$ shown in figure 8.12. It may be necessary to pad a pipeline with several registers in a row, depending on the latency of the other parallel paths.

Pipelining is a useful technique for improving the throughput of a circuit without adding much hardware. Sometimes, though, there is no substitute for a circuit with a shorter latency, no matter what its throughput. For example, a pipelined multiplier

*Performance Measures and Trade-offs*

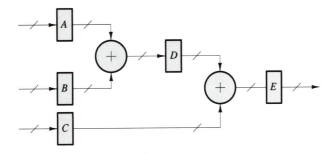

**Figure 8.11** A defective pipelined three-input adder.

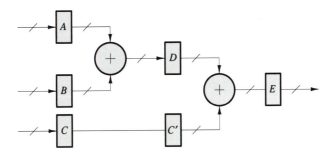

**Figure 8.12** A pipelined three-input adder.

can be built by recognizing it to be essentially an $N$-input adder, where $N$ is the number of bits in the multiplier and the inputs are the $N$ partial products to be summed. An example of this design, for the simple case $N = 4$, is shown in figure 8.13.

The operators labeled $A \cdot B$ in the figure compute the AND of the multiplicand with individual multiplier bits and thus form the partial products. The operators labeled $A + 2B$ and $A + 4B$ sum the partial products, with shifting to line them up properly. Neglecting the effect of addend size on the latencies of individual adder operators, a multiplier built in this fashion will exhibit a latency of $\Theta(\log N)$, where $N$ is the number of bits in the multiplier, and a throughput independent of $N$. (A variety of tricks can be used to speed the functioning of the pipelined multiplier by a constant factor, but none yields an improvement on its $\Theta(\log N)$ scaling behavior.)

This multiplier circuit will indeed perform as advertised, *provided* we can keep the pipeline full of pairs of numbers to be multiplied. But suppose we wish to use the circuit to compute $x^{(2^k)}$ by repeatedly squaring $x$ a total of $k$ times. There are certainly plenty of multiplications to do here, so a pipelined multiplier might seem like a good idea. Unfortunately, none of these multiplications can start until the previous one has been completed, since the result of that multiplication is the next number to be squared. Thus the pipeline will lie idle most of the time, in spite of

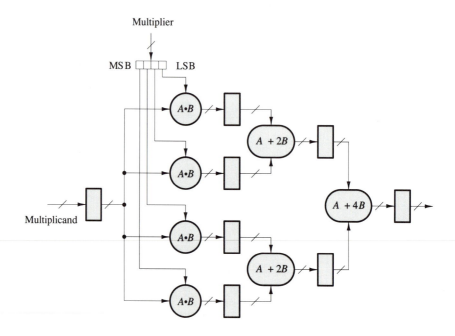

**Figure 8.13** A simple pipelined multiplier.

its potentially high throughput.

Of course, if we have several independent computations of $x^{(2^k)}$, for different values of $x$, it may still be possible to keep the pipeline full. But more often we are interested in using pipelined logic in the solution of just one problem. If that problem can be decomposed into enough concurrent operations, as would be the case, for example, in computing the element-by-element product of two vectors, then pipelining can result in a significant performance improvement. Many applications, however, resemble our $x^{(2^k)}$ example in that data dependencies make it difficult to generate enough concurrent activity to keep pipelines full. This is frequently the case in the central processors of general-purpose computers, where it is often difficult to unscramble the data dependencies in a program sufficiently to permit the most efficient use of a pipeline. Thus, while pipelining is an effective technique for increasing the throughput of a circuit, any proposed application must be scrutinized to ensure that it is sufficiently free of data dependencies that a real improvement will result.

## 8.2 Systematic Pipeline Construction

The design of simple pipelined systems lends itself to a modicum of engineering discipline aimed at ensuring their *well-formedness* in the sense that data from adjacent samples are not confused. As a foundation of our discipline, we define *k-pipelines*:

. . . . . . . . . . . . . . . . . . . . . . . . . . . . . . . . . . . . . . . . . . . . . . . . . . . . . . . .

A *k-**pipeline*** is an acyclic circuit consisting of combinational logic and registers, such that every path from an input to an output contains exactly $k$ registers.

. . . . . . . . . . . . . . . . . . . . . . . . . . . . . . . . . . . . . . . . . . . . . . . . . . . . . . . .

Note that this definition insists on equally many registers on each input-to-output path of the circuit; the reader should verify that this condition is both necessary and sufficient for proper operation of the pipelined circuits we have been considering.

We shall be focusing on *synchronous* $k$-pipelined circuits, in which a single clock serves each register. In general, we apply the inputs for a given computation during clock period $i$ and read their outputs during clock period $i + k$. The validity requirements for inputs and outputs depend on the placement of registers. Typically, we place registers at every *output* of a $k$-pipeline, so that inputs held valid during the entire $i$th clock period yield outputs valid during the entire $(i + k)$th period. Of course, the clock period must in every case be sufficiently long to accommodate the worst-case combinational delay between registers.

As a special case of the above definition, a 0-pipelined circuit is strictly combinational. The following rule offers, among other things, a technique for converting a combinational circuit to a pipeline that performs the same computation:

. . . . . . . . . . . . . . . . . . . . . . . . . . . . . . . . . . . . . . . . . . . . . . . . . . . . . . . .

***Pipeline rule 1***   A $k$-pipeline can be transformed into a $(k + 1)$-pipeline performing the same computation by adding a single register to each output node. Conversely, a $(k + 1)$-pipeline with at least one register on every output node can be transformed into a $k$-pipeline performing the same computation by deleting one register from each output node.

. . . . . . . . . . . . . . . . . . . . . . . . . . . . . . . . . . . . . . . . . . . . . . . . . . . . . . . .

Armed with this tool, we can create a $k$-pipeline from a combinational circuit by adding $k$ registers to each output. Although the result satisfies our definition (and, with an appropriate clock period, will perform the same computation as our original circuit), its particular distribution of registers offers no performance advantages. Our second pipeline construction tool gives us the flexibility necessary to overcome this situation:

. . . . . . . . . . . . . . . . . . . . . . . . . . . . . . . . . . . . . . . . . . . . . . . . . . . . . . . .

***Pipeline rule 2***   Given a $k$-pipeline $P$ containing a combinational element $E$, the result $P'$ of removing one register from each *output* of $E$ and adding one register to each *input* to $E$ is a $k$-pipeline performing the same computation as $P$. Conversely, the result of adding a register to each output of $E$ and removing a register from each of $E$'s inputs is again a $k$-pipeline performing the same computation as $P$.

. . . . . . . . . . . . . . . . . . . . . . . . . . . . . . . . . . . . . . . . . . . . . . . . . . . . . . . .

Rule 2 allows us to slide registers around in a pipelined circuit without violating the constraints necessary for well-formedness. The astute reader might verify that, given rule 2, rule 1 might as well have been written to allow adding/deleting registers at each *input* of a circuit rather than at each output. Note that each of the pipelined circuits appearing in this chapter can be constructed by applying rules 1 and 2 to their equivalent combinational circuits.

Typically rules 1 and 2 are used to distribute registers in a way that minimizes propagation delay over combinational paths, thus maximizing the usable clock frequency. Of course, the definition and rules of this section give no help in choosing between valid distributions, a topic to be explored in subsequent sections.

## 8.3 Cost-Performance Trade-offs and Options

Pipelining is an important technique that can be used to help squeeze the last ounce of performance from a given circuit configuration, assuming that the application is sensitive to the throughput of the circuit and not just to its latency. A given problem often admits of many solutions, with and without pipelining, that differ with respect to both cost and a number of performance criteria. The shape of this cost-performance space is heavily dependent on the nature of the particular problem being solved, and clever approaches exist that lead to important improvements in the implementations of many functions. Nevertheless, there are several implementation choices that almost always crop up: combinational vs. sequential, parallel vs. serial, and pipelined vs. nonpipelined. This section presents a case study in the consequences of choosing among these alternatives and describes some of the ways in which cleverness can be brought to bear on the problem we study. It should not be viewed as a prescription for creating a design with a certain cost-performance trade-off, but as an attempt to increase awareness of alternative possibilities and an illustration of the properties of different kinds of solutions.

For our example we choose the problem of building a circuit that sorts a sequence of numbers. We can imagine these numbers as being in binary representation and as being generated by some logic circuit or perhaps stored in some set of registers. We shall remain vague about several dimensions of the problem, such as how many numbers are to be sorted or how many bits long each number is, although of course such parameters show up in performance and cost figures. This problem is a less obvious choice for illustration than an arithmetic example such as multiplication; sorting has been chosen because it has an especially interesting solution space that can be explored without introducing methods that are particularly hard to understand. Furthermore, sorting is increasingly relevant to the data routing and distribution problems associated with building new multiprocessor systems.

Sorting a sequence of numbers may seem an uninteresting special case of the general problem of sorting a collection of data records according to the contents of some particular key field. However, if that key field is put at the head of the record and represented so that the desired sorting order corresponds to numeric order on the key bit string (an easy task in many cases), then numeric order on the entire set of records will be the same as the desired sort order. Thus we really are discussing a fairly general sorting problem.

**Figure 8.14** Basic comparator module.

To design any implementation as large as the sorting circuits we are going to examine, it is helpful to identify appropriate modular building blocks. A basic module convenient for our purposes is shown in figure 8.14. This module is a comparator and switch that takes two numbers as inputs at $A$ and $B$. The larger of these is produced at output $H$, and the smaller at output $L$. If $A$ and $B$ are the same, so are $H$ and $L$. We shall generally avoid examining the implementation of the comparator modules themselves, concentrating instead on ways of connecting them to make sorting circuits. Cost-performance trade-offs are also possible in the internal construction of the modules, of course, and these would figure in the overall cost and performance of a circuit. After an initial exploration of alternative interconnections of comparator modules, we shall look at some ways of changing the modules' specifications to make lower-cost implementations possible.

## 8.4 Implementations of Bubble Sort

The simplest strategy for sorting is the *bubble sort*, which consists of interchanging any pair of adjacent numbers that are out of order until no such pair remains. At this point, every adjacent pair, and hence the entire sequence, is in the desired order. The name comes from the fact that each number "bubbles" its way from one position to the next until it settles at its final location. This is a relatively inefficient sorting algorithm, but it is convenient for illustrative purposes; we shall have more to say about alternative sorting algorithms later. A bubble-sort circuit using our comparator module is shown in figure 8.15 for the case of sorting a sequence of eight numbers.

Each column of comparators "bubbles" to the top the maximum of all its inputs, which need not be further compared with any other numbers. The remaining numbers may still not be in order, and hence must be sorted by the remainder of the circuit, which operates on one fewer input.

A bubble-sort circuit for $N$ inputs requires

$$\sum_{i=1}^{N-1} i = \frac{(N-1)N}{2} = \Theta(N^2)$$

comparators. The longest path a signal could take from input to output goes through $2N - 3$ comparators (under what circumstances would a signal actually travel this worst-case path?), and hence the latency of this purely combinational sorter is $\Theta(N)$, giving a throughput of $\Theta(1/N)$. In order to improve this performance, we might try to use pipelining. To do this, we must put registers at appropriate places in the left-to-right flow of data to hold samples as they move through the

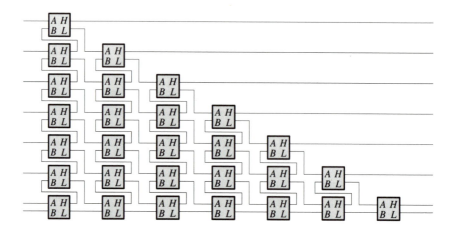

**Figure 8.15** Eight-input bubble-sort circuit.

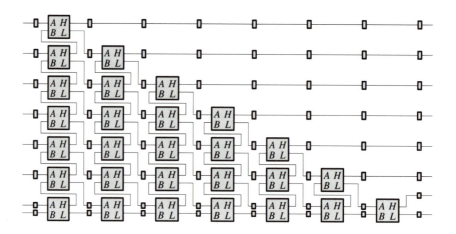

**Figure 8.16** An inferior pipelined bubble sorter.

circuit. An intuitively appealing place for these registers is between columns of comparators, as illustrated in figure 8.16. This way, as soon as one column has finished processing its inputs, another sample can be clocked in.

Note the padding along signal paths in the upper-right portion of the figure, to keep samples together as they proceed through the circuit. The speed at which we can clock data through this circuit is determined by the longest of the latencies of the combinational circuits between the banks of registers. This unfortunately is $\Theta(N)$, since we may have to wait for an input to bubble all the way from one end to the other before the outputs will all be valid. Thus, while we may be able to improve throughput by almost a factor of 2, it remains $\Theta(1/N)$. Furthermore, the latency of the circuit is now given by the clock period, which is $\Theta(N)$, times the number of stages, also $\Theta(N)$, so it has worsened to $\Theta(N^2)$. These results suggest

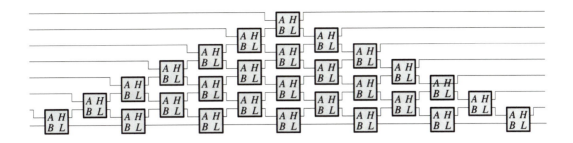

**Figure 8.17**  Redrawn eight-input bubble sorter.

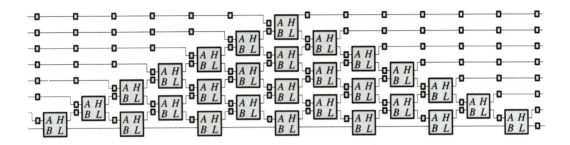

**Figure 8.18**  Improved pipelined bubble sorter.

that we have not done a good enough job of decomposing the sorter into stages. The problem is that each stage contains a long signal path, analogous to the carry chain in an adder, that slows it down. A better decomposition would have no such lateral chains to increase the latency of any stage. It is easier to visualize such a decomposition if we redraw our bubble-sort circuit so that data always flow from left to right. Figure 8.17 shows such a rearrangement of the circuit.

Identifying each vertical stripe of comparators as a stage leads to the pipeline implementation of figure 8.18. The delay in each stage has been reduced to just one comparator latency, so the throughput is now just the reciprocal of that, an improvement by a factor of $\Theta(N)$ over our previous pipelining scheme. The latency has also been improved back to $\Theta(N)$.

Figure 8.19 shows a minor additional improvement in the bubble sorter that will make it easier to discuss some further modifications. This form requires exactly the same number of comparators as before, but it has the advantage that they are organized into $N$ stages rather than the previous $2N - 3$. This does not affect the throughput of the pipelined forms, but it reduces the latency by approximately a factor of 2. The number of pipeline registers required is reduced by the same factor. The reader should verify that this arrangement still correctly sorts any sequence of input numbers.

Figure 8.19(c) shows a sorter that includes two comparator stages per pipeline stage. Such a circuit will have approximately half the throughput of the circuit in

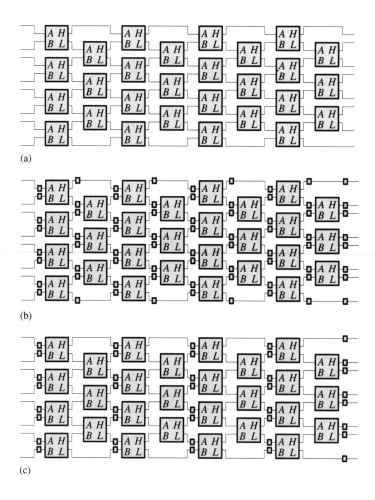

(a)

(b)

(c)

**Figure 8.19** Reorganized bubble sorters: (a) not pipelined; (b) one comparator delay per pipeline stage; (c) two comparator delays per pipeline stage.

figure 8.19(b), but it requires only half the number of pipeline registers. It also suggests an interesting implementation alternative. Since each pipeline stage is identical, we could take a piece of tracing paper on which the circuit has been drawn and roll it up into a cylinder until all the pipeline stages lie on top of each other, leading to the circuit shown in figure 8.20. In this circuit, instead of an input sample traveling through $N/2$ identical stages, it passes through the same stage $N/2$ times, at the end of which it has been fully sorted. Thus a sample to be sorted would be placed in the registers, the registers would be clocked $N/2$ times, and at the end the sorted sample could be read out of the same registers. This sequential bubble sorter requires only $N-1 = \Theta(N)$ comparators and still has $\Theta(N)$ latency, but the throughput is reduced to $\Theta(1/N)$ since only one sample can be active at a time.

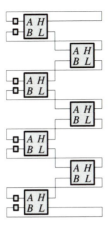

**Figure 8.20**  One-dimensional sequential bubble sorter.

This is the purest example so far of a cost-performance trade-off: A two-dimensional sorter requiring $\Theta(N^2)$ hardware can be reduced to a one-dimensional sorter requiring $\Theta(N)$ hardware at a cost of $\Theta(N)$ in throughput. If the application does not lend itself well to pipelining (for example, if there is only one sample to sort at a time), this reduction in throughput might not be a great concern, since the latency is still $\Theta(N)$; the one-dimensional implementation might then be the preferred way of building a bubble sorter.

The conversion from concurrent to sequential realization need not stop here; clearly, it is possible to sort any number of items using just one comparator and multiplexing it in sequence among all the comparisons that must be made. This reasoning leads to the "zero-dimensional" realizations shown in figure 8.21, each of which uses only one comparator module.

The elimination of all but one comparator module is accompanied by some increase in the complexity of control circuitry, which must now select in turn each pair of items to be compared and possibly interchanged. The register-and-multiplexer implementation of figure 8.21(a) includes quite a bit of extra hardware for selection of operands and distribution of results; however, most of this compli-cation can be hidden inside a RAM module that holds the items to be sorted, as shown in figure 8.21(b). This last figure also comes the closest to one final point on our spectrum of implementations: a general-purpose processor executing a sort program by operating on data stored in memory.

Since the bubble-sort algorithm requires $\Theta(N^2)$ comparisons to sort $N$ items, and the one-comparator circuit must perform all comparisons sequentially, the latency of the circuit is $\Theta(N^2)$. The circuit uses only one comparator but needs $N$ registers to hold the data, so in a very real sense it still requires $\Theta(N)$ hardware. Of course, a RAM capable of holding $N$ numbers may be considerably cheaper than a bank of $N$ comparators, so this solution may still be more economical.

Table 8.22 summarizes the characteristics of the different dimensionalities of bubble-sorter implementations we have examined so far. Choosing between two-

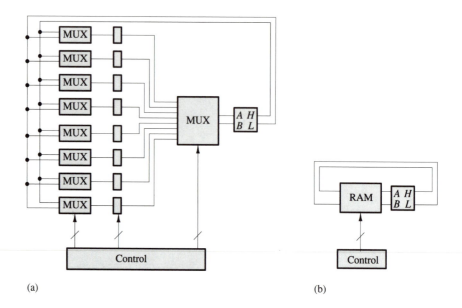

(a)                                                                 (b)

**Figure 8.21** Sorting circuits using only one comparator: (a) a circuit using multiplexers and registers; (b) a circuit using random-access memory.

**Table 8.22** Characteristics of implementations with different dimensionalities.

| Implementation | Figure | Number of comparators | Total hardware | Latency | Throughput |
|---|---|---|---|---|---|
| 2-D | 8.19(a) | $\Theta(N^2)$ | $\Theta(N^2)$ | $\Theta(N)$ | $\Theta(1/N)$ |
| 2-D pipelined | 8.19(b) | $\Theta(N^2)$ | $\Theta(N^2)$ | $\Theta(N)$ | $\Theta(1)$ |
| 1-D | 8.20 | $\Theta(N)$ | $\Theta(N)$ | $\Theta(N)$ | $\Theta(1/N)$ |
| 0-D | 8.21 | 1 | $\Theta(N)$ | $\Theta(N^2)$ | $\Theta(1/N^2)$ |

dimensional, one-dimensional, and zero-dimensional arrays of comparators is not the only degree of freedom open in designing a sorter, however; we can also pick among several ways of specifying the comparator modules themselves. Our implementations so far have assumed fully combinational implementations of the comparators, so that all input bits are presented simultaneously and all output bits become available in parallel. If the numbers to be sorted are $L$ bits long, this requires hardware of cost $\Theta(L)$ to build each comparator. Thus the true cost of the two-dimensional sorter is $\Theta(LN^2)$, a factor that becomes significant if we need to sort collections of long data records. (The latency also will increase somewhat with large $L$, since it takes longer to compare large numbers than small ones.)

An alternative way of building the comparator is to make it serial, like the serial adder discussed in chapter 7. Bits would be shifted in at the $A$ and $B$ inputs of

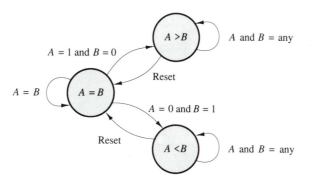

**Figure 8.23** State-transition diagram for the serial comparator.

the comparator, and the corresponding outputs shifted out at $H$ and $L$. This style requires that the comparator be able to determine the first several bits to be shifted out of $H$ and $L$ even before it has seen all the bits of the inputs $A$ and $B$. This in turn requires that the comparator decide which of $A$ and $B$ is greater with only partial knowledge of their values. This is possible if the data are shifted in most significant bit first. Then, as long as $A$ and $B$ remain identical, it does not matter which is sent to $H$ and which to $L$. As soon as a difference appears, the issue of which is larger is settled for good, and the remaining bits of $A$ and $B$ can be sent to the proper outputs. The serial comparator is thus a small sequential circuit, with an internal state recording its current belief about the relationship between $A$ and $B$. Figure 8.23 gives a state-transition diagram for the serial comparator. The only feature of this diagram not previously discussed is the provision of a reset input to return the comparator to its initial $A = B$ state before each new pair of numbers is applied at the $A$ and $B$ inputs.

Implementation of the serial comparator as a clocked sequential circuit is straight-forward; figure 8.24 shows one possible design. Note that the comparator module now has a clock input to mark the positions of successive bits in the input stream. In the diagrams to follow, the clock and reset inputs will usually not be shown explicitly; however, a common clock must be supplied to the clock input of every comparator.

Using this serial comparator module, we can implement the serial bubble sorter shown in figure 8.19(a), which accepts data input serially, most significant bit first, and supplies output data in the same format. The hardware cost of this circuit is $\Theta(N^2)$, no matter how long the items to be sorted are. To compute the latency of the circuit, we must take several factors into consideration. First of all, the period between clock pulses must be long enough to allow each bit to percolate all the way through the circuit. Since there are $N$ levels of comparators, the minimum clock period will be $\Theta(N)$. If each input number is $L$ bits long, $L$ clock periods are required to shift all input bits through the circuit. Thus the latency from when the first input bit is presented until the last output bit becomes available is $\Theta(LN)$. The throughput of the circuit is accordingly $\Theta(1/LN)$ samples per unit time.

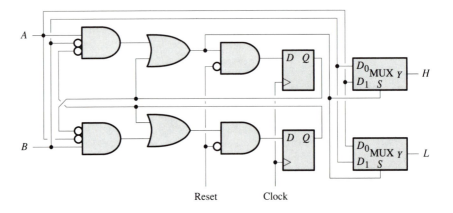

**Figure 8.24** Implementation of the serial comparator.

In order to achieve faster clock periods and hence higher performance, we can use a technique very much like pipelining, but usually called *reclocking* in the serial world. The obstacle to increasing the clock speed in figure 8.19(a) is the requirement that all input bits be able to propagate through the circuit and become valid outputs before the next clock pulse. If flip-flops were sprinkled throughout the circuit, in the manner of pipeline registers, then the distance a bit would have to travel before the next clock pulse would be reduced, and the interval between clock pulses could be shortened accordingly. This would increase the rate at which bits can be shifted through the network.

The extra hardware invested in reclocking, unlike pipelining, yields dividends in the form of both reduced latency *and* increased throughput. The circuit of figure 8.19(b) is a serial circuit with reclocking if we use serial comparators and, for each register, a single $D$ flip-flop sharing the clock line used by the comparator modules themselves. The clock period in this circuit can be reduced to a constant independent of $L$ and $N$ and dependent only on the propagation delays of individual circuit elements. Thus the latency depends only on how long it takes to shift one sample entirely through the circuit and is $\Theta(L + N)$. The throughput is simply $\Theta(1/L)$, since a new sample can start shifting through the circuit as soon as the last bit of the previous sample has gone in. (This assumes proper sequencing of resets for successive layers of comparators.) Reclocking can occur after every comparator stage, as in figure 8.19(b), or can be done at less frequent intervals, as in figure 8.19(c), depending on the chosen trade-off between cost and the magnitude of the delay.

One-dimensional layouts such as that of figure 8.20 can also be built using serial comparators, but since a comparator can only perform one comparison at a time, all the bits of a sample must be shifted through it and saved before the comparators can be reused for the next sorting step on the same sample. Thus each register in figure 8.20 must be replaced, not with one flip-flop, but with a shift register long enough to contain an entire data value, leading to an architecture like the one

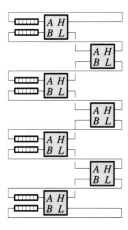

**Figure 8.25** A one-dimensional serial bubble sorter.

shown in figure 8.25.

This approach economizes on comparator hardware, relative to figure 8.20, but is likely to be significantly slower, depending on the difference in speed between parallel and serial comparators. Similarly, one could use a serial comparator in zero-dimensional architectures such as those of figure 8.21, but at this point our sense of engineering balance suggests that the comparator may have become a small enough part of the hardware cost that it is not worth seriously compromising its throughput to achieve further small economies.

Parallel and serial comparators are just two endpoints on a spectrum of implementation alternatives. Often, when a parallel circuit seems too expensive and a bit-serial implementation such as we have been discussing seems too slow, a design that handles bits shifted in in groups leads to the most desirable trade-off. For example, a serial comparator module might be designed to take two bits each of $A$ and $B$ input and supply two bits each at outputs $H$ and $L$. Such a module would use parallel logic to compare each pair of input bits and route data to the proper outputs, yet maintain state information as in the bit-serial implementation, allowing arbitrarily long input data to be handled. In real systems, two common choices for these parallel/serial implementations are *nibble-serial*, handling 4 input bits at a time, or *byte-serial*, in which 8 bits are handled at once. These particular choices are often favored by the sizes of modules available on integrated-circuit chips, the sizes of data commonly manipulated in digital systems, or both.

## 8.5 More Efficient Sorting Algorithms

Holding constant for the moment $L$, the number of bits in each input value, all the bubble-sort implementations we have discussed have cost/throughput ratios of $\Theta(N^2)$ or worse and latencies of $\Theta(N)$ or worse. Although the bubble sort is a fairly simple algorithm, these figures show that it is not particularly efficient; for example, algorithms exist that enable a sequential sorter to sort a set of $N$

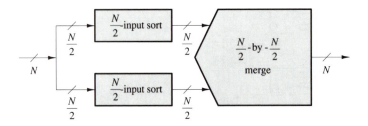

**Figure 8.26**   Recursive decomposition of an $N$-input sorter.

input values in time $\Theta(N \log N)$, rather than the $\Theta(N^2)$ time required by that configuration for a bubble sort. In this section we explore some of these algorithms, not with the idea of making a thorough study of the area, but to point out some alternatives and indicate how they can affect the design process.

The inefficiency of bubble sorting stems from the fact that, in general, every input item might have to be compared with every other input item before the whole list has been sorted. More efficient schemes avoid this by making better use of the information obtained from comparisons performed early in the sorting process. For example, in a sorting-by-merging scheme the input sample is arbitrarily divided into two smaller samples. Each subsample is then sorted (perhaps by recursively using the same sorting-by-merging approach), and the two resulting lists are then *merged* into a final sorted list. Only $N - 1$ comparisons are needed to merge two sorted sublists of size $N/2$ each, so by using the order of the sorted sublists to record the results of earlier comparisons, a number of potential comparisons between elements of the two sublists need never actually be made.

The sorting-by-merging approach can be used directly in the designs of the zero-dimensional sorters in figure 8.21, or it can be used to generate a more economical interconnection topology for a two-dimensional sorter. A useful way of deriving this topology is to do a recursive decomposition of the desired module into an interconnection of smaller modules. Using this approach, we can construct an $N$-input sorter out of two $N/2$-input sorters and a circuit capable of merging two sorted sequences of length $N/2$, as shown in figure 8.26.

As the basis of this recursive decomposition, a one-input sorter can be built trivially as a straight wire. However, the construction of merge modules must also be specified. A clever way of recursively constructing merge modules was discovered by Batcher [1968] and is depicted in figure 8.27. Proof that this method really works is not trivial; interested readers are referred to Batcher's paper. For our purposes, we simply accept it. Figure 8.28 shows merge networks of different sizes constructed according to this rule.

Using these merge networks, we can build up sorting networks as illustrated in figure 8.29. Even in these simple cases, both the total number of comparators and the number of levels of comparators through which an input signal may have to pass have been reduced relative to the bubble-sort implementation. As the number of inputs increases, the savings increase as well. In fact, an $N$-input sorter built

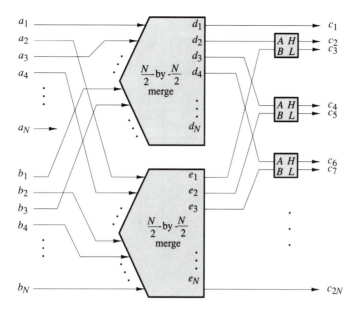

**Figure 8.27**  Recursive decomposition of an $N$-by-$N$ merger.

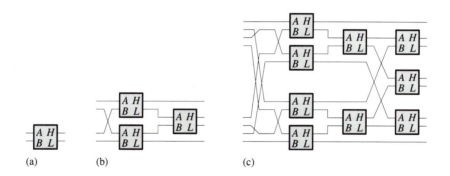

**Figure 8.28**  Merge networks: (a) 1-by-1; (b) 2-by-2; (c) 4-by-4.

in this fashion requires only $\Theta(N \log^2 N)$ comparators and has only $\Theta(\log^2 N)$ levels. This is a considerable improvement over an $N$-input bubble sorter and is, of course, still amenable to any of the pipelining and serial/parallel techniques discussed earlier. One minor sacrifice that has been made is that each level of the sorter is now different; thus there is no simple one-dimensional implementation analogous to figure 8.20.

A sorter with only one comparator can, of course, perform the same set of comparisons in sequence to sort $N$ numbers in $\Theta(N \log^2 N)$ comparisons. For this case, though, there exist better algorithms that will perform the sort in only $\Theta(N \log N)$ comparisons. Unfortunately, these algorithms cannot be used to build

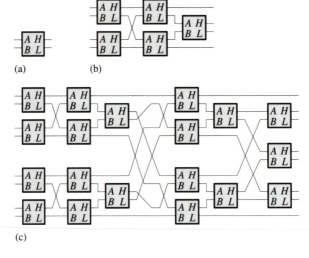

(a)     (b)

(c)

**Figure 8.29**   Sorting networks: (a) two-input; (b) four-input; (c) eight-input.

simple two-dimensional sorting networks with only $\Theta(N \log N)$ elements, because they use the sequentiality of a single processor to advantage.[2]

## 8.6  Summary

The sorter example we have used is somewhat outside the mainstream of computer architecture, although networks of this kind should become increasingly important with the increased interest in multiprocessor architectures. In developing this example, it was necessary to confront a variety of issues more or less specific to sorting. Indeed, any design problem one might pick is likely to have an associated body of specific folklore, and it is impossible to cover all of that here. Nevertheless, certain design issues are likely to arise in almost any context.

The first of these is the use of latency and throughput as performance measures, and recognition of their idiosyncrasies and limitations. Performance, as measured by these criteria, can often be traded off against cost over a wide range by varying the amount of hardware devoted to concurrent operations within a circuit. At one extreme of this spectrum lie maximally concurrent implementations, such as two-dimensional sorting networks. At the other extreme, all operations are done one after the other, sharing as much hardware as possible, much in the style of a single-sequence, general-purpose computer.

---

[2]  Ajtai, Komlos, and Szemeredi [1983] have shown how to solve this problem, constructing a network of depth $\Theta(\log N)$, containing $\Theta(N \log N)$ elements, that can sort $N$ numbers using an approach rather unlike conventional sequential sorting algorithms. The constant multiplicative factors on the size of the network are large enough to make this network larger in absolute size than the Batcher sorting network, however, except for extraordinarily large $N$.

The throughput of a concurrent circuit with several stages in series can be improved by the technique of pipelining; but this is done at the expense of additional hardware for pipeline registers. Also, several factors may limit the benefit obtainable by using pipelining. First, a poorly designed pipeline may have a latency considerably longer than that of the corresponding nonpipelined circuit. This can occur because of two kinds of mismatches: skew, which is a mismatch between the latencies along different paths in one stage of a pipeline, and variations in throughput between stages, which can force the faster stages to lie idle most of the time. Second, even a well-designed pipeline may be of limited utility if external data dependencies make it difficult to keep the pipeline full. This might well be true in many applications of our sorter example, suggesting that some other approach that saves hardware without increasing the latency too much, such as using serial comparators, might be more beneficial in this case.

A trade-off available in almost any circuit is the choice between doing each operation in a serial or parallel fashion or using a compromise such as a byte-serial implementation. This set of alternatives often offers a simple form of trade-off, in which the time required for an operation can be approximately halved by using twice as much hardware. In many cases a serial implementation uses a small fraction of the hardware required for a fully parallel implementation of an operator, thus making feasible the construction of large networks of operators, such as our sorting nets, that might otherwise be prohibitively expensive.

Finally, the performance of a circuit can often be improved, and its cost reduced as well, by using a better overall approach or algorithm (for example, merge sorting rather than bubble sorting). The improvement achievable in this fashion is independent, in principle, of that obtainable by the techniques discussed above, although the algorithm chosen will sometimes affect the applicability of these methods. At any rate, for many common problems there exist solution approaches that are more efficient than the immediately obvious algorithms.

In summary, in designing a digital-circuit implementation of an arbitrary function, an engineer should start by examining the algorithm to be used, to make sure that a strategic mistake has not been made at the top level. The engineer can then apply techniques such as replication of concurrent operators into one- or two-dimensional arrays, pipelining, and serial/parallel operator implementations to obtain a realization with acceptable performance and cost characteristics.

## 8.7 Context

The analysis of a system's performance borders on the theory of *computational complexity*, in which algorithms are analyzed to determine—quantitatively—their costs in both time and in space. There is a vast literature devoted to the subject; see, for example, Yeh [1976] for an introduction to complexity as well as several other theoretical topics of interest to the computer architect.

Pipelining is a standard topic of computer architecture texts and is treated in detail in Kogge [1981] and Stone [1987]. It will also be treated again in this text, particularly in chapter 17 which deals with pipelined processors. A category of digital design that stresses simple, synchronous, multidimensional pipelined structures is termed the *systolic array* [Kung 1982; Kung and Leiserson 1980], named by analogy to the pulsing flow patterns of the circulatory system.

Sorting networks such as those discussed in this chapter have become a topic of interest in architectural circles because of their potential applicability as flexible communication media. Their generalization as *communication networks* typically involves sorting *data packets* or *messages* rather than numbers. The comparisons are performed between an *address* portion of each message, which dictates its routing through the network. This general topic is revisited in chapter 9.

## 8.8 Problems

### Problem 8.1
Show that if $f(n)$ is $\Theta(g(n))$, then $g(n)$ is $\Theta(f(n))$.

### Problem 8.2   Order of Complexity:
Characterize each of the following functions in $\Theta(...)$ notation:

A. $N^2 + N$.

B. $3N^3$.

C. $N(N+1)/2$.

D. $N + \log N$.

### Problem 8.3
If all the operators in a pipeline require a fixed operation time and one can add arbitrarily fast buffers to the pipeline, is the steady-state throughput always equal to the reciprocal of the slowest operator's delay?

### Problem 8.4   Horner's Method:
The general polynomial evaluation

$$p(x) = a_n \cdot x^n + a_{n-1} \cdot x^{n-1} + \cdots + a_1 x + a_0$$

can be performed efficiently using *Horner's method*, that is,

$$p(x) = a_0 + x \cdot (a_1 + x \cdot (a_2 + x \cdot (a_3 + \cdots + x \cdot (a_{n-1} + x \cdot a_n)) \cdots)).$$

A convenient hardware module for evaluating polynomials using Horner's method is the *F module*, shown schematically below, which computes $F(A, B, C) = A + (B \cdot C)$.

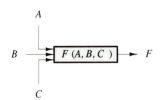

A. Several $F$ modules can be cascaded into the configuration shown below, in which the output $F$ of stage $i$ feeds the input $B$ of stage $i-1$. Assume that the $F$ modules are implemented in combinational logic.

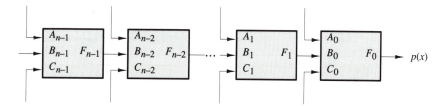

To evaluate the polynomial of the two equations above, what should be connected to the $C_i$ input of each module? What should be connected to the $A_i$ input of each module? What should be connected to input $B_{n-1}$?

B. If the latency of a combinational $F$ module is $\lambda$, what are the latency and throughput of the circuit shown above?

C. You are given a combinational multiplier with latency 100 ns, a combinational adder with latency 40 ns, and any number of clocked $D$ registers each with latency 10 ns. What is the fastest throughput attainable by a suitably pipelined $F$ module? Exhibit a design for an $F$ module that has this throughput. What is the latency of your pipelined $F$ module? Show your work in computing this latency.

D. Several pipelined $F$ modules with latency $\lambda$ and throughput $m/\lambda$ (for some positive integer $m$) are connected in a cascaded configuration like that shown above. We want to evaluate the same polynomial $p(x)$ for many different values of $x$; $x$ will vary, but the coefficients $a_0, a_1, ..., a_n$ may be thought of as constant. Show the kind of arrangement that is necessary to drive the $C_i$ inputs of the $F$ modules properly. Be specific about details like how many registers are required where.

E. What are the latency and throughput of the circuit discussed in part D? Answer in terms of $m$, $\lambda$, and $n$ (the degree of the polynomial).

F. Suppose now that you have only one pipelined $F$ module, whose output is fed back into its $B$ input, and that appropriate control and latching devices are available. Once again, as above, we want to evaluate the same polynomial $p(x)$ for many different values of $x$. Briefly outline a strategy for building a circuit that has a latency of $n\lambda$ and a throughput of $m/n\lambda$ for polynomials of degree $n$. You need not draw a circuit diagram, but do explain what provisions must be made for routing data to the proper place at the proper time.

### Problem 8.5  Circuit Synthesis of an Equation:
Consider the expression

$$\frac{(A \cdot_1 B +_1 C \cdot_2 D)}{(A \cdot_3 B +_2 C)}.$$

Assume that it is realized from three types of computational modules. The multiplier operates in 300 ns and the adder in 120 ns. The fast divider operates in 370 ns. Registers have a propagation delay of 40 ns. None of the operator modules are pipelined. Note also that since $\cdot_1$ and $\cdot_3$ compute the same function $(A \cdot B)$, we can take $\cdot_1 = \cdot_3$ and use only a single multiplier. The data-dependency graph for this circuit is as follows:

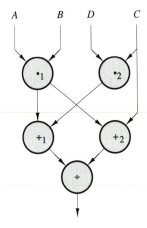

A. Show the data paths and registers to implement a pipelined circuit to compute the expression. Your circuit should have the highest throughput attainable.

B. Which paths need to be padded?

C. How often can you clock the pipeline?

D. What is the throughput?

E. Assume now that the fast divider is replaced with a slow divider that divides in 540 ns. What is the throughput? What is the latency?

F. Can you economize on registers in the slow divider circuit without compromising the throughput? Why? Show the data paths and registers in the economy model.

G. Assume now that the divider module itself is pipelined so that it has a latency of 580 ns and a throughput of 1/(290 nsec). A pipelined circuit is built to compute the expression with the maximum throughput. What will that throughput be? What will the latency time be?

### Problem 8.6  *Cartesian-to-Polar Conversion:*

An algorithm for converting a complex number $z$ from Cartesian coordinates, $z = x + jy$, to polar coordinates, $z = r(e^{j\theta})$, is

Convert($x$, $y$):
$$\theta = \arctan(x/y)$$
$$r = \sqrt{(x \cdot_1 x + y \cdot_2 y)}$$
return($\theta$, $r$)

The following operator modules are available, with the indicated execution times. You may use any quantity of these modules.

| Function performed | Execution time, ns |
|---|---|
| ADD | 50 |
| MULTIPLY | 110 |
| DIVIDE | 130 |
| SQUARE_ROOT | 80 |
| ARCTAN | 150 |

A. Draw the data-dependency graph for the Convert operation, assuming that only the above operators are available.

B. What are the latency and throughput of a maximally concurrent hardware implementation of this algorithm that uses only the above operators, input registers for $x$ and $y$, and output registers for $r$ and $\theta$? Assume that all registers have zero latency.

C. Show the data paths for a pipelined version of this algorithm that uses the same operators as shown above, but with only those extra registers required to maintain maximum throughput. What is the latency and throughput of this pipelined implementation? Once again, assume that all registers have zero latency.

### Problem 8.7  A Clipping Divider:

A position on a CRT screen can be represented as a point $(x, y)$ in a Cartesian coordinate system; line segments drawn on the screen can be represented by vectors of the form $((x_1, y_1), (x_2, y_2))$. The screen size is, of course, limited to a certain *window* characterized by maximum and minimum $X$ and $Y$ values. In order to display segments whose endpoints lie outside this window, the segments must be *clipped*; that is, new endpoints must be calculated that lie on the boundaries of the window. These endpoints must, of course, lie on the original segment, or the orientation of the segment will be changed. The clipping of a segment to fit a rectangular window can be performed in four separate operations, each of which clips the segment to one particular boundary of the window. Two of these operations will determine the intersection, if any, of the segment with vertical lines at $X_{\min}$ and $X_{\max}$, and the other two will use horizontal boundaries at $Y_{\min}$ and $Y_{\max}$. Any or all of these operations might be trivial, if the segment lies entirely on one side or the other of the designated boundary. In the particular case of a segment with both endpoints outside a boundary, the segment can be deleted.

The figure below illustrates the clipping of vectors against the "left-side" boundary. The $x$ coordinate of this line, hereinafter referred to as $X$, is thus the minimum $x$ coordinate any visible point can have. The diagram shows three vectors **A**, **B**, and **C** and the boundary $X$. Vector **A** must be deleted, and vector **C** can be left unchanged.

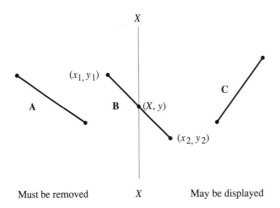

Must be removed        $X$        May be displayed

Vector **B**, however, must have its endpoint $(x_1, y_1)$ changed to $(X, y)$, where $y$ must be computed. The quantity $y$ can be computed by some formula such as

$$y = y_1 + (y_2 - y_1) \cdot \frac{X - x_1}{x_2 - x_1},$$

but there is an interesting way to do it, implemented in the C program shown below, that uses no multiplication or division (other than division by 2). This would probably not be a productive way to implement the clipping function in C, but in hardware, multiplication and division are much more expensive, and it is useful to be able to perform the function using only addition and division by 2 (which can be implemented as a simple binary shift right). The basic idea is to arrive at the answer by a process of successive approximation. Assume, without loss of generality, that $x_1 < X < x_2$. (If this is not true, either the segment does not cross the boundary or the conditions on $x_1$ and $x_2$ can be satisfied by swapping $(x_1, y_1)$ and $(x_2, y_2)$.) Then the midpoint of the line segment is easily computed by

$$(x_m, y_m) = \left( \frac{x_1 + x_2}{2}, \frac{y_1 + y_2}{2} \right).$$

Either $x_m = X$, in which case $y_m$ is the desired $y$; $x_m < X$, in which case the clipping computation can be repeated using $(x_m, y_m)$ as the left endpoint instead of $(x_1, y_1)$; or $x_m > X$, in which case the midpoint is substituted instead for the right-hand endpoint. In any case, the new line is only half as long as the current line, and this halving continues for each iteration of the algorithm. Thus, if originally $x_2 - x_1 < 2^n$, the clipping will be completed in at most $n$ iterations of the algorithm. High-performance graphics systems commonly incorporate a special-purpose unit, known as a *clipping divider*, that operates in this fashion.

Obviously, a clipping divider could be implemented in C as a simple loop, but the program below shows instead a recursive procedure Clip, which returns the integer value of $y$ given the vector $((x_1, y_1), (x_2, y_2))$ and a boundary value $X$. Clip assumes that $x_1 \leq X \leq x_2$.

```
int X, y;

int Clip(x1, y1, x2, y2);   /* The clipping procedure   */
 int x1, y1, x2, y2;
 {   int xm, ym;
     xm = (x1 + x2) / 2;
     ym = (y1 + y2) / 2;
     if (xm == X) return(ym);
     if (xm < X) return(Clip(xm, ym, x2, y2));
     else return(Clip(x1, y1, xm, ym));
 }


main()                        /* The main program        */
 {   X := 1000;
     y := Clip(840, 884, 1096, 116);
 }
```

One iteration of this function may be performed by a hardware module with the structure shown below. This "clipping-divider stage" contains three kinds of modules:

- an $(a+b)/2$ module, which is just an adder with its output shifted right one bit;

- an $a > b?$ module, which produces a 1 at its output if its $a$ input is greater than its $b$ input;

- a multiplexer module, which passes its $D_0$ inputs along to $Y$ if the $S$ input is 0, and its $D_1$ inputs otherwise.

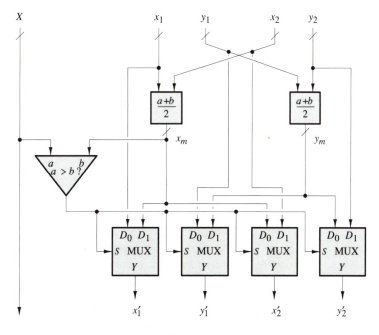

A. Assume that these are combinational (nonpipelined) modules. The propagation delay of an $(a+b)/2$ module is 90 ns, of an $a > b?$ module is 80 ns, and of a multiplexer is 30 ns. What will be the latency and throughput of the clipping-divider stage?

B. You have available a supply of registers with a propagation delay of 10 ns each. What is the maximum throughput attainable by a pipelined version of the clipping-divider stage? Give an implementation of the stage that achieves this throughput while using as few registers as possible. What is the latency of your circuit?

C. A faster version of the $a > b$? module, with a propagation delay of only 40 ns, becomes available. Is it possible to increase the throughput of your solution to that of part B by incorporating this new module? Why or why not? Is it possible to redesign your solution to part B, using the new module, so that its throughput is no less but its latency is less? If so, exhibit your design and give its latency. Continue to use as few registers as possible.

D. Consider again the combinational clipping-divider stage of part A, with the 80-ns $a > b$? module. A clipping divider can be built by providing some mechanism for feeding the $x_1'$, $y_1'$, $x_2'$, and $y_2'$ outputs back to the corresponding inputs, as shown below:

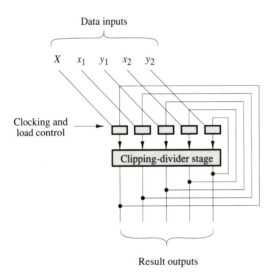

Result outputs

Although the clipping-divider stage contains no provision for making the completion check $x_m = X$, the correct output $y$ can be read off of output $y_1'$ if the circuit is simply allowed to perform a sufficient number of iterations $N$. If $x_1$ and $x_2$ are $k$-bit numbers, what is a large enough value for $N$? Using this value, what are the latency and throughput of this implementation of the clipping divider?

E. How likely would it be for the circuit of part D to work if the registers were removed from its feedback loop? What kinds of problems would arise?

F. Suppose we substitute the *pipelined* clipping-divider stage of part B into the circuit of part D. What are the latency and throughput of this configuration and what kinds of arrangements do we have to make in order to attain them? Be careful!

G. Describe how to build a clipping divider that has the same latency as the circuit in part F and the throughput you calculated in part B.

H. What is the cost of always doing $N$ iterations in the circuits of parts D and F, rather than using an explicit completion test $x_m = X$? How would you take advantage of the availability of such a completion test to improve on the circuit's performance? Would a similar approach be applicable to your solution to part G? Why or why not?

I. In order to reduce the cost of individual clipping-divider stages, we would like to implement them using serial arithmetic rather than parallel arithmetic. Should the data ($X$, $x_1$, etc.) be fed in least significant bit first or most significant bit first? What are the advantages and disadvantages of each approach for this application? Give an $\Theta(N)$-style estimate of the best latency and throughput you can expect out of a serial implementation of a clipping-divider stage, assuming $k$-bit input data. Briefly outline an implementation whose performance meets these latency and throughput specifications. How likely is this to be worth doing?

J. Can you see any way, given a large number of clipping-divider stages, to build a clipping divider with better throughput than that of part G? Explain what kind of approach could be used and what kind of throughput and latency characteristics it might have.

K. What is the running time of the procedure Clip, given particular values $x_1$ and $x_2$ for the arguments x1 and x2? Use the $\Theta(N)$ notation and give your answer in terms of $x_1$ and $x_2$. Assume the "worst case"—that is, that no fortuitous occurrence of $x_m = X$ will shortcut the computation, as it does in the example given with the definition of Clip. Explain any other assumptions you need to make.

### Problem 8.8  Cooker, Sizzler, and Grunter:

Partial Products, Inc., has hired you as its vice president in charge of marketing. Your immediate task is to determine the sale prices of three newly announced multiplier modules. The top-of-the-line Cooker is a pipelined multiplier. The Sizzler is a combinational multiplier. The Grunter is a slower sequential multiplier. Their performance figures are as follows ($T$ is some constant time interval):

|         | Throughput | Latency |
|---------|------------|---------|
| Cooker  | $1/T$      | $5T$    |
| Sizzler | $1/4T$     | $4T$    |
| Grunter | $1/32T$    | $32T$   |

Customers follow a single principle: *Buy the cheapest combination of hardware that meets my performance requirements.* These requirements may be specified as a maximum allowable latency time, a minimum acceptable throughput, or some combination of these. Customers are willing to try any paralleled or pipelined configuration of multipliers in an attempt to achieve the requisite performance. You may neglect the cost (both financial and as a decrease in performance) of any routing, latching, or other hardware needed to construct a configuration. Concentrate only on the inherent capabilities of the arrangement of multipliers itself.

It has been decided that the Cooker will sell for $1000. The following questions deal with determining the selling prices of Sizzlers and Grunters.

A. How much can you charge for Sizzlers and still sell any? That is, is there some price for Sizzlers above which any performance demands that could be met by a Sizzler could also be met by some combination of Cookers costing less? If there is no such maximum price, indicate a performance requirement that could be met by a Sizzler but not by any combination of Cookers. If there is a maximum selling price, give the price and explain your reasoning.

B. How little can you charge for Sizzlers and still sell any Cookers? In other words, is there a price for the Sizzler below which every customer would prefer to buy Sizzlers rather than a Cooker? Give and explain your answer, as above.

C. Is there a maximum price for the Grunter above which every customer would prefer to buy Cookers instead? As before, give the price, if it exists, and explain your reasoning in either case.

D. Is there a minimum price for the Grunter below which every customer would prefer to buy Grunters rather than a Cooker? Once again, give the price, if it exists, and explain your reasoning in either case.

E. Suppose that, as a customer, you have an application in which 64 pairs of numbers appear all at once, and their 64 products must be generated in as short a time as practicable. You have $1000 to spend. At what price would you consider using Sizzlers? At what price would you consider using Grunters?

### Problem 8.9 *Logarithmic Multiplier Design:*

This problem concerns the design of *logarithmic multiplier circuits* that multiply pairs of input numbers $A$ and $B$ by adding their logarithms; in other words, the circuits compute

$$A \cdot B = \log^{-1}(\log A + \log B).$$

Addition is performed by an adder module; the log and antilog operations are performed by table lookup in ROMs. Both ROMs and adder modules are combinational, and you have available a range of each type with different latencies $d$. Units with shorter latencies cost more, of course, as described below:

| Module type | Availability range of latencies, ns | Cost, $ |
|---|---|---|
| ROM | $50 \leq d \leq 500$ | $\dfrac{1000}{d} + 5$ |
| ADDER | $20 \leq d \leq 100$ | $\dfrac{500}{d} + 5$ |

Thus, for example, an adder module with a latency of 50 ns can be purchased for $15. You may assume that multiplexers and latches cost nothing and have no propagation delay.

The questions below will ask you to draw circuit diagrams of various implementations of logarithmic multipliers. In each case you need draw the *data paths only*; you need not draw any required control circuitry. However, if your data paths have control inputs whose sequencing is important to the correct operation of your circuit, be sure to explain what the proper sequencing is. In any of the questions below, you may use any quantity of ROMs, adders, latches, and multiplexers, subject only to the cost constraints stated in the question. Be sure to indicate the latency you have chosen for each ROM or adder module, and indicate for each ROM whether it is being used to look up values of the log function or the antilog function. You can use a given ROM to compute only the log function or the antilog function (ROMs big enough to hold both functions are too expensive).

A. If you may spend as much money as you like, how short can you make the latency of a logarithmic multiplier made up of the above modules? Give a circuit diagram of the *least expensive* implementation that has this latency. How much does your circuit cost?

B. What is the best throughput achievable by a circuit costing no more than $90? Show a diagram of a circuit costing $90 or less that has this throughput.

C. Given an unlimited amount of money, can you construct a logarithmic multiplier out of the components listed above, with the condition that the throughput be greater than $1/50$ ns$^{-1}$? If not, explain why not. If so, explain how you would construct such a circuit (you need not show a diagram) and *briefly* indicate how much you believe the throughput could be improved by using your approach.

D. Give a circuit diagram for a logarithmic multiplier whose throughput is at least $1/200$ ns$^{-1}$, whose latency is no greater than 400 ns, and whose cost is no greater than $40. (It is possible to solve this problem with a circuit cheaper than this; extra credit if your circuit costs less than $39.60 and still meets the performance goals.)

# 9 Communication: Issues and Structures

The hierarchical engineering approach outlined in chapter 1 structures each level of a complex digital system as a network of communicating modules, each of which performs a specified subtask. In this chapter we focus on issues and technologies relating to the communication portion of this recipe; that is, we assume preexisting *computation* modules and turn our attention to the development of similar modules for *communication*.

It should be observed that the distinction between computation and communication is largely an artifact of our engineering approach. While an OR gate is likely to be viewed as a tool for computation rather than communication, it in fact conveys information between its input and output terminals: To the extent that these are in different physical locations, the OR gate performs a communication function despite the fact that information is reorganized somewhat in the process of its transferal. Conversely, an open-collector (wired-OR) bus is characterized as a communication mechanism despite the fact that it also performs a logical function. The decisions of a digital engineer would be complicated considerably, though, if communication and logical functions had to be considered together at all levels; the choice of an ALU or ROM, for example, might reflect not only functional and timing specifications, but the physical displacement between input and output terminals. It is to avoid such complications that we usually treat the development of information and its physical relocation as separate subproblems.

## 9.1 Physical Limits and Constraints

Throughout this chapter we assume a system composed of $n$ separate computation modules, each of which takes input and produces output from time to time. Each output operation is presumed to correspond to an input operation at a different module, necessitating a communication transaction that conveys the output datum between the modules. We can identify the time taken by such a transaction as its *communication latency*, and the total rate of transactions as the *communication throughput* of the system.

We start by sketching two classes of fundamental constraints on these performance parameters of our communication system.

### 9.1.1 Physical Limits

Three of the most fundamental constraints imposed on the design of an information-processing system are taken, for the purposes of this text, as axioms of our physical universe:

- *Boundedness of information density.* We presume a physical limit on the number of bits of information that can be packed into a given volume.

- *Three-dimensionality of space.* The maximal volume of a region of space grows as the cube of its linear dimension.

- *Boundedness of the speed of information transfer.* No cause-and-effect relationship can exist between two events at different points in space unless the physical distance between the events divided by their time difference is less than the speed of light.

While these constraints may seem unrealistically removed from the world of practical engineering concerns, the parameters of modern digital technology are rapidly approaching them. The speed of light, for example, is about 1 ft/ns; this number is hardly negligible, given subnanosecond device-switching times. Indeed, loading and related physical effects inflate typical electrical communication times by a single-digit factor, allowing the communication time between a pair of components to become the limiting factor in computations involving both. While current technology may be several orders of magnitude away from basic limits on information density, that factor represents only a few years of technological progress in recent history.

One consequence of these physical constraints is that the number of bits of information that can interact in time $t$ grows as $t^3$, since at most $\Theta(t^3)$ bits can be stored within distance $\Theta(t)$ of each other. Conversely, time $\Theta(\sqrt[3]{n})$ is required for the computation of any function involving $n$ bits of information. Often this physical bound is overlooked in practical arguments. We tend to view the time taken by an $n$-bit logical OR operation, say, as $\Theta(\log n)$, since we can construct an $n$-bit OR gate as a $\Theta(\log n)$-depth tree of constant-time 2-bit gates. However, this logarithmic bound assumes that each of the communication links in the tree requires constant time—an assumption that becomes untenable for very large $n$.[1] Since we can at best pack the $\Theta(n)$ 2-bit gates into a sphere whose diameter is $\Theta(\sqrt[3]{n})$, distances and hence communication times must grow as $\sqrt[3]{n}$.

The interconnection of $n$ fixed-size modules likewise involves a $\Theta(\sqrt[3]{n})$ module-to-module communication time between at least some pairs of the modules. Of course, one reaction to this cost is to try to redistribute information in physical space so as to *localize* data that interact frequently: Ideally, the distribution of information and function among modules is such that each module actively communicates with only a few near neighbors.

---

[1] Logarithmic time cost may still be an appropriate model over practically interesting ranges of $n$ in a given application. However, it should be tempered with the realization that its assumptions break down for large $n$, yielding to a $\Theta(\sqrt[3]{n})$ asymptotic cost.

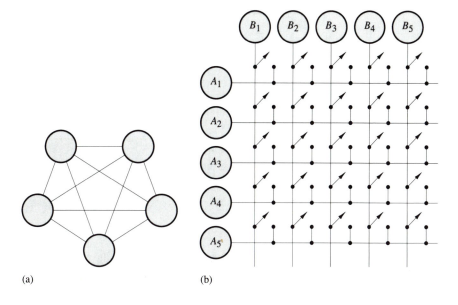

(a)                               (b)

**Figure 9.1**  Quadratic-cost communication topologies: (a) complete graph; (b) crossbar.

### 9.1.2 Communication Topology

A major factor in the communication costs of a system, both in hardware and in performance, is the topology chosen for the interconnection of modules. Often the best choice is fairly ad hoc, reflecting the intrinsic communication needs of the specific application being addressed. In other cases, the communication needs of a system are so unpredictable or poorly understood that the designer simply optimizes worst-case communication times, presumably within the constraints of a hardware budget. In this section, we sample several representative interconnect topologies commonly found in large digital systems. It should be noted that analysis of performance of communication topologies commonly assumes constant delay over communication links, even when this assumption is inconsistent with the physical realities discussed in the last subsection.

Consider the interconnection of $n$ subsystems in a *complete graph* as shown (for $n = 5$) in figure 9.1(a). In this scheme, each of the $n$ modules has a direct connection to each of the $n - 1$ remaining modules, for a total of $n(n - 1)/2$ connections. If we assume that each connection involves approximately constant hardware costs (for the receivers and drivers at each end, wiring, and logic), the cost of interconnecting $n$ modules grows as $n^2$, thus overshadowing the total cost of the modules themselves for sufficiently large $n$. The advantage of this extreme is that any module can communicate with any other module at any time, regardless of other simultaneous communications elsewhere in the system. Its disadvantage is quadratic cost, as well as the fact that the complexity of each module (that is, the number of connections to it) grows with the total system size.

A related interconnection scheme is the *crossbar* shown in figure 9.1(b). Cross-

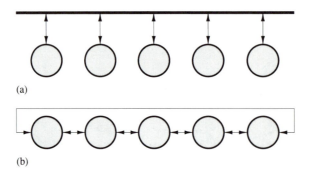

(a)

(b)

**Figure 9.2**   One-dimensional topologies: (a) shared bus; (b) store-and-forward.

bar interconnect schemes typically take the form of a two-dimensional array of switches, each capable of linking a module connected to a vertical bus to another connected to a horizontal bus. In this form, the crossbar provides interconnection paths between two sets of modules, one connected to horizontal buses and the other to vertical buses. At most one switch along any horizontal or vertical bus is enabled at any time, restricting each module to communication with at most one other module at a time. Typically the two classes of modules represent different system resources, such as processors and memories. As a special case, the two sets of modules may be identical—each module having both a horizontal and a vertical bus. Since the length of each bus (and hence the communication time) generally grows as $n$, the crossbar offers a $\Theta(n)$ latency; since it can accommodate $n$ simultaneous transactions, its throughput is constant.

Like the complete interconnect, the crossbar has a quadratic hardware-cost component since there are $n^2$ switches required for an $n$-by-$n$ crossbar. However, the quadratic cost is confined to switches and wires; the per-module cost of hardware to interface to bus lines, for example, is constant. Effective crossbar systems exploit inexpensive switch technology such as wired-OR or three-state drivers, keeping costs tractable even when scaled to reasonably large switching networks.

### Scalable-Cost Interconnect

The quadratic-cost communication approaches have the annoying feature that each module added to a system is more expensive than previously added ones, thus limiting expansion capability. In order to support configuration flexibility, and particularly growth potential, we would like to add hardware in constant-cost modules over a wide range. Ideally, each new module would include both a computational mechanism and a communication interface to the rest of the system.

Figure 9.2 shows two interconnections with the property that hardware costs scale linearly with the number of modules. Figure 9.2(a) depicts a *shared bus* scheme, in which a single communication path is used for intermodule communication among $n$ modules. The bus is basically a broadcast medium, allowing each module to transmit data to each of the remaining $n - 1$ modules. Since typical intermodule communications involve a specific pair of modules, the protocol surrounding bus usage generally dictates that all modules except the intended recipient of a datum ignore values broadcast on the bus. An example of such a protocol is described in section 9.2.

Since the bus can be carrying on at most one communication transaction at any time, it constitutes a scarce resource that must be shared among the attached modules. When several module pairs need to communicate simultaneously, an arbitration mechanism must be invoked to serialize the interactions. The time taken by each transaction—the communication *latency*—tends to increase in proportion to $n$, since physical distances (and hence communication time) scale with the number of modules. Moreover, as $n$ increases, the total communication capacity of the bus—its communication *throughput*—decreases as $1/n$, since each transaction is slower. This can become a bottleneck in large systems, since total communication throughput tends to increase with the number of modules. Thus an $n$-module shared bus offers a $\Theta(n)$ latency and $\Theta(1/n)$ throughput at $\Theta(n)$ cost.

Figure 9.2(b) shows an alternative one-dimensional communication scheme in which point-to-point connections link all $n$ modules in a linear chain.[2] Like the shared bus, this approach allows a constant-cost communication interface (supporting two connections) to be packaged with each module. Unlike the bus, it allows several—at most $\Theta(n)$—transactions to take place simultaneously; this is potentially a performance advantage. Communication between nonadjacent modules requires that data be forwarded by intermediate modules. For modules separated by $k$ intermediaries, communication requires $\Theta(k)$ steps, leading to a worst-case communication latency of $\Theta(n)$ for a chain of $n$ modules. This analysis suggests that a chain of store-and-forward modules is superior to the shared bus, offering similar, $\Theta(n)$, latency and improved throughput. However, the constant factors may distinguish strongly between the two approaches, since information propagates at electrical speeds on the bus but encounters logic delays in the store-and-forward case.

The approach of figure 9.2(b) can be generalized to several dimensions. Figure 9.3 shows two variants on the two-dimensional *mesh*, a sparsely connected network of modules, each of which supports a constant number of connections to local neighbors. Each mesh offers $\Theta(\sqrt{n})$ communication latency, since $n$ nodes can be arranged in a square array whose worst-case path involves $\Theta(\sqrt{n})$ intermediaries. Like the one-dimensional degenerate mesh of figure 9.2, the two-dimensional mesh can support $\Theta(n)$ simultaneous transactions, yielding a throughput proportional to $n$.

A three-dimensional mesh, although awkward to diagram (and similarly awkward to implement using two-dimensional media such as surfaces of silicon wafers or printed circuit boards) conforms ideally to the constraints imposed by our three-dimensional universe. One can, at least in theory, extend a three-dimensional

---

[2] The modules are shown connected in a *ring* rather than a *chain*, although this distinction is not important to our present discussion. The ring offers, among its advantages, a pleasant symmetry between the modules.

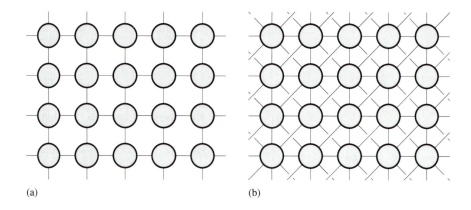

(a)                                              (b)

**Figure 9.3**  Two-dimensional mesh interconnects:  (a) four-neighbor;  (b) eight-neighbor.

mesh to arbitrary size while maintaining constant cost per node as well as constant communication time between neighbors. Of course, similar claims can be made for one- and two-dimensional meshes, but the $\Theta(n)$ and $\Theta(\sqrt{n})$ communication latencies of the lower-dimensionality meshes is inferior to the $\Theta(\sqrt[3]{n})$ latency offered by the three-dimensional mesh. Higher-dimensionality meshes cannot be arbitrarily extended without increasing the distance (and hence the time) between neighbors, owing to the speed-of-light constraints mentioned in section 9.1.1. In these respects, then, the three-dimensional mesh can be viewed as an optimal interconnect topology.[3]

### *Logarithmic Interconnect Schemes*

If speed-of-light limitations are ignored, allowing us to assume constant communication time between neighboring modules, higher-dimensionality meshes would seem to be worth considering. Indeed, a $k$-dimensional mesh requires a maximum of $\Theta(\sqrt[k]{n})$ forwarding steps to communicate between any pair out of $n$ modules, each of which has $\Theta(k)$ communication links. Of course, reconciling such networks with the constant-time assumption requires that we find a way to pack $s^k$ modules in a space $s$ on a side.

If our overriding concern is to minimize the number of forwarding steps in the worst-case path through a network of $n$ nodes, we can improve considerably on any mesh of constant dimensionality. Take, for example, the *binary tree*[4] shown

---

[3] The optimality of the three-dimensional mesh interconnect can be argued on fundamental grounds, since *any* communication network that can be implemented in our three-dimensional universe can in theory be simulated by such a mesh to within a constant factor of the network's actual real-time performance. The danger in such arguments lies in the unspecified "constant factor," which may sweep many orders of magnitude under the $\Theta(\sqrt[3]{n})$ carpet.

[4] The term *binary* here refers to the branching factor of the tree—the number of inferiors of each node—and has nothing to do with the binary number system.

*Communication: Issues and Structures*

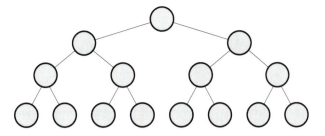

**Figure 9.4**   Binary tree interconnect.

in figure 9.4. Note that the worst-case path between a pair of nodes in the tree encounters a number of intermediary nodes that is about twice the depth of the tree, or $\Theta(\log n)$ for $n$ nodes. Thus the tree offers worst-case paths that grow logarithmically with the number of nodes, assuming constant-length paths between neighbors. Moreover, it achieves this bound with constant hardware cost per node, since the number of neighbors is constant (three for the binary case).

A drawback of tree topologies is their uneven distribution of communication traffic among the nodes. Note, for example, that about half of the node-node paths in a binary tree go through the tree's *root*, or topmost node. If every pair of nodes is equally likely to communicate, half of the communication transactions will involve the root as an intermediary; thus the root node becomes a bottleneck. The assumption that half of the tree's traffic goes through the root may be pessimistic, since it presumes little locality in the communication pattern. Nevertheless, *root congestion* exists even if we make much weaker assumptions about the portion of communication traffic involving the root.

The problem of root congestion can be avoided in a logarithmic time communication network at the cost of moderate (logarithmic) growth in node complexity with network size. The *n-cube* (or *hypercube*) topologies generalize a three-dimensional cube to arbitrarily many dimensions; figure 9.5 depicts hypercubes of one through four dimensions. Hypercubes of arbitrary dimension can be constructed by a simple induction: A 0-cube is a degenerate (single-node) network, and a binary $(n + 1)$-cube is constructed by taking two $n$-cubes and connecting corresponding nodes. Increasing the dimensionality of a binary hypercube thus doubles the number of nodes and adds 1 to the number of connections at each node. The maximal distance between nodes of a hypercube, measured by counting forwarding intermediaries, is the dimensionality of the cube; this number is consequently proportional to the logarithm of the network size. The result, again ignoring the constraints of section 9.1.1, is an $n$-node network that features $\Theta(\log n)$ communication latency at a hardware cost of $\Theta(n \log n)$.

### 9.1.3  Costs: Wires, Logic, and Time

Table 9.6 summarizes the cost and performance constraints imposed by the several sample topologies discussed in the preceding subsection. The table gives hardware

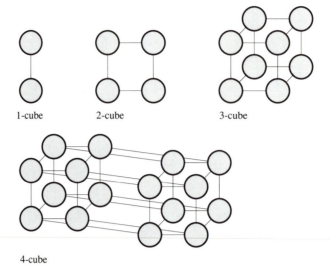

1-cube    2-cube    3-cube

4-cube

**Figure 9.5** Binary $n$-cubes.

**Table 9.6** Sample communication topology summary.

| Interconnect topology | Cost | Local traffic latency | Local traffic throughput | Distant traffic latency |
|---|---|---|---|---|
| 1-D bus | $\Theta(n)$ | $\Theta(n)$ | $\Theta(1/n)$ | $\Theta(n)$ |
| 1-D mesh (ring) | $\Theta(n)$ | $\Theta(1)$ | $\Theta(n)$ | $\Theta(n)$ |
| 2-D mesh | $\Theta(n)$ | $\Theta(1)$ | $\Theta(n)$ | $\Theta(\sqrt{n})$ |
| 3-D mesh | $\Theta(n)$ | $\Theta(1)$ | $\Theta(n)$ | $\Theta(\sqrt[3]{n})$ |
| Tree | $\Theta(n)$ | $\Theta(1)$ | $\Theta(n)$ | $\Theta(\log n)$ |
| $n$-cube | $\Theta(n \log n)$ | $\Theta(1)$ | $\Theta(n)$ | $\Theta(\log n)$ |
| Crossbar | $\Theta(n^2)$ | $\Theta(n)$ | $1$ | $\Theta(n)$ |
| Complete graph | $\Theta(n^2)$ | $\Theta(1)$ | $n$ | $\Theta(1)$ |

cost, latency, and throughput figures under strong locality assumptions (that is, for communication between adjacent nodes) and worst-case latencies for communication between remote nodes. Communication throughput involving remote nodes is omitted, since that parameter is generally dependent on application-specific details of communication patterns. Typically this throughput figure is limited by *contention* for scarce resources, such as the root-congestion problem noted for the tree topology.

Note that the figures in this table assume, as is common in such analyses, that the communication time between adjacent nodes is constant. This assumption ignores the physical limits discussed section 9.1.1, and consequently the usefulness of these performance characterizations does not extend to networks of arbitrary size. Moreover, this model discriminates against topologies (namely the bus and crossbar) that involve explicitly one-dimensional communication paths, since these are (accurately) reflected as $\Theta(n)$ latencies, whereas unspecified links (such as those of the complete graph) are optimistically assumed to have $\Theta(1)$ latencies.

Analysis at this abstract level is naive in other ways as well. Following a tradition stemming from the time when the cost of wiring was negligible compared with that of logic, the analysis ignores costs associated with the physical space occupied by signal conductors—quite likely the limiting factor in the physical realization of a communication network. Even if its nodes shrink to infinitesimal size, a tree network implemented on the surface of a silicon chip is constrained by lower bounds on the width of interconnection lines.

The characterization of communication networks by their asymptotic properties yields useful insight into their scaling behavior. As with other engineering approximations, however, the circumspect system designer must keep the limits of this abstraction in perspective.

## 9.2  Communication Buses

A common organizational approach to computers and other complex digital systems involves the centralization of all communication between major subsystems on a single shared bus.[5]  In this section we examine the technology of bus communication in moderate detail, both because of its specific importance and, more generally, to sample the engineering issues and protocols of a representative class of communication networks.

The major disadvantage of the shared bus is the poor way in which its performance scales with the size of the system—the $\Theta(n)$ latency and $\Theta(1/n)$ throughput noted earlier. To put these characteristics in perspective, however, we note that they derive primarily from the speeds at which electric signals propagate along conductors—typically fast phenomena compared with computation times. Bus-communication times can be on the order of tens of nanoseconds, providing an effective and versatile medium for interconnecting modules that take hundreds of nanoseconds to perform operations.

### 9.2.1  Circuit Nodes as Transmission Lines

A typical bus consists physically of a number of parallel conductors routed to every connected module. Although flexible ribbon cable with appropriate connectors can be used to extend the bus between modules, the most common bus-connector technology is a rigid *backplane* containing a row of multiconductor connectors whose corresponding pins are wired together as sketched in figure 9.7. System

---

[5] The single-bus approach to the architecture of computer systems was pioneered in the mid-1960s by the Digital Equipment Corporation, whose UNIBUS-based PDP-11 was elegantly simple and modular in comparison with its predecessors. The approach remains popular today.

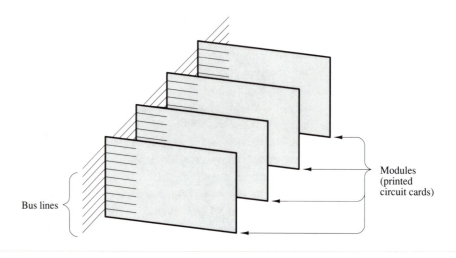

**Figure 9.7** Physical configuration of a backplane bus.

modules (typically each a printed circuit card) plug into the connectors, thereby sharing the backplane wiring.

Since each module is electrically connected to the same set of backplane wires, some logical protocol is required to avoid electrical conflicts (that is, multiple simultaneously enabled drivers); to this end, some bus conductors are dedicated to control signals, while others carry data. Bus lines may use *open-collector* technology, in which a passive pullup attached to each line provides a default value of, say, 1 and any active driver forces the value to 0, or they may depend on *three-state drivers* and a control discipline to ensure that one driver at most is active at any given time.

Unfortunately, the physical parameters of bus communication force us to deal with electrical issues hidden by the digital abstraction in ordinary logic design. The number of interconnected modules and the physical distances involved mean that considerable power must be devoted to driving bus lines and that signal propagation over bus lines must be considered as time-consuming rather than instantaneous. In effect, each bus conductor is a *transmission line* capable of propagating a wave front in each direction, at some finite speed, from the point at which it is driven. This speed, termed the *bus propagation velocity*, can approach the speed of light; typically it is on the order of fractions of an inch per nanosecond.

A variety of voltages may be seen at various points along a bus line at any time; at each point, the signal might be the superposition of several waves, perhaps moving in different directions. As a transmission line, the bus has a *characteristic impedance* that reflects its geometric properties. Impedance discontinuities along the bus—for example, at connectors or at its ends—tend to reflect some fraction of each wave front passing through them. Reflected signals contribute standing waves and other noise to the voltages seen by receiving modules, confounding the communication of data. Although discontinuities (and hence reflections) can be reduced considerably by use of *bus terminators* and careful connector design, such

*Communication: Issues and Structures*

fine tuning is tedious and expensive.

As a consequence of these complications, buses in all but the most performance-sensitive situations opt to compromise latency in favor of engineering simplicity. Worst-case latency can in theory be reduced to the time required for signal propagation over the physical length of the bus, which is the ratio of the physical bus length to the propagation velocity. However, typical bus designs accept a number interval several times this ratio—designated $t_{bus}$—as the time required for a signal asserted on some bus line by one module to become valid and stable at all other modules. This approach allows only sloppy attention to be paid to terminators and impedance matching, so that signals are reflected but there is a marked attenuation at each reflection. The theory behind choosing a conservative $t_{bus}$ is that all reflections will have been attenuated to an acceptable level after an appropriate interval, leaving a relatively clean logic level (established by the still-enabled driver) to be unambiguously read by all modules. It has the effect of allowing the complex transmission-line physics to be modeled, to a rough first approximation, as a simple rise/fall-time constant.

Despite this conservatism, however, surprises abound for the designer who is naive regarding the underlying physics of the bus. Significant noise can be introduced by *crosstalk*, or inductive effects between the parallel conductors. The accidental superposition of reflections can cause unanticipated fast voltage transients, spuriously activating edge-triggered devices. Propagation times are somewhat variable and may differ between lines of a bus, leading to *skew*: Closely timed edges may appear at a receiving module in the order opposite to that of their assertion. This can cause problems, for example, when the respective lines contain a changing data value and the clock signal to be used in loading the value.

Open-collector buses are plagued by the elusive *wired-OR glitch*, which occurs when two physically distant drivers are simultaneously pulling down a single line. The multiple drivers share the current sourced by pullups elsewhere on the line, although the current may not be split equally among them. When one driver suddenly releases the line, a voltage spike, whose magnitude is the product of the current discontinuity and the characteristic impedance of the bus, occurs at that point. The resulting "glitch" may be sufficient to appear as a momentary 1 on the line, even though the line should continue to read 0 by virtue of the other driver, which continues to pull the line down. When the glitch propagates to the other driver, it will be quenched, but modules between the two may be temporarily confused.

### 9.2.2 Bus Control and Timing Disciplines

Any of the timing disciplines discussed in section 7.1 can be adapted for use on a shared bus. Because of the complications mentioned in the last subsection, the use of an asynchronous locally timed discipline requires particular care to avoid spurious edges.[6] For this reason, the majority of buses choose a synchronous

---

[6] The *FutureBus*—IEEE 896—is an example of a bus using an ALT discipline [Borill and Theus 1984].

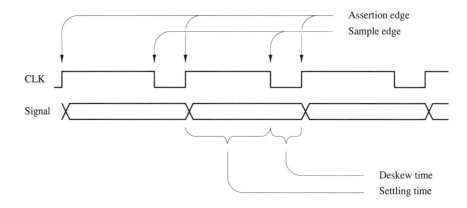

**Figure 9.8**  Clock timing on a synchronous bus.

discipline and incorporate a common clock among the control signals.

Figure 9.8 shows the nominal relationship between clock edges and signal transitions on a representative synchronous bus.[7]  A single bus line (designated CLK) carries the common clock signal and is driven by circuitry that constitutes, at least conceptually, part of the backplane itself. (Alternatively, a single module can be designated as the clock driver; the critical requirement is that there be exactly one driver.) In contrast to the synchronous clocking disciplines in chapter 7, in which only a single edge of the clock signal is used, the clocking scheme shown here uses two edges to time the transmission and reception of each signal independently. All signal lines on the bus are driven synchronously with the positive edge of CLK; this *assertion edge* marks the only times when drivers can be enabled or disabled. Signal lines are sampled (for example, clocked into registers) by each module on the opposite-polarity *sample edge*. The sample edge must follow the assertion edge by an interval greater than $t_{\text{bus}}$, to allow signal values to settle before they are sampled. The assertion edge follows the sample edge by a *deskew interval* sufficient to correct for any errors that might be introduced by differences in propagation time between the signal and clock lines.

Note that the time intervals required for settling and deskewing are in general different; this situation motivates the asymmetric clock waveform of figure 9.8. Typically, other timing parameters (such as driver propagation delay and receiver setup times) are allowed for in the clock-timing specification, so that these details need not be reconsidered in the context of each signal line.

### 9.2.3 Bus Transactions

Since most bus-based architectures are designed for configuration flexibility, locally

---

[7] These and other details in this section are based loosely on the *NuBus*, which originated at M.I.T. [Ward and Terman 1980] and evolved into the IEEE 1196 standard.

*Communication: Issues and Structures*

timed protocols are commonly used so as to accommodate modules with varying timing characteristics. As illustrated in the examples of chapter 7, the locally timed protocols involve the use of start and finish control lines to indicate the beginning and ending times of each communication transaction. We may view the two communicating modules in a transaction as having a master/slave relationship, with the master asserting the start line to initiate a transfer of data and the slave asserting finish to announce its completion. For an asynchronous bus, *edges* of the start and finish lines would signal the corresponding events. A synchronous bus would allow these lines (along with other signal lines) to be interpreted only on the sample edge of the common clock, thereby synchronizing start and finish events with the bus clock.

Most buses support several types of transactions, selected (by means of dedicated bus-control lines) by the master at the time of start. At minimum, the repertoire includes read and write transactions, whose semantics mimic the corresponding transactions with memory systems. This relationship is partly historical, in that early buses were seen primarily as communication paths to memory modules. However, the semantics associated with memory transactions extend neatly to the more general communication needs of a shared bus. Among other advantages, the availability of separate read and write transactions separates the issue of master and slave roles from the direction of information flow: The master module can cause information transfer in whatever direction it chooses.

Similarly, the notion of *address* has been inherited from semantics associated with memory systems. Each bus defines an *address space*—a range of natural (binary) numbers, each potentially associated with a unique datum. Typically the address space for a bus begins at 0 and extends through $2^k - 1$ for some $k$, where $k$-bit numbers are passed on the bus to represent addresses.

Figure 9.9 shows the lines of a typical synchronous bus and the connection of a single module. The bus contains $a$ address lines, $d$ data lines, and an unspecified number of operation lines, which carry information about the type of transaction to be performed; in addition, single-conductor start and finish lines and the centrally generated CLK signal are shown. Although the logic that interfaces the module to the bus is not shown, three-state *bus transceivers* are shown between the module's logic and bus lines. Transceivers provide a drive enable in the output direction and a buffer in the input direction, and they often contain registers to be clocked by one or the other edge of CLK, depending on the transfer direction.

Each potential slave module on a shared bus is preconditioned to respond to a particular set of addresses, with the constraint that no address be assigned to more than one slave.[8] When a master initiates a read or write operation, it broadcasts on the bus the address of the requested transfer; this address identifies both the module being addressed and a particular location within that module. A memory module with 100,000 locations might, for example, be assigned addresses between 200000 and 299999; a write to location 200037 would then change the contents of

---

[8] The preconditioning typically takes place via the setting of switches within the module itself, although more sophisticated alternatives allow the address assignments to be automatically configured.

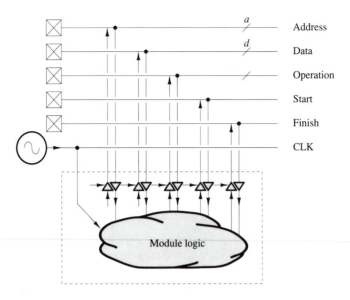

**Figure 9.9** Typical bus lines.

the thirty-eighth location within that module.

Figure 9.10 shows plausible timing of signals for a write transaction on a simple synchronous locally timed bus. We assume start and finish lines driven by the master and slave modules, respectively, as well as one or more transaction operation lines asserted by the master to signify the type of transaction (for example, read or write) it is requesting. Additional lines are dedicated to carrying address and data parameters for the transaction.

The write operation begins with the master's assertion of start simultaneously with a code signifying write on the operation lines and appropriate values on the address and data lines. The master then waits for completion of the requested transaction to be signaled via the finish line.

Each potential slave module detects the assertion of start at the sample edge following its assertion, latching the value on the address lines at that point. Each slave compares that latched address value with its assigned address range; the comparison is successful only at the addressed module. That slave reads the data lines, storing the value in the addressed location. Finally, the slave acknowledges completion of the transaction by asserting finish for a single clock cycle. On detecting the finish assertion, the master stops driving the bus lines and continues its computation. If the slave requires more time to perform its operation, it simply delays its response by an integral number of cycles.

It is noteworthy that, although address and data values are transmitted simultaneously by the master in the above scenario, the slave makes use first of the address values (to determine whether it is addressed by the transaction) and then of the data (to perform the actual operation). A common optimization of the bus architecture described above exploits this natural timing by multiplexing address

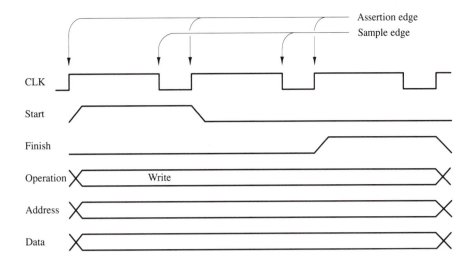

**Figure 9.10** Bus write transaction.

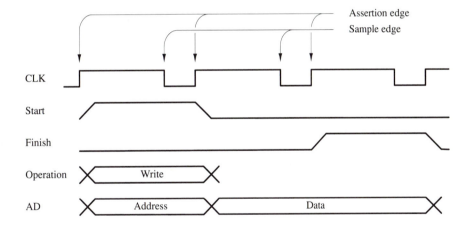

**Figure 9.11** Write transaction on a multiplexed bus.

and data, in sequence, onto a single set of lines.

Figure 9.11 shows the timing of a write transaction on a bus with multiplexed address and data lines, designated AD in the diagram. In this protocol, the address appears only during the clock cycle on which start is asserted; on subsequent cycles, the AD lines carry the value to be written. The slave will typically load the address into a register enabled by start, allowing it to remain locally available during the entire transaction. A minor variation of this protocol allows the data to be similarly asserted for only a single clock cycle, rather than requiring it to remain asserted until finish is seen by the master.

The timing of a typical read transaction on a multiplexed bus is depicted in figure

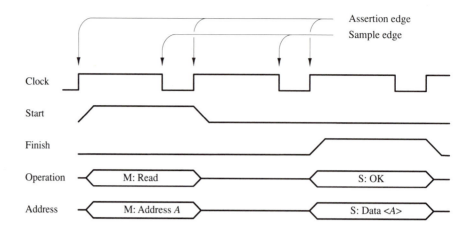

**Figure 9.12**  Read transaction on a multiplexed bus.

9.12. In contrast to the write operation, read requires that the slave drive AD with the data lines. In the course of the transaction, responsibility for driving AD thus shifts from the master (supplying the address) to the slave (supplying the contents of the addressed location). As shown in figure 9.12, there may be intervening cycles during which the bus is driven by neither master nor slave. A prefix M: or S: is used to indicate whether the master or the slave is driving the corresponding values onto the bus.

Other lines may similarly serve dual functions. The protocol of figure 9.12 shows the operation lines driven initially by the master to indicate a read operation, and subsequently by the slave (simultaneously with finish) to encode the *completion status* of the transaction. The convention suggested in this vignette allows the slave to report successful completion of the transaction (by the code OK) or an error condition (by driving the operation lines with alternative codes).

### 9.2.4  Error Conditions and Reporting

The ability of a bus slave to report other than normal execution of the requested operation contributes an important element of robustness to the communication scheme. A sophisticated master might respond to a read error from a memory (as detected perhaps by the parity mechanism described in section 2.6.1) by retrying the operation several times, in hopes that its cause was a passing transient. In the case of an error on memory write, the master might secure the data elsewhere, preventing a possibly irrecoverable loss of information.

An important class of errors, however, cannot depend on the slave for error reporting. These are cases in which the master specifies an address to which no slave responds, presumably reflecting a low-level misunderstanding between the master and the configuration of modules on the bus. In the absence of other provisions, the master would hang forever waiting for response by a nonexistent slave, generally causing an irrecoverable system crash. This situation is generally cir-

*Communication: Issues and Structures*

cumvented by circuitry that signals a *bus time-out* if a specified interval elapses between a start signal and the corresponding finish—in effect, behaving as a default slave that signals an error after the chosen time-out interval. The time-out mechanism effectively places an upper bound on the time that can be taken by a bus transaction, compromising slightly the flexibility of the locally timed bus protocol. However, it is generally a very long interval in comparison with the time allotted typical transactions, and it makes the diagnosis of a misbehaving system much more tractable.

### 9.2.5 Input/Output and Events

While the handling of read and write transactions by slave memory models is straightforward, the extension of these transactions to other devices (such as computational modules or devices performing input or output operations) requires some adaptation. A basic element of bus-based communication is the association of a bus address (and address-decoding logic) with a register, allowing it to be loaded and interrogated as a bus slave by means of write and read operations, respectively. Often, the slave bus logic causes device-specific side effects as a result of register read or write transactions, allowing the conceptual locations associated with the assigned bus addresses to have interesting semantic properties. A primitive interface to a square-root module, for example, might involve two special registers, each accessible via the bus, designated $SQRT_{in}$ and $SQRT_{out}$. The module interprets a write to $SQRT_{in}$ as a start signal, using the data written as the input to the operation. The computation might occupy a variable number of successive clock cycles, after which the result is loaded into a register for access via a subsequent bus read that addresses $SQRT_{out}$. Logic associated with the bus interface might delay response to the latter read to ensure that the most recent computation has completed; thus the bus write and read transactions not only communicate input and output data, but enforce precedence constraints as well.

There are a variety of common approaches to the interfacing of input/output devices via a shared bus. A natural first step is to associate read transactions with input operations and write transactions with output. A user terminal, for example, might be assigned the address $A$ on the bus of a computer system. Each write to address $A$ causes a character (whose code is the data written) to appear at the next screen location; each read causes the code corresponding to a character typed on the keyboard to be transferred to the master. This approach to I/O device interfacing, termed *memory-mapped I/O*, is popular in bus-based computer systems. A typical memory-mapped device associates bus addresses with one or more *device registers*, which behave as special memory locations for which read and write operations have prescribed side effects.

Memory-mapped I/O is complicated by the asynchronous timing of input/output devices, which is generally unrelated to the timing of computational modules communicating with them. The read of a user terminal module, for example, may occur when no character has been typed. Three possible reactions to this situation are

1. the slave hangs, not responding to the request (not asserting finish) until a character has been typed;

2. the slave responds immediately with a value reserved to signify "no input available," allowing the master to recognize that its request is premature; or

3. a mechanism is provided by which the master can be stimulated to perform reads only when data are actually available, so that the situation outlined above does not normally arise.

The first option ties up the entire communication system for arbitrarily long periods or, alternatively, runs afoul of the bus time-out mechanism; it is rarely used on practical buses. The second option motivates a master interested in input from an idle device to interrogate the device periodically (via bus reads) until legitimate data are returned; this practice is known as *polling*. While polling is practical in many situations, it requires continuous attention by the master and causes a certain amount of avoidable communication. Consequently, the third approach is provided for in most bus designs.

The key to avoiding polling is to provide a mechanism by which the I/O slave can notify the master that an interesting event (such as a character typed by the user) has occurred. This allows the master to devote its attention to other aspects of its operation, reading input (or writing output) only when assured by the affected device that it is appropriate to do so. (Typically this involves an interrupt mechanism, described in section 13.3.13, in the master. Bus transactions that lead to interrupts are commonly referred to as *interrupt requests*.) A wide variety of bus provisions have been developed to serve this purpose, involving dedicated lines and ad hoc protocols intimately tied to the details of host computer systems. In their most general form, the additional bus protocols support *event transactions*, in which a code associated with a particular event is either broadcast on the bus or directed to a particular module.

A particularly economical approach to event transactions, on buses that allow arbitrary modules to assume bus mastership, is simply to convey events by ordinary write operations. With this scheme, a master interested in input from a user terminal might preset a slave device register $E$ with a bus address $A$ of a device register on the master itself. The master then tends to other operations, awaiting a write operation to address $A$. When a key is struck by the user, the slave responds by executing a write operation to the address stored in its $E$ register, namely $A$. The write to $A$ has the side effect of interrupting the master's operation, causing it to interrogate the slave via a read that returns the code of the typed character.

### 9.2.6 Mastership and Arbitration

Although it is possible for a single module to be designated as the permanent bus master, modern buses allow bus mastership to change from one transaction to the next. Typically such buses treat all modules symmetrically as potential masters. Prior to each bus transaction, some form of arbitration is performed to select, from among participating modules, the master for the following transaction.

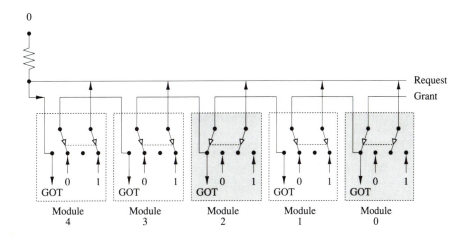

**Figure 9.13**  Daisy-chained bus arbitration.

One approach to bus arbitration is depicted in figure 9.13. The scheme dedicates two bus lines to the arbitration function: an open-collector request line and a specially wired grant line. The grant line differs from other bus lines in that it forms a *daisy chain* among the modules; rather than being wired directly to corresponding pins of each connector, it goes into each module via a grant$_{in}$ pin and out via a separate grant$_{out}$ pin. This configuration gives each module the option of intercepting the grant signal or passing it from left to right, depending on that module's role in the current arbitration contest.

The open-collector request line defaults to a value of 0, but becomes a 1 if one or more modules request the bus by driving request to 1. At the left end of the bus, request is used to drive grant, which propagates from left to right through each module until it is intercepted.

Figure 9.13 shows five modules, of which three (modules 1, 3, and 4) are requesting the bus. The arbitration logic on each module is represented as a double-pole switch. Modules not currently requesting the bus (modules 0 and 2 in the diagram) keep their switches in the left-hand position; they do not drive request and simply pass grant from left to right. Modules needing bus mastership move their switch to the right, driving request to the 1 state and intercepting the grant line by passing 0 as grant$_{out}$ regardless of the grant$_{in}$ value. The idea is that any module requesting the bus assures that request is asserted, and consequently that the leftmost end of the grant daisy chain carries a 1. Since nonrequesting modules simply pass grant to the right, the 1 will propagate to the leftmost requesting module; this module, seeing the asserted grant, will assume control of the bus for the next transaction. To ensure its sole mastership of the bus, it passes a 0 on the grant line to modules to its right.

Typically some timing constraints are necessary to ensure that the contesting modules agree on the winner, and that the new bus master does not take control until the previous transaction has been completed. The latter constraint can be satisfied by requiring all potential masters to pay attention to bus transactions initiated by other masters, keeping track (via start and finish) of whether a transaction is in progress. To ensure a consistent view of the arbitration process among modules, it is useful to constrain all participants in an arbitration contest to start simultaneously (on the same clock cycle for a synchronous bus); this can be effected, in the scheme just described, by requiring that a new request be asserted only when request was seen to carry 0 on the previous sample edge. Once a module asserts request, it is allowed to hold it until it is granted the bus. This rule yields a pattern of bus utilization in which bus requests are grouped as a sequence of distinct contests separated by at least one request = 0 cycle. Whenever request becomes 0 for a cycle, waiting masters enter the next contest by asserting request on the following assertion edge, thus preventing new contest entries during subsequent cycles. The contestants are then awarded the bus in sequence (from left to right), each releasing request (by changing its switches to the nonrequesting configuration) as it assumes bus mastership. When the last contestant has been served, the request line reverts to 0, which allows a new contest to begin as early as the following cycle. A desirable feature of this algorithm is its satisfaction of a minimal *fairness* property: No module can request the bus for a second cycle until all requesting modules have had at least one cycle. A fair bus arbitration scheme eliminates the possibility of "starvation" of a module by higher-priority modules, a characteristic pattern in heavily loaded buses whose arbitration is based on a rigid priority ordering.

Daisy-chained arbitration schemes are primitive in certain respects, but they are generally workable. A commonly cited disadvantage is their $\Theta(n)$ time penalty for $n$ contesting modules, because of the propagation delay along the daisy chain. This delay is mitigated somewhat by the ability to overlap arbitration with bus transactions: During each transaction, the mastership for the next transaction is determined. An alternative arbitration scheme dedicates a single request line to each module, connected to fast, centralized arbitration logic; this scheme can perform arbitration in a time of about $t_{\text{bus}}$. (Note that $t_{\text{bus}}$ still constitutes $\Theta(n)$ time, although it is often viewed as a constant in practice.)

The current bus arbitration scheme of choice is one requiring $\Theta(\log n)$ lines and $\Theta(t_{\text{bus}} \cdot \log n)$ time. The scheme involves assigning to each of (at most) $2^k - 1$ modules a unique $k$-bit *arbitration priority*. When an arbitration contest begins, each contesting module drives its priority onto $k$ open-collector lines, $A_{k-1} \cdots A_0$, dedicated to arbitration; the result is the bitwise logical OR of the binary priorities. As the arbitration progresses, each module monitors the arbitration lines and disables its drivers according to the following rule: Let $P_{k-1} \cdots P_0$ be the priority of a module, and let $a_{k-1} \cdots a_0$ be the binary value observed on the arbitration lines. If at any moment, for some $i$, $P_i = 0$ and $a_i = 1$, then drivers for each $P_j$, where $j < i$, are disabled. (They will be reenabled as soon as that condition no longer holds, perhaps because other modules disable their drivers as the arbitration progresses.) The effect of this rule is that the arbitration proceeds in stages from the high-order (leftmost) arbitration line to the low-order line. At each stage, the next lower bit of the winner's priority is determined and settles on the appropriate line. Since the time of each stage is bounded by $t_{\text{bus}}$, the total time

**Table 9.14** Binary-OR arbitration contest.

| Module | | | Bus |
| --- | --- | --- | --- |
| $A$ | $B$ | $C$ | values |
| 1010 | 1001 | 0110 | 1111 |
| 1000 | 1000 | 0000 | 1000 |
| 1010 | 1001 | 0000 | 1011 |
| 1010 | 1000 | 0000 | 1010 |

required is at most $k \cdot t_{bus}$.

Table 9.14 outlines an arbitration contest among three potential masters on a $k = 4$ configuration of this binary-OR scheme. The contestants have priorities 1010, 1001, and 0110, respectively, and begin arbitration by ORing these values onto the arbitration lines. After a $t_{bus}$ delay, the high-order arbitration line settles to the value of 1, where it will remain for the duration of this contest. By the above rule, module $C$ must disable its lower-order drivers, leaving it out of the competition. In the meantime, however, $C$'s highest-order 1 bit had the effect of disabling lower-order drivers in $A$ and $B$. After a second $t_{bus}$ delay, the value of $A_2$ returns to 0, whereupon $A$ and $B$ reenable their low-order drivers. It takes an additional $t_{bus}$ for $B$ to recognize the need to disable its low-order driver, which leads to a final value of 1010 on the four arbitration lines.

### 9.2.7 Block Transfers

The maximum throughput of a bus—the total number of data words it can transfer per second—is limited by the protocol overhead associated with each transaction. Each transfer requires arbitration for bus mastership, transmission of an address, and slave acknowledgment, in addition to the transfer of the actual data. Depending on details of the bus protocol, a typical transaction may take several clock cycles for a synchronous bus, or many times the $t_{bus}$ settling time on an asynchronous bus. In order to improve maximum transfer rates, some bus protocols provide for *block-transfer* transactions that effectively amortize the transaction overhead over larger data blocks.

Typically block-transfer operations provide for reads or writes to a number of consecutive locations, so that only the starting address and word count need be specified by the master. Figure 9.15 shows plausible timing for a primitive *block write* transaction. In this protocol, we assume that each word count and transfer type is associated with a distinct operation code asserted by the master at the start of the transaction; protocols may support, for example, block reads and writes of 2, 4, 8, and 16 consecutive data words.[9] We assume that the addressed slave device

---

[9] In this particular design, no provision is made for matching transfer sizes to application-related data structures. This choice reflects the view that block transfers are simply a performance improvement that

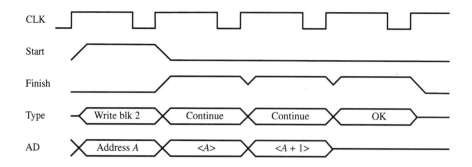

**Figure 9.15** Block-transfer write transaction.

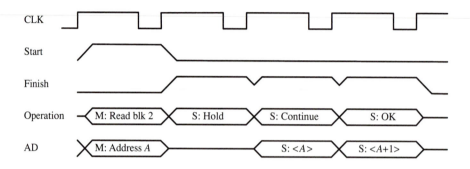

**Figure 9.16** Block-transfer read transaction.

controls the operation lines after the initial clock cycle, acknowledging its progress by driving a continue code and announcing successful completion by asserting OK. In keeping with our locally timed discipline, a hold code might be asserted by the slave to delay the transaction by one or more clock cycles, allowing it to pace the rate of incoming data to meet its needs.

The assertion of a hold code by the slave is illustrated in the context of a *block read* transaction in figure 9.16, which presumes that a clock cycle is needed between the start cycle and the first data transfer to access the data. This timing is typical of memory modules, whose access time is on the order of a clock cycle. Note that consecutive data transfers occur at the maximum bus-transfer rate of 1 word per clock cycle, also typical of memory modules, which use a variety of tricks to pipeline accesses to consecutive locations effectively.

### 9.2.8 Split-Transaction Buses

Accommodating relatively long access times on a shared bus usually requires ty-

---

is transparent at higher levels of system design; a 9-word transfer, for example, could be implemented using consecutive 8-word and 1-word transactions.

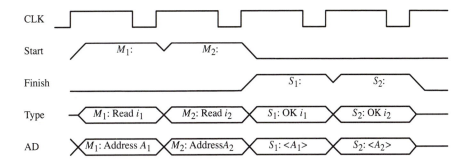

**Figure 9.17**  Split-transaction read operations.

ing up the bus, and hence the modules that share it, during the time the master is awaiting access. If a slow memory module has a 10-clock access time, for example, a read transaction might take a total of 12 or 13 cycles—the majority of which constitute idle time. To improve the efficiency of bus utilization under such circumstances, certain buses split conventional read operations into separate, lower-level request and response transactions. The intent of *split-transaction bus* designs is to relinquish the communication resource during the waiting period, allowing it to be used by other modules.

A scenario involving two read transactions between master-slave pairs $M_1$-$S_1$ and $M_2$-$S_2$ on a split-transaction bus is sketched in figure 9.17. Note that each read operation takes the form of two separate one-cycle transactions; between these transactions the bus is available for other communication. In this example, master $M_1$ initiates a read during the first cycle, immediately releasing the bus. This allows master $M_2$ to initiate another read, directed at a different slave module, during the second cycle. At this point there are two pending read transactions, a situation that is ruled out on conventional buses. On the third and fourth cycles, the addressed slaves respond with their respective data. In effect, the use of split-transaction protocols allows us to pipeline read operations over the bus.

A variety of complications must be addressed in the design of a workable split-transaction bus. Since a master is often unaware of which slave it is addressing, it is generally important that the protocols work even when several pending operations are directed at a single slave. Typically this involves pipelined operation of the slave itself. If the bus is to support flexible timing of slave responses, some additional means may be necessary to identify, in the response, the request being responded to; this might take the form of a module-identification code directing the response to a particular master. Figure 9.17 depicts such codes as $i_1$ and $i_2$ asserted on the operation lines by the respective masters during the request portion of each split transaction and reasserted by the slaves during the responses. It is noteworthy that if address and data are not multiplexed on the same lines, a split-transaction bus can accommodate *simultaneous* request and response transactions, with consequent performance improvement.

## 9.3 Serial Communication

Under many circumstances, particularly those involving nontrivial distances, it is important to minimize the number of wires between communicating modules. In general, this can be accomplished by decreasing the number of data lines, using a sequence of consecutive transactions to convey longer data words. In the limit, a single data line can be used to transmit *bit-serial data* at a corresponding degradation in communication throughput. At this extreme, separate control lines are eliminated as well; any necessary control functions are encoded into the single-bit data stream—for example, in the form of *packet headers*. This section briefly examines two popular technologies for bit-serial communication using a single signal line between communicating modules.

### 9.3.1 Asynchronous Clocking Technologies

The limitation of a single conductor between modules presents an interesting challenge in the choice of an intermodule timing discipline. Each of the timing disciplines introduced in chapter 7 seems to require a separate line to carry timing information: The synchronous (SGT and SLT) disciplines require a common clock signal, and the locally timed (SLT and ALT) disciplines require a start signal. In order to communicate using one wire it is necessary to convey a sequence of data values, along with the timing information necessary to sample it, in a single signal line. This trick of *self-clocking data* is the basis for single-line digital communication schemes.

The key to self-clocking schemes is that the communication modules must agree on a fixed clock frequency and have the ability (for example, through crystal-controlled oscillators local to each module) to independently generate local timing signals whose periods are closely matched. It remains to match the phase of the independent clocks, so that their edges coincide; if this can be done, the clock signals will be identical in each module, allowing them to be used as a common time base, as though they were generated from a single source. Given closely matched clock frequencies and a data stream whose transitions are synchronous with the remote clock, it is possible to deduce the remote-clock phase with reasonable accuracy. Once the phase relationship between the clocks is known, it needs only occasional corrections to account for *phase drift*, which is the gradual accumulation of error resulting from the inevitable slight frequency mismatch to yield a significant disparity in phases. These corrections can be made whenever a transition is seen on the data line, since such transitions are known to coincide with active transitions on the remote clock. In effect, this technique allows a replica of the remote clock to be produced locally on the basis of a known frequency and a phase deduced from data transitions. The remote-clock replica can then be used to sample the data stream at times that are "safe" with respect to the dynamic discipline, that is, at times known to be sufficiently far removed from transitions.

One technique for decoding self-clocked data is illustrated in figure 9.18. This scheme uses a local clock running at just four times the known frequency of the remote clock; thus we expect four active local-clock transitions during each *bit time* of the incoming asynchronous serial data stream. The data are sampled

*Communication: Issues and Structures*

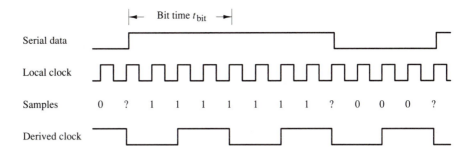

**Figure 9.18** Self-clocked data decoding.

at each local-clock cycle, generating a string of 0s and 1s that approximately characterize the sequence of input data values. Since input data transitions are asynchronous with respect to the local clock, this sampling process involves an arbitration problem and the possibility of metastable behavior. Fortunately, the sampled signals can be cleaned up by adding delays sufficient to make metastable values unlikely; we can, for example, delay the stream of sampled values by any multiple of four local-clock periods without significantly changing the algorithm used. After having been laundered, the stream of samples will show a 0 or 1, reflecting the serial input data value, except that samples taken near input transitions can choose between 0 and 1 at random.

Value changes in this sequence of samples reflect the times of active transitions of the input data to within about one local-clock period. We can thus estimate a safe sampling time as two local-clock periods (one half the bit time) beyond each such change, with assurance that these events are not within one local-clock period of an input transition. A local-clock signal (at the bit frequency) whose active edges correspond to these safe sampling times can be derived from the local clock by digital techniques such as a 2-bit counter. Occasionally clearing this counter at the time of a change in sampled data values will keep the active edges of its output near the center of each bit time.

The frequency at which such corrections are needed depends on the precision with which the local and remote clocks are coordinated; with precise frequency control, the decoder can run uncorrected for hundreds of bit times without drifting dangerously out of phase with the incoming signal. However, *some* periodic corrections must be provided for in any self-clocked data scheme, necessitating a requirement that the transmitted data have transitions at bounded intervals. Long strings of consecutive 0s, for example, must be avoided since they might allow the the derived clock to drift by a bit time or more, leading to confused interpretations of subsequent data.

Often this requirement is met by *recoding* input data so as to introduce artificial transitions. A simple example of such recoding is *Manchester encoding*, introduced in problem 6.7, in which each 0 and 1 of the input data is translated to a 01 or 10 sequence, respectively. While this inflates the number of bits by a factor of 2, it guarantees at least one transition for every two output bits. If clock corrections—

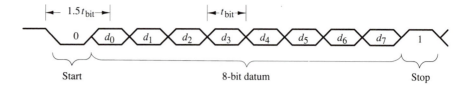

**Figure 9.19**  Asynchronous serial character transmission.

hence transitions—are needed less frequently, more efficient recoding techniques may be used.

### 9.3.2  Point-to-Point Serial Communication

A primitive form of self-clocked serial data transmission is commonly used for transmitting 8-bit character codes between terminals and computers. In order to facilitate the derivation of a clock signal, each 8-bit datum is recoded as a 10-bit sequence, as shown in figure 9.19. In addition to 8 bits of arbitrary data, the recoded sequence has a leading *start bit*, which is always a 0, and a trailing *stop bit*, which is always a 1. A module that sends and receives data in this format over a serial line is called a *universal asynchronous receiver transmitter*, or UART.

A UART typically derives a clock using techniques similar to those outlined above, taking as input a local clock that is some multiple of the nominal bit frequency. It adjusts the phase of its derived clock once per received character, at the leading edge of the start bit. Since 1 is the value read on an idle line as well as the last value transmitted as recoded data, there is guaranteed to be a $1 \rightarrow 0$ transition at the leading edge of the start bit. An idle UART, on detection of this transition, counts an interval of about 1.5 bit times using the local clock; this delay should expire near the middle of the interval assigned to the first data bit, which is sampled and stored in a register. Successive 1.0 bit time delays lead to safe sampling times for the remaining bits, which are loaded into consecutive register positions. After 8 data bits have been sampled, a complete 8-bit datum has been assembled and is transferred in parallel to other modules.

The serial line can remain in the 1 state for arbitrarily long intervals—not necessarily multiples of any clock period—between character transmission, since the clocking is resynchronized at the start bit of each character transmitted. Although the use of a continuously running local clock involves an arbitration problem at the start of each character, a UART can be designed to receive asynchronous characters *without arbitration* using approaches sketched in section 7.2.3. Under such circumstances, however, the UART finishes its receive operation asynchronously with respect to the system it is attached to, often postponing the arbitration problem to the interface between the UART and the system itself.

Many variations on this scheme are used for serial point-to-point communication. In order to improve communication throughput, *synchronous* serial schemes, in which the receiver remains synchronized to the transmitter continuously (once

*Communication: Issues and Structures*

synchrony is established), are often used to eliminate the overhead of start and stop bits.

### 9.3.3 Contention Networks

Much of the simplicity of the UART-based serial scheme derives from its dedication of an ad hoc point-to-point connection to a single unidirectional communication path. (Often such paths are bundled in pairs to allow bidirectional communication.) As a consequence, it avoids the arbitration mechanisms, addresses, and control lines that complicate the logic of backplane buses such as those sketched in section 9.2. Lest the reader draw the mistaken conclusion that these complications all derive from the parallel as opposed to serial data transfer of the bus, we provide a fleeting glimpse in this section of a popular serial-communication technology that has some of the same goals and complications as the shared bus.

Computers and input/output devices within a building are often interconnected in a *local area network* using a single signal line (often a coaxial cable) that can be driven and (simultaneously) sensed by each of the connected devices. To a good first approximation, this line can be viewed as an *open-collector bus line,* with transmission-line characteristics like those described in section 9.2.1. Like the shared bus, the cable can be used only for a single transaction at any time and is shared by a number of modules that must compete for its service. This necessitates arbitration and addressing provisions roughly comparable to those of the bus; the new complication, however, is that there are no additional signal lines to devote to these functions.

In order to convey control information, local area network protocols embed each communicated datum in a *packet* that includes both a string of bits representing the datum and a *packet header* containing an address and other control information. A sending module broadcasts such a packet on the bus, in hopes that the intended recipient will read the packet, recognize (by its embedded address) that the packet is destined for it, and assimilate the data portion of the packet appropriately. Often network transactions do work just that smoothly. Because the cable is a shared medium, though, two modules will occasionally decide to transmit packets at about the same time, causing *contention* for bus resources. If either module starts transmitting sufficiently in advance of the other, the later one will notice that the cable is busy and politely wait for an idle period to begin its packet; but if the decisions are closely timed, the modules will transmit their packets simultaneously and generate nonsense on the cable.

It is important that the random information resulting from such a conflict not be mistaken by receiving modules for legitimate packets; fortunately, this is a reasonably easy criterion to satisfy. Redundant information included in a packet header can be used to enable *error detection* with high reliability, using techniques such as those sketched in section 2.6.1. A primitive error-detection technique involves treating the packet as a series of $k$-bit binary numbers for some chosen $k$ and including the $k$-bit binary sum, or *checksum*, of these numbers in the header. If the checksum in the header of a received packet is inconsistent with the sum of the $k$-bit words as computed by the receiver, the packet is assumed to be corrupted and is ignored. If the checksum is consistent with the packet, the packet is presumed valid. Note that the choice of $k$ in this scheme effects a trade-off between communication overhead (since a $k$-bit checksum must accompany each packet) and error-detection reliability (since there is one chance in $2^k$ that a randomly garbled packet will still appear to have a valid checksum).

Since packets garbled by contention are ignored by all receivers, they must eventually be retransmitted by the transmitter. Commonly this is accomplished using a timer on the transmitting module, which causes periodic retransmission of a packet until the intended recipient acknowledges its receipt. The acknowledgment is effected by a special packet consisting of header (control) information only.

This discussion glosses over many important details of protocol, efficiency, and communication semantics that have been the object of considerable study over the past two decades. We refer the interested reader to the references in the next section for further study.

## 9.4 Context

Communication issues are fundamental to the processing of information, and many of the basic structures and constraints mentioned in this chapter recur throughout this text. It is important that the reader recognize that the several representative technologies sampled here constitute a far from complete treatment of existing communication schemes, which in turn constitute a tiny fraction of the infinite variety of untried but plausible approaches. Communication, generally recognized as the principal bottleneck faced by high-performance computers, is the central issue in much of today's research in computer architecture.

The term *bus* is applied to a wide variety of ad hoc data paths, although the emergence of shared buses as a general-purpose communication structure awaited the introduction of the UNIBUS [DEC 1972] in the late 1960s. The architecture of DEC's line of PDP-11 computers was elegantly modular compared with its predecessors, owing to its use of a single UNIBUS as the sole interconnect means between central processor, memory, and input/output subsystems. The single-bus organization remains popular today, despite the performance limitations it imposes. Further discussion of buses and bus technology can be found in Thurber et al. [1972], Sutherland and Mead [1977], Levy [1978], and Del Corso, Kirmann, and Nicoud [1986].

Local area networks serve a function similar to that of the shared bus, in the context of clusters of communicating computer systems. A major technological difference between buses and modern networks is the more flexible addressing structure of the latter, allowing networks to be interconnected via *gateways*. This element of scalability allows arbitrarily large numbers of geographically separated computers to communicate, promoting a view of them as a single *distributed system*. Relevant further reading on this topic includes Metcalf and Boggs [1976], Bertsekas and Gallager [1987], and Tanenbaum [1981].

More general communication networks have been the subject of intense study in recent years, motivated by the search for effective multiprocessor architectures;

further discussion of this topic appears in chapter 21. Many sophisticated communication networks resemble the sorting networks discussed in chapter 8, combining an array of logic switches in a way that provides flexible routing of traffic among a number of communicating modules. Examples include those of Batcher [1968] (discussed in chapter 8), the *omega networks* of Lawrie [1975], the *torus routing* of Dally [1987], and the *fat trees* of Leiserson [1984]. Further general discussion can be found in such advanced texts as Desrochers [1987], Kuck [1978], and Stone [1987].

## 9.5 Problems

### Problem 9.1
What is the relationship between the worst-case communication latencies of the four- and eight-neighbor two-dimensional meshes shown in figure 9.3?

### Problem 9.2
Show logic that can be used by module $A$ in table 9.14 for driving the four arbitration lines; you may build $A$'s priority into its design.

### Problem ★9.3
Show that, in a binary-OR arbitration scheme (see section 9.2.6), the combination of the arbitration-line logic from all the modules (taking each open-collector line as an OR gate) in table 9.14 yields a combinational circuit, that is, one without cycles. Discuss the practical significance of this observation.

### Problem 9.4   Fair Bus Arbitration:
Consider the following bus arbitration architecture:

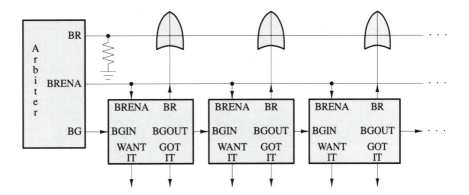

The arbiter output BRENA (bus request enable) is fed to every module's bus interface. The assertion of BRENA defines a window of time during which any interface is allowed to assert its BR (bus request) output. Specifically, a particular interface may assert BR when BRENA is asserted and up to 100 ns after it is deasserted.

Each interface's BR output is connected through a pullup to a common BR bus line, passively pulled down by a resistor, and fed to the arbiter as input. Thus BR is asserted whenever one or more interfaces assert BR. Finally, the arbiter's BG output is daisy-chained through each interface in such a fashion that the BGOUT (bus grant output) of one interface is fed to the BGIN (bus grant input) of the next.

A particular module interacts with its bus interface using a simple four-step handshake protocol on the WANT IT and GOT IT lines. When a module desires control of the bus, it asserts the WANT IT line to its bus interface. When the interface gains control of the bus, it tells the module by asserting GOT IT. The module is then free to use the bus. When finished, the module deasserts WANT IT, which causes the interface to drop GOT IT. It is assumed that a module will throttle its bus use so that WANT IT and GOT IT are both asserted for at most a limited length of time. If the module has more bus work to do, it must deassert WANT IT, wait for GOT IT to drop, and assert WANT IT again.

Each bus module's bus interface has the following circuit diagram:

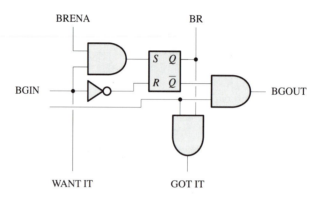

The bus arbiter is an asynchronous sequential circuit whose state-transition diagram is given below. Note that two arcs have a delay associated with them, meaning that their respective transitions occur only after the specified delay has transpired.

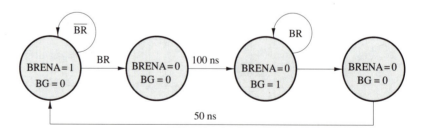

A. Draw a state-transition diagram that describes the behavior of the interface module. If we allow outputs for a given state to depend on inputs, there should be only two states, corresponding to the two states of the $R$-$S$ latch.

B. Is this bus arbitration scheme fair? Why or why not?

C. The 100-ns delay in the arbiter's transition diagram is to allow for resolution of metastable states. Give a specific example of bus timing that would cause such metastable states and improper operation if not for this delay.

D. The 50-ns delay in the arbiter's transition diagram is present because of the nonzero propagation time of the bus. Give a specific example of bus timing that would cause improper operation if not for this delay.

E. Suppose there is a significant amount of skew on the BRENA line. That is, changes in BRENA arrive significantly more quickly at some interfaces than at others. Would this cause a problem? Explain why or why not.

### *Problem ★9.5 Centralized Bus Arbitration:*

This problem involves the design of a centralized arbiter for a bus in a single-clock, synchronous system. We assume that each module has a WANT IT line, which it asserts at a rising clock edge when it wants access to the bus. All these request lines are connected to the centralized arbiter, which then outputs a separate GOT IT signal for each of the modules. On each rising clock edge, the arbiter examines its input lines and asserts only one GOT IT signal to a module that has a valid WANT IT signal. The module that receives the valid GOT IT signal is free to use the bus. When it is finished, it deasserts its WANT IT line. If other modules want access to the bus, the arbiter then asserts another GOT IT signal at the next rising clock edge. Otherwise, the arbiter deasserts all the GOT IT lines.

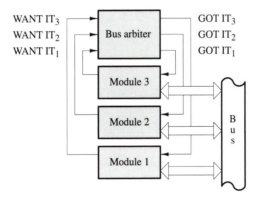

A. Can this bus arbiter be built using only (acyclic) combinational logic? Can it be built with a finite-state machine? Explain.

B. Design the simplest possible bus arbiter for three modules that satisfies the protocol above. (Show the Boolean logic equations if it is built from combinational logic; draw the state-transition diagram if it is a finite-state machine.)

C. If all three modules request access simultaneously, which module wins?

D. Describe a centralized bus arbiter strategy that would be fair to all modules.

E. How would you implement this strategy with a finite-state machine? Try to design your system to maximize the speed with which the arbiter switches control to the next module.

F. Suppose that the WANT IT requests were not synchronized to the system clock. Would this cause difficulties in your arbiter? How could you improve the arbiter performance in this case?

### Problem 9.6

Consider the role of acknowledgment packets in a contention network. Is it wise to require acknowledgment of acknowledgment packets themselves? Explain.

### Problem ⋆9.7

Suppose two modules on a contention network each retransmit at exactly 1-s intervals until an acknowledgment is received. What problem might occur if both modules decide to transmit packets at the same instant? Suggest an approach to mitigating such problems.

# 10　　Interpretation

In previous chapters, we developed a systematic technique for the implementation of finite-state-machine control circuitry for complex data paths. The FSM controller is typically implemented using a large ROM (or PLA) to generate the next-state information, leading to a view of the ROM contents as a digital *encoding* of the state-transition table of the FSM. In effect, the ROM contents specify much of the functionality of the resulting system; we can make relatively drastic changes in the system's behavior by reprogramming the ROM while preserving identical circuitry for both the data paths and control machine. The ability of this surrounding circuitry to emulate a variety of different FSMs, each dictated by a particular ROM configuration, constitutes a primitive form of *interpretation*: The circuit *interprets* an encoded representation of an abstract machine, emulating the behavior of that machine.

Interpretation is the fundamental mechanism of computers and the unifying principle of computer science. It allows us to deal with *representations* of machines rather than with the machines themselves, offering a wide range of advantages both in the implementation and in the formal analysis of machines. This chapter introduces interpreters as an engineering tool, and chapter 11 develops a first level of interpretive technology. Subsequent chapters add layers of interpretation, bringing the resulting model of computation closer to the level at which practical algorithms are conveniently expressed.

The design approaches discussed in these chapters are applicable to any digital module whose behavior is complicated enough to require a nontrivial set of internal data paths and registers and more than a simple finite-state machine to generate control signals for them.

## 10.1 Turing Machines and Computability

In order to explore a wider range of computations than those afforded by finite-state machines, the mathematician Alan Turing undertook, in the 1930s, to study a class of hypothetical machines that combine a finite-state machine with an infinite memory. The *Turing machine*, shown in figure 10.1, consists of an infinitely long tape containing a sequence of symbols from a finite alphabet and operating under the control of an FSM.

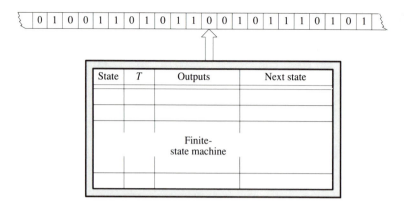

**Figure 10.1** A Turing machine.

The tape is interrogated and modified via a read/write head, which at any time is positioned at one of the infinite number of symbol positions on the tape; the symbol at the current head position provides some of the inputs dictating the FSM's next-state computation. Several FSM outputs are dedicated to tape motion, dictating that the head be moved one position to the left or right, or that it not be moved, at the completion of each FSM step.

Turing viewed the infinite tape as the machine's sole input/output organ as well as the memory for its intermediate results. The inputs for a Turing-machine computation are encoded as the initial configuration on its tape; the computation's outputs are encoded in the final tape configuration when the machine stops. Thus we may view each Turing machine $M$ as computing some function $M(T)$ of its input tape configuration $T$ and leaving the result as the final configuration of the tape. Encoding details, such as the representation of numbers and other data on the tape, are unimportant; we can assume that the tape contains binary information, with each position on the tape holding either a 0 or a 1.

Observe, however, that arbitrarily many data can be encoded on the tape. A simple example of such encoding is the representation of a pair of binary integers, $i$ and $j$, by placement of their successive bits in reverse order in alternate positions on the tape. Using this scheme, the Turing machine can read consecutive bits of $i$ by examining positions that are an even number of steps from the starting position, and consecutive bits of $j$ by examining the contents of odd positions. We shall denote a tape that encodes the independent data $i$ and $j$ in this fashion $\langle i, j \rangle$. Thus a Turing machine $M$ that performs binary addition might perform the operation $M(\langle i, j \rangle) = R$, where the resulting tape configuration $R$ contains the binary representation of $i + j$.

A major focus of the work of Turing and other pioneers of this period was the exploration of the class of computations that can be performed by Turing machines. Their approach was to study a wide variety of computation schemes and machine designs and then to devise for each a systematic way to construct a Turing machine that performed the same computation. This exercise led to a fundamental and surprising observation: *Any computation that can be performed in finitely many steps by a realizable machine of any known design, however large and complex, can be performed in finitely many steps by some Turing machine.*

In one sense, then, Turing machines are the most powerful computers we know how to build; the set of computations they can perform is identical to the set of computations that can be carried out on our most powerful supercomputers. It is important to recognize, however, that this sense of "power" completely ignores performance issues. It might literally take eons to perform on a simple Turing machine a computation that would require only seconds on a modern computer; this is one of two good reasons why Turing machines are not a viable approach to practical computation.

The second reason, of course, is the unrealizability of the Turing machine's infinite tape. It is important to understand the role of the tape in Turing's computational model: It serves simply to isolate the notion of computability from the issue of memory requirements. Since the result $R$ of a Turing-machine computation $M(T) = R$ is available on the tape only after the Turing machine stops, we are (as Turing was) interested only in computations that require finitely many steps; $M(T)$ must eventually reach a final (halting) state to present us with an answer. Since the machine can examine or modify only finitely many tape positions during these finitely many steps, it is evident that any *particular* finite computation requires only a *finite* tape of sufficient length. Thus the assertion that a given computation can be performed by a Turing machine is equivalent to the assertion that the computation can be performed on a realizable machine whose memory is sufficiently large.

The work of Turing and other mathematicians during this exciting period led to two fundamental results that serve as the foundation of the mathematics of computation. The first of these is the notion of *computability*: the distinction between functions that can be computed by some Turing machine and those that cannot. The discovery that Turing machines can perform any computation that can be executed on any known machine indicates that such computability is not narrowly related to limitations of Turing machines, but reflects computability by a much wider class of machines that includes all known computers. In fact, the widespread and unsuccessful search for realizable machines capable of a wider class of computations than those amenable to Turing machines has left as its residue an assumption that is nearly universally accepted:

. . . . . . . . . . . . . . . . . . . . . . . . . . . . . . . . . . . . . . . . . . . . . . . . . . . . . . . . . . .

***Church's thesis***    Every discrete function that can be computed by any realizable machine is computable by some Turing machine.

. . . . . . . . . . . . . . . . . . . . . . . . . . . . . . . . . . . . . . . . . . . . . . . . . . . . . . . . . . .

This assumption, named for the mathematician Alonzo Church, serves as an effective definition of *computability* for modern computer scientists. Church's thesis cannot be proved. There remains a remote possibility, however, that it might some day be disproved: Somebody could conceivably devise a computer capable of performing computations that are theoretically uncomputable on a Turing machine. But most experts are extremely skeptical about the likelihood of such a revolutionary development, leaving us reasonably secure in our acceptance of Turing-machine computability as the fundamental measure of computability.

## 10.2 Universality

The second fundamental result alluded to in the last section brings us back to the topic of *interpretation*. Recall that every Turing machine consists of an FSM coupled with a device capable of reading and writing an infinite tape; thus two distinct Turing machines differ from each other only in the structure (that is, in the state-transition diagram) of their respective FSMs. We have seen that the structure of an FSM can be represented by a ROM whose contents reflect both the assignment of particular values to state variables for each state and the computations that dictate the transitions between states. It should be plausible that the contents of such a ROM can be encoded into a finitely long string of bits that captures the entire behavior of the FSM. In effect, then, we can devise an encoding $e$ such that for any Turing machine $M$, $e(M)$ is a bit string that completely characterizes its behavior. There are many possibilities for the encoding function $e$; the interested or skeptical reader is invited to invent one.

The observation that we can encode the structure of an arbitrary Turing machine $M$ into a finite datum $e(M)$ allows us to consider computations that involve the manipulation of Turing-machine descriptions. Of particular interest is the possibility of a *universal* Turing machine $U$, whose input tape contains the description of an arbitrary Turing machine $M$ and an arbitrary input tape $T$, and which emulates the behavior of $M(T)$:

$$U(\langle e(M), T \rangle) \ = \ M(T).$$

The formalization of the universal Turing machine and the discovery that it is in fact computable (that is, the discovery that there exists a Turing machine $U$ that obeys the above specification) provided the foundation for the development of the general-purpose computer. $U$ is, in effect, an interpreter; given an encoded description $e(M)$ (its "program") and some input data $T$, it performs the computation dictated by $e(M)$.[1] The surprising power of $U$ is its ability to mimic the behavior of *any* Turing machine and hence (by Church's thesis) to perform *any* computation that can be performed by any other machine.

There are, in fact, infinitely many universal Turing machines; in addition to an obvious dependence on the particular encoding $e(M)$ used to format its input tape, there are infinitely many ways to perform any given computation. Following the discovery of the universal Turing machine, there was a flurry of activity directed toward the *simplest* universal machine. This work is noteworthy primarily because

---

[1] Since there are infinitely many choices for the encoding performed by $e$, we normally specify a particular encoding function $e_U$ for use in preparing the argument to a given machine $U$. $e_U$ in effect dictates the language interpreted by $U$.

it showed that even remarkably simple machines can offer the power of Turing universality; the simplest universal machines, although awkward to program, have FSMs with a mere handful of states.

Apart from memory limitations, every modern general-purpose computer has the power of a universal Turing machine. We are tempted to conclude from this observation that general-purpose computers differ, to a first approximation, only in their memory and performance parameters. Unfortunately, this view neglects what has become the most serious limitation on the practical assimilation of computer technology: the cost of software development and maintenance. The computer industry is under enormous pressure to decrease the cost of software; a machine's theoretical capacity to perform a given computation within a specified amount of time is of little practical interest if it requires an astronomical programming effort to translate the problem specification into a program.

This programmability constraint has had an important influence on the evolution of modern computers. It is fundamentally a human interface issue—the additional desiderata being that the structure of a computer's program reflect the programmer's conceptual structure of the problem being solved and that minor conceptual perturbations lead to minor program changes. It has stimulated the development of high-level programming languages, with the attendant implementation technologies of interpreters and compilers (which translate the programming language into a form suitable for direct interpretation by the computer). The former technology influences the computer architect toward a machine that directly interprets programs that are close to the language used by the programmer; the latter encourages machines whose programming can be readily mechanized by known algorithms.

At first glance, it seems that Turing universality might dismiss these programmability considerations, leaving us to focus on performance issues. If we provide a universal machine $U$ and programmers would prefer a more programmable machine $P$, they can, after all, program $U$ to mimic the behavior of $P$; we resort to the observation that $U(\langle e(P), T \rangle)$ is equivalent to $P(T)$. However, this layer of interpretation may cost dearly in performance: It may take 10 or 100 or 1000 computation steps of $U$ to emulate each step of $P$. Moreover, the unconstrained use of an interpretive mechanism leads to performance degradation that grows multiplicatively. If $P$ were to be used to emulate the behavior of some abstract machine $L$—for example, $e(L)$ might be a LISP interpreter emulating a LISP machine $L$—then the execution of $U(\langle e(P), \langle e(L), T \rangle \rangle)^2$ would suffer a performance overhead that is roughly the product of the overheads imposed by either interpretation alone.

Interpretation is the fundamental mechanism of computers, and ultimately the source of their power. Its major practical cost is performance (specifically, computation time), which limits its use, in modern computer systems, to a few interpretive "layers." The next block of chapters are devoted to the lowest interpretive layers of modern machines.

---

[2] In the general case, the encoding functions required by $P$ and $U$ will differ; for this reason, $U(\langle e_U(P), \langle e_P(L), T \rangle \rangle)$ is a more realistic model of two-level interpretation.

## 10.3 Uncomputable Functions

The foregoing sections have circumscribed the class of "computable functions"; ambitious readers may find themselves searching for an example of a function that is not computable. We provide in this section a fleeting glimpse of such a function.

Recall that a Turing-machine computation $M(T)$ proceeds for finitely many steps, after which it halts with its result $R$ left on the tape. The machine's *failure* to perform the desired computation may take either of two forms: It may halt with a wrong final tape configuration, or it may go on "computing" forever. It is easy to imagine a faulty machine that exhibits the latter behavior; it might, for example, simply move the tape left on even steps and right on odd ones.

There are legitimate computer programs whose termination is not obvious. Imagine a program $F$ to disprove Fermat's last theorem, the famous unproved conjecture that for no integers $n > 2$, $a$, $b$, and $c$ does the relation $a^n = b^n + c^n$ hold. The program might proceed by systematically enumerating values of $a$, $b$, $c$, and $n$ and evaluating the relation, halting when a solution is found. Knowing whether that program (or an equivalent Turing machine) halts is tantamount to proving or disproving Fermat's theorem: $F$ halts if and only if Fermat's last theorem is false.

It would be convenient for the resolution of this and other haunting questions if we had a systematic way of determining whether or not a given computation would terminate. We can, of course, simply run the program. If it halts, we have an answer to our question; but if it doesn't, we end up waiting forever. Thus our problem boils down to a reliable way of determining that a given program (or Turing machine) will *not* halt.

Using the notation of the last section, we might imagine a Turing machine $H$ that makes this determination. Given an input tape $\langle e(M), T \rangle$, it halts with a 1 at the final head position if $M(T)$ would terminate and a 0 at the final head position if the computation $M(T)$ would go on forever. An implementation of $H$ constitutes a solution to the *halting problem*: an algorithm for reliably determining whether an arbitrary computation will terminate. We can summarize $H$'s behavior as follows: For every Turing machine $M$ and input tape configuration $T$,

$$H(\langle e(M), T \rangle) = 1 \quad \text{if } M(T) \text{ terminates};$$
$$= 0 \quad \text{if } M(T) \text{ runs forever}.$$

$H$ is, alas, the best known of the uncomputable functions; we cannot, in principle, build a Turing machine or write a program that satisfies the above criteria.

The elegant proof of the unrealizability of $H$ proceeds as follows. Assume that we have a Turing machine (or, equivalently, a program) $H$ that behaves according to the above specification. Then we can certainly define a realizable machine $G$ such that for any Turing machine $F$, $G(e(F))$ halts if $H(\langle e(F), e(F) \rangle) = 0$ and runs forever if $H(\langle e(F), e(F) \rangle) = 1$. Since the execution of $G$ involves the computation of $H$, we might construct the machine $G$ by using a copy of $H$ as a component. Since $G$ is clearly realizable if $H$ is, it is (by Church's thesis) realizable by a Turing machine; thus, if we assume that the Turing machine $H$ exists, then $G$ exists also.

**Table 10.2** Abstractions.

| Abstraction | Language defined | Form of implementation |
|---|---|---|
| Digital abstraction | Logic diagrams | Electronic circuits |
| Finite-state machine | State-transition diagrams | Logic diagrams |
| Microcoding | Microcode | Logic diagrams |
| Machine language | Machine language | Microcode |
| LISP | LISP programs | Machine language |

Now consider the computation of $H(\langle e(G), e(G)\rangle)$. If $H(\langle e(G), e(G)\rangle)$ returns the value 1, this implies (by the specification of $H$) that the computation $G(e(G))$ halts; but our construction of $G$ ensures that $G(e(G))$ halts only if $H(\langle e(G), e(G)\rangle)$ returns 0. Alternatively, if $H(\langle e(G), e(G)\rangle)$ returns the value 0, then according to $H$'s definition, $G(e(G))$ runs forever; but $G$ is built to run forever only if $H(\langle e(G), e(G)\rangle)$ returns 1. Thus our pathological machine $G$ guarantees that either result $H$ may give for the input tape $\langle e(G), e(G)\rangle$ is wrong; since $H$ is specified to work for *any* encoded machine description and input tape, we conclude that no realizable $H$ can meet the above specifications.

To the uninitiated, the above proof may seem to be black magic. It is, in fact, an example of a *diagonal construction*, a term derived from a view of $H$ as an infinite, two-dimensional table whose $[i, j]$th entry is the value of $H(\langle i, j\rangle)$. The pathological $G$ is constructed in such a way as to differ from each function whose code is represented in the table, in that it deliberately violates the behavior predicted by $H$ along the diagonal of the table.

## 10.4 Interpretation versus Compilation

There are, generally speaking, two ways in which one abstraction can be built upon another: *interpretation* and *compilation*. To explore this distinction, it is useful to review a spectrum of abstractions involved in the execution of a program written in a high-level language. Table 10.2 shows the layers typical of the execution of a LISP program on a microcoded computer, with each abstraction seen as defining a *language* for describing systems and with each such language having a separate implementation. (Microcode is an interpretation-based technique often used in building processors; it is discussed in chapters 11 and 12.)

Along with defining a language, each abstraction can be viewed as defining an *abstract machine* with respect to which the semantics of the language can be understood. For example, the language of logic diagrams is understood as providing the interconnection rules for an abstract machine that pushes 0s and 1s through wires and through certain primitive operators such as AND gates. It matters not whether the logic diagram is implemented by electronic circuits or fluidics or simulation on a blackboard; the semantics of the logic diagram remain unchanged as long as the abstract machine is implemented correctly. Similarly, the language of microcode is understood with respect to an abstract machine that includes objects such as registers and an ALU. These parts can be implemented in many different ways—for example, using parallel or serial arithmetic—without changing the semantics of the microcode language.

*Interpretation* is an implementation technique in which the components of the abstract machine are built directly in terms of the underlying abstraction. This is the principal implementation technique that we have explored thus far. Our study of the digital abstraction furnishes one example: Standard electronic circuits are designed for each primitive logic gate type, and these circuits are then connected together as dictated by the logic diagram. Another good example is presented in the next chapter: The abstract machine in this case is the microarchitecture, which is implemented directly as a logic diagram.

*Compilation* is a less direct implementation technique. In compilation, a system $S_A$ described in the language of some abstraction $A$ (known as the *source* language) is implemented by *translating* it into a system $S_B$ described in the language of another (normally lower-level) abstraction $B$ (known as the *object* or *target* language). System $S_B$ is required to exhibit the same external behavior as $S_A$, but its internal organization may differ. In implementing the digital abstraction by compilation, a logic diagram would be translated into an equivalent electronic circuit (assuming a suitable mapping between analog and digital signals at the inputs and outputs). This might produce much the same electronic circuit as interpretation, but the compiled circuit could take advantage of patterns of interconnection in the logic diagram, such as $\overline{A \cdot B + C \cdot D}$, that can be implemented especially efficiently in the underlying abstraction. Compilation could be applied to microcode by translating a microprogram directly into a logic diagram that performs the specified computation, rather than building a universal interpreter (the microarchitecture) and simply inserting the microprogram into a ROM.

As these examples suggest, compilation offers the prospect of a more efficient implementation than may be available through interpretation, because each implementation can be custom-tailored, rather than being built on a standard abstract machine implementation that must serve all purposes. However, there are some other considerations:

- If the system is changed frequently, a compiled implementation may be less convenient since it is harder to change. For example, an interpreted microprogram can be changed simply by replacing a ROM, but a microprogram compiled into a logic diagram would have to be recompiled into a new logic diagram, which would then have to be physically laid out and built.

- If compilation is to achieve substantial efficiency gains over interpretation, the structure of the target language must be tractable enough that the compilation algorithm can be designed with a reasonable amount of effort. In other words, good algorithms for system design must be available in the target language. A target language that is loaded with exceptions, global interactions, and limiting cases is more difficult to compile to. This partly explains our use of interpretation for such relatively difficult-to-compile-to target languages as electronic circuits and logic diagrams.

The advantages of building complex systems using multiple levels of abstraction are considerable, but it is desirable to avoid the multiplicative performance penalties of layer upon layer of interpretation by using compilation wherever feasible. In practice, this means that the layers of abstraction should be designed so as to reach, at the lowest practicable level, a layer that is a suitable target for compilation. In most computer systems, that layer is the *machine language* of the computer (the subject of subsequent chapters). Thus we find that machine language is used in a qualitatively different way from our lower levels of abstraction: While each of our lower levels is intended for use by humans in designing an interpreter for the next-higher level, machine language is primarily a target language for compilers.

## 10.5 Context

Turing machines represent a *model of computation*, an abstract mechanism capable of effecting a general class of computations. While most models of computation are practically unrealistic (as with the infinite tape of the Turing machine), each presents a unique view of the computation process, together with a scheme for representing the computations to be performed. Just as interpretation is the fundamental mechanism of computers, models of computation are the intellectual bases for computer architecture.

Indeed, Turing machines shared the cradle of modern computer science with a number of other formalisms whose roles as models of computation have been notable. The *lambda calculi* of Alonzo Church [1941] continue to serve as the primary model for *applicative* or *functional programming*, terms applied to computation schemes whose primitives exclude side effects (such as assignment) and the notion of state. Church's system introduced an influential notation (the *lambda expressions* of LISP) as well as a simple syntactic paradigm that remains the standard for the semantics of variables in lexically scoped languages. Together with the related *combinatory logic*, the lambda calculus provides an implementation model for computation schemes that iteratively apply *reduction rules* to a program structure to deduce an irreducible result.

The production systems of Emil Post and others involve pattern matching and replacement rules applied to strings, providing elements of the models that underlie several string-manipulation languages and computer systems whose major activity involves making inferences using a set of rules. The *theory of recursive functions* developed by Kleene [1952] and others provides a linguistic basis, involving simple primitives and recursion, for the definition of every computable function. A number of other models of computation have been influential in computer science generally, and the conception and analysis of alternative models continues to be a driving force in computer architecture. Several of these are mentioned in chapter 21. Further information on this fascinating area can be found in Minsky [1967], a readable book whose depth and perspective ideally suit the student of computer architecture. Definitive treatments of particular models, such as Rogers [1967] on recursive function theory and Curry and Feys [1974] or Hindley and Seldin [1986] on combinatory logic and lambda calculus, are authoritative but dense.

## 10.6 Problems

### Problem ⋆10.1

Design a Turing machine that searches for (and stops at) the fifth 1 to the right of the initial head position. How many states are required for its FSM? How many states are required to revise your Turing machine so that it finds the $n$th 1 to the right of the initial position? Explain.

### Problem ⋆10.2

Design a Turing machine that searches for (and stops at) the $n$th 1 to the right of its initial head position, where $n$ is the exact number of 1s written to the *left* of the initial position. Assume that the tape to the left of the $n$ 1s contains 0s and that you may write on any portion of the tape you like.

### Problem ⋆10.3

Show that there are infinitely many correct answers to problem 10.2.

### Problem 10.4

Consider an $n$-state Turing machine that writes $k$ 1s on an initially blank tape (one with all 0s) and then halts. Is it possible for $k$ to be larger than $n$? Explain.

### Problem ⋆10.5

Describe a computation that can be performed on a Turing machine but not on any FSM.

### Problem ⋆10.6

Let $F$ be a Turing machine that computes some function $f(x)$; that is, given an initial tape containing the binary number $x$, $F$ halts with the binary number $f(x)$ on the tape. Let $G$ be a Turing machine that similarly computes the function $g(x)$. Give a careful argument, using Church's thesis, that there exists a Turing machine that computes $h(x) = f(g(x))$.

### Problem ⋆10.7

Prove the hypothesis of problem 10.6 *without* using Church's thesis. (*Hint:* Develop a general technique for composing machines of the form described in problem 10.6.)

### Problem ⋆10.8

Describe a scheme for encoding the state transitions of an arbitrary Turing machine as unique nonnegative integers.

### Problem ⋆⋆10.9

Consider a machine $HB$ that is similar to $H$, as described in section 10.3, except that it determines whether a Turing machine $M$ will halt if given a *blank* input tape rather than an arbitrary one. More precisely, given an initial tape containing $e(M)$, $HB$ halts on a 1 if $M$ would run forever on a blank tape and on a 0 if $M$ would eventually stop. Is there a Turing machine that conforms to the specifications for $HB$? Prove your result.

## Problem 10.10

Ben Bitdiddle's proposed Ph.D. thesis involves writing a program to compute a function $f(x)$ on a Cray supercomputer. Ben's advisor points out that $f$ cannot be computed on any Turing machine. Should Ben care? Why or why not?

## Problem 10.11

Discouraged by your answer to the last question, Ben has turned his attention to an alternative thesis topic. He now proposes to invent the universal FSM, which will be to FSMs what a universal Turing machine is to Turing machines. Ben's idea is to build an FSM that can be fed a sequence of inputs describing any other FSM and the inputs to that FSM. The universal FSM would then emulate the behavior of the described FSM on the specified inputs. Is Ben's idea workable? Why or why not?

## Problem 10.12

Let $T$ be the set of mathematical functions that can be computed by Turing machines, and let $F$ be the set of mathematical functions that can be computed by finite-state machines. Which, if any, of the following statements are true:

1. $F$ is a subset of $T$.
2. $F$ and $T$ are identical.
3. $T$ is a subset of $F$.

## Problem ⋆10.13

Syl Valle, a California entrepreneur, is promoting the idea of the Super Turing Machine (STM), which has two infinite tapes rather than one. Which, if any, of the following statements are true?

1. An STM has greater logical power than a regular Turing machine; that is, it can perform additional computations.
2. An STM has practical advantages over a regular Turing machine; that is, it provides a realistic solution to a greater number of practical problems.
3. An STM has neither formal nor practical advantages over a regular Turing machine.

# 11 Microinterpreter Architecture

This chapter describes a particular kind of architecture often used in digital systems designed to serve as the central processing unit (CPU) of general-purpose computers. The CPU is an interpreter for a *machine language* consisting of sequences of binary-coded *machine instructions* that constitute programs to be executed.

Our approach to the implementation of the machine-language interpreter is to construct a much simpler interpreter for a primitive language (called *microcode*) and then to program the higher-level interpreter in this primitive language. The execution of a machine-language program will then involve at least two levels of interpretation, since the interpretation of each machine-language instruction by the CPU will, in general, require the interpretation of several *microinstructions* by the microinterpreter within the CPU.

While this extra level of interpretation (as compared with the direct interpretation of machine language by hardware) typically entails some performance cost, it has important engineering advantages. First, it isolates the machine-language *design* and *implementation* issues, in that a wide range of machine-language instruction-set designs can be implemented using the same microinterpreter circuitry with differing microcode. Second, it provides flexibility, in that many high-level features can be incorporated into the machine-language instruction set at low cost. This economic advantage is one of the attractions of interpretation as an engineering technique: Beyond the cost of the interpreter itself, the marginal cost of adding a new function to the system is simply the cost of the memory necessary to hold the additional microcode that implements the function. This is typically much cheaper than adding hardware to implement the function directly.

Although the microarchitecture developed in this chapter is primarily an interpretive mechanism, we shall exploit some primitive compilation techniques in its use. In particular, certain design decisions regarding the microinterpreter that favor simple implementation at the cost of awkward microcode become acceptable if the resulting awkwardness is largely hidden from the microprogrammer by some low-level translation apparatus. To this end, we assume that a *microassembler* program is used to translate microprograms from a human-palatable form to the binary patterns that are directly interpreted by the microarchitecture.

The specific microarchitecture presented here is that of the MAYBE computer, a machine designed to illustrate representative technology and architectural approaches while remaining simple enough for student construction.

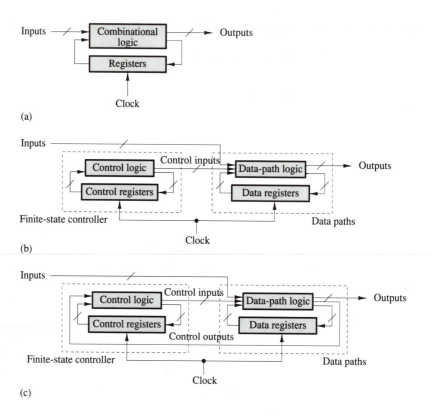

(a)

(b)

(c)

**Figure 11.1**  Models of processor architecture: (a) clocked sequential machine model; (b) finite-state controller plus data paths; (c) finite-state controller with control outputs.

## 11.1 Data Paths versus Control

We may think of a processor as being composed of a set of *registers* holding information on the current state of the processor and some combinational logic for transforming and moving data between registers, as shown schematically in figure 11.1(a). This is just the clocked sequential circuit model first discussed in chapter 6. Most processors, and most of the processors that we shall consider, are, in fact, clocked sequential machines with a single clock.

To gain further understanding of microcoded processor architecture, we must look for more structure than this. Some of the registers in a processor are usually reserved to hold intermediate data values relevant to computations being performed; we call these *data registers*. Together with the logic for combining these data values with each other and with input values to generate output values and new intermediate values, these registers comprise the *data paths* of the processor (as discussed in section 7.3), themselves a clocked sequential machine. The sequence of operations performed by the machine is determined by *control inputs* from another sequential machine, whose state is held in a set of *control registers* and whose output and next state are computed by some *control logic*. A processor of

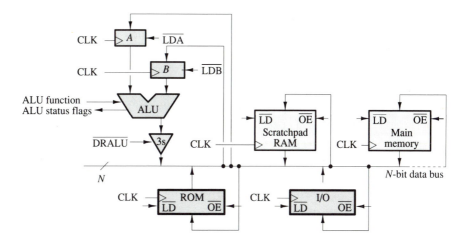

**Figure 11.2**  Microinterpreter data paths.

this sort is depicted in figure 11.1(b). Note that, in general, the control registers are clocked by the same signal as the data registers.

A machine of this type is capable of arbitrarily complex behavior, depending on the intricacy of the data paths and control machine. Note, however, that the control machine has no inputs other than the clock. Thus, although its behavior may be arbitrarily complex, it cannot be affected by anything in the data paths. In general, a processor needs to modify the sequence of operations it will perform according to the data being operated on; for example, some set of operations may be repeated until the value of some data register reaches zero. For this reason, a processor usually has *control outputs* from the data paths that can affect the sequence of states traversed by the control machine.

## 11.2  A Basic Data-Path Architecture

The structure of the MAYBE's control machine is the subject of section 11.4; our purpose here is to examine data paths, and our design goal is to allow for the convenient implementation, at a reasonable cost, of the various data manipulations a processor may be called on to perform. This is a very broad set of design objectives that is often well served by an organization of the general sort shown in figure 11.2.

At the heart of this set of data paths is an $N$-bit data bus that provides for communication of $N$-bit binary words among interconnected subsystems. We have chosen a *three-state bus* convention, in which each subsystem that drives the bus is capable of disabling its driver (allowing other subsystems to supply the data). The output circuitry that drives a three-state bus is often diagrammed as in figure 1.12. Note that an $N$-bit three-state driver has, in addition to the $N$ input data bits, an *output enable* control input; output enables are usually denoted OE if active high or $\overline{\text{OE}}$ if active low (as is often the case). When OE is active, the driver copies its $N$ input data bits onto the bus. When OE is inactive, the driver is effectively disconnected from the data bus, allowing it to be driven from elsewhere. As discussed in section 1.8.8, it is important to ensure that at most one driver is enabled on a three-state bus, to avoid interconnecting conflicting outputs.

Figure 11.2 shows several typical data-handling subsystems connected to the bus. Each subsystem has a number of additional control inputs, typically including an output enable and one or more *load enables*, the latter controlling the loading of registers. A common clock signal is available to each subsystem and clocks each register within the data paths. The inputs of each register connect to the data bus; each register whose load enable is asserted on an active clock edge will consequently be loaded with the data appearing on the bus at that edge.

The common clock thus reticulates time into a sequence of *clock cycles*, each of which is a single clock period beginning and ending with an active clock edge. For concreteness, we assume that the positive-going clock edge is active: throughout the system, registers are loaded and other state changes take place when the clock goes from low to high. During a typical cycle, a single $N$-bit datum is communicated via the bus; the driver of one subsystem (the data *source*) and the load input of one or more registers (the data *destinations*) are enabled during the cycle. At the end of the cycle, the valid data that have settled on the bus are loaded into the enabled registers.

One important subsystem shown in figure 11.2 is an $N$-bit *arithmetic and logic unit* (ALU) capable of performing various arithmetic and Boolean operations on its two input operands. The function performed by the ALU is dictated by a set of six control inputs labeled "ALU function select." Status bits generated by the ALU indicate such conditions as whether or not a result was negative or an arithmetic carry out was produced. These ALU outputs usually constitute the principal feedback from the data paths to the control machine. Table 11.3 gives the functions performed on $A$ and $B$ operands for each set of control input values. The table describes a 74181 integrated circuit, a commonly used part chosen to serve as a concrete example. The six control inputs that dictate the operation performed by this ALU are denoted $F_3 F_2 F_1 F_0 \overline{C} M$; the unique names for the latter two bits derive from special roles they play in the operation decoding. The $\overline{C}$ bit is the inverse of the carry input to the low-order bit position of arithmetic operations such as addition. The $M$ bit specifies a *mode*, distinguishing *arithmetic* operations (in which carries are propagated from one bit position to the next) from *logical* operations (which are performed bitwise with no carry propagation).

Because the $\overline{C}$ input is the *inverse* of the carry input, changing $\overline{C}$ from 1 to 0 in an arithmetic operation generally has the effect of adding 1 to the result. Table 11.3 need not be memorized; many of the 64 operations on $A$ and $B$ afforded by this ALU are of little use to us. For a starting tool kit, we list in table 11.4 a selection of useful input combinations.

In the MAYBE, the two ALU operands are routed to the ALU via separate $N$-bit *ALU operand registers* designated $A$ and $B$, providing, respectively, the $A$ and $B$ ALU operands. Thus an operation such as addition can be performed on two operands by loading them into the $A$ and $B$ registers on two successive cycles

**Table 11.3** Function decoding: 74181 ALU inputs and functions.

| $F_3$ $F_2$ $F_1$ $F_0$ | Function performed if $M = 0$ (arithmetic) | Function performed if $M = 1$ (logical) |
|---|---|---|
| 0 0 0 0 | $A + 1 - \overline{C}$ | $\overline{A}$ |
| 0 0 0 1 | $(A \text{ OR } B) + 1 - \overline{C}$ | $\overline{(A \text{ OR } B)}$ |
| 0 0 1 0 | $(A \text{ OR } \overline{B}) + 1 - \overline{C}$ | $\overline{A} \text{ AND } B$ |
| 0 0 1 1 | $-\overline{C}$ | $00000000$ |
| 0 1 0 0 | $A + (A \text{ AND } \overline{B}) + 1 - \overline{C}$ | $\overline{(A \text{ AND } B)}$ |
| 0 1 0 1 | $(A \text{ OR } B) + (A \text{ AND } \overline{B}) + 1 - \overline{C}$ | $\overline{B}$ |
| 0 1 1 0 | $A - B - \overline{C}$ | $A \text{ XOR } B$ |
| 0 1 1 1 | $(A \text{ AND } \overline{B}) - \overline{C}$ | $A \text{ AND } \overline{B}$ |
| 1 0 0 0 | $A + (A \text{ AND } B) + 1 - \overline{C}$ | $\overline{A} \text{ OR } B$ |
| 1 0 0 1 | $A + B + 1 - \overline{C}$ | $\overline{(A \text{ XOR } B)}$ |
| 1 0 1 0 | $(A \text{ OR } B) + (A \text{ AND } B) + 1 - \overline{C}$ | $B$ |
| 1 0 1 1 | $(A \text{ AND } B) - \overline{C}$ | $A \text{ AND } B$ |
| 1 1 0 0 | $A + A + 1 - \overline{C}$ | $11111111$ |
| 1 1 0 1 | $(A \text{ OR } B) + A + 1 - \overline{C}$ | $A \text{ OR } \overline{B}$ |
| 1 1 1 0 | $(A \text{ OR } \overline{B}) + A + 1 - \overline{C}$ | $A \text{ OR } B$ |
| 1 1 1 1 | $A - \overline{C}$ | $A$ |

**Table 11.4** Useful ALU functions.

| $F_3$ | $F_2$ | $F_1$ | $F_0$ | $\overline{C}$ | $M$ | Output |
|---|---|---|---|---|---|---|
| 0 | 0 | 1 | 1 | 1 | 1 | $00000000$ |
| 1 | 1 | 0 | 0 | 1 | 1 | $11111111$ |
| 1 | 1 | 1 | 1 | 1 | 1 | $A$ |
| 1 | 0 | 1 | 0 | 1 | 1 | $B$ |
| 1 | 1 | 1 | 1 | 1 | 0 | $A - 1$ |
| 0 | 0 | 0 | 0 | 0 | 0 | $A + 1$ |
| 1 | 0 | 0 | 1 | 1 | 0 | $A + B$ |
| 0 | 1 | 1 | 0 | 0 | 0 | $A - B$ |
| 1 | 0 | 1 | 1 | 1 | 1 | $A \text{ AND } B$ |
| 1 | 1 | 1 | 0 | 1 | 1 | $A \text{ OR } B$ |
| 0 | 1 | 1 | 0 | 1 | 1 | $A \text{ XOR } B$ |
| 0 | 0 | 0 | 0 | 1 | 1 | $\overline{A}$ (1's complement) |

and using a third cycle to perform the ALU operation. During this last cycle the appropriate ALU function must be selected on the ALU control inputs, the $\overline{\text{DRALU}}$ drive signal must be active to cause the result to appear on the bus, and a load enable for some destination register must be active to preserve the result in a register. Of course, the destination register may be $A$ or $B$, in which case the result will be available as an ALU input during the next cycle.

Several other data-path subsystems are shown in figure 11.2, albeit in less detail. In general, their interface to the data bus is identical to that of the ALU subsystem, using load-enable and output-enable control signals to effect communication over the bus. It is noteworthy that many modern integrated circuits, such as RAM and ROM chips, offer built-in three-state drivers and input registers; thus they conform to the bus-communication conventions without additional circuitry.

### 11.2.1 Data-Path Width and Data Size

Although the general structure depicted in figure 11.2 admits a variety of different data-path widths, the particular implementation we develop here has 8-bit data paths. Thus the data bus, the ALU, and the register inputs and outputs contain eight data lines each. It should be emphasized that the choice of data-path width is primarily a performance issue. Computers with 32-bit data paths frequently use these paths to manipulate 8-bit data (such as character codes); instructions that perform such manipulations typically ignore the unused data lines or set them to 0. Moreover, computers with 8-bit data paths (such as microprocessors) frequently manipulate longer data; they do so by using a sequence of 8-bit operations to emulate, say, a 32-bit operation. Indeed, any computer with the power of a universal Turing machine can manipulate data of arbitrary size.

Manipulating data of a variety of sizes can be awkward and slow if such manipulations are not anticipated in the machine design, and indeed modest provisions for several common data sizes are commonplace in modern computers. Our sample microarchitecture directly manipulates only 8-bit data, but we shall use it to implement a computer whose instruction set supports 1-, 2-, 4-, and 8-bit data. The physical width of the data path will be transparent to the programmer at this level.

### 11.2.2 Byte Addressing

One challenge for the computer architect is to design a memory that can efficiently store different kinds of data (such as characters, numbers, and instructions) and an instruction set that can efficiently perform the desired operations on each type of data. Many modern machines (for example, the IBM System/360 family and its descendants, the DEC PDP-11 and VAX-11 families, the Intel 8086, and the Motorola MC68000) deal with the memory-architecture question by having a memory composed of 8-bit locations known as *bytes*. Most data are too large to fit into a single byte and must be stored in a series of consecutive memory locations. This entails a level of complexity that could be avoided, to some extent, if each memory location were larger. On the other hand, the byte-addressed memory scheme offers a great deal of flexibility in representing several types of data, each in the most economical format.

Byte addressing might even be viewed as a step toward standardization among machines of different manufacturers, promoting a measure of program and data compatibility between, say, DEC and IBM computers. Unfortunately, this potential advantage is severely compromised by the lack of agreement on conventions for addressing multibyte data. On IBM machines, for example, a 16-bit integer is stored with its more significant byte at the lower of two consecutive addresses (this is known as the "big-Endian" approach); DEC machines, in contrast, store the *less* significant byte in the lower address (the "little-Endian" approach).[1] As a result, binary data transferred between IBM and DEC machines require considerable reinterpretation, even when the data represent communication between programs written in the same high-level language. For all of our illustrations in this chapter, we assume a little-Endian byte-addressed machine such as the DEC VAX-11.

The modern trend toward byte addressing dictates that many simple data, such as integers and pointers, occupy several consecutive (8-bit) locations. All but the most primitive processors support access to multibyte data in their instruction sets, typically for a variety of data sizes (such as 8-bit bytes, 16-bit words, and 32-bit longwords).

The philosophy, common in older designs, of organizing memory into fixed-length words longer than 8 bits does have some advantages. Notably, the data paths of a fixed-word-length computer can be simpler than data paths that must handle operands of varying size. Nevertheless, the difficulty of picking a word length that can efficiently accommodate all the different data types has relegated fixed-word-length designs to special niches, such as very-high-performance processors for numerical computing.

## 11.3 Typical Data-Path Subsystems and Uses

The data-path organization described thus far can be useful in a wide variety of contexts, including controllers, special-purpose computing elements, and the data handling of general-purpose computers of various sizes. In large, high-performance applications, the design is likely to be extended by a number of additional registers and devices such as multipliers. Often such machines include elaborate subsystems that perform ad hoc functions, such as the decoding of machine-language instructions fetched from memory. Thus, while the microarchitecture of a high-performance computer is isolated from the computer's instruction set by a level of interpretation (the microcode), it is apt to be tailored to the higher-level instruction set in a number of ways for performance reasons.

For simplicity of illustration, we focus on the "minimalist" end of the cost-versus-performance spectrum. The function of our MAYBE microarchitecture is to interpret microcode, which will in turn constitute the interpreter for the instruction set ("machine language") of the computer we are building. Within this context,

---

[1] This terminology results from a classic and entertaining paper by Danny Cohen [1981].

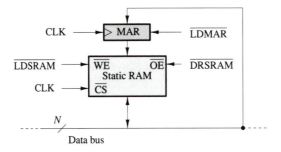

**Figure 11.5**  Static RAM subsystem.

each of the subsystems described in the following sections serves an important function.

### 11.3.1  Static RAM

In addition to $A$, $B$, and other data-path registers in which values can be stored, it is convenient to have locations in which temporary results and other data can be stored by the microprogram. To this end, we include on our data paths a *static RAM* (SRAM) subsystem, as shown in figure 11.5.

Note that we assume a static RAM with $N$ address bits and $N$ data bits; thus our microcode has available 256 8-bit locations, given our 8-bit data-path width. On read operations, the static RAM is much like a combinational circuit with integral three-state drivers; the microprogram can read a location by loading the desired address into the address register (MAR) and asserting the output enable of the SRAM on a subsequent cycle to drive the bus with the contents of the addressed location. Write operations are somewhat like memory loads; an enable line (denoted *write enable*) is asserted to cause data appearing on the bus to become the new contents of the addressed memory location. Note that the connection between the static RAM chip and the bus is bidirectional.

Our microcode will use static RAM extensively; the SRAM will hold a stack (for microsubroutine return addresses) as well as microprogram data. Among the data that will be stored here is the internal processor state of the machine whose instruction set is being interpreted by the microcode.

### 11.3.2  Microcode ROM

A read-only memory contains the microinstructions that are interpreted by the microarchitecture. Straightforward implementation of a ROM subsystem would be similar to the static RAM interface, omitting the provisions for writing addressed locations; it would feature an address register, loadable from the bus, and a ROM with its integral three-state driver. However, there are two modest complications that we cater to in our data-path design.

The first of these is an optimization stimulated by the intended use of the microcode ROM (or $\mu$ROM), which is fetching sequential microinstructions. We

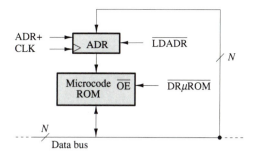

**Figure 11.6**  Microcode ROM subsystem.

expect that, during the execution of a typical microprogram, most ROM accesses will be to consecutive locations (fetching consecutive microinstructions). While we could use our ALU to generate the sequence of addresses (adding one to the previous address for each ROM access), this approach would be awkward to implement and very slow. We avoid these penalties by replacing the address register with a binary *counter*, which performs (in addition to the register functions) an increment operation governed by an additional enable line, as shown in figure 11.6. Note, in this diagram, that the address register ADR can be incremented at the end of a cycle by asserting the control signal ADR+ during that cycle.

The second complication we face is that the output width of the ROM corresponds nicely to our 8-bit data paths, but we require more than 256 ROM locations for our microcode. We can accommodate this need simply by expanding the ADR register, say to 16 bits; we could implement two data-path destinations, ADRHI and ADRLO, to provide high- and low-order address bits, respectively, to the ROM. Of course, the cost of this extension is that two cycles are required to reload the address; but, given the increment capability, ADR loads are required infrequently. Figure 11.7 depicts the minor variation of this plan that we adopt in the MAYBE. Two 8-bit registers, ADRHI and ADRLO, are used to hold the ROM address, but they are arranged to constitute a *single* data bus destination that requires two consecutive 8-bit loads to set a new 16-bit address. This alternative has the virtue that a single control line can be used to load both registers; it imposes the constraint that both registers must always be reloaded together and in the specified (high then low) order. This arrangement also introduces complications in incrementing the ADR register using the ADR+ signal. A carry signal (not shown in figure 11.7) goes from the ADRLO to the ADRHI register and acts as an "increment enable" for the latter; the net effect is that incrementing of ADRHI is disabled except when ADRLO "rolls over" from 11111111 to 00000000, ensuring that the ADR register, viewed as a whole, increments as one would expect.

### 11.3.3 Main-Memory Subsystem

The static RAM subsystem provides for the modest storage needs of our microcode, but we still need to provide access to more substantial memory that will serve as

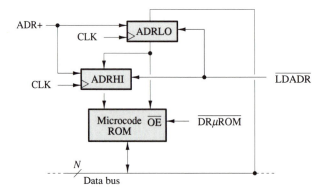

**Figure 11.7**  Microcode ROM with 16-bit address register.

the "main," or "primary," memory of our computer. The technology commonly used for main memory is dynamic rather than static RAM, because of the relatively low cost per bit and higher densities available with dynamic RAM (DRAM). A typical DRAM chip is designed to be used in large arrays; hence it is optimized for low pin count and small board area. A consequence of this goal is that such chips are less straightforward to interface than are typical static RAMs.

One complication is that modern DRAM chips have fewer address pins than the number of addressable locations. Each chip is a ($2^n$ by 1)-bit memory subsystem; hence it has a single *data-in* pin and another three-state *data-out* pin. Addressing a location requires a *sequence* of inputs, in which a *row* address and *column* address are applied in turn to a set of multiplexed address inputs. Row and column addresses may be viewed simply as high-order and low-order portions of a longer address; the terminology derives from the two-dimensional rectangular array of single-bit cells comprised by each DRAM chip. Control signals applied to the chip (*row-address strobe* and *column-address strobe*, or $\overline{\text{RAS}}$ and $\overline{\text{CAS}}$ for short) effect the loading (by the chip) of the corresponding portions of the address. A third control input, $\overline{\text{WRITE}}$, dictates whether a given operation is to be a memory read or write.

An additional complication introduced by the use of dynamic RAM is the need to periodically refresh its contents, since data are held as a stored charge that dissipates with time. An entire row can be refreshed simply by loading its row address and asserting $\overline{\text{RAS}}$; indeed, ordinary read and write operations perform this refresh function for the addressed row. However, to guarantee the integrity of stored data, *every* row must be refreshed at specified intervals; since we cannot depend on programmed memory access to conform to this refresh requirement, additional provisions are necessary. Often special-purpose hardware in the memory controller performs this function transparently. In our low-budget computer, however, we shall leave DRAM refresh to be performed by microcode.

Our simple DRAM subsystem, shown in figure 11.8, consists of eight (64K by 1)-bit RAM chips, thus implementing a 64K-byte main memory. Each chip has eight

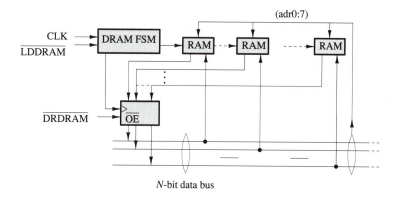

**Figure 11.8** Main-memory (dynamic RAM) subsystem.

address inputs, loaded consecutively with 8-bit row and column addresses to yield a 16-bit byte address. Interface circuitry consists of a single register (with three-state outputs), together with a primitive FSM controller that generates the required $\overline{\text{RAS}}$, $\overline{\text{CAS}}$, and $\overline{\text{WRITE}}$ signals routed to each chip. This interface implements a single 8-bit data source as well as a single destination, with corresponding load-enable ($\overline{\text{LDDRAM}}$) and drive-enable ($\overline{\text{DRDRAM}}$) control signals. The FSM's state transitions are governed by $\overline{\text{LDDRAM}}$, which it causes to behave like a special destination on the data bus. It responds to *sequences* of load enables on consecutive clock cycles in order to provide several different memory operations.

The FSM is designed in such a way that the following operations can be performed:

- *Read*. Loading values *adrlo* and *adrhi* on two consecutive clock cycles (and not writing to DRAM on the one immediately following) initiates a read operation, causing the addressed 8-bit value to be loaded into the data register in the DRAM interface. The value can be accessed in subsequent cycles by selecting this register as a data source, that is, by asserting its output-enable signal $\overline{\text{DRDRAM}}$.

- *Write*. Loading values *adrlo*, *adrhi*, and *data* on three consecutive clock cycles causes a write operation, loading *data* into the addressed location.

- *Refresh*. Loading a value *adrhi* on one cycle and not asserting $\overline{\text{LDDRAM}}$ on the following cycle causes the row addressed by *adrhi* to be refreshed.

It is essential that read and write operations use consecutive cycles; an intervening non-DRAM operation will cause the DRAM controller FSM to misinterpret the operation.

### 11.3.4 Communications Subsystem

Figure 11.9 sketches a typical interface to an input/output subsystem for communication with external devices such as user terminals or other computers. The heart of such an interface is a converter that translates data between the serial

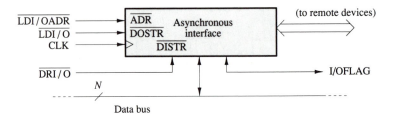

**Figure 11.9** Communications interface.

format used for external communications and the 8-bit binary words used by our machine. This circuitry is represented in the box labeled "asynchronous interface." In a typical computer system, this block might be a *universal asynchronous receiver/transmitter*, or UART, providing serial communications over an external line such as a telephone line. However, the organization we describe is applicable to a wide variety of bidirectional communication technologies and applications.

The UART contains a group of internal registers that hold data and control information. Incoming data bytes arrive and are translated by the interface; the translated data are loaded into a register within the UART. Similarly, characters to be output from the MAYBE must first be written into an internal UART register, from which the UART hardware causes them to be transmitted over the outgoing communication line. Other registers within the UART contain status information (Has a new character arrived since the last character read by the MAYBE? Is the UART currently busy transmitting a character?) and control selectable options such as the transmission rate in bits per second. I/OFLAG is a control output from the UART that can be tested by the MAYBE's control circuitry to see whether some condition that may merit attention (such as the arrival of a new input character or the completion of an output operation) has arisen.

Access to the UART's register set resembles access to static RAM: The UART contains an internal MAR indicating the register to be read to or written from the MAYBE's data bus. This MAR can be loaded from the data bus by asserting the $\overline{\text{LDI/OADR}}$ control signal. An internal UART register itself may be loaded from the data bus by first writing the register's address into the UART's MAR and then asserting $\overline{\text{LDI/O}}$ while the desired data are on the data bus. Similarly, the contents of a UART register may be driven onto the data bus by writing the register's address into the UART's MAR and then asserting $\overline{\text{DRI/O}}$ during a subsequent clock cycle. The detailed behavior of the UART is somewhat arcane and of little intellectual interest; the curious reader can glimpse these details by studying the microcode segments labeled `ioinit`, `iosend`, and `Mintest` in appendix 3.

### 11.3.5 Switches and Lights

Hollywood expects computers to have arrays of operator controls and flashing lights; indeed, such primitive input/output provisions can serve useful functions. We include a set of eight switches, $S_7$ through $S_0$, as a potential data source on

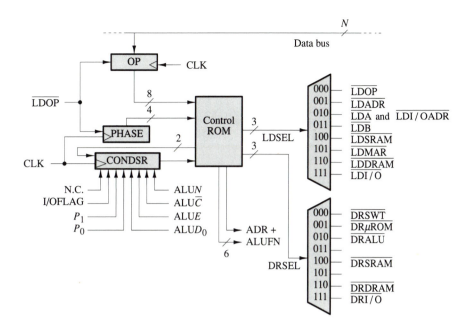

**Figure 11.10**  Microinterpreter control circuitry.

our bus; its interface is simply an 8-bit three-state driver. Similarly, we connect an array of eight lights to a register that can be loaded from the bus. Rather than adding a register to serve this purpose, we connect the lights to the $B$ input register to the ALU. Thus a microprogram can display a configuration in the lights by loading a bit pattern into $B$ and leaving it undisturbed for a period. Of course, when the computer is using $B$ to perform computations, the lights will change so fast as to blur each to a brightness level reflecting the average fraction of the time it contains a 1. It is typically necessary to program deliberate delays to convey useful information in the lights, Hollywood notwithstanding.

## 11.4  Control Subsystem

Figure 11.10 depicts the circuitry that controls the data paths of the MAYBE computer. The heart of the control circuit is a large combinational ROM, which takes a number of inputs (reflecting the state of devices on the data paths as well as the state associated with the control subsystem) and generates an appropriate combination of output signals. Two groups of three control ROM outputs are routed to decoders that generate the data-path load-enable and drive-enable signals, respectively; these six ROM outputs thus dictate the data-bus source and destination during each cycle.

The reader may note a minor detail in figure 11.10: the MAYBE's response to the embarrassment of having *nine* load-enable signals to drive but only eight outputs from the LDSEL decoder. Two of the $\overline{\mathrm{LD}\cdots}$ signals, $\overline{\mathrm{LDA}}$ and $\overline{\mathrm{LDI/OADR}}$, have

**Table 11.11**  Condition shift register control inputs.

| Inputs | | Action |
|---|---|---|
| $I$ | $S$ | |
| 0 | 0 | Load condition register |
| 0 | 1 | Shift condition register right |
| 1 | 0 | No change |
| 1 | 1 | No change |

been paired up and tied together. This decision has the curious consequence that it is impossible to avoid loading the UART's MAR when the ALU's $A$ register is loaded, and vice versa. This potential inconvenience in planning out the contents of the control ROM is usually minor, however, since ALU and UART functions are rarely of interest simultaneously.

### 11.4.1  Control-System State

The control system incorporates a certain amount of additional state, in new registers designated PHASE, OP, and COND. Each of these registers is clocked by the system clock, and consequently can change its value at the end of each clock cycle if appropriately enabled.

COND is an 8-bit shift register that can be loaded with various status bits from the data paths. The high-order bit of COND is an input to the control ROM; thus any of its inputs can be routed to the control ROM by a load followed by a number of shifts. This arrangement is a compromise, aimed at increasing the number of bits accessible as inputs to the control ROM without the expense of a vastly bigger ROM. The major cost of this compromise is the extra clock cycles necessary to access input bits at the low-order end of the shift register. Two control bits called $I$ and $S$ (connected to control ROM outputs) allow COND to be loaded, shifted right, or left unchanged during each cycle, as shown in table 11.11.

OP, an 8-bit register, provides a link between the data and control subsystems that is essential for the interpretation of microcode. Its name derives from its intended use: It will be loaded with an 8-bit code that dictates the *operation* to be performed by a microinstruction, and hence the sequence of control signals to be asserted during the interpretation of that microinstruction. Inputs to the OP register are connected to the data bus, from which OP can be loaded in the same way as data-path registers; however, its output goes only to the control ROM. In general, OP will be loaded once for each microinstruction executed; its contents will remain constant during the interpretation of that microinstruction, which may require several consecutive cycles. When the interpretation of a microinstruction has been completed, OP will be reloaded with a code corresponding to the next microinstruction to be executed.

The remaining control-system state is the contents of the PHASE register, a 4-bit counter whose contents increase by 1 at the end of each clock cycle. Its outputs go only to the control ROM; the sole but essential function of PHASE is to allow the control ROM to distinguish between the clock cycles of a multicycle operation.

The PHASE register has a control input that causes it to be cleared (to binary 0000). The control ROM is configured so that PHASE is cleared at the completion of each microinstruction; thus the interpretation of the next microinstruction will begin with a PHASE of zero. Since OP is always loaded with a new operation code at this time, we use a single control signal $\overline{\text{LDOP}}$ to clear PHASE and enable loading of OP.

In general, we encode each microinstruction as a sequence of one or more consecutive bytes in the microcode ROM, of which the first will be the new contents of the OP register (termed the *opcode* portion of the microinstruction). The interpretation of a microinstruction will begin immediately after a clock cycle during which $\overline{\text{LDOP}}$ is asserted; at the end of such a cycle, PHASE is cleared and OP is loaded with a new opcode from the microcode ROM.

### 11.4.2 Register-Transfer Notation

To describe machine operations concisely, it is convenient to adopt a simple *register-transfer language* whose statements closely resemble assignment statements of a C-like language. We shall use the informal notation $\alpha \leftarrow \beta$ to denote the transfer of the data $\beta$ to the destination $\alpha$; hence, if R is a register, then $R \leftarrow 237$ denotes the loading of R with the (binary representation of the) constant 237. Angle brackets $\langle \cdots \rangle$ denote *contents of*; hence $\langle R \rangle$ represents the contents of register R and $R1 \leftarrow \langle R2 \rangle$ loads register R1 with the contents of R2 (after which R1 and R2 have identical contents). In contexts involving addressable memory, addresses appear to the left of the arrow or within angle brackets; thus $100 \leftarrow \langle 123 \rangle$ denotes the loading of memory location 100 with the contents of memory location 123. It is important to note the asymmetry between the interpretation of the operands on either side of the arrow; the left operand specifies a *location*, while the right operand specifies a *value*. Additionally, we occasionally specify the *size* (in bytes, by default) of a datum or destination by means of a superscript; thus $100 \leftarrow \langle 123 \rangle^4$, $100^4 \leftarrow \langle 123 \rangle$, and $100^4 \leftarrow \langle 123 \rangle^4$ all denote copying the contents of the 4 bytes in memory starting at location 123 into the 4 bytes in memory starting at location 100.

### 11.4.3 Control-ROM Coding

The semantics of microinstructions, and consequently the programming model presented by our machine to the microprogrammer, is largely a function of the truth table we build into the control ROM of the microarchitecture. The reader may by now feel a bit lost: We have presented the hardware structure of a general-purpose computer virtually in its entirety, but we have not offered the slightest detail of how it is programmed or the structure of its microinstructions. This cloud will be lifted shortly, but it is noteworthy that virtually the entire programmer-visible structure

| Address increment | ALU inputs | | | | | | N.C. | COND S/L | | Drive select | | | Load select | | |
|---|---|---|---|---|---|---|---|---|---|---|---|---|---|---|---|
| ADR+ | $F_3$ | $F_2$ | $F_1$ | $F_0$ | $\overline{C}$ | $M$ | $X$ | $I$ | $S$ | $D_2$ | $D_1$ | $D_0$ | $L_2$ | $L_1$ | $L_0$ |

**Figure 11.12**  Control-ROM output word.

| Opcode | Phase | COND | = | ADR+ | ALU | CC | DRSEL | LDSEL | Comments |
|---|---|---|---|---|---|---|---|---|---|
| 00000001 | 0000 | 0 | = | 0 | 1100 01 | 11 | 010 | 101 | MAR ← 11111111 |
| 00000001 | 0000 | 1 | = | 0 | 1100 01 | 11 | 010 | 101 | MAR ← 11111111 |
| 00000001 | 0001 | 0 | = | 0 | 1111 11 | 11 | 100 | 010 | A ← SRAM |
| 00000001 | 0001 | 1 | = | 0 | 1111 11 | 11 | 100 | 010 | A ← SRAM |

**Figure 11.13**  A fragment of a nanoprogram.

of our machine is dictated by the contents of the control ROM. The specification of these contents is itself an activity not unlike programming, though it is subject to a variety of unusual and arcane restrictions, such as the maximum of 16 clock phases per opcode. Since the control-ROM code is at a level below even microcode, we shall refer to it as *nanocode*.

We can specify the control-ROM contents (that is, nanocode) by means of a truth table, specifying for each combination of control-ROM inputs a 16-bit output word in the format shown in figure 11.12. It is convenient to deal with small portions of the control-ROM coding at a time; for example, we shall specify only the portion of the control ROM that deals with a particular opcode. An example of a control-ROM fragment is shown in figure 11.13, which specifies the contents of four locations that deal with phases 0 and 1 of opcode 1.

Note that each line consists of a sequence of ROM input bits on the left, followed by an equal sign and a sequence of corresponding output bits on the right. Both the input and the output sequences are divided into columns corresponding to their functions in the MAYBE microarchitecture; the reader is urged to review the diagrams of preceding sections in which these functions are described.

Observe that the first two lines differ only in an input bit (the high-order bit from the COND shift register). Since they specify the same output, these lines dictate that the action to be taken on phase 0 of opcode 1 must be independent

| Opcode | Phase | COND | = | ADR+ | ALU | CC | DRSEL | LDSEL | Comments |
|--------|-------|------|---|------|-----|----|-------|-------|----------|
| 00000001 | 0000 | * | = | 0 | 1100 01 | 11 | 010 | 101 | MAR ← 11111111 |
| 00000001 | 0001 | * | = | 0 | 1111 11 | 11 | 100 | 010 | $A$ ← SRAM |

**Figure 11.14** Abbreviated nanoprogram fragment.

| Opcode | Phase | COND | = | ADR+ | ALU | CC | DRSEL | LDSEL | Comments |
|--------|-------|------|---|------|-----|----|-------|-------|----------|
| ******** | **** | * | == | 1 | 1111 11 | 11 | 001 | 000 | Opcode ← $\mu$ROM; ADR+ |

**Figure 11.15** Default control-ROM contents.

of the COND output bit. It is rather a nuisance to repeat the line for each unique input combination, so we afford ourselves the notational luxury of allowing an asterisk as a "wild-card" input bit. A line with an asterisk as an input bit specifies the contents of locations whose corresponding input is either 0 or 1; it is thus an abbreviation for two truth-table lines. Similarly, a line with $n$ asterisks abbreviates $2^n$ input lines. Using this notation, we can collapse figure 11.13 into the shorter nanoprogram of figure 11.14.

The two lines of nanocode in figure 11.14 specify two sets of control signals that appear during consecutive cycles. The first programs the ALU to generate the constant 11111111 (ALU function 110001), to place it on the bus (DRSEL selects the ALU), and to load it into the static RAM memory address register (LDSEL specifies the MAR). The second specifies that static RAM drive the bus and that $A$ be loaded. Thus the effect of the two-cycle sequence is to load the contents of SRAM location 11111111 into $A$.

It is useful to specify a *default* control-ROM output, a value to fill otherwise unspecified locations. One might wish, for example, to specify, as the default value for every location, the output combination that terminates the interpretation of each opcode. Figure 11.15 shows how this might be specified. Note that this single line specifies (default) contents for *every* ROM location, since an asterisk appears in each input bit position. We use the double equals to denote that the line specifies a default value that is possibly overridden by subsequently specified lines.

The line is a typical "begin next microinstruction" control state. It dictates that the OP register is to be loaded from microinstruction ROM, incrementing the

| $C_7$ | External communication $C_6$ | Push buttons $C_5$ | | ALU output condition bits | | | |
|---|---|---|---|---|---|---|---|
| | | | $C_4$ | $C_3$ | $C_2$ | $C_1$ | $C_0$ |
| N.C. | I/OFLAG | $P_1$ | $P_0$ | $D_0$ | $E$ | $\overline{C}$ | $N$ |

**Figure 11.16** Condition register.

microcode ROM address (specified by the 1 in the ADR+ column). Note that the new opcode will be fetched from the old value of ADR, which remains current until the end of the clock cycle; the incremented value will be used in subsequent fetches from microcode ROM.

### 11.4.4 Condition Register

Figure 11.16 diagrams the 8-bit word loaded into the condition register. Recall that this register may be rotated to the right; after one or more such rotates, the relative position of each bit has changed. Since the low-order bit ($C_0$) is a control-ROM input, its value may influence interpretation without further rotation.

The four low-order bits—$D_0$, $E$, $\overline{C}$, and $N$—reflect the ALU output data. $N$ is simply the high-order (sign) bit, $D_7$; it is 1 when the ALU's output value, viewed as an 8-bit 2's complement integer, is *negative*. Similarly, the low-order bit $D_0$ is 1 when the ALU's output value is *odd*. $\overline{C}$ is the inverted carry out of the high-order ALU bit. $E$, a bit produced by the ALU, is 1 if and only if the output word is all 1s; it is termed the *equal bit*, since with the ALU function $A - B - 1$, its value is 1 if and only if $A$ and $B$ are equal. $P_0$ and $P_1$ are connected to two momentary switches (push buttons); they serve as primitive user inputs that can be programmed (along with the eight switches on the data path) to serve as a low-level "operator's console." I/OFLAG comes from the MAYBE's communications interface. The final condition register bit, $C_7$, is unused and not connected to anything.

## 11.5 The Control Machine as an Interpreter

The control circuitry just presented can be viewed as an interpreter for the very primitive "program" contained in the control ROM. This view is justified by our implementation technology, which separates the subsystem into a small amount of fixed circuitry and an encoded representation of the desired subsystem behavior stored in the ROM. We have again applied the engineering lesson gleaned from the model of Turing universality: To build a complex system $A$, build a smaller subsystem $I$ that interprets a coded representation $A'$ of $A$.

The extra level of interpretation effected by the control ROM gives us a lot of flexibility to implement powerful features in the next level of interpretation, that is, in the structure of microcode. Indeed, our microarchitecture is quite programmable despite the modest amount of hardware needed to implement it, owing largely to the interpretive power of the control-ROM scheme. Of course, there is a performance cost associated with this extra interpretation; the machine could be made to execute microinstructions faster if they were interpreted directly by ad hoc hardware rather than by the interpreted control-ROM contents. For this reason, our machine is somewhat atypical of the contemporary computer spectrum; it sacrifices considerable performance to achieve high-level functionality with minimal hardware cost.

Along these lines, it is worth observing that one accepted approach to the engineering of high-performance computers involves eliminating the level of interpretation corresponding to our microcode rather than the control ROM's nanocode. *Reduced-instruction-set computers* (RISCs) present a machine-language programming model similar in level to our microcode, but they depend upon sophisticated compilers to translate programs directly to this level.

## 11.6 Context

Notes on the history of microprogramming and on its application in contemporary machines appear in section 12.5. The first major architecture oriented around byte addressing using 8-bit bytes was the IBM System/360 [Blaauw and Brooks 1964; Amdahl, Blaauw, and Brooks 1964]. Byte addressing has been used in almost every major architecture since, including subsequent IBM machines, the Digital Equipment PDP-11 and VAX-11 families [Strecker 1978], and virtually every existing microprocessor. The lamentable lack of consensus on representation of multiple-byte data is the subject of the readable and definitive paper by Cohen [1981].

## 11.7 Problems

### Problem 11.1

If we inadvertently switch connections to two data pins of the static RAM chip in the MAYBE, will operation be affected? Is your answer the same if we switch two data lines to the microcode ROM chip? If the answers are not the same, what constitutes the difference between the SRAM and the microcode ROM?

### Problem 11.2

A 16-bit DRAM address is transferred to the DRAM subsystem in two consecutive 1-byte transfers. What dictates whether the low-order or high-order address byte should be transferred first? That is, if we send the high-order byte first (and are consistent in doing so), will this be distinguishable from consistently sending the low-order byte first?

### Problem 11.3

What, if anything, prevents two drivers from putting conflicting data on the data bus of the MAYBE, ignoring transients during propagation delays? Can such conflicts happen if there are programming errors in the control ROM?

### Problem 11.4

Given a big enough control ROM, could the LDSEL and DRSEL decoders be eliminated (producing the load and drive signals directly as control ROM outputs)? If so, what advantage might this have? (*Hint:* Think about what limitations the decoders inflict on the LD and DR signals.) How many more outputs would the control ROM need to have to implement this?

### Problem 11.5

Given a big enough control ROM, could the condition shift register be eliminated (using the condition bits directly as control-ROM inputs)? If so, what advantage might this have? How many more (or fewer) outputs and inputs would the control ROM need to have to implement this? What would be the size (in bits) of the control ROM?

### Problem 11.6

Consider two alternative MAYBE improvements: (1) adding outputs to the control ROM to supply load and drive enables directly, eliminating the decoders (and the time they take); and (2) adding inputs to the control ROM to read bits from the COND register simultaneously, eliminating the need to shift them. Assume that the two changes each improve performance by about the same factor and that programming is not an issue. Which is likely to be less expensive to implement? Explain.

### Problem 11.7

One possible modification of the MAYBE machine is to replace the condition-code shift register with a regular register and a multiplexer, as shown in figure 11.17, which is a modified version of figure 11.10. Note that this circuit loads the register labeled CCREG when the three select bits CCA, CCB, and CCC coming out of the control ROM are all high. For this reason, the corresponding input to the CCMUX is unusable and is not connected to any signal. Why is the CCREG register needed? Why is the flip-flop on the output of the CCMUX needed?

### Problem 11.8

Suppose the microcode ROM is selected as a data source during a given clock cycle; that is, $\overline{DR\mu ROM}$ is asserted (low) during that cycle. Do the data that appear on the bus during that cycle depend on the value of the ADR+ signal (which increments ADR) during the *same* cycle? In other words, will the increment signal to the ADR register in the microcode ROM module cause the ADR register contents to increment on the same active clock edge on which the ADR+ is asserted, or does it increment on the *next* active clock edge?

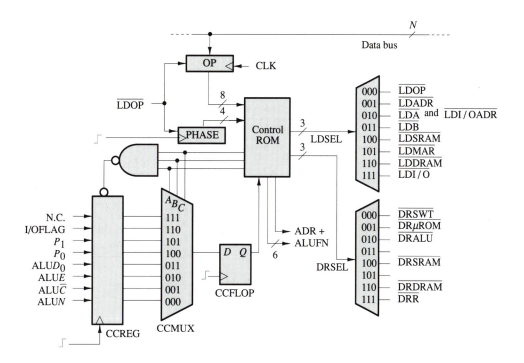

**Figure 11.17** Modified MAYBE condition-code logic.

### Problem 11.9

Figure 11.18 shows the data and control paths between the control ROM, the $\mu$ROM, and the SRAM in the existing MAYBE. The numbers in the boxes give the propagation delays of the individual circuit components, in nanoseconds. The clocks $Q_0$ and $\overline{Q_1}$ are constrained to have the periods, duty cycles, and phase relations shown in figure 11.19.

Assume that the critical path in the MAYBE (the path that limits the clock frequency of the machine) involves writing to the SRAM. Given that the rising edge of $Q_0$ starts the control-ROM access, generating the control signals for the write operation, estimate the time delay along this path. What is the maximum frequency of the system clock that avoids the possibility of a random write into the SRAM while the control signals are still in transition?

### Problem 11.10

How can you write a (perhaps infinite) loop in nanocode? (*Hint:* There are two different methods.)

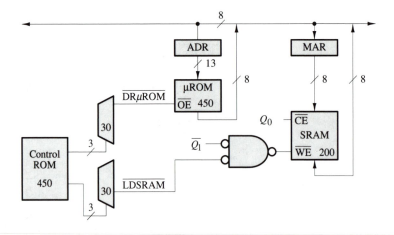

**Figure 11.18**  Current MAYBE (delays in nanoseconds).

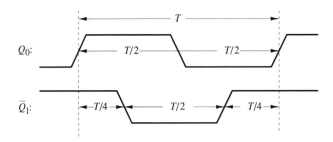

**Figure 11.19**  Clock timing.

# 12 Microprogramming and Microcode

A major engineering advantage of interpretive approaches is their tendency to isolate implementation details of the underlying interpreter from those of the programs being interpreted. Once a language interface has been agreed upon, the respective development of interpretive and interpreted mechanisms can proceed more or less independently. In the case of our microcoded processor, for example, we might eventually develop a new microinterpreter architecture (perhaps with vastly improved performance) compatible with the present one only in that it interprets the same microinstructions with the same meaning; this measure of compatibility allows us to preserve the entire machine-language implementation (in addition to software written in machine language and other, higher-level languages) while exploiting the advantages of the new microarchitecture. The pivotal element in this bipartite structure is an interface specification: the interpreted language.

In our present case, the interpreted language is composed of *microinstructions*, each of which is represented as a sequence of bytes stored at some address in the microcode ROM. Given a sufficiently careful specification of the microinstruction format and the meaning of the contents of each microinstruction field, the microinterpreter implementation could proceed concurrently with (and independently of) the development of the microcode it eventually will interpret. This observation suggests that the optimal way to design a microcoded system is to begin by specifying the microinstruction semantics and then to direct parallel efforts toward microcode and microinterpreter development.

This scenario, however, assumes that the language interface can be specified independently of both implementation issues and coding requirements, and this is rarely the case in practice. Typically both the interpreter design and coding efforts substantially influence the design of the interface language, which evolves into a series of compromises between implementation and programming pressures. The reader should, in fact, develop a healthy skepticism regarding extremists in the field of engineering methodology: In their pure forms, *top-down* (code → language → interpreter), *bottom-up* (interpreter → language → code), and *middle-out* (language → both interpreter and code) are all more or less unrealistic. A practical approach generally has elements of all three. In this regard, it should *not* be inferred from the bottom-up presentation in this text that microinterpreter design should precede microcoding; in fact, the particular designs presented here reflect numerous iterations through the language-design-code cycle.

## 12.1 Microcode Semantics

Although microcode is a low-level programming language, it is worth taking care to simplify the microprogramming environment as much as possible by isolating the microprogrammer from certain low-level architectural details. The extent to which this can be done depends on several architectural choices and largely determines the level of programmability enjoyed by the microcoder. Many machine architectures present more primitive programming models at the microcode level than that offered by the MAYBE machine; these machines tend to have "horizontal" microcode formats in which individual microinstruction bits correspond directly to control signals (much as in our control ROM). Indeed, it is the level of interpretation provided by the control ROM that allows us some flexibility in the interpretation of microinstructions.

We exploit this flexibility by hiding individual hardware registers from the microprogrammer. Thus the semantics of microinstructions will not be specified in terms of their effect on hardware registers, but at a slightly more abstract level. We use the static RAM as a collection of *virtual registers* available for use by the microcode, and we arrange to have each microinstruction take inputs from (and produce outputs in) these virtual registers. To remind us of this convention (and to distinguish static RAM locations from locations in main memory), we shall symbolically denote the $i$th static RAM location by R$i$ (for register $i$). Thus, when microprogrammers refer to R0 or R15, they are thinking of the first or sixteenth register of a many-register architecture; because of our intimacy with lower-level architectural details, however, we realize that they are actually dealing with SRAM locations 0 or 15.

Each microinstruction is coded into the microcode ROM as a sequence of one or more bytes, of which the first is the opcode loaded into the OP register to begin the microinstruction's execution. The interpretation of following microinstruction bytes depends on the particular opcode, but typically these additional bytes are register names (SRAM addresses) or program constants. An example of a typical microinstruction is add, which is encoded as the opcode 00001010 followed by the bytes $x$, $y$, and $z$ specifying the register names of two input operands and one output operand, respectively; thus this microinstruction performs the operation $z \leftarrow \langle x \rangle + \langle y \rangle$.

### 12.1.1 ALU Operations

The nanocode for the add operation is shown in figure 12.1. This segment of the control-ROM truth table dictates the control inputs of the data paths for seven consecutive cycles whose opcode input designates the add operation. Note that the sequence begins with phase 0 (immediately following the cycle that ends by loading the new opcode) and ends with a control state that loads the next opcode from the microcode ROM and clears the PHASE counter to begin its execution. (Recall from section 11.4.1 that the PHASE counter is automatically reset to 0 whenever the OP register is loaded.) Control outputs for phases 0–5 are thus devoted to execution of the add operation. They involve loading the $x$ value from the microinstruction stream (incrementing ADR in the process) into the MAR, fetching the contents of

| Opcode | Phase | COND | = | ADR+ | ALU | CC | DRSEL | LDSEL | Comments |
|--------|-------|------|---|------|--------|----|-------|-------|----------|
| 00001010 | 0000 | * | = | 1 | 1111 11 | 11 | 001 | 101 | MAR ← μROM; ADR+ |
| 00001010 | 0001 | * | = | 0 | 1111 11 | 11 | 100 | 010 | $A$ ← SRAM |
| 00001010 | 0010 | * | = | 1 | 1111 11 | 11 | 001 | 101 | MAR ← μROM; ADR+ |
| 00001010 | 0011 | * | = | 0 | 1111 11 | 11 | 100 | 011 | $B$ ← SRAM |
| 00001010 | 0100 | * | = | 1 | 1111 11 | 11 | 001 | 101 | MAR ← μROM; ADR+ |
| 00001010 | 0101 | * | = | 0 | 1001 10 | 00 | 010 | 100 | SRAM ← $A + B$; latch CCs |
| 00001010 | 0110 | * | = | 1 | 1111 11 | 11 | 001 | 000 | Opcode ← μROM; ADR+ |

**Figure 12.1** Nanocode for add($x,y,z$) microinstruction.

| Opcode | Phase | COND | = | ADR+ | ALU | CC | DRSEL | LDSEL | Comments |
|--------|-------|------|---|------|--------|----|-------|-------|----------|
| 00001011 | 0000 | * | = | 1 | 1111 11 | 11 | 001 | 010 | $A$ ← μROM; ADR+ |
| 00001011 | 0001 | * | = | 1 | 1111 11 | 11 | 001 | 101 | MAR ← μROM; ADR+ |
| 00001011 | 0010 | * | = | 0 | 1111 11 | 11 | 100 | 011 | $B$ ← SRAM |
| 00001011 | 0011 | * | = | 1 | 1111 11 | 11 | 001 | 101 | MAR ← μROM; ADR+ |
| 00001011 | 0100 | * | = | 0 | 1001 10 | 00 | 010 | 100 | SRAM ← $A + B$; latch CCs |
| 00001011 | 0101 | * | = | 1 | 1111 11 | 11 | 001 | 000 | Opcode ← μROM; ADR+ |

**Figure 12.2** Nanocode for cadd($cx,y,z$) microinstruction.

SRAM location $x$, similarly fetching $y$ from ROM and $\langle y \rangle$ from SRAM, loading $z$ into the MAR, and writing $\langle x \rangle + \langle y \rangle$ (from the ALU) into SRAM location $z$. During this latter cycle, in which ALU control inputs dictate an addition operation, the condition-code shift register is directed to load. Thus the ALU flags that reflect the result of the operation will be latched in the condition register for possible use by a subsequent conditional branch microinstruction. Close study of this fragment of control ROM is highly recommended.

The inclusion of program constants in the microinstruction stream is illustrated in figure 12.2, which shows nanocode that implements the cadd (*constant add*)

**Table 12.3** Selected data-handling microinstructions.

| Symbolic microinstruction | Control-ROM encoding | Operation performed |
|---|---|---|
| move($x$,$y$) | 0x05 $x$ $y$ | $y \leftarrow \langle x \rangle$ |
| cmove($cx$,$y$) | 0x06 $cx$ $y$ | $y \leftarrow cx$ |
| add($x$,$y$,$z$) | 0x0A $x$ $y$ $z$ | $z \leftarrow \langle x \rangle + \langle y \rangle$ |
| cadd($cx$,$y$,$z$) | 0x0B $cx$ $y$ $z$ | $z \leftarrow cx + \langle y \rangle$ |
| add2($x$,$y$,$z$) | 0x2C $x$ $y$ $z$<br>$x$+1 $y$+1 $z$+1 | $z^2 \leftarrow \langle x \rangle^2 + \langle y \rangle^2$ |
| cadd2($cx$,$y$,$z$) | 0x2D $cx$%256 $y$ $z$<br>$cx$/256 $y$+1 $z$+1 | $z^2 \leftarrow cx^2 + \langle y \rangle^2$ |
| sub($x$,$y$,$z$) | 0x1C $x$ $y$ $z$ | $z \leftarrow \langle x \rangle - \langle y \rangle$ |
| cmp($x$,$y$) | 0x1D $x$ $y$ | $\langle x \rangle - \langle y \rangle$ |
| and($x$,$y$,$z$) | 0x27 $x$ $y$ $z$ | $z \leftarrow \langle x \rangle \text{ AND } \langle y \rangle$ |
| or($x$,$y$,$z$) | 0x28 $x$ $y$ $z$ | $z \leftarrow \langle x \rangle \text{ OR } \langle y \rangle$ |
| xor($x$,$y$,$z$) | 0x29 $x$ $y$ $z$ | $z \leftarrow \langle x \rangle \text{ XOR } \langle y \rangle$ |
| not($x$,$y$) | 0x2A $x$ $y$ | $y \leftarrow \text{ NOT } \langle x \rangle$ (1's complement) |
| neg($x$,$y$) | 0x2B $x$ $y$ | $y \leftarrow (-\langle x \rangle)$ (2's complement) |

microinstruction. The cadd operation is nearly identical in coding and behavior to add; the sole difference is that the first argument byte $cx$ in a cadd microinstruction is a constant to be added rather than the address of an SRAM location containing the value to be added.

Other ALU operations follow the same pattern. In general, microinstructions that perform explicit arithmetic or logical operations are coded to load the condition-code register with bits that reflect the result of the operation; other microinstructions (with the exception of conditional branches) leave the condition register undisturbed. Our microinstruction encoding convention is that the opcode is followed by specifiers of the source operands, followed in turn by the SRAM location that is to hold the result. Table 12.3 summarizes a selection of simple operations; for a complete list, see appendix 2.

Certain conventions regarding the naming of MAYBE microinstructions are noteworthy. A single-digit suffix generally indicates the size of the source and destination data, in bytes; in the absence of such a suffix, single-byte data are manipulated. Thus add($x$,$y$,$z$) performs a 1-byte addition, while add2($x$,$y$,$z$) adds 2-byte data. ALU operations for which one source datum is a constant are denoted by adding a prefix "c" to the microinstruction name, as in the cadd microinstruction described earlier. These two conventions, used separately and in combination, yield a number of additional microinstructions that have been omitted from table 12.3 but whose meaning is apparent; cand, for example, is the microinstruction that performs a 1-byte logical AND operation between a constant and the contents of an SRAM location. As may be seen by consulting appendix 2, certain of these

| Opcode | Phase | COND | = | ADR+ | ALU | CC | DRSEL | LDSEL | Comments |
|--------|-------|------|---|------|---------|-----|-------|-------|----------|
| 00001100 | 0000 | * | = | 1 | 1111 11 | 11 | 001 | 010 | $A \leftarrow \mu$ROM; ADR+ |
| 00001100 | 0001 | * | = | 0 | 1111 11 | 11 | 001 | 001 | ADR $\leftarrow \mu$ROM |
| 00001100 | 0010 | * | = | 0 | 1111 11 | 11 | 010 | 001 | ADR $\leftarrow A$ |
| 00001100 | 0011 | * | = | 1 | 1111 11 | 11 | 001 | 000 | Opcode $\leftarrow \mu$ROM; ADR+ |

**Figure 12.4**  Nanocode for the jmp microinstruction.

microinstructions have been implemented by macroinstructions that expand to simpler forms rather than by direct control-ROM interpretation of a dedicated opcode. The move2 and ccmp microinstructions are examples of this latter category. Note that this implementation strategy decision is largely transparent to the microprogrammer, except to the extent that it affects the time performance and size of the translated microprogram.

### 12.1.2  Control Flow

An unconditional microinstruction jump (branch) instruction need only load a new value into the microcode ROM ADR register; in most cases, the new address is a constant that can be included in the microinstruction. Figure 12.4 shows nanocode that performs this operation, presuming that the jmp opcode is followed by the low- and high-order bytes, respectively, of the new microinstruction address. The only minor complication here is introduced by the fact that once the first byte has been loaded into ADR, the microcode ROM can no longer be used as a data source (since the two halves of its address input do not go together). This problem is avoided by using $A$ to store the first address byte fetched while fetching the second.

Figure 12.5 shows nanocode for a typical *conditional* transfer of control: The jnc microinstruction branches to the designated microinstruction address if the previously loaded condition register indicates no carry out of the ALU during the cycle in which it was loaded. The carry information is stored in *inverted* form in bit 1 of the condition register, so the register must be shifted once (during phase 1) for it to be presented as a control-ROM input. As with the jmp, the jnc opcode is followed by 2 bytes that specify the low- and high-order portions of the target microinstruction address. While the address bytes needn't really be fetched if the condition dictates that no jump is to take place, the ADR register *must* be incremented to avoid the subsequent interpretation of the unused address bytes as opcodes. Jump microinstructions are summarized in table 12.6.

Occasionally, it is useful to perform a *dispatch*, or $n$-way conditional branch,

| Opcode | Phase | COND | = | ADR+ | ALU | CC | DRSEL | LDSEL | Comments |
|--------|-------|------|---|------|-----|----|-------|-------|----------|
| 00010111 | 0000 | * | = | 1 | 1111 11 | 11 | 001 | 010 | $A \leftarrow \mu\text{ROM}$; ADR+ |
| 00010111 | 0001 | * | = | 0 | 1111 11 | 01 | 010 | 010 | Shift CCs |
| 00010111 | 0010 | 1 | = | 0 | 1111 11 | 11 | 001 | 001 | ADR $\leftarrow \mu\text{ROM}$ |
| 00010111 | 0011 | 1 | = | 0 | 1111 11 | 11 | 010 | 001 | ADR $\leftarrow A$ |
| 00010111 | 0100 | 1 | = | 1 | 1111 11 | 11 | 001 | 000 | Opcode $\leftarrow \mu\text{ROM}$; ADR+ |
| 00010111 | 0010 | 0 | = | 1 | 1111 11 | 11 | 001 | 010 | $A \leftarrow \mu\text{ROM}$; ADR+ |
| 00010111 | 0011 | 0 | = | 1 | 1111 11 | 11 | 001 | 000 | Opcode $\leftarrow \mu\text{ROM}$; ADR+ |

**Figure 12.5**  Nanocode for the jnc microinstruction.

**Table 12.6**  Jump microinstructions.

| Symbolic microinstruction | Control-ROM encoding | Operation performed |
|---------------------------|----------------------|---------------------|
| jmp($dst$) | 0x0C $dstlo$ $dsthi$ | Unconditional transfer: $\text{ADR} \leftarrow (dsthi, dstlo)$ |
| je($dst$) | 0x19 $dstlo$ $dsthi$ | jmp if ALU output was = 0b11111111 |
| jne($dst$) | 0x25 $dstlo$ $dsthi$ | jmp if ALU output was $\neq$ 0b11111111 |
| jmi($dst$) | 0x12 $dstlo$ $dsthi$ | jmp if ALU output was $< 0$ |
| jc($dst$) | 0x23 $dstlo$ $dsthi$ | jmp if carry |
| jnc($dst$) | 0x17 $dstlo$ $dsthi$ | jmp if no carry |
| jeven($dst$) | 0x22 $dstlo$ $dsthi$ | jmp if ALU output was even |
| jodd($dst$) | 0x16 $dstlo$ $dsthi$ | jmp if ALU output was odd |
| jready($dst$) | 0x14 $dstlo$ $dsthi$ | jmp if I/OFLAG is set |
| jp0($dst$) | 0x18 $dstlo$ $dsthi$ | jmp if $P_0$ is pressed |
| jp1($dst$) | 0x15 $dstlo$ $dsthi$ | jmp if $P_1$ is pressed |
| jnp0($dst$) | 0x24 $dstlo$ $dsthi$ | jmp if $P_0$ is not pressed |
| jnp1($dst$) | 0x21 $dstlo$ $dsthi$ | jmp if $P_1$ is not pressed |

dictated by the value of a datum; an important application of this capability is in the interpretation of machine instructions, where it is necessary to transfer control to one of $n$ different microinstruction sequences, depending on the value of an operation code fetched from the interpreted machine instruction. Efficient support for such constructs is effected by the dispatch microinstruction, described in table 12.7.

**Table 12.7** Dispatch microinstruction.

| Symbolic microinstruction | Control-ROM encoding | Operation performed |
|---|---|---|
| dispatch($x$,$tab$) | 0x80 $x$ $tabhi$ $tablo$ | $tab$ is taken as the $\mu$ROM address of a table of 2-byte $\mu$ROM addresses, each stored (low,high); the SRAM location $x$ contains an index into the table; jumps to the $\mu$ROM location given in the indexed entry. |

Note that *tab* is a 16-bit microcode ROM address giving the base (lowest address) of a 256-entry table whose entries each occupy 2 bytes; thus the microcode ROM address of the table entry denoted by $\langle x \rangle$ is $tab + \langle x \rangle + \langle x \rangle$. This microcode ROM location and the following one are presumed to contain *another* microcode ROM address to which control is transferred. The control-ROM coding of dispatch is tricky, owing to the 16-bit arithmetic involved in accessing the table element; the curious reader is referred to appendix 2.

### 12.1.3 Microsubroutines

The facility to code subroutines is a basic and important program-structuring tool at every programming level, but it is not included in all microprogramming languages. In its most primitive form, a subroutine is an instruction sequence that can be *called*, or invoked, from several points in a program; following the execution of the subroutine, control returns to the instruction following the call. The fundamental problem to be solved in the implementation of microsubroutines is the management of return addresses: A mechanism must be provided for remembering, during the execution of a microsubroutine, the address of the instruction to which control will return once the subroutine is completed.

The usual technique for managing return addresses on contemporary computers is the *stack*, whose first-in, last-out storage discipline nicely matches the need imposed by nested subroutine calls. We implement a modest "microstack" (so named to avoid confusion with stacks implemented in the machine-language instructions we shall consider in subsequent chapters) on the MAYBE using the high end of our static RAM to store return locations and reserving the topmost location (whose address is binary 11111111) as a *microstack pointer*, or $\mu$SP.

We adopt the convention that the microstack builds *down* in SRAM as new data are pushed and that the $\mu$SP will contain the address of the location that is to hold the next datum to be pushed. Thus a *push* operation requires loading the datum to be pushed into the SRAM location addressed by $\langle \mu SP \rangle$, then decrementing $\langle \mu SP \rangle$ by 1; conversely, a *pop* operation involves first incrementing $\langle \mu SP \rangle$, then accessing the contents of the newly addressed SRAM location. We can code a push microinstruction following this convention, as shown in figure 12.8. The

| Opcode | Phase | COND | = | ADR+ | ALU | | CC | DRSEL | LDSEL | Comments |
|--------|-------|------|---|------|-----|---|----|-------|-------|----------|
| 00000011 | 0000 | * | = | 0 | 1100 11 | 11 | 010 | 101 | MAR ←0xFF |
| 00000011 | 0001 | * | = | 0 | 1111 11 | 11 | 100 | 010 | A ←SRAM |
| 00000011 | 0010 | * | = | 0 | 1111 10 | 11 | 010 | 100 | SRAM ←A − 1 |
| 00000011 | 0011 | * | = | 1 | 1111 11 | 11 | 001 | 101 | MAR ←μROM; ADR+ |
| 00000011 | 0100 | * | = | 0 | 1111 11 | 11 | 100 | 011 | B ←SRAM |
| 00000011 | 0101 | * | = | 0 | 1111 11 | 11 | 010 | 101 | MAR ←A |
| 00000011 | 0110 | * | = | 0 | 1010 11 | 11 | 010 | 100 | SRAM ←B |
| 00000011 | 0111 | * | = | 1 | 1111 11 | 11 | 001 | 000 | Opcode ←μROM; ADR+ |

**Figure 12.8**  Nanocode for the push microinstruction.

alert reader can deduce from this nanocode that the push opcode is followed in the microinstruction by a single byte giving the address of the SRAM location containing the datum to be pushed.

Implementing microsubroutines is straightforward given this microstack mechanism. We need to provide a *call* microinstruction—similar to an unconditional branch except that it pushes the return address on the microstack—and a *return* microinstruction, which pops a microcode ROM address from the microstack and installs it in ADR. The latter is the simpler of the two, and its nanocode is shown in figure 12.9. Note that 2 bytes are required to hold a ROM address; consequently, two consecutive microstack pops are required. Note also that while we generally adopt a little-Endian approach, storing the least significant byte of a multibyte datum at the lowest address, the storage of the 2-byte microsubroutine return address follows a big-Endian convention, with the *more* significant byte at the lower address. This inconsistency in representation saves one or two clock cycles in the execution of the call and rtn microinstructions; the reader is invited to investigate the changes to call and rtn required if the pushed return address is to be stored in a little-Endian manner.

The design of the call microinstruction is complicated by the fact that the return address is not available on the data paths, since we have not provided drivers between ADR and the bus in our hardware design. This omission is a deliberate design decision and reflects a typical compromise between the cost of additional chips and the desire to provide direct support for programming constructs. Our compromise approach requires coding into the call microinstruction the return address in addition to the address of the called microsubroutine; at 2 bytes per address, the major cost of this scheme is an additional 2 microcode bytes in each

| Opcode | Phase | COND | = | ADR+ | ALU | CC | DRSEL | LDSEL | Comments |
|--------|-------|------|---|------|---------|----|-------|-------|----------|
| 00000010 | 0000 | * | = | 0 | 1100 11 | 11 | 010 | 101 | MAR ←0xFF |
| 00000010 | 0001 | * | = | 0 | 1111 11 | 11 | 100 | 010 | $A \leftarrow$ SRAM |
| 00000010 | 0010 | * | = | 0 | 0000 00 | 11 | 010 | 010 | $A \leftarrow A + 1$ |
| 00000010 | 0011 | * | = | 0 | 1111 11 | 11 | 010 | 101 | MAR $\leftarrow A$ |
| 00000010 | 0100 | * | = | 0 | 1111 11 | 11 | 100 | 001 | ADR ←SRAM |
| 00000010 | 0101 | * | = | 0 | 0000 00 | 11 | 010 | 010 | $A \leftarrow A + 1$ |
| 00000010 | 0110 | * | = | 0 | 1111 11 | 11 | 010 | 101 | MAR $\leftarrow A$ |
| 00000010 | 0111 | * | = | 0 | 1111 11 | 11 | 100 | 001 | ADR ←SRAM |
| 00000010 | 1000 | * | = | 0 | 1100 11 | 11 | 010 | 101 | MAR ←0xFF |
| 00000010 | 1001 | * | = | 0 | 1111 11 | 11 | 010 | 100 | SRAM $\leftarrow A$ |
| 00000010 | 1010 | * | = | 1 | 1111 11 | 11 | 001 | 000 | Opcode ←$\mu$ROM; ADR+ |

**Figure 12.9** Nanocode for the `rtn` microinstruction.

microsubroutine call. At first glance, the extra argument would seem to inconvenience the microprogrammer as well, but we shall shortly find that we can get around this slightly awkward detail by providing appropriate programming tools. Figure 12.10 shows nanocode implementing the `call` microinstruction, and table 12.11 summarizes microstack and subroutine microinstructions.

### 12.1.4 Miscellaneous Microinstructions

Table 12.12 describes some microinstructions that simply move data between SRAM locations. Note carefully the operations performed by the `imove` (indirect move) and `movei` (move indirect) microinstructions. Although these microinstructions may seem redundant at first glance, they provide for computations that treat SRAM addresses as variables (rather than as constants built into the microinstruction stream). The skeptical reader should consider their usefulness in the microcode implementation of, say, a second stack in SRAM (in addition to the microstack maintained by the microinstructions above).

Table 12.13 describes microinstructions that allow microcode access to the main-memory (DRAM) subsystem. These include straightforward load and store operations `l` and `s`, whose arguments include 16-bit main-memory addresses passed in two SRAM locations. The `refr` microinstruction refreshes six rows of dynamic RAM. It uses SRAM location 0xFE as a *refresh counter*, which is incremented as each row is refreshed; thus periodic execution of `refr` microinstructions will

| Opcode | Phase | COND | = | ADR+ | ALU | CC | DRSEL | LDSEL | Comments |
|--------|-------|------|---|------|-----|----|-------|-------|----------|
| 00000001 | 0000 | * | = | 0 | 1100 11 | 11 | 010 | 101 | MAR ←0xFF |
| 00000001 | 0001 | * | = | 0 | 1111 11 | 11 | 100 | 010 | $A$ ←SRAM |
| 00000001 | 0010 | * | = | 0 | 1111 11 | 11 | 010 | 101 | MAR ←$A$ |
| 00000001 | 0011 | * | = | 1 | 1111 11 | 11 | 001 | 100 | SRAM ←$\mu$ROM; ADR+ |
| 00000001 | 0100 | * | = | 0 | 1111 10 | 11 | 010 | 010 | $A$ ←$A-1$ |
| 00000001 | 0101 | * | = | 0 | 1111 11 | 11 | 010 | 101 | MAR ←$A$ |
| 00000001 | 0110 | * | = | 1 | 1111 11 | 11 | 001 | 100 | SRAM ←$\mu$ROM; ADR+ |
| 00000001 | 0111 | * | = | 0 | 1100 11 | 11 | 010 | 101 | MAR ←0xFF |
| 00000001 | 1000 | * | = | 0 | 1111 10 | 11 | 010 | 100 | SRAM ←$A-1$ |
| 00000001 | 1001 | * | = | 1 | 1111 11 | 11 | 001 | 010 | $A$ ←$\mu$ROM; ADR+ |
| 00000001 | 1010 | * | = | 0 | 1111 11 | 11 | 001 | 001 | ADR ←$\mu$ROM |
| 00000001 | 1011 | * | = | 0 | 1111 11 | 11 | 010 | 001 | ADR ←$A$ |
| 00000001 | 1100 | * | = | 1 | 1111 11 | 11 | 001 | 000 | Opcode ←$\mu$ROM; ADR+ |

**Figure 12.10**  Nanocode for the `call` microinstruction.

ensure that all 128 rows are refreshed after every 128/6 `refr` instructions.[1]   The fact that `refr` refreshes six rows (rather than some convenient power of 2) is simply due to constraints imposed by our 4-bit phase counter: Six happens to be the greatest number of refreshes that can conveniently be performed in 16 clock cycles.

The nanocode implementation of `refr` is shown in figure 12.14. Nanocode for the `l` and `s` microinstructions is straightforward; the load nanocode is shown in figure 12.15 as an illustrative example.

## 12.2  Symbolic Microprogramming

The goal of microprogramming is a truth table for a microinstruction ROM whose interpretation by the microarchitecture yields some desired behavior.  In its most

---

[1]  Actually, there are $2^8 = 256$ rows, since a row is designated by an 8-bit address, but each refresh operation actually refreshes *two* rows: The most significant bit of the row address given for the refresh operation is ignored, and the two rows that are refreshed are the ones whose addresses agree in their least significant 7 bits with the given row address. Thus 128 refresh operations to consecutive row addresses suffice to refresh an entire DRAM chip.

**Table 12.11**  Microstack and microsubroutine microinstructions.

| Symbolic microinstruction | Control-ROM encoding | Operation performed |
|---|---|---|
| push($x$) | 0x03 $x$ | Push SRAM $\langle x \rangle$ onto microstack: $\langle \mu SP \rangle \leftarrow \langle x \rangle$; $\mu SP \leftarrow \langle \mu SP \rangle - 1$ |
| pop($x$) | 0x04 $x$ | Pop microstack into SRAM $\langle x \rangle$: $\mu SP \leftarrow \langle \mu SP \rangle + 1$; $x \leftarrow \langle \langle \mu SP \rangle \rangle$ |
| call($s$) | 0x01 $rlo\ rhi\ slo\ shi$ | Microsubroutine call to microcode ROM address $s$; $r$ is the return location: $\langle \mu SP \rangle \leftarrow rlo$; $\mu SP \leftarrow \langle \mu SP \rangle - 1$; $\langle \mu SP \rangle \leftarrow rhi$; $\mu SP \leftarrow \langle \mu SP \rangle - 1$; $ADR \leftarrow shi$; $ADR \leftarrow slo$. |
| rtn() | 0x02 | Microsubroutine return: $\mu SP \leftarrow \langle \mu SP \rangle + 1$; $ADR \leftarrow \langle \langle \mu SP \rangle \rangle$; $\mu SP \leftarrow \langle \mu SP \rangle + 1$; $ADR \leftarrow \langle \langle \mu SP \rangle \rangle$. |

**Table 12.12**  Data-movement microinstructions.

| Symbolic microinstruction | Control-ROM encoding | Operation performed |
|---|---|---|
| move($x,y$) | 0x05 $x\ y$ | $y \leftarrow \langle x \rangle$ |
| cmove($cx,y$) | 0x06 $cx\ y$ | $y \leftarrow cx$ |
| imove($x,y$) | 0x0D $x\ y$ | $y \leftarrow \langle \langle x \rangle \rangle$ |
| movei($x,y$) | 0x0E $x\ y$ | $\langle y \rangle \leftarrow \langle x \rangle$ |

primitive form, microprogramming involves explicit decisions about each bit of the ROM contents, based on a detailed understanding of a microinterpreter's implementation and a well-defined sequence of control signals to be generated.

Specification of the control ROM is tedious, and such an approach is impractical for any but the most trivial of microprogramming tasks, since the complexity and interrelations between the lowest-level control signals become enormously burdensome. The microprogrammer escapes from this morass of detail into an *abstraction*, thinking in terms of (and designing instructions for) an abstract machine whose primitive elements include, perhaps, registers with names like R5 that can serve as sources or destinations, rather than the three-state buses and enable signals from which that abstract machine is constructed.

**Table 12.13** Dynamic RAM microinstructions.

| Symbolic microinstruction | Control-ROM encoding | Operation performed |
|---|---|---|
| l(*adrlo*,*adrhi*,*where*) | 0x0F *adrlo adrhi where* | *where* ← ⟨⟨*adrlo*⟩,⟨*adrhi*⟩⟩; loads contents of DRAM location whose address is contained in SRAM locations *adrlo* and *adrhi* into SRAM location *where*. |
| s(*where*,*adrlo*,*adrhi*) | 0x10 *where adrlo adrhi* | Stores contents of SRAM location *where* into DRAM location whose address is contained in SRAM locations *adrlo* and *adrhi*. |
| refr() | 0x11 | Refreshes six rows of dynamic RAM. |

The amenability of the machine to such an abstraction is, of course, not accidental; it has been a deliberate design goal of the microarchitecture. The basic format of the add microinstruction reveals in its structure much about the intended programming abstraction; for example, it segregates information about each of the two source operands and the single destination into separately encoded bytes. The process of producing a microinstruction that encodes some operation, say R1 ← 7 + ⟨R2⟩, might be viewed as translating each of the elements of the operation into a binary byte in a microinstruction. The sequence of bytes

11 7 2 1

(representing a cadd microinstruction) performs the indicated operation; its four consecutive bytes specify the operation, the two operands, and the desired location for the result. This encoding process relates various implementation details to elements of the abstraction; for example, the encoding of virtual register R1 as the value 00000001 or the *constant add* function by the value 11. It must also resolve such organizational details as the specific binary address of each microinstruction within the ROM.

Fortunately for the microprogrammer, such details are not essential to the abstraction. A microprogram can be specified in terms of symbolic names (such as R5) rather than binary codes for elements of the abstract machine, lifting the burden of remembering binary codes while reflecting the more important aspects of the program's structure. A clever engineer faced with the design of microcode for a machine like ours would probably divide the task into two phases: (1) microprogram design, using some symbolic shorthand to specify the function performed

| Opcode | Phase | COND | = | ADR+ | ALU | CC | DRSEL | LDSEL | Comments |
|--------|-------|------|---|------|-----|----|----|-------|----------|
| 00010001 | 0000 | * | = | 0 | 1100 11 | 11 | 010 | 010 | $A \leftarrow 0xFF$ |
| 00010001 | 0001 | * | = | 0 | 1111 10 | 11 | 010 | 101 | $MAR \leftarrow A - 1$ (= 0xFE) |
| 00010001 | 0010 | * | = | 0 | 1111 11 | 11 | 100 | 010 | $A \leftarrow SRAM$ |
| 00010001 | 0011 | * | = | 0 | 1111 11 | 11 | 010 | 110 | $DRAM \leftarrow A$ |
| 00010001 | 0100 | * | = | 0 | 0000 00 | 11 | 010 | 010 | $A \leftarrow A + 1$ |
| 00010001 | 0101 | * | = | 0 | 1111 11 | 11 | 010 | 110 | $DRAM \leftarrow A$ |
| 00010001 | 0110 | * | = | 0 | 0000 00 | 11 | 010 | 010 | $A \leftarrow A + 1$ |
| 00010001 | 0111 | * | = | 0 | 1111 11 | 11 | 010 | 110 | $DRAM \leftarrow A$ |
| 00010001 | 1000 | * | = | 0 | 0000 00 | 11 | 010 | 010 | $A \leftarrow A + 1$ |
| 00010001 | 1001 | * | = | 0 | 1111 11 | 11 | 010 | 110 | $DRAM \leftarrow A$ |
| 00010001 | 1010 | * | = | 0 | 0000 00 | 11 | 010 | 010 | $A \leftarrow A + 1$ |
| 00010001 | 1011 | * | = | 0 | 1111 11 | 11 | 010 | 110 | $DRAM \leftarrow A$ |
| 00010001 | 1100 | * | = | 0 | 0000 00 | 11 | 010 | 010 | $A \leftarrow A + 1$ |
| 00010001 | 1101 | * | = | 0 | 1111 11 | 11 | 010 | 110 | $DRAM \leftarrow A$ |
| 00010001 | 1110 | * | = | 0 | 0000 00 | 11 | 010 | 100 | $SRAM \leftarrow A + 1$ |
| 00010001 | 1111 | * | = | 1 | 1111 11 | 11 | 001 | 000 | Opcode $\leftarrow \mu$ROM; ADR+ |

**Figure 12.14** Nanocode for the `refr` microinstruction.

by individual microinstructions and the flow of control among them, and (2) the translation of the symbolic result to binary ROM contents. The latter translation process is historically referred to as *assembly* and is usually done automatically (by an *assembler program*) rather than by hand.

In this section, we develop such a symbolic shorthand, or *assembly language*, for our microarchitecture. The resulting notational tool relaxes considerably the amount that must be remembered about the microarchitecture in order to be able to program it. Assembly language differs from most high-level programming languages, however, in that the abstraction it provides is an ad hoc one: It is appropriate only on the machine for which it has been designed. While programs written in LISP or FORTRAN will run on any machines that support these languages, a program written in IBM System/370 assembly language will run only on an IBM System/370 computer.

The machine-specific nature of assembly languages reflects their close relation-

| Opcode | Phase | COND | = | ADR+ | ALU | CC | DRSEL | LDSEL | Comments |
|--------|-------|------|---|------|-----|----|-------|-------|----------|
| 00001111 | 0000 | * | = | 1 | 1111 11 | 11 | 001 | 101 | MAR ←μROM; ADR+ |
| 00001111 | 0001 | * | = | 0 | 1111 11 | 11 | 100 | 010 | A ←SRAM |
| 00001111 | 0010 | * | = | 1 | 1111 11 | 11 | 001 | 101 | MAR ←μROM; ADR+ |
| 00001111 | 0011 | * | = | 0 | 1111 11 | 11 | 010 | 110 | DRAM ←A (RAS) |
| 00001111 | 0100 | * | = | 0 | 1111 11 | 11 | 100 | 110 | DRAM ←SRAM (CAS) |
| 00001111 | 0101 | * | = | 1 | 1111 11 | 11 | 001 | 101 | MAR ←μROM; ADR+ |
| 00001111 | 0110 | * | = | 0 | 1111 11 | 11 | 110 | 100 | SRAM ←DRAM |
| 00001111 | 0111 | * | = | 1 | 1111 11 | 11 | 001 | 000 | Opcode ←μROM; ADR+ |

**Figure 12.15**  Nanocode for the l(*adrlo*,*adrhi*,*where*) microinstruction.

ship to the instruction set executed by the machines for which they are designed. In general, each machine instruction is encoded as a single symbolic assembly-language instruction. Consequently, the assembly-language encoding of a given algorithm reflects (among other details) the operations that can be performed by single instructions on the target machine.

### 12.2.1 Symbolic Assembly Language

Our symbolic notation is used to represent a sequence of binary data bytes that will eventually be loaded into microcode ROM. As a starting point, we shall allow such data to be specified by a sequence of constants separated by white space, such as the sequence

```
11  7  2  1
```

given previously as the representation of a particular cadd microinstruction. Constants appearing in the assembly program designate the contents of consecutive locations; thus the above line might be used to specify the contents of ROM locations 0 through 3; following lines would fill successive locations. Constants can be specified in *binary* by prefixing them with 0b or in *hexadecimal* (base 16) by prefixing them with 0x; thus the above 4 bytes could be specified by the equivalent line

```
0xB  0b111  2  0x1
```

*Constant expressions*—involving constants as well as the operators +, -, *, /, % (remainder), and & (bitwise logical AND)—may appear in place of simple constants. It is essential to understand that the operations implied by these expressions are performed in the process of translating the symbolic notation to executable microinstructions; they do *not* represent operations that will be performed by microcode. We are simply developing a convenient notation for specifying *constants* to be programmed into our ROM. Thus the fanciful assembly-language line

33/3   3 + 4   (2 * 5) − 8   17%16

is equivalent to the above two example lines and encodes precisely the same `cadd` microinstruction. The multiplications, divisions, etc., are performed at assembly time in computing the desired microcode ROM contents; the use of these assembly-language notations emphatically does *not* imply that the indicated multiplications, divisions, etc., will be performed during execution of the microprogram! (Indeed, the MAYBE cannot perform a multiplication or a division in a single microinstruction.)

It is particularly convenient to be able to associate symbolic names with constants. We can specify such an association in our assembly language by an expression of the form

*symbol = expression*

which sets the specified symbol to the value of *expression*. Valid symbols can be character strings of any length; the string must start with a letter and must contain only letters and digits. Symbols defined in this way may be used as constants, for example, in constant expressions. As an example, the assembly-language line

R1 = 1

might serve to associate the symbol R1, denoting a virtual register, with the SRAM address used to implement it.

A special symbol, "." (period), has a context-dependent meaning: It denotes the address of the *next* location to be filled. Thus, if our assembly-language program begins

.   . + 3   .   . − 2

it will fill the first four ROM locations with the values 0, 4, 2, and 1, respectively. The process of translating an assembly program to binary involves the notion of a *current location*, which begins at 0 and increases as consecutive symbolic expressions are translated to binary constants and assigned to ROM locations. The "." symbol gives the programmer access to this value.

A special notation is used to associate a symbol with the current location. A line beginning

*symbol*:

(that is, with a symbol followed by a colon) assigns the value of "." to *symbol*. Such symbols are called *tags* or *labels* and are used to label microinstructions so that their addresses can be referred to symbolically.

### 12.2.2 Macroinstructions

To complete our little assembly language we introduce a primitive *macroinstruction* capability, which allows us to define and name parameterized *templates* for specifying sequences of bytes. A line of the form

.macro $name(p_1, p_2, ...)$ *body*

*defines* the macroinstruction $name(p_1, p_2, \ldots)$, which may have any number (including zero) of formal parameters $p_i$. Once defined, the subsequent appearance of a *macro call* of the form

$name(v_1, v_2, ...)$

will be replaced by *body'*, where *body'* is the result of substituting, for each occurrence of a formal parameter $p_i$ appearing in *body*, the *value* of the corresponding actual parameter $v_i$. Note that we assume a call-by-*value* scheme in our macro expansion: Each actual parameter is evaluated when the macro call is encountered, and the resulting value is bound to the corresponding formal parameter symbol during the scan of the macro body. The text resulting from the expansion of a macro call is reinterpreted during the assembly process, allowing additional macro calls within the expansion to be further expanded. It is therefore meaningful (and useful) for macro calls to appear within the body of a macro definition.

### 12.2.3 Symbolic Microinstructions

We use the macroinstruction capability to provide a palatable symbolic representation for individual microinstructions. We define a macro for each microinstruction by an assembly-language line like

.macro cadd(cx, y, z) 0x0B cx y z

which defines a macro that generates instances of the cadd microinstruction previously described. Given this definition (and appropriate definitions of the symbols R1 and R2), the programmer can specify a microinstruction that performs the operation $R1 \leftarrow 7 + \langle R2 \rangle$ in the symbolic form

cadd(7, R2, R1)

rather than as the series of byte values to which the macro expands.

When dealing with machine translation of assembly language to binary (using an assembler program), it is convenient to gather the definitions of microinstruction macros and other basic symbols in a place separate from the actual microprogram. Often this is done by placing the definitions in a separate source file and including at the beginning of the microprogram source file a directive like

.include macros

which directs the assembler to behave as if the directive were replaced by the contents of the named file. Following this scheme, the microprogrammer is fairly isolated from the coding details of microinstructions and need never be concerned with the opcode value, say, of the cadd microinstruction. Moreover, the coding might be changed to correspond to a control-ROM improvement, and the change would be reflected in the definitions file rather than in actual microprogram source code.

An example of such a macro definition file is presented in figure 12.16 (a more extensive set of macro definitions appears in appendix 2). This file gives symbolic names to several SRAM locations, including the stack pointer, and contains macroinstructions that generate a number of microinstructions. Note that the macro WORD($x$) does not correspond to a microinstruction, but simply expands to a sequence of values that is required in a number of other contexts. The effect of WORD($x$) is to generate, from a 16-bit value $x$, two consecutive 8-bit values that represent the low- and high-order halves of $x$. WORD is used, for example, in the bodies of the call and jmp macros, which deal with 16-bit addresses.

Note in particular the coding of the call microinstruction, which includes the return location in the microinstruction stream transparently to the programmer. Thus the programmer can code a 5-byte call to a subroutine $s$ by the relatively humane notation call($s$); the macro definition supplies the address of the following microinstruction automatically as the return point.

## 12.3 Microcoding Examples

In later chapters, we shall use microcode extensively to implement the instruction sets of several machines. As a preview, we present a glimpse of microprogramming techniques here.

### 12.3.1 Microprogramming Conventions

A complete microprogram will in general begin with a set of definitions of macros and variables, as illustrated in figure 12.17. Note the use of comments (preceded by vertical bars) in the source code. Definitions of microinstruction macros reside in a separate file macros.uasm, which is conceptually included in the program by the line

```
.include macros      | Definitions of microinstructions.
```

Next are a series of variable definitions binding symbols like R1 to SRAM locations; typically such definitions, which represent general conventions, are collected in a macro definition file so that they needn't be entered in each microprogram. Our convention is that the first few static RAM locations serve as virtual registers for general use—holding temporary values, say, or passing arguments and return values to and from microsubroutines. Here we allow room for 32 such registers,

**Figure 12.16** Typical macro definitions.

```
| Definitions of macros corresponding to microinstructions.

.macro    WORD(x) x%256 x/256
.macro    move(x,y) 0x05 x y
.macro    cmove(cx,y) 0x06 cx y
.macro    call(s) 0x01 WORD(.+4) WORD(s)
.macro    rtn() 0x02
.macro    push(x) 0x03 x
.macro    pop(x) 0x04 x

.macro    add(x,y,z) 0x0A x y z
.macro    sub(x,y,z) 0x1C x y z
.macro    cadd(cx,y,z) 0x0B cx y z
.macro    addcy(x,y,z) 0x81 x y z
.macro    caddcy(cx,y,z) 0x82 cx y z
.macro    cand(cx,y,z) 0x83 cx y z
.macro    and(x,y,z) 0x27 x y z
.macro    or(x,y,z) 0x28 x y z
.macro    xor(x,y,z) 0x29 x y z
.macro    not(x,y) 0x2A x y
.macro    neg(x,y) 0x2B x y
.macro    cmp(x,y) 0x1D x y

.macro    jmp(adr) 0x0C WORD(adr)
.macro    jmi(x) 0x12 WORD(x)
.macro    jpl(a) 0x1E WORD(a)
.macro    jc(a) 0x23 WORD(a)
.macro    je(x) 0x19 WORD(x)
.macro    jne(a) 0x25 WORD(a)

.macro    pdisp(x,p00,p01,p10,p11) 0x08 x WORD(p00) WORD(p01)
                                            WORD(p10) WORD(p11)
.macro    pwrup() 0x09
.macro    dispatch(x,adr) 0x80 x adr/256 adr%256
```

beyond which we store microprogram variables (x and framis) that are specific to the particular microprogram and defined in its initial lines.

Recall that the microstack builds down from high SRAM; it is thus important that we avoid these locations in our allocation of microprogram variables. Usually 30 or 40 bytes of microstack is a lavish allocation, since it holds only microsubroutine return information and we don't anticipate seriously recursive microsubroutines.

The first few lines of actual microcode perform some basic initializations and are assembled into microcode ROM locations starting at address 0. When the machine is turned on, the ADR and PHASE registers are set to 0, and OP is loaded from microcode ROM location 0. This microinstruction fetch is slightly nonstandard, in that ADR is not incremented; thus on phase 0 of the first microinstruction executed after power-up, ADR still contains 0. The pwrup microinstruction is designed to accommodate this situation; it is a do-nothing opcode designed to adjust ADR

**Figure 12.17**   Beginning of a typical microprogram.

```
|  Beginning of a typical microprogram.

.include macros              |  Definitions of microinstructions.

|  Reserved static RAM locations:

SP             = 0xFF          |  Stack pointer.
RC             = 0xFE          |  Refresh counter.
SBASE          = 0xFD          |  Stack builds down from here.

R0             = 0             |  Some register definitions.
R1             = 1
R2             = 2
R3             = 3
x              = 32           |  Some microprogram variables.
framis         = 33
init:          pwrup()         |  Get things going.
               cmove(SBASE,SP) |  Initialize SP.
               jmp(top)        |  And jump to main program.

top:           . . .
               . . .
```

initially. The microstack pointer is then initialized to the base of the microstack, which is located to allow the topmost two SRAM bytes to serve as $\mu$SP and the DRAM refresh counter. Finally the actual microprogram—beginning at the microinstruction tagged top:—is entered via a jmp microinstruction.

### 12.3.2 Counting Loop

A simple microprogram that might appear following such an initial source-code segment is shown in figure 12.18. Its function is to count a register up whenever $P_1$ is pressed and down whenever $P_0$ is pressed, and it performs this function just fine. It has two major defects, however. First, it has no output, so that it is difficult to detect whether it is working; second, it ignores the need to refresh DRAM periodically.

To facilitate the microcoding of simple test programs of this sort, we include nanocode for a special microinstruction pdisp($x,p_{00},p_{01},p_{10},p_{11}$) that (1) loads a value from SRAM location $x$ into $B$, where it is displayed in the lights; (2) performs a DRAM refresh cycle; and (3) senses the $P_0$ and $P_1$ button states to effect a four-way conditional branch. pdisp will effect a jump to the microcode ROM location given by its argument $p_{ij}$, where $i$ is the state of $P_1$ and $j$ is the state of $P_0$; thus it jumps to $p_{00}$ if no buttons are pressed, $p_{10}$ if $P_0$ is pressed and $P_1$ is not, etc. Using this new microinstruction, we can improve our counter microprogram as shown in figure 12.19. pdisp is among the more complicated of

**Figure 12.18** Simple up/down counter microprogram.

```
|  Up/down counter microprogram.


count    = 32              |  Program variable: current count.


top:     cmove(0,count)    |  Start at zero.
loop:    jp0(down)         |  P0 pressed.
         jp1(up)           |  P1 pressed.
         jmp(loop)         |  Nothing pressed.


down:    cadd(-1,count)    |  Decrement count.
wait0:   jp0(wait0)        |  Wait for P0 release.
         jmp(loop)


up:      cadd(1,count)     |  Increment count.
wait1:   jp1(wait1)        |  Wait for P1 release.
         jmp(loop)
```

**Figure 12.19** Improved up/down counter microprogram.

```
|  Up/down counter microprogram.

count    = 32                           |  Program variable: currentcount.
top:     cmove(0,count)                 |  Start at zero.
wait:    pdisp(count,loop,wait,wait,wait)  |  Wait for no buttons pressed.
loop:    pdisp(count,loop,up,down,top)

down:    cadd(-1,count)                 |  Decrement count.
         jmp(wait)                      |  Return to wait loop.
up:      cadd(1,count)                  |  Increment count.
         jmp(wait)
```

our microinstructions, owing to its multiple functions; the curious reader is referred to appendix 2 for its control-ROM coding.

### 12.3.3 Multiple-Precision Arithmetic

It is possible to perform arithmetic on integers of 2 or more bytes using the microinstructions presented thus far. However, the microcoding of such operations is awkward and relatively inefficient; propagating the carry through a long add, for example, requires testing the carry after each byte and adjusting the higher-order sum accordingly. A number of multiple-precision operations (for example, 16-bit adds) can be implemented directly as microinstructions by adding nanocode. This approach would offer speed and be about as easy for the microprogrammer to use as the single-byte operations. There is clearly a limit, however, to the complexity

| Opcode | Phase | COND | = | ADR+ | ALU | CC | DRSEL | LDSEL | Comments |
|--------|-------|------|---|------|-----|-----|-------|-------|----------|
| 10000001 | 0000 | * | = | 1 | 1111 11 | 01 | 001 | 101 | MAR ← $\mu$ROM; ADR+; shift CCs |
| 10000001 | 0001 | * | = | 0 | 1111 11 | 11 | 100 | 010 | $A$ ← SRAM |
| 10000001 | 0010 | * | = | 1 | 1111 11 | 11 | 001 | 101 | MAR ← $\mu$ROM; ADR+ |
| 10000001 | 0011 | * | = | 0 | 1111 11 | 11 | 100 | 011 | $B$ ← SRAM |
| 10000001 | 0100 | * | = | 1 | 1111 11 | 11 | 001 | 101 | MAR ← $\mu$ROM; ADR+ |
| 10000001 | 0101 | $c$ | = | 0 | 1001 $c$0 | 00 | 010 | 100 | SRAM ← $A + B$ + carry; shift CCs |
| 10000001 | 0110 | * | = | 1 | 1111 11 | 11 | 001 | 000 | Opcode ← $\mu$ROM; ADR+ |

**Figure 12.20**  Nanocode for the `addcy` microinstruction.

of the operations we can encode in our maximum of 16 control states allocated to each microinstruction; we cannot, for example, manage 4- or 8-byte addition.

An interesting alternative is to provide simple nanocode support that facilitates the implementation of these operations at the microcode level. The `addcy` microinstruction, whose control states are shown in figure 12.20, is an example of such support. `addcy`$(x,y,z)$ is nearly identical to `add`$(x,y,z)$ with one important exception: Whereas `add` always uses a carry input of 0 (that is, $\overline{C} = 1$), `addcy` uses as carry input the value dictated by the $\overline{C}$ bit in the condition register. It thus propagates the carry bit from a previous `add` or `addcy`.

Note that phase 0000 of `addcy` shifts the condition register, bringing the $\overline{C}$ bit in as the control-ROM input condition bit. Phase 0101, which performs the addition operation, is coded using the notational convenience of a *variable*, $c$, which appears both on the input and on the output side of the table. This line is an abbreviation for two lines in which the variable $c$ is replaced by its two possible values: 0 and 1. It is important to recognize that $c$ is not a variable in the programming-language sense; its value does not change with time. It simply provides an abbreviation for a longer sequence of entries involving constant values.

Using the `addcy` microinstruction, we can code an $n$-byte add at the cost of $n$ single-byte adds by using one `add` microinstruction followed by $n - 1$ `addcy` microinstructions. Figure 12.21 shows a microsubroutine that can be called to add the 32-bit integer stored in R0 through R3 to another such integer stored in R4 through R7.

Since the time it takes to clear all of memory may be longer than the maximum interval between refreshes of each DRAM row, the routine has `refr` microinstructions in two places. It will be important in our future microcoding to ensure that

**Figure 12.21**  Multiple-precision addition microsubroutine.

```
|   4-byte addition microsubroutine:
|   Takes x in R0-3, y in R4-7, and returns their sum in R0-3.
|   Note: R0 and R4 are the LOW-ORDER ends of the long integers.

add4:     add(R0,R4,R0)         | Add low order; cin = 0.
          addcy(R1,R5,R1)       | Remaining adds use
          addcy(R2,R6,R2)       |   previous carry.
          addcy(R3,R7,R3)
          rtn()                 | Return to caller.
```

**Figure 12.22**  DRAM-clearing microprogram.

```
| Subroutine to clear DRAM to all zeros.

clrdram:  cmove(0,R2)           | Value to write.
          cmove(-1,R0)          | adr lo.
          cmove(-1,R1)          | adr hi.
          refr()                | For good measure.

clr1:     s(R2,R0,R1)           | Store a byte.
          cadd(-1,R0,R0)        | Next lower adr.
          je(clr2)              | Got back to 0xFF.
          refr()                | For good measure.
          jmp(clr1)

clr2:     cadd(-1,R1,R1)        | Decrement high byte
          je(clr3)              |   iff done.
          jmp(clr1)

clr3:     rtn()
```

long microinstruction sequences (and particularly loops) perform `refr` operations with sufficient frequency. Recall, however, that DRAM accesses (such as the store operations performed here) refresh the referenced row as a side effect. Thus, if we carefully engineer a loop that does memory accesses, we can avoid the need for explicit `refr` operations. Since each row must be refreshed at a given minimum frequency, however, we must guarantee that such a loop touches all rows at least once during each refresh interval. In the `clrdram` example of figure 12.22, it is likely that the refresh interval will be long compared with the inner loop time but short compared with the total execution time. The reader is challenged to determine whether this routine would meet the refresh criterion without `refr` microinstructions.

## 12.4 Summary

Thus far we have been developing fundamental computational abstractions and the engineering techniques necessary to model them in practice. We have progressed through combinational elements, finite-state machines, and universal Turing machines; the corresponding technologies have been logic gates, sequential circuits, and the general-purpose interpretive mechanism introduced in this chapter. In a sense, we have reached the end of this progression: Universal Turing machines (and the microarchitecture developed here) are in theory capable of performing every computation we know how to perform. There are, of course, a host of performance-related engineering issues that can be pursued much further, but the elements of interpretation now at our disposal are representative of today's most powerful computer systems.

Our arrival at this interpretive plateau exposes a number of new issues that are uniquely the province of computer science, namely, issues involving the representation and manipulation of algorithms. While the interpreted language of the microarchitecture presented here is sufficiently powerful to satisfy the formal criterion of Turing universality, it is structurally inadequate for the practical representation of algorithms beyond a modest complexity: The microcode itself becomes intractably complicated. Accordingly, the focus of the remaining chapters will be on the interpretation of successively higher-level representations of algorithms, each of which corresponds to an abstract machine whose structure is derived from a given programming methodology. The next chapter begins this progression with the development of the single-sequence machine.

## 12.5 Context

Microprogramming was first proposed in a paper by Wilkes [1951], and the idea was developed further by Wilkes and Stringer [1953]. Numerous past and present processors have been based on microprogramming, including the DEC PDP-11 and VAX-11 families [Strecker 1978], the IBM System/360 and System/370 families [Stevens 1964], and other processors as diverse as hand calculators and LISP machines [Moon 1985]. Integrated-circuit manufacturers have also developed and sold families of chips designed to facilitate the construction of custom-designed microprogrammed systems: The Am2900 family, described, along with several of the microprogrammed processors enumerated above, in Siewiorek, Bell, and Newell [1982], is a notable early representative of this genre.

## 12.6 Problems

### Problem 12.1

Consult the control ROM listing in appendix 2 to determine the behavior of the move2 microinstruction. Give a register-transfer-language description of the operation performed by the microinstruction move2(63,17).

## Problem 12.2

Referring again to appendix 2, how many bytes of microcode ROM does the microinstruction cadd2(-12,32,6) (and its operands) occupy?

## Problem 12.3

What single microinstruction has the same effect on static RAM locations as the sequence

$cmove(x, R5)$

$cadd(y, R5, R5)$

## Problem 12.4

Consider the push microinstruction, the nanocode for which is given in figure 12.8.

A. Explain why 0xFF is a better choice for the microstack pointer location than, say, 0x37.

B. What value is left in the $A$ register at the beginning of the next microinstruction after push?

C. Explain in words what value is carried by the data bus during clock phase 0111 of the execution of the push microinstruction.

D. How many 16-bit control ROM locations are filled by the lines of nanocode in figure 12.8?

## Problem 12.5

Rewrite the nanocode for the call and rtn microinstructions (shown in figures 12.10 and 12.9, respectively) so that the return address stored on the microstack is stored in a little-Endian (rather than the current big-Endian) format.

## Problem 12.6

Consider the nanocode given in figure 12.23, which specifies the operation of a hypothetical ex microinstruction.

A. How many bytes of microinstruction-stream operands are required by this microinstruction?

B. What opcode (in hexadecimal) is assigned to the ex microinstruction?

C. Give a register-transfer-language expression describing the value loaded into $A$ at the end of clock phase 4 of the ex microinstruction.

D. Give a register-transfer-language expression describing the value left in the MAR after execution of the ex microinstruction.

E. Describe *concisely* the effect of executing $ex(x, y)$.

F. Would the ex microinstruction continue to work as before if the ALU FUNC code for phase 0 were changed from 1111 to 1010?

| Opcode | Phase | COND | = | ADR+ | ALU | CC | DRSEL | LDSEL | Comments |
|--------|-------|------|---|------|-----|----|----|-------|----------|
| 01010101 | 0000 | * | = | 1 | 1111 11 | 11 | 001 | 010 | $A \leftarrow \mu\text{ROM}$; ADR+ |
| 01010101 | 0001 | * | = | 0 | 1111 11 | 11 | 001 | 101 | MAR $\leftarrow \mu$ROM |
| 01010101 | 0010 | * | = | 0 | 1111 11 | 11 | 100 | 011 | $B \leftarrow$ SRAM |
| 01010101 | 0011 | * | = | 0 | 1111 11 | 11 | 010 | 101 | MAR $\leftarrow A$ |
| 01010101 | 0100 | * | = | 0 | 1111 11 | 11 | 100 | 010 | $A \leftarrow$ SRAM |
| 01010101 | 0101 | * | = | 0 | 1010 11 | 11 | 010 | 100 | SRAM $\leftarrow B$ |
| 01010101 | 0110 | * | = | 1 | 1111 11 | 11 | 001 | 101 | MAR $\leftarrow \mu$ROM; ADR+ |
| 01010101 | 0111 | * | = | 0 | 1111 11 | 11 | 010 | 100 | SRAM $\leftarrow A$ |
| 01010101 | 1000 | * | = | 1 | 1111 11 | 11 | 001 | 000 | Opcode $\leftarrow \mu$ROM; ADR+ |

**Figure 12.23**   Nanocode for ex($x$, $y$) microinstruction.

## Problem 12.7

A *conditional return* microinstruction rtne() is proposed. This instruction is conditionalized in the same way as the je($x$) instruction. If the condition is met, it should behave exactly like the rtn() microinstruction. If the condition is not met, then microinstruction processing continues normally with the next instruction. Write a control-ROM segment to implement the microinstruction rtne(). Assume that the opcode for this microinstruction is 0x1A. Be sure to comment your nanocode!

## Problem 12.8

The conditional jump microinstructions (table 12.6) of the MAYBE take the jump address as an argument. Implement an indirect conditional jump microinstruction jei($x$) that takes as a 1-byte argument the address into static RAM. The jump address is stored in locations $x$ and $x + 1$ of SRAM (the high-order byte in location $x$, the low-order byte in location $x + 1$). The jump condition for the jei microinstruction is the same as that for the je microinstruction. Write a control-ROM segment to implement the jei microinstruction. Assume that the opcode for this microinstruction is 0x1A. Be sure to comment your nanocode!

## Problem 12.9

Because of the frequent need to increment 4-byte values, we decide to invent a new microinstruction, written inc4($x$), that directly performs a 4-byte increment on the value stored in SRAM locations $x$ through $x + 3$, where the least significant byte is in location $x$. Write a (symbolic) nanocode segment to implement this new microinstruction. You do not need to limit it to 16 cycles. How many cycles does your nanocode take?

### Problem 12.10

Dissatisfied with the speed of 4-byte incrementing, we decide to try a different microinstruction inc44($a,b,c,d$), where inc44 is a new opcode and $a$, $b$, $c$, and $d$ are four 1-byte quantities. It is the programmer's responsibility to supply $x$, $x + 1$, $x + 2$, and $x + 3$ for the four parameters if the same effect as inc4($x$), defined in problem 12.9, is desired. Write (symbolic) nanocode to implement this new microinstruction. How many cycles does your nanocode take?

### Problem 12.11

Write a macro inc4($x$) (see problem 12.9) that expands into an instance of the inc44 microinstruction discussed in problem 12.10.

### Problem 12.12

Still dissatisfied with the speed of 4-byte incrementing, we try to throw a little hardware support at it. Borrowing ideas from the operation of the ADR register, we convert the MAR register into an 8-bit, parallel-loadable *counter*. MAR now has two control signals: $\overline{\text{LDMAR}}$, which loads 8 bits off the data bus as before, and MAR+, which increments MAR by 1. We drive MAR+ from the unused control-ROM output bit. How would you extend the symbolic nanocode notation to include this new control signal? Write (symbolic) nanocode to implement the inc4 microinstruction (defined in problem 12.9) using this new hardware design. How many cycles does your nanocode take?

### Problem 12.13

Write a macro l2($adr$,$where$) that expands into an l microinstruction that takes its source operands from SRAM locations $adr$ and $adr + 1$.

### Problem 12.14

Frequently we want to read a value out of SRAM whose address is in the $\mu$ROM. In the current implementation (figure 11.18), this requires reading the address out of the $\mu$ROM and loading it into the MAR on one cycle. The value in SRAM is not available until the next cycle. To speed things up we might want to add a direct path from the $\mu$ROM to SRAM by adding a multiplexer that chooses either the address from the MAR or the address from the $\mu$ROM, as shown in the modified MAYBE circuit diagram of figure 12.24. The ASEL signal comes from the previously unused control-ROM output bit.

A. Rewrite the nanocode for the add microinstruction (figure 12.2). Give both the binary representation and the symbolic notation for each line of code. What is the ratio of execution times (measured in cycles of the MAYBE's clock) of the rewritten instruction to those of the original instruction?

B. What additional constraints does the modification shown in figure 12.24 impose on the the clock cycle time? Estimate the new cycle time of the machine.

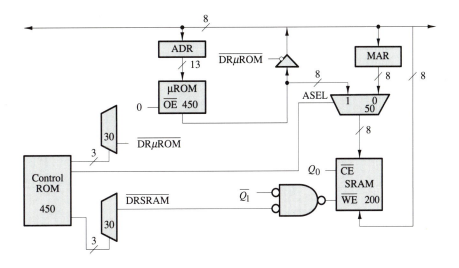

**Figure 12.24** Modified MAYBE (delays in nanoseconds).

Note that duty-cycle and phase-relation constraints on the two clocks (shown in figure 11.19) still hold.

C. Suppose that the effect of the modification shown in figure 12.24 on microinstruction execution times can be modeled as follows: Microinstructions either benefit from the modification and now run in three-fourths the number of cycles, or they are unchanged and require the same number of cycles as the original machine. Assuming minimum clock periods (as computed in parts A and B) for both the original and the modified machines, what fraction of executed microinstructions must benefit from the modification if the modified machine is to run faster than the original machine?

### Problem 12.15

A. Explain in words how to perform conditional jumps using the condition-code logic of figure 11.17 instead of that of figure 11.10.

B. Write nanocode for the **add** microinstruction, using the condition-code logic of figure 11.17 instead of that of figure 11.10.

C. Write nanocode for the **jodd** microinstruction, using the condition-code logic of figure 11.17 instead of that of figure 11.10.

### Problem 12.16

How many conditional jump microinstructions are there? Do all of them take the same number of cycles to execute? If not, explain why.

### Problem 12.17

You are examining the MAYBE hardware and nanocode to see if you can prefetch microinstructions in parallel with other computation. In the control-ROM listing you notice three things:

- The last phase of every microinstruction's nanocode always contains the nanoinstruction Opcode $\leftarrow$ $\mu$ROM; ADR+.

- The second-to-last phase of every microinstruction's nanocode *usually* contains an instruction that does not read from the microcode ROM.

- The OP register is never loaded from anywhere except the microcode ROM.

You figure that most of the time, the OP register could be loaded simultaneously with the heretofore second-to-last nanoinstruction phase, instead of taking an additional clock cycle. You realize that for this to happen you must provide an additional path on which data can flow from the $\mu$ROM to the opcode register, simultaneously with whatever data are being transferred on the data bus during the last opcode's final phase. Before actually changing the nanocode, however, you work out the details of this new data path.

Using only eight three-state buffers and no other gates, show how to modify the MAYBE hardware to provide a dedicated data path between the microcode ROM and the OP register. (In the resulting machine, the OP register will be loadable *only* from the microcode ROM; it will no longer be loadable from the data bus.) The resulting circuit must still work with the old nanocode and will not yet provide any performance gain. (Note that while the OP register is never loaded from anywhere except the $\mu$ROM, the $\mu$ROM is sometimes used as a source for other destinations. Thus it must still be able to drive the data bus when $\overline{\text{DR}\mu\text{ROM}}$ is asserted.)

### Problem 12.18

Looking for a way to activate the new data path you designed in problem 12.17 in parallel with the execution of another nanoinstruction, you spy an N.C. (not connected) control-ROM output bit. Show how, with only a single added gate, this ROM output bit could be used to activate the new data path (that is, load the OP register and clear the phase counter). Your change should be compatible with the original nanocode; in other words, the assertion of $\overline{\text{LDOP}}$ should still cause the OP register to load and the phase counter to clear. (Note that the original nanocode always drives the N.C. pin high.)

### Problem 12.19

Show how you would modify the nanocode of the add microinstruction (figure 12.2) so that it can take advantage of the new circuitry introduced in problems 12.17 and 12.18.

### Problem 12.20

Show how you would write nanocode for the move microinstruction to take advantage of the new circuitry introduced in problems 12.17 and 12.18.

### Problem 12.21

Show how you would write nanocode for the je microinstruction to take advantage of the new circuitry introduced in problems 12.17 and 12.18.

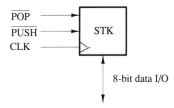

POP
PUSH
CLK
STK
8-bit data I/O

**Figure 12.25**  Stack chip interface.


## Problem 12.22

About how much improvement might you reasonably expect in the performance of your MAYBE computer as a result of the new circuitry introduced in problems 12.17 and 12.18? (*Hint:* What is the average number of nanoinstructions per microinstruction?)

## Problem 12.23

You have spent government funds on a boxcar full of 8-bit stack chips whose interface is shown in figure 12.25. The STK chip has a CLK input and active low $\overline{\text{PUSH}}$ and $\overline{\text{POP}}$ inputs. At most one of $\overline{\text{PUSH}}$ and $\overline{\text{POP}}$ can be asserted (low) at a time. If $\overline{\text{PUSH}}$ is asserted at the time of an active clock edge, data on the eight data lines are pushed onto a stack stored inside the chip. If $\overline{\text{POP}}$ is asserted at the time of an active clock edge, data from the top of the stack are popped off and driven onto the eight data lines.

You propose to use STK modules to implement the microstack of the MAYBE machine. The 8 data bits of the STK module are connected to the MAYBE's data bus, and $\overline{\text{PUSH}}$ and $\overline{\text{POP}}$ control inputs are connected to outputs of the load-select and drive-select decoders, respectively. Thus STK can be used as either a source or a destination for the MAYBE microarchitecture.

A. Give nanocode for the `push` and `pop` microinstructions using the new stack device. Use symbolic notation, as in the comment field of figure 12.8; STK may appear as either a source or destination.

B. You have likewise modified the `call` and `rtn` microinstructions to save the return point on the STK module. Since the capacity of the STK modules is quite large, you consider a microcode calling convention in which arguments to microsubroutines are passed on the microstack. Briefly explain why this proposal is awkward.

## Problem 12.24

Many digital music synthesizers use *wave tables* to produce sounds. A wave table is simply a small array of numbers. By outputting successive elements of this array at the proper intervals, the synthesizer can produce notes of a desired frequency. By changing the contents of the wave table, the user controls the timbre of the sound produced.

```c
char  Table[256];
sawtooth(tab)
 char *tab;    /* A pointer to the start of the table */
               /* (guaranteed to be a multiple of 256) */
 { int index;
   for (index = 0; index < 256; index = index + 1)
     tab[index] = index;
 }
```

**Figure 12.26**   Program to fill a sawtooth-waveform table.

Our wave tables contain 256 8-bit values, and they always start at a DRAM address whose low-order 8 bits are 0. Figure 12.26 shows such a program, written in C, for storing a "sawtooth" pattern in a wave table. For now, assume that characters in C require 1 byte, while integers occupy 4 bytes, or 32 bits. The declaration char Table[256]; allocates an array of 256 bytes. Note also that pointers to characters and arrays of characters are interchangeable in C. The statements tab[index] = index; and Table[index] = index; are equivalent if tab is a pointer to the start of Table.

Let's create a new microinstruction called sawfill(adrhi). The instruction takes a 1-byte argument that is the high-order byte of the table's starting address. (Remember, we know that the low-order byte is 0.) The macro we need to use this instruction is

```
.macro sawfill(adrhi) 0x68 adrhi 0x69
```

The nanocode for opcode 0x68 has the following comments:

```
| B ← μROM; ADR+
| A ← 0; latch CCs
| Opcode ← μROM; ADR+
```

Write the nanocode comments for opcode 0x69. Each iteration of your loop should fill one location in the wave table. (*Hint:* Consider the solution to problem 11.10.)

### Problem 12.25

The nanocode from your solution to problem 12.24 wastes many clock cycles. Suggest an alternative way of writing the sawfill(adrhi) microinstruction that does not waste any clock cycles. Write this improved nanocode program. How many clock cycles does this nanoprogram take to fill the wave table?

### Problem 12.26

Will the DRAM refresh timing specifications be met if the refr instructions are removed from the microprogram shown in figure 12.22? (Assume that the MAYBE clock frequency is 1 MHz and that each DRAM row must be accessed once every 2 ms in order to guarantee that no data are lost.) If the DRAM refresh timing specifications will not be met, is there a way to revise the program so that no refr instructions are necessary? Explain.

```
byte multiplier,multiplicand,product,mask;
multiply()
{
 product = 0;
 mask = 0b00000001;
 while (mask != 0b00010000)
    {
     if (multiplier & mask) product = product + multiplicand;
     multiplicand = multiplicand + multiplicand;
     mask = mask + mask;
    }
}
```

**Figure 12.27**   A 4-bit by 4-bit multiply subroutine.

### *Problem 12.27*

The program in figure 12.27 shows how to multiply two 4-bit unsigned numbers to produce an 8-bit unsigned result. Code this multiply routine in the MAYBE's symbolic microcode. Assume that the four single-byte variables `multiplier`, `multiplicand`, `product`, and `mask` are simply fixed locations in SRAM, say addresses 0 to 3. The calling program will place the 4-bit multiplier and multiplicand into the appropriate SRAM locations before calling the multiply routine and will expect to find the result at a fixed place in the SRAM. Other temporary variables may be placed anywhere in SRAM. Don't forget to comment your microcode.

### *Problem 12.28*

If it is known that the multiplier in the program of figure 12.27 is frequently 0, we can potentially speed up the routine by testing for this special case. Modify the multiply routine developed in problem 12.27 so that if the multiplier is 0, it returns a result of 0 without much computation (and if the multiplier is not 0, it simply performs the full multiply as before).

### *Problem 12.29*

The value of optimizing for 0, as in problem 12.28, depends on the frequency of 0 as a multiplier operand. For the purpose of computing execution times, assume that each microinstruction takes the same amount of time. Compute the number of microinstructions executed for (1) the unmodified routine (from problem 12.27), (2) the modified routine (from problem 12.28) with the multiplier equal to 0, and (3) the modified routine with the multiplier not equal to 0. Suppose that from empirical measurements of typical multiply operands we find that about 10 percent of the time the multiplier is 0. Will the modification be beneficial on average?

### *Problem 12.30*

In machine-language interpreters it is useful to store a 4-byte "program counter" in four consecutive SRAM locations. Let us designate these locations PC, PC+1, PC+2, and PC+3, from least to most significant byte. A frequent operation on the program counter is to increment it by 1. Write a microsubroutine that increments the program counter by 1. (Remember, this is a 4-byte addition.) How many clock cycles does your microsubroutine take?

### Problem 12.31

Write a microsubroutine that performs the same function as the `sawtooth` subroutine in figure 12.26. Your program should accept a 2-byte pointer to the beginning of the wave table in a register. Remember that the low-order byte of this pointer is guaranteed to be 0. Try to be as efficient as possible, but don't make your code overly tricky.

### Problem 12.32

How many clock cycles will your solution to problem 12.31 take to run?

# 13 Single-Sequence Machines

The design of any abstraction is necessarily a compromise between the user's requirements and the constraints imposed by the medium in which the abstraction is to be implemented. User requirements are chiefly of a *semantic* nature: The user wants the abstraction to include certain kinds of objects and certain ways of combining these objects into systems. The constraints imposed by the implementation medium tend primarily to influence *performance*: Once the rather minimal threshold of Turing universality is reached, *any* semantics that avoids issues of uncomputability can be implemented, but the structure of the implementation medium usually leads to strong performance advantages for certain kinds of semantics.

An important characteristic of an abstraction, therefore, is the degree to which user requirements and implementation constraints have each affected its design. As we look at the levels of abstraction we have explored so far (the digital abstraction, finite-state machines, and microarchitectures), it is clear that each abstraction has been abundantly influenced from both directions. However, there is a progression toward increasing emphasis on the semantic elegance of the abstraction and decreasing influence of the nature of the implementation medium. In this chapter, we continue this trend with another layer of abstraction, which we shall call *machine language*.

## 13.1 Machine Language as an Abstraction

Machine language represents a qualitative break with the previous approaches. Our previous abstractions were all designed to have other abstractions built on top of them, primarily via the technique of interpretation. The machine-language abstraction is principally designed to serve as a target language for compilation. This goal exerts a strong influence on machine-language design; the important criterion is not the performance that can be achieved by a programmer programming directly in the machine language, but the performance that can be achieved when a compiler translates a higher-level-language program into the machine language. It is thus desirable for machine languages to be "easy to compile to," not in the sense that the compilation process is trivial, but in the sense that known compilation algorithms are capable of exploiting the potential performance of the machine-language architecture. This emphasis on compilation thus favors machine-language constructs that can be exploited automatically over those whose exploitation requires human intelligence. A secondary objective of the machine-language interface is to support operating-system functions such as protection of information and management of resources such as processors and memory. The many demands on machine-language architecture tend to lead to a complexity of specification considerably beyond what we have considered up to now, and the power of microcode as an implementation medium proves very useful.

Machine languages allow us largely to ignore the underlying implementation technologies (such as electronics, logic gates, and microarchitecture) and solve subsequent problems in terms of the higher-level operations they provide. Machine language is, of course, not the highest-level abstraction we shall encounter; indeed, the principal function of modern machine languages is to provide a basis for higher-level languages such as LISP, Pascal, Ada, and C. It is, however, a particularly important abstraction, in that it bridges the gap between hardware architecture and what is conventionally considered to be software technology.

As with any powerful abstraction, the simplicity afforded by the machine language comes at the expense of decreased implementation flexibility. Each machine-language instruction comprises an aggregate of lower-level operations that together constitute a higher-level machine-language operation, but only a small fraction of the possible lower-level combinations are chosen to be represented as machine-language instructions. The major criteria by which we select functions for machine-language instructions are the goals of conceptual simplicity of the machine and utility in achieving high performance in code compiled from higher-level-language programs.

A major sacrifice that we make in the interest of conceptual simplicity is the omission of conventions for representing explicit parallelism. We choose to design the machine so that it interprets a single *sequence* of machine-language instructions, each corresponding to a single higher-level operation. For this reason, we apply the term *single-sequence machines* to the class of computers considered here. It should be mentioned that there are plausible alternatives to the single-sequence abstraction as the basis for a machine-language design, although these are rare in practice and predominantly experimental. Several such alternatives are briefly discussed in chapter 21.

In this chapter, we explore various factors, such as the need to implement higher-level languages, that influence machine-language design. Subsequent chapters examine several popular approaches to machine-language design and provide three extended case studies that will illustrate many of the concepts we discuss.

## 13.2 Gross Organization of the Single-Sequence Machine

The single-sequence machine model we shall use in this chapter is an accurate description of the vast majority of computer systems in existence today. Disregarding, for now, connections between a machine and the outside world, we can see that a single-sequence machine has two principal components: a *processor* and a *memory*. The processor can be viewed as a finite-state machine with a certain amount of state stored in *processor registers*. Generally, the number of processor registers is relatively small.

The memory consists of a series of *locations*, each of which can be thought of as a register containing some number of bits. The number of these bits is known as the *word size* of the computer and is an important architectural parameter. Each location has a unique numerical *address* by which it can be designated. The size of these addresses determines the maximum number of memory locations that the computer can handle; this is another important architectural parameter. For example, if a given computer uses 12-bit addresses, its *address space* is only $2^{12} = 4096$ locations, which limits it to relatively "toy" applications. On the other hand, 32-bit addresses allow an address space of $2^{32} = 4,294,967,296$ locations, which may seem effectively infinite. The history of computing has seen progressive expansion of address spaces as memory has become less expensive and computers have been used in more ambitious ways. Currently, many sectors of the computer community have converged on 32-bit addresses, which is the default assumption throughout our examples.

Memory locations can be both read and written (though many computers include some amount of read-only memory). They are used for storing numbers, programs, and any other data on which the computer operates. One such type of data is addresses of other locations in memory. The need to handle such *pointers* would suggest, for example, that a memory with 32-bit addresses would need to have a word size of at least 32 bits. It seems wasteful, though, to devote an entire 32-bit word to store what might be a small integer. One solution to this dilemma is the *byte-addressing* approach discussed in section 11.2.2. The *S* and *G* machines we shall discuss in later chapters are both byte-addressed machines.

Programs on the single-sequence machine are composed of *instructions* stored in the memory. The processor reads one instruction after another and *executes* each one. Instruction execution will typically cause state changes in the processor registers and often will cause the contents of one or more memory locations to be changed as well. A key element of the processor state is the *program-counter register*, or PC, which holds the address of the next instruction to be executed.

## 13.3 Influences on Machine-Language Design

In this section, we explore several aspects of modern higher-level languages and of operating systems that are relevant to the design of machine languages. It should be borne in mind, of course, that higher-level languages have evolved in response to the needs of computer users; thus we are really exploring how the design of computers is affected by what people want to do with them.

### 13.3.1 Data Structures and Typing

One feature of almost all higher-level languages is the ability to deal with a variety of different types of data. We distinguish between simple and compound data types. Typical *simple data types* are

- *numbers*, both integer and floating point, often with various possible precisions;
- *characters*, for input and output of human-readable data; and
- *pointers* to items in memory.

Pointers can be used to build complex data structures by threading together small items, each of which may reference other items via pointers.

There are two common *compound data types*:

- *Arrays* are collections of *elements* of a single type. A given element of an array $A$ may be designated by using a numerical counter $i$ in notation such as $A[i]$. For example, if $A$ is an array of floating-point numbers, $A[3]$ will denote one of those numbers and $A[4]$ will denote another. Arrays of characters can be used to represent printed documents within the computer.

- *Structures*, or *records*, are collections of elements that can be of different types. An example might be a set of data about an employee of a corporation. The structure might include character strings giving the employee's name and address, along with integers giving the employee's age and salary. A common notation for selection of an element from a structure is an infix dot; thus, if $S$ is a structure containing employee information, $S$.name and $S$.age would denote specific elements of that structure.

The representation of aggregate data structures such as arrays of numbers most commonly involves an allocation of consecutive locations to hold the respective array elements. Thus a 10-element array $A$ of 32-bit integers might be stored in memory locations 101 through 140 on a byte-addressed machine; a reference to the $i$th element $A[i]$ of $A$ would be translated by a compiler to access the 32-bit integer stored beginning at location $101 + 4i$. Similarly, structures are usually stored in several consecutive locations.

### 13.3.2 Data Types

At some level of implementation, the data manipulated by most computers take the form of *binary words*, perhaps in several different lengths. At some higher level (perhaps in the mind of the programmer), these words constitute the representation of some problem-specific value such as a number, a person's name, the coordinates of a point in space, or an instruction to be executed. The degree and style of architectural support for such representations is a complex and interesting issue in machine design.

Conventions for the representation of certain types of data, such as integers, floating-point numbers, machine instructions, and addresses, must be fixed in the architecture of the instruction set to the extent that its operations manipulate the data in type-specific ways. The logic (or microcode) that adds two floating-point numbers, for example, must differentiate between the fraction and exponent portion of each number, and it consequently establishes a convention for the representation of floating-point numbers as binary words. However, the fact that a given binary word represents a floating-point number (rather than, say, an integer or the address of some location) may not be apparent from the configuration of bits in the word itself; a given binary word might be interpreted as a floating-point number, a (different) integer, or a string of characters. Some bookkeeping is necessary to avoid misinterpretation.

Most commonly, the requisite data-type bookkeeping is left to higher-level software or to the programmer. In this case, all data are effectively of type "binary word," perhaps qualified by a length specification such as "binary byte" or "binary longword"; the *interpretation* of a word (for example, as an integer or floating-point number) depends on the particular operations applied to it. Accordingly, the instruction repertoire of typical machines includes an *integer add* operation, which treats its operands as 2's complement representations of integers and produces a 2's complement sum, as well as a *floating-point add* operation that interprets its inputs and output differently. Machine-language programs must be organized so that appropriately typed operations are performed on each datum. This responsibility is usually assumed by an interpreter or compiler for a higher-level language. To accommodate this, most languages (for example, C, Pascal, or ALGOL) include *declarations* by which the programmer must specify the type of every datum used in the program. An interpreter or compiler will then have the information it needs to pick the appropriately typed operators.

### 13.3.3 Tagged-Data Architectures

A few machine architectures provide means for the automatic discrimination of data types during program execution. In general, run-time type discrimination requires distinct representations for different types of data. In other words, the type of datum stored in a binary word in a tagged architecture can be determined simply by examining the bits in the word, in contrast to the situation in the untagged architectures discussed above. This is usually accomplished by adding type-encoding *tag bits* to each data word. A simple tagged architecture might manipulate 34-bit data words of the form

| tag | . . . data . . . |
|-----|------------------|
| 2 bits | 32 bits |

in which a 2-bit tag dictates the appropriate interpretation of the attached 32-bit binary word. The four possible tag-bit combinations might denote, say, integer, floating-point, machine instruction, or pointer typed data. (Most architectures would have more options and a longer tag field.)

Although tagged architectures increase the size of data representations and require an additional mechanism in the processor implementation, they offer a number of important advantages. The most obvious of these is that they avoid the need to proliferate instructions for manipulating different representations of similar data types: A single *generic* ADD instruction can be applied to integers, floating-point numbers, or a mixture of the two. The microcode responsible for ADD would determine the types of its operands, perform the appropriate operation after making necessary representation changes, and produce a tagged result. In addition to relieving the higher-level software of the bookkeeping burden, the generic ADD might provide for automatic recovery from certain error conditions; if the sum of two integer operands exceeds 32 bits, for example, it could produce a nearly accurate floating-point result.

Certain advanced languages, such as LISP, are designed on the assumption of tagged-data representations; their semantics demands generic operators as well as garbage-collected heap-storage allocation, both of which require run-time type discrimination. Implementations of such languages on conventional (untagged) machines thus require run-time software to maintain the tags, leading to a significant computational overhead. Such languages benefit the most from tagged architectures, since microcode support for tagged data is rather more efficient than building the corresponding mechanism using an untagged machine language.

A disadvantage of tagged architectures, apart from their additional implementation cost, is that they tend to bind at the machine-language level the choice of data types and representations available to higher-level software. In this respect, they become specialized to the particular programming languages and methodologies anticipated by their designers, often limiting the breadth of their appeal and hence their commercial marketability. As a consequence, tagged machines have never been spectacularly successful as products, despite their technical appeal. This probably reflects more the lack of consensus on language and data representation issues among computer users than any inherent limitations of tagged machines and may change as the computer industry matures.

Examples of tagged architectures include the LISP machine developed by the Artificial Intelligence Laboratory at M.I.T., a tagged machine motivated by the goal of efficient LISP execution, and the Burroughs B6700 and its predecessors, specialized to the execution of ALGOL programs.

### 13.3.4 Procedures

Among the frequently used features common to almost all programming languages, the *procedure* is probably the most complex. Because of the importance of procedures, almost all machine architectures provide some specialized support for them. In the next few pages we shall explore, in general terms, the requirements of implementing procedures for most modern higher-level programming languages, including Pascal, C, Ada, and LISP.

We shall concentrate on the organization and operations that are necessary to support procedures, whether or not they are directly supported in a machine's instruction set. Our programming examples will be kept simple so that we can focus our attention on implementation questions rather than on the analysis of algorithms.

The microsubroutines of the MAYBE microarchitecture (see section 12.1.3) are a primitive kind of procedure; however, procedures in modern higher-level languages provide many capabilities—including the passing of arguments, return of values, allocation of private (local) variables, and recursion—whose implementation should be considered in machine-language design. An example of some of these facilities in action is given in figure 13.1, a program written in the algebraic language C,

```
/* Procedure to compute the greatest common divisor of
 *   two integers, using Euclid's algorithm.
 */

int GCD(a,b)
  int a,b;
  {   int rem;         /* Allocate a local variable rem.   */
      rem = a % b;     /* Calculate the remainder          */
                       /*    of dividing a by b.           */
      if (rem == 0)    /* Test the remainder:              */
        return b;      /* If rem is 0, the GCD is just b,  */
        else return GCD(b,rem);  /*   else recurse.        */
  }


/* Procedure to compute the least common multiple of two integers;
 * it divides their product by their GCD.
 */

int LCM(a,b)
int a,b;
  {     return (a * b) / GCD(a,b);
  }


/* Main program: */

Main_Program()
  {     int j;
            .
            .
            .
        j = LCM(78,16);
            .
            .
            .

  }
```

**Figure 13.1**  Illustration of procedures.

which is a cousin to Pascal and ALGOL. A brief introduction to C may be found
in appendix 1.

### 13.3.5 Stacks

*Stacks*, introduced in section 12.1.3, play a central role in the implementation of
modern higher-level languages. The usual stack implementation at the machine-
language level uses a contiguous region of memory to hold the stack contents and
dedicates a processor register (called the *stack pointer*, or SP) to the task of remembering the number of stacked items. Thus we may view the allocated storage as an
array Stack[StackSize] and SP as counting the number of stacked items, which

occupy the first SP array elements. The operation of *pushing* a datum $D$ on the stack corresponds to the sequence `Stack[SP] = `$D$`; SP = SP+1;` and *popping* the datum $D$ from the stack corresponds to `SP = SP-1;` $D$` = Stack[SP];`. Note that pushing data causes this stack to build toward higher addresses, in contrast to the MAYBE microarchitecture's microstack, which builds toward lower addresses. Both directions of stack growth are used in contemporary machine-language designs; we see growth toward higher addresses as slightly more intuitive and hence have selected it for our illustrative machine architectures.

At any given point, the most recently pushed item still on the stack is referred to as being on the *top* of the stack. The *bottom* of the stack is the other end of the stack region (that is, the location `Stack[0]`). At the machine-language level, the SP is usually represented as a *pointer* to the location where the next datum to be pushed would be put, rather than as an index relative to the base of the allocated stack region. This simply amounts to offsetting the SP by the address of the stack in order to save run-time arithmetic in push and pop operations.

One function for which the stack is used almost universally in modern architectures, just as in the MAYBE microarchitecture, is storing linkage information for procedure calls. In the simplest of cases, a *call* to a procedure involves pushing the return address (the address of the instruction following the call) on the stack; the corresponding *return* pops the return address and installs it in the program counter. Additional processor-state information is often stacked as well, to be similarly reinstalled on return. A stack is useful for the storage of procedure return addresses, since it provides a simple means for nesting calls to a depth limited only by the amount of memory allocated to the stack. Stacks are applicable for storing procedure-linkage information because procedures obey *stack discipline*, which means that all the storage allocated when a procedure is entered can be deallocated when the procedure exits.

### 13.3.6 Stack Frames

The stack discipline that must be followed by a called procedure allows arbitrarily many data to be pushed on the stack during its execution, so long as SP is returned to its entry-point value before exit. The procedure might, for example, save the contents of several processor registers on entry (by pushing them on the stack) and restore their original values immediately prior to the return instruction that exits from the procedure (by corresponding pops), thus preserving any essential data that may have been left in them by the calling program.

The convention of stack discipline reserves the space occupied by these stacked register contents between the time of the push and the time of the corresponding pop. Additional space can be reserved for use by the procedure simply by adding a constant $n$ to the stack pointer (which is equivalent to pushing $n$ bytes of random data); stack discipline then requires that a corresponding subtraction of $n$ be executed at procedure exit to deallocate the storage. This scheme is commonly used to allocate storage space for local variables of procedures; the *extent* of these variables (the period during which their value is guaranteed to be preserved) consequently does not persist beyond a single invocation of the procedure. Such variables are

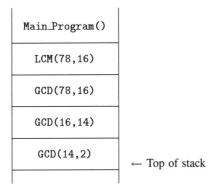

```
Main_Program()

LCM(78,16)

GCD(78,16)

GCD(16,14)

GCD(14,2)          ← Top of stack
```

**Figure 13.2**  Stack frames from execution of the program in figure 13.1.

often termed *automatic*, meaning that they are allocated for the duration of a single procedure invocation; *static* variables, in contrast, are permanently allocated.

Such use of the stack causes its contents to be segmented into sections, termed *stack frames* or *activation records*, each of which corresponds to the storage associated with a single procedure call. Each time a procedure is entered, a stack frame, typically comprising several words of information, will be pushed on the stack. When the procedure is exited, the stack frame will be popped off the stack. Figure 13.2 gives a snapshot of the stack frames at a particular point in the execution of the program in figure 13.1. Each frame is labeled with the procedure call that caused it to be created.

Some of the information in a stack frame is no longer needed after execution of the procedure is complete. This information is discarded. Other parts of the stack frame are used to restore parts of the processor's internal state (such as saved register contents) to the values that were saved at the time when the procedure was called. In more detail, virtually every stack frame has three parts:

- *local variables* used during the execution of the procedure;
- *arguments*, or parameters, passed to the procedure; and
- *saved processor state* (such as the saved program counter value) and other bookkeeping information.

A stack frame for the procedure GCD might look like figure 13.3.

### 13.3.7 Communication between Caller and Procedure

Activation and termination of a procedure are accomplished via a protocol with four distinguishable parts:

- The *calling sequence* is executed by the caller. Typically this involves pushing the argument values on the stack and saving some part of the processor state. The calling sequence terminates when control is transferred to the procedure.

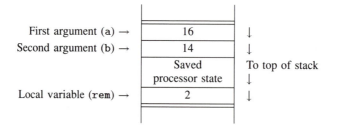

**Figure 13.3** Stack frame for GCD(16,14).

- The *entry sequence* is executed at the beginning of the procedure. This involves saving any additional processor state and then allocating space on the stack for local variables.

- The *exit sequence* is executed at the end of the procedure. It deallocates the local variable storage and restores some or all of the saved processor state. It must also provide for any returned value from the procedure to be put where it is accessible to the caller. The exit sequence terminates when control is returned to the procedure's caller.

- The *return sequence* is executed by the caller upon return from the procedure. Typically it will be responsible for popping the argument values off the stack and disposing properly of the value, if any, returned from the procedure.

Implementations differ widely in the details of internal stack-frame structure. They also differ in the division of responsibility between calling and entry and between exit and return sequences. Whether or not a machine includes special instructions for procedure calling, however, the operations described above will have to be performed.

### 13.3.8 *Lexical Scoping and Free Variables

Most programming languages allow communication to and from procedures by means of *free-variable references*, or simply *free references* (references to variables that are neither arguments nor local variables of the procedure from which they are referenced), as well as by means of explicit arguments and return values. There are three common policies for dealing with free-variable references:

- All free references refer to statically allocated variables accessible from anywhere within the program. This is essentially the policy followed by FORTRAN and C.

- Free references in a procedure are interpreted in the context of its caller. Thus a free reference to $i$ in procedure $P$ refers to the local variable $i$ of the most recent procedure in the chain of calls to $P$ that had a local variable called $i$. Thus, of all the local variables called $i$ that are located in different frames on

```
int g()
{       int y;

        int f(x)
         int x;
          {     if (x < y)
                    return x+f(x+1);
                    else return x;
          }

        y = 7;
        return f(5);
}
```

**Figure 13.4**  Program with free-variable reference.

the stack, a free reference $i$ always refers to the local variable $i$ that is closest to the top of the stack. This policy is called *dynamic scoping* and is followed by many dialects of LISP.

- A free reference in a procedure definition (or *block* in ALGOL terminology) is interpreted in the context of the *lexically* (textually) enclosing procedure definition or block. Here a free reference to $i$ in procedure $P$ is taken to refer to the local variable $i$ of the procedure $Q$ that is the innermost block that has a local variable called $i$ and also encloses the definition of procedure $P$. This policy is known as *lexical scoping* and is followed by most languages that allow procedure definitions to be nested inside other procedure definitions—for example, Pascal, ALGOL, and Scheme (a dialect of LISP). (The fact that procedure $Q$ has a local variable called $i$ is often expressed by saying that $Q$ contains a *declaration* of $i$. In C, a declaration of variables $x$ and $y$ is accomplished by a statement such as int $x,y;$.)

Lexical scoping is a particularly important policy for dealing with free references, and its requirements have influenced many computer architectures, including the ones that we discuss. Consider, for example, the program shown in figure 13.4. (The official definition of C does not allow for procedure definitions to be nested inside other procedure definitions. For the purposes of our examples, we extend the C programming language in the obvious way in order to allow this.)

The procedure f contains a free reference to the variable y declared in its lexically containing block. Since the storage for y is allocated from the stack, its address is not fixed; it depends on the contents of the stack pointer at the call to g. Moreover, the address of y is not a constant offset from either the current frame or the current top of stack at the time of its reference by f, since the recursive function f can intersperse a variable number of stack frames (each corresponding to an invocation of f) between the frame containing y and the current frame. Figure 13.5 gives a plausible snapshot of the stack after several invocations of f.

Each frame in figure 13.5 has a pointer known as the *static link*, which contains the information needed to support lexical scoping. The static link always points

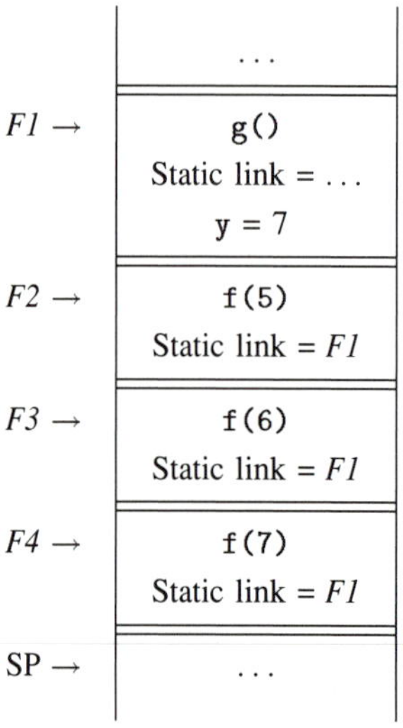

**Figure 13.5** Stack frames for the program of figure 13.4.

to the stack frame that corresponds to the lexically enclosing procedure. Since the procedure g encloses the definition of the procedure f, all the static links of stack frames for f point to the stack frame for g (frame *F1*). As figure 13.5 illustrates, this is not necessarily the stack frame immediately preceding the current frame.

Whenever the procedure f is being executed, the stack frame containing y may be found by starting with the current stack frame (which is a frame for f) and examining its static link. The static link points to the stack frame containing y (which is a frame for g). The offset of the variable y in the stack frame for g (which is a constant that the compiler can calculate) can be used with this pointer to access the memory location containing the value of y.

If the procedure f were *two* levels of nesting inside g, instead of one, then the static link in a stack frame for f would point to a stack frame for the intervening procedure h; the static link of this frame, in turn, would point to a stack frame for g. Thus a reference to the variable y from the procedure f would require two hops down the chain of static links (the "static chain") to reach the stack frame containing y. This mechanism generalizes to references from arbitrary lexical depths. In general, if $d$ levels of nesting separate a reference to a variable from its declaration, then $d$ hops down the static chain will yield a pointer to the stack frame where the variable is stored. Significantly, both $d$ (the nesting depth) and the offset of the variable in its stack frame can be computed at compile time and inserted as constants into the machine-language program, making lexical scoping cheaper to support than if run-time calculations were required.

The static chain is clearly a useful data structure for the implementation of lexical scoping, but it does not appear by magic. Every time a stack frame is created (that is, every time a procedure is called), the static link for that stack frame must be set appropriately. The static link for a stack frame for a procedure $P$ should point to the stack frame corresponding to $P$'s immediately enclosing procedure. In order to give all the information needed to build a stack frame when a procedure is called, a procedure value for a procedure $P$ really has two components: the address of the machine code for $P$ and a pointer to the stack frame that lexically encloses $P$. (This combination is known as a *closure*.) The stack-frame pointer in a closure for $P$ will be used to initialize the static link of any stack frame created by a call to $P$.

Just as in the case of simple variables, every *procedure* in a program can be treated as having been *declared* in some enclosing procedure. (We can hypothesize a "global procedure" to enclose outermost procedures.) For example, in figure 13.4, the procedure f is declared within procedure g. In such a case, the closure for f may be treated as a local variable of g, to be initialized when g is entered. The proper initialization sets the machine-code pointer in the closure for f to the address of the machine code that implements f and sets the stack-frame pointer in the closure for f to point to the newly created stack frame for g, the procedure that is in the process of being entered. The reader should consider why this algorithm always results in a static chain structure that mirrors the lexical nesting structure of the program.

Procedures with no free-variable references constitute an important special case. For such procedures, the static-link value is immaterial, since it will never be used. A simplified calling sequence can be used in this case, as we shall see with the `scall` instruction of the $S$ machine.

### 13.3.9 Storage Classes

Programming languages offer several *classes* (allocation disciplines) for storage. These classes differ mainly in the lifetime (or *extent*) of items of that class and in the degree to which responsibility for allocation and deallocation of storage is assumed implicitly by the system (as opposed to being left to the programmer). The personality of a programming language is strongly influenced by the selection of storage classes it supports; indeed, it may be argued that this selection is at the root of the differences between such disparate languages as LISP, Pascal, and FORTRAN.

We list briefly the commonly occurring storage classes:

- *Static storage* is allocated at the time a program is written, compiled, or loaded. This is the simplest allocation strategy and requires no run-time mechanism; its major drawback is that storage requirements must be anticipated in advance of program execution and are typically fixed at the source-program level. The FORTRAN language is designed to use static storage exclusively; consequently, it is always possible to analyze a FORTRAN program and determine the amount of main memory it requires for execution. This level of predictability is a practical asset, in that it allows a compile-time guarantee that a given program will run on a particular machine configuration; but it eliminates from FORTRAN the possibility of certain programming constructs (such as recursive procedures) whose space requirements cannot be bounded at compile time. This contrasts with LISP and ALGOL programs, which can exploit recursion and thus specify algorithms whose space requirements are unbounded. In a formal sense, ALGOL programs correspond to Turing machines while FORTRAN programs correspond to finite-state machines.

- *Stack*, or *automatic, storage* is allocated from a common processor stack. This is the most common *dynamic* storage allocation scheme; it allows program modules to allocate, at run time, arbitrary-sized regions of contiguous memory from a single pool (the stack) and to return them to the pool (*deallocate* them) when they are no longer needed. The major limitation of stack storage is that it requires allocation and deallocation to follow *stack discipline*, according to which the deallocation of a region $B$ must precede the deallocation of $A$ if the allocation of $A$ preceded the allocation of $B$. Stack discipline, and the pattern of storage management it induces, leads to the characteristic block structure of languages such as Pascal, Ada, and C.

- *Program-managed heap storage* refers to a variety of techniques developed for managing free-storage pools that avoid imposing stack discipline on allocation and deallocation. Such pools are often termed *heaps*. The simplest of these techniques involve explicit allocation and deallocation of each block of storage. Program-managed storage pools are often supported as library extensions to languages whose primary storage management is stack-oriented.

- *Garbage-collected heap storage* allows unconstrained allocation of blocks of storage, requires no explicit deallocation, and is the most general of the storage management techniques. It is available in advanced languages, such as LISP, whose data structures are sufficiently flexible as to make explicit deallocation infeasible. The automatic reclamation (*garbage collection*) of unused storage is fairly expensive, requiring a mechanism for a considerable amount of run-time management.

### 13.3.10  Operating-System Requirements

The preceding sections have discussed abstraction mechanisms, notably procedures and data types, that are included in modern high-level languages and whose implementation requirements influence the design of machine languages. The use of these mechanisms by a high-level-language programmer is generally discretionary—the programmer can benefit from employing them but is not forced to do so. When several users or applications share a computing machine, it is usually desirable to shield the management of the machine's physical resources—memory, input/output devices, and the processor itself—behind nondiscretionary abstraction barriers so that no user program, whether malicious or merely buggy, can prevent the machine from serving other programs correctly. Since virtually all computing environments, save some instances of single-user workstations or dedicated control processors, are shared, it is important for machine-language design to include any "hooks" necessary for implementing such nondiscretionary abstraction barriers.

These hooks generally consist of mechanisms for restricting a processor's *domain*—the set of operations the processor can perform while under the control of a particular program. Typically, this entails completely prohibiting the processor from executing certain *privileged operations* and restricting the regions of memory that can be accessed by the remaining unprivileged operations. Chapters 16 and 18 will discuss particular mechanisms for implementing and managing these restrictions; here we discuss some of the relevant issues at a higher level.

Although execution of ordinary users' programs may be subject to restrictions, the detailed restrictions (for example, which regions of memory can be accessed) will differ among programs. Moreover, a processor must be able to execute *operating-system software*, which normally runs with a higher level of privilege, to manage the machine's physical resources and orchestrate the execution of user programs, among other functions. (The innermost layer of the operating system, which directly manages the machine's physical resources, is often known as the *operating-system kernel*.) Transitions between user and system software domains, or between one user domain and another, must be performed carefully so that needed communication can occur without allowing any program to circumvent the restrictions under which it is supposed to operate.

Management of privileges is typically supported by specific items of *context information*, stored in the processor, that indicate the domain of the currently executing program. This information is consulted whenever a question of privilege arises—for example, before any memory access or attempt to execute a privileged operation. This context information is in addition to other items of processor state, such as the current program counter and stack pointer values, that are used in managing the processor's computational activities. Since a simple procedure call does not mark a transition from one domain to another, context information need not be saved or restored when performing an ordinary procedure call or return. Consequently, although a processor's context information is referenced frequently, it is relatively seldom modified.

Although privilege management is an important part of virtually any processor design, the infrequency with which context information is explicitly manipulated allows us pretty much to ignore it in the early phases of our study of processor design (chapters 14 and 15). The subject cannot be ignored completely, however, even in the early stages, for we cannot completely ignore the mechanisms that cause transitions between domains. These mechanisms are *instruction traps*, *faults*, and *interrupts*. Although, as we discuss in the following sections, there are differences among these three mechanisms, there are also a great many similarities, and it is often useful to discuss them collectively. For this purpose, we adopt the term *trap* to refer to any of the instruction-trap, fault, or interrupt mechanisms.

### 13.3.11 Instruction Traps

Given a layer of abstraction separating a user program's domain from the domain used for executing system software that manages shared resources, perhaps the most obvious requirement is for some mechanism that a user program can employ to request system software to perform operations requiring the privileges of the

| User-accessible processor state |
| Context information |

**Figure 13.6**  Processor-state information saved when processing a trap.

system software's domain. Such operations are typically requested by means of a special *instruction trap*, or *supervisor call*. Instruction traps effectively allow the operating system to reinterpret certain instructions and thereby create for user programs the appearance of an extended machine instruction set. An instruction trap is much like an ordinary procedure call except that it entails a change of domain as well as the customary deviation from straight-line execution. The *context switch* to the system software's domain requires the processor state pertaining to the user domain to be saved (typically on a stack) and new context information specifying the system software's domain to be loaded.

The basic operation of an instruction trap is as follows: The current processor state (for example, register contents) is saved in memory, and a new processor state (which might come from some block of reserved memory locations) is installed in the processor. Then execution resumes, fetching instructions from the instruction stream identified by the newly installed value of the program counter; these instructions typically are part of the operating-system software. Eventually, the operating-system software executes a privileged *trap-return* instruction, which reinstalls in the processor the saved processor state, following which the user program resumes execution immediately after the trap-causing instruction.

The processor state that is saved and reinstalled during a context switch includes not only the items of user-accessible processor state, such as the program counter, that are saved during a procedure call (diagrammed as part of the stack frame shown in figure 13.3) but also the additional context information needed to specify fully the processor's current privileges, as shown in figure 13.6. Typically, this context information includes a *processor status word*, or PSW, containing various key items of processor state, such as a bit indicating whether or not the processor is currently allowed to execute privileged instructions. In addition to the PSW, the context information may include details regarding the regions of memory that can be accessed; further discussion of this issue appears in chapters 16 and 18.

Modern computers typically reserve a block of main memory for the storage of *trap vectors*. Each such vector may be thought of as a processor-state block, of the form shown in figure 13.6, whose contents are loaded into the processor when the corresponding instruction-trap event occurs. (For efficiency in storage use, the vectors are often not represented exactly in this form. Instead, some of the information is omitted from the trap vector and loaded from some default source when a trap occurs; some registers in the processor, such as those where programs

```
handler(state)
 struct MState *state;
 {
        .
        .                       /* (body of the handler definition) */
        .
        userSP = state->SP;  /* Read trapped program's SP.      */
        .
        .


 }
```

**Figure 13.7** General form of a trap handler.

are intended to keep intermediate results, may not be loaded at all.) Thus some fixed address, say 100, might be allocated to the trap vector for supervisor calls; during operating-system initialization, this trap vector is filled with the processor-state and context information that should be loaded when a supervisor call occurs (for example, the part of the trap vector where the program counter is held is initialized to be the address of the supervisor-call trap-handler routine). A supervisor call will then cause the state of the interrupted program to be saved, after which the processor-state information at location 100 is installed; this causes the supervisor-call handler to be invoked.

Since an instruction trap can be thought of as a kind of procedure call (which happens to be combined with a context switch), a trap handler $H$ could use a user program $P$'s stack during $H$'s execution, with the usual proviso that it restore the stack to its prior state before returning. As long as the execution of $H$ maintains stack discipline and ultimately has no net effect on the number of items stacked, its use of $P$'s stack is completely invisible to $P$. On the other hand, by using $P$'s stack, $H$ leaves itself open to sabotage—for example, $P$ might load an invalid memory address into the stack pointer and then execute a supervisor-call instruction. For this reason, trap handlers commonly use their own dedicated and preallocated stack area, and the processor state loaded when a trap occurs typically includes a fresh stack-pointer value pointing to this area.

It is conventional on stack-based processors for the state of the interrupted program to be saved on the stack of the *handler* program, that is, to be pushed on the stack identified by the stack pointer in the trap vector. To the handler, the saved state is effectively an argument; thus a handler is effectively a procedure, as shown in figure 13.7, where `struct MState` refers to a definition of the format of the saved state information shown in figure 13.6. (Note that an asterisk is C syntax for "points to" and is used both in declarations of pointers and as a dereferencing operator. Thus `struct MState *state` declares the argument `state` as a pointer to—that is, the address of—an `MState` structure, while the expression `*state` is a reference to the structure to which `state` points.)

One difference between this handler and an ordinary procedure is in how returns occur. As mentioned previously, a trap handler needs to finish by executing a trap-return instruction, reinstalling the stacked processor state as the current processor state and causing a return to the interrupted program. During the execution of the handler, it may access the state of the interrupted program via references to `MState` components such as `state->SP` (which is synonymous with `(*state).SP`, the SP component of the `MState` structure pointed to by the pointer variable `state`). Indeed, it may *change* components of its `state` argument, and these changes will be reflected in the interrupted user program when execution of the latter resumes. Such references are useful for communication, that is, for passing arguments from the interrupted program to the trap handler and returning results.

### 13.3.12 Faults

Instruction execution is prone to error conditions or *faults* (also known as *exceptions*) such as arithmetic overflows, attempts to reference nonexistent memory locations, or attempts to execute invalid or privileged operations. Such faults are little different from the instruction traps just discussed in that faults, like traps, arise out of the execution of an instruction that somehow requires operating-system intervention. Because of this similarity, the mechanisms for handling faults differ little from those for handling traps—each kind of fault is associated with a particular *fault vector* at a predetermined address, the same trap-return instruction that is used for returning from a trap handler is used for returning from a fault handler, and so on. On the other hand, instruction traps are expected—they are programmed in with the express intent of invoking the operating system—whereas faults are typically unplanned and occur in instructions that, given other inputs, might well execute without causing a fault. The unplanned nature of faults makes communication between an interrupted program and the fault handler different from communication with a trap handler: Typically, in the case of a fault, some information generated by the processor's hardware (for example, the address of the memory location to which an invalid reference was attempted) is saved and may be accessed by the fault handler in diagnosing and possibly repairing the cause of the fault. We shall see some uses of faults and fault handlers in chapter 16.

### 13.3.13 Interrupts

A third stimulus, quite different from both faults and instruction traps in that it can cause a context switch, is an *interrupt* from an external source (such as an input/output device). Interrupts are useful as a way of invisibly inserting a call to an operating-system subroutine between any two instructions of user-program execution so that the operating system can respond to some external event (such as a key being pressed on a user's keyboard). Typically, a processor has one or more *interrupt-request* input signals. An external device requests an interrupt by asserting one of these signals and typically keeping it asserted until (either by actions of the interrupt's software handler or by means of an explicit *interrupt-acknowledge* signal) the device is informed that the requested interrupt has occurred.

Interrupts differ from faults and traps in that the cause of the interrupt does not arise from the instruction that is executing when the interrupt occurs, and therefore the details of what that instruction was doing are irrelevant to handling the interrupt in most cases. The `MState` of the computation in progress must still be saved, to prevent it from being damaged during execution of the interrupt handler, but there is usually no need for communication between the interrupt handler and the execution of the interrupted instruction. Aside from this difference, interrupts are handled much like faults and instruction traps: An *interrupt vector* found at a predetermined location associated with the cause of the interrupt contains the new `MState` to be loaded, and the `PC` component of this `MState` contains the address of an interrupt-handler routine similar to the trap handler shown in figure 13.7.

Since interrupts come from external and asynchronous sources, they can occur at any moment, and careful coding alone cannot prevent the occurrence of an interrupt as it can prevent the occurrence of a fault or instruction trap. There are times (for example, during updates to a data structure accessed by an interrupt handler) when it is important to be able to "lock out" or postpone the occurrence of an interrupt until a convenient time. This is sometimes accomplished through an *interrupt-enable mask* that forms part of the processor's context information (typically, part of the PSW). Interrupts will only occur when enabled by this mask; if an interrupt request arrives while interrupts are disabled by the mask, the occurrence of the interrupt request is noted and the interrupt occurs as soon as interrupts are reenabled. More common than interrupt-enable masks is the use of *interrupt-priority systems*, which associate a priority with each possible interrupt and also with the current processor state (this latter priority is typically stored in the PSW). A particular interrupt is enabled if and only if its priority is higher than the processor's current priority. Interrupt-priority systems are discussed further in chapter 20.

## 13.4 Implementation Considerations

### 13.4.1 Transparency

A major design goal for computer architectures is the independence of machine-language specifications from the details of their implementation. It is extremely valuable, for example, to be able to upgrade the implementation of a processor to provide improved performance without making existing software for the machine obsolete; such transparent upgrades can always be made as long as they maintain the identical interface (machine-language) semantics.

The advantages of implementation-independent machine-language semantics are demonstrated, for example, by IBM's System/360 series computers and their successors. This series is a compatible *family* of computers, sharing the same machine-language interface, with widely different cost and performance characteristics. System/360 customers can consequently upgrade their computation resources in steps, maintaining their software investments through each performance improvement.

It is not easy to design a good machine language for implementation on a wide spectrum of machines. The machine language must be simple enough to allow a low-cost implementation, but at the same time it must avoid features that make high-performance implementations difficult. Such features include overspecification of the sequence of operations in instruction execution, which makes it harder to use parallelism within a high-performance processor design.

### 13.4.2 Storage Levels

Most machine architectures provide several levels of storage implementation technology that differ in their performance characteristics; these typically include

- several active registers in the processor, consisting of high-speed registers or RAM;
- main (addressable) memory, usually composed of lower-speed directly addressable semiconductor memory; and
- a much larger volume of *secondary* storage such as magnetic disks.

This distinction between storage implementation technologies is often reflected directly in the way the machine language deals with storage at each level. Many machines provide a separate addressing mechanism for registers, and very few machines support absolutely uniform addressing over all three storage levels.

A common example of the reflection of memory implementation technologies in the machine architecture is the *general-register* organization, in which some number (say, 8 or 16) of active registers are available for explicit use by programs to hold frequently accessed data. Such machines typically distinguish strongly between access to registers and access to main memory, for example, by providing short instruction formats restricted to the manipulation of data in registers rather than main memory.

Proponents of the general-register organization cite two relatively independent arguments in its favor:

- *Performance*. The faster accessibility of data stored in active registers motivates their use for heavily referenced variables. The general-register architecture allows the programmer (or, in the case of a compiled higher-level language, the compiler) to explicitly allocate registers for the storage of selected critical data.
- *Compactness of code*. Since there are many fewer registers than main-memory locations, instructions that access only registers can be encoded in fewer bits than those capable of referencing arbitrary locations.

These are indeed sound practical arguments, and they account for the existence of general registers in the majority of extant computers. However, equally compelling objections to the general-register scheme can be raised:

- *Lack of implementation transparency*. The particular mixture of storage technologies used in a particular machine may properly be viewed as an implementation detail that should not be visible in the machine-language design. In a general-register machine, the number of general registers is effectively "frozen" in the machine-language specification; a higher-performance implementation, offering a greater number of registers, will require modification of the machine language and hence of the software designed for it.

- *Programming difficulty.* The need to allocate registers to variables complicates the programming task. Moreover, *automating* the process of register allocation (as is necessary in the construction of compilers producing code for general-register machines) requires an additional compiler mechanism and performs imperfectly even then.

There are alternatives to the general-register organization that offer, at some additional implementation cost, its performance and compactness advantages while avoiding the above objections. Storage of frequently accessed data in fast registers can be effected transparently by means of *cache-memory* techniques, which use program execution patterns to select the most profitable words to buffer in fast registers. The code compactness of register operations can be approached by means of tricks for address encoding, in which frequently accessed locations require fewer instruction-stream bits than infrequently accessed ones. We shall see examples of both techniques in this and the next chapter.

### 13.4.3 Very-High-Performance Processors

At the highest end of the performance spectrum, the use of parallelism and pipelining within the processor design become very important for achieving high instruction throughput. Examples of machines in this category include the CDC 7600 and CYBER series and the Cray family of computers. Consideration of these processors, with their heavy internal use of parallelism, as single-sequence machines requires us to sharpen our definition of the single-sequence machine. The sense in which these processors are still single-sequence machines is that they preserve the *appearance* of sequential instruction execution: Even though many instructions may simultaneously be in some phase of execution, the end result produced by the computer is guaranteed to be the same as if instructions had been executed one by one, in the order in which they appear in the program.

Broadly speaking, there are two principal ways in which parallelism is used in high-performance processors:

- *Pipelining.* Each instruction in a program goes through a number of phases in its execution: instruction fetch, instruction decode, operand fetch, execution, and result storage. These phases are discussed in more detail in section 13.5.2, but we note here that whereas a moderate-performance processor might go through these phases one after another, a high-performance processor typically includes a pipeline capable of working simultaneously on several instructions in various phases of execution.

- *Multiple execution units.* Often, the execution phase of the instruction pipeline will contain multiple execution units. One job of preceding pipeline stages in such a system is to allocate each instruction to a suitable execution unit. One goal of such systems is to uncover available parallelism in the instruction stream by effectively computing "on the fly" a data-dependency graph showing the relationship between results produced by instructions and the inputs required by subsequent instructions.

Both of these techniques for using parallelism in processor design produce especially good results for instruction sets that have a simple, regular structure and that make it easy to analyze dependencies between instructions. Simple instruction-set structure helps keep the instruction pipeline full by minimizing the amount of work that needs to be done on an instruction before the location in memory of its successor can be known (allowing the fetch and decode of the successor to begin). Easily analyzed dependencies between instructions make it easier to uncover enough potential parallelism in the instruction stream to keep multiple execution units busy. Detailed consideration of these issues is a fascinating exploration in computer architecture that is, unfortunately, beyond the scope of our present discussion. Nevertheless, amenability to high-performance implementation is an important criterion for an instruction set designed for a broad family of machines.

## 13.5 The von Neumann Machine

The general organizational characteristics of conventional digital computers is generally credited to John von Neumann, whose classic 1946 description [Burks, Goldstine, and von Neumann 1946] articulates the structure of addressable memory, stored programs, input/output devices, and other familiar organs of today's computers. In deference to his classic work, conventional machines (including the vast majority of commercially available computers) are categorized as *von Neumann architectures*. We explore typical characteristics of such machines in this section.

### 13.5.1 The Stored-Program Model

Modern computers (including those considered in this chapter) are termed *stored-program computers* since the programs they execute are stored in memory along with the data manipulated by those programs. The alternative to the stored-program model is one in which the program is built into the computer architecture at a lower level, for example, by wiring it in via a patch panel or even building it into the underlying circuitry (much as the behavior of our microarchitecture is designed into its implementation).

The issue is the level at which the structure of the program is bound. The stored-program organization leads us to view programs as relatively transient; they can be changed on an hour-to-hour or even minute-to-minute basis, as they might be during debugging. Moreover, the stored-program organization is conducive to the construction of layered systems in which one program generates or otherwise manipulates another.

It would be a mistake to conclude, however, that a program is as variable as the data it manipulates. Although self-modifying programs (which treat *themselves* as data) are occasionally written, the practice is rare and frowned upon by most programming disciplinarians. In general, we consider the program itself to be constant, *at least* during any single execution, and modern computers often provide a mechanism that prevents regions of storage containing programs from being casually modified.

### 13.5.2 Microcoded Implementation of Machine Language

In order to orient the reader, we briefly preview here the implementation strategy we shall follow in the construction of our machines. The microarchitecture developed in chapter 12 will be used to interpret programs that are themselves interpreters for the machine-language instruction sets described in the following subsections. To each microprogrammed interpreter, both the machine-language instructions being interpreted and the data manipulated by the machine-language instructions are data. The typical gross operation of the microcode will proceed in the following steps:

- *Instruction fetch*. Read from main memory the next machine-language instruction to be executed. We shall allocate one register of the microarchitecture to serve as the machine's *program counter*, in which we maintain the address of the *next* machine-language instruction to be executed. In general, immediately after an instruction is fetched, the program counter will be incremented to address the location containing the following instruction.

- *Instruction decode*. The microcode will inspect the bits of the newly fetched machine-language instruction word and dispatch to a sequence of microcode appropriate to that class of instruction. Thus our microcode may have one section devoted to the interpretation of ADD instructions, another devoted to MULTIPLY, and so on.

- *Operand fetch*. If the machine-language instruction requires source operands to be fetched from memory, the microcode will perform the requisite bus cycles and store temporarily (in the microarchitecture's registers) the operand values.

- *Execution*. The microprogram will then perform the operation (such as ADD, AND, or MULTIPLY) dictated by the machine-language instruction. This may require a number of microinstruction executions, as, for example, in the interpretation of a machine-language MULTIPLY instruction.

- *Result storage*. If the instruction specifies a memory location as the destination for the result, an appropriate bus cycle will be executed by the microcode.

The above steps are repeated indefinitely, executing one machine-language instruction on each iteration through the loop. It is important to observe that, in the general case, a number of microinstruction executions are necessary for the interpretation of each machine-language instruction; thus the single-sequence machine runs more slowly, in terms of instructions per second, than does the microarchitecture. Some, but not all, of this speed difference is accounted for by the difference in *level* between machine-language and microinstructions: Machine-language instructions such as MULTIPLY may specify operations whose microcode implementation would require many microinstruction executions, and we would expect them to take correspondingly many microcycle times for their interpretation. However, there is an additional time overhead associated with the interpretive mechanism itself (the fetching of instructions, dispatching on their bit patterns, and so on) that is simply the price we pay for the abstraction afforded by the extra level of interpretation.

It is crucial to the understanding of microcoded machine organization that one not confuse aspects of microcode interpretation with corresponding aspects of the

| Operation code | Source1 address | Source2 address | Destination address |
|---|---|---|---|

**Figure 13.8**  Three-address instruction format.

interpretation of single-sequence machine instructions. For example, microinstructions and machine-language instructions have little similarity; they generally have different lengths and use entirely different encoding conventions. Most importantly, the interpretation of *addresses* at the microcode level generally has no relation to machine addresses. We use addresses in microcode to identify locations in the microcode ROM and consequently to identify microinstructions; addresses manipulated at the machine-language level are interpreted by slaves of bus transactions and usually reference locations in main memory.

### 13.5.3  Instruction Formats

The binary representation of each machine-language instruction must encode the operation to be performed as well as the locations of its input and output data. An ADD instruction on a typical machine, for example, requires two *source* operands (the numbers to be added) and one *destination* specifying where the sum is to be stored. A simple approach to encoding such operations involves the allocation within each instruction word of four fields, containing, respectively, a binary operation code, or *opcode* (identifying an operation such as ADD or MULTIPLY), and three address fields specifying the locations of the two sources and one destination operand.

Figure 13.8 depicts a typical three-address instruction format. The operation-code field must be large enough to allow a unique binary code for each different machine operation; 5 bits, allowing 32 operations, is perhaps a typical number. In the absence of special address-encoding mechanisms (discussed later), each of the three operand fields must be large enough to contain an $n$-bit address (where $2^n$ is the address space size). For a machine with 16-bit addresses, this instruction format requires 48 bits of address information in each instruction. A three-address instruction such as

| ADD | 20 | 40 | 123 |
|---|---|---|---|

adds the contents of location 20 to the contents of location 40, putting the result into location 123.

Three-address instruction architectures are rare, primarily because of the cost associated with their long instruction format. A common compromise is the *two-address* format, in which one of the two specified operands serves both as a source and as a destination. Thus, in a typical two-address machine (such as the DEC PDP-11), the instruction

| ADD | 20 | 40 |
|---|---|---|

causes the sum of the contents of location 20 and the contents of location 40 to be stored in location 40 (replacing the original contents of location 40). One might suspect that this scheme would be awkward, since performing an operation such as ADD on two operands invariably overwrites one of them, making it unavailable for subsequent operations. In fact, it is quite workable in practice, owing to the temporary nature of computed values: The results of most operations are used exactly once before being discarded. In the relatively rare circumstance in which both operands of an operation must be preserved for subsequent computation, one must be copied to a temporary location where it (the copy) can be replaced by the result.

A historically important format, which was nearly ubiquitous in the days when a fast register was a major component of processor cost, is the *single-address* instruction. Single-address machines typically feature a single general register, historically termed an *accumulator*, which serves as one source and the destination for most operations. Thus the single-address instruction

| ADD | 123 |
|-----|-----|

would cause the contents of location 123 to be added to the contents of register $A$ (the accumulator), the sum replacing the contents of $A$. Such machines offer single-address LOAD and STORE instructions that move data between the addressed location and the accumulator.

A final category of architectures includes the "zero-address" architectures, which feature instructions such as

| ADD |
|-----|

in which the location of *both* operands is implicit. Typically, such architectures rely on a stack for storage of operands and temporary results; thus the ADD instruction would pop two numbers off the stack, add them, and push the sum back onto the stack. An extended example of a zero-address architecture, the $S$ machine, will be presented in the next chapter.

For purposes of illustration, consider a machine language whose instructions are each encoded as a series of consecutive 8-bit bytes. Specifically, each instruction consists of a 1-byte operation code (denoting *add*, *negate*, *halt*, an so on) followed by zero or more operand addresses. In the case of a 32-bit computer, the operand addresses might each occupy four consecutive bytes, so that the three-address instruction ADD 20,40,123 would require 13 instruction bytes, as indicated in figure 13.9. We assume here that the operation code 34 specifies a three-address add operation and that the machine uses a byte-addressing scheme in which multibyte data (such as 32-bit addresses) are stored with their least significant bytes at the lowest memory addresses. Thus, if the above instruction is stored in memory locations beginning at address 100, the last byte of the instruction occupies location 112. Moreover, the contents of (byte) locations 102–104, 106–108, and 110–112 are 0s, since these are the high-order bytes of small (less than 256)

| | Byte 0 | Bytes 1–4 | | | | Bytes 5–8 | | | | Bytes 9–12 | | | |
|---|---|---|---|---|---|---|---|---|---|---|---|---|---|
| | opcode | adr1 | | | | adr2 | | | | adr3 | | | |
| Instruction parts | 34 | 20 | | | | 40 | | | | 123 | | | |
| Instruction bytes | 34 | 20 | 0 | 0 | 0 | 40 | 0 | 0 | 0 | 123 | 0 | 0 | 0 |

**Figure 13.9**  Instruction bytes for ADD 20,40,123.

addresses. The instruction to be executed following execution of the ADD would be stored in locations beginning at address 113.

Typical machine languages utilize several instruction formats; for example, the operation code 35 might, in our sample machine, denote a two-address *negate* (2's complement) operation whose operands are its source and destination addresses, respectively. It is important to recognize that the format of a particular machine instruction is implied by the operation-code byte; having fetched the first byte of an instruction, the machine-language interpreter can determine how many operand bytes are to be fetched and the operation to be performed using them.

We may view a machine-language program in this case as a stream of instruction bytes, which are parsed into individual instructions by the machine during program execution. In the usual implementation of such a machine, a program-counter (PC) register in the processor contains the address of the next instruction byte to be fetched. As consecutive instruction-stream bytes are fetched and decoded by the processor during execution of an instruction, the PC is incremented to point to the following byte; at the completion of an instruction execution, the address of the following instruction can be found in the PC.

Machines using byte addressing commonly offer instructions that manipulate data of several different sizes; the size of the data manipulated by an instruction is commonly implied by the operation code of that instruction. To help keep things straight, we adopt the convention, throughout the remainder of this text, of suffixing each operation code with a number indicating the size of the data that it operates on. Thus ADD4 is an instruction that adds 4-byte (32-bit) numbers, while ADD2 works on 2-byte numbers and ADD1 works on 1-byte numbers.

Some typical instructions are summarized in table 13.10. Note that the JUMP (transfer control) instruction simply loads the program counter (PC) with the specified address, causing subsequent instruction fetches to begin at that address. The address $A$ in the JUMP instruction thus differs subtly from the addresses in the other instructions, in that the JUMP instruction moves the address itself (rather than the contents of the addressed memory location) as its data value.

The ASH4 (arithmetic-shift) instruction uses the second operand $\langle B \rangle$[1] as a *shift count* controlling the direction and magnitude of an arithmetic shift to be applied to the second operand. Rather than providing separate left- and right-shift instructions (as many machines do), we combine these functions in a single operation and use the sign of the shift count to determine the shift direction. Thus the result stored into $C$ by ASH4 $A,B,C$ is $\langle A \rangle \cdot 2^{\langle B \rangle}$ (ignoring truncation effects). ASH4 furnishes

**Table 13.10** Typical machine instructions.

| Operation | Operand addresses | Function performed |
|---|---|---|
| ADD4 | $A, B, C$ | $C^4 \leftarrow \langle A \rangle^4 + \langle B \rangle^4$ |
| SUB4 | $A, B, C$ | $C^4 \leftarrow \langle A \rangle^4 - \langle B \rangle^4$ |
| MULT4 | $A, B, C$ | $C^4 \leftarrow \langle A \rangle^4 \cdot \langle B \rangle^4$ |
| MOVE4 | $A, B$ | $B^4 \leftarrow \langle A \rangle^4$ |
| NEG4 | $A, B$ | $B^4 \leftarrow (-\langle A \rangle^4)$ |
| JUMP | $A$ | $PC^4 \leftarrow A^4$ |
| ASH4 | $A, B, C$ | $C^4 \leftarrow$ the result of shifting $\langle A \rangle^4$ left (right) $\langle B \rangle^1$ $(-\langle B \rangle^1)$ places |
| MOVE1 | $A, B$ | $B^1 \leftarrow \langle A \rangle^1$ |
| ADD1 | $A, B, C$ | $C^1 \leftarrow \langle A \rangle^1 + \langle B \rangle^1$ |
| HALT | | Stop the machine |

an example of how a single instruction can deal with more than one data format. Since the source and destination locations $A$ and $C$ are considered by the ASH4 instruction to be 4 bytes long, any shift count outside the range $-31$ through $+31$ will completely shift out all the significant bits of $\langle A \rangle$. A 1-byte value is thus sufficient to represent all interesting shift counts. Consequently, ASH4 specifies a 1-byte operand for the shift count, even though the source and destination operands are each 4 bytes long.

### 13.5.4 Assembly Language

As is the case with microcoding, serious programming at the machine-language level is virtually always done using symbolic notation rather than by direct manipulation of instruction bits. Translation from symbolic to binary representation of a machine-language program, referred to as program *assembly*, is performed by a low-level-language processing program called an *assembler*. The symbolic representation of a machine-language program is thus termed *assembly language*; it differs from higher-level languages in that its statements correspond nearly one for one with machine-language instructions of the target machine. Thus, while the translation of a 100-statement C program might yield 1000 or more machine instructions, a 100-statement assembly-language program will result in about 100 machine instructions.

An assembly-language programmer must know the instruction repertoire of the machine being programmed but needs no specific knowledge of either the bit patterns of its instruction formats or the numerical operation codes assigned to various functions. Assemblers can be quite sophisticated and machine-specific, making a range of low-level decisions that can include selection of appropriate machine instructions in cases where several alternatives exist. At the less sophisticated end

```
| Simple assembly-language program for hypothetical machine
|    using 4-byte direct addressing.

START:  MOVE4  LONG(DATA)   LONG(TEMP)                    | 1st element of array
        ADD4   LONG(TEMP)   LONG(DATA+4)  LONG(TEMP)  | + 2nd element
        ADD4   LONG(TEMP)   LONG(DATA+8)  LONG(TEMP)
        ADD4   LONG(TEMP)   LONG(DATA+12) LONG(TEMP)
        HALT                                                           | Sum of 4 data elements
                                                                       |    in TEMP.

DATA:   LONG(1)  LONG(2)  LONG(3)  LONG(4)          | Data to be added.
TEMP:   LONG(0)                                                    | Space for temp use.
```

**Figure 13.11**  Sum of four array elements on a hypothetical machine.

of the spectrum, a minimal but serviceable assembler simply provides symbolic names for tags, opcodes, and other values.

The microassembly language described in section 12.2 exemplifies the primitive end of this spectrum. We extend it (via macroinstruction definitions) to serve as our machine-level assembly language as well. For example, a typical three-address assembly-language instruction to add the contents of locations 120 and 140 and place the result in memory location 100 might be written as

ADD4  LONG(120) LONG(140) LONG(100) | 100 ← $\langle 120 \rangle + \langle 140 \rangle$

rather than as the string of 13 binary bytes corresponding to the ADD4 opcode followed by the addresses of the three operands (see figure 13.9). We assume here that LONG has been defined as a macroinstruction that assembles a 4-byte constant (similar to the WORD macro used in figure 12.16).

Figure 13.11 illustrates the use of this primitive assembly language to construct a program for our hypothetical computer. The program simply adds up the elements of a 4-word array at location DATA and halts with the sum in location TEMP. Note the use of arithmetic *expressions* such as DATA+4, rather than numeric constants, in addresses. Since we are dealing with longword (4-byte) operations on a byte-addressed machine, DATA is the address of a longword containing the integer 1, DATA+4 is the address of a longword containing the integer 2, and so on. Since the size and location of the DATA array are built into the instructions at assembly time, the program in figure 13.11 is of little interest other than to illustrate assembly-language features. More realistic approaches to array manipulation require additional addressing mechanisms and are illustrated in later chapters.

## 13.6 Perspectives and Trends

Machine-language instruction-set design remains a discipline in which aesthetic issues play a considerable role, and there are many points on which reasonable people disagree. In the following chapters, we present not one, but three, machine-language architectures—the $S$, $G$, and $R$ machines—reflecting the diverse state of the art. There is general agreement that the principal purpose of machine language is to serve as the target language for compilation. However, there are many different source languages for compilers and many different application areas. These factors conspire to make it very difficult to define any universal standard by which instruction sets can be compared objectively. The design of a machine language and the engineering of an implementation are still, therefore, quite definitely an artistic pursuit. The goal of this chapter has been to build a foundation for giving some representative examples of this art in practice and exploring the fundamental principles and constraints that guide the artist's work.

Many trends are at work in processor architecture, some clear and others as yet unrecognized. We can nevertheless make some general comments on current areas of activity and their relationship to the material in this and subsequent chapters:

- *RISC architectures.* If anything, the similarities between the $S$ and $G$ machines to be presented in the following two chapters are stronger than the typical degree of similarity between contemporary machine-language architectures. To plumb the depths of controversy regarding processor architecture, consider the current debate between advocates of reduced-instruction-set computers (RISC) and the so-called complex-instruction-set computers (CISC). Both the $S$ and $G$ machines qualify for the CISC family; RISC machine languages are closer in level to the MAYBE microarchitecture and are designed to be simple enough so that the microcode level of abstraction can be skipped in their design, leading to some increase in performance. RISC architectures are more primitive and incorporate fewer features specifically motivated by higher-level languages. They can thus be more challenging to compile to, though RISC advocates argue that the needed compiler techniques are known and that the result is a more cost-effective engine for running higher-level-language programs. RISC architectures have made major inroads in the market in recent years, because of the relatively spectacular cost/performance ratios of several recently introduced RISC machines. RISC architectures are explored, using the vehicle of the $R$ machine, in chapter 17.

- *Microarchitecture extensions.* Space limitations and the goal of allowing implementation with very few parts bias our sample microarchitecture, the MAYBE, toward simplicity in all design decisions. Some real processors have been implemented using a general-purpose microarchitecture such as the MAYBE, although even in these cases parts are added to increase performance. In most cases, however, performance considerations lead to the incorporation of several highly specialized features into the microarchitecture. For example, most machines have some specialized hardware for instruction fetch, decoding, and dispatch, rather than performing these functions in microcode. Because VLSI makes it practical to devote increasing amounts of hardware to processor design, the use of specialized microarchitecture extensions to enhance performance of those processors still following the CISC model is likely to increase.

- *Parallel computing.* As hardware becomes progressively cheaper, hardware-intensive design techniques such as pipelining, pioneered by designers of high-performance processors, are increasingly finding their way into medium- and even small-scale computing machines. This trend is bound to continue. An interesting question is how long the single-sequence machine abstraction itself will survive this process. As parallelism is increasingly used within processor implementations, the pressure will grow to allow the programmer direct access to the parallel facilities of the underlying hardware. The principal obstacle to this process today is a lack of good programming languages and design methods for parallel algorithms and programs; but if these problems can be solved, we may find that computer science in the future will deal largely with parallel architectures. A good guess is that the single-sequence abstraction still has many years of life left, even though multiprocessor and other parallel architectures are already taking a rapidly increasing share of the market.

## 13.7  Context

This chapter has introduced the von Neumann model of computation, roughly as articulated in Burks, Goldstine, and von Neumann [1946]. While most commercial computers conform to this description, some looming alternatives are sketched in chapter 21. A fascinating history of pre–von Neumann machines is given by Randell [1973].

### 13.7.1  Programming Languages

Many higher-level programming languages have been mentioned in this chapter. The first among them, historically, was FORTRAN, motivated primarily by the requirements of numerical computing and developed in the late 1950s; its early history is chronicled by Sammet [1969]. ALGOL 60, described in the seminal report edited by Naur [1963], put the definition of programming languages on a much sounder footing and introduced the concept of lexical scoping in the form of the "copy rule." ALGOL 60 allows procedures to be passed as arguments of other procedures, but it is predicated on the idea of maintaining stack discipline in the allocation and deallocation of stack frames and consequently does not allow procedures to be returned as values by other procedures. A thorough discussion of implementation considerations pertaining to ALGOL 60 is given by Randall and Russell [1964].

Also developed during the late 1950s was LISP [McCarthy et al. 1965], motivated primarily by the requirements of symbolic computing. LISP was another seminal programming language, but its impact was confined largely to academic circles until the 1980s, when LISP dialects such as Common Lisp [Steele 1984] and Scheme [Abelson and Sussman 1985; Rees and Clinger 1986] became widely used. LISP was the first higher-level programming language to rely on a garbage-collected heap for allocation of data not allocated in a stack-disciplined manner. LISP's Scheme dialect has popularized the aggressive use of lexical scoping and "procedures as first-class values"—allowing procedures not only to be passed as arguments to other procedures, but also to be returned as values and generally treated like any other sort of data. Synopses of FORTRAN, ALGOL 60, and LISP 1.5, along with several other early (and in many cases still widely used) programming languages such as COBOL, PL/I, SNOBOL4, and APL, appear in Pratt [1975].

The needs of system programming have encouraged a family of programming languages that stay fairly close to operations performed at the machine instruction-set level but avoid some of the pain and inefficiency of writing programs directly in assembly language. An early representative of this family is BCPL [Richards 1969], which is an ancestor of C [Kernighan and Ritchie 1978], chosen for examples in this book precisely because it facilitates the description of programs at a level fairly close to the subject of much of this book: machine instruction sets.

Recent times have seen further development of constructs for modularity and structure in programs. Pascal [Jensen and Wirth 1974] includes record structures and user-defined data types. Ada [Wegner 1980] goes further in defining modularity constructs such as *packages*. The designers of both Pascal and Ada were careful, however, not to include any capabilities (such as the ability to return procedures from other procedures, as is possible in Scheme) that would violate stack discipline in the allocation and deallocation of stack frames. Pascal and Ada are also concerned with *safety* in the sense that they strive to make as many programming errors as possible detectable at compile time rather than run time. In contrast to BCPL and C, therefore, they tend to exclude questionable constructs whose use may be meaningful and correct in some cases but error-prone in others.

The development of new programming languages shows no sign of abating. Many are variants on the languages mentioned above, but some are quite different; Prolog [Clocksin and Mellish 1981; Kowalski 1979], for example, encourages a view of program execution as the proof of a theorem, while *functional languages* categorically exclude side effects such as assignment statements. An interesting perspective on languages appears in Wulf, Shaw, and Hilfinger [1981], which emphasizes data structures and their relation to control mechanisms.

### 13.7.2 Processor Architecture

While many of the processor-architecture issues raised in this chapter are elaborated on in the following chapters, some themes will not recur. One is the idea of processors that handle tagged data. Such processors have never made it into the mainstream of computer architecture, though they have been present rather persistently at its outskirts. Early representatives of such architectures were the Burroughs B6500/B7500 [Hauck and Dent 1968] and B6700/B7700 [Organick 1973] systems. A more recent exemplar is the Symbolics 3600 LISP machine [Moon 1985].

Another issue briefly touched on was the construction of high-performance computers. A common theme here is the aggressive use of pipelining in the processor. Chapter 17 revisits this issue in the context of reduced-instruction-set computers; this use of pipelining is also explored by Kogge [1981] and Stone [1987]. Early high-performance computers such as the IBM System/360 Model 91, the CDC 6600 and CDC 7600, and the Control Data CYBER series are described in Siewiorek, Bell, and Newell [1982]. The development of the Cray-1 [Russell 1978] marked a watershed in the history of such "supercomputers." Subsequent machines in the

Cray-1 mold include the Cray-X/MP, the Cray-Y/MP, the Cray-2, the NEC SX series, and the Fujitsu VP series.

## 13.8 Problems

### Problem 13.1

There are four possible conventions for implementing a stack using a segment of memory and a stack pointer (SP). The stack can grow toward either increasing or decreasing addresses, and the SP can point either to the top element on the stack or to the first empty location past the top of stack. The following are register-transfer-language descriptions of the routines Push(x), Pop(x), and Access(x,n) for the convention in which the SP points to the first empty element and the stack grows downward (toward low addresses).

```
| Stack grows down; SP points to first empty element.

Push(x)    <SP> <- <x>              | Store contents of x on TOS.
           SP   <- <SP> - 1         | Decrement SP.

Pop(x)     SP   <- <SP> + 1         | Increment SP.
           x    <- <<SP>>           | Store value in x.

Access(x,n)  x <- <<SP> + n + 1> | Retrieve nth element from TOS.
```

Write register-transfer-language descriptions of the routines Push(x), Pop(x), and Access(x,n) for the other three conventions.

### Problem 13.2

Consider the arithmetic expression $(A + B) * (C + D - E)$. Give a sequence of instructions to compute this value on each of three-, two-, one-, and zero-address (stack) machines. Make reasonable assumptions about the instruction sets of the machines.

# 14 Stack Architectures: The $S$ Machine

We begin our study of actual machine-language architectures with a typical "zero-address" stack-machine architecture. Such architectures are not in the majority at present, although they are by no means rare. We begin with stack machines because they provide direct support for conventional block-structured compiled languages, which represent the bulk of modern programming. The run-time mechanism and conventions associated with stack machines are reflected, to varying extents, in nearly all current computers.

Most modern computers support a processor stack for procedure-linkage information and for the allocation of local storage; but they usually provide general registers in the processor, in conjunction with two- and three-address instructions, so that most data manipulations are performed without affecting the stack pointer. *Pure* stack machines, by contrast, consolidate the addressing of data at arbitrary places in memory into a very few *data-access* instructions. Intermediate results are stored on the stack, and the majority of instructions on the pure stack machine take inputs from and produce outputs on the processor stack. The ADD instruction of a typical stack machine, for example, will pop two addends from the stack, sum them, and push the result back on the stack. Constants may be pushed on the stack by means of a CONST instruction, whose operation code is followed in the instruction stream by a representation of the value to be pushed on the stack. This induces a programming style similar to that of the "reverse Polish notation" family of pocket calculators (such as those manufactured by Hewlett Packard) and of certain low-level programming languages such as FORTH and the typesetting language Postscript.

The value of the expression $(-36) \cdot (17 + 24)$ would be computed by a stack-machine code fragment such as the following:

```
          | Stack is initially empty.
CONST  36 | Stack contains 36.
NEG       | Stack contains -36.
CONST  17 | Stack contains -36, 17 (bottom to top).
CONST  24 | -36, 17, 24
ADD       | -36, 41
MULT      | -1476
```

Accesses to an arbitrary location in main memory can be performed by pushing the location's address onto the stack (for example, using a CONST instruction) and then using a LOAD or STORE instruction. The LOAD instruction pops an address off the stack and pushes the contents of the addressed memory location. LOAD thus corresponds to one $\langle ... \rangle$ step in our register-transfer notation. The STORE instruction pops a value, then an address, then stores the value at the designated address. STORE thus implements the register-transfer operation $address \leftarrow value$. The register-transfer operation $100 \leftarrow \langle 120 \rangle + 1$ would be performed by the following stack-machine code sequence:

```
                | Stack contents (bottom to top):
CONST    100    | 100
CONST    120    | 100, 120
LOAD            | 100, <120>
CONST    1      | 100, <120>, 1
ADD             | 100, <120>+1
STORE           | (empty).
```

We now describe a particular hypothetical stack-machine design, the $S$ machine, which illustrates a representative set of design choices. The $S$ machine is a stack machine in the pure sense (that is, most of its instructions are zero-address). It uses byte addressing on a 32-bit address space and provides direct (machine-language instruction) support for data widths of 1, 2, 4, and 8 bytes (which we refer to as *bytes*, *words*, *longwords*, and *quadwords*, respectively). Data are untagged: Their interpretation and size are implied by the choice of operators applied to them. Multibyte data are stored in consecutive memory locations, with the least significant bytes at the lowest addresses. The instruction stream of the machine comprises instructions of various lengths and formats, each consisting of an *opcode byte* followed by zero or more additional bytes. The length and format of each instruction can be determined by examining its opcode byte.

The $S$-machine processor state consists of four 32-bit words: a *program counter* (PC), a *stack pointer* (SP), a *base-of-frame pointer* (B), and a *processor status word* (PSW). For our immediate purposes, we consider only the program counter and stack pointer. We revisit B in section 14.7 and PSW in section 14.9.

## 14.1 Basic Instructions

All arithmetic and logical operations in the $S$ machine are performed by addressless instructions whose principal inputs and outputs are data at the top of the stack. We shall refer to this class of instructions as *stack-machine operators*, or simply *operators*, to distinguish them from other instruction formats recognized by the machine. Each operator is encoded as a single 8-bit byte in the instruction stream.

A representative sample of these instructions is shown in table 14.1. There are four different versions of each operation, corresponding to the four possible operand sizes. To differentiate, we suffix to the symbolic name of each operation a 1, 2, 4, or 8 to indicate the size (in bytes) of its input and output data words. For brevity, we abbreviate in the table the four lines corresponding to sadd1, sadd2, sadd4, and sadd8 by the notation sadd$\alpha$, where $\alpha$ is a metavariable ranging over the values 1, 2, 4, and 8. Because of character-set limitations, the symbol @ ("at" sign) is used occasionally in place of $\alpha$ in comments within programs.

**Table 14.1** Typical $S$-machine operators.

| Instruction | Stack before $\rightarrow$ after | Operation |
|---|---|---|
| $\texttt{sadd}\alpha$ | $a^{\alpha},\ b^{\alpha} \rightarrow (a+b)^{\alpha}$ | 2's complement add |
| $\texttt{ssub}\alpha$ | $a^{\alpha},\ b^{\alpha} \rightarrow (a-b)^{\alpha}$ | 2's complement subtract |
| $\texttt{smult}\alpha$ | $a^{\alpha},\ b^{\alpha} \rightarrow (a \cdot b)^{\alpha}$ | 2's complement multiply |
| $\texttt{sdiv}\alpha$ | $a^{\alpha},\ b^{\alpha} \rightarrow (a \div b)^{\alpha}$ | 2's complement divide |
| $\texttt{srem}\alpha$ | $a^{\alpha},\ b^{\alpha} \rightarrow (a \bmod b)^{\alpha}$ | 2's complement remainder |
| $\texttt{sand}\alpha$ | $a^{\alpha},\ b^{\alpha} \rightarrow (a \text{ AND } b)^{\alpha}$ | Bitwise logical AND |
| $\texttt{sash}\alpha$ | $a^{\alpha},\ s^{1} \rightarrow (a \cdot 2^{s})^{\alpha}$ | Arithmetic left (right) shift $s$ $(-s)$ places |
| $\texttt{sneg}\alpha$ | $a^{\alpha} \quad \rightarrow (-a)^{\alpha}$ | 2's complement negation |
| $\texttt{ssext}\alpha$ | $a^{\alpha} \quad \rightarrow a^{2\alpha}$ | Sign-extend |
| $\texttt{slow}\alpha$ | $a^{2\alpha} \quad \rightarrow a^{\alpha}$ | Keep only least significant $\alpha$ bytes |
| $\texttt{shalt}$ | $\cdots \quad \rightarrow \cdots$ | Stop the machine |

The second column of the table gives the number and sizes of stack operands, both inputs and outputs. Each of its entries is of the form $xxx \rightarrow yyy$, where $xxx$ is a list of source operands popped from the stack by the operation and $yyy$ is a list of destination operands (results) pushed onto the stack. Where $xxx$ or $yyy$ includes several operands, they are listed so that the rightmost operand is the one at the top of the stack. Superscripts indicate operand sizes, in bytes.

Several of the operators deviate from the typical pattern of $\alpha$-byte stacked inputs and outputs. Arithmetic shifts, for example, are performed by the $\texttt{sash}\alpha$ operator, which takes a second argument (in addition to the datum to be shifted): a single signed byte $s^{1}$ specifying the number of bits by which the first argument $a^{\alpha}$ is to be shifted. As with the three-operand $\texttt{ASH4}$ instruction discussed in section 13.5.3, the $S$ machine's $\texttt{sash}\alpha$ yields approximately $2^{s} \cdot a$.

The $\texttt{ssext}\alpha$ and $\texttt{slow}\alpha$ instructions provide for conversion between different operand lengths. For example, the $\texttt{ssext2}$ instruction will convert a 2-byte 2's complement integer to the 4-byte 2's complement representation of the same integer. (This is done by extending its sign bit through the extra 2 bytes.) The $\texttt{slow}\alpha$ instruction performs the inverse transformation, converting an integer that is $2\alpha$ bytes in length to its $\alpha$-byte representation, by discarding the most significant $\alpha$ bytes. This operation may, of course, change the value of the operand if it is too big to fit in $\alpha$ bytes, but this is an overflow condition that the programmer must anticipate and avoid. The $\texttt{ssext}\alpha$ and $\texttt{slow}\alpha$ instructions are useful for converting operands to conformable representations before they are, for example, added. Any machine with multiple data representations will include such instructions for converting, or *coercing*, data from one representation to another.

In general, access to a datum at an arbitrary location in memory in our stack machine involves two steps. The first *locates* the datum, pushing its absolute (4-byte) address on the stack; the second is the actual load or store (read or write)

**Table 14.2**  Basic data-access instructions.

| Instruction | Stack before $\rightarrow$ after | Operation |
|---|---|---|
| $\mathrm{sc}\alpha(b^\alpha)$ | $\rightarrow b^\alpha$ | Push constant $b^\alpha$: <br> $\langle\mathrm{SP}\rangle^\alpha \leftarrow b^\alpha \; ; \; \mathrm{SP} \leftarrow \langle\mathrm{SP}\rangle + \alpha$ |
| $\mathrm{sl}\alpha$ | $a^4 \quad \rightarrow \langle a\rangle^\alpha$ | Load: <br> $\mathrm{SP} \leftarrow \langle\mathrm{SP}\rangle - 4 \; ; \; temp^4 \leftarrow \langle\langle\mathrm{SP}\rangle\rangle^4$ <br> $\langle\mathrm{SP}\rangle \leftarrow \langle\langle temp\rangle\rangle^\alpha \; ; \; \mathrm{SP} \leftarrow \langle\mathrm{SP}\rangle + \alpha$ |
| $\mathrm{ss}\alpha$ | $a^4, \, b^\alpha \rightarrow$ | Store: <br> $\mathrm{SP} \leftarrow \langle\mathrm{SP}\rangle - \alpha \; ; \; temp^\alpha \leftarrow \langle\langle\mathrm{SP}\rangle\rangle^\alpha$ <br> $\mathrm{SP} \leftarrow \langle\mathrm{SP}\rangle - 4 \; ; \; \langle\langle\mathrm{SP}\rangle\rangle^\alpha \leftarrow \langle temp\rangle^\alpha$ |

operation, which moves data between the top of stack and the addressed location. Instructions that perform these functions are listed in table 14.2.

The $\mathrm{sc}\alpha$ instructions push $\alpha$-byte constants from the instruction stream onto the stack. It is convenient to define each as a macroinstruction whose argument gives the constant, namely,

```
.macro sc1(C) 0x10 C      | sc@(const): Load @-byte constant
.macro sc2(C) 0x11 WORD(C) |   onto stack.
.macro sc4(C) 0x12 LONG(C)
```

In our $S$-machine assembly language, instructions that require additional constants in the instruction stream are defined as macroinstructions, taking the constants as arguments, as above. Instructions that take no instruction-stream arguments are defined simply as symbols, as in

```
sadd4  = 0x22   | 4-byte S-machine addition instruction
```

We can collect macroinstruction and symbol definitions for the $S$-machine instruction set in a single file that we can include (using the assembler .include directive) at the beginning of each $S$-machine assembly-language program.

The $\mathrm{sc}\alpha$ instructions provide a starting point for other operations. The instructions $\mathrm{sl}\alpha$ and $\mathrm{ss}\alpha$ provide the actual load and store mechanisms. They typically follow instructions (such as sc4(X)) that push the address of a variable. The operation performed by our sample three-address machine instruction ADD4 120,140,100 would thus be performed on the $S$ machine by a sequence of instructions such as is shown in figure 14.3.

The binary representation of certain elements in this program must be deduced from their context. For example, the constant in each sc4 opcode is translated to 4 bytes, as dictated by its macroinstruction definition. As a concrete example of the assembly process for the $S$ machine, we give in table 14.4 the machine-code bytes corresponding to the program of figure 14.3. We have assumed that the program

```
sc4(100)        | Destination address.
sc4(120)        | Address of first addend.
sl4             | Push <120>.
sc4(140)
sl4             | Push <140>.
sadd4           | Compute <120>+<140>.
ss4             | Then store it at address 100.
```

**Figure 14.3**  *S*-machine code sequence equivalent to ADD4 120,140,100.

**Table 14.4**  Assembled code for the program of figure 14.3.

| Location | Bytes |     |     |     |     |
|----------|-------|-----|-----|-----|-----|
| 300      | *sc4* | 100 | 0   | 0   | 0   |
| 305      | *sc4* | 120 | 0   | 0   | 0   |
| 310      | *sl4* |     |     |     |     |
| 311      | *sc4* | 140 | 0   | 0   | 0   |
| 316      | *sl4* |     |     |     |     |
| 317      | *sadd4* |   |     |     |     |
| 318      | *ss4* |     |     |     |     |

starts at address 300 and have used the abbreviations *sc4*, *sl4*, *sadd4*, and *ss4* to stand for the numerical opcodes of the sc4, sl4, sadd4, and ss4 instructions, respectively.

The reader should not jump to the conclusion that the stack machine is far inferior because it takes seven instructions to do what the three-address machine can do in a single instruction. Each stack-machine instruction does much less; hence it is reasonable to expect it to execute more quickly. A count of the number of bytes occupied by the instruction sequence (a reasonable predictor of execution time on many machines) gives 19 for the *S* machine, as opposed to 13 for the three-address machine. Thus the *S* machine is probably a less efficient architecture for this particular operation. However, *S*-machine instructions are more "unbundled" than three-address instructions: Each instruction does just one thing. The resulting flexibility in constructing *S*-machine instruction sequences is useful in more complicated situations. For example, an *S*-machine program equivalent to the one in figure 13.11 is given in figure 14.5. The *S*-machine program has more instructions than that of figure 13.11, but it occupies only 34 bytes, as opposed to 49 bytes. (In fairness, it should be noted that most three-address machines, such as the *G* machine discussed in chapter 15, have features that make them look better in this comparison.)

## 14.2  *S*-**Machine Instruction Coding**

Figure 14.6 shows assembler definitions for several *S*-machine instructions.  (A

```
START:  sc4(TEMP)        | Address for result.
        sc4(DATA)
        sl4              | Load first operand.
        sc4(DATA+4)
        sl4              | Load second operand.
        sadd4            | Add first two operands.
        sc4(DATA+8)
        sl4
        sadd4            | Add in the third operand.
        sc4(DATA+12)
        sl4
        sadd4            | Add in the fourth operand.
        ss4              | Store the sum in TEMP.
        shalt


DATA:   LONG(1)          | The four operands.
        LONG(2)
        LONG(3)
        LONG(4)
TEMP:   LONG(0)          | Space for the result.
```

**Figure 14.5**  $S$-machine program to sum four array elements.

more complete set of definitions appears in appendix 4.) Since nearly every operation must be implemented for each of our supported data sizes (that is, for 1-, 2-, 4-, and 8-byte quantities), we use a systematic representation in which the 2 low-order bits of each opcode specify the datum length, and the remaining 6 bits dictate the operation to be performed. The 2 low-order opcode bits have values 00, 01, and 10 to indicate 1-, 2-, and 4-byte data, respectively; we reserve 11 for 8-byte data, a straightforward extension of our implementation that we do not pursue here.

## 14.3 *MAYBE Implementation

For the sake of an example, we offer an overview of a plausible implementation of the $S$ machine on the MAYBE microarchitecture. Appendix 4 includes a complete listing of a microcoded $S$-machine implementation for the MAYBE machine; the reader is invited to peruse this appendix while studying the material presented here.

In the microcoded implementation of the $S$ machine, we choose to dedicate certain locations in the microarchitecture's static RAM to storing processor-state information. Table 14.7 summarizes the conventions for $S$-machine processor-state representation within the microinterpreter. Note that these dedicated registers are allocated beginning at SRAM location 32, thus allowing the low SRAM locations to serve as temporary storage and for passing arguments to microsubroutines. The particular SRAM addresses are chosen to conform to requirements imposed by the $G$ machine presented in chapter 15, and they should be considered arbitrary for the present.

```
| Definitions for assembly of a few S-machine instructions.

.macro WORD(x) x%256 x/256                | Low byte followed by high byte.
.macro LONG(x) WORD(x) WORD(x/0x1000)     | Low word followed by high word.


| S opcode macros ...

.macro sc1(C)    0x04    C        | sc@(C) - push @-byte constant onto stack.
.macro sc2(C)    0x04+1  WORD(C)
.macro sc4(C)    0x04+2  LONG(C)


| S opcode remaining instructions

sl1     = 0x0C             | sl@ - @-byte fetch from user memory (i.e., DRAM).
sl2     = 0x0C+1
sl4     = 0x0C+2


ss1     = 0x10             | ss@ - @-byte store into user memory (i.e., DRAM).
ss2     = 0x10+1
ss4     = 0x10+2


sadd1   = 0x14             | sadd@ - @-byte addition.
sadd2   = 0x14+1
sadd4   = 0x14+2


ssub1   = 0x18             | ssub@ - @-byte subtraction.
ssub2   = 0x18+1
ssub4   = 0x18+2
```

**Figure 14.6**  Assembler definitions for $S$-machine interpreter.


Figure 14.8 shows microassembly-language definitions that give symbolic names
to these SRAM locations. Several additional SRAM locations are allocated here
for use during the interpretation of individual $S$-machine instructions; they include
MCond, which will contain temporary copies of a simulated condition-code byte,
and three 4-byte SRAM locations, Op1, Op2, and Op3, for temporarily holding data
values. Unlike B, PC, and SP, these locations are not part of the defined $S$-machine
state (as visible to the $S$-machine programmer); they hold transient data during
the interpretation of a single $S$-machine instruction, but their contents are not used
between $S$-machine instructions. Thus, at the level of the $S$ machine (where each
machine instruction is viewed as a single, "atomic" action), the machine's state is
completely specified by the contents of B, PC, SP, and main memory.

Figure 14.8 also defines a macroinstruction $\text{fetch}(x)$, which copies a single
byte from the instruction stream, incrementing $\langle PC \rangle$ accordingly, into the SRAM
location whose address is $x$. Since our MAYBE implementation supports only
16-bit main-memory addresses, we optimize the $\text{fetch}$ operation slightly by incrementing only the 2 low-order bytes of our 4-byte program counter.

**Table 14.7**  Static RAM allocation for $S$-machine implementation.

| SRAM location | Contents | Dedicated use |
|---|---|---|
| 0x5C | $\langle PC \rangle$ | Machine's program counter (address of next instruction byte) |
| 0x58 | $\langle SP \rangle$ | Machine's stack pointer (address for next pushed data) |
| 0x60 | $\langle PSW \rangle$ | Processor status word (status bits; see section 14.9) |
| 32=0x20 | $\langle B \rangle$ | Base-of-frame pointer (address of current stack frame) |

**Figure 14.8**  Assembler definitions for microcoded $S$-machine interpreter.

```
    | 32-bit S-machine architecture: microcode support.

    | Some SRAM registers are reserved for particular purposes.
    | Machine-level register definitions:
    |    Each is 4 bytes long.

    B      = 32           | Base-of-frame pointer.
    SP     = 0x58         | Stack pointer.
    PC     = 0x5C         | Program counter.
    PSW    = PC+4         | Processor status word (4 bytes).
                          | Note: Don't change SP and PC:
                          |    They are "hard-wired" into "sim"!

    MCond  = PSW+4        | Temporary location for condition codes
    Spare  = MCond+1      |    (unused for now).

    Op1    = Spare+1      | Temporary results and operands
    Op2    = Op1+4        |    (each 4 bytes wide!).
    Op3    = Op2+4

    | Fetch a byte from S-machine's instruction stream into SRAM x.
    | Increments PC.

    .macro fetch(x) l(PC, PC+1, x)  cadd2(1, PC, PC)
```

The reader will notice such optimizations throughout the microcoded MAYBE implementation of our machines, which are capable, at the machine-language level, of dealing with main-memory addresses greater than 16 bits. When actual DRAM references are made, only the 2 low-order address bytes are used; the high-order bytes are simply ignored. A somewhat cleaner (though slower) approach would involve checking the high-order bytes at each main-memory access, generating an error if they are nonzero. Such an implementation would provide a measure of error detection, flagging certain programs that exceed the MAYBE's memory capacity rather than simply computing incorrect results. While this approach is clearly preferable from a semantic standpoint, it is not followed here because of the substantial coding and performance overheads it introduces.

### 14.3.1 *Basic Instruction Fetch/Execute Loop

The microprogram in figure 14.9 contains the basic read/dispatch loop that is the heart of the interpretive mechanism for the $S$ machine. The execution of a new machine instruction begins at the microinstruction labeled NextInst, which uses the fetch macroinstruction to fetch the opcode byte addressed by the machine's program counter and increment the PC to point to the byte following the opcode byte. The microinstruction dispatch(R0,ITab) effects a 256-way branch to one of the microcode ROM locations given in ITab, according to the 8-bit opcode.

In general, each ITab entry identifies a sequence of microinstructions implementing a particular $S$-machine opcode. The forty-first entry of ITab (that is, the one taken when ⟨R0⟩ is 40, or 0x28 using C-syntax hexadecimal notation) thus contains the microcode address hsadd1, which handles the $S$-machine sadd1 operation. In general, we use the convention that the microcode address for the sequence of microinstructions that handle an instruction bears a tag that is the instruction's name with an h prefix; the microcode sequence is referred to as the *handler* for that machine instruction. The tag hii identifies a handler for *illegal instructions* and appears in table entries corresponding to unassigned opcodes.

After performing the indicated operation, instruction-handler sequences such as the one at hsadd1 could simply jump back to NextInst to fetch and execute the following $S$-machine instruction. However, we prefer to view NextInst as a microsubroutine that executes a single $S$-machine instruction and then returns to its caller; accordingly, each instruction handler executes a rtn microinstruction when it has completed interpretation of the current $S$-machine instruction.

The continuous execution of $S$-machine instructions might be effected by a microprogram loop that calls the NextInst microsubroutine, as shown in figure 14.10. Note that this loop is coded to include enough dynamic RAM refresh operations to ensure integrity of DRAM contents. A preferable (but more tedious) approach to DRAM refresh would be to distribute the refr operations among the microinstructions that interpret $S$-machine instructions, carefully taking microinstruction timings into account to ensure sufficient, but not redundant, attention to refresh.

We have chosen the microsubroutine organization, rather than direct jumps, partly to allow machine-instruction handlers to be available for internal use as

**Figure 14.9** Skeletal fetch/execute microcode for the $S$ machine.

```
| Main S-instruction fetch/execute microsubroutine.
| Dispatches to an S-instruction handler, which returns to caller
|   of NextInst via a rtn() microinstruction.


NextInst:
        fetch(R0)                 | Get opcode of next S-instruction.
        dispatch(R0, ITab)        | Dispatch through instruction table.
                                  | Note: dispatch(...) uses 2*<R0> for
                                  |   offset.


| This is the 256-entry instruction dispatch table.


| Note: "hhalt," "hbpt," and "hii" are prefixed by "h"
|   (as opposed to "hs") because these are generic instructions
|   that will be used by both the S and G machines.


        | The tags (loc0x??) are used merely to facilitate
        |   lookup by humans of table locations.
        |   (Remember: Location 2X corresponds to opcode X.)
ITab:
loc0x00:  WORD(hhalt)    WORD(hslla)    WORD(hslaa)    WORD(hsalloc)
loc0x08:  WORD(hsc1)     WORD(hsc2)     WORD(hsc4)     WORD(hii)
          . . .

loc0x28:  WORD(hsadd1)   WORD(hsadd2)   WORD(hsadd4)   WORD(hii)
          . . .
```

**Figure 14.10** Plausible $S$-machine instruction-execution loop microcode.

```
Go:    refr()          | Refreshes 54 rows per machine instr,
       refr()          |    assuming about 1 ms/instruction.
       refr()          | Slower instrs must add refr() calls.
       refr()          | Note: refr()s should preferably be
       refr()          |    distributed in the code!
       refr()
       refr()
       refr()
       refr()


       call(NextInst)  | Execute machine instruction.
       jmp(Go)
```

utility microsubroutines. The handler for ssub2, for example, can contain microsubroutine calls to sneg2 and sadd2 rather than duplicating the details of their arithmetic and stack manipulation. We show an example of this technique presently.

### 14.3.2 *Utility Microsubroutines

A number of basic operations recur frequently in our microcode, justifying their support as microsubroutines. Table 14.11 lists several microsubroutines we use. Once again, the suffixed $\alpha$ denotes a digit (1, 2, or 4) giving the length (in bytes) of the datum handled by the routine; thus get4 fetches a 32-bit longword from memory, while put1 stores a single byte at the specified memory location. Note that we have extended our register-transfer language slightly to distinguish dynamic RAM (main-memory) locations from the static RAM locations used by the microcode. The notation $\langle x \rangle$ is used in table 14.11 to denote the contents of the *static* RAM location whose address is $x$; the form $\text{DRAM}[x, y]$ denotes the DRAM location whose 2-byte address has $x$ as its low-order byte and $y$ as its high-order byte. Thus the contents of DRAM location 5 are denoted $\langle \text{DRAM}[5, 0] \rangle$. Recall that the static RAM locations containing the $S$ machine's stack pointer are SP and SP+1, so that their respective contents are $\langle \text{SP} \rangle$ and $\langle \text{SP}+1 \rangle$. Thus the location (in dynamic RAM) to which the SP points is denoted by the somewhat cryptic $\text{DRAM}[\langle \text{SP} \rangle, \langle \text{SP}+1 \rangle]$, and the contents of that location are $\langle \text{DRAM}[\langle \text{SP} \rangle, \langle \text{SP}+1 \rangle] \rangle$. We shall find it convenient to abbreviate the form $\text{DRAM}[\langle x \rangle, \langle x+1 \rangle]$, using our superscript notation, to the shorter $\text{DRAM}[\langle x \rangle^2]$. Thus the contents of the location pointed to by the $S$ machine's stack pointer will be designated $\langle \text{DRAM}[\langle \text{SP} \rangle^2] \rangle$. Of course, our use of 2-byte addresses for DRAM locations reflects the main-memory capacity of our MAYBE implementation. On a larger machine, these superscripts might be 3 or 4.

Note that the arguments to these microsubroutines include *addresses* of static RAM locations from or to which data are transferred. Thus, for example, put4 takes the 16-bit address $d$ of a dynamic RAM location in R0 and R1 and an 8-bit address $s$ of a static RAM location in R2; it then copies 4 data bytes from SRAM locations $s$ through $s + 3$ into DRAM locations $d$ through $d + 3$.

We adopt the implementation convention that temporary storage of data in SRAM locations (for example, in Op1) always occupies a full 4-byte longword, thereby greatly reducing the number of special cases that have to be treated by our microcode implementation. Thus conversion between the datum size specified by the programmer (and encoded into the low-order opcode bits) and our internal 4-byte representation takes place when operands are copied between main memory and SRAM. To facilitate this scheme, we arrange for the microsubroutines get$\alpha$, fetch$\alpha$, and pop$\alpha$ to extend the $\alpha$-byte datum to a 4-byte representation in the indicated static RAM location. Since we shall be dealing primarily with 2's complement quantities, the conversion of a smaller datum to the internal 4-byte representation is a *sign extension*—that is, the additional high-order bytes are filled with the sign bit of the shorter datum being converted. In this way, a 1-byte representation of $-37$ is extended to a 4-byte representation of $-37$ for internal purposes. A call to pop1, for example, will pop a single byte from the $S$-machine stack (adjusting $\langle \text{SP} \rangle$ by 1), sign-extend the popped datum to 4 bytes, and store the result in the four consecutive SRAM locations whose addresses begin at $\langle \text{R2} \rangle$. As is our convention throughout the text, low-order data bytes of multibyte data will be stored at lower addresses. Figure 14.12 shows an implementation of the get2 microsubroutine; similar code is used for operands of other lengths.

**Table 14.11** Utility microsubroutines for $S$-machine implementation.

| Name | Function performed | Temporary register usage | Description |
|------|--------------------|--------------------------|-------------|
| get$\alpha$ | $\langle R2 \rangle^4 \leftarrow \langle DRAM[\langle R0 \rangle^2] \rangle^\alpha$ <br> (sign-extended for $\alpha < 4$); <br> $R2 \leftarrow \langle R2 \rangle + 4$; <br> $R0^2 \leftarrow \langle R0 \rangle^2 + \alpha$ | | Memory read <br> (bumps $R0^2$, R2) |
| put$\alpha$ | $DRAM[\langle R0 \rangle^2]^\alpha \leftarrow \langle \langle R2 \rangle \rangle^\alpha$; <br> $R2 \leftarrow \langle R2 \rangle + 4$; <br> $R0^2 \leftarrow \langle R0 \rangle^2 + \alpha$ | | Memory write <br> (bumps $R0^2$, R2) |
| push$\alpha$ | $DRAM[\langle SP \rangle^2]^\alpha \leftarrow \langle \langle R2 \rangle \rangle^\alpha$; <br> $SP^2 \leftarrow \langle SP \rangle^2 + \alpha$ | R0, R1, R2 | Push datum on <br> processor stack |
| pop$\alpha$ | $SP^2 \leftarrow \langle SP \rangle^2 - \alpha$; <br> $\langle R2 \rangle^4 \leftarrow \langle DRAM[\langle SP \rangle^2] \rangle^\alpha$ <br> (sign-extended for $\alpha < 4$) | R0, R1, R2 | Pop datum from <br> processor stack |
| fetch$\alpha$ | $\langle R2 \rangle^4 \leftarrow \langle DRAM[\langle PC \rangle^2] \rangle^\alpha$ <br> (sign-extended for $\alpha < 4$); <br> $PC^2 \leftarrow \langle PC \rangle^2 + \alpha$ | R0, R1, R2 | Fetch datum from <br> instruction stream |

In a programming environment as primitive as our microarchitecture, which provides, for example, no well-structured mechanism for passing parameters to subroutines, one must pay particularly careful attention to a variety of low-level bookkeeping and documentation details. Among these are the side effects of microsubroutine invocation, which tend to be inescapable in situations (such as the present one) where there is limited temporary storage (such as our R0, R1, ...) to be shared among many program modules. If microsubroutine $M$ uses R5 to store an intermediate value during its computation (for example, to pass an argument to another microsubroutine), previous contents of R5 are lost. It is consequently crucial that the *caller* to $M$ avoid leaving anything in R5 that it expects to use upon return from $M$. The temporary storage usage of a subroutine thus constitutes an important part of its functional specification; table 14.11 includes a column for such information, and it should generally be included in the descriptive comment that appears at the beginning of the source code for each microsubroutine. In general, the set of registers used by a microsubroutine $M$ includes those used by any subroutines *called* by $M$.

This problem can be mitigated somewhat by the use of the stack (in the present example, the microstack) to preserve and restore the previous contents of temporary

**Figure 14.12**  get2 microsubroutine.

```
| Get a 2-byte operand from main memory.

| Copies operand from main-memory location given by R0,1 to SRAM
|    location whose address is <R2>.
| Sign-extends operand to 4 bytes.
| Increments <R2> by 4, <R0,1> by length.


get2:   push(R4) push(R3)     | Save registers for temporary use.
        call(getdatum)
        call(getdatum)
| Set R4 for sign extension and sign-extend 2-bytes ...
getx2:  cadd(0, R4, R4)       | Check sign of byte (set ALU flags).
        cmove(0, R4)          | Extend with zeros
        jpl(extend2)          |    iff positive,
        cmove(-1, R4)         | else extend with ones.
        jmp(extend2)          | Use common code.


| Microsubroutine used to copy and update 1 byte's worth of data.
getdatum: l(R0, R1, R4)       | Get data byte.
        movei(R4, R2)         | Store it away.
        cadd(1, R2, R2)       | Update <R2>.
        cadd2(1, R0, R0)      | Update <R0,1>.
        rtn()


| Microsubroutine for sign-extending 2 bytes using R4.
extend2: movei(R4, R2)        | Extend to high-order bytes.
        cadd(1, R2, R2)
        movei(R4, R2)
        cadd(1, R2, R2)
        pop(R3) pop(R4)       | Restore registers.
        rtn()
```

locations, as is done in get$\alpha$ with R3 and R4. Indeed, a programming discipline that takes this approach uniformly—preserving the contents of each register not used for communication with the caller—probably results in the cleanest program structure. However, this extreme usually involves some time and storage overhead, since many of the values thus preserved are of no interest to the caller. Often a compromise discipline is established, wherein a designated subset of the temporary locations is uniformly preserved, while the remaining ones are assumed to be lost during the invocation of any subroutine. At the microcode level, where performance and storage issues are particularly sensitive, an ad hoc approach (in which each subroutine may follow different conventions) is common. While this allows certain low-level optimizations, it is another detail the programmer must keep in mind.

The implementation of the remaining utility microsubroutines appears in appendix 3, to which the reader is urged to refer. These routines are used freely

**Figure 14.13** Macro definitions for utility microsubroutines.

```
| Some handy operations, defined as macros.

.macro  PUSH1(x)        cmove(x, R2)    call(push1)
.macro  PUSH2(x)        cmove(x, R2)    call(push2)
.macro  PUSH4(x)        cmove(x, R2)    call(push4)


.macro  POP1(x)         cmove(x, R2)    call(pop1)
.macro  POP2(x)         cmove(x, R2)    call(pop2)
.macro  POP4(x)         cmove(x, R2)    call(pop4)


.macro  FETCH1(x)       cmove(x, R2)    call(fetch1)
.macro  FETCH2(x)       cmove(x, R2)    call(fetch2)
.macro  FETCH4(x)       cmove(x, R2)    call(fetch4)
```

in the microcode implementations that follow. To make the calls to these utility routines slightly more transparent, we can define macros to handle common cases; examples appear in figure 14.13.

Note that each of these macros takes a constant argument that is an SRAM location; thus POP2(Op1) has the effect of popping a 2-byte datum from the $S$-machine stack, sign-extending it to 4 bytes, and leaving the result in SRAM locations Op1 through Op1+3.

### 14.3.3 *Operator Handlers

Figure 14.14 shows the microcode that implements the $S$-machine sadd2 operator. Very similar code is executed for other members of the sadd$\alpha$ family, namely, sadd1 and sadd4. The two POP2 operations (macroinstructions that expand to calls to pop2) pop appropriately sized (2-byte) arguments from the $S$-machine stack into Op1 through Op1+3 and Op2 through Op2+3, each sign-extended to 4 bytes. The add2 microinstruction computes a 2-byte sum, which is left in Op2 and Op2+1. The PUSH2 pushes the 2-byte sum onto the $S$-machine stack, and the operation is complete.

The microprogram of figure 14.15 shows one possible implementation of the sneg2 (2's complement) operator, which could be made less awkward by the control-ROM implementation of a negcy (negate with carry input) microinstruction.

Given sneg$\alpha$ and sadd$\alpha$, concise implementations of ssub$\alpha$ instructions might exploit our implementation of instruction handlers as microsubroutines, as in figure 14.16, where jmp(hsadd2) is a hand-optimization of the two-microinstruction sequence call(hsadd2) rtn(). While cute, this implementation of ssub2 introduces considerable unnecessary performance overhead; a more realistic implementation appears in the listing in appendix 4.

**Figure 14.14**  sadd2 instruction-handler microcode.

```
| sadd2 -- push(pop()+pop()), operands of length 2.

hsadd2: POP2(Op1)
        POP2(Op2)
        add2(Op1, Op2, Op2)
        PUSH2(Op2)
        rtn()
```

**Figure 14.15**  sneg2 instruction-handler microcode.

```
| sneg2(n) -- 2's complement.

hsneg2: POP2(Op2)
        not(Op1, Op1)            | Complement argument.
        not(Op1+1, Op1+1)
        cadd2(1, Op1, Op1)       | Then add 1.
        PUSH2(Op1)
        rtn()
```

**Figure 14.16**  Concise ssub2 instruction-handler microcode.

```
hssub2: call(hsneg2)    | Negate second argument on stack,
        jmp(hsadd2)     |   then add to first argument.
```

The constant loading instructions sc$\alpha$ use FETCH$\alpha$ to fetch and sign-extend a
constant from the instruction stream; a typical handler microsubroutine is shown
in figure 14.17, along with typical handlers for the load and store instructions sl$\alpha$
and ss$\alpha$. Both sl$\alpha$ and ss$\alpha$ pop a 4-byte memory address from the stack. Since
our MAYBE implementation has only $2^{16}$ bytes of main memory, the high-order
address bytes are unused; they are pushed and popped by the $S$ machine simply to
maintain machine-language compatibility with more grandiose implementations.

## 14.4 Compilation Techniques for Stack Machines

One of the attractions of the pure stack-machine architecture is its amenability to
automatic code generation. Stack-machine code is so convenient for a compiler
to generate that it is often used as an intermediate representation of a program

**Figure 14.17** `sc2`, `sl2`, and `ss2` instruction-handler microcode.

```
| sc2 -- Load 2-byte constant from instruction stream onto stack.

hsc2:    FETCH2(Op1)            | Fetch constant into Op1.
         PUSH2(Op1)             | Push it onto stack.
         rtn()                  | And we're done!


| sl2 -- Load 2-byte datum from main memory;
|        uses 4-byte address from stack.

hsl2:    POP4(Op1)              | Pop the 4-byte address.
         move2(Op1, R0)         |   (Ignores 2 top bytes!)
         cmove(Op1, R2)         | Load 2-byte value into Op1,
         call(get2)
         PUSH2(Op1)             |   then push it onto stack.
         rtn()



| ss2 -- Store 2-byte datum into main memory;
|        takes 2-byte datum, 4-byte address from stack.

hss2:    POP2(Op2)              | Pop the 2-byte datum from stack.
         POP4(Op1)              | Pop the 4-byte address.
         move2(Op1, R0)         |   (Ignores 2 top bytes!)
         cmove(Op2, R2)         | Store @-byte value from Op2
         call(put2)             |   into main memory.
         rtn()
```

by compilers whose ultimate target machine has a conventional general-register architecture. In this section, we sketch some primitive techniques for the translation of constructs of an algebraic language (such as FORTRAN, Pascal, or C) to stack-machine code.

A principal syntactic element of most high-level languages is the *expression*, containing variables, constants, and operators. Algebraic languages deal with expressions (such as $A \cdot B + C$) in the usual *infix* form, in which binary operators (such as $+$) appear *between* their operands. A major task of a compiler for such languages is the translation of infix expressions to machine code that computes their value. On a stack machine, the operands of an operator must be loaded onto the stack before the operator instruction is executed. Thus, assuming all integers are represented using 4 bytes, the following stack-machine code evaluates the expression $14 + 37$ and leaves the result on the stack:

```
sc4(14)
sc4(37)
sadd4
```

*Stack Architectures: The S Machine*

We might translate each variable $V$ as a reference to a memory location whose contents represent the value of $V$, whence the expression $A + 3$ might be evaluated by the stack-machine code:

```
sc4(A)          | Address of A.
sl4             | Contents of A.
sc4(3)
sadd4
```

If we treat each operand and operator as a separate token in the source program and assume that it is read from left to right, we notice that successive tokens must be processed by the stack machine in an order somewhat different from their sequence in the original program. In particular, the *infix* expression 14, $+$, 37 must be translated to the *postfix* form 14, 37, $+$, which corresponds more directly to the sequence of generated stack-machine instructions. The term *postfix* refers to the fact that operators follow their arguments, as opposed to the *infix* form of mathematics and the *prefix* expressions of LISP. Fortunately, it is quite easy to translate infix expressions to postfix form; it simply means moving operator tokens to the right, past their second operands.

One simple translation technique establishes an *operator stack* on which to store the deferred operators. The compilation of stack-machine expressions then involves reading successive source-language tokens and processing them as follows:

- If the token is a constant $c$, output the instruction $\mathtt{sc4}(c)$.

- If the token is a variable $X$, output the instruction $\mathtt{sc4}(X)$ followed by $\mathtt{sl4}$.

- If the token is an operator, push it on the operator stack.

- If the token is an end-of-expression delimiter, successively pop each token from the operator stack and output the corresponding machine instruction.

Using this translation scheme, the expression $A + B \cdot C$ would produce the code

```
sc4(A)
sl4
sc4(B)
sl4
sc4(C)
sl4
smult4
sadd4
```

This translation scheme glosses over a number of important problems, however. One complication arises from the ambiguity of infix expressions of the form $a \cdot b + c$, the conventional interpretation of which is $(a \cdot b) + c$ rather than $a \cdot (b + c)$. The above translation scheme would produce the code

```
sc4(A)
sl4
sc4(B)
sl4
sc4(C)
```

```
sl4
sadd4
smult4
```

whose result is unlikely to be what the programmer expected. In general, the scheme causes operators to associate to the right, because it defers (on the operator stack) all operator instructions until each operand has been stacked. Thus, for example, an input expression $A - B - C$ would be translated to the postfix form $A, B, C, -, -$, which computes $A - (B - C)$ rather than $(A - B) - C$. The reader is encouraged to devise (before reading the next paragraph) a fix to the translation algorithm that will cause operators to be popped from the operator stack and output as machine instructions at the *earliest* workable point; such an algorithm constitutes the extreme in which all operators associate to the left. The left-associative extreme has the advantage that the code produced requires less stack space, since stacked constants and variable values are used as operands as soon as possible after they are stacked. Conventional usage dictates that most operators (such as subtraction) associate to the left; we would like our translation scheme to treat $A - B - C$ as $(A - B) - C$ while treating $A - B \cdot C$ as $A - (B \cdot C)$.

The usual method of dealing with this problem is to associate a *precedence* (perhaps represented as a small integer) with each operator and to arrange that the precedence of the multiply and divide operators (for example) be higher than those of the add and subtract operators. Then, before each operator $O$ is placed on the operator stack, previously stacked operators whose precedence is greater than or equal to that of $O$ are popped and their machine instructions are output. Under this revised translation scheme, $A \cdot B + C$ produces the code

```
sc4(A)
sl4
sc4(B)
sl4
smult4
sc4(C)
sl4
sadd4
```

which produces more satisfactory results than the previous translation. This revised translation scheme represents a compromise between the previous extremes, in which the decision as to how long to defer an operator is made "on the spot" by considering the operator and its context (namely, nearby operators in the expression); its output reflects operator precedence, defaulting to left-associativity for operators of equal precedence. It may be extended in a variety of ways—for example, to allow certain operators (such as exponentiation) to associate to the right while others (such as subtraction) associate to the left.

Assignment statements of the form $A = E$ can be compiled into stack-machine code of the form

```
sc4(A)
...
(code to compute the value of expression E)
```

Note that the compilation of the variable to the *left* of the assignment operator produces code to compute the *address* of the corresponding variable, rather than its contents.

There is well-established technology for dealing with parentheses, procedure calls, and array references within expressions, as well as with the compilation of other language constructs; however, these are beyond our current scope. Compilation technology is among the most highly developed branches of computer science; it bears a close and complementary relationship to the architecture of processors, and the reader with serious interests in computer architecture is strongly encouraged to pursue it further.

## 14.5 Flow of Control on the $S$ Machine

Normally, execution of programs by the $S$ machine proceeds from each instruction to the instruction that immediately follows it in memory. The program counter is automatically incremented during each instruction execution to point to the next instruction. Some program constructs (such as loops) require a departure from this sequential flow of control. To accomplish this, the $S$ machine includes the sjmp instruction, which pops a 4-byte operand off the stack and stores it in the program counter, as described in table 14.18. Transfer of control to a designated location TARGET can be effected using the sequence

```
sc4(TARGET)
sjmp
```

An alternative to this design for the sjmp instruction would be to include the target address directly in the instruction, so that the above sequence would be replaced by the single instruction sjmp(TARGET), as in the three-address machine discussed in section 13.5.3. However, it is sometimes convenient to *calculate* the address of the instruction to jump to. For example, a program might use the character code of a character just read from the terminal as an index into a table containing the addresses of handler routines for different categories of input characters. This is analogous to the dispatch capability of our microarchitecture and would be effectively precluded if each sjmp instruction directly included a specific address to jump to.

Although unconditional transfers of control, such as the sjmp instruction provides, are necessary, *conditional* transfers of control are also needed (for example, for if tests in programs). Recall that the results of an operation such as an add performed in the ALU of our micromachine include several *condition-code bits* in addition to the 32-bit data word output. The $S$ machine includes a family of scmp$\alpha$ instructions that perform arithmetic comparisons between the top two $\alpha$-byte items on the stack. These items, $a^\alpha$ and $b^\alpha$, are popped off the stack by scmp$\alpha$, which then pushes a single *condition-code byte* that includes status bits resulting from the subtraction $a^\alpha - b^\alpha$. This byte can be used by a class of *conditional jump* machine

**Table 14.18**  Machine-language branch conditions.

| Mnemonic | Branches on | Description |
|----------|-------------|-------------|
| ne  | $\overline{Z}$ | Not equal (to zero) test |
| e   | $Z$ | Equal |
| ge  | $\overline{S}$ | Signed $\geq$ |
| lt  | $S$ | Signed $<$ |
| gt  | $\overline{Z \text{ OR } S}$ | Signed $>$ |
| le  | $Z \text{ OR } S$ | Signed $\leq$ |
| hi  | $C \text{ AND } \overline{Z}$ | Higher (unsigned $>$) |
| los | $\overline{C} \text{ OR } Z$ | Low or same (unsigned $\leq$) |
| his | $C$ | Higher or same (unsigned $\geq$) |
| lo  | $\overline{C}$ | Lower (unsigned $<$) |

instructions (`sjne`, `sje`, `sjlt`, and so on, corresponding to the 10 branch conditions listed in table 14.18) to control the flow of program execution. The condition-code byte produced by an `scmp`$\alpha$ instruction upon comparing two operands $a^\alpha$ and $b^\alpha$ (where $b^\alpha$ is the operand that was at the top of the stack) contains three useful bits:

- $Z$ (zero), set to 1 if $a^\alpha = b^\alpha$;

- $S$ (sign), set to 1 if $a^\alpha < b^\alpha$ when $a^\alpha$ and $b^\alpha$ are viewed as signed 2's complement $\alpha$-byte numbers; and

- $C$ (carry), set to 1 if the binary addition $a^\alpha + (-b^\alpha)$ yields a carry out of the most significant bit, where $-b^\alpha$ denotes the 2's complement negative of $b^\alpha$ (interestingly, this occurs if and only if $a^\alpha \geq b^\alpha$ when $a^\alpha$ and $b^\alpha$ are viewed as unsigned binary $\alpha$-byte numbers).

The leftmost column of table 14.18 gives the usual mnemonic for each of the 10 arithmetic conditions, and the rightmost column contains a brief English description of the relation it tests. This description should be interpreted as the relation of $x$ to $y$ following an `scmp`$\alpha$ applied to $x$ and $y$ (for example, `sc4(x)`; `sc4(y)`; `scmp4`). Thus, in the code fragment

```
sc2(5)
sc2(6)
scmp2
sc4(target)
sjge
...
```

the branch to `target` will *not* be taken since the relation $5 \geq 6$ does not hold. The center column of table 14.18 tells how the condition can be evaluated from

**Table 14.19** Jump and test instructions.

| Instruction | Stack before $\rightarrow$ after | Operation |
|---|---|---|
| scmp$\alpha$ | $a^\alpha,\ b^\alpha \rightarrow cc^1$ | Arithmetic compare |
| stest$\alpha$ | $a^\alpha \quad \rightarrow cc^1$ | Compare to zero |
| sdup$\alpha$ | $a^\alpha \quad \rightarrow a^\alpha, a^\alpha$ | Duplicate the datum at the top of the stack |
| sjmp | $a^4 \quad \rightarrow$ | Jump unconditionally:<br>$\text{SP} \leftarrow \langle \text{SP} \rangle - 4 \ ; \ \text{PC}^4 \leftarrow \langle \langle \text{SP} \rangle^4 \rangle$ |
| sj$cond$ | $cc^1, a^4 \rightarrow$ | Jump on condition:<br>$\text{SP} \leftarrow \langle \text{SP} \rangle - 4 \ ; \ temp^4 \leftarrow \langle \langle \text{SP} \rangle^4 \rangle$<br>$\text{SP} \leftarrow \langle \text{SP} \rangle - 1 \ ; \ cctemp^1 \leftarrow \langle \langle \text{SP} \rangle^4 \rangle$<br>if $cond$ matches $\langle cctemp \rangle^1$, then $\text{PC} \leftarrow \langle temp \rangle^4$ |

the bits of the condition-code byte stacked by the scmp$\alpha$ instruction.[1]

The signed tests appearing in table 14.18 (ge, lt, gt, and le) are obviously useful for comparisons involving signed integers represented in 2's complement format. The unsigned tests (hi, los, his, and lo) are, of course, useful for comparing unsigned integers represented in unsigned binary format, but they are also useful in comparing addresses of memory locations (for example, to determine whether a given address falls within the bounds of a given data structure): The lowest memory address is conventionally thought of as being 0, and hence an address of the form $1\cdots$ is conventionally thought of as being greater than any address of the form $0\cdots$, even though the 2's complement view would lead to the opposite conclusion. Obscure program bugs are sometimes traced to the (improper) use of signed comparisons on addresses when a data structure occupies a range of memory locations crossing the address boundary between $011\cdots111$ and $100\cdots000$.

Conditional jump instructions are summarized under the category sj$cond$ in table 14.19, which also includes the instructions stest$\alpha$ and sdup$\alpha$. stest$\alpha$ compares the $\alpha$-byte datum at the top of the stack to 0 and pushes the resulting condition-code byte. The instruction stest$\alpha$ has the same effect as the sequence

sc$\alpha$(0)
scmp$\alpha$

---

[1] The observant reader will notice that the condition-code bits appearing in this column (namely, $S$, $C$, and $Z$) are not exactly the $N$, $C$, and $E$ status bits derived from the 74LS181 arithmetic logic unit of the MAYBE microarchitecture. This issue is pursued in the following section.

```
sc4(a)          | Push address of a.
sl4             | Load a's value.
sc4(b)
sl4             | Load b's value.
scmp4           | Set condition codes from a - b.
sc4(here)       | Where to go if a > b:
sjgt            |   Go to here if a > b,
sc4(there)
sjmp            |   else go to there.
```

**Figure 14.20**  Some conditional jumps.

The $\text{sdup}\alpha$ instruction simply duplicates the $\alpha$-byte datum at the top of the stack. This is sometimes useful in connection with the $\text{scmp}\alpha$ and $\text{stest}\alpha$ instructions.

A C statement such as

```
if (a>b) goto here; else goto there;
```

can be translated as in the $S$-machine program of figure 14.20.

Many processors have comparison instructions and a separate family of conditional jump instructions, as the $S$ machine does, but differ from the $S$ machine in that the compare instructions do not produce an explicit result. Instead, they set condition-code bits within the processor state, which may be queried by subsequent conditional jump instructions. We explore this option later, in our discussion of the $G$ machine.

### 14.5.1 *Implementation of Test and Branch Instructions

Unfortunately, the ALU status bits of the MAYBE provide insufficient information to discriminate the 10 arithmetic conditions listed in table 14.18; consequently, the microcoded handler for the $\text{scmp}\alpha$ instruction must manipulate the ALU outputs into a more usable form. The machine-language condition-code byte produced by a $\text{scmp}\alpha$ instruction applied to $x$ and $y$ takes the form

| $S$ | $C$ | $Z$ | 0 | 0 | 0 | 0 | 0 |
|-----|-----|-----|---|---|---|---|---|

As discussed in the previous section, the $Z$ bit is 1 if $x - y$ is 0. The $C$ bit is the carry out from the subtraction $x - y$; it is the inverse of the $\overline{C}$ bit produced by an ALU subtract operation. Thus $C$ will be 1 after the subtractions $4 - 3$ or $4 - 4$, but 0 after the subtraction $3 - 4$. The $S$ bit is the sign of the difference $x - y$, where $x$ and $y$ are interpreted as (signed) 2's complement integers. It differs from the $N$ bit produced by the ALU in one important respect: Unlike $N$, which is simply the high-order (sign) bit of the result word, $S$ is adjusted to account for arithmetic overflow in the computation $x - y$. When $x$ is a large positive $n$-bit number and $y$ is a large negative $n$-bit number, for example, the representation of their difference may require $n + 1$ bits. The $n$-bit result of the naive subtraction $x - y$ will appear to be negative, despite the fact that their real difference is clearly positive. We can correct for this situation by detecting this overflow—namely, cases in which the signs of $x$ and $y$ differ but the sign bit of $x - y$ is different from that of $x$—and inverting the sign of the result (the ALU $N$ bit) on overflow to yield $S$.

One possible implementation of the scmp$\alpha$ handler microsubroutine is illustrated in figure 14.21. The comparison operation begins by popping arguments and performing an $\alpha$-byte subtraction in a straightforward manner. Immediately following the subtraction, the microinstruction cond(MCond) is performed; this copies the condition register of the microarchitecture into the static RAM variable MCond. Recall that the microarchitecture condition byte has the form $N\overline{C}XXXXXX$, where $N$ is the high-order bit of the result and $\overline{C}$ is the inverted carry output. ($X$ designates condition bits that are not relevant to the scmp$\alpha$ implementation.) This byte, now in MCond, will subsequently be manipulated into the desired $SCZ00000$ machine-language condition code.

The or microinstruction following cond leaves in R1 a single byte that is zero if and only if the $\alpha$-byte subtraction resulted in zero. The xor instructions followed by branches conditioned on the sign bit of the result are a convenient method for testing whether two values have like signs; note that, in each case, the most significant of the $\alpha$ bytes of each datum (whose high-order bit is the sign of that datum) are xored. If overflow is detected, control passes to McmpV, where the $N$ bit of the ALU status previously saved in MCond is flipped, effecting the overflow adjustment described earlier. At McmpX, the high-order MCond bit has been adjusted to yield the desired $S$-machine-level condition bit. The following instructions mask irrelevant bits from MCond, invert the ALU $\overline{C}$ bit to yield the machine-level C bit, and set the $Z$ bit if the result was zero (as indicated by $\langle$R1$\rangle$). Finally, the resulting single-byte condition code is pushed onto the stack.

The microsubroutine in figure 14.22 shows the straightforward implementation of the unconditional jump instruction. The implementation of conditional transfers is illustrated in figure 14.23, which shows microcode for the sje and sjne handlers (together with much of the mechanism for other conditional jumps). Note the use of an internal microsubroutine, popcond, which is shared by the other conditional jump handlers. The implementations of the remaining conditional jumps are given in appendix 4; the principal activity of each of these handlers is to apply the appropriate logical function to the 3 bits of the condition code.

## 14.6 *Relative Addressing and Position-Independent Code

Use of sc4 instructions to generate a location's address binds the absolute address of that location into the instruction stream. Thus, in general, a program that is assembled into locations 100–200, say, will not work properly if its binary instructions are copied from locations 100–200 to locations 300–400 and executed there. Its addresses will still refer to locations in the old range and must be adjusted if the program is moved.

Consider, for example, a sequence of five instructions to take the absolute value of a 4-byte integer $i$ on the stack, shown in figure 14.24. If these instructions are assembled at location 100 (for example, if they are immediately preceded by a .=100 pseudo-operation when assembled), then the symbol POS will be assigned the

**Figure 14.21** scmp2 handler microsubroutine.

```
| 2-byte compare instruction.
|   Compute x-y, leaving condition byte SCZ00000 on the stack.
|   (Note that the ALU E bit is of little use in multiprecision!)
| Note that when doing x - y (no carry-in), the C bit from the ALU
|   indicates x < y.
| To test for zero, result bytes are ORed into R1 (which is zero
|   if result is zero).
| Arithmetic overflow occurs if x and y have different signs
|   and the sign of the result is not the sign of x.
| The following code segment branches to hscmpX on no overflow and
|   to hscmpV on overflow.

hscmp2: POP2(Op1)                  | y
        POP2(Op2)                  | x

        sub2(Op2, Op1, Op3)        | Compute <Op2> - <Op1>.
        cond(MCond)                | Save ALU conditions.
        or(Op3, Op3+1, R1)         | OR bytes for zero test,
                                   |    leaving OR in R1.
        xor(Op1+1, Op2+1, R2)      | Like signs?
        jpl(hscmpX)                | Yup, no overflow.
        xor(Op3+1, Op2+1, R2)      | Sign of x = sign of result?
        jpl(hscmpX)                | Yup, no overflow.
        jmp(hscmpV)                | Else, overflow!

| On overflow, flip the N bit from the result to produce the S bit:

hscmpV: cxor(0x80, MCond, MCond)

| Here with ALU condition byte (used for S, C bits)
|   in MCond, ORed bytes in R1:

hscmpX: cand(0xC0,MCond,MCond)     | Mask to SC000000.
        ccmp(0, R1)                | Test for zero ...
                                   |    we left OR in R1, remember?
        jne(xcmp)                  | Not zero, so just exit,
        cor(0x20, MCond, MCond)    |    else set Z bit.
xcmp:   PUSH1(MCond)               | Push 1-byte condition
                                   |    code onto stack.
        rtn()
```

value 109 since the intervening five instructions total 9 bytes in length. The address of the instruction at POS: ... (that is, 109) will appear in the sc4 instruction assembled at locations 102–106. When moved to locations beginning at 300, the sjge will still address location 109 rather than 309, causing the relocated program to misbehave.

**Figure 14.22** sjmp handler microsubroutine.

```
| sjmp(x): ALWAYS jump.

hsjmp:  POP4(PC)        | Pop the target address,
        rtn()           |   install as <PC>.
```

We might, of course, move the program to location 300 by changing its .=100 pseudo-operation to specify 300 and reassembling. However, such reassembly imposes considerable overhead on the relocation process: It involves several passes over the source file, building a symbol table, retranslating each instruction, and so on. In many applications where storage for a number of programs is allocated dynamically, say on a real-time demand basis, this overhead is not acceptable.

One solution to this problem is to specify the addresses of locations that are to be relocated along with the program in a *PC-relative* way. Such addresses would be given not as absolute numbers but as *offsets* from the location of the current instruction to the addressed location. These offsets will remain the same even if the program as a whole is moved. Code that scrupulously uses PC-relative addressing for all references to locations that are relocated along with the program is termed *position-independent*, meaning that it can be copied to an arbitrary set of contiguous memory locations and executed there. Position-independent programs can be shuffled around in memory to suit the convenience and allocation requirements of an operating system, largely without regard to the details of the instruction streams they comprise.

The $S$ machine supports PC-relative addressing by means of the $slr\alpha$ (for "load-relative") instructions shown in table LastFigNum. An $slr\alpha$ instruction computes and stacks a PC-relative address from a signed $\alpha$-byte offset in the instruction stream. The metavariable $\alpha$ dictates not the width of the value produced by $slr\alpha$, which is always a 4-byte address, but rather the width of the signed offset $r^\alpha$ specified in the instruction stream. We provide *three* instructions—slr1, slr2, and slr4—simply to allow compact encoding of references to nearby locations.

The assembly-language notation for a PC-relative reference to location $X$ is of the form $slr\alpha(X)$. It is understood that the value $r^\alpha$ actually assembled into the instruction stream will be the *offset* from the current $\langle PC \rangle$ (the address of the instruction following the $slr\alpha$) to location $X$. Thus the program of figure 14.24 can be made position-independent by substituting the instruction slr1(POS) for sc4(POS). PC-relative addressing tends to be the preferred means to address locations whose offset from the reference is constant—in particular, for references to nearby locations in the instruction stream, where PC-relative addressing saves significant space over direct addressing.

Implementation of the $slr\alpha$ instructions is straightforward; a (sign-extended) offset is read from the instruction stream, added to the PC, and used as the argument to a push4 call. Figure 14.26 shows the microcode for slr2.

**Figure 14.23** `sje` and `sjne` handler microsubroutines.

```
| A couple of microsubroutines for handling conditional jumps.

jiff0:  ccmp(0, R0)           | Jump iff <R0>=0, else don't.
        jne(jmpno)            | R0 nonzero.
                              | Else fall through...
jmpyes: move4(Op2,PC)         | Install new PC value
jmpno:  rtn()                 |   and return.


jiffn0: ccmp(0, R0)           | Jump iff <R0> nonzero,
        jne(jmpyes)           |   else don't.
        rtn()


| Conditional jump instructions.

| sje(x): jump iff equal.
hsje:   call(popcond)         | Pop target addr into Op2
                              |   and Cond Code to MCond.
        cand(0x20, MCond, R0) | Fetch Z bit.
        jmp(jiffn0)           | Jump iff set.

| sjne(x): jump iff not equal.
hsjne:  call(popcond)         | Pop target addr into Op2
                              |   and Cond Code to MCond.
        cand(0x20, MCond, R0) | Fetch Z bit.
        jmp(jiff0)            | Jump iff not set.

| Internal microsubroutine for conditional jumps.
| Pop 4-byte target address into Op2;
|    then pop the single cond byte into MCond.

popcond:
        POP4(Op2)             | Pop jump target location,
                              |   hold in Op2.
        cadd2(-1, SP, SP)     | Decrement SP.
        l(SP, SP+1, MCond)    | Fetch the condition code.
        rtn()
```

This microcode simply calls the appropriate $\mathtt{fetch}\alpha$ to obtain the offset $r^\alpha$ from the instruction stream and adds that offset to the current $\langle \mathrm{PC} \rangle$ to generate the address to put on the stack. Since the offset $r^\alpha$ is to be a *signed* integer, it should be sign-extended to a length of 32 bits before being added to $\langle \mathrm{PC} \rangle$; conveniently, FETCH2 performs this operation already. Note that the $\mathtt{slr}\alpha$ instructions, as implemented here, add the offset to the PC value *after* fetching the offset from the instruction stream. Thus the offset should be stated relative to the location of the instruction that *follows* the $\mathtt{slr}\alpha$ instruction.

```
        sdup4      | Get another copy of i.
        stest4     | Compare i to 0.
        sc4(POS)   | Target for jump if i ≥ 0.
        sjge       | Skip sneg4 if i ≥ 0.
        sneg4      | Replace i by −i.
POS:    ...        | Absolute value of i now on stack.
```

**Figure 14.24** $S$-machine program to compute absolute value.

**Table 14.25** PC-relative load instructions.

| Instruction | Stack before→after | Operation |
|---|---|---|
| $\text{slr}\alpha(r^\alpha)$ | $\rightarrow a^4$ | Load PC-relative address: $\langle SP \rangle^4 \leftarrow \langle PC \rangle^4 + r^\alpha \; ; \; SP \leftarrow \langle SP \rangle + 4$ ($\alpha = 1,\ 2,\ \text{or } 4$) |

**Figure 14.26** PC-relative load instruction handler.

```
| slr2(n) instruction: Load PC-relative address.

hslr2:  FETCH2(Op1)                  | Fetch the 2-byte signed offset.
        add2(Op1, PC,    Op1)        | Add in the PC (signed addition).
        addcy(Op1+2, PC+2, Op1+2)
        addcy(Op1+3, PC+3, Op1+3)
        PUSH4(Op1)                   | Push the result.
        rtn()
```

## 14.7 Stack Frames and Procedure Linkage

The processor stack for the $S$ machine builds *upward* in memory, with consecutively pushed data occupying successively higher addresses. The stack contains procedure-linkage information, procedure arguments, and local storage for each active procedure. The processor state includes two registers dedicated to stack management:

- The *base-of-frame pointer* B contains the address of the lowest byte in the current stack frame. The contents of B change only when the program environment changes, that is, on procedure or block entry and exit.

- The *stack pointer* SP contains the address of the first *unused* byte beyond the current top of stack; in other words, SP will always contain $1 + a$, where $a$ is the highest byte address containing currently stacked data. The contents of the

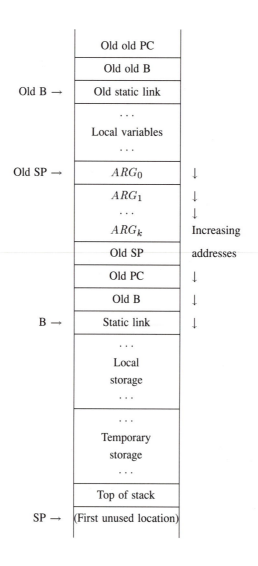

| Old old PC |
| Old old B |
| Old static link |
| $\cdots$ <br> Local variables <br> $\cdots$ |
| $ARG_0$ |
| $ARG_1$ <br> $\cdots$ <br> $ARG_k$ |
| Old SP |
| Old PC |
| Old B |
| Static link |
| $\cdots$ <br> Local <br> storage <br> $\cdots$ |
| $\cdots$ <br> Temporary <br> storage <br> $\cdots$ |
| Top of stack |
| (First unused location) |

Old B →

Old SP →

B →

SP →

Increasing addresses

**Figure 14.27**  Stack organization for the $S$ machine.

stack pointer consequently always reflect the address of the current top of stack and change at nearly every instruction execution.

Figure 14.27 illustrates the organization of stack frames in the $S$ machine. Note that the local variables of the current stack frame are accessible at fixed offsets with respect to the contents of B; thus the $n$th byte of local storage can always be found at address $\langle B \rangle + 4 + n$. The constant 4 in the offset from B reflects our somewhat arbitrary decision regarding which of the words of stacked linkage information B should point to. The important characteristic of B is its fixed relation to the linkage information and to the local storage in a stack frame, providing the microcode with a simple and uniform mechanism for accessing that storage.

Each new stack frame is constructed during a procedure call and is deallocated at the corresponding procedure return (restoring the stack to its configuration prior to the call). The caller of a procedure $P$ pushes $P$'s arguments on the stack and then executes an `scall` instruction that pushes the linkage information that will be necessary to return to the caller. This latter information is effectively a copy of the processor state pertaining to the caller; in particular, it contains

- the *stack pointer* contents immediately prior to the procedure call (these contents are adjusted to point to the base of the argument area, as shown in figure 14.27, for reasons discussed below);
- a *program counter* value that identifies the address of the next instruction following the procedure call; and
- the contents of B at the time of the procedure call, identifying the base of the caller's stack frame.

Thus the complete processor state, including copies of each register, is stored in every stack frame. Although B is called the "base-of-frame pointer," it is not convenient to think of the current stack frame as starting at the location pointed to by B. It is more convenient to think of a stack frame as starting with the first argument byte (the location pointed to by "Old SP") and ending where the next stack frame starts. Unless otherwise noted, this is the definition of stack frame that we use.

The stack frame entry labeled "Static link" is reserved for lexical-scoping support and may be ignored for now; the `scall` instruction described below always sets the static link to 0.

### 14.7.1 Procedure-Linkage Instructions

Table 14.28 summarizes procedure call and return instructions for the $S$ machine. The `scall` and `srtn`$\alpha$ instructions perform the essential stack-management functions corresponding to activation and deactivation of procedures. The `scall` instruction is executed by a program *after* any arguments to be passed to the called procedure—as well as the entry address for the procedure— have been stacked, and it includes as a constant in the instruction stream the number of argument bytes that have been stacked. Note that the incorporation of this number into the instruction stream rules out the situation in which the number of arguments passed by a particular call instruction is not known at compile time, a situation that arises very infrequently in practice and is ruled out by most high-level programming languages. *Distinct* calls to the same routine may, of course, pass different numbers of arguments, if the called procedure can deduce the presence of each $i$th argument based on information contained in the first $i - 1$ arguments. This ability to code *polymorphic functions* is quite convenient in certain applications—for example, in formatted input/output procedures whose first argument is a character string specifying the number, type, and external representation of the remaining arguments.

**Table 14.28** `scall` and `srtn` instructions.

| Instruction | Stack before | →after | Operation* |
|---|---|---|---|
| `scall`$(n^2)$ | $a_1 \cdots a_n,\ p^4$→ | $\cdots$ | Procedure call, $n$ arguments: |
| | | | $temp^4 \leftarrow pop4[\ ]$ |
| | | | $push4[\langle SP \rangle - n]$ |
| | | | $push4[\langle PC \rangle]$ |
| | | | $push4[\langle B \rangle]$ |
| | | | $B \leftarrow \langle SP \rangle^4$ |
| | | | $push4[0^4]$ |
| | | | $PC \leftarrow \langle temp \rangle^4$ |
| `srtn`$\alpha$ | $\cdots r^\alpha$ | →$r^\alpha$ | Return from procedure, $\alpha$-byte result |
| | | | $(\alpha = 0,\ 1,\ 2,\ 4,\ 8):$ |
| | | | $temp^\alpha \leftarrow pop\alpha[\ ]$ |
| | | | $SP \leftarrow \langle\langle B \rangle - 12 \rangle^4$ |
| | | | $PC \leftarrow \langle\langle B \rangle - 8 \rangle^4$ |
| | | | $B \leftarrow \langle\langle B \rangle - 4 \rangle^4$ |
| | | | $push\alpha[\langle temp \rangle^\alpha]$ |

\*$push\alpha[x]$ means $\langle SP \rangle^\alpha \leftarrow x$;  $SP \leftarrow \langle SP \rangle + \alpha$.
$x \leftarrow pop\alpha[\ ]$ means $SP \leftarrow \langle SP \rangle - \alpha$;  $x \leftarrow \langle\langle SP \rangle\rangle^\alpha$.

In operation, the `scall` instruction first pops a 4-byte longword, which is the address of the procedure to call. Then `scall` uses the information contained in the argument byte count $n^2$ to construct a pointer $\langle SP \rangle - n$ to the first stacked argument, which is then stacked as part of the saved processor state. This pointer is referenced to compute the address of each argument; thus, if the number of argument bytes passed by the caller disagrees with the number expected by the callee, the first few arguments (upon which the caller and callee have a consistent view) will be passed correctly. In addition, the presence of this information on the stack allows the detection of accesses to arguments that have not, in fact, been passed by the caller, providing (at minimum) an error report rather than erroneous program behavior. Finally, saving $\langle SP \rangle - n$ rather than $\langle SP \rangle$ makes it easier to pop all the arguments off the stack automatically during the procedure's exit sequence. Note that the constant $n$ in the `scall` instruction *must* reflect the number of argument bytes actually passed, although it may be different from the number the callee expects. This poses no serious programming problem, since $n$ and the stacked arguments are both supplied by code in the caller.

On completion of its task, the called procedure will execute one of the `srtn`$\alpha$ instructions, the principal effect of which is to deallocate the stack frame of the called procedure and reinstate that of the caller as current. However, each `srtn`$\alpha$

**Table 14.29**  Data-access instructions.

| Instruction | Stack before→after | Operation |
|---|---|---|
| $\mathtt{slla}(n^2)$ | $\rightarrow a^4$ | Load local address ($n^2$ is the offset): $push4[\langle\mathrm{B}\rangle + n + 4]$ |
| $\mathtt{slaa}(n^2)$ | $\rightarrow a^4$ | Local $arg_n$ address ($n^2$ is the offset): $push4[\langle\langle\mathrm{B}\rangle - 12\rangle + n]$ |
| $\mathtt{salloc}(n^2)$ [for $n \geq 0$] | $\rightarrow ?^n$ | Allocates space: $\mathrm{SP} \leftarrow \langle\mathrm{SP}\rangle + n$ |
| $\mathtt{salloc}(n^2)$ [for $n < 0$] | $?^n \rightarrow$ | Deallocates space: $\mathrm{SP} \leftarrow \langle\mathrm{SP}\rangle + n$ |

for $\alpha > 0$ also provides for the return of an $\alpha$-byte value to the caller. This *return value* is popped off the stack as the first action of the $\mathtt{srtn}\alpha$ instruction. After the stack frame has been deallocated, the return value is pushed back onto the stack (now as part of the *caller's* stack frame). Immediately following the return, then, the calling program can expect to have had its stacked arguments stripped from the stack and an $\alpha$-byte result pushed in their place. The $\mathtt{srtn0}$ instruction can be used if the procedure has no value to return to the caller.

### 14.7.2 Variable-Access Instructions

Some of the instructions for accessing variables in stack frames on the $S$ machine are summarized in table 14.29. The instructions $\mathtt{slla}$ and $\mathtt{slaa}$ generate the absolute addresses corresponding to offsets of local variables and arguments, respectively, in the relevant parts of the current stack frame. Thus $\mathtt{slla}$ computes the address of a local variable in the current (topmost) stack frame, and $\mathtt{slaa}$ computes the address of an argument to the currently active procedure. Note that the offset $n^2$ in each of these cases is in *bytes*; if one or more of the local variables or arguments is a multibyte word, the calculation of $n^2$ must take this into account.

The $\mathtt{salloc}$ instruction contains a 2-byte constant $n^2$ in the instruction stream. Here $n$ is interpreted as a signed 2's complement integer to be added to the stack pointer. Thus $\mathtt{salloc}(n)$, for positive $n$, can be used to reserve an area of $n$ bytes at the current stack top to use, for example, for local variables of a procedure. On the other hand, $\mathtt{salloc}(n)$, for negative $n$, can be used to deallocate previously $\mathtt{salloced}$ areas on the stack, although the astute reader will notice that this is not necessary just before a procedure return.

```
int fib(n)
 int n;
 { if (n < 2) return n;
       else return fib(n-1) + fib(n-2);
 }
```

**Figure 14.30**   Fibonacci procedure.


```
fib:    slaa(0)    | Fetch n (arg. 0, local frame).
        sl4
        sc4(2)     | Compare with 2.
        scmp4
        sc4(smalln)
        sjlt       | n < 2.

        slaa(0)    | Prepare for fib(n-1) call.
        sl4        | Fetch n.
        sc4(1)     | Constant 1, to
        ssub4      |   compute n-1.
        sc4(fib)   | Address of the procedure fib.
        scall(4)   | Call fib(n-1) with 4 arg bytes.

        slaa(0)    | Now prepare for fib(n-2).
        sl4
        sc4(2)
        ssub4
        sc4(fib)
        scall(4)   | fib(n-2).
        sadd4      | fib(n-1) + fib(n-2).
        srtn4      | Return that to our caller.

smalln: slaa(0)    | Return n.
        sl4
        srtn4
```

**Figure 14.31**   *S*-machine code for the Fibonacci procedure of figure 14.30.


### 14.7.3  Example Program

As a simple illustration of the use of the $S$ machine, consider the recursive procedure to compute the $n$th element of the Fibonacci sequence, shown in figure 14.30. The procedure takes a single integer argument and produces an integer value; it has no local variables.

A straightforward translation to $S$-machine code is shown in figure 14.31. In this translation we have used 4-byte representation for all integers. The argument n to fib is addressed via an slaa(0) instruction, indicating zero offset in the local argument frame (the first argument).

**Figure 14.32** `scall` instruction-handler microsubroutine.

```
| scall(n) -- call subroutine with n arguments (n < 2^16).

hscall: POP4(Op2)                | The subroutine entry point (new <PC>).

        FETCH2(Op1)              | The argument count, n.
        sub(  SP,   Op1,   Op1)  | <SP> - n.
        subcy( SP+1, Op1+1, Op1+1)
|       csubcy(SP+2, 0,     Op1+2)  | (These bytes are ignored...
|       csubcy(SP+3, 0,     Op1+3)  |  this is for upward compatibility!)

        PUSH4(Op1)               | Push <SP>-n.

        PUSH4(PC)                | Push the PC.
        PUSH4(B)                 | Push the B register.
        move4(SP, B)             | New B value.

        cmove4(0, Op1)
        PUSH4(Op1)               | And a constant zero.
        move4(Op2, PC)           | Install new PC.
        rtn()                    | And we're done!
```

### 14.7.4 *Implementation of Procedure-Linkage Instructions

Figure 14.32 contains the microcode for `scall`, whose major task is to stack a previous machine state and construct a new stack frame. Recall that at the point where $\text{scall}(n^2)$ is executed, $n$ bytes of arguments have already been pushed by the calling program onto the stack. However, the "old SP" to be stacked with the processor-state information is the SP contents *prior* to the stacking of arguments; thus some arithmetic must be done by the `scall` handler before this value can be stacked. Next, the remaining processor state (PC and B contents) must be stacked.

At this point, the SP points to the base of the new frame, and its contents are installed as the new $\langle B \rangle$. Finally, the quantity $0^4$ is placed in the unused static-link slot. On completion of the `scall` code, the SP points to the location just beyond the 4-byte static link. The new stack frame contains a static link, just above the arguments and saved processor state, but no local storage has been allocated within the newly created stack frame.

The $\text{srtn}\alpha$ handler performs, roughly, the inverse of the above. It must return an $\alpha$-byte result to the stack of the calling procedure. Figure 14.33 shows the $\text{srtn}\alpha$ handler microsubroutine, the bulk of which is devoted to saving the return value (in `Op1`) and then unstacking the previous processor state and installing it in the appropriate registers. Note that restoring the "old SP" effectively pops the current frame off the stack. The return value is then pushed on the stack for use by the caller. The `srtn0` instruction, which doesn't return a value, is similarly coded.

**Figure 14.33**   srtn$\alpha$ instruction-handler microsubroutine.

```
| srtn2 -- return 2-byte value.

hsrtn2: POP2(Op1)          | The argument.
        move2(B, R0)       | Temporary copy of B (low bytes).

        cadd2(-12, R0, R0) | Find <B> - 12 (only keeps 2 bytes).

        cmove(SP, R2)      | Restore previous values of
        call(get4)         |   <SP>, <PC>, and <B>
        cmove(PC, R2)      |   (4 bytes each).
        call(get4)
        cmove(B, R2)
        call(get4)

        PUSH2(Op1)         | Push 2-byte return value.
        rtn()
```

**Figure 14.34**   slla (load local address) instruction-handler microsubroutine.

```
| slla(n) -- load local address.

hslla:  FETCH2(Op1)       | Fetch a 2-byte offset.
        cadd2(4, Op1, Op1) | Compute offset+4.
        add2( B, Op1, Op1) | Add in <B>... but only 2 bytes.
        PUSH4(Op1)        | Push the result.
        rtn()
```

The slla handler microsubroutine, which computes and stacks a variable address, is shown in figure 14.34. It fetches the offset $n^2$ from the instruction stream, adds the constant 4 and frame base $\langle B\rangle$ (to accommodate the 4-byte static link), and pushes the resulting address on the stack.

The salloc handler microsubroutine, shown in figure 14.35, is straightforward. Notice that it treats $n^2$ as a *signed* integer when adding it to the stack pointer, so that negative values of $n$ may be used to deallocate storage.

## 14.8  *Lexical-Scoping Support

This section discusses features of the $S$-machine instruction set that facilitate the implementation of programs that use lexical scoping. Our motivation is twofold: (1) Many higher-level languages feature lexical scoping and commonly use mech-

**Figure 14.35** `salloc` instruction-handler microsubroutine.

```
| salloc(+/- n) -- adjust SP to allocate/deallocate local storage.

hsalloc:
        FETCH2(Op2)        | Fetch signed 2-byte adjustment.
        add2(Op2, SP, SP)  | Add it to <SP>.
        rtn()
```

anisms similar to those described here, and (2) the lexical-scoping support of the $S$ machine furnishes a good example of machine-language design that is guided by the implementation needs of higher-level languages.

In a lexically scoped language, a variable reference is associated with two quantities: the *depth* of its containing stack frame in the current environment (that is, the number of hops down the static chain) and its position within that stack frame (that is, its address relative to the base of that frame). Accordingly, the `sla` instruction, described in table 14.36, takes two parameters in the instruction stream: a lexical depth $d^1$ and an offset $n^2$. It uses the lexical depth to take $d$ hops down the static chain and then applies the offset $n$ in that frame (in a manner completely analogous to the operation of the `slla` instruction) to calculate the actual address of the referenced variable. The `saa` instruction similarly takes $d$ hops down the static chain to locate the proper stack frame and then applies the same algorithm as `slaa` to calculate the address of the $n$th argument byte in that frame. `saa` is useful for free references that refer to *arguments*, rather than local variables, of lexically enclosing procedures. Note that `slla` and `slaa` are special cases of `sla` and `saa` for which the depth $d$ is zero; thus `slla`($n$) and `slaa`($n$) are equivalent to `sla`($0,n$) and `saa`($0,n$), respectively.

In order to construct a stack frame with the correct static link for use with the above instructions, we introduce the `spdcall` instruction. It differs from `scall` in two respects:

- The topmost operand on the stack is the address of a *procedure descriptor*, or PD, rather than the address of the $S$-machine code for the procedure. The procedure descriptor is an 8-byte data structure. The first 4 bytes contain the address of a stack frame, and the last 4 bytes contain the address of the $S$-machine code for the procedure. The procedure descriptor is thus a *closure*, indicating both the address of the machine code for the procedure and the address of the lexically enclosing stack frame.
- `spdcall` builds a stack frame in which the static link has a useful value (in fact, it is a copy of the stack-frame address in the procedure descriptor), rather than zero, as in the case of the `scall` instruction.

In all other respects, `spdcall` and `scall` behave identically. In particular, the formats of the stack frames they build are identical.

**Table 14.36** Lexical-scoping support instructions.

| Instruction | Stack before | →after | Operation |
|---|---|---|---|
| $\texttt{sla}(d^1, n^2)$ | | →$a^4$ | Load address ($d^1$ is the lexical depth and $n^2$ is the offset): $temp^4 \leftarrow \langle \text{B} \rangle$; repeat $d$ times: $temp \leftarrow \langle \langle temp \rangle \rangle$ $push4[\langle temp \rangle + n + 4]$ |
| $\texttt{saa}(d^1, n^2)$ | | →$a^4$ | Load $arg_n$ address ($d^1$ is the lexical depth and $n^2$ is the offset): $temp^4 \leftarrow \langle \text{B} \rangle$; repeat $d$ times: $temp \leftarrow \langle \langle temp \rangle \rangle$ $push4[\langle \langle temp \rangle - 12 \rangle + n]$ |
| $\texttt{spdcall}(n^1)$ | $a_1 \cdots a_n, p^4$→$\cdots$ | | Procedure call: $temp^4 \leftarrow pop4[\ ]$ $push4[\langle \text{SP} \rangle - n]$ $push4[\langle \text{PC} \rangle]$ $push4[\langle \text{B} \rangle]$ $\text{B} \leftarrow \langle \text{SP} \rangle^4$ $push4[\langle \langle temp \rangle \rangle^4]$ $\text{PC} \leftarrow \langle \langle temp \rangle + 4 \rangle^4$ |
| $\texttt{spdcons}$ | $procp^4$ | →$pd^8$ | Construct procedure descriptor based on current frame: $temp^4 \leftarrow pop4[\ ]$ $push4[\langle \text{B} \rangle]$ $push4[\langle temp \rangle]$ |

A fourth instruction is useful to support lexical scoping. The $\texttt{spdcons}$ instruction builds procedure descriptors. Given the address of the $S$-machine code for a procedure $P$, $\texttt{spdcons}$ pops that address off the stack, saves it, pushes the address of the current stack frame, then pushes the saved address of the machine code for procedure $P$. A pointer to the $S$-machine code for $P$ is thus converted to a procedure descriptor for $P$, specifying the current stack frame as the lexically enclosing stack frame. This is an appropriate step to take upon entering the procedure $Q$ in which $P$ is declared. The resulting procedure may be stored where desired, using the $\texttt{ss8}$ instruction. Alternatively, if $\texttt{spdcons}$ is called in the process of building the stack frame for $Q$, the newly created procedure descriptor may be left just where it is, to take its place among the local variables of $Q$.

```
G:        salloc(4)    | Allocate space for y.
          sc4(F)
          spdcons      | Make the PD for f.

          slla(0)      | Address of y.
          sc4(7)
          ss4          | Assign y = 7.

          sc4(5)       | Argument for f.
          slla(4)      | Address of PD for f.
          spdcall(4)   | Call f(5), with 4 argument bytes.
          srtn4        | Return the value of f(5).

F:        slaa(0)      | Address of x.
          sl4          | The value of x.
          sla(1,0)     | Address of y.
          sl4          | The value of y.
          scmp4        | Compare: x < y?
          sc4(LESS)
          sjlt         | Go to LESS if x < y.

          slaa(0)
          sl4
          srtn4        | Return x.

LESS:     slaa(0)
          sl4          | Value of x.
          slaa(0)
          sl4
          sc4(1)
          sadd4        | x + 1.
          sla(1,4)     | Address of the PD for f.
          spdcall(4)   | Call f(x+1).
          sadd4        | Add to x, making x + f(x+1),
          srtn4        |   and return that value.
```

**Figure 14.37** *S*-machine code for the program of figure 13.4.

### 14.8.1 *Compilation of Lexically Scoped Procedures

As an example of the use of the lexical-scoping support on the *S* machine, figure 14.37 shows *S*-machine code that implements the procedure g in figure 13.4. In this example, we use 4-byte values to represent all integers. The procedure g in this program has two pieces of data in the local-variable portion of its stack frame: the integer y (at offset 0, and hence accessed by instructions such as slla(0)) and the procedure descriptor for f (at offset 4, accessed by instructions such as slla(4)). Note that g initially performs an salloc(4) to make space for y, and it then performs an spdcons to construct the procedure descriptor for f right at the place in g's stack frame where it belongs.

Other things to note about the program of figure 14.37 are its use of spdcall,

```
Print(n, Output)                        /* n is an integer.      */
 int n,Output();                        /* Output is a procedure.  */
{ if (n > 9) Print(n/10, Output);
      Output((n % 10) + '0');
}
```

**Figure 14.38**  Decimal print procedure.

instead of `scall`, for the calls to `f` and the use of the `sla` instruction within `f`.
Where `y` is referenced from `f`, this is clearly a free reference to a variable declared
one nesting level out, so that the form `sla(1,0)` is suitable for accessing it (lexical
depth = 1, offset in `g`'s stack frame = 0). However, the recursive call to `f` is also
technically a free reference, since the declaration of `f` is done in procedure `g`. In
implementation terms, recursive calls to `f` must use the procedure descriptor that
was constructed in `g`'s stack frame, or else the static link will not be set properly.
Therefore, the recursive calls to `f` are done via `spdcall`, which is supplied with
a pointer to the procedure descriptor for `f` that is stored in `g`'s stack frame and is
obtained by the instruction `sla(1,4)`.

### 14.8.2 *Handling Free Variables

The real power of our variable-binding mechanism becomes apparent in situations
involving the invocation of procedures from environments other than the one in
which they are defined. (This frequently occurs in connection with the use of procedures as arguments to other procedures.) Many programming languages (such as
FORTRAN and C) specifically restrict the use of procedures to permit simpler variable handling in their implementation; others, such as LISP, promote procedures
to the status of a first-class data type, allowing them to be passed as arguments,
stored in data structures, and otherwise manipulated during program execution.
Such capabilities constitute important tools in modern programming techniques;
they allow abstract data types to be implemented, for example, using data structures containing procedures for each of their primitive operations. As a simple
application of nonlocal-variable reference, consider the construction of a decimal
print routine shown in figure 14.38. The procedure $Print(n, Output)$ produces a
sequence of ASCII characters corresponding to the decimal representation of the
integer $n$, calling $Output(c)$ for each successive character $c$ in the sequence. Here
the form `(n%10)+'0'` is used to convert the integer `(n%10)` to the ASCII representation of the corresponding digit, which is the form required, for example, by
a printer device ($a\%b$ is a C expression denoting the remainder of dividing $a$ by
$b$). If the output device were *always* the same printer, the `Print` procedure might
have been constructed to take only the argument `n` and call a printer driver routine
directly, in place of the procedure `Output` specified by the caller. The present formulation provides additional flexibility in that the same `Print` procedure can be
used to format output characters for a variety of destinations, according to `Print`'s
second argument. The programmer might thus have a repertoire of character-output
routines, corresponding to line printer, CRT terminal, and file output, and use the
`Print` routine with each.

```
n = 0        | Argument offsets in the stack frame of Print.
Output = 4


Print:  slaa(n)        | Is n > 9?
        sl4            | Fetch n.
        sc4(9)
        scmp4
        sc4(Print1)
        sjle           | Jump if n is not greater than 9.


        slaa(n)        | Prepare to call
        sl4            |    Print(n/10, Output).
        sc4(10)
        sdiv4          | Gives quotient n/10.
        slaa(Output)
        sl4
        sc4(Print)
        scall(8)       | Call Print(n/10, Output).


Print1: slaa(n)
        sl4
        sc4(10)
        srem4          | Compute (n mod 10).
        sc4(48)        | ASCII '0'.
        sadd4          | Make ASCII digit.
        slaa(Output)   | Get Output PD pointer
        sl4            |    from second argument.
        spdcall(4)     | Call Output((n mod 10)+'0').


        srtn0          | All done!
```

**Figure 14.39** *S*-machine translation of the procedure `Print` in figure 14.38.

Figure 14.39 shows the translation of the `Print` procedure into *S*-machine code. Note the use of the assembler pseudo-operation **=** to give mnemonic names to the offsets of variables within the stack frame. The instruction `slaa(Output)` is simply a more readable equivalent of `slaa(4)`. Note also the use of `scall` for the recursive call to `Print`, which reflects the fact that the definition of `Print` contains no references to nonlocal variables and hence requires no static link. The procedure argument `Output` is implemented by passing a *pointer* to its procedure descriptor as the second argument to `Print`, rather than the procedure descriptor itself; this choice simply reflects the relative economy of stacking a 4-byte pointer argument rather than an 8-byte procedure descriptor.

Next, consider a program requiring that an integer be converted to a sequence of ASCII characters in memory rather than being sent directly to an output device, perhaps so that further formatting of the characters (for example, margin justification) can be performed. Such a program can exploit the flexibility of `Print` by supplying a second argument that disposes of characters by storing them into consecutive elements of a character array.

```
Main_Program()
{     int nchar;
      char Buffer[100];

      Save(c)
       char c;
        {     nchar = nchar + 1;
              Buffer[nchar] = c;
        }

      ...
      nchar = 0;
      ...

      Print(27,Save);

      ...
}
```

**Figure 14.40**   Procedure with free variables.

A plausible approach to this use of `Print` is sketched in figure 14.40, where the locally defined procedure `Save(c)` is constructed to store its character argument in the next available element of the character array `Buffer`. Note that the body of `Save` contains references to the variables `Buffer` and `nchar`, which are not local to `Save` but are bound in its lexical environment and hence accessible (given lexical-scoping rules). We depend on the static links stored in the stack frames to resolve these free-variable references.

The call `Print(27,Save)` passes two arguments to the `Print` routine, the second of which identifies the procedure descriptor of `Save`. It should be emphasized that, in our language, the value `Save` passed as an argument is a datum of type *procedure* that can be invoked during the execution of `Print`; it is not itself an invocation of `Save`. On execution of the program, we expect the call `Print(27,Save)` to store the two ASCII characters (2 and 7) in consecutive elements of `Buffer` and to have the side effect of incrementing `nchar` by 2.

*S*-machine code for this calling program is shown in figure 14.41. Note that the code for the internal procedure `Save` uses the form `sla(1,nchar)` to access the variable `nchar` in its lexically enclosing stack frame. It is important to recognize that the lexical depth (in this case, the 1 in the `sla(1,nchar)` instruction) is a constant determined by the lexical structure of the program and is independent, in particular, of the dynamics of program execution: Because of the recursive nature of `Print`, the various calls to `Save` for successive characters to be output will in fact generate stack frames at different distances relative to the frame containing `nchar` and `Buffer`, but the latter stack frame will always be at the same *lexical* depth from any of `Save`'s stack frames.

Note that `Save`'s procedure descriptor is in the stack frame of `Main_Program` and that its contents cannot be calculated at compile time. This procedure descriptor

```
nchar  = 0       | Local variable offsets in the
SavePD = 4       |    stack frame of Main_Program.
Buffer = 12
LSize  = 112     | Total bytes of local storage.


Example:  salloc(LSize) | Allocate local storage.

          slla(SavePD)  | Location for procedure descriptor.
          sc4(Save)
          spdcons       | Make PD for Save.
          ss8           | Store PD in frame of Main_Program.
          ...
          slla(nchar)   | Assign nchar = 0.
          sc4(0)
          ss4
          ...
          sc4(27)       | Prepare for call to Print.
          slla(SavePD)
          sc4(Print)
          scall(8)      | Call Print(27,Save).
          ...


| Here is the code for the procedure Save.
Save:   sla(1,nchar)  | nchar is in outer stack frame.
        sla(1,nchar)
        sl4
        sc4(1)
        sadd4
        ss4            | nchar = nchar + 1.

        sla(1,nchar)  | Get new nchar value
        sl4           |    for use as index into
        sla(1,Buffer) |    the character array.
        sadd4         | Compute address of Buffer[nchar].
        slaa(0)
        sl4           | Fetch argument character c.
        slow2
        slow1         | Reduce it to 1 byte in length.
        ss1           | Store it into Buffer[nchar].

        srtn0         | Return from Save.
```

**Figure 14.41** *S*-machine code with free-variable references.


must be constructed on entry to Main_Program. The procedure descriptor is treated as a local variable whose storage is allocated on the stack and initialized with pointers to the enclosing stack frame and to the entry point of the procedure's body. In contrast to our previous example, this procedure constructs the procedure descriptor and then stores it (using ss8) at the appropriate place in the stack frame of Main_Program.

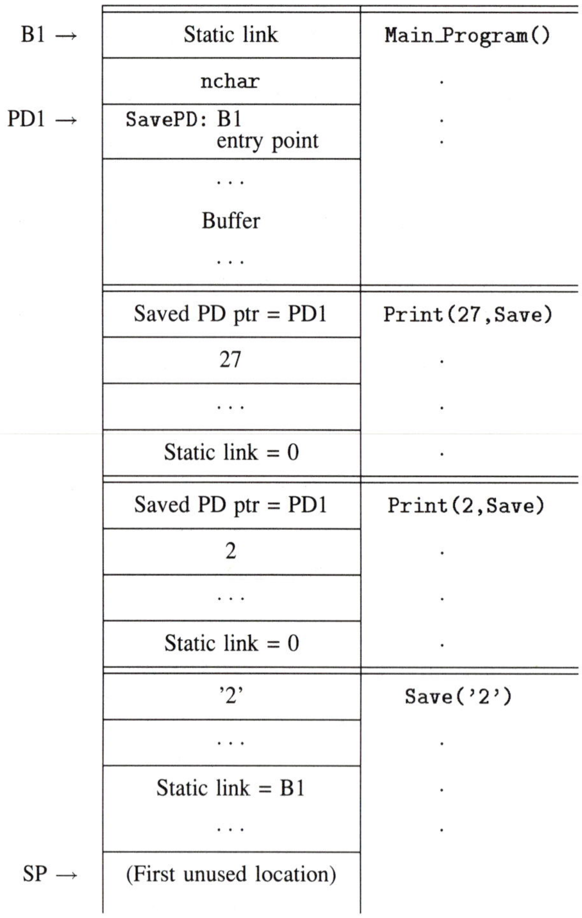

| | |
|---|---|
| B1 → | Static link | Main_Program() |
| | nchar | . |
| PD1 → | SavePD: B1<br>entry point | . |
| | . . . | . |
| | Buffer | |
| | . . . | |
| | Saved PD ptr = PD1 | Print(27,Save) |
| | 27 | . |
| | . . . | . |
| | Static link = 0 | . |
| | Saved PD ptr = PD1 | Print(2,Save) |
| | 2 | . |
| | . . . | . |
| | Static link = 0 | . |
| | '2' | Save('2') |
| | . . . | . |
| | Static link = B1 | . |
| | . . . | . |
| SP → | (First unused location) | |

**Figure 14.42** Stack snapshot during Print(27, Save).

The contents of the stack during the first call to Save are sketched in figure 14.42; note that the Save frame is separated from the outer frame by frames corresponding to two recursive invocations of Print. On each execution, however, the static link stored in the Save frame is extracted from the procedure descriptor and identifies the base B1 of the outer frame. Thus the code in the body of Save may access variables in that frame using the constant lexical depth of 1.

## 14.9 Traps

An instruction-trap mechanism is provided in the $S$ machine by the ssvc instruction described in table 14.43. We assume here that the context information depicted in figure 13.6 is all contained in a single processor status word PSW (containing, perhaps, an interrupt priority or interrupt-enable mask indicating which interrupts

**Table 14.43** Supervisor call and trap-return instructions.

| Instruction | Stack before → after | Operation |
|---|---|---|
| $\mathtt{ssvc}(code^1)$ | $\rightarrow \mathrm{PC}^4, \mathrm{SP}^4, \mathrm{B}^4, \mathrm{PSW}^4, code^1$ | Supervisor call: |
| | | $temp \leftarrow \langle \mathrm{SP} \rangle^4$ |
| | | $\mathrm{SP} \leftarrow \langle \mathtt{SSVCVEC} + 4 \rangle^4$ |
| | | $push4[\langle \mathrm{PC} \rangle]$ |
| | | $push4[\langle temp \rangle]$ |
| | | $push4[\langle \mathrm{B} \rangle]$ |
| | | $push4[\langle \mathrm{PSW} \rangle]$ |
| | | $push1[code^1]$ |
| | | $\mathrm{PC} \leftarrow \langle \mathtt{SSVCVEC} \rangle^4$ |
| | | $\mathrm{B} \leftarrow \langle \mathtt{SSVCVEC} + 8 \rangle^4$ |
| | | $\mathrm{PSW} \leftarrow \langle \mathtt{SSVCVEC} + 12 \rangle^4$ |
| | | |
| $\mathtt{strtn}$ | $\mathrm{PC}^4, \mathrm{SP}^4, \mathrm{B}^4, \mathrm{PSW}^4 \rightarrow$ | Trap return: |
| | | $\mathrm{PSW} \leftarrow pop4[\,]$ |
| | | $\mathrm{B} \leftarrow pop4[\,]$ |
| | | $temp \leftarrow pop4[\,]$ |
| | | $\mathrm{PC} \leftarrow pop4[\,]$ |
| | | $\mathrm{SP} \leftarrow \langle temp \rangle^4$ |

are enabled and a *privilege bit* indicating whether privileged instructions may be executed), which joins PC, SP, and B as a fourth processor-state register of the $S$ machine. When the $S$ machine executes an $\mathtt{ssvc}$ instruction, it picks up a new batch of processor-state information (that is, new values for PC, SP, B, and PSW) from a 4-longword trap vector that starts at memory location SSVCVEC. (In the concrete $S$-machine implementation of $\mathtt{ssvc}$, SSVCVEC is some numerical constant—such as 256—"wired" into the microcode for the $\mathtt{ssvc}$ instruction.) The trapping program's state is saved by pushing it on the stack indicated by the SP value loaded from SSVCVEC.

Typically, an operating system provides several different services (for example, read a character from a file or write a character to a file). The 1-byte *code* following the $\mathtt{ssvc}$ operation code is useful in distinguishing among these services. If different codes are associated with requests for different services, we can use the one $\mathtt{ssvc}$ instruction for requesting any service; by examining the code, the $\mathtt{ssvc}$ handler can conveniently determine which service is being requested in any particular instance. The $S$ machine's $\mathtt{ssvc}$ instruction helpfully fetches this code and pushes it on the handler's stack, but a more minimalist design could skip this step and let the $\mathtt{ssvc}$ handler fetch the code explicitly using the PC value saved during the $\mathtt{ssvc}$ trap.

```
ssvcHandler(code,state)
 struct MState *state;
 char code;
 {
        (body of handler definition)
 }
```

**Figure 14.44**  ssvc handler procedure.


```
/* Structure definition for active S-machine state. */

struct MState

 {      int PC;        /* Program counter.        */
        int SP;        /* Stack pointer.          */
        int B;         /* Base of frame.          */
        int PSW;       /* Processor status word.   */
 };
```

**Figure 14.45**  Machine-state data structure.


When the trap has been handled, the strtn instruction can be executed to restore the processor-state information saved by ssvc, thus returning control to the trapping program. (Note that the ssvc code must be popped before the strtn instruction is executed.) On most processors, trap-return instructions such as strtn are *privileged* in that they allow changes in parts of the processor state (such as the privilege bit itself in the PSW) that unprivileged programs are not normally permitted to modify.

The program in figure 14.44 outlines a handler for the ssvc trap; it differs from the general form of the program in figure 13.7 only in the addition of the explicit *code* argument saved by the ssvc instruction.

The struct MState referenced by this procedure describes the format of the state information saved by ssvc; it is shown in figure 14.45.

The interface between the ssvc trap mechanism and the handler procedure ssvcHandler consists of a short assembly-language *stub* such as that shown in figure 14.46. The stub is necessary because ssvcHandler, like any other higher-level-language procedure that returns no value, will return using an srtn0 instruction, but the return from the ssvc trap must use the strtn instruction, since ssvc saves a different collection of state information than scall. The stub gives ssvcHandler a place to return to, from which an strtn instruction will properly restore the state of the interrupted program.

Figure 14.46 is best understood in conjunction with the contents of the ssvc trap vector at SSVCVEC. Accordingly, figure 14.47 shows the assembly code that would properly initialize this trap vector. (The assembler directive .=SSVCVEC sets ".", the assembler's location counter, to SSVCVEC just before this code is assembled.) HStack is the address of the region of memory that has been set aside for the ssvc

```
ssvcStub:    slla(0)              | Push pointer to saved state.
             sc4(ssvcHandler)
             scall(5)             | Call ssvcHandler(code,state).
             strtn
```

**Figure 14.46**  Stub for `ssvc` handler.

```
.=SSVCVEC

| The following code goes at location SSVCVEC:

LONG(ssvcStub)     | New PC.
LONG(HStack)       | New SP.
LONG(HStack-4)     | New B.
LONG(.....)        | New PSW.
```

**Figure 14.47**  Initialization of the `ssvc` trap vector.

handler's stack.

The new B value loaded from this trap vector creates the appearance, upon beginning to execute `ssvcStub`, of a stack frame with 16 bytes of local variables that have been initialized with the saved processor state. This sham causes the `slla(0)` instruction at `ssvcStub` to push the address of the saved processor state on the stack. The following call to `ssvcHandler` thus passes 5 bytes of local variables on the stack: the 1-byte code pushed by the `ssvc` instruction itself plus the 4-byte pointer pushed by the `slla` instruction. Upon return from `ssvcHandler`, all 5 bytes have been popped from the stack, following our usual $S$-machine calling convention, leaving exactly the 16 bytes of saved processor state on the stack in just the right configuration for return to the interrupted program via `strtn`.

Faults can be handled on the $S$ machine by a mechanism very similar to that just outlined for instruction traps. Instead of the 1-byte *code* pushed by the `ssvc` instruction, the occurrence of a fault could push a block of information indicating the nature and cause of the fault. Compensating adjustments would be made in the details of the fault handler's stub and the definition of the fault-handling procedure itself. The `strtn` instruction would continue to be suitable for return from the fault (assuming that the cause of the fault can be repaired by the fault handler in such a way that resuming execution of the faulting program makes sense).

Interrupts can be handled by a similar mechanism. A typical interrupt would cause only the basic processor state listed in figure 14.45 to be saved, without pushing any additional information analogous to the `ssvc` code or fault information. The interrupt's handler would then be expected to do whatever detective work is required to determine the cause of the interrupt and the action that should be taken.

## 14.10 Summary

This chapter has explored in some detail the architecture of the $S$ machine, a typical zero-address processor, indicating the major constituents of such a machine and supplementing the general discussion of design issues in chapter 13 with a detailed case study. In conjunction with the microcoded implementation given in appendix 4, this chapter also furnishes a case study in the implementation of a representative processor architecture. The $S$ machine was chosen as our first case study because its simplicity and elegance introduce a minimal amount of intellectual clutter into our exploration of design and implementation issues; however, zero-address machines are not the most prevalent variety of processor architecture, and the engineering of the $S$ machine suffers from a variety of performance weaknesses, notably its extreme reliance on main memory (the stack) for storing even the most transient intermediate results. To cover a larger part of the space of contemporary processor design approaches, and to explore some of these performance weaknesses and some possible remedies to them, we now turn to case studies of two machines that illustrate contrasting processor design approaches.

## 14.11 Context

Stack-oriented (zero-address) processors have never made it into the mainstream of computer architecture but have been present rather persistently at its outskirts. The first commercial stack-based architecture to be delivered to customers was the Burroughs B5000 [Lonergan and King 1961]. The Burroughs B6500/B7500 [Hauck and Dent 1968] and B6700/B7700 [Organick 1973] systems are other early examples; a more recent instance is the Symbolics 3600 LISP machine [Moon 1985].

Stack instruction sets have enjoyed another kind of existence as *bytecodes*—instruction sets of virtual processors that are implemented by interpreters written in the instruction set of some other processor rather than in microcode. Among the systems that have used bytecodes are Smalltalk-80 [Goldberg and Robson 1983] and "P-code" [Nori et al. 1981; Brinch Hansen 1985]. Use of bytecodes often allows quick implementation of a new programming language (or of an old programming language on a new processor), though its performance will not be as good as that of an implementation that compiles the language directly to the processor's native instruction set.

The compilation of higher-level-language code to stack-machine or "postfix-notation" code, along with almost every other imaginable issue relating to compilation, is discussed in Aho, Sethi, and Ullman [1986].

## 14.12 Problems

### Problem 14.1
Write a MAYBE microcode handler for an `sinc2` (2-byte increment) $S$-machine instruction that pops a 2-byte value off the stack, adds 1 to it, and pushes the 2-byte result back onto the stack.

```
int f(n)
    int n;
{
    int ans;
    ans = n;
    if (n > 1)
        ans = ans + f(n-1);
    return(ans);
}
```

**Figure 14.48**  A C program.


## Problem 14.2

Write a MAYBE microcode handler for an `sclr4` (4-byte clear) *S*-machine instruction that pops a 4-byte address *A* off the stack and writes zero into the 4-byte location addressed by *A*.


## Problem 14.3

Write a MAYBE microcode handler for the `sadd8` (8-byte add) *S*-machine instruction defined in table 14.1.


## Problem 14.4

Write a MAYBE microcode handler for an `sswap4` (4-byte swap) *S*-machine instruction that pops two 4-byte addresses *A* and *B* off the stack and interchanges the contents of the 4-byte locations addressed by *A* and *B*.


## Problem 14.5

In general, can a computer with many levels of abstraction, like the MAYBE, execute complex instruction sets with very little hardware? Explain.


## Problem 14.6

In general, does designing a computer using many levels of abstraction result in a fast, efficient implementation of the top-level abstraction? Explain.


## Problem 14.7

The MAYBE executes about 100,000 microinstructions, or about 1000 *S*-machine instructions, per second. Consider an interpreter for MAYBE microcode written in *S*-machine language—that is, an *S*-machine program that interprets microinstructions. Is the most plausible rate of microinstruction execution (in microinstructions per second) for this new layer of interpretation equal to 100,000, 1000, 10, 0.1, or 0.0001? Explain.


## Problem 14.8

If the interpreter described in problem 14.7 were given the microcode for the *S* machine, it would be able to interpret *S*-machine instructions. Is the most plausible rate of *S*-machine instruction execution (in instructions per second) for this new layer of interpretation equal to 100,000, 1000, 10, 0.1, or 0.0001? Explain.

```
1000    f:      salloc(4)                            | int ans;
1003            slla(0)   slaa(0) sl4       ss4     | ans = n;
1011            slaa(0)   sl4     sc4(1)    scmp4   | if (n > 1)
1021            sc4(done) sjle
1027            slla(0)                              | push address of ans
1030            slla(0)   sl4                        | push value of ans
1034            slaa(0)   sl4     sc4(1)    ssub4   | ???
1044            sc4(f)    scall(4)                   | ???
1052            sadd4                                |      push(pop() + pop())
                                                     | i.e., push(ans + f(n-1))
1053            ss4           .                      | ???
1054    done:   slla(4)   sl4     srtn4             | return(ans);
```

**Figure 14.49**  Translation of figure 14.48 into $S$-machine code.

## Problem 14.9

Figure 14.49 gives a translation of the C program in figure 14.48 into $S$-machine code. This translation is annotated with addresses (in decimal) that indicate where each line begins in memory.

A. How is the stack changed by the execution of the four instructions starting at location 1034? Answer this question with a brief comment in the same style as the comments on the other lines of figure 14.49.

B. How is the stack changed by the execution of the two instructions starting at location 1044? (*Hint:* Consider only the execution of these two instructions. Do not consider the execution of any instructions in the procedure f.)

C. How is the stack changed by the execution of the instruction at location 1053?

## Problem 14.10

The function f (as defined in figure 14.48) is called with an argument of 10. Figure 14.50 shows a snapshot of the stack during one of the recursive calls. Addresses (in decimal) are located on the left.

A. What is the value of the argument ($n$) to the current call?

B. What will the SP register contain immediately following execution of the next instruction from the snapshot in figure 14.50?

C. What value is stored at location 2008 in figure 14.50?

D. What value is stored at location 2012?

E. What value is stored at location 2024?

## Problem 14.11

A. Give the $S$-machine assembly code for the GCD procedure defined in figure 13.1. Assume that all integers and addresses are 32 bits long. Give your code in a style similar to that of the program in figure 14.31. Be sure to comment your assembly code, as in figure 14.31, to show the correspondence between C-language and assembly-language constructs. Also give the actual $S$-machine

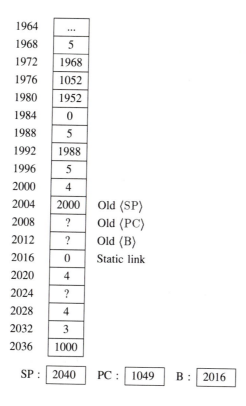

| 1964 | ... |
| 1968 | 5 |
| 1972 | 1968 |
| 1976 | 1052 |
| 1980 | 1952 |
| 1984 | 0 |
| 1988 | 5 |
| 1992 | 1988 |
| 1996 | 5 |
| 2000 | 4 |
| 2004 | 2000 | Old ⟨SP⟩ |
| 2008 | ? | Old ⟨PC⟩ |
| 2012 | ? | Old ⟨B⟩ |
| 2016 | 0 | Static link |
| 2020 | 4 |
| 2024 | ? |
| 2028 | 4 |
| 2032 | 3 |
| 2036 | 1000 |

SP : 2040    PC : 1049    B : 2016

**Figure 14.50**   Stack snapshot for f (figure 14.48).

instructions, in hexadecimal notation, for your assembly-language program. Be sure to identify which assembly-language statement corresponds to each byte of hexadecimal *S*-machine code.

B. Assume that the GCD routine was originally called (don't worry about where it was called from) with arguments 422 and 172. How many times will GCD be called recursively, and with what arguments?

C. Figure 14.51 gives a snapshot of the top of the stack during one of the recursive calls to GCD resulting from the initial call GCD(422,172). It shows the state of the stack immediately following the computation of the statement rem = a%b; in GCD. (*Note:* Addresses are in decimal.) What are the values of Old SP, Old PC, and Old B in this frame? What are the arguments to the current call? What is the return address for the recursive calls to GCD? What address holds the value of the local variable rem for this call?

D. Show a snapshot of the top of the stack following execution of the statement rem = a%b; during the call to GCD that occurs next when execution proceeds from the state shown in figure 14.51.

E. Starting from the state shown in figure 14.51, what is the largest value that the contents of B (the base pointer) reaches before the original call to GCD returns?

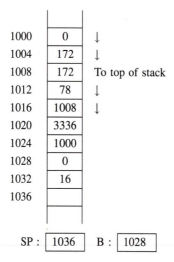

| 1000 | 0 | ↓ |
| 1004 | 172 | ↓ |
| 1008 | 172 | To top of stack |
| 1012 | 78 | ↓ |
| 1016 | 1008 | ↓ |
| 1020 | 3336 | |
| 1024 | 1000 | |
| 1028 | 0 | |
| 1032 | 16 | |
| 1036 | | |

SP : 1036    B : 1028

**Figure 14.51**  Stack snapshot for f (figure 14.48).

F. How many instructions are fetched from the beginning to the end of the execution of GCD(422,172)? The *S*-machine implementation on the MAYBE fetches 1 byte at a time: How many instruction *bytes* are fetched during execution?

G. What is the total number of stack reads and writes (in terms of bytes) during the execution of GCD(422,172)?

### *Problem 14.12*

Here is a fragment of a C program that will execute on the *S* machine:

```
{     int a, b, c, x;
          . . .
      x = a + b * c;          /* assignment statement  */
          . . .
}
```

Assume that integers are stored as 4-byte longwords. The *S*-machine instructions to perform the assignment statement above are

```
slla(x)
slla(a)     sl4
slla(b)     sl4
slla(c)     sl4
smult4
sadd4
ss4
```

For simplicity, we have written the slla instructions so they refer to the variables by their symbolic names rather than by offset.

For the purposes of this problem, we define a stack transaction as any push of a (4-byte) longword onto the stack or any pop of a longword from the stack. An instruction in the $S$ machine may perform one or more stack transactions during its execution. The `sadd4` instruction, for example, performs three stack transactions.

Draw up a table like the one started below. Fill in this table by following these instructions for each $S$-machine instruction in the above program fragment.

1. Check the "Push onto stack" column if the instruction pushes either a datum or an address onto the stack.

2. Check the "Pop from stack" column if the instruction removes either a datum or an address from the stack.

3. Indicate whether the entry pushed or popped is a value (datum) or an address by checking either the "Value" or the "Address" column.

4. If the instruction performs several stack transactions, indicate each on a separate line in the table. List the stack transactions in the order in which they occur. (*Hint:* No instruction makes more than three stack transactions.)

| Instruction | Push onto stack | Pop from stack | Value | Address |
|---|---|---|---|---|
| slla(x) | | | | |
| slla(a) | | | | |
| " | | | | |
| sl4 | | | | |
| " | | | | |

Assume that the width of the path between the processor and main memory is 1 longword. Each stack transaction transfers a longword to or from the stack. How many accesses to main memory are performed by the stack transactions in your answer?

### Problem 14.13

Ben Bitdiddle has written a recursive procedure `Square` that computes the square of a number without doing any multiplications. The procedure, written in C, is

```
int Square (N)
  int N;
    { if (N == 0) return (0);
      return (Square(N-1) + N + N - 1);
    }
```

All integers are 4 bytes long. Write $S$-machine code for `Square`. Be sure to comment your code.

### Problem 14.14

The C procedure `coeff` in figure 14.52 calculates the coefficient of the $m$th term in the binomial expansion $(x + y)^n$.

A. Translate `coeff` into $S$-machine assembly code using the general approach of figure 14.31.

B. How many bytes will the assembly-code procedure you wrote for part A assemble into?

```
coeff(m, n)
  int m, n;                        /* int is 4 bytes. */
{ int c1, c2;
  if(m <= 0) return(1);
  else if(m > n) return(0);
  else {
    c1 = coeff(m - 1, n - 1);
    c2 = coeff(m, n - 1);
    return(c1 + c2);
  }
}
```

**Figure 14.52** Program to calculate binomial coefficients.

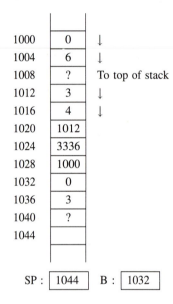

**Figure 14.53** Stack snapshot for `coeff` (figure 14.52).

## Problem 14.15

This problem uses the stack-frame conventions of the $S$ machine and the `coeff` procedure in figure 14.52. Note that the $S$-machine stack grows toward increasing addresses and that the SP points to the first empty location. Assume that the `coeff` routine was originally called (don't worry about where it was called from) with arguments 3 and 5. Figure 14.53 shows a snapshot of the top of the stack during one of the recursive calls to `coeff`. It shows the state of the stack immediately following the computation of the statement `c1 = coeff(m - 1, n - 1);` in the routine. (*Note:* Addresses are in decimal.)

A. What are the values of old SP, old PC, and old B in this frame? What are the arguments to the current call? What addresses hold the values of the local variables `c1` and `c2` for this call?

B. Draw a snapshot of the top of the stack following execution of the statement

*Stack Architectures: The S Machine*

```
/* Reverse the first n characters of string A. */

Reverse (n,A)
  char A[];
  int n;
    {int i;
     char temp[1000];
     for (i=0, i<n; i = i + 1)
       temp[i] = A[i];               /* Copy from A into temp      */

     for (i=0; i<n; i = i + 1)
       A[i] = temp[n - i - 1];       /*    and copy back, reversed. */
    }
```

**Figure 14.54**   Program to reverse characters in a string.

c1 = coeff(m - 1, n - 1); during the call to coeff that occurs when execution proceeds from the state diagrammed in figure 14.53.

C. In the scenario of the figure, what is the largest value that the content of B (the base pointer) reaches before the original call to coeff(3,5) returns?

### Problem 14.16

The C procedure Reverse given in figure 14.54 reverses the first n characters in a given string A. Translate Reverse into *S*-machine assembly code using the general approach of figure 14.31. Be sure to comment your assembly code, as in figure 14.31, to show the correspondence between C-language and assembly-language constructs. Note that the arguments passed on the stack to Reverse will be the number n and the *address* of the first character of A.

### Problem 14.17

A. Write an *S*-machine procedure that performs the sawtooth function, as described by figure 12.26. It should accept a single 4-byte quantity as an argument that is a pointer to the first byte in the wave table.

B. Roughly estimate how many clock cycles it will take to fill the wave table using your solution to part A. Show how you arrived at this estimate. Compare this number with your solutions to problems 12.32 and 12.25. What conclusions do you draw about the costs and benefits of layers of interpretation? Explain your reasoning.

### Problem 14.18

Figure 14.55 shows a microcode handler for a new *S*-machine instruction sxxx.

A. What value is left in R6 after execution of the first microinstruction of this handler? Use register-transfer-language notation.

B. What is the significance of the value left in R6 and R7 by the sxxx handler, in terms of the *S*-machine programming model?

**Figure 14.55** sxxx instruction-handler microsubroutine.

```
| Constants relating to S-machine implementation:

B = 32          | SRAM location of B register
Op1 = 0x62      | SRAM location for temporary storage (4 bytes)

hsxxx:  cadd2(-12, B, R6)
        move2(R6, R0)              | Copy 2-byte quantity...
        cmove(Op1, R2)
        call(get2)                 | <R2> <- <DRAM[<R0>,<R1>]>
                                   | Load DRAM locations whose adr is in
                                   |  R0, R1 into SRAM locations
                                   |   <R2>, <R2>+1.

        sub2(Op1, R6, Op1)         | Op1 <- <Op1> - <R6>, 2-byte data.
        PUSH2(Op1)                 | Macro that expands into
                                   |  cmove(Op1, R2)  call(push2).

        rtn()
```

C. Give a register-transfer-language expression for the value that is pushed on the S-machine stack by the sxxx instruction.

D. What is the significance of the value returned by the sxxx instruction, in terms of the S-machine programming model?

### Problem 14.19

A frequent operation in the S machine is to load the *value* of a local variable. This requires two S-machine operations: slla(n) and sl$\alpha$, where $\alpha$ is the number of bytes needed to hold the value of the local variable. To speed up this process, we can write a new S-machine instruction sllv$\alpha$(n) (load local value), which does the job of both previous instructions. Its specification is:

| Instruction | Stack before→after | Operation |
|---|---|---|
| sllv$\alpha$ | →$v^\alpha$ | $push[\langle\langle B\rangle + n + 4\rangle]$ |

Below is a partial implementation of the handler for the 1-byte version of this instruction. What values should ??1, ??2, and ??3 contain?

```
hsllv1: FETCH2(R0)
        add2(??1, B, R0)
        cadd2(??2, ??3, R0)
        l(R0, R0+1, Op1)
        PUSH1(Op1)
        rtn()
```

```
int g()
{
    int x, y;
    int f()
    {
        y = 3;
    }
    x = 4;
    f();
}
```

**Figure 14.56** A procedure with nonlocal variable references.

### Problem 14.20
Write the handler `hsllv2` for the `sllv2` instruction, as defined in problem 14.19.

### Problem 14.21
Are the STK modules shown in figure 12.25 appropriate for use as $S$-machine stack, assuming that they are sufficiently large? Explain why or why not.

### Problem 14.22
Are the following statements true or false? Explain your reasoning in each case.

A. One advantage of the $S$ machine is that, because of implicit operand specification, the instructions are relatively short.

B. A Turing machine that can interpret any $S$-machine program must be a universal Turing machine.

C. We can use *any* Turing machine and an appropriate input tape to compute the same function as a given $S$-machine program.

### Problem 14.23
Trace through a call to $g()$ in the program in figure 14.37. Draw the stack as it appears just before executing the `srtn4` instruction in the call to $f(7)$.

### Problem 14.24
Translate the program in figure 14.56 into $S$-machine code. Be sure to comment your code.

### Problem 14.25
Translate the program in figure 14.57 into $S$-machine code. Be sure to comment your code.

### Problem 14.26
Give a snapshot of the entire stack resulting from a call to `Square(5)` (figure 14.57) as it appears just after executing the statement `accum = accum + amount;` in the call to `Update(3)`.

```
int Square(x)
  int x;
    { int accum;

      Update(amount)
        int amount;
          { accum = accum + amount;}

      SquareFrom(i)
        int i;
          { if (i < x)
              {Update (2*i + 1);
               SquareFrom (i + 1);
              }
          }

      accum = 0;
      SquareFrom(0);
      return(accum);
    }
```

**Figure 14.57** Squaring using lexical scoping.

```
/* Read an n-digit integer.  Calls GetDigit() to read each successive
/*   digit; GetDigit is assumed to return an integer between 0 and 9
/*   for each digit.
*/
int ReadNum(GetDigit, n)
  int GetDigit();                        /* First arg: procedure.       */
  int n;                                 /* Second arg: integer.        */
  {  int value, i;                       /* Local variables.            */
     value = 0;                          /* Start with zero.            */
     for (i=0; i<n; i = i+1)             /* Loop over all digits,       */
       value = value*10 + GetDigit();    /*   updating value for each.  */
     return(value);
  }
```

**Figure 14.58** Device-independent numerical input program.

## Problem 14.27

Figure 14.58 shows a C program to read an integer from one of several input sources. It uses a procedural argument to achieve a measure of device independence. Assume that all integers (ints) are 4 bytes long. Note that the two arguments to ReadNum are a procedure and an integer, respectively. The for loop serves to call the argument procedure n times, fetching each of the n digits of the decimal number to be read. Translate ReadNum into $S$-machine assembly code using the general approach of the program in figure 14.31. Be sure to comment your assembly code, as in that figure, to show the correspondence between C-language and assembly-language constructs.

```
/* Convert an array of n consecutive bytes, containing
/* the binary-coded-decimal representation of an integer,
/* into the corresponding binary integer.  Successive bytes
/* starting at *s contain binary values of the n corresponding
/* consecutive digits.
*/
StringToNum(s, n)
char *s;                          /* The character array arg. */
int n;                            /* Number of digits in s.   */
{   int index = 0;                /* Index into string.       */

    int NextDigit()               /* Internal fn to return    */
      { int ans = s[index];       /*    next digit from s.     */
        index = index+1;
        return ans;
      }

    return ReadNum(NextDigit, n);  /* Use ReadNum.            */
}
```

**Figure 14.59**  Binary-coded-decimal conversion procedure.

### Problem 14.28
Consider the program in figure 14.59, which uses ReadNum. Translate this program into $S$-machine assembly code using the same style as in problem 14.27.

### Problem 14.29

A. The $S$-machine instruction slaa(4) appears in figure 14.59 within the translation of StringToNum. What is the significance of the value pushed on the stack by this instruction?

B. The $S$-machine instruction sla(1,0) appears in figure 14.59 within the translation of NextDigit. What is the significance of the value pushed on the stack by this instruction?

### Problem 14.30
Figure 14.60 gives a snapshot of the $S$ machine's stack taken during execution of a call to StringToNum (figure 14.59). The program counter, at the time of this snapshot, points to an srtn4 instruction within the procedure NextDigit.

A. What value is about to be returned from NextDigit?

B. What is the value in the 4 bytes starting at address 1972 in figure 14.60?

C. What is the address in the figure of the local variable index?

D. What value will be returned by StringToNum when execution proceeds from the state shown in the figure?

E. What are the values of the arguments to StringToNum in the figure?

| | | |
|---:|:---:|:---|
| 1904 | 1000 | |
| 1908 | 2 | |
| 1912 | 1904 | |
| 1916 | . . . | |
| 1920 | . . . | |
| 1924 | 0 | |
| 1928 | 2 | |
| 1932 | 1924 | |
| 1936 | 4000 | |
| 1940 | 1932 | |
| 1944 | 2 | |
| 1948 | 1940 | |
| 1952 | . . . | |
| 1956 | 1924 | |
| 1960 | 0 | |
| 1964 | 3 | |
| 1968 | 1 | |
| 1972 | ? | |
| 1976 | 30 | |
| 1980 | 1980 | ← Old SP |
| 1984 | 4444 | ← Old PC |
| 1988 | 1960 | ← Old B |
| B → 1992 | 1924 | ← Static link |
| 1996 | 7 | |
| 2000 | 7 | |
| 2004 | . . . | |
| SP → 2004 | | ← Top of stack |

**Figure 14.60**  Stack snapshot for StringToNum (figure 14.59).

F. What is the value located in the byte at address 1001 in the figure?

G. What is the instruction located at 4444 in the figure? (*Hint:* Where does "Old PC" point?)

## Problem 14.31

Ben Bitdiddle argues that the examples used in section 14.8 to motivate the use of static links can be handled using statically allocated variables rather than all the new *S*-machine instructions presented in table 14.36. Ben points out that access to static variables is easy to translate, even if they are free references contained in an internal procedure. He proposes that all such troublesome variables be statically allocated (like outer-level C variables) to eliminate access problems. Show how to translate the programs of figures 14.38 and 14.40 to *S*-machine code without using the instructions of table 14.36. You may give modifications to the *S*-machine code shown in figures 14.39 and 14.41 rather than completely rewriting the programs. Explain, in a sentence or two, how your approach differs from that of the programs in figures 14.39 and 14.41.

## Problem 14.32

Invent an example (using extended C code) for which the approach used in solving the last problem is unsuitable. Explain why your example can't be recoded using static storage to solve the free-variable access problems. (*Hint:* Consider cases, such as recursion, in which static variable allocation cannot be used.)

# 15  Register Architectures: The $G$ Machine

In this chapter we return to the two- and three-address machines introduced in chapter 13 and explore the elaborations on these ideas that have been made in modern architectures. Our basis for exploration is the $G$ (general-register) machine, which happens to be a close relative of the DEC PDP-11 and especially the VAX-11 family of machines, though many machines, ranging from the IBM System/360 and System/370 families to the Motorola MC68000 microprocessor family, are based on the same principles.

The naive implementation of our $S$ machine in chapter 14 took little advantage of the availability of fast storage (that is, registers or static RAM) in the processor, and it used main memory for virtually all data storage, even for temporary results. For most of the history of computers, including the present era, the interface to main memory has been one of the principal bottlenecks in computer systems. Architectures that can take maximum advantage of a limited amount of high-speed storage in the processor itself are therefore desirable, because they will be less constrained by the performance of the processor/main-memory interface.

In chapter 16 we shall explore ways of using high-speed storage in the processor to improve performance without changing the machine language. Some of these techniques are specific to stack-based architectures such as the $S$ machine, while others are more generally applicable, but all of them work by using extra amounts of fast storage in a *transparent* fashion. In other words, the machine-language programmer does not explicitly call for the use of fast storage: It is used, in a way that does not disturb the semantics of the machine language, in places where the machine designers have predicted it will yield the greatest performance improvement for "typical" programs of interest. For example, the topmost several items on the $S$-machine stack might actually be kept in processor registers (a "top-of-stack cache") rather than in memory. This would improve performance because a large fraction of the $S$ machine's memory references are to the data at the top of the stack.

While entirely reasonable, such implicit use of high-speed storage in the processor requires some extra complexity in the processor. There may also be situations in which the program writer or compiler implementor feels able to specify a discipline for the use of fast processor registers that is better than the discipline wired into the hardware. For these reasons, and other historical ones, the majority of today's machine-language architectures include a selection of *general registers* that are visible to the machine-language programmer and are normally implemented as high-speed storage within the processor.

General registers allow the machine-language program to designate explicitly the data that should be kept in processor registers. Use of general registers in a program economizes on main-memory accesses for frequently used data. Also, most general-register machines provide shortened forms of instructions for operating on data in general registers. Thus use of general registers can shorten programs and reduce the number of main-memory accesses needed to fetch the program itself.

It should be emphasized that stack architectures are not mere laboratory curiosities and that many of the advantages cited above for general-register architectures can also, by suitable design, be obtained in stack architectures. Furthermore, the explicit visibility of fast processor registers in general-register architectures reduces the flexibility available in picking different cost-performance trade-offs in implementation and complicates the task of generating machine-language code. We shall be in a better position to consider such issues after studying a representative general-register architecture.

## 15.1 Addressing Modes

Although the sample instruction formats in section 13.5.3 identified each operand by including its address explicitly in the instruction stream, most computers offer alternative means for locating operands. To accommodate registers and other addressing mechanisms, it is necessary to encode into the instruction stream the *addressing mode* to be used to access each operand—for example, whether the operand is stored in main memory or in a processor register. The addressing modes of operands can be implied by the operation code: We might add to our machine, for example, an *add-register* opcode (say, 36) whose three operands occupy registers specified in subsequent instruction-stream bytes.

A more flexible addressing structure arises from generalizing the operand address fields to include *address-mode* bits that specify the number and interpretation of remaining operand bytes, in much the same way as the operation-code byte indicates the number and processing of subsequent operands. Following this approach, we replace each operand address in our illustrative machine language by a *general address* GA of the form:

| Mode $M$ | Register $R$ | Additional information $X$ (optional) |
|----------|--------------|---------------------------------------|
| 4 bits   | 4 bits       | (mode dependent)                      |

This scheme provides for a maximum of 16 registers and 16 addressing modes. We assign a distinct 4-bit code to each addressing mode. For example, we use a code of 0 to denote register addressing. A general address that specifies an operand located in a register occupies a single instruction-stream byte, containing 0 in its high (address-mode) 4 bits and the number of the addressed register in its low 4 bits. Thus a three-address instruction gadd4 r(2) r(3) r(4) that adds the contents of register R2 to the contents of register R3 and places the result in register R4 would be coded as

| Byte | Contents | Description |
|------|----------|-------------|
| 0 | 00100010 | gadd4 opcode |
| 1 | 00000010 | First GA: mode 0 (register), register R2 |
| 2 | 00000011 | Second GA: mode 0 (register), register R3 |
| 3 | 00000100 | Third GA: mode 0 (register), register R4 |

Note that the above instruction requires 4 bytes, since the opcode and the three operands each require a single byte. Also, our convention for symbolic names for *G*-machine instructions prefixes each with a **g** to distinguish them from similar *S*-machine or microcode instruction names.

Certain addressing modes require additional information in the general address. The simplest of these is the *direct-addressing* mode, in which the additional information is simply the address of the operand in main memory. In the *G* machine, we indicate direct addressing by a mode $M = 2$; the value $X$ given in the following 4 bytes is taken as the memory address of the operand. Thus an instruction `gadd4 dir(10) r(4) dir(14)` that adds the contents of memory location 10 to the contents of register R4 and stores the result in memory location 14 would be coded as

| Byte | Contents | Description |
|------|----------|-------------|
| 0 | 00100010 | gadd4 opcode |
| 1 | 00100000 | First GA: mode 2 (direct address) |
| 2 | 00001010 | Low-order byte of first address (10 decimal) |
| 3 | 00000000 | High-order bytes of first address |
| 4 | 00000000 | |
| 5 | 00000000 | |
| 6 | 00000100 | Second GA: mode 0 (register), register R4 |
| 7 | 00100000 | Third GA: mode 2 (direct address) |
| 8 | 00001110 | Low-order byte of third address (14 decimal) |
| 9 | 00000000 | High-order bytes of third address |
| 10 | 00000000 | |
| 11 | 00000000 | |

Modern computers offer a variety of alternative addressing modes that differ in several important respects:

- *Extent to which the location of an operand is built into the program.* Including explicit addresses in the instruction stream fixes the location of the addressed data for the life of the program, assuming (as is conventional) that the instruction stream is read-only and hence constant. Certain alternative addressing modes perform address calculations using register contents or other run-time data, alleviating this inflexibility.

- *Time performance.* Operand addressing mechanisms differ considerably in their execution-time overhead. Complex addressing modes may require several ref-

**Table 15.1** Some typical addressing modes.

| Addressing mode | Instruction stream | Assembler syntax | Source datum $V$ | Destination address $E$ |
|---|---|---|---|---|
| Immediate | $X$ | $\texttt{imm}(X)$ | $V = X$ | |
| Direct | $X$ | $\texttt{dir}(X)$ | $V = \langle X \rangle$ | $E = X$ |
| Register | $R$ | $\texttt{r}(R)$ | $V = \langle R \rangle$ | $E = R$ |
| Indirect | $X$ | $\texttt{i}(X)$ | $V = \langle\langle X \rangle\rangle$ | $E = \langle X \rangle$ |
| Indirect register | $R$ | $\texttt{ir}(R)$ | $V = \langle\langle R \rangle\rangle$ | $E = \langle R \rangle$ |
| Indexed | $R, X$ | $\texttt{ix}(X, R)$ | $V = \langle\langle R \rangle + X \rangle$ | $E = \langle R \rangle + X$ |
| Stack push | | $\texttt{push()}$ | | $E = \langle \text{SP} \rangle$ ; $\text{SP} \leftarrow \langle \text{SP} \rangle + \alpha$ |
| Stack pop | | $\texttt{pop()}$ | $\text{SP} \leftarrow \langle \text{SP} \rangle - \alpha$ ; $V = \langle\langle \text{SP} \rangle\rangle$ | |
| SP-relative | $X$ | $\texttt{ix}(X,\text{SP})$ | $V = \langle\langle \text{SP} \rangle + X \rangle$ | $E = \langle \text{SP} \rangle + X$ |

erences to main memory to access the referenced operand, while faster modes confine their accesses to processor registers.

- *Code compactness.* Addressing forms differ in the number of bits required to encode them in the instruction stream. A simple reference to a processor register, for example, can generally be coded into many fewer instruction bits than are required to hold a full $n$-bit address. Note that an instruction that uses no registers, such as ADD4 20,40,123 from section 13.5.3 (which would be gadd4 dir(20) dir(40) dir(123) on the $G$ machine), occupies 16 bytes on the $G$ machine, as opposed to 13 bytes on the simple three-address architecture described earlier. The extra space is occupied by address-mode bytes indicating direct addressing. The simple three-address machine requires no address-mode bytes, since it offers no alternative to direct addressing. The extra space occupied by the mode bytes on the $G$ machine is counterbalanced by its extra flexibility: If half of the general addresses on the $G$ machine designate registers rather than memory (not an unreasonable goal), then the average general address on the $G$ machine will only occupy 3 bytes, whereas *every* operand specification on the simple three-address machine takes 4 bytes.

Table 15.1 lists some typical addressing modes found on modern computers. Each addressing mode requires a characteristic amount of additional information in the instruction stream to make a complete general address. For the examples in this table, these include possibly a register $R$ (whose number occupies the least significant 4 bits of the address-mode byte on the $G$ machine) and possibly a constant $X$ (which on the $G$ machine is always a 4-byte integer immediately following the address-mode byte). The second column of the table notes the additional instruction-stream information required by each addressing mode. The third column gives the assembler syntax we use for the addressing modes, each of which will be defined as a macroinstruction.

In most cases, a general address can be used as either a source (in which case it designates an operand value) or as a destination (in which case it designates a location into which a result may be stored). Table 15.1 gives the meaning of each addressing mode as either a source or a destination. A useful concept in working with addressing modes is the notion of *effective address*. For general addresses that are meaningful as both sources and destinations, the value as a source is $\langle E \rangle$, where $E$ (the effective address) is the location designated by the same general address if used as a destination. Most addressing modes can be fully described by specifying the additional information required in the instruction stream, plus the algorithm for using that information to calculate an effective address.

Each addressing mode generally caters to some class of software needs, and consequently the addressing structure of a machine tends to reflect the languages and programming disciplines anticipated by its designer. In the remainder of this section we briefly summarize the typical uses of the addressing modes listed in table 15.1.

1. *Immediate addressing* allows constants to be incorporated into the instruction stream. Since we consider the instruction stream itself to be read-only, immediate addressing is only useful for source operands.

2. In *direct addressing*, an explicit address $X$ in the instruction stream specifies the location of the datum to be accessed. This mode is used for access to variables of storage class *static*, and its use is illustrated in the sample instructions of section 13.5.3. Note the similarity between a direct address designating location $L$ and the $S$-machine instruction sequence sc4($L$) sl4. Figure 14.3 gives a more extended example of this correspondence.

3. *Register addressing* is like direct addressing, except that the referenced location is restricted to be one of the (relatively few) processor registers.

4. *Indirect addressing* differs from direct addressing in that the explicit address $X$ contained in the instruction stream is not the address of the operand, but rather the address of a location *containing* the address of the operand. Indirect addressing provides the fundamental capability to *compute* the address of a datum rather than fixing it as a constant in the program. $X$ might be the address of a program variable whose contents are the result of an arbitrary computation; thus the range of locations that an indirect reference through $X$ might access cannot, in general, be determined by inspecting the program.

The indirect addressing mode described in table 15.1 provides this capability in a pure and primitive form. In fact, many other addressing modes (such as *indexed* addressing, discussed below) contain an element of indirection and can be viewed as elaborations of indirect addressing that serve particular software requirements. Moreover, one can define additional addressing modes by adding levels of indirect addressing to existing ones; for example, *indirect register* and *indirect indexed* are modes often supported by modern instruction sets. Each additional level of indirection adds a $\langle \ldots \rangle$ step to the address calculation; thus an *indirect register* effective address is given by $E = \langle R \rangle$.

The sl$\alpha$ instruction of the $S$ machine is an example of indirection in its purest

```
gmove4   dir(J)    r(0)              | R0 <- <J>
gmult4   imm(4)    r(0)    r(0)      | R0 <- <R0> * 4
gmove4   ix(A,0)   r(1)              | R1 <- <<R0> + A>
```

**Figure 15.2**  Code to access the Jth element of the array A.

form: If a sequence $Q$ of $S$-machine instructions pushes a value $E$ on the stack, then the sequence $Q$ $\text{s}l\alpha$ will push the value $\langle E \rangle$. Thus an extra level of indirection is achieved on the $S$ machine by simply appending an $\text{s}l\alpha$ instruction to an existing instruction sequence.

5. *Indexed addressing* combines a level of indirect addressing (through a register) with the run-time addition of a constant offset. The address of the operand is thus the sum of two terms: a *constant* $X$ from the instruction stream and a *variable* held at run time in the register $R$. We use the assembler syntax $\text{ix}(X, R)$ to denote indexed mode, with an effective address $E = X + \langle R \rangle$. There are two common classes of use for this mode, differing in the interpretations given to the quantities $X$ and $\langle R \rangle$:

- *Constant base, variable offset.* This is typically used to reference elements of an array statically allocated at addresses beginning with $X$. In this case, the constant $X$ in the instruction stream is the base address of an area of storage; the offset within this area of the element to be accessed is calculated at run time and is loaded into the register $R$. If the aggregate is an array, the array index must often be scaled by the size of each array element to calculate a suitable offset. On a byte-addressed machine, for example, the Jth element of an array of 32-bit integers might be accessed by an instruction sequence like that of figure 15.2.

- *Constant offset, variable base.* This is typically used for accessing elements of dynamically allocated structures or records. In this case, the run-time contents of the register $R$ address the base $B$ of an area of storage. The constant $X$ in the instruction stream specifies the offset from $B$ of a particular element in the storage area.

For an example of such use, consider accessing an element of a data structure (such as the MState structure of figure 14.45, or its rather larger $G$-machine counterpart) whose format is known in advance but whose location is not known until run time. If R2 contains a pointer p to such a structure, and a particular component SP is located 4 bytes from the beginning of the structure, then a reference such as p->SP refers to the word at $\langle \langle R2 \rangle + 4 \rangle$ and can be compiled as the indexed address $\text{ix}(4,2)$. In general, a reference such as p->C, where p is a pointer to a structure and C is the name of one of the structure's components, can be compiled into an indexed general address $\text{ix}(X, R)$, where $X$ is the offset of the component C from the beginning of the structure and $R$ is the number of a register containing the value of p. The degenerate indexed address $\text{ix}(0, R)$ is equivalent to *indirect register* addressing; a clever programmer or compiler might exploit that equivalence on a machine offering both addressing modes.

Note that the use of an indexed address $\text{ix}(X, R)$ in this fashion is confined to

```
gmove4   dir(J)   r(0)             | R0 <- <J>
gmult4   imm(4)   r(0)   r(0)      | R0 <- 4 * <R0>
gadd4      r(2)   r(0)   r(0)      | R0 <- <R2> + <R0>
gmove4    ir(0)   r(1)             | R1 <- <<R0>>
```

**Figure 15.3**  Code to access the Jth element of an array pointed to by R2.

situations in which the offset from the address in $R$ is a constant known at compile time. This is likely when accessing elements of a structure, as illustrated by our example, but it is less likely in the case of arrays. To access the Jth element of an array whose base address is contained in R2, we may need to write code like that in figure 15.3 (assuming an array of 32-bit integers on a byte-addressed machine), where the gadd4 instruction performs an address calculation that cannot be stated as a simple indexed address.

When higher-level languages are implemented on a general-register machine, one of the machine's registers is usually dedicated to holding the address of the current stack frame, analogously to the B register of the $S$ machine. Indexed addresses using this register will then reference data at specific offsets within the current stack frame. This is an important example of the constant-offset, variable-base usage of indexing. Note the similarity between the calculation performed for an indexed address and the calculation performed by the slla instruction of the $S$ machine.

The one plausible combination of base and offset that simple indexed addressing does not furnish directly is variable-base, variable-offset. Figure 15.3 illustrates this situation (selecting an element of an array, where the array starts at an address that is computed dynamically). An instance of this arises in accessing arrays allocated in stack frames, where the address of the array depends on the location of the stack frame. To handle such accesses in one instruction, some machines (for example, the Motorola MC68000, IBM System/360, and IBM System/370 families) have an indexed addressing mode that specifies *two* registers rather than one. Extending our assembly-language notation conventions, we may write an address of this sort as $ix2(X, RA, RB)$, where $RA$ and $RB$ are registers and $X$ is a constant in the instruction stream. The effective address denoted by this specification is $E = X + \langle RA \rangle + \langle RB \rangle$. All three elements of this address ($X$, $RA$, and $RB$) are useful in accessing an element of an array in a stack frame. Although this addressing mode is useful, we do not include it in the $G$ machine.

The idea of indexing can be extended in many ways. For example, at least one machine (the IBM Series/1) has an addressing mode that we might be tempted to write $ix(X, ix(Y, R))$, whose instruction stream includes *two* constants $X$ and $Y$, as well as a register $R$. The corresponding effective address is $E = X + \langle Y + \langle R \rangle \rangle$. If $X$ and $Y$ are the offsets of components X and Y in their respective structures, this addressing mode can be used to express a "chained" structure reference (p->Y)->X in a single general address!

Indexed addressing is often combined with indirection to offer additional addressing modes. Performing the indexing and indirection operations in different orders yields different results, a common topic of confusion among machine-language programmers. Thus an *indirect indexed* effective address would be given by $E = \langle\langle R \rangle + X\rangle$. Alternatively, an *indexed indirect* mode would perform the *indirection* operation to $X$ *before* the indexing, yielding the effective address $E = \langle R \rangle + \langle X \rangle$. The former mode is occasionally useful when dealing with an array of *pointers*, accessing the word addressed by element $A[i]$ in a single instruction. Indexed indirect addressing is useful for accessing elements of dynamically allocated arrays, as an alternative to the $\texttt{ix2}(X, RA, RB)$ mode discussed above.

6. *Stack addressing* provides implicit push and pop operations in the addressing structure and is convenient for the storage of temporary results during expression evaluation. Note that the use of a stack addressing mode as a source or destination has the side effect of modifying the stack pointer. Furthermore, its use as a source operand causes an implicit pop, while its use as a destination causes a push. The push operation requires a combination of indirect register addressing (through SP) with a *postincrement* to modify $\langle SP \rangle$; that is, after the address of the operand is computed, the use of the addressing mode has the side effect of incrementing $\langle SP \rangle$. This is an example of a *postincrement* addressing mode, which we implement in a more general way shortly. Similarly, a stack pop addressing mode requires a *predecrement* of $\langle SP \rangle$ before indirectly addressing through it. Thus the following code sequence might be used to perform $R0 \leftarrow \langle R0 \rangle \cdot (\langle R0 \rangle + \langle R1 \rangle)$:

```
gadd4    r(0)    r(1)    push()   | push[<R0> + <R1>]
gmult4   r(0)    pop()   r(0)     | R0 <- <R0> * pop[]
```

Using `push()` as a source or `pop()` as a destination is clearly contrary to common conventions for stack usage.

7. *SP-relative addressing* is simply a special case of indexed addressing in which the register is the stack pointer. It can be used for accessing temporary values near, but not at, the top of the stack, without the need for popping the occluding data, as strict stack discipline (and the stack addressing modes noted above) would require. SP-relative addressing can also be used for accessing local variables in the current stack frame, whose offset from the SP is usually computable at compile time. However, if the stack pointer is very dynamic (as it might be as a result of the pushing and popping of temporary values), the SP offset required to access a particular local variable changes from one instruction to the next, and the compile-time bookkeeping burden can become heavy. For this reason, many compilers allocate a *base-of-frame register* for reference to local variables, as discussed above, rather than using the more volatile SP.

## 15.2 The $G$ Machine

Now we illustrate, in the context of the $G$ machine, the incorporation of a representative variety of addressing modes into a realistic machine-language design. The approach we follow is patterned after the addressing structure of the DEC PDP-11 and VAX-11, machines whose addressing structure is considered exemplary by many compiler implementors. The DEC scheme is noteworthy for its economy of mechanism: It supports a rich variety of addressing capabilities using a small number of underlying address manipulations. Two key ideas are heavily exploited in this regard:

- The program counter (PC) and stack pointer (SP) are available as general registers. This structure provides, for example, SP-relative addressing as a special case of indexed addressing. The $G$ machine dedicates registers R14 and R15 to serve as SP and PC, respectively; in our assembler syntax, we shall treat SP and PC as synonymous with the register names R14 and R15.

- The machine includes indirect register addressing modes that, as a side effect of the address computation, modify the contents of the specified register. Specifically, a *postincrement* addressing mode, written as posti($n$), addresses the memory location whose address is contained in the specified register R$n$, as in indirect register mode addressing, but the contents of R$n$ are then incremented to point to the next datum in memory. Thus an array of consecutive data may be referenced through successive postincrement-mode addresses, assuming that the specified register has been initialized to point to the base of the array. The machine has instructions that manipulate both byte and longword data, so we arrange for the register contents to be incremented by 1 in the context of a byte-manipulation instruction (such as gmove1), by 4 in the context of a longword-manipulation instruction (such as gmove4), and in general by $\alpha$ in the context of an instruction that manipulates data of length $\alpha$; thus consecutive items of size 1, 2, 4, or 8 may be accessed.

    A complementary *predecrement* addressing mode, written pred($n$), *subtracts* the datum size $\alpha$ from the contents of the specified register and uses the result to address the data. The asymmetry between these two modes (that is, the fact that the *previous* register contents are used to address the data in postincrement mode, whereas the *new* register contents are used in predecrement mode) is motivated by their use in stack addressing. Indeed, these modes may be viewed as generalizations of the push and pop stack addressing modes discussed previously.

It should be emphasized that neither of the above characteristics is *necessary* in implementing the addressing modes outlined in the previous section; indeed, there is some controversy among computer architects as to whether, for example, addressing modes should be allowed to have side effects. Such side effects tend to be particularly troublesome in high-performance pipelined implementations, where the side effects called for by a particular addressing mode must be understood before any further operand fetches can be performed.

The first byte of a general address in the $G$ machine contains a 4-bit addressing mode and a 4-bit register number. This scheme allows for 16 program-accessible registers, of which R0 through R13 are general-purpose registers, R14 is the processor stack pointer, and R15 is the program counter. Tables 15.4 and 15.5 summarize the addressing modes of the $G$ machine. Note that the modes in the latter table are simply instances of the modes in the first table, specifying the program counter or stack pointer as the general register. Immediate mode, for example, addresses

**Table 15.4** Fundamental address modes of the $G$ machine.

| Addressing mode | $M$ field | Effective address | Assembler syntax |
|---|---|---|---|
| Register | 0 | $E = \mathrm{R}n$ | $\mathtt{r}(n)$ |
| Indirect register | 1 | $E = \langle \mathrm{R}n \rangle$ | $\mathtt{ir}(n)$ |
| Direct | 2 | $E = X$ | $\mathtt{dir}(X)$ |
| Indirect | 3 | $E = \langle X \rangle$ | $\mathtt{i}(X)$ |
| Indexed | 4 | $E = X + \langle \mathrm{R}n \rangle$ | $\mathtt{ix}(X, n)$ |
| Indirect indexed | 5 | $E = \langle X + \langle \mathrm{R}n \rangle \rangle$ | $\mathtt{iix}(X, n)$ |
| Postincrement | 6 | $E = \langle \mathrm{R}n \rangle$ ; $\mathrm{R}n \leftarrow \langle \mathrm{R}n \rangle + \alpha$ | $\mathtt{posti}(n)$ |
| Indirect postincrement | 7 | $E = \langle \langle \mathrm{R}n \rangle \rangle$ ; $\mathrm{R}n \leftarrow \langle \mathrm{R}n \rangle + \alpha$ | $\mathtt{iposti}(n)$ |
| Predecrement | 8 | $\mathrm{R}n \leftarrow \langle \mathrm{R}n \rangle - \alpha$ ; $E = \langle \mathrm{R}n \rangle$ | $\mathtt{pred}(n)$ |
| Indirect predecrement | 9 | $\mathrm{R}n \leftarrow \langle \mathrm{R}n \rangle - \alpha$ ; $E = \langle \langle \mathrm{R}n \rangle \rangle$ | $\mathtt{ipred}(n)$ |

**Table 15.5** Derived address modes of the $G$ machine.

| Addressing mode | $M$ field | General register | Effective address | Assembler syntax |
|---|---|---|---|---|
| Immediate | 6 | PC | $E = \langle \mathrm{PC} \rangle$ ; $\mathrm{PC} \leftarrow \langle \mathrm{PC} \rangle + \alpha$ | $\mathtt{imm}\alpha(X)$ |
| SP-relative | 4 | SP | $E = X + \langle \mathrm{SP} \rangle$ | $\mathtt{ix}(X, \mathtt{SP})$ |
| Indirect SP-relative | 5 | SP | $E = \langle X + \langle \mathrm{SP} \rangle \rangle$ | $\mathtt{iix}(X, \mathtt{SP})$ |
| Stack (push) | 6 | SP | $E = \langle \mathrm{SP} \rangle$ ; $\mathrm{SP} \leftarrow \langle \mathrm{SP} \rangle + \alpha$ | $\mathtt{push}()$ |
| Stack (pop) | 8 | SP | $\mathrm{SP} \leftarrow \langle \mathrm{SP} \rangle - \alpha$ ; $E = \langle \mathrm{SP} \rangle$ | $\mathtt{pop}()$ |
| PC-relative | 4 | PC | $E = \langle \mathrm{PC} \rangle + X$ | $\mathtt{rel}(X)$ |

data in the instruction stream, using postincrement mode to adjust the PC so that the data will not subsequently be fetched as an instruction. PC-relative addressing, which (like the $\mathtt{slr}\alpha$ instructions of the $S$ machine) allows us to write position-independent code, involves using the program counter as an index register. And stack pushes and pops are instances of postincrement and predecrement address modes, which use the stack pointer as the specified register.

It must be emphasized that the general registers of the machine-language $G$-machine model are not to be confused with the similarly named temporary storage locations ("virtual registers") used at the microcode level. The two sets of registers play similar roles, but at different interpretive levels: The R0 used by microcode has nothing to do with the R0 used by $G$-machine programs, just as the microstack is completely independent of the stack used by the $G$ machine. The general registers (and other $G$-machine state) are implemented using static RAM locations, which appear as variables to the microcode that interprets $G$-machine instructions. We

| Addressing-mode macros:

```
.macro  r(R)            R               | Register.
.macro  ir(R)           0x10+R          | Indirect register.
.macro  dir(X)          0x20 LONG(X)    | Direct.
.macro  i(X)            0x30 LONG(X)    | Indirect.
.macro  ix(X, R)        0x40+R LONG(X)  | Indexed.
.macro  iix(X, R)       0x50+R LONG(X)  | Indirect indexed.
.macro  posti(R)        0x60+R          | Postincrement.
.macro  iposti(R)       0x70+R          | Indirect postincrement.
.macro  pred(R)         0x80+R          | Predecrement.
.macro  ipred(R)        0x90+R          | Indirect predecrement.


| Special "derived" addressing modes:

| Immediate modes.  Note that the length MUST agree with that in
|    the containing instruction or disaster will result; a more
|    sophisticated assembler would handle this automatically.


.macro  imm1(X) posti(PC) X             | Byte immediate.
.macro  imm2(X) posti(PC) WORD(X)       | Word immediate.
.macro  imm4(X) posti(PC) LONG(X)       | Long immediate.


.macro  rel(X)  ix(X-.-1,PC)            | PC-relative.
.macro  push()  posti(SP)               | Stack push.
.macro  pop()   pred(SP)                | Stack pop.
```

**Figure 15.6**  Macroinstruction definitions for addressing modes.

allocate 4 static RAM bytes to hold the contents of each *G*-machine register; in addition, we need a few other static RAM locations to hold temporary results during instruction execution.

Figure 15.6 shows the definition of macroinstructions corresponding to the addressing modes of our *G* machine. We emphasize again that these definitions are appropriate for the assembly of *G*-machine programs and will not be used for the assembly of microcode (such as the microcode that *interprets* the *G*-machine programs). We have defined the macros push() and pop() to provide *G*-machine assembly-language alternatives to the less mnemonic posti(SP) and pred(SP) forms; the reader should be careful about distinguishing these macros from the definitions of push(x) and pop(x) used in microcode to designate push and pop microinstructions that access the microstack.

### 15.2.1 Stack Management

As on the *S* machine, the three principal uses of the processor stack on the *G* machine are (1) storage of temporary values, for example, during expression evaluation; (2) call/return linkage to procedures; and (3) allocation of local storage in a block-structured environment. Not surprisingly, stack manipulation on the *G* machine is performed using address modes that specify the SP as the register.

```
gadd4      r(0)      r(1)     push()   | Stack <R0>+<R1>.
gash4      pop()    imm1(-1)  push()   | Shift right.
gsub4  ix(-4,SP)     r(0)     r(0)     | Subtract from R0.
gsub4      pop()     r(1)     r(1)     | Subtract from R1
                                       |   (and discard).
```

**Figure 15.7**  Program to subtract $\frac{\langle R0 \rangle - \langle R1 \rangle}{2}$ from R0 and R1.

A simple example of use of the stack for temporary storage is the three-instruction sequence

```
gmove4   r(0)   push()  | Swap <R0>, <R1>: push <R0>.
gmove4   r(1)   r(0)
gmove4   pop()  r(1)    | Pop into <R1>.
```

which swaps the contents of registers R0 and R1 without disturbing the other registers. Here we have used the more humane syntax push() and pop() for the addressing modes posti(SP) and pred(SP), respectively. Note that SP is incremented (by 4, since gmove4 is a 32-bit operation) by the first instruction, leaving SP pointing to the address immediately *following* the locations containing the newly pushed R0 contents. The third instruction restores SP to its original contents and copies the stacked R0 contents into R1.

A more interesting example of temporary stack storage is shown in figure 15.7. We assume that R0 and R1 contain numbers that are to be adjusted so that their average is zero; we accomplish this by subtracting their average from both R0 and R1. So as not to disturb the other registers (which may contain values needed in subsequent computation), the average is computed in the stack by the first two instructions. Note that the gash4 instruction performs a 1-bit right-shift, owing to its first source operand of imm1(-1); note also that this operand is always a 1-byte rather than an $\alpha$-byte quantity—hence the imm1(-1) rather than imm4(-1) general address. The addressing modes of the remaining gash4 source and its destination imply a pop of the number to be shifted, followed by a push of the result. The general address ix(-4,SP) in the third instruction refers to the topmost longword on the stack, containing the average to be subtracted from R0 and R1. The fourth instruction refers to this same word using pop()—alternative syntax for pred(SP)—which has the side effect of popping the average from the stack, restoring $\langle SP \rangle$ to its value at the start of the sequence.

This technique for managing temporary stack storage leads to straightforward translations of many $S$-machine instructions as single $G$-machine instructions. For example, the $S$-machine instruction sadd4 can be written as gadd4 pop() pop() push() on the $G$ machine. Similarly, the $S$-machine instruction sl4 can be translated as gmove4 ipred(SP) push(), and ss4 can be translated as gmove4 pop() iposti(SP). Finally, if we assume that, in $G$-machine implementations of higher-level languages, the address of the current stack frame is kept in R13, then the $S$-machine instruction slla($n$) can be translated as gadd4 imm4($n$+4) r(13) push().

Since the $S$ machine is exceptionally easy to compile code for, translations such as these offer a quick path to generating working code for a general-register machine. The code is quite inefficient, however, since it virtually ignores the general registers and resorts to main memory (the stack) for almost all operations. Furthermore, the address modes of the $G$ machine are powerful enough that the function equivalent to several $S$-machine instructions can usually be implemented as a single $G$-machine instruction. Making optimum use of general registers and address modes when generating code adds significant complication to a compiler but is an interesting and important part of modern compiler technology.

The other uses of the stack on the $G$ machine (procedure linkage and local-variable storage) are quite similar to the corresponding uses on the $S$ machine. They are discussed in section 15.5.

### 15.2.2 Instruction Repertoire of the $G$ Machine

As a beginning, we can take the instruction repertoire of the $G$ machine to be the same as that of our three-address machine, given in table 13.10. This table, with several additions, has been adapted into table 15.8, where the notations $E_A$, $E_B$, and $E_C$ represent the effective addresses corresponding to operands $A$, $B$, and $C$, respectively. We have also used the $\alpha$ notation introduced with the $S$ machine to note instructions that have several forms to handle operands of different sizes. Appearances of $\alpha$ in table 15.8 should be taken to mean 1, 2, 4, or 8; as in the case of the $S$ machine, our illustrative implementation deals with 1-, 2-, and 4-byte data only, for reasons of brevity. Extending the implementation to include 8-byte data is straightforward, assuming that general registers are expanded to 64 bits.

Instructions that perform tests and jumps are listed in table 15.9. Note that the operation of gjmp $A$ is given as PC $\leftarrow E_A$ rather than PC $\leftarrow \langle E_A \rangle$. This is convenient for various reasons, not the least being the intuitive appeal of writing "gjmp dir($X$)" when we want to transfer control directly to the instruction located at address $X$. However, it means that gjmp instructions treat their addresses as *destinations*, in that they use $E_A$ rather than $\langle E_A \rangle$, which would correspond to treatment as sources. Thus an instruction like gjmp imm4($X$) is nonsense.

Furthermore, some destinations do not make much sense as targets for gjmp instructions. For example, gjmp r(0) would direct a transfer of control to an instruction located *in R0*, but this would require us to put the *address* of R0 into the program counter. R0 is not a location in main memory and hence has no numerical address, which presents a problem. For this reason, we outlaw instructions of the form gjmp r($n$). (If R0 contains the *address* of an instruction to jump to, the instruction gjmp ir(0) will easily handle the situation.) Some machines (such as the DEC PDP-10 family) give numerical addresses to the general registers and allow the execution of instructions located in registers, but most machines follow the $G$ machine in this respect.

Our earlier three-address example was only a partial machine and did not confront several issues we would like to discuss now in the context of general-register machines. Notable among these issues are conditional jumping and procedure linkage. The $S$-machine scmp$\alpha$ and sj*cond* instructions furnish an example of explicit communication from comparison instructions to conditional jump instruc-

**Table 15.8** Typical $G$-machine instructions.

| Operation | Operand addresses | Function performed |
|---|---|---|
| gmove$\alpha$ | $A, B$ | $E_B^\alpha \leftarrow \langle E_A \rangle^\alpha$ |
| gadd$\alpha$ | $A, B, C$ | $E_C^\alpha \leftarrow \langle E_A \rangle^\alpha + \langle E_B \rangle^\alpha$ |
| gsub$\alpha$ | $A, B, C$ | $E_C^\alpha \leftarrow \langle E_A \rangle^\alpha - \langle E_B \rangle^\alpha$ |
| gmult$\alpha$ | $A, B, C$ | $E_C^\alpha \leftarrow \langle E_A \rangle^\alpha * \langle E_B \rangle^\alpha$ |
| gdiv$\alpha$ | $A, B, C$ | $E_C^\alpha \leftarrow \langle E_A \rangle^\alpha \div \langle E_B \rangle^\alpha$ |
| grem$\alpha$ | $A, B, C$ | $E_C^\alpha \leftarrow \langle E_A \rangle^\alpha \bmod \langle E_B \rangle^\alpha$ |
| gneg$\alpha$ | $A, B$ | $E_B^\alpha \leftarrow -\langle E_A \rangle^\alpha$ |
| gand$\alpha$ | $A, B, C$ | $E_C^\alpha \leftarrow \langle E_A \rangle^\alpha \text{ AND } \langle E_B \rangle^\alpha$ |
| gor$\alpha$ | $A, B, C$ | $E_C^\alpha \leftarrow \langle E_A \rangle^\alpha \text{ OR } \langle E_B \rangle^\alpha$ |
| gxor$\alpha$ | $A, B, C$ | $E_C^\alpha \leftarrow \langle E_A \rangle^\alpha \text{ XOR } \langle E_B \rangle^\alpha$ |
| gcom$\alpha$ | $A, B$ | $E_B^\alpha \leftarrow \text{NOT } \langle E_A \rangle^\alpha$ |
| gash$\alpha$ | $A, B, C$ | Arithmetically shift $\langle E_A \rangle^\alpha$ left (right) $\langle E_B \rangle^1$ $(-\langle E_B \rangle^1)$ places; store in $E_C$ |
| glsh$\alpha$ | $A, B, C$ | Logically shift $\langle E_A \rangle^\alpha$ left (right) $\langle E_B \rangle^1$ $(-\langle E_B \rangle^1)$ places; store in $E_C$ |
| ghalt | | Stop the machine |

tions, using condition-code bytes produced by the comparison instructions. On the $G$ machine we explore the opposite design decision: *implicit* communication of condition information through a condition-code register CC (which can be thought of as part of the $G$ machine's PSW) in the processor state.

As in the $S$ machine, we provide explicit gcmp$\alpha$ and gtest$\alpha$ instructions, which set the CC register to an appropriate $SCZ00000$ value; other $G$-machine instructions leave $\langle CC \rangle$ unchanged. We make this choice because of the considerable extra overhead required in the MAYBE microarchitecture to compute the $SCZ00000$ condition codes. However, an alternative (and preferable) ALU design would generate these status bits "for free" as a by-product of every ALU operation. In this case, we might choose to have most $G$-machine instructions that perform ALU operations set the CC register as a side effect, eliminating the necessity for many of the explicit gcmp$\alpha$ and gtest$\alpha$ instructions that otherwise must appear in our $G$-machine programs. This latter approach is common in modern general-register machines.

Conditional jumping is performed by the gj*cond* family of instructions, where *cond* is one of the condition names listed in table 14.18 (that is, the same condition names that can be used for conditional jumps by the $S$ machine). The gcmp$\alpha$ and gtest$\alpha$ instructions operate similarly to their $S$-machine counterparts, except that their results are left in the processor register CC rather than being stored in main memory. The higher-level-language statement

**Table 15.9** Condition test and jump instructions.

| Operation | Operand addresses | Sets CC? | Function performed |
|---|---|---|---|
| gcmp$\alpha$ | $A, B$ | Yes | Set $S$, $Z$, and $C$ bits in CC according to the result of the operation $\langle E_A \rangle^\alpha - \langle E_B \rangle^\alpha$ |
| gtest$\alpha$ | $A$ | Yes | Set $S$, $Z$, and $C$ bits in CC according to the result of $\langle E_A \rangle^\alpha - 0$ |
| gjmp | $A$ | No | $\text{PC}^4 \leftarrow E_A{}^4$ |
| gj$cond$ | $A$ | No | If $cond$ matches $\langle \text{CC} \rangle$, then $\text{PC}^4 \leftarrow E_A{}^4$ |

```
            gmove4   imm4(1)   dir(i)             | Initialize loop counter.

LOOP:       gmult4   dir(A)    dir(A)    dir(A) | Do A = A * A.
            gadd4    dir(i)    imm4(1)   dir(i) | Increment loop counter.
            gcmp4    dir(i)    imm4(4)          | Done with loop yet?
            gjle     dir(LOOP)                  |   (If no, go around again.)
```

**Figure 15.10**  $G$-machine code to compute $A^{16}$.

```
if (a>b)  goto here;  else goto there;
```

whose $S$-machine code is given in figure 14.20, can be translated on the $G$ machine as

```
gcmp4   dir(a)    dir(b)   | Set CC from a - b.
gjgt    dir(here)          | Go to here if a > b,
gjmp    dir(there)         |   else go to there.
```

A higher-level-language program might compute the power $A^{16}$ by a loop such as

```
for (i = 1; i ≤ 4; i = i+1) A = A * A;
```

A straightforward translation of this into $G$-machine code is given in figure 15.10.

A clever compiler (or human programmer) might recognize the value of using a general register, say R0, for the loop counter. Moreover, the loop counter could be changed to count down from 4 rather than up from 1; this might lead to the slightly improved program in figure 15.11, which has the same number of instructions as the program in figure 15.10 but makes fewer accesses to main memory. On a machine whose subtract instruction sets the condition codes, the gtest$\alpha$ instruction can be eliminated. The reader can doubtless devise further improvements to this program.

```
        gmove4    imm4(4)       r(0)          | Initialize loop counter.

LOOP: gmult4     dir(A)       dir(A)  dir(A)  | Do A = A * A.
        gsub4      r(0)        imm4(1)  r(0)   | Decrement loop counter.
        gtest4     r(0)
        gjgt     dir(LOOP)                     | (Haven't gone 4 times yet.)
```

**Figure 15.11**  Optimized version of figure 15.10.

## 15.3 *MAYBE Implementation

The MAYBE microcode for the G machine is similar in its gross structure to that of the S machine, discussed in chapter 14 and given in detail in appendix 4. Complete details of the G-machine implementation on the MAYBE are given in appendix 5; in this section, we offer an overview of its structure.

Figure 15.12 shows conventions for use of static RAM in our microcode implementation. Note that SRAM locations allocated to the G machine's general registers are named GRn, to distinguish them from the SRAM locations Rn used for temporary storage and arguments to microsubroutines. As with the S-machine implementation, we allocate G-machine-specific locations starting at SRAM address 32, to leave room for our microprogram temporaries.

### 15.3.1 *Effective-Address Computation

The G-machine implementation follows a pattern similar to that of the S machine and uses identical microcode to fetch and dispatch on opcodes. Not surprisingly, a major implementation difference involves the implementation of the general addressing modes (which have no S-machine counterpart). For convenient access to operands by G-machine instruction handlers, we provide several microsubroutines that are central to the G machine's mechanism: Meff, which fetches and decodes the effective address of the next operand from the G-machine instruction stream, and LoadGA$\alpha$ and StoreGA$\alpha$, which handle source and destination addressing modes, respectively. Notice that certain effective-address computations (for example, those for autoincrement mode) require the operand size as an input.

Figure 15.13 shows the skeleton of the Meff microsubroutine. Meff is called with no arguments. It fetches a general address from the instruction stream, decodes it (performing any indicated postincrement or predecrement side effects), and leaves the effective address in three SRAM locations reserved for that purpose.

The effective address may identify an SRAM location (corresponding to one of the general registers) or a DRAM location (corresponding to a main-memory reference by the G-machine program). The single-byte SRAM location MAdrFlag indicates which kind of reference the most recently decoded effective address requires. In the case of a register-mode operand, MAdrFlag is set to SRAM (a mnemonic for the numerical value 0) and the SRAM address of the effectively addressed register is left in the SRAM location MEAdr. If a main-memory location is addressed,

**Figure 15.12**   Definitions for microcoded *G*-machine implementation.

```
| 32-bit G-machine architecture: microcode support.

| Machine-level register definitions:
|    Each is 4 bytes long.
GR0      = 32
GR1      = GR0+4
GR2      = GR1+4
GR3      = GR2+4
GR4      = GR3+4
GR5      = GR4+4
GR6      = GR5+4
GR7      = GR6+4
GR8      = GR7+4
GR9      = GR8+4
GR10     = GR9+4
GR11     = GR10+4
GR12     = GR11+4
GR13     = GR12+4
GR14     = GR13+4
GR15     = GR14+4
SP       = GR14          | G machine's stack pointer.
PC       = GR15          | G machine's program counter.

| Some SRAM registers reserved for particular purposes:
Op1      = 0x60          | Temporary results and operands.
Op2      = Op1+4
Op3      = Op2+4
Op4      = Op3+4
Op5      = Op4+4
Op6      = Op5+4

MCond    = Op6+4         | G machine's condition codes.
MLen     = MCond+1       | Current operand length.
MOp      = MCond+2       | Current opcode.

MReg     = MOp+1         | Register number of current operand.
MMode    = MOp+2         | Current addressing mode.

MAdrFlag = MMode+1       | Flags whether the eff adr is a DRAM or SRAM adr.
MEAdr    = MMode+2       | Effective addresses may be 2 bytes wide
MEAdr2   = MMode+3       |    (DRAM adrs).

| Fetch a byte from machine's instruction stream into SRAM address x.
| Increments PC.
.macro fetch(x) l(PC,PC+1,x)  cadd2(1,PC,PC)
```

MAdrFlag is set to DRAM (a mnemonic for the numerical value 1) and the 2-byte DRAM effective address is left in MEAdr and MEAdr+1.

The microcode shown in figure 15.13 fetches the mode-and-register byte of the

**Figure 15.13** $G$-machine effective-address computation: fetch/dispatch microcode.

```
| Microsubroutines to compute the effective address of an operand
|   specified by the next general address in the G instruction
|   stream.  Performs any register modifications implied by the
|   general address encoding (such as postincrement and predecrement).
| Sets MAdrFlag to "SRAM" if the operand is in SRAM
|   (else sets it to "DRAM"), where "SRAM" and "DRAM" are
|   arbitrarily chosen constants.


SRAM = 0        | These are defined as constants to be used to "flag"
DRAM = 1        |   whether the effective address is an SRAM or DRAM adr.


| MEAdr, MEAdr+1 are set to the effective address
|   (for SRAM adrs, MEAdr+1 is ignored
|   since these are 1-byte addresses).
| Clobbers Op3, temporary registers R0-R4.
| Assumes that MLen is preset to the appropriate operand length.


| Extracts the register number and mode specified into MReg and MMode,
|   respectively.

MEff:   fetch(MOp)                     | The mode/register byte.
        move(MOp, MReg)                | Copy, for register number.
        cand(0x0F, MReg, MReg)         | Mask off register number bits.
        rotl2(MReg, MReg)              | Multiply by 4
                                       |   (4-byte-wide registers).

        cadd(GR0, MReg, MReg)          | Add base address in SRAM where
                                       |   the registers begin to get
                                       |   the SRAM adr of the specified
                                       |   register.

        move(MOp, MMode)               | Copy, for adr mode.
        rotr4(MMode, MMode)            | Extract the mode bits.
        cand(0x0F, MMode, MMode)
        dispatch(MMode, AdrTab)


| 16-entry mode dispatch table.

AdrTab:
        WORD(hr)        WORD(hir)       WORD(hdir)      WORD(hi)
        WORD(hix)       WORD(hiix)      WORD(hposti)    WORD(hiposti)
        WORD(hpred)     WORD(hipred)    WORD(GAerr)     WORD(GAerr)
        WORD(GAerr)     WORD(GAerr)     WORD(GAerr)     WORD(GAerr)
```

general address, translates the register portion of this byte (its 4 low-order bits) to the SRAM address of the corresponding GR$n$ variable (left in SRAM location MReg), and dispatches through the table AdrTab to a microcode sequence specific

**Figure 15.14**  Effective-addressing microcode for r(R) and ir(R) addressing modes.

```
| Register mode handler: all operand sizes.

hr:     move(MReg, MEAdr)       | Rn is effective address.
        cmove(SRAM, MAdrFlag)   |   (Remember that it is in SRAM.)
        rtn()


| Indirect register mode handler:
|   Use 2-byte register contents as DRAM adr.

hir:    move(MReg, R0)          | Low 2 bytes of Rn into MEAdr.
        imove(R0, MEAdr)        | Low adr is  <R0>   (= <MReg>).
        cadd(1, R0, R0)         | High adr is <R0>+1 (= <MReg>+1).
        imove(R0, MEAdr+1)
        cmove(DRAM, MAdrFlag)   | Eff. adr is in DRAM, adr <MEAdr>.
        rtn()
```

**Figure 15.15**  Effective-addressing microcode for ix(X, R) addressing modes.

```
| Indexed mode handler.

hix:    move(MReg, R1)          | Fetch low 2 bytes of register
        imove(R1, R3)           |   into R3, R4.
        cadd(1, R1, R1)
        imove(R1, R4)

        FETCH4(Op3)             | Fetch 4-byte offset.
        add2(R3,Op3,MEAdr)      | Add in register contents.
        cmove(DRAM, MAdrFlag)   | Eff. adr is in DRAM, adr <MEAdr>.
        rtn()
```

to the addressing mode.

The microprogram in figure 15.14 shows the handling of register (mode 0) and indirect register (mode 1) effective-address computations. The addressing mode r(n) results in an effective SRAM address GRn, which is simply copied from MReg to MEAdr. Note that in each of the other modes, a DRAM location is addressed; hence MAdrFlag is nonzero. The effective-address computation for indirect register mode (mode 1), for example, begins at the tag hir: in figure 15.14. Note that the 2 low-order bytes of the indicated general register are copied to MEAdr, and MAdrFlag is set to DRAM (that is, 1), indicating a DRAM location.

Figure 15.15 shows the relatively straightforward implementation of indexed addressing. Note that Op3 is used to hold, temporarily, the 4-byte offset fetched

**Figure 15.16**  Effective-addressing microcode for `iix`$(X, R)$ addressing modes.

```
| Indirect indexed mode handler.

hiix:   move(MReg, R1)              | Fetch low 2 bytes of register
        imove(R1, R3)               |   into R3,4.
        cadd(1, R1, R1)
        imove(R1, R4)

        FETCH4(Op3)                 | Fetch 4-byte offset.
        add2(R3,Op3,MEAdr)          | Add in register contents.

| Fall through to...

| Following handler executes one level of
|   indirection on MEAdr, MEAdr+1, i.e., implements
|       MEAdr, MEadr+1  <-  <DRAM[ <MEAdr>, <MEAdr+1> ]>

hind:   l(MEAdr, MEAdr+1, R0)       | The indirection: first adr byte.
        cadd2(1, MEAdr, MEAdr)
        l(MEAdr, MEAdr+1, MEAdr+1)  | Second adr byte.
        move(R0, MEAdr)
        cmove(DRAM, MAdrFlag)       | Eff. adr is in DRAM, adr <MEAdr>.
        rtn()
```

from the instruction stream. As we observed in connection with 4-byte addresses in the *S*-machine implementation, the 4-byte addressing mechanism goes beyond what is needed for our little machine; it is provided for machine-language compatibility with larger, more expensive implementations.

Figure 15.16 shows the indirect indexed mode effective-address computation, which performs the same calculation as the indexed mode microcode, then passes control to `hind:` where the indirect addressing, $\texttt{MEAdr} \leftarrow \langle \text{DRAM}[\langle \texttt{MEAdr} \rangle^2] \rangle$, is applied.

The postincrement and predecrement addressing modes rely upon internal microsubroutines `increg` and `decreg`, respectively, which increment or decrement the register specified by the mode-and-register byte by an amount dictated by the operand length passed in the static RAM location `MLen`. The curious reader can find the implementation of these routines in appendix 5. Figure 15.17 shows the implementation of indirect postincrement addressing; note that since we are dealing with a *post*increment addressing mode, the effective address is computed *before* the call to `increg`. The reader is referred to the listing in appendix 5 for the complete implementation of the effective-address microsubroutine.

**Figure 15.17**   Microcode for indirect postincrement effective-address computation.

```
| Indirect postincrement handler.

hiposti: move(MReg, R0)      | Fetch low 2 bytes of register
         imove(R0, MEAdr)    |   into MEAdr.
         cadd(1, R0, R0)
         imove(R0, MEAdr+1)


         call(increg)        | Increment the register.
         jmp(hind)           | Indirect through MEAdr.
```

### 15.3.2 *Operand Access

Once the effective-address computation for an operand has been performed by
`Meff`, $G$-machine instruction handlers will typically need to fetch and/or store data
at the effectively addressed location. We provide the support microsubroutines
LEff$\alpha$ and SEff$\alpha$ to facilitate such access. (Figure 15.18 shows the implementations of LEff1 and SEff1 as examples.) Note that these microsubroutines call the
get$\alpha$ and put$\alpha$ utility microsubroutines described in table 14.11.

We provide top-level operand-access microsubroutines LoadGA$\alpha$ and StoreGA$\alpha$
(figure 15.19 shows LoadGA1 and StoreGA1), which combine the effective-address
computation (via `Meff`) with the fetch or store of the addressed location. Note
that LoadGA$\alpha$ and StoreGA$\alpha$ load and store operands into/from the 4-byte Op1
temporary location. To support operators with several source operands, LoadGA$\alpha$
moves the previous Op1 contents to Op2 before reloading Op1 with the fetched
operand. Thus two consecutive LoadGA$\alpha$ operations leave the first operand stored
in Op2 and the second in Op1. Since LoadGA$\alpha$ calls get$\alpha$, each source operand is
sign-extended to 4 bytes as it is fetched. Except for special cases (such as jumps)
that require effective-address computation but not access to an operand, LoadGA$\alpha$
and StoreGA$\alpha$ provide the standard interface to our address-mode microcode.

### 15.3.3 *$G$-Machine Instruction Handlers

Microcoding of instruction handlers for the $G$ machine is similar to that for the
$S$ machine. A typical handler for a three-address arithmetic operation, gadd4, is
shown in figure 15.20. Other three-address operators are equally straightforward,
using LoadGA$\alpha$ to fetch source operands and StoreGA$\alpha$ to store the result.

We have observed that a general-register machine may have several alternative
instruction formats for the same operation, using distinct opcodes to distinguish
among them. We might provide, for example, *two-address* versions of the gadd$\alpha$
instructions in addition to the three-address ones. One approach to the microcode
implementation of a putative two-address instruction g2add$\alpha$ is shown in figure 15.21. The source operands are copied into Op1 and Op2 via LoadGA$\alpha$, as in

**Figure 15.18**  LEff1 and SEff1 microsubroutines

```
| Microsubroutines to store @-byte operand in SRAM<<R0>> into the
|   current effective address.
| Destroys R0, R1, R2.

SEff1:  ccmp(SRAM, MAdrFlag)  | Is it in SRAM?
        je(SSRAM)             | Yes, so jump.
        move(R0, R2)          | Source SRAM address.
        move2(MEAdr, R0)      | Target DRAM address.
        jmp(put1)             | Copy SRAM<<R2>> -> DRAM<MEAdr> & rtn.


SSRAM:  move(MEAdr, R1)       | Target SRAM address.
        jmp(imovei4)          | Copy SRAM<<R0>> -> SRAM<MEAdr> & rtn.



| Microsubroutines to load @-byte operand into SRAM<<R0>> from the
|   current effective address.

LEff1:  ccmp(SRAM, MAdrFlag)  | Is it in SRAM?
        je(LSRAM)             | Yes, so jump.
        move(R0, R2)          | Target SRAM address.
        move2(MEAdr, R0)      | Source DRAM address.
        jmp(get1)             | Copy DRAM<<MEAdr>> -> SRAM<R1> & rtn.


LSRAM:  move(R0, R1)          | Target SRAM address.
        move(MEAdr, R0)       | Source SRAM address.
        jmp(imovei4)          | Copy SRAM<MEAdr> -> SRAM<<R1>> & rtn.

| Indirect @-byte SRAM copy:
|   Copy @-byte word from SRAM locations beginning at address <R0> to
|     SRAM locations beginning at address <R1>.
|   Increments <R0>, <R1> by @-1.

imovei4: push(R2)             | Used as a temporary.
        call(fetchnstore)
        call(fetchnstore)
        call(fetchnstore)
        call(fetchnstore)
        pop(R2)               | Restore temporary register.
        rtn()

fetchnstore: imove(R0, R2)    | Fetch a byte's worth of data.
        movei(R2, R1)         | Store it away.
        cadd(1, R0, R0)       | Increment source address.
        cadd(1, R1, R1)       | Increment destination address.
        rtn()
```

**Figure 15.19** LoadGA1 and StoreGA1 microsubroutines.

```
| Microsubroutine to load an operand specified by the next general
|    address in the M instruction stream.  Returns the operand in
|    Op1 after having copied previous Op1 contents to Op2.
|
| Note: Sign-extends operand to 4 bytes.

LoadGA1: move4(Op1, Op2)              | Save previous Op1.
         cmove(1, MLen)               | In case of posti or pred mode.
         call(MEff)                   | Decode general address.
         cmove(Op1, R0)               | Fetch <EA> into Op1.
         jmp(LEff1)


| Microsubroutine to store Op1 into an operand specified by the next
|    general address in the G-machine instruction stream.
|
| This code follows a pattern similar to LoadGA1 above.


StoreGA1:
         cmove(1, MLen)               | In case of posti or pred mode.
         call(MEff)
         cmove(Op1, R0)               | Store <Op1> into EA.
         jmp(SEff1)
```

**Figure 15.20** *G*-machine gadd4 handler.

```
| gadd4(x y z): three-address add, 4 bytes wide.
| z <- <x> + <y>

hgadd4: call(LoadGA4)              | Fetch 1st operand.
        call(LoadGA4)              | Fetch 2nd operand.
        add2( Op1,   Op2,   Op1)   | Add all 4 bytes.
        addcy(Op1+2, Op2+2, Op1+2)
        addcy(Op1+3, Op2+3, Op1+3)
        call(StoreGA4)
        rtn()
```

the three-address gadd$\alpha$ handler. However, the result of the addition is stored by means of a call to SEff$\alpha$ rather than StoreGA$\alpha$. The SEff$\alpha$ call reuses the effective address left in MAdrFlag and MEAdr by the second LoadGA$\alpha$ call; thus the result is stored in the location from which the second source operand was fetched. Note that this approach evaluates the second general address only once, despite the fact that it is used twice (once as a source and once as a destination).

**Figure 15.21**    Two-address add instruction-handler microcode.

```
| g2add4(x y): two-address add, 4 bytes wide.
| y <- <x> + <y>

hg2add4:call(LoadGA4)              | Fetch 1st operand.
        call(LoadGA4)              | Fetch 2nd operand.
        add2(Op1, Op2, Op1)        | Add all 4 bytes.
        addcy(Op1+2, Op2+2, Op1+2)
        addcy(Op1+3, Op2+3, Op1+3)
        call(SEff)                 | Store, reusing second effective address.
        rtn()
```

Microcode implementation of instructions that transfer control is illustrated in figure 15.22. Note that `Meff` rather than `LoadGAα` is called to evaluate the general address, reflecting our decision that the effective address of the operand (rather than the *contents* of that effective address) should be the `gjmp` target. Conditional jumps follow a similar pattern; we have chosen a condition-code format identical to that of the $S$ machine, so the logic involved is that of the $S$-machine conditional jumps. An important difference, however, is that the $G$-machine conditional jumps take the condition code from the CC register, which constitutes part of the $G$ machine's processor state, whereas $S$-machine conditional jumps take an explicit condition-code input on the stack. Thus the contents of the static RAM location `MCond` is to be considered part of the processor state (along with the general registers) of the $G$ machine, whereas it is simply a temporary variable in the $S$-machine implementation. Likewise, the $G$ machine's `gcmpα` instructions perform the same calculations as the corresponding $S$-machine instructions, but they leave their condition-code result byte in CC (implemented as `MCond`) rather than on the stack. The remaining $G$-machine instruction handlers are straightforward extensions of the examples above and of the corresponding handlers given for the $S$ machine; the complete sampling appears in appendix 5.

## 15.4 Other General-Register Architectures

The $G$-machine architecture is exceptionally uniform and "clean" compared with most general-register architectures that exist in reality. Most of the departures from the simple philosophy of the $G$ machine accommodate specific needs that can be served efficiently by ad hoc instructions. Accommodations that are frequently made for efficiency reasons include

- *Short-form address modes.* Many machines offer address modes that are intermediate between the long modes (such as indexed and immediate modes) and the very short register addressing modes. For example, many indexed references of the form `ix(X,R)` use a fairly small integer $X$. A "short index" mode that

**Figure 15.22**  *G*-machine jump instruction-handler microcode.

```
| gjmp x -- unconditional jump to target address x.

hgjmp:  cmove(4, MLen)        | 4-byte jump address.
        call(MEff)            | Compute effective address.
        ccmp(DRAM, MAdrFlag)  | Had better be a DRAM location...
        jne(adrerr)           | It is.


jmpx:   move2(MEAdr, PC)      | Copy effective address into PC.
        rtn()



        ...


| ERROR: Illegal address in call, jump, or handler declaration.


adrerr: ...
```

only has (for example) a 1-byte constant $X$ in the instruction stream could be used in many cases to make programs more compact. Another common optimization is to introduce a "short immediate" mode to capitalize on the fact that most immediate operands of the form imm4($X$) incorporate a small constant $X$, despite the necessity, in our $G$ machine, for the size of the immediate constant to agree with the datum size specified in the instruction's opcode. We emphasize that an instruction like gadd4 imm1(1) dir(A) dir(A) does not serve the goal of short immediate mode addressing (or, for that matter, any other reasonable goal); the skeptical reader is encouraged to analyze the serious misbehavior of this instruction.

- *Short-form instructions.* Certain operations are so common that special abbreviated instructions are introduced to specify them more compactly. For example, the form gadd$\alpha$ $A$ imm$\alpha$(1) $A$ (where $A$ is a general address) is so common that many computers include an *increment* instruction ginc$\alpha$ $A$ that performs the same function. Another common instruction is gclear$\alpha$ $A$ for gmove$\alpha$ imm$\alpha$(0) $A$.

A different kind of observation leads to another optimization. Many jump instructions transfer control to locations that are not far away. (The slr1 instruction of the $S$ machine capitalizes on this.) Therefore, many machines have a special category of control-transfer instructions, which we shall call *branch instructions* (this terminology is not universal). Branch instructions include a short *offset* from the current PC value to designate the target location; they are thus a special (limited) case of PC-relative addressing, using short offsets. Branches can be used only for control transfers that do not go farther than the distance that can be expressed as a short offset.

- *Variable instruction formats.* This is really a variant of short-form instructions. Often, the full flexibility of the three-address format is not needed. For example, the operation $A = A + B$ can be written as gadd4 dir($A$) dir($B$) dir($A$), but it can also be written as g2add4 dir($B$) dir($A$) by using a two-address format for gadd4. Because a two-address form is often sufficient, some machines (for example, the VAX-11) offer *both* two- and three-address forms of many instructions. Many other machines offer *only* the two-address forms.

- *Reduced orthogonality.* The $G$ machine's architecture is highly *orthogonal*, in the sense that any addressing form can be used with any instruction. In the quest to provide shorter encodings for frequently occurring operations, many designers place restrictions on the addressing forms that can be used in various contexts. For example, many machines require that one or both operands of most instructions be in a register, offering the most general addressing modes only in expanded-format load and store instructions. Orthogonality is highly prized by compiler implementors because it means that preparing an operand for, say, a multiplication need not be performed differently from preparing an operand for an addition: Wherever the operand is located, it will be equally accessible to either instruction.

Incorporating these optimizations into general-register machines makes higher performance possible, but at the cost of increased complexity, both in the processor hardware and in the algorithm for generating machine code from higher-level languages. In practice, the pressure for performance is strong enough to force a number of these compromises on any real architecture.

## 15.5 Procedure Linkage

The machine instructions gcall and grtn, listed in table 15.23, provide the necessary mechanism for procedure linkage. The instruction gcall pushes the contents of the program counter (which points to the instruction following the gcall) onto the stack and then branches to the specified address. Control is returned to the calling program via a grtn instruction, which pops the return address and reinstalls it in the program counter. Thus the last instruction executed by a procedure will, in general, be a grtn. Note that it is vital that the procedure maintain stack discipline so that the return address popped by the grtn will be the pointer to the instruction following the gcall.

This set of procedure-linkage instructions includes much less protocol than the procedure-linkage instructions of the $S$ machine. Although many general-register machines have more elaborate procedure-linkage instructions than the $G$ machine, they tend to be simpler than the $S$-machine instructions. One reason for the complexity of the procedure support on the $S$ machine is that the $S$ machine's only medium for communication between caller and procedure is the stack. This becomes awkward unless special instructions such as srtn$\alpha$ are provided to perform the necessary shuffling of data on the stack. General-register machines, however, can use registers for communication. Thus procedure linkage on general-register machines is more likely to involve user-defined conventions that pass information

**Table 15.23** Procedure-linkage instructions.

| Operation | Operand addresses | Function performed |
|-----------|-------------------|--------------------|
| gcall | $A$ | $push4[\langle\mathrm{PC}\rangle];$ $\mathrm{PC}^4 \leftarrow E_A$ |
| grtn | | $\mathrm{PC} \leftarrow pop4[\ ]$ |

```
| The main program:

main:   ...
        gmove4  imm4(A)   r(1)   | Address of array in r(1).
        gmove4  imm4(N)   r(2)   | Number of elements in r(2).
        gcall   dir(sum)         | To compute sum.
        gmove4    r(0)    ...    | Return from sum; result in r(0).
        ...


A:      LONG(1)                  | Array of values to be added.
        LONG(37)
        ...


| The subroutine:

sum:    gmove4  imm4(0)   r(0)        | Accumulator <- 0.

loop:   gadd4   posti(1)  r(0) r(0) | Add in next array element.
        gsub4   r(2)    imm4(1) r(2) | Count down number of elements.
        gtest4  r(2)                 | Any left?
        gjgt    dir(loop)            | If so, keep looping.

        grtn                         | Else return to caller.
```

**Figure 15.24** Subroutine-call example on the $G$ machine.

through registers, rather than the wired-in, stack-oriented protocol of the $S$ machine. A simple subroutine to compute the sum of an array of consecutive longwords, and a program fragment that calls it, are shown in figure 15.24. Note that the subroutine takes its two arguments (the address of the array and the number of words of data it contains) in registers R1 and R2, respectively, and leaves its result (the sum) in R0.

This argument-passing convention, and indeed the coding of the subroutine itself, is typical of hand-coded assembly-language programming in that it exploits specific properties of the program at hand to improve code efficiency and compactness. Passing parameters in registers, for example, is workable only as long as the number of parameters does not exceed the number of available registers; hence compilers typically use the more general convention of passing parameters on the stack. Similarly, the use of postincrement addressing to access consecutive array elements is feasible only as long as the addressing structure of the machine closely matches the size and layout of the array; hence a more general (and less efficient) array-indexing scheme is likely to be found in compiled code.

The gap between the efficiencies of compiled and hand-coded programs presents a continuing challenge to compiler designers, and a number of sophisticated compilers that rival the coding efficiency of assembly-language wizards have been produced. Such compilers typically recognize the special cases exploited by the assembly-language coder (such as the efficiency, in a particular case, of passing arguments in registers) as well as the idiosyncrasies of the target machine, taking advantage of them where applicable.

The value of such highly optimizing compilers remains controversial, however, since their most effective use requires the high-level-language programmer to be aware of the program structures that can be heavily optimized. This requires some sophistication regarding the target machine as well as the internal structure of the compiler, a qualification that belies considerably the purported advantages of high-level-language programming.

A more satisfactory approach to closing the efficiency gap between compiled and hand-produced code is, in large part, the responsibility of computer architects. The design of simple, uniform machine languages to serve well-understood code-generation algorithms tends to decrease the importance of assembly-language wizardry in the production of efficient programs; indeed, the interests of both the computer industry and its consumers would be well served if the implementation of a compiler were a required step in every new machine design.

In the typical compiled implementation in which arguments and local variables are kept on the stack, rather than in registers, indexed addressing modes may be used to access them efficiently. In our sample machine, a general address of the form $ix(-n,SP)$ can be used to refer to the $n$th byte from the top of the stack; by keeping track of the address of each local variable relative to the current SP contents, a compiler can use SP-relative addressing to access local variables. If the stack is used to store temporary results during expression evaluation, however, this approach has the disadvantage that the distance from a particular local variable to the top of the stack varies with the number of temporary results currently on the stack; a new offset $n$ must be computed for each reference to the variable, taking into account the number of stacked temporaries at the point of that reference.

While many compilers perform this bookkeeping and implement SP-relative access to local variables, a simpler scheme dedicates a general register, say R13, as a *base-of-frame pointer*. At procedure entry, the SP is copied into this register, whose contents then remain constant throughout the execution of the procedure. Each local variable can then be referred to by a general address of the form $ix(n,13)$, where $n$ is a constant. Similarly, if we adopt the convention that procedure arguments are pushed by the calling procedure immediately prior to the gcall, arguments can be accessed by fixed (negative) offsets from R13.

```
int AddUp(A, n)
 int *A,n;
  {    int sum, j;
       sum = 0;
       for (j = 0; j < n; j = j+1) sum = sum + A[j];
       return sum;
  }
```

**Figure 15.25**  Procedure to sum the $n$ elements of an array $A$.

Figure 15.25 shows a simple procedure AddUp that takes two arguments and has two local variables. A simple compiler that passes arguments on the stack (pushing them in order from left to right) might produce the assembly-language code for this procedure given in figure 15.26. The four symbol definitions at the start of this figure define offsets from R13 that correspond to the addresses containing the arguments and local variables. Note that the procedure's value is returned in R0 and that the called procedure preserves the contents of all other registers; R13, in particular, is saved on the stack and restored prior to the procedure return. Note also that the array $A$ is passed to AddUp as a *pointer* to the array in memory: The program avoids copying the data in the array onto the stack.

Figure 15.27 depicts the stack during the execution of the procedure. It shows a stack frame for the procedure AddUp that resembles the stack frames of procedures on the $S$ machine. The exit sequence in the compiled code for AddUp deallocates all of the stack frame except for the arguments A and n, leaving to the caller the responsibility for popping these. Figure 15.28 shows code for a typical call to AddUp.

Major issues relating to the subroutine call interface on general-register machines include the following:

- *How are arguments passed?*  We have seen that the most general argument-passing scheme is to push the arguments on the stack, but it is also possible to use hybrid schemes in which the first few arguments are passed in registers and the remainder on the stack, in an effort to make better use of the registers and reduce stack manipulations.

- *Who performs stack maintenance?*  If arguments are pushed on the stack, then they must be popped off sometime. Responsibility for this may be allocated to the exit sequence of the subroutine (as in the srtn$\alpha$ instruction of the $S$ machine) or to the return sequence of the caller (as in figure 15.28 and perhaps the majority of general-register machines).

- *Who saves registers?*  If a register is used for different purposes by both caller and subroutine, its value must be saved during the subroutine call so that its value in the context of the caller can be restored upon procedure return. Perhaps the most common register-save discipline is for a subroutine to save (in its entry sequence) and restore (in its exit sequence) any registers that it uses (though some compiled language implementations explicitly identify certain registers as scratch registers that can be used by a procedure without being saved). An

```
          | Offsets from base of frame for AddUp:

          A       =       -16     | First argument offset.
          N       =       -12     | Second argument offset.
          SUM     =       0       | Offset for sum.
          J       =       4       | Offset for j.

          B       =       13      | Register used as base-of-frame pointer.

          | The code for the procedure AddUp:

ADDUP:    gmove4     r(B)      push()          | Save old R13 to use as
          gmove4    r(SP)        r(B)          |    base-of-frame pointer.
          gadd4   imm4(8)       r(SP)   r(SP)  | Allocate space for sum j.
          gmove4  imm4(0)  ix(SUM,B)           | sum = 0.
          gmove4  imm4(0)    ix(J,B)           | j = 0.

LOOP:     gcmp4      ix(J,B)    ix(N,B)                | End test for loop.
          gjge    dir(BREAK)                           | j >= n; break loop.
          gash4      ix(J,B)    imm1(2)        push()  | Push j*4 to use
                                                       |   as a word-array index.
          gadd4      ix(A,B)      pop()        push()  | Compute address of A[j].
          gadd4    ipred(SP)  ix(SUM,B)    ix(SUM,B)   | sum = sum+A[j].
          gadd4      imm4(1)    ix(J,B)      ix(J,B)   | j = j+1.
          gjmp    dir(LOOP)

BREAK:    gmove4  ix(SUM,B)       r(0)         | Leave sum in R0 as result.
          gsub4       r(SP)    imm4(8)  r(SP)  | Deallocate local variables.
          gmove4      pop()       r(B)         | Restore previous R13 contents.
          grtn                                 | Exit.
```

**Figure 15.26** Simple compiled $G$-machine code for the program in figure 15.25.

| | | |
|---|---|---|
| | | |
| | (Caller's local variables) | |
| | (Caller's temporaries) | |
| ix(-16,B) | First argument: A | |
| ix(-12,B) | Second argument: n | |
| | Return address | ↓ |
| | Saved R13 | ↓ |
| ix(0,B) | sum | ↓ |
| ix(4,B) | j | increasing |
| | Temporaries | addresses |
| ix(0,SP) | (First unused location) | ↓ |

**Figure 15.27** Stack during execution of the program in figure 15.26.

```
        ...
        gmove4   imm4(ARRAY)  push()  | Address of the argument array.
        gmove4      imm4(5)    push()  | Number of elements in the array.
        gcall    dir(ADDUP)            | Call AddUp.
        gsub4       imm4(8)    r(SP)   | Pop the args off the stack.
        gmove4        r(0)      ...    | Value is returned in R0.
        ...


ARRAY:  LONG(1)               | The array to add up.
        LONG(4)
        LONG(9)
        LONG(16)
        LONG(25)
        ...
```

**Figure 15.28**  *G*-machine code to call AddUp(ARRAY,5).

equally tenable discipline is for the *caller* of a procedure to save any register values it will still need when the procedure returns. The only registers that really need to be saved are those used by *both* caller and procedure, but this information varies from one procedure call to the next; it is thus easier to adopt one of the more conservative strategies listed above.

This concern with saving and restoring registers is a noticeable complication to the business of calling procedures on the *G* machine. The price that we pay for the explicit availability of high-speed storage in the processor (that is, registers) is this explicit visibility of the details of managing the contents of that storage.

## 15.6 Register Allocation by Compilers

The program in figure 15.26 is quite unsophisticated in its use of the general registers. Registers R0, R13, and SP are used where required by the subroutine-call conventions, but where the address of $A[j]$ must be computed within the procedure, it is computed on the stack. The explicit visibility of registers in general-register machines is intended to encourage the use of fast storage within the processor where possible, as an alternative to the continual access to main memory that is implied by stack operations. This potential advantage can only be realized, however, if compilers for general-register machines generate code that actually uses the registers. Thus the simple compilation techniques discussed in the context of the *S* machine, although applicable to general-register machines, do not make effective use of such machines.

The principal new problem that arises in compiler design for general-register machines is the problem of *register allocation*. This problem is complicated by the fact that registers are a finite resource with multiple competing uses. Often, it is further complicated by a nonuniform register set, containing some registers that can be used only for certain purposes. The compiler must decide which registers to use for temporary results while evaluating expressions and which to reserve for longer-term use (examples of the latter are holding pointers to frequently accessed data structures). On top of this, if the register set is not uniform, the compiler must try to plan ahead so that results will be computed in registers from which they can be used directly, without first having to be copied into other registers. A substantial portion of modern compiler theory is devoted to solving these problems.

## 15.7 Traps

The hardware and microcode provisions for trap handling on general-register machines are typically quite minimalistic, in the same spirit as the `gcall` and `grtn` instructions. Typically, only a minimum amount of necessary data is saved immediately upon the occurrence of a trap, and responsibility for saving and restoring processor state is relegated to software wherever possible. Nevertheless, the context switches associated with these activities require somewhat more elaborate support than is required by procedure linkage. A typical supervisor-call instruction `gsvc`, modeled after the $S$ machine's `ssvc`, would load new values for the PC, SP, and PSW (including condition codes) from a designated trap vector, installing these new values after saving the PC, SP, and PSW pertaining to the user program. Often these values are saved by pushing them on the stack pointed to by the new SP value being loaded from the trap vector, just as in the case of `ssvc`. The trap-return instruction `gtrtn` would then restore the user's PC, SP, and PSW by popping them off the trap handler's stack. The $G$ machine has much more processor state than just the PC, SP, and PSW registers: to wit, all the other general registers. Typically, however, the saving and restoring of these registers is left up to the trap handler's software.

As in the $S$ machine, a trap handler for the $G$ machine will often consist of an assembly-language *stub* containing a call to a procedure that conducts the main business of handling the trap. In the case of the $G$ machine, this stub will be responsible for saving and restoring general registers, as well as calling the handler procedure and finally executing a `gtrtn` instruction to resume execution of the trapping program. As in the case of the $S$ machine, fault and interrupt handling on the $G$ machine differ little from instruction trap handling.

The $G$-machine trap-handling strategy just described is quite viable, but many variants are in common use. Perhaps most common, but somewhat more complex than the strategy just described, is a scheme using *two* stack-pointer registers, one for unprivileged user programs and the other for privileged operating-system code. In such a scheme, the stack-pointer register that currently serves as the SP is selected by a bit in the PSW (perhaps the same bit that indicates whether privileged instructions can be executed). Traps save and load only the PC and PSW; the SP in use will change if the newly loaded PSW selects a different stack-pointer register than the previously loaded PSW value. This scheme facilitates building a structure in which one stack is shared by all operating-system functions; the scheme in which the SP is loaded from the trap vector requires a separate stack area to be allocated for each different source of traps, if a trap can occur while the handler for another trap is running.

Traps and trap handling will be discussed in greater length in later chapters, but those discussions will be at the level of the trap-handling procedures shown in figures 13.7 and 14.44; for this reason, the details of operation of the `gsvc` and `gtrtn` instructions, and of the $G$ machine's fault and interrupt mechanisms, need not concern us any further here.

## 15.8 High-Performance Implementation Considerations

Architectures such as the $G$ machine pose a major challenge to high-performance pipelined processor implementors. Brief examination of some of the reasons for this will help us understand the kinds of instruction sets that are best for high-performance implementation. Basically, the $G$-machine instruction set strongly favors a sequential, rather than parallel, implementation. There are two major reasons for this:

- *Flexible instruction formats*. There are many different instruction formats on the $G$ machine, depending on the opcode and addressing modes used. This means that an instruction-fetch unit has to understand the opcode (so that it knows how many general addresses follow) and address-mode bytes (so that it knows how many bytes long each general address is). Although the $G$ machine's instruction-format flexibility offers great expressive power, it is easier to build a high-performance instruction-fetch unit as an automaton that knows which words to fetch from memory based on some very simple decision such as looking at a couple of bits in the opcode.

- *Side effects of address calculation*. Postincrement and predecrement addressing modes cause special problems because of instructions like `gadd4 ix(8,SP)` `pred(SP) ix(8,SP)` in which the two general addresses `ix(8,SP)` refer to different memory locations! Address modes such as postincrement or predecrement, which change register contents as a side effect of address calculation, force the specification of an evaluation order (for example, left to right), which must then be respected by all implementations. This leads to data dependencies that prevent parallel calculation of operand addresses (or at least require a preliminary check for pathological cases). High-performance machines will usually be seen not to have addressing modes that involve side effects.

Unfortunately, these negative comments apply precisely to some of the features of the $G$ machine that give it its notable expressive power and economy of mechanism, underscoring the constant tension in computer architecture between the user's requirements and the constraints of the implementation medium.

## 15.9 Summary

We have now covered the considerable distance between the technology of electronic digital components and the implementation of representative processors of contemporary design, and students with a good grasp of this body of material are entitled to feel confident that they know what modern computers are made of. However, the focus of chapters 10–15 on general-purpose processor design belies somewhat the more fundamental methodology they explore. An underlying theme of these chapters has been the use of *interpretation* as a technique for the implementation of complex systems. This is a tool of vastly wider applicability than just to the construction of general-purpose computers. Interpretive mechanisms play an important role in endless numbers of special-purpose systems, ranging from washing machines to radio communications equipment. They are a technology that belongs in every engineer's repertoire.

Now that we have explored two representative processor architectures—the $S$ and $G$ machines—and their microcoded implementation, we have seen some of the goals these abstractions are intended to achieve and the application of interpretation to their implementation. In chapter 16 we turn our attention to the architecture of memory systems—a central component of all von Neumann architectures. Following that (in chapter 17), we consider the $R$ machine, which illustrates an alternative approach to processor design: simplifying the machine language so that it can be implemented directly in hardware, skipping the step of microcode interpretation. We then turn to several topics more properly in the domain of *operating systems* and explore their impact on the design of computing hardware.

## 15.10 Context

The best-known and most influential commercial computers have been based on general-register architectures. These architectures may be said to have evolved, on the one hand, from three-address memory-oriented architectures by the addition of special fast registers that can serve as sources and destinations and, on the other hand, from one-address accumulator-based architectures by the addition of more accumulators or index registers, followed by rationalization and systematization of the resulting architecture. The IBM System/360 family of computers [Blaauw and Brooks 1964; Stevens 1964] brought general-register architectures into prominence, only to be succeeded by the IBM System/370 and later architectures [Siewiorek, Bell, and Newell 1982, pp. 829–855], all in essentially the same mold. Another notable general-register architecture was the Digital Equipment Corporation PDP-10 and its successors [Bell, Mudge, and McNamara 1978].

The DEC PDP-11 series [Bell et al. 1970; Bell, Mudge, and McNamara 1978] introduced several innovations on the general-register motif, such as the use of the program counter and stack pointer as general registers. These ideas were further elaborated in the DEC VAX-11 series [Strecker 1978; Bell, Mudge, and McNamara 1978], whose treatment of addressing modes furnishes the most direct inspiration for the addressing modes of the $G$ machine.

The development in the mainframe and minicomputer markets away from ad hoc multiple-register architectures and toward flexible general-register architectures has been recapitulated in the microcomputer domain. The processor that, more than any other, launched the microcomputer revolution was the Intel 8008, introduced in 1972. This was followed by increasingly complex, sophisticated, and regular general-register microprocessors: in 1974, the 8080, and then in 1978 the 8086 [Liu and Gibson 1984], used in the influential IBM personal computer. This evolution, which continues to this day as improved variants on the 8086 are released, is chronicled in Siewiorek, Bell, and Newell [1982, pp. 615–646]. Other manufacturers' microprocessors, such as the Motorola MC68000, the National 32032, and their descendants, have gone even further in the direction of the regular, general-register architectures typified by the $G$ machine.

Register allocation is a major challenge in compiling good code for general-register architectures; register-allocation techniques are thoroughly discussed in Aho, Sethi, and Ullman [1986].

## 15.11 Problems

### Problem 15.1
One of the purported advantages of the $G$ machine is that special-purpose registers such as SP and PC are implemented as part of the general-register set of the machine. One implication of this is that instructions that make implicit use of these registers (such as jumps and calls/returns) are really just variations on the gmove$\alpha$ instruction. Write a single gmove instruction to replace the jump instruction gjmp dir(destination).

### Problem 15.2
Does the $G$-machine instruction gmove4 dir(A) dir(B) do the same thing as gmove4 iposti(PC) LONG(A) iposti(PC) LONG(B)? Explain.

### Problem 15.3
Does the $G$-machine instruction gmove1 dir(A) dir(B) do the same thing as gmove1 iposti(PC) LONG(A) iposti(PC) LONG(B)? Explain.

### Problem 15.4
Write an $S$-machine code fragment that produces an equivalent result in main memory and the stack as the $G$-machine instruction gadd4 dir(1000) imm4(3) posti(SP).

### Problem 15.5
Write an $S$-machine code fragment that produces an equivalent result in main memory and the stack as the following $G$-machine instruction sequence:

```
gmove4 imm4(300) r(6)
gadd4  posti(6)  ir(6)  ipred(SP)
```

### Problem 15.6
Give a sequence of $S$-machine instructions that has the same effect on memory as the following $G$-machine instruction sequence. (You need not worry about mimicking the effect on R5.)

```
gmove4    dir(300)  r(5)
gadd2     imm2(77)  ix(100,5) ix(200,5)
```

**Table 15.29** `slta` instruction.

| Instruction | Stack before→after | Operation |
|---|---|---|
| `slta`$(n^2)$ | $\rightarrow a^4$ | Load temporary address ($n^2$ is a 16-bit 2's complement offset from SP): $push4[\langle \text{SP} \rangle + n]$ |

## Problem 15.7

Give a single $G$-machine instruction that has the same effect on memory as the following $S$-machine instruction sequence. (You need not worry about mimicking the effect on the stack.)

```
sc4(100)
sl4
sc4(200)
sl4
sc4(300)
sadd4
ss4
```

## Problem 15.8

Which $G$-machine addressing mode is used to specify an immediate (instruction-stream constant) source operand? What happens if this addressing mode is used as a destination operand?

## Problem 15.9

Which, if any, of the following instructions cause a transfer of control to location 3? (Be careful. There may be more than one that works!) For each instruction that does not work, briefly explain what's wrong.

```
gjmp     dir(3)
gjmp     imm4(3)
gjmp     r(3)
gmove1   imm1(3)    r(15)
gmove4   imm4(3)    r(15)
gmove1   dir(3)     pred(15)
```

## Problem 15.10

Assume that the $S$ machine's instruction set is augmented with the `slta` instruction described in table 15.29. Using this instruction, show a fragment of $S$-machine code equivalent to the following $G$-machine code, which does not use any registers except PC and SP:

```
gadd4 pop() imm4(23) i(1000)
```

Explain why the `slta` instruction is useful in writing this $S$-machine code.

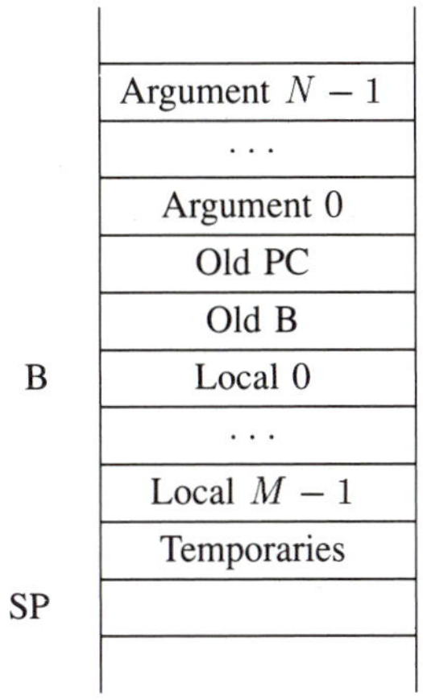

**Figure 15.30** A possible $G$-machine stack-frame format.

### Problem 15.11

The putative $G$-machine instruction $\texttt{gsext}\alpha$ $A,B$ sign-extends $\langle E_A \rangle^\alpha$ to a quantity of length $2\alpha$ and stores the result in the $2\alpha$-byte location at $E_B$. The sign extension is done in the same manner as by the $S$ machine's $\texttt{ssext}\alpha$ instruction (see table 14.1). Write a microcode handler for $\texttt{gsext1}$.

### Problem 15.12

Write a microcode handler for a putative $G$-machine instruction $\texttt{gffo4}$ $A,B$ (find first one), which performs the operation $E_B^1 \leftarrow FFO(\langle E_A \rangle^4)$, where $FFO(X)$ is the number of the lowest-numbered bit position in $X$ that contains a 1. In other words, $FFO(1) = 0$, $FFO(2) = 1$, $FFO(4) = 2$, $FFO(5) = 0$, $FFO(6) = 1$, and so on.

### Problem 15.13

The putative $G$-machine instruction $\texttt{gsubcc}\alpha$ $A,B,C$ performs the same operation $E_C^\alpha \leftarrow \langle E_A \rangle^\alpha - \langle E_B \rangle^\alpha$ as is performed by $\texttt{gsub}\alpha$, except that $\texttt{gsubcc}\alpha$ also sets the $S$, $Z$, and $C$ bits of the condition-code register CC according to the result of the subtraction, as $\texttt{gcmp}\alpha$ does. Write a microcode handler for $\texttt{gsubcc2}$.

### Problem 15.14

Another putative $G$-machine instruction, $\texttt{gjle}\alpha$ $A,B,C$, performs the operation $\text{PC}^4 \leftarrow E_C^4$ if $\langle E_A \rangle^\alpha \leq \langle E_B \rangle^\alpha$; otherwise, it just continues to the next instruction. Write a microcode handler for $\texttt{gjle1}$.

### Problem 15.15

Write a sequence of two $\texttt{gmove}\alpha$ instructions to replace the call instruction $\texttt{gcall}$ $\texttt{dir(subroutine)}$.

### Problem 15.16

Write a single $\texttt{gmove}\alpha$ instruction to replace the return instruction $\texttt{grtn}$.

## Problem 15.17

A C compiler for the $G$ machine uses the stack-frame structure shown in figure 15.30. The calling procedure pushes the arguments onto the stack in *reverse* order, then executes a gcall instruction to transfer control. Register 13 (R13) is reserved by the compiler to serve as a base pointer (B). Registers 14 and 15 hold, as always, the SP and PC, respectively.

A. What should a procedure's entry sequence look like?

B. Given this stack-frame organization, does it make more sense (for example, does it take fewer memory references) for the caller or the callee to pop the arguments from the stack at the time of subroutine return? Or does it make no difference? Explain your reasoning.

C. To allocate space for $M$ bytes of local variables, the $S$-machine instruction salloc($M$) is used. With the given stack-frame organization, what $G$-machine instruction can perform this function? (Include opcode and operands.)

D. Which instruction from the list below might a compiler generate to load the value of a local variable into R2? (For this and the following parts, assume the stack-frame organization of figure 15.30.)

```
1.  gmove4 ix(0,B) r(2)

2.  gmove4 iix(0,B) r(2)

3.  gmove4 ix(-4,B) r(2)

4.  gmove4 ix(-12,B) r(2)

5.  gmove4 iix(-12,B) r(2)

6.  gmove1 ix(2000,3) r(2)

7.  gmove4 imm4(1000) r(2)

8.  gmove4 dir(1000) r(2)

9.  gadd4 dir(2000) r(3) r(2)

10. gadd4 r(B) imm4(-12) r(2)
```

E. Which instruction from the list might be used to load the value of an argument into R2?

F. Which instruction from the list might be used to load the value of a static (global) variable into R2?

G. Which instruction from the list might be used to load the $i$th element of a statically allocated array of characters into a register, where $i$ is a variable whose value is in a register?

H. Which instruction from the list might be used to load the address of an argument into a register?

```
struct Employee
  {    int Salary;
       int YearsOfService;
       char Name[32];
  }



          .
          .
          .


struct Employee *(A[N]);
struct Employee *temp;
int I, J;



          .
          .
          .


for (I = 1; I < N; I = I + 1)
 {
  /* Invariant: A[0..I-1] is sorted */
  /* Goal: sift A[I] down to its */
  /*       proper place in A[0..I-1] */
  J = I;
  while ((J > 0) && (A[J-1]->Salary > A[J]->Salary)) do
    {
      temp = A[J];
      A[J] = A[J-1];
      A[J-1] = temp;
      J = J - 1;
    }
 }
```

**Figure 15.31**  Program to sort a data base of employee records.

### Problem 15.18

The C procedure `coeff` given in figure 14.52 calculates the coefficient of the $m$th term in the binomial expansion $(x + y)^n$. Translate `coeff` into $G$-machine assembly code. Explain the interface to your $G$-machine code—that is, where the arguments are put, where the return result is found, and which register contents are left undisturbed by a call to `coeff`. Be sure to comment your code.

### Problem 15.19

How many bytes will the assembly-code procedure you wrote for the last problem assemble into?

### Problem 15.20

Figure 15.31 shows some code for sorting data bases of employee records using a certain $O(N^2)$ algorithm. (The array A to be sorted is an array of N *pointers* to Employee records; it is thus declared as `struct Employee *(A[N]);`).

A. Describe the layout in the $G$ machine's storage of the `Employee` structure, assuming that each `int` is allocated 4 bytes. (You may wish to refer to the description of structures in C in appendix 1.) ·

B. The program sorts the pointers in the array `A[0...N-1]` in order of increasing salaries by starting with the sorted subarray `A[0...0]` and then inserting the elements `A[1]` through `A[N-1]` in the correct position in that subarray. (This is an "in-place" algorithm in that it mutates the original array rather than allocating a new array for the result.) The array `A` and the `Employee` structures to which `A`'s elements point are stored in the MAYBE machine's DRAM memory. Write a $G$-machine subroutine for the sort described above.

1. Assume that when your routine is called, the size `N` of the array is stored in register R1. (`N` is a 4-byte number.)

2. Assume that the $G$-machine assembler has allocated space for the array starting at address `A` of DRAM memory. Thus, to refer to element `A[j]` of the array, use the addressing mode `ix(A,Rj)`, where the contents of register `Rj` are computed from the current value of $j$.

3. You may use any $G$-machine registers, but you must save the old contents of those registers and restore them on exit from the routine.

4. Since arguments are passed to this routine in registers, rather than on the stack, you need not be concerned with the structure of the $G$-machine stack frame.

C. Repeat part B, assuming instead of point 2 above that your routine is called with a second argument, in register R2. The address in this register is a pointer to the start of the array `A` in DRAM. Since the array could be located anywhere in memory, you must use pointers in registers to access array elements. What addressing mode will you use here? Write the program using this addressing mode. Which approach (this one or that of part B) leads to a more compact program?

D. Explain what specific changes must be made to the $G$-machine programs of parts B and C if we want to sort employees in increasing order of years of service instead of salaries.


## Problem 15.21

Typical procedure-linkage conventions for general-register machines require the caller (rather than the callee) to pop procedure arguments from the stack on return. Why is it awkward for the callee to perform this step?


## Problem 15.22

Late one night in the lab you hear a strange noise. "Whrrr, click click click dmp." You glance around, but no one else is there. Nervously you return to your machine and notice a strange line of text in the middle of the screen:

```
!retupmoc eht edisni deppart m'I   !pleh esaelP
```

The message is clear, but the order of the characters has been reversed. Write a *G*-machine program that will take a message such as this one and decode it. You can assume that (1) the string you must reverse is stored in DRAM memory; (2) the address of the string's first byte is given to you in R0; and (3) the address of the string's last byte is given to you in R1. Your program should reverse the string "in place"; that is, the reversed string should occupy the same memory locations as the original string.

### Problem 15.23

Suppose we use a calling convention in the *G* machine similar to that of the *S* machine:

- We reserve R13 to be a base register and call it B, as in the *S* machine.
- The caller pushes a block of arguments onto the stack.
- The caller pushes old SP and old B onto the stack. Old SP should point to the first byte in the block of arguments.
- The caller executes the usual `gcall` instruction.
- The callee sets B to point to the current top of the stack.
- The callee allocates space for local variables on the stack, as in `salloc(+n)`.
- The callee executes its code, computing a result on the top of the stack.
- The callee copies the result from the top of the stack down over the first argument.
- The callee pops the stack up to and including its locals, as in `salloc(−n)`.
- The callee executes the standard `grtn` instruction.
- The caller restores its old B and adjusts the SP so that the result of the call is at the top of the stack.

Consider the following C function and corresponding call:

```
int f(a,b)
  int a, b;
    { int j;       /* Only one local variable. */
      . . .

    }

f(23, 37);
```

Assume that all integers are 4 bytes long. Show the *G*-machine code executed by the *caller* for steps 2, 3, 4, and 11. (In other words, show the code for a call to f.) Also show the *G*-machine code executed by the *callee* for steps 5, 6, 8, 9, and 10. (In other words, show f's entry and exit sequences.) Comment your code, indicating which steps are performed by which instructions.

### Problem 15.24

Will the calling conventions established in the last problem work for the following C procedure? Explain.

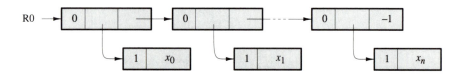

**Figure 15.32** A list structure.

```
int g()
  {......}
```

## *Problem 15.25*

Consider doing operations on lists and trees stored in memory. To build the lists and trees we shall use two different types of nodes (which are just record structures in memory):

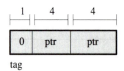

The first type of node has a 1-byte tag field that contains the number 0, followed by two 4-byte fields that contain either other memory addresses (`car` and `cdr` pointers) or −1 to indicate a `nil` pointer. The second type of node has a 1-byte tag field, which contains the number 1, followed by a 4-byte integer.

Consider the structure shown in figure 15.32. The `car` of a list node always points to an integer node; the `cdr` of a list node is either `nil` or points to another list node.

A. The program of figure 15.33 takes a pointer to the head of the list and returns the sum of all the $x_i$. The argument is passed in R0, and the sum is returned in R1. What will be the maximum stack depth due to this procedure? (You cannot give a number here, but you can give the maximum depth in terms of some property of the list.)

B. Suppose we replace the last two instructions in `list_sum` with the single instruction

    gjmp dir(do_next)

Will the program still correctly compute the sum? Why or why not? With this modification, what will be the maximum stack depth?

```
list_sum: gmove4 imm4(0) r(1)        | Intialize R1.

 do_next: gcmp4 r(0) imm4(-1)        | nil?
          gjne dir(add_x)            | If no, add and recurse.
          grtn                       | If yes, done, return.

   add_x: gmove4 ix(1,0) r(2)        | car pointer to R2.
          gadd4 ix(1,2) r(1) r(1)    | R1 ← <R1> + xj.
          gmove4 ix(5,0) r(0)        | cdr pointer to R0.
          gcall dir(do_next)         | Recursive call.
          grtn                       | Return.
```

**Figure 15.33**  Program to sum the elements of a list.

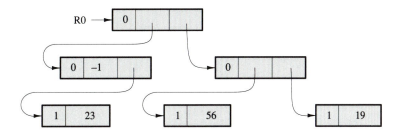

**Figure 15.34**  A tree structure.

### Problem 15.26

Consider tree structures with internal nodes of the type we have tagged with a 0 and leaves of the type tagged 1; figure 15.34 shows an example. We want to write a recursive program with three specifications: (1) It should have one argument—a pointer to the root of the tree passed in R0; (2) it should return the sum of all the leaves in R1; and (3) it should work on trees of any depth, not just on our specific example. Complete the following code at the "···" so that the program meets the specifications. Comment your code. Add no more than 10 instructions.

```
Tree_sum:    gcmp4 r(0) imm4(-1)       | nil?
             gjne dir(LeafOrNode)      | If no, then jump.

Nil:         gmove4 imm4(0) r(1)       | If yes, return 0.
             grtn

LeafOrNode:  gcmp1 ir(0) imm1(0)       | Node type?
             gjeq dir(Node)            | If internal node, jump.

Leaf:        gmove4 ix(1,0) r(1)       | If leaf, return value.
             grtn

Node:
                 .
                 .
                 .

             grtn
```

# 16 Memory Architectures

Nearly every successful contemporary computer is a form of the classic *von Neumann machine* shown in figure 16.1, which separates the computation and memory functions into physically distinct hardware modules. Interactions between processor and memory are based on a model of the entire memory as a uniformly accessible array of constant-sized *words*, consecutively numbered with unique *addresses*. This set of addresses provides the lowest-level mechanism for *naming* stored data; a stored datum may be accessed by reference to the address of the memory location at which it is stored. The resulting single, global name space (*address space*) is a key element of the von Neumann model.

This arrangement has a number of clear advantages. First, the functional partitioning of a computer into processor and memory serves the important engineering goal of breaking large systems into component subsystems, each having clear specifications. The characterization of a memory subsystem in terms of addresses and locations is concise, unambiguous, and relatively easy to deal with conceptually.

Second, the von Neumann model is straightforward to implement. Typically, a single mechanism (for example, a *memory bus* consisting of three-state address, data, and control lines) is used for processor-memory communications. The cost of this single mechanism can be amortized over a number of memory modules, leading to a small cost per bit in computer systems with large amounts of primary memory. It is quite easy to conceive of and implement a scheme for deducing the physical location of a memory element (say, on a circuit board) from its address, thereby providing natural schemes for decoding addresses and producing local control signals for each element.

Finally, the uniform access time of each memory word makes the performance of von Neumann machines highly predictable and reasonably fast. Alternative schemes using serial-access memory (such as magnetic tape and rotating drums) have been explored but then mostly discarded because of the much higher average memory access time they require for typical computations.

Despite these advantages and the ubiquity of von Neumann machines, there is an emerging consensus among computer architects that the *von Neumann bottleneck* (as it is sometimes called) between processor and memory modules is the major stumbling block in the evolution of high-performance computers. The limitations imposed on current machines by this traditional processor-memory interface fall in two classes:

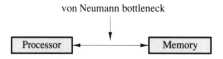

**Figure 16.1** A von Neumann machine.

- *Speed.* A single interface to the entire memory of a large computer typically dictates that processor-memory transactions be *serialized*, since at most one transaction can be going on at any time. The communication link itself establishes an upper bound on the rate at which data can be exchanged between processor and memory, which limits the potential for exploiting concurrency in either or both of these modules. For example, if the memory interface described in chapter 9 is capable of at most one transaction every microsecond, the machine will be unable to exceed about 1 million instructions per second, no matter how fast we make the processor itself.

- *Size.* The global address space of the von Neumann machine leads to the run-time representation of locations (that is, addresses) as fixed-size binary integers, where the size is chosen to hold the largest anticipated memory address. Since instructions, registers, and data structures must include space for memory addresses, the maximum address size becomes a constant that is built into a machine's architecture in a fundamental way. Thus every von Neumann machine has a fixed address-space size, which limits the amount of memory it (and any of its successors that claim program compatibility) can support.

Primarily as a result of these considerations, a major current research goal in computer architecture is the development of alternative computer organizations that distribute memory elements among processors rather than concentrating memory in a single physical module. One popular criterion for such systems is that multiple transactions between independent processing elements and their local memories be concurrent, thereby improving performance through the exploitation of parallelism. A related research goal is the development of a scheme for naming stored data that avoids the global address space of the von Neumann machine and hence the constraints on the total amount of addressable storage in a system. Unfortunately, no one has demonstrated a clear solution to these problems, and so the von Neumann machine and its variants remain the state of the art.

These research efforts have, however, a basis for optimism. In contrast to the uniformly accessible global address space of the von Neumann model, high-level programs and data structures exhibit a rich structure, with accessibility requirements that vary widely among different storage accesses. Programs are typically organized into small modules (for example, as *procedures*), each of which needs access to a tiny fraction of the total system storage. Modern programming languages are designed to encourage such modularity and to make explicit the requirements of each module for communication with external program and data modules. It would seem that an appropriately organized machine could exploit this structure, perhaps by physically localizing each procedure and its little subuniverse of data, promoting both parallelism and local rather than global naming conventions. Researchers are currently looking in this general direction (as well as others) for a viable alternative to the von Neumann organization; their success might well constitute a revolutionary development in the field of computer architecture.

While awaiting this revolution, system architects have pursued related but slightly less lofty goals with considerable success. In this chapter we shall examine some accepted, successful, and widely used approaches to exploiting the high-level structure of programs and data *within* the basic von Neumann model. They represent compromises, in that they achieve some of the performance advantages sought by proponents of nonstandard machine organizations while maintaining compatibility with the conceptual basis and programming methodology that surround present-day computers.

The approach described in this chapter embraces the von Neumann model as an interface specification rather than an implementation; it allows liberties to be taken with the implementation of memory as long as they conform, at the programming level, to the semantics associated with a single, uniformly accessible address space. Thus we use the analogy with physical memories to define a *memory abstraction*, or *virtual memory*, that admits a variety of implementations along the cost/performance trade-off.

The virtual memory of the machines described in chapters 14 and 15 consists of $2^{32}$ bytes that can be read or written. That is, the processor can read or write a byte at any one of $2^{32}$ distinct addresses. It is uncommon, however, for all of the 4 *billion* bytes represented to be implemented out of the fastest memory technology—even present-day semiconductor memory costs about a dollar per 4K bytes, so the price of such a memory would be *at least* a million dollars. Fortunately, as we shall see, the behavior required by the processor can be simulated by less expensive schemes.

The size and cost problem is intimately tied to the performance problem, since one can buy for the same price either a small amount of fast memory or a larger amount of slower memory. Given this trade-off, reducing the access time entails either decreasing the memory size or increasing the total cost. The techniques described in this chapter effectively "change the rules of the game": By adding some complexity to a memory system, we can dramatically reduce the cost of a memory of a given size and performance level. These techniques all have one thing in common: They exploit knowledge about the typical behavior of programs to achieve better average memory system performance.

## 16.1 Locality of Reference and Other Regularities of Memory Access

Programs do not access memory locations at random. If, for a typical program running on a conventional computer, we plot the memory addresses accessed against time, we are likely to observe a substantial clustering of data points, as suggested in figure 16.2. Such clustering indicates that during short time intervals of a pro-

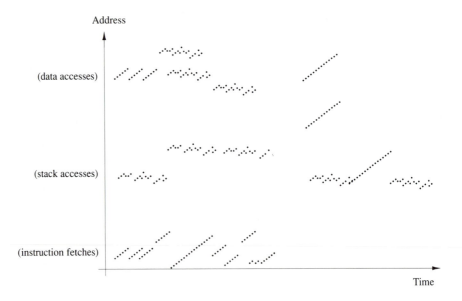

**Figure 16.2** Typical memory-reference patterns.

gram's execution, its memory accesses tend to be concentrated in a small number of small regions of the address space.

The phrase *locality of reference* refers to this tendency. The phenomenon of locality of reference is not a mystical principle, but rather a result of machine features and standard programming techniques. The bulk of memory references for our $S$, $G$, and $R$ machines, for example, fall into one of three categories: instruction fetches, accesses to local variables and temporaries, and accesses to data structures not in the current stack frame. At any point in a program's execution, we are likely to observe repeated memory accesses to several independent regions corresponding, say, to the locations of the instructions for the current procedure, the current stack frame, and perhaps one or two data structures currently being manipulated.

One of the most predictable patterns of memory access arises from the instruction stream. Since jumps are relatively rare—the average number of instructions executed between jumps may range between two or three for tight loops or complicated conditionals to several hundred for lengthy numerical calculations—it is highly probable that the next, say, 5–10 bytes after the location currently addressed by the program counter will be needed by the processor in the near future. Tight program loops show up on our diagram as regular sawtooth patterns, but even relatively undisciplined programs laden with local branching still generate sequences of references to consecutive addresses, punctuated by occasional discontinuities. Generally, an instruction fetch from address $x$ implies that, with very high probability, the next instruction fetch will be from address $x + 1$. Moreover, the probability of instruction fetches in the near future from locations $x + n$ for small $n$ is con-

*Memory Architectures*

siderably enhanced, since the likelihood of a jump among the next $n$ instructions decreases as $n$ becomes small. The probability of instruction fetches from locations $x - n$ is increased as well, owing to loops and similar program structures. These phenomena create a "hot spot" of frequent accesses in the vicinity of the current program counter value. Of course, other memory accesses to data locations, often following relatively unrelated patterns of their own, will be intermixed with instruction fetches.

In contemporary programming, most data accesses involve local variables and consequently reference locations within the local stack frame. In addition, the stack is often used for transient data such as temporary values computed during expression evaluation. These two classes of access lead to a second "hot spot" in the reference patterns of a running program, located at a region surrounding the current top-of-stack address. This region tends to change in a relatively continuous way as call and return instructions are executed.

Accesses to external data are not nearly as constrained by the architecture of the machine as are stack and instruction accesses. Nonetheless, they typically exhibit considerable regularity. Consider an array, for example. A programmed operation (such as clearing, transposing, or array multiplication) that accesses one element of the array is likely to access other elements as well; since the array occupies contiguous storage, this tendency directly reinforces our locality observation. Other data structures, such as payroll records and character strings, tend to be referenced in similar activity clusters.

Generalizing from these observations, we can summarize the locality principle qualitatively as follows:

· · · · · · · · · · · · · · · · · · · · · · · · · · · · · · · · · · · · · · · · · · · · · · · · · · · · · · · · · ·

***Locality of reference*** Reference to location $X$ at time $t$ implies that the probability of access to location $X + \Delta X$ at time $t + \Delta t$ increases as $\Delta X$ and $\Delta t$ approach zero.

· · · · · · · · · · · · · · · · · · · · · · · · · · · · · · · · · · · · · · · · · · · · · · · · · · · · · · · · · ·

It is common to think of this locality as consisting of two components: *temporal* locality, which refers to the propensity for repeated references to the *same* location, and *spatial* locality, which refers to the likelihood of accesses to *different* but nearby locations within small time delays $\Delta t$.

Another important regularity exhibited by most processors is that writes are much less frequent than reads. One reason is that all instruction fetches are reads. Another reason is that many processor operations (such as addition) read more operands than they write results. A ratio of reads to writes of at least 2:1 is to be expected; greater ratios are often observed.

The following sections discuss a variety of techniques that exploit such regularities. These memory architectures are tuned to work well for common patterns of memory access but not for accesses made at random or made in unusual patterns.

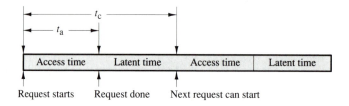

**Figure 16.3** Timing of successive accesses to noninterleaved memory.

## 16.2 Interleaved Memory Modules

The technique of *memory interleaving* exploits the timing of typical memory devices. The access cycle of devices used for primary memory in a computer (usually dynamic RAM chips) is divided into two phases. The first phase consists of the time from the initial access request made by the processor until the completion of the processor's role in that access. For a read, this occurs when the value is copied by the processor; for a write, when the memory has copied the value to be written. The second phase consists of *latent time* needed by the memory for housekeeping before it can be available for another access. For many memory devices, including dynamic RAM, a read is destructive—the accessed memory cell is cleared—so the memory's read circuitry must write back the accessed data after it is read. It is also common for a memory to acknowledge a write once the data are stably latched in the memory module but before completion of the (relatively slower) process of updating the actual cell. The time for the two phases of a memory access is called the *cycle time* $t_c$ (read and write cycle times differ, but for contemporary memories they are typically in the 100–500 ns range). The time for the first phase is called the *access time* $t_a$. The ratio of access time to cycle time is often about 1:2.

Suppose a processor needs to fetch a long operand stored in two consecutive memory locations. It will make two references to memory, one for location $X$ and one for location $X + 1$. If the locations are stored in the same memory module, the minimum time the processor must wait for these values to be available will be $t_c + t_a$, as shown in figure 16.3.

If locations $X$ and $X + 1$ are in different memory modules, the accesses to memory can be overlapped in time. That is, once location $X$ is copied by the processor, the access to location $X+1$ can be started while the module containing $X$ is still executing the second phase of its cycle, as shown in figure 16.4. If the processor is very fast, the time needed to make these two accesses will approach $2t_a$, a considerable improvement.

A memory organization that implements this improvement is shown in figure 16.5. This organization is called *two-way interleaving*, because the memory modules have in effect been "shuffled" together, so that consecutive memory locations are contained in alternate memory modules. In figure 16.5 the memory module $A$ contains locations with even addresses, while module $B$ contains locations with odd addresses. The implementation of two-way interleaving is simple:

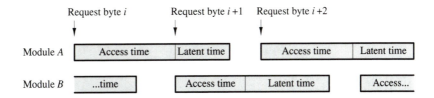

Figure 16.4 Overlapping of cycles in interleaved memory.

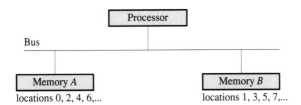

Figure 16.5 Organization of two-way interleaved memory.

The low-order bit of the address is used to select one of the two memory modules, while the higher-order bits are used to address the location within the module. Although each memory module can perform at most one operation every $t_c$ seconds, both together can provide *successive* data at a sustained rate of one every $t_a$ seconds (provided that $t_c \leq 2t_a$), which, as noted above, can be a substantial improvement. More generally, an *N-way* interleaved memory system has $N$ memory modules and shuffles addresses so that module number $k$ contains all locations whose addresses are equal to $k$ plus a multiple of $N$. When $N$ is a power of 2, such a memory system can be implemented easily by letting the least significant $\log_2 N$ bits of the address select a memory module and letting the remaining address bits designate the specific location to be accessed within that module.

In a situation like the one discussed above, in which the processor's need for the data in location $X + 1$ is not contingent on the result of reading location $X$, a cleverly designed processor using an interleaved memory system will begin a read operation from location $X + 1$ *before* it has received the value read from location $X$. *Vector processors* such as the Cray-1 and its descendants exploit this idea to achieve an $N$-fold increase in their bandwidth to memory by having up to $N$ memory accesses active concurrently, supporting this operation by an $N$-way memory interleaving. These machines often use 16-way, 32-way, and even 512-way interleaving (in the NEC SX-2 supercomputer).

Even if accesses do not always alternate between memory banks, the rate of memory accesses in an interleaved memory system should never be worse than one access every $t_c$ seconds. This worst case is sustained only during long runs of accesses to locations all in one memory module—presumably a rare occurrence. Interleaving is a way of introducing more concurrency into the operations of the memory system. In this case, the result is a memory that is *on the average* faster, but in the worst case no faster, than the ordinary memory organization.

## 16.3 Instruction Prefetch

The high predictability of instruction-fetch patterns makes this an attractive candidate for special treatment to exploit locality. Some instructions leave the memory idle for long periods of time. Multiply and divide in a contemporary machine, for example, might well take longer than the cycle time of the memory. Conversely, during an instruction fetch, the processor must wait, doing very little, for the memory to provide the next opcode and successive bytes of the instruction. This creates an opportunity to improve the processor's utilization of memory. Whenever the processor is busy doing work that does not involve accessing the memory, it can be simultaneously fetching successive bytes of memory at locations just beyond the current program counter value. Then the memory and processor can run concurrently, rather than alternately as in the simple case. This is an example of pipelining, accessing the next instruction in the memory while processing the previous instruction. The strategy is usually called *instruction prefetch*.

Prefetch is only advantageous, of course, when execution proceeds sequentially through the instruction stream. Transfers of control (jumps, calls, and returns) must carefully ignore prefetched bytes. Transfers of control are thus more expensive in a prefetch scheme, because extra memory accesses are performed.

Prefetch is usually performed by a special hardware unit. Typical prefetch hardware contains a queue that can operate asynchronously from the processor. The hardware prefetch unit must be carefully designed to provide properly for transfers of control and for memory references outside the instruction stream.

## 16.4 Top-of-Stack Cache

An important property of stack usage is that instructions that push data are often immediately followed by instructions that pop data. This memory-reference pattern allows the choice of keeping, or *caching*, some of the top elements of the stack in fast processor registers rather than in memory. Suppose, for example, that the processor has one register TOS that can hold the top element of the stack and a flag TOSFull that keeps track of whether the top element of the stack is currently in TOS or in memory. We can redefine the Push and Pop operations as in figure 16.6.

Now if the sequence Push;Push;Pop;Pop;Push;Pop is executed starting with TOS empty, two memory accesses are required (for the second Push and the second Pop), rather than the six required if there were no top-of-stack cache. In general, if a sequence of $N$ Pushes follows one or more Pops, the Pushes will require only $N - 1$ memory accesses. Similarly, if a sequence of $N$ Pops follows one or more Pushes, the Pops will require only $N - 1$ memory accesses. If the average length of runs of Pushes or Pops is $r$, then the average number of memory references required per stack operation will be $1 - 1/r$. If $r$ is small, the savings will be significant.

```
int     TOS;            /* Top-of-stack cache.              */
int     TOSFull = 0;    /* Boolean flag: Is cache full?     */

Push(a)
 int a;
 {      if (TOSFull)    /* Is cache nonempty?               */
           *(SP-1) = TOS; /*  (Yes, store it away.)         */
         SP = SP + 1;   /* Increment stack pointer.         */
         TOS = a;       /* Cache the newly pushed datum     */
         TOSFull = 1;   /*  and set flag.                   */
 }


int Pop()
 {      SP = SP - 1;    /* Decrement stack pointer.         */
         if (!TOSFull)  /* Is cache empty?                  */
           TOS = *SP;   /*  (Yes, load it up.)              */
         TOSFull = 0;   /* Cache always empty after pop.    */
         return TOS;    /* Return current TOS value.        */
 }
```

**Figure 16.6**   Push and Pop for a one-element top-of-stack cache.

The technique can be generalized by keeping more than one of the top elements of the stack in the cache. Management of a cache for several stack elements is complicated by the need to remember how many of the top stack elements are currently cached, and where in the cache registers they are located, rather than just whether or not a stack element is in the cache. Decisions about when to transfer data between the cache and memory are also more complicated, but there are no fundamental obstacles.

There is also a phenomenon of diminishing returns; the $(n + 1)$st stack-cache register will never yield an incremental improvement in performance greater than that provided by the $n$th register. Given a set of cost and performance constraints, it is thus possible to adjust the size of a top-of-stack cache to best meet them. Significantly, the ramifications of this design decision are transparent to software, which will execute without change on any machine that supports the same instruction set, regardless of the number of fast internal registers the machine devotes to top-of-stack cache storage. The use of fast registers for a top-of-stack cache in a stack architecture such as the $S$ machine has the considerable advantage over their use for general registers in an architecture such as the $G$ machine that the number of fast processor registers is hidden from view and hence is easy to change in a program-transparent fashion.

## 16.5 Multilevel Memory

The top-of-stack cache is a special case of a general technique for exploiting locality of reference using *multilevel memory systems*. The basic idea is to organize a small amount of fast-access memory and a large amount of slower-access memory so that most of the accesses go to the small, fast memory. The average access time of such a memory system may approximate that of the small, fast memory, while its effective size is that of the large memory. Let the fast memory's access time be $t_{af}$, its size be $M_f$, and its cost per bit be $c_f$. Similarly, let the access time of the slow memory be $t_{as}$, its size be $M_s$, and its cost per bit be $c_s$. Then the effective size of the memory will be approximately $M_s$, and its cost will be $c_f \cdot M_f + c_s \cdot M_s$. If $\alpha$ is the fraction of all memory accesses that address only the fast memory, then the average access time of the memory as a whole will be

$$t_a = \alpha \cdot t_{af} + (1 - \alpha) \cdot t_{as}.$$

If $\alpha$ is close to 1, then $t_a$ will be close to $t_{af}$. In multilevel-memory jargon, $\alpha$ is called the *hit ratio*, or *hit rate*. The complementary *miss ratio* $1 - \alpha$ reflects the fraction of memory transactions that require access to the slower memory. (For this equation we assume that both the fast and slow memory accesses can be started at the same time; if the slow memory access does not begin until it is found that the desired datum is not in the fast memory, then $t_{as}$ must include the time for the probe of fast memory as well as the access time of the slower memory in order for the equation to be valid.)

The top-of-stack cache of the previous section uses one cell of fast memory and many cells of slow memory to hold the stack. For most programs, however, even a small amount of fast memory will give $\alpha > 1/2$, so that

$$t_a < \frac{t_{af} + t_{as}}{2}.$$

This is the same substantial performance improvement noted in the previous section.

## 16.6 Cache Memory

A common form of multilevel memory system is *cache memory*, or *lookaside buffer memory*. A cache memory is a relatively small, specialized memory device placed between the processor and memory, as shown in figure 16.7. The cache memory holds *copies* of words from memory that seem likely to be accessed by the processor. The cache is faster than main memory; thus, if frequently accessed locations are found in the cache, $\alpha$ will be high and the average memory access time will be small. The strategy followed by the cache is to hold data at or near locations recently accessed by the processor. The locality of reference exploited by this strategy is the propensity of memory accesses, over short periods of time, to cluster in small regions of memory.

Cache-memory locations are redundant, in the sense that each is used to provide a more accessible copy of information also stored in slower main memory (although, in some cases, the main-memory copy may contain obsolete information). Thus the total addressable memory size, as seen by the programmer, is not increased by the presence of a cache. Rather, the cache provides, in a program-transparent way, an improvement in the average memory access time.

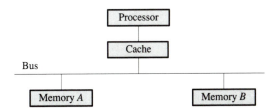

**Figure 16.7** Memory system with cache.

Because the cache is much smaller than main memory, only a minority of the main-memory locations can be cached at any one time. Consequently, in the general case each location in the cache, or *cache line*, conceptually has two parts: a *tag* field and a *contents* field. When a read or write operation is requested, the accessed location's address is compared with the tag field of selected cache lines. If a match is found, the contents field of the cache line containing the matching tag is read or written. There is no need to access main memory. This is known as a *cache hit*.

If the address does not match any tag, a *cache miss* occurs. If the cache misses on a read, the datum is fetched from main memory, returned to the processor, and also stored in one of the cache lines (by setting the selected cache line's tag to the address accessed and the selected cache line's contents to the value received from main memory). Since the cache is of limited size, this updating must replace some value already stored there. The *replacement strategy* for choosing which of these values to replace affects the effectiveness of the cache.

It is useful to think about replacement strategies in terms of the time $\tau_i$ of the *next* reference to each line $i$ currently in the cache. It is generally impossible for the cache implementation to know $\tau_i$, since knowing $\tau_i$ requires an ability to predict the future, but $\tau_i$ is nevertheless a crucial parameter, since our goal is to maximize the probability that subsequent references to data already loaded into the cache will lead to cache hits. The optimal replacement strategy, which we shall call *OPT*, replaces the line $i$ for which $\tau_i$ is the greatest: In other words, OPT replaces the line whose next reference is the longest into the future.[1]

If a cache cannot know $\tau_i$ with certainty, then it must effectively estimate $\tau_i$ from whatever information it can collect. A common strategy, suggested by our locality observations, is to estimate that $\tau_i$ equals the amount of time that has elapsed since the *most recent* access to cache line $i$. Applying this estimate results in replacing the cache line whose most recent reference was the longest time in the past. This replacement strategy is referred to as *least recently used*, or LRU, implying that on a cache miss the cache line whose contents were accessed least recently is selected to hold the newly fetched data.

---

[1] The optimality of OPT is intuitively plausible, but its formal proof is tedious; the reader is referred to Mattson et al. [1970] or to the summary by Stone [1987, pp. 53–54].

For a memory write, both the cache and main memory must eventually be updated. Many cache-memory systems update main memory immediately. This technique is called *memory write-through*. The processor need not wait for the write to main memory to complete before proceeding; the write to main memory can proceed concurrently with subsequent cache reads. Another commonly used technique is to defer the main-memory write until the modified cache line is replaced. This approach is more complicated but usually reduces the number of write operations to main memory, which is important when bandwidth to main memory is a critical resource.

The most commonly used performance indicator for a cache is the hit ratio $\alpha$, the ratio of cache hits to total memory accesses (typically expressed as a percentage). Cache systems on modern computers usually yield hit ratios above 95 percent, resulting in an average access time $t_a$ nearly equal to the cache access time $t_{af}$. As in the case of a top-of-stack cache, the performance of a cache-memory system obeys a law of diminishing returns. Once a certain minimum cache size has been reached that suffices to contain all the different data that would be accessed during the execution of a few instructions, the incremental benefit (as measured by the increase in hit ratio) of each additional cache line is less than that of the previous one, though it does continue to be appreciable over a considerable range of cache sizes. (The miss ratio $1 - \alpha$ is often found to be inversely proportional to powers of the cache size $M_f$ that lie between $M_f^{0.5}$ and $M_f$, for cache sizes up to several hundred thousand bytes.) Thus, as in the case of the top-of-stack cache, a particular cost/performance objective will dictate a certain optimum cache size, typically determined by simulating the system for different cache sizes and job mixes in order to measure the resulting hit ratios experimentally.

### 16.6.1 Fully Associative Cache

When a cache miss occurs, the cache line selected to hold the data read from main memory can in general be any cache line, if a replacement strategy such as LRU is in use. Since the contents of a given main-memory location might reside in any cache line, it is necessary to examine the tag field of *each* line in the cache to determine whether a given memory access constitutes a cache hit.

Although the inspection of cache tag fields could conceivably be performed sequentially, performance considerations generally require that all tag fields be simultaneously compared with an incoming address, delaying access on a hit by one comparison time rather than by $\Theta(N)$ comparison times. This parallelism involves $\Theta(N)$ hardware cost, since an independent comparator is required for each cache line, as sketched in figure 16.8. Note that the incoming address from the processor (shown at the top left of the figure) is bussed to $N$ comparators, each associated with one of the $N$ cache lines. We assume that the cache contents are maintained so as to avoid duplicate tag fields; thus the incoming address will match at most one of the tags. If there is such a match (that is, if there is a cache hit), then a HIT output line is pulled active, and a driver is enabled to assert the *contents* portion of the corresponding cache line on the output data bus.

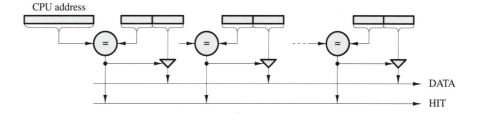

**Figure 16.8** Fully associative cache organization.

If location 123 is resident in the cache, some cache line will contain 123 in its tag field and ⟨123⟩ (the contents of memory location 123) in its contents field. A read of address 123 by the processor (or CPU) will lead to a match at the comparator associated with that cache line, driving HIT active and asserting ⟨123⟩ as the cache output data. The CPU (or associated logic) will interpret the cache output data as the result of the read operation, and no further memory access will be required. If, on the other hand, no cache line contains ⟨123⟩, then no tag will match and HIT will not be asserted. In this case, cache management circuitry (not shown in the diagram) must fetch ⟨123⟩ from main memory, replacing a selected cache line with the tag 123 and contents ⟨123⟩.

This cache may be viewed as a memory system in which locations are named by a portion of their contents (the tag) rather than by addresses fixed to each location. Such systems are termed *content-addressable* or *associative* memories and constitute an abstraction whose usefulness goes beyond the construction of caches. In general, an associative memory of size $N$ embodies, in a simple abstraction, an $N$-way parallel search. Truly associative memories can be and have been made; however, their cost remains quite high because of the replication of comparison logic. As a result, fully associative caches of the type sketched here are rarely constructed in practice. Practical cache approaches almost invariably achieve lower cost by compromising the degree of parallelism employed.

### 16.6.2 Nonassociative (Direct-Mapped) Cache

While a fully associative cache of reasonable size is prohibitively expensive, it can be made very much cheaper by sacrificing parallelism so as to allow the use of ordinary RAMs as the storage medium. An extreme example of this approach is sketched in figure 16.9, which illustrates a cache that examines a single location of an ordinary RAM to determine whether a processor access causes a cache hit. The cache is therefore not associative; it is sometimes referred to as a *direct-mapped cache*, since main-memory addresses are mapped into cache-memory addresses in a straightforward way.

Note that the direct-mapped cache uses *low-order* bits of the incoming memory address to dictate the address within the cache to examine for a hit. Thus memory location $A$ can *only* reside in the cache line whose address is the low $k$ bits of $A$, a substantial constraint compared with the fully associative alternative. It is

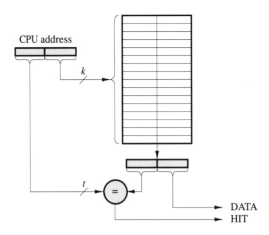

**Figure 16.9** Nonassociative cache.

this constraint—the discipline that the address used within the cache is dictated by the main-memory address to be cached—that allows the use of addressable RAM rather than associative memory. (Observe that, since the low-order bits of a main-memory address $A$ are implicit in the identity of the direct-mapped cache line that holds $\langle A \rangle$, it is unnecessary to include these bits in the stored tag or in the comparison.)

The constraint implies, however, that memory locations that share the same $k$ low-order address bits also share the same cache line. Among other limitations, such a cache cannot support an LRU replacement strategy; indeed, the cache line to be replaced on a miss is dictated entirely by the new address to be cached. This inadequacy of the direct-mapped cache exhibits itself when two or more simultaneous "hot spots" in the memory access pattern of an executing program— say, the instruction addresses of a tight loop and the addresses of data manipulated by that loop—compete for the same cache lines. The result is frequent replacement of cached data about to be accessed, with a dramatic drop in the hit ratio.

The chances of such a collision between hot spots decreases as the total size of the cache grows. Since a nonassociative cache uses ordinary (albeit fast) RAMs, it can be made quite large for the cost of even a small fully associative cache. While the collision probability never becomes negligible, a large direct-mapped cache can perform remarkably well; it is often the cache of choice on a performance/cost basis. Its major drawback is the unpredictability of its performance: A seemingly trivial program change can redistribute addresses so as to cause (or cure) a serious collision problem, making a conspicuous and unnerving difference in the running time of the program.

### 16.6.3 Set-Associative Cache

A commonly used intermediate point on the cache associativity spectrum is the *N-way set-associative cache* sketched in figure 16.10. Such a cache may be viewed

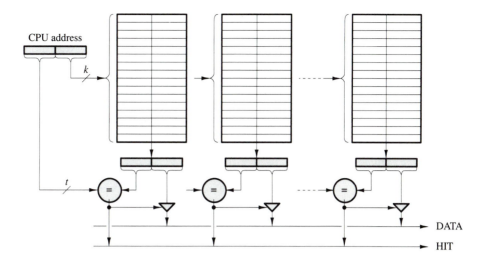

**Figure 16.10**  Set-associative cache.

as $N$ nonassociative caches operating in parallel. The incoming address is bussed to each of the $N$ comparators, while its low-order bits dictate single locations in each of $N$ RAMs to be accessed. Thus every main-memory location might reside in any of $N$ cache lines, one in each independent RAM module. Typical values of $N$ are 2 or 4, yielding a modest amount of associativity (parallelism) while using ordinary addressable RAMs.

The set-associative cache combines most of the cost advantages of the nonassociative cache with sufficient associativity to avoid collisions in typical programs. Since reference patterns of typical programs contain only a few independent hot spots at any time, a four-way set-associative cache of sufficient size will typically eliminate the danger of serious collisions, since four independent ranges of consecutive addresses can be cached simultaneously.

A "pure" LRU replacement strategy cannot be used by a set-associative cache, since the replacement choice is highly constrained by the incoming main-memory address. However, it is possible to implement a quasi-LRU strategy that chooses the least recently used location from among the candidate lines. An alternative is simply to choose the cache line to be replaced at random from among the candidates. The random replacement strategy is generally cheap to implement and, remarkably, has been shown to perform nearly as well as LRU in most circumstances.

### 16.6.4  Blocked Caches

Cache capacity can be increased without increasing the hardware cost associated with tags and comparators by expanding the contents portion of each cache line to hold several data words. In effect, such a cache deals with an increased effective data-word size by treating *blocks* of, say, $2^B$ words as a single datum. In a *blocked cache*, each line holds $2^B$ consecutive words aligned on a $2^B$-word address boundary. Figure 16.11 shows a direct-mapped cache in which $B = 2$ and the block size is therefore $2^2 = 4$. Note that the $B$ low-order address bits are used to indicate the offset of the addressed word within the addressed block, while the remaining address bits are used in much the same way as in the direct-mapped cache shown in figure 16.9.

Much of the appeal of this scheme is that the cost of the added cache capacity is little more than the cost of the added data RAM. On the other hand, a blocked cache of this sort introduces the significant constraint that every access to main memory must transfer an entire block of data rather than a single word. Thus a cache miss at address $A$ causes the entire block containing $A$ to be fetched, which may require substantially more time than simply accessing $A$. Although spatial locality suggests that other locations within the block are likely to be referenced in the near future, some fraction of these additional words will not be. Thus the blocked cache *prefetches* some memory locations but introduces a potential inefficiency, in that the prefetched memory locations will not all be used.

In general, a blocked cache is best suited to circumstances in which the $2^B$-word block can be transferred in less than $2^B$ times the transfer time of a single word. A memory system with $2^B$-way interleaving, for example, might allow an entire block to be accessed in one memory cycle time by exercising $2^B$ independent memory modules simultaneously; in this case, a blocked cache is likely to be very advantageous. Less extreme examples include memory busses that provide some performance advantage for the transfer of $N$ consecutive words but still require some added time per additional word accessed. Such cases may favor a blocked cache with moderate block size, but it is difficult to defend convincingly a particular choice of block size (or any other cache parameter) without simulation results.

## 16.7 Paging and Virtual Memory

*Paging*, another common application of multilevel memory techniques, allows us to create large virtual memories using a main memory and slower storage devices such as magnetic disks. The disparity between the access times of a disk (on the order of tens of milliseconds) and those of main memory (on the order of tenths of microseconds) is severe, but the locality of reference of most programs is good enough that the average access time to a paged memory system consisting of, say, a few million bytes of main memory and a billion bytes of disk memory (about $2^{30}$ bytes in all) will usually be little longer than the main-memory access time.

The essence of the paging technique is similar to that of a cache memory. For paging, main memory contains copies of recently accessed data. If the data for a read or write operation are present in main memory, a hit occurs, and the operation is performed there. Otherwise, the data are copied from disk into main memory and then accessed. Such a two-level memory architecture breaks the simple correspondence that exists in one-level memory schemes between the addresses issued by the processor and the addresses ultimately used to locate data in the machine's physical memory. It is therefore useful in discussing paging systems to refer to the former as *virtual addresses* and to the latter as *physical addresses*.

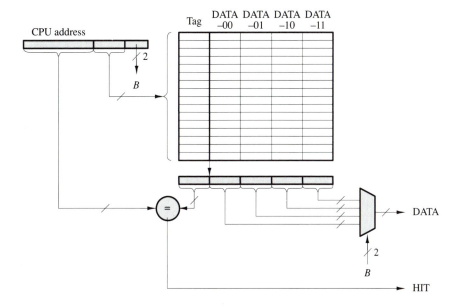

**Figure 16.11** Blocked, direct-mapped cache.

Using this language, we can discuss the operation of paging more precisely. Whenever a processor attempts a memory access, it issues the *virtual address* of the memory datum to be accessed. This datum may currently be present in main memory, or it may currently reside only on disk. In the former case, the virtual address is translated into the *physical address* in main memory where the datum is currently located. In the latter case, a *page fault* occurs, and a page-fault handler, normally implemented in software, causes the accessed datum to be copied from its location on disk to some location in main memory. The faulting access is then performed again, avoiding a second page fault since the datum to be accessed is now in main memory.

Data (both in main memory and on disk) are organized into fixed-size blocks called *pages*. The page, which is analogous to a block in a blocked cache, is the unit of transfer between disk and main memory. Typically, the number of bytes in a page is some power of 2, ranging from 256 ($2^8$) to 4096 ($2^{12}$). The size chosen depends on several factors, such as the kind of disk and the size of main memory. The physical locations of pages of the virtual memory are stored in a *page table*. Each reference to virtual memory (using a virtual address) entails a reference to the page table to determine the physical address of the desired page, followed by a reference to the page itself.

The page table can be kept in a special fast memory located in the processor or in main memory itself. Page tables for processors with small address spaces are not too large and can be kept fairly economically in dedicated memories within the processor. Page tables for modern processors with address spaces of $2^{32}$ bytes or more, however, are very large and hence are usually kept in main memory. Page

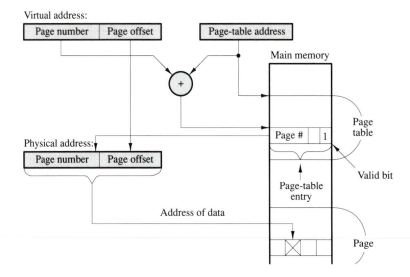

**Figure 16.12** Page-lookup algorithm.

tables located in main memory cannot be accessed as quickly as can those in a dedicated fast memory, but a caching technique known as *translation lookaside buffers*, discussed below, can restore most of the lost performance. Consequently, we shall base our discussion of paging on the assumption that page tables are located in main memory.

For purposes of page-table lookup, a virtual address is considered to be composed of two parts: a *virtual page number* and a *page offset*. On a byte-addressed machine, if the page size is $2^P$ bytes, then the least significant $P$ bits of the virtual address are the page offset, and the remaining bits of the virtual address form the virtual page number. The page table is an array of *page-table entries*, one corresponding to each virtual-memory page. When a virtual address needs to be translated to a physical address, the *page-table entry*, or PTE, corresponding to the virtual address is located by indexing into the page table using the virtual page number as the index, as illustrated in figure 16.12. The PTE contains a *valid bit* and a *physical page number*. The PTE usually also contains some other status information such as a *dirty bit*, discussed later. The valid bit indicates whether the page in question is currently located in main memory. If it is, then the physical page number is concatenated with the page offset (from the virtual address) to form the physical address corresponding to the original virtual address, as shown in the figure.

Each PTE needs to be large enough to accommodate the physical page number, along with the valid bit and a few other status bits. In most systems, this means that a PTE will fit into 32 bits but not into 16; consequently, we shall assume in our examples that each PTE is represented as a 4-byte longword. To locate the relevant PTE, then, the virtual page number is multiplied by 4 and added to the *page-table address*, typically kept in a processor register. This computation gives

```
VMap(Context, VAddress)
 {    int VPageNum = VPAGENUM(VAddress);
      int PTEPAddress = Context + 4 * VPageNum; /* Physical PTE address. */
      int PTE = PGet(PTEPAddress);             /* Read the PTE.          */

      if (VALIDBIT(PTE) == 0)
              PageFault(Context, VAddress);    /* (if invalid)           */

      return MAKEPADDR(PPAGENUM(PTE), VPAGEOFFSET(VAddress));
 }                                             /* Assemble the physical address. */
```

**Figure 16.13**  One-level page-table address-translation algorithm.

the physical address of the desired PTE, which can then be read to determine the physical address of the datum the processor is attempting to access.

Keeping the page-table address in a processor register, rather than "wiring" it into the processor hardware, is convenient because it allows operating-system code to maintain several independent page tables, corresponding to several independent, customized address spaces, and to switch easily from one to another just by reloading the page-table address register. Thus, for example, each of several users sharing a machine can be given a separate virtual address space, and the operating system can be given yet another virtual address space. The ramifications of this capability are discussed in chapter 18; for now, we observe simply that this opportunity exists and that, if it is to be exploited, the page-table address register must be part of the context information saved and restored when a trap occurs, so the proper page table will be in use at all times. To highlight this perspective on the page-table address register's role, we refer to it henceforth as the *addressing-context register*.

Another way of viewing this translation process is shown in figure 16.13, which is a C-language description illustrating the details of this address-translation scheme (a realistic implementation would, of course, use microcode or hardware rather than C). The procedure VMap receives the relevant addressing context as its `Context` argument and the virtual address in question as its argument `VAddress`. VMap returns the corresponding physical address, or invokes the procedure `PageFault` if some step of the translation failed because a needed page was not in main memory.

VMap invokes several subsidiary procedures to do small jobs for it. For example, VPAGENUM($A$) returns the virtual page number of the virtual address $A$; VPageNum thus becomes the virtual page number of VAddress. Likewise, VPAGEOFFSET($A$) returns the page offset of the virtual address $A$. Assuming $V$-bit virtual and physical addresses and a page size of $2^P$ bytes, VPAGEOFFSET will extract the low-order $P$ bits and VPAGENUM will extract the top $V - P$ bits of the virtual address. Thus VPAGENUM can return values from 0 to $2^{V-P}$, and VPAGEOFFSET can return values from 0 to $2^P$.

PGet($A$) reads and returns the 4-byte longword at physical address $A$. VALID-BIT(PTE) and PPAGENUM(PTE) return the valid bit and physical page number, respectively, of the page-table entry PTE. MAKEPADDR($N$,$Q$) concatenates the physical page number $N$ and the page offset $Q$ to produce a physical address.

The virtual-to-physical address-mapping algorithm is implemented in hardware or microcode because it is performed for every memory access requested by the processor. Even so, this mapping algorithm as described has considerable cost: Even when there is no page fault, every access to a datum in virtual memory leads to *two* physical memory accesses—one for address mapping and one to access the datum itself. This cost can be mitigated through caching. Programs tend to show excellent locality of reference at the page level—the set of pages accessed during a short period of a computation is quite small. Therefore, recently computed translations of virtual page numbers to physical page numbers can be remembered in a *translation lookaside buffer*, or TLB, which operates like a cache. Whenever a virtual address *VA* needs to be translated to a physical address, the TLB is first checked for an entry containing the same virtual page number as *VA*. If such an entry is found, its physical page number is read out and used to form the desired physical address immediately; otherwise, a *TLB miss* occurs and the full address-mapping algorithm must be executed.

Because of the excellent locality that programs usually show at the page level, quite small TLBs—in the range of 16–64 entries—often show hit ratios in excess of 95 percent. Thus, if a TLB is used, typically fewer than 5 percent of virtual memory accesses require two physical memory accesses, and in most cases an access to a datum in virtual memory requires only the one physical memory access to the actual datum—the performance that would be achieved by storing the entire page table in a dedicated fast memory within the processor.

Note that a change in the contents of the addressing-context register implies a change in the correspondence between virtual addresses and physical addresses. If the addressing-context register is reloaded (as might occur on a trap), all entries in the TLB must therefore be invalidated. An alternative approach is for the TLB to cache correspondences between (addressing context, virtual page number) *pairs* and physical page numbers. In this latter case, TLB entries need to be invalidated only when a page formerly resident in memory is replaced.

TLBs are usually implemented separately from the data caches discussed in section 16.6. Although the two kinds of cache are based on very similar principles and can be unified, they are used at different stages in the processing of a memory reference, and keeping them separate can lead to a simpler design, as well as allowing both caches to be in use at the same time (for example, in a high-performance processor) for different purposes.

### 16.7.1 Page Faults

If a referenced page is not in main memory, a *page fault* occurs, as mentioned above: Interpretation of the current instruction (whose execution has resulted in the fault) is aborted, the state of the processor is saved, and the processor transfers control to a software *page-fault handler*—similar to the `ssvc` handler of figure 14.44—to read in the missing page, after which the faulting instruction is transparently reexecuted. By relegating page-fault handling to software rather than hardware, an architecture avoids committing to a specific policy for handling page faults at hardware design time. Moreover, the machine instruction set is usually a better implementation medium than hardware or microcode for the requisite paging strategy decisions and the mechanics of performing the necessary disk operations.

Finally, the time taken by a page-fault-induced disk access—on the order of tens of milliseconds—is large enough to dwarf the execution time of software page-fault handlers, meaning that page-fault handling in hardware would not improve performance significantly.

The job of the page-fault handler is to move the referenced datum into main memory, where it can be accessed using the built-in mechanisms discussed above. As in the case of caches, it may first be necessary to remove a page currently in main memory in order to make room for the newly referenced page. It is not practical for paged memories to use write-through, since that would insert a disk-access delay into every virtual-memory write. Thus a page in main memory that is a candidate for being replaced may have been modified since it was loaded from the disk, in which case it must first be written back out to disk. Paging hardware usually includes a *written*, or *dirty*, *bit* in each page's PTE that is set by hardware mechanisms whenever there is a write into that page. A page-fault handler can use this bit to skip an unnecessary disk write when a read-only page is replaced.

Several kinds of facilities must be available to the page-fault handler if it is to do its job. First, it must be able to determine the cause of the fault (that is, which page is missing); thus it should be able to find out what virtual address was being accessed. The page-fault handler needs to know how to compute, from this virtual address, the location on disk of the desired page; often the page's address on disk is stored in the otherwise unused bits of a PTE whose valid bit is 0. The page-fault handler must have access to read and update the page table so that it can record the pages that it has read from or written to the disk.

When a page fault occurs, a trap sequence much like that followed by the $S$ machine's supervisor-call instruction `ssvc` (see table 14.43) is followed, including the loading of processor state registers from a page-fault trap vector and the saving of the old values of processor state registers on a new stack for use by the page-fault handler. It is important that page faults not occur while the page-fault handler itself is executing; therefore, the stack and machine code for the page-fault handler must be located in "wired pages" that are never removed from main memory. The state information saved when a page fault occurs must suffice to allow correct restarting of the instruction that caused the page fault once the requested page has been brought into main memory. The software page-fault handler must use this saved information, plus other statistics it may be able to gather, to decide which page to remove from main memory, read the requested page from disk, and update the page table to contain the physical address of the new page.

Finally, there must be a mechanism for resuming execution of the program that suffered the page fault. This can be tricky, since an instruction might go through several steps of its execution before encountering a page fault. A "back-out" procedure must be executed to restore the original values of any internal registers or memory locations modified prior to the point at which the page fault occurred, so that execution of the instruction can be resumed from the beginning after the cause of the page fault has been remedied. Alternatively, the page-fault handler must be given some way of resuming an aborted instruction in midstream so that no part of it will appear to have been executed twice. This latter approach requires saving additional state information (beyond the usual information saved for a trap) when a page fault occurs, so that instruction execution can resume where it left off. This is unattractive both because it requires data paths that can capture and later insert the extra state information wherever in the processor it resides and because it exposes a very low-level view of the processor's internal implementation, compromising the integrity of the machine-language abstraction. Nevertheless, the difficulty of implementing certain instructions to allow back-out leads to a hybrid strategy in many machines, allowing back-out of simple instructions and providing intermediate checkpoints for restarting instructions for which backing out is infeasible.

If we take the $S$ machine as a case study, the problems that arise most often in backing out of the execution of an instruction concern restoring the PC and SP values that prevailed at the beginning of the instruction's execution; this can be accomplished by saving their values at the beginning of each instruction's execution, just in case that instruction should encounter a page fault. A worse problem occurs for instructions that can take a page fault after writing over their input values in memory. The `scall` instruction, for example, writes over its procedure address operand before building its new stack frame. If a page fault occurs during the building of the stack frame, it is difficult to regenerate the state existing before the `scall` instruction so that the instruction can be successfully reexecuted. In general, instructions are hard to back out of once they have written to memory.

The easiest strategy for allowing restarting of instructions that can take a page fault after writing to memory is to verify that all the pages they will touch are in main memory before doing any writes. Reading all the bytes to be read or written before doing any writes will ensure that any page fault to be taken by the instruction will happen before any modifications to memory are made. This strategy can be thought of as a "dry run" of the instruction's execution. If we make sure that all instructions that write into memory do such a dry run, then aborting an instruction in the case of a page fault can be done simply by restoring SP and PC (and any other affected registers, such as the $S$ machine's B register) to the values they had when the instruction began. Machines that implement paged virtual memories usually follow these two general strategies to allow instructions that take page faults to be aborted: recording vital pieces of the processor state at the start of each instruction, and doing a dry run for memory-modifying instructions that would otherwise be difficult to restart.

### 16.7.2 *Multilevel Page Tables

The astute reader will have noticed that an implementation of virtual memory for a 32-bit machine as a $2^{32}$-byte virtual memory of even rather large $2^{12}$-byte pages would require a page table of $2^{20}$ entries! This in itself quite possibly requires more main memory than we would wish to buy for the machine. Real machines that implement paged virtual memories as large as $2^{32}$ bytes incorporate additional levels of page-table lookup so that parts of the page table itself can be paged out to disk. Such approaches typically promote the page table to a tree of, say, two or three levels, of which only one has dedicated physical memory. If the page tables

```
VMap(Context, VAddress)
{   int VPageNum = VPAGENUM(VAddress);
    int PTEVAddress, PTEPAddress, PTE;

    if ((VPageNum == 0) && (Context == 0))  /* Terminate.            */
            return VAddress;
    PTEVAddress = Context + 4 * VPageNum;   /* Virtual PTE address.  */
    PTEPAddress = VMap(0, PTEVAddress);     /* Physical PTE address. */
    PTE = PGet(PTEPAddress);                /* Read the PTE.         */

    if (VALIDBIT(PTE) == 0)
            PageFault(Context, VAddress);   /* (if invalid)          */

    return MAKEPADDR(PPAGENUM(PTE), VPAGEOFFSET(VAddress));
}                                           /* Assemble the physical address. */
```

**Figure 16.14** Multilevel page-table address-translation algorithm.

are themselves stored in paged virtual memory, several accesses may be required to translate a virtual address to an appropriate physical address. (As we show below, most of these accesses can be eliminated by using a translation lookaside buffer, so the scheme is not as expensive as it sounds. For simplicity, however, we first present the use of multilevel page tables without using a TLB.)

One approach to multilevel page tables is to keep page tables in *kernel virtual space*—the virtual address space in which privileged operating-system code executes—rather than in physical address space. This involves a change in the interpretation of the addressing-context register (ACR) from containing the *physical* address of the page table to holding a *virtual* address in the operating system's (or *kernel*'s) virtual address space. This reinterpretation threatens an infinite recursion, however: If the ACR holds a virtual address in kernel virtual space even when the current addressing context *is* kernel virtual space, then how do we ever arrive at the physical address of any page-table entry? This threat can be countered in various ways; we solve the problem here by "hard-wiring" virtual page 0 of addressing context 0 to physical page 0 and declaring that kernel virtual space corresponds to addressing context 0. Figure 16.14 is a C-language description, modeled after figure 16.13, illustrating the details of this address-translation scheme; a realistic implementation would, as before, use microcode or hardware rather than C. The procedure VMap is a straightforward implementation of the design just described. PTEVAddress is the virtual address of the PTE that must be fetched, whose physical address PTEPAddress is computed by a recursive call to VMap, after which the page-table entry itself can be loaded into PTE using PGet.

The most notable aspect of this algorithm is the recursive call to VMap to compute the physical address of the page-table entry that dictates the physical address of the referenced location. The basis for the recursion is the statement commented Terminate, which handles virtual page 0 of addressing context 0 as a special case. Again assuming 32-bit virtual and physical addresses and a page size of $2^{12}$ bytes, we see that we can have up to $2^{20}$ virtual pages in one addressing context. Since the page size is $2^{12}$ bytes, the page table alone for one addressing context will occupy $2^{10}$ virtual pages (remember, page-table entries are 4 bytes long); thus there are $2^{10}$ page-table entries for pages comprising this page table. But $2^{10}$ page-table entries fit conveniently into a single page. In the case of context 0, this page (page 0, context 0) is permanently resident starting at physical location 0. (Note that in any memory mapping scheme, there always has to be at least one page that is permanently resident in order to provide a point of reference. There may be several additional such "wired pages" resulting from operating-system constraints. Aside from those containing trap vectors and the code and stack for the page-fault handler, discussed previously, time-critical system services may need to have their code and data be permanently memory-resident.)

Assuming a page size of $2^{12}$ bytes and a 32-bit virtual address for each context, we note that the depth of recursive calls can go up to three: The original call maps an arbitrary addressing context to context 0, the first recursive call reduces an arbitrary virtual address in context 0 to a virtual address less than $2^{22}$, the second call reduces this address further to be less than $2^{12}$, and the final call recognizes this address as being in page 0 of context 0 and consequently returns it unchanged. At any stage of this process, a page fault may occur if a needed page is not in memory, but such an event will be rare at the deeper recursive levels of VMap because the set of different pages touched at these levels by a program will be quite small. Using this scheme, a switch of addressing context requires only a change in the addressing-context register; page faults will bring in the needed pages after this point.

A translation lookaside buffer can greatly improve the performance of multilevel page tables—indeed, it is only with a TLB that the performance of such systems is even marginally acceptable. It is very important in this system for the TLB to cache mappings from (addressing context, virtual page number) pairs to physical page numbers, since two different contexts are used for mapping any virtual address that does not start out in context 0. If a change of addressing context required the TLB to be invalidated, *every* lookup not starting from context 0 would invalidate the TLB, and the TLB would never be of much use. Assuming that the TLB is properly designed for this application, then after a change in addressing context, cache misses and page faults caused by references to addresses in the new context will force the necessary page-table entries and pages to be loaded on demand into the TLB and main memory, respectively. The desired result is a "gradual" context switch, which loads only the few pages actually referenced.

### 16.7.3 *Implementation of Paging

Using the $S$ machine as a case study, we can explore the impact of paging (specifically, of the address translation associated with paging) on processor design. The addition of address translation to the $S$ machine sounds simple enough and is not difficult in principle; however, modifications must be made throughout our register-transfer-level instruction descriptions to account for the memory-mapping function that now must be applied to every virtual address. In practice, microsubroutines analogous to get4, put4, and others defined in appendix 3 could be written to accept virtual addresses and map them to physical addresses before performing the memory operations, so modifications to other parts of the microcode need not be

**Table 16.15** Impact of address translation on the definition of sl$\alpha$.

| Without memory mapping | With memory mapping |
|---|---|
| $SP^4 \leftarrow \langle SP \rangle - 4$ | $SP^4 \leftarrow \langle SP \rangle - 4$ |
| $temp \leftarrow \langle\langle SP \rangle\rangle^4$ | $temp \leftarrow \langle VMap[\langle ACR \rangle, \langle SP \rangle]\rangle^4$ |
| $\langle SP \rangle \leftarrow \langle\langle temp \rangle\rangle^\alpha$ | $VMap[\langle ACR \rangle, \langle SP \rangle] \leftarrow \langle VMap[\langle ACR \rangle, \langle temp \rangle]\rangle^\alpha$ |
| $SP^4 \leftarrow \langle SP \rangle + \alpha$ | $SP^4 \leftarrow \langle SP \rangle + \alpha$ |

major. (Of course, the extra processing does add somewhat to the cost of each memory operation.) For use in register-transfer-level descriptions, we introduce the notation $VMap[c, VA]$ to denote the physical address corresponding to the virtual address $VA$ in the addressing context $c$. The impact of address translation on a typical member of the $S$-machine instruction set, the sl$\alpha$ instruction, is illustrated in table 16.15, where ACR is the processor's addressing-context register.

### 16.7.4 *Paging and Caching

Caches (other than TLBs) are frequently used in systems that also feature paging, resulting in a three-level memory structure: a relatively small, very fast cache memory backed up by a larger, slower main memory, backed up by a relatively enormous and much slower disk memory. In such systems, there are two interesting ways to integrate the cache memory with the address-translation activities associated with paging, according to whether virtual addresses or physical addresses are supplied as the "CPU address" shown in figures 16.8–16.11.

If virtual addresses are supplied to the cache, then address translation only needs to occur when there is a cache miss, making the normal processing of cache hits faster and simpler. Unfortunately, a virtual-address cache must generally be invalidated whenever there is a change in addressing context or the page table for the current addressing context is updated, since the correspondence between virtual and physical addresses then changes. Moreover, it is possible to configure a page table to map more than one virtual address to the same physical address, a situation known as *aliasing*. Aliasing does not occur if we use paging simply as a way to emulate a large virtual memory by means of a large amount of disk memory and a smaller amount of main memory, but some operating systems have found uses for aliased structures to implement various forms of data sharing. A virtual-address cache is incompatible with aliasing, since it is difficult to know all the virtual addresses that might be affected by a write to a single, possibly aliased location. Therefore, systems that use virtual-address caches generally avoid aliasing or restrict its use to situations in which the invalidation problem does not come up (for example, read-only locations).

It is usually more elegant to supply physical addresses to the cache, avoiding the problems discussed in the last paragraph. Unfortunately, memory-referencing performance usually suffers when this approach is used, since address translation must now be performed before it can even be determined whether or not a given memory reference will hit in the cache. Both virtual-address caches and physical-address caches are in fairly wide use.

### 16.7.5 Costs and Benefits of Paging

The major benefit of paging is, of course, that the programs running on the processor need not be aware of the actual size of main memory and that programs can be run even if they require more virtual memory than the entire amount of main memory on the machine. But there are also costs. First, every access to the virtual memory requires extra accesses to main memory to read the page table. This cost can be reduced by using a translation lookaside buffer.

Another cost of paging is in the complexity of the processor. The extra care needed to record the machine state at the beginning of each instruction execution, and to perform dry runs where necessary so that aborting any instruction is safe, adds a significant cost in complexity and can reduce the speed of the processor.

The fact that modern large-scale processors and many personal computers support paging despite its costs indicates the great value of hiding the main memory size. Indeed, several recent generations of high-end microprocessor designs (such as the Motorola 680X0 and Intel 80X86 families) have as a goal the ability to support paging. Unfortunately, early designs of these processors were not entirely able to avoid the pitfalls associated with the mechanism for aborting instructions (section 16.7.1), rendering them largely useless for applications requiring virtual memory. The fact that several major American integrated-circuit manufacturers have blundered in this respect underscores the importance for hardware architects of understanding the system functions, such as paging, that their hardware should support.

## 16.8 Summary

In this chapter we have discussed four techniques for organizing the memory of a computer system to improve the overall performance of the system—memory interleaving, instruction prefetch, top-of-stack cache, and multilevel memory. Each of these techniques relies on observed regularities in the memory-access patterns of programs running on the processor. There are many possible variations of these techniques that we have not discussed in detail; but the details are far less important than the key idea of observing regularities and exploiting them. As new memory technologies are developed and new machine organizations are devised, it is likely that different strategies for exploiting regularities in memory-access patterns will be found. Nonetheless, the *idea* of exploiting the regularities will continue to be important.

## 16.9 Context

Memory interleaving is widely used in mainframe computer systems, and instruction prefetch is widely used in computer systems of all types. Top-of-stack caches are not very prevalent because of the limited market penetration of stack-oriented processors; however, top-of-stack caches were used as far back as the Burroughs B5000 [Lonergan and King 1961], which had a two-word top-of-stack cache. Descendants of the B5000, such as the B6500 and B7500 [Hauck and Dent 1968], also had small top-of-stack caches. More recent processor designs incorporating top-of-stack caches include the Symbolics 3600 LISP machine [Moon 1985] and the CRISP microprocessor [Ditzel and McLellan 1987].

The idea of generalized multilevel memory systems first appeared in the virtual memory system of the Atlas computer constructed at Manchester University [Kilburn et al. 1962]. The application of this idea to cache memory can be traced to Wilkes [1965]. Smith [1982] gives a thorough and authoritative summary of cache design techniques and performance characteristics. Stone [1987] includes a good discussion of models for cache-memory performance and techniques for determining the performance of proposed cache-memory designs.

The Multics operating system and its Honeywell 645 host machine pioneered many virtual-memory concepts now widely used, including the use of segmentation and translation lookaside buffers. This system is described by Organick [1972]. A more recent virtual memory system is that of the DEC VAX-11/780, which features both a translation lookaside buffer and a two-level page table [Clark and Emer 1985]. Denning [1970] provides a classic overview of virtual memory and segmentation systems, and Denning [1980] reviews the history of virtual-memory techniques.

## 16.10 Problems

### Problem 16.1
Computer $A$ performs more memory accesses executing a given program $P$ than does computer $B$ while executing the same program. The machines are identical except that one machine uses instruction prefetch. Which machine uses prefetch?

### Problem 16.2
The following statements apply to a single-longword top-of-stack (TOS) cache implemented as in figure 16.6. Make each of these statements true by choosing the correct word from the triple in parentheses.

A. The TOS cache register (always, sometimes, never) contains the TOS longword after a push stack transaction.

B. The TOS cache register (always, sometimes, never) contains the TOS longword after a pop stack transaction.

C. A push transaction (always, sometimes, never) writes a stack longword into main memory.

D. A pop transaction (always, sometimes, never) reads a stack longword from main memory.

E. A push transaction that follows a pop transaction (always, sometimes, never) writes into main memory.

F. A pop transaction that follows a push transaction (always, sometimes, never) reads from main memory.

## Problem 16.3

Rework problem 14.12, assuming a one-element top-of-stack (TOS) cache implemented as in figure 16.6. How does the number of main-memory accesses in the presence of this TOS cache compare with your answer to problem 14.12?

## Problem 16.4

Consider the implementation of top-of-stack caches for the $S$ machine. The operation of a simple one-element cache is described in figure 16.6.

A. If initially SP $= 100$ and TOSFull $= 0$, what sequence of memory accesses will be performed during execution of the following sequence: Push(1); Push(2); Push(3); a=Pop(); b=Pop(); Push(4); c=Pop(); d=Pop()? What values will be assigned to the variables a, b, c, and d?

B. Write a pair of procedures Push and Pop that implement an $N$-element top-of-stack cache. Let TOS be a globally declared array with indices ranging from 1 to $N$. Explain what other global variables you need, and make sure your Push and Pop procedures never perform any unnecessary memory accesses.

C. If $N$ is 2, what sequence of memory accesses will be performed by your Push and Pop procedures for the sequence of Push and Pop operations given in part A? What is the minimum value of $N$ for which *no* memory accesses will be needed (assuming an initially empty cache)?

D. What problems arise in using a large top-of-stack cache (with, say, 100 elements) in the $S$ machine when a procedure is called using the scall instruction? Suggest a solution, and mention any other $S$-machine instructions that need similar treatment.

E. It has been suggested that a top-of-stack cache might benefit from prefetch— using idle time to fetch elements near the top of the stack that would fit in the cache but are not currently there. Briefly, what advantages and disadvantages does this idea have? (The answer has nothing to do with the scall instruction problems of part D.)

## Problem 16.5

Consider the performance of a one-element top-of-stack (TOS) cache. Assume that an access to main memory requires $10T$ time units. Assume also that we classify data accesses into four categories: (1) reads from main memory, (2) writes to main memory, (3) pushes on the stack, and (4) pops off the stack.

A. How long would a noncache system take to execute fib(3) using the definitions of fib given in figures 14.30 and 14.31? Do not include instruction fetch time or execution time in your answer; only count time for data accesses.

B. Recalculate the time for `fib(3)` using a one-element (4-byte) TOS cache. Assume that a cache access takes $T$ time units. What is the increase (if any) in performance over that calculated in part A?

C. If we count instruction fetch times, our numbers change drastically. Why?

D. Would a larger cache increase performance even more?

E. Describe briefly how you would manage a TOS cache consisting of four registers (elements).

## Problem 16.6

A cache memory can speed up computation by eliminating some references to main memory. Does its use require clever programming techniques? Explain.

## Problem 16.7

Will a four-way set-associative cache capable of holding 1K data bytes always have a better hit ratio than a direct-mapped cache capable of holding 1K data bytes? Explain.

## Problem 16.8

Will a completely associative cache using LRU replacement and capable of holding 1K data bytes always perform as well as or better than a direct-mapped cache of 1K data bytes? Explain.

## Problem 16.9

In caches, is an LRU replacement stategy always better than a last-in/first-out strategy (that is, replacing the cache line *most* recently brought into the cache)? Explain.

## Problem 16.10

A performance fanatic has tried three different ideas for a machine, with the following results:

1. Four top-of-stack registers doubled the speed.

2. Instruction prefetch doubled the speed.

3. Cache memory doubled the speed.

Our fanatic now proposes to implement all of these features at once, in hopes of improving performance by a factor of 8. Give at least two reasons why this expectation might be unrealistic.

## Problem 16.11

For this problem, assume that you have a processor with a cache connected to main memory via a bus. A successful cache access by the processor (a hit) takes 1 cycle. On an unsuccessful access (a miss), an entire cache block must be fetched from main memory over the bus. A bus transaction consists of one cycle to send the address to memory, four cycles of idle time for main-memory access, and then one cycle to transfer each word in the block to the cache. (Assume that the processor continues execution only after the last word of the block has arrived.) In other words, if the block size is $B$ words (at 32 bits/word), a cache miss will cost $1 + 4 + B$ cycles. The following table gives the average cache miss rates of a 1 Mbyte cache for various block sizes:

| Block size ($B$) | Miss ratio ($m$), % |
| --- | --- |
| 1 | 3.4 |
| 4 | 1.0 |
| 16 | 0.4 |
| 64 | 0.25 |
| 256 | 0.19 |

A. Write an expression for the average memory access time for a 1-Mbyte cache and a $B$-word block size (in terms of $m$ and $B$).

B. What block size yields the best average memory access time?

C. If bus contention adds three cycles to the main-memory access time, which block size yields the best average memory access time?

D. If bus width is doubled to 64 bits, what is the optimal block size?


## Problem 16.12

Consider the performance of several alternative cache designs with a selection of test programs on a general-register machine with 8-bit data paths and byte addressing (much like the MAYBE). Each cache has a 1-byte block size. Each cache is used for *all* memory references, *including instruction fetches*. The cache designs are as follows:

$W$: a nonassociative, 4096-byte cache,

$X$: a two-way set-associative cache, of *total* size 2048 bytes, with random replacement,

$Y$: a four-way set-associative cache, of *total* size 1024 bytes, with random replacement,

$Z$: a fully associative cache, of *total* size 512 bytes, with LRU replacement.

Recall that a one-way set-associative cache of total size $N$ bytes is a nonassociative cache and that an $N$-way set-associative cache of total size $N$ bytes is a fully associative cache.

A. Briefly explain why cache $W$ uses low-order (rather than high-order) address bits to choose a cache location.

B. The following simple loop (test A) was run using each cache design:

```
A:      gaddi    imm1(1)  r(0)     r(0)     | R0 <- <R0> + 1.
        gjmp     rel(A)                     | Loop forever.
```

Ignoring cache misses on the first few thousand iterations, for which cache designs (if any) would you expect the hit ratio to be less than 100 percent on this test? Explain.

C. Next, the four designs are tested with the following code (test B):

```
B:      gcmp4   r(0)        imm4(1500)      | If (<R0> >= 1500) ...
        gjlt    rel(B1)
        gmove4  imm4(0)  r(0)               |    ... then R0 <- 0.
B1:     gmove1  imm1(1)  ix(tab, 0)         | tab[<R0>] <- 1.
        gadd4   imm4(1)  r(0)     r(0)      | Increment R0.
        gjmp    rel(B)                      | Loop forever.
```

Note that `tab` is a constant specifying the address of a byte array. Assume that R0 initially contains 0. After the first few thousand iterations, it is found that only one of the cache designs gives a perfect hit ratio. Which cache design yields this hit ratio? Explain.

D. Suppose the location `tab` is changed. Might the hit ratio of the cache you identified in part C fall below 100 percent? Explain.

E. Again suppose the location `tab` is changed. Might the hit ratios of any of the *other* cache designs reach a perfect 100 percent? If so, name them and explain why.

F. Which, if any, of the cache designs might result in a hit ratio below 75 percent with test B? Explain.

G. The final test program is shown below:

```
C:      gcmp4   r(0)        imm4(100)       | If (<R0> >= 100) ...
        gjlt    rel(C1)
        gmove4  imm4(0)  r(0)               |    ... then R0 <- 0.
C1:     gmove1  ix(taba, 0)  ix(tabb, 0)    | tabb[<R0>] <- <taba[<R0>]>.
        gadd4   imm4(1)  r(0)     r(0)      | Increment R0.
        gjmp    rel(C)                      | Loop forever.
```

Note that `taba` and `tabb` each denote byte arrays. Again assume that the initial contents of R0 are 0. Which, if any, of the cache designs are *guaranteed* to yield a perfect hit ratio after the first several thousand iterations of this test? Explain.

H. Which, if any, of the cache designs *might* achieve a perfect hit ratio after the first several thousand iterations of test C, assuming a favorable assignment of the addresses of `taba` and `tabb`? Explain.

I. Is it possible to devise a test program on which cache $Y$ is likely to outperform cache $Z$? Explain.

### Problem 16.13

Two processors $A$ and $B$ share the same bus, as shown below:

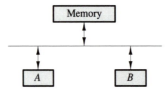

The bus is capable of transferring 1 byte (either from or to memory) every 500 ns. For a particular instruction mix, the average instruction executed is 1 byte long and causes three additional bus transactions: two reads and one write. The detailed instruction timing for both processors is as follows:

1. Fetch opcode byte.
2. Compute for 250 ns.
3. Read one data byte.
4. Read another data byte.
5. Compute for 750 ns.
6. Write a data byte.
7. [Go back to step 1.]

To improve the performance of the system, a cache is added to processor $B$:

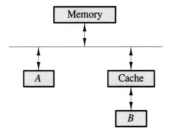

Two caches are proposed. Cache 1 has a hit ratio of 80 percent and a cache access time of 100 ns; cache 2 has a hit ratio of 90 percent and a cache access time of 200 ns. (*Cache access time* is the access time to a datum when a cache hit occurs; it includes all decoding and searching time to determine if the datum was in the cache.) Assume that no overhead is imposed by the cache when a cache miss occurs, and ignore the effects of write-through or copying of data into the cache after a cache miss.

Which cache should be used? Consider both the effect on the speed of execution of instructions on processor $B$ and the effect on the average bus loading (which will affect the execution speed of processor $A$). Give an argument in favor of your choice and justify your argument with numerical performance figures.

## Problem 16.14

In this problem we consider the relative performance improvement obtained by running a particular program with various caches installed between the memory and the CPU. Consider the following C subroutine:

```
char a[512], b[512];

add_arrays()
{
        register int i;

        for (i = 0; i < 511; i = i + 1)
                a[i+1] = a[i] + b[i];                /* Work. */
}
```

(The `register` keyword persuades the C compiler to reserve a register for the variable i; let's assume it keeps i in R0. The `char` keyword allocates character arrays at fixed locations in memory, using 1 byte per character.) When translated to *G*-machine code, the line labeled `Work` yields the following *G*-machine instruction:

```
gadd1 ix(a,0) ix(b,0) ix(a+1,0)
```

For the following questions, assume that two separate memory systems are used, one for instruction fetches and the other for data accesses. Execution of instructions, however, occurs in a sequential fashion (that is, accesses to the two memories do not overlap in time). Each memory can read or write 1 byte at a time.

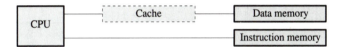

A. Suppose that the CPU is directly connected to the two memory systems (no cache is used) and that the access time of each memory is 100 ns. How many nanoseconds of the above instruction's execution will be spent waiting for memory?

B. Suppose that a 512-byte fully associative cache with the following characteristics is inserted between the CPU and the data memory. A cache hit has an access time of 20 ns, while a cache miss requires 120 ns. A write-through strategy is used, with 120 ns for each data write, and a least-recently-used (LRU) strategy is used to manage the cache. The cache is initially empty before the program begins. Does the cache help any? If so, on average, what is the new "memory overhead" (time spent waiting for memory) for this instruction?

C. Suppose that a 256-byte cache is used. Will the cache still be useful? What is the smallest LRU fully associative cache that would still be useful?

D. Suppose that we insert a 512-byte direct-mapped cache between the CPU and the data memory. Assume the cache timing specifications of part B. Assume that arrays a and b are adjacent in data memory. Does this cache help any? What is the average memory overhead now for this instruction?

E. Suppose we use a 2-way, 256-set (that is, 512-byte), set-associative cache with a block size of 1 byte. The timing specifications are the same as in part B. A quasi-LRU replacement strategy is used, replacing the least recently used element within the set. Does this cache help any? What is the average memory overhead now for this instruction?

F. Suppose we change the block size of the cache of part E to 2 bytes, maintaining a total data capacity of 512 bytes. A cache hit requires 20 ns. A cache miss, however, now requires 220 ns to read 2 bytes from main memory. Writing a byte requires 120 ns. Has cache performance improved? Under what circumstances is this cache design better than the one in part E?

### *Problem 16.15*

Adverbs Unlimited is considering a computer system based loosely on the MAYBE. Five designs have been proposed, each of them similar to the MAYBE except for a cache between the 8-bit processor data bus and the main-memory subsystem. Like the MAYBE, each machine deals with 16-bit main-memory addresses, for a total address space of $2^{16}$ bytes. The machines' caches differ only in the parameters of associativity, size, and writeback. The caches can be nonassociative (direct-mapped), two-way set-associative, or four-way set-associative. All follow an LRU replacement strategy within each set. The total number of data bytes (exclusive of addresses, valid bits, and so on) varies from cache to cache. Finally, certain caches are write-through (always writing to main memory on a write operation), while others are write-back (writing only on line replacement). The five models are outlined below.

| Model | Associativity | Total data size, bytes | Write- |
|---|---|---|---|
| DEFINITELY | four-way | $2^{16}$ | back |
| CERTAINLY | direct-mapped | $2^{16}$ | back |
| HOPEFULLY | four-way | $2^{10}$ | through |
| PERHAPS | two-way | $2^{10}$ | back |
| DOUBTFULLY | direct-mapped | $2^{10}$ | back |

A. How many bits are required for the *tag* portion of each cache entry in the HOPEFULLY model?

B. How many bits are required for the *tag* portion of each cache entry in the DOUBTFULLY model?

C. How many 4-bit comparators are needed to build the HOPEFULLY cache?

D. Address lines from the CPU are designated $A_{15}, ..., A_1, A_0$, where $A_0$ is the low-order address bit. Which of these CPU address lines are used as address inputs to the SRAMs of the cache in the PERHAPS model?

Engineers at AU are evaluating each of the proposals in terms of cost and performance. Cost for each cache is estimated by considering only SRAM (at 1 cent per byte) and comparators (at 10 cents per byte). Performance evaluations are made using three benchmark programs: $A$ does only writes, cycling through addresses $0, 1, ..., 2^{12}, 0, ...$; $B$ reads locations 0, 1024, 2048, 1, 1025, 2049, 0, 1024, ...; $C$ reads randomly from all addresses. The goal of this evaluation is to enumerate the respects in which each cache is superior to the others. In the next several questions, you are asked to indicate the ways in which one cache is preferable to another. You should answer each question with some combination of $A$, $B$, $C$, and $, to indicate your reasons for preferring the first cache to the second. Answering $A$, $B$, and $C$ indicates that the corresponding program demonstrates a better hit rate; a dollar sign indicates a cost advantage. Answer "none" if none of the other answers ($A$, $B$, $C$, or $) is applicable. Explain your reasoning in each case.

E. In what ways is the CERTAINLY preferable to the DEFINITELY model?

F. In what ways is the DEFINITELY preferable to the CERTAINLY model?

G. In what ways is the DEFINITELY preferable to the HOPEFULLY model?

H. In what ways is the PROBABLY preferable to the HOPEFULLY model?

I. In what ways is the PERHAPS preferable to the PROBABLY model?

J. In what ways is the HOPEFULLY preferable to the PERHAPS model?

K. In what ways is the PERHAPS preferable to the DOUBTFULLY model?

L. Suppose that address lines $A_0$ and $A_{10}$ were inadvertently interchanged in the cable between the DOUBTFULLY CPU and its cache. Which, if any, of the following statements best describes the effect(s) of this change, assuming that other hardware and software remain unmodified?
  1. The machine would no longer work.
  2. The machine would continue to work as before.
  3. The machine would continue to work, but at a reduced performance level.
  4. The machine would continue to work, at an improved performance level.

### Problem 16.16
As a highly trained consultant, you have been hired by companies $A$, $B$, and $C$ to recommend cache designs for their respective general-register machines. Each company's product is a clone of the original $G$ machine and executes an identical instruction set. For the sake of variety, you have recommended a different cache to each manufacturer as follows:

$A$: one-way (direct-mapped) write-through cache, 4K bytes total size, 4 data bytes per line;

$B$: two-way set-associative write-through cache, 4K bytes total size, 4 data bytes per line;

$C$: four-way set-associative write-through cache, 4K bytes total size, 4 data bytes per line.

Note that (for the sake of consistency) you have recommended a write-through cache dealing with a total of 1K 4-byte data blocks in each case. Each uses a quasi-LRU replacement strategy that chooses the least recently used line from among the candidate lines.

Each of the companies is outraged to learn that you consulted for the others, and you are being threatened with numerous lawsuits. To placate your clients, you stress to each the strategic need for product differentiation, and assure each company that its machine now outperforms the others in certain applications. Unconvinced, each manufacturer demands to see a benchmark $G$-machine program that achieves a better hit ratio on its machine than on the other two. Your challenge is to find three appropriate programs.

Write three small $G$-machine loops that run forever, each of which performs best (in the sense of hit ratio) on one of the three machines. Assume that the path to main memory is 8 bits wide; that is, access to a 4-byte word takes the form of four consecutive 1-byte memory transactions. For each of your three program fragments, give the following information:

1. the memory reference string, that is, the sequence of addresses referenced during execution of the loop (the sequence is, of course, an infinite cycle; use ellipses as appropriate);

2. for each machine, an indication of whether each reference misses the cache (that is, results in a main-memory transaction);

3. the hit ratio for each cache.

You should provide this information in the following format:

```
Program A:    ...
              (G-machine loop)
              ...


ref string: 1  37  42  1025  1 37 42 1025 ...
   cache A: -  H   H    -     - H  H   -  ... (HR = 0.5)
   cache B: -  H   -    -     - H  -   -  ... (HR = 0.25)
   cache C: -  -   -    -     - -  -   -  ... (HR = 0)
```

## Problem 16.17

You are designing a controller for a tiny cache that is fully associative but has only three words in it. The cache has an LRU replacement policy. A reference record module (RRM) monitors references to the cache and always outputs the binary value 1, 2, or 3 on two output signals to indicate the least recently used cache entry. The RRM has two signal inputs, which can encode the number 0 (meaning no cache reference is occurring) or 1, 2, or 3 (indicating a reference to the corresponding word in the cache).

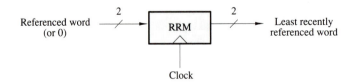

A. What hit ratio will this cache achieve if faced with a repeating string of references to the following addresses: 100, 200, 104, 204, 200?

B. The RRM can be implemented as a finite-state machine. How many states does the RRM need to have? Why?

C. How many state bits does the RRM need to have?

D. Draw a state-transition diagram for the RRM.

E. Consider building an RRM for a 15-word fully associative cache. Write a mathematical expression for the number of bits in the ROM required in a ROM-and-register implementation of this RRM. (You need not calculate the numerical answer.)

F. Is it feasible to build the 15-word RRM of part E using a ROM and register in today's technology? Explain why or why not.

### Problem 16.18
If a TLB is implemented as a set-associative cache, how would you recommend determining the TLB slots examined by VMap(*context*, *addr*)? Why?

### Problem 16.19
Consider a multilevel page table scheme following the algorithm of figure 16.14 but using a TLB. Estimate the average time required for a memory access by such an implementation. Assume a TLB cache hit rate of 90 percent, 100-ns TLB cache lookup time (for either a hit or a miss), and a 1-$\mu$s main-memory access time. Ignore page faults and any minor overhead timing; consider only time spent in cache and memory references.

### Problem 16.20
If the program in figure 16.14 is used for a page size $2^P = 2^{10}$ and virtual addresses are $V = 32$ bits long, how deeply can the recursive calls to VMap go?

### Problem 16.21
Explain how to construct the cache tags of a virtual-address cache so that a switch of addressing context does not require invalidation of the cache. Assume that aliasing does not occur.

### Problem 16.22
Assume that you have a cache designed as specified in the last problem. Explain how the function of a TLB can be integrated into this cache; in other words, explain how to use just this cache, with no TLB, to achieve the same kind of performance improvement as is achieved by using a TLB for the address-translation procedure VMap of figure 16.14.

### Problem 16.23
It is possible to arrange a set-associative physical address cache so that the page-table entry for a location can be fetched concurrently with a cache lookup for the same location. The trick is to ensure that the address bits that select the cache

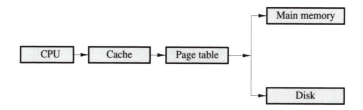

**Figure 16.16** A CPU and its memory system.

entry are unmapped—that is, that selection of the cache entries to examine is based only on bits from the offset portion of the virtual address. Devise a scheme that exploits this potential parallelism. What constraint does this approach impose on the relation between the page size and the cache lookup mechanism? Explain.

### Problem 16.24

Must a user program written for use with a nonpaged memory system be modified in order to be used with a paged memory system? Explain.

### Problem 16.25

Explain how a paged memory system depends on locality of reference for efficient operation.

### Problem 16.26

A paged memory system has 16-bit virtual addresses and pages that are 1024 locations long. How many entries must the page table have?

### Problem 16.27

Figure 16.16 shows a CPU and its memory system. The computer features a single process; 32-bit virtual addresses; a cache of $2^{10}$ lines that is four-way set-associative, has 8-byte data blocks, and is write-through; a main memory of $2^{26}$ bytes; and a page size of $2^{12}$ bytes.

A. Does this system cache virtual or physical addresses?

B. How many bytes of *data* from memory can the cache hold? (Don't count tags.)

C. In the cache, each block of data must have a tag associated with it. How many bits long are these tags?

D. How many comparators are needed to build this cache?

E. How many entries are there in the page table? (Assume a one-level page table.)

F. At any one time, what is the greatest number of page-table entries that can have their valid bit set to 1?

### Problem 16.28

Consider two possible page-replacement strategies: LRU (the least recently used page is replaced) and FIFO (the page that has been in the memory longest is

*Memory Architectures*

replaced). The merit of a page-replacement strategy is judged by its hit ratio.

Assume that, after space has been reserved for the page table, the interrupt service routines, and the operating-system kernel, there is only sufficient room left in the main memory for *four* user-program pages. Assume also that initially virtual pages 1, 2, 3, and 4 of the user program are brought into physical memory in that order.

A. For each of the two strategies, what pages will be in the memory at the end of the following sequence of virtual page accesses? Read the sequence from left to right: $(6, 3, 2, 8, 4)$.

B. Which (if either) replacement strategy will work best when the machine accesses pages in the following (stack) order: $(3, 4, 5, 6, 7, 6, 5, 4, 3, 4, 5, 6, 7, 6, ...)$?

C. Which (if either) replacement strategy will work best when the machine accesses pages in the following (repeated sequence) order: $(3, 4, 5, 6, 7, 3, 4, 5, 6, 7, ...)$.

D. Which (if either) replacement strategy will work best when the machine accesses pages in a randomly selected order, such as $(3, 4, 2, 8, 7, 2, 5, 6, 3, 4, 8, ...)$.

## Problem 16.29

Program $A$ consists of 1000 consecutive ADD instructions, while program $B$ consists of a loop that executes a single ADD instruction 1000 times. You run both programs on a certain machine and find that program $B$ consistently executes faster. Give two plausible explanations.

## Problem 16.30

If virtual addresses are $V$ bits long, physical addresses are $A$ bits long, the page size is $2^P$ bytes, and a one-level page table is used, give an expression for the size of the page table.

## Problem 16.31

Consider a paging system that uses a one-level page table with a virtual memory size of $2^V$ bytes, a physical memory size of $2^M$ bytes, and a page size of $2^P$ bytes. Assume that the machine has byte addressing and that the entire page table resides in the main memory. The paging scheme is diagrammed in figure 16.17, and the virtual address has the format:

| virtual page number | offset in page |
| --- | --- |

A. How many pages can be stored in physical memory at once?

B. How many entries are there in the page table?

C. Assume that $V = 24$, $M = 21$, and $P = 10$. How many bits are necessary per entry in the page table? (Assume that the page-table entry contains the physical page number, a "valid" bit, and a "dirty" bit.)

D. With the variable values specified in part C, approximately (ignoring integer round-off problems) how many pages does the page table require?

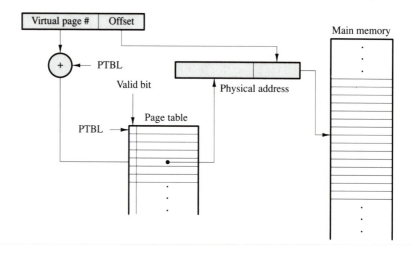

**Figure 16.17** A one-level page-table scheme.

E. A portion of the page table is given below. If $P = 10$, what is the physical address corresponding to the decimal virtual address 4980? (*Hint:* $2^{10} = 1024$.)

| Virtual page number | Valid bit | Physical page number |
|---|---|---|
| 0 | 0 | 7 |
| 1 | 1 | 9 |
| 2 | 0 | 6 |
| 3 | 1 | 3 |
| 4 | 1 | 5 |
| 5 | 0 | 5 |
| 6 | 0 | 4 |
| 7 | 1 | 1 |
| ... | ... | ... |

### Problem 16.32

Consider implementing a $2^{32}$-byte virtual memory on a $2^{20}$-byte primary memory. Assume that we need at least five pages in memory at all times: Page 1 is the page table, page 2 is a page trap handler, page 3 is a page trap stack, and pages 4 and 5 are user data and instruction pages. Can we implement this system? If so, give the page size and number of pages. If not, explain why not.

Now assume that because of communication and hit-ratio issues we decide that the optimum page size is $2^{12}$ bytes. What major problem arises? Propose some solutions to this problem. (Changing the size of the memory or page is not acceptable.) Your answer should be in the range of 2–3 paragraphs.

## Problem 16.33

Consider a *G* machine with virtual memory in which an instruction that encounters a page fault is simply retried from the beginning (PC is backed up) after the page fault has been handled. For the following *G*-machine instructions, what are the ranges of virtual addresses that must be in physical memory to avoid page faults? Assume that each instruction is stored beginning at location 1000. You may use register names in giving your answers.

A. `gcmp1 pop() i(2000)`

B. `gadd4 r(3) iix(1000,4) push()`

C. `gjne dir(Foo)`

## Problem 16.34

We have seen the need to *abort* instructions if their execution causes a page fault. One scheme for ensuring proper restart of an aborted instruction is to save the SP and PC at the beginning of each instruction and merely reload the saved values to abort the instruction. This scheme will not work for some *S*-machine instructions.

A. What are these instructions? (You may confine your attention to instructions that are discussed in chapter 14.)

B. Propose a scheme for correctly aborting each of these instructions.

C. What is undesirable about an instruction-specific scheme for aborting instructions?

## Problem 16.35

A simple strategy for aborting *G*-machine instructions when page faults occur would be simply to reset the *G* machine's program counter and stack pointer to the values they had when the current instruction began to execute. List as many problems as you can find with this strategy.

## Problem 16.36

A paged memory with a one-level page table has the following parameters: The pages are $2^P$ bytes long; virtual addresses are $V$ bits long, organized as follows:

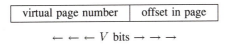

| virtual page number | offset in page |

$$\leftarrow \leftarrow \leftarrow V \text{ bits} \rightarrow \rightarrow \rightarrow$$

the page-table starts at physical address PTBL; and each page-table entry is a 4-byte longword, so that, given a virtual address, the relevant page-table entry can be found at $\text{PTBL} + (\text{page number}) \cdot 4$.

A. How many bits long is the "offset in page" field? How many bits long is the "virtual page number" field? How many entries does the page table have, and what is the highest address occupied by a page-table entry? How many pages long is the page table? Answer in terms of the parameters $P$ and $V$.

B. What is the smallest value of $P$ such that the page table fits into one page?

C. What relationships, if any, must hold between $P$, $V$, and the size of physical memory?

D. You are now given the additional information that page-table entries have the following format:

| valid bit | physical page address |
|---|---|

$\leftarrow \leftarrow \leftarrow 32$ bits $\rightarrow \rightarrow \rightarrow$

The valid bit is 1 if the page is present in primary memory and 0 if the page is absent. If a page is present in primary memory, then the physical address of a byte in that page is the sum of the "physical page address" in the page-table entry plus the "offset in page" from the original virtual address.

Give a register-transfer-level description of the procedure $PA = pmap[VA]$ for calculating the physical memory address $PA$ corresponding to a virtual address $VA$. Be sure to indicate the circumstances under which there will be a page fault. Use the forms $A \div 2^i$ and $A \cdot 2^i$ to denote right and left shifts, respectively, of $A$ by $i$ bits. Use $A \bmod 2^i$ to denote the low-order $i$ bits of $A$. You can test the high-order bit of a quantity $A$ by a statement such as "if $A$<0 then ... else ...". Use any other notation that is convenient, but be sure to explain the meaning of any nonstandard notation you use.

## Problem 16.37

Adverbs Unlimited has recently added a new product, the VIRTUALLY, to the product line discussed in problem 16.15. The VIRTUALLY has a $2^{10}$-byte, two-way set-associative cache, $2^{20}$ bytes of physical memory, 16-bit virtual addresses, and a $2^6$-entry page map. The VIRTUALLY will be used to support multiuser time-sharing. The page map holds the address translation for a single (current) process and must be reloaded (by the kernel) at each process switch. The cache is located between the page map and main memory.

A. What is the page size?

B. Which address lines provide address inputs to the RAM in the page map?

C. Can the cache and page-map RAMs be read simultaneously? Explain in a single sentence.

D. Under what circumstances, if any, must the cache be invalidated (that is, its entries marked as invalid)?

# 17    Reduced-Instruction-Set
        Computers

After several generations of computers offering ever more sophisticated and ornate instruction-set architectures, a strong trend has developed toward the minimalist end of the complexity spectrum. This movement bears the popular name RISC (for *reduced-instruction-set computer*) and is represented by a growing number of modern high-performance machines.[1]    Exactly what constitutes a RISC machine is the subject of some debate, but such machines generally share three biases:

- Simplicity of implementation takes precedence over direct support for a high-level language or programming model.

- Stress is laid on compilation rather than on interpretive mechanisms. For example, language constructs are translated to primitive instruction sequences rather than being supported by high-level instructions interpreted by microcode.

- Hardware is dedicated to increased performance rather than to increased semantics; cache and pipelining, for example, are preferred to additional instructions.

A typical RISC provides a machine language at a level close to that of the MAYBE microcode. It is designed to exploit software sophistication (primarily in the compiler) rather than incur hardware costs. In so doing, it reduces the interpretive overhead, with consequent performance improvements. A side effect is that the value of the RISC machine language as an abstraction is compromised relative to higher-level alternatives; it provides less isolation from hardware details than an instruction-set architecture at the level, say, of the $S$ machine. This compromise is mitigated by bundling the compiler as an inseparable part of the architecture: The purveyor of RISCs advances the compiler source language, rather than machine language, as the major interface to the abstract programming model.

Specific characteristics common to most machines of this minimalist category include:

- fixed-length instructions, using very few different formats, simplifying instruction fetch and decode;

---

[1] The term *RISC* was proposed by Patterson and Ditzel [1980] and popularized by the RISC project at the University of California, Berkeley [Patterson and Sequin 1982]; see section 17.10 for further background.

- fixed time per instruction execution (typically, one instruction executed during each clock period);

- pipelined instruction fetch/execute unit;

- general-register architecture, with a substantial number of registers;

- most operations limited to register operands; limited load/store instructions (with very simple addressing modes) for access to main memory;

- direct hardware execution of machine-language instructions rather than their interpretation by microcode; and

- compiler code generation specialized to the timing details and idiosyncrasies of the architecture (for example, to the length and organization of the instruction pipeline).

This chapter sketches the $R$ machine, a hypothetical RISC-style architecture designed to illustrate some of the issues glossed over by our MAYBE-based examples.

## 17.1 Basic Data Pipeline

In compliance with the RISC bias toward compromises in the hardware-level programming model to achieve simplicity and speed, we begin by focusing on the basic performance-critical path within the processor. In most RISC machines, this path is the one necessary to perform basic arithmetic and logical operations on register operands, for example, B ← $\langle A \rangle$ OP $\langle B \rangle$ on a two-address machine, or C ← $\langle A \rangle$ OP $\langle B \rangle$ using a three-address format. A general goal is to execute one such instruction during every clock period, where the clock period is trimmed to what is needed to fetch a single operand from a static RAM register file.

Since each such operation requires fetching *two* register operands, the single-cycle goal demands that the register file be able to supply two independently addressed source operands during the same cycle. Such memories are referred to as *dual-port* and feature multiple copies of addressing logic so that two words can be read from the same array of static RAM cells. Since these ports support only read operations, each may be viewed as a multiplexer that routes the contents of a chosen register to a set of output data lines. Each such port has an address input (corresponding to the multiplexer select lines) and a data output.[2] Since the result of the typical register operation is to be written into a register, a write port is needed in addition to the two read ports.

Figure 17.1 shows the basic data paths of a simple pipelined machine in sufficient detail to follow the gross operation of an instruction of the form B ← $\langle B \rangle$ OP $\langle A \rangle$. We assume a single two-address, 16-bit instruction format, comprising a 6-bit opcode field and two 5-bit operand (register) addresses. Although our discussion is generally independent of data-path width (and, for that matter, of instruction

---

[2] One implementation of two-port register files, found on some early machines, used two ordinary static RAMs whose contents were maintained to be identical. Modern approaches vary the design of the static RAM itself by replicating only the addressing logic, eliminating the redundant storage cells.

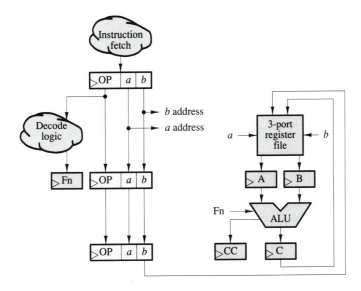

**Figure 17.1**  Basic four-stage data pipeline.

size and format), we further assume a 32-bit data path for concreteness. Note that the symbols $a$ and $b$ are used to designate bit fields of the instruction word that specify operand locations in the register file, while A and B denote actual data-path registers that hold the operands and present them as the left and right inputs, respectively, to the ALU.

The execution of B $\leftarrow$ $\langle$B$\rangle$ OP $\langle$A$\rangle$ follows a four-stage pipeline; these stages are

- *instruction fetch* (IF), in which a 16-bit instruction word is fetched from instruction memory (which may be main memory, cache, or dedicated instruction memory);
- *operand fetch/instruction decode* (OF/ID), in which the source operands are fetched from the register file into A and B registers and the opcode is decoded to generate control signals (Fn) to be used in subsequent stages;
- *arithmetic and logic unit* (ALU), in which the actual operation is performed, the result being stored in the C register; and
- *operand store* (OS), in which the result is rewritten into the register file.

There are, of course, registers at points where each data or control signal crosses a pipeline boundary. The first of these is the instruction register, filled by the *instruction-fetch unit* (the first pipeline stage) and passed down to successive stages.[3]  The second (operand fetch/instruction decode) stage routes the A and

---

[3] Although we show the original instruction word passed to each of the following stages, some of its fields (such as the A address) are unnecessary and could be eliminated.

Instruction

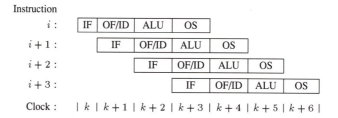

**Figure 17.2** Four-stage pipeline timing.

B addresses to the read ports of the register file, allowing the addressed operands to be fetched and loaded into the A and B registers. Meanwhile, combinational logic decodes the opcode field of the instruction to produce control signals, notably function-code input Fn for the ALU operation to be performed during the following clock cycle. The third stage takes A, B, and function-code inputs from their respective registers, performs the indicated computation, and produces a result that is loaded into the C register. During the last pipeline stage, this result is routed (along with the B address) to the write port of the register file.

## 17.2 Pipeline Timing

The pipeline in figure 17.1 comprises four stages and follows our synchronous, single-clock SGT timing discipline. Four consecutive cycles are needed for an instruction execution; an instruction is completed during every clock cycle, and consequently during every clock cycle four instructions are in progress in various stages.

It is convenient to visualize the timing of instruction-execution stages in two dimensions, where several consecutive instructions occupy descending positions and where the horizontal coordinate of each operation stage reflects the time at which it is performed. Figure 17.2 shows the execution of four consecutive instructions as they propagate through the $R$-machine pipeline.

### 17.2.1 Pipeline Interlocks and Load Delays

The pipelining of instruction execution makes certain sequences of instructions awkward to implement. Consider the execution of the two consecutive $R$-machine instructions

```
radd(1,3)        | R3  <-  <R3> + <R1>
rsub(3,5)        | R5  <-  <R5> - <R3>
```

which involve a data dependency concerning the value passed through register 3. If we examine the timing of the respective execution stages of this sequence (shown in figure 17.3), we discover that the R3 source operand of the rsub instruction is read from the register file during clock cycle $k + 2$, while it is not written by the

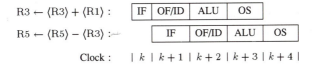

$$R3 \leftarrow \langle R3 \rangle + \langle R1 \rangle : \quad \boxed{IF} \; \boxed{OF/ID} \; \boxed{ALU} \; \boxed{OS}$$

$$R5 \leftarrow \langle R5 \rangle - \langle R3 \rangle :- \quad \boxed{IF} \; \boxed{OF/ID} \; \boxed{ALU} \; \boxed{OS}$$

Clock :  | $k$ | $k+1$ | $k+2$ | $k+3$ | $k+4$ |

**Figure 17.3** Pipeline data-dependency conflict.

earlier `radd` until clock cycle $k+3$. Thus, if implemented naively, the `rsub` would simply fetch the wrong value for its source operand.

There are three commonly used approaches to dealing with such conflicts between data dependencies and pipeline timing:

- *Pipeline interlock hardware* detects instructions whose source operands are destinations of instructions further down the pipe. Detection of this situation causes the instruction whose source is not available—and any following instructions—to be delayed by enough clock cycles to resolve the conflict. (Often this is done by freezing early pipeline stages while running the later ones, filling the resulting gap with *no-operation* instructions.) Thus this approach maintains the integrity of the programming model by inserting judicious delays in the execution of the instruction stream.

- *Bypass*, or *pass-around*, *paths* detect conflicts and circumvent them by routing data through ad hoc paths between pipe stages. In the example of figure 17.3, dedicated hardware in the operand-fetch circuitry might recognize that the current A address is identical to the B address of the following instruction and load the A register directly from the C register rather than from the register file. This approach also maintains the programming model, avoiding the introduction of additional delays. It tends to be expensive, though, since it complicates the hardware design with additional data paths (and multiplexers) as well as the conflict-detection circuitry.

- *Programming model compromises* recognize the pipeline structure and timing and require compiled code to accommodate its idiosyncrasies. In our example, the compiler would be required either to reorder instructions so as to avoid the conflict or to insert explicit `rnop` (*no-operation*) instructions as necessary to delay loading of the conflicting value. Such *load delays* incur a performance penalty similar to that associated with the use of hardware interlocks. This approach is the least expensive, requiring no hardware changes. However, it increases the dependency of the architecture on machine-specific compiler technology.

Often a given system will depend on elements of all three strategies. Even where hardware cost is not a critical issue, the use of pass-around paths (the most expensive solution) may be ruled out by fundamental data-dependency constraints—the required data may not yet have been produced by the ALU, for example. In such cases, interlocks may be provided to include the delays necessary to preserve the programming model. However, clever compilers may still contrive to reorder instructions so as to avoid interlock delays and maximize performance.

### *Load Delays*

Using the data paths of figure 17.1, we must reflect the pipeline timing in the programming model by forbidding use of the previous instruction's destination as a source operand. The alert reader will notice that this implies that our register file must properly handle the case in which one or both read addresses are identical to the write address; that is, it implies that the data being written will also be routed to the read data ports, if required, during the same clock cycle. This result may be a natural consequence of the design of the multiport register file; if not, it may require bypass paths within the register file itself.

The software approach opens the door to considerable cleverness on the part of the compiler. Consider a (forbidden) sequence of machine code that contains two pipeline conflicts of the form illustrated by the previous example:

```
radd(1,3)        | R3  <-  <R3> + <R1>
rsub(3,5)        | R5  <-  <R5> - <R3>
radd(1,4)        | R4  <-  <R4> + <R1>
rsub(4,6)        | R6  <-  <R6> - <R4>
```

This sequence can be converted to working code simply by padding it with `rnop` instructions at the critical points:

```
radd(1,3)        | R3  <-  <R3> + <R1>
rnop             |   (no operation)
rsub(3,5)        | R5  <-  <R5> - <R3>
radd(1,4)        | R4  <-  <R4> + <R1>
rnop             |   (no operation)
rsub(4,6)        | R6  <-  <R6> - <R4>
```

The execution time of the resulting code is increased by 50 percent. A more sophisticated compiler, though, might discover that the original four instructions can simply be reordered to preserve their effect while avoiding the need for delays, as follows:

```
radd(1,3)        | R3  <-  <R3> + <R1>
radd(1,4)        | R4  <-  <R4> + <R1>
rsub(3,5)        | R5  <-  <R5> - <R3>
rsub(4,6)        | R6  <-  <R6> - <R4>
```

Such a reordering is, of course, not always possible; the compiler must be prepared to insert `rnop`s under unfavorable circumstances. It is noteworthy that similar compiler optimizations are valuable even for machines that have hardware interlocks, because they circumvent unnecessary delays in instruction-stream execution (and also make the code more compact).

*Reduced-Instruction-Set Computers*

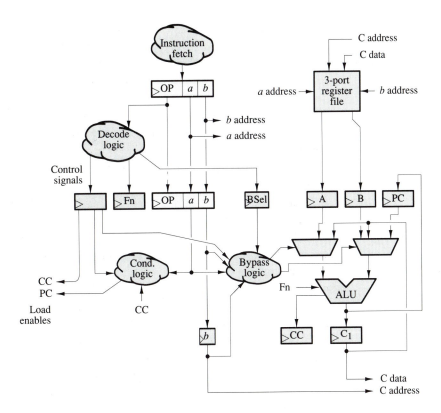

**Figure 17.4** Pipeline with bypass paths.

### Pipeline Pass-Around Paths

Figure 17.4 sketches a four-stage pipelined processor with bypass paths that make load-delay rules unnecessary and other features that will be discussed in the next section. In this design, multiplexers have been inserted at each input of the ALU, allowing the ALU output from the previous instruction—held in the register labeled $C_1$—to be selected as either or both ALU inputs. These multiplexers are controlled by *bypass logic* whose inputs include both operand fields from the current instruction and the destination operand field from the previous instruction. The bypass logic contains comparators that detect whether either current operand field is identical to the destination specified for the previous instruction; in such cases, the bypass path (from $C_1$) is selected rather than the contents of the A or B register that holds a stale value from the register file.

## 17.3 Interface Issues

While the diagram of figure 17.1 supports simple two-address register-to-register operations, some additional mechanism is necessary to support branches, calls, and access to main memory. To facilitate these operations, several additional registers are added to the data paths and dedicated to specific functions. These registers include the program counter (PC), perhaps an up/down counter to serve as the stack pointer (SP), and address and data registers constituting an interface to a main-memory bus (which might also support input/output devices). In a similar fashion, the PC amounts to an interface to the instruction-fetch unit, itself a finite-state machine designed to supply the stream of 16-bit instructions. Note that, since the instruction-fetch unit is normally fetching an instruction somewhat beyond the one currently dictating the operation of subsequent pipeline stages, the contents of the PC are usually offset from the address of the instruction at each pipeline stage by different constants. This issue is discussed in section 17.5.

One option is to integrate these registers into the register file, making them accessible as general registers in much the way that the $G$ machine allows general access to the PC as R15. Although this approach is simple conceptually (that is, from the programmer's standpoint), it is somewhat awkward because of the ad hoc data paths that must access each of these dedicated registers, which is inconsistent with the structure of a conventional register file. Consequently, we revise the data paths so as to allow additional registers to be selected as the ALU operands by the multiplexers between the A and B registers and the ALU. The PC is shown interfaced in this manner in figure 17.4, allowing it to be selected as the right-hand ALU operand. To control the selection of alternative ALU operands, we use the register ASel to pass multiplexer select inputs from the decode logic through the bypass logic to the right-hand multiplexer. Note that the bypass paths are selected by the bypass logic only when the $a$ or $b$ field of the current instruction matches the $b$ field of the previous instruction and, in the case of a $b$ match, BSel selects the register source. The loading of the PC (and other similarly interfaced registers) is also governed by decode logic outputs, again delayed until the ALU stage of instruction execution. Thus the additional registers are loaded simultaneously with the $C_1$ register.

## 17.4 Instruction-Stream Constants

Instruction-stream constants play several important roles in an architecture. In addition to the instantiation of explicit program constants, they provide the basis for direct addressing, indexed and offset addressing, branches, calls, and numerous other implicit uses. Typically constants are provided for either by general addressing modes (as in our $G$ machine) or by alternative instruction formats. The RISC bias rules out the former approach, but it also strongly discourages the latter, since additional formats complicate the machine's implementation. As a result, efficient handling of instruction-stream constants in RISCs motivates some interesting and creative compromises.

It is reasonably straightforward to include immediate-mode instruction formats in which a short portion of the instruction word constitutes a constant operand; for example, certain $R$-machine instructions interpret the contents of the $a$ operand field as a 5-bit constant operand rather than the location where a full 32-bit operand is to be found. Longer immediate constants can be similarly accommodated, but they often require either allocation of a dedicated constant field to *every* instruction

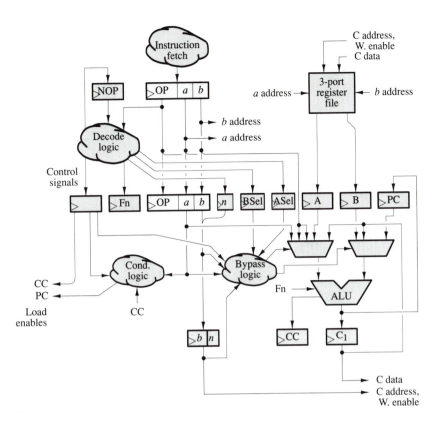

**Figure 17.5** Incomplete $R$-machine pipeline with constant paths.

(ignored in many cases) or multiple instruction formats. This choice reflects, to some degree, a trade-off between simplicity and code compactness.

The approach taken by the $R$ machine illustrates, in primitive form, both approaches. First, it provides for short immediate constants (called *quick constants*) as source operands, within the 16-bit two-address instruction format. Second, it provides for longer (16-bit) constants interspersed between instructions. While the latter can be viewed as adding new instruction formats, it does so in a way that is specific to the $R$-machine pipeline design and hence involves very little additional hardware cost. Figure 17.5 sketches incomplete $R$-machine data paths, including support for both 5- and 16-bit constants.

Note the addition of several new alternatives that can be selected by the multiplexer at the A input of the ALU, together with a new register ASel that conveys the selection in a manner analogous to BSel. The sources of the A operand are now:

- the 5-bit constant $a$ from the current instruction word itself, which allows quick instruction formats having short immediate constants as source operands; examples are rmoveq($c$,$r$), which copies the 5-bit constant $c$ to register $r$, and raddq($c$,$r$), which adds a short constant to the register;

- the 16-bit word that is the literal instruction word from the previous pipeline stage, that is, the immediately following 16-bit instruction;

- the following 16-bit instruction word, left-shifted by 16 bits, provided to facilitate the building of 32-bit constants;

- the contents of the A register, reflecting the addressed location of the register file; and

- the bypass path from the $C_1$ register, selected when the specified A source operand is the destination operand from the previous instruction.

The $R$ machine thus allows an instruction to appropriate the following instruction in the pipeline as a constant. An additional mechanism must be provided to prevent such a constant from being executed as an instruction. This need is fulfilled by the 1-bit NOP register attached to the decode logic: When NOP is set during a cycle, the decode logic always treats the instruction currently being decoded as an `rnop` instruction, which performs no operation. Conversely, when the decode logic loads ASel with a code selecting a 16-bit constant, it simultaneously sets NOP so that the following instruction will be disabled.

It is necessary that subsequent pipeline stages be able to identify disabled instructions, in order to avoid such undesirable side effects as storage of meaningless data in the register file or unwarranted invocations of bypass paths. To this end, an additional bit $n$ is passed by the decode logic along with the $b$ address field to successive stages. The $n$ bit indicates a NOP (disabled) instruction and ultimately generates an enable signal that causes a write operation in the register file. Moreover, it serves to identify disabled instructions to the bypass logic, avoiding confusion that could arise if the portion of a constant corresponding to the $b$ instruction field happened to match a source address in a following instruction.

## 17.5 Instruction Fetch and Branch Control

The PC shown in figure 17.5 is a counter, configured to increment at each clock cycle. (As with our previous machines, we assume byte addressing; thus the PC is incremented by 2.) The *instruction-fetch unit* (IFU) fetches, during each cycle, the 16-bit instruction word addressed by the PC and passes it to the OF/ID pipeline stage for execution. In the general case, then, the value in the PC is offset from an instruction's original location during its execution by a different amount at each pipeline stage. The PC contains $a + 2$ while the instruction fetched from $a$ is in the OF/ID stage, $a + 4$ while it is in the ALU stage, and so on. These offsets must be accommodated, for example, in PC-relative addressing.

The fixed relationship between the contents of the PC and the address of the instruction at each stage in the pipeline is violated temporarily during transfers of control. In particular, no constant relationship exists between $\langle PC \rangle$ and the address of instructions in the pipeline following loading of the PC as a result of a branch instruction. This issue is discussed in section 17.5.3.

### 17.5.1 Instruction-Stream Data Rate

High-performance RISCs tend to stress instruction execution speed rather than code compactness, and this leads to demand for instruction-stream data at a rate that is difficult to reconcile with simple main-memory accesses. A complicating factor is that instruction fetches compete for memory bandwidth with data accesses, necessitating some arbitration between requests via the bus interface and those originated by the instruction-fetch circuitry.

RISCs mitigate the memory-bandwidth bottleneck by a variety of techniques, often involving fetching instructions from a separate memory so as to eliminate contention. In the *Harvard architecture*, a separate instruction memory is an explicit feature of the programming model. This approach leads to two entirely separate address spaces, devoted to instructions and data, respectively; often the former is constrained to be read-only.

Alternatively, the use of a separate high-speed instruction memory is made transparent by the *cache* techniques described in chapter 16. An *instruction-stream cache* consisting of a small, fast memory is often incorporated into the instruction-fetch subsystem; this allows the majority of instruction fetches to be satisfied by local memory references, with only an occasional need to fetch new instructions from main memory. An instruction-fetch unit following this approach would keep pace with the processor (providing one instruction per cycle) as long as main-memory references could be avoided, introducing delays otherwise.

Various other tricks can be used to optimize the instruction-fetch data rate. If the memory word is 32 bits (as is likely on a 32-bit RISC) and the instruction word is only 16 bits, a pair of instructions can be fetched during each memory cycle. Interleaved memory modules (discussed in chapter 16) and related techniques allow even wider paths to memory, proportionately increasing the data rate of the instruction stream.

### 17.5.2 Transfer of Control

Several $R$-machine instructions effect branches by loading a new value into the PC at the end of their ALU stage. For example, the instruction rjmpr(delta) uses the 16-bit instruction-stream constant delta to specify a PC-relative jump target. The decode logic causes this instruction to add delta—sign-extended—to $\langle PC \rangle$, storing the result back into the PC. Notice that during the ALU stage, the A and B operands to the ALU are the 16-bit constant and the PC, respectively. Although a following 16-bit constant word is used to convey delta, the $a$ and $b$ operand fields of the instruction are unused.

Conditional branches share the same opcode, taking the form rjmprc(cond, delta), where the 5-bit instruction-stream constant cond dictates the branch conditions, using the codes defined for the $S$ and $G$ machines (table 14.18). The cond value is coded into the otherwise unused $a$ operand field of the instruction, from which it is routed to the conditional logic in the ALU stage. That logic combines the current condition-code information from the CC register with the specified branch condition and generates a load enable to the PC register if the branch is to be taken.

Instruction

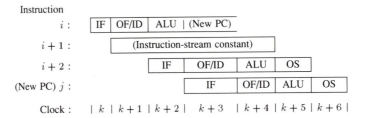

**Figure 17.6** Branch instruction timing.

In the interests of implementation simplicity, the $R$ machine provides no explicit `rcall` instruction. Compiled code must therefore use explicit, lower-level instructions to save $\langle PC \rangle$ (for example, on an explicitly maintained stack) and execute a jump to the called subroutine.

### 17.5.3 Branch Timing and Delays

A pipelined execution path complicates the timing (and often the semantics) of branches. Consider the situation diagrammed in figure 17.6. Instruction $i$ is an `rjmprc` instruction, which causes the PC to be reloaded at the completion of its ALU cycle. Since that instruction uses the following instruction word (`delta`) as an instruction-stream constant, the cycle following the loading of the PC will execute no operation. However, the instruction $i + 2$ will have been loaded by the IFU during the cycle in which the `rjmprc` takes effect. This instruction has thus entered the pipeline, despite the fact that its execution is contrary to the usual sequential-machine semantics.

The most conventional fix for this problem is to perform a *pipeline flush* at each branch instruction, removing (or changing to "no operation") each partially executed instruction that remains in the pipe. This strategy preserves the single-sequence machine semantics but incurs some costs in hardware and in performance (since idle cycles are introduced at each branch).

An alternative popular in RISCs is to shift the burden to the compiler by explicitly documenting the idiosyncratic sequence of instruction executions surrounding a branch and insisting that the compiler cope with it. In particular, the $R$-machine language semantics dictate that the instruction following an `rjmprc` *always* be executed, whether or not the branch takes place. The compiler writer has the option to put a useful instruction in that position, if possible; otherwise the `rjmprc` must be followed by an `rnop` instruction.

The execution of instruction $i + 2$ may be further complicated by the fact that its address has no fixed relationship to the various values in the program counter as the instruction passes down the pipeline.[4] As a result, aspects of instruction

---

[4] Note that instruction $i + 1$ would face a similar quandary, avoided because the $R$ machine devotes

*Reduced-Instruction-Set Computers*

execution that depend on this relationship will fail to work for instruction $i + 2$ unless additional steps are taken. These include PC-relative addressing and the use of a following 16-bit instruction-stream constant. The former would compute an address relative to the branch target rather than the address of instruction $i + 2$, while the latter would use an instruction word fetched from the new address as the constant. (A clever programmer might find useful ways to exploit this peculiarity of the machine—for example, to implement dispatch tables.)

The burden of this problem can be shifted to the compiler writer as well, placing restrictions on the form of the instruction that can follow a branch. We adopt this strategy for the $R$ machine, requiring that an instruction following a branch avoid using a 16-bit constant word (which implies, in the case of the $R$ machine, the avoidance of PC-relative addressing). An alternative solution is to provide multiple copies of the PC register, effectively passing down the pipeline the location from which each instruction is fetched. While the latter approach requires additional hardware, it substantially simplifies the programming model presented by a pipelined machine.

## 17.6 Main-Memory Timing Conflict

The $R$ machine provides several simple load and store instructions for access to main-memory locations. Of these, the most basic are

```
rload(a,b)          | Load main-memory <<a>> into register b.
```

and

```
rstore(a,b)         | Store <a> into main memory location b.
```

which offer what might be viewed as register indirect mode access to main memory. The implementation plan assumes a memory-bus interface having data and address registers BDATA and BADR. The memory access is started and BADR is loaded during the ALU stage of a load or store instruction; the data are supplied in that same cycle on a store or arrive several cycles later on a load. (The choice of the ALU stage rather than the earlier operand-fetch stage to specify the address allows use of the ALU in its computation, for example, for indexed mode or PC-relative addressing.)

Access to main-memory locations is typically somewhat slower than access to operands in the register file, even when the caching techniques described in chapter 16 are used to improve apparent memory speed. This difference in timing is problematic in a pipelined architecture, particularly in the case of a load instruction. The problem is that the memory access takes several clock cycles, returning the value to be loaded (into the register file) *after* the operand-store cycle of the load instruction. Thus the write to the register file for a load operation happens at a

---

this instruction-stream word to holding a constant to specify the branch address. In the general case, however, every word fetched between the fetch of the branch instruction and the consequent change to $\langle PC \rangle$ will be executed with abnormal PC contents during one or more pipeline stages.

different time relative to, say, instruction fetch than other instructions: The normal operand store happens at the fourth pipeline stage, but the load instructions require a store into the register file on perhaps a fifth cycle of the instruction. Unfortunately, the write port of the register file is likely to be occupied during that cycle by the operand-store portion of the following instruction, unless that instruction is a load as well. This situation corresponds to an ill-formed pipeline whose various paths encounter different numbers of stages: Some computations (instructions) get to the operand-store phase in four clock cycles, others get to it in five. The result is a conflict.

There are several ways to circumvent this problem. One is to provide yet another independent port to the register file, dedicated to writes resulting from main-memory load operations. Another is to require the compiler to replace the conflicting instruction following each `rload` with an `rnop` instruction and modify the data paths so that a load usurps the operand-store phase of the next instruction. A third alternative, and the one we select for the $R$ machine, is to pad the shorter paths through the pipeline with extra stages: We execute all $R$-machine instructions in a five-stage pipeline, despite the fact that many (all but loads) could be executed in four stages.

Figure 17.7 shows the complete data paths of the $R$ machine, in which a fifth pipeline stage has been added between the ALU and operand-store stages. This stage is devoid of logic; its only function is to provide sufficient delay that main memory can respond in time for the operand-store phase of load instructions. The expanded pipeline timing diagram is shown in figure 17.8.

The interface to memory uses two bus registers, BADR and BDATA. BADR is loaded at the end of the ALU phase of a load or store instruction, beginning a memory read or write operation, respectively. (One of the control bits generated by the decode logic specifies the memory operation and is routed to the bus interface.) In the case of a store instruction, BDATA is loaded at the same time as BADR; a special path between the A data output of the register file to BDATA is provided for this purpose. Thus the only datum that can be written directly into main memory is the contents of a register.

In the case of a load instruction, the fetched datum (the contents of the addressed main-memory location) is required to appear in BDATA during the operand-store cycle, after the intervening wait phase. Thus the memory has between one and two cycles to respond, depending on what constraints are placed on the timing of the C data input by the register file. Clearly, additional wait stages could be added to the pipeline to increase the delay.

We consider four $R$-machine load and store instructions, although other useful possibilites exist. Our selection is

```
rload(a,b)           | b -> <<a>>
rloadx(a,delta,b)    | b <-  <<a>+delta>
rstore(a,b)          | <b> <- <a>
rstorex(a,delta,b)   | <b>+delta <- <a>
```

which includes the `rload` and `rstore` mentioned earlier, in addition to indexed versions `rloadx` and `rstorex`, which perform simple address arithmetic involving

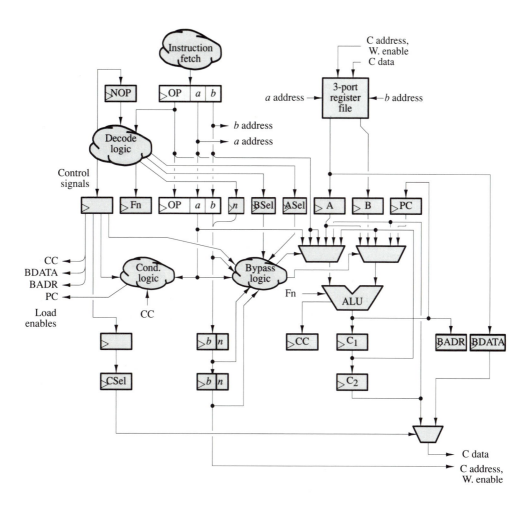

**Figure 17.7** *R*-machine data paths.

a 16-bit instruction-stream constant `delta`. No bypass paths or interlocks are provided for load instructions; hence the compiler must provide one or two load delays, depending on the type of load instruction.

Referring to figure 17.7, we note that the `rload` instruction can be effected by programming the ALU to pass its A operand through unchanged to be loaded into BADR and allowing the *b* instruction operand to specify the destination register. In this case, two load delays are required (that is, neither of the following two instructions may refer to the *b* register). The `rstore` instruction uses the contents of the register addressed by *a* to supply (via an ad hoc path) the input to BDATA, while the *b* operand specifies a register whose contents are passed through the ALU to be loaded into BADR.

For the `rloadx` and `rstorex` instructions, the following instruction is selected as a 16-bit constant offset to be added to the contents of a register to yield the address. In the case of the `rstorex` instruction, the contents of the *a* register are

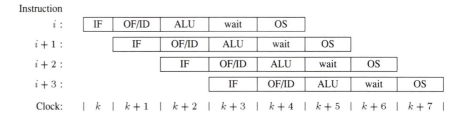

**Figure 17.8** Five-stage $R$-machine pipeline.

routed to BDATA, so that the $b$ register must be used as an index register. Its contents, along with the 16-bit constant offset, are routed to the ALU and added; the result is loaded into BADR.

In the case of the `rloadx` instruction, the $b$ register must serve as the destination and hence cannot specify the index register without introducing an awkward programming constraint. However, the left-hand ALU operand, normally the path for the contents of the $a$ register, is occupied by the 16-bit constant; hence we provide a path from the A register to the B input multiplexer of the ALU, allowing us to route the contents of the register addressed by $a$ into the right-hand ALU input. The ALU output is thus $\langle a \rangle + \text{delta}$, reserving the $b$ operand field of the instruction as the destination for the data. Since the `rloadx` instruction uses the following instruction word as a constant (`delta`), it reduces the effective load delay from two cycles to one.

As with pipeline dependencies, the main-memory delay requirements can be detected and enforced with hardware interlocks or be left as a software responsibility. Thus the most economical hardware implementation would simply return erroneous data should the program access the destination of an `rload` without sufficient time for the memory to respond, while a somewhat more forgiving approach would delay execution until the data became available. The argument for hardware memory interlocks is somewhat more compelling than that for pipeline interlocks, since external memory is usually a subsystem independent from the processor. Separating memory timing from the programming model allows memory timing to vary, as it might, for example, as a result of contention with other devices or external caches.

## 17.7 Impact of Lengthened Pipeline

Although additional pipeline stages provide more time per instruction without reducing throughput, they can increase hardware costs and degrade performance in other ways. Note, in figure 17.7, that the bypass paths needed to avoid load delays in register operations have doubled: Because of the longer pipeline, conflicts are possible with the previous two instructions instead of just the previous one. This approximately doubles the cost of the bypass approach: Not only are the additional paths necessary, but additional comparisons must be performed to detect the

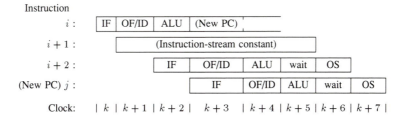

Instruction

| $i:$ | IF | OF/ID | ALU | (New PC) | | | |

| $i+1:$ | (Instruction-stream constant) |

| $i+2:$ | | IF | OF/ID | ALU | wait | OS |

| (New PC) $j:$ | | | IF | OF/ID | ALU | wait | OS |

Clock:  | $k$ | $k+1$ | $k+2$ | $k+3$ | $k+4$ | $k+5$ | $k+6$ | $k+7$ |

**Figure 17.9**  Branch delay on five-stage pipeline.

additional conflicts. Alternatively, if load delays are used in lieu of bypass paths, a performance degradation due to extra rnops is likely. While a good compiler can follow a load with a single useful instruction most of the time, it typically has trouble filling several such gaps.

The extra stage has no impact on branch delays. Since the new stage comes after the ALU phase in which the PC is loaded with the new address, the number of clock cycles between the instruction fetch and the PC load is unchanged; you can see this in the timing shown in figure 17.9. Thus only a single 16-bit instruction will be executed following a branch (since one following instruction is usurped as a branch address).

## 17.8  Alternatives and Issues

A number of neighboring architectural schools share elements with the RISC approach. Simple processors have been proposed that offer a single operation—*move*—and attach operator semantics to specialized source and destination locations. (See Lipovski [1976] for one such design.) Instructions on such machines have no opcode, encoding simply source and destination locations. The 32-bit Inmos Transputer [Whitby-Strevens 1985; Barron 1983] reduces the instruction coding to another extreme, utilizing a single 8-bit instruction format.

More conventional microcoded architectures have softened the machine-language boundary by means of *writable control store*, which makes microcode accessible as a programming interface. Compilers that directly produce microcode have been written for various of these machines, allowing direct execution of compiler output in much the manner of RISCs. (The Lambda processor, made by the now-defunct Lisp Machines, Inc., is an interesting example in this regard. Although running counter to the RISC bias in most regards, its architecture is specifically tailored to the execution of compiler-generated microcode.) Typically only performance-critical regions of application software are compiled to microcode, since control store size is usually limited; thus such machines exhibit a mixture of direct execution and microcoded interpretation of user programs.

Other tricks have been used effectively to exploit RISC performance advantages while conforming to more traditional programming models. One class of machines—exemplified by the Harris HCX series and the earlier Computer Consoles, Inc., machines on which they are based—utilizes an instruction-fetch unit that fetches instructions from a conventional instruction set (similar to that of our $G$ machine) and translates them, on the fly, to equivalent RISC-like instructions that are passed to a simple, high-performance pipelined processor for execution. Since the relatively complex IFU translation is a potential performance bottleneck, an instruction cache is incorporated *between* the IFU and the processor. Thus *translated* instructions are cached, and small loops can be repeatedly executed without being repeatedly retranslated from the original machine code.

## 17.9 Summary

This chapter has provided a glimpse of a trend that might be viewed as reactionary: RISC is the back-to-basics movement in computer architecture. Although a variety of its technical specifics will remain controversial for years to come, the undeniable impact of RISC comes from the fundamental message it delivers: the value of simplicity. Current RISC machines are enjoying a demonstrable cost/performance edge over their more conventional alternatives—not because of what their designers have included, but because of what they have left out. The simpler machines are more tractable from both cost and engineering standpoints. The design is manageable; performance bottlenecks are visible; improvements are straightforward. The result is a generally higher level of engineering, with consequent practical payoff.

## 17.10 Context

The roots of the RISC movement are generally acknowledged to be a 1970s project at IBM's Watson Research Center that developed the experimental 801 computer under the direction of John Cocke [Radin 1982]. The 801 combines a fast clock, pipelined execution, simple instructions, and a sophisticated compiler.

The wave of momentum currently enjoyed by RISC processors, along with the popularization of the name RISC, awaited the Berkeley RISC project [Patterson and Sequin 1982] and the MIPS project at Stanford [Hennessy et al. 1982], whose advocates aggressively challenged the architectural obesity of commercially successful processors from such established sources as DEC and IBM. Although the Berkeley processors have a number of specific characteristics that remain controversial, their general design priorities won an immediate following and have stimulated a generation of lean designs; many of these are successful commercial products.

Occasionally the RISC development is characterized as a technical debate between the advocates of RISCs and CISCs, the latter short for *complex-instruction-set computers*. That debate, to the extent that it exists, is largely one-sided: it is difficult to find a CISC advocate for the same reason that one rarely encounters a crusader for obesity. On the contrary, the current vogue has motivated even relatively complex architectures to be labeled as RISCs by their promoters. While there are substantive controversies regarding RISC, each involves a trade-off involving a particular mechanism whose value to the computation model is offset by additional hardware complexity (such as run-time tags and type-checking hardware) rather than an attack on the minimalist bias in general. Further reading on RISCs includes Hennessy [1984], Patterson [1985], Colwell et al. [1985], and Patterson and Hennessy [1985].

It should be observed, finally, that the fundamental mechanism explored in this chapter is pipelined architectures. Pipelined machines substantially predate the RISC wave, having been standard techniques in high-performance machines since the 1960s; classic examples are described by Thornton [1970] and Russell [1978]. The RISC idiom and the $R$ machine provide a convenient vehicle for illuminating pipelined execution for the same reason that RISCs bring these techniques to inexpensive processors: They minimize the extent to which the pipeline is encumbered by unrelated but complicating factors. Further general information on pipelined execution can be found in Ramamoorthy and Li [1977], Kogge [1981], and Stone [1987].

## 17.11 Problems

### Problem 17.1
Describe details of the implementation of the `rload` and `rloadx` instructions, specifying for each the operation details (such as control signals asserted) at each pipeline stage.

### Problem 17.2
Describe a plausible implementation of a PC-relative `rloadr` instruction:

```
rloadr(delta,b)    | <<PC>+delta> -> b
```

Can `rloadr` be implemented using the data paths of figure 17.7, assuming appropriate combinational logic in the unspecified circuitry?

### Problem 17.3
Suppose the $R$-machine bypass logic ignored the $n$ bit and assumed that every instruction word is valid (enabled). Describe a scenario in which this naive variant will give results that differ from those likely to be anticipated by the programmer. Outline a programming discipline that avoids the need for $n$.

### Problem ⋆17.4   Design of R-Machine Stack-Pointer Support:
Add stack-pointer hardware to the data paths of figure 17.7, using an *up/down counter* as the register component. Assume that this clocked register has a *count-enable* input as well as an *up/down* input and that it increments, decrements, or remains unchanged on the basis of their values. In other respects it serves as an ordinary register; its *load enable* allows parallel loading, and its contents are available continuously at output terminals.

Your design should provide for (1) program loading of the SP register, (2) program access to ⟨SP⟩, and (3) simple subroutine linkage via `rcall` and `rrtn` instructions that maintain the return ⟨PC⟩ on the stack. Sketch the implementation of

*R*-machine instructions that perform these functions, identifying portions of each operation with pipeline stages in a diagram patterned after figure 17.8.

# 18    Processes and
Processor Multiplexing

In this chapter we move beyond the single-sequence machine to consider one further level of abstraction from which we can view computing systems. As with all our levels of abstraction, it is motivated by the twin desires to provide a more congenial environment for the user of the abstraction (the programmer) and to allow a greater degree of flexibility to the implementor of the abstraction.

The single-sequence machine is an abstraction powerful enough to enable the expression of all manner of computational algorithms, and its emphasis on strict sequentiality of operations avoids a potential source of complexity and confusion for the programmer. Nevertheless, when a digital system must interact with the physical world, when improved performance may be achievable by carrying out several operations simultaneously, and for other organizational reasons, it is useful to be able to deal conveniently with concurrency.

For example, a digital system might be called upon to serve as part of a telephone switching system, connected to a multitude of individual customers. At any particular time, several customer lines could be in various states of activity. For another example, a system could be connected to several printers and be required to keep each of them busy printing the appropriate data. In each of these cases, an ad hoc program *could* be written for a single-sequence machine to do the job. Such a program would have to record explicitly the status of the various devices or activities to be managed and shift its attention from one to another as required. Writing such a program for a single-sequence machine has much in common with trying to express an inherently recursive algorithm in FORTRAN: It is possible, but it requires explicit management of information that would be handled implicitly by a more appropriate abstraction.

An alternative to employing a single-sequence machine for one of these applications would be to use several processors, one for each task to be performed (for example, one for each telephone line or each printer). Then a relatively simple single-sequence program on each processor would equip the system to perform its function. Given the previously mentioned advantages of expressing algorithms as single-sequence programs, this approach has much to recommend it; in fact, it may be viewed as the most conservative extension of the single-sequence abstraction to situations that the unadorned single-sequence paradigm does not handle well.

However well it may work and however pleasing its structure, though, such a multiprocessor system is rarely the most cost-effective solution to a problem.

Individual processors may be idle much of the time, waiting for external events. Moreover, dedicating a separate processor to each task leads to inflexibility: A change in the system's specification that adds new functionality, for example, may require additional processors as well as revised software.

Some way is needed to take advantage of the conceptual simplification afforded by the multiprocessor solution without our being forced to dedicate a physical processor to each task. This is accomplished by the *process abstraction*. We use the term *process* to describe the action of a virtual processor, which executes a program as though that program had a physical processor entirely to itself. Instead of actually devoting a physical processor to each process, though, we can program a single physical processor to multiplex itself among several processes, allowing the implementation of systems comprising fewer physical processors than the number of processes they contain.

An important special case, and a basis for building more complex systems, is the implementation of a group of processes on just one physical processor. This chapter explores the implementation of processes on single-sequence machines. As it happens, processes are useful in many more situations than the rather elementary scenarios just discussed; some of these applications are described, along with the additional mechanisms needed to support them.

## 18.1 The Process Abstraction

Along with its program and data in memory, a physical processor has a certain amount of internal state information, such as a stack pointer, program counter, and PSW. In order to implement a virtual processor, copies of this information must be supplied, and an interpreter must emulate the effects of the virtual machine instructions on the contents of these registers and main memory. To support several processes on one physical processor, a special area of main memory might be reserved to store one copy of the internal state information for each virtual processor. Software could then read the instruction stream of a virtual processor and perform the requisite operations on internal state and main-memory contents.

This technique is really applied when a processor is simulated using the hardware of another processor, but this software-level emulation is usually grossly inefficient relative to a microcode- or hardware-level implementation. Fortunately, for the special case in which the virtual processor to be emulated has the same instruction set as the underlying processor, a modest amount of additional microcode and/or hardware support permits an efficient and satisfactory implementation. The trick, not surprisingly, is to use the machine instruction set already supported by microcode to do the bulk of the emulation, with the virtual state registers of the currently executing process loaded into the physical state registers of the processor. A small amount of additional mechanism—essentially the machine's trap mechanism—is needed to support switching from one process to another, which requires saving away the current internal state registers at a designated place in main memory and loading these registers with a new set of values found at another designated place in main memory.

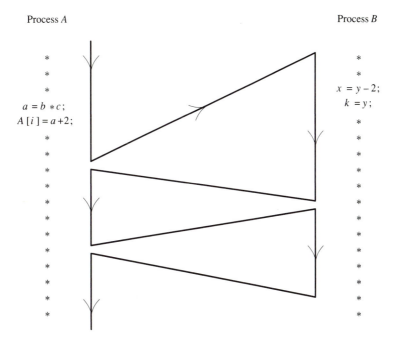

Process A                                                    Process B

**Figure 18.1** Two-process time-slicing.

In order to support several virtual processors on one physical processor, some kind of "time-slicing" technique must be used, wherein the physical processor devotes its attention to emulating one virtual processor for some (possibly very short) interval, then shifts its attention to another. Figure 18.1 illustrates the sharing of a single processor between two independent programs, each of which constitutes a process comprising a sequence of instruction executions. The arrows between the two processes depict the switching of the processor's attention from one program to the other, leading to a characteristic "dovetail" pattern of control flow: Some number of process $A$'s instructions are executed; then some number of process $B$'s instructions are executed; then control passes back to process $A$ for the next few instruction executions; and so on.

A key element of the process abstraction is that the time-slicing mechanism is entirely transparent to each of the processes, maintaining for each the illusion that it has the entire resources of the processor; this transparency allows the programs executed in each process to be written independently of the details of the time-slicing. The transparency requirement dictates that every piece of program-visible processor state information be maintained between time slices of each process. In effect, each of the processes $A$ and $B$ has an associated *context* that includes variable values, a program counter, and other processor states. To be invisible to the programs sharing a processor, time-slicing requires more than just occasionally passing control from one program to the other; it requires a complete *context switch* in which the processor state corresponding to one program's execution is

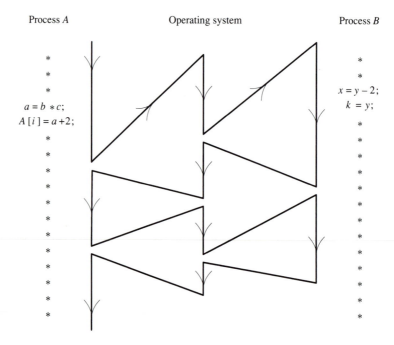

Process A    Operating system    Process B

```
*                                              *
*                                              *
*                                    x = y - 2;
a = b * c;                           k = y;
A [ i ] = a + 2;                               *
*                                              *
*                                              *
*                                              *
*                                              *
*                                              *
*                                              *
*                                              *
*                                              *
*                                              *
*                                              *
*                                              *
*                                              *
```

**Figure 18.2**   Operating-system intervention in time-slicing.

saved away in memory (to be reinstalled when execution of that program resumes) and the processor state associated with execution of the other program is installed in its place.

The *mechanism* to support such context switching is already present in any processor that supports traps, but there is also a need for *strategy* decisions to be made regarding when to switch processes and which process to switch to next. The considerations that enter into formulating this strategy are sufficiently complex and variable from one use to another that they are not usually implemented in hardware or microcode. Rather, it is more common to provide just enough hardware and microcode support so that these strategy decisions can be made and carried out by operating-system software written in the machine's instruction set. Typically, hardware and microcode support for time-slicing provides (through the trap mechanism) a limited mechanism for context switching, sufficient to interrupt a running process $A$, save certain essential elements of $A$'s context, and pass control to the operating system. The operating system then saves away the remainder of $A$'s context, selects a process $B$ to run next, installs $B$'s context, and executes a machine instruction that completes the context switch by resuming execution of $B$. In effect, the operating system is an additional process whose execution is interspersed with that of the processes it manages. Figure 18.2 illustrates, schematically, the intervention of the operating system in the administration of time-slicing between two processes.

The use of time-slicing as an implementation strategy determines some of the

*Processes and Processor Multiplexing*

```
/* Structure definition for active machine state:      */

struct MState
{       int PC, SP, B, PSW;      /* Active registers.      */
};


/* Structure definition for process descriptor block:   */

struct PDB
{       struct MState state;     /* Active registers.      */
        ...                      /* Various other stuff.   */
} ProcList[NPROC];               /* All processes.         */
```

**Figure 18.3**   Process-descriptor-block declaration.

properties of the process abstraction. In the absence of more specific information about the scheduling strategies in use (and it is usually unsafe to rely on any such "information"), it must be assumed that execution of a process may be suspended for an indefinite period after the execution of any instruction and that arbitrary numbers of instructions from other processes may be executed in the interim. The process abstraction thus makes no guarantees about the real-time behavior of a program: Arbitrary time intervals may intervene between the execution of any pair of instructions. Furthermore, in cases where processes can communicate with one another, programs must be written so that they will work correctly for any interleaved order of executing instructions in the various processes. This requirement leads to some interesting problems that we shall explore in chapter 19.

## 18.2 Process Management

We have noted that the time-sliced emulation of several virtual processors on a single physical machine requires that state or context information for each virtual processor be remembered between its successive time slices. For this purpose we devise a data structure called a *process descriptor block* (or PDB), which is used by operating-system software to record the state of each process. Figure 18.3 gives the declaration of a skeletal PDB structure for use with the $S$ machine. Subsequent sections augment this structure at the "..." line to store additional information about each process.

Figure 18.3 contains two declarations, each of which defines (effectively as a new data type) an aggregate data format. The first of these is the MState structure, seen previously in figure 14.45, which contains the actual state information maintained in registers by the processor and with which the processor's trap mechanism deals directly. In the case of a general-register machine such as the $G$ machine of chapter 15, the MState data structure would contain copies of the general registers in addition to implicit machine state such as the PSW.

The second declared data structure in figure 18.3 is the PDB itself, one of whose components is a saved machine state (in the format of an MState data structure).

```
int CurProc;              /* Number of the current process.          */

Scheduler(old)                        /* The scheduler procedure.     */
 struct MState *old;                   /* arg is pointer to saved MState.*/
 {     ProcList[CurProc].state = *old; /* Save away old state...        */
       CurProc = (CurProc+1) % NPROC;  /* ... find a new one to run...  */
       *old = ProcList[CurProc].state; /* and install its state.        */
 }
```

**Figure 18.4**  Round-robin scheduler.

In addition to defining the format of the PDB, this second declaration establishes an *array* of process descriptor blocks, ProcList[NPROC], which will be used to hold information about each of the virtual machines emulated by the system. Thus, if $i$ indicates the position in the ProcList array where the state of some suspended process $P$ is kept, ProcList[$i$].state.PC, ProcList[$i$].state.B, and so on, reflect the various register contents associated with $P$ at the time of its suspension.

Note that the **state** component of a PDB is exactly the saved state information that is received by a trap handler. The access that a trap handler has to this stacked state provides the basis for the process-management functions of an operating system. Assume, for example, that we arrange for a hardware clock circuit to interrupt the processor's execution periodically (say, once every 10 ms), save the state of the interrupted program, and invoke a *scheduler* procedure that we provide in the operating system. The implementation of such a *clock interrupt* might be identical to that of an instruction trap (including an assembly-language stub like that in figure 14.46 to call the handler), except that (1) it is invoked by an external clock signal rather than the execution of a supervisor-call instruction and (2) it invokes the procedure **Scheduler** rather than the supervisor-call trap handler.

A simple scheduler is sketched in figure 18.4. Recall the declaration in figure 18.3 of the array ProcList of process descriptor blocks, one for each of the processes to be managed; the index of a process's descriptor in this array effectively defines a unique *process number* for that process. The integer variable CurProc holds the process number of the process that is currently running.

When the scheduler is invoked, it receives (as the argument old) a *pointer* (just as in the handler procedures of figures 13.7 and 14.44) to an MState data structure containing the saved processor state of the currently running process, which was interrupted by the clock signal. The scheduler starts by copying this state information into the ProcList entry assigned to that process: The assignment ProcList[CurProc].state = *old has the effect of copying each element of the MState structure addressed by old into its corresponding element of the indexed ProcList entry.

In our example, the selection of a new process to run simply involves cycling to the next process in the table; this strategy is termed *round-robin scheduling*. (The C expression (CurProc+1)%NPROC increments CurProc modulo NPROC, the latter being an integer constant specifying the number of processes supported by the system.) Once the number of the next process is known, the scheduler re-

*Processes and Processor Multiplexing*

places the state information on the stack (still pointed to by `old`) with the `MState` from the newly selected `ProcList` entry, so that upon return from the clock interrupt the state of the new process (rather than that of the interrupted process) will be restored. Thus the assignment `*old = ProcList[CurProc].state` followed by the procedure return installs the state contained in another process's process descriptor block and continues the execution of that process.

## 18.3  Operating-System Services

Often the hardware protocols for interaction with physical input/output devices attached to a processor are cumbersome and fail to adhere to any particular standard. Furthermore, several processes in a system may all want to access a particular device. For example, a magnetic tape drive may be used first by one process to read one tape and then by another process for a different purpose. In order to hide, or abstract, from user-level programs the frequently messy details of physical dealings with input/output hardware, as well as to allow for the appropriate coordination of accesses to shared devices, it is customary for operating-system software to provide virtual processors with a way of dealing with physical devices that is more uniform and streamlined than the actual hardware protocols themselves. Thus the virtual machine seen by user programs executing on virtual processors may be viewed as an *extension* of the underlying virtual machine, including not only the basic virtual instruction set but also special "instructions" whose executions cause input/output or other operations to be performed by operating-system software. These additional instructions, introduced in sections 13.3.11, 14.9, and 15.7, are known as *system calls*, or *supervisor calls*.

We have now encountered two kinds of functions that are usually performed by operating-system software: the basic scheduling and emulation that create several virtual processors on one physical processor, and the emulation of additional instructions by which a process can interact with its environment. A big part of the art of operating-system design is specifying these extensions to the basic virtual machine so that the ensemble forms a simple, clean, and powerful set of primitives for dealing with parallelism and communication. Additional details to consider include provisions for protecting users from each other and the system from users and mechanisms for resource control and allocation. Even a cursory study of these problems is beyond our scope; the intent of this chapter is to concentrate on some of the ways in which these demands can affect processor architecture.

In most operating systems, there is an identifiable *kernel* of software that implements the fundamental process abstraction. Often additional layers of software within the operating system provide many of the remaining facilities. Beyond this level of detail, however, it is difficult to generalize, since there are many different philosophies of operating-system construction, and the particular hardware architecture on which an operating system is built frequently has a major impact on the kinds of system organizations that are feasible.

In many simple operating systems, the operating-system kernel is simply a collection of handlers for various interrupts, traps, and faults that may occur, along with support routines and data structures shared by these handlers. Often this body of kernel software shares a single virtual address space and a single stack; it nearly always is *privileged* in the sense that it is allowed to execute instructions (for example, to perform low-level input and output) that cause illegal-instruction faults when executed by user-level programs.

### 18.3.1 Supervisor Calls

Let us use the $S$ machine for a case study in supervisor calls. Recall from section 14.9 the ssvc supervisor-call instruction, whose opcode is followed in the instruction stream by a single byte *code* that dictates the service to be performed by the kernel. When ssvc causes an instruction trap, the ssvc trap handler invokes one of 256 ssvc *subhandlers* within the kernel, selected by the second byte of the ssvc instruction. The ssvc instructions are *interpreted* by their kernel-level handlers as requests for various services; thus ssvc(0) might invoke a kernel handler that reads a character from the user's keyboard, ssvc(1) might cause a character to be typed, and so on.

An ssvc trap causes the current machine state to be saved on the stack and a new stack frame to be built for the handler invocation in the same way as for a clock interrupt; thus control may be returned to the process via the trap-return instruction strtn or to another process via an assignment to the stacked machine state before the trap return.

Frequently, a user program will want to do more than merely cause a trap to the kernel; it will also want to communicate some arguments and possibly receive some results. It is thus desirable for the kernel to be able to fetch arguments off the user's stack and push results back onto it. To accomplish this we implement, as support routines within the kernel, procedures POPPS$\alpha$($s$) and PUSHPS$\alpha$($s$, *datum*), which perform pop and push operations, respectively, on the stack associated with the machine state $s$. The argument $s$ is passed as a pointer to an MState structure from which these procedures can access and modify the previous (interrupted) stack. Figure 18.5 shows implementations of POPPS1 and PUSHPS1 as examples.

### 18.3.2 An Example of Supervisor-Call Handling

We have hypothesized that supervisor call number 0 reads a character from a teletype and is handled by a routine called ReadCh, and that supervisor call number 1 types a character out on the teletype and is handled by a routine called TypeCh. A supervisor-call handler for such a system is shown as the procedure ssvcHandler in figure 18.6; it is essentially the supervisor-call handler of figure 14.44 expanded with some detail in its body. (The switch statement used in ssvcHandler is described in appendix 1. As used here, it dispatches on the value of code, going to the label case $n$: when the value of code is $n$.)

Figure 18.6 also shows how the ReadCh and TypeCh subhandlers might be written. We assume the existence of kernel routines TTYRead and TTYWrite that perform the appropriate low-level manipulations of the physical devices to cause the input or output to happen. We assume that several terminals (formerly known as

```
POPPS1(s)
 struct MState *s;
 {      char *p;
        s->SP = s->SP - 1;    /* Decrement user's stack pointer. */
        p = s->SP;            /* Address of user's top-of-stack. */
        return *p;            /* Read and return the byte there. */
 }


PUSHPS1(s, datum)
 struct MState *s;
 char datum;
 {      char *p;
        p = s->SP;
        *p = datum;           /* Store byte at user's top-of-stack. */
        s->SP = s->SP + 1;    /* Increment user's stack pointer. */
 }
```

**Figure 18.5**   Simple implementations of POPPS1 and PUSHPS1.

```
ssvcHandler(code,p)                    /* The main ssvc handler. */
 struct MState *p;
 char code;
  {
        switch (code)
         { case 0:  ReadCh(p); return;
           case 1:  TypeCh(p); return;

                 .
                 .
                 .

         }
  }

ReadCh(p)                              /* Read a character from the TTY. */
 struct MState *p;
 {      PUSHPS1(p, TTYRead(ProcList[CurProc].TTYNumber));
 }

TypeCh(p)                              /* Type a character to the TTY. */
 struct MState *p;
 {      TTYWrite(ProcList[CurProc].TTYNumber, POPPS1(p));
 }
```

**Figure 18.6**   Typical supervisor-call handlers.

*teletypes*, or TTYs) can be connected to the computer (so that, for example, users of a time-sharing system can each interact through their own terminal); consequently, the kernel routines take an integer argument specifying on which terminal the read or write operation is to be performed. Thus TTYRead($n$) returns a character read from terminal number $n$, and TTYWrite($n,c$) types the character whose ASCII

```
Loop:   ssvc(0)   | Read a character from the terminal,
        ssvc(1)   |   type it out on the terminal,
        sc4(Loop)
        sjmp      |   and loop back to do it again!
```

**Figure 18.7**  User-level terminal echo program.

code is $c$ on terminal number $n$.

In choosing the terminal number $n$ to be passed to the physical input/output routines, the kernel performs a simple mapping function that isolates the user program from the details of device selection. Note in particular that the ReadCh and TypeCh supervisor-call instructions do *not* specify the terminal to be used; in effect, users each have a single *virtual* terminal (the one at which they are sitting), and all interactions via ReadCh and TypeCh are directed to that device. Thus a user can run the same program on another day from a different terminal without changing its supervisor calls to reflect the move. To effect this mapping, the PDB structure for a process, defined in figure 18.3, is augmented with a field called TTYNumber to store the terminal number associated with the process. This field is referenced in the above handlers by the form ProcList[CurProc].TTYNumber. Figure 18.7 gives a simple assembly-language example of how a user program might use the ReadCh and TypeCh supervisor calls. The program is a trivial echo loop that types out every character it reads in.

The procedures given in figure 18.6 illustrate supervisor-call handling but are rather simplistic in other respects. They assume, for instance, the existence of a subroutine TTYRead that will return a new character from a terminal whenever it is called. In fact, some time may well elapse from when a process requests a new character until the character is actually typed in by the user. The procedure TTYRead will wait for a character to be typed in before returning, wasting time that could be used for execution of some other process.

To deal with this problem, we need some mechanism by which the kernel can detect the fact that the current process is about to wait for physical input or output and switch the attention of the processor to another user process. To determine the status of the physical input/output devices, we assume low-level kernel procedures TTYReadOK($n$) and TTYWriteOK($n$), which return *false* if the corresponding single-character input/output operation on console $n$ would cause waiting because the device is not currently ready for a new input/output transaction. The use of these routines is illustrated in the ReadCh and TypeCh subhandlers of figure 18.8.

These handlers are similar to the preceding ones, except that they invoke the scheduler to run another process if the indicated operation would result in waiting for physical input or output. In such cases, the program counter is adjusted before the scheduler is called, so that the next time the process is scheduled the same supervisor call will be executed again. The purpose of backing up the program counter is to restore the user process's state in every respect to that existing just prior to the troublesome supervisor call, so that reexecution of the call later on will not yield any anomalous results (in particular, so that it will not appear to the user

```
ReadCh(p)
 struct MState *p;
 {      if (TTYReadOK(ProcList[CurProc].TTYNumber))
                PUSHPS1(p, TTYRead(ProcList[CurProc].TTYNumber));
        else
                {       p->PC := p->PC - 2;
                        Scheduler(p);
                }
 }


TypeCh(p)
 struct MState *p;
 {      if (TTYWriteOK(ProcList[CurProc].TTYNumber))
                TTYWrite(ProcList[CurProc].TTYNumber, POPPS1(p))
        else
                {       p->PC := p->PC - 2;
                        Scheduler(p);
                }
 }
```

**Figure 18.8**   Improved supervisor-call subhandlers.


process that the supervisor call was executed twice).

In general, backing up the PC as in figure 18.8 is only the first step that may be needed to restore the user's state. For example, if the supervisor-call handler had performed manipulations on the user's stack before deciding that it could not continue, all those manipulations would have to be undone. This is one reason why the TypeCh handler does not pop its character argument off the user's stack until after a call to TTYWriteOK has assured that a TTYWrite will work. If the character had been popped earlier, it would have to be pushed back on before returning; otherwise the next attempt to execute the TypeCh would not only type the wrong character, but would also leave the user's stack 1 byte shorter than it ought to be. This general theme of not performing any irreversible side effects until it is certain that a supervisor call can be completed successfully is reminiscent of the considerations applicable to aborting and restarting instructions when page faults occur, as discussed in section 16.7.1.

Our simple kernel has no way to determine what a process is waiting for, other than starting the process up and seeing whether it continues to run or immediately returns because it is attempting a supervisor call that still cannot be completed. This tactic is simple, but in many real situations it is grossly inefficient. Even in our simple operating system, some overhead attends restarting a process; the machine state assignment and trap-return mechanisms must be invoked, the restarted process must execute a supervisor call, and finally the subhandler must determine whether the supervisor call can now be satisfied.

In most systems, this *context-switching* overhead is substantial and may involve paging traffic and other kinds of activity. Furthermore, large time-sharing systems typically support a large number of processes, of which usually only a small fraction are not waiting for something. Restarting each process in round-robin fashion is an expensive way to find a process that is capable of proceeding. Therefore, most systems store additional state information in their equivalent of the PDB—recording, for example, that the reason a process was suspended was that it requested terminal input and none was available. Then the scheduler can check, without going through the overhead of actually restarting a process, whether the condition that caused it to wait is still true. In fact, even the overhead of repeated checking can often be avoided by maintaining lists of runnable processes and of processes waiting for various conditions. Instead of repeatedly checking the status of a process, the operating system can simply move it from one list to another upon the occurrence of events that affect its eligibility to execute.

## 18.4 Memory Mapping

As described thus far, our mechanisms for emulating multiple virtual processors on one physical processor create an environment quite different in at least one respect from that created when several physical processors are used: All of our virtual processors share a single physical memory and address space, whereas multiple physical processors would not necessarily share physical memory. Sharing of memory between virtual processors is undesirable in many respects. Every process needs to have a private area of main memory (for its stack, for example) that will be undisturbed by other processes. When all processes share a common address space, they must each agree to use a different part of it. This creates a severe lack of modularity, since a process cannot know which area of memory is safe for it to use without knowing about the memory use of all other processes in the system.

The situation might be tolerable if, at execution time, a process could request the system to assign it a free area of memory; then all knowledge of different processes' memory use could be encapsulated within the kernel. Unfortunately, various memory addresses associated with a program's execution (for example, subroutine addresses) are often determined when the machine code is generated, well before the program is actually executed. Thus a program tends to be "rooted" at a particular memory address.

A more desirable semantics for the virtual processor abstraction would be for each virtual processor to have its own virtual memory covering some specified range of addresses. Then each of the many virtual processors that might exist on a system could have, for example, its own virtual location 0, and this location would be private to each virtual processor, rather than being globally shared among all virtual processors. In the emulation of virtual processors on a physical processor, it is thus important to consider not only the issue of multiplexing the physical *processor*, but also the need for multiplexing physical *memory* to emulate a collection of virtual memories, one for each virtual processor.

Schemes for implementing such virtual memories fall under the general heading of *memory mapping*. Generally speaking, a memory-mapping scheme takes a *virtual address* generated by a program and applies a mapping function to convert it to the *physical address* actually used to access the physical memory. In order for each virtual processor to have its own virtual memory, the memory-mapping

*Processes and Processor Multiplexing*

function must be different for each virtual processor, so that the same virtual address will generate a different physical address for each different process.

Many kinds of memory-mapping schemes are viable, and many have been used in real computer systems. The reader should recognize the address-translation mechanism associated with paging and discussed in section 16.7 as a memory-mapping scheme. Indeed, the hardware and software used for paging are often pressed into service for the memory-mapping functions necessary to provide a distinct virtual memory for each virtual processor. This is a fortuitous example of one mechanism serving two needs, but this sharing of a mechanism should not confuse the reader about the quite distinct nature of the two needs: In section 16.7 we explored the use of page tables as a tool for *expanding* virtual memory beyond the size of main memory via two-level memory techniques; the purpose of memory mapping here is to provide *isolation* (or, more precisely, *controlled sharing*) between the address spaces of different virtual processors.

Paging hardware is not a precondition to achieving this interprocess isolation—systems that do not support paging can support and have supported interprocess isolation using other memory-mapping schemes. Thus, although systems often find it useful in practice to piggyback their support for interprocess isolation on top of their paging support, we begin our exploration by considering interprocess isolation apart from paging.

### 18.4.1 Segmented Address Spaces

From the point of view of a user program, a convenient virtual-memory abstraction presents virtual memory as a collection of *memory segments*, where each segment is a sequence of memory words with consecutive addresses. Each segment can thus be characterized by its *base* (the virtual address of its first word) and its *bound* (the virtual address of its last word). Supervisor calls are typically provided to *create* a new segment starting at a designated base address (frequently, base addresses cannot be chosen arbitrarily, but must be multiples of some designated power of 2), to *change* the bound of an existing segment (again, the bound is often restricted to be a multiple of some designated power of 2), and to *destroy* an existing segment.

Valid addresses in segmented virtual memory are not necessarily contiguous, as they are in a single "linear" address space. If a segment beginning at virtual address 0 has a length of 1024 bytes, for example, a segmented virtual memory would have a "gap" between location 1024 and the starting address of the next segment. Since each segment has its own base and bound, the segments can be created, destroyed, expanded, and contracted independently.

A process would typically devote one memory segment to holding the program it is running, a second to its stack (which can thus be expanded and contracted as stack storage requirements dictate), and a third to other data storage needs, such as heap storage; on the other hand, if a system's hardware severely limits the number of segments that a process can have, some of these segments might be coalesced.

In the absence of paging hardware, segmented address spaces can be implemented by means of hardware that examines each virtual address issued by the processor, determines in which of the current process's segments the virtual address falls (signaling a fault if the reference does not fall within the bounds of *any* existing segment of the current process), and then *maps* the virtual address to the corresponding physical address in the region of physical memory where the segment is actually stored.

In the presence of paging hardware, the "physical address" resulting from the memory-mapping process described in the preceding paragraph could then be used as a "virtual address" by the paging mechanisms described in section 16.7 to produce the real physical address in main memory of the referenced datum. *Two* address translations are thus cascaded in series: one due to segmentation (to present processes with an elegant virtual-memory abstraction) and the other due to paging (to permit virtual memory to be larger than a machine's main memory).

The expense of performing two address-translation steps in sequence every time a processor accesses a memory location is not pleasing. In a moment we shall explore ways to reduce this cost at some sacrifice of elegance and modularity in the implementation, but let us linger for a moment to consider the sources and significance of faults in the simpler world of two cascaded translations. Faults can occur in either the segmentation or the paging step of address translation. A fault in the segmentation step indicates a genuine programming error: A program has attempted to access a virtual address that it has not requested in its address space. This *segmentation fault* should be treated much like an attempted division by zero or execution of an illegal instruction: Execution of the process should be suspended or terminated and some user-visible fault action, such as invoking a debugger, should be taken. A fault in the *paging* step, however, has quite a different meaning: A process has accessed a location that is quite properly in its address space but is currently located on disk rather than in main memory. The desired action in this case is the user-*transparent* action of moving the accessed page from disk to main memory and then resuming execution of the process.

For efficiency, we prefer to minimize the number of address-translation steps that must occur on every memory reference, even at the cost of more complex procedures to set up processes' addressing contexts. To this end, we can "fold" together the address-translation steps associated with segmentation and paging into one step performed by precisely the memory-mapping hardware associated with paging, described in section 16.7. The trick is to require segments to start and end on page boundaries and to maintain a separate page table—effectively, a separate *addressing context*—for each process. This context (represented perhaps by the base address of its page table in kernel virtual memory) becomes part of each process's state information and must be added to the MState structure defined in figure 18.3.

While building the page table for a process $A$, we *precompute* the physical address $P$ that will ultimately result from applying the two conceptually separate address-translation steps to the virtual address $V$ of each page in $A$'s address space. $A$'s page table is then set up to map each such $V$ directly to the corresponding physical address $P$ in main memory. Memory-management software must be designed cleverly to update the page tables of the affected processes whenever the set of pages in main memory changes in response to a page fault *or* whenever a process executes a supervisor call to change the configuration of its address space. This software must also maintain the tables needed to classify address-translation faults as either page faults or segmentation faults and handle them accordingly.

Complete isolation of processes can be achieved by using disjoint areas of physical memory to hold pages belonging to different processes' segments. Kernel virtual memory can be similarly arranged to be disjoint from the virtual memories of any of the other processes. Thus a system can be constructed that protects processes from other malfunctioning or malicious processes and that cannot be "crashed" by any user process. This isolation of the effects of a misbehaving process to the process itself is a desirable characteristic for an operating system, and it is important that the underlying machine instruction set not have "holes" that make such isolation impossible. Unfortunately, the implementation of practical operating systems that do not have such "holes" at higher levels is definitely a nontrivial enterprise. Protection issues are discussed further in section 18.5; here we simply note that sound instruction-set mechanisms are a necessary, but far from sufficient, condition for the implementation of a secure operating system.

The existence of separate addressing contexts for different processes, and the existence of yet another addressing context for the kernel itself, has far-reaching consequences for the design of kernel software that accesses data structures in processes' virtual memories. When separate addressing contexts are used, the kernel can no longer read an address $A$ out of a process's address space and use it directly to obtain the contents of the associated location: The kernel's addressing context is likely to associate a completely different physical address with $A$ than the process's addressing context does. Kernel procedures such as PUSHPS$\alpha$ and POPPS$\alpha$ (see figure 18.5) must be revised carefully to use the proper addressing context for each memory access. To make this possible, the operating-system kernel must provide facilities for kernel routines to perform the address translation appropriate for an arbitrary addressing context and then to access the location associated with the resulting physical address.

### 18.4.2 Other Memory-Mapping Strategies

We have illustrated one representative and powerful approach to memory management, but there are many popular alternatives. At one extreme is the class of simple operating systems that offer *no* memory mapping whatsoever: The various processes simply reside within a single address space. This primitive scheme places the burden of memory management on the user programs themselves. Their designers typically preallocate regions of the address space to the various tasks and build this allocation into each program as a constant. While such preallocation is too inflexible for use in general-purpose time-sharing systems, it is common practice in specialized real-time applications.

A degenerate version of segmentation, sometimes implemented where a modest interprocess isolation mechanism is desired at minimal hardware cost, is to provide just one segment, constrained to begin at virtual address 0 but with a variable bound. This scheme is known as base-and-bound memory mapping.

At the more sophisticated end of the memory-management spectrum are schemes that allow processes to *share* regions of physical memory by mapping portions of the virtual address space of several processes to the same physical locations (implemented, for example, by mapping different processes' memory segments to the same regions of physical memory). In a general-purpose time-sharing system, commonly used system programs (such as an editor or LISP interpreter) can be organized so that a single copy of their "pure" (read-only) portions—machine code and read-only data—can serve a number of simultaneous user processes. Some systems allow processes to share read/write physical memory, providing a high-bandwidth communication path between processes: Process $A$ might change a data structure in shared memory, so that the changes become immediately apparent to process $B$. Such situations require mechanisms for synchronizing the activities of the respective processes—for example, to prevent process $B$ from inspecting the shared data in the midst of a change by process $A$ and drawing erroneous conclusions based on a transient inconsistency. The need for and the mechanism of such process synchronization are discussed in chapter 19.

Our approach has been to build the process-related memory management *on top of* a paged memory system. There are a variety of plausible alternatives to this organization. Some segmented-memory systems, for example, invert our hierarchy and build a paging mechanism on top of an underlying segmentation scheme, using a separate page map for each segment. Systems may provide paging without segmentation, segmentation without paging, both, or neither. The structure, implementation, and use of segmented virtual memory is a complex and interesting topic, but further discussion of it is beyond our current scope. The interested reader is referred to the literature describing exemplary segmented-memory systems such as those of MULTICS or the Burroughs B6700.

## 18.5 Protection

An important function of the process abstraction is the isolation it provides between the activities of a program on one virtual processor and those on another. A general-purpose time-sharing system, for example, effectively guarantees to each user the environment of a virtual machine dedicated to that user's purposes, regardless of what programs other users of the system may be running. To do this, each user's program must be *protected* from the activities of other programs, so that, for example, the program bugs of one user do not endanger the service provided to another. Such guarantees are provided by means of constraints on each user program. One common mechanism for providing such constraints is the memory map, which the kernel can use to ensure that one user program will not interfere with the operation of another by tampering with the contents of its memory.

In fact, the memory map often provides the basis for a much wider range of protection functions. Input/output devices connected to the machine's bus, for example, are commonly designed to respond to reserved physical addresses as if they were memory locations; writing a byte to a particular physical address might thus, using this *memory-mapped input/output scheme*, cause a character to be printed on a typewriter device. The process-related memory-management mechanism need not distinguish between such device register addresses and normal memory addresses. A process can thus be prevented from accessing a particular memory-mapped input/output device simply by excluding that device's register addresses from the range of physical addresses accessible through the process's memory map.

Certain machine instructions perform functions that are necessary for the kernel but would allow user programs to influence one another directly, violating the desired isolation characteristic. Thus the trap-return instruction strtn, for example, should distinguish between kernel and user processes, affording the kernel certain privileges not available to the user (such as changing the current addressing context). Typically, processors distinguish between *user* and *supervisor* modes of operation, using a *privilege bit* in the PSW to indicate mode, and cause illegal-instruction faults when a privileged instruction is executed by a program running in user mode. Typically the privilege bit is set to 1 (indicating the privileged supervisor mode) on power-up and (through being loaded from a trap vector's PSW) on entry to a trap handler; moreover, strtn and other "dangerous" instructions cause a fault if an attempt to execute them is made while the privilege bit is 0.

At the kernel operating-system level, protection issues become somewhat more complex. Although the kernel may perform a wide variety of services on behalf of each user program, it must carefully protect each nonconsenting program from interfering requests made by others. Thus a system that offers the capability of shared read/write memory between processes must provide a corollary mechanism by which a process can *protect* its memory from being accessed by arbitrary processes. Security and protection apparatus at the operating-system level has been the subject of a variety of interesting proposals, implementations, and research. While discussion of modern approaches to protection is beyond the scope of this text, we note that each approach depends ultimately on mechanisms built into the processor for constraining the privileges of a running program and trapping its attempted violations of this constraint.

## 18.6 Summary

The process abstraction and its implementation furnish yet another example of the use of *interpretation* in computer architecture to provide "things that are virtual"— to support abstractions, such as the illusion of multiple processors, on hardware that does not look much like the abstractions, such as a single physical processor. The power of these "virtual things"—virtual processors, virtual memory, and so on—to decouple the conceptual structure of systems from the physical structure of their underlying hardware implementations is difficult to overestimate, but efficient implementation is always a concern as well. The mechanisms discussed in this chapter offer several practical case studies in resolving this tension between elegance of abstractions and efficiency of implementation. For example, they show how a virtual processor can be implemented efficiently by executing most instructions directly on the physical processor, as long as "hooks" such as supervisor calls allow the instruction set of the virtual processor to be an *extension* of that of the physical processor, where certain sensitive "instructions" of the virtual processor, such as those for managing input and output, can be interpreted by operating-system software. Similarly, segmented virtual memory—an attractive but potentially expensive abstraction—can be supported (albeit at the cost of some complexity in the kernel's memory-management software) at no greater cost per virtual-memory access than a simple paged memory (whose cost per virtual-memory access, as we saw in chapter 16, can in turn be minimized using a translation lookaside buffer).

The specific techniques explored in this chapter—time-slicing, supervisor calls, memory segmentation, and so on—are important and widely used, but the equally important larger lesson is that careful design allows an abstraction to be virtualized without unacceptable implementation costs.

## 18.7 Context

The first time-sharing system was CTSS [Corbato et al. 1962]. Supervisor calls have their roots in the "extracodes" of the Manchester Atlas machine [Kilburn et al. 1962]. A subsequent landmark system that developed elaborate protection and address-space management mechanisms was MULTICS [Organick 1972]. Perhaps the most widely used time-sharing operating system in history is UNIX [Ritchie and Thompson 1974]. Many of UNIX's design features were inspired by the earlier MULTICS experience of its designers, but UNIX contains a much more minimal set of features, befitting the "small machine" status of UNIX's original host machine, the DEC PDP-11.

Exemplary segmented-address-space architectures include MULTICS's Honeywell 645 and 6180 host machines and the Burroughs B6700 and its relatives [Organick 1973]. Segmented addressing mechanisms of more modest pretensions (typically, each address space may contain only a strictly limited number of segments) appear in many architectures, such as the Intel 8086 and 80286 [Liu and Gibson 1984].

The subject of protection in operating systems has been much studied, and considerable lore has accumulated regarding protection issues. An outline of the subject is given by Janson [1985], who also includes a substantial bibliography of further references on particular protection issues.

## 18.8 Problems

### Problem 18.1

Suppose we had $n$ programs, each of which computes for a time $t_c$ (its *compute time*) and then spins idly (busy-waits for an I/O device) for a time $t_i$ (its *idle time*). Suppose we ran these $n$ programs one after the other. (That is, suppose we ran the first program to completion, immediately followed by the second, immediately followed by the third, and so on.) What is the *utilization* of the machine, where utilization is defined as the ratio of total compute time to total time.

*Processes and Processor Multiplexing*

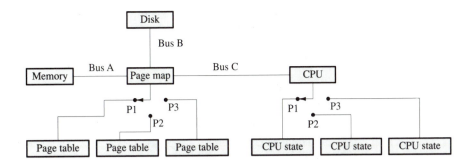

**Figure 18.9** Cache Flow time-shared computer.

### Problem 18.2

A process runs for a time $t_a$ dictated by an "alarm clock." When the time is up, the alarm clock requests an interrupt, which causes a trap into the kernel. The kernel saves the current process state, sets up the next process, sets the alarm clock to $t_a$, and returns from the interrupt, which allows the next process to run. The processes are scheduled in a round-robin manner. Let $t_k$ be the time spent in the kernel during the process switch. Assume that the time for the trap into the kernel and the time to set the alarm clock and return from the interrupt are negligible. In terms of $t_k$ and $n$, $t_c$, and $t_i$ (defined in problem 18.1), give the time $t_a$ that maximizes utilization of the machine. Explain your answer.

### Problem 18.3

Given the scenario of problem 18.1 and assuming that $t_a$ is set as calculated in problem 18.2, how large should $n$ be (how many programs should there be) in order for there to be no idle time? Call this value $n_{crit}$. Give an expression for the utilization of the machine when $n < n_{crit}$. Give an expression for the utilization of the machine when $n > n_{crit}$.

### Problem 18.4

Cache Flow, Inc., markets a three-process time-shared computer whose structure is shown in figure 18.9. The three-way switch modules are arranged to step together to a new position every millisecond, thus switching the processor from one process to the next. All lines in the figure correspond to bus interconnections. The page-map module performs the address translation needed for paging, using the currently selected page table.

A. Which bus between memory and CPU in the diagram deals with *physical* addresses? Which bus deals with *virtual* addresses? Explain.

B. What problems are encountered if a single cache is added to the Cache Flow machine between the page map and the CPU? Explain *briefly*, giving a simple example of the difficulty.

C. How can a single cache be added to the Cache Flow system so as not to require any further changes to the hardware or software? If memory access time is

1 $\mu$s, the page map adds 0.1 $\mu$s to the time required for an access to memory (when no page fault occurs), and the cache-memory time is 0.2 $\mu$s for a hit but delays memory access by 0.1 $\mu$s on a miss, give the access times for cache hits and misses in the resulting machine, assuming no page faults.

D. Augment the Cache Flow machine using three cache memories such that one cache is devoted to each virtual address space. You may use additional three-way switch modules. Using the same assumptions about the speeds of system components as in part C, give the access times for cache hits and misses in the resulting machine, again assuming no page faults.

## Problem 18.5

Trace the events that occur when a supervisor call implemented by a handler in figure 18.8 cannot be completed because of input/output delays, and therefore the scheduler is entered instead. Scheduler first updates the saved state on the stack and then returns to its caller (in this case, a supervisor-call handler), whose further return to its caller eventually causes execution of a trap-return instruction. Explain why executing this trap-return instruction resumes execution of the new process. Then give a scenario for how control can return to the suspended process so that its supervisor call can be completed. Explain the steps involved in detail.

## Problem 18.6

You are to add a new supervisor call to the *S*-machine operating system. This supervisor call, to which we assign the code ssvc(2), is a "type character string" service handled by a kernel procedure TypeSt, similar to the procedures ReadCh and TypeCh of figure 18.6. To invoke the TypeSt supervisor call, a user program pushes the address of a string of characters onto its stack. The TypeSt handler should pop the address, print out all the characters, and then return. The string of characters is stored in consecutive bytes in memory, followed by a byte containing zero. Here is an example of the usage of this call to print IHTFP on the user's terminal:

```
String: 'I'  'H'  'T'  'F'  'P'  0
        . . .
        sc4(String)
        ssvc(2)
        . . .
```

Write a simple version of TypeSt in the style of figure 18.6. Don't worry about the possibility of the terminal being busy or about scheduling other users. You will need some mechanism for obtaining a byte located at a designated memory address; assume the existence of a routine FetchByte for this purpose, so that *byte* = FetchByte(*addr*) assigns to *byte* the value stored in memory location *addr*.

## Problem 18.7

Extend your implementation of TypeSt in problem 18.6 to deal with the possibility of the terminal being busy; design the program so that it will switch to another process in that case. Your solution should be in the style of figure 18.8. What issues do you have to worry about when the terminal becomes busy after some,

```
/* This all executes in the kernel context...           */
char WaitingChar,       /* Character code sent by producer. */
     Flag = 0;          /* Flag: nonzero iff char waiting.  */

/* This handler takes a character off the calling process's stack,
 *   sending it to the receiver.
 */
SendHandler(s)
 struct MState *s;
 {   if (Flag > 0)
       { s->PC = s->PC - 2;
       }
     else
       { WaitingChar = POPPS(s);   /* Pop the argument.    */
         Flag = 1;                 /* Show that we have it. */
       }
 }


/* This handler accepts a character from the sender and pushes it
 *   onto the calling process's stack.
 */
RcvHandler(s)
 struct MState *s;
 {   if (???)
       { s->PC = s->PC - 2;
       }
     else
       { PUSHPS(s, WaitingChar);
         Flag = 0;
       }
 }
```

**Figure 18.10**  Send and Rcv supervisor-call subhandlers.

but not all, of the characters in the argument string have been typed? How does your procedure deal with these issues?

### Problem 18.8

Figure 18.10 shows the proposed implementation of supervisor calls for communication between producer and consumer processes without explicitly shared memory. The new supervisor calls are Send(c), executed by the producer process, which passes the character c to the consumer, and c=Rcv(), executed by the consumer process, which accepts a previously passed character.

A. Note that the supervisor-call handlers shown in figure 18.10, like all kernel code, are uninterruptible. What should appear in place of the ??? in the RcvHandler code?

B. What is the significance of the constant 2 in s->PC = s->PC - 2;?

C. These supervisor calls are used by the two processes shown in figure 18.11,

```
Producer:                             Consumer:
-------------------------             -------------------------
int i;                                int i;
for (i=0; i<100; i = i+1)             int j = 0;
   Send(i);                           for (i=0; i<100; i = i+1)
                                          j = j + Rcv();
```

**Figure 18.11**  Communicating processes using Send and Rcv.

```
Producer:                                 Consumer:
-----------------------------             -----------------------------

      int i;                                    int i;
loop: for (i=0; i<100; i = i+1)                 int j = 0;
         Send(i);                         loop: for (i=0; i<100; i = i+1)
                                                { j = j + Rcv();
      compute 100 seconds;                         compute .5 seconds;
      goto loop;                                 }
                                                goto loop;
```

**Figure 18.12**  Compute-intensive communicating processes.

which transfer a total of 100 characters during their operation. Assume that the time-sharing system time-slices between these processes with a 1-s quantum; that is, an alarm-clock interrupt (which invokes the scheduler) occurs once per second. The alarm-clock interrupt request is honored only in user mode, that is, when one of the processes (rather than a kernel handler) is running. If an alarm-clock interrupt request occurs when the kernel is running, response to it is deferred until user mode is reentered. Assuming that all computation times are negligible, estimate the total real time that elapses between invocation of these processes and their completion.

D. Suggest a one-statement addition to each of the handlers in figure 18.10 that dramatically reduces the elapsed time you calculated in part C.

E. If the producer and consumer processes shown in figure 18.12 are invoked (using the Send and Rcv handlers in figure 18.10), how many characters per second will be transferred, on the average, between these processes?

### Problem 18.9

Consider a simple multiprocessing system in which all processes run in a single address space. Suppose we want to implement a primitive mail facility between processes using supervisor calls. We first enlarge process descriptor blocks with three new fields, as shown in figure 18.13. When process $i$ wants to send mail to process $j$, it pushes the value $j$ and a pointer to the message on its stack and

```
struct PDB
{   struct MState state;      /* as before */
    char *Mailbox;            /* pointer to a message */
    int  MailFrom             /* sender's process number */
    int  MailArrived          /* 1 if previous two fields are valid,
                                  0 if not */
    ...                       /* various other stuff, as before */
} ProcList[NPROC] ;           /* all processes */
```

**Figure 18.13**   Process descriptor block with mailbox entry.

```
SendMail(p)
struct MState *p;
{
 int j;
 j = POPPS4(p);
 if (ProcList[j].MailArrived == 0)
 { ProcList[j].Mailbox    = POPPS4(p);
   ProcList[j].MailFrom    = curproc;
   ProcList[j].MailArrived = 1;        }
 else
 { p->PC = p->PC - 2;
   Scheduler(p); }
}
```

**Figure 18.14**   Defective SendMail supervisor-call subhandler.

executes ssvc(23). The handler, shown in figure 18.14, waits until the Mailbox
for process $j$ is empty before sending the message. Interrupts are *disabled* while
this handler executes.

A. What is the problem with this code?

B. Give one line of code just preceding the Scheduler call in figure 18.14 that
   will make it work correctly.

C. A process that wants to receive its mail executes ssvc(24), which waits until
   mail has arrived, then leaves the message pointer and the sender's name (process
   number) on its stack. Write a handler for ssvc(24), following the style of
   figure 18.14.

### Problem 18.10
Write a register-transfer-level description of the sl$\alpha$ instruction on an $S$ machine
with base-and-bound memory mapping and no paging hardware.

### Problem 18.11
Consider the implementation of the TypeSt supervisor-call handler (see problem 18.6) on a machine with base-and-bound memory mapping but no paging
hardware. Assume that FetchByte(*addr*) fetches the contents of *physical* location *addr* (no mapping is applied). Assume further that the MState structure has
been augmented with a field called Base, which gives the physical address corresponding to virtual address 0 of the process in question, and a field called Bound

```
1  EmulateL8(p)
2  struct MState *p;
3  {      int a;
4         a = POPPS4(p);
5         PUSHPS4(p,Get4(p,a));      /* low-order 4 bytes  */
6         PUSHPS4(p,Get4(p,a+4));    /* high-order 4 bytes */
7  }
```

**Figure 18.15**  Emulator for the s18 instruction.

such that all valid virtual addresses for the process in question are less than Bound. Write a routine UFetchByte, to be used instead of FetchByte by the TypeSt handler, that performs the proper mapping. Assume the usage

$$byte = \text{UFetchByte}(p, addr),$$

where $p$ points to an MState structure and $addr$ is the address in the user's address space. What does it mean if TypeSt passes to UFetchByte an address bigger than the user's bound? What would be a reasonable strategy for handling this case? (You need not implement the strategy.)

### Problem 18.12

Consider an $S$ machine without hardware support for the s18 or ss8 instructions. Operating-system routines catch the illegal instruction faults generated by attempts to execute these instructions and then emulate the instructions. The following utility routines are available:

- POPPS4($s$): A 4-byte longword is popped off the stack of the process whose MState is *s, and that longword is returned as the value of POPPS4.

- PUSHPS4($s,n$): The 4-byte longword $n$ is pushed onto the stack of the process whose MState is *s.

- Get4($s,a$): The 4-byte longword at virtual address $a$ of the process whose MState is *s is fetched and returned as the value of Get4.

- Put4($s,a,n$): The 4-byte longword $n$ is stored at virtual address $a$ of the process whose MState is *s.

A. Using these routines, the s18 instruction can be emulated by the C procedure shown in figure 18.15. Write the procedure EmulateS8 that emulates the ss8 instruction.

B. Write PUSHPS4. Use Get4 and Put4 as needed. Use p->SP to denote the stack pointer of struct MState *p. Note that any necessary address translation is performed inside Get4 and Put4 (this is the reason for passing them the parameter *p), so you need not concern yourself with the address-translation scheme used by this machine.

C. If this machine supports paging, then a page fault might occur during execution of line 4, 5, or 6 of the EmulateL8 routine given in figure 18.15. (Assume that the machine code and stack for EmulateL8 itself are always kept in main memory; thus page faults can only arise from missing pages belonging to the user process.) It is possible to avoid page faults during the execution of EmulateL8 if certain pages, covering certain ranges of virtual addresses in the user process, are already in primary memory. What ranges of virtual address must these pages cover (that is, which virtual addresses in the user process will be accessed by EmulateL8)?

D. If any of the locations enumerated in your answer to part C refers to a page not currently in main memory, a page fault will occur. What must be done to ensure that the user process is restored to its state on entry to EmulateL8 if a page fault occurs during execution of line 4? What about during execution of line 5? Finally, what about during execution of line 6?

### Problem 18.13

A computer system has multiple terminals and multiple users. Each terminal has registers for testing status and for reading and writing characters. The addresses for these registers can be set by the manufacturer, who is weighing several options for providing input/output facilities to programmers:

- Option 1: Give the programmer a supervisor call that returns the addresses of the terminal's registers. The programmer can then read and write to the terminal directly.

- Option 2: Give the programmer a supervisor call that returns the addresses of the terminal's registers and standard subroutines that use these addresses to read and write the terminal's registers.

- Option 3: Give the programmer supervisor calls that test the status of the device and read and write a character.

A. Under which, if any, of these options will users have to rewrite their *source* programs if we move the terminal device registers to new locations?

B. Under which, if any, of these options will users have to rewrite their *source* programs if we replace the terminal device with a new one that has different protocols?

C. Under which, if any, of these options will users' *object* programs be affected if we replace the terminal device with a new one that has a different protocol for testing its status?

D. Suppose a user's program wants to read a character before one is available. Under which, if any, of these options is it possible for the user's program to avoid checking the device multiple times?

E. Under which of these options will users' programs be able to respond fastest to an input character?

F. Under which, if any, of these options can we protect a user's terminal from other users' processes? (Assume that all user processes run in the same address space.)

# 19 Process Synchronization

Because processes must sometimes interact with input/output devices or with other processes, we need to be able to synchronize events in a process with events outside the process. For example, the process of reading a character from a terminal cannot proceed until that character has been typed in, while the process of writing a character to a terminal must wait until the terminal is finished transmitting previously written characters. Similarly, a set of cooperating processes implementing a computation will need to communicate, and such communication also requires synchronization. In this chapter we discuss some general mechanisms for synchronizing events in a process with events outside the process. We shall limit ourselves, though, to a few examples of the problem and only one technique for solving it. There is an enormous literature on this topic, and many synchronization-related research problems are still open.

We start with a discussion of the two main classes of process-synchronization constraints, giving simple practical examples that arise in doing input and output. Next, we introduce *semaphores*, an abstract mechanism for enforcing process-synchronization constraints, and explore several ways of implementing them. We conclude with a discussion of *fairness* and *deadlocks*, two issues that complicate the implementation and use of semaphores and other synchronization constructs.

## 19.1 Process-Synchronization Constraints

There are two kinds of synchronization constraints. A *precedence constraint* between two events is a requirement that one of the events occur before the other. We express such a constraint that event $X$ must precede event $Y$ by $X \preceq Y$. As discussed in section 7.3.2, this definition can be extended to two *operations* $A$ and $B$ by defining $A \preceq B$ to mean $A^F \preceq B^S$. Precedence constraints generally stem from data dependencies: A constraint $A \preceq B$ results when $A$ produces data required by $B$. In reading from a terminal, for example, the constraint that the process not return a character until one is received is a precedence constraint. Similarly, in writing to the terminal, the constraint that a process wait for the previous character to be transmitted is also a precedence constraint.

A *mutual-exclusion constraint* between two operations is a requirement that they not overlap in time. It does not matter which operation begins first, but whichever does begin first must finish before the other starts. If operations $X$ and $Y$ are mutually exclusive, the mutual-exclusion constraint says that either $X \preceq Y$ or $Y \preceq X$. In section 7.3.7 we introduced the notation $X \bowtie Y$ to signify a mutual-exclusion constraint between $X$ and $Y$.

Mutual-exclusion constraints typically arise from a shared resource, such as a printer or data base. If two processes can use a resource, they must coordinate their use to avoid undesirable interactions—for example, to avoid intermingling two unrelated streams of output on the same page of print-out. Enforcing such constraints among processes usually requires some form of arbitration. Requests to use shared resources occur at arbitrary times in each process. In a system in which two processes requesting a resource can actually execute concurrently (for example, if the processes are executing on different physical processors), this arbitration will ultimately depend on some physical arbiter. However, if the concurrency among processes is simulated (many processes on a single processor), mutual-exclusion constraints can be enforced without a hardware arbiter: The needed arbitration is effectively performed in advance by the scheduler in deciding which process will run next and consequently will have the first shot at some shared resource.

## 19.2 Semaphores and Precedence Constraints

Both precedence and mutual exclusion can be enforced by using the primitive mechanism of *semaphores*. A semaphore $S$ is a data object that includes an integer count and supports the two primitive operations `wait(S)` and `signal(S)`. In general, a semaphore is *initialized* to an integer value and subsequently subjected to a sequence of `wait` and `signal` operations performed by various processes. These operations behave roughly as follows:

- `wait(S)` delays the process performing it until the count in $S$ is greater than 0, at which point it decrements the count by 1 and returns. Thus `wait` can introduce arbitrarily long delays into the progress of a process.
- `signal(S)` increments the count in $S$ and returns. Thus `signal` does not delay the calling process and can have the side effect of allowing other processes that have been delayed by `wait(S)` to proceed.

The fundamental semantic constraint imposed by a semaphore can be summarized as follows:

. . . . . . . . . . . . . . . . . . . . . . . . . . . . . . . . . . . . . . . . . . . . . . . . . . . . . . . . . . . . . . . .

***Semaphore semantics*** A semaphore $S$ initialized to the value $n$ enforces the constraint

$$\mathtt{signal}_i(S)^{\mathrm{S}} \preceq \mathtt{wait}_{i+n}(S)^{\mathrm{F}},$$

where $\mathtt{signal}_i(S)^{\mathrm{S}}$ denotes the start of the $i$th `signal` operation on $S$ and $\mathtt{wait}_j(S)^{\mathrm{F}}$ denotes the completion of the $j$th `wait` operation to complete on $S$.

. . . . . . . . . . . . . . . . . . . . . . . . . . . . . . . . . . . . . . . . . . . . . . . . . . . . . . . . . . . . . . . .

```
/* Sketch of three-process solution to Print(f(x,y))   */

float x, y, z;             /* Shared variables.         */
semaphore Sx=0,Sy=0,Sz=0;  /* Shared semaphores.        */

/*********************************************************/

Process A:      |   Process B:    |   Process C:
...             |   ...           |   ...
x = ...;        |   wait(Sx);     |   wait(Sz);
signal(Sx);     |   wait(Sy);     |   Print(z);
...             |   z = f(x,y);   |   ...
y = ...;        |   signal(Sz);   |
signal(Sy);     |   ...           |
...             |   ...           |
```

**Figure 19.1**   Semaphores to enforce precedence.

## 19.3 Semaphores for Precedence

Figure 19.1 sketches a somewhat silly implementation of a pipeline consisting of three processes. The processes share variables x, y, and z as well as semaphores Sx, Sy, and Sz in order to perform the computation Print(f($x$,$y$)) for some pair of computed values $x$ and $y$. The division of labor among the three processes requires process $A$ to compute the values of x and y, process $B$ to apply f to these values and to leave the result in the shared variable z, and process $C$ to do the actual printing.

There are three essential precedence constraints resulting from data dependencies: (Compute x) $\preceq$ f(x,y), (Compute y) $\preceq$ f(x,y), and (Compute z) $\preceq$ Print. These constraints are enforced by semaphores Sx, Sy, and Sz, respectively. Since each semaphore is initialized to 0, each enforces the constraint that its first (and, perhaps, only) signal operation precede the completion of its first wait operation. The three semaphores thus enforce exactly the three constraints we have noted. We can, in effect, make the above program into a precedence graph by adding constraint edges from each signal to its corresponding wait. This simple example is somewhat artificial, but we shall see a more realistic application of these principles shortly.

## 19.4 Semaphores for Mutual Exclusion

Shared resources often lead to mutual-exclusion constraints. The sharing of a printer, for example, might lead to garbled output unless its users arrange (at the very least) that the output of unrelated processes not be mixed on the same page. Conceptually, this requires assignment of exclusive use of the resource to a process for a period of time sufficient for it to perform a critical set of operations, after which it presumably relinquishes the resource to other waiting processes. One user's process might, for example, request exclusive access to a printer for a period

```
/* Sharing of a printer resource by two processes.         */
semaphore Sp=1;          /* Shared mutual-exclusion semaphore.  */


/*************************************************************/

Process A:                    |   Process B:
...                           |   ...
/* Begin critical region.  */ |   /* Begin critical region. */
wait(Sp);      /* Assign it. */ |   wait(Sp);
Print(...)     /* Use it.    */ |   for (...) Print(...);
...                           |   signal(Sp);
Print(...)                    |   /* End critical region.   */
signal(Sp);    /* Release it. */ |   ...
/* End critical region.     */ |   ...
...                           |
```

**Figure 19.2** Two processes using a semaphore for mutual exclusion.

long enough to print a report without being contaminated by the program listing required by another user.

The usual approach to such exclusivity requirements is the identification of *critical regions* of code that are not to be run in parallel. In general, two mutually exclusive critical regions may be run in either order; however, any overlap of their execution is forbidden. This constraint can be enforced for by means of a semaphore whose initial value is 1. Consider the example of figure 19.2, which depicts the sharing of a printer by two processes.

Note that the critical region of each process initially executes `wait(Sp)` and ends with `signal(Sp)`. The effect of this pair of operations is to decrement the value of Sp during execution of the critical region. Because Sp is initialized to 1, its value will thus be 0 while either process is executing code within its critical region. The semantics of `wait` are such that `wait(Sp)` will delay its process as long as Sp remains 0; thus the *second* `wait(Sp)` to be executed will be delayed until the process executing the first `wait(Sp)` performs a corresponding `signal` to restore Sp to a nonzero value.

The mutual-exclusion semantics can be generalized somewhat by initialization of the semaphore to values other than 1. In general, a semaphore $S$ initialized to the value $n$ can be viewed as an allocator for a pool of $n$ resources. The first $n$ requesters (who express their requests via `wait(S)` operations) will proceed undelayed, having been allocated one of the resources. Eventually each will return its resource to the pool via a `signal(S)`, making it available for future reallocation. Note that the $(n + 1)$st requester will encounter a value of zero in $S$ (unless one of the first $n$ has already finished) and will be delayed until some process executes a `signal`. In fact, there can be many simultaneously `waiting` processes, patiently awaiting the availability of a resource; each `signal` will allow exactly one of them to proceed.

## 19.5 Producer-Consumer Synchronization

A common synchronization problem concerns two communicating processes: a *producer process* and a *consumer process*. The former produces a sequence of data (say, characters), and the latter processes those data in the order in which they have been produced. For example, the producer process might be formatting the listing of a program, and the consumer process might be driving a printer device.

The processes may not produce and consume data at a steady pace. For example, the producer might rapidly generate an entire line of characters, then pause while it determines the format for the next line. Similarly, the consumer may take longer to handle some data (such as the command to advance the printer's paper to a new page) than others. It is desirable to implement a "pipe" for passing data from the producer process to the consumer process that can store some number of data, allowing the producer process (at least temporarily) to get ahead of the consumer so that a backlog of already produced data is available for consumption even if the producer temporarily slows its rate of producing data. Such a pipe must enforce two synchronization constraints: (1) No datum can be consumed before it is produced, and (2) if only a finite amount of storage is available within the pipe (the usual case), the producer must be prevented from getting too far ahead of the consumer, or there will be no place to store the data produced.

Figure 19.3 shows an implementation of such a pipe for the case in which the data being produced and consumed are characters. The producer process periodically produces characters and puts them into the pipe by calling the procedure `write`. The consumer can read the next character out of the pipe by calling `read`. Before either the producer or the consumer begins to run, the status of the pipe is initialized by calling `init`.

Communication between the producer process (`write`) and the consumer process (`read`) is effected by two semaphores (`Chars` and `Holes`) and the shared first-in/first-out (FIFO) buffer `buf`. This example follows the standard practice of implementing a FIFO buffer as a *circular buffer*: an array (`buf`) and two pointers (the array indices `InPtr` and `OutPtr`). At any time, `InPtr` contains the index of the array element that is to receive the next datum to be added, while `OutPtr` contains the index of the next element to be extracted. Thus `InPtr = OutPtr` when the buffer is empty, since the next element to be extracted has yet to be entered. Inserting or removing a character from the buffer involves an access to the element of `buf` specified by the appropriate index, followed by a *circular increment* (that is, an increment modulo the buffer size) of that index. Thus the elements are filled (and emptied) in the order `buf[0]`, `buf[1]`, ..., `buf[98]`, `buf[99]`, `buf[0]`, .... During operation, `OutPtr` and `InPtr` chase each other around modulo 100, as characters are asynchronously inserted and extracted by the producer and consumer processes, respectively. Consequently, when the buffer is *full* (contains 100 characters), `InPtr = OutPtr`, exactly as when the buffer is empty.

To prevent *buffer underflow* (consumption of a "character" that has not yet been produced), we must guarantee that the *i*th buffer *insert* operation precedes the *i*th *extract* operation. The `Chars` semaphore enforces this constraint. The value stored in `Chars` at any moment is the number of characters currently in the buffer. The

```
char buf[100];          /* 100-character buffer.     */
int InPtr, OutPtr;
semaphore Chars, Holes;


init()                  /* Once-only initialization.  */
{     InPtr = OutPtr = 0;
      Chars = 0; Holes = 100;
}


/* Procedure for consumer to call: */
char read()
{             char c;
              wait(Chars);                /* Need a character.   */
              c = buf[OutPtr];            /* Read the character. */
              OutPtr = (OutPtr+1) % 100;  /* Circular increment. */
              signal(Holes);              /* We've added a hole. */
              return c;
}


/* Procedure for producer to call: */
write(c)
 char c;
{             wait(Holes);                /* Need a hole.        */
              buf[InPtr] = c;             /* Insert character.   */
              InPtr = (InPtr+1) % 100;    /* Circular increment. */
              signal(Chars);              /* We've added a char. */
}
```

**Figure 19.3**  Producer-consumer communication using a circular buffer.


producer process executes signal(Chars) after inserting each character, thus incrementing the semaphore. The consumer process executes wait(Chars) before extracting each character, decrementing Chars. If the buffer is empty when the consumer is ready for a character, Chars will have the value 0, and the consumer process will hang in the wait operation until the producer process inserts a character and executes signal(Chars). This producer-consumer relationship illustrates the typical and most natural application of general semaphores to process synchronization. The producer and consumer processes are allowed to proceed asynchronously, as long as the producer process stays at least one step ahead of the consumer process.

The Chars semaphore does nothing to prevent *buffer overflow*. It ensures that the producer process stays ahead of the consumer, but it allows the producer to get arbitrarily far ahead of the consumer (which would require arbitrarily large amounts of buffer space to store the data that have been produced but not yet consumed). In addition to the precedence constraint $insert_i \preceq extract_i$ enforced by the Chars semaphore, we must constrain the production of characters so that $extract_i \preceq insert_{i+100}$, reflecting the boundedness of our buffer size. wait and signal operations on the Holes semaphore, whose value at any moment reflects the number of empty spaces in the buffer, enforce this constraint.

This elegant solution to the buffer-overflow problem follows directly from the *dual* view of the above producer-consumer relationship, in which the commodity being produced and consumed is empty buffer spaces ("holes") rather than data characters. From this standpoint, the consumer process is the producer (each time it removes a character from the buffer, it produces a hole), and the producer process is the consumer (each character insertion uses up a hole). This duality between data and holes is closely analogous to that between electrons and holes in semiconductor physics. We may view data characters as flowing from the producer to the consumer process, while holes flow from the consumer to the producer. We use the `Holes` semaphore to keep the production of holes at least one step ahead of their consumption, in exactly the way we use the `Chars` semaphore to constrain the consumption of characters. Note that the `Chars` and `Holes` semaphores are initialized to 0 and 100, respectively, reflecting the initial buffer contents (all holes).

One other aspect of the program design merits a brief note. The producer process can *insert* characters into the buffer but can never remove any. It therefore modifies only `InPtr`, never `OutPtr`. The consumer process likewise modifies only `OutPtr`. Since each of these variables is updated by only one process, no special synchronization is required to protect such updates, as would be required if there were multiple producer processes or multiple consumer processes.

## 19.6  Binary Semaphores

A special case of the semaphore, in which the count is constrained to take on values of only 0 or 1, is called the *binary semaphore*. It is primarily of interest because (1) it satisfies directly a useful subset of semaphore applications (such as mutual exclusion), and (2) it provides the basis for software implementation of general semaphores and other synchronization constructs. Binary semaphores have the virtue that they require only a single bit of storage, and they are often chosen as the primitive synchronization mechanism to be supported in hardware.

## 19.7  Implementing Semaphores

A simple approach to the implementation of semaphores, shown (for the $G$ machine) in figure 19.4, follows directly from the informal description given earlier. It uses a 4-byte integer variable to represent each semaphore; `signal` is simply an increment instruction, and `wait` follows an appropriate test-and-wait loop by a decrement instruction.

Unfortunately, this implemention is naive in two ways. The first is simply an inefficiency: It uses *busy-waiting* to waste processor time until the semaphore has a value greater than 0. The only objection to the busy-waiting approach is that it wastes processor cycles that might be spent profitably elsewhere (for example, running some other process). Sometimes this is not an issue, and then busy-waiting is appropriate.

```
| Translation of wait(S):
    w:      gtest4      dir(S)                      | Is it zero?
            gjle        dir(w)                      | Yes, keep waiting.
            gsub4       dir(S) imm4(1) dir(S)       | No, decrement it.
            ...


| Translation of signal(S):
            gadd4       dir(S) imm4(1) dir(S)       | Add 1 to its value.
            ...
```

**Figure 19.4**   Naive semaphore implementation.

The second objection to this implementation is more serious. The problem stems from the fact that, in a multiprocess environment, activities of other processes may be timed so as to corrupt the behavior of the sequence of primitive operations executed by the code. Consider the gtest4 instruction, which performs a memory access (to fetch the operand S) and sets the processor's condition codes according to its value. The subsequent gjle instruction acts on the result of this test, the intention being that the following gsub4 will be executed if and only if the value in S is greater than 0. The semaphore should *never* have a negative value; it should be decremented only if the *result* of the decrement operation will be 0 or greater. The assumption made at the time of the gsub4 instruction is that the value in S is greater than 0; this assumption derives from the earlier gtest4.

The logic of this sequence breaks down if another process intervenes and changes the value in S between the gtest4 and the gsub4 instructions. Consider, for example, a semaphore S whose initial value is 1 and two processes $A$ and $B$ that are "racing" to be the first to perform a wait operation on S. $A$ might reach the gtest4 instruction at w (seeing that S $= 1$) before $B$, but be suspended by an alarm-clock interrupt immediately after executing the gtest4. $B$ might then run, reach the gtest4 instruction, see S $= 1$, decrement S to 0, and continue. If $B$ is now suspended and $A$ resumes its execution, $A$ will make a decision based on the previously seen (and no longer accurate) value 1 of S. $A$ will accordingly decrement S again (to $-1$) and also continue. The (erroneous) result is that *two* wait operations succeed where the initial value of S should have allowed only one.

### 19.7.1 Atomicity

The failure of the naive semaphore implementation of figure 19.4 underscores the need for a primitive mutual-exclusion mechanism on which to base semaphores and higher-level synchronization approaches. In effect, we require a way to make sequences of instructions *atomic* in the sense that they execute as single, uninterruptible operations. A key to fixing our naive wait implementation is to ensure that no foreign process will intervene between the testing of the semaphore and the modification of its value. Ultimately, we recognize that wait is capable of performing an arbitration function; we need to identify a basis for that arbitration. Close examination of particular computers virtually always reveals primitive

```
| Translation of wait(S):
    w:      (Enable alarm-clock interrupts)
            (Disable alarm-clock interrupts)
            gtest4    dir(S)                    | Is S zero?
            gjle      dir(w)                    | Yes, keep waiting.
            gsub4     dir(S) imm4(1) dir(S)     | No, decrement it.
            (Enable alarm-clock interrupts)
            ...


| Translation of signal(S):
            gadd4     dir(S) imm4(1) dir(S)  | Add 1 to its value.
            ...
```

**Figure 19.5**  Semaphore implementation with interrupts disabled.

means for ensuring such atomicity. Any multiprocess environment that supports shared memory must include some means for arbitrating between simultaneous accesses to a location by several processes. Thus we assume (at minimum) that individual memory read and write transactions are atomic. Although it is far from obvious, Dijkstra [1968a] showed that this assumption is sufficient to effect mutual exclusion, given an elaborate set of protocols and conventions. While interesting in theory, this approach is awkward in practice and consequently is primarily of academic interest.

Most practical architectures provide some primitive mechanism intended specifically to support atomic sequences of operations. In the case of a single processor that is time-shared by a number of processes using alarm-clock interrupts and a scheduler, as discussed in chapter 18, any sequence of instructions executed by a process can be made atomic simply by disabling alarm-clock interrupts for the duration of the sequence. This insight leads to a fix for the bugs in figure 19.4; the solution is shown in figure 19.5.

The disabling of alarm-clock interrupts during the gtest4-gjle-gsub4 sequence guarantees that, once a process has observed S > 0 using gtest4, no other process will intervene to change S (or do anything else!) until the gsub4 decrementing S has completed. Interrupts are enabled briefly at w to allow deferred alarm-clock interrupt requests to be granted; if this were not done, a process $A$ looping at w waiting for some other process $B$ to perform a signal operation on S would wait forever, because the alarm-clock interrupt allowing $B$ to run (and execute its signal operation) would never occur. Note that it is not necessary to disable interrupts in the implementation of signal in figure 19.5. This is because interrupt requests are only granted *between* instruction executions; thus *any* single instruction defines an atomic sequence of operations. If interrupts could occur in the middle of executing a gadd4 instruction (say, after reading the operand values but before storing the result) and if a gadd4 instruction interrupted in that way could resume where it left off, then it would in fact be necessary to disable alarm-clock interrupts around the implementation of signal as well as that of wait.

Although the disabling of alarm-clock interrupts is a path to fixing the bugs in figure 19.4, there are two problems with this approach. First, giving user code the unrestricted ability to disable interrupts is tantamount to giving user code the unrestricted ability to "crash" the entire system, because a malicious or buggy user process could disable interrupts and then enter an infinite loop. Without interrupts enabled, there would be no way to seize control of the machine back from that process. We are thus motivated to find solutions to the problem of correctly implementing semaphores that involve lesser grants of power to user processes.

The second problem with the interrupt-disabling approach is that it does not extend to true multiprocessors—machines with two or more independent processors sharing a common memory. On such systems, two processes running on different processors can execute concurrently, allowing a more or less arbitrary interleaving of their individual computational steps, even if one or both of those processes disable interrupts. This is because concurrent execution of several processes is now performed directly by the hardware; it is no longer an illusion created by a scheduler. Obtaining atomicity on multiprocessors by disabling interrupts is thus futile. In fact, there is a more serious problem: Even the atomicity of individual instructions, exploited in figure 19.5 to implement `signal`, is not generally preserved. The individual memory read and write operations performed by separate processors can be interleaved in arbitrary ways, without regard to instruction boundaries. Thus the `gadd4` instructions of two nearly simultaneous `signal` operations performed by two different processors might each read a given value $v$ of a semaphore $S$, compute $v + 1$, and then store $v + 1$ into $S$. The result is that only one `signal` operation appears to have occurred, even though two were performed.

To solve this problem, true multiprocessors generally provide some hardware support for *locking* a memory bus for two or more consecutive transactions, thus preventing intervening operations by other processors. This memory locking is often tied to the execution of particular instructions designed for semaphore implementation, allowing such instructions to behave as atomic operations even in the presence of other processors competing for access to shared memory locations.

Instructions useful as a basis for implementing semaphores (and other synchronization primitives) perform, at minimum, an atomic operation including a *test* of the contents of some memory location followed by a *modification* of its value. The execution of the instruction thus returns some information to the processor about the status of the location and simultaneously changes the contents of the location so that subsequent executions of that instruction by other processors will return different information. These elements are necessary to arbitrate a contest among processors competing for access to a resource. Such instructions are often referred to as *test-and-set instructions*, named after one common atomic instruction design.

In fact, almost any instruction that has this dual function can serve as a basis for semaphores if implemented so as to guarantee atomicity. For example, an atomic increment or decrement instruction that sets condition codes can be used. Consider figure 19.6, where we hypothesize an atomic instruction `gccsub4` that is just like `gsub4` except that it sets the condition codes CC of the $G$ machine according to the result of the subtraction. (Such instructions are fairly common in general-register architectures.)

```
| Translation of wait(S):
    w:      gccsub4  dir(S) imm4(1) dir(S)    | Atomic; sets CCs.
            gjge     dir(OK)                   | (Result was >= 0.)
            gadd4    dir(S) imm4(1) dir(S)     | (Atomic) restore value
            gjmp     dir(w)                    |    ... and keep waiting.
    OK:     ...                                | Go here when wait succeeds.
```

**Figure 19.6** wait using atomic decrement.

This approach depends on (1) the atomicity of the instructions that *change* $S$, (2) the atomic *testing and modification* of the value of $S$ by the gccsub4 instruction; and (3) the acceptability of temporarily negative values in $S$. The latter arise because the initial gccsub4 decrements $S$ independently of its initial value; some of these operations will occur when the semaphore's value is already 0 (or less) and must be corrected for by the subsequent gadd4. The briefly negative value is often tolerable since it gives (at worst) a pessimistic estimate of the available resources and will never cause a waiting process to proceed inappropriately.

On the other hand, problems can arise when many processes are simultaneously waiting for the same semaphore. In this case, about half of those processes are likely to be between the gccsub4 and gadd4 instructions at any given moment; consequently, if $N$ processes are waiting for $S$, the value observed in $S$ at any given moment is likely to be about $N/2$ less than $S$'s true value. If $S$'s true value is 0 (as is likely if many processes waiting for it have accumulated), then a signal operation on $S$ should allow exactly one of the waiting processes to proceed; however, it is possible that *none* of those processes will ever proceed, since all the other waiting processes are continuously decrementing $S$ and so no process will ever observe that the true value of $S$ is now greater than 0. Such a semaphore implementation must therefore be used with caution and restricted to situations in which this pathology can be guaranteed not to arise.

### 19.7.2 Implementing Binary Semaphores

Because of the problems encountered in the program shown in figure 19.6, other semaphore implementation approaches are typically used. The most common entails adding an atomic test-and-set instruction to the machine instruction set, as mentioned above. Although all (or nearly all) instructions are defined to be atomic with respect to interrupts, and hence can be considered to be atomic on a single-processor time-shared system, this test-and-set instruction is often the *only* instruction that is guaranteed to be atomic (by using bus locking or similar technology) on a multiprocessor system as well. In the context of the $G$ machine, we illustrate this approach by adding an atomic instruction to test a 1-byte memory location, setting the condition codes CC according to the result, and then setting the contents of the tested memory location to 0. We name this instruction "test and clear" and give it the mnemonic gtc1. It is further described in table 19.7.

There is no obvious way to use a test-and-set instruction such as gtc1 to implement a *general* semaphore directly, but it is quite straightforward to implement

**Table 19.7**  Test-and-clear instruction.

| Operation | Operand addresses | Sets CC? | Function performed |
|---|---|---|---|
| gtc1 | $A$ | Yes | Set $S$, $Z$, and $C$ bits in CC according to the result of $\langle E_A \rangle^1 - 0$ and then *atomically* set $E_A{}^1 \leftarrow 0$ |

```
| Translation of wait(S):
    w:    gtc1    dir(S)          | Was semaphore zero?
          gjeq    dir(w)          | (Yes, keep waiting.)
          ...                     | No, but it is now!  Proceed!

| Translation of signal(S):
          gmove1  imm1(1)  dir(S) | Add 1 to its value
                                  | (which is known to have been 0).
          ...
```

**Figure 19.8**  Binary-semaphore implementation using test-and-clear instruction.

*binary* semaphores in this way, as shown in figure 19.8. Since the only two legal values of a binary semaphore are 0 and 1, the **wait** operation will always leave the semaphore (which must have contained 1 immediately before the **wait**) with the value 0. The **signal** operation likewise must occur when the semaphore's value is 0 and therefore must leave the semaphore with the value 1. This restriction thus eliminates the need for arithmetic, and the implementation of a binary semaphore consists simply of move operations (with the appropriate testing atomically bundled in, in the case of gtc1). The problems of the program in figure 19.6 have disappeared along with the need for arithmetic, since a gtc1 instruction that fails because the semaphore already contains 0 does not alter the state of the semaphore and consequently requires no compensating action before another gtc1 attempt.

The apparent loss of power in having implemented only binary semaphores rather than general semaphores is largely illusory. Given a correct implementation of binary semaphores, a general semaphore $S$ can be implemented as a combination of a counter $C$ and a binary semaphore $B$, as shown in figure 19.9. The basic idea is to use $B$ to ensure mutual exclusion among processes attempting to modify $C$. If only one process modifies $C$ at a time, no bugs due to race conditions will arise.

Figure 19.9 demonstrates that general semaphores—and, by extension, any of the large variety of higher-level synchronization operations that can be implemented using them—can be implemented even if the simple gtc1 instruction is the only atomic operation available. This fact is satisfying, but in reality the power of binary semaphores suffices for most applications; in such cases, the extra complexity of figure 19.9 is gratuitous and the semaphore implementation of figure 19.8 can be used directly. Therefore, we confine our attention to binary semaphores for the

*Process Synchronization*

```
| Translation of wait(S):
    w:    gtc1    dir(B)            | Was binary semaphore zero?
          gjeq    dir(w)            | (Yes, keep waiting.)


          gtest4  dir(C)            | Is counter zero?
          gjgt    dir(win)          | (No, decrement it and proceed.)
          gmove1  imm1(1) dir(B)    | Yes, signal(B)
          gjmp    dir(w)            |   and go try it all again.


  win:    gsub4   dir(C) imm4(1) dir(C) | Decrement S's value.
          gmove1  imm1(1) dir(B)    | signal(B)
            . . .


| Translation of signal(S):
  sig:    gtc1    dir(B)            | Was binary semaphore zero?
          gjeq    dir(sig)          | (Yes, keep waiting.)


          gadd4   dir(C) imm4(1) dir(C)  | Increment S's value.
          gmove1  imm1(1) dir(B)    | signal(B)
            . . .
```

**Figure 19.9**  General-semaphore implementation using a binary semaphore.

remainder of this chapter, except where otherwise noted.

Many other mechanisms have been used as bases for synchronization primitives, including indirect addressing, shift and rotate operations, and instruction-stream modification. Modern computers, however, typically include one atomic mechanism, such as a test-and-set instruction, that is specifically targeted toward correctly and efficiently implementing binary semaphores and similar locking operations.

### 19.7.3 The Waiting in wait(S)

As noted earlier, the use of busy-waiting is often undesirable in time-sharing systems because the process that is busy-waiting ties up the processor while not executing any useful instructions. If another process $Q$ is going to signal a semaphore $S$ for which a process $P$ is waiting, there is no point in $P$ looping: It would be much more efficient to allow $Q$, the process that will signal $S$, to run.

Under a round-robin scheduler, passing control to the next process in the process list is a more productive use of time than busy-waiting. We might postulate a supervisor call, say gsvc(10), that we label yield(), whose handler is just a call to Scheduler, terminating the quantum of execution of the currently executing process and passing control to the next process. When the current process regains control, it will start at the instruction after the gsvc(10). Figure 19.10 shows how to revise the implementation of wait given in figure 19.8 along these lines to improve its efficiency.

Ai even more efficient, but more complex, implementation of the waiting part of wait is often used. In this implementation, the process list is divided into two sets: runnable processes and waiting processes. A process that is waiting

```
| Translation of wait(S):
    w:     gtc1      dir(S)        | Was semaphore zero?
           gjne      dir(win)      | (No, succeeded!)
           gsvc(10)                | Else YIELD to other processes,
           gjmp      dir(w)        |    then try again.

    win:   ...
```

**Figure 19.10**  Invocation of scheduler within wait.

for a semaphore places itself in the waiting class. The scheduler never looks at waiting processes: It just runs the runnable processes in turn. When a signal($S$) operation is done, the signaling process, after setting $S = 1$, looks to see if any processes are waiting for $S$. If so, one of the processes waiting for $S$ is moved from the waiting set into the runnable set. The implementation of this technique requires remembering, along with each waiting process, the name of the semaphore for which it waits. Time is saved, however, in the common case in which most of the processes in the process list are waiting. The round-robin scheduler would repeatedly run each waiting process, even if no signals have occurred. Here a waiting process never runs until a signal happens.

### 19.7.4  Fairness

All of the semaphore implementations discussed thus far are potentially *unfair* in how they choose which of several waiting processes will proceed when another process signals a semaphore. In these implementations, a wait operation on a semaphore whose value is 0 just tests the semaphore repeatedly, hoping to catch it during an interval when it is nonzero. A signal operation on a semaphore whose value is 0 simply changes the semaphore's value to 1, without explicitly notifying any of the waiting processes. The next waiting process to proceed is thus chosen "at random" to be whichever waiting process first observes the change made by signal. The choice is not based on the length of time that each process has been waiting or any other such criterion that might strike one as being "fair."

First-come/first-served (select the process that has been waiting on the semaphore for the longest time) is intuitively the "fairest" policy for ordering the waiting processes, but an adequate formal definition of what it means for a semaphore to be fair can be much weaker:

. . . . . . . . . . . . . . . . . . . . . . . . . . . . . . . . . . . . . . . . . . . . . . . . . . . . . . . . . . . . . . .

***Fair semaphores***   A semaphore $S$ is *fair* if every wait operation on $S$ eventually terminates (assuming that a sufficient number of signal operations are performed on $S$).

. . . . . . . . . . . . . . . . . . . . . . . . . . . . . . . . . . . . . . . . . . . . . . . . . . . . . . . . . . . . . . .

In other words, a semaphore is fair if a particular wait operation cannot be arbitrarily discriminated against, in the sense of being bypassed by an unbounded number of `signal` operations on the semaphore.

This fairness standard will be met by our semaphore implementations (at least in a probabilistic sense) if the choice of the next waiting process to proceed is *truly* random; unfortunately, in real systems, many factors usually conspire to produce systematic biases. For example, with a round-robin scheduler, if process number $N$ performs a `signal` operation on a semaphore $S$, process number $N + 1$ is highly likely to be the next to proceed if, in fact, it is performing a `wait` operation on $S$. If a particular collection of processes is structured so that process number $N$ performs all the `signal` operations on $S$ and many processes are waiting on $S$, process number $N - 1$ (the last process to be scheduled after $N$ has run) is very likely to `wait` forever.

Fairness of semaphores is related to the question of fairness of bus arbitration, discussed in section 9.2.6. In a bus-based multiprocessor, for example, it will be hard to build *any* fair higher-level mechanism in the absence of fairness in low-level mechanisms such as bus arbitration. Fairness at the low level, however, is only a necessary, not a sufficient, condition for fair implementations of higher-level constructs such as semaphores.

Detailed discussion of the importance of fairness is beyond our current scope, but it does not take much imagination to picture the difficulty of building a reliable system based on a `wait` operation that is not guaranteed ever to finish! Detailed exploration of mechanisms for achieving fairness would likewise take more space than is available here. We content ourselves with a brief sketch of one method for building fair semaphores: associating a first-in/first-out *queue* of waiting processes with each semaphore. If a `signal` operation is performed on a semaphore with a nonempty queue of waiting processes, the `signal` operation simply removes the waiting process at the head of the queue and reactivates it. If a process attempts to perform a `wait` operation on a semaphore whose value is currently 0, the process is suspended and placed at the tail of the semaphore's queue. This structure ensures that waiting processes will be reactivated in first-come/first-served order and thus guarantees fairness. It has the further advantage, shared with other queue-based schemes such as the one outlined at the end of section 19.7.3, of avoiding busy-waiting, but its implementation is more complex than the simple semaphore implementations of figures 19.8–19.10.

## 19.8 Deadlock

A problem arising from the indiscriminate use of semaphores (or any other mutual-exclusion construct) is illustrated in the classic *five dining philosophers problem*. This problem is stated as follows. Consider five philosophers, $P_0$ through $P_4$, seated at a round table such that philosopher $P_{((i+1) \bmod 5)}$ is just to the right of philosopher $P_i$. To the left of each philosopher $P_i$ (and therefore to the right of philosopher $P_{((i-1) \bmod 5)}$) is a fork $F_i$. In the center of the table is a large bowl of spaghetti so tangled that it requires two forks to eat.

Each philosopher periodically becomes hungry and at that time executes the following algorithm:

1. Pick up fork to the left.
2. Pick up fork to the right.
3. Eat spaghetti.
4. Put both forks back where they were found.

Hungry philosopher $P_i$ picks up fork $F_i$ and then fork $F_{((i+1) \bmod 5)}$ and holds both forks for a period of time before putting them back. If a fork is momentarily unavailable (because some other philosopher is holding it), $P_i$ waits until it is available before proceeding to the next step of the algorithm. In particular, if fork $F_{((i+1) \bmod 5)}$, required in step 2 of the algorithm, is currently unavailable, philosopher $P_i$ continues to hold fork $F_i$, acquired during step 1 of the algorithm, until fork $F_{((i+1) \bmod 5)}$ can be picked up. This is where the trouble starts: If hunger pangs attack all five philosophers at approximately the same time, all five may complete step 1 of the algorithm before any of them has a chance to begin step 2. The result is that each philosopher $P_i$ is stubbornly holding onto fork $F_i$ and waiting for fork $F_{((i+1) \bmod 5)}$ to become available. The system becomes stuck in a state known as *deadlock*, from which it will never emerge.

Deadlock is a computational equivalent of the gridlock that plagues traffic-filled city streets. The key feature of both situations is a directed *cycle* in the graph of interprocess dependencies. In other words, some process (or automobile) $A_1$ is waiting for some resource $R_2$ (either a fork or space in an intersection), which it must acquire in order to make progress. But $R_2$ is currently held by some other process $A_2$, which in turn is waiting for some other resource $R_3$, which it must acquire in order to make progress and eventually release $R_2$. In a deadlocked situation, this chain continues until at some point it reaches a resource $R_1$ that is currently held by $A_1$.

Although our philosophers' problem is somewhat whimsical, deadlock is a very serious threat to all kinds of practical systems that use mutual exclusion. For example, updates to a bank account can be performed atomically by first `waiting` on a semaphore associated with the bank account, then performing the update, then `signaling` the semaphore. Imagine a procedure `Transfer(A,B,M)` that transfers an amount of money $M$ from account $A$ to account $B$ by debiting $A$'s balance and crediting $B$'s balance. The transfer should be done after waiting for both $A$'s and $B$'s semaphores, to avoid any third process from observing a state of affairs in which, for example, $A$'s account has been debited but $B$'s has not yet been credited, so that an amount of money $M$ appears to have disappeared into thin air.

A plausible and straightforward implementation of `Transfer` is shown in figure 19.11. Unfortunately, if a process $P_1$ attempts a `Transfer(A_1,A_2,M_1)` at about the same time that another process $P_2$ attempts a `Transfer(A_2,A_1,M_2)`, deadlock can occur, with $P_1$ holding semaphore $A_1$->`sema` and waiting for semaphore $A_2$->`sema` while $P_2$ holds semaphore $A_2$->`sema` and waits for $A_1$->`sema`. This is an exact analog, on a smaller scale, of the five dining philosophers problem.

Deadlock is clearly the enemy of the concurrent-system builder. Techniques for preventing parts of a system from "locking up" permanently as a result of deadlock fall into two general categories: *deadlock avoidance* and *deadlock recovery*. Dead-

```
Transfer(A,B,M)
 struct BankAccount *A,*B;
 int M;
 {      wait(A->sema);                 /* Get exclusive access to A. */
        wait(B->sema);                 /* Get exclusive access to B. */
        A->balance = A->balance - M;   /* Perform the updates.       */
        B->balance = B->balance + M;
        signal(A->sema);               /* Release resources.         */
        signal(B->sema);
 }
```

**Figure 19.11**   Deadlock-prone bank-account-transfer program.

lock avoidance involves imposing some discipline on the way in which resources are accumulated by a process, so that deadlock becomes impossible. The strategy of deadlock recovery, in contrast, allows deadlocks to happen but provides a mechanism for detecting when a deadlock has occurred and "backing out" of some operation, releasing resources that it had already accumulated so that other tasks needing those resources can proceed to completion. The backed-out process then resumes execution at a later time. Both deadlock avoidance and deadlock recovery are widely used in real systems. The full range of such techniques far exceeds the scope of our treatment, but we shall give some glimpses of typical methods.

A typical deadlock-avoidance technique is to put all the resources (for example, semaphores) into some numerical order and then require that programs always acquire resources in increasing numerical order; in other words, require a program never to attempt to acquire a resource numbered $i$ if it is already holding another resource whose number is greater than $i$. To modify the philosophers' algorithm to implement this technique, we need only assign a unique number to each fork (it does not matter how these numbers are assigned) and change the algorithm as follows:

1. Pick up the *lower-numbered* adjacent fork.
2. Pick up the *higher-numbered* adjacent fork.
3. Eat spaghetti.
4. Put both forks back where they were found.

A similar modification could be applied to the program in figure 19.11. The directed cycles that cause deadlock are impossible when the philosophers use the new algorithm because if any philosopher $P$ is waiting for some resource (fork) $R$, any resources $P$ is already holding must have lower numbers than $R$. There can be no philosopher $P'$ who holds $R$ but is waiting (directly or indirectly) for some resource held by $P$, since all of those resources have lower numbers than $R$. Thus, in contrast to the situation produced by the original algorithm, there can be no situation in which any philosophers are indirectly blocking themselves from making further progress.

This scheme for deadlock avoidance is limited to situations in which the resources that will be required by a transaction are always known before any of the resources are acquired. In such a situation, the full set of resources required can be put into the proper numerical order and then acquired in that order. If the identity of some of the needed resources cannot be known until other resources have already been acquired, there is a chance that a transaction will find that it needs to acquire a resource with a lower number than the resources it has already acquired, thus risking deadlock if it attempts to acquire the resource. Other deadlock-avoidance schemes encounter similar problems in such situations.

If deadlocks cannot be avoided, then it is important to be able to recover from them by "backing up" some process involved in a deadlock and releasing the resources it holds so that other processes can acquire those resources and proceed. This mechanism is reminiscent of the back-out that must occur when a machine-language instruction encounters a page fault in midexecution. All visible effects of the instruction must be undone if the instruction is to be transparently restartable after the cause of the page fault is remedied. Likewise, the main problem in backing up a process $P$ to break a deadlock is that any visible side effects performed by $P$ after the point to which it is being backed up must be undone so that $P$ can be transparently restarted from that point. Operationally, this means that $P$ should avoid performing side effects (other than the inevitable side effects inherent in wait operations) until all needed resources have been acquired. If this policy is followed, then a backup can be performed simply by backing up the program counter to the first wait operation and signaling all semaphores that have been acquired.

## 19.9  Summary

Interprocess synchronization is an important topic with a large literature. It is especially vital to the proper functioning of on-line data bases such as bank and airline records. Semaphores are a relatively classic synchronization mechanism, but they are only one member of a very large set of synchronization mechanisms that have been studied and are in use. Even within the restricted domain of semaphores, this chapter has explored only a small fraction of the relevant issues and implementation ideas. Our study has been directed by two goals: (1) to illustrate the need for hardware to support primitive atomic instructions if synchronization operations are to be implemented correctly, and (2) to describe one representative and flexible synchronization construct in enough detail that it can be used to illustrate the role of synchronization in operating-system design. The reader continuing on to a study of operating systems will find synchronization mechanisms to be a subject whose richness this chapter only hints at.

## 19.10  Context

Semaphores were developed by Dijkstra [1968a], who used the names $P$ and $V$ where we use wait and signal. A wealth of alternative synchronization mechanisms have been described in the literature, including conditional critical regions [Brinch Hansen 1972; Hoare 1972], monitors [Hoare 1974], path expressions [Campbell and Habermann 1974], and eventcounts and sequencers [Reed and Kanodia 1979], all of which have been inspired by interprocess synchronization problems that come up in general applications involving concurrent processes. A separate, though not completely independent, thread of development has involved concurrency-control mechanisms for transaction processing in on-line data bases such as airline reservation systems and banking systems. The concurrency-control requirements of these applications center around making atomic updates to data bases, as in the example of figure 19.11. Bernstein and Goodman [1981] survey many of the synchronization mechanisms used in this area. General discussions of synchronization mechanisms and their role in operating-system design can be found in textbooks such as Finkel [1986] and Janson [1985].

The lore of famous synchronization problems is rich and colorful. Aside from the producer-consumer problem discussed in section 19.5, there is the *readers-writers problem* [Courtois and Parnas 1971], which concerns synchronizing access to a shared, readable, and updatable object. An early description of the five dining philosophers problem was given by Dijkstra [1971]. A closely related, and colorfully stated, synchronization problem is the *cigarette smokers' problem* [Parnas 1975]. The deadlock-avoidance technique of numbering resources and acquiring them in increasing numerical order is credited to Havender [1968]. Alternative deadlock-avoidance techniques include the *banker's algorithm* [Habermann 1969], first implemented in the THE operating system [Dijkstra 1968b]. Deadlock-recovery techniques are legion and are used mostly in the realm of transaction processing on data bases [Bernstein and Goodman 1981].

A variety of atomic instructions have been proposed and implemented to serve as the basis for synchronization operations. Aside from the test-and-set operation, discussed in section 19.7.2, there are the *compare-and-swap operation* (implemented on many processors and discussed by Stone [1987]) and the *fetch-and-add operation* [Gottlieb et al. 1983].

## 19.11 Problems

### Problem 19.1

Draw a precedence graph for the constraints imposed on the operations U, V, W, X, and Y in figure 19.12.

### Problem 19.2

A. What initial values should the three semaphores S1, S2, and S3 have so that the processes shown in figure 19.13 cooperate to print BITBITBITBI...?

B. What initial values should the three semaphores S1, S2, and S3 have so that the processes cooperate to print ITBITBITBI...?

C. Suppose that initially S2 = 3, S1 = 0, S3 = 0. Is it possible that the output string begins with TTIBTTI?

```
Shared memory
------ ------
semaphore SemA=0, SemB=0;

Process 1                    Process 2
---------                    ---------
U;                           wait(SemA);
signal(SemA);                X;
V;                           wait(SemB);
signal(SemB);                Y;
W;
```

**Figure 19.12**  Two synchronizing processes.

```
Process 1            Process 2            Process 3
----------------     ----------------     ----------------
L1: wait(S3);        L2: wait(S1);        L3: wait(S2);
    print("B");          print("I");          print("T");
    signal(S1);          signal(S2);          signal(S3);
    goto L1;             goto L2;             goto L3;
```

**Figure 19.13**  Three synchronizing processes.

### *Problem 19.3*

Three processes—*A*, *B*, and *C*—must cooperate in transmitting a sequence of values each of which is 1 greater than the previous value. A skeletal version of the code executed by each process is given in figure 19.14. The variables x and y are shared by all three processes. The procedure call `transmit(y)` in process *C* causes the value y to be transmitted. You may assume that this includes any necessary synchronization with the output device.

A. In order for the processes to cooperate properly, various `signal` and `wait` operations must be added. Draw a precedence graph that shows the constraints on ordering of operations that are necessary to produce the correct output sequence. Use the name *assign* for the operation y = x in process *A*, *incr* for x = y + 1 in process *B*, and *transmit* for `transmit(y)` in process *C*. You need not show the `goto` operations. Subscript operation names as $assign_1$, $assign_2$, and so on, to indicate which repetition of an operation is meant. Draw out the nodes for the first three repetitions of each operation, and indicate by ellipsis how the precedence graph continues. Be sure not to include any nonessential constraints!

B. Add appropriate semaphores, and `signal` and `wait` operations, to the program so that it operates correctly. *Do not* add any statements other than `signal` and `wait`. Indicate the initial value of each semaphore you add.

C. By adding semaphore operations differently than in part B, can you make the

*Process Synchronization*

```
Process A:                  Process B:                Process C:
------------------          -----------------         ------------------

LoopA:                      LoopB:                    LoopC:

    y = x;                      x = y + 1;                transmit(y);

    goto LoopA;                 goto LoopB;               goto LoopC;
```

**Figure 19.14**  Three communicating processes.

```
Process P:                          Process Q:
---------------------               ----------------------------

        N = 5;
        Sqr = 0;

loopP:                              loopQ:

        if (N == 0)                     Sqr = Sqr +  2*N + 1;
            goto endP;

        N = N - 1;                      goto loopQ;

        goto loopP;

endP:

        print(Sqr);
```

**Figure 19.15**  Squaring using communicating processes.

program type out a sequence of values each of which is 2 greater than the previous value? Write a program or explain why it cannot be done. Give an initial value for each semaphore, adding only `signal` and `wait` statements.

## *Problem 19.4*

Figure 19.15 shows two processes that must cooperate in computing $N^2$ by taking the sum of the first $N$ odd numbers. Add appropriate semaphores and `signal` and `wait` statements to these programs so that the proper value Sqr = 25 will be printed out. Indicate the initial value of every semaphore you add. Insert the semaphore operations so as to preserve the maximum degree of concurrency between the two processes; do not put any nonessential constraints on the ordering of operations. (*Hint:* Two semaphores suffice for a simple and elegant solution.)

```
Process A:                        Process B:
--------------------------        --------------------------
        . . .                             . . .

A1:     tempA = counter + 1;      B1:     tempB = counter + 2;
A2:     counter = tempA;          B2:     counter = tempB;


        . . .                             . . .
```

**Figure 19.16**  Concurrent increment of a counter.

## Problem 19.5

Add a new semaphore to the program in figure 19.12 to ensure that the operations W and Y can never be performed concurrently. Your change should constrain the order of operations *as little as possible*.

## Problem 19.6

Figure 19.16 shows a pair of processes that share a common set of variables: counter, tempA, and tempB. The variable counter initially has the value 10 before either process begins to execute.

A. What different values of counter are possible when both processes have finished executing? Give an order of execution of statements from processes A and B that would yield each of the values you give. (For example, the execution order A1, A2, B1, B2 would yield the value 13.)

B. Modify the program by adding appropriate signal and wait operations on a semaphore SYNC such that the only possible final value of counter is 13. Indicate the initial value of SYNC.

C. Draw a precedence graph that describes all the possible orderings of executions of statements A1, A2, B1, and B2 that yield the final value counter = 11.

D. Modify the program by adding semaphores and signal and wait operations to guarantee that the final result of executing the two processes will be counter = 11. Give the initial values for every semaphore you introduce. Try to put the minimum number of constraints on the ordering of statements. In other words, don't just pick one ordering that will yield 11 and enforce that one by means of semaphores; instead, enforce only the essential precedence constraints marked in your solution to part C.

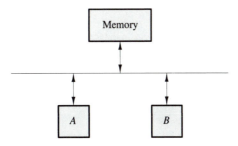

**Figure 19.17**   Dual-processor system with shared memory.

```
int Allocate(Who);
 int Who;
 {      int i;
        for (i = 1; i < Size; i = i+1)
                        if (Owner[i] == 0) goto Found;
        error("No free blocks");
Found:
        Owner[i] = Who;
        Allocate = i;
 }
```

**Figure 19.18**   Allocator for shared memory blocks.

### Problem 19.7

Two processors, $A$ and $B$, share the same memory, as shown in figure 19.17, and must therefore coordinate their use of memory. We assume a shared array `Owner` of integers such that $Owner[i] = 0$ if the $i$th memory block is unallocated, 1 if it is allocated to processor $A$, and 2 if it is allocated to processor $B$. Each processor can call the `Allocate` subroutine shown in figure 19.18 to allocate a new memory block for itself: Processor $A$ would call `Allocate(1)`, and processor $B$ would call `Allocate(2)`. Explain why `Allocate` will occasionally return the same memory block number to both processors, and explain how to fix `Allocate` to cure this problem.

### Problem 19.8

In the scenario outlined in problem 18.9, there is a problem if interrupts are *enabled* while `SendMail` is executed. This problem could be solved if access to `SendMail` were guarded by a semaphore. What is this problem?

### Problem 19.9

A. How many Cs are printed when the set of processes in figure 19.19 runs?

B. How many Ds are printed when this set of processes runs?

```
/* Initializations: L = 3; R = 0 */

Process 1:          Process 2:          Process 3:
--------------      -------------       --------------

l1:                 l2:                 l3:

    wait(L);            wait(R);            wait(R);
                       type('A');
    type('C');          type('B');          type('D');
    signal(R);          signal(R);


    goto l1;            goto l2;            goto l3;
```

**Figure 19.19**  Three interacting processes.

C. What is smallest number of As that might be printed when this set of processes runs?

D. Is CABABDDCABCABD a possible output sequence when this set of processes runs?

E. Is CABACDBCABDD a possible output sequence when this set of processes runs?

F. Add an additional semaphore Mutex to the program in figure 19.19 to prevent the A and B printed by process 2 from being separated by a D printed by process 3. (Add appropriate signals and waits to process 2 and process 3. Be sure to initialize the Mutex semaphore.)

## Problem 19.10
Give the values of InPtr, OutPtr, Chars, and Holes after 255 calls to write and 155 calls to read in the program of figure 19.3 have completed successfully. How do these values change if the next event is a call to read? What happens if, instead, the next event is a call to write?

## Problem 19.11
Consider a situation in which several producer processes can call the procedure write in figure 19.3. Each process is producing a sequence of characters, and the desired behavior is that those sequences should be interleaved, in the order of their arrival, and the interleaved sequence should appear at the other end of the pipe. If the program is used in this way, the result will not necessarily conform to this specification. Give a scenario in which the output sequence is not an interleaving of the input sequences, and explain how this misbehavior occurs.

## Problem 19.12
Using one additional semaphore, you should be able to fix the misbehavior of the program in figure 19.3 in the multiple-producer case. Show how to modify the program so that the interleaving is done properly. Explain what steps you have taken to eliminate unnecessary waiting for synchronization.

```
      int Sem[100];                  /* Room for 100 semaphores. */

      WaitSVC(p)
       struct MState *p;
       {   int s;                     /* The semaphore number.   */

again:  s = POPPS4(p);
          if (Sem[s] <= 0)            /* Is value zero?          */
           { PUSHPS4(p, s);           /* Yes, keep waiting.      */
             p->PC = p->PC - 2;       /* Back up.                */
             Scheduler(p);
            }
          else Sem[s] = Sem[s] - 1;   /* No, decrement and return.*/
       }
```

**Figure 19.20**  Wait supervisor-call subhandler.

### Problem 19.13

Suggest a modification to the program in figure 18.10 that will minimize the number of process switches (that is, calls to Scheduler) that occur when the processes of the program in figure 18.12 run. An explanation of your approach will suffice; you need not write out the actual code for your solution.

### Problem 19.14

Modify the general semaphore implementation of figure 19.9 to avoid busy-waiting by inserting calls to the yield supervisor call gsvc(10) as in figure 19.10. Explain why each yield is necessary and why you had to place it where you did.

### Problem 19.15

Figure 19.20 shows the implementation of a supervisor call that performs a Wait semaphore operation for user-mode programs. Both the handler code and the Sem array are located in kernel (operating-system) memory.

A. How would the behavior of the Wait supervisor call be changed if the statement commented "Back up" were deleted from the handler code?

B. What is the minimal atomicity assumption that suffices for the implementation of Wait shown in the figure to work properly on a single-processor system?

C. What is the minimal atomicity assumption that suffices for the implementation of Wait to work properly on a system in which any of several processors might be executing the WaitSVC code simultaneously?

D. If the call to Scheduler in WaitSVC were changed to goto again, how would the behavior of the Wait supervisor call change?

E. What would be the effect of adding a call to Scheduler(p) as a new last statement in WaitSVC (following the else clause)?

F. Ben Bitdiddle suggests moving the semaphore storage (Sem) from kernel memory to the virtual memory of user processes performing the Wait supervisor calls. Comment on the practicality of Ben's suggestion.

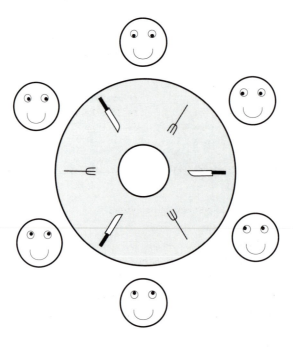

**Figure 19.21**  Six feasting gourmands.

### Problem 19.16

An interesting variant of the five dining philosophers problem has recently been discovered. Six gourmands are seated around a table with a large hunk of roast beef in the middle. Forks and knives are arranged as shown in figure 19.21. Each gourmand obeys the following algorithm:

1. Grab the closest knife.

2. Grab the closest fork.

3. Carve and devour a piece of beef.

4. Put down knife and fork where they used to be.

Can deadlock ever occur in this situation? Why or why not?

### Problem 19.17

Consider implementing producer-consumer communication on a system that supports binary semaphores but has no direct support for general semaphores.

A. Show how to modify figure 19.3 so that `Chars` and `Holes` are simple integer values rather than semaphores and an additional binary semaphore `Mutex` is added for synchronization. Be sure to show the needed changes to `init` as well as to `read` and `write`. Explain what steps you have taken to prevent your system from deadlocking if, for example, `read` is called when the buffer is empty or `write` is called when the buffer is full.

B. Modify your code from part A to invoke a system call `yield()` (in the spirit of figure 19.10) to allow the scheduler to run another process if a process attempting a `read` or `write` is currently prevented from making progress.

C. Looking over your code for parts A and B, you find that you are doing extra work: The increments and decrements to `Chars` and `Holes` precisely mirror each other; moreover, they precisely mirror the increments to `InPtr` and `OutPtr`. In fact, you notice that, in between calls to `read` and `write`, the following invariants are always true:

$$\texttt{Chars} \equiv (\texttt{InPtr} - \texttt{OutPtr}) \bmod 100,$$
$$\texttt{Holes} \equiv (\texttt{OutPtr} - \texttt{InPtr}) \bmod 100.$$

These facts can be used to avoid the cost of maintaining `Chars` and `Holes` as separate variables; instead, whenever their values are needed, they can be computed from the values of `InPtr` and `OutPtr`. The only problem occurs when `InPtr = OutPtr`, which is consistent with either `Chars = 0` and `Holes = 100` or `Holes = 0` and `Chars = 100`. We can avoid this ambiguity by restricting `write` so that `Holes` never drops below 1. Revise your code from parts A and B to eliminate the variables `Chars` and `Holes`. Explain how your solution works.

D. In search of the ultimate economy of mechanism, you consider eliminating the binary semaphore `Mutex` from your solution to part C. (This can work only for situations in which there is just a single producer process and a single consumer process.) Explain how this can be done without creating any timing races, and show the resulting code. What constraints on how `InPtr` and `OutPtr` are updated must your program observe in order to be correct?

# Interrupts, Priorities, and Real Time

One common application of producer-consumer communication routines such as the `read` and `write` routines illustrated in figure 19.3 is as "middlemen" handling output from a user program. The user program in this case is the producer, calling `write` every time it has another character to output. The consumer is a simple process of the kind illustrated in figure 20.1. This program is simply an infinite loop that calls `read` to obtain each character for output and then calls `transmit`, which is assumed to contain the device-dependent code needed to make the character available to the output device (say, a terminal). Typically, `transmit` would write the character into an "output holding register" associated with the device. This scenario assumes that synchronization between the terminal server process and the output device is mediated by two semaphores, TREADY and TSTART. When `transmit` has sent a character to the device, a `signal` operation on TSTART causes the device to proceed and output the character; when the device has finished, it performs a `signal` operation on TREADY to indicate its readiness for another output character. We may thus imagine the device as repeatedly executing the sequence of operations `wait(TSTART)`; *output the character*; `signal(TREADY)`.

Although the philosophy of the program in figure 20.1 is quite tenable, certain optimizations lead to substantial implementation economies as well as more efficient operation. Most of the time, we would expect the terminal server process to be waiting either for the production of a new output character by the user process or for the output device to reach the point at which it is ready for a new character. In typical operation, the terminal server process thus operates in short bursts of activity, punctuated by `wait`s on either TREADY (to wait for the device) or the `Chars` semaphore in `read` (to wait for the producer process to generate a new character). The computation performed between these points of synchrony is time-bounded, consisting primarily of removing a buffered character and transmitting it to the output device.

The semaphores TREADY and `Chars` rely on an underlying time-sharing mechanism to apply their waiting time to executing other processes. As we have seen, a simple busy-waiting semaphore implementation can apportion the waiting time between the blocked server process and other processes; a more sophisticated scheme (for example, using `yield`) would interact with the time-sharing scheduler so as to recover nearly all of the wasted time. While the latter approach can lead to more efficient processor utilization than the former approach, both involve considerable

```
while (true) do
  { wait(TREADY);
    transmit(read());
    signal(TSTART);
  }
```

**Figure 20.1**  Terminal server process.

scheduling and process-management overhead.

A popular alternative approach to the scheduling of device server processes uses the mechanism of *interrupts*. In this approach, an event (such as a `signal` on `TREADY`) signaled by an input/output device stimulates a process swap with no intervention by the operating-system kernel; the server process is effectively invoked on demand by the device with which it interfaces. As discussed in section 13.3.13, the implementation of interrupts is virtually identical to that of supervisor calls or illegal-instruction faults; the major difference is that the "trap" is caused by an incoming digital signal rather than by the execution of a particular instruction. The clock interrupt, which we have already postulated to drive the scheduler portion of our kernel operating system, is an example of a simple interrupt mechanism.

By using an interrupt-driven server for input/output devices, we can entirely avoid the use of kernel scheduling and other time-sharing mechanisms for buffered input and output services. The server process of the previous example reduces to a single procedure, which is invoked on demand as a result of the interrupt. Invocation of the server procedure requires interrupting the currently executing program (hence the term *interrupt*), preserving its state on, say, the kernel stack. The server is invoked (in our case, as a kernel procedure) and runs to completion, returning control to the previous (interrupted) program.

Figure 20.2 illustrates a typical interrupt-driven buffered output system. Note that the terminal server process of the multiprocess scheme has been replaced by the `ttyint` interrupt-handler procedure. We assume here that the device asserts a single status bit `TREADY`, corresponding to the semaphore `TREADY` of the previous example, to indicate that it is ready to accept a new character. Note also that `ttyint` does not receive a `state` argument, as the trap handler of figure 14.44 does, because the occurrence of an input/output interrupt is not correlated with the execution of any particular instruction of the interrupted program, and therefore the current state of the interrupted program is not relevant. We assume that the stubs for input/output interrupts simply call the handler procedure without passing a pointer to the saved processor state as an argument.

The device maintains an *interrupt-enable flag* that is set and cleared, respectively, by the `Enable` and `Disable` statements in figure 20.2. Interrupts are stimulated by the conjunction of the enable flag and `TREADY`: Whenever interrupts are enabled *and* `TREADY` = 1, the currently executing program is interrupted, interrupts are disabled, and `ttyint` is invoked. Normally `ttyint` extracts a character from the buffer, transmits it to the device, reenables interrupts, and returns to the interrupted program. The user-program interface, `type(c)`, simply inserts its argument character $c$ into the buffer as before.

In the absence of semaphore protection against buffer overflow and underflow,

```
char buf[100];
int InPtr, OutPtr;


/* One-time only initialization code:                  */

init()
{       InPtr = OutPtr = 0;
}



/* The interrupt handler: Invoked by TREADY == 1.       */

ttyint()
{       if (InPtr != OutPtr)                /* Buffer not empty.      */
        {       transmit(buf[OutPtr]);      /* Send next character.   */
                OutPtr = (OutPtr+1) % 100; /* Update buffer.         */
                signal(TSTART);             /* Start physical output. */
                (Enable TTY Output Interrupts)
        }
        else
        {
                (Disable TTY Output Interrupts) /* Buffer is empty.  */
        }
}


/* User side: Type the character c.                     */

type(c)
char c;
{       int i;
        i = (InPtr+1) % 100;                /* New InPtr value.       */
        while (i == OutPtr) ;               /* Wait for buffer not full. */
        buf[InPtr] = c;                     /* Insert character.      */
        InPtr = i;                          /* Install new InPtr.     */
        (Enable TTY Output Interrupts)  /* In case buffer was empty. */
}
```

**Figure 20.2**  Interrupt-driven buffered output.


each of the procedures `ttyint` and `type` compares InPtr with OutPtr to avoid placing the buffer into an inconsistent state. `type` begins by computing the new InPtr value but does not install it as the value of InPtr until it has verified that doing so will not cause buffer overflow. If the buffer is full—that is, if the new InPtr value is identical to the current OutPtr value—`type` busy-waits until an interrupt-driven `ttyint` invocation makes a new buffer space. It is important that the interrupts be enabled for this busy-waiting to work; if `type` were not interruptible by `ttyint`, OutPtr would never change and the user process would busy-wait forever. Note also that the busy-waiting occurs only when the user process fills the output buffer. A more sophisticated implementation might avoid this wasted CPU time by arranging to schedule another process instead of looping.

A similar check for buffer *under*flow is built into `ttyint`. Note that interrupts are disabled during `ttyint` execution; `ttyint` effectively takes priority over the execution of the user process and will never be interrupted for execution of a user procedure. Thus the busy-waiting approach illustrated in `type` is not an appropriate reaction by `ttyint` to its invocation with an empty buffer. Moreover, if it simply reenables interrupts and returns without transmitting another character to the typewriter, it will be reinvoked immediately when interrupts are reenabled, since `TREADY` will remain set. This new invocation will then reenable interrupts and return again, only to be immediately interrupted once more. The resulting loop will effectively preclude any user-process instruction executions and hang up the system.

Consequently, `ttyint` returns with the interrupt disabled when it finds the buffer to be empty. When the user process executes a subsequent `type`($c$), the character $c$ is inserted into the (empty) buffer, and interrupts are explicitly reenabled.

## 20.1 Mutual-Exclusion Requirements

The relationship between the interrupt handler and the user process illustrates a special case of multiprocessing in which the execution of one process takes priority over the execution of another. Whenever `ttyint` is active, it runs to completion; its invocation stems from external inputs and is entirely asynchronous with respect to the (user) process that it interrupts. Although its invocation and return are generally transparent to the interrupted process (whose state is faithfully restored after the interrupt), the sharing of variables (such as `InPtr` and `OutPtr`) between the user process and the interrupt handler makes the occurrence of an interrupt potentially visible to the user process.

In particular, the shared variable `OutPtr` may be modified by an invocation of `ttyint`. Since this may happen asynchronously with respect to the user process, the user-process `type` procedure must anticipate changes in `OutPtr` value at any time (that is, between any pair of instruction executions). Note that the single reference to `OutPtr` in the `type` procedure is made to guarantee that at least one space is available in the buffer. Since changes to `OutPtr` resulting from `ttyint` invocations can only *increase* the number of available buffer slots, the assumption (of remaining buffer space) made on the basis of the `OutPtr` value can never be made obsolete by additional `ttyint` invocations; thus `type` is "safe" with respect to the class of asynchronous `OutPtr` changes made by the interrupt handler. In fact, `type` depends on such a change to break out of its busy-waiting loop.

In more complex interrupt situations, it is often necessary to take steps to preclude interrupts during certain *critical regions* of user-program execution. For example, the extraction of a character from `buf` by a user-level process would involve a comparison of `InPtr` and `OutPtr` to ensure that the buffer is nonempty, followed by an access to `buf[OutPtr]` and an increment of `OutPtr`. If an interrupt occurs between the test and the `OutPtr` increment, `ttyint` may extract the last character from the buffer *after* the user process decides that the buffer is nonempty but *before* it removes the character. The user process will then attempt to extract a character from the empty buffer, resulting in an inconsistent buffer state.

In such situations it is necessary to add a synchronization mechanism to ensure the mutual exclusion of critical code regions. In effect, the above buffer manipulations must be combined into an *atomic* operation that cannot be interfered with by asynchronous `ttyint` calls. In full multiprocess situations, such mutual exclusion can be enforced by semaphores; interrupt handlers, however, can be excluded by the simple expedient of disabling the interrupt mechanism. Thus, in order to guarantee that a region of user-process code will not be interrupted by `ttyint` invocations, it is sufficient to disable the TTY interrupt at the beginning of the region and reenable it at the end.

A major complication in the development of interrupt-based device-handler software is the detection and mutual exclusion of such critical regions. System bugs resulting from undetected critical regions are exasperatingly hard to find, because their symptoms are highly dependent on transient and uncontrollable timing details (such as whether the TTY chooses to request an interrupt between a critical pair of instruction executions). The best solution to this problem is the avoidance of critical regions altogether, as is done in figure 20.2, by the careful isolation of variables manipulated by the interrupt handler from those changed by the user process. Where this isolation is not practical (and unfortunately it rarely is), careful analysis of the necessary critical interactions and their mutual-exclusion requirements is the only alternative.

## 20.2  Enable/Disable Mechanism

Under normal circumstances, the disabling of interrupts causes interrupt requests by the corresponding device to be deferred rather than ignored. Thus, if the TTY output device becomes ready while its interrupt is disabled (for example, during a `ttyint` invocation), the TREADY flag will remain set, causing an interrupt immediately when the interrupt mechanism is reenabled. This fact allows the user process, for example, to turn off interrupts temporarily for mutual-exclusion purposes without endangering the integrity of the output.

The ability to disable interrupts is exploited by the program in figure 20.2 for two relatively independent purposes. First, the interrupt handler `ttyint` explicitly disables interrupts when it finds that the buffer is empty, since it is unable to reset the TREADY device flag by transmitting another character. Second, interrupts are disabled on entry to the interrupt handler in order to prevent the handler itself from being interrupted before it can take action to remedy the cause of the interrupt (in this case, by transmitting the next character).

The first of these functions is device-specific and reflects the fact that the device is idle by virtue of having printed all of the requested output. If we interface several interrupt-driven devices to a machine, we would prefer that each have its own enable/disable mechanism, so that the line printer, for example, can continue printing even though the TTY output device is idle and has had its interrupts disabled. In most machines, this device-specific interrupt control is provided in the hardware of the device interface itself, rather than as part of the processor.

The second function is more fundamental and reflects a need to have *exactly one* invocation of the interrupt handler for each external event signaled. Under most circumstances, we would like to use the positive transition of TREADY, for example, to stimulate an invocation of ttyint. Each positive edge signals the device's readiness to accept an additional single character, and each invocation of ttyint provides one. Indeed, some computers accommodate this one-to-one correspondence by providing an edge-triggered interrupt mechanism in which each positive transition of an incoming interrupt-request line causes exactly one interrupt.

As discussed in section 13.3.13, it is usual to provide some categorical means for interrupt disabling within the processor itself, in addition to the device-specific mechanism. This typically takes the form of one or more status bits within the processor state that, if zero, inhibit the processor's response to interrupt requests. Typically such bits are packed into the processor status word (PSW). For concreteness, let us imagine the PSW as containing a 1-bit variable ENAB specifying whether interrupts are enabled. An alternative, and common, approach, introduced briefly in section 13.3.13, is a *priority-interrupt* system, in which the PSW (or equivalent) contains a numerical *priority* that can be set so as to disable "low-priority" interrupts while leaving higher-priority interrupts enabled. Such systems are discussed further in section 20.6.

Note that the PSW (including our new ENAB bit) is saved and restored on interrupt service. Thus the ENAB bit, loaded from the interrupt vector, can be set to 0 on entry to the interrupt handler, disabling interrupts; it will be automatically restored to a 1, reenabling interrupts, when the handler returns control to the interrupted program.

## 20.3 Interrupts and Stack Discipline

Several asynchronous processes that individually maintain proper stack discipline fail, in general, to maintain stack discipline when viewed as an aggregate; this is the principal reason for our association of a separate stack with each process. However, the scheduling asymmetry of the interrupt mechanism allows a single stack to be shared by all interrupt handlers, as long as interrupt handlers require *no* stack space *between* invocations. Thus, if a process $P$ is interrupted for an invocation of handler $H$, then $P$ will execute no instructions (and hence make no changes in the state of its stack) until $H$ returns. It is reasonable for $H$ to use $P$'s stack during $H$'s execution, of course with the proviso that it restore the stack to its prior state before returning. As long as the execution of each interrupt handler maintains stack discipline and ultimately has no net effect on the number of stacked data, the handler's use of $P$'s stack is completely transparent to $P$. Thus we needn't associate a separate stack with each interrupt handler, as would be required were the handlers implemented as general processes.

In the context of a multiprocessing system, there are several options for the stacks to be used by interrupt handlers. Certain systems, primarily those engineered for dedicated applications in which protection against incorrect or malicious programs is not important, allow interrupt handlers to use the stack of the interrupted process, thus saving context-switching overhead. For protection reasons, interrupt handlers generally avoid user programs' stacks. Instead, in many systems, they share the kernel stack and memory map; they may best be viewed as portions of the kernel "process." Note, however, that interrupt handlers cannot share a stack with the kernel if kernel-mode programs can be interrupted and if the stack pointer for an interrupt handler is loaded from the interrupt vector. For interrupt handlers to share the kernel stack, a system of separate user and kernel stack pointers, such as the one described in section 15.7, must be used.

## 20.4 Implementation of Interrupts

The implementation of interrupts requires that some input to the machine, perhaps a logic level on a dedicated *interrupt-request* wire, cause a trap to an operating-system kernel handler procedure. A simple approach to interrupts is to provide, in the microarchitecture, for sampling the interrupt-request status and branching conditionally to an appropriate microcode interrupt-handling sequence. This function could be performed, for example, by an additional branch condition irq in the microinstruction conditional-branch repertoire, with a corresponding jirq(ADDR) microinstruction to branch to ROM address ADDR if a device is requesting an interrupt. (This approach is not followed in the MAYBE implementation given in appendix 2; however, the jready conditional-branch microinstruction, which branches if the I/OFLAG signal from the MAYBE's communication interface is asserted, is a close analog of the hypothetical jirq.)

The rest of the interrupt mechanism can be implemented in microcode. Microinstructions can be added to the instruction fetch/dispatch loop (for example, at the address labeled NextInst) to test the ENAB bit (in the PSW) and the irq condition, branching to an interrupt-causing microinstruction sequence if both are set. This microcode executes the interrupt sequence, which has much in common with the operation of faults and instruction traps:

- The interrupting device is identified (if there are multiple interrupt sources); this may involve interrogating a number of device-status flags in sequence until a 1 is found.

- The memory address $m$ of the interrupt vector associated with the interrupting device is computed. Recall that this is the location in which the operating system has stored a struct MState identifying the entry point of the interrupt handler for that device.

- The stack pointer is fetched from the SP component of the MState structure located at $m$ and is used to push the current machine state on the stack of the interrupt handler.

- The machine state stored at $m$, including the (modified) stack pointer, is installed as the current machine state; that is, it is copied into appropriate registers of the microarchitecture.

- Execution of machine instructions is resumed (by branching to microaddress NextInst).

The MState structure in an interrupt vector will usually contain an ENAB bit of 0, so that interrupts are disabled during the processing of an interrupt request. An incoming interrupt request (signaled by a logical 1 on the interrupt-request line) will be ignored until the currently executing machine instruction is completed. If at that time ENAB is set, the state of the current process will be saved and the kernel interrupt handler will be entered with its ENAB bit off (in the usual case); when service is completed, the handler will execute a trap-return instruction such as the strtn instruction of the $S$ machine. Microcode interpretation of the latter instruction causes the stacked MState to be reinstalled in microarchitecture registers, restoring the state of the interrupted program (including, typically, the enabling of interrupts).

## 20.5 Weak Priorities

It should be clear to the reader that we can interface several interrupt-driven devices to a computer by replicating the mechanism discussed in the preceding section for each device. The detection of interrupts might thus involve several consecutive microinstructions, each of which samples a given device's request line. The order in which the request lines are tested establishes the way in which simultaneous requests are resolved: The device whose request line is tested first will be served first. We term the resulting ordering of devices a *weak priority* system.

The categorical disabling of interrupts via ENAB during the execution of interrupt handlers prevents a new interrupt from a device until service of the current interrupt from that device has been completed, usually a desirable constraint. It also prevents interrupts from *other* devices from occurring while any interrupt is being serviced, which may or may not be desirable, depending on the devices involved.

Certain devices impose "hard" real-time constraints on their use. An input device, for example, might read a stream of characters at a rate fixed by some physical consideration (such as the rotational speed of a magnetic disk). If the interface to such a device has a single-character buffer, it is essential that each character be extracted from the buffer before the next character is ready to be stored. If the availability of a character is signaled to the computer by an interrupt, this places a bound on the length of time that can elapse between the interrupt request and the execution of the handler. If the deadline is missed, characters will be lost. The time that elapses between an interrupt request and the start of execution of the appropriate handler is termed *interrupt latency* and is a central parameter in the support of time-critical devices.

Suppose, for example, that a time-critical disk memory system demands response to an interrupt request within 500 $\mu$s. If we interface such a disk to our machine along with an interrupt-driven printer, we must guarantee that the interrupt handler for the printer takes somewhat less than 500 $\mu$s to execute, since the disabling of interrupts during that execution precludes interrupt service for the disk. If there are several additional devices, we might establish a weak priority among them that

**Table 20.3**  Weak priority assignment.

| Task (device) | Service time | Assigned priority | Worst-case latency |
|---|---|---|---|
| $A$ | 3 | 3 (highest) | 5 |
| $B$ | 4 | 2 | 8 |
| $C$ | 5 | 1  (lowest) | 7 |

favors the disk over every other device; this guarantees that disk service won't be delayed by more than one other device service, but still allows response to a disk interrupt to be delayed by as much as the longest interrupt service (handler execution) time. In the worst case, a disk interrupt request may occur just *after* the interrupt handler for some other device has been entered; since the interrupt handler is not itself interruptible, disk service must be delayed by its entire execution time.

Guaranteeing that the constraints imposed by time-critical devices will be met generally requires careful analysis of the worst-case timing relationships that can arise in the containing system. In the case of multiple devices arranged in a weak priority interrupt system, the worst-case interrupt response for each device is the sum of the maximum service times of higher-priority devices *plus* the longest service time among the lower-priority devices. This number reflects the least favorable situation, in which the interrupt request is issued just after service of a lower-priority device begins and every higher-priority device requests service while the lower-priority device is being serviced. We are assuming here that interrupt requests are sufficiently infrequent that we need not consider multiple requests from a single higher-priority device while a lower-priority interrupt request is still pending.

Consider, for example, a three-device weak priority interrupt system whose characteristics are summarized in table 20.3. The highest-priority interrupt handler, $A$, can suffer a delay of 5 time units since its service can be delayed by an invocation of $C$'s handler. The devices $B$ and $C$ can have their interrupt service delayed by each of the other service times, yielding worst-case latency times of 8 and 7, respectively.

## 20.6  Processor Priorities

The interrupt latencies obtainable using weak priority systems are unsatisfactory for certain demanding devices, since even the highest-priority interrupt service can be delayed by the longest device-service time. To accommodate the most time-critical devices, we might consider adding an entirely separate *high-priority* interrupt system, similar to the existing one but having its own request line and HENAB bit in the processor status. If we connect the time-critical device $D$ to the new request line and leave the other devices on the old (lower-priority) system, we can allow $D$'s requests to interrupt the handler for another device, since the old interrupts would clear ENAB but not the new HENAB bit. Moreover, we can

**Table 20.4**  Weak vs. strong priority assignments.

| Task (device) | Service time | Assigned priority | Worst-case latencies | |
| --- | --- | --- | --- | --- |
| | | | Weak priority | Strong priority |
| A | 3 | 3 (highest) | 5 | 0 |
| B | 4 | 2 | 8 | 3 |
| C | 5 | 1 (lowest) | 7 | 7 |

arrange to have the new interrupt mechanism clear *both* of the interrupt bits, so that $D$'s handler will never be interrupted to serve some other device. Our special treatment of the device $D$ results in a worst-case latency time of nearly zero for $D$'s interrupt requests, since under no circumstances will $D$'s service be deferred for other processing.

This mechanism generalizes to an $n$-level *strong* priority interrupt system, in which the handler for a device connected to interrupt level $i$ can be interrupted for service of a device connected to level $j$ if and only if $j > i$. Strong priority orderings are *preemptive* in that the higher-priority task can preempt service of lower-priority requests. In effect, each level constitutes a separate interrupt mechanism of the type already discussed, except that an interrupt at level $i$ disables all interrupts at levels $i$ and lower. Rather than using $n$ ENAB bits of which only the leftmost $i$ are 1s (for priority $n - i$), the current processor priority is included in the processor status word as a binary number. The storage of this *processor priority* as part of the processor state is the key to the operation of strong priority interrupts, in that it allows the interrupt decision to reflect the priority of the device *currently* being served rather than simply the priorities of simultaneously requesting devices. Most modern computers offer a mixture of strong and weak priority systems, typically a small number (perhaps four) of strong priority levels, each of which may connect to an arbitrary number of devices arranged in a weak subordering. Thus a device connected to interrupt level 2 will always preempt service of a device at priority level 1 and will never preempt service of a device at level 2 or higher. Several pending interrupts at level 2 will be resolved in favor of the device whose priority is highest in the level 2 subordering.

Table 20.4 shows the worst-case interrupt latencies of the previous three-device example, using both weak and strong priority interrupt systems. Note that, if the overhead of the actual interrupt processing is ignored (as it is here), the worst-case latencies achieved by the more preemptive strong priority scheme are no greater than (and may be much lower than) the corresponding latencies in the weak priority scheme.

## 20.7 Scheduling and Priority Assignments

The assignment of priorities to interrupt handlers is an example of the more general class of *scheduling problems*, which arise when $n$ physical processors need to be allocated among $m$ tasks, with $m > n$. There is a considerable body of literature devoted to the subject, documenting a number of useful techniques and a greater number of intractability proofs. It is important to recognize that scheduling problems arise in many multiprocessing contexts, that they are notoriously difficult to deal with formally, and that the invention of workable scheduling algorithms for particular applications is viewed as something of a black art.

While even a competent introduction to the subject of scheduling is beyond our present scope, we present informally an example of one-processor priority assignments for a typical real-time computer application. Consider the use of an on-board microprocessor dedicated to controlling a number of automobile functions, each served by an interrupt-driven handler. The right-hand portion of table 20.5 lists the devices to be controlled and their characteristics, and the left-hand portion gives a plausible priority assignment with the actual worst-case performance guarantees it provides. The devices to be controlled include:

- an instrument panel display, which is refreshed every millisecond in response to an interrupt generated by a 1-kHz clock signal; the interrupt handler for this device requires 200 $\mu$s (maximum) to execute;

- an impact sensor, which generates an interrupt when, say, the automobile hits a tree; such an interrupt must be responded to within 100 $\mu$s to activate safety devices; the interrupt service time is not important since, in the presumably rare event of an impact, we are willing to forgo other services;

- an engine fuel system control, requiring 1-ms service at most 500 times per second;

- an ignition system control, requiring 100 $\mu$s of computation at most 500 times per second;

- an engine temperature monitor system, driven by an interrupt that must be responded to within 300 ms; and

- the air-conditioning system, which has no critical response time requirements but which requests a 100-ms interrupt service at most once per second.

The required maximum latency in the table is the maximum interrupt response time for each device. The maximum frequency is the maximum rate at which each device may request new interrupts, and the service time is the maximum CPU time required to service each such interrupt. The rightmost column gives the product of the interrupt frequency and service time for each device; this number represents the maximum CPU *load* imposed by the device. For example, the display update service will account for 20 percent of the processing capacity of the computer, since it requires 200 $\mu$s of service out of each 1000 $\mu$s of real time. A good first step in the design of an interrupt system is to compute the total load imposed by the devices to be interfaced; if this total exceeds 100 percent, there is simply no feasible single-processor interrupt system that meets the requirements. In the current example, the load totals 95 percent, which falls just short of full processor loading.

Consider now the assignment of (strong) interrupt priorities to the various ser-

**Table 20.5** Interrupt-analysis example.

| Loading factor | Actual worst-case latency | Priority | Device | Required maximum latency | Service frequency | Service time | Load |
|---|---|---|---|---|---|---|---|
| | 0 | 4 | Display | 1000 $\mu$s | 1000 s$^{-1}$ | 200 $\mu$s | .2 |
| | 0 | 5 | Impact | 100 $\mu$s | 0 | | |
| .8 | 300 $\mu$s | 3 | Fuel | 2 ms | 500 s$^{-1}$ | 1 ms | .5 |
| .80 | 1.4 ms | 3 | Ignition | 1.5 ms | 500 s$^{-1}$ | 100 $\mu$s | .05 |
| .25 | 1.5 ms | 2 | Engine temp. | 300 ms | 1 s$^{-1}$ | 100 ms | .1 |
| .15 | 400 ms | 1 | A/C | None | 1 s$^{-1}$ | 100 ms | .1 |
| .5 | 800 ms | 0 | Background (idle time) | | | | |

vices. We assume that the processor offers a six-level strong priority interrupt system (the highest priority being 5) and that several devices may be connected to a given priority level in a weak subordering. Examining the right-hand portion of table 20.5, we note that the 100-$\mu$s latency requirement of the impact sensor can be satisfied only if that device is alone at the highest priority level, since its maximum response time precludes delaying its service by any other service time. For this reason, we assign priority 5 to the impact sensor.

We assign the next most time-critical device, the display, to priority level 4 to guarantee that its 1-ms latency requirement will be met (except following an impact). The actual worst-case latency in the table is the maximum delay between an interrupt request and entry to the corresponding service routine; for the display, this is nearly zero if we disregard impacts.

Assignment of the fuel system to priority level 3 implies that service of a fuel system interrupt can be delayed by the service of a display interrupt, yielding a maximum latency of 200 $\mu$s (which is well within the specified 2-ms limit). We may thus add ignition service to level 3 as well,, allowing either of the level-3 interrupt-service routines to be delayed by the other. This arrangement yields a worst-case interrupt response time of 300 $\mu$s for the fuel system (since it can be delayed by an ignition and a display service, in the worst case) and 1400 $\mu$s for the ignition system (since it can be delayed by one fuel-system interrupt service and *two* display updates), as the reader should verify.

Note that, from the standpoint of worst-case interrupt response times, the weak priority ordering we choose for the two devices at priority level 3 is immaterial. In general, weak priority assignments become significant only when they include three or more tasks, since weak priority systems allow service to be delayed by at least one other service time regardless of its relative weak priority.

The worst-case interrupt response time for the engine-temperature system, assigned to priority level 2, includes delays arising from one fuel-system service, one ignition-system service, and two display updates, for a total interrupt latency of 1.5 ms.

Note that the worst-case analysis at each priority level must take into account every device at that and higher priority levels but is independent of activity at lower priorities. As interrupt systems become more complex, detailed worst-case analysis at lower priority levels can become impossibly cumbersome, motivating their replacement by statistical approximations. For example, the worst-case interrupt latency at priority level 1 (to which we have assigned the air-conditioning system) must consider the 100-ms engine-temperature service time, during which a myriad of higher-priority interrupts might be served. Rather than exploring in painful detail the possible scenarios, we approximate the effect of higher-level interrupt activity by lumping it into a *loading factor* specified for each level in the leftmost column of table 20.5. The 80 percent loading factor specified for level 3, for example, reflects the fact that 20 percent of the processor time is spent servicing higher-level (display) interrupts, leaving approximately 80 percent of the processor capacity for service at priorities 3 and lower. Thus the 1-ms fuel-system service time may be prolonged to about $1/.80$, or 1.25 ms of *real* time, since only 80 percent of the processor capacity is effectively available. By similar arguments, the 100-ms engine-temperature service may be prolonged to approximately 400 ms in view of the 25 percent remaining CPU capacity at level 2; thus the worst-case interrupt response time at level 1 is about 400 ms.

This approximation technique is based on the *average* number of higher-level interrupts during the execution of a service routine and is consequently accurate only when that number is large and relatively constant. It would be inappropriate to conclude, for example, that the level 0 worst-case response time is 100 ms/0.15, or 667 ms, under the assumption that the air-conditioner service time is executed with an 85 percent loaded processor; this number reflects the *average* number of engine-temperature interrupts encountered during air-conditioner service. In fact, the actual number of engine-temperature interrupts is 0 in the best case and 1 in the worst case; the average number (0.4) is a poor approximation of the worst case.

A more accurate worst-case latency for priority 0 accounts for delays due to engine-temperature service (400 ms, loaded) and air-conditioner service (400 ms, loaded) for a total of 800 ms. Note that in our example no useful function is performed at level 0; the program running at this lowest priority would likely be a simple loop that uses idle time in the absence of interrupt activity. We would expect at least 5 percent of the processor time to be spent in this idle loop, from the 5 percent loading factor derived for level 0; moreover, because of interrupt load, we might expect as much as 800 ms of real time to elapse between consecutive executions of instructions at level 0.

## 20.8 Summary

Chapters 18–20 have provided a brief glimpse into the structure and management of *processes*, a topic that brings us to the threshold of higher-level technologies conventionally dealt with by courses in operating systems and higher-level programming languages. The reader should be aware that approaches to process management and its subproblems vary widely, because of differences in operating-system design goals as well as disparate levels of architectural support. The process-management technology presented here is neither broad enough to be viewed as a complete introduction to operating systems nor sufficiently detailed to constitute a case study. It serves primarily to raise the major issues confronted at the interface between architecture and operating system, and secondarily to outline one of several plausible strategies for structuring an operating-system kernel.

## 20.9  Context

The use of priority interrupts to schedule input/output activities is ubiquitous in contemporary computers. The roots of this approach to limited multitasking go back at least as far as the early 1960s, when the DEC PDP-1 computer introduced *sequence break*, a primitive interrupt scheme.

Alternative approaches to input/output processing include simple polling of devices by software and dedicated I/O processing hardware. Polling, while requiring even less hardware support than the modest architectural demands of an interrupt system, requires explicit periodic interrogation by the active program to detect requests for processor services. Consequently, the polling approach necessitates a compromise between response time to device requests and the organizational simplicity of application software. For this reason, it is most commonly used on simple microprocessors that are dedicated to a single application and whose single program can be carefully riddled with device interrogations.

The dedication of hardware to process input/output transactions is more costly than interrupt-based schemes but potentially delivers higher performance, since a single processor need not be multiplexed between the application program and I/O operations. Typically the hardware involved is a processor specialized to the transfer of data between a device and main memory, an activity referred to as *direct memory access* or DMA. Large mainframes often have a number of ports to which various high-performance I/O devices (such as magnetic tapes and disks) can be connected, each associated with a dedicated special-purpose processor. In the jargon of mainframes, such a port is sometimes called a *data channel* and the corresponding processor a *data-channel controller*. Alternatively, a reasonably general-purpose processor can be dedicated as a *peripheral processor* to manage the activities of each device; the advent of the high-performance, mass-produced microprocessor has increased the cost-effectiveness of this approach relative to the special-purpose data-channel controller.

The general topic of input/output systems raises the issue of *real time*, since the performance of devices is sensitive to the responsiveness of the computer to their status. The use of a single processor to service several devices is effectively a resource-allocation problem and is addressed by a substantial body of literature devoted to the theory of *real-time scheduling*. The more general formulations of scheduling problems involve a pool of $n$ processors serving $m$ tasks having independent deadlines, perhaps with dependencies among the tasks. Special-case scheduling problems deal with single-processor systems and priority-interrupt schemes such as described in this chapter. Sadly, most of the theoretical results

**Table 20.6**   Interrupt characteristics and requirements.

| Device | Interrupt service time, $\mu s$ | Interrupt frequency, $s^{-1}$ | Response-time requirement, $\mu s$ |
|---|---|---|---|
| Printer | 1000 | 500 | 1000 |
| Disk | 300 | 1000 | 200 |
| Keyboard | 2000 | 10 | 2000 |
| Display | 100 | 1000 | 200 |

on scheduling problems are negative: In most cases there is no tractable algorithm that guarantees that the specified deadlines will be met. Two well-known exceptions are *rate-monotonic priority assignment* [Liu and Layland 1973] and *earliest deadline scheduling* [Mok and Dertouzos 1978], each of which provides a practical algorithm for dealing with a restricted set of scheduling problems.

## 20.10 Problems

### Problem 20.1

A computer system is interfaced to four devices: a printer, a disk, a keyboard, and a display. The characteristics of the devices are summarized in table 20.6.

A. A program $P$, which performs only computation (no input/output), takes 100 s to run when no input/output is being performed. How long will it take for $P$ to run when all of the above devices are operating at their maximum speeds?

B. Suppose that the interrupt system enforces a nonpreemptive (weak) priority ordering printer>disk>keyboard>display among interrupt requests. Assuming the characteristics given in table 20.6, what is the maximum time that might elapse between a disk interrupt request and execution of the first instruction of its handler? Assume that the time taken for state save and context switch is negligible.

C. Can the requirements given in table 20.6 be met using a *weak* priority ordering among the interrupt requests? If so, give such an ordering; if not, explain.

D. Can the requirements given in table 20.6 be met using a *strong* priority ordering among the interrupt requests? If so, give such an ordering; if not, explain.

### Problem 20.2

A computer must service three devices whose interrupting frequencies, service times, and assigned priorities are given in table 20.7.

A. Assuming a *strong* priority system, compute for each device the maximum time between service request and the *completion* of service for that device.

B. What percentage of the processor's time is devoted to servicing D1?

C. What percentage of the processor's time is left for noninterrupt programs?

**Table 20.7** An interrupt-handling scenario.

| Device | Service time, ms | Maximum frequency, ms$^{-1}$ | Priority |
|--------|------------------|------------------------------|----------|
| D1 | 10 | 1/100 | 3 (highest) |
| D2 | 50 | 1/1000 | 2 |
| D3 | 200 | 1/5000 | 1 (lowest) |

D. Assume that if a device interrupts again before a pending interrupt on that same device has been serviced, the later interrupt is ignored (lost). Will the system outlined in table 20.7 lose interrupts using a *strong* priority scheme (with priorities as given)?

E. Under the assumption of part D, will the system outlined in table 20.7 lose interrupts using a *weak* priority scheme (with priorities as given)?

## Problem 20.3

A computer system designed for use on board a spacecraft has been assigned three real-time tasks: sense engine conditions and adjust the fuel flow for correct (and safe!) operation, monitor the on-board gyroscopes and update the spacecraft's records of its current position, and monitor and control the air pressure in the crew cabin. To service each task, the processor is periodically interrupted and requested to execute a service routine for that task. Execution of the service routine must be *completed* before a deadline occurring a specified amount of time after each interrupt. (Note that this differs slightly from the concept of latency discussed in this chapter, which refers to the time that elapses until the *start* of execution of the service routine.) Table 20.8 gives the minimum period between interrupts, the maximum execution time of the service routine, and the maximum allowable deadline for the completion of each kind of task.

A. If a weak priority interrupt system is used, what is the maximum service time for the cabin-pressure task that still allows all constraints to be met? Explain why this is the maximum and give a weak priority ordering on these tasks that meets the constraints in this case. In your solution, assuming all interrupt requests are occurring at their maximum allowable rate, what fraction of the time will the processor spend idle? What will be the actual worst-case delays from the occurrence of each kind of interrupt to completion of the corresponding service routine?

B. If a strong priority interrupt system is used in this scenario, what is the maximum service time for the cabin-pressure task that still allows all constraints to be met? Explain why this is the maximum and give a strong priority ordering of these tasks that meets the constraints in this case. In your solution, assuming that all interrupt requests are occurring at their maximum allowable rate, what fraction of the time will the processor spend idle? What will be the actual worst-

**Table 20.8**  Spacecraft interrupt-system scenario.

| Task | Period, ms | Service time, ms | Deadline, ms |
|---|---|---|---|
| Fuel flow | 30 | 5 | 25 |
| Gyroscopes | 40 | 10 | 20 |
| Cabin pressure | 100 | ? | 100 |

**Table 20.9**  Priority-interrupt scenario.

| Task | Service time, ms | Maximum allowed latency, ms | Maximum frequency, ms |
|---|---|---|---|
| A | 30 | 500 | 1/3000 |
| B | 20 | 70 | 1/1000 |
| C | 50 | 25 | 1/500 |
| D | 10 | 10 | 1/50 |

case delays from the occurrence of each kind of interrupt to completion of the corresponding service routine?

C. A design change increases the service time for the fuel-flow task from 5 to 15 ms. Explain why a weak priority system can no longer be used.

D. Solve part B again for the case in which the fuel-flow service time is 15 ms instead of 5 ms.

## Problem 20.4

A. Can you use a weak priority scheme for the scenario outlined in table 20.9? Explain.

B. Assume that all the interrupts listed in table 20.9 occur at their maximum frequency. What percent of the processor's time is used to handle interrupts?

C. Assume a strong priority system in which 3 is the highest priority, 0 the lowest. Assign a unique priority to each task in table 20.9 to meet the specifications given. Show the maximum time between interrupt and *completion* of service for each of the tasks if your priority scheme is used.

# 21 Architectural Horizons

While the emphasis of preceding chapters of this text has been on fundamentals, the examples and specific approaches have overwhelmingly reflected the mainstream of computer architecture. This final chapter ventures into more speculative territory, identifying controversial but interesting alternative architectural approaches whose practical merits have been hypothesized but not convincingly demonstrated.

An ever-present challenge for next-generation computer systems is to deliver improved functionality and performance at reduced cost. The most conservative way for a computer architect to address this challenge is to keep upgrading existing architectures to use newer and faster logic technology. In fact, positions close to this reactionary extreme have fared well in the past: Over the course of the history of general-purpose computers, nearly all of the observed price/performance improvement has been attributable to the phenomenal evolution of the underlying logic devices. Beyond parametric adjustments, such as increased address sizes to accommodate larger memories, architectural innovation has played an identifiable but modest role in the computer revolution. Although a bleak thought for most computer architects (the authors included), it is distinctly possible that the future holds a similarly minor role for new developments on the architectural front. Perhaps in two decades the state of the art will remain based on von Neumann machines, selling for tens of dollars and executing billions of instructions per second.

Yet there are compelling reasons to look elsewhere for tomorrow's revolutionary improvements in the price/performance ratio. First, looming fundamental barriers—the speed of light, for example, and the diminishing number of electrons used to represent a bit in a RAM cell—seem to foretell a limit to the rampaging technological progress experienced in recent decades. Second, traditional computers are so rigidly sequential that only a tiny fraction of their components are actively computing at any instant; moreover, that fraction diminishes as the size of the computer system increases.

These considerations have led many researchers to the conviction that the next revolution in computer architecture—if there is to be one—will involve machines that can carry on many parallel activities, thereby regaining a large performance factor lost in conventional single-sequence machines. Some researchers take vague but compelling reassurance from the structure of the brain, which seems to make up for the slowness of its technological elements by their vast number. Study of important and computationally intensive problems, such as the fluid-dynamics simulations inspired by weather-forecasting applications, underscores the unfair computational advantage enjoyed by the physical situation over the computer simulating it: Interactions that happen in parallel in nature must be considered sequentially on a single-sequence machine simulating nature.

## 21.1 Models of Computation

The von Neumann model of computation, which underlies virtually every successful computer architecture, is often cited as a reactionary influence on the development of innovative approaches to computer design. Indeed, the temptations to stay within the traditional single-sequence programming model are great: It is familiar and proven; it builds on existing software, languages, and programming methodology; and its implementation is supported by a substantial body of engineering experience. Consequently, much of the progress in computer architecture has been incremental: "tuning" the model with alternative instruction sets and data representations. The more significant architectural developments, such as caches and virtual memory, have hidden radical hardware changes under a carpet of software transparency. Thus the programming model, much of our software, and our view of computation remain relatively unperturbed.

It may well be the case, however, that dramatic and revolutionary architectural developments require a different programming model, one unlikely to be reached by conservative incrementalism. A minority of researchers in computer architecture address this possibility by exploring machines that support a model of computation that deviates, to varying extents, from the von Neumann standard. The alternative models range from minor extensions of the single-sequence machine to its complete abandonment in favor of a radical alternative. Examples include:

- *Multiple sequential processes* interacting via semaphores, shared variables, or a number of alternative communication and synchronization primitives. This conservative adaptation of the single-sequence programming model (which was discussed in chapters 18 and 19) is the approach to parallel computation taken by most multiprocessor computers as well as by time-shared single-processor systems. A variety of programming constructs and models have been proposed to deal with communicating processes; the one suggested by Hoare [1978] is among the best known.

- *Message-passing systems*, which model computation as a heterarchy of *objects* that communicate by directing packets of data, or *messages*, to one another. The receipt of a message by an object stimulates that object to perform some computational step, usually resulting in the transmission of additional messages to other objects. Although the activities of each object are typically sequential, the message-passing model stresses parallelism, since many objects can be simultaneously active.

- *Data-flow systems*, which are close relatives of the message-passing systems. In the data-flow model a representation of the data-dependency graph of a computation is used as a program. Nodes (operators) of the graph serve as destinations for messages containing operand values; when a node has its requisite operands, it performs the associated operation and ships the result to dependent nodes. Data-flow machines stress fine-grained parallelism, allowing individual operations to be scheduled as independent tasks.

- *Graph-reduction architectures*, which distribute a data structure, often representing the parse tree of an expression or program, over a network of processing elements. Portions of the data structure are examined in parallel, applying "reduction rules" to substitute reduced versions where appropriate. Thus the graph representing (2+3)*(4+5) might be reduced to 5*9 in a single time step, then to 45, which is the desired result. This approach can be extended to arbitrary general-purpose computation by the use of sufficiently powerful reduction rules. Often a *combinatory logic*, a relative of the *lambda calculi*, provides the underlying computational model. These remarkable formalisms offer a small set of operators (called *combinators*) that can be composed in various ways to yield every computable function. Combinatory logic and the lambda calculus were mentioned briefly in section 10.5; the ambitious reader is referred to Hindley and Seldin [1986], Church [1941], and Curry and Feys [1974].

- *Logical-inference architectures* based on the class of *logic programming languages*, the best known of which is Prolog [Clocksin and Mellish 1981; Kowalski 1979]. These languages have stimulated interest in computers tailored to their declarative, logic-based model. Although such machines have to date been fairly conventional architecturally (at least by the standards of this section), they emphasize mechanisms for efficiently performing simple logical inferences, *backtracking* control structures used in searches for proofs of propositions, and a generalized string-matching operation called *unification*. See section 13.7 for a relevant discussion.

- *Cellular automata*, which are arrays of identical finite-state machines that operate synchronously. The input to the FSM at each cell is just the set of state variables from FSMs at neighboring cells. Thus the state of a cell during clock period $i + 1$ reflects only the states of neighboring cells during clock period $i$. The "programming" of a cellular automaton involves forcing the states of its cells into a prescribed initial configuration, from which it evolves autonomously. The dimensionality and topology of the array, as well as the transition diagram of each FSM, determine the characteristics of the automaton. The best-known cellular automaton is John Horton Conway's LIFE [Gardner 1971–1972], which involves an infinite two-dimensional array of two-state FSMs in nine-neighbor cells. (This means that each cell's next state reflects its own previous state as well as that of eight adjacent cells. It is customary to count a cell as part of its own neighborhood if its inputs include its own state variables; interestingly, the latter need not be the case.) LIFE, along with many other cellular automata, can (given an appropriate initial configuration) simulate a universal Turing machine and hence be used to perform general computation. Cellular automata are of potential practical interest in simulation and image-processing applications; they have also been proposed as a discrete model for our physical universe. See Toffoli and Margolus [1987] and Wolfram [1986] for further discussion.

- *Trainable automata* and *learning machines*, which are at the fringe of the spectrum of computer architectures. These include a disparate collection of machines that are not programmed in any conventional sense; rather than executing explicit instructions, they react in complex and indirect ways to environmental stimuli. Modest representatives of this collection include simple adaptive control systems and trainable automata. Less well understood (and, perhaps by virtue of their mystery, more glamorous) alternative models crop up at regular intervals. Recently in vogue have been a number of proposed *neural networks*, in which simple devices (typically *threshold logic* elements) are interconnected to perform such tasks as pattern classification.

The above list is neither exhaustive nor even representative; typical nonstandard architectures are much more conservative than the majority of the above examples in their deviation from conventional computational models.

## 21.2 The Multiprocessor Challenge

Performance through parallelism is a deceptively simple catechism that offers a notorious garden path for the unwary computer designer. The trap is laid by the characterization of a computer's performance by its instruction-execution rate—typically in MIPS, or millions of instructions per second. If a 2-MIPS computer can be built for a cost of $1000, reasons the naive architect, then the interconnection of 100 such computers yields a 200-MIPS computer at a cost of roughly $100,000. The latter machine, being 100 times as powerful as the former, should be able to execute programs 100 times faster. The generalization of this reasoning is that the performance of a computer system scales proportionately to its number of processors, which is in turn proportional to the system's cost.

The most glaring problem with this analysis is the naive assumption that programs can, in general, be split among $n$ processors for an $n$-fold speedup. This is similar to arguing that nine women should be able to get together and have a baby in one month. While most algorithms can be reworked to exploit a certain amount of parallel processing, there is no general technique for distributing algorithms among $n$ processors with proportionate speedup. Computations with pathologically sequential data-dependency graphs, such as $f(f(f(f(f(f(n))))))$, admit no performance improvement by parallel execution of their subcomputations. Other computations offer limited potential for parallelism; while they might involve two or three or ten subcomputations that can be profitably performed simultaneously, they cannot exploit $n$-processor systems for arbitrarily large $n$. These observations are, of course, relative to the granularity at which subcomputations are considered. If $f$ in the pathological example given above is itself a complex of simpler operations (such as adds and multiplies), some of which can be performed simultaneously, then it might be fruitful to split the computation of each $f$ among several processors so as to exploit parallel execution of the component instructions.

In addition to algorithmic constraints (such as data dependencies) that limit the systematic application of multiprocessors to achieve proportional performance gains, there are important engineering obstacles. The most obvious of these is the overhead of communication cost incurred when components of a program are split among physically separated processors: In general, the subcomputations must interact at least occasionally. This imposes the hardware (and hence cost) requirement that some provision be made for communication among the processors; it also introduces a time overhead to account for the latency required by such communications. Even ignoring algorithmic constraints on the potential for parallel execution, these overhead factors undermine the goal of strictly linear scaling of multiprocessor performance with cost.

A somewhat more subtle stumbling block to scalability is the issue of reliability. Digital engineers generally enjoy the luxury of assuming reliable components, designing systems whose reliable operation is assured as long as each component behaves properly. Put negatively, however, the typical digital system will fail if *any* component fails; assuming constant component reliability, the reliability of a large, complex computer system is lower than that of a simple one, simply because of component count. If reliability specifications for a computer system are constant (for example, in the form of an acceptable value for minimum mean time between failures), then an $n$-processor system that depends on all $n$ processors functioning correctly is bound to become unacceptably failure-prone for sufficiently large $n$.

Despite these obstacles, the development of multiprocessors that offer nearly linear performance/cost characteristics remains the utopian goal of the avant garde in both research and industry. Lest the reader conclude that the fundamental problems sketched above—algorithms, communications, and reliability—lead to a dim prognosis, we hasten to observe, in the following sections, grounds for considerable optimism on all three fronts.

### 21.2.1 Algorithmic Constraints on Parallelism

Algorithmic constraints on parallelism yield to two attacks: (1) decrease *grain size*, that is, the level of operation at which the algorithm is expressed, thereby exposing more operations and more potential parallelism; and (2) identify alternative algorithms that produce the same result but offer more potential for parallelism. The practical exploitation of fine-grain parallelism is primarily an architectural challenge, since the performance overhead associated with distributing tiny operations among processors and arranging their intercommunication can easily outweigh potential gains from parallel execution.

The development of alternative algorithms more amenable to parallelism is being actively pursued at several different levels. The first is the study of the fundamental bounds on the time complexity of algorithms. Interesting discoveries include *chaotic relaxation* algorithms derived from more rigid relatives by dropping certain of their precedence constraints. A simple example is the solution of Laplace's equation using a two-dimensional array of processors, each maintaining a single value corresponding to a point in a scalar field. Each processor repeatedly updates its value with the average of the values of its four orthogonal neighbors; even if the activities of the processors are completely asynchronous, the array of values converges appropriately. (For further discussion, see Baudet [1978].)

At another level, sophisticated compilers are able to recognize and eliminate gratuitous precedence constraints introduced into programs as an artifact of the programming language. The assignment statements A=3 and B=4 in C or FORTRAN, for a trivial example, can be executed in parallel despite the requirement by these languages that they be coded so as to imply a precedence between them. This technique of extracting parallelism from existing programs has the attractive potential of preserving an investment in existing software through use of automatic algorithmic transformations that allow the software to exploit modern multiprocessor systems effectively.

### 21.2.2 Communication and Locality

Communication issues and technologies such as those discussed in chapter 9 are hot topics among multiprocessor system designers, owing to the critical impact of interprocessor communication efficiency on the performance of programs whose instructions are distributed among several processors. Much attention has been devoted to communication networks and topologies that minimize the communication latency and maximize the throughput between nodes of a multiprocessor network. Typically these efforts focus on improving the *worst-case* communication performance, for example, between the two most distant processors in a multiprocessor system. As observed in chapter 9, however, there are physical limits on the worst-case communication performance achievable in an $n$-node network, assuming constant-sized nodes. These factors assure us that worst-case processor-to-processor communication latency will grow as the number of processors increases, eliminating any hope of linear performance scaling if a constant fraction of the computation steps suffer worst-case communication delays.

The strong ray of hope on the communications front, therefore, is to *avoid* worst-case communication paths rather than (or, perhaps, in addition to) optimizing them. The trick is to arrange for program and data objects that interact frequently to reside on the same or neighboring processors and hence communicate efficiently, while unrelated objects are allowed to be widely separated. The efficacy of this approach depends on *locality of communications*—the tendency of each program or data module to interact intensely with only a small number of closely related program and data modules—a phenomenon closely related to the locality of reference exploited by the caching techniques of chapter 16. Assuming that a program exhibits locality of communications, the problem is to distribute the modules on a network of processors in such a way that the structure of the program's critical communication paths matches the physical structure of the processor network. This may involve preliminary analysis of the program and static allocation of its components to processors, or observation of the communication patterns of the running program and dynamic reallocation of its modules.

Like locality of reference, locality of communcations is a statistical property; it is possible to devise a program whose modules each communicate with every other module at every computation step. Clever distribution of the modules of this pathological program offers no communication advantage, except possibly for their concentration on a single processor to eliminate interprocessor communication overhead entirely. Indeed, the extent to which large, complex, and highly parallel computations exhibit locality in their communication patterns is currently the subject more of speculation than of science: The architecture of parallel computer systems is at such a primitive state that we have neither sound analytic models nor significant empirical data from which to extrapolate.

### 21.2.3 Fault Tolerance

A simple approach to maintaining acceptable reliability as the complexity of a system increases is to insist on increasingly reliable components, thereby keeping the probability of a component failure below the acceptable system failure rate. This approach has obvious appeal to system architects, allowing them to work within the comfortable abstraction that deals with ideal components. Indeed, often the most practical route to achieving system reliability goals is improvement of component reliability. However, more reliable components are likely to cost more, compromising cost/performance scaling. Moreover, there are probably practical limits to component reliability characteristics, imposing corresponding limits on the size of a system that can be constructed with acceptably low probability of component failure.

An alternative route to system reliability that shifts the burden from the component supplier to the system architect is to design systems that continue to function despite some number of component failures. We might envision a system with 10,000 small processors embedded in a communications network, with the system having the ability to detect malfunctioning processors and circumvent them in the distribution of computation tasks. Such a *fault-tolerant system* might continue to perform well as long as a substantial majority of the processors are operational, exhibiting only a minor performance degradation with each new failure.

The engineering of fault-tolerant systems, although critical to our more ambitious goals for next-generation computers, is not currently well understood. A crudely unsophisticated but effective approach to improving the apparent reliability of a device is to replicate it, giving each copy of the device identical inputs and comparing their outputs. Dissimilar outputs at any point signal a component error; if three or more devices run redundant computations in parallel, surrounding *voting circuitry* selects the most popular result as the likely correct answer. This technique, called *triple modular redundancy*, affords correction of errors due to single component failures at something exceeding a threefold increase in cost.

With this or other approaches to fault tolerance, there is a question as to the level at which the redundancy—and hence the error correction—is applied. At one extreme, an entire computer system can be replicated three times, supplying identical inputs and voting among their outputs. Such a system masks single failures, reducing the probability of apparent system failure to the (much lower) probability that two of the component systems fail simultaneously. Alternatively, a single computer system can be constructed of triply replicated components, each equipped with voting circuitry. In addition to masking single component failures, the latter approach will survive multiple component failures, as long as no two failures occur in the same replicated triple. Although each approach requires a threefold redundancy in the constituent logic components, the component-level redundancy offers the possibility of significantly higher reliability. Unfortunately, this superficial analysis ignores both the cost of the voting circuitry, which is higher in the latter scheme, and the possibility of its failure. Indeed, one can actually degrade the reliability characteristics of a system by naively adding an error-correction mechanism, since new hardware carries with it new possibilities for failure.

The cost penalties associated with brute-force modular redundancy approaches are prohibitive except in the most reliability-sensitive applications. Fortunately, error-correction techniques requiring much less redundancy show promise of reducing the costs of fault tolerance to tractable levels. The techniques alluded to in section 2.6.2, typically applied to memory and communication systems, offer single error correction at roughly logarithmic costs. While not directly applicable to the correction of errors introduced by arbitrary logic circuitry, they suggest similarly economical approaches to the correction of errors in other computer subsystems. For an overview of fault-tolerance techniques, the reader is referred to Su and Hsieh [1982].

## 21.3 Taxonomy of Multiprocessors

Michael Flynn [1972] distinguished multiprocessor computers along two orthogonal dimensions, reflecting parallelism in their instruction stream and in their data paths, respectively. Flynn's terminology, which has become standard jargon for computer researchers, classifies the traditional single-sequence machine as *single instruction stream, single data stream*, or SISD, reflecting the fact that it executes a single instruction and processes a single datum at a time. Interesting multiprocessors include the following:

- *Single instruction stream, multiple data stream.* SIMD machines use a single sequence of instructions to control multiple independent (but usually identical) data paths. The MAYBE architecture could be converted into a simple SIMD machine, for example, roughly by replicating the data paths and feeding signals from the control-ROM decoders to corresponding control inputs on each set of data paths.[1] Each replicated set of data paths would include an ALU, registers, and static RAM; each ALU would always perform the same operation, but different ALUs would use different data. Such a modification might be motivated by the desire to handle vector data, such as $(X, Y)$ pairs representing points on a plane, more efficiently; if it were arranged that one data path carried $X$ values and the other $Y$ values, then a simple add operation on the MAYBE

---

[1] We gloss over some important issues, of course; these include control signals that go *from* the existing MAYBE data paths *to* the control circuitry. A case in point is the ALU condition codes; presumably an SIMD version of the MAYBE would handle these somewhat differently. Similarly, facilities for permuting information among the data streams and selectively enabling individual data paths, as discussed in section 21.6, might be included.

would perform vector addition. Such a machine would be a simple SIMD *vector machine*, using replicated data paths to deal with vector rather than scalar data.

- *Multiple instruction stream, multiple data stream.* MIMD machines feature multiple independent data paths, each controlled by an independent stream of instructions. An MIMD system is, in effect, a group of interconnected single-sequence machines performing independent (but usually related and interacting) tasks. An MIMD system can present a programming environment very similar to that of a multiprocess (time-shared) computer, as discussed in chapter 18, except that the MIMD system uses multiple processors to achieve *real* parallelism, whereas the time-shared machine multiplexes a single processor to *simulate* parallelism. A primitive MIMD machine might be fashioned by somehow interconnecting several MAYBE computers and programming them to cooperate on a task.

- *No instruction, multiple data stream.* NIMD multiprocessors are our extension to Flynn's taxonomy to cover cellular automata, neural networks, and other machines that exhibit no identifiable instruction stream.

The distinctions among these classes relate closely to differences in the models of computation they support. SIMD machines, by virtue of their single instruction stream, can be viewed as single-sequence machines. They provide the most conservative extension of the conventional programming model by hiding the parallelism in the data paths. The impact on the programmer is an enriched set of primitive data types: Where an SISD machine handles a binary number, an SIMD machine handles an $n$-element vector.

An MIMD machine, in contrast, exposes the parallelism and challenges the programmer to control it. On the one hand, an MIMD system relaxes the SIMD constraint that all data paths must perform the same operation at every instant; on the other hand, this new freedom complicates the programmer's task enormously. As a consequence, sophisticated MIMD architectures are generally coupled with languages, programming methodology, and run-time support tools that both focus and leverage the efforts of the software developer.

NIMD machines, not being programmable in the conventional sense, avoid the issue of a programming model. As a category, they present something of a philosophical enigma: Their nonprogrammability implies, in a sense, that they can do only one thing; yet that one thing, at some futuristic extreme, might be to decide what needs to be done and then do it. A nonprogrammable machine might have the power of a universal Turing machine, perhaps mimicking other computers after having observed their behavior.

## 21.4 Hiding Parallelism: Concurrent SSM Execution

The most conservative approach to parallel computation is to hide it from the programmer, presenting a completely conventional programming model but exploiting parallelism in its implementation. Pipelining, as illustrated in the examples of chapter 17, is one powerful technique for achieving modest performance gains by parallel execution within a single sequence of instructions. As observed in that chapter, however, precedence constraints inherent in the sequence limit these gains to a factor of 3 or 4. While pipelining is used by virtually every high-performance computer, additional parallelism must be uncovered to reach the hundreds or thousands of MIPS needed to merit supercomputer status.

In addition to the main instruction-stream pipeline, individual operations can exploit dedicated pipelined hardware. A pipelined multiplier, for example, might be used to accommodate a sequence of consecutive multiplication instructions even in cases where the latency of a single multiplication is slower than the instruction-execution period. Similar engineering attention may be paid to subsystems (*functional units*) dedicated to other operations such as division and shifting, with the goal of reaching the same throughput for each subsystem. This strategy allows a constant instruction-execution rate, regardless of the particular mix of instructions being executed.

As an alternative to pipelining functional units, they may be replicated to increase throughput. Two multiplier units, each having a throughput of half the instruction-execution rate, could be called into service alternately during a stream of consecutive multiplication operations. While the use of multiple functional units requires additional data paths and control logic, it generally allows pipelined instruction throughput to exceed the throughput of individual functional units.

Replication and pipelining of functional units can be combined and generalized in a variety of ways. A pipelined instruction-fetch unit might prefetch a number of instructions, analyze their data dependencies (possibly even reordering them to accommodate local bottlenecks), and assign their operations to functional units. In this way a number of consecutive instructions can be executed simultaneously, as long as (1) hardware resources (such as functional units) are available and (2) data dependencies among the instructions allow parallel execution. The transparency of such approaches for the programmer requires automatic recognition of data dependencies, which are enforced by means similar to pipeline interlocks and bypass paths. At the extreme, these techniques amount to the on-the-fly construction of the data-dependency graph for a "window" of consecutive instructions. Classic machines incorporating these techniques include the IBM 360/91 [Tomasulo 1967; IBM 1967] and the CDC 7600 [Bonseigneur 1969]. The data-flow machines (see, for example, Dennis, Leung, and Misunas [1979]) can be viewed as descendants of these techniques.

## 21.5 Data Parallelism

The use of pipelining and multiple functional units adds commensurate expense and capacity to a processor; the expense is clearly unjustified unless the capacity is effectively used. The execution of conventional instructions, such as those of the $S$ and $G$ machines, typically generates at most one operation to be performed on a functional unit per instruction fetched; thus the rate of operation execution is typically bounded on such machines by the rate at which instructions can be fetched. Although the techniques of the preceding section can be used to guarantee that the rate of instruction execution is not limited by the functional-unit throughput, the utilization of the functional units is typically limited by the rate at which the instruction stream generates new operations.

An effective way to relax this bottleneck is to include machine instructions that generate multiple operations to be performed, preferably operations that can be executed in parallel. This is commonly done by extending the instruction set to include *vector operations*, as alluded to in the discussion of SIMD machines in section 21.3. Generally, the use of $n$-element vector data allows at most an $n$-fold increase in the amount of computation implied by each instruction. While a three-address scalar instruction `add a,b,c` implies only a single operation $c \leftarrow \langle a \rangle + \langle b \rangle$, a vector `vadd n,A,B,C` can generate the set of $n$ scalar operations $c \leftarrow \langle a \rangle + \langle b \rangle$, $c+1 \leftarrow \langle a+1 \rangle + \langle b+1 \rangle$, ..., $c+n-1 \leftarrow \langle a+n-1 \rangle + \langle b+n-1 \rangle$.

A primitive approach to parallel implementation of a vector instruction set, hinted at in section 21.3, is to fix $n$ at the number of parallel functional units and establish a one-to-one correspondence between vector elements and functional units. While this approach can be useful in machines designed for applications with particular vector requirements (for example, 2-vectors for dealing with points and lines on a display, or 3-vectors for physical calculations involving points in space), it is usually desirable to unhinge data sizes and formats from the implementation parameters of the machine. Thus high-performance vector machines use vector instructions as a compact encoding of a number of similar but independent operations, to be distributed among functional units or routed to pipelined arithmetic processors as these resources become available. Classic machines of this category include the CDC STAR [Hintz and Tate 1972], the TI ASC [Watson 1972], and the Cray-1 [Russel 1978]. Virtually every modern supercomputer offers vector operations and requires their use to achieve full utilization of processing capacity.

The addition of vector operations hides hardware parallelism in new primitives, namely, the vector operations; moreover, vector machines must continue to support scalar operations. In theory, these factors minimize the impact of their programming model on software structure and on programming. In practice, however, vector supercomputers provide outstanding performance only when executing programs that carefully exploit vector operations, thereby keeping pipelines full and functional units profitably occupied. The performance difference between execution of vector and scalar operations is sufficiently dramatic that supercomputer programmers devote much of their energy to the *vectorization* of programs—finding clever ways to substitute vector operations for groups of scalar instructions.

## 21.6 Other SIMD Approaches

A number of SIMD alternatives involve more radical changes to the programming model, by exposing explicitly parallel processing elements to the programmer. Such machines generally involve a network of processing elements (each consisting of roughly the data paths of a simple computer) communicating via some programmer-visible topology and synchronously executing a single sequence of instructions.

The earliest and best known of these is the ILLIAC IV [Bouknight et al. 1972], whose 64 processing elements are interconnected in an 8-by-8 two-dimensional array that allows each to communicate directly with its four orthogonal neighbors. Each processing element has state (including four registers) and some associated local memory. Although each instruction is routed to every processing element for execution, *processor enable bits* in each processing element's state dictate whether each processor will execute or ignore instructions. These bits are set by local data-dependent tests, allowing some data-dependent criterion to dictate the set of processors that executes a given instruction. For example, an instruction sequence might first test the contents of register 2, setting the enable bits of those processors having negative numbers in that register, then execute a `negate <R2>` operation on the selected processors. The net effect is to replace the contents of each `R2` with its absolute value.

Begun in the early 1960s, the ILLIAC IV was a pioneering effort in SIMD multiprocessors, but it was plagued by reliability and software problems. Modern descendants, such as the Connection Machine [Hillis 1981, 1985], have pushed the SIMD architecture much further and with greater practical success. The Connection Machine offers a 64K array of very simple processors, embedded in a logarithmic-cost communication network similar to those described in section 9.1.2 as well as a two-dimensional interconnection mesh. Both processing and communication are bit-serial; thus both the cost and the performance of each processor are minuscule, even by microprocessor standards. Much of the success of the Connection Machine stems from the extreme at which it trades processor numbers for processor power: It depends heavily on massive parallelism to balance the stark simplicity of its processors.

Another class of SIMD machines is the *associative array processors*, typified by the Sanders OMEN [Higbie 1972] and the Goodyear STARAN [Batcher 1977]. These computers couple an array of processors, typically bit-serial, to some form of associative memory. In the OMEN, for example, a 64-bit-wide memory array is coupled to 64 single-bit elements in such a way that during a single cycle the processors can each access either a single bit of 64 consecutive words or successive bits of a single word. Interprocessor communication is typically facilitated further by additional interconnections, often in the form of an array of switches reminiscent of the sorters depicted in chapter 8. Such a machine can be programmed to act as a uniprocessor with 64-bit-wide data paths, or as a 64-processor SIMD machine with bit-serial data paths. It can even vacillate between these personalities during the execution of a program.

## 21.7 Shared-Memory Multiprocessors

The communication and synchronization requirements of parallel processes can be met by shared memory locations, using techniques such as those discussed in chapters 18 and 19. An MIMD multiprocessor can thus take the form of a number of conventional processors and memory modules embedded in a communication network that allows any of the processors to access locations in any of the memory

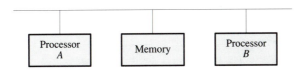

**Figure 21.1**   Simple shared-memory multiprocessor.

modules. Typically this approach involves a physical address space shared by the processors in such a way that memory read and write requests can be routed to the appropriate memory modules by simple hardware means. The sharing of memory, like other resource sharing, opens the possibility of contention among the processors for memory access; hence an allocation policy and an arbitration mechanism are required.

### 21.7.1 Bus-Based MIMD Multiprocessors

Any of the communications topologies discussed in section 9.1.2 can be used for the interconnection; a popular formula involves several processors and memory modules plugged into a backplane bus such as described in section 9.2. Figure 21.1 shows a bus-based multiprocessor in which a pair of processors share a single memory module.

In such a configuration, arbitration for bus mastership among the processors determines which of the processors is allowed to access the memory at any instant. The bus, and hence access to the memory, is thus potentially reallocated among the processors on a transaction-by-transaction basis. Modern processors often provide one or more synchronization instructions (such as the *test-and-clear* instruction described in chapter 19) that require atomicity for a sequence of several consecutive memory transactions. The atomicity requirement is typically accommodated by simply not relinquishing bus mastership in the midst of such instructions, thereby excluding other processors from the shared memory during the critical period. Using this simple expedient and ordinary memory transactions, we can meet fundamental synchronization and communication needs; semaphores and other higher-level programming constructs can be provided as software extensions.

The simplicity of this approach is offset by severe performance limitations. At the extreme depicted in figure 21.1, where the processor-memory traffic for each processor must compete for shared communication and memory resources, system performance is constrained by the communication bandwidth of the bus. As the number of processors is increased in such a system, it quickly reaches a performance threshold beyond which adding more processors does not increase overall performance; rather, it simply divides available bus cycles among a greater number of contending modules. The performance is similarly unaffected by additional memory modules, since at most one can be addressed via the bus during any transaction.

### 21.7.2 Mitigating the Shared-Bus Bottleneck

Alternative topologies for the communication network can alleviate the single-bus communication bottleneck, at additional hardware cost, by providing parallel paths between different processor-memory pairs. For example, the use of a crossbar, such as the one depicted in section 9.1.2, allows $p$ processors to access any of $m$ memory modules. As long as each processor accesses a different memory module, processor-memory transactions can be simultaneous, thus reducing contention for memory access. In the best case, contention can be eliminated except where memory accesses address semaphores or shared variables for explicit synchronization or communication purposes.

Some of the same performance improvement can be obtained on bus-based multiprocessors by adding local memory or a cache to each processor module. Blocks of memory can be interfaced to each processor via a private bus, allowing each processor to access local memory directly (without a system bus transaction) and use the system bus only for access to shared ("global") memory. The local memory at each processor can be private—accessible only to that processor—or it can be interfaced as a slave on the system bus as well as being accessible to the attached processor via a private bus. In the latter case, each processor-resident memory module is potentially shared; every memory location is accessible to every processor, although access time will substantially favor access to local memory locations.

The use of local memory, together with a strategy for allocating it appropriately to high-traffic programs and unshared data, can substantially reduce each processor's load on the shared bus and hence eliminate contention, except where explicitly shared structures are involved. Typically, the vast majority of memory accesses are to private structures, even among cooperating processes; thus, if care is taken to identify and segregate memory uses that require sharing, the bulk of the contention in the naive system of figure 21.1 can be eliminated. The shared bus remains a potential bottleneck even after this improvement; but since it restricts communication only to shared structures, it constrains processor interaction rather than the independent activities of each processor.

### 21.7.3 Cache Coherence

Similar advantages can be obtained without the tedium of software reorganization by the use of transparent caches on each processor, as depicted in figure 21.2. In such a system, the memory-access patterns of each processor cause frequently referenced programs and data to be copied to its local cache; repeated access to cached locations requires no additional bus traffic.

Unfortunately, the use of caches on shared-memory multiprocessors introduces an additional complication, termed the *cache-coherence* or *cache-consistency* problem. Suppose processor $A$ in figure 21.2 reads memory location $X$, causing the pair $X$ and $\langle X \rangle$ to be loaded into $A$'s cache. If processor $B$ then writes $X$, the value of $\langle X \rangle$ stored in $A$'s cache becomes obsolete; subsequent reads of $X$ by $A$ will continue to result in cache hits, naively returning the previous "stale" value to the program. Note that this problem occurs regardless of whether or not a write-through

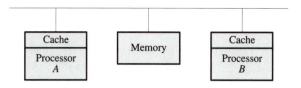

**Figure 21.2** Shared-memory system with caches.

strategy is used by $B$; the value of $\langle X \rangle$ stored in the shared memory module will, however, be valid if write-through is used. The general problem is that cached copies of shared memory locations become obsolete whenever the locations are written, but they are not marked as invalid. Caches in such a multiprocessor thus become *incoherent*, in that different caches have inconsistent images of the contents of main memory.

The cache-coherence problem occurs only when shared read/write locations are cached by one or more processors; it can be avoided by segregating such locations and arranging that they not be cached. This can be done, for example, by designing a cached virtual-memory system so that certain virtual addresses are never cached; access to these addresses will always result in a transaction on the system bus. If shared structures are segregated and allocated to these uncached virtual addresses, the cache will apply to read-only storage (such as programs) and private structures and continue to yield performance benefits without confusing the semantics of memory sharing. (Provision for uncached locations is valuable also for memory-mapped I/O devices.) High-traffic shared locations, however, will cause bus contention and tend to limit performance; a frequently accessed global semaphore, for example, may prove to be a critical bottleneck.

An alternative approach to solving the cache-coherence problem is to design cache hardware that is more sophisticated about invalidating its entries. With a write-through policy, the processors of figure 21.2 can detect when cached locations are written by eavesdropping on bus transactions. A cache that invalidates or updates its entries based on observation of bus traffic—called a *snoopy cache*—maintains cache coherence even in the presence of shared variables and synchronization structures. A processor waiting on a global semaphore, for example, might repeatedly interrogate the semaphore location in a busy-waiting loop; no bus traffic will result during this period, however, since the semaphore value will be locally cached. When some processor eventually signals on that semaphore, its new value will be written; the resulting bus transaction will be noticed by the snoopy cache of the waiting processor, and the cache line containing the semaphore value will be invalidated. The next read of the semaphore by the waiting processor will cause a cache miss, and the new value will then be fetched from shared memory.

Hardware approaches to cache coherence can be extended to other communication networks, although the invalidation of cached copies of stale data becomes more complicated in the absence of the "broadcast" characteristic of the shared bus.

## 21.8 Distribution of Subcomputations

Algorithms vary in the communication patterns they exhibit as well as in their potential for parallel computation; there is consequently a strong motivation for computer architects to understand the structure of the algorithms their machine is intended to run well, and to accommodate that structure in the communication topology and other aspects of the machine design. Most parallel machines have been developed in the context of such analyses and are shown off in their best light when applied to the algorithms considered during their design. A number of simple but commercially important algorithms (such as matrix operations, Fourier transforms, and numerical solutions to simple partial differential equations) provide traditional fodder for performance analysis, and researchers are developing a corpus of "parallel algorithms" whose amenability to concurrent attack is reasonably well understood.

Most commonly, the distribution of parts of a parallel algorithm over the elements of a multiprocessor system is carefully prearranged to match the structure of the system to the structure of the problem. This approach biases both SIMD and MIMD machines toward a relatively static distribution of programs and data structures over processing elements, but it allows algorithms amenable to such analysis to be efficiently supported. In the extreme, individual processors may be dedicated during the machine design to very specific functions, effectively using processors as data-path components rather than as general-purpose programmable devices.

Certain approaches to parallel computation associate hardware with computations in a much more dynamic fashion, allocating processors to tasks on the basis of run-time supply and demand. The data-flow machines illustrate this extreme. These machines dynamically instantiate a tiny data structure, describing the operation and carrying operand values for each operation to be performed. This packet of information is routed to an available processing element, where its execution typically generates a value to be routed to a structure representing another operation. This latter routing generally follows the data-dependency graph of the program, allowing each operation to be performed as soon as its essential data dependencies are satisfied (assuming, of course, that processing elements are available).

Data-flow computers depend on the mobility of information packets describing each operation and require special hardware to assemble the packets and route them appropriately. This mobility affords a strong measure of flexibility, since the task of distributing the computation over processing elements is assumed by the hardware. Moreover, the hardware is designed to support the allocation of processor resources at the level of individual instructions, potentially exploiting fine-grain parallelism, which is unavailable in systems that allocate processors to larger tasks such as processes. Like the parallelism approaches described in section 21.4, data-flow machines depend on latent parallelism to generate a sufficient volume of operations to keep processing elements busy. They also share a relative inability to exploit locality of communications, since every operation is pumped through the high-performance data-flow mill of assembling and routing technology independently of its context. A very simple "hot spot," such as a small intense loop that can perform at blazing speeds if confined to a single-chip processor, invokes the heavyweight mechanism necessary to funnel its component operations through the pool of processing elements.

Architectures that have the best potential to exploit locality tend to mix processing and memory functions with fine granularity, allowing sufficient resources to sustain physically localized hot spots. Neural nets and cellular automata are extreme points along this dimension, providing a nearly homogeneous matrix in which memory and computation are difficult to distinguish. More conventional architectures based on communication networks with a strong sense of locality—which somehow reward interactions that are "nearby" by some metric—can exploit this locality if processors and memories are intermixed so that every processor has "nearby" memory and vice versa. This can be effected, for example, by a mesh of processors, each having local memory: Computations that fit within one processor/memory node can operate without the overhead of internode communications, and computations that require only a few nodes can be localized so as to exploit the nearness of the nodes with which they interact.

The nature of communication locality and the rate at which it can be traded for other advantages (such as those attainable only through heavyweight processor technology) are not well understood. It seems likely, though, that multiprocessors whose performance scaling is nearly linear with configuration size must recognize and physically localize communicating modules. In many interesting cases, this distribution of modules can be the result of preliminary analysis—either by hand or by a sophisticated compiler. Many programs, however, confound such analyses by unpredictable communication patterns or patterns that change as the computation progresses. The exploitation of locality in general may require run-time mobility of program and data objects, together with sufficient run-time analysis to recognize patterns as they develop and redistribute objects to accommodate them.

## 21.9 Summary

Computer architecture is properly regarded as a branch of engineering, encompassing a body of intellectual tools for the analysis of systems and recipes for their development. An engineering discipline is the result of a sufficiently thorough understanding of a circumscribed class of systems to allow a systematic approach to their synthesis; such disciplines surround, for example, combinational circuits and finite-state machines. The computer architect uses these tools to design subsystems, to evaluate them and make incremental improvements, and to leverage these efforts by applying the methods and abstractions established by previous generations of architects.

Like the architecture of buildings, however, computer architecture combines engineering with art. At the core of an innovative computer design is a new idea—a new model of computation, or a new approach to implementation, that falls outside the range of existing engineering disciplines. Such an idea often stems from mental searches that are unruly by engineering standards—crossing the boundaries of abstractions, exploring possibilities selected not by recipe but by aesthetic judgment and subtle analogy. The most dramatic of these insights provide an alternative view of the problem, casting it in a light that reveals new structure and suppresses complications. Although successful creative leaps are strongly tempered by engineering sophistication, no engineering discipline can systematize their generation. By their nature, perhaps even by definition, they represent revolutionary deviations from established discipline. The circumspect engineering student recognizes this distinction, aware that the powerful truths of an engineering discipline are not necessarily absolute—that they stem in part from artificial constraints and structures to which there may be alternatives.

It is important that this perspective be applied to the issues and approaches sampled in this chapter, which reflect the chaotic search for a new discipline rather than the structure of a mature one. General approaches to the exploitation of parallel computation—and the consequent ability to trade hardware cost for performance—constitute a largely unsolved problem despite growing commercial and intellectual pressure. While it is plausible that continued evolution of some existing approach will yield a replacement to the ubiquitous von Neumann machine, it is also possible that such a revolution awaits an entirely new model of computation based on ideas foreign to current practice. There are many engineering lessons to be learned from the topics of this chapter, but they should be approached more as lessons in art: Rather than structure and constraints, their message is creative stimulation and exploration of new ground.

## 21.10  Context

The idea of massively parallel architectures is not new. The human brain has supplied a natural inspiration; indeed, McCulloch and Pitts [1943] established the link between computation and networks of elements inspired by neurons, laying the groundwork for that fringe of nonstandard computer architectures labeled *neural networks*. Early devotees of neural models of computation included Rosenblatt [1962], whose *perceptrons* developed an enthusiastic following apparently based on the hope that they would somehow exhibit intelligent behavior such as learning better than conventional computers. This hope was deflated by Minsky and Papert [1969], whose substitution of careful analysis for enthusiasm revealed that, at least in the perceptrons studied, the magic isn't there. More recently, Hopfield [1982] and others have stimulated a rebirth of interest in neural models of computation, and a number of mechanisms that substitute "fuzzy" or statistical methods for deterministic logic are enjoying considerable attention. While a measure of careful skepticism is in order when evaluating radical claims for any new model of computation, the vast diversity of unexplored structures almost certainly holds exciting discoveries in store for future researchers. The interested reader is referred to Minsky [1967], who introduces neural nets in the context of other classic models of computation. More recent readings on this subject can be found, among many other places, in the books of the Parallel Distributed Processing Group [Rumelhart et al. 1987].

Somewhat more conventional parallel architectures were proposed prior to 1960. A fascinating but problematic proposal by Holland [1959] describes a general-purpose machine that shares with cellular automata the distribution of programs over a mesh of processing elements. ILLIAC IV and its predecessor SOLOMON [Slotnick et al. 1962; Bouknight et al. 1972] represent a serious pioneering effort that, despite practical problems, remains a major landmark in computer history. Subsequent SIMD machines of note include PEPE [Vick 1978], the Goodyear STARAN [Batcher 1977], the Massively Parallel Processor [Batcher 1982], and the Connection Machine [Hillis 1985].

Early experimental shared-memory MIMD machines include the crossbar-based C.mmp [Wulf, Shaw, and Hilfinger 1981] and Cm* [Swan et al. 1977], whose communications are based on a hierarchy of buses. The viability of bus-based MIMD machines awaited the 1980s, when a snoopy cache proposed by Goodman [1983] stimulated a number of variations [Sweazey and Smith 1986] and commercial products. Bus-based multiprocessors with hardware support for cache coherence are currently available in configurations that offer tens of processors sharing an address space; see, for example, Thakkar, Gifford, and Fielland [1987].

The use of data-flow graphs as a basis for computer programming goes back to at least the 1960s and continues as an active research area today; see Dennis [1979], Arvind and Kathail [1981], and Gurd, Kirkham, and Boehm [1987] for a representative sampling. Message-passing semantics are developed as a computation model in the seminal *actor* systems of Hewitt [Hewitt 1977; Agha 1986], which inspired a lambda-calculus-like formalism (the *mu calculus*) by Ward and Halstead [1980]. The MuNet [Halstead and Ward 1980] is a scalable MIMD multiprocessor based on this model and prototyped at M.I.T.; it incorporates a topology-independent scheme for dynamically distributing a system of program and data objects on a processor mesh. The Cosmic Cube [Seitz 1985] and its commercial descendant, the Intel iPSC [Ashbury, Frison, and Roth 1985], use a message-based communication network involving 64 processors in a binary 6-cube. The latter machines exploit a prescribed (static) distribution of program components over their processors, but they offer considerable flexibility owing to their logarithmic-time communication costs. They have been used to explore the distribution of parallel algorithms.

Multiprocessors and related issues are the subject of a substantial body of literature; in addition, many advanced textbooks treat these topics in greater depth. The reader is referred to Stone [1987], Desrochers [1987], and Kuck [1978] for further detail and perspective. Dongarra [1987] describes some recent experimental architectures, and Babb [1988] summarizes a number of current commercial parallel computers.

# A1    The C Language:
# A Brief Overview

The text uses the C language, developed at Bell Telephone Laboratories, for the informal presentation of algorithms and program fragments. C is quite typical of modern compiled languages, and any reader with some programming experience should find the examples fairly readable. This appendix is provided as an aid to understanding the simple C programs presented in the text. It falls far short of a complete introduction to the language, for which the interested reader is referred to Kernighan and Ritchie [1978].

C is a relatively low-level language, designed to be easily translated to efficient object code for many modern computers. Unlike LISP, for example, the semantics of C strongly reflect the assumption of compiled (rather than interpreted) implementations and a bias toward simplicity and efficiency of the translated program rather than flexibility and generality of the source language. In these respects, C is typical of languages in widespread use for production programming; other examples include FORTRAN, Pascal, and PL/1.

## A1.1  Simple Data Types and Declarations

C offers several representations of integer data, differing in the number of bits used. The data types char, short, and long designate, respectively, 8-, 16-, and 32-bit signed integer data. The type int designates signed integer data of an implementation-dependent size; it is equivalent to short in some C implementations (typically those for 16-bit machines) and to long in others.

Every variable in C has an associated compile-time type. Unlike some interpreted languages (for example, LISP), the type information in C is used only to make compile-time decisions regarding the object code (machine instructions) to be generated; the type information is not manipulated during program execution. A variable may be *declared* in C by declarations of the form:

```
short x, y, z;    /* Declare three 16-bit integers. */
long a, b = 13;   /* Declare two 32-bit integers.   */
```

This C program fragment includes two declarations, signaling to the compiler that 16-bit storage locations are to be reserved for the storage of x, y, and z and that a and b require 32-bit storage. The "= 13" clause in the declaration of b specifies an initial value; if absent, the initial value will be random. Note the use of "/* ⋯ */" syntax to incorporate comments into the source program.

The keyword `unsigned` may precede the type in a declaration; it serves as an adjective to notify the compiler that the declared variables represent natural numbers rather than signed integers. This information affects the compiler's choice of instructions in certain operations, such as comparisons and right shifts.

C programs use integer data to represent Boolean (true/false) conditions. In general, zero is taken to mean *false* and nonzero represents *true*.

Typed *pointers* can be manipulated in C. A pointer to a datum is represented at run time by a word containing the machine address of that datum; if the datum occupies multiple (consecutive) bytes, the pointer contains the *lowest* address occupied by the data to which it points. Pointer variables are declared using one or more asterisks preceding the variable name. Thus the declaration

```
long a, *b, **c;
```

notifies the compiler that the variable `a` will have as its value a 32-bit integer, `b` will have as its value a *pointer* to a 32-bit integer (that is, the address of a memory location containing a long integer), and `c`'s value will be a pointer to a location containing a pointer to a long integer.

A *procedure* in C may return a value and is declared with a type corresponding to the value returned. The following is a typical procedure declaration:

```
long add1(a)
 long a;
 {
      return a+1;
 }
```

Note that the name `add1` of the procedure is preceded by the type of its returned value; this may be omitted if the procedure returns no value. Following the procedure name is a list of dummy arguments, separated by commas and surrounded by parentheses; these names become variables whose declaration immediately follows the argument list and whose scope is the *body* of the function, enclosed in braces.

## A1.2 Expressions

The simplest C expressions consist of single constants or variables; 123 and x are each valid C expressions (assuming that x has been declared as a variable). More complicated expressions can be constructed using C *operators*, such as +, −, *, and /, which designate the usual arithmetic operations. Thus x/3+4 is an expression whose *value* (computed during program execution) is four plus the quotient of the value of x and three. Examples of expressions using C operators are given in table A1.1.

In this table, $a$, $b$, $f$, and $p$ may be replaced by valid expressions, while $x$ must be a variable (since the storage location associated with it is referenced). $c$ is a structure component name (see section A1.5). Note that = dictates assignment but

**Table A1.1**  C expressions and operators.

| Expression | Value |
|---|---|
| $a+b$ | Addition |
| $a-b$ | Subtraction |
| $-a$ | 2's complement (negative) |
| $a*b$ | Multiplication |
| $a/b$ | Division |
| $a\%b$ | Modulus (remainder from $a/b$) |
| $(a)$ | Value of $a$; parentheses used for grouping |
| $a<b$ | True (nonzero) if $a$ is less than $b$, else false |
| $a>b$ | True (nonzero) if $a$ is greater than $b$ |
| $a<=b$ | Less-than-or-equal-to comparison |
| $a>=b$ | Greater-than-or-equal-to comparison |
| $a==b$ | Equal-to comparison (don't confuse with assignment =) |
| $a!=b$ | Not-equal-to comparison |
| $!a$ | True (nonzero) if $a$ is false (zero); Boolean *not* |
| $a\&\&b$ | Wordwise AND: false (zero) if either $a$ or $b$ is false |
| $a||b$ | Wordwise OR: true (nonzero) if either $a$ or $b$ is true |
| $\tilde{}a$ | Bitwise complement of $a$ |
| $a\&b$ | Bitwise AND |
| $a|b$ | Bitwise OR |
| $a>>b$ | Integer $a$ shifted right $b$ bit positions |
| $a<<b$ | Integer $a$ shifted left $b$ bit positions |
| $x\ =\ a$ | Assignment: has value $a$, but sets the current value of $x$ to the value of $a$ (don't confuse with equal-to comparison ==) |
| $\&x$ | Address of the variable $x$ |
| $*p$ | Contents of the location whose address is $p$ |
| $f(a,b,\ldots)$ | Procedure call |
| $p[a]$ | Array reference: element $a$ of array $p$ |
| $x.c$ | Component $c$ of structure $x$ |
| $p\text{->}c$ | Component $c$ of structure pointed to by $p$ |
| `sizeof` $x$ | Size, in bytes, of the representation of $x$ |

is syntactically an operator; thus simple expressions such as 3*(x=x+1) may have side effects as well as values.

The unary operators * and & can be used for referencing through and creating pointers. Thus, if $a$ is an expression of type $t$, &$a$ is an expression of type *pointer to t*. Conversely, if $a$ is of type *pointer to t*, then *$a$ is an expression of type $t$.

The form $f(a,b,\ldots)$ denotes a *procedure call* and is an expression whose type is that declared for the function $f$. C procedure arguments are passed by value; thus the *values* (rather than the addresses) of the arguments ($a$, $b$, and so on) are bound to the formal parameters of $f$ during its execution.

## A1.3 Statements and Programs

A *statement* in C is a single imperative or declarative command. Unlike an expression, a statement has no value; its purpose in the program stems from the effect it has, either during compilation or during execution. We have seen variable declarations, which typify the declarative class; the simplest example of an imperative statement is an expression followed by a semicolon:

```
a = b+3;
```

This causes the evaluation of the given expression during program execution. Such a statement is of interest to the programmer, of course, because its execution causes the *side effect* of changing a's value. While a side-effect-free expression such as a+3 can be made into a syntactically valid C statement by appending a semicolon, the exercise is clearly silly.

Compound statements can be constructed by using braces to enclose a sequence of component statements that are to be treated as a syntactic unit. Thus

```
{ temp=a; a=b; b=temp;
}
```

is a statement that has the effect of exchanging the values of a and b; we assume, of course, that a, b, and temp have been appropriately declared. Note that the body of a procedure, as specified in a procedure declaration, is just such a compound statement.

Each compound statement is, in fact, a program *block* and may begin with declarations of variables that are local to that block. Thus the exchange of values in the above example might better be written as

```
{ int temp;
  temp = a;
  a = b;
  b = temp;
}
```

Here the temporary location is local to the block, minimizing externally visible side effects. Note that variables declared inside a block are *dynamic*; they are allocated (from the stack) when the block is entered and are deallocated on exit from the block. Variables declared outside any block are *static*; they are effectively allocated at compile time and retain their values during the entire program execution. Variables declared with initial values (using the "= *constant*" declaration syntax) are initialized at allocation; a dynamic variable with a specified initial value is thus reinitialized at each entry to the block.

Conditional execution can be specified using an if statement, optionally including an else clause, as follows:

```
if (a < b) biggest = b;
  else biggest = a;
```

```
/* Fibonacci -- recursive version              */
long rfib(n)
long n;
{       if (n>1) return rfib(n-1) + rfib(n-2);
        else return n;
}


/* Fibonacci -- iterative version              */
long ifib(n)
long n;
{
        if (n<2) return n;
        else    { long val0, val1=0, val2=1, i;
                    for (i=1; i<n; i = i+1)
                        {       val0 = val2;
                                val2 = val2 + val1;
                                val1 = val0;
                        }
                    return val2;
                }
}
```

**Figure A1.2**   Illustration of conditional and iteration constructs.

The condition in the `if` statement is enclosed in parentheses and immediately follows the keyword `if`. At execution time, the conditional expression is evaluated; if it is true (nonzero), then the statement following the condition (the *then clause* of the `if` statement) is executed; otherwise it is skipped. The body of an `else` clause is executed if and only if the then clause of the immediately preceding `if` statement is skipped. Of course, the then clause and the `else` clause bodies may each be (and often are) program blocks.

We shall use two C constructs for program loops:

`while` (*cond*) *statement*;

and

`for` (*init*; *test*; *increment*) *statement*;

The `while` statement repeatedly evaluates the conditional expression *cond*, executing *statement* once after each evaluation of *cond* until *cond* evaluates to false (zero). The `for` statement is semantically equivalent to

*init*;
`while` (*test*)
  {     *statement*;
        *increment*;
  }

and provides a syntactically compact form for small loops.

A C *program* consists of a set of declarations of procedures and data. Figure A1.2 is a simple example, using two versions of the Fibonacci function to illustrate these constructs.

*The C Language: A Brief Overview*                                                629

```
/* Fibonacci -- "quick" (for small argument) version */
long qfib(n)
long n;
{       switch (n)
        {       case 0:
                case 1: return n;
                case 2: return 1;
                case 3: return 2;
                case 4: return 3;
                case 5: return 5;
                case 6: return 8;
                default:        return ifib(n);
        }
}
```

**Figure A1.3**   Illustration of the `switch` statement.

C provides a multiway branch construct, the `switch` statement, allowing a given expression to be tested for a fixed number of constant values. The syntax of `switch` is illustrated in figure A1.3, yet another Fibonacci function, which uses `switch` to handle certain commonly occurring arguments quickly. The `case` labels identify statements in the `switch` block to which control is transferred for various values of the `switch` expression; the value in each `case` label must be a compile-time constant. Control is transferred to the statement bearing the label `default:` if the switch value matches none of the `case` constants; in the example, the default action is to call one of the alternative Fibonacci procedures.

Several additional C statements are provided for low-level control. We have seen that `return` *expr*; returns from the innermost enclosing procedure with the optional value *expr*; `break`; can be used in a similar way to exit the innermost enclosing `for` or `while` loop or `switch` block. A `continue`; statement within a loop terminates the current iteration, effectively jumping to the end of the loop body to perform the indicated *increment* and *test* operations and continue with the next iteration, if appropriate. A `goto` *tag*; statement, where the label *tag*: identifies a statement local to the procedure, provides the lowest-level control mechanism. It is occasionally convenient (for example, to exit several nested loops), as illustrated in figure A1.4.

Figure A1.4 includes several notable features. First, it illustrates the use of *procedure* names as arguments; the procedures passed as `f` and `g` are presumed to be defined elsewhere in the program. (The actual arguments are, in fact, *pointers* to procedures; some C implementations require the somewhat inscrutable declaration syntax "`int (*f)();`" to reflect this fact.) Second, the end test in the outer `for` loop requires application of one of the argument procedures; to avoid redundant evaluation of `f(x)` within the loop body, the resulting value is assigned to a local variable. The end test of this loop thus contains an *assignment*; it is important to distinguish between the assignment `fx=f(x)` and the syntactically similar equality test `fx==f(x)`. The corresponding end test of the inner `for` statement is left blank, resulting in two consecutive semicolon characters delimiting an empty expression.

```
/* See if an x,y pair exists for which f(x) = g(y);
 * search each function's domain between 1 and the value for
 * which it returns 0.                                          */
Search(f, g)
 int f(), g();
 {      int x, y, fx, gy;
        for (x=0;  (fx = f(x)) != 0; x = x+1)
        {       for (y=0; ; y=y+1)
                {       if ((gy = g(y)) == 0) break;
                        if (fx != gy) continue;
                        else goto GotOne;    /* Found an answer!   */
                }
        }
        return 0;                            /* No answer found.   */
GotOne: return 1;                            /* Found an x,y pair. */
 }
```

**Figure A1.4**  Illustration of procedure parameters and `goto`.

In this context, the missing conditional expression is equivalent to a nonzero constant expression, causing the loop to iterate forever unless other provisions are made. Execution of this inner loop is terminated by the explicit `if` statement within its body, which performs the assignment and test functions of the end test in the outer loop. The `break` statement in this conditional exits one level (back to the body of the outer loop) when `g(y)` evaluates to zero. The `continue` statement in the following `if` ends execution of the current iteration of the containing loop, continuing that loop with the next value of `y` if the `fx` and `gy` values differ. The `goto` in the `else` statement is used to exit both loops when a solution is found. In this example, the statement `goto GotOne;` could be replaced by a simple `return 1;`. Indeed, the latter coding is to be preferred since proliferation of `goto` statements can make program logic difficult to follow. In more complicated cases (for example, those involving substantial computation at `GotOne:` that is to be entered from a variety of different places), `goto` may be the most natural solution.

Table A1.5 summarizes a set of useful C statement types.

## A1.4  Arrays and Pointers

In addition to simple scalar and pointer data, C provides two mechanisms for handling aggregate data objects stored in contiguous memory locations. The first of these is the single-dimensioned *array* or *vector*, declared using a bracketed constant following the variable name:

```
/* 100-employee payroll record     */
long    Salary[100];
char    *Name[100];
```

This fragment declares two 100-element arrays, comprising 100 consecutive 32-bit and 8-bit locations, respectively. The brackets serve also as the C operator for referencing an array element; thus `Salary[37]` designates element 37 of the `Salary`

**Table A1.5**  Summary of C statements.

| Statement type | Use |
|---|---|
| *expr*; | Evaluate expression *expr* |
| if (*test*) *statement*; | Conditional test |
| else *statement*; | Optionally follows if statement |
| switch(*expr*) | $N$-way branch (dispatch) |
| { case $C_1$: ... | (each $C_i$ is a constant) |
| case $C_2$: ... | |
| ... } | |
| while (*test*) *statement*; | Iteration |
| for (*init*; *test*; *incr*) *statement*; | |
| return *expr*; | Procedure return; *expr* is optional |
| break; | Break out of loop or switch |
| continue; | Continue to next loop iteration |
| *tag*: | Define a label for goto |
| goto *tag*; | Transfer control |

array. C arrays are *zero-indexed*, meaning that the first element of Salary is Salary[0]; thus Salary[37] is, in fact, the thirty-eighth element. Salary[100] is an out-of-bounds array reference since it refers to the 101st element of a 100-element array.

Using the array indexing operator, the Salary array might be cleared as follows:

```
{ int i;
  for (i=0; i<100; i=i+1) Salary[i] = 0;
}
```

From a type standpoint, C treats arrays as pointers; thus Salary will be treated in subsequent statements as a variable of type *pointer to* long. However, the declaration long Salary[100]; has the additional effect of reserving 400 bytes of storage for the Salary array and permanently binding the value of Salary to the beginning (lowest) address of the reserved storage. Similarly, the declaration char *Name[100]; causes Name to be treated in subsequent statements as if it had been declared char **Name, except that Name permanently identifies the start of a reserved memory block of sufficient size to hold 100 pointers. Since C views an array as a pointer to the first element of consecutive similarly typed data, it also allows a pointer to a block of memory to be used as an array. Thus, if a variable p is declared char *p and is set to point to a block of consecutive bytes of memory, references of the form p[*i*] can be used to access the *i*th element of p.

Arrays declared using the "[ $\cdots$ ]" syntax must have sizes that are compile-time constants. However, available library procedures allocate variable-size contiguous regions of memory dynamically (that is, during program execution) and return pointers to them; such library routines allow more flexible and efficient use of memory. The `Salary` array in the above example could be allocated at run time rather than at compile time by rewriting it as

```
long    *Salary; /* Simple pointer variable */
...
/* Allocate storage (N elements) for array: */
Salary = malloc(N*sizeof *Salary);
/* Use array: */
for (i=0; i=100; i=i+1) Salary[i] = 0;
...
/* Return array to free storage pool:     */
free(Salary);
```

In this example, the storage for the `Salary` array is allocated by an executable statement (that is, at run time) rather than by a declaration. This technique makes convenient use of C's happy confusion between pointers and arrays; the identical syntax (for example, `Salary[i]`) can be used to reference the elements of `Salary` independently of the means by which its storage is allocated. The library procedures `malloc` and `free` are used in this example to deal with a program-managed heap storage pool like the one described in section 13.3.9: `p=malloc(s)` allocates an s-byte region and returns a pointer to its first location, while `free(p)` returns a previously allocated block to the pool.

Textual data are naturally represented in C as arrays of characters. Thus a text-string variable `text` would be declared `char *text`, and the $i$th character of its current (string) value can be referred to as `text[i]`. Constant text strings can be designated in C using the double-quote character "; thus `"fungus"` is a C constant of type `char *`.

## A1.5 Structures

In addition to arrays, which have homogeneous type but variable size, C supports *structures*, which are fixed-size records of heterogeneous data. A structure declaration provides a useful way to localize related data; our payroll data, for example, might naturally be given the type:

```
struct Employee
{       char *Name;     /* Employee's name.    */
        long Salary;    /* Employee's salary.  */
};
```

This fragment describes a structure type and gives it the name `Employee`. Subsequent declarations can treat `struct Employee` as a valid C type; for example,

```
struct Employee Payroll[100];
```

declares an array of 100 structures, each devoted to some employee's records.

It should be understood that a structure declaration provides the compiler with a prototype for the interpretation of blocks of memory. In particular, each region of memory identified to the compiler as a `struct Employee` will begin with a pointer to a character string that holds the employee's name (occupying, say, the first 4 bytes of the region) and will contain in the immediately following 4 bytes a binary integer giving the employee's salary. The C syntax for referring to the components of a structure is "*str.cname*," where *str* designates a structure and *cname* is the name of one of its components. The salary of the fourth employee, for example, is referenced by `Payroll[3].Salary`.

It is often both convenient and efficient to manipulate pointers to structures rather than structures themselves. This is particularly true when some `struct` type must contain another value of the same type. We might, for example, wish to expand our little payroll data base to include the supervisor of each employee:

```
struct Employee
{     char *Name;                /* Employee's name.     */
      long Salary;               /* Employee's salary.   */
      struct Employee *Supervisor; /* Employee's boss.    */
} Payroll[100];
```

Our goal here is to identify in each payroll record the record of the employee's supervisor. While it is perfectly legal in C to declare a structure component that is itself a `struct` type, the result is that the containing structure type is enlarged by the size of the contained structure. If the supervisor component were declared to be type `struct Employee` rather than a pointer to `struct Employee`, C would complain. We would have asked it to allocate a structure large enough for several elements, one of which is the same size as itself!

We circumvent such difficulties by referencing the supervisor through a pointer to the appropriate payroll record. In addition, it is usually far preferable from a performance standpoint to pass pointers to structures (for example, as procedure arguments) rather than copies of the structures themselves. Since access to structures through pointers is so common, C provides the special syntax "*p->cname*" to reference component *cname* of the structure that *p* points to. Use of structure pointers is illustrated by the silly program in figure A1.6.

```
struct Employee
{       char *Name;                 /* Employee's name.     */
        long Salary;                /* Employee's salary.   */
        long Points;                /* Brownie points.      */
        struct Employee *Supervisor; /* Employee's boss.    */
}


/* Annual raise program.    */
Raise(p)
  struct Employee p[100];
{       int i;
        for (i=0; i<100; i=i+1)     /* Consider each employee. */
        { p->Salary =
                p->Salary           /* Salary adjustment:    */
                + 100               /*   cost-of-living term, */
                + p->Points;        /*   merit term.         */
          p->Points = 0;            /* Start over next year! */
          p = p+1;                  /* On to next record!    */
          Check(p);                 /* Make sure no disparities. */
          }
}


/* Make sure employee is getting less than boss:            */
Check(e)
  struct Employee *e;               /* Pointer to record.   */
{
        if (e == e->Supervisor)     /* Ignore the president */
                return;             /*  (pres. is own boss). */
        if (e->Salary <             /* Problem here?        */
            (e->Supervisor)->Salary)
                return;             /* Nope, leave happy.   */
        /* When e's boss is making no more than e is,
         * give boss a raise, then check that boss's
         * new salary causes no additional problems:
         */
        (e->Supervisor)->Salary =
                1 + e->Salary;      /* Now boss makes more. */
        Check(e->Supervisor);       /* Check further.       */
}
```

**Figure A1.6**  Use of structures.

# A2     MAYBE Microarchitecture Summary

This appendix documents the structure and implementation of the MAYBE computer, to the level of interpreted microcode.

## A2.1 Control-ROM Bit Fields

Tables A2.1–A2.7 summarize the details and interpretation of MAYBE control signals output by the control ROM.

**Table A2.1**   Control-ROM output word.

| Address increment | ALU inputs | | | | | | N.C. | COND S/L | | Drive select | | | Load select | | |
|---|---|---|---|---|---|---|---|---|---|---|---|---|---|---|---|
| ADR+ | $F_3$ | $F_2$ | $F_1$ | $F_0$ | $\overline{C}$ | $M$ | $X$ | $I$ | $S$ | $D_2$ | $D_1$ | $D_0$ | $L_2$ | $L_1$ | $L_0$ |

**Table A2.2**   Condition shift register control inputs.

| Inputs | | Action |
|---|---|---|
| $I$ | $S$ | |
| 0 | 0 | Load condition register |
| 0 | 1 | Shift condition register right |
| 1 | 0 | No change |
| 1 | 1 | No change |

**Table A2.3**  Function decoding: 74181 ALU inputs and functions.

| Control inputs | | | | Function performed if $M = 0$ (arithmetic) | Function performed if $M = 1$ (logical) |
|---|---|---|---|---|---|
| $F_3$ | $F_2$ | $F_1$ | $F_0$ | | |
| 0 | 0 | 0 | 0 | $A + 1 - \overline{C}$ | $\overline{A}$ |
| 0 | 0 | 0 | 1 | $(A \text{ OR } B) + 1 - \overline{C}$ | $\overline{(A \text{ OR } B)}$ |
| 0 | 0 | 1 | 0 | $(A \text{ OR } \overline{B}) + 1 - \overline{C}$ | $\overline{A} \text{ AND } B$ |
| 0 | 0 | 1 | 1 | $-\overline{C}$ | 00000000 |
| 0 | 1 | 0 | 0 | $A + (A \text{ AND } \overline{B}) + 1 - \overline{C}$ | $\overline{(A \text{ AND } B)}$ |
| 0 | 1 | 0 | 1 | $(A \text{ OR } B) + (A \text{ AND } \overline{B}) + 1 - \overline{C}$ | $\overline{B}$ |
| 0 | 1 | 1 | 0 | $A - B - \overline{C}$ | $A \text{ XOR } B$ |
| 0 | 1 | 1 | 1 | $(A \text{ AND } \overline{B}) - \overline{C}$ | $A \text{ AND } \overline{B}$ |
| 1 | 0 | 0 | 0 | $A + (A \text{ AND } B) + 1 - \overline{C}$ | $\overline{A} \text{ OR } B$ |
| 1 | 0 | 0 | 1 | $A + B + 1 - \overline{C}$ | $\overline{(A \text{ XOR } B)}$ |
| 1 | 0 | 1 | 0 | $(A \text{ OR } B) + (A \text{ AND } B) + 1 - \overline{C}$ | $B$ |
| 1 | 0 | 1 | 1 | $(A \text{ AND } B) - \overline{C}$ | $A \text{ AND } B$ |
| 1 | 1 | 0 | 0 | $A + A + 1 - \overline{C}$ | 11111111 |
| 1 | 1 | 0 | 1 | $(A \text{ OR } B) + A + 1 - \overline{C}$ | $A \text{ OR } \overline{B}$ |
| 1 | 1 | 1 | 0 | $(A \text{ OR } \overline{B}) + A + 1 - \overline{C}$ | $A \text{ OR } B$ |
| 1 | 1 | 1 | 1 | $A - \overline{C}$ | $A$ |


**Table A2.4**  Useful ALU functions.

| Control inputs | | | | | | Output |
|---|---|---|---|---|---|---|
| $F_3$ | $F_2$ | $F_1$ | $F_0$ | $\overline{C}$ | $M$ | |
| 0 | 0 | 1 | 1 | 1 | 1 | 00000000 |
| 1 | 1 | 0 | 0 | 1 | 1 | 11111111 |
| 1 | 1 | 1 | 1 | 1 | 1 | $A$ |
| 1 | 0 | 1 | 0 | 1 | 1 | $B$ |
| 1 | 1 | 1 | 1 | 1 | 0 | $A - 1$ |
| 0 | 0 | 0 | 0 | 0 | 0 | $A + 1$ |
| 1 | 0 | 0 | 1 | 1 | 0 | $A + B$ |
| 0 | 1 | 1 | 0 | 0 | 0 | $A - B$ |
| 1 | 0 | 1 | 1 | 1 | 1 | $A \text{ AND } B$ |
| 1 | 1 | 1 | 0 | 1 | 1 | $A \text{ OR } B$ |
| 0 | 1 | 1 | 0 | 1 | 1 | $A \text{ XOR } B$ |
| 0 | 0 | 0 | 0 | 1 | 1 | $\overline{A}$ (1's complement) |

**Table A2.5**  Drive-select signals.

| $D_2$ | DRSEL $D_1$ | $D_0$ | Source |
|---|---|---|---|
| 0 | 0 | 0 | Switch register |
| 0 | 0 | 1 | Microcode ROM |
| 0 | 1 | 0 | ALU output |
| 0 | 1 | 1 | Not connected |
| 1 | 0 | 0 | Static RAM |
| 1 | 0 | 1 | Not connected |
| 1 | 1 | 0 | Dynamic RAM output register |
| 1 | 1 | 1 | Input/output data |

**Table A2.6**  Load-select signals.

| $D_2$ | LDSEL $D_1$ | $D_0$ | Destination |
|---|---|---|---|
| 0 | 0 | 0 | OP (opcode) register |
| 0 | 0 | 1 | Microcode ROM ADR |
| 0 | 1 | 0 | ALU *A* input *and* I/O address |
| 0 | 1 | 1 | ALU *B* input |
| 1 | 0 | 0 | Static RAM data |
| 1 | 0 | 1 | Static RAM address (MAR) |
| 1 | 1 | 0 | Dynamic RAM |
| 1 | 1 | 1 | Input/output data |

**Table A2.7**  Condition register.

| $C_7$ | External communication $C_6$ | Push buttons $C_5$ | $C_4$ | ALU output condition bits $C_3$ | $C_2$ | $C_1$ | $C_0$ |
|---|---|---|---|---|---|---|---|
| N.C. | I/OFLAG | $P_1$ | $P_0$ | $D_0$ | $E$ | $\overline{C}$ | $N$ |

## A2.2 Circuit Details

The schematic diagrams in figures A2.8–A2.17 show the design of a complete MAYBE computer, which may be constructed from readily available parts. These diagrams focus on details useful in the construction of a MAYBE (for example, integrated-circuit packages and pin numbers) rather than the architectural structure of the machine; for insight into the latter, the reader will fare much better using the diagrams in chapter 11.

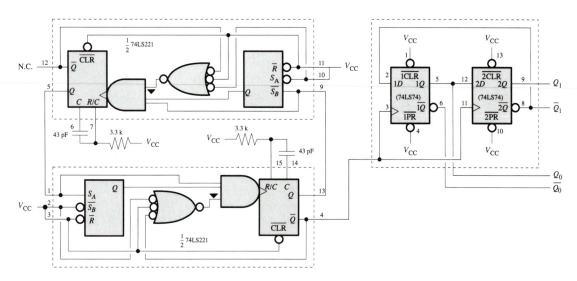

**Figure A2.8** Left: System clock (nominal frequency is 3.7 MHz). Right: Gray-code counter.

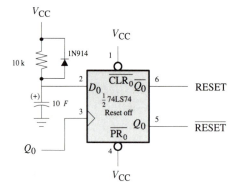

**Figure A2.9** Reset circuitry.

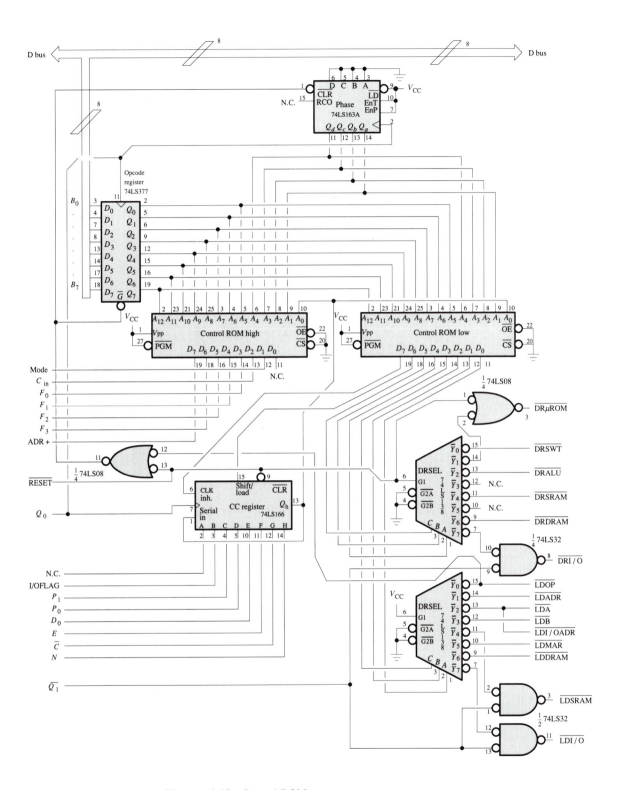

**Figure A2.10**  Control ROM.

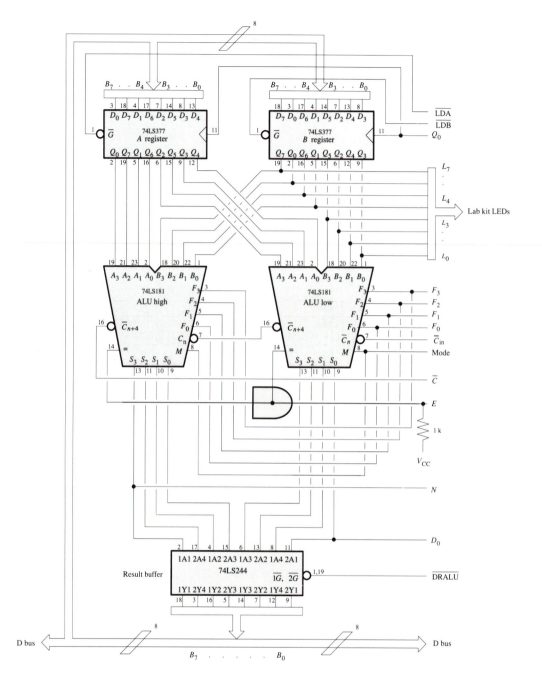

**Figure A2.11** Arithmetic logic unit (PC card).

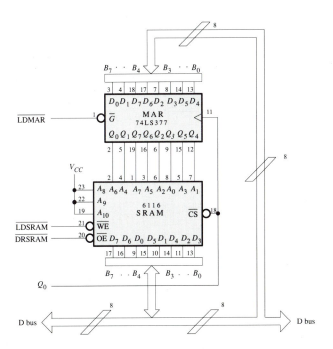

**Figure A2.12**  Static RAM (PC card).

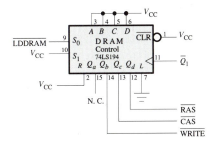

**Figure A2.13**  Dynamic RAM controller.

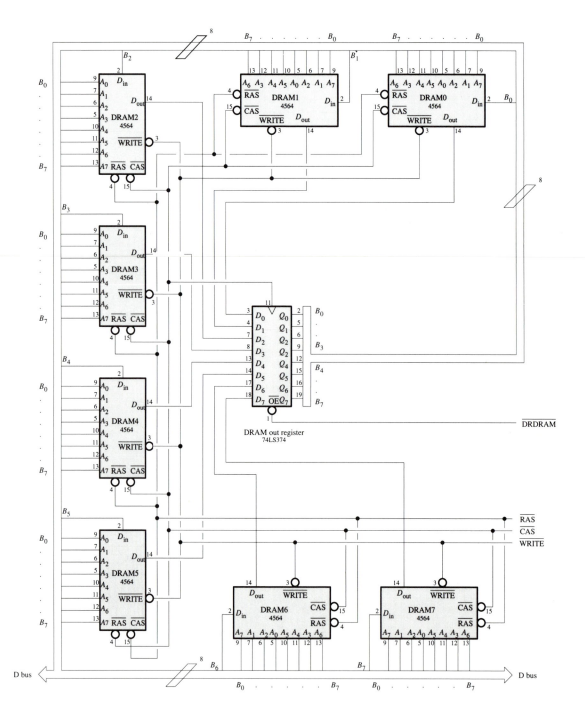

**Figure A2.14** Dynamic RAM (PC card).

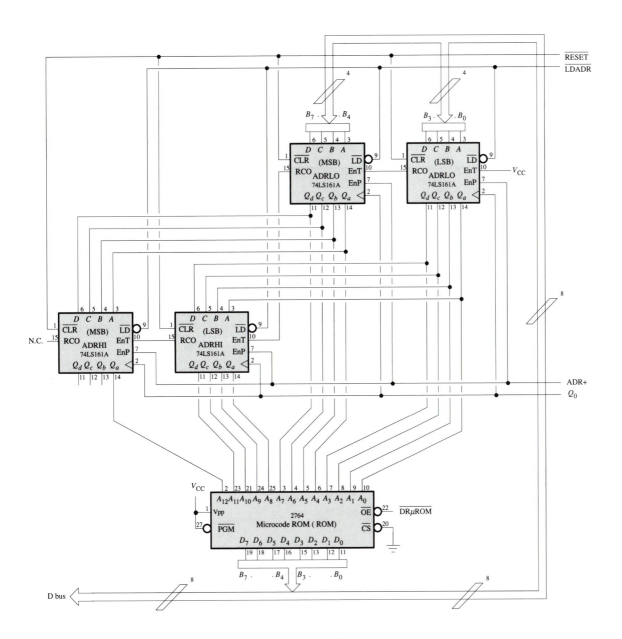

**Figure A2.15** Microcode ROM (PC card).

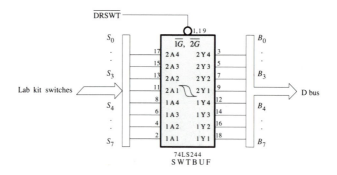

**Figure A2.16**  Switch buffer.

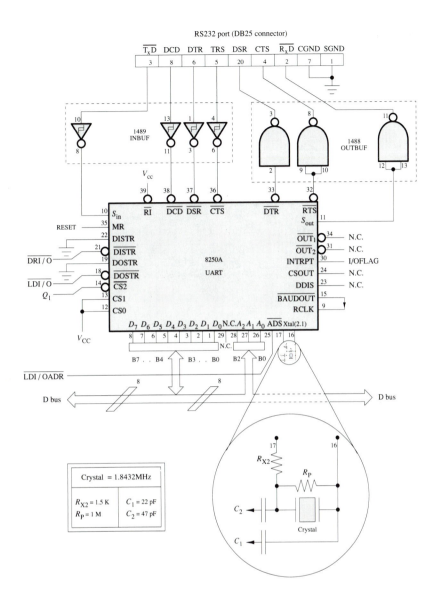

**Figure A2.17** Serial interface (PC card).

## A2.3 Microinstruction Set

Tables A2.18–A.2.24 summarize, in symbolic form, the basic set of MAYBE microinstructions.

**Table A2.18**   Data-movement microinstructions.

| Symbolic microinstruction | Control-ROM encoding | Operation performed |
|---|---|---|
| $\texttt{move}(x,y)$ | 0x05 $x$ $y$ | $y \leftarrow \langle x \rangle$ |
| $\texttt{cmove}(cx,y)$ | 0x06 $cx$ $y$ | $y \leftarrow cx$ |
| $\texttt{imove}(x,y)$ | 0x0D $x$ $y$ | $y \leftarrow \langle\langle x \rangle\rangle$ |
| $\texttt{movei}(x,y)$ | 0x0E $x$ $y$ | $\langle y \rangle \leftarrow \langle x \rangle$ |

**Table A2.19** ALU operation microinstructions.

| Symbolic microinstruction | Control-ROM encoding | Operation performed |
|---|---|---|
| $\texttt{add}(x,y,z)$ | 0x0A $x$ $y$ $z$ | $z \leftarrow \langle x \rangle + \langle y \rangle$ |
| $\texttt{cadd}(cx,y,z)$ | 0x0B $cx$ $y$ $z$ | $z \leftarrow cx + \langle y \rangle$ |
| $\texttt{sub}(x,y,z)$ | 0x1C $x$ $y$ $z$ | $z \leftarrow \langle x \rangle - \langle y \rangle$ |
| $\texttt{cmp}(x,y)$ | 0x1D $x$ $y$ | $\langle x \rangle - \langle y \rangle$ |
| $\texttt{and}(x,y,z)$ | 0x27 $x$ $y$ $z$ | $z \leftarrow \langle x \rangle$ AND $\langle y \rangle$ |
| $\texttt{or}(x,y,z)$ | 0x28 $x$ $y$ $z$ | $z \leftarrow \langle x \rangle$ OR $\langle y \rangle$ |
| $\texttt{xor}(x,y,z)$ | 0x29 $x$ $y$ $z$ | $z \leftarrow \langle x \rangle$ XOR $\langle y \rangle$ |
| $\texttt{not}(x,y)$ | 0x2A $x$ $y$ | $y \leftarrow$ NOT $\langle x \rangle$ (1's complement) |
| $\texttt{neg}(x,y)$ | 0x2B $x$ $y$ | $y \leftarrow (-\langle x \rangle)$ (2's complement) |
| $\texttt{add2}(x,y,z)$ | 0x2C $x$ $y$ $z$ <br> $x{+}1$ $y{+}1$ $z{+}1$ | $z^2 \leftarrow \langle x \rangle^2 + \langle y \rangle^2$ |
| $\texttt{cadd2}(cx,y,z)$ | 0x2D $cx\%256$ $y$ $z$ <br> $cx/256$ $y{+}1$ $z{+}1$ | $z^2 \leftarrow cx^2 + \langle y \rangle^2$ |
| $\texttt{sub2}(x,y,z)$ | 0x2E $x$ $y$ $z$ <br> $x{+}1$ $y{+}1$ $z{+}1$ | $z^2 \leftarrow \langle x \rangle^2 - \langle y \rangle^2$ |
| $\texttt{cmp2}(x,y)$ | 0x2F $x$ $y$ $x+1$ $y+1$ | $\langle x \rangle^2 - \langle y \rangle^2$ |
| $\texttt{caddcy}(cx,y,z)$ | 0x82 $cx$ $y$ $z$ | $z \leftarrow cx + \langle y \rangle +$ saved ALU $C$ flag |
| $\texttt{cand}(cx,y,z)$ | 0x83 $cx$ $y$ $z$ | $z \leftarrow cx$ AND $\langle y \rangle$ |
| $\texttt{rotl}n(x,y)$ | 0x88$+n$ $x$ $y$ | $y \leftarrow \langle x \rangle$ rotated left $n$ places $(1 \leq n \leq 7)$ |
| $\texttt{rotr}n(x,y)$ | 0x90$-n$ $x$ $y$ | $y \leftarrow \langle x \rangle$ rotated right $n$ places $(1 \leq n \leq 7)$ |

**Table A2.20** Jump microinstructions.

| Symbolic microinstruction | Control-ROM encoding | Operation performed |
|---|---|---|
| jmp($dst$) | 0x0C $dstlo$ $dsthi$ | Unconditional transfer: $\text{ADR} \leftarrow (dsthi, dstlo)$ |
| je($dst$) | 0x19 $dstlo$ $dsthi$ | jmp if ALU output was = 0b11111111 |
| jne($dst$) | 0x25 $dstlo$ $dsthi$ | jmp if ALU output was $\neq$ 0b11111111 |
| jmi($dst$) | 0x12 $dstlo$ $dsthi$ | jmp if ALU output was < 0 |
| jc($dst$) | 0x23 $dstlo$ $dsthi$ | jmp if carry |
| jnc($dst$) | 0x17 $dstlo$ $dsthi$ | jmp if no carry |
| jeven($dst$) | 0x22 $dstlo$ $dsthi$ | jmp if ALU output was even |
| jodd($dst$) | 0x16 $dstlo$ $dsthi$ | jmp if ALU output was odd |
| jready($dst$) | 0x14 $dstlo$ $dsthi$ | jmp if I/OFLAG is set |
| jp0($dst$) | 0x18 $dstlo$ $dsthi$ | jmp if $P_0$ is pressed |
| jp1($dst$) | 0x15 $dstlo$ $dsthi$ | jmp if $P_1$ is pressed |
| jnp0($dst$) | 0x24 $dstlo$ $dsthi$ | jmp if $P_0$ is not pressed |
| jnp1($dst$) | 0x21 $dstlo$ $dsthi$ | jmp if $P_1$ is not pressed |

**Table A2.21** Dispatch microinstruction.

| Symbolic microinstruction | Control-ROM encoding | Operation performed |
|---|---|---|
| dispatch($x$,$tab$) | 0x80 $x$ $tabhi$ $tablo$ | $tab$ is taken as the $\mu$ROM address of a table of 2-byte $\mu$ROM addresses, each stored (low,high); the SRAM location $x$ contains an index into the table; jumps to the $\mu$ROM location given in the indexed entry. |

**Table A2.22** Microstack and microsubroutine microinstructions.

| Symbolic microinstruction | Control-ROM encoding | Operation performed |
|---|---|---|
| push($x$) | 0x03 $x$ | Push SRAM $\langle x \rangle$ onto microstack: $\langle \mu SP \rangle \leftarrow \langle x \rangle;\ \mu SP \leftarrow \langle \mu SP \rangle - 1$ |
| pop($x$) | 0x04 $x$ | Pop microstack into SRAM $\langle x \rangle$: $\mu SP \leftarrow \langle \mu SP \rangle + 1;\ x \leftarrow \langle\langle \mu SP \rangle\rangle$ |
| call($s$) | 0x01 $rlo\ rhi\ slo\ shi$ | Microsubroutine call to microcode ROM address $s$; $r$ is the return location: $\langle \mu SP \rangle \leftarrow rlo;\ \mu SP \leftarrow \langle \mu SP \rangle - 1;$ $\langle \mu SP \rangle \leftarrow rhi;\ \mu SP \leftarrow \langle \mu SP \rangle - 1;$ $ADR \leftarrow shi;\ ADR \leftarrow slo.$ |
| rtn:() | 0x02 | Microsubroutine return: $\mu SP \leftarrow \langle \mu SP \rangle + 1;\ ADR \leftarrow \langle\langle \mu SP \rangle\rangle;$ $\mu SP \leftarrow \langle \mu SP \rangle + 1;\ ADR \leftarrow \langle\langle \mu SP \rangle\rangle.$ |

**Table A2.23** Dynamic RAM microinstructions.

| Symbolic microinstruction | Control-ROM encoding | Operation performed |
|---|---|---|
| l($adrlo,adrhi,where$) | 0x0F $adrlo\ adrhi\ where$ | $where \leftarrow \langle\langle adrlo \rangle, \langle adrhi \rangle\rangle$; loads the contents of the DRAM location whose address is contained in SRAM locations $adrlo$ and $adrhi$ into SRAM location $where$. |
| s($where,adrlo,adrhi$) | 0x10 $where\ adrlo\ adrhi$ | Stores the contents of the SRAM location $where$ into the DRAM location whose address is contained in SRAM locations $adrlo$ and $adrhi$. |
| refr() | 0x11 | Refreshes six rows of dynamic RAM. |

**Table A2.24**  Miscellaneous microinstructions.

| Symbolic microinstruction | Control-ROM encoding | Operation performed |
|---|---|---|
| pwrup() | 0x09 | Initialization |
| pdisp($x, p_{00}, p_{01}, p_{10}, p_{11}$) | 0x08 $x$ WORD($p_{00}$)<br>WORD($p_{01}$)<br>WORD($p_{10}$)<br>WORD($p_{11}$) | Display $\langle x \rangle$ in lights;<br>refresh one DRAM row;<br>transfer to $p_{ij}$, where $i, j$ are states of<br>buttons $P_0, P_1$ |
| cond($x$) | 0x31 $x$ | $x \leftarrow$ condition register |
| swt($x$) | 0x07 $x$ | $x \leftarrow$ switches |
| urom($l, h, dst$) | 0x26 $l$ $h$ $dst$ | Loads the contents of the microcode ROM<br>location whose address is contained in SRAM<br>locations $l$ and $h$ into SRAM location $dst$;<br>then performs a rtn() operation. |

# A2.4  Control-ROM Listing

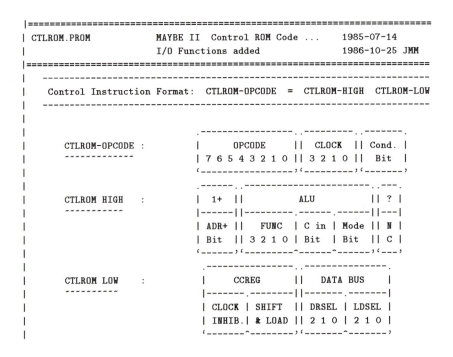

```
|    ------------------------------------------------------------------
|                    DATA BUS device decoder implementation ...
|    ------------------------------------------------------------------
|
|
|                          .--------------..---------------..---------.
|    DRIVER SELECT (DRSEL): | S2 | S1 | SO || DRIVER DEVICE ||  ABBR.  |
|    ~~~~~~~~~~~~~~~~~~~     |--------------||---------------||---------|
|                           | 0  | 0  | 0  ||   SWITCHES    ||  DRSWT  |
|                           | 0  | 0  | 1  ||   uCODE ROM   || DRuROM  |
|                           | 0  | 1  | 0  ||  ALU output   ||  DRALU  |
|                           | 0  | 1  | 1  ||  ????????     || ( NOP ) |
|                           | 1  | 0  | 0  ||  Static RAM   || DRSRAM  |
|                           | 1  | 0  | 1  ||  ????????     || ( NOP ) |
|                           | 1  | 1  | 0  ||  Dynamic RAM  || DRDRAM  |
|                           | 1  | 1  | 1  || External Comm.||  DRI/O  |
|                           '----^----^----)'---------------)'---------)
|
|                          .--------------..-------------------..--------.
|    LOADER SELECT (LDSEL): | S2 | S1 | SO ||   LOADER DEVICE   ||  ABBR. |
|    ~~~~~~~~~~~~~~~~~~~     |--------------||-------------------||--------|
|                           | 0  | 0  | 0  || CTLROM OPCODE Reg.||  LDOP  |
|                           | 0  | 0  | 1  ||  uROM  Addr. Reg. || LDADR  |
|                           | 0  | 1  | 0  ||   ALU "A" Reg.    ||  LDA   |
|                           | 0  | 1  | 1  ||   ALU "B" Reg.    ||  LDB   |
|                           | 1  | 0  | 0  || Static RAM datum  || LDSRAM |
|                           | 1  | 0  | 1  || Memory Addr.Reg.  || LDMAR  |
|                           | 1  | 1  | 0  ||   Dynamic RAM     || LDDRAM |
|                           | 1  | 1  | 1  ||  External Comm.   || LDI/O  |
|                           '----^----^----)'-------------------)'--------)
|    ------------------------------------------------------------------
| Note:  LDA is also tied to LDI/OADR so that loading the ALU A register
|    also loads the I/O address register.
|    ------------------------------------------------------------------
|
| SRAM allocation conventions:
|----------------------------
|      0xFF      Stack pointer.  Points to top stack element.
|      0xFE      Refresh counter.
|      0xFD-F0   Reserved, e.g., for microinstruction temporaries.
|      0xEF down Microstack.
|
|>>>>>>>>>>>><<<<<<<<<
|>>> UNUSED OPCODE <<<  Opcode  00000000 is reserved for an I/O hack opcode.
|>>>>>>>>>>>><<<<<<<<<
|
|               C      A      M      I
|               o      D ALU  Co     nS DR  LD    |
|  OPCODE  CLOK n  ==  R FUNC id N   h/ SEL SEL   | COMMENTS
|  76543210 3210 d      + 3210 ne C  bL 210 210   |
|
| call(rtnlo, rtnhi, subrlo, subrhi)
   00000001 0000 *  = 0 1100 11 1   11 010 101   | MAR <- 0xFF
   00000001 0001 *  = 0 1111 11 1   11 100 010   | A   <- SRAM
   00000001 0010 *  = 0 1111 11 1   11 010 101   | MAR <- A
   00000001 0011 *  = 1 1111 11 1   11 001 100   | SRAM <- uROM; ADR+
   00000001 0100 *  = 0 1111 10 1   11 010 010   | A   <- A-1
   00000001 0101 *  = 0 1111 11 1   11 010 101   | MAR <- A
   00000001 0110 *  = 1 1111 11 1   11 001 100   | SRAM <- uROM; ADR+
   00000001 0111 *  = 0 1100 11 1   11 010 101   | MAR <- 0xFF
   00000001 1000 *  = 0 1111 10 1   11 010 100   | SRAM <- A-1
```

```
    00000001 1001 *  = 1 1111 11 1    11 001 010   | A    <- uROM; ADR+
    00000001 1010 *  = 0 1111 11 1    11 001 001   | ADR  <- uROM;
    00000001 1011 *  = 0 1111 11 1    11 010 001   | ADR  <- A
    00000001 1100 *  = 1 1111 11 1    11 001 000   | OPCODE <- uROM; ADR+

| rtn()
| Note: This opcode (2) is built into ctlrom code for urom(), below.
| DO NOT CHANGE IT without modifying urom code.
    00000010 0000 *  = 0 1100 11 1    11 010 101   | MAR  <- 0xFF
    00000010 0001 *  = 0 1111 11 1    11 100 010   | A    <- SRAM
    00000010 0010 *  = 0 0000 00 1    11 010 010   | A    <- A+1
    00000010 0011 *  = 0 1111 11 1    11 010 101   | MAR  <- A
    00000010 0100 *  = 0 1111 11 1    11 100 001   | ADR  <- SRAM
    00000010 0101 *  = 0 0000 00 1    11 010 010   | A    <- A+1
    00000010 0110 *  = 0 1111 11 1    11 010 101   | MAR  <- A
    00000010 0111 *  = 0 1111 11 1    11 100 001   | ADR  <- SRAM
    00000010 1000 *  = 0 1100 11 1    11 010 101   | MAR  <- 0xFF
    00000010 1001 *  = 0 1111 11 1    11 010 100   | SRAM <- A
    00000010 1010 *  = 1 1111 11 1    11 001 000   | OPCODE <- uROM; ADR+

| push(x)
    00000011 0000 *  = 0 1100 11 1    11 010 101   | MAR  <- 0xFF
    00000011 0001 *  = 0 1111 11 1    11 100 010   | A    <- SRAM
    00000011 0010 *  = 0 1111 10 1    11 010 100   | SRAM <- A-1
    00000011 0011 *  = 1 1111 11 1    11 001 101   | MAR  <- uROM; ADR+
    00000011 0100 *  = 0 1111 11 1    11 100 011   | B    <- SRAM
    00000011 0101 *  = 0 1111 11 1    11 010 101   | MAR  <- A
    00000011 0110 *  = 0 1010 11 1    11 010 100   | SRAM <- B
    00000011 0111 *  = 1 1111 11 1    11 001 000   | OPCODE <- uROM; ADR+

| pop(x)
    00000100 0000 *  = 0 1100 11 1    11 010 101   | MAR  <- 0xFF
    00000100 0001 *  = 0 1111 11 1    11 100 010   | A    <- SRAM
    00000100 0010 *  = 0 0000 00 1    11 010 010   | A    <- A+1
    00000100 0011 *  = 0 1111 11 1    11 010 100   | SRAM <- A
    00000100 0100 *  = 0 1111 11 1    11 010 101   | MAR  <- A
    00000100 0101 *  = 0 1111 11 1    11 100 010   | A    <- SRAM
    00000100 0110 *  = 1 1111 11 1    11 001 101   | MAR  <- uROM; ADR+
    00000100 0111 *  = 0 1111 11 1    11 010 100   | SRAM <- A
    00000100 1000 *  = 1 1111 11 1    11 001 000   | OPCODE <- uROM; ADR+

| move(x, y)    [move value]   y <- <x>
    00000101 0000 *  = 1 1111 11 1    11 001 101   | MAR  <- uROM; ADR+
    00000101 0001 *  = 0 1111 11 1    11 100 010   | A    <- SRAM
    00000101 0010 *  = 1 1111 11 1    11 001 101   | MAR  <- uROM; ADR+
    00000101 0011 *  = 0 1111 11 1    11 010 100   | SRAM <- A
    00000101 0100 *  = 1 1111 11 1    11 001 000   | OPCODE <- uROM; ADR+

| cmove(cx, y)  [move constant]  y <- cx
    00000110 0000 *  = 1 1111 11 1    11 001 010   | A    <- uROM; ADR+
    00000110 0001 *  = 1 1111 11 1    11 001 101   | MAR  <- uROM; ADR+
    00000110 0010 *  = 0 1111 11 1    11 010 100   | SRAM <- A
    00000110 0011 *  = 1 1111 11 1    11 001 000   | OPCODE <- uROM; ADR+

| swt(x)        x <- switches
    00000111 0000 *  = 1 1111 11 1    11 001 101   | MAR  <- uROM; ADR+
    00000111 0001 *  = 0 1111 11 1    11 000 100   | SRAM <- SWT
    00000111 0010 *  = 1 1111 11 1    11 001 000   | OPCODE <- uROM; ADR+
```

```
| pdisp(x, p00, p01, p10, p11)
| Displays <x> in the lights.  Dispatches to (2-byte) location
|   pyz, where y is state of P0 and z is state of P1.
| Does not put data other than <x> in lights, hence suitable for
|   tight "prompt" loop.
  00001000 0000 *  = 1 1111 11 1   00 001 101   | Latch CCs;MAR <- uROM;ADR+
  00001000 0001 *  = 0 1111 11 1   01 100 011   | B <- SRAM; shift CCs
  | Following 3 states shift P0 into CCs and load 0xFE (refresh counter adr)
  |    into SRAM MAR.
  00001000 0010 *  = 0 1100 11 1   01 010 010   | Shift CCs; A <- 0xFF
  00001000 0011 *  = 0 1111 10 1   01 010 101   | Shift CCs; MAR<-A-1 (=0xFE)
  00001000 0100 *  = 0 1111 11 1   01 010 010   | Shift CCs
  | In either P0 case, they refresh one DRAM column.
  | If P0=1, uROM adr is incremented 4 times as well to point to p10 in uROM.
  00001000 0101 n  = n 1111 11 1   11 100 010   | if P0, ADR+; A <- SRAM
  00001000 0110 n  = n 1111 11 1   11 010 110   | if P0, ADR+; DRAM <- A
  00001000 0111 n  = n 0000 00 1   11 010 100   | if P0, ADR+; SRAM <- A+1
  00001000 1000 n  = n 1111 11 1   01 010 010   | if P0, ADR+; Shift CCs

  00001000 1001 n  = n 1111 11 1   11 010 010   | if P1, ADR+ (else NOP)
  00001000 1010 n  = n 1111 11 1   11 010 010   | if P1, ADR+ (else NOP)

  00001000 1011 *  = 1 1111 11 1   11 001 010   | A   <- uROM; ADR+
  00001000 1100 *  = 0 1111 11 1   11 001 001   | ADR <- uROM
  00001000 1101 *  = 0 1111 11 1   11 010 001   | ADR <- A
  00001000 1110 *  = 1 1111 11 1   11 001 000   | OPCODE <- uROM; ADR+


| pwrup()
  00001001 **** * == 1 1111 11 1   11 001 000   | OPCODE <- uROM; ADR+
  00001001 0000 *  = 1 1111 11 1   11 010 010   | A   <- A; ADR+


| add(x, y, z)
  00001010 0000 *  = 1 1111 11 1   11 001 101   | MAR <- uROM; ADR+
  00001010 0001 *  = 0 1111 11 1   11 100 010   | A   <- SRAM
  00001010 0010 *  = 1 1111 11 1   11 001 101   | MAR <- uROM; ADR+
  00001010 0011 *  = 0 1111 11 1   11 100 011   | B   <- SRAM
  00001010 0100 *  = 1 1111 11 1   11 001 101   | MAR <- uROM; ADR+
  00001010 0101 *  = 0 1001 10 1   00 010 100   | SRAM <- A+B, Latch CCs
  00001010 0110 *  = 1 1111 11 1   11 001 000   | OPCODE <- uROM; ADR+


| cadd(cx, y, z)
  00001011 0000 *  = 1 1111 11 1   11 001 010   | A   <- uROM; ADR+
  00001011 0001 *  = 1 1111 11 1   11 001 101   | MAR <- uROM; ADR+
  00001011 0010 *  = 0 1111 11 1   11 100 011   | B   <- SRAM
  00001011 0011 *  = 1 1111 11 1   11 001 101   | MAR <- uROM; ADR+
  00001011 0100 *  = 0 1001 10 1   00 010 100   | SRAM <- A+B, Latch CCs
  00001011 0101 *  = 1 1111 11 1   11 001 000   | OPCODE <- uROM; ADR+


| jmp(adrlo, adrhi)
  00001100 0000 *  = 1 1111 11 1   11 001 010   | A   <- uROM; ADR+
  00001100 0001 *  = 0 1111 11 1   11 001 001   | ADR <- uROM
  00001100 0010 *  = 0 1111 11 1   11 010 001   | ADR <- A
  00001100 0011 *  = 1 1111 11 1   11 001 000   | OPCODE <- uROM; ADR+


| imove(x, y)   [move indir value]   y <- <<x>>
  00001101 0000 *  = 1 1111 11 1   11 001 101   | MAR <- uROM; ADR+
  00001101 0001 *  = 0 1111 11 1   11 100 101   | MAR <- SRAM
  00001101 0010 *  = 0 1111 11 1   11 100 010   | A   <- SRAM
  00001101 0011 *  = 1 1111 11 1   11 001 101   | MAR <- uROM; ADR+
```

```
          00001101 0100 *  = 0 1111 11 1    11 010 100   | SRAM <- A
          00001101 0101 *  = 1 1111 11 1    11 001 000   | OPCODE <- uROM; ADR+

 | movei(x, y)    [move value indir]    <y> <- <x>
          00001110 0000 *  = 1 1111 11 1    11 001 101   | MAR <- uROM; ADR+
          00001110 0001 *  = 0 1111 11 1    11 100 010   | A   <- SRAM
          00001110 0010 *  = 1 1111 11 1    11 001 101   | MAR <- uROM; ADR+
          00001110 0011 *  = 0 1111 11 1    11 100 101   | MAR <- SRAM
          00001110 0100 *  = 0 1111 11 1    11 010 100   | SRAM <- A
          00001110 0101 *  = 1 1111 11 1    11 001 000   | OPCODE <- uROM; ADR+

 | l(adrlo, adrhi, where) -- DRAM load
          00001111 0000 *  = 1 1111 11 1    11 001 101   | MAR <- uROM; ADR+
          00001111 0001 *  = 0 1111 11 1    11 100 010   | A   <- SRAM
          00001111 0010 *  = 1 1111 11 1    11 001 101   | MAR <- uROM; ADR+
          00001111 0011 *  = 0 1111 11 1    11 010 110   | DRAM <- A (RAS)
          00001111 0100 *  = 0 1111 11 1    11 100 110   | DRAM <- SRAM (CAS)
          00001111 0101 *  = 1 1111 11 1    11 001 101   | MAR <- uROM; ADR+
          00001111 0110 *  = 0 1111 11 1    11 110 100   | SRAM <- DRAM
          00001111 0111 *  = 1 1111 11 1    11 001 000   | OPCODE <- uROM; ADR+

 | s(value, adrlo, adrhi) -- DRAM store
          00010000 0000 *  = 1 1111 11 1    11 001 101   | MAR <- uROM; ADR+
          00010000 0001 *  = 0 1111 11 1    11 100 011   | B   <- SRAM (value)
          00010000 0010 *  = 1 1111 11 1    11 001 101   | MAR <- uROM; ADR+
          00010000 0011 *  = 0 1111 11 1    11 100 010   | A <- SRAM (row)
          00010000 0100 *  = 1 1111 11 1    11 001 101   | MAR <- uROM; ADR+
          00010000 0101 *  = 0 1111 11 1    11 010 110   | DRAM <- A (row)
          00010000 0110 *  = 0 1111 11 1    11 100 110   | DRAM <- SRAM (CAS)
          00010000 0111 *  = 0 1010 11 1    11 010 110   | DRAM <- B
          00010000 1000 *  = 1 1111 11 1    11 001 000   | OPCODE <- uROM; ADR+

 | refr() - refresh 6 DRAM rows.
          00010001 0000 *  = 0 1100 11 1    11 010 010   | A <- 0xFF
          00010001 0001 *  = 0 1111 10 1    11 010 101   | MAR <- A-1 (= 0xFE)
          00010001 0010 *  = 0 1111 11 1    11 100 010   | A   <- SRAM

          00010001 0011 *  = 0 1111 11 1    11 010 110   | DRAM <- A
          00010001 0100 *  = 0 0000 00 1    11 010 010   | A <- A+1

          00010001 0101 *  = 0 1111 11 1    11 010 110   | DRAM <- A
          00010001 0110 *  = 0 0000 00 1    11 010 010   | A <- A+1

          00010001 0111 *  = 0 1111 11 1    11 010 110   | DRAM <- A
          00010001 1000 *  = 0 0000 00 1    11 010 010   | A <- A+1

          00010001 1001 *  = 0 1111 11 1    11 010 110   | DRAM <- A
          00010001 1010 *  = 0 0000 00 1    11 010 010   | A <- A+1

          00010001 1011 *  = 0 1111 11 1    11 010 110   | DRAM <- A
          00010001 1100 *  = 0 0000 00 1    11 010 010   | A <- A+1

          00010001 1101 *  = 0 1111 11 1    11 010 110   | DRAM <- A
          00010001 1110 *  = 0 0000 00 1    11 010 100   | SRAM <- A+1

          00010001 1111 *  = 1 1111 11 1    11 001 000   | OPCODE <- uROM; ADR+

 | Conditional jumps CLOBBER CCs!
```

```
| jmi(adrlo, adrhi) -- jump if N set.
    00010010 0000 * = 1 1111 11 1   11 001 010  | A <- uROM; ADR+

    00010010 0001 1 = 0 1111 11 1   11 001 001  | ADR <- uROM
    00010010 0010 1 = 0 1111 11 1   11 010 001  | ADR <- A
    00010010 0011 1 = 1 1111 11 1   11 001 000  | OPCODE <- uROM; ADR+

    00010010 0001 0 = 1 1111 11 1   11 001 010  | A <- uROM; ADR+
    00010010 0010 0 = 1 1111 11 1   11 001 000  | OPCODE <- uROM; ADR+

| jextra(adrlo, adrhi) -- jump if extra (i.e., undefined) flag set.
    00010011 0000 * = 1 1111 11 1   00 001 010  | A <- uROM; ADR+; latch CCs

    00010011 0001 * = 0 1111 11 1   01 010 010  | Shift CCs
    00010011 0010 * = 0 1111 11 1   01 010 010  | Shift CCs
    00010011 0011 * = 0 1111 11 1   01 010 010  | Shift CCs
    00010011 0100 * = 0 1111 11 1   01 010 010  |
    00010011 0101 * = 0 1111 11 1   01 010 010  | Shift CCs
    00010011 0110 * = 0 1111 11 1   01 010 010  | Shift CCs
    00010011 0111 * = 0 1111 11 1   01 010 010  | Shift CCs

    00010011 1000 1 = 0 1111 11 1   11 001 001  | ADR <- uROM
    00010011 1001 1 = 0 1111 11 1   11 010 001  | ADR <- A
    00010011 1010 1 = 1 1111 11 1   11 001 000  | OPCODE <- uROM; ADR+

    00010011 1000 0 = 1 1111 11 1   11 001 010  | A <- uROM; ADR+
    00010011 1001 0 = 1 1111 11 1   11 001 000  | OPCODE <- uROM; ADR+

| jready(adrlo, adrhi) -- jump if I/O flag set; refresh one row.
    00010100 0000 * = 0 1100 11 1   00 010 010  | A <- 0xFF

    00010100 0001 * = 0 1111 10 1   01 010 101  | Shift CCs; MAR<-A-1 (=0xFE)
    00010100 0010 * = 0 1111 11 1   01 100 010  | Shift CCs; A <- SRAM
    00010100 0011 * = 0 1111 11 1   01 010 110  | Shift CCs; DRAM <- A
    00010100 0100 * = 0 0000 00 1   01 010 100  | Shift CCs; SRAM <- A+1
    00010100 0101 * = 1 1111 11 1   01 001 010  | Shift CCs; A <- uROM; ADR+
    00010100 0110 * = 0 1111 11 1   01 010 010  | Shift CCs

    00010100 0111 1 = 0 1111 11 1   11 001 001  | ADR <- uROM
    00010100 1000 1 = 0 1111 11 1   11 010 001  | ADR <- A
    00010100 1001 1 = 1 1111 11 1   11 001 000  | OPCODE <- uROM; ADR+

    00010100 0111 0 = 1 1111 11 1   11 001 010  | A <- uROM; ADR+
    00010100 1000 0 = 1 1111 11 1   11 001 000  | OPCODE <- uROM; ADR+

| jp1(adrlo, adrhi) -- jump if P1 pressed.
    00010101 0000 * = 1 1111 11 1   00 001 010  | A <- uROM; ADR+; latch CCs

    00010101 0001 * = 0 1111 11 1   01 010 010  | Shift CCs
    00010101 0010 * = 0 1111 11 1   01 010 010  | Shift CCs
    00010101 0011 * = 0 1111 11 1   01 010 010  | Shift CCs
    00010101 0100 * = 0 1111 11 1   01 010 010  | Shift CCs
    00010101 0101 * = 0 1111 11 1   01 010 010  | Shift CCs

    00010101 0110 1 = 0 1111 11 1   11 001 001  | ADR <- uROM
    00010101 0111 1 = 0 1111 11 1   11 010 001  | ADR <- A
    00010101 1000 1 = 1 1111 11 1   11 001 000  | OPCODE <- uROM; ADR+

    00010101 0110 0 = 1 1111 11 1   11 001 010  | A <- uROM; ADR+
```

```
   00010101 0111 0  = 1 1111 11 1    11 001 000    | OPCODE <- uROM; ADR+

| jodd(adrlo, adrhi) -- jump if low ALU bit set.
   00010110 0000 *  = 1 1111 11 1    11 001 010    | A <- uROM; ADR+

   00010110 0001 *  = 0 1111 11 1    01 010 010    | Shift CCs
   00010110 0010 *  = 0 1111 11 1    01 010 010    | Shift CCs
   00010110 0011 *  = 0 1111 11 1    01 010 010    | Shift CCs

   00010110 0100 1  = 0 1111 11 1    11 001 001    | ADR <- uROM
   00010110 0101 1  = 0 1111 11 1    11 010 001    | ADR <- A
   00010110 0110 1  = 1 1111 11 1    11 001 000    | OPCODE <- uROM; ADR+

   00010110 0100 0  = 1 1111 11 1    11 001 010    | A <- uROM; ADR+
   00010110 0101 0  = 1 1111 11 1    11 001 000    | OPCODE <- uROM; ADR+

| jnc(adrlo, adrhi) -- jump if carry bit not set
   00010111 0000 *  = 1 1111 11 1    11 001 010    | A <- uROM; ADR+

   00010111 0001 *  = 0 1111 11 1    01 010 010    | Shift CCs

   00010111 0010 1  = 0 1111 11 1    11 001 001    | ADR <- uROM
   00010111 0011 1  = 0 1111 11 1    11 010 001    | ADR <- A
   00010111 0100 1  = 1 1111 11 1    11 001 000    | OPCODE <- uROM; ADR+

   00010111 0010 0  = 1 1111 11 1    11 001 010    | A <- uROM; ADR+
   00010111 0011 0  = 1 1111 11 1    11 001 000    | OPCODE <- uROM; ADR+

| jp0(adrlo, adrhi) -- jump if P0 pressed.
   00011000 0000 *  = 1 1111 11 1    00 001 010    | A <- uROM; ADR+; latch CCs

   00011000 0001 *  = 0 1111 11 1    01 010 010    | Shift CCs
   00011000 0010 *  = 0 1111 11 1    01 010 010    | Shift CCs
   00011000 0011 *  = 0 1111 11 1    01 010 010    | Shift CCs
   00011000 0100 *  = 0 1111 11 1    01 010 010    | Shift CCs

   00011000 0101 1  = 0 1111 11 1    11 001 001    | ADR <- uROM
   00011000 0110 1  = 0 1111 11 1    11 010 001    | ADR <- A
   00011000 0111 1  = 1 1111 11 1    11 001 000    | OPCODE <- uROM; ADR+

   00011000 0101 0  = 1 1111 11 1    11 001 010    | A <- uROM; ADR+
   00011000 0110 0  = 1 1111 11 1    11 001 000    | OPCODE <- uROM; ADR+

| je(adrlo, adrhi) -- jump if equal to 11111111 (0xFF).
   00011001 0000 *  = 1 1111 11 1    11 001 010    | A <- uROM; ADR+

   00011001 0001 *  = 0 1111 11 1    01 010 010    | Shift CCs
   00011001 0010 *  = 0 1111 11 1    01 010 010    | Shift CCs

   00011001 0011 1  = 0 1111 11 1    11 001 001    | ADR <- uROM
   00011001 0100 1  = 0 1111 11 1    11 010 001    | ADR <- A
   00011001 0101 1  = 1 1111 11 1    11 001 000    | OPCODE <- uROM; ADR+

   00011001 0011 0  = 1 1111 11 1    11 001 010    | A <- uROM; ADR+
   00011001 0100 0  = 1 1111 11 1    11 001 000    | OPCODE <- uROM; ADR+

|>>>>>>>>>>><<<<<<<<<<<
|>>> UNUSED OPCODES <<<   Opcodes 00011010 & 00011011 are NOT currently used.
|>>>>>>>>>>><<<<<<<<<<<                                                ===
```

```
| sub(x, y, z) -- z <- x - y
  00011100 0000 *  = 1 1111 11 1    11 001 101   | MAR <- uROM; ADR+
  00011100 0001 *  = 0 1111 11 1    11 100 010   | A   <- SRAM
  00011100 0010 *  = 1 1111 11 1    11 001 101   | MAR <- uROM; ADR+
  00011100 0011 *  = 0 1111 11 1    11 100 011   | B   <- SRAM
  00011100 0100 *  = 1 1111 11 1    11 001 101   | MAR <- uROM; ADR+
  00011100 0101 *  = 0 0110 00 1    00 010 100   | SRAM <- A-B, latch CCs
  00011100 0110 *  = 1 1111 11 1    11 001 000   | OPCODE <- uROM; ADR+

| cmp(x, y) --   x-y-1; latch CCs
| This operation only affects the condition codes.
| After the cmp(x,y), the significance of the condition codes is:
|       E:     1 iff <x> = <y>
|      -C:     0 iff <x> > <y> (unsigned) (i.e., it is asserted active low)
  00011101 0000 *  = 1 1111 11 1    11 001 101   | MAR <- uROM; ADR+
  00011101 0001 *  = 0 1111 11 1    11 100 010   | A   <- SRAM
  00011101 0010 *  = 1 1111 11 1    11 001 101   | MAR <- uROM; ADR+
  00011101 0011 *  = 0 1111 11 1    11 100 011   | B   <- SRAM
  00011101 0100 *  = 0 0110 10 1    00 010 010   | A <- A-B-1, latch CCs
  00011101 0101 *  = 1 1111 11 1    11 001 000   | OPCODE <- uROM; ADR+

| jpl(adrlo, adrhi) -- jump if N not set.
  00011110 0000 *  = 1 1111 11 1    11 001 010   | A <- uROM; ADR+

  00011110 0001 0  = 0 1111 11 1    11 001 001   | ADR <- uROM
  00011110 0010 0  = 0 1111 11 1    11 010 001   | ADR <- A
  00011110 0011 0  = 1 1111 11 1    11 001 000   | OPCODE <- uROM; ADR+

  00011110 0001 1  = 1 1111 11 1    11 001 010   | A <- uROM; ADR+
  00011110 0010 1  = 1 1111 11 1    11 001 000   | OPCODE <- uROM; ADR+

| jnextra(adrlo, adrhi) -- jump if extra (i.e., undefined) flag not set.
  00011111 0000 *  = 1 1111 11 1    00 001 010   | A <- uROM; ADR+; latch CCs

  00011111 0001 *  = 0 1111 11 1    01 010 010   | Shift CCs
  00011111 0010 *  = 0 1111 11 1    01 010 010   | Shift CCs
  00011111 0011 *  = 0 1111 11 1    01 010 010   | Shift CCs
  00011111 0100 *  = 0 1111 11 1    01 010 010   | Shift CCs
  00011111 0101 *  = 0 1111 11 1    01 010 010   | Shift CCs
  00011111 0110 *  = 0 1111 11 1    01 010 010   | Shift CCs
  00011111 0111 *  = 0 1111 11 1    01 010 010   | Shift CCs

  00011111 1000 0  = 0 1111 11 1    11 001 001   | ADR <- uROM
  00011111 1001 0  = 0 1111 11 1    11 010 001   | ADR <- A
  00011111 1010 0  = 1 1111 11 1    11 001 000   | OPCODE <- uROM; ADR+

  00011111 1000 1  = 1 1111 11 1    11 001 010   | A <- uROM; ADR+
  00011111 1001 1  = 1 1111 11 1    11 001 000   | OPCODE <- uROM; ADR+

| jnready(adrlo, adrhi) -- jump if I/O ready flag not set; refresh 1 row.
  00100000 0000 *  = 0 1100 11 1    00 010 010   | A <- 0xFF

  00100000 0001 *  = 0 1111 10 1    01 010 101   | Shift CCs; MAR<-A-1 (=0xFE)
  00100000 0010 *  = 0 1111 11 1    01 100 010   | Shift CCs; A <- SRAM
  00100000 0011 *  = 0 1111 11 1    01 010 110   | Shift CCs; DRAM <- A
  00100000 0100 *  = 0 0000 00 1    01 010 100   | Shift CCs; SRAM <- A+1
  00100000 0101 *  = 1 1111 11 1    01 001 010   | Shift CCs; A <- uROM; ADR+
  00100000 0110 *  = 0 1111 11 1    01 010 010   | Shift CCs
```

```
        00100000 0111 0  = 0 1111 11 1    11 001 001   | ADR <- uROM
        00100000 1000 0  = 0 1111 11 1    11 010 001   | ADR <- A
        00100000 1001 0  = 1 1111 11 1    11 001 000   | OPCODE <- uROM; ADR+

        00100000 0111 1  = 1 1111 11 1    11 001 010   | A <- uROM; ADR+
        00100000 1000 1  = 1 1111 11 1    11 001 000   | OPCODE <- uROM; ADR+

| jnp1(adrlo, adrhi) -- jump if P1 not pressed.
        00100001 0000 *  = 1 1111 11 1    00 001 010   | A <- uROM; ADR+; latch CCs

        00100001 0001 *  = 0 1111 11 1    01 010 010   | Shift CCs
        00100001 0010 *  = 0 1111 11 1    01 010 010   | Shift CCs
        00100001 0011 *  = 0 1111 11 1    01 010 010   | Shift CCs
        00100001 0100 *  = 0 1111 11 1    01 010 010   | Shift CCs
        00100001 0101 *  = 0 1111 11 1    01 010 010   | Shift CCs

        00100001 0110 0  = 0 1111 11 1    11 001 001   | ADR <- uROM
        00100001 0111 0  = 0 1111 11 1    11 010 001   | ADR <- A
        00100001 1000 0  = 1 1111 11 1    11 001 000   | OPCODE <- uROM; ADR+

        00100001 0110 1  = 1 1111 11 1    11 001 010   | A <- uROM; ADR+
        00100001 0111 1  = 1 1111 11 1    11 001 000   | OPCODE <- uROM; ADR+

| jeven(adrlo, adrhi) -- jump if low ALU bit not set.
        00100010 0000 *  = 1 1111 11 1    11 001 010   | A <- uROM; ADR+

        00100010 0001 *  = 0 1111 11 1    01 010 010   | Shift CCs
        00100010 0010 *  = 0 1111 11 1    01 010 010   | Shift CCs
        00100010 0011 *  = 0 1111 11 1    01 010 010   | Shift CCs

        00100010 0100 0  = 0 1111 11 1    11 001 001   | ADR <- uROM
        00100010 0101 0  = 0 1111 11 1    11 010 001   | ADR <- A
        00100010 0110 0  = 1 1111 11 1    11 001 000   | OPCODE <- uROM; ADR+

        00100010 0100 1  = 1 1111 11 1    11 001 010   | A <- uROM; ADR+
        00100010 0101 1  = 1 1111 11 1    11 001 000   | OPCODE <- uROM; ADR+

| jc(adrlo, adrhi) -- jump if carry bit set.
        00100011 0000 *  = 1 1111 11 1    11 001 010   | A <- uROM; ADR+

        00100011 0001 *  = 0 1111 11 1    01 010 010   | Shift CCs

        00100011 0010 0  = 0 1111 11 1    11 001 001   | ADR <- uROM
        00100011 0011 0  = 0 1111 11 1    11 010 001   | ADR <- A
        00100011 0100 0  = 1 1111 11 1    11 001 000   | OPCODE <- uROM; ADR+

        00100011 0010 1  = 1 1111 11 1    11 001 010   | A <- uROM; ADR+
        00100011 0011 1  = 1 1111 11 1    11 001 000   | OPCODE <- uROM; ADR+

| jnp0(adrlo, adrhi) -- jump if P0 not pressed.
        00100100 0000 *  = 1 1111 11 1    00 001 010   | A <- uROM; ADR+; latch CCs

        00100100 0001 *  = 0 1111 11 1    01 010 010   | Shift CCs
        00100100 0010 *  = 0 1111 11 1    01 010 010   | Shift CCs
        00100100 0011 *  = 0 1111 11 1    01 010 010   | Shift CCs
        00100100 0100 *  = 0 1111 11 1    01 010 010   | Shift CCs

        00100100 0101 0  = 0 1111 11 1    11 001 001   | ADR <- uROM
```

```
        00100100 0110 0  = 0 1111 11 1   11 010 001  | ADR <- A
        00100100 0111 0  = 1 1111 11 1   11 001 000  | OPCODE <- uROM; ADR+


        00100100 0101 1  = 1 1111 11 1   11 001 010  | A <- uROM; ADR+
        00100100 0110 1  = 1 1111 11 1   11 001 000  | OPCODE <- uROM; ADR+

| jne(adrlo, adrhi) -- jump if not equal to 11111111 (0xFF)
        00100101 0000 *  = 1 1111 11 1   11 001 010  | A <- uROM; ADR+

        00100101 0001 *  = 0 1111 11 1   01 010 010  | Shift CCs
        00100101 0010 *  = 0 1111 11 1   01 010 010  | Shift CCs

        00100101 0011 0  = 0 1111 11 1   11 001 001  | ADR <- uROM
        00100101 0100 0  = 0 1111 11 1   11 010 001  | ADR <- A
        00100101 0101 0  = 1 1111 11 1   11 001 000  | OPCODE <- uROM; ADR+


        00100101 0011 1  = 1 1111 11 1   11 001 010  | A <- uROM; ADR+
        00100101 0100 1  = 1 1111 11 1   11 001 000  | OPCODE <- uROM; ADR+

| urom(adrlo, adrhi, x)
| Reads ucode uROM[SRAM[adrlo], SRAM[adrhi]] into SRAM[x], then forces a
| rtn(). Note: This code MUST change iff the opcode for RTN changes!
        00100110 0000 *  = 1 1111 11 1   11 001 101  | MAR <- uROM; ADR+; adrlo
        00100110 0001 *  = 0 1111 11 1   11 100 010  | A   <- SRAM; <adrlo>
        00100110 0010 *  = 1 1111 11 1   11 001 101  | MAR <- uROM; ADR+; adrhi
        00100110 0011 *  = 0 1111 11 1   11 100 011  | B   <- SRAM; <adrhi>
        00100110 0100 *  = 1 1111 11 1   11 001 101  | MAR <- uROM; ADR+; x
        00100110 0101 *  = 0 1010 11 1   11 010 001  | ADR <- B; <adrhi>
        00100110 0110 *  = 0 1111 11 1   11 010 001  | ADR <- A; <adrlo>
        00100110 0111 *  = 0 1111 11 1   11 001 100  | SRAM <- uROM; <adrlo,adrhi>
        00100110 1000 *  = 0 0011 11 1   11 010 010  | A    <- 0
        00100110 1001 *  = 0 0000 00 1   11 010 010  | A    <- A+1 (= 1)
        00100110 1010 *  = 0 0000 00 1   11 010 010  | A    <- A+1(=2, RTN opcode)
        00100110 1011 *  = 0 1111 11 1   11 010 000  | OPCODE <- A; force RTN

| and(x, y, z)
        00100111 0000 *  = 1 1111 11 1   11 001 101  | MAR <- uROM; ADR+
        00100111 0001 *  = 0 1111 11 1   11 100 010  | A   <- SRAM
        00100111 0010 *  = 1 1111 11 1   11 001 101  | MAR <- uROM; ADR+
        00100111 0011 *  = 0 1111 11 1   11 100 011  | B   <- SRAM
        00100111 0100 *  = 1 1111 11 1   11 001 101  | MAR <- uROM; ADR+
        00100111 0101 *  = 0 1011 11 1   00 010 100  | SRAM <- A&B, Latch CCs
        00100111 0110 *  = 1 1111 11 1   11 001 000  | OPCODE <- uROM; ADR+

| or(x, y, z)
        00101000 0000 *  = 1 1111 11 1   11 001 101  | MAR <- uROM; ADR+
        00101000 0001 *  = 0 1111 11 1   11 100 010  | A   <- SRAM
        00101000 0010 *  = 1 1111 11 1   11 001 101  | MAR <- uROM; ADR+
        00101000 0011 *  = 0 1111 11 1   11 100 011  | B   <- SRAM
        00101000 0100 *  = 1 1111 11 1   11 001 101  | MAR <- uROM; ADR+
        00101000 0101 *  = 0 1110 11 1   00 010 100  | SRAM <- A|B, latch CCs
        00101000 0110 *  = 1 1111 11 1   11 001 000  | OPCODE <- uROM; ADR+

| xor(x, y, z)
        00101001 0000 *  = 1 1111 11 1   11 001 101  | MAR <- uROM; ADR+
        00101001 0001 *  = 0 1111 11 1   11 100 010  | A   <- SRAM
        00101001 0010 *  = 1 1111 11 1   11 001 101  | MAR <- uROM; ADR+
        00101001 0011 *  = 0 1111 11 1   11 100 011  | B   <- SRAM
        00101001 0100 *  = 1 1111 11 1   11 001 101  | MAR <- uROM; ADR+
```

```
   00101001 0101 *  = 0 0110 11 1    00 010 100   | SRAM <- A xor B, latch CCs
   00101001 0110 *  = 1 1111 11 1    11 001 000   | OPCODE <- uROM; ADR+

| not(x, y)
   00101010 0000 *  = 1 1111 11 1    11 001 101   | MAR <- uROM; ADR+
   00101010 0001 *  = 0 1111 11 1    11 100 010   | A    <- SRAM
   00101010 0010 *  = 1 1111 11 1    11 001 101   | MAR <- uROM; ADR+
   00101010 0011 *  = 0 0000 11 1    00 010 100   | SRAM <- not A; latch CCs
   00101010 0100 *  = 1 1111 11 1    11 001 000   | OPCODE <- uROM; ADR+

| neg(x, y)
   00101011 0000 *  = 1 1111 11 1    11 001 101   | MAR <- uROM; ADR+
   00101011 0001 *  = 0 1111 11 1    11 100 010   | A    <- SRAM
   00101011 0010 *  = 1 1111 11 1    11 001 101   | MAR <- uROM; ADR+
   00101011 0011 *  = 0 0000 11 1    00 010 010   | A    <- not A
   00101011 0100 *  = 0 0000 00 1    00 010 100   | SRAM <- A+1; latch CCs
   00101011 0101 *  = 1 1111 11 1    11 001 000   | OPCODE <- uROM; ADR+

| Following are a few 2-byte operators:

| add2(xlo, ylo, zlo, xhi, yhi, zhi) -- 16-bit add.
   00101100 0000 *  = 1 1111 11 1    11 001 101   | MAR <- uROM; ADR+
   00101100 0001 *  = 0 1111 11 1    11 100 010   | A <- SRAM
   00101100 0010 *  = 1 1111 11 1    11 001 101   | MAR <- uROM; ADR+
   00101100 0011 *  = 0 1111 11 1    11 100 011   | B <- SRAM
   00101100 0100 *  = 1 1111 11 1    11 001 101   | MAR <- uROM; ADR+
   00101100 0101 *  = 0 1001 10 1    00 010 100   | SRAM <- A+B, latch CCs
   00101100 0110 *  = 1 1111 11 1    01 001 101   | MAR <- uROM;ADR+;shift CCs
   00101100 0111 *  = 0 1111 11 1    11 100 010   | A <- SRAM
   00101100 1000 *  = 1 1111 11 1    11 001 101   | MAR <- uROM; ADR+
   00101100 1001 *  = 0 1111 11 1    11 100 011   | B <- SRAM
   00101100 1010 *  = 1 1111 11 1    11 001 101   | MAR <- uROM; ADR+
   00101100 1011 c  = 0 1001 c0 1    00 010 100   | SRAM <- A+B+c, latch CCs
   00101100 1100 *  = 1 1111 11 1    11 001 000   | OPCODE <- uROM;  ADR+

| cadd2(cxlo, ylo, zlo, cxhi, yhi, zhi) -- 16-bit add.
   00101101 0000 *  = 1 1111 11 1    11 001 010   | A <- uROM; ADR+
   00101101 0001 *  = 1 1111 11 1    11 001 101   | MAR <- uROM; ADR+
   00101101 0010 *  = 0 1111 11 1    11 100 011   | B <- SRAM
   00101101 0011 *  = 1 1111 11 1    11 001 101   | MAR <- uROM; ADR+
   00101101 0100 *  = 0 1001 10 1    00 010 100   | SRAM <- A+B, latch CCs
   00101101 0101 *  = 1 1111 11 1    01 001 010   | A <- uROM;ADR+;shift CCs
   00101101 0110 *  = 1 1111 11 1    11 001 101   | MAR <- uROM; ADR+
   00101101 0111 *  = 0 1111 11 1    11 100 011   | B <- SRAM
   00101101 1000 *  = 1 1111 11 1    11 001 101   | MAR <- uROM; ADR+
   00101101 1001 c  = 0 1001 c0 1    00 010 100   | SRAM <- A+B+c, latch CCs
   00101101 1010 *  = 1 1111 11 1    11 001 000   | OPCODE <- uROM;  ADR+

| sub2(xlo, ylo, zlo, xhi, yhi, zhi) -- 16-bit subtract.
   00101110 0000 *  = 1 1111 11 1    11 001 101   | MAR <- uROM; ADR+
   00101110 0001 *  = 0 1111 11 1    11 100 010   | A <- SRAM
   00101110 0010 *  = 1 1111 11 1    11 001 101   | MAR <- uROM; ADR+
   00101110 0011 *  = 0 1111 11 1    11 100 011   | B <- SRAM
   00101110 0100 *  = 1 1111 11 1    11 001 101   | MAR <- uROM; ADR+
   00101110 0101 *  = 0 0110 00 1    00 010 100   | SRAM <- A-B, latch CCs
   00101110 0110 *  = 1 1111 11 1    01 001 101   | MAR <- uROM;ADR+;shift CCs
   00101110 0111 *  = 0 1111 11 1    11 100 010   | A <- SRAM
   00101110 1000 *  = 1 1111 11 1    11 001 101   | MAR <- uROM; ADR+
   00101110 1001 *  = 0 1111 11 1    11 100 011   | B <- SRAM
```

```
        00101110 1010 *  = 1 1111 11 1   11 001 101   | MAR <- uROM; ADR+
        00101110 1011 c  = 0 0110 c0 1   00 010 100   | SRAM <- A-B-c, latch CCs
        00101110 1100 *  = 1 1111 11 1   11 001 000   | OPCODE <- uROM; ADR+

| cmp2(xlo, ylo, xhi, yhi) -- 16-bit compare.
| This operation only affects the condition codes.
| After the cmp(x,y), the significance of the condition codes is:
|        E:    1 iff <x> = <y>
|       -C:    0 iff <x> > <y> (unsigned) (i.e., it is asserted active low)
        00101111 0000 *  = 1 1111 11 1   11 001 101   | MAR <- uROM; ADR+
        00101111 0001 *  = 0 1111 11 1   11 100 010   | A <- SRAM
        00101111 0010 *  = 1 1111 11 1   11 001 101   | MAR <- uROM; ADR+
        00101111 0011 *  = 0 1111 11 1   11 100 011   | B <- SRAM

        00101111 0100 *  = 0 0110 10 1   00 010 010   | A <- A-B-1, latch CCs
        00101111 0101 *  = 1 1111 11 1   01 001 101   | MAR <- uROM;ADR+;shift CCs
        00101111 0110 *  = 0 1111 11 1   11 100 010   | A <- SRAM
        00101111 0111 *  = 1 1111 11 1   11 001 101   | MAR <- uROM; ADR+
        00101111 1000 *  = 0 1111 11 1   11 100 011   | B <- SRAM

        00101111 1001 c  = 0 0110 c0 1   00 010 010   | A <- A-B-c, latch CCs
        00101111 1010 *  = 1 1111 11 1   11 001 000   | OPCODE <- uROM; ADR+

| count(x) -- counts down <x>, setting flags.
| Doesn't disturb <B>, hence lights.
        00110000 0000 * = 1 1111 11 1   11 001 101   | MAR <- ROM; ADR+
        00110000 0001 * = 0 1111 11 1   11 100 010   | A   <- SRAM
        00110000 0010 * = 0 1111 10 1   00 010 100   | SRAM <- A-1; latch CCs
        00110000 0011 * = 1 1111 11 1   11 001 000   | OP <- UROM; ADR+

| cond(x) -- copies condition register into SRAM<x>.
|                         .------------------------------------------.
|      CC Format:   ctl ROM <-  | N | -C | E | D0 | P0 | P1 | I/0 | ?? |
|                         '------------------------------------------'
|
|                              <---   Direction of shift   <---

  00110001 0*** 0 = 0 1100 10 1   01 010 010   | A  <- A+A (Shift in 0)
  00110001 0*** 1 = 0 1100 00 1   01 010 010   | A  <- A+A+1 (Shift in 1)
  00110001 1000 * = 1 1111 11 1   11 001 101   | MAR <- ROM; ADR+
  00110001 1001 * = 0 1111 11 1   11 010 100   | SRAM<x> <- A
  00110001 1010 * = 1 1111 11 1   11 001 000   | OP  <- UROM; ADR+

| negcy(x, y) - negate with carry input.
        00110010 0000 *  = 1 1111 11 1   11 001 101   | MAR <- uROM; ADR+
        00110010 0001 *  = 0 1111 11 1   11 100 010   | A   <- SRAM
        00110010 0010 *  = 1 1111 11 1   11 001 101   | MAR <- uROM; ADR+
        00110010 0011 *  = 0 0000 11 1   01 010 100   | A   <- not A; shift CCs
        00110010 0100 c  = 0 0000 c0 1   00 010 100   | SRAM <- A+c; latch CCs
        00110010 0101 *  = 1 1111 11 1   11 001 000   | OPCODE <- uROM; ADR+

| subcy(x, y, z) -- z <- x - y with carry input.
        00110011 0000 *  = 1 1111 11 1   01 001 101   | MAR <- uROM;ADR+;shift CCs
        00110011 0001 *  = 0 1111 11 1   11 100 010   | A   <- SRAM
        00110011 0010 *  = 1 1111 11 1   11 001 101   | MAR <- uROM; ADR+
        00110011 0011 *  = 0 1111 11 1   11 100 011   | B   <- SRAM
        00110011 0100 *  = 1 1111 11 1   11 001 101   | MAR <- uROM; ADR+
        00110011 0101 c  = 0 0110 c0 1   00 010 100   | SRAM <- A-B-1+C, latch CCs
        00110011 0110 *  = 1 1111 11 1   11 001 000   | OPCODE <- uROM; ADR+
```

```
| readio(r,y) --  y <- [r]; [N] means "contents of I/O internal reg N."
  00110100 0000 *  = 1 1111 11 1    11 001 010   | A, I/O ADR <- uROM; ADR+
  00110100 0001 *  = 1 1111 11 1    11 001 101   | MAR  <- uROM; ADR+
  00110100 0010 *  = 0 1111 11 1    11 111 100   | SRAM <- I/O
  00110100 0011 *  = 1 1111 11 1    11 001 000   | OPCODE <- uROM; ADR+

| ireadio(x,y) --  y <- [<x>]; [N] means "contents of I/O internal reg N."
  00110101 0000 *  = 1 1111 11 1    11 001 101   | MAR  <- uROM; ADR+
  00110101 0001 *  = 0 1111 11 1    11 100 010   | A, I/O ADR <- SRAM
  00110101 0010 *  = 1 1111 11 1    11 001 101   | MAR  <- uROM; ADR+
  00110101 0011 *  = 0 1111 11 1    11 111 100   | SRAM <- I/O
  00110101 0100 *  = 1 1111 11 1    11 001 000   | OPCODE <- uROM; ADR+

| writeio(x,r) --  io r <- <x>     (i.e., <x> into I/O reg referenced by y)
| >>>>> NOTE  <<<<<  ARGUMENTS ARE REVERSED BY MACRO (see macros.uasm)
  00110110 0000 *  = 1 1111 11 1    11 001 010   | A, I/O ADR <- uROM;ADR+(r)
  00110110 0001 *  = 1 1111 11 1    11 001 101   | MAR <- uROM; ADR+      (x)
  00110110 0010 *  = 0 1111 11 1    11 100 111   | I/O <- SRAM
  00110110 0011 *  = 1 1111 11 1    11 001 000   | OPCODE <- uROM; ADR+

| writeioi(x,y) --  io <y> <- <x>   (i.e., <x> into I/O reg referenced by y)
| >>>>> NOTE  <<<<<  ARGUMENTS ARE REVERSED BY MACRO (see macros.uasm)
  00110111 0000 *  = 1 1111 11 1    11 001 101   | MAR <- uROM; ADR+      (y)
  00110111 0001 *  = 0 1111 11 1    11 100 010   | A, I/O ADR <- SRAM
  00110111 0010 *  = 1 1111 11 1    11 001 101   | MAR <- uROM; ADR+      (x)
  00110111 0011 *  = 0 1111 11 1    11 100 111   | I/O <- SRAM
  00110111 0100 *  = 1 1111 11 1    11 001 000   | OPCODE <- uROM; ADR+


|>>>>>>>>>>><<<<<<<<<<
|>>> UNUSED OPCODES <<<   Opcodes 0011100 - 01111111 are NOT currently used.
|>>>>>>>>>>><<<<<<<<<<                                      ===

| dispatch(x, tabhi, tablo)
| Takes (tabhi, tablo) as the address in uROM of a dispatch table
|   whose consecutive entries are each 2-byte uROM addresses stored
|   (low, high).  Uses contents of SRAM register x as an index into
|   this table, and jumps to the indexed entry.  Note that the
|   uROM address of the entry is adr+x+x, since entries are 2 bytes
|   each; phases 0 thru 1011 compute this value and load it into
|   ADR.  Note use of SRAM location beyond stack as a temporary.
|
| Note nonstandard order of (tabhi, tablo) arguments.
  10000000 0000 *  = 1 1111 11 1    11 001 101   | MAR <- uROM (= x); ADR+
  10000000 0001 *  = 0 1111 11 1    11 100 010   | A   <- SRAM (= <x>)
  10000000 0010 *  = 0 1100 11 1    11 010 101   | MAR <- 0xFF
  10000000 0011 *  = 0 1111 11 1    11 100 101   | MAR <- SRAM (= <0xFF>)
  10000000 0100 *  = 0 1100 10 1    00 010 011   | B<-A+A (=<x>+<x>);latch CCs
  10000000 0101 *  = 1 1111 11 1    01 001 010   | A<-uROM; ADR+;shift (tabhi)
  10000000 0110 c  = 0 0000 c0 1    11 010 100   | SRAM<-A+Carry    (tabhi+C1)
  10000000 0111 *  = 1 1111 11 1    11 001 010   | A   <-uROM; ADR+     (tablo)
  10000000 1000 *  = 0 1001 10 1    00 010 011   | B <-A+B;latch CCs(x+x+tablo)
  10000000 1001 *  = 0 1111 11 1    01 100 010   | A <-SRAM;shift CCs(tabhi+C1)
  10000000 1010 c  = 0 0000 c0 1    11 010 001   | ADR <-A+carry  (tabhi+C1+C2)
  10000000 1011 *  = 0 1010 11 1    11 010 001   | ADR <-B           (x+x+tablo)
  10000000 1100 *  = 1 1111 11 1    11 001 010   | A   <- uROM; ADR+
  10000000 1101 *  = 0 1111 11 1    11 001 001   | ADR <- uROM
  10000000 1110 *  = 0 1111 11 1    11 010 001   | ADR <- A
  10000000 1111 *  = 1 1111 11 1    11 001 000   | OPCODE <- uROM; ADR+
```

```
| addcy(x, y, z)
| Like add(x, y, z), but adds in the incoming carry bit.
  10000001 0000 *  = 1 1111 11 1    01 001 101   | MAR <- uROM; ADR+; shift CCs
  10000001 0001 *  = 0 1111 11 1    11 100 010   | A   <- SRAM
  10000001 0010 *  = 1 1111 11 1    11 001 101   | MAR <- uROM; ADR+
  10000001 0011 *  = 0 1111 11 1    11 100 011   | B   <- SRAM
  10000001 0100 *  = 1 1111 11 1    11 001 101   | MAR <- uROM; ADR+
  10000001 0101 c  = 0 1001 c0 1    00 010 100   | SRAM <- A+B+carry, latch CCs
  10000001 0110 *  = 1 1111 11 1    11 001 000   | OPCODE <- uROM;  ADR+

| caddcy(cx, y, z)
| Like cadd, but adds in the incoming carry bit.
  10000010 0000 *  = 1 1111 11 1    01 001 010   | A   <- uROM; ADR+ shift CCs
  10000010 0001 *  = 1 1111 11 1    11 001 101   | MAR <- uROM; ADR+
  10000010 0010 *  = 0 1111 11 1    11 100 011   | B   <- SRAM
  10000010 0011 *  = 1 1111 11 1    11 001 101   | MAR <- uROM; ADR+
  10000010 0100 c  = 0 1001 c0 1    00 010 100   | SRAM <- A+B+carry, latch CCs
  10000010 0101 *  = 1 1111 11 1    11 001 000   | OPCODE <- uROM;  ADR+

| cand(cx, y, z)
  10000011 0000 *  = 1 1111 11 1    11 001 010   | A   <- uROM; ADR+
  10000011 0001 *  = 1 1111 11 1    11 001 101   | MAR <- uROM; ADR+
  10000011 0010 *  = 0 1111 11 1    11 100 011   | B   <- SRAM
  10000011 0011 *  = 1 1111 11 1    11 001 101   | MAR <- uROM; ADR+
  10000011 0100 *  = 0 1011 11 1    00 010 100   | SRAM <- A&B, latch CCs
  10000011 0101 *  = 1 1111 11 1    11 001 000   | OPCODE <- uROM;  ADR+

|>>>>>>>>>>>><<<<<<<<<<<
|>>> UNUSED OPCODE  <<<  Opcode 10001000 is NOT currently used.
|>>>>>>>>>>>><<<<<<<<<<<                         ===

| rotl1(x, y) -- left rotate x 1 position.
  10001001 0000 *  = 1 1111 11 1    11 001 101   | MAR <- uROM; ADR+
  10001001 0001 *  = 0 1111 11 1    11 100 010   | A   <- SRAM
  10001001 0010 *  = 1 1111 11 1    00 001 101   | MAR <- uROM; ADR+; latch CCs

  10001001 0011 0  = 0 1100 10 1    00 010 100   | SRAM <- A+A+C; latch CCs
  10001001 0011 1  = 0 1100 00 1    00 010 100   | SRAM <- A+A+C; latch CCs

  10001001 0100 *  = 1 1111 11 1    11 001 000   | OPCODE <- uROM;  ADR+

| rotl2(x, y) -- left rotate x 2 positions.
  10001010 0000 *  = 1 1111 11 1    11 001 101   | MAR <- uROM; ADR+
  10001010 0001 *  = 0 1111 11 1    11 100 010   | A   <- SRAM
  10001010 0010 *  = 1 1111 11 1    00 001 101   | MAR <- uROM; ADR+; latch CCs

  10001010 0011 0  = 0 1100 10 1    00 010 010   | A    <- A+A+C; latch CCs
  10001010 0100 0  = 0 1100 10 1    00 010 100   | SRAM <- A+A+C; latch CCs

  10001010 0011 1  = 0 1100 00 1    00 010 010   | A    <- A+A+C; latch CCs
  10001010 0100 1  = 0 1100 00 1    00 010 100   | SRAM <- A+A+C; latch CCs

  10001010 0101 *  = 1 1111 11 1    11 001 000   | OPCODE <- uROM;  ADR+

| rotl3(x, y) -- left rotate x 3 positions.
  10001011 0000 *  = 1 1111 11 1    11 001 101   | MAR <- uROM; ADR+
  10001011 0001 *  = 0 1111 11 1    11 100 010   | A   <- SRAM
  10001011 0010 *  = 1 1111 11 1    00 001 101   | MAR <- uROM; ADR+; latch CCs
```

```
           10001011 0011 0  = 0 1100 10 1    00 010 010   | A    <- A+A+C; latch CCs
           10001011 0100 0  = 0 1100 10 1    00 010 010   | A    <- A+A+C; latch CCs
           10001011 0101 0  = 0 1100 10 1    00 010 100   | SRAM <- A+A+C; latch CCs

           10001011 0011 1  = 0 1100 00 1    00 010 010   | A    <- A+A+C; latch CCs
           10001011 0100 1  = 0 1100 00 1    00 010 010   | A    <- A+A+C; latch CCs
           10001011 0101 1  = 0 1100 00 1    00 010 100   | SRAM <- A+A+C; latch CCs

           10001011 0110 *  = 1 1111 11 1    11 001 000   | OPCODE <- uROM;  ADR+

  | rotl4(x, y) -- left rotate x 4 positions.
           10001100 0000 *  = 1 1111 11 1    11 001 101   | MAR <- uROM; ADR+
           10001100 0001 *  = 0 1111 11 1    11 100 010   | A    <- SRAM
           10001100 0010 *  = 1 1111 11 1    00 001 101   | MAR <- uROM; ADR+; latch CCs

           10001100 0011 0  = 0 1100 10 1    00 010 010   | A    <- A+A+C; latch CCs
           10001100 0100 0  = 0 1100 10 1    00 010 010   | A    <- A+A+C; latch CCs
           10001100 0101 0  = 0 1100 10 1    00 010 010   | A    <- A+A+C; latch CCs
           10001100 0110 0  = 0 1100 10 1    00 010 100   | SRAM <- A+A+C; latch CCs

           10001100 0011 1  = 0 1100 00 1    00 010 010   | A    <- A+A+C; latch CCs
           10001100 0100 1  = 0 1100 00 1    00 010 010   | A    <- A+A+C; latch CCs
           10001100 0101 1  = 0 1100 00 1    00 010 010   | A    <- A+A+C; latch CCs
           10001100 0110 1  = 0 1100 00 1    00 010 100   | SRAM <- A+A+C; latch CCs

           10001100 0111 *  = 1 1111 11 1    11 001 000   | OPCODE <- uROM;  ADR+

  | rotl5(x, y) -- left rotate x 5 positions.
           10001101 0000 *  = 1 1111 11 1    11 001 101   | MAR <- uROM; ADR+
           10001101 0001 *  = 0 1111 11 1    11 100 010   | A    <- SRAM
           10001101 0010 *  = 1 1111 11 1    00 001 101   | MAR <- uROM; ADR+; latch CCs

           10001101 0011 0  = 0 1100 10 1    00 010 010   | A    <- A+A+C; latch CCs
           10001101 0100 0  = 0 1100 10 1    00 010 010   | A    <- A+A+C; latch CCs
           10001101 0110 0  = 0 1100 10 1    00 010 010   | A    <- A+A+C; latch CCs
           10001101 0101 0  = 0 1100 10 1    00 010 010   | A    <- A+A+C; latch CCs
           10001101 0111 0  = 0 1100 10 1    00 010 100   | SRAM <- A+A+C; latch CCs

           10001101 0011 1  = 0 1100 00 1    00 010 010   | A    <- A+A+C; latch CCs
           10001101 0100 1  = 0 1100 00 1    00 010 010   | A    <- A+A+C; latch CCs
           10001101 0101 1  = 0 1100 00 1    00 010 010   | A    <- A+A+C; latch CCs
           10001101 0110 1  = 0 1100 00 1    00 010 010   | A    <- A+A+C; latch CCs
           10001101 0111 1  = 0 1100 00 1    00 010 100   | SRAM <- A+A+C; latch CCs

           10001101 1000 *  = 1 1111 11 1    11 001 000   | OPCODE <- uROM;  ADR+

  | rotl6(x, y) -- left rotate x 6 positions.
           10001110 0000 *  = 1 1111 11 1    11 001 101   | MAR <- uROM; ADR+
           10001110 0001 *  = 0 1111 11 1    11 100 010   | A    <- SRAM
           10001110 0010 *  = 1 1111 11 1    00 001 101   | MAR <- uROM; ADR+; latch CCs

           10001110 0011 0  = 0 1100 10 1    00 010 010   | A    <- A+A+C; latch CCs
           10001110 0100 0  = 0 1100 10 1    00 010 010   | A    <- A+A+C; latch CCs
           10001110 0101 0  = 0 1100 10 1    00 010 010   | A    <- A+A+C; latch CCs
           10001110 0110 0  = 0 1100 10 1    00 010 010   | A    <- A+A+C; latch CCs
           10001110 0111 0  = 0 1100 10 1    00 010 010   | A    <- A+A+C; latch CCs
           10001110 1000 0  = 0 1100 10 1    00 010 100   | SRAM <- A+A+C; latch CCs
```

```
        10001110 0011 1  = 0 1100 00 1   00 010 010  | A    <- A+A+C; latch CCs
        10001110 0100 1  = 0 1100 00 1   00 010 010  | A    <- A+A+C; latch CCs
        10001110 0101 1  = 0 1100 00 1   00 010 010  | A    <- A+A+C; latch CCs
        10001110 0110 1  = 0 1100 00 1   00 010 010  | A    <- A+A+C; latch CCs
        10001110 0111 1  = 0 1100 00 1   00 010 010  | A    <- A+A+C; latch CCs
        10001110 1000 1  = 0 1100 00 1   00 010 100  | SRAM <- A+A+C; latch CCs

        10001110 1001 *  = 1 1111 11 1   11 001 000  | OPCODE <- uROM;  ADR+

| rotl7(x, y) -- left rotate x 7 positions.
        10001111 0000 *  = 1 1111 11 1   11 001 101  | MAR <- uROM; ADR+
        10001111 0001 *  = 0 1111 11 1   11 100 010  | A    <- SRAM
        10001111 0010 *  = 1 1111 11 1   00 001 101  | MAR <- uROM; ADR+; latch CCs
| Following states shift in sign bit (remember, Cin is asserted low):
        10001111 0011 0  = 0 1100 10 1   00 010 010  | A    <- A+A+C; latch CCs
        10001111 0100 0  = 0 1100 10 1   00 010 010  | A    <- A+A+C; latch CCs
        10001111 0101 0  = 0 1100 10 1   00 010 010  | A    <- A+A+C; latch CCs
        10001111 0110 0  = 0 1100 10 1   00 010 010  | A    <- A+A+C; latch CCs
        10001111 0111 0  = 0 1100 10 1   00 010 010  | A    <- A+A+C; latch CCs
        10001111 1000 0  = 0 1100 10 1   00 010 010  | A    <- A+A+C; latch CCs
        10001111 1001 0  = 0 1100 10 1   00 010 100  | SRAM <- A+A+C; latch CCs

        10001111 0011 1  = 0 1100 00 1   00 010 010  | A    <- A+A+C; latch CCs
        10001111 0100 1  = 0 1100 00 1   00 010 010  | A    <- A+A+C; latch CCs
        10001111 0101 1  = 0 1100 00 1   00 010 010  | A    <- A+A+C; latch CCs
        10001111 0110 1  = 0 1100 00 1   00 010 010  | A    <- A+A+C; latch CCs
        10001111 0111 1  = 0 1100 00 1   00 010 010  | A    <- A+A+C; latch CCs
        10001111 1000 1  = 0 1100 00 1   00 010 010  | A    <- A+A+C; latch CCs
        10001111 1001 1  = 0 1100 00 1   00 010 100  | SRAM <- A+A+C; latch CCs

        10001111 1010 *  = 1 1111 11 1   11 001 000  | OPCODE <- uROM;  ADR+

|>>>>>>>>>>>><<<<<<<<<<
|>>> UNUSED OPCODES <<<  Opcodes 10001111 - 11111110 are NOT currently used.
|>>>>>>>>>>>><<<<<<<<<<                              ===

| bpt() --  a do-nothing opcode that has been put in to allow explicit
|    breakpoints in the simulator.
        11111111 0000 *  = 1 1111 11 1   11 001 000  | OPCODE <- uROM;  ADR+
```

## A2.5 Macro Definitions for Microinstructions

```
| Definitions of macros corresponding to ctlrom opcodes for MAYBE II.

| Reserved static RAM locations:

uSP     = 0xFF                    | Microstack pointer.
uRC     = 0xFE                    | Refresh counter.

_DEBUG  = 0xFD                    | Nonzero iff debugging under simulator.
_RESERV = 0xFC                    | Reserved for future uses.

| These SRAM locations are reserved for temporary use by microinstruction
|    macros:

T3      = 0xFB                    | 4 bytes; T0 is lowest address.
```

```
T2       = T3-1
T1       = T2-1
T0       = T1-1

SBASE    = T0-1                              | Base of microstack (builds down).

.macro WORD(x) x%256 x/256                   | Low-byte followed by high-byte.
.macro LONG(x) WORD(x) WORD(x >> 16)         | Low-word followed by high-word.


| Opcode 0 not used for now (reserved for an I/O hack opcode later).

.macro call(s)                  0x01 (.+4)%256 (.+3)/256 WORD(s)
.macro rtn()                    0x02
.macro push(x)                  0x03 x
.macro pop(x)                   0x04 x
.macro move(x,y)                0x05 x y
.macro cmove(cx,y)              0x06 cx y
.macro swt(x)                   0x07 x
.macro pdisp(x,p00,p01,p10,p11) 0x08 x WORD(p00) WORD(p01) WORD(p10) WORD(p11)
.macro pwrup()                  0x09
.macro add(x,y,z)               0x0A x y z
.macro cadd(cx,y,z)             0x0B cx y z
.macro jmp(adr)                 0x0C WORD(adr)
.macro imove(x,y)               0x0D x y
.macro movei(x,y)               0x0E x y


| Copy n-byte SRAM values:

.macro move2(x,y)    move(x,y)    move(x+1,y+1)
.macro move4(x,y)    move2(x,y)   move2(x+2,y+2)


.macro cmove2(cx,y) cmove((cx)%256,y) cmove((cx)/256,y+1)
.macro cmove4(cx,y) cmove2(cx,y)      cmove2(cx >> 16,y+2)

.macro l(adrlo,adrhi,x)         0x0F adrlo adrhi x
.macro s(x,adrlo,adrhi)         0x10 x adrlo adrhi
.macro refr()                   0x11

.macro jmi(x)                   0x12 WORD(x)
.macro jextra(x)                0x13 WORD(x)
.macro jready(x)                0x14 WORD(x)
.macro jp1(x)                   0x15 WORD(x)
.macro jodd(x)                  0x16 WORD(x)
.macro jnc(x)                   0x17 WORD(x)
.macro jp0(x)                   0x18 WORD(x)
.macro je(x)                    0x19 WORD(x)


| Opcodes 0x1A and 0x1B are not used.

.macro sub(x,y,z)               0x1C x y z
.macro cmp(x,y)                 0x1D x y


| Following macros demonstrate an alternative to composing countless
|   nanoinstructions. All could have been written as explicit nanocodes,
|   but at the cost of 1 opcode each and much effort in pounding out
|   the nanobits. Note, however, that each of these expands into
|   2 nanoinstruction calls. You have to pay for your laziness.

.macro ccmp(cx,y)      cmove(cx,T0)   cmp(T0,y)   | Constant compare.
```

```
.macro cor(cx,y,z)     cmove(cx,T0)    or(T0,y,z)   | Constant OR (inclusive).
.macro cxor(cx,y,z)    cmove(cx,T0)   xor(T0,y,z)   | Constant XOR.
.macro csub(x,cy,z)    cmove(cy,T0)    sub(x,T0,z)  | Constant subtract.
.macro csubcy(x,cy,z) cmove(cy,T0) subcy(x,T0,z)    | Constact sub w/borrow.


.macro jpl(a)                  0x1E WORD(a)
.macro jnextra(a)              0x1F WORD(a)      | Extra condition bit.
.macro jnready(a)              0x20 WORD(a)
.macro jnp1(a)                 0x21 WORD(a)
.macro jeven(a)                0x22 WORD(a)
.macro jc(a)                   0x23 WORD(a)
.macro jnp0(a)                 0x24 WORD(a)
.macro jne(a)                  0x25 WORD(a)
.macro urom(l,h,dst)           0x26 l h dst
.macro and(x,y,z)              0x27 x y z
.macro or(x,y,z)               0x28 x y z
.macro xor(x,y,z)              0x29 x y z
.macro not(x,y)                0x2A x y
.macro neg(x,y)                0x2B x y


| 16-bit operations. Operands use 2 consecutive SRAM locations.

.macro add2(x,y,z)             0x2C x y z x+1 y+1 z+1
.macro cadd2(cx,y,z)           0x2D cx%256 y z cx/256 y+1 z+1
.macro sub2(x,y,z)             0x2E x y z x+1 y+1 z+1
.macro cmp2(x,y)               0x2F x y   x+1 y+1


.macro ccmp2(cx,y) cmove2(cx,T0) cmp2(T0,y)


.macro count(x)                0x30 x
.macro cond(x)                 0x31 x


| Opcodes 0x32 & 0x33 are negcy & subcy(x,y,z) below (for no good reason).

| Opcodes 0x34 - 0x39 implement the I/O functions
|.macro iowrite(x)             0x34 x
|.macro ioread(x)              0x35 x
.macro iowrite(x)             writeio(x, 0)
.macro ioread(x)              readio(0, x)
.macro cwriteio(cx, r)        cmove(cx,T0) writeio(T0, r)
.macro readio(r, x)           0x34 r x
.macro ireadio(x, y)          0x35 x y
.macro writeio(x, r)          0x36 r x | NOTE ARG REVERSAL [see ctlrom]
.macro writeioi(x, y)         0x37 y x | NOTE ARG REVERSAL [see ctlrom]


| Opcodes 0x37 - 0x7F not used (for no good reason).

.macro dispatch(x,adr)         0x80 x adr/256 adr%256
.macro addcy(x,y,z)            0x81 x y z
.macro negcy(x, y)             0x32 x y
.macro subcy(x,y,z)            0x33 x y z
.macro caddcy(cx,y,z)          0x82 cx y z
.macro cand(cx,y,z)            0x83 cx y z


| Opcodes 0x84 - 0x88 not used (for no good reason).

.macro rotr7(x,y)              0x89 x y         | Right rotations.
.macro rotr6(x,y)              0x8A x y
.macro rotr5(x,y)              0x8B x y
```

```
.macro rotr4(x,y)              0x8C x y
.macro rotr3(x,y)              0x8D x y
.macro rotr2(x,y)              0x8E x y
.macro rotr1(x,y)              0x8F x y

.macro rotl7(x,y)              0x8F x y            | Left rotations.
.macro rotl6(x,y)              0x8E x y
.macro rotl5(x,y)              0x8D x y
.macro rotl4(x,y)              0x8C x y
.macro rotl3(x,y)              0x8B x y
.macro rotl2(x,y)              0x8A x y
.macro rotl1(x,y)              0x89 x y

| Following added for debugging under the simulator:

.macro bpt() 0xFF              | Breakpoint.
```

# A3 MAYBE Microcode Support for Interpreters

This appendix contains listings of MAYBE microcode common to the MAYBE implementations of the *S* and *G* machines.

## A3.1 Switch Console

```
| Simple switch-based "operator's console" for MAYBE.
|       Original code                             Fall 1984 SAW
|       PRIMITIVE I/O FUNCTIONS           [I/O]   Spring-1986 ~Ziggy
|       TERMINAL FUNCTION                 [TERM]   Fall---1986 ~JMM
|       terminal loop is power-up default          21-Feb-87 Kenmac
|       new interrupt structure                     28-Mar-87 Kenmac

| On entry: Flashes 11110000, 00001111 in lights; responds to P0, P1
|    to effect simple SRAM examine/deposit loop (same as function 1, below):

| P1:           Examine current SRAM location;
|                   when released, increment current address.
|                   Displays contents while P1 down, else address.
| P1, P0:       Deposit switches in current location.
|     P0:       Set current location from switches, display contents.
| P0, P1:       Dispatch on function code in data switches.

| Internally defined symbols:
| hhalt: Halt handler: returns to caller, flashing 11100111, 00011000 (cons).
| hii:   Illegal instruction handler: flashes 10000001,01111110.
| error: General error handler: flashes <R0>, 00000000.
| hbpt:  Breakpoint handler; simply returns (causes breakpoint in simulator).

| Externally defined symbols:
| MInit:    Machine (virtual S or G) Init, prepare for program execution.
| NextInst: Microsubroutine to execute a single virtual machine instr.

| Gross allocation of SRAM locations:
|      0-15:    Rn temporaries, used as microregisters
|     16-31:    Reserved for use by operator's console code (see below)
|     32-12?:   Reserved for use by machine emulators (S, G ucode, q.v.)
|  128?-SBASE:  Reserved for microstack.
| SBASE-255:    Reserved for microinstruction implementations
|                   (uSP, refresh counter, etc).

.include macros
```

```
R0      = 0                 | Temporaries, used throughout ucode.
R1      = 1
R2      = 2
R3      = 3
R4      = 4
R5      = 5
R6      = 6
R7      = 7


| Some SRAM locations used by console:

MInstCount = 16     | 4-byte count of virtual (S or G) machine instr execs.

sadr    = 20                | Current SRAM adr.
dadrlo  = 21                | Low  current DRAM adr.
dadrhi  = 22                | High current DRAM adr.
BREAK   = 23                | Flag location to tell when halt is encountered.


| Entry point, on power-up.
| This microcode starts at uROM address zero.


| Initialize MAYBE machine and jump to terminal loop

init:   pwrup()

        cmove(SBASE, uSP)      | Initialize micro SP.
        cmove(-1, sadr)        | Initial display in lights.
        cmove(0, _DEBUG)       | Not running under simulation (default).
        call(ioinit)           | Initialize I/O device.
        jmp(remote)            | Enter the I/O-interface remote loop.


|       TERMINAL FUNCTION                    [TERM]  Fall-1986 JMM
| added S- and G-machine I/O hooks                   14-Jan-1987 Kenmac


ioadr   = 24                | Current I/O register address [I/O].
sum     = 25                | Used to store checksum results.
count   = 26                | Used to keep track of bytes sent or received.
inchar  = 27                | Byte read from HP.
oldp0   = 28                | Old state of p0.
intp0   = 29                | Set on falling edge of p0; signals an interrupt.


| Commands used to communicate with the HP:

| 1. From the HP:

MAYBE_STOP      = 0x80      | Stop running program (from HP).
MAYBE_SYNC      = 1         | Echo a sync character.
MAYBE_ECHO      = 2         | Enter echo loop (debug tool).
MAYBE_WR_DRAM   = 3         | Write DRAM, given address, count, data cksum.
MAYBE_RD_DRAM   = 4         | Read DRAM, given address, count.
MAYBE_WR_SRAM   = 5         | Write SRAM, given address, count, data cksum.
MAYBE_RD_SRAM   = 6         | Read SRAM, given address, count.
MAYBE_INIT      = 7         | Initialize machine.
MAYBE_RUN       = 8         | Run program in dram.
MAYBE_SSTEP     = 9         | Single-step program in DRAM.

| 2. To the HP:

MAYBE_HALT      = 0x80      | Halt instruction executed.
```

```
MAYBE_BPT      = 0x81      | Breakpoint instruction executed.
MAYBE_II       = 0xFF      | Illegal instruction executed.
MAYBE_OVF      = 0x82      | HP overflowed input buffer.
MAYBE_ACK      = 0x83      | Acknowledge a character when running.
MAYBE_MODERR   = 0x84      | Bad G-machine general address mode.
MAYBE_ADRERR   = 0x85      | Bad call/jump effective address (G).


| Some constants defined for ease of reading:

BLINK   = 0x30        | Blink constant for light display.
ESC     = 27          | Definition of the constant ESC.


| Definitions of the I/O card internal registers:
RBR     = 0     | Receiver buffer register (read only).
THR     = 0     | Transmitter holding register (write only).
IER     = 1     | Interrupt enable register.
IIR     = 2     | Interrupt identification register (read only).
LCR     = 3     | Line control register.
MCR     = 4     | Modem control register.
LSR     = 5     | Line status register (read only).

ioinit: cwriteio(0b10000000, LCR)     | Set DLAB.
        cwriteio(12, 0)               | 9600 baudot (LSB).
        cwriteio( 0, 1)               |    "       (MSB).
        cwriteio(0b00000011, MCR)     | Set DTR and RTS.
        cwriteio(0b00000011, LCR)     | No parity; 1 stop bit; 8-bit words.
        rtn()


| Function 7: (pecho) primitive echo via LSR hand shake [PECHO].
| P0,P1: ABORT, dispatching on function in <switches>.

pecho: readio(LSR, R0)        | Read LSR.
       cand(0b01000001, R0, R0)| Mask off all but Xmitter Ready & Data Ready.
       ccmp(0b01000001, R0)   | Is Xmitter Empty (TEMT) & Data Ready (DR)?
       jne(pexit)             |    Nope: Check for exit
       ioread(R0)             |    Yup:  Read the byte
       iowrite(R0)            |             and echo back

pexit: pdisp(R0, pecho, pexit, pexit, fndsp) | Show read byte, loop or fndsp.

| Function 8: Terminal loop.
| Takes commmands from the Chipmonk and dispatches on them.
| Lights flash 10101010 01010101 to indicate terminal loop.
| Current commands are:

remote_table:
        WORD(remote)                  | Ignore this one.
        WORD(tsync)                   | Echo sync character.
        WORD(tpecho)                  | Debug echo loop.
        WORD(tlddram)                 | Write data to DRAM from HP.
        WORD(trddram)                 | Read data from DRAM to HP.
        WORD(tldsram)                 | Write data to SRAM from HP.
        WORD(trdsram)                 | Read data from SRAM to HP.
        WORD(tinit)                   | Initialize machine.
        WORD(texec)                   | Run program and return status.
        WORD(tsing)                   | Single-step and return status.

REMOTE_FUNCTIONS = 10
```

```
remote: cwriteio(1, IER)        | Interrupt on data available.
        cmove(1, R1)            | Light pattern for terminal mode.
        cmove(0, R2)            | Direction of blink.
        cmove(0, R3)            | Blink counters.
        cmove(BLINK / 8, R4)

termwt: pdisp(R1, term1, termwt, termwt, fndsp) | Exit if P0 and P1
term1:  count(R3)              | Decrement count.
        jne(term10)            | If zero, inc next byte.
        count(R4)              | Decrement high byte.
        jne(term10)            | If not one, continue.
        cmove(BLINK / 8, R4)   | Reinitialize blink count.

        count(R2)              | Test direction bit.
        jne(term105)           | Jump if heading right.
        cmove(0, R2)           | Keep heading left.
        rotl1(R1,R1)           | Move left one.
        jpl(term10)            | Continue, if not time to turn.
        cmove(42,R2)           | Turn right.
        jmp(term10)

term105: rotr1(R1,R1)          | Move right one.
        jeven(term10)          | Continue if not time to turn.
        cmove(0,R2)            | Turn left.

term10: jnready(termwt)        | No byte ready at I/O, return termwait.
        ioread(R0)             | Read a byte from uart and put it in R0.
        ccmp(0, R0)
        jpl(termwt)            | Hack, test for negative codes.
        ccmp(REMOTE_FUNCTIONS, R0)
        jmi(termwt)            | Ignore errors.
        dispatch(R0, remote_table)  | Dispatch to remote function.

| texec executes the program located in DRAM, then returns to
|   the terminal loop.

texec:  cmove(0, BREAK)        | Initialize BREAK flag.
        cmove(0, inchar)       | Flush input buffer.
        cmove(0, oldp0)        | p0 must be 0.
        cmove(0, intp0)        | Flush p0 interrupt.

texgo:  call(Mintest)          | Check for interrupts.
        ccmp(0, BREAK)         | Test for exit conditions.
        jne(texit)             | Quit, return code if nonzero.

        call(SStep)            | Execute an instruction.
        ccmp(0, BREAK)         | Break execution?
        je(texgo)              | Exec another instruction.

texit:  cwriteio(2, IER)       | Interrupt on TFULL.
texdun: pdisp(R0, texdunc, texdun, texdun, remote)
texdunc:jnready(texdun)        | Wait for xmit buffer empty.
        iowrite(BREAK)         | Return exit code.
        jmp(remote)            | Done.

| tsing executes a single program instruction stored in MAYBE DRAM.

tsing:  cmove(0x00, BREAK)     | Initialize BREAK flag.
        call(SStep)            | Execute one instruction,
```

```
        cwriteio(2, IER)        | Interrupt on TFULL.
tsing1: pdisp(R0, tsing2, tsing1, tsing1, remote)
tsing2: jnready(tsing1)         | Can we send result?
        iowrite(BREAK)          | Return result.
tsing3: pdisp(R0, tsing4, tsing3, tsing3, remote)
tsing4: jnready(tsing3)         | Ready to transmit?
        iowrite(PC)             | Send program counter low.
tsing5: pdisp(R0, tsing6, tsing5, tsing5, remote)
tsing6: jnready(tsing5)         | Ready to transmit?
        iowrite(PC+1)           | Send program counter high.
        jmp(remote)             | Return to terminal loop.


| tinit initializes the state of the MAYBE, preparing the machine for
| execution of a program.

tinit:  call(MInit)             | Initialize state of the MAYBE.
        cmove4(0, MInstCount)   | Clear the instruction execution count.
        jmp(remote)             | Return to terminal loop.


| tsync is used to let the HP know it is on the same wavelength as
| the MAYBE.  The HP sends a character, and the MAYBE is supposed
| to return the same character!

tsync:  pdisp(R0, tsync1, tsync, tsync, fndsp)
tsync1: readio(LSR, R0)         | Look at the status register.
        cand(0b01000001, R0, R0)| Strip all but data ready & transmit empty.
        ccmp(0b01000001, R0)    | Data ready & transmit empty?
        jne(tsync)              | Not ready yet, return to sync.
        ioread(R0)              | Got it!
        iowrite(R0)             | Now send it back and we are done here!
        jmp(remote)             | Return to terminal loop.


| Primitive echo loop test via LSR hand shake [PECHO].
| P0 and P1: ABORT, returning to terminal loop.
| Software abort occurs when two successive <CR>s are received.
|   R0    => data received and displayed in lights.
|   R1    => Status register.
|   BREAK => Exit flag.

tpecho: cmove(0b01101101, R0)   | Put a pattern in lights to know we're here.
tprloop:cmove(0, BREAK)         | Initialize done flag.
tploop: pdisp(R0, tploop1, tploop, tploop, remote)
                                | Show read byte, loop, or dun.
tploop1:readio(LSR, R1)         | Read LSR.
        cand(0b01000001, R1, R1)| Mask off all but Xmitter Ready & Data Ready.
        ccmp(0b01000001, R1)    | Is Xmitter Empty (TEMT) & Data Ready (DR)?
        jne(tploop)             |   Nope: Loop again.
        ioread(R0)              |   Yup:  Read the byte
        iowrite(R0)             |            and echo back.
        ccmp(13, R0)            | Is this the exit condition?
        jne(tprloop)            | Nope, keep going, but reset flag.
        ccmp(13, BREAK)         | Was last character a <CR>?
        je(remote)              | Yup, We're done with the echo test.
        cmove(13, BREAK)        | Nope, store the <CR> as a flag.
        jmp(tploop)             | Loop, but don't reset flag.


| tlddram will load the DRAM starting at DRAM address
| <addrlo> <addrhi> with <count> bytes of data.  <count> = 0
| implies count is 256.  A simple, one-byte, additive checksum is computed
```

```
| and returned to the sender when transfer is completed.
| Registers are defined as:
|   R0:     Byte sent to or received from the I/O board.
|   count:  Count of remaining bytes to receive.
|   dadrlo: <adrlo> in DRAM.
|   dadrhi: <adrhi> in DRAM.
|   sum:    Additive checksum for simple check.


tlddram:cwriteio(1, IER)       | Interrupt on data available.
        cmove(0, sum)          | Initialize checksum.
tldlo:  pdisp(R0, tldlo1, tldlo, tldlo, remote)
tldlo1: jnready(tlddram)       | No byte available, wait up.
        ioread(dadrlo)         | Put <adrlo> into dadrlo.
tldhi:  pdisp(dadrlo, tldhi1, tldhi, tldhi, remote)
tldhi1: jnready(tldhi)         | Waiting ...
        ioread(dadrhi)         | Put <adrhi> into dadrhi.
tldcnt: pdisp(dadrhi, tldcnt1, tldcnt, tldcnt, remote)
tldcnt1:jnready(tldcnt)        | Waiting ...
        ioread(count)          | Put <count> into count.
tldrc:  pdisp(dadrhi, tldrc1, tldrc, tldrc, remote)
tldrc1: jnready(tldrc)         | Waiting ...
        ioread(R0)             | Get a byte.
        add(R0, sum, sum)      | Simple checksum!
        s(R0, dadrlo, dadrhi)  | Store byte in DRAM.
        cadd2(1, dadrlo, dadrlo)| Increment <addrlo> and <addrhi>.
        count(count)           | Decrement count.
        ccmp(0, count)
        jne(tldrc1)            | Have we received correct number of bytes?
        cwriteio(2, IER)       | Interrupt on transmitter empty.
tldrcw: pdisp(count, tldrcw1, tldrcw, tldrcw, remote)
tldrcw1:jnready(tldrcw)        | Waiting ...
        iowrite(sum)           | Yep, send the checksum to sender.
        jmp(remote)            | And exit!

| trddram sends <count> data to the requester starting at <adrlo> <adrhi>.
| After it has finished, a simple, additive checksum is sent and the
| requester may do whatever with this information.
| Registers are defined as:
|   R0:     Byte sent to or received from the I/O board.
|   count:  Count of remaining bytes to send.
|   dadrlo: <adrlo> in DRAM.
|   dadrhi: <adrhi> in DRAM.
|   sum:    Additive checksum for simple check.

trddram:cmove(0, sum)          | Initialize checksum.
        cwriteio(1, IER)       | Interrupt on data ready.
trdlo:  pdisp(R0, trdlo1, trdlo, trdlo, remote)
trdlo1: jnready(trddram)       | No byte, wait up.
        ioread(dadrlo)         | Put <adrlo> into R2.
trdhi:  pdisp(R2, trdhi1, trdhi, trdhi, remote)
trdhi1: jnready(trdhi)         | Waiting ...
        ioread(dadrhi)         | Put <adrhi into dadrhi.
trdcnt: pdisp(dadrhi, trdcnt1, trdcnt, trdcnt, remote)
trdcnt1:jnready(trdcnt)        | Waiting ...
        ioread(count)          | Put <count> into count.
        cwriteio(2, IER)       | Interrupt on transmitter empty.
trdsd:  pdisp(dadrhi, trdsd1, trdsd, trdsd, remote)
trdsd1: jnready(trdsd)         | Waiting ...
        l(dadrlo, dadrhi, R0)  | Load byte from DRAM in R0.
```

```
        iowrite(R0)              | Send a byte.
        add(R0, sum, sum)        | Simple checksum!
        cadd2(1, dadrlo, dadrlo)| Increment <addrlo> and <addrhi>.
        count(count)             | Decrement count.
        ccmp(0, count)           | Equal to zero?
        jne(trdsd1)              | Have we sent enough bytes?
trdsdw: pdisp(count, trdsdw1, trdsdw, trdsdw, remote)
trdsdw1:jnready(trdsdw)          | Can we send the checksum?
        iowrite(sum)             | Yep, send the checksum to sender.
        jmp(remote)              | And exit!


| tldsram will load the SRAM starting at SRAM address <addr> with
| <count> bytes of data.  <count> = 0 implies count is 256.
| A simple, one-byte, additive checksum is computed and returned to
| the sender when transfer is completed.
| Registers are defined as:
|   R0:    Byte sent to or received from the I/O board.
|   count: Count of remaining bytes to receive.
|   sadr:  <adr> in SRAM.
|   sum:   Additive checksum for simple check.

tldsram:cwriteio(1, IER)         | Interrupt on data available.
        cmove(0, sum)            | Initialize checksum.
tlsadr: pdisp(R0, tlsadr1, tlsadr, tlsadr, remote)
tlsadr1:jnready(tldsram)         | No byte available, wait up.
        ioread(sadr)             | Put <adrlo> into dadrlo.
tlscnt: pdisp(sadr, tlscnt1, tlscnt, tlscnt, remote)
tlscnt1:jnready(tlscnt)          | Waiting ...
        ioread(count)            | Put <count> into count.
tlsrc:  pdisp(sadr, tlsrc1, tlsrc, tlsrc, remote)
tlsrc1: jnready(tlsrc)           | Waiting ...
        ioread(R0)               | Get a byte.
        add(R0, sum, sum)        | Simple checksum!
        movei(R0, sadr)          | Store byte in SRAM.
        cadd(1, sadr, sadr)      | Increment <addrlo> and <addrhi>.
        count(count)             | Decrement count.
        ccmp(0, count)           | Equal to zero?
        jne(tlsrc1)              | Have we received correct number of bytes?
        cwriteio(2, IER)         | Interrupt on transmitter empty.
tlsrcw: pdisp(count, tlsrcw1, tlsrcw, tlsrcw, remote)
tlsrcw1:jnready(tlsrcw)          | Waiting ...
        iowrite(sum)             | Yep, send the checksum to sender.
        jmp(remote)              | And exit!


| trdsram sends <count> data to the requester starting at <adr>.
| After it has finished, a simple, additive checksum is sent, and
| the requester may do whatever with this information.
| Registers are defined as:
|   R0:    Byte sent to or received from the I/O board.
|   count: Count of remaining bytes to send.
|   sadr:  <adr> in SRAM.
|   sum:   Additive checksum for simple check.

trdsram:cmove(0, sum)            | Initialize checksum.
        cwriteio(1, IER)         | Interrupt on data ready.
trsadr: pdisp(R0, trsadr1, trsadr, trsadr, remote)
trsadr1:jnready(trdsram)         | No byte, wait up.
        ioread(sadr)             | Store SRAM address.
trscnt: pdisp(sadr, trscnt1, trscnt, trscnt, remote)
```

```
trscnt1:jnready(trscnt)              | Waiting ...
        ioread(count)                | Put <count> into count.
        cwriteio(2, IER)             | Interrupt on transmitter empty.
trssd:  pdisp(dadrhi, trssd1, trssd, trssd, remote)
trssd1: jnready(trssd)               | Waiting ...
        imove(sadr, R0)              | Load byte from SRAM in R0.
        iowrite(R0)                  | Send a byte.
        add(R0, sum, sum)            | Simple checksum!
        cadd(1, sadr, sadr)          | Increment <sadr>.
        count(count)                 | Decrement count.
        ccmp(0, count)               | Equal to zero?
        jne(trssd1)                  | Have we sent enough bytes?
trssdw: pdisp(count, trssdw1, trssdw, trssdw, remote)
trssdw1:jnready(trssdw)              | Can we send the checksum?
        iowrite(sum)                 | Yep, send the checksum to sender.
        jmp(remote)                  | And exit!


| Function 9: I/O INIT
| ioinit intializes the I/O card to operate at the correct baud, etc.
| Note: Card is initialized on power up, so this is not required.


reinit: call(ioinit)
        jmp(console)


| General routine to send information to the HP. These
| assume that the HP is attached and capable of receiving;
| if it's not, the routine will hang (but may be switch-reset).
| iosend sends the character in R0 to the HP.
| ioack sends an acknowledgement to the HP.


ioack:  cmove(MAYBE_ACK, R0)         | Ack character (fall through to iosend).


iosend: cwriteio(2, IER)             | Interrupt on transmitter empty.
iosloop:pdisp(R0, ioscont, ioscont, ioscont, remote) | Does a refresh.
ioscont:jnready(iosloop)             | Waiting ...
        iowrite(R0)                  | Send the byte.
        rtn()


| Console loop functions. Can be entered by escaping from terminal loop.
| This is also what happens when P0, P1 sequence is entered from
| terminal loop.


| Function dispatch table, used on P0, P1 sequence.


contab: WORD(con0)                   | 00000000: Initialize DRAM, machine, then run.
        WORD(con1)                   | 00000001: SRAM examine/deposit loop.
        WORD(con2)                   | 00000010: DRAM examine/deposit loop.
        WORD(con3)                   | 00000011: Initialize DRAM, machine.
        WORD(con4)                   | 00000100: Initialize machine.
        WORD(con5)                   | 00000101: Single machine instruction step.
        WORD(con6)                   | 00000110: Run program.
        WORD(pecho)                  | 00000111: Primitive I/O echo test.
        WORD(remote)                 | 00001000: I/O remote-control driver [TERM].
        WORD(reinit)                 | 00001001: Init I/O             [INIT].
CONFNS  = 10                         | Total number of console functions defined.


| Here on P0, P1 sequence; dispatch on a function code in switches.


fndsp:  swt(R0)                      | Get function code from switches.
```

```
            ccmp(CONFNS, R0)         | Make sure it's in range...
            jmi(fnerr)               | Oops, operator blew it.


            pdisp(R0, fndsp1, fndsp, fndsp, fndsp)
    fndsp1: dispatch(R0, contab)     | The dispatch.


    fnerr:  cmove(0xCC, R0)          | Gritch about undefined function call.
            cmove(0x33, R1)          | (Make pretty flashing lights.)
            jmp(error1)

    | Main console function:
    | Flashes 11110000, 00001111 pattern, awaits buttons. When any button
    |   is pressed, dispatches to con1 (i.e., interprets buttons
    |   as in SRAM examine/deposit loop)

    console: cmove(0xF0, R0)         | 11110000, 00001111 light pattern.
             cmove(0x0F, R1)         | (Make pretty flashing lights.)
             jmp(error1)


    | Function 0: Initialize DRAM and machine, run to completion:
    con0:   call(DLoad)
            call(MInit)              | Initialize virtual (S or G) machine state.
            cmove4(0, MInstCount)    | Clear instruction execution count.
            jmp(Go)                  | Run program.

    | Function 1: (default function) -- SRAM examine/deposit.
    | ---    Display current SRAM address.
    | P1:    Examine current location; when released, increment current address.
    |        Displays contents while P1 down, else address.
    | P1,P0:Deposit switches in current location.
    | P0:    Set current location from switches, display contents.
    | P0, P1: Dispatch on function.

    | Here on no buttons pressed: Display <sadr> (current SRAM address),
    |   wait for a button:

    |                        ---     P1      P0      P1,P0
    con1:   pdisp(sadr,      con1,   con11,  con10,  fndsp)


    | Here when P1 pressed: Display <<sadr>>, await buttons:

    con11:  imove(sadr, R0)
    con11L: pdisp(R0,       con11X, con11L, con10,  con110)


    con11X: cadd(1, sadr, sadr)      | P1 released: step to next SRAM adr.
            jmp(con1)


    con110: swt(R0)                  | P1,P0 pressed: deposit <SWT> in <sadr>.
            movei(R0, sadr)

    | Wait until buttons released, then back to con1:
    con1X:  pdisp(R0,       con1,   con1X,  con1X,  con1X)

    | Here on P0 pressed: set sadr from <SWT>, display <sadr>, wait.
    con10:  swt(sadr)
            imove(sadr, R0)
    con10L: pdisp(R0,       con1,   con11,  con10L, fndsp)
```

```
| Function 2: DRAM examine loop; similar in form to SRAM loop.
| P1:    Examine current location; when released, increment current address.
|        Displays contents while P1 down, else LOW ORDER address.
| P1,P0:Deposit switches in current location.
| P0:    Returns to SRAM loop, with current SRAM adr set to point to 2-byte
|        current DRAM adr (making it convenient -- well, possible -- to
|        change the DRAM address).

|                            ---      P1       P0       P1,P0
con2:   pdisp(dadrlo,   con2,    con21,   con20,   fndsp)


con21:  l(dadrlo, dadrhi, R0)
con21L: pdisp(R0,       con21X, con21L,  con20,   con210)
con21X: cadd(  1, dadrlo, dadrlo)
        caddcy(0, dadrhi, dadrhi)
        jmp(con2)


con210: swt(R0)
        s(R0, dadrlo, dadrhi)


| Wait until buttons released, then back to con1:
con2X:  pdisp(R0,       con2,   con2X,   con2X,   con2X)


con20:  pdisp(R0,       con20Y, con20,   con20,   fndsp)
con20Y: cmove(dadrlo, sadr)
        jmp(con1)



| Function 3: Load DRAM from ROM, fall through to function 4:
con3:   call(DLoad)             | Initialize DRAM from uROM.


| Function 4: Initialize machine.
con4:   call(MInit)             | Initialize virtual (S or G) machine state.
        cmove4(0, MInstCount)   | Clear instruction execution count.
        jmp(console)            | Return to console.



| Function 5: Single-step machine program: calls NextInst to execute instr.
con5:   call(SStep)             | Execute single machine instruction,
        jmp(console)            |   then return to console.


| Function 6: Run program to completion ... a.k.a. GO.
| Also determines the correct BREAK returned and
| places the appropriate pattern for display in the lights.
| The usage of BREAK is as follows:
|       BREAK = 00000000        Initial value when executing.
|       BREAK = 10000000        HALT executed.
|       BREAK = 10000001        Breakpoint encountered.
|       BREAK = 11111111        Illegal instruction encountered.

Go:
con6:   cmove(0x00, BREAK)      | Clear BREAK FLAG.
con61:  call(SStep)
        ccmp(0x00, BREAK)       | BREAK Execution?
        je(con61)               | Nope, continue.
        ccmp(MAYBE_BPT, BREAK)  | Break for BPT?
        je(con61)               | Ignore Bpt().
        ccmp(MAYBE_HALT, BREAK) | Break for halt?
```

```
            jne(con62)              | Yup, display lights.
            cmove(0xE7, R0)         | Pattern for lights to say we're done.
            cmove(0x18, R1)         |
            jmp(error1)             | Flash away!
con62:      ccmp(MAYBE_II, BREAK)   | Illegal instruction? or bad halt code.
            cmove(0x81, R0)         | No jcond since we're through checking.
            cmove(0x7E, R1)         | Pattern for lights.
            jmp(error1)             | Flash away!
```

| Microsubroutine to execute a single machine instruction; calls
|   NextInst to do the work.
| Counts instructions executed in MInstCount (4-byte counter);
|   does some DRAM refresh before calling NextInst.

| Uses contents of reserved SRAM location _DEBUG to allow refresh and
|   simulator breakpoints to be disabled or enabled:
|   Bits of _DEBUG (SRAM location 11111101) have following effects:
|           Bit 0:       Disables refresh, for faster simulation.
|           Bit 1:       Causes breakpoint to be hit for every instruction.
| Normally <_DEBUG>=0, enabling DRAM refresh and disabling breakpoints.

```
SStep:   cand(1, _DEBUG, T1)     | Test bit 0 of _DEBUG...
         ccmp(0, T1)             |   Should we refresh?
         jne(SStep1)             | Nope, skip it.

         refr()                  | Refreshes 54 rows per machine instr;
         refr()                  | this assumes about 1 ms/instruction.
         refr()                  | Slower instrs must add refr() calls.
         refr()                  | Note: refr()s should preferably be
         refr()                  |   distributed in the code!
         refr()
         refr()
         refr()
         refr()


SStep1:  cand(2, _DEBUG, T1)     | Test bit 2 of _DEBUG...
         ccmp(0, T1)             |   Should we skip the breakpoint?
         je(SStep2)              | Yes, don't single step.

         bpt()                   | Breakpoint instruction, for simulator.

SStep2:  call(NextInst)          | Execute machine instruction.

         cadd2( 1, MInstCount,   MInstCount)| Count machine instructions.
         caddcy(0, MInstCount+2, MInstCount+2)
         caddcy(0, MInstCount+3, MInstCount+3)

         rtn()
```

| Microsubr: Initialize DRAM from uROM locations between IDRAM and EDRAM.

```
IDRAM    = 0x1C00               | Last 1K bytes of uROM are user program bits.
EDRAM    = 0x2000

DLoad:   cmove(IDRAM%256, R0)
         cmove(IDRAM/256, R1)
         cmove(0, R2)
```

```
                cmove(0, R3)
                cmove(EDRAM%256, R5)              | For end test.
                cmove(EDRAM/256, R6)

DLoad1:  call(DLoad2)                     | Fetch byte from uROM into R4.
         s(R4, R2, R3)
         cadd2(1, R2, R2)
         cadd2(1, R0, R0)
         refr()
         cmp(R0, R5)                      | LSB match end address?
         jne(DLoad1)
         cmp(R1, R6)                      | MSB match end address?
         jne(DLoad1)

         rtn()                            | Yup: done downloading.

DLoad2:  urom(R0, R1, R4)


| Error handler:
| jmp(error) with an error code in R0. Blinks error code in lights.
| To alternate between two patterns in lights, load R0 and R1, jmp(error1).
| Waits any button, then goes to con1 to interpret buttons.

| ERROR CODES:
| ===========
|       Pattern 1    Pattern 2     MEANING
|       ---------    ---------     -------
|       11110000     00001111      Top-level console loop prompt
|       11100111     00011000      Halt
|       11001100     00110011      Bad function call [See contab:]
|       10000001     01111110      Illegal machine instruction
|       10101010     01010101      Terminal mode
|
|       Additional error codes for G-machine ONLY ...
|
|       11111111     00000000      Bad general address mode
|
|       11000011     00111100      Bad CALL target effective address
|       11011011     00100100      Bad JUMP target effective address

error:   cmove(0, R1)           | The off-period light display.
error1:  cmove(BLINK, T1)       | Initialize blink counter.
errorx:  cmove(SBASE, uSP)      | Reinitialize micro SP.

         | For simulator: get <R0> in lights, hit breakpoint.
         pdisp(R0, errory, errory, errory, errory)
errory:  bpt()                  | Breakpoint for debugging.

| First: wait for switches to be released ...
|                         ---    P1     P0      P1,P0
erro1:   pdisp(R0,     erro2, erro1x, erro1x, erro1x)
erro1x:  call(err1)
         jmp(erro1)

| Switches released, wait for button.
erro2:   pdisp(R0,     erro2x, con1, con1, con1)
erro2x:  call(err1)
         jmp(erro2)
```

```
| Subroutine to flash lights between values in <R0> and <R1>.
| Uses T0, T1 as counters, T3 as a temporary.

err1:   refr()
        refr()
        count(T1)
        je(err11)
err12:  rtn()
err11:  count(T2)
        jne(err12)
        cmove(BLINK, T2)        | The blink period time constant.
        move(R0, T3)            | Swap R0, R1.
        move(R1, R0)
        move(T3, R1)
        rtn()


| Handler for HALT: Return BREAK = 10000000.

hhalt:  bpt()                   | Stop, if simulating.
        cmove(0x80, BREAK)      | Set BREAK FLAG.
        rtn()                   | Return, let caller figure out what to do!

| Handler for Illegal Instruction error: Return BREAK = 11111111.

hii:    bpt()                   | Stop, if simulating.
        cmove(0xFF, BREAK)      | Set BREAK = ERROR.
        rtn()                   | Return, let caller figure out what to do!

| Handler for BREAKPOINT: Return BREAK = 10000001.

hbpt:   bpt()
        cmove(0x81, BREAK)      | Set BREAK = HALT.
        rtn()                   | Return, let caller figure out what to do!

| Mintest is the common interrupt checking routine. It checks for any
| interrupts, and if an interrupt should occur (it is both being requested
| and its priority is higher than the processor's current priority),
| it calls the Mint routine (defined in s.uasm or g.uasm) with the address
| of the appropriate interrupt vector.

| Three interrupts are currently available. In order of priority:
|
| 1. Receive-interrupt, generated when a character is received.
| 2. PO-interrupt, generated when PO RELEASED.
| 3. Clock-interrupt, generated after a given number of instructions.

| Interrupt vector addresses (in DRAM, of course!).
| Interrupt vector contents depend on the machine (S or G).

SSVCVEC         = 0x100         | Supervisor call trap vector address.
RECIVEC         = 0x110         | Receive interrupt vector address.
POVEC           = 0x120         | PO interrupt vector address.
CLKVEC          = 0x130         | Clock interrupt vector address.

| Interrupt priorities (in SRAM location "Prty" in the PSW):

MAXPRI          = 0x7F          | The maximum possible priority.
RECIPRI         = 6            | Receive interrupt priority.
```

```
POPRI          = 4            | P0 interrupt priority.
CLKPRI         = 2            | Clock interrupt priority.

| SRAM space used by the interrupt handlers:

Minth          = 0xC0         | 2-byte temp to pass the vector address.
Mclkcount      = Minth + 2    | 4-byte counter, signals clk-int when < 0.

| Interrupt initialization: Clears all the flags. This is called
| by Minit in s.uasm or g.uasm.

Mintinit:
        cmove4(0, Mclkcount)    | Clear clock-interrupt counter.
        rtn()

| Mintest is called before each SStep to see if an interrupt
| condition has arisen and to do housekeeping with the I/O
| devices. If an interrupt condition is true, the interrupt has
| a handler, and interrupts are enabled, then Mint, defined
| by s.uasm or g.uasm, is called with the interrupt vector
| address in Minth.
|
| Mintest returns status in the BREAK flag. if BREAK is nonzero, the
| calling routine should exit.

Mintest: refr()                | For time spent in this loop.

| Check for any new data on the serial port. This is partly for
| information to the running program (the character is put into inchar)
| and partly for housekeeping, in case the interface has sent a
| STOP command.

        cwriteio(1, IER)             | Interrupt on Data Available.
        jnready(Mintest_no_new)      | New data ?
        ioread(R0)                   | Get the data.
        ccmp(MAYBE_STOP,R0)          | Test for exit command from HP.
        je(Mintest_exit)             | Exit if true.

| If a character HAS been read, check that inchar is empty. If not,
| then the interface program on the HP has screwed up. It is supposed
| to wait for each normal character to be individually acknowledged
| so that the interface can be kept clear for other purposes.

        ccmp(0, inchar)       | Test if character already read.
        jne(Mintest_bad)      | Bad exit if true.
        move(R0, inchar)      | Save the character and fall through.
Mintest_no_new:

| More housekeeping: Check the p0 switch and compare the value
| to oldp0. If the switch has just been released, the p0-interrupt
| may be called. This is signaled by setting intp0.

        jp0(Mintest_p0_set)
        ccmp(0, oldp0)        | Check if p0 was zero before.
        je(Mintest_skip_p0)   | Exit if it was and is zero.

        cmove(0, oldp0)       | Was 1, is 0: Reset oldp0...
        cmove(1, intp0)       | ... and signal a possible interrupt.
        jmp(Mintest_skip_p0)
```

```
Mintest_p0_set:
        ccmp(0, oldp0)          | Check if p0 was one before.
        jne(Mintest_skip_p0)    | Exit if it is was and is one.

        cmove(1, oldp0)         | Was 0, is 1: Set oldp0...
        cmove(0, intp0)         | ... and reset the interrupt, if any.

Mintest_skip_p0:

| At this point, the housekeeping is done.
| Now test to see if there is a character for the receive-interrupt.

        ccmp(0, inchar)         | Test if character exists.
        je(Mintest_no_recint)   | Skip if no data.
        ccmp(RECIPRI-1, Prty)   | Is interrupt pri <= processor pri?
        jmi(Mintest_no_recint)  | (Yes, then interrupt is disabled.)

        cmove2(RECIVEC, Minth)  | Pointer to receive-interrupt vector.
        jmp(Mintest_do_int)

| If there is no receive-interrupt, check for a P0 interrupt.

Mintest_no_recint:
        ccmp(0, intp0)          | Test if a p0 just released.
        je(Mintest_no_p0int)    | Skip if not.
        ccmp(P0PRI-1, Prty)     | Is interrupt pri <= processor pri?
        jmi(Mintest_no_p0int)   | (Yes, then interrupt is disabled.)

        cmove2(P0VEC, Minth)    | Pointer to P0-interrupt vector.
        cmove(0, intp0)         | Reset for next interrupt.
        jmp(Mintest_do_int)

| Finally, if the other two conditions don't exist, decrement the clock
| and, if it is zero, try a clock-interrupt.

Mintest_no_p0int:
        ccmp(0,Mclkcount+3)     | Is clock-count negative?
        jmi(Mintest_clkint)     | (Yes, request clock interrupt.)

        csub(Mclkcount, 1, Mclkcount)    | (No, decrement clock count.)
        csubcy(Mclkcount+1, 0, Mclkcount+1)
        csubcy(Mclkcount+2, 0, Mclkcount+2)
        csubcy(Mclkcount+3, 0, Mclkcount+3)

Mintest_rtn:                    | Come here when no intr work left.
        rtn()                   | Done; return.

Mintest_clkint:                 | Here to request a clock interrupt.
        ccmp(CLKPRI-1, Prty)    | Is interrupt pri <= processor pri?
        jmi(Mintest_rtn)        | (Yes, then interrupt is disabled.)

        cmove2(CLKVEC, Minth)   | Pointer to clock-interrupt vector.

| Here is where the call to Mint is made. After the call, the Mintest
| routine simply returns to the caller.

Mintest_do_int:
        jmp(Mint)               | Call Mint, let it rtn to our caller.
```

```
        | Tell the caller to exit. This is jumped to if a STOP code is
        | received by the serial card.

Mintest_exit:
        cmove(MAYBE_STOP, BREAK) | Signal exit.
        rtn()

        | Tell the caller to exit with bad status. This is jumped to
        | if the serial buffer is overrun.

Mintest_bad:
        cmove(MAYBE_OVF, BREAK) | Signal overrun.
        rtn()
```

## A3.2 Microsubroutines

```
        | Some utility subroutines for emulation of 32-bit machines on MAYBE.

        | Naming convention:
        | get@:         Fetch DRAM<R0,1> into SRAM<R2>; extend to 4 bytes.
        | put@:         Store SRAM<R2> into DRAM<R0,1>.
        | push@:        Push datum from <R2> on main stack.
        | pop@:         Pop datum from main stack into <R2>.
        | fetch@:       Fetch @-byte datum from instr stream into <R2>.
        | imovei@:      Copy @-byte longword in SRAM: <R1> <- <<R0>>.

        | shift:        4-byte shifter, Op1=data, Op2=kount, Op3=sign adjust.
        | multiply:     4x4->8-byte: multiplicand * multiplier = product.
        | divide:       4-byte: dividend / divisor = quotient (and remainder).

        | Handy macros to access above utilities:

.macro  PUSH1(x)        · cmove(x, R2)     call(push1)
.macro  PUSH2(x)          cmove(x, R2)     call(push2)
.macro  PUSH4(x)          cmove(x, R2)     call(push4)

.macro  POP1(x)           cmove(x, R2)     call(pop1)
.macro  POP2(x)           cmove(x, R2)     call(pop2)
.macro  POP4(x)           cmove(x, R2)     call(pop4)

.macro  FETCH1(x)         cmove(x, R2)     call(fetch1)
.macro  FETCH2(x)         cmove(x, R2)     call(fetch2)
.macro  FETCH4(x)         cmove(x, R2)     call(fetch4)

        | Get an @-byte operand from main memory.
        |   Copies operand from main memory location given by R0,1 and
        |   copies to SRAM location whose address is <R2>.
        | Sign-extends operand to 4 bytes.
        | Increments <R2> by 4, <R0,1> by length.

get1:   push(R4) push(R3)      | Save registers for temporary use.
        call(getdatum)
        | Now set R4 for sign extension and sign-extend 3 bytes ...
getx1:  cadd(0, R4, R4)        | Check sign of byte (set ALU flags).
        cmove(0, R4)           | Extend with zeros
        jpl(extend3)           |     iff positive.
```

```
                cmove(-1, R4)              | Else extend with ones.
                jmp(extend3)

get2:    push(R4) push(R3)          | Save registers for temporary use.
                call(getdatum)
                call(getdatum)
                | Set R4 for sign extension and sign-extend 2 bytes ...
getx2:   cadd(0, R4, R4)            | Check sign of byte (set ALU flags).
                cmove(0, R4)               | Extend with zeros
                jpl(extend2)               |    iff positive.
                cmove(-1, R4)              | Else extend with ones.
                jmp(extend2)               | Use common code.

get4:    push(R4) push(R3)          | Save registers for temporary use.
                call(getdatum)
                call(getdatum)
                call(getdatum)
                call(getdatum)
                pop(R3) pop(R4)            | Restore registers.
                rtn()


| Microsubroutine used to copy and update 1 byte's worth of data.
getdatum: l(R0, R1, R4)            | Get data byte.
                movei(R4, R2)              | Store it away.
                cadd(1, R2, R2)            | Update <R2>.
                cadd2(1, R0, R0)           | Update <R0,1>.
                rtn()


| Microsubroutine for sign-extending 2 or 3 bytes using R4.
extend3: movei(R4, R2)             | Extend to high-order bytes.
                cadd(1, R2, R2)
extend2: movei(R4, R2)
                cadd(1, R2, R2)
                movei(R4, R2)
                cadd(1, R2, R2)
                pop(R3) pop(R4)            | Restore registers.
                rtn()


| Put an @-byte operand into main memory.
|   Copies operand into main-memory location given by R0,1;
|   copies from SRAM location whose address is <R2>.
| Increments <R2>, <R0,1> by length.

put1:    push(R4) push(R3)          | Save registers for temporary use.
                call(putdatum)
                pop(R3)  pop(R4)           | Restore registers.
                rtn()

put2:    push(R4) push(R3)          | Save registers for temporary use.
                call(putdatum)
                call(putdatum)
                pop(R3)  pop(R4)           | Restore registers.
                rtn()

put4:    push(R4) push(R3)          | Save registers for temporary use.
                call(putdatum)
                call(putdatum)
                call(putdatum)
                call(putdatum)
```

```
        pop(R3)  pop(R4)              | Restore registers.
        rtn()

| Microsubroutine used by above to store a 1 byte's worth of data.
putdatum: imove(R2, R4)              | get data byte.
        s(R4, R0, R1)                | store it away.
        cadd(1, R2, R2)              | update <R2>
        cadd2(1, R0, R0)             | update <R0,1>
        rtn()

| Microsubroutines to push and pop operands.
| Push value onto machine stack; value is fetched from consecutive SRAM
|   locations starting with the SRAM address contained in R2.
| DESTROYS R0, R1, R2.

push1:  move2(SP, R0)                | DRAM address to write.
        call(put1)
        move2(R0, SP)                | Replace SP with incremented version.
        rtn()

push2:  move2(SP, R0)                | DRAM address to write.
        call(put2)
        move2(R0, SP)                | Replace SP with incremented version.
        rtn()

push4:  move2(SP, R0)                | DRAM address to write.
        call(put4)
        move2(R0, SP)                | Replace SP with incremented version.
        rtn()

| Similar; pops operand into consecutive SRAM locations beginning at <R0>.
| DESTROYS R0, R1, R2.

pop1:   cmove(1, R0)                 | Put length in bytes into R1, R0.
        cmove(0, R1)                 | Subtract length in bytes from SP.
        sub2(SP, R0, SP)
        move2(SP, R0)                | DRAM address to read.
        jmp(get1)                    | Read into <R2>, sign-extend.

pop2:   cmove(2, R0)                 | Put length in bytes into R1, R0.
        cmove(0, R1)                 | Subtract length in bytes from SP.
        sub2(SP, R0, SP)
        move2(SP, R0)                | DRAM address to read.
        jmp(get2)                    | Read into <R2>, sign-extend.

pop4:   cmove(4, R0)                 | Put length in bytes into R1, R0.
        cmove(0, R1)                 | Subtract length in bytes from SP.
        sub2(SP, R0, SP)
        move2(SP, R0)                | DRAM address to read.
        jmp(get4)                    | Read into <R2>, sign-extend.

| Fetch an @-byte constant from instruction stream, updating <PC>.
|   Stores into SRAM <R2>, sign-extending to 4 bytes.
| DESTROYS R0, R1, R2.

fetch1: move2(PC, R0)                | Fetch constant from instr stream.
        call(get1)                   | (Sign-extends.)
        move2(R0, PC)                | Update PC to reflect fetch.
        rtn()
```

```
fetch2: move2(PC, R0)              | Fetch constant from instr stream.
        call(get2)                 | (Sign-extends.)
        move2(R0, PC)              | Update PC to reflect fetch.
        rtn()

fetch4: move2(PC, R0)              | Fetch constant from instr stream.
        call(get4)                 | (Sign-extends.)
        move2(R0, PC)              | Update PC to reflect fetch.
        rtn()

| Indirect @-byte SRAM copy:
|   Copy @-byte word from SRAM locations beginning at address <R0> to
|    SRAM locations beginning at address <R1>.
|   Increments <R0>, <R1> by @-1.

imovei1: push(R2)                  | Used as a temporary.
         call(fetchnstore)
         pop(R2)                   | Restore temporary register.
         rtn()

imovei2: push(R2)                  | Used as a temporary.
         call(fetchnstore)
         call(fetchnstore)
         pop(R2)                   | Restore temporary register.
         rtn()

imovei4: push(R2)                  | Used as a temporary.
         call(fetchnstore)
         call(fetchnstore)
         call(fetchnstore)
         call(fetchnstore)
         pop(R2)                   | Restore temporary register.
         rtn()

fetchnstore: imove(R0, R2)         | Fetch 1 byte's worth of data.
         movei(R2, R1)             | Store it away.
         cadd(1, R0, R0)           | Increment source address.
         cadd(1, R1, R1)           | Increment destination address.
         rtn()

| Shift operations:
| rshift is used by shifts, multiplies, and divides;
| shift does both sash@, slsh@.

| rshift shifts Op1 one position right, inserting a 0 at bit 31.

rshift:
         refr()
         rotr1(Op1, Op1)           | Rotate low byte.
         cand(0x7F, Op1, Op1)      | Clear top bit.
         cadd(0, Op1+1, Op1+1)     | Test second byte.
         jeven(rshiftskip1)        | Skip if no carry.
         cor(0x80, Op1, Op1)       | Set top bit if carry.
rshiftskip1:
         rotr1(Op1+1, Op1+1)       | Rotate second byte.
         cand(0x7F, Op1+1, Op1+1)
         cadd(0, Op1+2, Op1+2)
         jeven(rshiftskip2)
```

```
              cor(0x80, Op1+1, Op1+1)
rshiftskip2:
              rotr1(Op1+2, Op1+2)      | Rotate third byte.
              cand(0x7F, Op1+2, Op1+2)
              cadd(0, Op1+3, Op1+3)
              jeven(rshiftskip3)
              cor(0x80, Op1+2, Op1+2)
rshiftskip3:
              rotr1(Op1+3, Op1+3)      | Rotate top byte.
              cand(0x7F, Op1+3, Op1+3) | Zero top bit.
              refr()
              rtn()                    | Result in Op1.

| shift shifts Op1 left or right by the amount
| specified by Op2. The result is put back
| on the stack. Shifts left for positive numbers, right for
| negative. The lowest byte of Op3 is ANDed to the top byte
| of the data after each right shift. This is intended to allow
| sign correction so that the shifter can
| function as either an arithmetic or a logical shifter.
| Note the insertion of refr() instructions in shift and
| rshift above; this IS a loop and may take a long time.

shift:  cadd(0, Op2, Op2)        | Test amount.
        jmi(shiftnegloop)        | Go to second half if negative.

shiftposloop:
        csub(Op2, 1, Op2)        | Decrement count.
        jmi(shiftexit)           | Quit if done shifting.
        refr()                   | Maintain DRAM.
        add2(Op1, Op1, Op1)      | Shift left.
        addcy(Op1+2, Op1+2, Op1+2)
        addcy(Op1+3, Op1+3, Op1+3)
        jmp(shiftposloop)        | Continue looping.

shiftnegloop:
        call(rshift)             | Shift right (does refr).
        or(Op3, Op1+3, Op1+3)    | Adjust for arith/log shift.
        cadd(1, Op2, Op2)        | Increment (negative) count.
        jmi(shiftnegloop)        | Continue if not done.

shiftexit:
        rtn()

| Multiplication and division using a shifting algorithm.
| mult performs a 4-byte multiplication, returning an 8-byte
| result. Calling routines decide which parts to load.
| Similarly div performs a 4-byte divide, returning a 4-byte
| quotient and a 4-byte remainder. Extra refr() calls are
| made to account for the loop nature of the algorithm.

| These symbols are defined for interface to calling routines.

multiplier = Op1             | 4-byte
multiplicand = Op2           | 4-byte (8-byte internal)
product = Op4                | 8-byte result

divisor = multiplier         | 4-byte
dividend = multiplicand      | 4-byte (8-byte internal)
```

```
        quotient = product            | 4-byte result
        remainder = multiplicand + 4  | 4-byte result

        kount   = Op6                 | (1-byte internal)
        thesign = Op6+1               | (1-byte internal)
        remsign = Op6+2               | (1-byte-internal)


        | Sign-handling is done by determining the sign from the original
        | numbers (XOR of signs), then stripping the sign from the numbers
        | before multiplying or dividing. The correct sign is reapplied
        | before returning. Sign of the remainder in division is determined
        | solely by the sign of the dividend.


        | savesigns determines thesign of the result and strips
        | signs from the multiplier/divisor and multiplicand/dividend.

savesigns:
        cand(0x80, Op1+3, thesign)    | Sign of 1st number.
        jpl(savesignskip1)            | No negate if positive.
        not(Op1, Op1)                 | Make 1st positive.
        not(Op1+1, Op1+1)
        not(Op1+2, Op1+2)
        not(Op1+3, Op1+3)
        cadd2(1, Op1, Op1)
        caddcy(0, Op1+2, Op1+2)
        caddcy(0, Op1+3, Op1+3)
savesignskip1:
        cand(0x80, Op2+3, R0)         | Sign of 2nd number.
        jpl(savesignskip2)
        not(Op2, Op2)                 | Make 2nd positive.
        not(Op2+1, Op2+1)
        not(Op2+2, Op2+2)
        not(Op2+3, Op2+3)
        cadd2(1, Op2, Op2)
        caddcy(0, Op2+2, Op2+2)
        caddcy(0, Op2+3, Op2+3)
savesignskip2:
        xor(R0, thesign, thesign)     | Produce the result sign.
        refr()                        | Long instruction.
        rtn()


        | restoresigns uses thesign to decide whether or not to negate the
        | product/quotient and then, if yes, does so.

restoresigns:
        cadd(0, thesign, thesign)     | Test thesign.
        jpl(restoresignexit)          | Quit if positive.
        not(Op4, Op4)                 | 8-byte negate.
        not(Op4+1, Op4+1)
        not(Op4+2, Op4+2)
        not(Op4+3, Op4+3)
        not(Op4+4, Op4+4)
        not(Op4+5, Op4+5)
        not(Op4+6, Op4+6)
        not(Op4+7, Op4+7)
        cadd2(1, Op4, Op4)
        caddcy(0, Op4+2, Op4+2)
        caddcy(0, Op4+3, Op4+3)
        caddcy(0, Op4+4, Op4+4)
```

```
                    caddcy(0, Op4+5, Op4+5)
                    caddcy(0, Op4+6, Op4+6)
                    caddcy(0, Op4+7, Op4+7)
                    refr()
restoresignexit:
                    rtn()


| shiftcand is an 8-byte left-shift operations used by the multiply
| and divide routines to shift the multiplicand/dividend.

shiftcand:
                    add2(Op2, Op2, Op2)                 | Left-shift = doubling.
                    addcy(Op2+2, Op2+2, Op2+2)
                    addcy(Op2+3, Op2+3, Op2+3)
                    addcy(Op2+4, Op2+4, Op2+4)
                    addcy(Op2+5, Op2+5, Op2+5)
                    addcy(Op2+6, Op2+6, Op2+6)
                    addcy(Op2+7, Op2+7, Op2+7)
                    refr()
                    rtn()


| mult is the generic, 4x4 -> 8-byte multiply. It uses the fact that
| a multiplication of a 32-bit multiplicand by a 32-bit multiplier
| can be expanded to 32 additions (one for each bit in the
| multiplier) of the multiplicand, suitably shifted according to
| the position of the multiplier bit being tested.
|
| a four-bit example:
|
| 9 * 5 ->        1001 *      0101          (1001 is the multiplier)
|
| expanded:          1 *      0101  -> 00000101
|              +    0  *      0101  -> 00000000
|              +    0  *      0101  -> 00000000
|              +    1  *      0101  -> 00101000
|                                     ----------
|                                     00101101   (32+8+4+1 = 45)
|
| On each pass through the loop, the lowest bit of the multiplier
| is tested to check whether to add the multiplicand onto the accumulator.
| Then the multiplier is shifted right one position and the
| multiplicand (8-byte internally) is shifted left one position.

mult:     call(savesigns)          | Strip signs.

          cmove4(0, Op4)           | Clear accumulator . . .
          cmove4(0, Op4+4)         |   all 8-bytes of it.
          cmove4(0, Op2+4)         | Clear upper part of 'cand.

          cmove(32, kount)         | Set up counter.

          ccmp(0, Op1+3)           | Test top byte of multiplier.
          jne(multloop)            | Directly to loop if not 0.
          cmove(24, kount)         | Reduce count if 0.
          ccmp(0, Op1+2)           | Test next byte of multiplier.
          jne(multloop)            | Directly to loop if not 0.
          cmove(16, kount)         | Reduce count if 0.
          ccmp(0, Op1+1)           | Test next byte of multiplier.
          jne(multloop)            | Go to loop if > 255.
```

*MAYBE Microcode Support for Interpreters*

```
            cmove(8, kount)        | Reduce count if 0.

    multloop:
            refr()
            csub(kount, 1, kount)  | Decrement count.
            jmi(multexit)          | Quit if done.

            cadd(0, multiplier, multiplier) | Test lowest bit.
            jeven(multskip)                 | No addition if not set.
            add2(Op2, Op4, Op4)             | Simple addition.
            addcy(Op2+2, Op4+2, Op4+2)
            addcy(Op2+3, Op4+3, Op4+3)
            addcy(Op2+4, Op4+4, Op4+4)
            addcy(Op2+5, Op4+5, Op4+5)
            addcy(Op2+6, Op4+6, Op4+6)
            addcy(Op2+7, Op4+7, Op4+7)
    multskip:
            call(rshift)           | Shift multiplier one right.
            call(shiftcand)        | Shift multiplicand one left.
            jmp(multloop)          | Continue looping.

    multexit:
            call(restoresigns)     | Reattach sign to product.
            rtn()                  | 8-byte result in product.


| divide is the generic, 4x4 -> 4,4-byte divide producing both a
| quotient and a remainder. It implements the binary version of
| long division. As the 'decimal point' is moved right one position
| (effectively a left-shift), an attempt is made to subtract the
| divisor from the dividend/remainder. If the subtract is
| 'successful,' leaving a positive result, then the dividend/remainder
| is updated with this result, and a 1 is put into the quotient
| for this position. If the subtract goes negative, then the
| dividend/remainder is left unchanged, and a 0 is put into the
| quotient for the position.
|
| A 4-bit example:
|
| 13 / 5 -> 1101 / 0101
|
|
|            ----------
|      0101 ) 0001101  (start shifted by one)
|             0101                subtract fails,   -> 0
|             0011010  (shifted original)
|             0101                subtract fails,   -> 0
|             0110100  (shifted original)
|             0101                subtract works,   -> 1
|             0011000  (subtract, then shift)
|             0101                subtract fails,   -> 0
|             0011     <- this is the remainder
|
| So the quotient is 0010 = 2 and the remainder is 0011 = 3, as expected.
|
| divide plays the same games with the sign as multiply, stripping
| it before dividing, then restoring sign to the result. The sign
| of the remainder is always the same as the sign of the dividend.

divide: cand(0x80, dividend+3, remsign) | Store remainder sign.
        call(savesigns)        | Save and strip signs.
```

```
        cmove4(0, Op4)          | Clear quotient.
        cmove4(0, Op3)          | Clear remainder.

        cmove(32, kount)        | Set up counter.

divideloop:
        refr()
        csub(kount, 1, kount)   | Decrment counter.
        jmi(dividexit)          | Quit if done.

        call(shiftcand)         | Shift dividend up one.
        add(Op4, Op4, Op4)      | Shift quotient up one.
        addcy(Op4+1, Op4+1, Op4+1)
        addcy(Op4+2, Op4+2, Op4+2)
        addcy(Op4+3, Op4+3, Op4+3)       | (Lowest bit is a zero.)

        refr()
        sub(Op3, Op1, Op5)      | Attempt subtract
        subcy(Op3+1, Op1+1, Op5+1) | of divisor from remainder
        subcy(Op3+2, Op1+2, Op5+2) | (result to temporary storage).
        subcy(Op3+3, Op1+3, Op5+3)
        jmi(divideloop)          | If negative, continue shifting.

        cor(1, Op4, Op4)         | If positive, add a one to the quotient
        move4(Op5, Op3)          |   and reduce the remainder.
        jmp(divideloop)          | Continue looping.

dividexit:
        call(restoresigns)       | Reattach sign to quotient.
        cadd(0, remsign, remsign) | Test for remainder sign.
        jpl(dividedone)          | No negation if positive.

        refr()
        not(Op3, Op3)            | Negate remainder if
        not(Op3+1, Op3+1)        |   dividend was negative.
        not(Op3+2, Op3+2)
        not(Op3+3, Op3+3)
        cadd2(1, Op3, Op3)
        caddcy(0, Op3+2, Op3+2)
        caddcy(0, Op3+3, Op3+3)

dividedone:
        rtn()
```

# A4    *S* **Machine**
# **Summary**

This appendix begins with a section giving a complete description of the *S* machine instruction set (including some instructions not discussed elsewhere in the text) for convenient reference. Subsequent sections reproduce the *S* machine's machine-language definition file, an example of an *S*-machine program, and a complete listing of the MAYBE microcode that implements the *S* machine. These items are included for reference and for use with the MAYBE software tools.

## A4.1 Instruction-Set Details

Tables A4.1–A4.6 give a complete summary of the *S*-machine instruction set as implemented on the MAYBE machine.

**Table A4.1**  *S*-machine operators.

| Instruction | Stack before $\rightarrow$ after | Operation |
|---|---|---|
| sadd$\alpha$ | $a^{\alpha},\ b^{\alpha} \rightarrow (a+b)^{\alpha}$ | 2's complement add |
| ssub$\alpha$ | $a^{\alpha},\ b^{\alpha} \rightarrow (a-b)^{\alpha}$ | 2's complement subtract |
| smult$\alpha$ | $a^{\alpha},\ b^{\alpha} \rightarrow (a \cdot b)^{\alpha}$ | 2's complement multiply |
| sdiv$\alpha$ | $a^{\alpha},\ b^{\alpha} \rightarrow (a \div b)^{\alpha}$ | 2's complement divide |
| srem$\alpha$ | $a^{\alpha},\ b^{\alpha} \rightarrow (a \bmod b)^{\alpha}$ | 2's complement remainder |
| sand$\alpha$ | $a^{\alpha},\ b^{\alpha} \rightarrow (a\ \mathrm{AND}\ b)^{\alpha}$ | Bitwise logical AND |
| sash$\alpha$ | $a^{\alpha},\ s^{1} \rightarrow (a \cdot 2^{s})^{\alpha}$ | Arithmetic left (right) shift $s$ $(-s)$ places |
| sneg$\alpha$ | $a^{\alpha} \rightarrow (-a)^{\alpha}$ | 2's complement negation |
| ssext$\alpha$ | $a^{\alpha} \rightarrow a^{2\alpha}$ | Sign-extend |
| slow$\alpha$ | $a^{2\alpha} \rightarrow a^{\alpha}$ | Keep only least significant $\alpha$ bytes |
| shalt | $\cdots \rightarrow \cdots$ | Stop the machine |
| semult$\alpha$ | $a^{\alpha},\ b^{\alpha} \rightarrow (a \cdot b)^{2\alpha}$ | 2's complement extended precision multiply |
| sediv$\alpha$ | $a^{\alpha},\ b^{\alpha} \rightarrow$ $(a \div b)^{\alpha}, (a \bmod b)^{\alpha}$ | 2's complement extended divide |
| sor$\alpha$ | $a^{\alpha},\ b^{\alpha} \rightarrow (a\ \mathrm{OR}\ b)^{\alpha}$ | Bitwise logical OR |
| sxor$\alpha$ | $a^{\alpha},\ b^{\alpha} \rightarrow (a\ \mathrm{XOR}\ b)^{\alpha}$ | Bitwise logical XOR |
| slsh$\alpha$ | $a^{\alpha},\ s^{1} \rightarrow (a \cdot 2^{s})^{\alpha}$ | Logical left (right) shift $s$ $(-s)$ places |
| szext$\alpha$ | $a^{\alpha} \rightarrow a^{2\alpha}$ | Extend with zeros |
| shigh$\alpha$ | $a^{2\alpha} \rightarrow a^{\alpha}$ | Keep only most significant $\alpha$ bytes |

**Table A4.2**  Jump and test instructions.

| Instruction | Stack before $\rightarrow$after | Operation |
|---|---|---|
| scmp$\alpha$ | $a^{\alpha}$, $b^{\alpha}\rightarrow cc^{1}$ | Arithmetic compare |
| stest$\alpha$ | $a^{\alpha}$ $\rightarrow cc^{1}$ | Compare to zero |
| sdup$\alpha$ | $a^{\alpha}$ $\rightarrow a^{\alpha}, a^{\alpha}$ | Duplicate the datum at the top of the stack |
| sjmp | $a^{4}$ $\rightarrow$ | Jump unconditionally:<br>$\text{SP} \leftarrow \langle\text{SP}\rangle - 4$ ; $\text{PC}^{4} \leftarrow \langle\langle\text{SP}\rangle^{4}\rangle$ |
| sj$cond$ | $cc^{1}, a^{4}\rightarrow$ | Jump on condition:<br>$\text{SP} \leftarrow \langle\text{SP}\rangle - 4$ ; $temp^{4} \leftarrow \langle\langle\text{SP}\rangle^{4}\rangle$<br>$\text{SP} \leftarrow \langle\text{SP}\rangle - 1$ ; $cctemp^{1} \leftarrow \langle\langle\text{SP}\rangle^{4}\rangle$<br>if $cond$ matches $\langle cctemp\rangle^{1}$, then $\text{PC} \leftarrow \langle temp\rangle^{4}$ |

**Table A4.3**  Machine-language branch conditions.

| Mnemonic | Branches on | Description |
|---|---|---|
| ne | $\overline{Z}$ | Not equal (to zero) test |
| e | $Z$ | Equal |
| ge | $\overline{S}$ | Signed $\geq$ |
| lt | $S$ | Signed $<$ |
| gt | $\overline{Z \text{ OR } S}$ | Signed $>$ |
| le | $Z \text{ OR } S$ | Signed $\leq$ |
| hi | $C \text{ AND } \overline{Z}$ | Higher (unsigned $>$) |
| los | $\overline{C} \text{ OR } Z$ | Low or same (unsigned $\leq$) |
| his | $C$ | Higher or same (unsigned $\geq$) |
| lo | $\overline{C}$ | Lower (unsigned $<$) |

**Table A4.4**  Procedure-linkage instructions.

| Instruction | Stack before | →after | Operation* |
|---|---|---|---|
| $\texttt{scall}(n^2)$ | $a_1 \cdots a_n,\ p^4$ | →$\cdots$ | Procedure call, $n$ arguments: |
| | | | $temp^4 \leftarrow pop4[\,]$ |
| | | | $push4[\langle SP \rangle - n]$ |
| | | | $push4[\langle PC \rangle]$ |
| | | | $push4[\langle B \rangle]$ |
| | | | $B \leftarrow \langle SP \rangle^4$ |
| | | | $push4[0^4]$ |
| | | | $PC \leftarrow \langle temp \rangle^4$ |
| $\texttt{srtn}\alpha$ | $\cdots r^\alpha$ | →$r^\alpha$ | Return from procedure, $\alpha$-byte result: |
| | | | $(\alpha = 0,\ 1,\ 2,\ 4,\ 8)$ |
| | | | $temp^\alpha \leftarrow pop\alpha[\,]$ |
| | | | $SP \leftarrow \langle\langle B \rangle - 12 \rangle^4$ |
| | | | $PC \leftarrow \langle\langle B \rangle - 8 \rangle^4$ |
| | | | $B \leftarrow \langle\langle B \rangle - 4 \rangle^4$ |
| | | | $push\alpha[\langle temp \rangle^\alpha]$ |
| $\texttt{spdcall}(n^1)$ | $a_1 \cdots a_n,\ p^4$ | →$\cdots$ | Procedure call: |
| | | | $temp^4 \leftarrow pop4[\,]$ |
| | | | $push4[\langle SP \rangle - n]$ |
| | | | $push4[\langle PC \rangle]$ |
| | | | $push4[\langle B \rangle]$ |
| | | | $B \leftarrow \langle SP \rangle^4$ |
| | | | $push4[\langle\langle temp \rangle\rangle^4]$ |
| | | | $PC \leftarrow \langle\langle temp \rangle + 4 \rangle^4$ |
| $\texttt{spdcons}$ | $procp^4$ | →$pd^8$ | Construct procedure descriptor |
| | | | based on current frame: |
| | | | $temp^4 \leftarrow pop4[\,]$ |
| | | | $push4[\langle B \rangle]$ |
| | | | $push4[\langle temp \rangle]$ |

*$push\alpha[x]$ means $\langle SP \rangle^\alpha \leftarrow x$; $SP \leftarrow \langle SP \rangle + \alpha$.
$x \leftarrow pop\alpha[\,]$ means $SP \leftarrow \langle SP \rangle - \alpha$; $x \leftarrow \langle\langle SP \rangle\rangle^\alpha$.

**Table A4.5** Data-access instructions.

| Instruction | Stack before $\rightarrow$ after | Operation |
|---|---|---|
| $\mathtt{sc}\alpha(b^\alpha)$ | $\rightarrow b^\alpha$ | Push constant $b^\alpha$: $\langle\mathrm{SP}\rangle^\alpha \leftarrow b^\alpha$ ; $\mathrm{SP} \leftarrow \langle\mathrm{SP}\rangle + \alpha$ |
| $\mathtt{sl}\alpha$ | $a^4 \quad \rightarrow\langle a\rangle^\alpha$ | Load: $\mathrm{SP} \leftarrow \langle\mathrm{SP}\rangle - 4$ ; $temp^4 \leftarrow \langle\langle\mathrm{SP}\rangle\rangle^4$ $\langle\mathrm{SP}\rangle \leftarrow \langle\langle temp\rangle\rangle^\alpha$ ; $\mathrm{SP} \leftarrow \langle\mathrm{SP}\rangle + \alpha$ |
| $\mathtt{ss}\alpha$ | $a^4,\ b^\alpha\rightarrow$ | Store: $\mathrm{SP} \leftarrow \langle\mathrm{SP}\rangle - \alpha$ ; $temp^\alpha \leftarrow \langle\langle\mathrm{SP}\rangle\rangle^\alpha$ $\mathrm{SP} \leftarrow \langle\mathrm{SP}\rangle - 4$ ; $\langle\langle\mathrm{SP}\rangle\rangle^\alpha \leftarrow \langle temp\rangle^\alpha$ |
| $\mathtt{slr}\alpha(r^\alpha)$ | $\rightarrow a^4$ | Load PC-relative address: $\langle\mathrm{SP}\rangle^4 \leftarrow \langle\mathrm{PC}\rangle^4 + r^\alpha; \mathrm{SP} \leftarrow \langle\mathrm{SP}\rangle + 4$ $(\alpha = 1,\ 2,\ \text{or } 4)$ |
| $\mathtt{slla}(n^2)$ | $\rightarrow a^4$ | Load local address ($n^2$ is the offset): $push4[\langle\mathrm{B}\rangle + n + 4]$ |
| $\mathtt{slaa}(n^2)$ | $\rightarrow a^4$ | Local $arg_n$ address ($n^2$ is the offset): $push4[\langle\langle\mathrm{B}\rangle - 12\rangle + n]$ |
| $\mathtt{salloc}(n^2)$ [for $n \geq 0$] | $\rightarrow ?^n$ | Allocates space: $\mathrm{SP} \leftarrow \langle\mathrm{SP}\rangle + n$ |
| $\mathtt{salloc}(n^2)$ [for $n < 0$] | $?^n\rightarrow$ | Deallocates space: $\mathrm{SP} \leftarrow \langle\mathrm{SP}\rangle + n$ |
| $\mathtt{sla}(d^1,n^2)$ | $\rightarrow a^4$ | Load address ($d^1$ is lexical depth and $n^2$ is the offset): $temp^4 \leftarrow \langle\mathrm{B}\rangle;$ repeat $d$ times: $temp \leftarrow \langle\langle temp\rangle\rangle$ $push4[\langle temp\rangle + n + 4]$ |
| $\mathtt{saa}(d^1,n^2)$ | $\rightarrow a^4$ | Load $arg_n$ address ($d^1$ is lexical depth and $n^2$ is the offset): $temp^4 \leftarrow \langle\mathrm{B}\rangle;$ repeat $d$ times: $temp \leftarrow \langle\langle temp\rangle\rangle$ $push4[\langle\langle temp\rangle - 12\rangle + n]$ |

**Table A4.6**  Supervisor-call and trap-return instructions.

| Instruction | Stack<br>before $\rightarrow$ after | Operation |
|---|---|---|
| $\mathtt{ssvc}(code^1)$ | $\rightarrow \mathrm{PC}^4, \mathrm{SP}^4, \mathrm{B}^4, \mathrm{PSW}^4, code^1$ | Supervisor call:<br>$temp \leftarrow \langle \mathrm{SP} \rangle^4$<br>$\mathrm{SP} \leftarrow \langle \mathtt{SSVCVEC} + 4 \rangle^4$<br>$push4[\langle \mathrm{PC} \rangle]$<br>$push4[\langle temp \rangle]$<br>$push4[\langle \mathrm{B} \rangle]$<br>$push4[\langle \mathrm{PSW} \rangle]$<br>$push1[code^1]$<br>$\mathrm{PC} \leftarrow \langle \mathtt{SSVCVEC} \rangle^4$<br>$\mathrm{B} \leftarrow \langle \mathtt{SSVCVEC} + 8 \rangle^4$<br>$\mathrm{PSW} \leftarrow \langle \mathtt{SSVCVEC} + 12 \rangle^4$ |
| $\mathtt{strtn}$ | $\mathrm{PC}^4, \mathrm{SP}^4, \mathrm{B}^4, \mathrm{PSW}^4 \rightarrow$ | Trap return:<br>$\mathrm{PSW} \leftarrow pop4[\,]$<br>$\mathrm{B} \leftarrow pop4[\,]$<br>$temp \leftarrow pop4[\,]$<br>$\mathrm{PC} \leftarrow pop4[\,]$<br>$\mathrm{SP} \leftarrow \langle temp \rangle^4$ |

# A4.2  Language Definition

```
| This is where the S-machine instruction encoding is defined. Note that the
|   hexadecimal number (0x??) after each declaration defines the encoding
|   for that S instruction. Organized to correspond to dispatch table rows.

.macro WORD(x) x%256 x/256            | Low-byte followed by high-byte.
.macro LONG(x) WORD(x) WORD(x >> 16)  | Low-word followed by high-word.

| S opcode macros:
.macro slla(n)   0x00+1 WORD(n) | slla(n) - Push local address n.
.macro slaa(n)   0x00+2 WORD(n) | slaa(n) - Push argument address n.
.macro salloc(n) 0x00+3 WORD(n) | salloc(n)-Allocate/deallocate +/- n bytes.

.macro sc1(C)    0x04   C        | sc@(C) - Push @-byte constant onto stack.
.macro sc2(C)    0x04+1 WORD(C)
.macro sc4(C)    0x04+2 LONG(C)

.macro slr1(n)   0x08   n        | slr@ - Push PC-relative adr, @-byte offset.
.macro slr2(n)   0x08+1 WORD(n)
.macro slr4(n)   0x08+2 LONG(n)
```

```
| S Opcode remaining instructions
sl1     = 0x0C             | sl@ - @-byte fetch from user memory (i.e., DRAM).
sl2     = 0x0C+1
sl4     = 0x0C+2


ss1     = 0x10             | ss@ - @-byte store into user memory (i.e., DRAM).
ss2     = 0x10+1
ss4     = 0x10+2


sadd1   = 0x14             | sadd@ - @-byte addition.
sadd2   = 0x14+1
sadd4   = 0x14+2


ssub1   = 0x18             | ssub@ - @-byte subtraction.
ssub2   = 0x18+1
ssub4   = 0x18+2


sneg1   = 0x1C             | sneg@ - @-byte negation (2's complement).
sneg2   = 0x1C+1
sneg4   = 0x1C+2


scmp1   = 0x20             | scmp@ - @-byte comparison.
scmp2   = 0x20+1
scmp4   = 0x20+2


sjmp    = 0x24             | Unconditional jump.
sje     = 0x24+2           | =    Jump iff equal.
sjne    = 0x24+3           | ~=   Jump iff not equal.


sjle    = 0x28             | <=   Jump iff less or equal     (signed).
sjgt    = 0x28+1           | >    Jump iff greater than      (signed).
sjlt    = 0x28+2           | <    Jump iff less than         (signed).
sjge    = 0x28+3           | >=   Jump iff greater or equal  (signed).


sjlos   = 0x2C             | LS   Jump iff lower or same     (unsigned).
sjhi    = 0x2C+1           | H    Jump iff higher            (unsigned).
sjlo    = 0x2C+2           | L    Jump iff lower             (unsigned).
sjhis   = 0x2C+3           | HS   Jump iff higher or same    (unsigned).


| Alternate conditional jump mnemonics for use with siostat:

sjda    = sjlt             | Jump if data available (S bit set).
sjnda   = sjge             | Jump if data not available (S bit reset).

sjp1    = sjlo             | Jump if P1 pressed (C bit set).
sjnp1   = sjhis            | Jump if P1 not pressed (C bit reset).

sjp0    = sje              | Jump if P0 pressed (Z bit set).
sjnp0   = sjne             | Jump if P0 not pressed (Z bit reset).

.macro scall(n) 0x30 WORD(n)
                          | scall(n) - Call subr with n arguments.
.macro spdcall(n) 0x31 WORD(n)
                          | Procedure call (through descriptor) with n args.
spdcons = 0x32            | Procedure-descriptor constructor.

srtn0   = 0x34            | Valueless return.
.macro sla(d,n) 0x35 d WORD(n)   | Address of local n at lexical depth d.
```

*S Machine Summary*

```
.macro saa(d,n) 0x36 d WORD(n)    | Address of argument n at lexical depth d.

srtn1    = 0x38            | srtn@ - Return @-byte value.
srtn2    = 0x38+1
srtn4    = 0x38+2


| Encodings 3C-43 left blank for sarraysize@ and sarray@.

sdiv1    = 0x44           | sdiv@ - @-bit division with @-bit quotient.
sdiv2    = 0x45
sdiv4    = 0x46

srem1    = 0x48           | srem@ - @-bit modulo with @-bit remainder.
srem2    = 0x49
srem4    = 0x4A

sediv1   = 0x4C           | sediv@ - @-bit division with @-bit quotient
sediv2   = 0x4D           |               and @-bit remainder
sediv4   = 0x4E

sand1    = 0x50           | sand@ - @-bit bitwise-logical AND function.
sand2    = 0x51
sand4    = 0x52

sor1     = 0x54           | sor@ - @-bit bitwise-logical OR function.
sor2     = 0x55
sor4     = 0x56

sxor1    = 0x58           | sxor@ - @-bit bitwise-logical XOR function.
sxor2    = 0x59
sxor4    = 0x5A

scom1    = 0x5C           | scom@ - @-bit bitwise complement.
scom2    = 0x5D
scom4    = 0x5E

sash1    = 0x60           | sash@ - @-bit arithmetic shift (+ left, - right).
sash2    = 0x61
sash4    = 0x62

slsh1    = 0x64           | slsh@ - @-bit logical shift (+ left, - right).
slsh2    = 0x65
slsh4    = 0x66

ssext1   = 0x68           | ssext@ - 2@-bit result of sign-extension.
ssext2   = 0x69
ssext4   = 0x6A

szext1   = 0x6C           | szext@ - 2@-bit result of zero-extend.
szext2   = 0x6D
szext4   = 0x6E

slow1    = 0x70           | slow@ - low @-bits of a 2@-bit number.
slow2    = 0x71
slow4    = 0x72

shigh1   = 0x74           | shigh@ - high @-bits of a 2@-bit number.
shigh2   = 0x75
shigh4   = 0x76
```

```
        stest1  = 0x78          | stest@ - @-bit compare with zero (see scmp@).
        stest2  = 0x79
        stest4  = 0x7A

        sdup1   = 0x7C          | sdup@ - Duplicate top @ bits on stack.
        sdup2   = 0x7D
        sdup4   = 0x7E

        smult1  = 0x80          | smult@ - @-bit multiplication with @-bit product.
        smult2  = 0x81
        smult4  = 0x82

        semul1  = 0x84          | semul@ - @-bit multiplication with 2@-bit product.
        semul2  = 0x85
        semul4  = 0x86

        | I/O instructions:

        siostat = 0x88          | Get SIO, P0, P1 status.
        sioget  = 0x89          | Read a byte.
        sioput  = 0x8A          | Send a byte.

        .macro ssvc(C)  0x8C C  | ssvc(C) - Supervisor call with code C.
        strtn   = 0x8D          | Return from trap or interrupt.
        ssetclk4 = 0x8E         | Set alarm-clock timer.

        | DO NOT REASSIGN THESE ENCODINGS: They are "hard-wired" into the simulator.

        shalt   = 0x00          | Stop machine (flash: 111..111 <=> ...11...).
        sbpt    = 0xFF          | Breakpoint (for debugging using simulator).
```

## A4.3  Sample *S*-Machine Program

```
        | Test instructions for S machine.

                .include smach          | S-machine definitions.

        | The entry point:

                sc4(3)                  | Argument: 3.
                sc4(fib)
                scall(4)
                shalt
                shalt
                shalt
                shalt

        fib:    slaa(0)
                sl4
                sc4(2)
                scmp4
                sc4(tiny)
                sjlo

                slaa(0)
                sl4
```

```
                sc4(-1)
                sadd4
                sc4(fib)
                scall(4)                        | fib(n-1)

                slaa(0)
                sl4
                sc4(-2)
                sadd4
                sc4(fib)
                scall(4)                        | fib(n-2)

                sadd4                   | fib(n-1)+fib(n-2)
                srtn4

        tiny:   slaa(0)                 | Return n.
                sl4
                srtn4
```

## A4.4  Complete MAYBE *S*-Machine Microcode

Following is a listing of complete MAYBE microcode for the *S* machine, exclusive
of the utility microsubroutines listed in appendix 3 and the operator's console
microcode listed in appendix 3.

```
| 32-bit S-machine architecture: Microcode support.

| Some SRAM registers reserved for particular purposes.
| Machine-level register definitions (each is 4 bytes long).

B       = 32             | Base-of-frame pointer.
SP      = 0x58           | Stack pointer.
PC      = 0x5C           | Program counter.
                         | Don't change PC and SP: They are "hard-wired into
                         |   "sim"!
PSW     = PC+4           | Processor status word (4 bytes).
Prty    = PSW+3          | Priority is high-order byte of PSW.

MCond   = PSW+4          | Temporary location for condition codes.
Spare   = MCond+1        | Unused, for now.

Op1     = Spare+1        | Temporary results and operands (each 4 bytes wide).
Op2     = Op1+4
Op3     = Op2+4
Op4     = Op3+4
Op5     = Op4+4
Op6     = Op5+4


| Fetch a byte from S-machine's instruction stream into SRAM x.
| Increments PC.

.macro fetch(x) l(PC, PC+1, x)  cadd2(1, PC, PC)
| S machine: Microcode implementation for MAYBE.

| Each instruction is encoded as an opcode byte followed by zero or more
|   operands.  For opcodes that may have differing lengths of operands, we
```

```
|   have followed the convention that the low 2 bits of each opcode specify
|   operand length, as follows:
|   00      1 byte
|   01      2 bytes (low, high)
|   10      4 bytes
|   11      (unused, at present)


STACK    = 0x1000              | Base of stack (grows UP from here!).


| Microsubroutine to initialize virtual S-machine state:

MInit:  cmove4(0, PC)                | Start at beginning.
        cmove4(STACK, SP)            | Base of stack.
        cmove4(0xBBBBBBBB, B)        | Initial (dummy) <B>.
        cmove(MAXPRI, Prty)          | Initially disable interrupts.
        jmp(Mintinit)                | goto interrupt initialization.

| Interrupt handler. If an interrupt condition is recognized by the
| Mintest routine, then Mint is called with the address of the interupt
| vector in Minth.  Mint loads a new SP from the vector, then saves the
| old PC, SP, B, and PSW (in that order) by pushing them on the new
| stack.  Writes Op3, Op4, and Op5 but leaves Op1 and Op2 undisturbed.

Mint:
        refr()  refr()  refr()  | 54 refreshes (this routine is as long
        refr()  refr()  refr()  |   as an instruction).
        refr()  refr()  refr()

        move4(PC, Op3)          | Save interrupt-time PC
        move4(SP, Op4)          |   and stack pointer.

        move2(Minth, R0)        | Prepare to read from interrupt vector.
        cmove(PC, R2)           | First get4 goes into the PC.
        call(get4)              | PC <- <vector_address + 0>.
        cmove(SP, R2)           | Next get4 goes into the SP.
        call(get4)              | SP <- <vector_address + 4>.
        move2(R0, Op5)          | Op5 <- vector_address + 8.

        PUSH4(Op3)              | Save old PC on new stack.
        PUSH4(Op4)              | Save old SP on new stack.
        PUSH4(B)                | Save old B on new stack.
        PUSH4(PSW)              | Save old PSW on new stack.

        move2(Op5, R0)          | R0 <- vector_address + 8.
        cmove(B, R2)            | Next get4 goes into the B.
        call(get4)              | B <- <vector_address + 8>.
        cmove(PSW, R2)          | Next get4 goes into the PSW.
        call(get4)              | PSW <- <vector_address + 12>.

        rtn()                   | Continue with instruction fetch.

| Main S instruction fetch/execute microsubroutine.
| Dispatches to an S instruction handler, which returns to caller
|   of NextInst via a rtn() microinstruction.

NextInst:
        fetch(R0)               | Get opcode of next S instruction.
        dispatch(R0, ITab)      | Dispatch through Instruction Table,
                                | Note: dispatch(...) uses 2*<R0> for offset.
```

| This is the 256-entry instruction dispatch table:

| Note: hhalt, hbpt, and hii are prefixed by "h" (as opposed to "hs")
|   since these are generic instructions that will be used by both the S
|   and the G machines.

| The tags (loc0x??) are used merely to facilitate lookup by humans
|   of table locations. (REMEMBER: location 2X corresponds to opcode X.)

```
ITab:
loc0x00:        WORD(hhalt)     WORD(hslla)     WORD(hslaa)     WORD(hsalloc)
loc0x08:        WORD(hsc1)      WORD(hsc2)      WORD(hsc4)      WORD(hii)
loc0x10:        WORD(hslr1)     WORD(hslr2)     WORD(hslr4)     WORD(hii)
loc0x18:        WORD(hsl1)      WORD(hsl2)      WORD(hsl4)      WORD(hii)
loc0x20:        WORD(hss1)      WORD(hss2)      WORD(hss4)      WORD(hii)
loc0x28:        WORD(hsadd1)    WORD(hsadd2)    WORD(hsadd4)    WORD(hii)
loc0x30:        WORD(hssub1)    WORD(hssub2)    WORD(hssub4)    WORD(hii)
loc0x38:        WORD(hsneg1)    WORD(hsneg2)    WORD(hsneg4)    WORD(hii)
loc0x40:        WORD(hscmp1)    WORD(hscmp2)    WORD(hscmp4)    WORD(hii)
loc0x48:        WORD(hsjmp)     WORD(hii)       WORD(hsje)      WORD(hsjne)
loc0x50:        WORD(hsjle)     WORD(hsjgt)     WORD(hsjlt)     WORD(hsjge)
loc0x58:        WORD(hsjlos)    WORD(hsjhi)     WORD(hsjlo)     WORD(hsjhis)
loc0x60:        WORD(hscall)    WORD(hspdcall)  WORD(hspdcons)  WORD(hii)
loc0x68:        WORD(hsrtn0)    WORD(hsla)      WORD(hsaa)      WORD(hii)
loc0x70:        WORD(hsrtn1)    WORD(hsrtn2)    WORD(hsrtn4)    WORD(hii)
loc0x78:        WORD(hii)       WORD(hii)       WORD(hii)       WORD(hii)
loc0x80:        WORD(hii)       WORD(hii)       WORD(hii)       WORD(hii)
loc0x88:        WORD(hsdiv1)    WORD(hsdiv2)    WORD(hsdiv4)    WORD(hii)
loc0x90:        WORD(hsrem1)    WORD(hsrem2)    WORD(hsrem4)    WORD(hii)
loc0x98:        WORD(hsediv1)   WORD(hsediv2)   WORD(hsediv4)   WORD(hii)
loc0xA0:        WORD(hsand1)    WORD(hsand2)    WORD(hsand4)    WORD(hii)
loc0xA8:        WORD(hsor1)     WORD(hsor2)     WORD(hsor4)     WORD(hii)
loc0xB0:        WORD(hsxor1)    WORD(hsxor2)    WORD(hsxor4)    WORD(hii)
loc0xB8:        WORD(hscom1)    WORD(hscom2)    WORD(hscom4)    WORD(hii)
loc0xC0:        WORD(hsash1)    WORD(hsash2)    WORD(hsash4)    WORD(hii)
loc0xC8:        WORD(hslsh1)    WORD(hslsh2)    WORD(hslsh4)    WORD(hii)
loc0xD0:        WORD(hssext1)   WORD(hssext2)   WORD(hssext4)   WORD(hii)
loc0xD8:        WORD(hszext1)   WORD(hszext2)   WORD(hszext4)   WORD(hii)
loc0xE0:        WORD(hslow1)    WORD(hslow2)    WORD(hslow4)    WORD(hii)
loc0xE8:        WORD(hshigh1)   WORD(hshigh2)   WORD(hshigh4)   WORD(hii)
loc0xF0:        WORD(hstest1)   WORD(hstest2)   WORD(hstest4)   WORD(hii)
loc0xF8:        WORD(hsdup1)    WORD(hsdup2)    WORD(hsdup4)    WORD(hii)
loc0x100:       WORD(hsmult1)   WORD(hsmult2)   WORD(hsmult4)   WORD(hii)
loc0x108:       WORD(hsemul1)   WORD(hsemul2)   WORD(hsemul4)   WORD(hii)
loc0x110:       WORD(hsiostat)  WORD(hsioget)   WORD(hsioput)   WORD(hsioswt)
loc0x118:       WORD(hssvc)     WORD(hstrtn)    WORD(hssetclk4) WORD(hii)
loc0x120:       WORD(hii)       WORD(hii)       WORD(hii)       WORD(hii)
loc0x128:       WORD(hii)       WORD(hii)       WORD(hii)       WORD(hii)
loc0x130:       WORD(hii)       WORD(hii)       WORD(hii)       WORD(hii)
loc0x138:       WORD(hii)       WORD(hii)       WORD(hii)       WORD(hii)
loc0x140:       WORD(hii)       WORD(hii)       WORD(hii)       WORD(hii)
loc0x148:       WORD(hii)       WORD(hii)       WORD(hii)       WORD(hii)
loc0x150:       WORD(hii)       WORD(hii)       WORD(hii)       WORD(hii)
loc0x158:       WORD(hii)       WORD(hii)       WORD(hii)       WORD(hii)
loc0x160:       WORD(hii)       WORD(hii)       WORD(hii)       WORD(hii)
loc0x168:       WORD(hii)       WORD(hii)       WORD(hii)       WORD(hii)
loc0x170:       WORD(hii)       WORD(hii)       WORD(hii)       WORD(hii)
loc0x178:       WORD(hii)       WORD(hii)       WORD(hii)       WORD(hii)
```

```
loc0x180:       WORD(hii)       WORD(hii)       WORD(hii)       WORD(hii)
loc0x188:       WORD(hii)       WORD(hii)       WORD(hii)       WORD(hii)
loc0x190:       WORD(hii)       WORD(hii)       WORD(hii)       WORD(hii)
loc0x198:       WORD(hii)       WORD(hii)       WORD(hii)       WORD(hii)
loc0x1A0:       WORD(hii)       WORD(hii)       WORD(hii)       WORD(hii)
loc0x1A8:       WORD(hii)       WORD(hii)       WORD(hii)       WORD(hii)
loc0x1B0:       WORD(hii)       WORD(hii)       WORD(hii)       WORD(hii)
loc0x1B8:       WORD(hii)       WORD(hii)       WORD(hii)       WORD(hii)
loc0x1C0:       WORD(hii)       WORD(hii)       WORD(hii)       WORD(hii)
loc0x1C8:       WORD(hii)       WORD(hii)       WORD(hii)       WORD(hii)
loc0x1D0:       WORD(hii)       WORD(hii)       WORD(hii)       WORD(hii)
loc0x1D8:       WORD(hii)       WORD(hii)       WORD(hii)       WORD(hii)
loc0x1E0:       WORD(hii)       WORD(hii)       WORD(hii)       WORD(hii)
loc0x1E8:       WORD(hii)       WORD(hii)       WORD(hii)       WORD(hii)
loc0x1F0:       WORD(hii)       WORD(hii)       WORD(hii)       WORD(hii)
loc0x1F8:       WORD(hii)       WORD(hii)       WORD(hii)       WORD(hbpt)
| Microcoded instruction handlers for MAYBE S-machine instruction set.

| c@ -- Load @-byte constant from instruction stream onto stack.

hsc1:   FETCH1(Op1)             | Fetch constant into Op1.
        PUSH1(Op1)              | Push it onto stack.
        rtn()                   | And we're done!

hsc2:   FETCH2(Op1)             | Fetch constant into Op1.
        PUSH2(Op1)              | Push it onto stack.
        rtn()                   | And we're done!

hsc4:   FETCH4(Op1)             | Fetch constant into Op1.
        PUSH4(Op1)              | Push it onto stack.
        rtn()                   | And we're done!


| l@: Load @-byte datum from main memory; uses 4-byte address from stack.

hsl1:   POP4(Op1)               | Pop the 4-byte address.
        move2(Op1, R0)          | (Ignores 2 top bytes!)
        cmove(Op1, R2)          | Load 1-byte value into Op1,
        call(get1)              |   sign-extending to 4 bytes.
        PUSH1(Op1)              | Then push it onto stack.
        rtn()

hsl2:   POP4(Op1)               | Pop the 4-byte address.
        move2(Op1, R0)          | (Ignores 2 top bytes!)
        cmove(Op1, R2)          | Load 2-byte value into Op1,
        call(get2)              |   sign-extending to 4 bytes.
        PUSH2(Op1)              | Then push it onto stack.
        rtn()

hsl4:   POP4(Op1)               | Pop the 4-byte address.
        move2(Op1, R0)          | (Ignores 2 top bytes!)
        cmove(Op1, R2)          | Load 4-byte value into Op1,
        call(get4)              |   sign-extending to 4 bytes.
        PUSH4(Op1)              | Then push it onto stack.
        rtn()


| s@: Store @-byte datum into main memory.
| Takes @-byte datum, 4-byte address from stack.
```

```
hss1:    POP1(Op2)              | Pop the 1-byte datum from stack.
         POP4(Op1)              | Pop the 4-byte address.
         move2(Op1, R0)         | (Ignores 2 top bytes!)
         cmove(Op2, R2)         | Store 1-byte value from Op2
         call(put1)             |   into main memory.
         rtn()

hss2:    POP2(Op2)              | Pop the 2-byte datum from stack.
         POP4(Op1)              | Pop the 4-byte address.
         move2(Op1, R0)         | (Ignores 2 top bytes!)
         cmove(Op2, R2)         | Store 2-byte value from Op2
         call(put2)             |   into main memory.
         rtn()

hss4:    POP4(Op2)              | Pop the 4-byte datum from stack.
         POP4(Op1)              | Pop the 4-byte address.
         move2(Op1, R0)         | (Ignores 2 top bytes!)
         cmove(Op2, R2)         | Store 4-byte value from Op2
         call(put4)             |   into main memory.
         rtn()


| add@ -- push(pop()+pop()).

hsadd1:  POP1(Op1)
         POP1(Op2)
         add(Op1, Op2, Op2)
         PUSH1(Op2)
         rtn()

hsadd2:  POP2(Op1)
         POP2(Op2)
         add2(Op1, Op2, Op2)
         PUSH2(Op2)
         rtn()

hsadd4:  POP4(Op1)
         POP4(Op2)
         add2( Op1,    Op2,    Op2)
         addcy(Op1+2, Op2+2, Op2+2)
         addcy(Op1+3, Op2+3, Op2+3)
         PUSH4(Op2)
         rtn()

| sub@ -- push(pop()-pop())

hssub1:  POP1(Op2)
         POP1(Op1)
         sub(Op1, Op2, Op1)
         PUSH1(Op1)
         rtn()

hssub2:  POP2(Op2)
         POP2(Op1)
         sub2(Op1, Op2, Op1)
         PUSH2(Op1)
         rtn()
```

```
hssub4: POP4(Op2)
        POP4(Op1)
        sub2(Op1, Op2, Op1)
        subcy(Op1+2, Op2+2, Op1+2)
        subcy(Op1+3, Op2+3, Op1+3)
        PUSH4(Op1)
        rtn()

| neg@ -- 2's complement.

hsneg1: POP1(Op1)
        neg(Op1, Op1)          | Negate.
        PUSH1(Op1)
        rtn()

hsneg2: POP2(Op1)
        not(Op1, Op1)          | Negate.
        not(Op1+1, Op1+1)
        cadd2(1, Op1, Op1)
        PUSH2(Op1)
        rtn()

hsneg4: POP4(Op1)
        not(Op1, Op1)          | Negate.
        not(Op1+1, Op1+1)
        not(Op1+2, Op1+2)
        not(Op1+3, Op1+3)
        cadd2(1, Op1, Op1)
        caddcy(0, Op1+2, Op1+2)
        caddcy(0, Op1+3, Op1+3)
        PUSH4(Op1)
        rtn()

| Compare instructions.
| Compute x - y, leaving condition byte SCZ00000 on the stack.
|    (Note that the ALU E bit is of little use in multiprecision!)
| Note that when doing x - y (NO carry-in), the C bit from the ALU
|    indicates x < y.
| To test for zero, result bytes are ORed into R1 (which is zero
|    if result is zero).
| Arithmetic overflow occurs if x and y have different signs and
|    the sign of the result is not the sign of x. Following code
|    segments branch to hscmpX on no overflow, to hscmpV on overflow.

hscmp1: POP1(Op1)        | y
        POP1(Op2)        | x

hstest1entry:
        sub(Op2, Op1, R1)      | Compute <Op2> - <Op1>.
        cond(MCond)            | Save ALU conditions.
        xor(Op1, Op2, R2)      | Like signs?
        jpl(hscmpX)            | Yup, no overflow.
        xor(Op2, R1, R2)       | Sign of x = sign of result?
        jpl(hscmpX)            | Yup, no overflow.
        jmp(hscmpV)            | Else, overflow!

hscmp2: POP2(Op1)        | y
        POP2(Op2)        | x
```

```
hstest2entry:
        sub2(Op2, Op1, Op3)     | Compute <Op2> - <Op1>.
        cond(MCond)             | Save ALU conditions.
        or(Op3, Op3+1, R1)      | OR bytes for zero test, leaving OR in R1.
        xor(Op1+1, Op2+1, R2)   | Like signs?
        jpl(hscmpX)             | Yup, no overflow.
        xor(Op3+1, Op2+1, R2)   | Sign of x = sign of result?
        jpl(hscmpX)             | Yup, no overflow.
        jmp(hscmpV)             | Else, overflow!

hscmp4: POP4(Op1)           | y
        POP4(Op2)           | x

hstest4entry:
        sub2( Op2, Op1,  Op3)   | Compute <Op2> - <Op1>.
        subcy(Op2+2,Op1+2,Op3+2)
        subcy(Op2+3,Op1+3,Op3+3)
        cond(MCond)             | Save ALU conditions.
        or(Op3+3,Op3+2,R1)      | OR bytes for zero test.
        or(Op3+1, R1, R1)
        or(Op3, R1, R1)         | Leave OR of byte in R1.
        xor(Op1+3, Op2+3, R2)   | Like signs?
        jpl(hscmpX)             | Yup, no overflow.
        xor(Op3+3, Op2+3, R2)   | Sign of x = sign of result?
        jpl(hscmpX)             | Yup, no overflow.
        jmp(hscmpV)             | Else, overflow!

| On overflow, flip the N bit from the result to produce S bit:

hscmpV: cxor(0x80, MCond, MCond)

| Here with ALU condition byte (used for S, C bits) in MCond, ORed bytes in
|   R1:

hscmpX: cand(0xC0,MCond,MCond)  | Mask to SC000000.
        ccmp(0, R1)             | Test for zero. We left OR in R1, remember?
        jne(xcmp)               | Not zero, so just exit.
        cor(0x20, MCond, MCond) | Else set Z bit.
xcmp:   PUSH1(MCond)            | Push 1-byte condition code onto stack.
        rtn()

| stest instructions. These instructions are nearly identical to the
| compare instructions except that they compare a single number to zero.
| This implementation loads the appropriate OPx registers, then jumps
| into the compare code (above).

hstest1:
        POP1(Op2)                       | Single argument in 2-reg.
        cmove(0, Op1)                   | Zero as other argument.
        jmp(hstest1entry)               | Do compare.

hstest2:
        POP2(Op2)                       | Single argument in 2-reg.
        cmove2(0, Op1)                  | Zero as other argument.
        jmp(hstest2entry)               | Do compare.

hstest4:
        POP4(Op2)                       | Single argument in 2-reg.
        cmove4(0, Op1)                  | Zero as other argument.
```

```
            jmp(hstest4entry)                    | Do compare.

| call(n) - Call subr with n argument(s), where n < 256.

hscall: POP4(Op2)                                | The subr entry point (new <PC>).

        FETCH2(Op1)                              | The argument count n.
        sub(SP, Op1, Op1)                        | <SP> - n.
        subcy(SP+1, Op1+1, Op1+1)
|       csubcy(SP+2, 0, Op1+2)                    | (These bytes are ignored...
|       csubcy(SP+3, 0, Op1+3)                    |   this is for upward compatibility!)

        PUSH4(Op1)                               | Push <SP> - n.

        PUSH4(PC)                                | Push the PC
        PUSH4(B)                                 |   the B register,
        move4(SP, B)                             |   new B value,

        cmove4(0, Op1)
        PUSH4(Op1)                               |   and a constant zero.
        move4(Op2, PC)                           | Install new PC,
        rtn()                                    |   and we're done!

| rtn0 -- Return, with no value. Used below as a subr for popping old frame.

hsrtn0: move2(B, R0)                             | Temporary copy of B (low bytes).

        cadd2(-12, R0, R0)                       | Find <B> - 12 (only keeps 2 bytes).

        cmove(SP, R2)                            | Restore previous values of
        call(get4)                               |   <SP>, <PC>, and <B>
        cmove(PC, R2)                            |   (4 bytes each).
        call(get4)
        cmove(B, R2)
        call(get4)

        rtn()


| rtn@ -- Return @-byte value.

hsrtn1: POP1(Op1)                                | The argument.
        call(hsrtn)                              | Pop off old stack frame.
        PUSH1(Op1)                               | Push 1-byte return value.
        rtn()

hsrtn2: POP2(Op1)                                | The argument.
        call(hsrtn)                              | Pop off old stack frame.
        PUSH2(Op1)                               | Push 2-byte return value.
        rtn()

hsrtn4: POP4(Op1)                                | The argument.
        call(hsrtn)                              | Pop off old stack frame.
        PUSH4(Op1)                               | Push 4-byte return value.
        rtn()


| lr@(n) microinstruction: Load PC-relative address.
```

```
hslr1:   FETCH1(Op1)                  | Fetch the 1-byte signed offset.
         add2(Op1, PC,    Op1)        | Add in the PC (signed addition).
         addcy(Op1+2, PC+2, Op1+2)
         addcy(Op1+3, PC+3, Op1+3)
         PUSH4(Op1)                   | Push the result.
         rtn()

hslr2:   FETCH2(Op1)                  | Fetch the 2-byte signed offset.
         add2(Op1, PC,    Op1)        | Add in the PC (signed addition).
         addcy(Op1+2, PC+2, Op1+2)
         addcy(Op1+3, PC+3, Op1+3)
         PUSH4(Op1)                   | Push the result.
         rtn()

hslr4:   FETCH4(Op1)                  | Fetch the 4-byte signed offset.
         add2( Op1,   PC,    Op1)     | Add in the PC.
         addcy(Op1+2, PC+2, Op1+2)
         addcy(Op1+3, PC+3, Op1+3)
         PUSH4(Op1)                   | Push the result.
         rtn()


| lla(n) -- load local address.

hslla:   FETCH2(Op1)                  | Fetch a 2-byte offset.
         cadd2(4,Op1, Op1)            | Compute offset+4.
         add2(B, Op1, Op1)            | Add in <B>, but only 2 bytes.
         PUSH4(Op1)                   | Push the result.
         rtn()

| laa(n) -- load argument address.
| Computes <<B>-12>+n

hslaa:   move2(B, R0)                 | <B>
         cadd2(-12, R0, R0)           | <B>-12
         cmove(Op1, R2)
         call(get4)                   | Fetch <<B>-12> into Op1.

         FETCH2(Op2)                  | Fetch a 2-byte offset.
         add2(Op2, Op1, Op1)          | <<B>-12>+n
         PUSH4(Op1)                   | Push the result.
         rtn()

| alloc(+/- n): Adjust SP to allocate/deallocate local storage for 2-byte n.

hsalloc:
         FETCH2(Op2)                  | Fetch signed 2-byte adjustment.
         add2(Op2, SP, SP)            | Add it to <SP>
         rtn()


| jmp(x): ALWAYS jump.
hsjmp:   POP4(PC)                     | Pop the target address, install as <PC>.
         rtn()


| A couple of microsubroutines for handling conditional jumps:
jiff0:   ccmp(0, R0)                  | Jump iff <R0>=0, else don't.
         jne(jmpno)                   | R0 nonzero.
```

```
                | Else fall through...
jmpyes: move4(Op2,PC)           | Install new PC value
jmpno:  rtn()                   |   and return.

jiffn0: ccmp(0, R0)             | Jump iff <R0> nonzero, else don't.
        jne(jmpyes)
        rtn()

| Conditional jump instructions.

| je(x): Jump iff equal.
hsje:   call(popcond)    | Pop target addr into Op2 & Cond Code to MCond.
        cand(0x20, MCond, R0)   | Fetch Z bit.
        jmp(jiffn0)             | Jump iff set.

| jne(x): Jump iff not equal.
hsjne:  call(popcond)    | Pop target addr into Op2 & Cond Code to MCond.
        cand(0x20, MCond, R0)   | Fetch Z bit.
        jmp(jiff0)              | Jump iff not set.

| jle(x): Jump iff less than or equal (signed).
hsjle:  call(popcond)    | Pop target addr into Op2 & Cond Code to MCond.
        cand(0xA0, MCond, R0)   | Fetch S, Z bits.
        jmp(jiffn0)             | Jump iff set.


| jgt(x): Jump iff greater than (signed).
hsjgt:  call(popcond)    | Pop target addr into Op2 & Cond Code to MCond.
        cand(0xA0, MCond, R0)   | Fetch S, Z bits.
        jmp(jiff0)              | Jump iff not set.

| jlt(x): Jump iff less than (signed).
hsjlt:  call(popcond)    | Pop target addr into Op2 & Cond Code to MCond.
        cand(0x80, MCond, R0)   | Fetch S bit.
        jmp(jiffn0)             | Jump iff set.

| jge(x): Jump iff greater than or equal (signed).
hsjge:  call(popcond)    | Pop target addr into Op2 & Cond Code to MCond.
        cand(0x80, MCond, R0)   | Fetch S bit.
        jmp(jiff0)              | Jump iff not set.

| jlos(x): Jump iff lower or same (unsigned).
hsjlos: call(popcond)    | Pop target addr into Op2 & Cond Code to MCond.
        cand(0x60, MCond, R0)   | Fetch C, Z bits: C=1 -> (x < y) unsigned.
        jmp(jiffn0)             | Jump iff either set.

| jhi(x): Jump iff higher (unsigned).
hsjhi:  call(popcond)    | Pop target addr into Op2 & Cond Code to MCond.
        cand(0x60, MCond, R0)   | Fetch C, Z bits: C=1 -> (x < y) unsigned.
        jmp(jiff0)              | Jump iff neither set.

| jlo(x): Jump iff lower (unsigned).
hsjlo:  call(popcond)    | Pop target addr into Op2 & Cond Code to MCond.
        cand(0x40, MCond, R0)   | Fetch C bit: C=1 -> (x < y) unsigned.
        jmp(jiffn0)             | Jump iff set.

| jhis(x): Jump iff lower (unsigned).
hsjhis: call(popcond)    | Pop target addr into Op2 & Cond Code to MCond.
        cand(0x40, MCond, R0)   | Fetch C bit: C=1 -> (x < y) unsigned.
```

```
        jmp(jiff0)                      | Jump iff not set.


| Internal microsubroutine for conditional jumps. Pop 4-byte target
|   address into Op2, then pop the single cond byte into MCond.

popcond:
        POP4(Op2)                       | Pop jump target location, hold in Op2.
        cadd2(-1, SP, SP)               | Decrement SP.
        l(SP, SP+1, MCond)              | Fetch the condition code.
        rtn()

| Stack-data manipulation instructions:
| sdup@, slow@, shigh@, ssext@ szext@.

| sdup@ duplicates the top of the stack.

hsdup1: POP1(Op1)                       | Get data from the stack,
        PUSH1(Op1)                      |   put it back,
        PUSH1(Op1)                      |   and duplicate it.
        rtn()


hsdup2: POP2(Op1)                       | Get data from the stack,
        PUSH2(Op1)                      |   put it back,
        PUSH2(Op1)                      |   and duplicate it.
        rtn()


hsdup4: POP4(Op1)                       | Get data from the stack,
        PUSH4(Op1)                      |   put it back,
        PUSH4(Op1)                      |   and duplicate it.
        rtn()

| slow@ pops 2@ bytes from the stack and puts back the lowest @.

hslow1: POP1(Op1)                       | Get high bits.
        POP1(Op2)                       | Get low bits.
        PUSH1(Op2)                      | Put back the low bits.
        rtn()


hslow2: POP2(Op1)                       | Get high bits.
        POP2(Op2)                       | Get low bits.
        PUSH2(Op2)                      | Put back the low bits.
        rtn()


hslow4: POP4(Op1)                       | Get high bits.
        POP4(Op2)                       | Get low bits.
        PUSH4(Op2)                      | Put back the low bits.
        rtn()

| shigh@ pops 2@ bytes from the stack and puts back the highest @.

hshigh1:POP1(Op1)                       | Get high bits.
        POP1(Op2)                       | Get low bits.
        PUSH1(Op1)                      | Put back the high bits.
        rtn()


hshigh2: POP2(Op1)                      | Get high bits.
        POP2(Op2)                       | Get low bits.
        PUSH2(Op1)                      | Put back the high bits.
```

```
        rtn()

hshigh4:POP4(Op1)                | Get high bits.
        POP4(Op2)                | Get low bits.
        PUSH4(Op1)               | Put back the high bits.
        rtn()


| ssext@ sign-extends the quantity on the stack to a 2@-byte result.

hssext1: POP1(Op1)               | Get the number.
        PUSH1(Op1)               | Put it back.
        cmove(0, Op2)            | Zero extension bits.
        cadd(0, Op1, R1)         | Check sign of number.
        jpl(hssext1skip)         | Use 0 if positive.
        cmove(-1, Op2)           | Use -1 if negative.
hssext1skip:
        PUSH1(Op2)               | Push extension bits.
        rtn()


hssext2: POP2(Op1)               | Get the number.
        PUSH2(Op1)               | Put it back.
        cmove2(0, Op2)           | Zero extension bits.
        cadd(0, Op1+1, R1)       | Check sign of number.
        jpl(hssext2skip)         | Use 0 if positive.
        cmove2(-1, Op2)          | Use -1 if negative.
hssext2skip:
        PUSH2(Op2)               | Push extension bits.
        rtn()


hssext4: POP4(Op1)               | Get the number.
        PUSH4(Op1)               | Put it back.
        cmove4(0, Op2)           | Zero extension bits.
        cadd(0, Op1+3, R1)       | Check sign of number.
        jpl(hssext4skip)         | Use 0 if positive.
        cmove4(-1, Op2)          | Use -1 if negative.
hssext4skip:
        PUSH4(Op2)               | Push extension bits.
        rtn()


| szext@ zero-extends the quantity on the stack to 2@-bytes
| (this is the same as pushing @-bytes of zero onto the stack).

hszext1: cmove(0,Op1)            | Make a zero.
        PUSH1(Op1)               | Put it on the stack.
        rtn()

hszext2: cmove2(0,Op1)           | Make a zero.
        PUSH2(Op1)               | Put it on the stack.
        rtn()

hszext4: cmove4(0,Op1)           | Make a zero.
        PUSH4(Op1)               | Put it on the stack.
        rtn()


| Lexical-scoping support: spdcons, spdcall, sla, saa.

| spdcons constructs a procedure descriptor given a pointer to
|   the procedure code and the current stack frame.
```

```
hspdcons:
        POP4(Op1)                       | Pop code pointer temporarily.
        PUSH4(B)                        | Put B register onto stack.
        PUSH4(Op1)                      | Put code pointer back.
        rtn()

| spdcall(n) -- Call procedure with n argument(s), where n < 256.

hspdcall: POP4(Op2)                     | Pointer to procedure descriptor.

        FETCH2(Op1)                     | The argument count n.
        sub(  SP,    Op1,   Op1)        | <SP> - n.
        subcy( SP+1, Op1+1, Op1+1)
|       csubcy(SP+2, 0,     Op1+2)      | (These bytes are ignored...
|       csubcy(SP+3, 0,     Op1+3)      |  this is for upward compatibility!)

        PUSH4(Op1)                      | Push <SP> - n.

        PUSH4(PC)                       | Push the PC.
        PUSH4(B)                        | Push the B register.
        move4(SP, B)                    | New B value.

        move2(Op2, R0)                  | Pointer to procedure descriptor.
        cmove(Op1, R2)                  | Put result of get in Op1.
        call(get4)                      | Get <<Op2>>.
        PUSH4(Op1)                      | Static link from procedure desc.

        move2(Op2, R0)                  | Pointer to procedure descriptor.
        cadd2(4, R0, R0)                | Advance pointer to second part.
        cmove(PC, R2)                   | Put code pointer into PC.
        call(get4)                      | Get <<Op2> + 4>.
        rtn()                           | And we're done!

| tracestack is used by hsla and hsaa to follow the stack back up
| a set number of frames. The number of frames is passed in Op2,
| and the pointer to the desired frame is returned in Op1. Op2 is
| modified.

tracestack:
        move2(B, Op1)                   | Get pointer to static link.

tracestackloop:
        csub(Op2, 1, Op2)               | Decrement and set flags.
        jmi(tracestackexit)             | Quit if < 0.

        move2(Op1, R0)                  | Pointer to static link.
        cmove(Op1, R2)                  | Put result in Op1.
        call(get4)
        refr()                          | This loop might last awhile.
        refr()                          | get4 is long enough to need 2.
        jmp(tracestackloop)

tracestackexit:
        rtn()

| sla(d,n) -- Load local address at depth d.

hsla:   FETCH1(Op2)                     | Fetch depth d.
        call(tracestack)                | Follow stack to depth d (Op1=ptr).
```

```
                FETCH2(Op2)                     | Fetch a 2-byte offset.
                cadd2(4,Op2, Op2)               | Compute offset+4.
                add2(Op1, Op2, Op2)             | Add in ptr to frame at depth d.
                PUSH4(Op2)                      | Push the result.
                rtn()

    | saa(d,n) -- Load argument address at depth d.
    | Computes <<B> - 12> + n.

hsaa:           FETCH1(Op2)                     | Fetch depth d.
                call(tracestack)                | Follow stack to depth d (Op1=ptr).
                move2(Op1, R0)                  | <ptr>
                cadd2(-12, R0, R0)              | <ptr> - 12
                cmove(Op1, R2)                  | Put result back into Op1.
                call(get4)                      | Fetch <<ptr>-12> into Op1.

                FETCH2(Op2)                     | Fetch a 2-byte offset.
                add2(Op2, Op1, Op1)             | <<ptr> - 12> + n
                PUSH4(Op1)                      | Push the result.
                rtn()


    | Logical instructions: sand@, sor@, sxor@, scom@.

    | and@ -- push(pop()&pop())

hsand1:  POP1(Op2)
         POP1(Op1)
         and(Op1, Op2, Op1)
         PUSH1(Op1)
         rtn()

hsand2:  POP2(Op2)
         POP2(Op1)
         and(Op1, Op2, Op1)
         and(Op1+1, Op2+1, Op1+1)
         PUSH2(Op1)
         rtn()

hsand4:  POP4(Op2)
         POP4(Op1)
         and(Op1, Op2, Op1)
         and(Op1+1, Op2+1, Op1+1)
         and(Op1+2, Op2+2, Op1+2)
         and(Op1+3, Op2+3, Op1+3)
         PUSH4(Op1)
         rtn()

    | or@ -- push(pop()|pop())

hsor1:   POP1(Op2)
         POP1(Op1)
         or(Op1, Op2, Op1)
         PUSH1(Op1)
         rtn()

hsor2:   POP2(Op2)
         POP2(Op1)
         or(Op1, Op2, Op1)
```

*S Machine Summary*

```
                or(Op1+1, Op2+1, Op1+1)
                PUSH2(Op1)
                rtn()

    hsor4:      POP4(Op2)
                POP4(Op1)
                or(Op1, Op2, Op1)
                or(Op1+1, Op2+1, Op1+1)
                or(Op1+2, Op2+2, Op1+2)
                or(Op1+3, Op2+3, Op1+3)
                PUSH4(Op1)
                rtn()


    | xor@ -- push(pop()^pop())

    hsxor1:     POP1(Op2)
                POP1(Op1)
                xor(Op1, Op2, Op1)
                PUSH1(Op1)
                rtn()

    hsxor2:     POP2(Op2)
                POP2(Op1)
                xor(Op1, Op2, Op1)
                xor(Op1+1, Op2+1, Op1+1)
                PUSH2(Op1)
                rtn()

    hsxor4:     POP4(Op2)
                POP4(Op1)
                xor(Op1, Op2, Op1)
                xor(Op1+1, Op2+1, Op1+1)
                xor(Op1+2, Op2+2, Op1+2)
                xor(Op1+3, Op2+3, Op1+3)
                PUSH4(Op1)
                rtn()


    | com@ -- 1's complement.

    hscom1:     POP1(Op1)
                not(Op1, Op1)              | Complement argument.
                PUSH1(Op1)
                rtn()

    hscom2:     POP2(Op1)
                not(Op1, Op1)              | Complement argument.
                not(Op1+1, Op1+1)
                PUSH2(Op1)
                rtn()

    hscom4:     POP4(Op1)
                not(Op1, Op1)              | Complement argument.
                not(Op1+1, Op1+1)
                not(Op1+2, Op1+2)
                not(Op1+3, Op1+3)
                PUSH4(Op1)
                rtn()


    | sash@ does an arithemtic shift (retains sign) using shift.
```

```
| THESE ROUTINES EXPECT POP@ TO DO SIGN-EXTENSION.

hsash1:  POP1(Op2)                | Shift-control.
         POP1(Op1)                | Get data.
         cand(0x80, Op1, Op3)     | Store sign-adjustment byte.
         call(shift)              | Do the shift.
         PUSH1(Op1)               | Put data back.
         rtn()

hsash2:  POP1(Op2)                | Shift-control.
         POP2(Op1)                | Get data.
         cand(0x80, Op1+1, Op3)   | Store sign-adjustment byte.
         call(shift)              | Do the shift.
         PUSH2(Op1)               | Put data back.
         rtn()

hsash4:  POP1(Op2)                | Shift-control.
         POP4(Op1)                | Get data.
         cand(0x80, Op1+3, Op3)   | Store sign-adjustment byte.
         call(shift)              | Do the shift.
         PUSH4(Op1)               | Put data back.
         rtn()

| slsh@ does a logical shift (zero-extends) using shift.

hslsh1:  POP1(Op2)                | Shift-control.
         POP1(Op1)                | Get data.
         cmove(0, Op3)            | Clear adjustment byte.
         cmove(0, Op1+1)          | Clear upper bytes.
         cmove2(0, Op1+2)
         call(shift)              | Do the shift.
         PUSH1(Op1)               | Put data back.
         rtn()

hslsh2:  POP1(Op2)                | Shift-control.
         POP2(Op1)                | Get data.
         cmove(0, Op3)            | Clear adjustment byte.
         cmove2(0, Op2+2)         | Clear upper bytes.
         call(shift)              | Do the shift.
         PUSH2(Op1)               | Put data back.
         rtn()

hslsh4:  POP1(Op2)                | Shift-control.
         POP4(Op1)                | Get data.
         cmove(0, Op3)            | Clear adjustment byte.
         call(shift)              | Do the shift.
         PUSH4(Op1)               | Put data back.
         rtn()

| Actual multiply and divide instructions just use the
| general code above regardless of the size of the operands.
| smult@, semul@, sdiv@, srem@, sediv@
| THESE ROUTINES RELY ON POP@() SIGN-EXTENDING 1- AND 2-BYTE NUMBERS.

| smult@ is signed multiplication of @-byte numbers producing
| an @-byte result.

hsmult1: POP1(multiplier)         | Multiplier.
         POP1(multiplicand)       | Multiplicand.
```

```
                      call(mult)              | Do the multiply.
                      PUSH1(product)          | 1-byte result.
                      rtn()

    hsmult2:  POP2(multiplier)                | Get operands.
              POP2(multiplicand)
              call(mult)                      | Do multiply.
              PUSH2(product)                  | 2-byte result.
              rtn()

    hsmult4:  POP4(multiplier)                | Get operands.
              POP4(multiplicand)
              call(mult)                      | Do multiply.
              PUSH4(product)                  | 4-byte result.
              rtn()
```

| semul@ is signed multiplication of @-byte numbers producing
| a 2@-byte result. These routines just call the normal
| hsmult routines, then put the second half of the result onto
| the stack, a fortunate result of low-address/low-order
| convention.

```
    hsemul1:  call(hsmult1)                   | Usual multiply, 1-byte result.
              PUSH1(product+1)                | Add 2nd byte of result.
              rtn()

    hsemul2:  call(hsmult2)                   | Do multiply with 2-byte result.
              PUSH2(product+2)                | Add high word of result.
              rtn()

    hsemul4:  call(hsmult4)                   | Do multiply with 4-byte result.
              PUSH4(product+4)                | Add high longword of result.
              rtn()
```

| sdiv@ is signed division of @-byte numbers producing
| an @-byte result (quotient).

```
    hsdiv1:  POP1(divisor)                    | Get divisor (denominator).
             POP1(dividend)                   | Get dividend (numerator).
             call(divide)                     | Do the division.
             PUSH1(quotient)                  | Return 1-byte result.
             rtn()

    hsdiv2:  POP2(divisor)                    | Get operands.
             POP2(dividend)
             call(divide)
             PUSH2(quotient)                  | 2-byte quotient.
             rtn()

    hsdiv4:  POP4(divisor)                    | Get operands.
             POP4(dividend)
             call(divide)
             PUSH4(quotient)                  | 4-byte quotient.
             rtn()
```

| srem@ is signed division of @-byte numbers producing
| an @-byte result (remainder).

```
    hsrem1:  POP1(divisor)                    | Get divisor (denominator).
```

```
        POP1(dividend)              | Get dividend (numerator).
        call(divide)                | Do the division.
        PUSH1(remainder)            | Return 1-byte result.
        rtn()

hsrem2: POP2(divisor)               | Get operands.
        POP2(dividend)
        call(divide)
        PUSH2(remainder)            | 2-byte remainder.
        rtn()

hsrem4: POP4(divisor)               | Get operands.
        POP4(dividend)
        call(divide)
        PUSH4(remainder)            | 4-byte remainder.
        rtn()


| hsediv@ is signed division of @-byte numbers producing
| both an @-byte quotient and an @-byte remainder.

hsediv1: call(hsdiv1)               | Do normal divide.
        PUSH1(remainder)            | Add 1-byte remainder.
        rtn()

hsediv2: call(hsdiv2)               | Do divide.
        PUSH2(remainder)            | Add 2-byte remainder.
        rtn()

hsediv4: call(hsdiv4)               | Do divide.
        PUSH4(remainder)            | Add 4-byte remainder.
        rtn()


| I/O instructions:

| siostat reads the 8250 interface and the P0 and P1 switches, then
| returns a byte coded like an scmp or stest byte.
|
| The S bit (bit 7) is set if there are data available to read.
| The C bit (bit 6) is set if P1 is being pressed.
| The Z bit (bit 5) is set if P0 is being pressed.
|
| This is intended to be used with the conditional jump instructions
| that test these bits.
|

hsiostat:
        cmove(0, Op1)               | Make a zero.
        ccmp(0, inchar)             | Test if character has been read.
        je(hsiostat_nochar)         | Skip if no character.
        cmove(0x80, Op1)            | Set the S bit for data available.
hsiostat_nochar:

        jnp1(hsiostat_nop1)
        cor(0x40, Op1, Op1)         | Set C bit for P1 pressed.
hsiostat_nop1:

        jnp0(hsiostat_nop0)
        cor(0x20, Op1, Op1)         | Set Z bit for P0 pressed.
hsiostat_nop0:
```

```
           PUSH1(Op1)                  | Put the character on the stack.
           rtn()

| sioget reads a character from the HP, if there is one.
| A 0 will be returned if no character is available.

hsioget: PUSH1(inchar)                 | Put the character on the stack.
         ccmp(0, inchar)               | Skip if no character.
         je(hsiogetnochar)
         cmove(0, inchar)              | Signal the character as taken.
         call(ioack)                   | Acknowledge the character.
hsiogetnochar:
         rtn()

| sioput sends a character to the HP. The character is restricted
| to 7 bits so as not to interfere with control codes that the
| MAYBE may need to send.

hsioput: POP1(Op1)                     | Get the character.
         cand(0x7F, Op1, R0)           | Put it in R0 for call to iosend.
         call(iosend)                  | Send the character to the HP.
         rtn()

| sioswt reads the switches on the lab kit and returns a byte
| representing their value.

hsioswt: swt(Op1)                      | Read the byte.
         PUSH1(Op1)                    | Put it on the stack.
         rtn()

| ssvc -- Supervisor call.

hssvc:   FETCH1(Op1)                   | Fetch the 1-byte code from instr.
         cmove2(SSVCVEC, Minth)        | Trap vector address.
         call(Mint)                    | Go through the interrupt sequence.
         PUSH1(Op1)                    | Then additionally push the code.
         rtn()                         | Done!

| strtn -- Trap/interrupt return.

hstrtn: POP4(PSW)                      | Restore processor regs from
        POP4(B)                        |   current stack.
        POP4(Op1)                      | Old SP.
        POP4(PC)                       | Old PC.
        move4(Op1, SP)                 | Done popping, restore old SP.
        rtn()                          | Finished!

| ssetclk4 -- Pops 4-byte integer off stack and sets alarm-clock timer.

hssetclk4: POP4(Mclkcount)             | Just do it!
         rtn()                         | Then done!

| Symbol that tells us how much microcode ROM we're using:
END:
ENDHI = END/256                        | MAX VALUE: 0b11111 (= 31 decimal).
```

# A5 $G$ Machine Summary

This appendix begins with a section summarizing the $G$-machine instruction set for convenient reference. Subsequent sections reproduce the $G$ machine's machine-language definition file, an example of a $G$-machine program, and a complete listing of the MAYBE microcode that implements the $G$ machine. These items are included for reference and for use with the MAYBE software tools.

## A5.1 Instruction-Set Details

Tables A5.1–A5.3 summarize the $G$-machine instruction set as implemented on the MAYBE machine.

**Table A5.1** Typical $G$-machine instructions.

| Operation | Operand addresses | Sets CC? | Function performed |
|---|---|---|---|
| gmove$\alpha$ | $A, B$ | No | $E_B^\alpha \leftarrow \langle E_A \rangle^\alpha$ |
| gadd$\alpha$ | $A, B, C$ | No | $E_C^\alpha \leftarrow \langle E_A \rangle^\alpha + \langle E_B \rangle^\alpha$ |
| gsub$\alpha$ | $A, B, C$ | No | $E_C^\alpha \leftarrow \langle E_A \rangle^\alpha - \langle E_B \rangle^\alpha$ |
| gmult$\alpha$ | $A, B, C$ | No | $E_C^\alpha \leftarrow \langle E_A \rangle^\alpha * \langle E_B \rangle^\alpha$ |
| gdiv$\alpha$ | $A, B, C$ | No | $E_C^\alpha \leftarrow \langle E_A \rangle^\alpha \div \langle E_B \rangle^\alpha$ |
| grem$\alpha$ | $A, B, C$ | No | $E_C^\alpha \leftarrow \langle E_A \rangle^\alpha \bmod \langle E_B \rangle^\alpha$ |
| gneg$\alpha$ | $A, B$ | No | $E_B^\alpha \leftarrow -\langle E_A \rangle^\alpha$ |
| gand$\alpha$ | $A, B, C$ | No | $E_C^\alpha \leftarrow \langle E_A \rangle^\alpha \text{ AND } \langle E_B \rangle^\alpha$ |
| gor$\alpha$ | $A, B, C$ | No | $E_C^\alpha \leftarrow \langle E_A \rangle^\alpha \text{ OR } \langle E_B \rangle^\alpha$ |
| gxor$\alpha$ | $A, B, C$ | No | $E_C^\alpha \leftarrow \langle E_A \rangle^\alpha \text{ XOR } \langle E_B \rangle^\alpha$ |
| gcom$\alpha$ | $A, B$ | No | $E_B^\alpha \leftarrow \text{NOT } \langle E_A \rangle^\alpha$ |
| gash$\alpha$ | $A, B, C$ | No | Arithmetically shift $\langle E_A \rangle^\alpha$ left (right) $\langle E_B \rangle^1$ $(-\langle E_B \rangle^1)$ places; store in $E_C$ |
| glsh$\alpha$ | $A, B, C$ | No | Logically shift $\langle E_A \rangle^\alpha$ left (right) $\langle E_B \rangle^1$ $(-\langle E_B \rangle^1)$ places; store in $E_C$ |
| ghalt | | No | Stop the machine |
| gcall | $A$ | No | $push4[\langle \text{PC} \rangle]$; $\text{PC}^4 \leftarrow E_A$ |
| grtn | | No | $\text{PC} \leftarrow pop4[]$ |
| gcmp$\alpha$ | $A, B$ | Yes | Set $S$, $Z$, and $C$ bits in CC according to the result of the operation $\langle E_A \rangle^\alpha - \langle E_B \rangle^\alpha$ |
| gtest$\alpha$ | $A$ | Yes | Set $S$, $Z$, and $C$ bits in CC according to the result of $\langle E_A \rangle^\alpha - 0$ |
| gjmp | $A$ | No | $\text{PC}^4 \leftarrow E_A{}^4$ |
| gj$cond$ | $A$ | No | If $cond$ matches $\langle \text{CC} \rangle$, then $\text{PC}^4 \leftarrow E_A{}^4$ |
| gtc1 | $A$ | Yes | Set $S$, $Z$, and $C$ bits in CC according to the result of $\langle E_A \rangle^1 - 0$ and then *atomically* set $E_A{}^1 \leftarrow 0$ |

**Table A5.2**  Fundamental address modes of the $G$ machine.

| Addressing mode | $M$ field | Effective address | Assembler syntax |
|---|---|---|---|
| Register | 0 | $E = \mathrm{R}n$ | `r(n)` |
| Indirect register | 1 | $E = \langle \mathrm{R}n \rangle$ | `ir(n)` |
| Direct | 2 | $E = X$ | `dir(X)` |
| Indirect | 3 | $E = \langle X \rangle$ | `i(X)` |
| Indexed | 4 | $E = X + \langle \mathrm{R}n \rangle$ | `ix(X,n)` |
| Indirect indexed | 5 | $E = \langle X + \langle \mathrm{R}n \rangle \rangle$ | `iix(X,n)` |
| Postincrement | 6 | $E = \langle \mathrm{R}n \rangle$ ; $\mathrm{R}n \leftarrow \langle \mathrm{R}n \rangle + \alpha$ | `posti(n)` |
| Indirect postincrement | 7 | $E = \langle \langle \mathrm{R}n \rangle \rangle$ ; $\mathrm{R}n \leftarrow \langle \mathrm{R}n \rangle + \alpha$ | `iposti(n)` |
| Predecrement | 8 | $\mathrm{R}n \leftarrow \langle \mathrm{R}n \rangle - \alpha$ ; $E = \langle \mathrm{R}n \rangle$ | `pred(n)` |
| Indirect predecrement | 9 | $\mathrm{R}n \leftarrow \langle \mathrm{R}n \rangle - \alpha$ ; $E = \langle \langle \mathrm{R}n \rangle \rangle$ | `ipred(n)` |

**Table A5.3**  Derived address modes of the $G$ machine.

| Addressing mode | $M$ field | General register | Effective address | Assembler syntax |
|---|---|---|---|---|
| Immediate | 6 | PC | $E = \langle \mathrm{PC} \rangle$ ; $\mathrm{PC} \leftarrow \langle \mathrm{PC} \rangle + \alpha$ | `imm`$\alpha$`(X)` |
| SP-relative | 4 | SP | $E = X + \langle \mathrm{SP} \rangle$ | `ix(X,SP)` |
| Indirect SP-relative | 5 | SP | $E = \langle X + \langle \mathrm{SP} \rangle \rangle$ | `iix(X,SP)` |
| Stack (push) | 6 | SP | $E = \langle \mathrm{SP} \rangle$ ; $\mathrm{SP} \leftarrow \langle \mathrm{SP} \rangle + \alpha$ | `push()` |
| Stack (pop) | 8 | SP | $\mathrm{SP} \leftarrow \langle \mathrm{SP} \rangle - \alpha$ ; $E = \langle \mathrm{SP} \rangle$ | `pop()` |
| PC-relative | 4 | PC | $E = \langle \mathrm{PC} \rangle + X$ | `rel(X)` |

## A5.2 Language Definition

```
| Definitions for assembly of G-machine instructions.

.macro WORD(x)  x%256 x/256
.macro LONG(x)  WORD(x) WORD(x >> 16)

| G register names:
SP      = 14            | SP = General Register 14 (GR14).
PC      = 15            | PC = General Register 15 (GR15).

| G opcode macros:

gmove1  = 4             | gmove@ x y -- @-byte move: y <- <x>.
gmove2  = 4+1
```

```
gmove4  = 4+2

giostat = 8                     | giostat -- Get status of SIO, P0, P1.
gioget  = 9                     | gioget <addr> -- Read byte from serial port.
gioput  = 0xA                   | gioput <byte> -- Send byte to serial port.
gioswt  = 0xB                   | sioswt <addr> -- Read byte from switches.

.macro gsvc(C)   0xC C          | gsvc(C) - Supervisor call with code C.
gtrtn   = 0xD                   | Return from trap or interrupt.
gsetclk4 = 0xE                  | Set alarm-clock timer.

gand1   = 0x14                  | gand x y z -- Bitwise AND: z <- <x> & <y>.
gand2   = 0x15
gand4   = 0x16

gor1    = 0x18                  | gor x y z -- Bitwise OR: z <- <x> | <y>.
gor2    = 0x19
gor4    = 0x1A

gxor1   = 0x1C                  | gxor x y z -- Bitwise XOR: z <- <x> ^ <y>.
gxor2   = 0x1D
gxor4   = 0x1E

gadd1   = 0x20                  | gadd@ x y z -- @-byte addition: z <- <x> + <y>.
gadd2   = 0x20+1
gadd4   = 0x20+2

gsub1   = 0x24                  | gsub@ x y z -- @-byte subtraction: z <- <x> - <y>.
gsub2   = 0x24+1
gsub4   = 0x24+2

gneg1   = 0x28                  | gneg@ x y -- @-byte negation (2's complement):
gneg2   = 0x28+1                |            y <- -<x>.
gneg4   = 0x28+2

gcmp1   = 0x2C                  | gcmp@ x y -- @-byte comparison.
gcmp2   = 0x2C+1
gcmp4   = 0x2C+2

gtest1  = 0x30                  | gtest x -- Comparison with 0.
gtest2  = 0x31
gtest4  = 0x32

gcom1   = 0x34                  | gcom x y -- Bitwise complement: y <- ~<x>.
gcom2   = 0x35
gcom4   = 0x36

gmult1  = 0x38                  | gmult x y z -- Multiplication: z <- <x> * <y>.
gmult2  = 0x39
gmult4  = 0x3A

gdiv1   = 0x3C                  | gdiv x y z -- Division: z <- <x> / <y>.
gdiv2   = 0x3D
gdiv4   = 0x3E

gjmp    = 0x40                  | Unconditional jump.
gje     = 0x40+2                | =     Jump iff equal.
gjne    = 0x40+3                | ~=    Jump iff not equal.
```

```
gjle    = 0x44      | <=    Jump iff less or equal      (signed).
gjgt    = 0x44+1    | >     Jump iff greater than       (signed).
gjlt    = 0x44+2    | <     Jump iff less than          (signed).
gjge    = 0x44+3    | >=    Jump iff greater or equal    (signed).

gjlos   = 0x48      | LS    Jump iff lower or same      (unsigned).
gjhi    = 0x48+1    | H     Jump iff higher             (unsigned).
gjlo    = 0x48+2    | L     Jump iff lower              (unsigned).
gjhis   = 0x48+3    | HS    Jump iff higer or same      (unsigned).

| Alternate conditional jump mnemonics for use with giostat:

gjda    = gjlt      | Jump if data available (S bit set).
gjnda   = gjge      | Jump if data not available (S bit reset).

gjp1    = gjlo      | Jump if P1 pressed (C bit set).
gjnp1   = gjhis     | Jump if P1 not pressed (C bit reset).

gjp0    = gje       | Jump if P0 pressed (Z bit set).
gjnp0   = gjne      | Jump if P0 not pressed (Z bit reset).

gcall   = 0x4C      | gcall -- Call subroutine (arguments are on stack or
                    |         in registers).

grtn    = 0x50      | grtn -- Return from subroutine (results are on
                    |         stack or in registers).

grem1   = 0x54      | grem x y z remainder: z <- <x> % <y>.
grem2   = 0x55
grem4   = 0x56

gash1   = 0x58      | gash x y z arithmetic shift: z <- <x> << <y>.
gash2   = 0x59      |   (y is always a 1-byte quantity.)
gash4   = 0x5A      |   ash preserves the sign of x.

glsh1   = 0x5C      | glsh x y z logical shift: z <- <x> << <y>
glsh2   = 0x5D      |   (y is always a 1-byte quantity.)
glsh4   = 0x5E      |   lsh shifts in 0s always.


| DO NOT REASSIGN NEXT 2 ENCODINGS: They are "hard-wired" into simulator.

ghalt   = 0x00      | Stop machine (flash: 111..111 <=> ...11...).
gbpt    = 0xFF      | Breakpoint (for debugging using simulator).

| Addressing mode macros:

.macro  r(R)        R              | Register.
.macro  ir(R)       0x10+R         | Indirect register.
.macro  dir(X)      0x20 LONG(X)   | Direct.
.macro  i(X)        0x30 LONG(X)   | Indirect.
.macro  ix(X, R)    0x40+R LONG(X) | Indexed.
.macro  iix(X, R)   0x50+R LONG(X) | Indirect indexed.
.macro  posti(R)    0x60+R         | Postincrement.
.macro  iposti(R)   0x70+R         | Indirect postincrement.
.macro  pred(R)     0x80+R         | Predecrement.
.macro  ipred(R)    0x90+R         | Indirect predecrement.

| Special "derived" addressing modes:
```

```
| Immediate modes.  Note that the length MUST agree with that in
|    the containing instruction or disaster will result. A more
|    sophisticated assembler would handle this automatically.

.macro  imm1(X) posti(PC) X              | Byte immediate.
.macro  imm2(X) posti(PC) WORD(X)        | Word immediate.
.macro  imm4(X) posti(PC) LONG(X)        | Long immediate.


.macro  rel(X)  ix(X-.-1,PC)             | PC-relative.
.macro  push()  posti(SP)                | Stack push.
.macro  pop()   pred(SP)                 | Stack pop.
```

## A5.3 Sample *G*-Machine Program

```
| Test instructions for G machine.

        .include gmach                   | G-machine definitions.

| Takes n in R0 and returns fib(n) in R1, where ...
|
| fib(n) =
| {
|       if (n < 2) return(n);
|       else return(fib(n-1) + fib(n-2));
| }


| The entry point:
| Compute fibonacci of <r0>, leave in <r1>:

        gcall   rel(fib)
        ghalt

fib:    gcmp4   r(0) imm4(2)             | Is n < 2?
        gjlo    rel(tiny)                | Yup, just return n.

        gmove4  r(0) push()              | Save r0 for later.

        gsub4   r(0) imm4(1) r(0)        | Compute n - 1.
        gcall   rel(fib)                 | r(1) <- fib(n - 1).
        gmove4  r(1) push()              | Save fib(n - 1).

        gsub4   r(0) imm4(1) r(0)        | Compute n - 2.
        gcall   rel(fib)                 | r(1) <- fib(n - 2)
        gadd4   pop() r(1) r(1)          | r(1) <- fib(n - 1) + fib(n - 2).

        gmove4  pop() r(0)               | The saved copy of n.
        grtn

tiny:   gmove4  r(0) r(1)                | Return n.
        grtn
```

## A5.4 Complete MAYBE *G*-Machine Microcode

This section gives the complete MAYBE microcode for the *G* machine, exclusive of the utility microsubroutines listed in appendix 3 and the operator's console microcode listed in appendix 3.

```
| 32-bit G-machine architecture: Microcode support.

| Machine-level register definitions (each is 4 bytes long):

GR0       = 32
GR1       = GR0+4
GR2       = GR1+4
GR3       = GR2+4
GR4       = GR3+4
GR5       = GR4+4
GR6       = GR5+4
GR7       = GR6+4
GR8       = GR7+4
GR9       = GR8+4
GR10      = GR9+4
GR11      = GR10+4
GR12      = GR11+4
GR13      = GR12+4
GR14      = GR13+4
GR15      = GR14+4

SP        = GR14          | G machine's stack pointer.
PC        = GR15          | G machine's program counter.

| Some SRAM registers reserved for particular purposes:

Op1       = 0x60          | Temporary results and operands.
Op2       = Op1+4
Op3       = Op2+4
Op4       = Op3+4
Op5       = Op4+4
Op6       = Op5+4

PSW       = Op6+4         | Processor status word.
MCond     = PSW           | Condition codes are low-order byte of PSW.
Prty      = PSW+3         | Interrupt priority is high-order byte of PSW.

MLen      = PSW+1         | Current operand length.
MOp       = MLen+1        | Current opcode.

MReg      = MOp+1         | Register number of current operand.
MMode     = MOp+2         | Current addressing mode.

MAdrFlag = MMode+1        | "Flags" whether the eff adr is a DRAM or SRAM adr.
MEAdr     = MMode+2       | Effective addresses may be 2 bytes wide (DRAM adrs).
MEAdr2    = MMode+3

| Fetch a byte from machine's instruction stream into SRAM x.
| Increments PC.

.macro fetch(x) l(PC,PC+1,x)  cadd2(1,PC,PC)
```

```
| G machine: Microcode implementation for MAYBE.

| Each instruction is encoded as an OPCODE byte followed by zero or more
| operands.  For opcodes that may have differing lengths of operands, we
| have followed the convention that the low 2 bits of each opcode specify
| operand length, as follows:
| 00      1 byte
| 01      2 bytes (low, high)
| 10      4 bytes
| 11      (unused at present)

| Each OPERAND is encoded as a mode byte followed by zero or more bytes
| of modifier.  The mode byte is of the form MMMMRRRR, where MMMM is
| an encoded addressing mode and RRRR is a general register number
| (currently 0-15).

STACK   = 0x1000                | Base of stack (grows UP from here!).

| Microsubroutine to initialize machine state:

MInit:  cmove4(0, PC)           | Start at beginning.
        cmove4(STACK, SP)       | Base of stack.
        cmove(MAXPRI, Prty)     | Initially disable interrupts.
        jmp(Mintinit)           | Do interrupt initialization.

| Interrupt handler. If an interrupt condition is recognized by
| the Mintest routine, then Mint is called with the address of the
| interrupt vector in Minth.  Mint loads a new SP from the vector,
| then saves the old PC, SP, and PSW (in that order) by pushing
| them on the new stack.  Writes Op3, Op4, and Op5 but leaves Op1 and
| Op2 undisturbed.

Mint:
        refr()  refr()  refr()  | 54 refreshes (this routine is as long
        refr()  refr()  refr()  |   as an instruction).
        refr()  refr()  refr()

        move4(PC, Op3)          | Save interrupt-time PC
        move4(SP, Op4)          |    and stack pointer

        move2(Minth, R0)        | Prepare to read from intr vector.
        cmove(PC, R2)           | First get4 goes into the PC.
        call(get4)              | PC <- <vector_address + 0>.
        cmove(SP, R2)           | Next get4 goes into the SP.
        call(get4)              | SP <- <vector_address + 4>.
        move2(R0, Op5)          | Op5 <- vector_address + 8.

        PUSH4(Op3)              | Save old PC on new stack.
        PUSH4(Op4)              | Save old SP on new stack.
        PUSH4(PSW)              | Save old PSW on new stack.

        move2(Op5, R0)          | R0 <- vector_address + 8.
        cmove(PSW, R2)          | Next get4 goes into the PSW.
        call(get4)              | PSW <- <vector_address + 8>.

        rtn()

| Main G-instruction fetch/execute microsubroutine.
| Dispatches to a G-instruction handler, which returns to caller
```

```
         |    of NextInst via a rtn() microinstruction.

         | Main instruction fetch/execute loop:

NextInst: fetch(R0)                | Get opcode of next G instruction.
          dispatch(R0, ITab)       | Dispatch through instruction table.
                                   | Note: dispatch(...) uses 2*<R0> for offset.

         | This is the 256-entry instruction-dispatch table:

         | Note that hhalt, hbpt, and hii are prefixed by "h" (as opposed to "hg")
         | since these are generic instructions that are used by both the S and the
         | G machines.

         | The tags (loc0x??) are used merely to facilitate lookup by humans
         | of table locations. (REMEMBER: Location 2X corresponds to opcode X.)
ITab:
loc0x00:        WORD(hhalt)     WORD(hii)       WORD(hii)       WORD(hii)
loc0x08:        WORD(hgmove1)   WORD(hgmove2)   WORD(hgmove4)   WORD(hii)
loc0x10:        WORD(hgiostat)  WORD(hgioget)   WORD(hgioput)   WORD(hgioswt)
loc0x18:        WORD(hgsvc)     WORD(hgtrtn)    WORD(hgsetclk4) WORD(hii)    ||
loc0x20:        WORD(hii)       WORD(hii)       WORD(hii)       WORD(hii)    ||
loc0x28:        WORD(hgand1)    WORD(hgand2)    WORD(hgand4)    WORD(hii)
loc0x30:        WORD(hgor1)     WORD(hgor2)     WORD(hgor4)     WORD(hii)
loc0x38:        WORD(hgxor1)    WORD(hgxor2)    WORD(hgxor4)    WORD(hii)
loc0x40:        WORD(hgadd1)    WORD(hgadd2)    WORD(hgadd4)    WORD(hii)
loc0x48:        WORD(hgsub1)    WORD(hgsub2)    WORD(hgsub4)    WORD(hii)
loc0x50:        WORD(hgneg1)    WORD(hgneg2)    WORD(hgneg4)    WORD(hii)
loc0x58:        WORD(hgcmp1)    WORD(hgcmp2)    WORD(hgcmp4)    WORD(hii)
loc0x60:        WORD(hgtest1)   WORD(hgtest2)   WORD(hgtest4)   WORD(hii)
loc0x68:        WORD(hgcom1)    WORD(hgcom2)    WORD(hgcom4)    WORD(hii)
loc0x70:        WORD(hgmult1)   WORD(hgmult2)   WORD(hgmult4)   WORD(hii)
loc0x78:        WORD(hgdiv1)    WORD(hgdiv2)    WORD(hgdiv4)    WORD(hii)
loc0x80:        WORD(hgjmp)     WORD(hii)       WORD(hgje)      WORD(hgjne)
loc0x88:        WORD(hgjle)     WORD(hgjgt)     WORD(hgjlt)     WORD(hgjge)
loc0x90:        WORD(hgjlos)    WORD(hgjhi)     WORD(hgjlo)     WORD(hgjhis)
loc0x98:        WORD(hgcall)    WORD(hii)       WORD(hii)       WORD(hii)
loc0xA0:        WORD(hgrtn)     WORD(hii)       WORD(hii)       WORD(hii)
loc0xA8:        WORD(hgrem1)    WORD(hgrem2)    WORD(hgrem4)    WORD(hii)
loc0xB0:        WORD(hgash1)    WORD(hgash2)    WORD(hgash4)    WORD(hii)
loc0xB8:        WORD(hglsh1)    WORD(hglsh2)    WORD(hglsh4)    WORD(hii)
loc0xC0:        WORD(hii)       WORD(hii)       WORD(hii)       WORD(hii)
loc0xC8:        WORD(hii)       WORD(hii)       WORD(hii)       WORD(hii)
loc0xD0:        WORD(hii)       WORD(hii)       WORD(hii)       WORD(hii)
loc0xD8:        WORD(hii)       WORD(hii)       WORD(hii)       WORD(hii)
loc0xE0:        WORD(hii)       WORD(hii)       WORD(hii)       WORD(hii)
loc0xE8:        WORD(hii)       WORD(hii)       WORD(hii)       WORD(hii)
loc0xF0:        WORD(hii)       WORD(hii)       WORD(hii)       WORD(hii)
loc0xF8:        WORD(hii)       WORD(hii)       WORD(hii)       WORD(hii)
loc0x100:       WORD(hii)       WORD(hii)       WORD(hii)       WORD(hii)
loc0x108:       WORD(hii)       WORD(hii)       WORD(hii)       WORD(hii)
loc0x110:       WORD(hii)       WORD(hii)       WORD(hii)       WORD(hii)
loc0x118:       WORD(hii)       WORD(hii)       WORD(hii)       WORD(hii)
loc0x120:       WORD(hii)       WORD(hii)       WORD(hii)       WORD(hii)
loc0x128:       WORD(hii)       WORD(hii)       WORD(hii)       WORD(hii)
loc0x130:       WORD(hii)       WORD(hii)       WORD(hii)       WORD(hii)
loc0x138:       WORD(hii)       WORD(hii)       WORD(hii)       WORD(hii)
loc0x140:       WORD(hii)       WORD(hii)       WORD(hii)       WORD(hii)
loc0x148:       WORD(hii)       WORD(hii)       WORD(hii)       WORD(hii)
```

| loc0x150: | WORD(hii) | WORD(hii) | WORD(hii) | WORD(hii) |
|-----------|-----------|-----------|-----------|-----------|
| loc0x158: | WORD(hii) | WORD(hii) | WORD(hii) | WORD(hii) |
| loc0x160: | WORD(hii) | WORD(hii) | WORD(hii) | WORD(hii) |
| loc0x168: | WORD(hii) | WORD(hii) | WORD(hii) | WORD(hii) |
| loc0x170: | WORD(hii) | WORD(hii) | WORD(hii) | WORD(hii) |
| loc0x178: | WORD(hii) | WORD(hii) | WORD(hii) | WORD(hii) |
| loc0x180: | WORD(hii) | WORD(hii) | WORD(hii) | WORD(hii) |
| loc0x188: | WORD(hii) | WORD(hii) | WORD(hii) | WORD(hii) |
| loc0x190: | WORD(hii) | WORD(hii) | WORD(hii) | WORD(hii) |
| loc0x198: | WORD(hii) | WORD(hii) | WORD(hii) | WORD(hii) |
| loc0x1A0: | WORD(hii) | WORD(hii) | WORD(hii) | WORD(hii) |
| loc0x1A8: | WORD(hii) | WORD(hii) | WORD(hii) | WORD(hii) |
| loc0x1B0: | WORD(hii) | WORD(hii) | WORD(hii) | WORD(hii) |
| loc0x1B8: | WORD(hii) | WORD(hii) | WORD(hii) | WORD(hii) |
| loc0x1C0: | WORD(hii) | WORD(hii) | WORD(hii) | WORD(hii) |
| loc0x1C8: | WORD(hii) | WORD(hii) | WORD(hii) | WORD(hii) |
| loc0x1D0: | WORD(hii) | WORD(hii) | WORD(hii) | WORD(hii) |
| loc0x1D8: | WORD(hii) | WORD(hii) | WORD(hii) | WORD(hii) |
| loc0x1E0: | WORD(hii) | WORD(hii) | WORD(hii) | WORD(hii) |
| loc0x1E8: | WORD(hii) | WORD(hii) | WORD(hii) | WORD(hii) |
| loc0x1F0: | WORD(hii) | WORD(hii) | WORD(hii) | WORD(hii) |
| loc0x1F8: | WORD(hii) | WORD(hii) | WORD(hii) | WORD(hbpt) |

```
| General-address decoding routines for MAYBE.
| Implements the 10 addressing modes in tables 15.4.


| Uses 4-byte registers; HOWEVER, main-memory addresses (including
|   instruction-stream constants and offsets) are only 2 bytes.


| Microsubroutines to compute the effective address of an operand
|   specified by the next general address in the G instruction
|   stream. Performs any register modifications implied by the
|   general-address encoding (such as postincrement and predecrement).
| Sets MAdrFlag to "SRAM" if the operand is in SRAM (else sets it to "DRAM"),
|   where "SRAM" and "DRAM" are arbitrarily chosen constants (see code).
| MEAdr, MEAdr+1 are set to the effective address (for SRAM adrs, MEAdr+1 is
|   ignored since these are 1-byte addresses).
| Clobbers Op3, temporary registers R0-R4.
| ASSUMES that MLen is preset to the appropriate operand length.

SRAM = 0        | These are defined as constants to be used to "flag"
DRAM = 1        |   whether the effective address is an SRAM or DRAM adr.


| Extracts reg number and mode specified into MReg and MMode, respectively.


MEff:   fetch(MOp)                  | The mode/register byte.
        move(MOp, MReg)            | Copy for register number.
        cand(0x0F, MReg, MReg)     | Mask off the register number bits.
        rotl2(MReg, MReg)          | Multiply by 4 (4-byte-wide regs).
        cadd(GR0, MReg, MReg)      | Add base address in SRAM where the
                                   |   registers begin to get the SRAM
                                   |   adr of the specified register.

        move(MOp, MMode)           | Copy for adr mode.
        rotr4(MMode, MMode)        | Extract the mode bits.
        cand(0x0F, MMode, MMode)
        dispatch(MMode, AdrTab)

| 16-entry mode dispatch table:
```

```
AdrTab:
        WORD(hr)        WORD(hir)       WORD(hdir)      WORD(hi)
        WORD(hix)       WORD(hiix)      WORD(hposti)    WORD(hiposti)
        WORD(hpred)     WORD(hipred)    WORD(GAerr)     WORD(GAerr)
        WORD(GAerr)     WORD(GAerr)     WORD(GAerr)     WORD(GAerr)


| General-address error: Mark the error, then return to the caller.
| This may produce complete garbage somewhere, but, hey, c'est la vie.

GAerr:  cmove(MAYBE_MODERR, BREAK)
        cmove(Op1, MEAdr)               | Give Op1 as the fake address.
        cmove(SRAM, MAdrFlag)           | Op1 is in SRAM.
        rtn()


| Register mode handler: All operand sizes.

hr:     move(MReg, MEAdr)               | Rn is effective address
        cmove(SRAM, MAdrFlag)           |  ... remember that it is in SRAM.
        rtn()


| Indirect register mode handler: Use 2-byte register contents as DRAM adr.

hir:    move(MReg, R0)                  | Fetch low 2 bytes of Rn into MEAdr
        imove(R0, MEAdr)                | Low adr is <R0>    (= <MReg>).
        cadd(1, R0, R0)                 | High adr is <R0>+1 (= <MReg>+1).
        imove(R0, MEAdr+1)
        cmove(DRAM, MAdrFlag)           | Eff. adr is in DRAM, adr <MEAdr>.
        rtn()


| Direct mode handler: 16-bit absolute adr in instruction stream.

hdir:   FETCH4(Op3)                     | Fetch 4-byte address.
        move2(Op3, MEAdr)               | Use low 2 bytes.
        cmove(DRAM, MAdrFlag)           | Eff. adr is in DRAM, adr <MEAdr>.
        rtn()


| Indirect mode handler.

hi:     FETCH4(Op3)                     | Fetch 4-byte address.
        l(Op3,Op3+1,MEAdr)             | Read address from DRAM.
        cadd2(1,Op3,Op3)                | Increment to read 2-byte address.
        l(Op3,Op3+1,MEAdr+1)           | Load high-order adr byte.
        cmove(DRAM, MAdrFlag)           | Eff. adr is in DRAM, adr <MEAdr>.
        rtn()


| Indexed mode handler.

hix:    move(MReg, R1)                  | Fetch low 2 bytes of register
        imove(R1, R3)                   |    into R3, R4.
        cadd(1, R1, R1)
        imove(R1, R4)

        FETCH4(Op3)                     | Fetch 4-byte offset.
        add2(R3,Op3,MEAdr)             | Add in register contents.
        cmove(DRAM, MAdrFlag)           | Eff. adr is in DRAM, adr <MEAdr>.
        rtn()


| Indirect indexed mode handler.
```

```
hiix:    move(MReg, R1)              | Fetch low 2 bytes of register
         imove(R1, R3)               |   into R3, R4.
         cadd(1, R1, R1)
         imove(R1, R4)

         FETCH4(Op3)                 | Fetch 4-byte offset.
         add2(R3,Op3,MEAdr)          | Add in register contents.

| Fall through to...

| Following handler executes one level of indirection on MEAdr, MEAdr+1:
|   i.e., it implements:  MEAdr, MEadr+1  <-  <MEAdr>, <MEAdr>+1.

hind:    l(MEAdr, MEAdr+1, R0)       | The indirection: 1st adr byte.
         cadd2(1, MEAdr, MEAdr)
         l(MEAdr, MEAdr+1, MEAdr+1)  | 2nd adr byte.
         move(R0, MEAdr)
         cmove(DRAM, MAdrFlag)       | Eff. adr is in DRAM, adr <MEAdr>.
         rtn()

| Postincrement mode handlers.

hposti:  move(MReg, R0)              | Fetch low 2 bytes of register
         imove(R0, MEAdr)            |   into MEAdr.
         cadd(1, R0, R0)
         imove(R0, MEAdr+1)
         cmove(DRAM, MAdrFlag)       | Eff. adr is in DRAM, adr <MEAdr>.

| Fall through to ...

| Common code: Increment 4-byte general register at MReg by amount in MLen.

increg:  push(R1)                    | Saves registers...
         push(R2)
         push(R3)
         push(R4)

         cadd(1,MReg,R1)             | Get the other MReg addresses.
         cadd(2,MReg,R2)
         cadd(3,MReg,R3)

         imove(MReg,R4)              | Fetch low byte of register.
         add(MLen,R4,R4)            | Increment.
         movei(R4,MReg)             | Then put it back.

         imove(R1,R4)               | Next byte.
         caddcy(0,R4,R4)            | Propagate carry (if any).
         movei(R4,R1)              | Store it away.

         imove(R2,R4)               | Next byte.
         caddcy(0,R4,R4)            | Propagate carry (if any).
         movei(R4,R2)              | Store it away.

         imove(R3,R4)               | Next byte.
         caddcy(0,R4,R4)            | Propagate carry (if any).
         movei(R4,R3)              | Store it away.

         pop(R4)                    | Restore registers & return.
```

```
        pop(R3)
        pop(R2)
        pop(R1)
        rtn()


| Indirect postincrement handler.

hiposti: move(MReg, R0)              | Fetch low 2 bytes of register
        imove(R0, MEAdr)             |   into MEAdr.
        cadd(1, R0, R0)
        imove(R0, MEAdr+1)

        call(increg)                 | Increment the register.
        jmp(hind)                    | Indirect through MEAdr.

| Predecrement mode handler.

hpred:  call(decreg)                 | Decrement the register.

        move(MReg, R0)               | Fetch low 2 bytes of register
        imove(R0, MEAdr)             |   into MEAdr.
        cadd(1, R0, R0)
        imove(R0, MEAdr+1)
        cmove(DRAM, MAdrFlag)        | Eff. adr is in DRAM, adr <MEAdr>.
        rtn()

| Indirect predecrement handler.

hipred: call(decreg)                 | Decrement the register.

        move(MReg, R0)               | Fetch low 2 bytes of register
        imove(R0, MEAdr)             |   into MEAdr
        cadd(1, R0, R0)
        imove(R0, MEAdr+1)
        jmp(hind)

| Common code: Decrement the general register at MReg by amount in MLen.

decreg: push(R1)                     | Saves registers.
        push(R2)
        push(R3)
        push(R4)

        cadd(1,MReg,R1)              | Get the other MReg addresses.
        cadd(2,MReg,R2)
        cadd(3,MReg,R3)

        imove(MReg,R4)              | Fetch low byte of register.
        sub(R4,MLen,R4)             | Decrement.
        movei(R4,MReg)             | Then put it back.

        imove(R1,R4)               | Next byte.
        csubcy(R4,0,R4)            | Carry propagate.
        movei(R4,R1)              | Store it away.

        imove(R2,R4)               | Next byte.
        csubcy(R4,0,R4)            | Carry propagate.
        movei(R4,R2)              | Store it away.
```

```
            imove(R3,R4)                    | Next byte.
            subcy(R0,R4,R4)                 | Carry propagate.
            movei(R4,R3)                    | Store it away.

            pop(R4)                         | Restore registers & return.
            pop(R3)
            pop(R2)
            pop(R1)
            rtn()


| Microsubroutines to store @-byte operand in SRAM<<R0>> into the
|    current effective address.
| Destroys R0, R1, R2.

SEff1:  ccmp(0, BREAK)          | Test if a bad mode has been detected.
        jne(SErtn)             | If so, bug out and avoid writing garbage.
        ccmp(SRAM, MAdrFlag)        | Is it in SRAM?
        je(SSRAM)                   | Yes, so jump.
        move(R0, R2)                | Source SRAM address.
        move2(MEAdr, R0)            | Target DRAM address.
        jmp(put1)                   | Copy SRAM<<R2>>->DRAM<MEAdr> & rtn.

SEff2:  ccmp(0, BREAK)          | Test if a bad mode has been detected.
        jne(SErtn)             | If so, avoid writing garbage.
        ccmp(SRAM, MAdrFlag)        | Is it in SRAM?
        je(SSRAM)                   | Yes, so jump.
        move(R0, R2)                | Source SRAM address.
        move2(MEAdr, R0)            | Target DRAM address.
        jmp(put2)                   | Copy SRAM<<R2>>->DRAM<MEAdr> & rtn.

SEff4:  ccmp(0, BREAK)          | Test if a bad mode has been detected.
        jne(SErtn)             | If so, avoid writing garbage.
        ccmp(SRAM, MAdrFlag)        | Is it in SRAM?
        je(SSRAM)                   | Yes, so jump.
        move(R0, R2)                | Source SRAM address.
        move2(MEAdr, R0)            | Target DRAM address.
        jmp(put4)                   | Copy SRAM<<R2>>->DRAM<MEAdr> & rtn.

SSRAM:  move(MEAdr, R1)             | Target SRAM address.
        jmp(imovei4)                | Copy SRAM<<R0>>->SRAM<MEAdr> & rtn.

SErtn:  rtn()

| Microsubroutines to load @-byte operand into SRAM<<R0>> from the
|    current effective address.

LEff1:  ccmp(SRAM, MAdrFlag)        | Is it in SRAM?
        je(LSRAM)                   | Yes, so jump.
        move(R0, R2)                | Target SRAM address.
        move2(MEAdr, R0)            | Source DRAM address.
        jmp(get1)                   | Copy DRAM<<MEAdr>>->SRAM<R1> & rtn.

LEff2:  ccmp(SRAM, MAdrFlag)        | Is it in SRAM?
        je(LSRAM)                   | Yes, so jump.
        move(R0, R2)                | Target SRAM address.
        move2(MEAdr, R0)            | Source DRAM address.
        jmp(get2)                   | Copy DRAM<<MEAdr>>->SRAM<R1> & rtn.
```

```
LEff4:  ccmp(SRAM, MAdrFlag)          | Is it in SRAM?
        je(LSRAM)                     | Yes, so jump.
        move(R0, R2)                  | Target SRAM address.
        move2(MEAdr, R0)              | Source DRAM address.
        jmp(get4)                     | Copy DRAM<<MEAdr>>->SRAM<R1> & rtn.


LSRAM:  move(R0, R1)                  | Target SRAM address.
        move(MEAdr, R0)               | Source SRAM address.
        jmp(imovei4)                  | Copy SRAM<MEAdr>->SRAM<<R1>> & rtn.



| Microsubroutine to load an operand specified by the next general
|   address in the M instruction stream. Returns the operand in
|   Op1, after having copied previous Op1 contents to Op2.
|
| Note: Sign-extends operand to 4 bytes.

LoadGA1: move4(Op1, Op2)             | Save previous Op1.
         cmove(1, MLen)              | In case incr or decr mode.
         call(MEff)                  | Decode general address.
         cmove(Op1, R0)             | Fetch <EA> into Op1.
         jmp(LEff1)

LoadGA2: move4(Op1, Op2)             | Save previous Op1.
         cmove(2, MLen)              | In case incr or decr mode.
         call(MEff)                  | Decode general address.
         cmove(Op1, R0)             | Fetch <EA> into Op1.
         jmp(LEff2)

LoadGA4: move4(Op1, Op2)             | Save previous Op1.
         cmove(4, MLen)              | In case incr or decr mode.
         call(MEff)                  | Decode general address.
         cmove(Op1, R0)             | Fetch <EA> into Op1.
         jmp(LEff4)


| Microsubroutine to store Op1 into an operand specified by the next general
|   address in the M instruction stream.
|
| This code follows similar pattern to LoadGA, above.

StoreGA1:
         cmove(1, MLen)              | In case incr or decr mode.
         call(MEff)
         cmove(Op1, R0)             | Store Op1 into EA.
         jmp(SEff1)

StoreGA2:
         cmove(2, MLen)              | In case incr or decr mode.
         call(MEff)
         cmove(Op1, R0)             | Store Op1 into EA.
         jmp(SEff2)

StoreGA4:
         cmove(4, MLen)              | In case incr or decr mode
         call(MEff)
         cmove(Op1, R0)             | Store Op1 into EA.
         jmp(SEff4)
```

```
| Microcoded instruction handlers for MAYBE G-machine instruction set.

| move@ x y: x <- <y>.

hgmove1: call(LoadGA1)              | Source operand.
         call(StoreGA1)            | Copy to destination.
         rtn()                     | Back for next instruction.

hgmove2: call(LoadGA2)              | Source operand.
         call(StoreGA2)            | Copy to destination.
         rtn()                     | Back for next instruction.

hgmove4: call(LoadGA4)              | Source operand.
         call(StoreGA4)            | Copy to destination.
         rtn()                     | Back for next instruction.

| add@ x y z: z <- <x> + <y>.

hgadd1:  call(LoadGA1)              | Fetch 1st operand.
         call(LoadGA1)              | Fetch 2nd operand.
         add(Op1, Op2, Op1)        | Add ops.
         call(StoreGA1)
         rtn()

hgadd2:  call(LoadGA2)              | Fetch 1st operand.
         call(LoadGA2)              | Fetch 2nd operand.
         add2(Op1, Op2, Op1)       | Add 2 bytes.
         call(StoreGA2)
         rtn()

hgadd4:  call(LoadGA4)              | Fetch 1st operand.
         call(LoadGA4)              | Fetch 2nd operand.
         add2( Op1,   Op2,   Op1)| Add all 4 bytes.
         addcy(Op1+2, Op2+2, Op1+2)
         addcy(Op1+3, Op2+3, Op1+3)
         call(StoreGA4)
         rtn()

| sub@ x y z: z <- <x> + <y>.

hgsub1:  call(LoadGA1)              | Fetch 1st operand.
         call(LoadGA1)              | Fetch 2nd operand.
         sub(Op2, Op1, Op1)        | Subtract ops.
         call(StoreGA1)
         rtn()

hgsub2:  call(LoadGA2)              | Fetch 1st operand.
         call(LoadGA2)              | Fetch 2nd operand.
         sub2(Op2, Op1, Op1)       | Subtract 2-byte ops.
         call(StoreGA2)
         rtn()

hgsub4:  call(LoadGA4)              | Fetch 1st operand.
         call(LoadGA4)              | Fetch 2nd operand.
         sub2( Op2,   Op1,   Op1)| Subtract all 4 bytes.
         subcy(Op2+2, Op1+2, Op1+2)
         subcy(Op2+3, Op1+3, Op1+3)
         call(StoreGA4)
```

```
                rtn()

    | neg@ x y: y <- -<x> (2's complement negation).

    hgneg1: call(LoadGA1)           | Fetch operand.
            neg(Op1, Op1)           | Negate op.
            call(StoreGA1)
            rtn()

    hgneg2: call(LoadGA2)           | Fetch operand.
            not(Op1, Op1)           | Negate 2 bytes.
            not(Op1+1, Op1+1)
            cadd2(1, Op1, Op1)
            call(StoreGA2)
            rtn()

    hgneg4: call(LoadGA4)           | Fetch operand.
            not(Op1, Op1)
            not(Op1+1, Op1+1)
            not(Op1+2, Op1+2)
            not(Op1+3, Op1+3)
            cadd2(1, Op1, Op1)
            caddcy(0, Op1+2, Op1+2)
            caddcy(0, Op1+3, Op1+3)
            call(StoreGA4)
            rtn()

    | com x y: y <- ~<x> (bitwise complement).

    hgcom1: call(LoadGA1)           | Fetch operand.
            not(Op1, Op1)           | Complement op.
            call(StoreGA1)
            rtn()

    hgcom2: call(LoadGA2)           | Fetch operand.
            not(Op1, Op1)           | Complement 2 bytes.
            not(Op1+1, Op1+1)
            call(StoreGA2)
            rtn()

    hgcom4: call(LoadGA4)           | Fetch operand.
            not(Op1, Op1)
            not(Op1+1, Op1+1)
            not(Op1+2, Op1+2)
            not(Op1+3, Op1+3)
            call(StoreGA4)
            rtn()

    | and@ x y z: z <- <x> & <y>.

    hgand1: call(LoadGA1)           | Fetch 1st operand.
            call(LoadGA1)           | Fetch 2nd operand.
            and(Op1, Op2, Op1)      | Bitwise AND.
            call(StoreGA1)
            rtn()

    hgand2: call(LoadGA2)           | Fetch 1st operand.
            call(LoadGA2)           | Fetch 2nd operand.
            and(Op1, Op2, Op1)      | Bitwise AND.
```

```
            and(Op1+1, Op2+1, Op1+1)
            call(StoreGA2)
            rtn()

hgand4: call(LoadGA4)              | Fetch 1st operand.
        call(LoadGA4)              | Fetch 2nd operand.
        and(Op1, Op2, Op1)         | Bitwise AND.
        and(Op1+1, Op2+1, Op1+1)
        and(Op1+2, Op2+2, Op1+2)
        and(Op1+3, Op2+3, Op1+3)
        call(StoreGA4)
        rtn()

| or@ x y z: z <- <x> | <y>.

hgor1:  call(LoadGA1)              | Fetch 1st operand.
        call(LoadGA1)              | Fetch 2nd operand.
        or(Op1, Op2, Op1)          | Bitwise OR.
        call(StoreGA1)
        rtn()

hgor2:  call(LoadGA2)              | Fetch 1st operand.
        call(LoadGA2)              | Fetch 2nd operand.
        or(Op1, Op2, Op1)          | Bitwise OR.
        or(Op1+1, Op2+1, Op1+1)
        call(StoreGA2)
        rtn()

hgor4:  call(LoadGA4)              | Fetch 1st operand.
        call(LoadGA4)              | Fetch 2nd operand.
        or(Op1, Op2, Op1)          | Bitwise OR.
        or(Op1+1, Op2+1, Op1+1)
        or(Op1+2, Op2+2, Op1+2)
        or(Op1+3, Op2+3, Op1+3)
        call(StoreGA4)
        rtn()

| xor@ x y z: z <- <x> ^ <y>.

hgxor1: call(LoadGA1)              | Fetch 1st operand.
        call(LoadGA1)              | Fetch 2nd operand.
        xor(Op1, Op2, Op1)         | Bitwise XOR.
        call(StoreGA1)
        rtn()

hgxor2: call(LoadGA2)              | Fetch 1st operand.
        call(LoadGA2)              | Fetch 2nd operand.
        xor(Op1, Op2, Op1)         | Bitwise XOR.
        xor(Op1+1, Op2+1, Op1+1)
        call(StoreGA2)
        rtn()

hgxor4: call(LoadGA4)              | Fetch 1st operand.
        call(LoadGA4)              | Fetch 2nd operand.
        xor(Op1, Op2, Op1)         | Bitwise XOR.
        xor(Op1+1, Op2+1, Op1+1)
        xor(Op1+2, Op2+2, Op1+2)
        xor(Op1+3, Op2+3, Op1+3)
        call(StoreGA4)
```

```
                    rtn()

| Multiplication.
| First argument is the multipicand, second is the multiplier.
| These use the multiplier routine defined in subrs.uasm, which
| expects the multiplier to be in Op1 and the multiplicand in Op2.

hgmult1:
        call(LoadGA1)           | Fetch multiplicand.
        call(LoadGA1)           | Fetch multiplier.
        call(mult)
        move(product, Op1)
        call(StoreGA1)          | Put result.
        rtn()

hgmult2:
        call(LoadGA2)           | Fetch multiplicand.
        call(LoadGA2)           | Fetch multiplier.
        call(mult)
        move2(product, Op1)
        call(StoreGA2)          | Put result.
        rtn()

hgmult4:
        call(LoadGA4)           | Fetch multiplicand.
        call(LoadGA4)           | Fetch multiplier.
        call(mult)
        move4(product, Op1)
        call(StoreGA4)          | Put result.
        rtn()

| Division.
| These routines use the division subroutine defined in subrs.uasm,
| which expects the dividend to be in Op2 and the divisor in Op1,
| so the first argument becomes the dividend, and the second the
| divisor: div(x,y,z):  z <- <x> / <y>.

hgdiv1:
        call(LoadGA1)           | Fetch dividend.
        call(LoadGA1)           | Fetch divisor.
        call(divide)
        move(quotient, Op1)
        call(StoreGA1)          | Put result.
        rtn()

hgdiv2:
        call(LoadGA2)           | Fetch dividend.
        call(LoadGA2)           | Fetch divisor.
        call(divide)
        move2(quotient, Op1)
        call(StoreGA2)          | Put result.
        rtn()

hgdiv4:
        call(LoadGA4)           | Fetch dividend.
        call(LoadGA4)           | Fetch divisor.
        call(divide)
        move4(quotient, Op1)
        call(StoreGA4)          | Put result.
```

```
                    rtn()

        | Remainder.
        | These routines use the division subroutine defined in subrs.uasm,
        | which expects the dividend to be in Op2 and the divisor in Op1,
        | so the first argument becomes the dividend, and the second the
        | divisor: rem(x,y,z):  z <- <x> % <y>.

        hgrem1:
                call(LoadGA1)           | Fetch dividend.
                call(LoadGA1)           | Fetch divisor.
                call(divide)
                move(remainder, Op1)
                call(StoreGA1)          | Put result.
                rtn()

        hgrem2:
                call(LoadGA2)           | Fetch dividend.
                call(LoadGA2)           | Fetch divisor.
                call(divide)
                move2(remainder, Op1)
                call(StoreGA2)          | Put result.
                rtn()

        hgrem4:
                call(LoadGA4)           | Fetch dividend.
                call(LoadGA4)           | Fetch divisor.
                call(divide)
                move4(remainder, Op1)
                call(StoreGA4)          | Put result.
                rtn()

        | Shifting.
        | These routines use the shift subroutine defined in subrs.uasm,
        | which expects the number to shift in Op1 and the byte used for
        | shift-control in Op2. This is unfortunate, since LoadGA
        | would get the two numbers in the wrong registers.
        | ash(x,y,z): z <- <x> << <y>, arithmetic shift preserves sign.

        hgash1: call(LoadGA1)           | Data.
                cmove(1, MLen)          | Do most of LoadGA1.
                call(MEff)
                cmove(Op2, R0)          | But put it into Op2 instead.
                call(LEff1)
                cand(0x80, Op1, Op3)    | Store sign-adjustment byte.
                call(shift)
                call(StoreGA1)
                rtn()

        hgash2: call(LoadGA2)           | Data.
                cmove(1, MLen)          | Do most of LoadGA1.
                call(MEff)
                cmove(Op2, R0)          | But put it into Op2 instead.
                call(LEff1)
                cand(0x80, Op1+1, Op3)  | Store sign-adjustment byte.
                call(shift)
                call(StoreGA2)
                rtn()
```

```
hgash4:  call(LoadGA4)              | Data.
         cmove(1, MLen)             | Do most of LoadGA1.
         call(MEff)
         cmove(Op2, R0)            | But put it into Op2 instead.
         call(LEff1)
         cand(0x80, Op1+3, Op3)   | Store sign-adjustment byte.
         call(shift)
         call(StoreGA4)
         rtn()


| lsh(x,y,z): z <- <x> << <y>, logical shift shifts in zeros always.

hglsh1:  call(LoadGA1)              | Data.
         cmove(1, MLen)             | Do most of LoadGA1.
         call(MEff)
         cmove(Op2, R0)            | But put it into Op2 instead.
         call(LEff1)
         cmove(0, Op3)             | Clear adjustment byte.
         cmove(0, Op1+1)          | Clear upper bytes.
         cmove2(0, Op1+2)
         call(shift)
         call(StoreGA1)
         rtn()


hglsh2:  call(LoadGA2)              | Data.
         cmove(1, MLen)             | Do most of LoadGA1.
         call(MEff)
         cmove(Op2, R0)            | But put it into Op2 instead.
         call(LEff1)
         cmove(0, Op3)             | Clear adjustment byte.
         cmove2(0, Op1+2)         | Clear upper bytes.
         call(shift)
         call(StoreGA2)
         rtn()


hglsh4:  call(LoadGA4)              | Data.
         cmove(1, MLen)             | Do most of LoadGA1.
         call(MEff)
         cmove(Op2, R0)            | But put it into Op2 instead.
         call(LEff1)
         cmove(0, Op3)             | Clear adjustment byte.
         call(shift)
         call(StoreGA4)
         rtn()
```

| Compare instructions.
| Compute x - y, leaving condition byte SCZ00000 in MCond
| (Note that the ALU E bit is of little use in multiprecision!).
| Note that when doing x - y (NO carry-in), the C bit from the ALU
|    indicates x < y.
| To test for zero, result bytes are ORed into R1 (which is zero
|    if result is zero).
| Arithmetic overflow occurs if x and y have different signs and
|    the sign of the result is not the sign of x. Following code
|    segments branch to hgcmpX on no overflow, to hgcmpV on overflow.


| cmp@ x y                        | Compare two operands, set virtual CC.

```
hgcmp1:  call(LoadGA1)              | Fetch 1st operand (x).
```

```
          call(LoadGA1)           | Fetch 2nd operand (y).

          sub(Op2, Op1, R1)       | Compute <Op2> - <Op1>.
          cond(MCond)             | Save ALU conditions.
          xor(Op1, Op2, R2)       | Like signs?
          jpl(hgcmpX)             | Yup, no overflow.
          xor(Op2, R1, R2)        | Sign of x = sign of result?
          jpl(hgcmpX)             | Yup, no overflow.
          jmp(hgcmpV)             | Else, overflow!

hgcmp2:   call(LoadGA2)           | Fetch 1st operand (y).
          call(LoadGA2)           | Fetch 2nd operand (x).

          sub2(Op2, Op1,  Op3)    | Compute <Op2> - <Op1>.
          cond(MCond)             | Save ALU conditions.
          or(Op3, Op3+1, R1)      | OR bytes for zero test, leaving OR in R1.
          xor(Op1+1, Op2+1, R2)   | Like signs?
          jpl(hgcmpX)             | Yup, no overflow.
          xor(Op3+1, Op2+1, R2)   | Sign of x = sign of result?
          jpl(hgcmpX)             | Yup, no overflow.
          jmp(hgcmpV)             | Else, overflow!

hgcmp4:   call(LoadGA4)           | Fetch 1st operand (y).
          call(LoadGA4)           | Fetch 2nd operand (x).

          sub2( Op2, Op1,  Op3)   | Compute <Op2> - <Op1>.
          subcy(Op2+2,Op1+2,Op3+2)
          subcy(Op2+3,Op1+3,Op3+3)
          cond(MCond)             | Save ALU conditions.
          or(Op3+3,Op3+2,R1)      | OR bytes for zero test.
          or(Op3+1, R1, R1)
          or(Op3, R1, R1)         | Leave OR of byte in R1.
          xor(Op1+3, Op2+3, R2)   | Like signs?
          jpl(hgcmpX)             | Yup, no overflow.
          xor(Op3+3, Op2+3, R2)   | Sign of x = sign of result?
          jpl(hgcmpX)             | Yup, no overflow.
          jmp(hgcmpV)             | Else, overflow!


| On overflow, flip the N bit from the result to produce S bit:

hgcmpV: cxor(0x80, MCond, MCond)

| Here with ALU condition byte (used for S, C bits) in MCond, ORed bytes
|   in R1:

hgcmpX: cand(0xC0,MCond,MCond)  | Mask to SC000000.
        ccmp(0, R1)             | Test for zero; we left OR in R1, remember?
        jne(xcmp)               | Not zero, so just return.
        cor(0x20, MCond, MCond) | Else force Z bit.
xcmp:   rtn()                   | Done, so return.

| Test instructions are the same as the compare instructions except
|   that they compare a single argument to 0. Overflow is not possible.

hgtest1:
        call(LoadGA1)           | Fetch operand.
        csub(Op1, 0, R1)        | Compute <Op1> - 0, leave result in R1.
        cond(MCond)             | Save ALU conditions.
        jmp(hgcmpX)             | No overflow.
```

```
hgtest2:
        call(LoadGA2)           | Fetch operand.
        csub(Op1, 0, Op1)       | Compute <Op1> - 0.
        csubcy(Op1+1, 0, Op1+1)
        cond(MCond)             | Save ALU conditions.
        or(Op1, Op1+1, R1)      | OR bytes for zero test, leaving OR in R1.
        jmp(hgcmpX)             | No overflow.

hgtest4:
        call(LoadGA4)           | Fetch operand.
        csub(Op1, 0, Op1)       | Compute <Op1> - 0.
        csubcy(Op1+1, 0, Op1+2)
        csubcy(Op1+2, 0, Op1+2)
        csubcy(Op1+3, 0, Op1+3)
        cond(MCond)             | Save ALU conditions.
        or(Op1+3,Op1+2,R1)      | OR bytes for zero test.
        or(Op1+1, R1, R1)
        or(Op1, R1, R1)         | Leave OR of byte in R1.
        jmp(hgcmpX)             | No overflow.


| call x -- Call to subroutine at address x.

hgcall: cmove(4, MLen)          | 2-byte target address (better not matter!).
        call(MEff)              | Compute effective adr.
        ccmp(DRAM, MAdrFlag)    | Had better be a DRAM location.
        jne(adrerr)

        PUSH4(PC)               | Push old PC (recall we're using 4 bytes).
        move2(MEAdr, PC)        | Install new PC.
        rtn()

| ERROR: Illegal address in call, jump, or handler declaration.

adrerr: cmove(MAYBE_ADRERR, BREAK)
        rtn()

| rtn -- Return from subroutine.

hgrtn:  POP4(PC)                | Pop & restore PC.
        rtn()

| jmp x -- Unconditional jump to target address x.

hgjmp:  cmove(4, MLen)          | 4-byte jump address.
        call(MEff)              | Compute effective address.
        ccmp(DRAM, MAdrFlag)    | Had better be a DRAM location.
        jne(adrerr)             | It is.

jmpx:   move2(MEAdr, PC)        | Copy effective address into PC.
        rtn()

| A couple of microsubroutines for handling conditional jumps:
jiff0:  ccmp(0, R0)             | Jump iff <R0>=0, else don't.
        je(hgjmp)               | R0 zero, so jump.
        | Else fall through...

jmpno:  cmove(4, MLen)          | 4-byte addresses.
```

```
            call(MEff)                   | Fetch, decode, and ignore operand.
            rtn()

jiffn0:  ccmp(0, R0)                     | Jump iff <R0> nonzero, else don't.
         jne(hgjmp)
         jmp(jmpno)

| Conditional jump instructions.

| je x: Jump iff equal.
hgje:    cand(0x20, MCond, R0)   | Fetch Z bit.
         jmp(jiffn0)             | Jump iff set.

| jne x: Jump iff not equal.
hgjne:   cand(0x20, MCond, R0)   | Fetch Z bit.
         jmp(jiff0)              | Jump iff not set.

| jle x: Jump iff less than or equal (signed).
hgjle:   cand(0xA0, MCond, R0)   | Fetch S, Z bits.
         jmp(jiffn0)             | Jump iff set.


| jgt x: Jump iff greater than (signed).
hgjgt:   cand(0xA0, MCond, R0)   | Fetch S, Z bits.
         jmp(jiff0)              | Jump iff not set.

| jlt x: Jump iff less than (signed).
hgjlt:   cand(0x80, MCond, R0)   | Fetch S bit.
         jmp(jiffn0)             | Jump iff set.

| jge x: Jump iff greater than or equal (signed).
hgjge:   cand(0x80, MCond, R0)   | Fetch S bit.
         jmp(jiff0)              | Jump iff not set.

| jlos x: Jump iff lower or same (unsigned).
hgjlos: cand(0x60, MCond, R0)    | Fetch C,Z bits: C = 1 -> (x < y) unsigned.
         jmp(jiffn0)             | Jump iff either set.

| jhi x: Jump iff higher (unsigned).
hgjhi:   cand(0x60, MCond, R0)   | Fetch C,Z bits: C = 1 -> (x < y) unsigned.
         jmp(jiff0)              | Jump iff neither set.

| jlo x: Jump iff lower (unsigned).
hgjlo:   cand(0x40, MCond, R0)   | Fetch C bit: C = 1 -> (x < y) unsigned.
         jmp(jiffn0)             | Jump iff set.

| jhis x: Jump iff lower (unsigned).
hgjhis: cand(0x40, MCond, R0)    | Fetch C bit: C = 1 -> (x < y) unsigned.
         jmp(jiff0)              | Jump iff not set.


| I/O instructions:

| iostat reads the 8250 interface and the P0 and P1 switches, then
|   returns a byte coded like an scmp or stest byte.
|
| The S bit (bit 7) is set if there are data available to read.
| The C bit (bit 6) is set if P1 is being pressed.
| The Z bit (bit 5) is set if P0 is being pressed.
```

```
        |
        | This is intended to be used with the conditional jump instructions
        |    that test these bits.
        |

hgiostat:
            cmove(0, MCond)             | Make a zero.
            ccmp(0, inchar)            | Test if character has been read.
            je(hgiostat_nochar)        | Skip if no character.
            cmove(0x80, MCond)         | Set the S bit for data available.
hgiostat_nochar:

            jnp1(hgiostat_nop1)
            cor(0x40, MCond, MCond)    | Set C bit for P1 pressed.
hgiostat_nop1:

            jnp0(hgiostat_nop0)
            cor(0x20, MCond, MCond)    | Set Z bit for P0 pressed.
hgiostat_nop0:

            rtn()

        | ioget reads a character from the HP, if there is one.
        | A 0 will be returned if no character is available.

hgioget:
            move(inchar, Op1)          | Get character for store.
            ccmp(0, inchar)            | Skip if no character.
            je(hgiogetnochar)
            cmove(0, inchar)           | Signal the character as taken.
            call(ioack)                | Acknowledge the character.
hgiogetnochar:
            call(StoreGA1)             | Store the character.
            rtn()

        | ioput sends a character to the HP. The character is restricted
        |    to 7 bits so as to not interfere with control codes that the
        |    MAYBE may need to send.

hgioput:
            call(LoadGA1)              | Get the character.
            cand(0x7F, Op1, R0)        | Put it in R0 for call to iosend.
            call(iosend)               | Send the character to the HP.
            rtn()

        | ioswt reads the switches on the lab kit and returns a byte
        |    representing their value.

hgioswt:
            swt(Op1)                   | Read the byte.
            call(StoreGA1)             | Store it.
            rtn()

        | gsvc -- Supervisor call.

hgsvc:  FETCH1(Op1)                    | Fetch the 1-byte code from instr.
        cmove2(SSVCVEC, Minth)         | Trap vector address.
        call(Mint)                     | Go through the interrupt sequence.
        PUSH1(Op1)                     | Then additionally push the code.
```

```
                rtn()                          | Done!

    | gtrtn -- Trap/interrupt return.

    hgtrtn: POP4(PSW)                          | Restore regs from current stack.
            POP4(Op1)                          | Old SP.
            POP4(PC)                           | Old PC.
            move4(Op1, SP)                     | Done popping, restore old SP.
            rtn()                              | Finished!

    | gsetclk4 -- Pops 4-byte integer off stack and sets alarm-clock timer.

    hgsetclk4: call(LoadGA4)                   | Read 4-byte source operand into Op1
            move4(Op1, Mclkcount)              |   and set the alarm clock from it.
            rtn()                              | Then done!

    | Symbol that tells us how much microcode ROM we're using:
    END:
    ENDHI  = END/256                           | MAX VALUE: 0b11111 (= 31).
```

# Bibliography

Abelson and Sussman [1985]: Abelson, H., and G. Sussman, *Structure and Interpretation of Computer Programs*, MIT Press, Cambridge, MA, 1984.

Agha [1986]: Agha, G., *ACTORS: A Model of Concurrent Computation in Distributed Systems*, MIT Press, Cambridge, MA, 1986.

Aho, Sethi, and Ullman [1986]: Aho, A., R. Sethi, and J. Ullman, *Compilers: Principles, Techniques, and Tools*, Addison-Wesley, Reading, MA, 1986.

Ajtai, Komlos, and Szemeredi [1983]: Ajtai, M., J. Komlos, and E. Szemeredi, "Sorting in $c \log n$ Parallel Steps," *Combinatorica*, vol. 3, no.1, 1983, pp. 1–19.

Amdahl, Blaauw, and Brooks [1964]: Amdahl, G., G. Blaauw, and F. Brooks, "Architecture of the IBM System/360," *IBM Journal of Research and Development*, vol. 8, no. 2, April 1964, pp. 87–101.

Arvind and Kathail [1981]: Arvind and V. Kathail, "A Multiple Processor Dataflow Machine That Supports Generalized Procedures," *Proceedings of the 8th Annual Symposium on Computer Architecture*, 1981, pp. 291–302.

Ashbury et al. [1985]: Ashbury, R., S. G. Frison, and T. Roth, "Concurrent Computers Ideal for Inherently Parallel Problems," *Computer Design*, 1 September 1985.

Babb [1988]: Babb, R. G., *Programming Parallel Processors*, Addison-Wesley, Reading, MA, 1988.

Backus [1978]: Backus, J., "Can Programming Be Liberated from the von Neumann Style? A Functional Style and Its Algebra of Programs," *Communications of the ACM*, vol. 16, no. 8, August 1978.

Baer [1980]: Baer, J.-L., *Computer Systems Architecture*, Computer Science Press, Rockville, MD, 1980.

Barron [1981]: Barron, D., *Pascal—The Language and Its Implementation*, Wiley, Chichester, 1981.

Barron [1983]: Barron, I. M., et al., "The Transputer," *Electronics*, 17 November 1983, pp. 109ff.

Batcher [1968]: Batcher, K. E., "Sorting Networks and Their Applications," *Proceedings of the Spring Joint Computer Conference*, AFIPS, 1968, pp. 307–314.

Batcher [1977]: Batcher, K. E., "The Multi-dimensional Access Memory in STARAN," *IEEE Transactions on Computers*, vol. C-26, no. 2, February 1977, pp. 174–177.

Batcher [1982]: Batcher, K. E., "Bit-Serial Parallel Processing Systems," *IEEE Transactions on Computers*, vol. C–30, no. 5, May 1982.

Baudet [1978]: Baudet, G. M., *The Design and Analysis of Algorithms for Asynchronous Multiprocessors*, Ph.D. Thesis, Carnegie-Mellon University, April 1978.

Bell et al. [1970]: Bell, C. G., R. Cady, H. McFarland, B. DeLagi,J. O'Laughlin, R Noonan, and W. Wulf, "A New Architecture for Mini-Computers: The DEC PDP-11," *Proceedings of the Spring Joint Computer Conference*, AFIPS, 1970, pp. 657–675 (reprinted in Siewiorek, Bell, and Newell [1982]).

Bell and Newell [1971]: Bell, C. G., and A. Newell, *Computer Structures: Readings and Examples*, McGraw-Hill, New York, 1971.

Bell, Mudge, and McNamara [1978]: Bell, C. G., J. C. Mudge, and J. McNamara, eds., *Computer Engineering: A DEC View of Hardware Design*, Digital Press, Bedford, MA, 1978.

Bernstein and Goodman [1981]: Bernstein, P., and N. Goodman, "Concurrency Control in Distributed Database Systems," *ACM Computing Surveys*, vol. 13, no. 2, June 1981, pp. 185–221.

Bertsekas and Gallager [1987]: Bertsekas, D., and R. Gallager, *Data Networks*, Prentice-Hall, Englewood Cliffs, NJ, 1987.

Blaauw and Brooks [1964]: Blaauw, G., and F. Brooks, "The Structure of SYSTEM/360. Part I: Outline of the Logical Structure," *IBM Systems Journal*, vol. 3, no. 2, 1964, pp. 119–135 (reprinted in Siewiorek, Bell, and Newell [1982]).

Bonseigneur [1969]: Bonseigneur, P., "Description of the 7600 Computer System," *IEEE Computer Group News*, May 1969, pp. 11–15.

Borill and Theus [1984]: Borill, P., and J. Theus, "An Advanced Communication Protocol for the Proposed IEEE 896 Futurebus," *IEEE Micro*, August 1984, pp. 42–56.

Bouknight et al. [1972]: Bouknight, W. J., S. A. Denenberg, D. E. McIntyre, J. M. Randall, A. H. Sameh, and D. L. Slotnick, "The Illiac IV System," *Proceedings of the IEEE*, vol. 60, no. 4, April 1972, pp. 369–388.

Brinch Hansen [1972]: Brinch Hansen, P., "Structured Multiprogramming," *Communications of the ACM*, vol. 15, no. 7, July 1972, pp. 574–578.

Brinch Hansen [1985]: Brinch Hansen, P., *Brinch Hansen on Pascal Compilers*, Prentice-Hall, Englewood Cliffs, NJ, 1985.

Brooks [1975]: Brooks, F., *The Mythical Man-Month: Essays on Software Engineering*, Addison-Wesley, Reading, MA, 1975.

Burks, Goldstine, and von Neumann [1946]: Burks, A. W., H. H. Goldstine, and J. von Neumann, "Preliminary Discussion of the Logical Design of an Electronic Computing Instrument," *U.S. Army Ordinance Department Report*, 1946. Reprinted in *Collected Works of John von Neumann*, vol. 5, Macmillan, New York, 1963, pp. 34–79.

Campbell and Habermann [1974]: Campbell, R., and A. N. Habermann, "The Specification of Process Synchronization by Path Expressions," in Kaiser [1974], pp. 89–102.

Chaney [1979]: Chaney, T. J., "Comments on 'A Note on Synchronizer or Interlock Maloperation,' " *IEEE Transactions on Computers*, vol. C-28, October 1979, pp. 802–804.

Church [1941]: Church, A., "The Calculi of Lambda Conversion," *Annals of Mathematics Studies*, vol. 6, Princeton University Press, Princeton, NJ, 1941.

Clark et al. [1981]: Clark, D., R. Halstead, S. Keohan, J. Sieber, J. Test, and S. Ward, "The TRIX 1.0 Operating System," *IEEE Distributed Processing Quarterly*, vol. 1, no. 2, December 1981.

Clark and Emer [1985]: Clark, D., and J. Emer, "Performance of the VAX-11/780 Translation Buffer: Simulation and Measurement," *ACM Transactions on Computer Systems*, vol. 3, no. 1, February 1985, pp. 31–62.

Clocksin and Mellish [1981]: Clocksin, W., and C. Mellish, *Programming in Prolog*,

Springer-Verlag, Berlin, 1981.

Cody [1981]: Cody, W. J., "Analysis of Proposals for the Floating-Point Standard," *IEEE Computer*, vol. 14, March 1981, pp. 63–68.

Cohen [1981]: Cohen, D., "On Holy Wars and a Plea for Peace," *IEEE Computer*, vol. 14, no. 10, October 1981, pp. 48–54.

Colwell et al. [1985]: Colwell, R. P., C. Y. Hitchcock, E. D. Jensen, H. M. B. Sprunt, and C. P. Kollar, "Computers, Complexity, and Controversy," *IEEE Computer*, vol. 18, no. 9, September 1985, pp. 8–19.

Coonen [1980]: Coonen, J. T., "An Implementation Guide to a Proposed Standard for Floating Point Arithmetic," *IEEE Computer*, vol. 13, no. 1, January 1980, pp. 75–87.

Corbato et al. [1962]: Corbato, F., et al., "An Experimental Time Sharing System," *Proceedings of the Fall Joint Computer Conference*, vol. 21, AFIPS, pp. 335–344.

Couranz and Wann [1975]: Couranz, G. R., and D. F. Wann, "Theoretical and Experimental Behavior of Synchronizers Operating in the Metastable Region," *IEEE Transactions on Computers*, vol. C-24, June 1975, pp. 604–616.

Courtois and Parnas [1971]: Courtois, P., and D. Parnas, "Concurrent Control with Readers and Writers," *Communications of the ACM*, vol. 14, no. 10, October 1971, pp. 667–668.

Curry and Feys [1974]: Curry, H. B., and R. Feys, *Combinatory Logic*, North-Holland, Amsterdam, 1974.

Dally [1987]: Dally, W. J., *A VLSI Architecture for Concurrent Data Structures*, Kluwer, Deventer, 1987.

DEC [1972]: *Unibus Interface Manual*, Digital Equipment Corporation, Maynard, MA, 1972.

DEC [1975]: "UNIBUS Theory and Operation," *PDP-11 Peripherals Manual*, Digital Equipment Corporation, Maynard, MA, 1975.

Del Corso, Kirrmann, and Nicoud [1986]: Del Corso, D., H. Kirrmann, and J. D. Nicoud, *Microcomputer Buses and Links*, Academic Press, San Diego, 1986.

Denning [1970]: Denning, P. J., "Virtual Memory," *Computing Surveys*, vol. 2, September 1970, pp. 153–189.

Denning [1980]: Denning, P. J., "Working Sets Past and Present," *IEEE Transactions on Software Engineering*, vol. SE-6, pp. 64–84.

Dennis [1972?]: Dennis, J. B., *Class Notes for M.I.T. Course 6.032*, circa 1972.

Dennis [1979]: Dennis, J. B., "The Varieties of Data Flow Computers," *Proceedings of the 1st International Conference on Distributed Computing Systems*, October 1979, pp. 430–439.

Dennis and Misunas [1975]: Dennis, J. B., and D. P. Misunas, "Preliminary Architecture for a Basic Data–Flow Processor," *Proceedings of the 2nd Annual Symposium on Computer Architecture*, Houston, TX, January 1975, pp. 126–132.

Dennis, Leung, and Misunas [1979]: Dennis, J. B., C. K. C. Leung, and D. P. Misunas, *A Highly Parallel Processor Using a Data Flow Machine Language*, Laboratory for Computer Science, M.I.T., CSG Memo 134–1, June 1979.

Desrochers [1987]: Desrochers, G., *Principles of Parallel and Multiprocessing*, McGraw-Hill, New York, 1987.

Dijkstra [1968a]: Dijkstra, E., "Cooperating Sequential Processes," in Genuys [1968].

Dijkstra [1968b]: Dijkstra, E., "The Structure of the 'THE' Multi-Programming System," *Communications of the ACM*, vol. 11, no. 5, May 1968, pp. 341–346.

Dijkstra [1971]: Dijkstra, E., "Hierarchical Ordering of Sequential Processes," *Acta Infor-*

*matica*, vol. 2, no. 1, 1971, pp. 115–138.

Dijkstra et al. [1976]: Dijkstra, E. W., L. Lamport, A. J. Martin, C. S. Scholten, and E. F. M. Steffens, "On-the-Fly Garbage Collection: An Exercise in Co-operation," in *Language Hierarchies and Interfaces*, Lecture Notes in Computer Science, vol. 46, Springer-Verlag, New York, 1976.

Ditzel and McLellan [1987]: Ditzel, D., and H. R. McLellan, "The Hardware Architecture of the CRISP Microprocessor," *14th International Symposium on Computer Architecture*, Pittsburgh, PA, June 1987, pp. 309–319.

Dongarra [1987]: Dongarra, J. J., ed., *Experimental Parallel Computing Architectures*, North-Holland, Amsterdam, 1987.

Finkel [1986]: Finkel, R., *An Operating Systems Vade Mecum*, Prentice-Hall, Englewood Cliffs, NJ, 1986.

Finnila and Love [1977]: Finnila, C. A., and H. H. Love, "The Associative Linear Array Processor," *IEEE Transactions on Computers*, vol. C–26, no. 2, February 1977, pp. 112–125.

Flynn [1972]: Flynn, M. J., "Some Computer Organizations and Their Effectiveness," *IEEE Transactions on Computers*, vol. C-21, no. 9, September 1972, pp. 948–960.

Gardner [1971–72]: Gardner, M., "Mathematical Games," *Scientific American*, vol. 224, February 1971, pp. 112ff.; March 1971, pp. 106ff.; April 1971, pp. 114ff.; January 1972, pp. 104ff..

Garey and Johnson [1979]: Garey, M. R., and D. S. Johnson, *Computers and Intractability: A Guide to the Theory of NP-Completeness*, W. H. Freeman, San Francisco, CA, 1979.

Genuys [1968]: F. Genuys, ed., *Programming Languages*, Academic Press, New York, 1968.

Gibson [1985]: Gibson, G., "Draft SpurBus Specification," Computer Science Division, University of California at Berkeley, September 1985.

Goldberg and Robson [1983]: Goldberg, A., and D. Robson, *Smalltalk-80: The Language and Its Implementation*, Addison-Wesley, Reading, MA, 1983.

Goodman [1983]: Goodman, J. R., "Using Cache Memory To Reduce Processor-Memory Traffic," *10th International Symposium on Computer Architecture*, 1983.

Goodman and Chiang [1984]: Goodman, J., and M.-C. Chiang, "The Use of Static Column RAM as a Memory Hierarchy," *11th International Symposium on Computer Architecture*, 1984, pp. 167–174.

Gottlieb et al. [1983]: Gottlieb, A., B. D. Lubachevsky, and L. Rudolph, "The NYU Ultracomputer—Designing an MIMD Shared Memory Parallel Computer," *IEEE Transactions on Computers*, vol. C-32, no. 2, February 1983, pp. 175–189.

Greenblatt [1984]: Greenblatt, R. D., "The LISP Machine," in *Interactive Programming Environments*, McGraw-Hill, New York, 1984.

Gurd, Kirkham, and Boehm [1986]: Gurd, J., C. Kirkham, and W. Boehm, "The Manchester Dataflow Computing System," in Dongarra [1987], pp. 177–219.

Gurd, Kirkham, and Watson [1985]: Gurd, J., C. Kirkham, and I. Watson, "The Manchester Prototype Dataflow Computer," *Communications of the ACM*, vol. 28, no. 1, January 1985, pp. 34–52.

Gustavson [1984]: Gustavson, D. B., "Computer Buses: A Tutorial," *IEEE Micro*, August 1984, pp. 7–22.

Gustavson and Theus [1983]: Gustavson, D. B., and J. Theus, "Wired-OR Logic on Transmission Lines," *IEEE Micro*, June 1983, pp. 51–55.

Habermann [1969]: Habermann, A. N., "Prevention of System Deadlocks," *Communications of the ACM*, vol. 12, no. 7, July 1969, pp. 373–377.

Halstead [1981]: Halstead, R., "Architecture of a Myriaprocessor," in J. Solinsky, ed., *Advanced Computer Concepts*, La Jolla Institute, La Jolla, CA, 1981.

Halstead [1984]: Halstead, R., "Implementation of Multilisp: Lisp on a Multiprocessor," *ACM Symposium on LISP and Functional Programming*, Austin, TX, August 1984, pp. 293–298.

Halstead [1985]: Halstead, R., "Multilisp: A Language for Concurrent Symbolic Computation," *ACM Transactions on Programming Languages and Systems*, vol. 7, no. 4, October 1985, pp. 501–538.

Halstead and Ward [1980]: Halstead, R., and S. Ward, "The MuNet: A Scalable Decentralized Architecture for Parallel Computation," *Proceedings of the International Symposium on Computer Architecture*, La Baule, France, May 1980.

Hamming [1980]: Hamming, R. W., *Coding and Information Theory*, Prentice-Hall, Englewood Cliffs, NJ, 1980.

Hastings [1955]: Hastings, C., *Approximations for Digital Computers*, Princeton University Press, Princeton, NJ, 1955.

Hauck and Dent [1968]: Hauck, E., and B. Dent, "Burroughs' B6500/B7500 Stack Mechanism," *Proceedings of the Spring Joint Computer Conference*, AFIPS, 1968, pp. 245–251 (reprinted in Siewiorek, Bell, and Newell [1982]).

Havender [1968]: Havender, J., "Avoiding Deadlocks in Multi-Tasking Systems," *IBM Systems Journal*, vol. 7, no. 2, 1968, pp. 74–84.

Hennessy [1984]: Hennessy, J. L., "VLSI Processor Architecture," *IEEE Transactions on Computers*, vol. C-33, no. 12, December 1984, pp. 1221–1246.

Hennessy et al. [1982]: Hennessy, J. L., N. Jouppi, J. Gill, F. Baskett, A. Stong, T. Gross, C. Rowen, and J. Leonard, "The MIPS Machine," *Proceedings of the IEEE Compcon*, Spring 1982, pp. 2–7.

Hewitt [1977]: Hewitt, C., "Viewing Control Structures as Patterns of Passing Messages," *Journal of Artificial Intelligence*, vol. 8, no. 3, June 1977, pp. 324–364.

Higbie [1972]: Higbie, L. C., "The OMEN Computers: Associative Array Processors," *COMPCON '72 Digest*, 1972, pp. 287–290.

Hill and Peterson [1981]: Hill, F. J., and G. R. Peterson, *Introduction to Switching Theory and Logical Design*, Wiley, New York, 1981.

Hill and Peterson [1987]: Hill, F. J., and G. R. Peterson, *Digital Systems: Hardware Organization and Design*, Wiley, New York, 1987.

Hillis [1981]: Hillis, W. D., *The Connection Machine*, MIT Artificial Intelligence Laboratory Memo 646, September 1981.

Hillis [1985]: Hillis, W. D., *The Connection Machine*, MIT Press, Cambridge, MA, 1985.

Hindley and Seldin [1986]: Hindley, J. R., and J. P. Seldin, *Introduction to Combinators and Lambda-Calculus*, Cambridge University Press, Cambridge, U.K., 1986.

Hintz and Tate [1972]: Hintz, R. G., and D. P. Tate, "Control Data STAR-100 Processor Design," *Proceedings of the IEEE Compcon*, 1972, pp. 1–4.

Hoare [1972]: Hoare, C. A. R., "Towards a Theory of Parallel Programming," in Hoare and Perrot [1972], pp. 61–71.

Hoare [1974]: Hoare, C. A. R., "Monitors: An Operating System Structuring Concept," *Communications of the ACM*, vol. 17, no. 10, October 1974, pp. 549–557.

Hoare [1978]: Hoare, C. A. R., "Communicating Sequential Processes," *Communications of the ACM*, vol. 21, no. 8, August 1978, pp. 666–677.

Hoare and Perrot [1972]: Hoare, C. A. R., and R. Perrot, eds., *Operating System Techniques*, Academic Press, London, 1972.

Holland [1959]: Holland, J. H., "A Universal Computer Capable of Executing an Arbitrary Number of Sub-Programs Simultaneously," *Proceedings of the 1959 Eastern Joint Computer Conference*, pp. 108–113.

Hopcroft and Ullmann [1979]: Hopcroft, J. E., and J. D. Ullman, *Introduction to Automata Theory, Languages, and Computation*, Addison-Wesley, Reading, MA, 1979.

Hopfield [1982]: Hopfield, J. J., "Neural Networks and Physical Systems with Emergent Collective Computational Abilities," *Proceedings of the National Academy of Sciences*, vol. 79, 1982, pp. 2554–2558.

IBM [1967]: "System/360 Model 91," special issue of the *IBM Journal of Research and Development*, vol. 11, no. 1, January 1967.

Janson [1985]: Janson, P., *Operating Systems: Structures and Mechanisms*, Academic Press, London, 1985.

Jensen and Wirth [1974]: Jensen, K., and N. Wirth, *Pascal User Manual and Report*, Lecture Notes in Computer Science, vol. 18, Springer-Verlag, New York, 1974.

Kaiser [1974]: Kaiser, C., ed., *Operating Systems*, Springer-Verlag, Berlin, 1974.

Kernighan and Ritchie [1978]: Kernighan, B., and D. Ritchie, *The C Programming Language*, Prentice-Hall, Englewood Cliffs, NJ, 1978.

Kernighan and Ritchie [1989]: Kernighan, B., and D. Ritchie, *The C Programming Language*, second edition, Prentice-Hall, Englewood Cliffs, NJ, 1989.

Kilburn et al. [1962]: Kilburn, T., D. B. G. Edwards, M. J. Lanigan, and F. H. Sumner, "One-Level Storage System," *IRE Transactions on Electronic Computers*, vol. EC-11, no. 2, April 1962, pp. 223–235 (reprinted in Siewiorek, Bell, and Newell [1982]).

Kleene [1952]: Kleene, S., *Introduction to Metamathematics*, Van Nostrand, New York, 1952.

Kogge [1981]: Kogge, P., *The Architecture of Pipelined Computers*, McGraw-Hill, New York, 1981.

Kowalski [1979]: Kowalski, R., *Logic for Problem Solving*, North-Holland, Amsterdam, 1979.

Kuck [1978]: Kuck, D. J., *Computers and Computations*, Wiley, New York, 1978.

Kuck, Muraoka, and Chen [1972]: Kuck, D., Y. Muraoka, and S.-C. Chen, "On the Number of Simultaneously Executable in Fortran-Like Programs and Their Resulting Speedup," *IEEE Transactions on Computers*, vol. C-21, no. 12, December 1972, pp. 1293–1310.

Kuck et al. [1980]: Kuck, D. J., R. H. Kuhn, B. Leasure, and M. Wolfe, "Analysis and Transformation of Programs for Parallel Computation," *Proceedings of the 4th International Computer Software and Applications Conference*, October 1980.

Kung [1982]: Kung, H. T., "Why Systolic Architectures?," *IEEE Computer*, January 1982.

Kung and Leiserson [1980]: Kung, H. T., and C. E. Leiserson, "Algorithms for VLSI Processor Arrays," in Mead and Conway [1980], pp. 271–292.

Lawrie [1982]: Lawrie, D., "Alignment and Access of Data in an Array Processor," *IEEE Transactions on Computers*, vol. C-24, no. 12, December 1975, pp. 1145–1155.

Leiserson [1984]: Leiserson, C. E., "Fat-Trees: Universal Networks for Hardware-Efficient Supercomputing," *IEEE Transactions on Computers*, vol. C-34, no. 10, October 1985.

Levy [1978]: Levy, J., "Buses, the Skeleton of Computer Structures," in Bell, Mudge, and

McNamara [1978], pp. 269–299.

Lipovski [1976]: Lipovski, G. J., "The Architecture of a Simple, Effective Control Processor," in M. Sami, J. Wilmink, and R. Zaks, eds., *Microprocessing and Microprogramming*, North-Holland, Amsterdam, 1976.

Liu and Gibson [1984]: Liu, Y., and G. Gibson, *Microcomputer Systems: The 8086/8088 Family*, Prentice-Hall, Englewood Cliffs, NJ, 1984.

Liu and Layland [1973]: Liu, C. L., and J. W. Layland, "Scheduling Algorithms for Multiprogramming in a Hard Real-Time Environment," *Journal of the ACM*, vol. 20, no. 1, January 1973, pp. 46–61.

Lonergan and King [1961]: Lonergan, W., and P. King, "Design of the B 5000 System," *Datamation*, vol. 7, no. 5, May 1961, pp. 28–32 (reprinted in Siewiorek, Bell, and Newell [1982]).

Mattson et al. [1970]: Mattson, R., J. Gecsei, D. Slutz, and I. Traiger, "Evaluation Techniques for Storage Hierarchies," *IBM Systems Journal*, vol. 9, 1970, pp. 78–117.

McCarthy et al. [1965]: McCarthy, J., P. W. Abrahams, D. J. Edwards, T. P. Hart, and M. I. Levin, *LISP 1.5 Programmer's Manual*, second edition, MIT Press, Cambridge, MA, 1965.

McCulloch and Pitts [1943]: McCulloch, W. S., and W. Pitts,"A Logical Calculus of the Ideas Immanent in Nervous Activity," *Bulletin of Mathematical Biophysics*, no. 5, 1943, pp. 115–133.

Mead and Conway [1980]: Mead, C. A., and L. A. Conway, *Introduction to VLSI Systems*, Addison-Wesley, Reading, MA, 1980.

Metcalf and Boggs [1976]: Metcalf, R. M., and D. R. Boggs, "Ethernet: Distributed Packet Switching for Local Computer Networks," *Communications of the ACM*, vol. 19, no. 7, July 1976, pp. 395–404.

Minsky [1967]: Minsky, M., *Computation: Finite and Infinite Machines*, Prentice-Hall, Englewood Cliffs, NJ, 1967.

Minsky and Papert [1969]: Minsky, M., and S. Papert, *Perceptrons*, MIT Press, Cambridge, MA, 1969.

Mok and Dertouzos [1978]: Mok, A., and M. Dertouzos, "Multiprocessor Scheduling in a Hard Real-Time Environment," *Proceedings of the 7th Texas Conference on Computing Systems*, Houston, TX, October 1978.

Mok and Ward [1979]: Mok, A., and S. Ward, "Distributed Broadcast Channel Access," *Computer Networks*, vol. 3, no. 5, November 1979, pp. 327–335.

Monolithic Memories [1985]: *LSI Handbook*, Monolithic Memories, Santa Clara, CA, 1985.

Moon [1985]: Moon, D., "Architecture of the Symbolics 3600," *12th Annual Symposium on Computer Architecture*, Boston, MA, June 1985, pp. 76–83.

Multibus [1983]: *Multibus II Bus Architecture Specification Handbook*, Intel Corporation, 1983.

Naur [1963]: Naur, P., ed., "Revised Report on the Algorithmic Language ALGOL 60," *Communications of the ACM*, vol. 6, no. 1, January 1963, pp. 1–17.

Nori et al. [1981]: Nori, K., U. Ammann, K. Jensen, H. Nageli, and C. Jacobi, "Pascal P Implementation Notes," in Barron [1981], pp. 125–170.

Organick [1972]: Organick, E., *The Multics System: An Examination of Its Structure*, MIT Press, Cambridge, MA, 1972.

Organick [1973]: Organick, E., *Computer System Organization: The B5700/B6700 Series*, Academic Press, New York, 1973.

Parnas [1975]: Parnas, D., "On a Solution to the Cigarette Smokers' Problem," *Communications of the ACM*, vol. 18. no. 3, March 1975, pp. 181–183.

Patterson [1985]: Patterson, D. A., "Reduced Instruction Set Computers," *Communications of the ACM*, vol. 28, no. 1, January 1985, pp. 8–21.

Patterson and Ditzel [1980]: Patterson, D. A., and D. R. Ditzel, "The Case for the RISC," *Computer Architecture News*, vol. 8, no. 6, 15 October 1980, pp. 25–33.

Patterson and Hennessy [1985]: Patterson, D. A., and J. L. Hennessy, "Response to 'Computers, Complexity, and Controversy,' " *IEEE Computer*, vol. 18, no. 11, November 1985, pp. 142–143.

Patterson and Sequin [1982]: Patterson, D. A., and C. H. Sequin, "A VLSI RISC," *Computer*, vol. 15, no. 9, September 1982, pp. 8–22.

Peatman [1980]: Peatman, J. B., *Digital Hardware Design*, McGraw-Hill, New York, 1980.

Pechoucek [1976]: Pechoucek, M., "Anomalous Response Times of Input Synchronizers," *IEEE Transactions on Computers*, vol. C-25, February 1976, pp. 133–139.

Pratt [1975]: Pratt, T., *Programming Languages: Design and Implementation*, Prentice-Hall, Englewood Cliffs, NJ, 1975.

Radin [1982]: Radin, G., "The 801 Minicomputer," *Proceedings of the Symposium on Architectural Support for Programming Languages and Operating Systems*, Palo Alto, CA, March 1982, pp. 39–47.

Ramamoorthy and Li [1977]: Ramamoorthy, C. V., and H. F. Li, "Pipeline Architecture," *Computing Surveys*, March 1977, pp. 61–101.

Randall and Russell [1964]: Randall, B., and L. Russell, *ALGOL 60 Implementation*, Academic Press, New York, 1964.

Randell [1973]: Randell, B., *The Origins of Digital Computers: Selected Papers*, Springer Verlag, New York, 1973.

Reed and Kanodia [1979]: Reed, D., and R. Kanodia, "Synchronization with Eventcounts and Sequencers," *Communications of the ACM*, vol. 22, no. 2, February 1979, pp. 115–123.

Rees and Clinger [1986]: Rees, J., and W. Clinger, eds., "Revised[3] Report on the Algorithmic Language Scheme," *ACM SIGPLAN Notices*, vol. 21, no. 12, December 1986, pp. 37–79.

Rettberg [1979]: Rettberg, R., et al., "Development of a Voice Funnel System: Design Report," BBN Report 4088, Bolt, Beranek, and Newman, Cambridge, MA, August 1979.

Richards [1969]: Richards, M., "BCPL: A Tool for Compiler Writing and System Programming," *Proceedings of the Spring Joint Computer Conference*, AFIPS, 1969, pp. 557–566.

Ritchie and Thompson [1974]: Ritchie, D., and K. Thompson, "The Unix Time-Sharing System," *Communications of the ACM*, vol. 21, no. 2, February 1974, pp. 365–375.

Rogers [1967]: Rogers, H., *Theory of Recursive Functions and Effective Computability*, McGraw-Hill, New York, 1967.

Rosenblatt [1962]: Rosenblatt, F., *Principles of Neurodynamics*, Spartan, Rochelle Park, NJ, 1962.

Rudolph [1972]: Rudolph, J. A., "A Production Implementation of an Associative Array Processor—STARAN," *Proceedings of the Fall Joint Computer Conference*, AFIPS, 1972, pp. 229–241.

Rumelhart et al. [1987]: Rumelhart, D. E., J. L. McClelland, and the PDP Research Group, *Parallel Distributed Processing*, vol. 1, MIT Press, Cambridge, MA, 1987.

Russell [1978]: Russell, R., "The Cray-1 Computer System," *Communications of the ACM*, vol. 21, no. 1, January 1978, pp. 63–72 (reprinted in Siewiorek, Bell, and Newell [1982]).

Sammet [1969]: Sammet, J., *Programming Languages: History and Fundamentals*, Prentice-Hall, Englewood Cliffs, NJ, 1969.

Schwartz [1980]: Schwartz, J., "Ultracomputers," *ACM Transactions on Programming Languages and Systems*, vol. 2, no. 4, October 1980, pp. 484–521.

Seitz [1985]: Seitz, C. L., "The Cosmic Cube," *Communications of the ACM*, vol. 28, no. 1, January 1985, pp. 22–33.

Siewiorek, Bell, and Newell [1982]: Siewiorek, D., C. G. Bell, and A. Newell, eds., *Computer Structures: Principles and Examples*, McGraw-Hill, New York, 1982.

Shapiro [1983]: Shapiro, E. Y., "A Subset of Concurrent Prolog and Its Interpreter," Institute for New Generation Computer Technology technical report TR-003, January 1983.

Sherburne et al. [1984]: Sherburne, R. W., M. G. H. Katevenis, D. A. Patterson, and C. H. Sequin, "A 32-Bit NMOS Microprocessor with a Large Register File," *IEEE Journal of Solid-State Circuits*, vol. SC-19, no. 5, October 1984.

Slotnick et al. [1962]: Slotnick, D., W. Borck, and R. McReynolds, "The SOLOMON Computer," *Proceedings of the Fall Joint Computer Conference*, AFIPS, 1962, pp. 97-107.

Smith [1978]: Smith, B. J., "A Pipelined, Shared Resource MIMD Computer," *Proceedings of the International Conference on Parallel Processing*, 1978.

Smith [1982]: Smith, A. J., "Cache Memories," *ACM Computing Surveys*, vol. 14, no. 3, September 1982, pp. 473–530.

Steele et al. [1984]: Steele, G., et al., *Common Lisp Reference Manual*, Digital Press, Burlington, MA, 1984.

Stevens [1964]: Stevens, W., "The Structure of SYSTEM/360; Part II—System Implementations," *IBM Systems Journal*, vol. 3, no. 2, 1964, pp. 136–143 (reprinted in Siewiorek, Bell, and Newell [1982]).

Stewart and Ward [1988]: Stewart, W. K., and S. A. Ward, "A Solution to a Special Case of the Synchronization Problem," *IEEE Transactions on Computers*, vol. 37, no. 1, January 1988, pp. 123–125.

Stone [1987]: Stone, H., *High-Performance Computer Architecture*, Addison-Wesley, Reading, MA, 1987.

Strecker [1978]: Strecker, W., "VAX-11/780—A Virtual Address Extension to the DEC PDP-11 Family," *Proceedings of the National Computer Conference*, AFIPS, 1978, pp. 967–980 (reprinted in Siewiorek, Bell, and Newell [1982]).

Su and Hsieh [1982]: Su, S. Y. H., and Y. Hsieh, "Design and Diagnosis of Reconfigurable Modular Digital Systems," in S. P. Kartashev and S. I. Kartashev, eds., *Designing and Programming Modern Computers and Systems*, vol. I: *LSI Modular Computer Systems*, Prentice-Hall, Englewood Cliffs, NJ, 1982.

Sutherland and Mead [1977]: Sutherland, I. E., and C. A. Mead, "Microelectronics and Computer Science," *Scientific American*, vol. 237, no. 3, September 1977, pp. 210–228.

Swan et al. [1977]: Swan, R. J., S. H. Fuller, , and D. P. Siewiorek, "CM*: A Modular, Multi–Microprocessor," *Proceedings of the National Computer Conference,* AFIPS, 1977, pp. 637–644.

Sweazey and Smith [1986]: Sweazey, P., and A. J. Smith, "A Class of Compatible Cache-Consistency Protocols and Their Support by the IEEE Futurebus," *Proceedings of the 13th International Symposium on Computer Architecture*, Tokyo, June 1986, pp. 414–423.

Tanenbaum [1981]: Tanenbaum, A. S., *Computer Networks*, Prentice-Hall, Englewood Cliffs, NJ, 1981.

Tanenbaum [1984]: Tanenbaum, A. S., *Structured Computer Organization*, Prentice-Hall, Englewood Cliffs, NJ, 1984.

Thakkar, Gifford, and Fielland [1987]: Thakkar, S., P. Gifford, and G. Fielland, "Balance: A Shared Memory Multiprocessor," *Proceedings of the 2nd International Conference on Supercomputing*, Santa Clara, CA, May 1987.

Thornton [1970]: Thornton, J. E., *Design of a Computer: The Control Data 6600*, Scott, Foresman, Glenview, IL, 1970.

Thurber et al. [1972]: Thurber, K. J., L. A. Jensen, L. L. Jack, P. C. Kinney, P. C. Patton, and L. C. Anderson, "A Systematic Approach to the Design of Digital Bussing Structures," *Proceedings of the Fall Joint Computer Conference*, AFIPS, 1972, pp. 719–739.

TI [1984]: *The TTL Data Book for Design Engineers*, Texas Instruments, Dallas, TX, 1984.

Toffoli and Margolus [1987]: Toffoli, T., and N. Margolus, *Cellular Automata Machines: A New Environment for Modeling*, MIT Press, Cambridge, MA, 1987.

Tomasulo [1967]: Tomasulo, R. M., "An Efficient Algorithm for Exploiting Multiple Arithmetic Units," *IBM Journal of Research and Development*, vol. 11, no. 1, January 1967, pp. 25–33.

Turing [1936]: Turing, A. M., "On Computable Numbers, with an Application to the Entscheidungsproblem," *Proceedings of the London Mathematical Society*, vol. 2, no. 42, 1936–37, pp. 230–265.

Ungar [1984]: Ungar, D., "Generation Scavenging: A Non-disruptive High Performance Storage Reclamation Algorithm," *SIGPLAN Notices: Software Engineering Symposium on Practical Software Development Environments*, Pittsburgh, PA, April 1984.

Ungar et al. [1984]: Ungar, D., R. Blau, P. Foley, D. Samples, and D. Patterson, "Architecture of SOAR: Smalltalk on a RISC," *Proceedings of the 11th Annual IEEE Symposium on Computer Architecture*, 1984, pp. 188–197.

Veendrick [1980]: Veendrick, H. J. M., "The Behavior of Flip-Flops Used as Synchronizers and Prediction of Their Failure Rate," *IEEE Journal of Solid-State Circuits*, vol. SC-15, April 1980, pp. 604–616.

Vick [1978]: Vick, C. R., "PEPE Architecture—Present and Future," *Proceedings of the 1978 National Computer Conference*, AFIPS, pp. 981–992.

VME [1982]: *VMEbus Specification Manual*, Motorola Corporation, 1982.

Ward [1978]: Ward, S., "The MuNet: A Multiprocessor Message-Passing System Architecture," *Proceedings of the 7th Texas Conference on Computing Systems*, October 1978.

Ward [1980]: Ward, S., "TRIX: A Network-Oriented Operating System," *Proceedings of the Spring COMPCON*, San Francisco, CA, February 1980.

Ward and Halstead [1980]: Ward, S., and R. Halstead, "A Syntactic Theory of Message Passing," *Journal of the ACM*, vol. 27, no. 2, January 1980, pp. 365–383.

Ward and Terman [1980]: Ward, S., and C. Terman, "An Approach to Personal Computing," *Proceedings of the Spring COMPCON*, San Francisco, CA, February 1980.

Waser and Flynn [1982]: Waser, S., and M. J. Flynn, *Introduction to Arithmetic for Digital Systems Engineers*, Holt, Rinehart, and Winston, New York, 1982.

Watson [1972]: Watson, W. J., "The TI ASC—A Highly Modular and Flexible Super Computer Architecture," *Proceedings of the Fall Joint Computer Conference*, AFIPS, 1972, pp. 221–228.

Wegner [1980]: Wegner, P., *Programming with Ada*, Prentice-Hall, Englewood Cliffs, NJ, 1980.

Weste [1985]: Weste, N. H. E., *Principles of CMOS VLSI Design*, Addison-Wesley, Reading, MA, 1985.

Whitby-Strevens [1985]: Whitby-Strevens, C., "The Transputer," *Proceedings of the 12th Annual International Symposium on Computer Architecture*, Boston, MA, June 1985, pp. 292–300.

Wilkes [1951]: Wilkes, M., "The Best Way To Design an Automatic Calculating Machine," *Manchester University Computer Inaugural Conference*, Ferranti, Ltd., London, July 1951, pp. 15–16.

Wilkes [1965]: Wilkes, M., "Slave Memories and Dynamic Storage Allocation," *IEEE Transactions on Electronic Computers*, vol. EC-14, no. 2, February 1965, pp. 270–271.

Wilkes and Stringer [1953]: Wilkes, M., and J. Stringer, "Microprogramming and the Design of the Control Circuits in an Electronic Digital Computer," *Proceedings of the Cambridge Philosophical Society*, part 2, vol. 49, April 1953, pp. 230–238 (reprinted in Siewiorek, Bell, and Newell [1982]).

Wolfram [1986]: Wolfram, S., *Theory and Applications of Cellular Automata*, World Scientific, Singapore, 1986.

Wulf, Shaw, and Hilfinger [1981]: Wulf, W. A., M. Shaw, and P. N. Hilfinger, *Fundamental Structures of Computer Science*, Addison-Wesley, Reading, MA, 1981.

Xilinx [1986]: *The Programmable Gate Array Design Handbook*, Xilinx, Inc., San Jose, CA, 1986.

Yeh [1976]: Yeh, R., *Applied Computation Theory: Analysis, Design, Modeling*, Prentice-Hall, Englewood Cliffs, NJ, 1976.

# Index

indeterminacy, 187, 195
indeterminate behavior, 187
index register, 460
indirection, 433
inference, 277
infix form, 382
information, 2–3, 33
    amount of, 2–3
    flow of, 7
    speed of transfer, 238
    theoretical maximum rate of flow, 7
information content, 3
information density, 238
information representation
    by continuous variables, 3
    discrete, 3
    electronic, 2
information storage, 3
innovation, 621
    architectural, 605
input gating, 14–15
input/output (I/O), 253–254, 264, 291,
        348, 352, 356
    memory-mapped, 253, 548
input/output devices, 539, 542, 548, 600
    device registers, 253–254, 548
    interfacing, 253, 591
    memory-mapped, 619
instruction, 281, 286, 315, 336–337,
        356–357, 359
    address fields, 358
    atomic, 576–577
    branch, *see* instruction, conditional
        jump *or* instruction, unconditional
        jump
    comparison, 388, 625
    conditional jump, 385, 388–389, 449
    decoding, 287, 355, 357, 513, 515
    destination operand, 358
    execution, 355
    execution time, 337
    fetch, 355, 357, 474, 478, 513, 515
    fetch/dispatch loop, 593
    fetch/execute loop, 375–376
    generic, 339–340
    high-level, 513
    illegal, 375
    jump, 385, 451, 523–524
    load/store, 514
    no-operation, 517
    prefetch, 478, 496
    privileged, 408–409, 458, 539, 549
    source operands, 358
    supervisor-call, 491

test-and-clear, 569, 617
test-and-set, 568–569, 571
unconditional jump, 389
vector, 615
virtual machine, 534
instruction counter, *see* program counter
instruction-fetch unit (IFU), 515,
        522–525, 529, 614
instruction formats, 358–361
    flexible, 459
    immediate-mode, 520
    one-address, 359
    short, 354, 451
    stack (zero-address), 359
    three-address, 358, 451
    two-address, 358, 451
    variable, 451
instruction handlers as microsubroutines,
        380
instruction register, 515
instruction-set architecture, *see* architec-
        ture, instruction-set
instruction sets, 287, 547
    comparison of, 362
    extended, 349
    virtual, 539
instruction size, 514
instruction stream, 367–368, 373, 431,
        613
    arguments in, 370
    constants from, 370, 520–522
instruction traps, 349–352, 408, 411, 458,
        538, 540, 593
instructions per second, 357
    millions of (MIPS), 608, 613
integers, 45, 287
integrated circuit (IC), 21–24, 105, 120,
        134
    pin count, 107, 122, 289
    pins, 106
integrated-circuit chip, 8, 221
intelligence, 622
interleaving, *see* memory, interleaving
interlock delay, 517
interlocks, 526
International Business Machines (IBM),
        530
    Thomas J. Watson Research Center,
        530
interpretation, 269–279, 281, 325, 335,
        357, 459, 514, 529, 549
    cost, 273
    layers of, 269, 273, 276
    levels of, 275, 281, 287, 357
    of machine instructions, 307
    of microcode, 294
    overhead, 357, 513

rstorex, 526–527
rsub, 516
race condition, 79, 570
radiation, *see* noise
radio communications equipment, 459
random-access memory (RAM), 127–128, 134, 217, 354
  cell, 605
  chips, 286
  dynamic, *see* dynamic RAM
  SRAM, write enable input, 288
  static RAM (SRAM), 288–289, 292, 297, 304–306, 309, 311, 317, 319–320, 326–328, 372, 376, 442, 514
RAS, *see* dynamic RAM
read, 249, 253
read, 563, 582, 584–585, 587
read error, 252
read-only memory (ROM), 75, 110, 119–123, 126–128, 130, 133–134, 144–146, 174, 188–190, 269, 272, 276, 288, 337
  chips, 286
  erasable PROM (EPROM), 120
  field-programmable ROM, 120
  implementation, 120–123
  mask-programmed ROM, 120
  programmable ROM (PROM), 120, 129
ReadCh, 540, 542, 552
real time, 594, 597, 599–600
real-time application, 547
reclocking, 219–220
recoding, 261
recursion, 277, 403
recursive decomposition, 222
recursive functions, 345
  theory of, 277
reduction rule, 149, 277
Reed, D., xx
reflexivity, 179
  of $\preceq$, 179
register, 76, 78–86, 91, 93, 147–148, 171, 173–175, 178, 183–185, 188, 197, 269, 281, 286, 313, 337, 357, 514
  active, 354
  clock input, 85–86, 178
  clocked, 146, 174
  data input, 85–86
  fast, 359
  high-speed, 354
  load-enable input, 85–86, 175, 178, 184, 188

on bus, 253
processor, 336, 431
timing, 85–86
virtual, 304, 314, 317, 319, 436
register files, 127–128, 514–515, 518
  multiport, 518
  two-port, implementation of, 514
register load operation ($\leftarrow$), 184, 191
register set, nonuniform, 457
register-transfer notation, 295, 367, 376
  size of transfer, 295
  superscripts, 368
regular expression, 151–154
relation
  reflexive, 149, 179
  symmetric, 149
  transitive, 149, 179
relaxation, 149
  chaotic, 609
  optimistic, 149, 151
relaxation algorithm, 149
reliability, 609
replacement strategy, 481, 484–485
  least recently used (LRU), 481–482, 484–485
  optimal (OPT), 481
  optimality of OPT, 481
  random, 485
representation
  of information, 2
  of logical values, 6, 9
  of machines, 269
resistor, 14–15
resources
  conflict over, 183
  shared, 560–561
result storage, 355, 357
return sequence, *see* procedure linkage
return value, *see* procedure linkage
reverse Polish notation, 367
ribbon cable, 245
ring, 241
RISC, *see* architecture
rise time ($t_r$), 16–20, 247
ROM, *see* read-only memory
root, 243
root congestion, 243
rotl, 649
rotr, 649
routing, 226
  data, 212
  torus, 264
RTL, *see* logic families
run time, 365
run-time tags, 530
runt pulses, 88